SISCIS

La statistique est la première des sciences inexactes.

Goncourt Journals,
14 January 1861.

important source books for reference and research

Europe

Directory of European Associations: Part 1—National industrial, trade & professional associations.
Interests, activities and publications of c 9,000 organisations in Western and Eastern Europe. English, French & German indexes.

Directory of European Associations: Part 2—National learned, scientific & technical societies.
Interests, activities & publications of c 5,000 organisations in Western and Eastern Europe. English, French and German indexes.

European Companies: A Guide to Sources of Information.
Describes organisations and publications providing information about business enterprises in Western and Eastern Europe.

Statistics—Europe.
Describes organisations and publications providing statistical information for economic, social and market research in Western and Eastern Europe.

Current European Directories
Guide to international, national and specialised directories covering all countries of Europe.

Great Britain & Ireland

Directory of British Associations.
Interests, membership, activities & publications of c 8,500 British and Irish organisations.

Current British Directories.
Describes c 2,500 directories and lists published in Great Britain, Ireland, the Commonwealth and South Africa.

Councils, Committees & Boards.
Constitution, activities and publications of advisory, consultative, executive and similar bodies in British public life.

Overseas

Statistics—Africa.
Describes organisations and publications providing statistical information for economic, social and market research for all countries of Africa.

Current African Directories
Guide to directories and other sources of business information covering all countries of Africa

Statistics—America.
Describes organisations and publications providing statistical information for economic, social and market research in North, Central and South America.

Current Asian and Australasian Directories
Guide to international, national & specialised directories covering all countries in Asia, Australasia and Oceania.

Statistics—Asia & Australasia.
Describes organisations and publications providing statistical information for economic, social and market research for all countries in Asia, Australasia and Oceania.

Write for our complete descriptive catalogue

CBD Research Ltd
154 High Street, Beckenham, Kent, BR3 1EA, England
Telephone 01-650 7745.

 Member: European Association of Directory Publishers and Association of British Directory Publishers

SISCIS

Subject Index to Sources of Comparative International Statistics

Compiled by F C Pieper, BSc (Econ), FLA
at the University of Warwick Library
under a grant from the
Social Science Research Council

CBD Research Ltd
Beckenham, Kent, England

First published	1978 (Reprinted 1980)
Copyright ©	1978. The Library of the University of Warwick.
All rights reserved	No part of this book may be reproduced, stored in a retrieval system, or transmitted, in any form or by any means, electronic, mechanical, photocopying, recording or otherwise, without the prior permission of C.B.D. Research Ltd.
ISBN	900246 23 5.
Published by	C.B.D. Research Ltd, 154 High Street, Beckenham, Kent, BR3 1EA, England. Telephone 01-650 7745.

Printed in Great Britain by Page Bros (Norwich) Ltd

CONTENTS

Preface	vii
Note on method of compilation and use of SISCIS	ix
Publisher's note	xi
Abbreviations	xiii
Notes on monetary units	xvi
Notes on product classifications	xvi
Notes on indications of territorial coverage	xvii
Symbols indicating frequency	xviii
Alphabetical list of titles indexed	xix
Alphabetical SUBJECT INDEX	1
Appendices:	
1. Exports by product and destination	615
2. Imports by product and source	660
3. Index numbers	697
4. Global statistics	711
List of title codes	731

WARWICK STATISTICS SERVICE

University of Warwick Library
Coventry CV4 7AL

BUSINESS INFORMATION AND STATISTICS FOR INDUSTRY

Few librarians can hope to hold comprehensive collections, even of the literature of their core subjects, and yet more and more are being asked to cope with diversifying interests. In particular, many industrial librarians are facing increasing demands for commercial and market information. To collect all the materials required, and to pick up the experience in using it is not normally a practical proposition. There are many sources and organisations from where such information can be obtained if you have time to trail round, or in some cases, a very large budget.

A great deal of the data required is of a statistical nature—production figures, brand shares, company accounts, international trade, economic conditions, consumer data, prices and so on. The WARWICK STATISTICS SERVICE has one of the country's leading collections of such material with 10,000 titles including over 2,000 current statistical serials and a world wide coverage. It has deposit arrangements for the statistical output of thirty countries and most leading international organisations. Publications of other governments, of trade associations and of private research organisations are purchased. Being based in the University Library, the directory, monograph and journal literature provided for business and economic studies are at hand.

Experienced staff are available to answer your enquiries, and to help with sources and technical problems involved in their use. Enquiries can be made by telephone, telex or letter. Facilities for personal visits include study carrels, calculators and typewriters. A monthly newsletter, WARWICK STATISTICS NEWS, abstracts the business press, updates major economic indicators and reviews new sources of information.

Access to the service is by a modest annual subscription, though frequent users may make additional enquiries and will be charged on an hourly basis.

If you would like more information about the WARWICK STATISTICS SERVICE, telephone Colin Offor, Coventry (0203) 62530

PREFACE

The wide range of subjects for which detailed statistics are available is a matter of some surprise to many users. Perhaps the most useful publications are those which summarise data collected from original sources on a uniform and comparative basis for a large number of countries; it is mainly with this kind of source that this book is concerned.

Tracing specific series of published statistical data has long been a problem: specialists with a narrow subject field and limited range of sources know them well, but once outside that subject area they, like non-specialists, can spend much time and effort in sifting through a mass of unfamiliar publications seeking the exact series of data they require.

This problem has progressively become more acute with the increase in the number of publications now available on a regular basis. Although some useful guides to national official statistical series have appeared recently, few comprehensive, detailed subject-indexes exist to cover the vast store of statistics published by international and co-operative organisations, professional bodies and semi-official institutions throughout the world.

The need for an index of sources of comparative data convinced the undersigned of the potential value of a research project to fill the gap. The Library of the University of Technology, Loughborough, was known to possess a suite of computer programs, which we believed could be adapted for this purpose; previous attempts to subject-index statistical material by conventional methods had had little success, largely because of the wide range and kinds of data available and the daunting multiplicity of subject sub-headings to be handled.

For these reasons we approached the Social Science Research Council for financial support, suggesting that a computer-based system could offer an effective means at minimum cost for sorting and printing-out a very large number of entries. We are grateful to SSRC for funding this project over two-and-a-half years and also to Professor A J Evans, the Librarian at Loughborough, for making available the computer programs which had been set up for periodicals control. His advice and the assistance of his staff in the early stages of the idea were extremely helpful.

In April 1974 Frank Pieper, who for many years had had a great deal of experience in the field of statistics, was appointed to carry out this research work. The originators of the project wish to pay tribute to the painstaking work and planning put into the compilation of this book and believe that the finished publication is testimony enough of his efforts. Due to factors beyond our control, the completion of the project took longer than was originally contemplated.

P.E.Tucker	-	University Librarian
J. Fletcher	-	Economics & Business Studies Librarian
		University of Warwick

essential information for all concerned with business in Europe

Directory of EUROPEAN ASSOCIATIONS

Part 1: National industrial, trade & professional associations
over 9,000 trade associations, professional institutes, employers' associations, etc, classified by subject interest and subdivided by countries

2nd Edition, 1976.   £30; $65   634 pages, A4

Part 2: National learned, scientific & technical societies
over 5,000 academies, learned, scientific & technical societies and research associations, classified by subject interest and subdivided by countries

1st Edition, 1975.   £16.50; $45   365 pages, A4

Entries in each Part contain:
  name & authorised translations of name
  acronym or abbreviated name
  date of formation
  address, telephone & telex number
  membership data
  activities—especially conferences, information
    services, collection of statistics, etc
  publications

Each Part has the following indexes:
  complete alphabetical index of names and of
    authorised translations of names
  index of acronyms and abbreviated names
  subject indexes in English, French & German
Coverage:
  all European countries except Great Britain and
    the Republic of Ireland

CBD Research Ltd | **Gale Research Co**
Beckenham · Kent · England | Detroit · Michigan · USA

NOTE ON METHOD OF COMPILATION & USE OF SISCIS

In practice the indexing and compilation of SISCIS, which we hope will become a standard reference book for statistical sources, posed fewer problems than the research aspect of the project itself, namely the most appropriate methods of using computer technology to achieve this end.

Selection of Publications

Criteria had first to be drawn up to decide which publications among the many available deserved inclusion, so that the broad spectrum of economic subject matter in the widest sense was adequately covered in a balanced selection.

A thorough assessment of the importance, detail and relevance to contemporary problems and interest of published statistical series was carried out, taking first the publications on the shelves of the Statistics Collection in the Library of the University of Warwick. As far as possible sources giving a wide international coverage of comparative data, currently appearing on a regular basis, were chosen, although some occasional reports and research publications which may not be up-dated under the same title in the future were included, provided their contents were not known to be easily available elsewhere. Other special collections, including the Department of Industry's Statistics and Market Intelligence Library (SMIL), were sifted for additional publications which met the original criteria of selection.

As the project progressed, methods of indexing procedure were refined, cross-referencing was added and more publications were included. No restriction was placed on subject coverage, in fact almost all the tables of primary statistics in the chosen sources were indexed as computer input, which finally totalled over 53,000 entries under a large number of subject headings extracted from 358 publications.

The compiler was fortunate in being able to carry out this research project at the Library of the University of Warwick, not only because of the helpfulness of the staff, but because of the exhaustive stocks of publications in the field of economic subjects readily available on its shelves.

Method of Computer Input and Output

Modification of the computer programs was carried out in order to adapt them to the special requirements of the project. These changes allowed a sufficiently greater depth of indexing, so that the descriptive detail of the sub-headings was adequate to pin-point the precise nature of the statistics and, in addition, to add all other essential information needed, such as territorial coverage and the frequency of the data described.

Since manual indexing of the material was essential, the method used was firstly to commit the subject detail to punched cards as computer input; secondly, to validate these entries, as a check on the proper functioning of the amended programs; thirdly, to obtain output in tabulated form using the system of alphabetical sorting and the important functions of indenting the subject sub-divisions and of linking with a title code, and finally, to edit the results into a form suitable for conventional publication. It had become clear in the early stages that the use of photographic copy of computer printout, so much used these days, was impracticable in this particular case, because first-time accuracy and uniformity of indexing would be too time-consuming to achieve.

Method of Use of SISCIS

Users of this book should first decide on the main subject of the required statistics and look down the indented descriptions of data available on that subject until the required headings are found; they should then select the territories for which the information is needed and read off the title code which applies. The actual title of the publication in which the relevant statistics are printed is listed at the end of the book. No list of subject headings contained in SISCIS is necessary as adequate cross-references are printed in the text.

Acknowledgements

The compiler received a great deal of assistance and advice from many quarters, but would mention in particular the following who were especially helpful; the two originators of the project, who have kindly written the Preface, my two hard-working assistants, Beryl Wood and Marion Kendrick, and also Ian Drummond of the University of Warwick Computer Unit, who modified the computer programs and wrestled successfully with the technical difficulties of arranging output from the 1906A computer.

F.C. Pieper

what's new in economics? management?

Unpublished working papers contain the most up-to-date thinking of researchers, practitioners and academics from all over the world.

More than 2500 papers are listed each year in the semi-annual **Economics Working Papers Bibliography.**

The full texts of about 1500 papers are available on microfilm annually.

For further details of these services write to:

Trans-Media Publishing Company
154 Camden High Street
London NW1 0NE

For their EWP Brochure

PUBLISHER'S NOTE
Advice to users of SISCIS

Statistics are collected, published, and used in a very wide variety of forms; subjects are divided and cross-related in many, and often incompatible, ways; and all this makes the subject indexing of statistical tables notoriously difficult. These inherent difficulties in the task are compounded by the problems of computer handling. Inevitably there are, in this volume, incongruities in presentation, some of which did not emerge until the final stage of the project. The compilers and publishers feel that users should be aware of these difficulties. In particular, the enormous variations in terminology in the original tables have defied complete compression into mutually exclusive headings, with the result that some inconsistencies and overlaps occur.

The following suggestions are offered to the user:
1. Read the notes on page ix carefully.
2. Try all possible headings appropriate to the enquiry, and follow up all cross-references.
3. Scan all entries under these headings, and do not rely on conventional alphabetisation of entries. Note particularly that the regular indexing rule "NOTHING BEFORE SOMETHING" is frequently reversed, thus:
   Labour force employed at census dates
   Labour force employed by sex
   Labour force employed by status in building industry
   Labour force employed
4. Remember that headings may not be mutually exclusive - peaches, for example, will be found under FRUIT, FRESH; FRUIT, FRESH BY KIND; FRUIT, PROCESSED; and FRUIT, DRIED.

For all publications we maintain records of any errors brought to our notice after publication; we propose to extend this practice to SISCIS. We shall be grateful to receive notes of any mistakes discovered, and shall also do our best to help any purchaser who has difficulty in using the book.

As compilers of substantial reference works ourselves, we have a great deal of admiration for Frank Pieper's courage and stamina in undertaking and carrying out the enormous task of compiling SISCIS. We wish also to acknowledge the tremendous work of Mrs Jackie Smith, who typed very difficult copy with unfailing accuracy and cheerfulness.

CBD Research Ltd.

STATISTICS:

Sources for Social, Economic and Market Research

Joan M. Harvey

A series of four separate works:

Statistics—Europe
(covering both Western & Eastern Europe)
3rd edition, 1976. 467 pages. £15.00 (US$40.00)

Statistics—Africa
(covering the whole continent & adjacent islands)
2nd Edition for publication 1978

Statistics—America
(covering North, Central & South America)
1st Edition, 1973. 220 pages. £6.00 (US $22.50)

Statistics—Asia & Australasia
1st Edition, 1974. 236 pages. £8.00 (US $26.50)

giving, for each country:

    central statistical office: address, description of work, facilities offered

    other important organisations that collect & publish statistics

    principal libraries of statistical material

    information services provided in other countries particularly the UK, the USA, Canada & Australia

    bibliographies of statistics

    description of major publishing sources, arranged in the standard grouping: General — Production — External trade — Internal distribution — Population — Social — Finance — Transport & communications

CBD Research Ltd,
154 High Street, Beckenham, Kent, England
01-650 7745

ABBREVIATIONS

AASM	Associated African States & Madagascar (see notes page xvii)
ACP	African & Caribbean Countries & Pacific Is (see notes page xvii)
A$	Australian dollar
AFRA	average freight rate assessment
A.I.D.	Agency for International Development
ASch	Austrian Schilling
bhp	brake horse-power
bn	(with £ or $) billion
BRT	Brutto-Register-Tonnen; British [gross] registered tons
BTU	British thermal units
CACM	Central American Common Market (see notes page xvii)
C.A.P.	Common Agricultural Policy (EEC)
CARIFTA	Caribbean Free Trade Area (see notes page xvii)
cc	cubic centimetres
CECA	Communauté Européenne du Charbon et de l'Acier
c & f	cost & freight
cif	cost, insurance & freight
CIF	Community Investment Funds
cm	centimetres
cos	companies
CSA	Commonwealth Sugar Agreement
CST	Classification Statistique et Tarifaire (see notes page xvi)
cu ft	cubic feet
cwt	hundredweight
DAC	Development Assistance Committee (OECD)
DEG	Direchos especiales de giro (see notes page xvi)
DIY	Do-it-yourself
DKr	Danish kroner
DM	Deutsche Mark
doz	dozen
dwt	deadweight ton
E	East
EA Sh	East African shillings
ECAFE	Economic Commission for Asia & the Far East (see page xvii)
ECE	Economic Commission for Europe (see notes page xvii)
ECSC	European Coal & Steel Community
EDF	European Development Fund
EEC	European Economic Community (see notes page xvii)
EFTA	European Free Trade Association
eqpt	equipment
equiv	equivalent
Esc	Escudos
ESCAP	Economic & Social Commission for Asia & the Pacific (formerly ECAFE)
estim	estimated
excl	excluding

ABBREVIATIONS

FAO	Food & Agriculture Organization of the UN
FEOGA	Fonds Européen d'Orientation et de Garantie Agricole
Fl	Florin
Fmk	Finnish marks
fob	free on board
for	free on rail
Fr	Francs
FrB	Belgian francs
FrCFA	Francs, Communauté Financière Africaine
FrS	Swiss francs
ft	feet
GATT	General Agreement on Tariffs & Trade
GW	giga-watts
GWh	giga-watt-hours
ha	hectare
hp	horse-power
hr	hour
IATA	International Air Transport Association
IBRD	International Bank for Reconstruction & Development
ICA	International Coffee Agreement
IDA	International Development Association
IDB	Inter-American Development Bank
IFC	International Finance Corporation
IMF	International Monetary Fund
incl	including
IRSG	International Rubber Study Group
ISA	International Sugar Agreement
ISIC	International Standard Industrial Classification (see notes page xvi)
ISO	International Sugar Organisation
ITC	International Tin Council
IUOTO	International Union of Official Travel Organisations
IWA	International Wheat Agreement
kcal	kilocalories
kg	kilograms
km	kilometres
kV	kilovolts
kVa	kilovolt-amperes
kW	kilowatts
kWh	kilowatt-hours
LAFTA	Latin-American Free Trade Association (see notes page xvii)
lbs	pounds
Lit	Lire
LPG	liquefied petroleum gas
m	metres
m^2	square metres

ABBREVIATIONS

m³	cubic metres
m	(with £, $, Fr or DM) million
M$	Malaysian dollars
mm	millimetres
mrd	milliard
mth	month
MV	megavolts
MVa	megavolt-amperes
MW	megawatts
MWe	electron megawatts
MWh	megawatt-hours
N	North
NACE	(see notes page xvi)
NATO	North Atlantic Treaty Organisation (see notes page xvii)
NIMEXE	(see notes page xvi)
no	number
NST	(see notes page xvi)
OAS	Organization of American States (see notes page xvii)
ODA	Overseas Development Administration
OECD	Organization for Economic Cooperation & Development (see notes page xvii)
OPEC	Organization of Petroleum Exporting Countries (see notes page xvii)
oz	ounces
Rs	Rupees
Rep	Republic
S	South
SITC	Standard International Trade Classification (see notes page xvi)
SKr	Swedish kronor
sq ft	square feet
TEU	twenty-foot equivalent units
UA	Units of account (see notes page xvi)
UNICEF	United Nations Children's Fund
UNRWA	United Nations Relief & Works Agency
VAT	Value added tax
W	West, Western
wk	week
wt	weight
yd	yard
yr	year

NOTES ON MONETARY UNITS

DEG Units Direchos especiales de giro - a Latin American unit of account based on, but not at par with, the US $ and used to assess contribution of tourism to balances of payments.

UA Units of Account - a notional currency unit, fixed at intervals by the EEC Commission, based on the US $ value of approx. 0.89 grammes of fine gold. The UA is used primarily for budgeting and other internal financial calculations of the EEC, but also for evaluating trade between the EEC member countries and the AASM countries.

"in local currency" Used in the text to indicate that monetary values are given in the notional currencies of the countries listed under column headed "Territorial coverage".

NOTES ON PRODUCT CLASSIFICATIONS

CST "Classification statistique et tarifaire pour le commerce international" - the original classification of goods for purposes of recording international trade adopted by the EEC Commission but now largely replaced by the NIMEXE nomenclature. CST product groupings, however, are still used for trade statistics between EEC and ACP countries, e.g. in the EEC publications "Foreign Trade - Analytical tables" (Title codes E 21 and E 48). CST product groupings closely follow those listed in the SITC classification.

ISIC "International Standard Industrial Classification" - the main classification of goods and primary products used for comparative production statistics globally. Except for minor revisions the ISIC has been in general use since it was approved by the United Nations Organisation in 1948. Eurostat (Statistical Office of the European Community) has, however, recently finalised its own common harmonised nomenclature for production statistics (NIPRO), which will eventually replace the ISIC in Eurostat publications.

NIMEXE Acronym for "La Nomenclature harmonisée pour les statistiques des pays de la CEE" (Nomenclature of goods for the external trade statistics of the Community and statistics of trade between member states) (1973). This nomenclature was compiled, with the assistance of the statistical institutions of the original six member states of the EEC, by CCCN (Customs Co-operation Council for Nomenclature) within the harmonisation procedures envisaged by the Rome Treaty. NIMEXE remains a widely-used grouping of goods entering international trade and provides a more exact comparison than was possible under the CST system which it largely replaces. Minor changes have been embodied in annual revisions and additions authorised under Community legislation. NIMEXE classification has been used for import and export data published in Eurostat sources since January 1966.

Statistical publications of the EEC will in due course bring further harmonised classifications into use. NACE and NST are examples, both of which will dovetail into the NIMEXE classification.

NACE "Nomenclature générales des activités économiques dans les Communautés Européennes" (General industrial classification of economic activities within the European Communities).

NST "Nomenclature uniforme des marchandises pour les statistiques de transport" (Standard goods nomenclature for transport statistics).

NOTES ON INDICATIONS OF TERRITORIAL COVERAGE

The names of countries or regions listed under "Territorial coverage" are generally self-explanatory, but the following information may be found helpful:

AASM countries.	Countries in membership of Associated African States & Madagascar (= Etats Africains, Malgache et Mauricien Associés). Mainly the former French colonial territories in Africa, plus Madagascar and Mauritius.
ACP countries.	African & Caribbean Countries & Pacific Is. The developing countries in these areas which were signatories of the Lomé Convention of February 1975. Most African countries; Bahamas, Barbados, Grenada, Guyana, Trinidad & Tobago; Fiji, Tonga & Western Samoa.
Benin.	New name of Dahomey.
CACM countries.	Central American Common Market. Costa Rica, El Salvador, Guatemala, Honduras, Nicaragua.
CARIFTA.	Caribbean Free Trade Area - now replaced by Caribbean Common Market. Antigua, Barbados, Belize, Dominica, Grenada, Guyana, Jamaica, Montserrat, St Kitts-Nevis-Anguilla, St Lucia, St Vincent, Trinidad & Tobago.
Dahomey.	Former name of Benin.
ECAFE countries.	Area covered by the reports of the UN Economic Commission for Asia & the Far East (now UN Economic & Social Commission for Asia & the Pacific - ESCAP). All countries of Asia (incl China & Mongolia); Australia and its dependencies, New Zealand, the Philippines, Cook Is, Fiji, Gilbert Is, Nauru, Solomon Is, Tonga, Western Samoa.
ECE countries.	Area covered by the reports of the UN Economic Commission for Europe. All countries of Europe - East & West - including Greece, Turkey, USSR & Yugoslavia.
EEC countries.	European Economic Community. 1958-1972: Belgium, France, Germany, Italy, Luxembourg & the Netherlands. 1973-: also Denmark, Eire & UK.
Latin American countries.	Generally indicates reports covering all Central and South American countries, plus Barbados, Dominican Republic, Haiti, Jamaica, Mexico, Trinidad & Tobago.
LAFTA.	Latin American Free Trade Association. Argentina, Brazil, Chile, Colombia, Ecuador, Mexico, Paraguay, Peru, Uruguay, Venezuela.
Malagasy Republic.	Now again known as Madagascar.
NATO countries.	Member countries of the North Atlantic Treaty Organization. Belgium, Canada, Denmark, France, Greece, Germany (FR), Iceland, Italy, Luxembourg, the Netherlands, Norway, Portugal, Turkey, UK, USA.
OAS countries.	Member countries of the Organization of American States (= Organizacion de los Estados Americanos). Argentina, Barbados, Bolivia, Brazil, Chile, Colombia, Costa Rica, Dominican Republic, Ecuador, El Salvador, Grenada, Guatemala, Haiti, Honduras, Jamaica, Mexico, Nicaragua, Panama, Paraguay, Peru, Trinidad & Tobago, USA, Uruguay, Venezuela. Cuba was a member until 1968; Guyana is a 'permanent observer'.
OECD countries.	Member countries of the Organisation for Economic Co-operation & Development. Australia, Austria, Belgium, Canada, Denmark, Finland, France, Germany (BR), Greece, Iceland, Irish Republic, Italy, Japan, Luxembourg, the Netherlands, New Zealand, Norway, Portugal, Spain, Sweden, Switzerland, Turkey, UK & USA. Yugoslavia participates with a special status - i.e. data sometimes included in statistics.
OPEC countries.	Member countries of the Organisation of Petroleum Exporting Countries. Algeria, Gabon, Libya, Nigeria; Ecuador, Venezuela; Indonesia, Iran, Iraq, Kuwait, Qatar, Saudi Arabia, Utd.Arab Emirates.

SYMBOLS INDICATING FREQUENCY OF STATISTICS

The letters following Title codes in the Index indicate the frequency of the figures given in the tables contained in the publications indicated.

The following are used:-

- w   weekly
- m   monthly
- q   quarterly
- a2   twice annually, i.e. half-yearly
- a   annually

The absence of a letter after the title code indicates a frequency other than the above, i.e. where the figures given relate to a specific year, e.g. 1995 (as a projection) or a census frequency of 5 or 10 years.

Note: "See no.1, 2, etc" refers to the number of the monthly issue of title code U 27 (UN Monthly Bulletin of Statistics).

ALPHABETICAL LIST OF TITLES INDEXED
To identify titles from their title codes, see the List of Title Codes (page 731)

Advertising expenditure around the world - a survey. Z 4.
Agrarpreise. E 34.
Agricultural commodities - projections 1975-1985. A 1.
Agricultural & food statistics for the enlarged Community. B 1.
Agricultural statistics. (EEC) E 1.
Agricultural statistics 1955-1968. (OECD) D 1.
Agricultural trade in Europe - European market for fruit & vegetables. U 20.
America en cifras. Parts 1 to 6. N 11-20.
Analysis of world tanker tonnage. S 4.
Annuaire statistique - Afrique. U 44.
Annuaire de statistique agricole. (EEC) E 44.
Annuaire statistique des Etats Africains, Malgache et Mauricien Associés. E 41.
Annuaire des statistiques du commerce extérieur: Synthèse. E 45.
Annuaire de statistiques sociales. E 2.
Annual bulletin of electric energy statistics for Europe. U 1.
Annual bulletin of exports of chemical products. U 2.
Annual bulletin of gas statistics for Europe. U 3.
Annual bulletin of general energy statistics for Europe. U 4.
Annual bulletin of housing & building statistics for Europe. U 5.
Annual bulletin of statistics, & supplement. (International Tea Committee). C 1.
Annual bulletin of steel statistics for Europe. U 6.
Annual bulletin of transport statistics. U 8.
Annual coffee statistics. J 1.
Annual fertiliser review. A 2.
Annual forest products market review. Parts 1 & 2. A 24-25.
Annual report. (International Finance Corporation). M 2.
Annual review of oilseeds, oils, oilcakes & other commodities. P 1.
Annual statistical bulletin. (OPEC). C 3.
Annual summary of merchant ships launched in the world. S 1.
Annual survey of wages & working conditions, production & employment of the metal industry. C 2.
Aussenhandel der Gemeinschaft - Ergebnisse nach Mitgliederstaaten. E 5.

Balance of payments yearbook. F 1.
Balances of payments. (EEC). E 4.
Basic statistics of the Community. E 3.
The Belgian & international economy - synoptical tables. C 4.
Bilans énergétiques - situation et prévisions. E 14.
British machine tools in Europe - a study of competition. B 20.
Bulletin annuel des exportations de produits chimiques. U 2.
Bulletin annuel de statistiques de l'acier pour l'Europe. U 6.
Bulletin annuel de statistiques du logement et de la construction pour l'Europe. U 5.
Bulletin annuel de statistiques de transports pour l'Europe. U 8.
Bulletin du bois pour l'Europe. A 13.
Bulletin de la Chambre Syndicale de la Sidérurgie Française. C 5.

Bulletin of labour statistics. L 1.
Bulletin mensuel des statistiques générales. (EEC) E 26.
Bulletin of statistics on world trade in engineering products. U 9.
Bulletin de statistiques du commerce mondial des produits des industries mécaniques et électriques. U 9.
The Cement industry. (OECD) D 4.
The Chemical industry. (OECD) D 5.
Coal situation in Europe and its prospects. U 10.
Coal statistics for Europe. U 31.
Cocoa market report. P 2.
Cocoa statistics. (FAO) A 3.
Cocoa statistics. (Gill & Duffus) P 3.
Coconut situation. (FAO) A 4.
Commerce extérieur de la Communauté - résultats par états membres. E 5.
Commerce extérieur: statistiques mensuelles. (EEC) E 22.
Commerce extérieur: tableaux analytiques. (EEC) E 20, E 21, E 48.
Commodity bulletin series. (FAO) A 7, A 8, A 12, A 15, A 18.
Commodity data summaries. N 1.
Commodity reference series. (FAO) A 19, A 20.
Commodity review & outlook. (FAO) A 5.
Commodity survey. (UNCTAD) U 11.
Commodity trade statistics: Statistical papers, series D. U 12.
Compendio statistico. (Associazione Nazionale dell'Industria Chimica). C 6.
Compendium of housing statistics. U 13.
Comptes nationaux. (EEC) E 32.
Comptes sociaux dans la Communauté Européenne. E 6.
Conjoncture énergétique dans la Communauté. E 7.
Consumer price indices. (OECD) D 6.
Cost of social security. L 2.
Cotton - world statistics: quarterly bulletin. K 1.

Dairy produce: a review of production, trade, consumption & prices. B 4.
Demographic yearbook. U 14.
Developing countries economic indicators: Part 1. B 2.
Development co-operation - review. D 7.
Digest of statistics. (ICAO) S 5-11.
Direct & total wage costs for workers - international survey 1960-1970. C 7.
Direction of trade. F 3.
Direction of trade - annual supplement. F 2.

ECE Region in figures. U 15.
Economic handbook of the machine tool industry. J 2.
Economic situation in the Community. E 13.
Economic survey of Asia & the Far East. U 17.
Economic survey of Europe. U 16.
Economic survey of Latin America. U 18.
l'Economie Belge et Internationale - tableaux synoptiques. C 4.
Edible nut statistics. P 4.
EEC dairy facts & figures. B 3.
EEC internal information - crop production. E 12.
Electricity supply industry: achievements... forecasts. D 8.
Energia ed idrocarburi - sommario statistico. H 4.

xix

ALPHABETICAL LIST OF TITLES INDEXED

Energy balances - situation & forecasts. E 14.
Energy statistics. E 16.
Energy statistics - supplement. E 17.
Energy statistics yearbook. E 15.
Engineering industries in OECD member countries: new basic statistics 1963-70. D 9.
Estimated world requirements of narcotic drugs. U 19.
Etudes et enquêtes statistiques. (EEC) Vols. 1 & 2. E 39 & 40.
European cotton statistics. K 2.
European historical statistics 1750-1970. Z 1.
European Monetary Agreement: Annual report. D 10.
Examen de la situation mondiale des céréales. C 16.
Expenditure trends in OECD countries 1960-1980. D 11.
Exporter's guide to the wool textile markets of the world. K 3.

Farm prices. (EEC) E 34.
Financial statements of the general account & special drawing account. (IMF) F 4.
Financial statistics. (OECD) D 12.
Flow of resources to developing countries. D 13.
Fonds Européen de Développement - situation semestrielle des projets. E 19.
Food consumption statistics. D 14.
Forecasts of the dairy & beef situations in 1975 & 1978. D 15.
Foreign trade - analytical tables. (EEC) E 20, E 21, E 48.
Foreign trade - monthly statistics. (EEC) E 22, E 24.
Fruit intelligence. B 6.
Fruit - a review of production & trade. B 5.
Furniture industry in Western Europe: a statistical digest. C 8.

Grain bulletin. B 7.
Grain crops - a review. B 8.
Die grössten Unternehmen der Welt. H 1.
Growth of output 1960-1980. D 17.
Growth of world industry. Vols 1 & 2. U 21, U 22.

Handbook of international trade & development statistics. U 23.
Hides, skins & footwear industry in OECD countries. D 18.
Hides & skins quarterly. B 9.
Highway expenditures: road & motor vehicle statistics. S 13.

Indices des prix à la consommation. D 6.
Industrial fibres - a review of production, trade & consumption. B 10.
Industrial production. (OECD) D 19, D 20.
Industrial review to 1977. (NEDO) B 21-29.
Industrial statistics. (EEC) E 28.
Industrial statistics yearbook. (EEC) E 27.
l'Industrie chimique. (OECD) D 5.
l'Industrie du ciment. (OECD) D 4.
l'Industrie de l'électricité. (OECD) D 8.
l'Industrie des métaux non-ferreux. (OECD) D 21.
l'Industrie des pâtes et papiers. (OECD) D 40.
l'Industrie sidérurgique. (OECD) D 22.
Information on man-made fibres. K 4.
Informations sur les textiles synthétiques et cellulosiques. K 4.
International coal trade. N 2.
International cotton industry statistics. K 5.
International financial statistics. (IMF) F 5, F 6.

International market survey - cattle, sheep, pigs. C 9.
International steel statistics - world tables. T 1.
International survey of interest rates. M 7.
International tourism & tourism policy in OECD member countries. D 47.
International trade. (GATT) G 1.
International travel statistics. S 14.
International whaling statistics. C 10.
Inventory of taxes. E 31.
Investment in the Community coalmining & iron & steel industries. E 46.
Iron & steel industry - monthly bulletin. (BSC) T 2.
Iron & steel industry in... & trends in... (OECD) D 22.
Iron & steel statistics bi-monthly. (EEC) E 30.
Iron & steel yearbook. E 29.

Jahrbuch der Sozialstatistik. E 2.

Key figures of European securities. F 9.
Know more about oil: world statistics. T 3.

Labour force statistics. D 23, D 24.
Labour force & world population growth. L 3.
Latest information on national accounts of less-developed countries. D 25.
Lead & zinc statistics - monthly bulletin. U 24.
Lloyd's Register of Shipping - statistical tables. S 2.

Main economic indicators. D 26.
Man-made fibres: production, consumption, capacity. D 27.
Manuel de statistiques du commerce international et du développement. U 23.
Marchés agricoles - échanges commerciaux. E 47.
Maritime transport. D 28.
Market forecasts for 1975 for certain fruit & vegetables. D 29.
Market share reports - US participation in foreign markets. N 3.
Market trends & prospects for chemical products. Vols 1 & 2. U 25, U 26.
Meat & dairy produce bulletin. B 12.
Merchant shipbuilding return. S 3.
Meat: a review of production, trade, consumption & prices. B 11.
"Metal Bulletin" handbook. T 4.
Metal statistics. (American Metal Market) J 3.
Metal statistics. (Metallgesellschaft AG) H 2.
Metalli non ferrosi e ferroleghe statistiche. C 12.
Mineral industry surveys. N 4.
Minerals yearbook - vol.3. N 5.
Monthly bulletin of agricultural economics & statistics. A 9.
Monthly bulletin of statistics. U 27.
Monthly general statistics bulletin. (EEC) E 26.
Monthly statistical bulletin. (International Tin Council) C 20.
Monthly statistical summary. (International Tea Committee) C 11.
Monthly statistics. (Civil Aviation Authority) S 12.
Motor industry of Great Britain. V 1.

National accounts of OECD countries. D 30.
National accounts yearbook. E 32.
Newsprint data. J 4.
Non-ferrous metal & ferro-alloy statistics. C 12.
Non-ferrous metals industry. D 21.

ALPHABETICAL LIST OF TITLES INDEXED

Oil statistics: supply & disposal. D 31.
Oil - world statistics. C 13.
Oilseeds review. N 10.
Operations report. (AID) M 1.

Paper & board: consumption patterns...in OECD countries 1950-67. D 32.
Pâtes et papiers...stocks...production et livraisons. D 41.
Per caput fibre consumption. A 6.
Pétrole. (Comité Professionnel du Pétrole) C 14.
Phosphate rock statistics. C 15.
Plantation crops - a review. B 13.
La Population active et sa structure. C 28.
Population & employment. (EEC) E 33.
Population et population active. (EEC) E 33.
Population & vital statistics: statistical papers series A. U 28.
Preise, Löhne, Wirtschaftsrechnungen. R 1-4.
Price movements of basic commodities in international trade 1950-1970. U 29.
Prices of agricultural products & selected inputs in Europe. U 30.
Prices received by farmers. E 35.
Prix agricoles. E 34.
Prix reçus par les producteurs agricoles. E 35.
Processed fruit & vegetables. A 7.
Processed tropical fruit. A 8.
Production, consumption & foreign trade of fruit & vegetables in OECD countries. D 33-36.
Production of fruit & vegetables in OECD countries. D 37.
Production & marketing structures for horticultural produce in Australia & Italy. D 38.
Production yearbook. A 9.
Projections of the population of the Communist countries of Eastern Europe by age & sex. N 6.
Provisional oil statistics. D 39.
Public financing of research & development in the Community countries. E 36.
Pulp & paper industry in the OECD member countries. D 40.
Pulp & paper...stocks...production...trade & shipments of market pulp. (OECD) D 41.

Quarterly bulletin of statistics for Asia & the Far East. U 32.
Quarterly bulletin of steel statistics for Europe. U 7.

Rapport annuel sur les engrais. A 2.
Rates of change in economic data for ten industrial countries. N 7.
Recent developments of agricultural trade in Europe. U 33.
Recueil des statistiques de l'habitation. U 13.
Regional development in the Community - analytical survey. E 37.
Regional statistics yearbook. (EEC) E 38.
Répertoire mondial des usines d'assemblage de véhicules automobiles. V 2.
Report on output expenses & income of agriculture in European countries: Vol 3 - statistical annex. U 34.
Revenue statistics of OECD member countries. D 42.
Review. (Fearnley & Egers Chartering Co Ltd) S 15.
Review of the agricultural situation in Europe. Vols 1 & 2. U 35, U 36.

Review of fisheries in OECD member countries. D 43.
Review of maritime transport. U 37.
Review of the world grains situation. C 16.
Rice bulletin. (Commonwealth Secretariat). B 14.
Rice report. (FAO) A 10.
Role & place of engineering industries in national & world economics - Vol 2. (ECE) U 38.
Rubber market report. C 17, C 18.
Rubber statistical bulletin. C 18.

Schedule of par values. F 7.
Self-service. Z 2.
Shipping economics & statistics. S 17.
Shipping statistics: Monthly figures of shipping, ports & sea trade. S 16.
Sidérurgie annuaire. E 29.
Sidérurgie statistique bimestrielle. E 30.
Social accounts in the European Community. E 6.
Social statistics. (EEC) E 8-11, E 18, E 25.
Sozialstatistik. (EEC) E 8-11, E 18, E 25.
State of food & agriculture. A 11.
Statistical abstract of Latin America. J 5.
Statistical bulletin. (International Sugar Organisation) C 19.
Statistical bulletin for Latin America. U 40, U 41.
Statistical & economic information bulletin for Africa. U 39.
Statistical indicators of short-term economic changes in ECE countries. U 42.
Statistical review of the National Association of the Chemical Industry. C 6.
Statistical review of the world oil industry. C 24.
Statistical studies & surveys. (EEC) Vols 1 & 2. E 39, E 40.
Statistical summary of the mineral industry. B 15.
Statistical supplement. (British Sulphur Corporation) T 5.
Statistical yearbook. (UN Dept of Economic & Social Affairs) U 43.
Statistical yearbook. (UNESCO) U 62.
Statistical yearbook - Africa. U 44.
Statistical yearbook for Asia & the Far East. U 45.
Statistical yearbook of the Associated African, Malagasy & Mauritian States. E 41.
Statistical yearbook of the European jute industry. C 22.
Statistical yearbook of the Federal German Republic. R 5.
Statistical yearbook of the iron & steel industry. H 3.
Statistics. (International Union of Producers & Distributors of Electrical Energy) C 23.
Statistics of energy. (OECD) D 44.
Statistics of foreign trade. (OECD) D 16.
Statistics of the instrument industry. C 24.
Statistics on narcotics drugs & maximum levels of opium stocks. U 46.
Statistics of newspapers & other periodicals. U 63.
Statistics of road traffic accidents in Europe. U 47.
Statistics of students abroad. U 64.
Statistics of world trade in steel. U 48.
Statistik der Schiffahrt. S 16.
Statistique agricole. (EEC) E 1.
Statistiques des accidents de la situation routière en Europe. U 47.
Statistiques du commerce extérieur - bulletin mensuel. (OECD) D 16.
Statistiques fiscales. (EEC) E 42.

ALPHABETICAL LIST OF TITLES INDEXED

Statistiques industrielles. (EEC)　E 27, E 28.
Statistiques de la population active.　D 23, D 24.
Statistiques routières mondiales.　S 24.
Statistiques sociales. (EEC)　E 8-11, E 18, E 25.
Statistiques des télécommunications.　S 18.
Statistiques - Union Internationale des Producteurs et Distributeurs d'Energie Electrique.　C 23.
Statistisches Jahrbuch fur die Bundesrepublik Deutschland.　R 5.
Statistisches Jahrbuch der Eisen und Stahl Industrie.　H 3.
Steam boilers & boilerhouse plant - effects of UK entry into the EEC.　B 30.
The Steel market.　U 49.
The Stock Exchange fact book.　F 8.
Sugar yearbook.　C 25.
Superphosphate statistics.　C 26.
Survey of electric power equipment.　D 45.
Survey of Europe today, 1970.　Z 3.
Survey of export markets for sorghum.　A 12.
Survey of world iron ore resources 1968.　U 51.

Tax statistics yearbook.　E 42.
Tea statistics.　P 6.
Telecommunication statistics.　S 18.
Textile industry in OECD countries.　D 46.
Timber bulletin for Europe.　A 13.
Tobacco consumption in various countries.　B 16.
Tobacco intelligence.　B 17.
Trade by commodities. (OECD)　D 2, D 3.
Trade by commodity classes & main countries. (EEC)　E 23.
Trade in manufacture of developing countries.　U 52.
Trade yearbook. (FAO)　A 14.
Transport yearbook. (EEC)　E 43.
Transports - statistique annuelle. (EEC)　E 43.
Trends in developing countries.　M 4.
Trends in grain consumption.　C 27.
Tropical products quarterly.　B 18.
Tungsten statistics.　U 53.

UK - EEC machine tool competition 1971.　B 31.
Uranium production & short-term demand.　D 48.

Vegetable oils & oilseeds.　B 19.
Very large crude carriers in excess of 175,000 dwt.　S 19, S 20.

West Indies & Caribbean yearbook.　T 6.
Wood pulp statistics.　J 7.
The Working population & its structure.　C 28.

World air transport statistics.　S 21.
World automotive market.　V 3.
World banana economy.　A 15.
World Bank: annual report.　M 3.
World bank atlas.　M 5.
World bulk fleet.　S 22.
World currency charts.　M 8.
World economic survey: current economic developments.　U 54.
World energy supplies.　U 55.
World forest industry.　A 16.
World grain trade statistics.　A 17.
World health statistics annual.　W 1.
World health statistics report.　W 2.
World hides, skins, leather & footwear economy.　A 18.
World invisible trade.　M 9.
World market for electric power equipment.　T 7.
World market for iron ore.　U 56.
World merchant shipping laid up for lack of employment.　S 23.
World metal statistics.　C 30.
World military expenditure.　N 9.
World motor vehicle data.　V 4.
World motor vehicle production & registration.　N 8.
World rice economy in figures 1909-1963.　A 19.
World road statistics.　S 24.
World sugar economy in figures.　A 20.
World summary of statistics of motor vehicle production.　V 2.
World tables. (IBRD)　M 6.
World trade annual.　U 50.
World trade in steel & steel demand in developing countries.　U 57.
World wheat statistics.　C 29.
World wool digest.　K 6.
The World's telephones.　S 25.
Worldwide operating statistics of the hotel industry.　Z 5.

Yearbook: American Bureau of Metal Statistics.　J 6.
Yearbook of agricultural statistics.　E 44.
Yearbook of construction statistics.　U 58.
Yearbook of fishery statistics.　A 21, A 22.
Yearbook of foreign trade statistics: statistical abstract.　E 45.
Yearbook of forest products.　A 23.
Yearbook of international trade statistics. (UN)　U 59.
Yearbook of labour statistics.　L 4.
Yearbook of national account statistics.　U 60.

	Territorial coverage	Title codes
A.I.D. (US AGENCY FOR INTERNATIONAL DEVELOPMENT)		
Administrative & expenses appropriations in $		M 1-a
Alliance for progress loans in $	All recipient countries	M 1-a
Contingency fund in $		M 1-a
Development aid authorisations for agriculture in $m	All recipient countries	M 1-a
business promotion in $m	All recipient countries	M 1-a
education in $m	All recipient countries	M 1-a
health in $m	All recipient countries	M 1-a
industry & mining in $m	All recipient countries	M 1-a
public administration in $m	All recipient countries	M 1-a
social welfare in $m	All recipient countries	M 1-a
transportation in $m	All recipient countries	M 1-a
commitments by appropriation category in $m	All recipient countries	M 1-a
Emergency assistance grants (under food aid program) in $m	All recipient countries	M 1-a
Expenditure by category of assistance in $m	All recipient countries	M 1-a
on barter transactions against farm products in $m		M 1-a
on commodities: animal feeding stuffs in $m		M 1-a
chemical products & plastics in $m		M 1-a
engines & turbines in $m		M 1-a
farm tractors in $m		M 1-a
fertilisers in $m		M 1-a
foodstuffs & live animals in $m		M 1-a
machine tools in $m		M 1-a
machinery by type in $m		M 1-a
metal manufactures in $m		M 1-a
motor vehicles & replacement parts in $m		M 1-a
natural & synthetic rubber in $m		M 1-a
non-ferrous metals in $m		M 1-a
office machinery in $m		M 1-a
paper products & newsprint in $m		M 1-a
petroleum products in $m		M 1-a
railway equipment in $m		M 1-a
raw materials by kind in $m		M 1-a
steel products by kind in $m		M 1-a
textile yarns & fibres in $m		M 1-a
on emergency food aid in $m	Recipient countries	M 1-a
Total expenditure in $m	Recipient countries	M 1-a
Exports of soybean oil under relief programs: tonnage	USA	B 19-a
Food for peace agreements by commodities in detail in $m		M 1-a
Food sales agreements: repayable in foreign currencies in $m		M 1-a
repayable in US dollars		M 1-a
Foreign participants: no by country of origin & fields of activity		M 1-a
by fields of activity	All countries	M 1-a
engaged on aid programs & working engaged overseas		M 1-a
specialising in agricultural projects	All countries	M 1-a
atomic energy programs	All countries	M 1-a
educational projects	All countries	M 1-a
housing projects	All countries	M 1-a
industrial projects	All countries	M 1-a
public safety projects	All countries	M 1-a
sanitation projects	All countries	M 1-a
transport projects	All countries	M 1-a
no engaged under university contracts	All countries	M 1-a
Investment guaranties issued by kind of guaranty in $m	All countries	M 1-a
Loans approved as development assistance in $m	OAS member countries	N 16-a
by A.I.D. but administered by other agencies in $m		M 1-a
Loans granted to electric power industry in $m	Latin American countries	U 18-a
Loans & grants & famine relief contributions in $m	USA	F 1-a
Net loan commitments for development purposes in $m	All recipient countries	M 1-a
for supporting assistance in $m	All recipient countries	M 1-a
No of technicians working overseas & directly-employed by A.I.D.	All countries	M 1-a
engaged on aid programs	All countries	M 1-a
indirectly-employed by A.I.D.	All countries	M 1-a
on contract	All countries	M 1-a
Non-regional appropriations: Agency for Cancer Research in $m		M 1-a
Dependent Education Program in $m		M 1-a
International Atomic Energy Organisation in $m		M 1-a
special contributions to Vietnam in $m		M 1-a
UN Children's Fund in $m		M 1-a
UN Development Program in $m		M 1-a
UN Peacekeeping Fund for Cyprus in $m		M 1-a
UN Population Program in $m		M 1-a
UN Relief Agency in $m		M 1-a

	Territorial coverage	Title codes
A.I.D. continued		
Non-regional appropriations: UN Training & Research Program in $m		M 1-a
UN World Food Program in $m		M 1-a
Voluntary Relief Secretariat in $m		M 1-a
World Meteorological Organisation in $m		M 1-a
Sales agreements signed & currency allocations granted in $	All recipient countries	M 1-a
Status of development loans for specific projects in $	Worldwide	M 1-a
Supporting assistance appropriations in $m	All recipient countries	M 1-a
Technical assistance appropriations in $m	All recipient countries	M 1-a

ABACA
    see also   HEMP

	Territorial coverage	Title codes
Disposals ex USA stockpile: tonnage		U 11-a
Export prices in $ per 100 lbs fob	Philippines	U 17-m
of raw hemp at Manila in pesos fob	Philippines	U 32-m
in pesos	Philippines	A 9-a
Exports by value in $ per ton	Philippines	U 32-m
of manila hemp: tonnage	Philippines & Sabah	B 10-a
Unit value of exports of abaca in cents per kg ex main producing countries		U 11-a
Import prices of abaca shipped ex Manila in £ per ton cif at European ports		B 10-m
shipped ex Manila (grade 2) in £ per ton cif at UK ports		B 2-a
(non davao grade 2S) in Frs per kg tax-paid	France	R 2-m
(non davao grade G) in £ per ton cif	UK	R 2-m
Import prices in $	European countries & USA	A 9-a
Imports: tonnage	Main countries	A 5-a
Production: tonnage	Philippines	A 5-a U 11-a
Wholesale prices in $ per ton	Philippines	A 9-a
World production of manila hemp: tonnage	All countries	B 10-a K 4-a

Abalone   see   CRUSTACEANS & MOLLUSCS

ABATTOIRS

	Territorial coverage	Title codes
Labour costs as % of total costs	EEC countries	E 8-a
by status of employees in local currency	EEC countries	E 8-a
for all employees per hr	EEC countries	E 11-a
salaried staff per hr	EEC countries	E 11-a
salaried staff per mth	EEC countries	E 11-a
Labour force: no of salaried staff employed	EEC countries	E 11-a
wage earners & salaried staff employed	EEC countries	E 8-a
wage earners employed	EEC countries	E 11-a
No of hours worked per yr by salaried staff	EEC countries	E 11-a
by wage earners	EEC countries	E 11-a
per yr	EEC countries	E 8-a

ABORTION

	Territorial coverage	Title codes
No of deaths & death rates due to abortion	Main countries	W 1-a
of legally-induced abortions by age of women	All countries	U 14

ABRASIVES, ARTIFICIAL

	Territorial coverage	Title codes
Production by kind: tonnage	Canada & USA	B 15-a
Exports of corundum & carborundum: tonnage	All countries	B 15-a
Imports of corundum & carborundum: tonnage	All countries	B 15-a
World production tonnage of corundum	All countries	N 1-a

ABRASIVES, NATURAL
    see also   GARNET

	Territorial coverage	Title codes
Production by kind: tonnage	All countries	B 15-a
Consumption of bauxite in production of natural abrasives: tonnage	USA	T 4-a
Exports: tonnage	All countries	B 15-a
Imports: tonnage	All countries	B 15-a
Production: pumice & emery powders: tonnage	All countries	U 22-a
pumice in m³: tonnage	W Germany	U 5-a
& trade in corundum: tonnage	All countries	B 15-a
emery powders: tonnage	All countries	B 15-a
pumice: tonnage	All countries	B 15-a
World production of pumice: tonnage	Worldwide excl Communist Bloc	N 4-a

ABSENTEEISM
    see also   SHORT-TIME WORKING

	Territorial coverage	Title codes
As % possible no of working days by cause in coal mining industry	EEC countries	E 33-a
Coal mining: % absence for reasons of sickness or injury	EEC countries	E 15-a
Iron ore mining: due to accidents at work	EEC countries	E 29-a
agreed rest day periods	EEC countries	E 29-a
illness of labour force	EEC countries	E 29-a
lack of orders on mine	EEC countries	E 29-a
lock-outs by management	EEC countries	E 29-a
normal holiday periods	EEC countries	E 29-a
strikes by labour force	EEC countries	E 29-a
technical mining problems	EEC countries	E 29-a
transport difficulties	EEC countries	E 29-a
"unjustified" reasons	EEC countries	E 29-a

	Territorial coverage	Title codes	
Abura see HARDWOOD LOGS			

ACCELERATORS, ELECTRON & PROTON

	Territorial coverage	Title codes	
Imports by value in $m	All countries	U 38-a	
World export trade by value in $m		U 38-a	

ACCEPTANCE HOUSES

	Territorial coverage	Title codes	
Advances to local authorities in $m	All countries	F 5-m	F 6-q
to private sector in $m	All countries	F 5-m	F 6-q
Deposits of non-residents in $m	All countries	F 5-m	F 6-q
Volume of bills discounted	All countries	F 5-m	F 6-q
Investments in $m	All countries	F 5-m	F 6-q

Accessories, Automotive   see   AUTOMOTIVE ACCESSORIES

ACCIDENTS

see also   ACCIDENTS, AIRCRAFT
ACCIDENTS, FARM
ACCIDENTS, INDUSTRIAL
ACCIDENTS, MARITIME
ACCIDENTS, RAILWAY
ACCIDENTS, ROAD
FATALITY RATES
FIRES

	Territorial coverage	Title codes
Claims paid out against personal accident risks in local currency	OAS member countries	N 16-a
Fatality rates in building industry	All countries	L 4-a
No of fatalities through accidents of all kinds	OAS member countries	N 12-a
Premiums paid for personal accident insurance in local currency	OAS member countries	N 16-a

Accidents at Sea   see   ACCIDENTS, MARITIME

ACCIDENTS, AIRCRAFT

	Territorial coverage	Title codes
Claims paid out by insurance companies in local currency	OAS member countries	N 16-a
No of fatalities: aircrew & passengers	Worldwide	S 21-m
of injuries: aircrew & passengers	Worldwide	S 21-m

ACCIDENTS, FARM

	Territorial coverage	Title codes
No of persons killed & injured	Asian, Far East & Australasian countries	U 45-a

ACCIDENTS, INDUSTRIAL

	Territorial coverage	Title codes	
% share of social expenditure	All countries	L 2-a	
Claims paid out by insurance cos in local currency	OAS member countries	N 16-a	
Fatality rates at work	All countries	L 4-a	
in mining & quarrying	All countries	L 4-a	
Frequency by industrial sectors	EEC countries	E 2-a	
Injury rates in iron & steel industry per million man-hrs	EEC countries	E 3-a	
Injury rates per 100 employees by industrial sector	USA	J 2-a	
No of benefits paid out for disability	OAS member countries	N 18-a	
as result of fatalities	OAS member countries	N 18-a	
casualties (injuries & fatalities)	Asian, Far East & Australasian countries	U 45-a	
days work lost in iron & steel industry	EEC countries	E 2-a	E 3-a
fatalities in iron foundries	UK	B 25-a	
manufacturing industry	UK	B 25-a	
mechanical engineering industry	UK	B 25-a	
metal refining industry	UK	B 25-a	
steel industry per million man-hrs	EEC countries	E 3-a	
fatalities per 10,000 employees	W Germany	H 3-a	
non-fatal accidents in steel industry	EEC countries	E 2-a	
per 1m man-hrs of work	W Germany	H 3-a	
reported in iron foundries	UK	B 25-a	
manufacturing industry	UK	B 25-a	
mechanical engineering shops	UK	B 25-a	
metal refining industry	UK	B 25-a	
No of workers & staff insured	All countries	L 2-a	
Social benefit payments made in $	EEC countries	E 3-a	

ACCIDENTS, MARITIME

	Territorial coverage	Title codes
Claims paid out by insurance companies in local currency	OAS member countries	N 16-a
Shipping casualties & no of lives lost	Asian, Far East & Australasian countries	U 45-a
by flag of vessel	Worldwide	S 16-a
vessels & tonnage	Worldwide	S 2-a
cargo ships	Worldwide	D 28-a
due to collisions at sea	Worldwide	S 16-a
damage to equipment	Worldwide	S 16-a
fires & explosions	Worldwide	S 16-a
foundering by gale	Worldwide	S 16-a
strandings	Worldwide	S 16-a
weather damage sustained	Worldwide	S 16-a
no vessels missing (unexplained loss)	Worldwide	S 16-a
tankers: tonnage	Worldwide	D 28-a

ACCIDENTS, RAILWAY

	Territorial coverage	Title codes
Death rates	All countries	L 4-a

	Territorial coverage	Title codes
ACCIDENTS, ROAD		
% occurring during night-time	Main countries	S 24-a
in built-up areas	Main countries	S 24-a
Claims paid out by insurance companies in local currency	OAS member countries	N 16-a
Death rates per 100,000 population	All countries	W 2-m
No of accidents, no injured & no of fatalities	EEC countries	E 3-a
accidents in built-up areas	European countries, Cyprus & USA	U 47-a
injuries & of fatalities	Main countries	R 5-a
accidents involving personal injury	European countries, Cyprus & USA	U 47-a
	Main countries	S 24-a
road accident victims by age groups	EEC countries	E 43-a
accidents in towns & in countryside	EEC countries	E 43-a
fatalities & injured bus & tram users	EEC countries	E 43-a
cyclists	EEC countries	E 43-a
motorcyclists	EEC countries	E 43-a
motorists	EEC countries	E 43-a
pedestrians	EEC countries	E 43-a
truck drivers	EEC countries	E 43-a
& of injuries on roads	Asian, Far East & Australasian countries	U 45-a
in motor vehicle accidents	Main countries	W 1-a
infants 1-4 yrs of age	OAS member countries	N 12-a
on roads	Main countries	S 24-a
	European countries, Cyprus & USA	U 47-a
	OAS member countries	N 12-a
injuries sustained in accidents per million vehicle-km	Main countries	S 24-a
persons injured on roads	Main countries	S 24-a
serious injuries recorded	European countries, Cyprus & USA	U 47-a
ACCIDENTS, ROAD BY AGE		
No of fatalities by age & by kind of vehicle involved	European countries	U 47-a
of injured by age & by kind of vehicle involved	European countries	U 47-a
ACCIDENTS, ROAD BY CATEGORY		
No of fatalities: animal-drawn vehicles	European countries	U 47-a
bus passengers	European countries	U 47-a
car drivers	European countries	U 47-a
motorcyclists	European countries	U 47-a
tram passengers	European countries	U 47-a
transport drivers	European countries	U 47-a
injuries: animal-drawn vehicles	European countries	U 47-a
bus passengers	European countries	U 47-a
car drivers	European countries	U 47-a
motorcyclists	European countries	U 47-a
tram passengers	European countries	U 47-a
transport drivers	European countries	U 47-a
ACCIDENTS, ROAD BY CAUSE		
No of collisions between moving vehicles	European countries	U 47-a
with animals	European countries	U 47-a
obstructions	European countries	U 47-a
parked vehicles	European countries	U 47-a
pedestrians	European countries	U 47-a
accidents due to alcohol intake: car drivers	European countries	U 47-a
cyclists	European countries	U 47-a
lorry drivers	European countries	U 47-a
moped users	European countries	U 47-a
motorcyclists	European countries	U 47-a
pedestrians	European countries	U 47-a
fatalities due to alcohol intake	European countries	U 47-a
injuries due to alcohol intake	European countries	U 47-a
single vehicle accidents	European countries	U 47-a

Accommodation, rented   see   DWELLINGS

Accommodation   see   BOARDING HOUSES
　　　　　　　　　　　DWELLINGS
　　　　　　　　　　　HOTELS
　　　　　　　　　　　HOUSING

ACCOUNTING MACHINES

Production volume	All countries	U 38-a

Accumulators   see   BATTERIES & ACCUMULATORS

Acetaldehyde   see   CHEMICALS, ORGANIC
　　　　　　　　　　CHEMICAL PRODUCTS

Acetate fibres   see   CELLULOSIC FIBRES

Acetate filaments   see   RAYON YARN

Acetate staple   see   CELLULOSIC FIBRES

Acetic acid   see   CHEMICAL PRODUCTS
　　　　　　　　　VINEGAR

	Territorial coverage	Title codes

ACETYLENE
    see also HYDROCARBONS, ALIPHATIC

Consumption for organic synthesis: tonnage	OECD countries	D 5-a
tonnage	OECD countries	D 5-a
Production: tonnage from calcium carbide	European countries, Japan & USA	U 26-a
from coal	OECD countries	D 5-a
from hydrocarbons	European countries, Japan & USA	U 26-a
from oil & natural gas	OECD countries	D 5-a
tonnage	All countries	U 22-a
	European countries, Japan & USA	U 26-a

ACIDS, ORGANIC
    see also HYDROCHLORIC ACID
               PHOSPHORIC ACID
               SULPHURIC ACID

Exports by destination: halogenated acid by value in $	Main countries	U 2-a
nitrated acid by value in $	Main countries	U 2-a
sulfonated acid by value in $	Main countries	U 2-a
nitrosated acid derivatives by value in $	Main countries	U 2-a
polyacids & derivatives by value in $	Main countries	U 2-a
Production: sulphuric, nitric & hydrochloric acids: tonnage	All countries	U 43-a

Acreage subsidies   see SUBSIDIES, AGRICULTURAL

Acrilan   see MAN-MADE FIBRES
               NON-CELLULOSIC FIBRES

Acrylic fibres   see MAN-MADE FIBRES

Acrylic yarn   see YARN, NON-CELLULOSIC

Acrylo-nitrile   see CHEMICALS, ORGANIC

Actuarial tables   see EXPECTATION OF LIFE

Added value of industrial processing   see VALUE ADDED IN MANUFACTURING

Adding machines   see ELECTRONIC CALCULATORS, DESK-TYPE

ADDITIVES, ANTI-KNOCK

Lead consumption in manufacture of anti-knock chemicals: tonnage	European countries & USA	C 12-a

Adhesives   see GUMS, GLUES & SOLUTIONS

Administration, local   see LOCAL AUTHORITIES

ADMINISTRATION, PUBLIC SECTOR

A.I.D. grants to assist public administration in $m	All countries	M 1-a
Contribution to gross domestic product in local currency	African countries	U 44-a
Development aid funds in $m	All recipient countries	M 1-a
Labour force employed (total)	India & New Zealand	U 32-q
by sex (census data)	OAS member countries	N 18

Administrative costs (EEC)   see EXPENDITURE, ADMINISTRATIVE

Administrative staff   see SALARIED STAFF

ADULT EDUCATION

% of adult population attending recreational courses	W European countries	Z 3
vocational courses	W European countries	Z 3
taking correspondence courses	W European countries	Z 3
courses by social classes	W European countries	Z 3
No of establishments of adult education	Latin American countries	J 5-a
teachers & students by sex	Latin American countries	J 5-a
by sex employed in private schools	OAS member countries	N 19-a
in public schools	OAS member countries	N 19-a
employed in special schools by kind	OAS member countries	N 19-a

Advanced technology   see RESEARCH & DEVELOPMENT

ADVERTISING

% changes in expenditure reported	Main countries	Z 4-a
% of expenditure used on specific media	Main countries	Z 4-a
Expenditure as % of gross national product	Main countries	Z 4-a
in $m (estim)	World regions	Z 4-a
per capita (all media) in $	Main countries	Z 4-a
reported (measured media) in $m	Main countries	Z 4-a

ADVERTISING BY MEDIA

Expenditure in newspapers & magazines in $	Main countries	Z 4-a
print in $m	Main countries	Z 4-a
print per capita in $	Main countries	Z 4-a

	Territorial coverage	Title codes

ADVERTISING BY MEDIA, continued
    Expenditure on cinema advertising in $ — Main countries — Z 4-a
        direct advertising in $ — Main countries — Z 4-a
        display at point of sale in $ — Main countries — Z 4-a
        exhibitions & demonstrations in $ — Main countries — Z 4-a
        posters & billboards in $ — Main countries — Z 4-a
        posters on vehicles in $ — Main countries — Z 4-a
        radio per capita in $ — Main countries — Z 4-a
        radio programmes in $ — Main countries — Z 4-a
        reference book advertising in $ — Main countries — Z 4-a
        sales promotion in $ — Main countries — Z 4-a
        subsidised signs in $ — Main countries — Z 4-a
        television in $m — Main countries — Z 4-a
        television per capita in $ — Main countries — Z 4-a
    No of hrs of radio advertising broadcasts — All countries — U 62-a
        television advertising broadcasts — All countries — U 62-a

Advertising tax   see   TAXATION

ADVISORY SERVICES, OFFICIAL
    Assistance given by governments to agriculture in $ — ECE countries — U 34-a

Aeronautical instruments   see   SCIENTIFIC INSTRUMENTS

AEROSPACE EQUIPMENT INDUSTRY
    see also   AIRCRAFT INDUSTRY
    % usage of machine tools installed — EEC countries — B 20-a
    Labour costs as % total costs — EEC countries — E 8-a
        by status in local currency — EEC countries — E 8-a
    Labour force employed by status — EEC countries — E 8-a
    No of hrs worked per yr — EEC countries — E 8-a

AFRICAN DEVELOPMENT BANK
    Net flow of development aid as % of total aid — — M 4-a

AGGLOMERATES
    see also   BLAST FURNACES
                PIG IRON
    % by weight used in ore charge in blast furnaces — Main countries — U 49-a
    Consumption tonnage for pig iron production — All countries — U 49-a

AGRARIAN REFORM
    % of farms expropriated — Chile — U 18-a
    Area of expropriated irrigated farms in ha — Chile — U 18-a
                unirrigated farms in ha — Chile — U 18-a
    No of expropriated farms — Chile — U 18-a

AGRICULTURAL CONTRACTORS
    % farm holdings using contractors — EEC countries — E 3-a
    Value transport equipment hire — W Germany — U 34-a

Agricultural costs   see   FARM COSTS

AGRICULTURAL HOLDINGS
    As % national territory — Latin America — J 5-a
    By size of dairy herds kept — EEC countries — B 1-a
    By size - % distribution by ha areas — EEC countries — B 1-a
        acreage under rubber — Sri Lanka — B 13-a
        intercensal change in ha — OAS member countries — N 13-a
        no in ha size groupings — EEC countries — B 1-a
    No & area in ha: owner-operated — Latin American countries — J 5-a
        rented — Latin American countries — J 5-a
    % by means of traction: mechanised or horses — EEC countries — E 3-a
    % changes in no of holdings farmed by size in ha — EEC countries — B 1-a
    % distribution by form of tenure — OAS member countries — N 13-a
    % farmed by owners or tenant-farmers — EEC countries — E 3-a
    % of total according to no of workers employed — EEC countries — E 3-a
    % processing & packing own produce — EEC countries — E 3-a
    Area of arable land under crops or fallow in ha — Latin American countries — J 5-a
        as % total land area — OAS member countries — N 13-a
    Changes in no of farms by size groups in ha — EEC countries — E 44-a
    No & % of land wooded, farmed or fallow — EEC countries — E 3-a
        & area in ha by kind of tenure — Latin American countries — J 5-a
            ha by size groups — Latin American countries — J 5-a
            ha (world census data) — All countries — A 9-a
            ha by size of farms — EEC countries — E 44-a
            sq km — OAS member countries — N 13-a
        by form of tenure — OAS member countries — N 13-a
        by size & % by size — EEC countries — E 3-a
            intercensal change — OAS member countries — N 13-a

Agricultural implements   see   FARM IMPLEMENTS
                              IMPLEMENTS, MULTI-PURPOSE FARM

Agricultural income   see   FARM INCOME

	Territorial coverage	Title codes
AGRICULTURAL INPUTS		
see also FEEDING STUFFS		
SEEDS		
LIVESTOCK		
FERTILISERS		
Cost of animal feeding stuffs in £m	EEC countries	B 1-a
fertilisers & lime in £m	EEC countries	B 1-a
seeds in £m	EEC countries	B 1-a
Expenditure on gross input in £m	EEC countries	B 1-a
AGRICULTURAL LEVIES		
Receipts from betterment levies on land in £m	UK	E 42-a
Revenue in £m	EEC countries	E 42-a
Soft wheat in $ per ton	EEC countries	U 33-m

Agricultural machinery   see MACHINERY, AGRICULTURAL
                                     TRACTORS, AGRICULTURAL

Agricultural machinery industry   see FARM MACHINERY INDUSTRY

Agricultural mechanisation   see FARM TRACTION

Agricultural price review   see PRICE SUPPORTS

AGRICULTURAL PRODUCTION
    see also FOOD PRODUCTION

	Territorial coverage	Title codes	
As % of gross domestic product	All countries	U 60-a	
Less feed & store cattle - index nos	OECD countries	D 1-a	
Per capita - index nos	African countries	U 44-a	
	Latin American countries	J 5-a	
	Main countries	R 5-a	
	S American countries	U 40-a	
	World regions	U 23-a	U 43-a
% change as component in gross domestic product	All countries	U 60-a	
	S European countries	U 16-a	
% changes	Main developing countries	U 54-a	
% growth rates in food production per capita	All countries	M 6-a	
% growth rates	Developing countries	A 11-a	U 54-a
	E European countries & USSR	U 54-a	
% real growth rates	Main developing countries	M 3-a	
Contribution to gross domestic product	S American countries	U 41-a	
Food & all farm products - index nos	Worldwide	U 43-a	
Gross output by value & consumption	EEC countries	E 44-a	
by value at market prices in $m	ECE countries	U 34-a	
in £m	EEC countries	B 1-a	
Gross output - index nos (value basis)	ECE countries	U 15-a	
Growth rate as % gross domestic product	Developing world regions	A 1	
under economic plan	All countries	A 11-a	
Income distribution at factor cost	S American countries	U 41-a	
Index nos (quantum basis)	Main countries	C 4-a	
	S American countries	U 40-a	
Index nos (volume basis)	EEC countries	E 44-a	
Index nos	African countries	U 44-a	
	All countries	A 9-a	
	Asian, Far East & Australasian countries	U 45-a	
	Asian & Far East countries	U 32-a	
	Developed countries	A 11-a	
	Developing countries	A 11-a	
	EEC countries	B 1-a	
	Latin American countries	J 5-a	
	Main countries	E 3-a	R 5-a
	Main ECAFE countries	U 17-a	
	OAS member countries	N 13-a	
	OECD countries	D 1-a	
	World & world regions	A 1-a	U 23-a
	World economic areas	U 60-a	
	Continents	A 11-a	
Indirect taxes levied on agricultural turnover in $	S American countries	U 41-a	
Labour force employed in farming by status	Main countries	C 28	
Planned & % growth rates in output	E European countries & USSR	U 54-a	
Planned targets for farm output	Small African countries	U 39	

Agricultural productivity   see FARM PRODUCTIVITY

Agricultural products   see COMMODITIES, AGRICULTURAL

Agricultural raw materials   see RAW MATERIALS, AGRICULTURAL

Agricultural subsidies   see SUBSIDIES, AGRICULTURAL

Agricultural technology   see RESEARCH & DEVELOPMENT

Agricultural tractor industry   see FARM MACHINERY INDUSTRY

Agricultural tractors   see TRACTORS, AGRICULTURAL

	Territorial coverage	Title codes

AGRICULTURE

see also AGRARIAN REFORM
AGRICULTURAL HOLDINGS
COLLECTIVE FARMS
COMMODITIES, AGRICULTURAL
DEFICIENCY PAYMENTS
FARM COSTS
FARM SIZES
FARM TENURE
LAND DISTRIBUTION
LAND UTILISATION
LIVESTOCK FARMING
SUBSIDIES, AGRICULTURAL

	Territorial coverage	Title codes	
% change in crop production: main farm products	Latin American countries	U 18-a	
in gross output of crops	E European countries & USSR	U 16-a	
livestock	E European countries	U 16-a	
gross output	E European countries	U 16-a	
	Latin American countries	U 18-a	
in gross value of output - index nos	ECE countries	U 34-a	
in implicit price deflator for agriculture	Developing countries	D 25-a	
% contribution to gross domestic product	AASM countries	E 41-a	
	EEC countries	B 3-a	
	OECD countries	D 1-a	
% contribution to gross product: historical table from 1800 to national income	Main European countries	Z 1-a	
	Developing countries	D 25-a	
% of employed population 14-24 yrs working in agriculture	EEC countries	E 2-a	
% growth in output per capita projected to 1980	Main countries	D 17-a	
of farm labour force	ECAFE countries	U 17-a	
% growth rates in gross domestic product	Developing countries	D 25-a	
% of active population by region employed in agriculture	EEC countries	E 33-a	
over 60 yrs of age employed in agriculture	EEC countries	E 2-a	
employed in agricultural occupations	EEC countries	E 33-a	
	Main countries	M 4-a	
% of farms expropriated under agrarian reform	Chile	U 18-a	
% of government expenditure on farm modernisation	Main countries	R 5-a	
% of married women employed in agricultural occupations	EEC countries	E 2-a	
% of students enrolled studying agriculture	ECAFE countries	U 17	
% share embodied in economic planning for farm investment	All countries	A 11-a	
% share of capital investment overall	E European countries	U 16-a	
A.I.D. grants to promote food production & farming in $m	All recipient countries	M 1-a	
Area of expropriated irrigated holdings in ha	Chile	U 18-a	
unirrigated holdings in ha	Chile	U 18-a	
Capital consumption as % of value of gross output	ECE countries	U 15-a	
Capital equipment: funds available as aid from European Development Fund in $m		D 13-a	
Capital formation as % of gross farm product	EEC countries	B 1-a	
	ECE countries	U 34-a	
as % of gross output	ECE countries	U 34-a	
as % of gross domestic product	EEC countries	B 1-a	
farm buildings as % total farm investment	ECE countries	U 34-a	
farm improvements in local currency	OAS member countries	N 16-a	
as % of total capital investment	ECE countries	U 34-a	
in local currency	E European countries	U 34-a	
incl forestry & fishing in local currency	OAS member countries	N 16-a	
machinery as % of total farm investment	ECE countries	U 34-a	
machinery & equipment in $m	ECE countries	U 34-a	
Capital formation - index nos (value basis)	ECE countries	U 34-a	
Changes in farm labour input - index nos	ECE countries	U 34-a	
Changes in operating expenses in agriculture	ECE countries	U 34-a	
Consumption of electricity in farming in kWh	OECD countries	D 8-a	
fertilisers by kind: tonnage	Main countries	R 5-a	
(nitrogenous): tonnage	Main countries	R 5-a	
(phosphate): tonnage	Main countries	R 5-a	
(potash): tonnage	Main countries	R 5-a	
gas incl forestry in m³	European countries & USA	U 3-a	
materials on farms: tonnage	Czechoslovakia & E Germany	U 34-a	
petroleum products by kind: tonnage	OECD countries	D 31-a	
petroleum products & fuels: tonnage	EEC countries	E 16-q	E 15-a
sulphur compounds: tonnage	OECD countries	D 5-a	
Contribution to gross domestic product as % total	EEC countries	E 32-a	
	All countries	U 23-a	
at factor cost in local currency	African countries	U 44-a	
	Latin American countries	U 18-a	
Cost of electricity, fuel & lubricants in local currency	Hungary & Poland	U 34-a	
feeding stuffs in local currency	Hungary & Poland	U 34-a	
fertilisers in local currency	Hungary & Poland	U 34-a	
maintenance & repairs in local currency	Hungary & Poland	U 34-a	
pesticides in local currency	Hungary & Poland	U 34-a	
Depreciation allowances: changes in value	ECE countries	U 34-a	
in $m	ECE countries	U 34-a	
Depreciation as % of fixed capital formation	ECE countries	U 34-a	
Development aid authorisations in $m	All recipient countries	M 1-a	
Earnings (average) in local currency	All countries	L 4-a	
seasonal workers in local currency	All countries	L 4-a	
Electricity: consumption from own production in kWh	All countries	C 23-a	
from public supply in kWh	All countries	C 23-a	
Employment in farming & % change	EEC countries	E 26-a	
as % total labour force	Main OECD countries	D 24-q	D 1-a

AGRICULTURE, continued

	Territorial coverage	Title codes
Employment in farming by sex & status by areas	EEC countries	E 38-a
farming by sex	OECD countries	D 24-q
farming & forestry incl fishing	EEC countries	E 33-a
farming as % total employed population	EEC countries	E 33-a
incl forestry, fishing & hunting	ECE countries	U 15-a
Employment – index nos	OAS member countries	N 18-a
	OECD countries	D 1-a
Expenditure on electricity & fuel as % value of output	ECE countries	U 34-a
farm improvements under EEC budget	EEC countries	B 3-a
farm maintenance as % value of output	ECE countries	U 34-a
feeding stuffs as % value of output	ECE countries	U 34-a
fertilisers as % value of output	ECE countries	U 34-a
pesticides as % value of output	ECE countries	U 34-a
Farm employment incl forestry	Japan Philippines	U 32-q
Farm taxes levied on sales & turnover taxes	ECE countries	U 34-a
Frequency of accidents at work incl fisheries	EEC countries	E 2-a
Government aid to improve farm infra-structure	ECE countries	U 34-a
Government grants for capital formation	ECE countries	U 34-a
Government expenditure on research into new agricultural methods in $m	EEC countries	E 36-a
Gross fixed capital formation at current prices in $m	ECE countries	U 34-a
	EEC countries	E 32-a
in farm buildings	ECE countries	U 34-a
in machinery & equipment	ECE countries	U 34-a
in £m	EEC countries	B 1-a
Gross fixed capital formation – index nos	ECE countries	U 34-a
Gross income as component in national income in local currency	OAS member countries	N 16-a
Gross output as % gross domestic product	EEC countries	B 1-a
at factor cost in $m	ECE countries	U 34-a
at market prices in $m	ECE countries	U 34-a
Gross output, gross input & value added in £m	EEC countries	B 1-a
Gross output per labour unit – index nos	E European countries	U 34-a
	ECE countries	U 34-a
as % gross output at current prices	ECE countries	U 34-a
domestic product	ECE countries	U 34-a
as component of gross domestic product	Developing countries	D 25-a
at factor cost as % of gross output	ECE countries	U 34-a
in $m	ECE countries	U 34-a
at market prices in $m	ECE countries	U 34-a
changes at market prices in $m	ECE countries	U 34-a
Gross product, depreciation & net product in £m	EEC countries	B 1-a
in local currency	E European countries	U 34-a
incl forestry & fishing in local currency	OAS member countries	N 16-a
per capita in $	Main countries	A 11-a
per farm worker in £m	EEC countries	B 1-a
per labour unit – index nos	E European countries	U 34-a
	ECE countries	U 34-a
IBRD loans granted for farm improvement in $m	OAS member countries	N 16-a
Indirect taxation levied on farming sector	EEC countries	E 44-a
Labour force employed as % total employment by region	EEC countries	E 2-a
by sex at census dates	African countries	U 44-a
	OAS member countries	N 18
by sex	EEC countries	E 18-a
(total)	All countries	L 4-a
	EEC countries	E 18-a
Labour force employed – index nos	Main OECD countries	D 24-q
farm labour on co-operatives	E European countries	U 34-a
hired labour on collectives	E European countries	U 34-a
incl forestry by sex: historical table 1750-1969	Main European countries	Z 1-a
Labour force employed incl forestry, fishing & hunting	OECD countries	D 23-a
incl forestry: no of labourers	AASM countries	E 41-a
no of salaried staff	AASM countries	E 41-a
no of wage earners	AASM countries	E 41-a
Labour force employed: no of state farm workers	E European countries	U 34-a
Labour force employed	OECD countries	D 23-a
Labour input: estim changes – index nos	ECE countries	U 34-a
Loan advances from commercial banks in local currency	OAS member countries	N 16-a
Membership of agricultural co-operative societies	OAS member countries	N 18-a
Net income from farming in £m	EEC countries	B 1-a
Net material product in local currency	USSR	U 34-a
Net product at factor cost as % gross output	ECE countries	U 34-a
at current prices	ECE countries	U 34-a
in $m	ECE countries	U 34-a
at factor cost – index nos	ECE countries	U 34-a
per labour unit – index nos	E European countries	U 34-a
	ECE countries	U 34-a
No employed in farming occupations	OECD countries	D 1-a
No employers, wage earners & salaried staff	OECD countries	D 23-a
of family helpers as % of farm labour force	EEC countries	E 18-a
by sex by areas	EEC countries	E 38-a
full & part-time research workers	All countries	U 62-a
farm workers unemployed	All countries	L 4-a
farm co-operative societies	OAS member countries	N 18-a
farms expropriated under agrarian reform	Chile	U 18-a
hrs worked per week as family help on farms	EEC countries	E 33-a
by self-employed persons by sex	EEC countries	E 33-a
by sex	EEC countries	E 2-a E 18-a
		E 33-a

	Territorial coverage	Title codes
AGRICULTURE, continued		
No of salaried staff as % of labour force	EEC countries	E 2-a
self-employed persons as % of labour force	EEC countries	E 18-a
by sex by areas	EEC countries	E 38-a
students enrolled abroad by origin	All countries	U 64-a
on university courses	OAS member countries	N 19-a
university degrees granted in agricultural subjects	All countries	U 62-a
wage & salary earners as % of labour force	EEC countries	E 18-a
wage earners employed in farm occupations: 14-24 yrs age	EEC countries	E 3-a
in farm occupations: 60 yrs age & over	EEC countries	E 3-a
in farm occupations: by sex by areas	EEC countries	E 18-a E 38-a
Operating expenses at current prices in $	ECE countries	U 34-a
Output, income, value added taxes & subsidies	EEC countries	E 32-a
Planned % growth rates in output	Greece, Portugal, Spain & Turkey	D 17
% increase in crop production	E European countries & USSR	U 16-a
in farm output	E European countries & USSR	U 16-a
in livestock rearing	E European countries & USSR	U 16-a
% relationship between crops & livestock	E European countries	U 16-a
Production by value: crops as % of total output	E European countries	U 34-a
in local currency	E European countries	U 34-a
livestock as % of total output	E European countries	U 34-a
of crops & livestock - index nos (value basis)	ECE countries	U 34-a
tonnage: industrial crops by kind	OAS member countries	N 13-a
Production costs (in detail): banana industry	Main countries	A 15-a
Production targets by specific crops in plan	Small African countries	U 39
Productivity per capita - index nos	ECE countries	U 34-a
Ratio of net capital formation to net product	ECE countries	U 34-a
Unemployment as % of total labour force	Main OECD countries	D 24-q
Wage rates by occupation in local currency	OAS member countries	N 17-a
by sex of farm employee - index nos	W European countries	U 30-a
historical tables from 1770	Main European countries	Z 1-a
Wages by occupation hourly daily monthly in local currency	OAS member countries	N 17-a
cattle minders (hourly & daily) in local currency	OAS member countries	N 17-a
coffee plantation workers in local currency	OAS member countries	N 17-a
farm equipment drivers hourly & daily in local currency	OAS member countries	N 17-a
farm labourers (hourly & daily) in local currency	OAS member countries	N 17-a
milking staff (hourly & daily) in local currency	OAS member countries	N 17-a
paid to farm workers - index nos	EEC countries	E 44-a
sugar cane cutters (hourly & daily) in local currency	OAS member countries	N 17-a
Wages costs for hired labour - index nos	ECE countries	U 34-a
World bank loans & credits granted for farm projects in $m	Worldwide	M 3-a
AGRONOMY		
see also AGRICULTURE		
No of students enrolled on university courses	OAS member countries	N 19-a
Aid see DEVELOPMENT AID		
Aid appropriations see DEVELOPMENT AID		
Air & oil filters see REPLACEMENT PARTS		
AIR CONDITIONING EQUIPMENT		
Exports by destination by value in $m	Main countries	U 9-a
	OECD countries	D 9-a
by value in $m	All countries	U 38-a
by volume	OECD countries	D 9-a
Imports by value in $m	All countries	U 38-a
Production by volume	All countries	U 22-a
World export trade by value in $m	Worldwide	U 38-a
AIR FREIGHT		
Carried in ton-km	Worldwide	R 5-a
	Asian, Far East & Australian countries	U 32-a
incl transit shipments: tonnage	European countries	U 8-a
on scheduled flights: tonnage	Latin American countries	U 40-a
tonnage	EEC countries	E 43-a
Landed & forwarded by regional airports: tonnage	EEC countries	E 38-a
by airports: international freight: tonnage	Worldwide	S 9-a
% change in cargo tonnage carried by domestic airport	UK	S 12-m
Cargo carried in ton-km: domestic flights	OAS member countries	N 15-a
international flights	OAS member countries	N 15-a
on charter by route: tonnage	Worldwide	S 21-a
charter flights by Atlantic routes: tonnage		S 21-m
domestic scheduled IATA flights: tonnage	Worldwide	S 21-a
IATA membership aircraft: tonnage	Worldwide	S 21-a
international routes by each UK airline: tonnage	Worldwide	S 12-m
scheduled flights by Atlantic routes: tonnage		S 21-m
loaded & unloaded at airports: tonnage	AASM countries	E 41-a
	African countries	U 44-a
at domestic airports: tonnage	UK	S 12-m
by airline co: tonnage	Worldwide	S 11-a
off-loaded at US inland airports: tonnage	USA	S 21-m
at US East Coast airports: tonnage	USA	S 21-m
at US West Coast airports: tonnage	USA	S 21-m
Exports of agricultural products by kind: tonnage	European countries	U 8-a

	Territorial coverage	Title codes
AIR FREIGHT, continued		
Exports of chemical products: tonnage	European countries	U 8-a
food products: tonnage	European countries	U 8-a
fresh fruit & vegetables: tonnage	European countries	U 8-a
metals & metal products & light machinery: tonnage	European countries	U 8-a
raw materials: tonnage	European countries	U 8-a
Imports of agricultural products by kind: tonnage	European countries	U 8-a
chemical products: tonnage	European countries	U 8-a
food products: tonnage	European countries	U 8-a
fresh fruit & vegetables: tonnage	European countries	U 8-a
metals & metal products & light machinery: tonnage	European countries	U 8-a
raw materials: tonnage	European countries	U 8-a
Load factors as % of capacity by airline co	Worldwide	S 11-a
Loadings: charter flights by foreign cos at UK airports: tonnage	UK	S 12-m
by UK cos at UK airports: tonnage	UK	S 12-m
domestic flights by airport: tonnage	Worldwide	S 9-m
international flights by airport: tonnage	Worldwide	S 9-m
scheduled flights by airport: tonnage	Worldwide	S 9-m
scheduled services by foreign cos at UK airports: tonnage	UK	S 12-m
by UK cos at UK airports: tonnage	UK	S 12-m
Mail freight in ton-km: domestic flights	OAS member countries	N 15-a
international flights	OAS member countries	N 15-a
No of charter cargo flights by Atlantic routes		S 21-m
of scheduled cargo flights by Atlantic routes		S 21-m
of ton-km carried		R 5-a
of ton-km carried on international routes by UK airlines		S 12-m
Passengers flown in ton-km: domestic flights	OAS member countries	N 15-a
international flights	OAS member countries	N 15-a
Revenue of IATA airline cos in $m	Worldwide	S 21-a
Ton-km available by scheduled airlines: domestic flights	Worldwide	S 7-m
international flights	Worldwide	S 7-m
Ton-km carried: historical tables from 1920	Main European countries	Z 1-a
Ton-km flown by scheduled airlines: domestic flights	Worldwide	S 7-m
international flights	Worldwide	S 7-m
by non-scheduled airlines: domestic flights	Worldwide	S 10-a
international flights	Worldwide	S 10-a
Ton-km performance by scheduled airlines: domestic flights	Worldwide	S 7-m
international flights	Worldwide	S 7-m
Ton-km used for freight transport by UK airlines	UK	S 12-m
mail transport by UK airlines	UK	S 12-m
passenger transport by UK airlines	UK	S 12-m
Tonnage of goods carried on international scheduled flights	Worldwide	S 21-a
Traffic by airline co incl mail by route: tonnage	Worldwide	S 8-m
Unloadings: charter flights by foreign cos at UK airports	UK	S 12-m
charter flights by UK cos at UK airports	UK	S 12-m
domestic flights by airport: tonnage	Worldwide	S 9-m
international flights by airport: tonnage		S 9-m
scheduled services by foreign cos at UK airports: tonnage	UK	S 12-m
scheduled services by UK cos at UK airports: tonnage	UK	S 12-m
unscheduled flights by airport: tonnage	Worldwide	S 9-m
Weight-load factors for non-scheduled airlines: domestic flights		S 10-a
international flights		S 10-a

Air freight co-efficients   see   AIR TRANSPORT

AIR MAIL

Carried in ton-km	Worldwide	R 5-a
	Main countries	R 5-a
Loaded & unloaded: overseas mail by airports: tonnage	Worldwide	S 9-a
all mail: tonnage	Worldwide	S 9-a
Freight carried on charter by routes across Atlantic: tonnage		S 21-a
in ton-km: domestic flights	OAS member countries	N 15-a
international flights	OAS member countries	N 15-a
Loadings by airline cos: tonnage	Worldwide	S 11-a
domestic flights by airport: tonnage	Worldwide	S 9-m
international flights by airport: tonnage	Worldwide	S 9-m
scheduled flights by airport: tonnage	Worldwide	S 9-m
Ton-km carried by scheduled airlines: domestic flights	Worldwide	S 7-m
international flights	Worldwide	S 7-m
on international routes by each UK airline	UK	S 12-m
Tonnage carried by Atlantic routes (East and Westbound)		S 21-m
on IATA membership aircraft	Worldwide	S 21-a
on scheduled services by UK airlines	UK	S 12-m
Unloadings: domestic flights by airport: tonnage	Worldwide	S 9-m
international flights by airport: tonnage	Worldwide	S 9-m
unscheduled flights by airport: tonnage	Worldwide	S 9-m

Air passenger co-efficients   see   AIR TRANSPORT

AIR PASSENGER TRAFFIC
    see also   TOURISM

In passenger-km	Worldwide	R 5-a
In ton-km: domestic flights	OAS member countries	N 15-a
international flights	OAS member countries	N 15-a
% seat-km used for tours as % availability on UK airlines	UK	S 12-m
Excess baggage carried by airline in ton-km	Worldwide	S 7-m

	Territorial coverage	Title codes	
AIR PASSENGER TRAFFIC, continued			
Landings & departures at regional airports	EEC countries	E 38-a	
at main airports	EEC countries	E 43-a	
	AASM countries	E 41-a	
	African countries	U 44-a	
Load factors as % of total on IATA aircraft	Worldwide	S 21-a	
by airline companies by routes		S 8-m	
non-scheduled services of UK airlines		S 12-m	
scheduled services by route		S 21-a	
No aircraft-hrs flown: international routes	UK	S 12-m	
aircraft-km flown: international routes	UK	S 12-m	
No carried by scheduled airlines: all flights	Worldwide	S 7-m	
domestic flights	Worldwide	S 7-m	
international flights	Worldwide	S 7-m	
on charter flights by Atlantic routes		S 21-a	
on domestic scheduled flights	Worldwide	S 21-a	
No carried: economy class on domestic flights	UK	S 12-m	
on international flights	UK	S 12-m	
first class on domestic flights	UK	S 12-m	
on international flights	UK	S 12-m	
international scheduled flights	Worldwide	S 21-a	
N Atlantic route on IATA charter flights		D 47-a	
N Atlantic route: first class		D 47-a	
economy class		D 47-a	
non-scheduled domestic flights	UK	S 12-m	
international flights	UK	S 12-m	
regular services: historical table from 1920	Main European countries	Z 1-a	
scheduled flights by Atlantic routes		S 21-m	
No charter flights from UK airports by foreign airlines	UK	S 12-m	
by UK airlines	UK	S 12-m	
on Atlantic routes		S 21-a	
No disembarked at Canadian airports	Canada	S 21-a	
domestic flights by airport	Worldwide	S 9-m	
international flights by airport	Worldwide	S 9-m	S 9-a
scheduled flights by airport	Worldwide	S 9-m	
US airports (inland)	USA	S 21-m	
US East Coast airports	USA	S 21-m	
US West Coast airports	USA	S 21-m	
unscheduled flights by airport	Worldwide	S 9-m	
No embarked & disembarked by airport	Worldwide	S 9-a	
by airports: international traffic	Worldwide	S 9-a	
domestic flights by airport	Worldwide	S 9-m	
international flights by airport	Worldwide	S 9-m	
scheduled flights by airport	Worldwide	S 9-m	
unscheduled flights by airport	Worldwide	S 9-m	
No flights made on charter by route		S 21-a	
of passengers in transit	African countries	U 44-a	
of passenger-km flown: domestic flights	Worldwide	S 21-a	
international flights	Worldwide	S 21-a	
IATA aircraft	Worldwide	S 21-a	
total	Main countries	R 5-a	
by scheduled airlines	Worldwide	S 7-m	
No of passengers as % of seat availability	UK	S 12-m	
by countries of departure	Worldwide	S 12-m	
by domestic routes of UK airlines		S 12-m	
by route on charter flights of UK airlines		S 21-a	
on non-scheduled flights by UK airlines		S 12-m	
international routes by UK airlines from UK airports		S 12-m	
on scheduled flights by foreign airlines from UK airports		S 12-m	
by UK airlines from UK airports		S 12-m	
on unscheduled flights by foreign airlines from UK airports		S 12-m	
by UK airlines from UK airports		S 12-m	
on scheduled flights by routes	Worldwide	S 12-m	
per aircraft (average) on IATA aircraft	Worldwide	S 21-a	
of scheduled flights by Atlantic routes		S 21-m	
of seat-km available: scheduled airlines	Worldwide	S 7-m	
international routes	Worldwide	S 12-m	
scheduled services	UK	S 12-m	
used as % of availability	UK	S 12-m	
available	UK	S 12-m	
used: international routes	UK	S 12-m	
No of stage flights: international routes	UK	S 12-m	
No terminal passengers: British airlines at UK airports		S 12-m	
domestic flights at UK airports		S 12-m	
foreign airlines at UK airports		S 12-m	
international flights at UK airports		S 12-m	
ton-km available: international routes at UK airports		S 12-m	
ton-km used as % of availability on international routes		S 12-m	
ton-km used: international routes from UK airports		S 12-m	
transit passengers: foreign airlines at UK airports		S 12-m	
Passenger load factors by scheduled airlines	Worldwide	S 7-m	
Payload capacity by airline cos by routes	Worldwide	S 8-m	
Revenue of IATA airline cos in $m	Worldwide	S 21-a	
Seat-km available for tours by UK airlines	UK	S 12-m	
used for tours by UK airlines	UK	S 12-m	

	Territorial coverage	Title codes
AIR PASSENGER TRAFFIC, continued		
Ton-km available: advance charters on UK airlines	UK	S 12-m
for tours as % total	UK	S 12-m
by UK airlines	UK	S 12-m
performance by scheduled airlines	Worldwide	S 7-m
Transport capacity on N Atlantic route		D 47-a
AIR PASSENGER TRAFFIC, DOMESTIC		
No of arrivals & departures by airport	Worldwide	D 47-a
AIR PASSENGER TRAFFIC, INTERNATIONAL		
No of arrivals & departures by airport	Worldwide	D 47-a
AIR PASSENGER TRAFFIC BY AIRLINE		
No carried on scheduled & unscheduled flights	Worldwide	S 21-a
No carried	Worldwide	S 11-a
AIR PASSENGER TRAFFIC BY ROUTES		
No of passengers carried: economy class	Worldwide	S 21-a
first class	Worldwide	S 21-a
tourist class	Worldwide	S 21-a
to & from UK by airline	UK	S 12-m
% change to & from UK airports	UK	S 12-m
AIR POLLUTION		
IBRD loans approved for research in $m	OAS member countries	N 16-a
AIR ROUTE NETWORKS		
Length scheduled flight routes by airline in km		S 21-a
AIR TRAFFIC		
see also AIR PASSENGER TRAFFIC		
CIVIL AVIATION		
Aircraft movement: by airports	Worldwide	S 9-a
international routes by airports	Worldwide	S 9-a
Basic traffic coefficients on scheduled services	Worldwide	S 11-a
Departures by scheduled airlines: domestic flights	Worldwide	S 7-m S 10-a
international flights	Worldwide	S 7-m S 10-a
Distances of stage flights in km: non-scheduled services	Worldwide	S 12-m
scheduled services	Worldwide	S 12-m
Freight carried on IATA aircraft: tonnage	Worldwide	S 21-a
km flown by scheduled airlines: domestic flights	Worldwide	S 7-m S 10-a
international flights	Worldwide	S 7-m S 10-a
Mail freight carried on IATA aircraft: tonnage	Worldwide	S 21-a
No aircraft departures by IATA aircraft: scheduled services	Worldwide	S 21-a
unscheduled services	Worldwide	S 21-a
scheduled flights by airport	Worldwide	S 9-m
unscheduled flights by airport	Worldwide	S 9-m
non-scheduled airlines: domestic flights	Worldwide	S 10-a
international flights	Worldwide	S 10-a
domestic flights by airport	Worldwide	S 9-m
international flights by airport	Worldwide	S 9-m
scheduled flights by airport	Worldwide	S 9-m
unscheduled flights by airport	Worldwide	S 9-m
No flights by Atlantic routes (East & Westward)		S 21-m
No hrs flown by IATA aircraft (domestic & international routes)	Worldwide	S 21-a
scheduled services	Worldwide	S 21-a
unscheduled services	Worldwide	S 21-a
non-scheduled airlines: domestic flights	Worldwide	S 10-a
international flights	Worldwide	S 10-a
scheduled airlines: domestic flights	Worldwide	S 7-m S 10-a
international flights	Worldwide	S 7-m S 10-a
No km by stages of service (airport to airport)	Worldwide	S 8-m
No km flown by IATA aircraft: scheduled services	Worldwide	S 21-a
unscheduled services	Worldwide	S 21-a
domestic & international routes	Worldwide	S 21-a
No of aircraft movements at each domestic airport	UK	S 12-m
No of aircraft-km flown: non-scheduled services by UK airlines	UK	S 12-m
scheduled services by UK airlines	UK	S 12-m
No of stage flights: non-scheduled services of UK airlines	UK	S 12-m
No passengers carried by IATA aircraft	Worldwide	S 21-a
per IATA aircraft (average)	Worldwide	S 21-a
seat-km available on IATA aircraft	Worldwide	S 21-a
ton-km carried (incl baggage) on IATA aircraft	Worldwide	S 21-a
ton-km of excess baggage carried on IATA aircraft	Worldwide	S 21-a
Non-scheduled airlines: domestic flights in km	Worldwide	S 10-a
international flights in km	Worldwide	S 10-a
Passenger load factors as % total on IATA aircraft	Worldwide	S 21-a
Passenger-km flown by IATA aircraft	Worldwide	S 21-a
by non-scheduled airlines: domestic routes	Worldwide	S 10-a
international routes	Worldwide	S 10-a
by scheduled airlines: domestic routes	Worldwide	S 10-a
Passengers freight: scheduled services	Latin American countries	J 5-a
Seating capacity by Atlantic routes: economy class		S 21-m
first class		S 21-m

	Territorial coverage	Title codes

AIR TRAFFIC, continued
    Volume of traffic in ton-km (incl mail)

	ECE countries	U 15-a
	Latin American countries	U 40-a

AIR TRAFFIC BY AIRLINE
    No passenger seats available by routes   Worldwide   S 8-m
        passengers carried by routes   Worldwide   S 8-m
    Passenger load factors by routes   Worldwide   S 8-m

AIR TRAFFIC BY ROUTE
    No scheduled cargo flights   Worldwide   S 21-a
        passenger flights: economy class   Worldwide   S 21-a
                first class   Worldwide   S 21-a
                mixed classes   Worldwide   S 21-a
                tourist class   Worldwide   S 21-a
    Seating capacity: economy class   Worldwide   S 21-a
              first class   Worldwide   S 21-a
              tourist class   Worldwide   S 21-a

AIR TRANSPORT
        see also   AIR FREIGHT
                      AIR MAIL
                      AIR PASSENGER TRAFFIC
                      AIRLINE COMPANIES
                      AIRPORTS
                      CIVIL AVIATION

Cargo co-efficients as % usage of capacity	OAS member countries	N 15-a
Cargo uplifted in ton-km	OAS member countries	N 15-a
non-scheduled services by airport	UK	S 12-m
Consumption of aviation fuel: tonnage	EEC countries	E 14-a
of petroleum products by kind: tonnage	OECD countries	D 31-a
tonnage	EEC countries	E 16-q E 14-a
		E 15-a
Hrs of flight recorded in km: domestic traffic	OAS member countries	N 15-a
international traffic	OAS member countries	N 15-a
Length of air routes of national airlines in km	EEC countries	E 43-a
Licence operations of classes 2-7: domestic flights	UK	S 12-m
international flights	UK	S 12-m
tour charter services by airline co	UK	S 12-m
Movements: charter flights by British operators from UK airports		S 12-m
by foreign operators from UK airports		S 12-m
scheduled flights by British operators from UK airports		S 12-m
by foreign operators from UK airports		S 12-m
No of aircraft by type operated commercially by each airline co	Worldwide	S 5-a
aircraft-hrs flown: non-scheduled services by UK airlines		S 12-m
aircraft-km flown: non-scheduled services by UK airlines		S 12-m
cargo ton-km available	OAS member countries	N 15-a
flight & ground staff employed by national airlines	EEC countries	E 43-a
landings & departures of aircraft	EEC countries	E 43-a
diverted to UK domestic airports		S 12-m
passenger arrivals & departures at airports	EEC countries	E 43-a
passenger-km flown	OAS member countries	N 15-a
passengers carried: domestic flights	OAS member countries	N 15-a
international flights	OAS member countries	N 15-a
national airlines	EEC countries	E 43-a
non-scheduled services	UK	S 12-m
No seat-km available: non-scheduled services of UK airlines		S 12-m
No seat-km available	OAS member countries	N 15-a
used as % of no available on non-scheduled services		
of UK airlines		S 12-m
non-scheduled services by airport	UK	S 12-m
stage flights: non-scheduled services	UK	S 12-m
ton-km available: non-scheduled services of UK airlines		S 12-m
scheduled services of UK airlines		S 12-m
ton-km used: non-scheduled services by airport	UK	S 12-m
Passenger co-efficients as % usage of capacity	OAS member countries	N 15-a
Postal freight: tonnage	EEC countries	E 43-a

AIRCRAFT

% of world exports shipped to developed countries		U 38-a
developing countries		U 38-a
Exports by destination by value in $m	Main countries	U 9-a
by value in $m	All countries	U 38-a
(incl engines & parts) by value in $m	OECD countries	D 9-a
(incl parts) by NIMEXE classes: no & value in $m	All countries	E 20-a
by SITC classes: no & value in $m	All countries	U 50-a U 59-a
Imports by value in $m	All countries	U 38-a
(incl parts) by NIMEXE classes: no & value in $m	All countries	E 20-a
by SITC classes: no & value in $m	All countries	U 50-a U 59-a
Labour costs of production per hr (incl staff)	EEC countries	E 2-a
Load capacity available per plane in kg by airline	Worldwide	S 11-a
No of arrivals & departures at main airports	EEC countries	E 43-a
of commercially-operated aircraft by type in service	Countries of registration	S 5-a
by type, no engines & weight of aircraft in commercial operation	Worldwide	S 5-a

	Territorial coverage	Title codes
AIRCRAFT, continued		
No of departures by 2, 3 or 4-engined turbo-jets of IATA airlines	Worldwide	S 21-q
by piston-engined aircraft of IATA airlines	Worldwide	S 21-q
by turbo-prop-type aircraft of IATA airlines	Worldwide	S 21-q
No of flights (commercial) by domestic airport	UK	S 12-m
for local pleasure by domestic airport	UK	S 12-m
for test & training by domestic airport	UK	S 12-m
military planes by domestic airport	UK	S 12-m
non-commercial private aircraft by aero clubs by domestic airport	UK	S 12-m
non-commercial private planes by domestic airport	UK	S 12-m
of aircraft on charter by domestic airport	UK	S 12-m
No of hrs flown by 2, 3 or 4-engined turbo-jets of IATA airlines	Worldwide	S 21-q
by piston-engined aircraft of IATA airlines	Worldwide	S 21-q
by turbo-prop-type aircraft of IATA airlines	Worldwide	S 21-q
non-scheduled services by airline		S 11-a
scheduled services by airline		S 11-a
No in commercial use by airline	Country of registration	S 11-a
by manufacturer & identification nos	Worldwide	S 5-a
of multi-engined aircraft owned by private airlines	Worldwide	S 10-a
of km flown: non-scheduled services by airline	Worldwide	S 11-a
scheduled services by airline	Worldwide	S 11-a
operated by IATA airlines by type of aircraft	Worldwide	S 21-q
by national airlines by type of engine	EEC countries	E 43-a
of seats available per aircraft operated by each airline	Worldwide	S 11-a
of single-engined planes owned by private airlines	Worldwide	S 10-a
of operations of each IATA airline: domestic flights	Worldwide	S 21-a
international flights	Worldwide	S 21-a
scheduled flights	Worldwide	S 21-a
unscheduled flights	Worldwide	S 21-a
Production volume of cargo & passenger aircraft	All countries	U 22-a U 38-a
Registrations of aircraft by type, make & model	Country of registration	S 5-a
Size of operating fleets of IATA membership		S 21-a
Utilisation data: cargo load in kg by airline	Worldwide	S 11-a
distance flown per hr by airline	Worldwide	S 11-a
mail load by airline in kg	Worldwide	S 11-a
no of passengers carried per aircraft by airline co	Worldwide	S 11-a
passenger load by airline in kg	Worldwide	S 11-a
proportion of seats sold by airline	Worldwide	S 11-a
Value added in manufacture in $m	OECD countries	D 9-a
World export trade in $m		U 38-a
AIRCRAFT BY TYPE		
Exports by destination by SITC classes by value in $m	Main countries	D 2-q
by tonnage & value in $m	OECD countries	D 3-a2
incl parts by CST classes: tonnage & value in $m	EEC countries	E 48-a
Imports by source by SITC classes by value in $m	Main countries	D 2-q
by tonnage & value in $m	OECD countries	D 3-a2
by CST classes by source: tonnage & value in $m	EEC countries	E 21-a
Maximum take-off weight: tonnage by type of aircraft	Worldwide	S 10-a S 11-a
acquired & sold	Country of registration	S 11-a
in fleet: individual airlines	Worldwide	S 11-a
in service owned by UK airlines	UK	S 12-m
by each UK airline	UK	S 12-m
owned by each airline	Worldwide	S 11-a
used by airline cos by flight stages	Worldwide	S 8-m
of aircraft-km flown by UK airlines	UK	S 12-m
by each UK airline	UK	S 12-m
cargo stage flights by UK airlines	UK	S 12-m
by each UK airline	UK	S 12-m
cargo-hrs flown by each UK airline	UK	S 12-m
departures & % of total departures: IATA companies	Worldwide	S 21-q
per yr by airlines	Worldwide	S 11-a
hrs flown & % of total hrs flown: IATA companies	Worldwide	S 21-q
per yr & per day by airline	Worldwide	S 11-a
installed passenger seats in aircraft owned by each airline	Worldwide	S 11-a
passenger stage flights by UK airlines	UK	S 12-m
by each UK airline	UK	S 12-m
passenger-hrs flown by UK airlines	UK	S 12-m
passenger-km flown by UK airlines	UK	S 12-m
by each UK airline	UK	S 12-m
passengers carried by UK airlines	UK	S 12-m
by each UK airline	UK	S 12-m
Operating IATA fleet by make & type	Worldwide	S 21-a
Utilisation per aircraft by each UK airline in hrs	UK	S 12-m
per day in hrs	UK	S 12-m
AIRCRAFT, PISTON-ENGINED		
No of aircraft-hrs flown by airlines	Worldwide	S 11-a
chartered by each airline	Worldwide	S 11-a
operated by commercial air transport cos	Worldwide	S 5-a
IATA cos by type of aircraft	Worldwide	S 21-a
non-scheduled airlines	Worldwide	S 10-a
owned by each airline	Worldwide	S 11-a
AIRCRAFT, ROTARY-WING		
No of aircraft operated by commercial air transport cos	Worldwide	S 5-a

	Territorial coverage	Title codes
AIRCRAFT, TURBO-JET		
No of aircraft-hrs flown by airlines	Worldwide	S 11-a
of aircraft chartered by each airline	Worldwide	S 11-a
operated by commercial air transport cos	Worldwide	S 5-a
IATA cos by type	Worldwide	S 21-a
non-scheduled airlines	Worldwide	S 10-a
owned by each airline	Worldwide	S 11-a
AIRCRAFT, TURBO-PROP		
No of aircraft-hrs flown by airlines	Worldwide	S 11-a
chartered by each airline	Worldwide	S 11-a
operated by commercial air transport cos	Worldwide	S 5-a
by non-scheduled airlines	Worldwide	S 10-a
by type by IATA cos	Worldwide	S 21-a
owned by each airline	Worldwide	S 11-a
Aircraft accidents see ACCIDENTS, AIRCRAFT		
AIRCRAFT CO-EFFICIENTS		
see also AIR PASSENGER TRAFFIC		
AIR TRANSPORT		
Average per aircraft: capacity in seats per aircraft		S 7-m
capacity in seats per flight		S 7-m
no of passengers carried		S 7-m
no of seats available		S 7-m
payload capacity: tonnage		S 7-m
payload: tonnage		S 7-m
speed in km per hr		S 7-m
stage distances in km		S 7-m
Average per passenger: no km flown		S 7-m
weight in kg		S 12-m
Cargo uplifted by each UK airline: tonnage		S 12-m
of aircraft-hrs flown by each UK airline		S 12-m
aircraft-km flown by each UK airline		S 12-m
passengers carried: each UK airline		S 12-m
seat-km available: each UK airline		S 12-m
used: each UK airline		S 12-m
stage flights: each UK airline		S 12-m
ton-km available: each UK airline		S 12-m
used as % of availability: each UK airline		S 12-m
each UK airline		S 12-m
for cargo: each UK airline		S 12-m
mail: each UK airline		S 12-m
passengers: each UK airline		S 7-m
Weight-load factors: domestic flights		S 7-m
international flights		S 7-m
AIRCRAFT ENGINES		
Exports by destination by value in $m	Main countries	U 9-a
by value in $m	All countries	U 38-a
Imports by value in $m	All countries	U 38-a
Production volume of engines for aircraft	All countries	U 22-a U 38-a
World export trade by value in $m		U 38-a
AIRCRAFT INDUSTRY		
see also AEROSPACE EQUIPMENT INDUSTRY		
Labour costs: salaried staff per mth	EEC countries	E 11-a
all employees per hr	EEC countries	E 11-a
wage earners per hr	EEC countries	E 11-a
Labour force: no of salaried staff employed	EEC countries	E 11-a
wage earners employed	EEC countries	E 25-a
No of hrs worked per wk by area	Main countries	R 3-a
per wk	EEC countries	E 11-a
per yr: salaried staff	EEC countries	E 11-a
wage earners	EEC countries	E 25-a2
Wage rates in local currency per hr	Main countries	R 3-m
by sex in local currency per hr		
AIRCRAFT PERSONNEL		
see also AIRLINE PERSONNEL		
No of cabin attendants employed by airlines	Worldwide	S 11-a
cockpit personnel employed by airlines	Worldwide	S 11-a
employees by occupation by airlines	Worldwide	S 11-a
maintenance staff employed by airlines	Worldwide	S 11-a
pilots & co-pilots employed by airlines	Worldwide	S 11-a
Salary per mth: cabin attendants by airline	Worldwide	S 11-a
cockpit personnel by airline	Worldwide	S 11-a
pilots & co-pilots by airline	Worldwide	S 11-a
Aircraft tyres see TYRES, AIRCRAFT		
AIRLINE COMPANIES		
% change in ton-km capacity: scheduled flights of UK airlines	UK	S 12-a
unscheduled flights of UK airlines	UK	S 12-a

AIRLINE COMPANIES, continued	Territorial coverage	Title codes	
% of scheduled peak traffic utilised	Worldwide	S 21-a	
unscheduled peak traffic utilised	Worldwide	S 21-a	
% of ton-km capacity used by UK airlines	UK	S 12-a	
% weight-load factors on scheduled services	Worldwide	S 21-a	
Air mail freight carried in tons-km	Worldwide	R 5-a	
Assets & liabilities (in detail) by airline in $ & local currency	Worldwide	S 6-a	
Assets & deferred charges in $ & local currency	Worldwide	S 6-a	
ground eqpt (after depreciation) in $ & local currency	Worldwide	S 6-a	
investment in affiliated airlines in $ & local currency	Worldwide	S 6-a	
land owned by value in $ & local currency	Worldwide	S 6-a	
in $ & local currency	Worldwide	S 6-a	
Capacity of UK airlines in ton-km	UK	S 12-a	
Costs: aircraft fuel in cents per ton-km	Worldwide	S 6-a	
aircraft maintenance in cents per ton-km	Worldwide	S 6-a	
crew training in cents per ton-km	Worldwide	S 6-a	
depreciation of eqpt in cents per ton-km	Worldwide	S 6-a	
eqpt rental charges in cents per ton-km	Worldwide	S 6-a	
flight insurance in cents per ton-km	Worldwide	S 6-a	
general administration in cents per ton-km	Worldwide	S 6-a	
landing & departure fees in cents per ton-km	Worldwide	S 6-a	
passenger services in cents per ton-km	Worldwide	S 6-a	
salaries of flight crew in cents per ton-km	Worldwide	S 6-a	
ticket sales & promotion expenses in cents per ton-km	Worldwide	S 6-a	
Earnings (unappropriated & retained) in $ & local currency	Worldwide	S 6-a	
Employment: no of cabin attendants employed	Worldwide	S 21-a	
cockpit personnel employed	Worldwide	S 21-a	
maintenance personnel employed	Worldwide	S 21-a	
pilots & co-pilots employed	Worldwide	S 21-a	
traffic & sales personnel employed	Worldwide	S 21-a	
total labour force of IATA airlines	Worldwide	S 21-a	
Freight carried in tons-km	Worldwide	R 5-a	
Length of route network on scheduled services in km	Worldwide	S 21-a	
Liabilities: advances from affiliates in $ & local currency	Worldwide	S 6-a	
capital stock value in $ & local currency	Worldwide	S 6-a	
deferred credits in $ & local currency	Worldwide	S 6-a	
long-term debts in $ & local currency	Worldwide	S 6-a	
operating reserves in $ & local currency	Worldwide	S 6-a	
unearned transport revenue in $ & local currency	Worldwide	S 6-a	
in $ & local currency	Worldwide	S 6-a	
Names of largest US cos & % change in turnover	USA	H 1	
labour force employed	USA	H 1	
net profits or loss in $m	USA	H 1	
turnover in $m	USA	H 1	
No of aircraft departures: scheduled services	Worldwide	S 21-a	
unscheduled services	Worldwide	S 21-a	
of IATA airlines flying intra-European routes		S 21-a	
mid-Atlantic route		S 21-a	
north Atlantic route		S 21-a	
south Atlantic route		S 21-a	
hrs flown: scheduled services	Worldwide	S 21-a	
unscheduled services	Worldwide	S 21-a	
km flown: scheduled services of IATA airlines	Worldwide	S 21-a	
unscheduled services of IATA airlines	Worldwide	S 21-a	
km flown	Main countries	R 5-a	
	Worldwide	R 5-a	
passenger-km flown: scheduled services	Worldwide	R 5-a	S 21-a
passengers carried: scheduled services	Worldwide	S 21-a	
seat-km available: scheduled services	Worldwide	S 21-a	
staff employed by occupation by IATA airlines	Worldwide	S 21-a	
ton-km available on unscheduled services	Worldwide	S 21-a	
ton-km of performance: scheduled services	Worldwide	S 21-a	
unscheduled services	Worldwide	S 21-a	
Operating expenses: administrative costs in $m	Worldwide	S 21-a	
by airline in $ per ton-km (in detail)	Worldwide	S 6-a	
by kind of IATA aircraft in $m	Worldwide	S 21-a	
depreciation of eqpt in $m	Worldwide	S 11-a	S 21-a
flight operations in $m	Worldwide	S 11-a	S 21-a
ground costs in $m	Worldwide	S 21-a	
maintenance & overhaul expenses in $m	Worldwide	S 11-a	S 21-a
passenger services in $m	Worldwide	S 21-a	
sales promotion expenses in $m	Worldwide	S 21-a	
ticketing costs in $m	Worldwide	S 21-a	
total in $m	Worldwide	S 11-a	
Operating revenue in $m	Worldwide	S 11-a	
Profit & loss in $m	Worldwide	S 11-a	
Profits (after tax) in $m	Worldwide	S 6-a	
Revenue: air mail freight earnings per ton-km		S 6-a	
cargo freight earnings in cents per ton-km		S 6-a	
excess baggage charges in cents per ton-km		S 6-a	
express freight earnings in cents per ton-km		S 6-a	
on cargo & freight traffic in $m		S 21-a	
mail freight of IATA airlines in $m	Worldwide	S 21-a	
passenger fares in cents per ton-km	Worldwide	S 6-a	
of IATA airlines in $m	Worldwide	S 21-a	
scheduled services in cents per ton-km	Worldwide	S 6-a	
of IATA airlines in $m	Worldwide	S 21-a	
Weight-load factors: domestic flights	Worldwide	S 7-m	
international flights	Worldwide	S 7-m	

	Territorial coverage	Title codes
AIRLINE COMPANIES, NON-SCHEDULED		
Aircraft-km flown by airline company	Worldwide	S 10-a
Assets of each airline in $m	Worldwide	S 10-a
Capital & retained earning of each airline in $m	Worldwide	S 10-a
Flight eqpt owned less depreciation by value in $m	Worldwide	S 10-a
Liabilities & long-term debt in $m	Worldwide	S 10-a
No of aircraft owned by each airline	Worldwide	S 10-a
departures: domestic flights	Worldwide	S 10-a
international flights	Worldwide	S 10-a
hrs flown by airline	Worldwide	S 10-a
domestic flights	Worldwide	S 10-a
international flights	Worldwide	S 10-a
km flown: domestic flights	Worldwide	S 10-a
international flights	Worldwide	S 10-a
passenger-km flown: domestic flights	Worldwide	S 10-a
international flights	Worldwide	S 10-a
Operating revenue of each airline in $m	Worldwide	S 10-a
Traffic carried by each airline in ton-km	Worldwide	S 10-a
Weight-load factors: domestic flights	Worldwide	S 10-a
international flights	Worldwide	S 10-a

Airline company profits   see   PROFITS

Airline costs   see   OPERATING COSTS, AIRLINE

AIRLINE PERSONNEL

   see also   AIRCRAFT PERSONNEL

	Territorial coverage	Title codes
Costs: crew training in cents per ton-km	Worldwide	S 6-a
flight crew salaries in cents per ton-km	Worldwide	S 6-a
No employed by each airline	Worldwide	S 11-a
Salary (average): maintenance staff by airline	Worldwide	S 11-a
traffic controllers by airline	Worldwide	S 11-a

Airline staff   see   AIRCRAFT PERSONNEL
                             AIRLINE PERSONNEL

Airport traffic   see   AIR FREIGHT
                          AIR MAIL
                          AIR PASSENGER TRAFFIC
                          AIR ROUTE NETWORKS
                          AIR TRAFFIC
                          CIVIL AVIATION

AIRPORTS

	Territorial coverage	Title codes
IBRD loans approved for airport development in $m	OAS member countries	N 16-a
Passenger traffic through each main airport	EEC countries	E 43-a

AIRPORTS, DOMESTIC

	Territorial coverage	Title codes
% change in air transport movements	UK	S 12-a
no of terminal passengers	UK	S 12-a
total passenger movements	UK	S 12-a
% of passengers disembarking by airport	UK	S 12-a
No of air transport movements at UK airports	UK	S 12-a
movements: commercial air transport	UK	S 12-m
non-commercial air transport	UK	S 12-m
private aero-club flights	UK	S 12-m
test & training flights	UK	S 12-m
terminal passengers by airport	UK	S 12-a
Passenger movement (total) at UK airports	UK	S 12-a

Alcohol   see   ETHYL ALCOHOL
                    METHANOL

Alcohol sales taxes   see   LICENCE FEES

ALCOHOLIC DRINKS

   see also   BEVERAGES, ALCOHOLIC

	Territorial coverage	Title codes
% changes in retail sales: hard liquor	E European countries	U 16-a
Consumption per capita in litres	E European countries	U 16-a
Intervention prices: distilled spirits	EEC countries	E 44-a

ALCOHOLIC DRINKS INDUSTRY

	Territorial coverage	Title codes
Labour costs as % total costs	EEC countries	E 8-a
per hr: all employees	EEC countries	E 11-a
wage earners	EEC countries	E 11-a
salaried staff	EEC countries	E 11-a
Labour force employed: no of salaried staff	EEC countries	E 11-a
wage earners	EEC countries	E 11-a
wage earners & salaried staff	EEC countries	E 8-a
No of hrs worked per wk	OAS member countries	N 18-a
per yr	EEC countries	E 8-a
salaried staff	EEC countries	E 11-a
wage earners	EEC countries	E 11-a

Alcohols, acyclic & derivatives   see   METHANOL

	Territorial coverage	Title codes

Aldehydes　see　CHEMICALS, ORGANIC

Aldrin　see　INSECTICIDES

Ale　see　BEER

ALFALFA MEAL

Export prices in $ per ton	USA	A 9-a
Wholesale prices in $ per ton	USA	A 9-a

Aliphatics　see　HYDROCARBONS, ALIPHATIC

Alliance for progress program　see　DEVELOPMENT AID

Allocations, budgetary　see　BUDGET ACCOUNTS
　　　　　　　　　　　　　　　　EEC BUDGET

Alloy castings　see　CASTINGS, COPPER ALLOY

Alloy steel ingots　see　INGOTS, ALLOY STEEL

ALLOY STEEL

Deliveries to EEC area: tonnage	EEC countries	E 29-a	
Exports by destination by quality: tonnage	Main countries	T 4-a	
corrosion-resistant alloy steel: tonnage	EEC countries	E 29-a	
high-speed alloy steel: tonnage	EEC countries	E 29-a	
manganese alloy steel: tonnage	EEC countries	E 29-a	
silicon alloy steel: tonnage	EEC countries	E 29-a	
tonnage	EEC countries	E 5-q	E 29-a
Imports: blooms, billets & slabs: tonnage	European countries, Japan & USA	C 5-m	
by source by quality: tonnage	Main countries	T 1-a	
	Main countries	T 4-a	
corrosion-resistant steel: tonnage	EEC countries	E 29-a	
high-speed steels: tonnage	EEC countries	E 29-a	
manganese alloy steel: tonnage	EEC countries	E 29-a	
silicon alloy steel: tonnage	EEC countries	E 29-a	
tonnage: all alloy steels	EEC countries	E 5-q	E 29-a
Imports: coated steel sheets: tonnage	Main countries	T 1-a	
cold-rolled bars: tonnage	Main countries	T 1-a	
strip: tonnage	Main countries	T 1-a	
heavy plates over 3mm gauge: tonnage	All countries	T 1-a	
hot-rolled bars: tonnage	Main countries	T 1-a	
coils: tonnage	Main countries	T 1-a	
sheets under 3mm gauge: tonnage	All countries	T 1-a	
strip: tonnage	Main countries	T 1-a	
ingots: tonnage	Main countries	T 1-a	
light sections, angles & shapes: tonnage	Main countries	T 1-a	
tonnage	European countries, Japan & USA	C 5-m	
wire rod: tonnage	Main countries	T 1-a	
Production of castings as % all steel castings	UK	B 25-a	
tonnage & value in £m	UK	B 25-a	
excl stainless steel: tonnage	OECD countries	D 22-a	
special qualities by kind: tonnage	EEC countries		
tonnage	EEC countries	E 29-a	
	European countries	C 5-m	
Production by quality: tonnage	Main countries	T 4-a	
Receipts from EEC area: tonnage	EEC countries	E 29-a	
Usage of cobalt in production of alloy steel in lbs	USA	T 4-a	
of nickel in production of electrical resistance steel	USA	J 6-a	
of electro-plating anodes	USA	J 6-a	
of high-temperature alloy steel	USA	J 6-a	

Alloying elements　see　CHROMIUM
　　　　　　　　　　　　　FERRO-SILICON
　　　　　　　　　　　　　MANGANESE
　　　　　　　　　　　　　MOLYBDENUM
　　　　　　　　　　　　　NICKEL
　　　　　　　　　　　　　TITANIUM MINERALS
　　　　　　　　　　　　　TUNGSTEN
　　　　　　　　　　　　　VANADIAN

ALMONDS

Exports: tonnage	Main countries	P 4-m
Import prices by grade in £ per ton c & f UK port	UK	P 4-m
Imports: tonnage	Main countries	P 4-m
Production: tonnage (world crop shelled)	All countries	P 4-a

ALTERNATORS, HYDRAULIC

　　see also　GENERATORS, HYDRAULIC

Exports in mV	European countries, Japan & USA	D 45-a

ALTERNATORS, THERMAL

　　see also　GENERATORS, THERMAL

Exports in mV	European countries, Japan & USA	D 45-a

Alumina　see　BAUXITE

	Territorial coverage	Title codes
ALUMINA PHOSPHATE		
Production: tonnage of raw & dehydrated alumine phosphate	Senegal	E 41-a
ALUMINIUM		
% contribution to export earnings	Sierra Leone, Ghana & Cameroun	E 45-a
Consumption by building industry: tonnage	EEC countries, Japan & USA	C 12-a
chemical industry: tonnage	EEC countries, Japan & USA	C 12-a
electrical engineering industry: tonnage	EEC countries, Japan & USA	C 12-a
end-use: tonnage	Main countries	C 12-a H 2-a
	EEC countries, Japan & USA	C 12-a
iron & steel industry: tonnage	Main countries	C 12-a
mechanical engineering industry: tonnage	EEC countries, Japan & USA	C 12-a
metals industries: tonnage	EEC countries, Japan & USA	C 12-a
office appliances manufacturing industry: tonnage	EEC countries, Japan & USA	C 12-a
packaging industry: tonnage	EEC countries, Japan & USA	C 12-a
powder-using industry: tonnage	EEC countries, Japan & USA	C 12-a
in production of aluminium castings: tonnage	Main countries	C 12-a
of aluminium forgings: tonnage	Main countries	C 12-a
of aluminium powder: tonnage	Main countries	C 12-a
of aluminium wire: tonnage	Main countries	C 12-a
of plates, sheet & strip: tonnage	Main countries	C 12-a
of rods & sections: tonnage	Main countries	C 12-a
of semi-finished products: tonnage	Main countries	C 12-a
of primary & secondary grades: tonnage	All countries	C 30-a
	USA	J 6-a
of primary metal for secondary production: tonnage	All countries	C 12-a
historical table: tonnage	World regions	C 12-a
tonnage	EEC countries	C 12-a
	OECD countries	D 21-q
of secondary aluminium: tonnage	UK	C 30-a
of virgin aluminium: tonnage	UK	C 30-a
Consumption: tonnage & world total	Main countries	B 2-a
tonnage - index nos	EEC countries	C 12-a
tonnage	Brazil & Mexico	U 18-a
	OAS member countries	N 17-a
	USA	N 1-a
Deliveries to building construction industry: tonnage	OECD countries	D 21-a
domestic & office appliances industry: tonnage	OECD countries	D 21-a
electrical engineering industry: tonnage	OECD countries	D 21-a
iron & steel industry: tonnage	OECD countries	D 21-a
mechanical engineering industry: tonnage	OECD countries	D 21-a
metal industries: tonnage	OECD countries	D 21-a
packaging industry: tonnage	OECD countries	D 21-a
vehicle & transport eqpt industry: tonnage	OECD countries	D 21-a
Disposals ex US government stockpile: tonnage	US	U 11-a
Export prices - index nos (weighted average main sources)		U 29-q
Exports (incl alumina) by value in $m	Developing countries	U 11-a
(incl aluminium alloys): tonnage	Main countries	H 2-a
by destination of primary metal: tonnage	OECD countries	D 21-q
tonnage (total) & to EEC area: tonnage & value in UA	Cameroun	E 41-a
tonnage & value in $m	Ghana & Cameroun	E 45-a
unwrought metal: tonnage	Main countries	C 12-a
	OECD countries	D 21-a
Government stockpile: tonnage	USA	N 1-a
Imports (incl alloys) by source: tonnage	Main countries	H 2-a
by source of primary metal: tonnage	OECD countries	D 21-q
tonnage of unwrought metal	Main countries	C 12-a
Plant production capacity tonnage by company	Main countries	C 12-a
Producer prices of aluminium ingots in local currency	W Germany, UK & USA	H 2-m
Production capacity tonnage	All countries	N 1-a
& consumption of secondary metal: tonnage	All countries	H 2-a
& consumption: tonnage	All countries	H 2-a
sales, supply & stock: tonnage	USA	J 6-m
& world total: tonnage	All countries	R 5-a
	All countries	U 27-m U 43-a
from ore & scrap: tonnage	Main European countries	Z 1-a
historical tables from 1892: tonnage	AASM countries	E 41-a
primary aluminium: tonnage	EEC countries	C 12-a
	OECD countries	D 21-q
	World regions	D 21-q C 12-a
semi-manufactured products: tonnage	EEC countries	E 28-q E 27-a
unwrought aluminium: tonnage	All countries	U 22-a
virgin metal & semi-manufactured products: tonnage	EEC countries	E 26-m
tonnage	All countries	B 15-a C 30-a
	Main countries	E 3-a
	OAS member countries	N 14-a
	USA	J 3-m
Sales ex government stockpile: tonnage	USA	N 1-a
Stock changes: tonnage	EEC countries, Japan & USA	C 12-a
Wholesale prices (average) at London in £ per ton	UK	C 12-a
Milan in lire per kg	Italy	C 12-a
New York in cents per lb	USA	C 12-a
per lb or ton in local currency	Canada, UK & USA	J 6-m
aluminium ingots in $ per ton	Norway, UK & USA	U 27-m
secondary ingots at New York in cents per lb	USA	J 3-m
virgin ingots at New York in cents per lb	USA	J 3-m
in local currency	Main countries	T 4-w
World consumption of primary refined aluminium: tonnage	Worldwide	C 30-a

	Territorial coverage	Title codes
ALUMINIUM, continued		
World consumption: tonnage	Main countries	J 3-a J 6-a
tonnage (historical table)	Worldwide	C 12-a
World prices: virgin metallic ingots in cents per lb	Canada	T 4-m
World production: primary & refined metal: tonnage	Worldwide	C 30-a
primary metal: tonnage	All countries	J 3-a J 6-a
unalloyed ingots: tonnage	Worldwide	N 4-a
World reserves (estimated): tonnage	Worldwide	N 1-a
ALUMINIUM, PRIMARY		
Consumption (industrial) by use: tonnage	Main countries	T 4-a
tonnage	All countries	C 12-a
Export prices in cents per lb	Canada	R 2-m
Exports by destination: tonnage	Main countries	T 4-a
Import prices ex Canada in cents per lb	European countries	R 2-m
Imports by source: tonnage	Main countries	T 4-a
Production, consumption & trade: tonnage	All countries	H 2-a
Production: tonnage	All countries	C 12-a
World export trade: tonnage	Main countries	T 4-a
ALUMINIUM ALLOYS		
Consumption of magnesium in production of alloys: tonnage	USA	T 4-a
Aluminium castings see CASTINGS, ALUMINIUM		
ALUMINIUM FOIL		
see also COPPER FOIL		
LEAD FOIL		
TIN FOIL		
Consumption: tonnage	UK	T 4-a
Despatches: tonnage	OECD countries	D 21-a
	UK	C 30-a
Exports by destination: tonnage	Main countries	T 4-a
Imports by source: tonnage	Main countries	T 4-a
Production: tonnage	Japan	T 4-a
Aluminium ingots see INGOTS, ALUMINIUM		
Aluminium ore see BAUXITE		
Aluminium oxide see CHEMICAL PRODUCTS		
ALUMINIUM POWDER & PASTE		
Consumption: tonnage	UK & USA	T 4-a
Despatches: tonnage	UK	C 30-a
Exports: tonnage	USA	T 4-a
Sales (incl aluminium flake): tonnage	USA	J 6-a
ALUMINIUM PRODUCTS, SEMI-FINISHED		
see also SLABS & BLOCKS, ALUMINIUM		
STRIP IN COIL, ALUMINIUM		
TUBES, ALUMINIUM		
WIRE, ALUMINIUM		
WIRE-DRAWING RODS, ALUMINIUM		
Despatches by kind: tonnage	UK	C 30-a
Domestic sales: tonnage	Main countries	H 2-a
Exports: bars, plates & sheets: tonnage	USA	J 6-a
by kind: tonnage	Canada	J 6-a
by type: tonnage	Main countries	H 2-a
Imports: bars, plates & sheets: tonnage	USA	J 6-a
Imports by type: tonnage	Main countries	H 2-a
Sales: aluminium foil: tonnage	OECD countries	D 21-a
cast products by kind: tonnage	USA	J 6-a
wrought products by kind: tonnage	USA	J 6-a
castings: tonnage	OECD countries	D 21-a
extruded shapes: tonnage	USA	J 6-a
forgings: tonnage	OECD countries	D 21-a
plates & sheets: tonnage	OECD countries	D 21-a
rolled shapes: tonnage	USA	J 6-a
tubes (extruded): tonnage	OECD countries	D 21-a
wire: tonnage	OECD countries	D 21-a
Wholesale prices in £ per ton	UK	T 4-q
in lire per ton	Italy	C 12-m
World production: tonnage	Main countries	T 4-a
ALUMINIUM SCRAP		
Arisings & recovery: tonnage of pure metal & alloy	UK	C 30-a
Consumption by secondary smelters: tonnage	UK	C 30-a T 4-a
Dealer buying prices: cast scrap in cents per lb	USA	J 3-m
clippings in cents per lb	USA	J 3-m
Exports by destination: tonnage	Main countries	T 4-a
by kind: tonnage	All countries	B 15-a
tonnage	USA	J 6-a
Imports by source: tonnage	Main countries	H 2-a T 4-a
tonnage	USA	J 6-a

	Territorial coverage	Title codes

ALUMINIUM SCRAP, continued

Production: tonnage	Main European countries	T 4-a
Wholesale prices: aluminium crankcases in $ per lb	USA	J 6-m
clippings & old sheets in local currency per ton	Main countries	T 4-q
ingot scrap in local currency per ton	Main countries	T 4-q
new aluminium clippings per ton	USA	J 6-m
scrap (all types) in lire per kg	Italy	C 12-m

Aluminium strip   see   STRIP IN COIL, ALUMINIUM

Aluminium tubes   see   TUBES, ALUMINIUM

Aluminium wire   see   WIRE, ALUMINIUM

Amblygonite   see   LITHIUM MINERALS

Ambulances   see   SERVICE VEHICLES

Aminoplastics   see   PLASTICS

AMMONIA
    see also   NITROGEN, FIXED

Exports of ammonia (anhydrous or aqueous) by destination: tonnage	Main countries	U 2-a
tonnage	ECE countries	U 15-a
	European countries, Japan & USA	U 25-a
Imports: tonnage	ECE countries	U 15-a
	European countries, Japan & USA	U 25-a
	All countries	U 22-a
Production: tonnage	ECE countries	U 15-a
	European countries, Japan & USA	U 25-a
Wholesale prices in $ per ton	USA	N 1-a

AMMONIA, SYNTHETIC

Consumption for production of chemical products: tonnage	OECD countries	D 5-a	
nitrogen fertilisers: tonnage	OECD countries	D 5-a	
Exports: tonnage	OECD countries	D 5-a	
Imports: tonnage	OECD countries	D 5-a	
Production tonnage: % by electrolysis	OECD countries	D 5-a	
% from coal by-products	OECD countries	D 5-a	
natural gas	OECD countries	D 5-a	
petroleum products	OECD countries	D 5-a	
Production capacity in tons of nitrogen	EEC countries	E 26-m	
Production: tonnage based on nitrogen content	Belgium & USA	B 15-a	
Production: tonnage	EEC countries	E 28-q	E 27-a
	Main countries	E 3-a	

Ammonium molybdate   see   MOLYBDENUM COMPOUNDS

Ammonium nitrate   see   FERTILISERS

Ammonium phosphate   see   FERTILISERS

Ammonium sulphate   see   FERTILISERS

Ammunition   see   ARMS & AMMUNITION

Amortisation   see   DEBT SERVICING
                        DEPRECIATION
                        FINANCIAL RATIOS, CORPORATE

Amosite   see   ASBESTOS

Amsterdam   see   CHEESE BY VARIETY

Analytical instruments   see   ELECTRONIC EQUIPMENT

Anchovies   see   SARDINES & ANCHOVIES

ANDALUSITE
    see also   KYANITE
                      SILLIMANITE

Imports & exports by source & destination: tonnage	All countries	B 15-a
Production: tonnage	S Korea & S Africa	B 15-a

Anglers   see   CATTLE BY BREED

Angles, shapes & sections, steel   see   HEAVY SECTIONS, STEEL
                                                         LIGHT SECTIONS, STEEL

ANIMAL FATS & OILS
    see also   BEEF FATS
                      FATS & OILS
                      FATTY OILS

	Territorial coverage	Title codes	

ANIMAL FATS & OILS, continued
 % changes in retail sales   E European countries & USSR   U 16-a
 Consumption production of margarine & cooking fats: tonnage   USA   A 4-a
          soap & detergents: tonnage   Japan & UK   A 4-a
 Consumption per capita in kg   E European countries   U 16-a
 Export prices - index nos (weighted average)   Worldwide   U 29-q
 Exports to EEC & non-EEC area by value in $m   EEC countries   E 24-a
 Imports from EEC & non-EEC area by value in $m   EEC countries   E 24-a

ANIMAL FATS & OILS BY KIND
 Production tonnage stocks & consumption   OECD countries   D 14-a
                    All countries   P 1-a
 Retail prices in local currency   OAS member countries   N 17-a
 World production: tonnage   N 10-a
 World supply: tonnage   B 19-a

ANIMAL FEED MILLS
  see also   FLOUR MILLING INDUSTRY
 No in operation by tonnage of deliveries   UK   P 5-a

Animal feeding stuffs   see   BARLEY
               FEEDING STUFFS
               OATS

Animal fertiliser   see   MANURE

Animal fodder   see   FEEDING STUFFS

Animal husbandry   see   CATTLE

Animal products   see   LIVESTOCK PRODUCTS

Animal protein   see   PROTEIN, ANIMAL

Animal skins   see   HIDES

Animals, live   see   LIVESTOCK

ANNUITIES
  see also   LIFE INSURANCE
 Amounts paid out by insurance companies in local currency   OAS member countries   N 16-a

ANODES
 Consumption of cadmium in production of plating anodes: tonnage   UK   T 4-a
        nickel in production of plating anodes: tonnage   USA   J 6-a   T 4-a
 Sales of cast magnesium anodes: tonnage   USA   J 6-a

Anthracene   see   CHEMICALS, ORGANIC

ANTHRACITE
 Consumption: tonnage   Main countries   N 2-a
                       OAS member countries   N 17-a
                       USA   N 1-a
 Exports by destination: tonnage   EEC countries   E 5-q
 Imports by source: tonnage   EEC countries   E 5-q
                      Main countries   N 2-a
 Production: tonnage (incl low volatile coals)   EEC countries   E 16-m   E 15-(
     tonnage per man-day at mines   USA   N 1-a
     tonnage   All countries   B 15-a
                      Main countries   N 1-a
 Shipments (domestic) by rail: tonnage   USA   N 1-a
          by road carriers: tonnage   USA   N 1-a
 Stocks at coking plants: tonnage   USA   N 1-a
   at electricity undertakings: tonnage   USA   N 1-a
   held by retail trade: tonnage   USA   N 1-a
 Wholesale prices in $ per ton   USA   N 1-a
 World production: tonnage   Main countries   N 1-a   N 4-c

ANTI-FRICTION METALS
 Consumption of lead in production of bearings: tonnage   USA   J 6-a
        in production of anti-friction metals: tonnage   USA   T 4-a
                        European countries & USA   C 12-a
     of tin in production of anti-friction metals:
                    tonnage   France & W Germany   C 12-a
                         UK   C 20-m
 Wholesale prices in lire per kg at Milan   Italy   C 12-m

Anti-knock additives (to motor spirit)   see   ADDITIVES, ANTI-KNOCK

ANTIBIOTICS
 Exports by destination: penicillin & streptomycin by value in $ Main countries   U 2-a

	Territorial coverage	Title codes	
ANTIMONY			
Consumption by end-use: tonnage	USA	J 3-a	
Consumption in production of oxides & sulphides: tonnage	UK & USA	C 12-a	
ammunition: tonnage	UK	C 12-a	
antimonial lead: tonnage	USA	C 12-a	T 4-a
antimonial lead: tonnage	UK	C 30-m	
batteries: tonnage	UK & USA	T 4-a	
	UK	C 30-m	T 4-a
	UK & USA	C 12-a	
bearings: tonnage	UK	C 30-m	C 12-a
	UK & USA	T 4-a	
cable covering: tonnage	USA	C 12-a	T 4-a
castings: tonnage	USA	C 12-a	
ceramics & glass: tonnage	USA	C 12-a	
fireworks: tonnage	USA	C 12-a	
flame-proof chemicals: tonnage	USA	C 12-a	
oxides & sulphides of antimony: tonnage	UK	T 4-a	
pigments: tonnage	USA	C 12-a	
plastics: tonnage	USA	C 12-a	
regulus metal: tonnage	USA	C 12-a	
rubber products: tonnage	USA	C 12-a	
solder: tonnage	USA	C 12-a	
tubes & foils: tonnage	USA	C 12-a	
type metal: tonnage	USA	C 12-a	T 4-a
Consumption of primary & secondary metal: tonnage	USA	N 1-a	
of primary metal: tonnage	USA	J 6-a	
Exports: antimony metal by destination: tonnage	Main countries	T 4-a	
Government stockpile: tonnage	USA	N 1-a	
Import prices: regulus metal in £ per ton cif	UK	C 12-m	
Imports by source: antimony metal: tonnage	Main countries	T 4-a	
Imports & exports by source & destination: tonnage	Main countries	B 15-a	
Production tonnage based on metal content of ore	All countries	B 15-a	U 22-a
		U 43-a	
Production tonnage: antimony metal	African countries	U 44-a	
primary metal at mines	USA	J 6-a	
primary metal at smelter plants	USA	J 6-a	
secondary metal	USA	J 6-a	
Production: tonnage	Latin American countries	U 40-a	
	Main countries	J 6-a	
Sales ex government stockpile: tonnage	USA	N 1-a	
Stocks of antimony metal: tonnage	USA	T 4-a	
Wholesale prices: antimony in cents per lb	USA	N 1-a	
antimony in yen per ton	Japan	T 4-w	
regulus metal in lire per kg	Italy	C 12-m	
World production: tonnage	All countries	C 12-a	N 4-a
		T 4-a	
World production tonnage based on metal content of ore		C 30-a	
World reserves: tonnage (estim)		N 1-a	
ANTIMONY, UNWROUGHT			
Imports by source: tonnage	Italy & USA	C 12-a	
Exports by destination: tonnage	Italy	C 12-a	
ANTIMONY COMPOUNDS			
Consumption of antimony in production of compounds: tonnage	UK	C 12-a	
in production of pigments: tonnage	UK	C 30-m	
of antimony sulphides: tonnage	UK	C 30-m	
Imports by source: antimony oxides: tonnage	Italy	C 12-a	
Production tonnage: oxides & sulphides	Italy	C 12-a	
ANTIMONY ORE			
Export prices: lump sulphide ore in $ per ton	European countries	T 4-m	
Exports by destination: tonnage	Main countries	T 4-a	
Imports by source: tonnage	Main countries	T 4-a	
Production: tonnage	Italy	C 12-a	
	OAS member countries	N 14-a	
Wholesale prices: lump sulphide in $ per ton on London market	UK	C 12-m	
World export trade: tonnage	Main countries	T 4-a	
World production: tonnage based on metal content of ore	Worldwide	C 12-a	
tonnage	Main countries	N 1-a	T 4-a
World reserves: tonnage	Main countries	N 1-a	
ANTIMONY SCRAP			
Consumption: tonnage	UK	C 30-m	
for production of antimonial lead: tonnage	UK	C 30-m	

Antimony-lead alloy   see   REGULUS METAL

Apartments   see   DWELLINGS

Apatite   see   PHOSPHATE ROCK

Apparel industry   see   CLOTHING INDUSTRY

Apples   see   FRUIT, FRESH

	Territorial coverage	Title codes

Appliances, domestic   see   DOMESTIC EQUIPMENT

APPLIANCES, ELECTRICAL
    see also DOMESTIC EQUIPMENT
               ELECTRIC COOKERS
                ELECTRIC IRONS
                ELECTRIC MOTORS
                ENGINEERING PRODUCTS, ELECTRICAL
                HEATING APPLIANCES, ELECTRIC
                KETTLES, ELECTRIC
                MACHINERY, ELECTRICAL
                MEASURING APPARATUS, ELECTRICAL
                POWER TOOLS
                RAZORS, ELECTRIC
                SWITCHGEAR, ELECTRIC
                VACUUM CLEANERS

% contribution to export earnings	Barbados	E 45-a
Consumption of mercury in production of electrical goods: in flasks	USA	T 4-a

APPLIANCES, ELECTRICAL BY KIND

Exports by destination by CST classes: tonnage & value in $	EEC countries	E 48-a	
by SITC classes: tonnage & value in $	OECD countries	D 3-a2	
by value in $	Main countries	D 2-q	
NIMEXE classes by value in $	All countries	E 20-a	
SITC classes by value in $	All countries	U 50-a	U 59-a
Imports by NIMEXE classes by value in $	All countries	E 20-a	
SITC classes by value in $	All countries	U 50-a	U 59-a
source by CST classes: tonnage and value in $	EEC countries	E 21-a	
SITC classes: tonnage & value in $	OECD countries	D 3-a2	
by value in $	Main countries	D 2-q	

APPLIANCES, ELECTRO-MAGNETIC

Imports by value in $m	All countries	U 38-a
World export trade by value in $m	All countries	U 38-a

APPLIED SCIENCES
    see also MEDICAL SCIENCE
                NATURAL SCIENCES
                SOCIAL SCIENCES

No of new book titles published on scientific subjects	All countries	U 62-a

Apprenticeship tax   see   TAXATION

APPRENTICESHIP

No of apprentices: collieries, mines & in steel industry	EEC countries	E 3-a
iron & steel industry	EEC countries	E 30-m
	EEC area	E 29-a
	OECD countries	D 22-a
	W Germany	H 3-a
iron ore mining	EEC area	E 29-a
	EEC countries	E 30-m
machine tools industry	UK	B 26-a

Appropriations   see   BUDGET ACCOUNTS
                          DEVELOPMENT AID
                          EEC BUDGET
                          EUROPEAN DEVELOPMENT FUND

Apricots   see   FRUIT, FRESH

Aquatic animal fats & oils   see   FISH OILS & FATS
                                      WHALE OIL

AQUATIC ANIMAL PRODUCTS

Production of pearls & corals	All countries	A 22-a

AQUATIC PLANTS

Production: seaweeds by kind: tonnage	All countries	A 22-a

Arabicas, mild   see   COFFEE BY GRADE

Arable land   see   LAND UTILISATION

Architecture   see   FINE ARTS

Area of land   see   HORTICULTURAL AREAS
                        LAND AREA

Area under crops   see   LAND UTILISATION

Area under glass   see   HORTICULTURAL AREAS

ARGON

Wholesale prices (as gas or liquid) in $ per ton	USA	N 1-a
World production: tonnage	All countries	N 1-a

	Territorial coverage	Title codes

ARMED FORCES
    see also   GOVERNMENT EXPENDITURE
                    PENSIONS, WAR

Expenditure on pay & allowances from public funds	EEC countries	E 32-a
No of military service personnel by sex	OECD countries	D 23-a
military service personnel	All countries	L 4-a
	Main countries	N 9-a

ARMS & AMMUNITION
    see also   MILITARY EQUIPMENT

Consumption of lead in production of ammunition: tonnage	USA	J 6-a

Aromatics   see   HYDROCARBONS, AROMATIC

ARSENIC

Imports & exports by source & destination: tonnage	Main countries	B 15-a	
Production tonnage: white arsenic & ores	All countries	B 15-a	
white arsenic	Brazil, Mexico & Peru	U 40-a	
	Main countries	N 1-a	
Wholesale prices: powdered metallic arsenic in cents per lb	USA	N 1-a	
World production & reserves of white arsenic: tonnage		N 1-a	
World production: metallic white arsenic: tonnage		N 4-a	T 4-a
World reserves: metallic white arsenic: tonnage (estim)		N 1-a	

ART & CRAFT INDUSTRIES

Loan advances to arts & crafts from banks in local currency	OAS member countries	N 16-a

ARTICHOKES

Production tonnage, area harvested & yield per ha	All countries	A 9-a

Articulated vehicles   see   COMMERCIAL VEHICLES, ARTICULATED

Artificial fabrics   see   WOVEN CELLULOSIC FABRICS
                             WOVEN CELLULOSIC SPUN YARN FABRICS

Artificial fibres   see   CELLULOSIC FIBRES

Artificial fibres industry   see   MAN-MADE FIBRES INDUSTRY

ARTIFICIAL INSEMINATION

% cows over 2 yrs old inseminated	EEC countries	B 3-a
No of inseminations carried out on beef cows	EEC countries	B 3-a
on dairy cows	EEC countries	B 3-a

Artificial resins   see   PLASTICS

Artificial yarns   see   MAN-MADE FIBRE YARN
                          YARN, CELLULOSIC

ARTISTS' COLOURS
    see also   PAINTS & VARNISHES
                      WATER PAINTS

Exports: tonnage & value in $	OECD countries	D 5-a
Imports: tonnage & value in $	OECD countries	D 5-a
Production: tonnage	OECD countries	D 5-a
unit value in $ per ton	OECD countries	D 5-a

Asbestos cement   see   BUILDING MATERIALS

ASBESTOS

% contribution to export earnings	Swaziland	E 45-a	
Consumption: tonnage	USA	N 1-a	
Exports by destination incl products by CST classes: tonnage & value in $	EEC countries	E 48-a	
SITC classes by value in $	Main countries	D 2-q	
tonnage & value in $	OECD countries	D 3-a2	
Government stockpile of amosite: tonnage	USA	N 1-a	
chrysotile: tonnage	USA	N 1-a	
crocidolite: tonnage	USA	N 1-a	
Imports by source incl products by CST classes: tonnage & value in $	EEC countries	E 21-a	
by SITC classes by value in $	Main countries	D 2-q	
tonnage & value in $	OECD countries	D 3-a2	
Imports & exports by source & destination: tonnage	Main countries	B 15-a	
Production tonnage & world total	All countries	R 5-a	
tonnage of asbestos fibres & powder	All countries	U 43-a	
tonnage	All countries	B 15-a	U 22-a
	Main countries	N 1-a	
	OAS member countries	N 14-a	
Sales of amosite ex government stockpile: tonnage	USA	N 1-a	
crocidolite ex government stockpile: tonnage	USA	N 1-a	
Wholesale prices in $ per ton at mine (average)	USA	N 1-a	
World production: tonnage		N 1-a	N 4-a
World reserves: tonnage (estim)		N 1-a	

	Territorial coverage	Title codes
ASIAN DEVELOPMENT BANK		
Net flow of development aid as % of total aid		M 4-a
Asphalt see BITUMEN		
ASPHALT ROCK		
Production: tonnage	Angola, France, W Germany & Italy	B 15-a
Asphalt roofing sheets see BUILDING MATERIALS		
Assembly of vehicles see MOTOR VEHICLES		
PASSENGER CARS		
Asset formation see CAPITAL FORMATION		
ASSETS & LIABILITIES		
see also BALANCE OF PAYMENTS		
BALANCE SHEETS		
CAPITAL ACCUMULATION		
CAPITAL FORMATION		
FOREIGN ASSETS		
FOREIGN DEBT		
Airline companies (specific) in $m	Worldwide	S 10-a
in $m & local currency	Worldwide	S 6-a
Assets: chemical manufacturing corporations as % of liabilities	USA	J 2-a
engineering corporations as % of liabilities	USA	J 2-a
machine tool corporations as % of liabilities	USA	J 2-a
manufacturing corporations as % of liabilities	USA	J 2-a
motor vehicles corporations as % of liabilities	USA	J 2-a
Astronomical instruments see SCIENTIFIC INSTRUMENTS		
Atmospheric research see RESEARCH & DEVELOPMENT		
Atomic weights see ELEMENTS		
Aubergines see EGGPLANTS		
Auction prices see WHOLESALE PRICES		
Authorities see LOCAL AUTHORITIES		
REGIONAL AUTHORITIES		
Automated production trains see TRANSFER MACHINES		
Automatic lathes see LATHES, AUTOMATIC		
AUTOMATIC VENDING MACHINES		
Exports by value in $m	OECD countries	D 9-a
AUTOMATION		
see also COMPUTER SCIENCE		
LATHES, AUTOMATIC		
TRANSFER MACHINES		
Public expenditure on research in $m	EEC countries	E 39-a
Automobile industry see MOTOR VEHICLES INDUSTRY		
Automobiles see PASSENGER CARS		
AUTOMOTIVE ACCESSORIES		
see also REPLACEMENT PARTS		
Exports by volume & value in $m	USA	V 3-a
Trade between Canada & USA by value in $m fob		G 1-a
Automotive chassis see CHASSIS, AUTOMOTIVE		
Automotive electrics see ELECTRICAL EQUIPMENT, AUTOMOTIVE		
Autoroutes see MOTORWAYS		
Auxiliary engines see ENGINES, AUXILIARY		
Aviation see AIR TRANSPORT		
AVIATION FUEL		
Consumption by Italian international air services: tonnage	Italy	H 4-a
in air transportation: tonnage	EEC countries	E 14-a
	OECD countries	D 31-a
	Main countries	C 14-a
Deliveries, home consumption & exports: tonnage	OECD countries	D 39-q D 31-a

	Territorial coverage	Title codes	
AVIATION FUEL, continued			
Imports by source: tonnage	OECD countries	D 31-a	
Imports & exports by source & destination: tonnage	Main countries	B 15-a	
Prices posted at specific ports in cents per gallon	Worldwide	C 3-a	
Production & consumption: tonnage	OECD countries	D 31-a	D 44-a
Production by volume in m³	OAS member countries	N 14-a	
Production: tonnage	African countries	U 39-a	
	All countries	U 22-a	
	EEC countries	E 26-m	E 28-q
		E 27-a	
	European countries, USSR & USA	U 4-a	
	Main countries	B 15-a	E 3-a
Production tonnage, imports & supply	OECD countries	D 39-q	D 31-a
AVOCADOS			
Production: tonnage	All countries	A 9-a	

Axles, automotive   see   REPLACEMENT PARTS

Axles, steel   see   WHEELS TYRES AXLES, STEEL

Ayrshires   see   CATTLE BY BREED

	Territorial coverage	Title codes	
BABASSU KERNELS			
Exports: tonnage	Brazil	B 19-a	
BABASSU OIL			
Exports: tonnage	Brazil	B 19-a	
Imports: tonnage	USA	B 19-a	
World production: tonnage		A 4-a	A 5-a
		N 10-a	
BABBIT'S METAL			
Consumption of tin in production of Babbit's metal: tonnage	All countries	C 20-m	
	Italy & USA	C 12-a	
of tin scrap in production of Babbit's metal: tonnage	USA	J 6-a	
Production: tonnage	USA	T 4-a	
Wholesale prices: ingots by grade in lire per kg	Italy & USA	C 12-a	
	Italy	C 12-m	

Baby carriages   see   PERAMBULATORS & PUSH-CHAIRS

Baby foods   see   DIETETIC FOODS

BACON

   see also   HAM

	Territorial coverage	Title codes
% share of world imports & world exports	Main countries	B 1-a
Consumption per capita (incl ham) in lbs per yr	UK	B 12-a
in lbs per yr	UK	B 11-a
Export prices - index nos (weighted average main sources)		U 29-q
Export prices in local currency	Denmark, Eire & Poland	A 9-a
Exports by value (incl ham) as % value of total exports	Main countries	B 11-a
(incl ham) by destination: tonnage	EEC countries	E 47-a
(incl ham) : tonnage	Main countries	B 11-a
Import prices in £ per ton	UK	A 9-a
Imports by source: tonnage	UK	B 11-a
Inter-EEC shipments of bacon & lard: tonnage	EEC countries	E 47-m
Production for export: tonnage	Main producing countries	B 12-a
Production: dried pig meat & ham: tonnage	All countries	U 22-a
	EEC countries	B 1-a
Requirements & allocation for market sharing: tonnage	EEC area	B 11-a
Retail prices (comparative): bacon (smoked & sliced) per kg	EEC countries	Z 3-a
bacon (sliced & salted) in local currency	OAS member countries	N 17-a
Supply of home-produced & imported bacon by source: tonnage	UK	B 12-w
Supply, production, consumption & trade: tonnage	EEC countries	B 1-a
Wholesale prices: home-produced & imported bacon in £ per ton	UK	B 12-m
English, Danish, Irish & Polish bacon in £ per cwt	UK	B 11-m
salted bacon in local currency per ton	OAS member countries	N 17-a
in local currency	Denmark & UK	U 27-m
	UK & USA	A 9-a
World exports in value by $m	World regions	A 5-a
World market prices: Danish bacon per 100 kg (on London market)		E 34-m
BACON FACTORIES		
No of pigs slaughtered for bacon curing	Denmark	B 12-m
Receipts of pigs by volume for processing into bacon	Eire	B 12-m

Bagasse pulp   see   WOOD PULP

Bags & sacks   see   JUTE MANUFACTURES

Bags, paper   see   PACKING CONTAINERS

	Territorial coverage	Title codes	
BAKING & CONFECTIONERY INDUSTRY			
Costs: salaried staff per mth	EEC countries	E 11-a	
Investment in buildings in $m	EEC countries	E 40-a	
land purchase in $m	EEC countries	E 40-a	
machinery in $m	EEC countries	E 40-a	
Labour costs: all employees	EEC countries	E 11-a	
Labour costs as % of total costs	EEC countries	E 8-a	
by status of employees in local currency	EEC countries	E 8-a	
wage earners	EEC countries	E 11-a	
Labour force by status: no wage earners & salaried staff employed	EEC countries	E 8-a	
No of hrs worked per yr	EEC countries	E 8-a	
salaried staff	EEC countries	E 11-a	
wage earners	EEC countries	E 11-a	
salaried staff employed	EEC countries	E 11-a	
wage earners employed	EEC countries	E 11-a	
Wage rates per hr by sex	Main countries	R 3-m	
per hr in A.Sch	Austria	R 4-a	
BALANCE OF PAYMENTS			
see also BANK DEPOSITS			
COMPENSATION PAYMENTS			
DEBT SERVICING			
DRAWING RIGHTS (IMF)			
FOREIGN EXCHANGE			
FOREIGN LOANS			
GOLD HOLDINGS			
GOVERNMENT BONDS			
INVESTMENT, DIRECT			
INVESTMENT, PRIVATE OVERSEAS			
INVISIBLE TRADE			
OVERSEAS INVESTMENT INCOME			
TRADE BALANCES			
TRANSFER PAYMENTS			
In local currency: historical table from 1816	Main European countries	Z 1-a	
Allocation of drawing rights in $m	OAS member countries	N 16-a	
	Latin American countries	U 18-a	
Amortisation payments in $m	OAS member countries	N 16-a	
	Latin American countries	U 18-a	
Assets, liabilities & reserves in $m	OAS member countries	N 16-a	
	All countries	F 1-a	
Balance of Latin America by item with USA in $m		U 40-q	
Capital flows & assets by sector in $m	OAS member countries	N 16-a	
Capital & monetary sector debits in $m	EEC countries	E 26-q	
Capital transfers of government in $m	All countries	F 1-a	
in $bn	ECAFE countries	U 17-a	
in $m	OECD countries	D 10-a	
(private) in $m	Latin American countries	U 18-a	
Central bank liabilities in $m	ECAFE countries	U 17-a	
	OAS member countries	N 16-a	
Changes in reserves (special drawing rights) in $m	All countries	F 1-a	
Compensation payments received in $m	Japan	G 1-a	
	OAS member countries	N 16-a	
Current account balances in $m	All countries	F 1-a	
	OECD countries	D 10-a	
	All countries	M 6-a	
	OAS member countries	N 16-a	
	Latin American countries	U 18-a	
Direct investment income in $m	OAS member countries	N 16-a	
	All countries	F 1-a	
Direct investment in $m	Latin American countries	U 18-a	
Expenditure of tourism in $m	OECD countries	D 47-a	
	USA	D 47-a	
Exports of goods & services in $m	Latin American countries	U 18-a	
External financing (net) in $m	OAS member countries	N 16-a	
Foreign balances projected to 1980 in $m	OECD countries	D 11	
Geographical balances for specific world regions in $m	EEC countries	E 4-a	
Global balances in $m	Japan & USA	E 4-a	
Goods & services component in $m	OAS member countries	N 16-a	
	Main countries	E 3-a	
	ECAFE countries	U 17-a	
Government transfer payments in $m	OAS member countries	N 16-a	
	All countries	F 1-a	
Imports of goods & services by value in $m	Latin American countries	U 18-a	
Income from capital flows in $m	All countries	F 5-m	F 6-q
from freight payments in $m	OAS member countries	N 16-a	
	All countries	F 5-m	F 6-q
		F 1-a	
(net) from trade in $ m	All countries	F 1-a	
from government investment in $m	All countries	F 5-m	F 6-q
investments overseas in $m	OAS member countries	N 16-a	
invisible trade in $m	All countries	F 1-a	
private investment in $m	All countries	F 5-m	F 6-q
tourism in $m	OAS member countries	N 16-a	
	All countries	F 1-a	
trade credits in $m	OAS member countries	N 16-a	
	All countries	F 5-m	F 6-q

	Territorial coverage	Title codes
BALANCE OF PAYMENTS, continued		
Income of banking & monetary sectors in $m	OAS member countries	N 16-a
International liquidity as % of imports	ECAFE countries	U 17-a
Invisible balance: historical table from 1816 in local currency	Main European countries	Z 1-a
Liabilities of public & private sectors in $m	OAS member countries	N 16-a
(short-term) in $m	EEC countries	E 26-q
Long & medium-term loans received in $m	Latin American countries	U 18-a
Long-term loans received in $m	Latin American countries	U 18-a
	OAS member countries	N 16-a
	All recipient countries	F 1-a
Money deposits in banks in $m	ECAFE countries	U 17-a
Net external financing in $m	Latin American countries	U 18-a
Net external investment income in $m	Latin American countries	U 18-a
Net flows by components in $m	OAS member countries	N 16-a
	Main countries	E 3-a
Net income on imports & exports in $m	OAS member countries	N 16-a
	All countries	F 1-a
Net long-term capital account in $m	Japan	G 1-a
Net outflow of long-term capital in $m	OAS member countries	N 16-a
	USA	U 16-a
Net payments, profit & interest in $m	Latin American countries	U 18-a
Net private transfer payments in $m	Latin American countries	U 18-a
Net short-term capital account in $m	Japan	G 1-a
Net trade & long-term capital account in $m	OECD countries	D 26-q
Official settlements in $bn	OECD countries	D 10-a
Official transfer payments in $m	OAS member countries	N 16-a
	Latin American countries	U 18-a
Outflow as foreign liabilities in $m	OAS member countries	N 16-a
	USA	U 16-a
military transactions in $m	USA	U 16-a
long & short-term financing in $m	OAS member countries	N 16-a
long-term financing in $m	USA	U 16-a
short-term financing in $m	USA	U 16-a
Private transfers from abroad in $m	All countries	F 1-a
(net) in $m	OAS member countries	N 16-a
Receipts & disbursements by kind in $m	OAS member countries	N 16-a
	EEC countries	E 4-a
	OECD countries	D 30-a
Receipts from tourism in $m	Main countries	S 14-a
	OECD countries	D 47-a
	USA	D 47-a
from US flag carriers in $m	USA	D 47-a
Services, payments & other transfers in $m	Japan	G 1-a
Surpluses & deficits per capita in $	All countries	M 6-a
Trade balances with E European bloc in $m	USA	U 16-a
W European bloc in $m	USA	U 16-a
rest of world in $m	USA	U 16-a
Trade in general merchandise by value in $m	Japan	G 1-a
Visible trade balance: historical table from 1816 in local currency	Main European countries	Z 1-a
BALANCE OF PAYMENTS BY COMPONENT		
In local currency	Main countries	R 5-a
In $m	OAS member countries	N 16-a
Breakdown (in detail) in $m	All countries	U 43-a
	EEC countries	E 4-a
	Asian, Far East & Australasian countries	U 45-a
By type of account in $m	EEC countries	E 4-a
	OAS member countries	N 16-a
	USA	U 54-a
Capital changes by kind in local currency	African countries	U 44-a
Commercial banks: assets in local currency	African countries	U 44-a
liabilities in local currency	African countries	U 44-a
Global balances in $m	EEC countries	E 4-a
Goods, services & transfers in $m	EEC countries	E 26-q
Income & debts in $m	OAS member countries	N 16-a
	All countries	F 5-m F 6-q
from services in local currency	African countries	U 44-a
Investment income in local currency	African countries	U 44-a
Trade balances in local currency	African countries	U 44-a
Transfer payments by kind in local currency	African countries	U 44-a

Balance of trade   see   TRADE BALANCES

BALANCE SHEETS

    see also   ASSETS & LIABILITIES

Airline companies' assets & liabilities in local currency & $	Worldwide	S 6-a
Assets, liabilities, profits & losses of major companies	W European countries	F 9-a

BALERS

Production: volume	EEC countries	E 28-q	E 27-a

BALL BEARINGS

Exports: ball & roller bearings by value in $	OECD countries	D 9-a

Ballast   see   WEIGHTS & BALLAST

Balsam   see   NATURAL GUMS

	Territorial coverage	Title codes
BAMBOO		
Production & exports: tonnage	All countries	A 23-a
Bamboo pulp see WOOD PULP		
BANANAS		
% contribution to export earnings	Jamaica, Somali Rep, Tonga & W Samoa	E 45-a
Area under crop in acres	Main countries	B 5-a
in ha	Main countries	A 15-a
Consumption: tonnage	OAS member countries	N 13-a
Distribution cost patterns	Main countries	B 2-a
Excise duties: rates charged	Main countries	A 15-a
Export prices – index nos	EEC countries	E 31-a
Exports as % of total exports (value basis)	S American countries	U 40-q
by value in $	Main countries	A 15-a
tonnage & value in $m	Cook Is, W Samoa & Tonga	U 32-m
tonnage	Jamaica & Somalia	E 45-a
total & to EEC area: tonnage & by value in UA	All countries	B 6-a
unit value in $ per kg	AASM countries	E 41-a
Import demand: projections to 1975	OAS member countries	N 15-a
Import prices ex Jamaica on London market in £ per 21lb box	Main importing regions	A 1
in $ per ton	UK	B 2-a
	France, W Germany, UK & USA	A 5-a
	France, W Germany & USA	A 9-a
Imports: banana products, banana flour, puree & powder: tonnage	Main countries	A 5-a
by source: tonnage	OECD countries	D 37-a
	Main countries	B 6-m
of dried bananas: tonnage	Main countries	A 5-a
tonnage	USSR	U 20-a
unit value in $ per ton	W European countries	U 20-a
Prices (minimum shipside) for export per box	Main countries	A 15-a
Producer prices received	Brazil & Guatemala	A 9-a
Production: tonnage incl world total	Main countries	B 2-a
tonnage area under crop & yield per ha	Latin American countries	J 5-a
tonnage by main producing regions	Main countries	A 15-a
	AASM countries	E 41-a
	Latin American countries	U 40-a
	Main countries	B 5-a
Supply, production, consumption & trade: tonnage	OAS member countries	N 13-a
Supply sources & % world market share taken each major company	EEC countries	B 1-a
Wholesale prices: bananas shipped from Caribbean & Canary Is	Worldwide	A 15-a
per box	UK	B 5-m A 9-a
World exports by value in $m	World regions	A 5-a
tonnage	Main countries	A 5-a
unit value in $ per ton	Worldwide	U 11-a
World market prices based ex Martinique in Fr per kg		E 41-a
BANK ADVANCES		
see also CREDIT		
Borrowing by agriculture in local currency	OAS member countries	N 16-a
art & craft industries in local currency	OAS member countries	N 16-a
coffee plantations in local currency	OAS member countries	N 16-a
commercial & financial undertakings in local currency	OAS member countries	N 16-a
financial institutions in local currency	OAS member countries	N 16-a
forestry undertakings in local currency	OAS member countries	N 16-a
housing construction undertakings in local currency	OAS member countries	N 16-a
livestock farming in local currency	OAS member countries	N 16-a
manufacturing companies in local currency	OAS member countries	N 16-a
mining & quarrying companies in local currency	OAS member countries	N 16-a
provincial & municipal authorities in local currency	OAS member countries	N 16-a
public bodies & official organisations in local currency	OAS member countries	N 16-a
public institutions in local currency	OAS member countries	N 16-a
public utility undertakings in local currency	OAS member countries	N 16-a
real estate companies in local currency	OAS member countries	N 16-a
service industries in local currency	OAS member countries	N 16-a
trading & industrial companies in local currency	OAS member countries	N 16-a
transport & communications companies in local currency	OAS member countries	N 16-a
Borrowings: changes in volume of private sector loans	OECD countries	D 26-q
domestic loans in $m	Asian, Far East & Australasian countries	U 45-a
loans to individuals & firms by areas	EEC countries	E 38-a
personal loans in local currency	OAS member countries	N 16-a
to customers in $m	ECE countries	U 42-m
private & business short-term loans in $	EEC countries	E 26-m
volume of loans & trade credits in $m	OECD countries	D 12-a
BANK CLEARINGS		
Volume of cheques et al passed through clearing banks	All countries	F 5-m F 6-q
BANK DEPOSITS		
see also NATIONAL SAVINGS		
As credit factor in payment balances	All countries	F 1-a
Held by 100 world's largest banks in FrS	Worldwide	H 1
10 largest British banks in £m	UK	H 1
10 largest French banks in Frm	France	H 1
10 largest Italian banks in Lit	Italy	H 1

	Territorial coverage	Title codes	
BANK DEPOSITS, continued			
Held by 20 largest German banks in DMm	W Germany	H 1	
20 largest Swiss banks in FrS	Switzerland	H 1	
5 largest Canadian banks in $m	Canada	H 1	
Bank deposits: historical tables from 1848 in local currency	Main European countries	Z 1-a	
in local currency	Main countries	R 5-a	
in $m	ECAFE countries	U 17-a	
% rates of interest paid on deposits per annum	Main countries	R 5-a	
changes in domestic deposits in $m	OECD countries	D 26-q	
demand & time deposits in $m	All countries	F 5-m	F 6-q
foreign currency held by foreign banks in $m	All countries	F 5-m	F 6-q
foreign sterling deposits by source in $m	All countries	F 5-m	F 6-q
savings deposits: historical tables from 1817 in local currency	Main European countries	Z 1-a	
sight & time deposits by areas in $m	EEC countries	E 38-a	

Bank investments   see   BANKING & INSURANCE

Bank loans   see   BANK ADVANCES

BANK PROFITS

	Territorial coverage	Title codes
Net trading profit of largest 5 Canadian banks in $m	Canada	H 1
10 British banks in £m	UK	H 1
10 French banks in Fr m	France	H 1
10 Italian banks in Lit	Italy	H 1
20 German banks in DM m	W Germany	H 1
20 Swiss banks in FrS	Switzerland	H 1
30 US banks in $m	USA	H 1

BANK RATE

    see also   MINIMUM LENDING RATE (after October 1972)

	Territorial coverage	Title codes	
% rate of interest of Central Bank for loans	All countries	F 5-m	F 6-q
Changes over last 8 yrs by Bank of England		P 1	

BANKING & INSURANCE

    see also   CREDIT FINANCE

	Territorial coverage	Title codes	
Breakdown of costs of banking institutions	EEC countries	E 9-a	
insurance companies	EEC countries	E 9-a	
Gross product (incl real estate) in local currency	OAS member countries	N 16-a	
Income contribution to gross domestic product	EEC countries	E 32-a	
	S American countries	U 41-a	
Income distribution at factor cost in $m	S American countries	U 41-a	
Indirect tax revenue of government in $m	S American countries	U 41-a	
Labour costs of banking per mth in local currency	EEC countries	E 9-a	
insurance companies per mth in local currency	EEC countries	E 9-a	
per salary earner per mth	EEC countries	E 3-a	
Labour force employed at yr-end	EEC countries	E 2-a	E 33-a
by status	Main countries	C 28-ir	
(incl real estate cos)	OECD countries	D 23-a	
No of hrs worked per wk	Main countries	R 3-m	
per yr by banking employees	EEC countries	E 9-a	
by employees of insurance cos	EEC countries	E 9-a	
No of hrs worked: tellers	Main countries	L 1-a	
Salaries paid to tellers & machine operators	All countries	L 1-a	
Salary costs per mth	EEC countries	E 2-a	
Wage rates by sex in local currency per hr	Main countries	R 3-m	
	Australia	R 4-a	

Banknotes   see   MONEY SUPPLY

Banks   see   CENTRAL BANKS
                    CLEARING BANKS
                    COMMERCIAL BANKS
                    FOREIGN BANKS

BARGES

    see also   TUGS

	Territorial coverage	Title codes
% distribution by type & by yr of construction	European countries	U 8-a
% of total capacity covered by barges of specific age groups	European countries	U 8-a
Deliveries: volume of new barges by type	Netherlands	S 16-a
by engine hp capacity & yr of construction	EEC countries	E 43-a
load capacity: self-propelled craft	European countries	U 8-a
type on inland waterways	European countries	U 8-a
using inland waterways & tonnage of craft	EEC countries	E 43-a
without own engine & using waterways	Main countries	R 5-a

Barite   see   BARIUM MINERALS

BARIUM MINERALS

	Territorial coverage	Title codes
Consumption of barytes: tonnage	OAS member countries	N 17-a
ground or crushed barite: tonnage	USA	N 1-a
Imports & exports by source & destination: tonnage	All countries	B 15-a
Production: tonnage of barytes at mines: tonnage	Main countries	N 1-a
	All countries	B 15-a
	OAS member countries	N 14-a

		Territorial coverage	Title codes	

BARIUM MINERALS, continued
    Wholesale prices in $ per ton at mine   USA   N 1-a
    World reserves: tonnage   N 1-a

Barium sulphate   see   BARIUM MINERALS

Bark for tanning   see   TANNING BARK

Barley, roasted   see   MALT

BARLEY

Item	Territorial coverage	Title codes	
Area under crop in acres	Main countries	B 8-a	
ha & harvested: tonnage	Main countries	R 5-a	
ha: historical tables from 1815	Main European countries	Z 1-a	
ha, production tonnage & yield per ha	All countries	A 9-a	
ha	All countries	C 16-a	
	EEC countries	B 1-a	E 44-a
	OAS member countries	N 13-a	
	OECD countries	D 1-a	
Area under winter & spring barley in ha	EEC countries	E 12-a	
Consumption & consumption per capita per day	OECD countries	D 14-a	
as animal feed: tonnage	EEC countries	E 44-a	
	Main countries	B 8-a	
for industrial processing: tonnage	UK	B 7-a	
for milling & malting: tonnage	UK	B 7-a	
per capita in kg	Main countries	B 8-a	
	EEC countries	B 1-a	E 44-a
Consumption requirements as human food: tonnage	UK	B 7-a	
Consumption: tonnage	OAS member countries	E 44-a	
	EEC countries	E 44-a	
Crop yield in cwt per acre	Main countries	B 8-a	
in kg per ha	EEC countries	B 1-a	E 3-a
	Main countries	R 5-a	
	OAS member countries	N 13-a	
	OECD countries	D 1-a	
in quintals per ha	E European countries & USSR	U 16-a	
winter & spring barley in 100 kg per ha	EEC countries	E 12-a	
Deliveries by farmers: tonnage	Main countries	B 7-a	
EEC levy per ton on imported barley shipped from non-EEC sources		B 7-m	
Ex-farm prices: domestic grain for malting in £ per ton	UK	B 8-a	
Export prices (average) by grade	Denmark & USA	B 8-a	
barley for animal feed	Argentine & Canada	B 8-a	
for malting in £ per ton	Australia	B 8-a	
for milling in £ per ton	Australia	B 8-a	
by grade as fodder in local currency	Canada & USA	R 2-m	
in $ per ton fob	Canada	U 35-a	
	Canada & USA	C 16-m	
		U 29-q	
Export prices - index nos (weighted average main sources)			
Export prices in local currency per ton	Argentine, Australia, Canada, Sweden & UK	A 9-a	
Export subsidies per ton	EEC countries	B 8-a	
Exports by destination: tonnage	E European countries, China & USSR	A 17-a	
	Main countries	A 17-a	B 8-a
by value & as % of exports of agricultural products	W European countries	U 20-a	
in $m	W European countries	U 33-a	
tonnage incl world total	Main countries	C 16-a	
	All countries	A 17-a	
	European countries	U 35-a	
Feed price ratios per quintal for pigs: live wt	W European countries	U 30-a	
Government expenditure on price guarantees in £m	UK	P 5-a	
Import prices ex Argentine, S Africa & USA in £ per ton	UK	B 8-m	
ex USA at European ports in $ per ton		U 35-a	
for animal feed in £ per ton cif	UK	B 7-m	
at UK & North Sea ports in $ per ton		A 9-a	
Imports by port of entry: tonnage	UK	B 7-m	P 5-a2
source: tonnage	EEC area	B 8-a	
value & as % of imports of agricultural products	W European countries	U 20-a	
value in $m	W European countries	U 33-a	
for production of animal feeding stuffs: tonnage	UK	P 5-a	
into E European countries & USSR: tonnage	Non-Communist countries	A 17-a	
tonnage	All countries	A 17-a	
	European countries	U 35-a	
	W European countries, Japan & UK	B 8-a	
Industrial usage for distilling spirits: tonnage	UK	C 27-a	
for malting purposes: tonnage	UK	C 27-a	
for processing: tonnage	World regions	C 27-a	
Intervention price per ton	EEC countries	B 8-a	E 44-a
Prices in EEC area as % of world market prices		E 44-a	
Prices paid by farmers for barley as animal feed	E European countries	U 30-a	
	W European countries	U 30-a	
Producer prices in £ per cwt	EEC countries	B 1-a	
% change over previous yr	EEC countries	E 34-a	
in prices received	W European countries	U 30-a	
Producer prices & fixed basic prices	W European countries	U 30-a	
for barley sold as animal feed per 100 kg in			
local currency	European countries	E 35-a	
in local currency per kg	EEC countries	E 34-m	E 44-a
per ton	OECD countries	D 1-a	
per 100 kg	EEC countries	B 3-a	
	W European countries	E 35-a	

	Territorial coverage	Title codes	
BARLEY, continued			
Producer prices in £ equiv per 100 kg	EEC countries	B 3-a	
in $ per bushel	USA	E 35-a	
received by farmers per ton	All countries	A 9-a	
Producer prices - index nos	EEC countries	B 3-a	
in $ per ton	E European countries	U 30-a	
Production by value at current prices	EEC countries	E 44-a	
Production harvested: tonnage	EEC countries	E 12-m	
Production, stocks, industrial usage & consumption as fodder & seed	OECD countries	D 14-a	
Production: tonnage & value of output in £m	EEC countries	B 1-a	
& yield per 100 ha	Latin American countries	J 5-a	
by areas	EEC countries	E 38-a	
historical tables	Main European countries	Z 1-a	
tonnage	Main countries	B 7-a	
	OECD countries	D 1-a	
	African countries	U 44-a	
	All countries	U 43-a	
	European countries	U 35-a	
	E European countries & USSR incl Ukraine	U 16-a	
	EEC countries	E 12-a	E 44-a
	European countries, Canada, Japan, USA & USSR	E 44-a	
	Main countries	B 7-a	B 8-a
		E 3-a	P 5-a
	OAS member countries	N 13-a	
	S American countries	U 40-a	
tonnage: winter & spring crop	EEC countries	E 12-a	
Proportion of harvest exported	Main exporting countries	B 8-a	
Sales by growers in England & Scotland: tonnage		B 7-a	
ex farm: tonnage	EEC countries	E 12-m	
Self-sufficiency ratios	EEC countries	B 1-a	
Stocks at wholesalers' premises: tonnage	EEC countries	E 12-m	
end-season tonnage	Argentine, Canada & USA	B 8-a	
	Main countries	C 16-a	
	Main exporting countries	B 7-a	
Stocks on farms at end-season: tonnage	Main countries	B 7-a	
at end-month: tonnage	EEC countries	E 12-m	
left unsold at end-season: tonnage	UK	B 7-a	
Supply & disposal by purpose: tonnage	Main countries	B 8-a	
Supply, production & required imports: tonnage (estim)	UK	B 7-a	
Supply, production, consumption & trade: tonnage	EEC countries	B 1-a	
Supply (production plus net imports): tonnage	Main countries	B 8-a	
Target, intervention, & threshold prices in £ per cwt	EEC countries	B 1-a	
Wholesale prices: % change over previous yr	EEC countries	E 34-m	
by grade in local currency per kg	OAS member countries	N 17-a	
home-grown for pig-feed - index nos	EEC countries	C 9-m	
in local currency per kg	EEC countries	E 34-m	
in local currency	Main countries	A 9-a	
World production: tonnage		C 16-a	
Barrows see PIGS			
BARS & RODS, BERYLLIUM-COPPER			
Wholesale prices in £ per lb	UK	T 4-w	
Bars & rods, magnesium see MAGNESIUM PRODUCTS, SEMI-FINISHED			
BARS, RODS & SECTIONS, ALUMINIUM			
Production: tonnage	All countries	U 22-a	
BARS, RODS & SECTIONS, COPPER			
Production: tonnage	All countries	U 22-a	
BARTER AGREEMENTS			
A.I.D. barter under development aid programs	Worldwide	M 1-a	
Agreements covering wheat & flour: tonnage	USA	C 16-a	

Barytes see BARIUM MINERALS

Basic bessemer plants see STEELWORKS

Basic economic indicators see ECONOMIC INDICATORS, BASIC

Basic metals see METALS, BASIC

Basic organic chemicals see ORGANIC CHEMICALS

Basic slag see FERTILISERS, PHOSPHATE
FURNACE SLAG

Bastnaesite see RARE EARTH MINERALS

Bath facilities, fixed see DWELLINGS

		Territorial coverage	Title codes	
BATTERIES & ACCUMULATORS				
% demand increase projected to 1977		UK	B 23	
% share of world trade (value basis)		Main countries	B 23-a	
Consumption of antimony in production of batteries: tonnage		UK	C 12-a	T 4-a
of lead in production of batteries: tonnage		European countries	C 12-a	
		Main countries	T 4-a	
of silver in production of batteries in oz		USA	T 4-a	
Demand projected to 1980		E African countries	U 38	
Exports by destination: no & value in £m		UK	V 1-a	
by value in $m		Main countries	U 9-a	
value in $m		Main countries	U 38-a	
Imports by source: no & value in £m		UK	V 1-a	
value in $m		All countries	U 38-a	
Production by volume: accumulators		African countries	U 44-a	
for vehicles		All countries	U 38-a	
		EEC countries	E 28-q	E 27-a
Production by volume		All countries	U 22-a	
World export trade by value in $m			U 38-a	

Battery oxides   see   PIGMENTS, MINERAL

BAUXITE

	Territorial coverage	Title codes	
% contribution to export earnings of shipments of aluminium ore	Guyana & Jamaica	E 45-a	
% share of estim world reserves	Latin American region	U 18-a	
Consumption for industrial purposes: tonnage	USA	T 4-a	
tonnage	OAS member countries	N 17-a	
	USA	N 1-a	
		U 29-q	
Export prices - index nos (weighted average main sources)	African, Caribbean countries & Pacific Is	E 45-a	
Exports: tonnage & value in $m	Main countries	T 4-a	
by destination: tonnage	Developing countries	U 11-a	
by value in $m	Guyana, Jamaica & Surinam	B 2-a	
tonnage & value in $m	All importing countries	D 28-a	
Freight: tonnage by cargo source			
Government stockpile of bauxite (metal & refractory grades): tonnage	USA	N 1-a	
Imports by source: tonnage	Main countries	H 2-a	T 4-a
Production: tonnage incl world total	Main countries	B 2-a	
alumina	Guyana, Jamaica & Surinam	U 18-a	
crude ore mined	All countries	U 27-m	U 22-a
		U 43-a	
dry calcined alumina	Guyana & Surinam	U 18-a	
dry ore	Brazil, Guyana, Jamaica & Surinam	U 18-a	
historical table from 1901	Main European countries	Z 1-a	
from 1913	All countries	C 4-a	
	EEC countries & USA	C 12-a	
tonnage - index nos	All countries	B 15-a	C 12-a
tonnage		H 2-a	J 6-a
		R 5-a	
	EEC countries	E 28-q	E 27-a
	Latin American countries	J 5-a	U 40-a
	Main countries	E 3-a	
	OAS member countries	N 14-a	
Shipments through Panama Canal westwards: tonnage		D 28-a	
Stocks at producers' & consumers' premises: tonnage	USA	N 1-a	
excl govt stockpile: tonnage	USA	B 2-a	
Wholesale prices by quality in Frs per ton	France	T 4-m	
in $ per ton (at mine)	USA	N 1-a	
World export trade: tonnage	Main countries	T 4-a	
World production: tonnage	Main countries	N 1-a	
tonnage: historical table		C 12-a	
tonnage (incl alumina)		N 4-a	
	All countries	C 30-a	J 3-a
		J 6-a	
World reserves: tonnage (estim)		N 1-a	

Beans   see   DRY BEANS

Beans, green   see   PEAS & BEANS

Bearings metals   see   ANTI-FRICTION METALS

BEARINGS

	Territorial coverage	Title codes	
% share held of world exports in ball & roller bearings	UK	B 27-a	
Consumption of antimony in bearings production: tonnage	UK	T 4-a	
	UK & USA	C 12-a	
of silver in bearings production in oz	USA	T 4-a	
Exports: ball & roller bearings by value in $m	All countries	U 38-a	
Exports by value & destination in $m	Main countries	U 9-a	
Imports by value in $m	All countries	U 38-a	
Production: tonnage of anti-friction bearings	EEC countries	E 28-q	E 27-a
World export trade in ball & roller bearings by value in $m		U 38-a	

Beaujolais   see   WINE

Bedclothes   see   HOUSEHOLD TEXTILES

Beds   see   HOSPITALS
            HOTELS
            TOURIST ACCOMMODATION

	Territorial coverage	Title codes

Bedspreads & quilts   see   HOUSEHOLD TEXTILES

Beef cattle   see   LIVESTOCK

BEEF FATS

Consumption in production of cooking fats: tonnage	USA	B 19-a
margarine: tonnage	USA	B 19-a

BEEF

% contribution to export earnings	Chad	E 45-a	
Availability for consumption: tonnage	Main countries	B 11-a	
Consumption (incl veal) as % meat consumption	Main countries	B 11-a	
per capita (incl veal) in kg per yr	European countries	U 36-a	
	OECD countries	D 1-a	
	EEC countries	B 1-a	
	UK	B 12-a	
	Main countries	B 11-a	
tonnage & consumption per capita in kg per yr	EEC countries	E 1-a	
tonnage (incl veal) projected to 1978	OECD countries	D 15-a	
Export availability & import needs (incl veal) projected to 1978	OAS member countries	N 17-a	
	OECD countries	D 15-a	
Export prices: chilled & frozen beef in $ per ton	Main countries	A 9-a	
index nos (weighted average main sources)		U 29-q	
index nos	S American countries	U 40-q	
Exports by destination (incl veal): tonnage	Main countries	B 12-m	B 11-a
	Netherlands & W Germany	C 9-m	
Exports (incl veal) by value as % of total exports	Main countries	B 11-a	
tonnage	European countries & USSR	U 36-a	
Import prices ex Argentine of chilled beef in pence per kg	UK	U 33-q	
Imports & exports: dried or salted beef: tonnage	EEC countries	E 1-a	
fresh or frozen beef: tonnage	EEC countries	E 1-a	
Imports (incl veal) by source: tonnage	EEC countries	B 11-a	
fresh, salted or chilled	Main countries	B 11-a	
tonnage	European countries & USSR	U 36-a	
Intervention price fixed by EEC commission	EEC area	E 44-a	
Price factors in EEC trade: export levies in pence per lb	EEC countries	C 9	
import duties in % ad val	EEC countries	C 9	
import subsidies in pence per lb	EEC countries	C 9	
Prices in EEC area as % of world market prices	EEC countries	E 44-a	
Producer prices in DKr per kg	Denmark	D 1-a	
Production: chilled or frozen beef: tonnage	Main countries	B 12-a	
by areas: tonnage	EEC countries	E 38-a	
from indigenous cattle: tonnage	AASM countries	E 41-a	
Production, imports, exports & net domestic supply: tonnage	EEC countries	E 1-a	
stocks, & consumption per capita per day: tonnage	OECD countries	D 14-a	
	EEC countries	E 26-m	B 1-a
(incl veal) in dressed carcase wt: tonnage	OECD countries	D 1-a	
	Main countries	B 11-a	
	African countries	U 44-a	
	European countries	U 36-a	
	Main countries	B 11-a	
	All countries	A 9-a	
	European countries, Japan, USSR & USA	E 44-a	
	Latin American countries	U 40-a	
	OAS member countries	N 14-a	
Production projected to 1978: tonnage	OECD countries	D 15-a	
slaughterings of beef animals: tonnage	EEC countries	E 1-a	
Retail prices by cut of animal in local currency	OAS member countries	N 17-a	
(comparative): boned sirloin in $ per kg	EEC countries	Z 3-a	
Self-sufficiency ratios (incl veal)	EEC countries	B 1-a	E 3-a
		E 44-a	
Stocks & change in stocks on previous yr (at 1st July): tonnage	France & W Germany	E 1-a	
Stocks: imported frozen beef held in cold storage: tonnage	UK	B 12-w	
Supply, production, consumption, imports & exports: tonnage	EEC countries	B 1-a	
Surplus of production (incl veal) over needs projected to 1978: tonnage	OECD countries	D 15-a	
Wholesale prices by cuts of animal at central markets in pence per lb	UK	B 12-w	
by kind (incl veal) in local currency	OAS member countries	N 17-a	
by quality	Main countries	A 9-a	
English, Australian & Argentinian beef - index nos	UK	B 11-q	
English & imported at Smithfield in pence per lb	UK	B 11-m	
hindquarters ex Argentine in pence per kg	UK	U 20-q	
Wholesale prices (incl veal) - index nos	EEC countries	C 9-m	
in local currency per lb at London & New York markets	UK & USA	R 2-m	
in local currency	Denmark & UK	U 27-m	
World exports (incl veal) by value in $m	World regions	A 5-a	
World market prices: hindquarters (ex Argentine) per 100 kg		E 34-m	
World market prices - index nos		G 1-a	
World production: tonnage (incl veal)	World regions	A 5-a	

BEER

% changes in volume of retail sales	E European countries & USSR	U 16-a
Consumption in litres per yr	OAS member countries	N 17-a
per capita in kg per yr	OECD countries	D 1-a
in litres per yr	E European countries & USSR	U 16-a

	Territorial coverage	Title codes
BEER, continued		
Excise duties: rates charged	EEC countries	E 31-a
Production & consumption per capita in kg per yr	OECD countries	D 14-a
Production by volume of beer made from malt in hectolitres	All countries	U 22-a
historical table in hectolitres from 1750	Main countries	Z 1-a
in hectolitres	AASM countries	E 41-a
	African countries	U 44-a
	EEC countries	E 28-q E 27-c
	OAS member countries	N 14-a
in proof gallons	W Indies & Caribbean countries	T 6-a
	Latin American countries	U 40-a
of malted liquors	All countries	U 43-a
Retail prices (comparative) of light ale per 0.33 litre measure	EEC countries	Z 3-a
in local currency	OAS member countries	N 17-a
Revenue from taxation on beer in $m	OECD countries	D 42-a

Beet   see   SUGAR BEET
                   FODDER BEET

Beet sugar   see   SUGAR, BEET

BELTING, INDUSTRIAL

Consumption of fibres by kind in production of belting: tonnage	EEC countries	K 4-a
of rubber in production of belting: tonnage	France, Japan & UK	C 18-a

Bending & forming machines   see   MACHINE TOOLS

Benefits, National Health   see   DEATH BENEFITS
                                     INJURY & DISABLEMENT BENEFITS
                                     MATERNITY BENEFITS
                                     SICKNESS BENEFITS
                                     SOCIAL SECURITY BENEFITS
                                     UNEMPLOYMENT BENEFITS
                                     WIDOW'S & ORPHAN'S BENEFITS

BENTONITE

    see also   FULLER'S EARTH

Imports & exports by source & destination: tonnage	Main countries	B 15-a
Production: tonnage	USA	N 1-a
	Main countries	B 15-a

BENZENE

    see also   CHEMICAL PRODUCTS
                       HYDROCARBONS, AROMATIC

Consumption: tonnage (total) & for organic synthesis	OECD countries	D 5-a
Exports: tonnage	European countries, Japan & USA	U 26-a
Imports: tonnage	European countries, Japan & USA	U 26-a
Production: tonnage from coal derivatives	OECD countries	D 5-a
	Main countries	U 26-a
oil & natural gas	Main countries	U 26-a
	OECD countries	D 5-a
tonnage	European countries, Japan & USA	U 26-a
Refining capacity installed in tons per yr	EEC countries	B 30-a

Benzole   see   CHEMICAL PRODUCTS

BERYL

Imports & exports by source & destination: tonnage	Main countries	B 15-a
Production: tonnage	All countries	B 15-a
World production: tonnage		N 4-a

BERYLLIUM

Consumption: tonnage	USA	N 1-a
Government stockpile: tonnage	USA	N 1-a
Production: tonnage	Main countries	N 1-a
	Zaire	E 41-a
Stocks at consumers' premises: tonnage	USA	N 1-a
Wholesale prices: beryllium metal in $ per lb	USA	N 1-a

BERYLLIUM CONCENTRATES

Production: tonnage	USA	J 6-a

BERYLLIUM ORE

Exports by destination: tonnage	Brazil	T 4-a
Import prices: cobbed lump in $ per ton	European countries	T 4-m
Imports by source: tonnage	USA	T 4-a
Wholesale prices of imported ore in $ per 20 lbs	USA	N 1-a
World export trade: tonnage		T 4-a
World production: tonnage (incl concentrates)		C 30-a
tonnage	Main countries	T 4-a

Beryllium-copper ingots   see   INGOTS, BERYLLIUM-COPPER ALLOY

Beryllium-copper rods   see   RODS & BARS, BERYLLIUM-COPPER

	Territorial coverage	Title codes

Beryllium-copper sheets   see   SHEETS, BERYLLIUM-COPPER

Beryllium-copper strip   see   STRIP, BERYLLIUM-COPPER

Beryllium-copper wire   see   WIRE, BERYLLIUM-COPPER

Bespoke tailoring   see   CLOTHING, READY-MADE

Bessemer plants   see   STEELWORKS

Bessemer steel   see   CRUDE STEEL

Betterment levies   see   AGRICULTURAL LEVIES

BETTING & GAMBLING

Rates of taxation on betting & lotteries	EEC countries	E 31-a
Revenue from taxes on betting & gambling	EEC countries	E 42-a
	OECD countries	D 42-a

Betting & gaming taxes   see   TAXATION

BEVERAGES

see also   BEER
          COCOA
          COFFEE
          TEA
          WINE

As source of calorie intake per capita per day in grammes	OAS member countries	N 17-a
fat intake per capita per day in grammes	OAS member countries	N 17-a
protein intake per capita per day in grammes	OAS member countries	N 17-a
Consumption cost of non-alcoholic drinks: tea & coffee	EEC countries	E 32-a
Consumption expenditure (private) in local currency	OAS countries	N 16-a
Earnings from sales in international hotels per room in $	World regions	Z 5-a
tourist hotels per room in $	World regions	Z 5-a
Excise duties: rates charged	EEC countries	E 31-a
Exports of coffee, tea & cocoa by value in $m	OECD countries	D 1-a
(incl tobacco) as % of total agricultural trade	W European countries	U 20-a
to EEC & non-EEC area by value in $m	EEC countries	E 24-a
Imports of coffee, tea & cocoa by value in $m	OECD countries	D 1-a
ex EEC & non-EEC area by value in $m	EEC countries	E 24-a
(incl tobacco) as % of total agricultural trade	W European countries	U 20-a
Production of mineral waters, lemonade & soda water	AASM countries	E 41-a
Production - index nos (quantum basis)	S American countries	U 40-a
World market prices: coffee, cocoa & tea - index nos		U 23-a

BEVERAGES, ALCOHOLIC

% of households consuming spirits & liqueurs	W European countries	Z 3
% contribution to export earnings	Bahamas, Guyana & Jamaica	E 45-a
Consumption expenditure: private sector in local currency	OAS member countries	N 16-a
	EEC countries	E 32-a
Consumption: volume in litres	OAS member countries	N 17-a
Exports: tonnage & value in $m	African & Caribbean countries & Pacific Is	E 45-a
Production: distilled drinks & spirits	All countries	U 22-a
	W Indies & Caribbean countries	T 6-a
Receipts of taxes on beer, wines & spirits	EEC countries	E 42-a
Retail prices by kind in local currency	OAS member countries	N 17-a
(comparative) of whisky per 0.75 litre measure	EEC countries	Z 3-a
Wholesale prices in local currency	OAS member countries	N 17-a

BEVERAGES BY KIND

% changes in retail sales	E European countries & USSR	U 16-a	
Exports by destination by CST classes: tonnage & value in $m	EEC countries	E 48-a	
by SITC classes by value in $m	Main countries	D 2-q	
by SITC classes: tonnage & value in $m	OECD countries	D 3-a2	
(incl tobacco by kind) by value in $m	All countries	U 12-a	
Exports by NIMEXE classes by value in $m	All countries	E 20-a	
SITC classes by value in $m	All countries	U 50-a	U 59-a
Imports by NIMEXE classes by value in $m	All countries	E 20-a	
SITC classes by value in $m	All countries	U 50-a	U 59-a
source by CST classes: tonnage & value in $m	EEC countries	E 21-a	
by SITC classes by value in $m	Main countries	D 2-q	
by SITC classes: tonnage & value in $m	OECD countries	D 3-a2	
Retail prices in local currency	OAS member countries	N 17-a	

Bicycles   see   CYCLES & MOPEDS

BILATERAL AID

see also   INVESTMENT, PRIVATE OVERSEAS
          INVESTMENT, PUBLIC OVERSEAS
          DEVELOPMENT AID

Received in $m	Recipient countries	D 7-a
Capital commitments in $m	China, E European countries & USSR	U 43-a
Disbursements (gross) by type of aid given in $m	OECD countries	D 13-a
(public) in $m	Main countries	D 7-a
to developing countries in $m	Recipient countries	U 43-a
as grants, loans, relief & food aid in $m	OECD countries	D 13-a

	Territorial coverage	Title codes
BILATERAL AID, continued		
Loans as development assistance in $m	Worldwide	M 3-a
(official) granted to developing countries in $m	Worldwide	M 4-a
(private) granted to developing countries in $m	Worldwide	M 4-a
Milk powder shipments as food aid: tonnage	EEC countries	B 3-a
Portfolio investment in overseas bonds: value in $m	Worldwide	M 3-a

Bill discounting   see   ACCEPTANCE HOUSES

Billets, steel   see   INGOTS, STEEL
　　　　　　　　　　　STEEL, SEMI-FINISHED

Bills of exchange   see   ACCEPTANCE HOUSES

Bills of exchange tax   see   TAXATION

Binoculars   see   OPTICAL INSTRUMENTS

BIRD'S FEATHERS

Exports by value in local currency	S Vietnam	U 32-m

BIRTH RATES

Per 1000 population projected to yr 2000	Developed world regions	M 4-a	
	Developing world regions	M 4-a	
historical table 1750-1969	Main European countries	Z 1-a	
by areas	EEC countries	E 38-a	
in 5-yr periods	Main countries	R 5	
	World average excl USSR	R 5	
Per 1000 population	All countries	W 1-q	M 6-a
	E European countries	N 6-a	
	EEC countries	E 2-a	
	OECD countries	D 23-a	
No of births & birth rates per 1000	All countries	U 14-a	U 28-a
per 1000 population by sex	OAS member countries	N 12-a	
per 1000 population	Latin American countries	J 5-a	
of registrations per 1000 population	Main countries	U 27-m	

Births   see   LIVE BIRTHS

BISCUITS

Production: tonnage by kind	EEC countries	E 28-q	E 27-a
tonnage	All countries	U 22-a	

BISMUTH

Consumption for production of alloys: tonnage	USA	T 4-a
of fusible alloys: tonnage	USA	T 4-a
of metallic additives: tonnage	USA	T 4-a
of pharmaceuticals: tonnage	USA	T 4-a
Consumption: tonnage	USA	N 1-a
Export prices in $ per lb cif	USA	T 4-m
Exports by destination of bismuth metal: tonnage	Main countries	T 4-a
Government stockpile: tonnage	USA	N 1-a
Imports & exports by source & destination: tonnage	Main countries	B 15-a
Production: bismuth ore & concentrates: tonnage	All countries	B 15-a
from tungsten-bismuth ores: tonnage	S Korea	U 53-a
tonnage	Bolivia, Mexico & Peru	U 40-a
	Main countries	N 1-a
Stocks at consumers' & dealers' premises: tonnage	USA	N 1-a
Wholesale prices ex warehouse per kg	Japan & UK	T 4-m
in $ per lb	USA	N 1-a
World production: tonnage	Reporting countries only	C 30-a
	Main countries	N 1-a
	USA	T 4-a
tonnage (excl US production)		N 4-a
World reserves: tonnage (estim)	Main countries	N 1-a

BITUMEN

Consumption for construction of roads & airfields: tonnage	OECD countries	D 31-a	
tonnage	Main countries	C 14-a	
from own plants: tonnage	Italy	H 4-a	
Deliveries, home consumption & exports: tonnage	OECD countries	D 31-a	
Imports by source: tonnage	OECD countries	D 31-a	
Imports & exports by source & destination: tonnage	All countries	B 15-a	
Production: tonnage of natural asphalt	African countries	U 44-a	
	All countries	U 22-a	
	Main countries	B 15-a	
tonnage	All countries	U 43-a	
	EEC countries	E 28-q	E 27-a
	Latin American countries	J 5-a	
Refinery output, imports & supply: tonnage	OECD countries	D 31-a	

Bituminous coal   see   ANTHRACITE
　　　　　　　　　　　　COAL
　　　　　　　　　　　　COKING COAL
　　　　　　　　　　　　HARD COAL BRIQUETTES
　　　　　　　　　　　　LIGNITE

	Territorial coverage	Title codes	

Black lead   see   GRAPHITE

Blackplate   see   TINPLATE

BLANKETS
   see also   HOUSEHOLD TEXTILES

Consumption of wool for production of blankets in kg	Main countries	K 6-a	
Demand (domestic) projected to 1977 in million lbs	UK	B 29	
Exports in kg	Belgium, Greece, Italy, Spain & UK	K 6-a	
Imports in kg	France, Netherlands, Syria, UK & USA	K 6-a	
Production by kind of textile fibre used	EEC countries	K 4-a	
volume (incl rugs & bedspreads)	All countries	U 22-a	
Retail prices in local currency	OAS member countries	N 17-a	

BLANKS FOR TUBES, STEEL

Consumption: tonnage	EEC countries	E 29-a	
Deliveries for seamless tube production: tonnage	ECE countries	U 7-q	U 6-a
	Main countries	H 3-a	
for home & export sales: tonnage	OECD countries	D 22-a	
Exports by destination: tonnage	Main countries	T 4-a	
	EEC area	E 5-q	
Imports by source: tonnage	Main countries	T 4-a	
	EEC countries	E 5-q	
Prices (net less tax) at main centres	EEC countries	E 30-a	
Production: tonnage of tube ingots & solids	All countries	T 1-a	
	EEC countries	E 30-m	E 28-q
		E 27-a	E 29-a
	ECE countries	U 7-m	U 6-a
	Main countries	H 3-a	T 4-a
	OECD countries	D 22-a	

Blast furnace alloys   see   PIG IRON

BLAST FURNACE GAS

Calorific value (average)	European countries & USA	U 3-a	
Changes in stocks in coal equiv tonnage	EEC countries	E 14-a	
Consumption by electricity supply plants	EEC countries	U 1-a	
industrial sectors	EEC countries	E 14-a	
iron & steel industry	EEC countries	E 14-a	E 29-a
	OECD countries	D 44-a	
of coke oven coke in production of gas	OECD countries	D 44-a	
for industrial purposes in m³	EEC countries	E 16-q	E 15-a
for producing power & energy in m³	EEC countries	E 16-q	E 15-a
in electricity generation in m³	EEC countries	E 16-q	E 14-a
		E 15-a	
in m³	European countries, USSR & USA	U 4-a	
Deliveries to steel industry in coal equiv tonnage	EEC countries	E 29-a	
Distribution losses in calorific value	EEC countries	E 16-q	E 15-a
by volume in m³	OECD countries	D 44-a	
Production in calorific value	EEC countries	E 16-q	E 15-a
	European countries & USSR	U 4-a	
	EEC countries	E 14-a	
in coal equiv tonnage	ECE countries	U 6-a	U 7-a
volume in m³	Main countries	H 3-a	
	OECD countries	D 44-a	
Resources ex indigenous production	EEC countries	E 14-a	
Sales by volume in m³ by steelworks	ECE countries	U 6-a	U 7-a
	Main countries	H 3-a	

BLAST FURNACES
   see also   PIG IRON

% of agglomerates in ore charge	Main countries	U 49-a	
Consumption: coke in pig iron production: tonnage	All countries	U 49-a	
	ECE countries	U 6-a	U 7-a
	EEC countries	E 14-a	
	Main countries	H 3-a	T 1-a
iron ore for pig iron production: tonnage	Main countries	T 1-a	
scrap for pig iron production: tonnage	Main countries	T 1-a	U 49-a
sinter in blast furnaces: tonnage	UK	T 2-m	
Investment by regions in UA million	EEC countries	E 46-a	
on new equipment in blast furnace plants in $m	Main countries	U 49-a	
No of blast furnaces installed & no in operation	France	C 5-m	

Blister copper   see   COPPER, BLISTER

Blockboard   see   PLYWOOD & BLOCKBOARD

Blooming mills   see   STEEL RE-ROLLING PLANTS

Blooms   see   INGOTS, STEEL
              STEEL, SEMI-FINISHED

Blouses   see   CLOTHING

Blue-vein   see   CHEESE BY VARIETY

	Territorial coverage	Title codes

BOARDING HOUSES
    see also   HOTELS
                   INNS
                   MOTELS

No of beds available for visitors & tourists	OECD countries	D 47-a
tourist & lodging establishments	OAS member countries	N 15-a
rooms & no of beds available	OAS member countries	N 15-a

Boars   see   PIGS

BOILERHOUSE PLANT
    see also   BOILERS
                   POWER GENERATING EQUIPMENT

% share of imports by source	EEC countries	B 30-a
Exports: boiler auxiliaries by value in $m	Main European countries	B 30-a
replacement parts by value in $m	Main European countries	B 30-a
steam condensers by value in $m	Main European countries	B 30-a
Imports by value in $m	EEC countries	B 30-a
condensers by value in $m	All countries	U 38-a
Production by value in £m	EEC countries	B 30-a

BOILERHOUSE PLANT BY KIND

% of exports by destination	EEC countries	B 30-a
% of imports by source	EEC countries	B 30-a
Exports by value in £m	EEC countries	B 30-a
in $m	France, W Germany & UK	B 30-a
Imports by value in £m	EEC countries	B 30-a
Production by value in £m	EEC countries	B 30-a

BOILERS
    see also   BOILERHOUSE PLANT

% share of world exports of boilerhouse plant	UK	B 27-a
Consumption of electric power in industrial boilers in kWh	All countries	C 23-a
Deliveries by boiler sizes in ton-hr capacity	European countries, Japan & USA	D 45-a
Exports as % of production	European countries, Japan & USA	D 45-a
steam boilers in tons-hr capacity	European countries, Japan & USA	D 45-a
Imports by value (incl machinery) in local currency	Iran	U 32-m
New orders & orders on hand	European countries, Japan & USA	D 45-a
Production capacity in ton-hrs of steam	W European countries, Japan & USA	D 45-a

BOILERS, MARINE

Production by value in million yen	Japan	S 16-a

BOILERS, STEAM
    see also   ALTERNATORS, THERMAL
                   BOILERHOUSE PLANT
                   GENERATORS, THERMAL
                   POWER GENERATING EQUIPMENT

% of exports by destination	EEC countries	B 30-a
% of imports by source	EEC countries	B 30-a
% share of exports by kind of steam boiler	EEC countries	B 30-a
of imports by source	EEC countries	B 30-a
Exports by destination by value (in detail) in £m	EEC countries	B 30-a
value in £m	EEC countries	B 30-a
Imports by source by value (in detail) in £m	EEC countries	B 30-a
value in £m	EEC countries	B 30-a
in $m	EEC countries	B 30-a
Production by value in £m	EEC countries	B 30-a
in $m	All countries	U 22-a

BOILERS, WATERTUBE

Exports by destination by value (in detail) in £m	EEC countries	B 30-a
Imports by source by value (in detail) in £m	EEC countries	B 30-a
Production by value in £m	EEC countries	B 30-a

BOILERS BY KIND

% of exports by destination	EEC countries	B 30-a
% of imports by source	EEC countries	B 30-a
Exports by value in £m	EEC countries	B 30-a
Imports by source by value in £m	EEC countries	B 30-a
Production by value in £m	EEC countries	B 30-a

Bond yields, corporate   see   INTEREST RATES

Bond yields, government   see   INTEREST RATES

BONDS
    see also   GOVERNMENT BONDS
                   MUNICIPAL BONDS
                 PRIVATE BONDS

By type of issue & kind of investors by value in $m	OECD countries	D 12-a
Sold on stock exchanges (incl securities) by value in local currency	OAS member countries	N 16-a
% interest rates per annum & yields by maturity dates	OECD countries	D 12-a
No of international issues by currency of issue	OECD countries	D 12-a

	Territorial coverage	Title codes
BOOK TRANSLATIONS		
No & name of most-translated authors	All countries	U 62-a
published by original language & subject group	All countries	U 62-a
	OAS member countries	N 19-a
	Main countries	U 43-a
by subject	All countries	U 43-a U 62-a
in foreign languages	All countries	U 62-a
on fine arts	OAS member countries	N 19-a
pure & applied sciences	OAS member countries	N 19-a
social sciences	OAS member countries	N 19-a
BOOKBINDING INDUSTRY		
Wage rates of bookbinders in FrS	Switzerland	R 4-a
BOOKS		
see also BOOK TRANSLATIONS		
NOVELS, PAPERBACK		
PAMPHLETS		
PRINTING & PUBLISHING		
Exports by NIMEXE classes by value in $	All countries	E 20-a
by SITC classes by value in $	All countries	U 50-a U 59-a
Imports by NIMEXE classes by value in $	All countries	E 20-a
by SITC classes by value in $	All countries	U 50-a U 59-a
No of new titles published per 1 million population	World regions	U 62-a
of titles published by language	Main countries	U 43-a
by subject groups	Latin American countries	J 5-a
	Main countries	U 43-a
	OAS member countries	N 19-a
	Asian, Far East & Australasian countries	U 45-a
on fine arts	OAS member countries	N 19-a
geography & history	OAS member countries	N 19-a
literature	OAS member countries	N 19-a
philosophy	OAS member countries	N 19-a
religion	OAS member countries	N 19-a
social sciences	OAS member countries	N 19-a
school textbooks	All countries	U 62-a
No of titles published	Latin American countries	J 5-a
Production volume by broad subject groups	All countries	U 62-a
no of new titles published (estim)	World regions	U 62-a
BOOKS BY KIND		
% adults buying & reading books by social classes	W European countries	Z 3
BOOKS BY LANGUAGE		
Production in national & foreign languages	All countries	U 62-a
BOOKS BY SUBJECT		
No of first editions published by content	All countries	U 62-a
Production (in detail) by content	All countries	U 62-a
BOOKS FOR CHILDREN		
No of copies published	All countries	U 62-a
	OAS member countries	N 19-a
of titles published	All countries	U 62-a
	OAS member countries	N 19-a
Boot & shoe manufacturing industry see FOOTWEAR INDUSTRY		
Boots & shoes see FOOTWEAR		
BORATE		
Imports & exports by source & destination: tonnage	Main countries	B 15-a
Production: tonnage of crude borate	Argentine, Turkey & USA	B 15-a
Borax, Pentahydrate see BORON		
Borer-millers, horizontal see MACHINE TOOLS		
BORING MACHINES		
see also MACHINE TOOLS		
Deliveries by industrial sector by value in $m	USA	J 2-a
Exports by volume & value in $m	USA	J 2-a
Imports by volume & value in $m	USA	J 2-a
Inter-EEC trade by value in $m incl % growth rates		B 20-a
Production, imports, exports, & home sales by value in $m	EEC countries	B 20-a
BORING MACHINES, AUTOMATIC		
Production of numerically-controlled type by volume	EEC countries	B 20-a
BORING MACHINES BY TYPE		
Sales by volume & value in $m	USA	J 2-a

	Territorial coverage	Title codes
BORON		
Wholesale prices: pentahydrate borax in $ per ton	USA	N 1-a
World production: tonnage (at mines)	Main countries	N 1-a
World reserves: tonnage (estim)	Main countries	N 1-a
Bottled fruits see CANNED & BOTTLED FRUIT		
BOTTLES & CONTAINERS, GLASS		
Production volume	All countries	U 22-a
	Zaire	E 41-a
Bottling machinery see PACKAGING MACHINERY		
Bottom-blown plants see STEELWORKS		
Box calf & sides see LEATHER		
Box-board, folding see PAPER & PAPERBOARD		
Boxing matches see SPORTS		
Brake & clutch linings see REPLACEMENT PARTS		
BRASS		
see also INGOTS, BRASS		
Consumption in production of castings: tonnage	UK	J 6-a
rods, bars & sections: tonnage	UK	J 6-a
sheet plate & strip: tonnage	UK	J 6-a
tubes: tonnage	UK	J 6-a
wire: tonnage	UK	J 6-a
of lead in production of brass & bronze: tonnage	USA	T 4-a
tin in production of brass & bronze: tonnage	USA	J 6-a
zinc in production of brass: tonnage	Main countries	T 4-a
	UK	J 6-a
Exports by destination of rolled brass: tonnage	USSR	T 4-a
Producer prices in DM	W Germany	H 2-m
Production: tonnage	France & Italy	C 12-a
Wholesale prices: heavy yellow brass in local currency per ton	Main countries	T 4-m
Brass castings see CASTINGS, BRASS		
BRASS PRODUCTS, SEMI-FINISHED BY KIND		
Imports by source: tonnage	USA	J 6-a
of tubes (seamless) by source: tonnage	USA	J 6-a
Production: tonnage	France & Italy	C 12-a
Wholesale prices	Main countries	T 4-w
Wholesale prices: rods per ton	Main countries	T 4-w
sheets per ton	Italy	C 12-m
	Main countries	T 4-w
tubes by size per ton	UK	T 4-w
per ton	Italy	C 12-m
	Main countries	T 4-w
wire per kg	Italy	C 12-m
ton	Main countries	T 4-w
BRASS SCRAP		
Exports in bars, plates & sheets: tonnage	USA	J 6-a
in ingot form: tonnage	USA	J 6-a
of pipe tubing & fittings scrap: tonnage	USA	J 6-a
wire scrap: tonnage	USA	J 6-a
Imports: tonnage	USA	J 6-a
Wholesale prices: heavy rods, ends & swarf in £ per ton	UK	T 4-w
red composition brass per ton	Main countries	T 4-w
yellow brass scrap & turnings per ton	Main countries	T 4-w
Brass sheets see BRASS PRODUCTS, SEMI-FINISHED		
Brass tubes see BRASS PRODUCTS, SEMI-FINISHED		
Brass wire see BRASS PRODUCTS, SEMI-FINISHED		
BRAZIL NUTS		
Import prices of medium kernels in £ per ton cif	UK	P 4-m
Imports: tonnage in shell & unshelled	Main countries	P 4-m
BRAZING METALS		
see also SOLDER		
WHITE METAL		
Consumption of silver in production of brazing metals & solder in oz	USA	T 4-a
Production: tonnage	UK	C 30-m

	Territorial coverage	Title codes

BREAD
- Consumption cost to private sector at current prices — EEC countries — E 32-a
- per capita: bread grain products in kg — USSR — C 27-a
- Production tonnage: bakers' wares — All countries — U 22-a
- Retail prices by kind in local currency — OAS member countries — N 17-a
- (comparative) for white loaves in cents per kg — EEC countries — Z 3-a

BREAD GRAINS
    see also   WHEAT
                   RYE
- Area under crop in ha — OECD countries — D 1-a
- Consumption tonnage & consumption per capita in kg — OECD countries — D 14-a
- as animal feed: tonnage — OECD countries — D 1-a
- per capita in kg per yr — OECD countries — D 1-a
- Production: stocks (industrial) & usage for fodder: tonnage — OECD countries — D 14-a
- mixed bread grains: tonnage — OECD countries — D 1-a
- State procurement: tonnage — E European countries & USSR — U 16-a

Breakfast cereals   see   CEREAL PREPARATIONS

Brewing & malting   see   DISTILLING & MALTING

BREWING INDUSTRY
    see also   DISTILLING & MALTING
                   MALT
- Investment in buildings in local currency — EEC countries — E 40-a
- machinery in local currency — EEC countries — E 40-a
- Wage rates in local currency — OAS member countries — N 17-a
- per hr by occupation — Austria — R 4-a
- by sex in local currency — Main countries — R 3-m

Bricks   see   BUILDING MATERIALS

Bright flat steel   see   PLATES, UNIVERSAL

BRIGHT STEEL BARS
    see also   MERCHANT BARS, STEEL
- Deliveries to EEC area: tonnage — EEC countries — E 29-a
- to user industries: tonnage — ECE countries — U 7-q   U 6-a
- — Main countries — H 3-a
- tonnage — EEC countries — E 30-m
- Exports by destination: tonnage — EEC countries — E 5-q   E 29-a
- — Main countries — T 4-a
- Imports by source: tonnage — EEC countries — E 5-q   E 29-a
- — Main countries — T 4-a
- Production: tonnage — EEC countries — E 30-m   E 28-q
-     — E 27-a   E 29-a
- — Latin American countries — U 40-a
- — Main countries — T 4-a
- Receipts from EEC area: tonnage — EEC countries — E 29-a

BRIMSTONE
    see also   PYRITES
                   SULPHUR
- Production: tonnage — All countries — T 5-a

Brine   see   SALT

Briquettes   see   HARD COAL BRIQUETTES

BRIQUETTING PLANTS
- Capital expenditure by regions in UA million — EEC countries — E 46-a
- Costs for salaried staff per mth — EEC countries — E 11-a
- Investment in buildings (incl lignite mines) in local currency — EEC countries — E 40-a
- land purchase in local currency — EEC countries — E 40-a
- machinery incl lignite mines in local currency — EEC countries — E 40-a
- Labour costs as % of total costs — EEC countries — E 8-a
- by status of employee in local currency — EEC countries — E 8-a
- per hr all employees — EEC countries — E 11-a
- wage earners — EEC countries — E 11-a
- Labour force: no of salaried staff employed — EEC countries — E 11-a
- wage earners employed — EEC countries — E 11-a
- wage earners & salaried staff — EEC countries — E 8-a
- No of hrs worked by labour force per yr — EEC countries — E 8-a
- salaried staff per yr — EEC countries — E 11-a
- wage earners per yr — EEC countries — E 11-a

Bristle fibre   see   COIR FIBRE

British funds   see   GOVERNMENT BONDS

	Territorial coverage	Title codes

BRITISH STANDARDS

    Specification requirements: iron & steel products   T 4
                                 non-ferrous metal alloys   T 4
                                 non-ferrous metal products   T 4
                                 steel alloys   T 4

BROAD BEANS, DRIED

Area under crop in ha	OAS member countries	N 13-a
Crop yield in kg per ha	OAS member countries	N 13-a
Production: tonnage	African countries	U 44-a
	OAS member countries	N 13-a

Broad-leaved timber   see   TIMBER, DECIDUOUS

Broadcasting   see   RADIO STATIONS

Broadcasting equipment   see   ELECTRONIC EQUIPMENT

Broadcasting transmitters   see   RADIO STATIONS

Broilers   see   POULTRY

Brokerage commissions   see   INVISIBLE TRADE

BROMIDE

Consumption: tonnage	USA	N 1-a
Imports & exports by source & destination: tonnage	Main countries	B 15-a
Production: tonnage (incl compounds)	All countries	B 15-a
	Main countries	N 1-a
Wholesale prices: purified bromide in cents per lb	USA	N 1-a
World production: tonnage	Main countries	N 1-a

Bronchitis   see   DISEASES

BRONZE

         see also   COPPER ALLOYS

Consumption of tin in production of bronze, brass & gunmetal: tonnage	UK	C 20-m
of tin scrap in production of bronze & brass: tonnage	USA	T 4-a
Deliveries incl brass ingots to user industries: tonnage	USA	J 6-m
Production: tonnage	France & Italy	C 12-a

Bronze castings   see   CASTINGS, BRONZE

BRONZE SCRAP BY GRADE

Wholesale prices in lire per kg	Italy	C 12-m

Brown coal   see   LIGNITE

BROWN COAL BRIQUETTES

         see also   HARD COAL BRIQUETTES

Consumption of coke in production of briquettes: tonnage	ECE countries	U 6-a	U 7-a
	Main countries	H 3-a	

BUCKWHEAT

Area harvested in ha, production tonnage & yield per ha	All countries	A 9-a
under crop in ha: historical tables from 1815	Main European countries	Z 1-a
Consumption: tonnage	OAS member countries	N 17-a
Production, consumption & usage for fodder & seed: tonnage	OECD countries	D 14-a
Production harvested: historical tables: tonnage	Main European countries	Z 1-a

BUDGET ACCOUNTS

         see also   EEC BUDGET
                           GOVERNMENT EXPENDITURE
                           INVESTMENT

% increases in central government expenditure	EEC countries	E 13-a
central government revenue	EEC countries	E 13-a
Capital expenditure in Fr CFA milliard	AASM countries	E 41-a
in local currency	Latin American countries	U 18-a
on education in $m	All countries	U 62-a
Central bank operations in local currency	Latin American countries	U 18-a
Consolidated fund in local currency	Latin American countries	U 18-a
Education costs as % of public expenditure	Latin American countries	J 5-a
Expenditure by FEOGA on EEC price intervention in £m	EEC area	B 1-a
type of disbursement in £m	EEC countries	B 1-a
in Fr CFA milliard	AASM countries	E 41-a
local currency	Latin American countries	U 18-a
on overseas food aid in £m	EEC countries	B 1-a
research & development in £m	EEC countries	B 1-a
running expenses in £m	EEC countries	B 1-a
social welfare in £m	EEC countries	B 1-a
Government expenditure as % of gross national product	EEC countries	E 13-a
by categories in $m	Latin American countries	J 5-a
on public health in $m	Latin American countries	J 5-a

	Territorial coverage	Title codes
BUDGET ACCOUNTS, continued		
Government income & expenditure in local currency	W Indies & Caribbean countries	T 6-a
Income & capital account in local currency	Latin American countries	U 18-a
Internal financing in local currency	Latin American countries	U 18-a
Public expenditure & capital account	EEC countries	E 13-a
Receipts & expenditure in $m	Main countries	U 43-a
Surpluses & deficits in local currency	EEC countries	E 13-a
Buffalo hides see HIDES		
BUFFALOES		
Nos slaughtered	All countries	A 9-a
Population of buffaloes	All countries	A 9-a
BUILDING BLOCKS, CONCRETE		
Wholesale prices - index nos	European countries	U 5-a
BUILDING BLOCKS, STONE		
Wholesale prices - index nos	Greece & Malta	U 5-a
BUILDING CONSTRUCTION		
see also BUILDING INDUSTRY		
PUBLIC WORKS		
STEEL FABRICATION INDUSTRY		
(Total & residential) - index nos	OECD countries	D 26-m
As % of fixed investment	All countries	M 6-a
gross domestic product	All countries	U 60-a
gross capital formation	Main countries	E 3-a
As factor in fixed capital formation	ECE countries	U 15-a
By type: floor areas in m²	Main countries	U 43-a
By type - index nos	Main countries	U 43-a
By type: new completions	Main countries	U 27-m U 43-a
no of permits granted by value in local currency	OAS member countries	N 14-a
By type	Asian, Far East & Australasian countries	U 45-a
By wood-working industry in local currency	EEC countries	E 40-a
(Excl buildings) as factor in capital formation in $m	African countries	U 44-a
% change as component of gross domestic product	S European countries	U 16-a
	All countries	U 60-a
	Latin American countries	U 18-a
% change in implicit price deflator	Developing countries	D 25-a
nominal wages in building industry	E European countries	U 16-a
output per employee in building industry	E European countries	U 16-a
productivity in building industry	E European countries	U 16-a
unit wage costs	E European countries	U 16-a
% contribution to gross domestic product	All countries	U 23-a
national product: historical table from 1850	Main European countries	Z 1-a
national income	Developing countries	D 25-a
% of dwellings constructed by co-operatives	E European countries	U 16-a
by state agencies	E European countries	U 16-a
by private enterprise companies	E European countries	U 16-a
% of new dwellings financed by state agencies	European countries	U 5-a
by private enterprise companies	European countries	U 5-a
% growth rate in expenditure	Developing countries	D 25-a
in gross product of building industry	Developing countries	D 25-a
investment projected to 1980 by building industry	OECD countries	D 11
% of employed population working in building industry	EEC countries	E 33-a
% share of total capital investment	E European countries	U 16-a
investment in construction of dwellings	Developing countries	U 57-a
in construction of office building	Developing countries	U 57-a
in other types of construction work	Developing countries	U 57-a
Activity as % change over previous yr	Main countries	D 4-a
Activity - index nos	Main countries	U 58-a
Area of buildings completed in m²	OAS member countries	N 14-a
Capital formation as % gross national product	All countries	U 13-a
	European countries & USA	U 5-a
in building industry as % total capital formation	ECE countries	U 15-a
	European countries	U 5-a
by areas in $m	EEC countries	E 38-a
in local currency	African countries	U 44-a
Civil engineering projects completed by value in $m	OAS member countries	N 16-a
Civil engineering projects - index nos	Main countries	U 58-a
Consumption of electricity by areas in kWh	Main countries	U 58-a
of electricity in kWh	EEC countries	E 38-a
Contracts awarded by value in $m	EEC countries	E 15-a
Contribution to gross domestic product in $m	USA	J 3-m
	African countries	U 44-a
in local currency	Latin American countries	U 18-a
	S American countries	U 41-a
Costs - index nos	Main W European countries, Japan & USA	R 5-a
	OAS member countries	N 14-a
Earnings per hr (average) in building industry	EEC countries	E 3-a
by areas	EEC countries	E 38-a
Employment as % of total by region	EEC countries	E 2-a
by areas	EEC countries	E 38-a
status of employees & by areas	EEC countries	E 38-a

BUILDING CONSTRUCTION, continued

	Territorial coverage	Title codes
Employment - index nos	EEC countries	E 26-m
	OAS member countries	N 18-a
Expenditure as % of gross domestic product	Developing countries	D 25-a
Expenditure in local currency	Developing countries	D 25-a
Fatality rates for accidents in building industry	All countries	L 4-a
Floor area of new dwellings completed in m²	Main countries	U 58-a
Frequency of accidents at work in building industry	EEC countries	E 2-a
Gross product at current prices in local currency	OAS member countries	N 16-a
Housing space completed in million m²	E European countries	U 16-a
IDA loans approved in $m	OAS member countries	N 16-a
Income contribution to gross domestic product	EEC countries	E 32-a
	Main countries	D 25-a
Income distribution at factor cost in $m	S American countries	U 41-a
Index nos of activity in building industries	Main countries	U 49-a
	World economic areas	U 60-a
Indirect taxes levied on building activity in $m	S American countries	U 41-a
Investment in buildings by baking & confectionery industry in local currency	EEC countries	E 40-a
brewing industry in local currency	EEC countries	E 40-a
building materials industry in local currency	EEC countries	E 40-a
cement & plaster industry in local currency	EEC countries	E 40-a
ceramics industry in local currency	EEC countries	E 40-a
chemical industry in local currency	EEC countries	E 40-a
clothing industry in local currency	EEC countries	E 40-a
coal mining industry in local currency	EEC countries	E 40-a
cotton textile industry in local currency	EEC countries	E 40-a
distilleries in local currency	EEC countries	E 40-a
electrical engineering industry in local currency	EEC countries	E 40-a
electronic industry in local currency	EEC countries	E 40-a
engineering industries in local currency	EEC countries	E 40-a
farm machinery industry in local currency	EEC countries	E 40-a
flour milling industry in local currency	EEC countries	E 40-a
food processing industry in local currency	EEC countries	E 40-a
footwear industry in local currency	EEC countries	E 40-a
fur manufacturing industry in local currency	EEC countries	E 40-a
gas supply industry in local currency	EEC countries	E 40-a
glass industry in local currency	EEC countries	E 40-a
iron & steel industry in local currency	EEC countries	E 40-a
jewellery industry in local currency	EEC countries	E 40-a
jute products industry in local currency	EEC countries	E 40-a
knitting mills in local currency	EEC countries	E 40-a
leather goods industry in local currency	EEC countries	E 40-a
leather tanneries in local currency	EEC countries	E 40-a
lignite & briquetting industry in local currency	EEC countries	E 40-a
locomotive & rolling stock industry in local currency	EEC countries	E 40-a
machine tools industry in local currency	EEC countries	E 40-a
man-made fibres industry in local currency	EEC countries	E 40-a
manufacturing industry in local currency	EEC countries	E 40-a
marine engineering industry in local currency	EEC countries	E 40-a
mechanical engineering industry in local currency	EEC countries	E 40-a
metals industry in local currency	EEC countries	E 40-a
motor cycle industry in local currency	EEC countries	E 40-a
musical instruments industry in local currency	EEC countries	E 40-a
non-ferrous metals industry in local currency	EEC countries	E 40-a
non-metallic metals industry in local currency	EEC countries	E 40-a
office machinery industry in local currency	EEC countries	E 40-a
optical instruments industry in local currency	EEC countries	E 40-a
ore mining industry in local currency	EEC countries	E 40-a
paper & board industry in local currency	EEC countries	E 40-a
petroleum & natural gas industry in local currency	EEC countries	E 40-a
petroleum refineries in local currency	EEC countries	E 40-a
plastics industry in local currency	EEC countries	E 40-a
power stations in local currency	EEC countries	E 40-a
printing & publishing in local currency	EEC countries	E 40-a
public utilities in local currency	EEC countries	E 40-a
rubber processing industry in local currency	EEC countries	E 40-a
shipyards in local currency	EEC countries	E 40-a
silk-using industry in local currency	EEC countries	E 40-a
sugar refining industry in local currency	EEC countries	E 40-a
textile machinery industry in local currency	EEC countries	E 40-a
timber & sawmill industry in local currency	EEC countries	E 40-a

	Territorial coverage	Title codes	
BUILDING CONSTRUCTION, continued			
Investment in buildings by toys & sports goods industries in local currency	EEC countries	E 40-a	
watch-making industry in local currency	EEC countries	E 40-a	
wire & cable industry in local currency	EEC countries	E 40-a	
woollen textile industry in local currency	EEC countries	E 40-a	
in coke ovens in local currency	EEC countries	E 40-a	
Labour costs: manual workers in building industry per hr	EEC countries	E 3-a	
costs per hr in building industry	EEC countries	E 2-a	
in building industry by areas	EEC countries	E 38-a	
force employed at census dates	OAS member countries	N 18	
by sex: historical table 1750-1969	Main European countries	Z 1-a	
by status in building industry	Main countries	C 28-ir	
force employed	EEC countries	E 2-a	
	All countries	L 4-a	
	Australia & main Far East countries	U 32-q	
	ECE countries	U 15-a	
No of buildings completed by type	EEC countries	E 28-q	E 27-a
by size	Argentina	U 40-a	
by value in $m	Main countries	U 58-a	
buildings & dwellings started by type	EEC countries	E 28-q	E 27-a
started by floor area in m²	Chile	U 40-a	
dwellings completed per 1000 population	ECE countries	U 15-a	
	All countries	U 13-a	
per 100,000 population	E European countries	U 16-a	
dwellings completed	E European countries & USSR	U 16-a	
	All countries	U 13-a	
	European countries, Canada & USA	A 24-a	
	OAS member countries	N 14-a	
hrs worked per wk in building industry	All countries	L 4-a	
	EEC countries	E 26-a2	
per yr in building industry	EEC countries	E 2-a	
new dwellings completed by no of floors	European countries	U 5-a	
under construction	European countries	U 5-a	
permits issued by value in local currency	OAS member countries	N 14-a	
for dwellings construction	Main countries	U 58-a	
rooms completed in new dwellings	Main countries	E 3-a	
& no per 1000 population	ECE countries	U 15-a	
Output, employment & wages in building industry	Main countries	U 43-a	
Production - index nos	EEC countries	E 28-q	E 27-a
Unemployment in building industry	All countries	L 4-a	
	ECE countries	U 42-m	
Unfilled vacancies in building industry	EEC countries	U 42-m	
Value of buildings constructed as % of gross national product (per capita basis)	Main countries	U 57-a	
BUILDING CONSTRUCTION, AGRICULTURAL			
see also CAPITAL FORMATION			
Capital formation in $m	E European countries	U 34-a	
	ECE countries	U 34-a	
BUILDING CONSTRUCTION, NON-RESIDENTIAL			
As % capital formation	All countries	U 13-a	
As % gross domestic product	All countries	U 13-a	
By value in $m	All countries	U 13-a	
% change in investment	USA	G 1-a2	
Activity - index nos	Main countries	U 58-a	
Area completed in m²	OAS member countries	N 14-a	
Capital formation as % value of construction	European countries	U 5-a	
Commercial building activity in $m	USSR	U 58-a	
Educational building activity in $m	USSR	U 58-a	
Floor area by type in m²	Main countries	U 58-a	
in m²	Main countries	U 58-a	
	Japan & S Korea	U 32-q	
Industrial building activity in $m	USSR	U 58-a	
Investment in $bn	USA	G 1-a2	
No of buildings completed	OAS member countries	N 14-a	
	Main countries	U 58-a	
permits granted	AASM countries	E 41-a	
	Philippines	U 32-q	
Tender values in $m	Main countries	U 58-a	
BUILDING CONSTRUCTION, PRIVATE			
No of units built by commercial enterprises	All countries	U 13-a	
BUILDING CONSTRUCTION, PUBLIC			
No of units built by government agencies	All countries	U 13-a	
BUILDING CONSTRUCTION, RESIDENTIAL			
see also DWELLINGS			
HOUSING			
As % of total building construction	All countries	U 13-a	
capital formation	All countries	U 13-a	
gross domestic product	All countries	U 13-a	
As factor in capital formation in $m	ECE countries	U 15-a	
By value in $m	All countries	U 13-a	

	Territorial coverage	Title codes	
BUILDING CONSTRUCTION, RESIDENTIAL, continued			
% growth rate projected to 1980	OECD countries	D 11	
Activity – index nos	Main countries	U 58-a	
Area completed in m²	OAS member countries	N 14-a	
Capital formation as % value of construction	ECE countries	U 15-a	
Cost per m² (average) in local currency	OAS member countries	N 14-a	
per unit (average) in local currency	OAS member countries	N 14-a	
Floor area in m²	Main countries	U 58-a	
New dwellings completed: value in $	Main countries	U 58-a	
No of new dwellings completed	ECAFE area	U 32-q	
	ECE countries	U 15-a	
	OAS member countries	N 14-a	
	Main countries	U 58-a	
of permits granted	AASM countries	E 41-a	
Tender values in $m	Main countries	U 58-a	
BUILDING INDUSTRY			
see also BUILDING CONSTRUCTION			
STEEL FABRICATION INDUSTRY			
Activity – index nos	OAS member countries	N 14-a	
Consumption of alloy sheets: tonnage	USA	J 6-a	
aluminium: tonnage	Main countries	T 4-a	
	EEC countries, Japan & USA	C 12-a	
brass mill products: tonnage	USA	J 6-a	
copper rods & alloy wire: tonnage	USA	J 6-a	
copper tubes for plumbing: tonnage	USA	J 6-a	
iron castings: tonnage	UK	B 25-a	
plastics as % of total usage of plastics	European countries	U 26-a	
Costs & annual changes – index nos	Main countries	R 2-m	
Costs for labour wages – index nos	OAS member countries	N 14-a	
materials – index nos	OAS member countries	N 14-a	
overheads – index nos	OAS member countries	N 14-a	
salaried staff per mth	EEC countries	E 11-a	
(total) – index nos	OAS member countries	N 14-a	
Earnings in local currency per hr	Main countries	L 4-a	R 3-a
		U 58-a	
Electricity: consumption from public supply in kWh	All countries	C 23-a	
Employment – index nos	European countries & USA	U 5-a	
Gross additions to fixed assets in $m	Main countries	U 58-a	
Gross output by value in $m	Main countries	U 58-a	
Incidence of strikes or lock-outs	Main countries	R 3-a	
Investment in buildings in local currency	EEC countries	E 40-a	
land purchase in local currency	EEC countries	E 40-a	
machinery in local currency	EEC countries	E 40-a	
Labour costs as % of total costs	EEC countries	E 8-a	
by status of employee in local currency	EEC countries	E 8-a	
per hr: all employees	EEC countries	E 11-a	
wage earners	EEC countries	E 11-a	
Labour force employed by sex at census dates	African countries	U 44-a	
by sex	EEC countries	E 18-a	
(total)	Main countries	R 5-a	U 58-a
salaried staff	EEC countries	E 11-a	
wage earners & salaried staff	EEC countries	E 8-a	
wage earners	EEC countries	E 11-a	
Loan advances from banking system in local currency	OAS member countries	N 16-a	
New construction by value in $m	Main countries	U 58-a	
No of dwellings completed by value in $m	Main countries	U 58-a	
employees involved in strikes	Main countries	R 3-a	
hrs worked by labour force per yr	EEC countries	E 8-a	
wage earners per wk	EEC countries	E 33-a	
sex per wk	EEC countries	E 33-a	
per wk	Main countries	R 3-a	
	OAS member countries	N 18-a	
by sex per wk	EEC countries	E 18-a	
by area per wk	EEC countries	E 25-a	
salaried staff per yr	EEC countries	E 11-a	
wage earners per yr	EEC countries	E 11-a	
employees engaged	Main countries	U 58-a	
firms comprising the industry	Main countries	U 58-a	
wage & salary earners employed by sex by area	EEC countries	E 18-a	
working days lost per employee	UK	B 29-a	
lost through strikes	Main countries	R 3-a	
Receipts of aluminium products: tonnage	OECD countries	D 21-a	
Repairs & maintenance work done by value in $m	Main countries	U 58-a	
Unemployment – index nos	European countries & USA	U 5-a	
Value added in construction work in $m	Main countries	U 58-a	
Wage rates (average) in local currency per hr	EEC countries	E 25-a2	
by grade of employee per day	Portugal	R 4-q	
by sex in local currency per hr	Main countries	R 3-m	C 7-a
carpenters in local currency per hr	OAS member countries	N 17-a	
electricians in local currency per hr	OAS member countries	N 17-a	
labourers in local currency per hr	OAS member countries	N 17-a	
	Canada & Switzerland	R 4-a	
masons in local currency per hr	OAS member countries	N 17-a	
painters in local currency per hr	OAS member countries	N 17-a	
plumbers in local currency per hr	OAS member countries	N 17-a	
skilled & unskilled workers in local currency per hr	Main countries	R 4-q	
index nos	Main countries	R 3-a	

	Territorial coverage	Title codes

BUILDING MATERIALS
    see also BUILDING BLOCKS, CONCRETE
                BUILDING BLOCKS, STONE
                CEMENT
                CLINKER
                GLASS & GLASS PRODUCTS
                IRON PRODUCTS
                SAND & GRAVEL
                SHEETS, GALVANISED
                SOFTWOOD, SAWN
                WOOD-BASED PANELS

Coastal shipping: tonnage	EEC countries	E 43-a
Consumption of crude gypsum: tonnage	USA	N 1-a
Exports by sea, inland waters, road & rail: tonnage	European countries	U 8-a
Exports - index nos (quantum & value bases)	OECD countries	D 16-q
Gypsum: stocks at producers' stockyards: tonnage	USA	N 1-a
Imports & exports by rail: tonnage	EEC countries	E 43-a
road: tonnage	EEC countries	E 43-a
sea: tonnage	EEC countries	E 43-a
Imports by sea, inland waters, road & rail: tonnage	European countries	U 8-a
Imports - index nos (quantum & value bases)	OECD countries	D 16-q
Imports & exports of gypsum: tonnage	Main countries	B 15-a
Labour costs of production per hr	EEC countries	E 2-a
Production: asphalt roofing in m²	USA	U 5-a
bricks & blocks by volume in million	All countries	U 22-a
bricks by kind by volume in million	European countries & USA	U 5-a
by volume in million	EEC countries	E 26-m
	OAS member countries	N 14-a
	Main countries	E 3-a
concrete (ready-mixed) in m³	UK	U 5-a
crushed stone in m³	E Germany & Malta	U 5-a
hardwood flooring in m³	USA	U 5-a
plate glass in m²	European countries	U 5-a
pumice in m³	W Germany	U 5-a
roofing materials in m²	Ukraine	U 5-a
roofing tiles of cement by volume in million	European countries	U 5-a
of clay by volume	European countries	U 5-a
sawnwood in m³	Yugoslavia	U 5-a
sheet glass in m²	European countries	U 5-a
softwood flooring in m³	USA	U 5-a
tiles (glazed) in m²	France	U 5-a
(mosaic) in m²	Spain	U 5-a
Production: asbestos cement: tonnage	Spain	U 5-a
bitumen felt: tonnage	Yugoslavia	U 5-a
calcareous stone: tonnage	All countries	U 22-a
ceramics: tonnage	Yugoslavia	U 5-a
clay bricks: tonnage	All countries	U 22-a
clay roofing tiles: tonnage	All countries	U 22-a
concrete pipes: tonnage	All countries	U 22-a
gravel & crushed stone: tonnage	All countries	U 22-a
gypsum: tonnage	Main countries	B 15-a N 1-a
	African countries	U 44-a
gypsum & sulphur anhydrite: tonnage	OECD countries	D 5-a
lime (anhydrous): tonnage	E Germany	U 5-a
lime (hydraulic): tonnage	W Germany	U 5-a
lime (ordinary): tonnage	Main European countries	U 5-a
limestone: tonnage	W Germany	U 5-a
natural stone: tonnage	W Germany	U 5-a
particle board: tonnage	Sweden	U 5-a
plaster: tonnage	Luxembourg & W Germany	U 5-a
quicklime: tonnage	All countries	U 22-a
roofing slates: tonnage	France	U 5-a
rough freestone: tonnage	France	U 5-a
sand & gravel: tonnage	Cyprus	U 5-a
tiles, gypsum & lime: tonnage	EEC countries	E 28-q E 27-a
Production: vitreous flooring in m²	France	U 5-a
Production - index nos	ECE countries	U 42-m
Rail freight: inland & abroad: tonnage	EEC countries	E 43-a
Retail prices - index nos	EEC countries	E 26-m
Road transport over frontiers: tonnage	EEC countries	E 43-a
Seaborne freight: tonnage by kind of material	EEC countries	E 43-a
Wholesale prices: bricks - index nos	European countries & USA	U 5-a
	OAS member countries	N 14-a
cement - index nos	European countries & USA	U 5-a
	OAS member countries	N 14-a
concrete products - index nos	European countries & USA	U 5-a
glass - index nos	European countries & USA	U 5-a
hydraulic lime - index nos	OAS member countries	N 14-a
lime - index nos	European countries & USA	U 5-a
reinforcing rods - index nos	OAS member countries	N 14-a
roofing tiles - index nos	European countries & USA	U 5-a
sand - index nos	European countries	U 5-a
	OAS member countries	N 14-a
timber - index nos	European countries	U 5-a
	OAS member countries	N 14-a
window glass - index nos	OAS member countries	N 14-a
wood panels - index nos	European countries	U 5-a
Wholesale prices of crude gypsum in $ per ton	USA	N 1-a

	Territorial coverage	Title codes	

BUILDING MATERIALS
    Wholesale prices of crushed stone in $ per ton   USA   N 1-a
                           dimension stone in $ per ton   USA   N 1-a
    Wholesale prices - index nos   Australia   U 32-m
                       EEC countries   E 26-m
                       European countries   A 13-a
                       Main countries   R 2-m   R 5-a
                       OAS member countries   N 17-a
    World production: tonnage of gypsum   Worldwide   N 4-a
                       Main countries   N 1-a
    World quarry production of crushed stone: tonnage   Main countries   N 1-a

BUILDING MATERIALS BY KIND
    Exports by destination by CST classes: tonnage   EEC countries   E 48-a
                     SITC classes: tonnage & value in $ OECD countries   D 3-a2
                     SITC classes by value in $ Main countries   D 2-q
            by NIMEXE classes: tonnage & value in $ All countries   E 20-a
            by SITC classes: tonnage & value in $ All countries   U 50-a   U 59-a
    Imports by NIMEXE classes: tonnage & value in $ All countries   E 20-a
            by SITC classes: tonnage & value in $ All countries   U 50-a   U 59-a
            by source by CST classes: tonnage   EEC countries   E 21-a
                     SITC classes by value in $ Main countries   D 2-q
                     SITC classes: tonnage & value in $ OECD countries   D 3-a2
    Production: tonnage   European countries & USA   U 5-a
    Wholesale prices - index nos   European countries & USA   U 5-a
                       OAS member countries   N 14-a

BUILDING MATERIALS INDUSTRY
        see also   CEMENT & PLASTER INDUSTRY
                      GLASS INDUSTRY
    % share of total capital investment   E European countries   U 16-a
    Costs for salaried staff   EEC countries   E 11-a
    IDA loans approved in $m   OAS member countries   N 16-a
            to expand concrete production in $ OAS member countries   N 16-a
    Investment in buildings in local currency   EEC countries   E 40-a
             in land purchase in local currency   EEC countries   E 40-a
             in machinery in local currency   EEC countries   E 40-a
    Labour costs as % of total costs   EEC countries   E 8-a
            by status of employees in local currency   EEC countries   E 8-a
            of labour force per hr   EEC countries   E 11-a
            of wage earners per hr   EEC countries   E 11-a
    Labour force employed: no of salaried staff   EEC countries   E 11-a
                      no of wage earners   EEC countries   E 11-a
                      no of wage earners & salaried staff   EEC countries   E 8-a
    No of hrs worked by labour force   EEC countries   E 8-a
            by area per wk   EEC countries   E 25-a
            salaried staff   EEC countries   E 11-a
            wage earners   EEC countries   E 11-a
    Wage rates (average) in local currency per hr   EEC countries   E 25-a2
            by sex per hr   Main countries   C 7-a

BUILDING PERMITS
        see also   SHIPPING FLEETS
    Floor areas covered by permits in m²   Main countries   U 58-a
            dwellings in m²   Main countries   U 58-a
            industrial buildings in m²   OAS member countries   N 14-a
            non-residential buildings in m²   Main countries   U 58-a
            office buildings in m²   OAS member countries   N 14-a
            residential housing units in m²   OAS member countries   N 14-a
    No issued by floor area in m²   S American countries   U 40-a
            for commercial buildings   Main countries   U 58-a
                commercial office buildings   OAS member countries   N 14-a
                construction work (all kinds)   African countries   U 44-a
                                 ECE countries   U 42-m
                                 Main countries   U 58-a
                educational buildings   Main countries   U 58-a
                industrial buildings   Main countries   U 58-a
                                 OAS member countries   N 14-a
                non-residential buildings   Main countries   U 58-a
                residential housing units   Main countries   U 58-a
                                 European countries & USA   U 5-a
                                 OAS member countries   N 14-a

BUILDING SCIENCES
    No of students enrolled on civil engineering courses   OAS member countries   N 19-a

BUILDING SOCIETIES
    % interest rates charged on mortgages   OECD countries   D 12-a

Building stones   see   BUILDING BLOCKS, CONCRETE
                                BUILDING BLOCKS, STONE
                                GRANITE

Buildings, commercial   see   BUILDING CONSTRUCTION,
                                        NON-RESIDENTIAL

	Territorial coverage	Title codes	
Buildings, educational see BUILDING CONSTRUCTION, NON-RESIDENTIAL			
Buildings, industrial see BUILDING CONSTRUCTION, NON-RESIDENTIAL			

BULK CARRIERS
    see also   CARGO SHIPS
                  TANKERS
                  WORLD FLEETS

	Territorial coverage	Title codes	
Acquisitions new & second-hand: no & tonnage by flag	Worldwide	U 37-a	
Age of carriers afloat in 5 yr age groups	Worldwide	U 37-a	
Bulk freight carried per dwt in ton-miles	Worldwide	U 37-a	
Carrying capacity: tonnage afloat of iron ore carriers	Worldwide	U 56-a	
Combination fleet afloat: dry cargo freight: tonnage	Worldwide	S 17-m	
oil freight: tonnage	Worldwide	S 15-a	
Deliveries: no & tonnage of bulk carriers	Worldwide	S 17-m	
combined cargo & oil carriers	Worldwide	S 17-m	
combined ore & oil carriers	Worldwide	S 17-m	
specialised ore carriers	Worldwide	S 17-m	
standard bulk carriers	Worldwide	S 17-m	
Deliveries scheduled for new bulk carriers by size	Worldwide	S 17-m	
combined carriers by size	Worldwide	S 17-m	
ore carriers by size	Worldwide	S 17-m	
Distances per loaded voyage of dry cargo in miles	Worldwide	S 16-a	
Draft distribution in ft by tonnage classes	Worldwide	S 22-a	
Exports of wet & dry carriers: no & tonnage	OECD countries	D 9-a	
Freight: tonnage carried in million ton-miles: alumina & bauxite	Worldwide	D 28-a	
coal, grain, iron ore & phosphates	Worldwide	D 28-a	
Labour costs: ore-loading & unloading	Worldwide	U 56-a	
New orders: no & tonnage of bulk carriers	Worldwide	S 15-a	
combined cargo oil carriers	Worldwide	S 17-m	
combined ore oil carriers	Worldwide	S 17-m	
specialised ore carriers	Worldwide	S 17-m	
standard bulk carriers	Worldwide	S 17-m	
tonnage	Country of build	D 28-a	
No afloat (total)	Country of registration	S 22-a	
by size groups by flag	Worldwide	U 56-a	
(over 10,000 dwt) for bulk cargo	Worldwide	S 22-a2	
for ore cargo	Worldwide	S 22-a2	
No & tonnage afloat	OAS member countries	N 15-a	
No & tonnage afloat: chemical carriers by flag	Worldwide	S 2-a	
combination fleet carrying cargo & oil	Worldwide	S 17-a2	
ores & oil	Worldwide	S 17-a2	
combined ore & oil carriers in fleet	Norway	S 15-a	
liquefied gas carriers by flag	Worldwide	S 2-a	
ore carriers by flag	Worldwide	S 2-a	
ore carriers in fleet	Norway	S 15-a	
ore carriers	Worldwide	S 17-m	
steamships incl ore carriers by flag	Worldwide	S 2-a	
motorships incl ore carriers by flag	Worldwide	S 2-a	
completed	Country of build	S 3-q	
delivered to Norwegian companies	Norway	S 15-a	
fixtures by kind of cargo	Worldwide	S 17-m	
laid up by flag	Worldwide	S 16-a	
launched	Country of build	S 3-q	S 1-a
new orders (not yet started)	All countries	S 3-q	S 15-a
new orders on hand	Country of registration	S 22-a	
under construction	All countries	S 3-q	
No of new construction completed: tonnage	World regions	U 37-a	
No of ton-miles of bulk cargo carried	Worldwide	U 37-a	
Operating costs by size of vessels in $ per day	Worldwide	U 56-a	
crew & victualling in $ per day	Worldwide	U 56-a	
deck stores & radio in $ per day	Worldwide	U 56-a	
engine stores & bunkers in $ per day	Worldwide	U 56-a	
fuel used by tonnage size of vessels in $ per day	Worldwide	U 56-a	
repairs & maintenance in $ per day	Worldwide	U 56-a	
Ore-loading & unloading costs: maintenance of equipment	Worldwide	U 56-a	
power, for equipment	Worldwide	U 56-a	
Prices ex shipyards by tonnage sizes in £m	Worldwide	S 16-a2	
Productivity of shipping space in ton-miles	Worldwide	U 37-a	
Sales by name of carrier, tonnage, age, speed, price to buyers & sellers	Worldwide	S 17-m	
Seaborne freight carried in ton-miles	UK	S 16-a	
Service speed of iron ore ships by size in knots		U 56-a	
Tonnage afloat & as % total shipping	Worldwide	D 28-a	U 37-a
(all carriers)	Country of registration	S 22-a	
by flag	Worldwide	S 4-a	
by size classes	Worldwide	D 28-a	
in million dwt	Worldwide	U 37-a	
forward estimates	Worldwide	S 15-a	
liquefied gas carriers	Worldwide	D 28-a	
contracted for building	Worldwide	S 15-a	
on order by year of agreed delivery	Worldwide	S 22-a2	
(incl combined carriers)	Worldwide	S 22-a2	
over 10,000 tons by size classes	Worldwide	S 22-a2	
over 10,000 tons	Country of build	S 22-a2	

	Territorial coverage	Title codes	
BULK CARRIERS BY AGE			
No by yr of construction: tonnage	Worldwide	S 22-a	
& tonnage groups afloat	Worldwide	S 17-m	
ore carriers afloat	Worldwide	U 56-a	
ore carriers laid up	Worldwide	S 17-m	
tweendeckers laid up	Worldwide	S 17-m	
BULK CARRIERS BY SIZE			
Classes afloat: tonnage	Worldwide	S 22-a	
New orders for combined carriers: tonnage	Worldwide	D 28-a	
No & tonnage of completions: combined carriers	Worldwide	S 17-m	
all types of bulk carriers	Japan & world regions	S 17-m	
(incl ore carriers) by age afloat	All countries	S 2-a	
new construction: iron ore carriers	Worldwide	U 56-a	
& completions by type	Poland	S 16-q	
scheduled deliveries by type	Worldwide	S 17-m	
ore carriers by engine hp afloat	Worldwide	U 56-a	
Tonnage afloat: combined carriers	Worldwide	D 28-a	
BULLDOZERS			
see also EXCAVATING MACHINES			
GRADERS & LEVELLERS			
SCRAPERS			
Production volume	All countries	U 22-a	
	European countries, Japan, UK & USA	U 38-a	
BULLION			
see also GOLD			
Exports by destination: silver bullion in oz	USA	T 4-a	
Imports by source: silver bullion in oz	UK & USA	T 4-a	
Imports & exports: gold bullion in oz	All countries	B 15-a	
silver bullion in oz	All countries	B 15-a	
World exports: gold bullion in kg	Main countries	T 4-a	
silver bullion in oz	All countries	T 4-a	
World imports: gold bullion in kg	Main countries	T 4-a	

Bulls   see   CATTLE

Bunker capacity   see   CARGO SHIPS

BUNKERS

    see also   PETROLEUM PRODUCTS

	Territorial coverage	Title codes	
Coal & other fuels sold as bunkers in coal equiv tonnage	All countries	U 55-a	
Consumption: diesel oil as ships' supplies: tonnage	Main countries	C 14-a	
fuel oils as ships' supplies: tonnage	Italy	H 4-a	
	Main countries	C 14-a	
hard coal as ships' supplies: tonnage	OECD countries	D 44-a	
oil products as ships' supplies: tonnage	Main countries	C 14-a	H 4-a
petroleum products as ships' supplies: tonnage	EEC countries	E 16-q	E 15-a
Diesel oil sold as ships' supplies: tonnage	OECD countries	D 39-q	D 31-a
Exports of coal: for sale as ships' supplies: tonnage	All countries	B 15-a	
Price increases: diesel oil as ships' supplies in $ per ton	World regions	S 16-q	
fuel oil as ships' supplies in $ per ton	World regions	S 16-q	
gas oil as ships' supplies in $ per ton	World regions	S 16-q	
Prices of fuel oil (bunker C grade) in cents per gallon	Main countries	C 3-a	H 4-a
		U 18-a	
at main ports by grade	EEC countries	E 17-q	
as ships' supplies posted at specific ports in cents per gallon	Worldwide	C 3-a	
Refined liquid fuels sold as ships' supplies: tonnage	All countries	U 55-a	
	OECD countries	D 39-q	D 31-a
Sale of kerosenes, gasolenes & fuel oil as ships' supplies: tonnage	All countries	U 55-a	
lubricating oil as ships' supplies: tonnage	OECD countries	D 31-a	
petroleum products as ships' supplies: tonnage	OECD countries	D 31-a	
BURLAP			
Imports by source of hessian cloth: tonnage	USA	B 10-a	
Wholesale prices of hessian cloth in Rs per 100 metres	India	U 32-m	
of burlap	France, India & USA	U 27-m	

Burley   see   TOBACCO

BUSES & COACHES

    see also   TRANSPORT SERVICES

	Territorial coverage	Title codes	
Assembly by make by overseas subsidiaries	Main countries	V 2-a	
model by overseas subsidiaries	Main countries	V 2-a	
Distance covered in km per yr (estim)	Main countries	S 24-a	
Exports by destination: no & value in £m	UK	V 1-a	
	European countries, Japan & USA	V 1-a	
by volume by destination	USSR	V 1-a	
by volume	All countries	S 24-a	V 4-a
(incl trucks & lorries) by volume	OECD countries	D 9-a	
Length of passenger routes in vehicle-km	EEC countries	E 43-a	
No of coaches crossing frontiers & no crossing empty	European countries	U 8-a	

	Territorial coverage	Title codes
BUSES & COACHES, continued		
No of foreign-owned coaches crossing frontiers	European countries	U 8-a
km run (estim)	European countries	U 47-a
new registrations	All countries	S 24-a
	European countries & USA	U 47-a
	N Ireland	V 1-q
by seating capacity	UK	V 1-q
	UK	V 1-a
(incl taxis) by area	Eire	V 1-a
(incl taxis)	Main countries	V 4-a
	All countries	N 8-a
of registered vehicles in service (incl world total)	Main countries	R 5-a S 24-a
in use		V 1-a
	European countries & USA	U 47-a
	EEC countries	E 43-a
	UK	V 1-a
in use (incl taxis)	World areas	N 8-a
(incl world total)	EEC countries	E 38-a
by areas	European countries	U 8-a
seating capacity	UK	V 1-a
licensed by seating capacity & age	UK	V 1-a
public transport vehicles	Main countries	V 2-a
No locally-assembled	UK	V 1-m
Production volume: single & double-decker buses	All countries	N 8-a S 24-a
(total)		U 22-a U 38-a
	EEC countries	E 28-q E 27-a
Traffic volume in million vehicle-km	Main countries	S 24-a

Business enterprises   see   COMMERCIAL UNDERTAKINGS

Business losses   see   LOSSES, COMMERCIAL

BUSINESS STUDIES
No of students enrolled on university courses	OAS member countries	N 19-a

BUSINESS TRAVEL
% of households which includes a foreign business traveller	W European countries	Z 3

BUTADIENE
Exports: tonnage	European countries, Japan & USA	U 26-a
Imports: tonnage	European countries, Japan & USA	U 26-a
Production capacity: tonnage by plant	European countries, Japan & USA	U 26-a
Refining capacity: tonnage per yr	EEC countries	B 30-a

Butane   see   NATURAL GAS LIQUIDS

BUTANOL
Production, imports & exports: tonnage	European countries, Japan & USA	U 26-a

BUTTER
      see also   COCOA BUTTER
               CREAMERIES

% change in producer prices	W Germany	E 34-m
retail sales	E European countries & USSR	U 16-a
wholesale prices ex dairies	EEC countries	E 34-m
% of production from dairy co-operatives	EEC countries	B 3-a
% of production exported	Main producing countries	B 4-a
% share of world imports & world exports	Main countries	B 1-a
Change in stocks of butter: tonnage	EEC countries	E 44-a
Commonwealth share of UK imports: tonnage		B 4-a
Consumption cost to private sector incl oils & fats	EEC countries	E 32-a
: tonnage	EEC area	B 4-a
	OAS member countries	N 17-a
	EEC countries	B 3-a E 44-a
of milk for production of butter in gallons	Main countries	B 4-a
tonnage	EEC countries	E 44-a
per capita in kg per yr	European countries	U 35-a
	European countries, Canada, Japan & USA	E 44-a
	OECD countries	D 1-a
	E European countries & USSR	U 16-a
	EEC countries	B 1-a B 3-a
		E 44-a
in lbs per yr	Main countries	B 19-a
	UK	B 12-a B 19-a
butter fat content in kg per yr	OECD countries	D 1-a
	Main countries	E 3-a
Consumption projected to 1978: tonnage	OECD countries	D 15-a
Export availability & import needs projected to 1978	OECD countries	D 15-a
Export prices ex dairy in local currency per kg	Denmark & Netherlands	R 2-m
unit value in $ per 100 lb	New Zealand	U 32-m
- index nos (weighted average main sources)	Worldwide	U 29-q
in local currency	Australia, Eire, Netherlands & New Zealand	A 9-a
Export subsidies by zone per 100 kg	EEC area	B 4-a
Exports by destination: tonnage	Main countries	B 12-m B 4-a
by value & as % exports of farm products	W European countries	U 20-a

	Territorial coverage	Title codes	
BUTTER, continued			
Exports by value in $m	OECD countries	D 1-a	
	New Zealand	U 32-m	
	W European countries	U 33-a	
by value to E Europe in $m	W European countries	U 20-a	
tonnage & EEC area share as % of world exports		B 3-a	
tonnage	Main countries	B 4-a	
historical table from 1830: tonnage	Denmark	Z 1-a	
Farm gate purchase price for export per lb	New Zealand	B 4-a	
Import prices ex Denmark & Australasia in £ per ton	UK	R 2-m	
ex New Zealand (salted) in £ per cwt	UK	U 33-a	
in £ per ton	UK	A 9-a	
Import quotas in lbs	USA	B 4-a	
tonnage authorised by source	UK	B 4-a	
Imports by source: tonnage	Main countries	B 12-m	
value & as % imports of farm products	W European countries	U 20-a	
ex E Europe in $m	W European countries	U 20-a	
value in $m	OECD countries	D 1-a	
	W European countries	U 33-a	
Imports & exports: tonnage	European countries	U 35-q	
Imports: tonnage & EEC area share as % of world imports		B 3-a	
tonnage	Main countries	B 4-a	P 1-a
Inter-EEC imports & exports: tonnage	EEC countries	B 3-a	B 12-a
Intervention & threshold prices in £ per cwt	EEC countries	B 1-a	
prices fixed by Commission	EEC area	E 44-a	
(82 % fat) in £ per ton	Denmark, Eire & UK	B 3-a	
in local currency per 100 kg	EEC countries	B 12-m	B 3-a
Net trade: tonnage	EEC countries	B 4-a	
Prices in EEC area as % of world market prices		E 44-a	
Producer prices in £ per cwt	EEC countries	B 1-a	
ex dairies in FrB per kg	Belgium	D 1-a	
in DM per 100 kg	W Germany	E 34-m	
ex farm in FrB per kg	Belgium	D 1-a	
in local currency	All countries	A 9-a	
Production, imports, exports, stocks & consumption: tonnage	EEC countries	E 44-a	
stocks & consumption per capita per day	EEC countries	E 44-a	
supply, trade, consumption & stocks: tonnage	OECD countries	D 14-a	
ex dairies: tonnage	EEC countries	B 3-a	
ex factories: tonnage	Main countries	B 12-m	
ex farms & dairies: tonnage	Main countries	B 3-a	
historical tables from 1903: tonnage	OECD countries	D 1-a	
(incl butter oil): tonnage	Main European countries	Z 1-a	
(incl farm butter): tonnage	EEC countries	B 1-a	
Production: fat content of butter: tonnage	EEC countries	B 3-a	
projected to 1978: tonnage	OECD countries	D 1-a	
tonnage	OECD countries	D 15-a	
	All countries	A 9-a	U 22-a
	Australia & New Zealand	P 1-a	
	European countries & USSR	U 35-a	
	E European countries & USSR	U 16-a	
	EEC countries	E 26-m	E 28-q
		E 27-a	
	European countries, Canada, Japan, USSR & USA	E 44-a	
	Latin American countries	J 5-a	
	Main countries	A 5-a	B 4-a
		E 3-a	P 1-a
		R 5-a	U 43-a
Purchase price by Commodity Credit Corp in cents per lb	USA	B 4-a	
Retail prices: butter by kind in local currency	OAS member countries	N 14-a	
(comparative) in $ per kg	OAS member countries	N 17-a	
in local currency	EEC countries	Z 3-a	
	Main countries	B 4-a	
Retail sales - index nos	UK	B 12-m	
Self-sufficiency ratios	EEC countries	E 3-a	E 44-a
Stocks at beginning of yr, at end-Aug & at end-yr: tonnage	EEC countries	B 3-a	
end-Jan & end-July: tonnage	Main countries	B 4-a2	
end-yr: tonnage	Main countries	A 5-a	A 11-a
end-month: tonnage	Main countries	B 12-m	
butter & other milk products: tonnage	EEC countries	E 44-a	
creamery butter at end-mth: tonnage	Eire	B 12-m	
tonnage	Main W European countries	U 35-q	
Subsidy payments to cover sale at low prices to manufacturers in £ per ton	EEC countries	B 3-a	
Subsidy payments: non-profit sales to institutions	EEC area	B 3-a	
package sales to consumers in £ per ton	EEC countries	B 3-a	
private storage costs in EEC area in £ per ton		B 3-a	
Supply, production, consumption & trade: tonnage	EEC countries	B 1-a	
imports & exports: tonnage	EEC countries	B 4-a	
Surplus of production over requirements projected to 1978	OECD countries	D 15-a	
Wholesale prices by grade in £ per cwt on London provision exchange	UK	B 12-m	
by kind in £ per ton equiv	Main countries	B 12-w	
of butter ex Australia on London Provision Exchange in £ per cwt	UK	U 32-m	
ex dairies in local currency per 100 kg	W European countries	U 35-a	
	EEC countries	E 34-m	
ex New Zealand (salted) on London Provision Exchange in £ per 56 lbs	UK	U 20-q	
normal grade (average) in local currency	Main countries	B 4-a	

	Territorial coverage	Title codes

BUTTER, continued

Wholesale prices in local currency (average)	Canada, France, W Germany, UK & USA	A 9-a
by kind in local currency	OAS member countries	N 17-a
in £ per ton	Denmark & Netherlands	U 27-m
World exports by value in $m	UK	B 12-m
unit value in $ per ton	World regions	A 5-a
		A 11-a
World market prices based ex Denmark per 100 kg on London Provision Exchange		E 34-m
based ex New Zealand per 100 kg on London Provision Exchange		E 34-m
World market prices - index nos		G 1-a
production: tonnage for ensuing yr (estim)		A 1
tonnage		A 5-a N 10-a
stocks at end-yr: tonnage		G 1-a
supply: tonnage		B 19-a

Butter-oil   see   MILK FAT, ANHYDROUS

Buttermilk   see   MILK PRODUCTS

Butyl   see   SYNTHETIC RUBBER

Butyl alcohol   see   BUTANOL
                              CHEMICAL PRODUCTS

BUTYLENE
    see also   HYDROCARBONS, ALIPHATIC

Consumption: tonnage	OECD countries	D 5-a
Production: tonnage from oil & natural gas	OECD countries	D 5-a
tonnage	European countries, Japan & USA	U 26-a

By-products of solid fuels   see   COAL BY-PRODUCTS
                                            COKE BY-PRODUCTS
                                            LIGNITE BY-PRODUCTS

C.A.P. price factors   see   EXPORT LEVIES (EEC)
                                      EXPORT RESTITUTION PAYMENTS (EEC)
                                      IMPORT LEVIES (EEC)
                                      IMPORT SUBSIDIES (EEC)

CECA   see   COMMUNITY INVESTMENT FUNDS
                  IRON & STEEL COMMUNITY (EEC)

Cabbages & cauliflowers   see   VEGETABLES, FRESH

Cabin attendants   see   AIRCRAFT PERSONNEL

Cables   see   INSULATED WIRE & CABLES
                  WIRE ROPE & CABLES

Cabs   see   TAXI CABS

CADMIUM

Consumption in production of artists' colours: tonnage	UK	C 30-q	
cadmium alloy: tonnage	UK	C 30-q	C 12-a
cadmium-copper: tonnage	UK	C 30-q	
cadmium-copper alloys: tonnage	UK	T 4-a	
colours & pigments: tonnage	UK	C 12-a	T 4-a
plating anodes: tonnage	UK	C 30-q	C 12-a
		T 4-a	
plating salts: tonnage	UK	C 30-q	T 4-a
solder: tonnage	UK	C 30-q	C 12-a
		T 4-a	
tonnage	All countries	C 30-a	
	UK & USA	T 4-a	
	USA	N 1-a	
Exports by destination of cadmium metal: tonnage	Main countries	T 4-a	
unwrought & finished metal: tonnage	Italy	C 12-a	
Government stockpile & sales: tonnage	USA	N 1-a	
Import prices: cadmium ingots in $ per lb cif	UK	C 12-m	
cadmium sticks in £ per lb cif	UK	T 4-m	
in $ per lb cif	UK	C 12-m	
Imports by source of cadmium metal: tonnage	Main countries	T 4-a	
	UK	C 30-q	
of unwrought metal & scrap: tonnage	Italy	C 12-a	
Imports & exports by source & destination: tonnage	Main countries	B 15-a	
Producer prices in $ per lb on New York Metal Market	USA	C 12-m	
in local currency per lb	UK & USA	H 2-a	
Production in lbs	Main countries	J 6-a	
Production: historical table: tonnage	Italy	C 12-a	
(incl compounds): tonnage	All countries	B 15-a	

	Territorial coverage	Title codes

CADMIUM, continued
   Production: tonnage

	Zaire	E 41-a
	All countries	C 30-q
Stocks at producers' & dealers' premises: tonnage	UK	C 30-q
Stocks: tonnage (excl strategic pile)	USA	N 1-a
Wholesale prices: cadmium sticks in £ per lb	USA	T 4-a
in local currency	UK	T 4-m
in lire per kg	Main countries	T 4-m
electrolytic metal in Fr per kg	Italy	C 12-m
in $ per lb	France	T 4-m
	USA	N 1-a
World consumption: tonnage		C 30-a
	Main countries	C 12-a
export trade: tonnage	Main countries	T 4-a
production: tonnage		C 30-a N 4-a
	All countries	C 12-a
	Main countries	N 1-a T 4-a
reserves: tonnage (estim)	Main countries	N 1-a

Caerphilly   see   CHEESE BY VARIETY

Caesium ore   see   CESIUM ORE

Caffeine   see   OPIUM ALKALOIDS

Calcium arsenate   see   INSECTICIDES

Calcium carbide   see   CHEMICAL PRODUCTS

Calcium carbonate   see   CHALK

Calcium compounds   see   BUILDING MATERIALS
                                         CHALK
                                         CHEMICAL PRODUCTS
                                         FERTILISERS
                                         INSECTICIDES

Calcium cyanamide   see   FERTILISERS

Calcium nitrate   see   FERTILISERS, NITROGENOUS

Calcium oxide (quicklime)   see   BUILDING MATERIALS

CALCIUM SILICIDE

Consumption in ferro-alloy production: tonnage	UK	T 4-a

CALCULATORS, DESK-TYPE
         see also   ELECTRONIC CALCULATORS, DESK-TYPE

Exports by destination by value in $m	Main countries	U 9-a
by value in $m	Main countries	U 38-a
Imports by value in $m	All countries	U 38-a
Production by volume: adding machines	All countries	U 38-a
calculators	All countries	U 22-a U 38-a
	EEC countries	E 28-q E 27-a
World export trade by value in $m		U 38-a

CALFSKINS
         see also   FOOTWEAR UPPERS, LEATHER
                            HIDES

% consumption of light leather products for production of footwear uppers	USA	A 18-a
Consumption: tonnage (salted wt)	OECD countries	D 18-a
for leather production: tonnage	Main countries	B 9-a
Exports by destination: tonnage	OECD countries	D 18-a
	Main countries	B 9-m
(incl kips): tonnage	OECD countries (in Europe)	D 18-a
tonnage	Main exporting countries	B 2-a
	Main producing countries	A 18-a
Imports by source by value in $	OECD countries	D 18-a
tonnage	OECD countries	D 18-a
ex non-OECD countries (salted wt)	OECD countries	D 18-a
(incl kips): tonnage	Main countries	B 9-m
Intra-European trade: tonnage	European economic areas	D 18-a
Production of leather from calfskins: tonnage	Main countries	B 9-a
cattle hides (untanned): tonnage	OAS member countries	N 14-a
(salted wt): tonnage	OECD countries	D 18-a
volume	Main countries & world regions	A 18-a
Wholesale prices (8 lb & under) in pence per kg	UK	B 2-a
light calfskins – index nos	OECD countries	D 18-a

Call money rates   see   MONEY MARKET RATES

Calorie intake   see   FOOD
                             NUTRITION
                             PROTEIN

	Territorial coverage	Title codes	
CALORIFIC VALUE			
Calorific value of food consumed per capita	Main countries	E 3-a	
gas production by kind	European countries & USA	U 3-a	
heat equivalents of fuels by type compared with petroleum		C 21	
no of calories, nutrients, proteins & fats contained by food item		D 14-a	
CALVES			
see also CATTLE			
LIVESTOCK			
VEAL			
Auction prices in local currency per kg (live wt)	EEC countries	C 9-m	
Reference prices in pence per lb (live wt)	EEC countries	C 9-m	
Slaughterings & average carcase weight in kg	EEC countries	E 44-a	
& production tonnage of veal	EEC countries	E 1-a	
by volume & % change	EEC countries	C 9-m	
tonnage (carcase wt)	Main countries	B 12-m	B 11-a
	European countries	U 36-a	
CAMELS			
Population: no of head	AASM countries	E 41-a	
	African countries	U 44-a	
	All countries	A 9-a	
Camembert see CHEESE BY VARIETY			
Cameras see PHOTOGRAPHIC APPARATUS			
CAMPING SITES			
No of camping sites in use	OECD countries	D 47-a	
of places available for tourists on sites	OECD countries	D 47-a	
Camps see HOUSING, TEMPORARY			
Canals see INLAND WATERWAYS			
KIEL CANAL			
PANAMA CANAL			
ST LAWRENCE SEAWAY			
CANARY SEED			
Production tonnage & area harvested in ha & yield per ha	All countries	A 9-a	
Cancer see DISEASES			
Cane sugar see SUGAR, CANE			
Cannabis see DRUGS & MEDICINES			
CANNED & BOTTLED FRUIT			
see also CITRUS FRUITS, CANNED			
Consumption per capita: apricots in kg	Main countries	A 7-a	
peaches in kg	Main countries	A 7-a	
Consumption: tonnage	OECD countries	D 37-a	
Exports of apricots: tonnage	All countries	A 7-a	
by destination: peaches: tonnage	Main countries	A 7-a	
by value in $m	W European countries	U 33-a	
of peaches: tonnage	All countries	A 7-a	
tonnage	Main countries	B 5-a	
Imports of apricots: tonnage	Main countries	A 7-a	
by source: tonnage & value in £	UK	B 6-a	
by value in $m	W European countries	U 33-a	
of peaches: tonnage	Main countries	A 7-a	
tonnage	Main countries	B 6-a	
Production: stocks & consumption: tonnage	OECD countries	D 14-a	
apricots: tonnage	All countries	A 7-a	
canned peaches: tonnage	All countries	A 7-a	
canned pears: tonnage	OECD countries	D 35-a	
	Australia	D 34-a	
tonnage	All countries	B 5-a	U 22-a
	EEC countries	E 28-q	E 27-a
CANNED & BOTTLED FRUIT BY KIND			
Exports by destination: tonnage	Main European countries	B 6-m	
Import prices in £ per cwt	UK	B 6-a	
Imports preserved in syrup: tonnage	UK	B 5-a	
Production: tonnage	Main countries	B 5-a	
	Japan	B 6-a	
Retail prices in local currency	OAS member countries	N 17-a	
Canned baby foods see DIETETIC FOODS			

	Territorial coverage	Title codes
CANNED FISH		
Consumption of fish (fresh) for canning: tonnage	OECD countries	D 43-a
sardines: tonnage	OAS member countries	N 17-a
tuna fish: tonnage	OAS member countries	N 17-a
Exports: tonnage & value in local currency & in $m	OECD countries	D 43-a
Imports: tonnage & value in local currency in $m	OECD countries	D 43-a
Production of heat-processed fish products: tonnage	All countries	U 22-a
of herrings & tuna fish: tonnage	African countries	U 44-a
stocks & consumption per capita in kg: tonnage	OECD countries	D 14-a
tonnage	EEC countries	E 28-q E 27-a
Wholesale prices by quality in $	USA	A 9-a
CANNED FISH BY KIND		
Production: tonnage	Main countries	U 43-a
Retail prices in local currency	OAS member countries	N 17-a
World production (incl crustaceans & molluscs): tonnage		A 21-a

Canned fruit juices   see   FRUIT JUICES

CANNED MEAT

see also   MEAT PREPARATIONS

	Territorial coverage	Title codes
% share of world import & export trade	Main countries	B 1-a
Availability for consumption tonnage	Main countries	B 11-a
Consumption per capita in lbs per yr	Main countries	B 11-a
	UK	B 12-a
Exports by destination: tonnage	Main countries	B 11-a
Imports of preserved meat: tonnage	European countries	U 36-a
tonnage	Main countries	B 11-a
Production: tonnage	All countries	U 22-a
	EEC countries	E 28-q E 27-a
	Main countries	B 12-m B 11-a
Retail prices: corned beef in local currency	OAS member countries	N 17-a
Shipments to UK & USA: tonnage	Argentine	C 9-m
World exports by value in $m	World regions	A 5-a
CANNED MEAT BY KIND		
Exports: tonnage	European countries	U 36-a
Imports of canned pork products: tonnage	UK	B 11-a
poultry: tonnage	UK	B 11-a
veal: tonnage	UK	B 11-a
corned beef: tonnage	UK	B 11-a
(incl meat preparations): tonnage	UK	U 36-a
of tongues of beef & pork: tonnage	UK	B 11-a
Production (incl meat products): tonnage	W Germany	U 36-a
tonnage	UK	B 12-a U 36-a
CANNED SOUP		
Production & consumption per capita per day	OECD countries	D 14-a

Canned tomatoes   see   TOMATO PRODUCTS

	Territorial coverage	Title codes
CANNED VEGETABLES		
Consumption tonnage	OAS member countries	N 17-a
Imports incl dried & frozen: tonnage	UK	B 6-a
Production & consumption per capita	OECD countries	D 14-a
Production: tinned or bottled vegetables	All countries	U 22-a
tonnage	EEC countries	E 28-q E 27-a
	OECD countries	D 37-a
CANNED VEGETABLES BY KIND		
Production tonnage	Japan	B 6-a
Retail prices in local currency	OAS member countries	N 17-a
CANS, METAL		
Exports of metal storage containers: tonnage	OECD countries	D 9-a
Production: tonnage	All countries	U 22-a

Capacitors   see   ELECTRONIC COMPONENTS

Capacity   see   PLANT CAPACITY

Capital   see   SHARE CAPITAL

CAPITAL ACCUMULATION

see also   CAPITAL FORMATION

	Territorial coverage	Title codes
Savings & consumption as % total capital accumulation	All countries	U 60-a
CAPITAL CONSUMPTION		
Capital consumption in agriculture as % value gross output	ECE countries	U 15-a
Fixed capital consumed by value in $m	All countries	U 60-a

Capital duty   see   CORPORATION TAX

	Territorial coverage	Title codes

Capital expenditure   see   BUDGET ACCOUNTS
                                     INVESTMENT

Capital flows   see   BILATERAL AID
                           EUROPEAN DEVELOPMENT FUND
                           EUROPEAN INVESTMENT BANK
                           INTERNATIONAL FINANCE CORPORATION
                           INVESTMENT, PRIVATE OVERSEAS
                           INVESTMENT, PUBLIC OVERSEAS
                           MULTILATERAL AID
                           TRANSFER PAYMENTS

Capital flows, private   see   INVESTMENT, PRIVATE OVERSEAS

Capital flows, public   see   INVESTMENT, PUBLIC OVERSEAS

CAPITAL FORMATION

       see also   CAPITAL ACCUMULATION
                          CAPITAL OUTPUT RATIOS
                          DEPRECIATION
                          NET MATERIAL PRODUCT

Subheading	Territorial coverage	Title codes	
Arising from changes in inventories	AASM countries	E 41-a	
ownership of dwellings	ECE countries	U 15-a	
services rendered	ECE countries	U 15-a	
As % of disposal of total gross domestic product	Main countries	E 3-a	
expenditure on gross domestic product	All countries	U 43-a	U 60-a
gross domestic product	EEC area	E 13-a	
output in agriculture	ECE countries	U 34-a	
product in agriculture	ECE countries	U 34-a	
net material product	All countries	U 60-a	
	E European countries	U 16-a	
	E European countries, Cuba & Yugoslavia	U 43-a	
product in agriculture	ECE countries	U 34-a	
As component in financing of capital	Latin American countries	J 5-a	
in national accounts	All countries	F 5-m	F 6-q
of gross domestic product in $m	Main countries	U 27-a	
national product in local currency	Developing countries	D 25-a	
in $m	S American countries	U 41-a	
By government & corporate activity	EEC countries	E 32-a	
By industrial sectors at constant prices	ECE countries	U 15-a	
	E European countries	U 16-a	
	Main countries	U 21-a	
By industry	Asian, Far East & Australasian countries	U 45-a	
By kind of economic activity & composition	EEC countries	E 32-a	
	S American countries	U 41-a	
	OECD countries	D 30-a	
By main sectors of investment	E European countries & USSR	U 16-a	
By source of funds (state or co-ops)	E European countries	U 34-a	
By type of asset: buildings & equipment	Main countries	E 3-a	
buildings & machinery in local currency	OAS member countries	N 16-a	
	EEC countries	E 32-a	
of capital goods in local currency	Main African countries	U 44-a	
	OAS member countries	N 16-a	
of purchaser in local currency	OAS member countries	N 16-a	
By use: agricultural improvements in local currency	OAS member countries	N 16-a	
agriculture, forestry & fishing in local currency	OAS member countries	N 16-a	
banking, insurance & real estate in local currency	OAS member countries	N 16-a	
building construction in local currency	OAS member countries	N 16-a	
livestock farming in local currency	OAS member countries	N 16-a	
manufacturing industry in local currency	OAS member countries	N 16-a	
mining & quarrying in local currency	OAS member countries	N 16-a	
public administration in local currency	OAS member countries	N 16-a	
public utilities in local currency	OAS member countries	N 16-a	
service industries in local currency	OAS member countries	N 16-a	
transportation & warehousing in local currency	OAS member countries	N 16-a	
wholesale & retail trade in local currency	OAS member countries	N 16-a	
In agriculture & forestry at cost in $m	E European countries	U 34-a	
as % of gross farm product	EEC countries	B 1-a	
of gross output	ECE countries	U 34-a	
of gross domestic product	EEC countries	B 1-a	
	ECE countries	U 34-a	
at current prices in $m	ECE countries	U 34-a	
	EEC countries	E 44-a	
In agriculture, forestry & fishing in £m	EEC countries	B 1-a	
forestry, fishing & hunting in $m	ECE countries	U 15-a	
in local currency	E European countries	U 34-a	
- index nos (value basis)	ECE countries	U 34-a	
farm buildings & land improvements in $m	ECE countries	U 34-a	
machinery & equipment - index nos	ECE countries	U 34-a	
forestry at current prices	EEC countries	E 44-a	
general building construction in $m	ECE countries	U 15-a	
industry in $m	Main countries	U 25-a	
local currency & % change	All countries	U 13-a	
machinery & equipment at constant prices in $m	ECE countries	U 15-a	
non-corporate private sector in local currency	OAS member countries	N 16-a	
(Gross & net) in local currency	E European countries & USSR	U 16-a	
(Incl value of stock increases) in $m	Latin American countries	J 5-a	

CAPITAL FORMATION, continued

	Territorial coverage	Title codes
% change in building activity	European countries & USA	U 16-a
construction of dwellings	European countries & USA	U 16-a
gross fixed capital	E European countries	U 16-a
implicit price deflator	Developing countries	D 25-a
machinery purchase	European countries & USA	U 16-a
net fixed capital investment	E European countries	U 16-a
% change on previous year	EEC countries	E 13-a
% distribution: buildings & farm machinery	ECE countries	U 34-a
% financed by saving & deficits	Latin American countries	J 5-a
% of gross national product spent on fixed capital investment	ECE countries	U 15-a
% growth rates in expenditure	Developing countries	D 25-a
	All countries	U 60-a
% of total arising from house ownership	ECE countries	U 15-a
from services	ECE countries	U 15-a
% of total by type of use at current prices in $m	ECE countries	U 15-a
% of total invested in agriculture	E European countries	U 16-a
agriculture & forestry	ECE countries	U 15-a
construction	E European countries	U 16-a
housing	E European countries	U 16-a
industry	E European countries	U 16-a
industry & building construction	ECE countries	U 15-a
transport	E European countries	U 16-a
% share: building materials industry	E European countries	U 16-a
chemicals & rubber industry	E European countries	U 16-a
electric power industry	E European countries & USSR	U 16-a
engineering industry	E European countries & USSR	U 16-a
food processing industry	E European countries	U 16-a
fuel industry	E European countries & USSR	U 16-a
metallurgical industry	E European countries	U 16-a
textiles, clothing & footwear industries	E European countries	U 16-a
wood pulp paper industry	E European countries	U 16-a
Building construction as % gross national product	European countries & USA	U 5-a
as % total investment	European countries & USA	U 5-a
	ECE countries	U 15-a
industry in $m	Main countries	U 58-a
- index nos	ECE countries	U 34-a
industry investment in machinery & transport eqpt in $m	Main countries	U 58-a
(residential) as % total investment	ECE countries	U 15-a
Buildings at purchasers' value in local currency	African countries	U 44-a
Chemical industry in $m	European countries, Japan & USA	U 25-a
Construction (other than buildings) in local currency	African countries	U 44-a
	OAS member countries	N 16-a
Depreciation allowances in current values	EEC countries	E 32-a
Expenditure as % of gross domestic product	Developing countries	D 25-a
of gross national product	All countries	U 23-a
at current prices in local currency	OAS member countries	N 16-a
by sector as % of gross domestic product	Greece, Portugal & Spain	D 17-a
in local currency	Developing countries	D 25-a
on building construction in local currency	Developing countries	D 25-a
on machinery & eqpt in local currency	Developing countries	D 25-a
Farm buildings as % of total capital investment in agriculture	ECE countries	U 34-a
in local currency	E European countries	U 34-a
improvements by own resources by value in $m	ECE countries	U 34-a
machinery & eqpt on replacement value basis in $m	E European countries	U 34-a
as % of total capital investment in agriculture	ECE countries	U 34-a
in local currency	E European countries	U 34-a
Financial provision by government agencies in local currency	OAS member countries	N 16-a
by private companies in local currency	OAS member countries	N 16-a
by public corporations in local currency	OAS member countries	N 16-a
Fixed capital additions by government in local currency	African countries	U 44-a
	AASM countries	E 41-a
by private households	AASM countries	E 41-a
by private companies	AASM countries	E 41-a
investment - index nos	EEC countries	E 32-a
& % changes	EEC countries	E 26-a
as component in gross domestic product	African countries	U 44-a
by industrial sector	EEC countries	E 32-a
in industry	E European countries	U 16-a
(new) as % total investment	E European countries	U 16-a
(new) in industry in $m	E European countries	U 16-a
in $m	E European countries	U 16-a
	Asian, Far East & Australasian countries	U 45-a
	ECE countries	U 15-a
	OECD countries	D 30-a
	EEC countries	E 32-a
	S American countries	U 41-a
Historical tables from 1850 in local currency	Main European countries	Z 1-a
House building as % of total capital formation	European countries & USA	U 5-a
total building construction	European countries	U 5-a
gross national product	All countries	U 13-a U 43-a
	European countries & USA	U 5-a
Index nos (volume basis)	EEC countries	E 26-a
	World economic areas	U 60-a
Industry & building construction in $m	ECE countries	U 15-a
Investment by co-operative farms in $m	E European countries	U 34-a
in state agriculture in $m	E European countries	U 34-a
(uncompleted) as % total	E European countries	U 16-a

	Territorial coverage	Title codes
CAPITAL FORMATION, continued		
Land & dwellings in local currency	OAS member countries	N 16-a
Land improvement in local currency	E European countries	U 34-a
Machinery & ancillary equipment in local currency	African countries	U 44-a
Machinery as % of total investment	Developing countries	U 38-a
in local currency	OAS member countries	N 16-a
Manufacturing industry in $m	Main countries	U 25-a
Motor vehicles industry as % of capital formation in manufacturing		
industry	UK	B 28
Motor vehicles industry - index nos	UK	B 28
Non-residential building as % of all building construction	European countries	U 5-a
in local currency	OAS member countries	N 16-a
in $m	All countries	U 13-a
Private construction in local currency	OAS member countries	N 16-a
Public construction in local currency	OAS member countries	N 16-a
Public, private & government enterprises in $m	Latin American countries	J 5-a
Repairs to equipment in local currency	OAS member countries	N 16-a
Residential housing construction as % total construction	ECE countries	U 15-a
in $m	All countries	U 13-a
Supply of fixed capital in $m	E European countries & USSR	U 16-a
Transport equipment as % of total capital formation	Developing countries	U 38-a
	African countries	U 44-a
in local currency	OAS member countries	N 16-a
CAPITAL GAINS		
see also REVENUE		
Government receipts from taxes	EEC countries	E 42-a
	OECD countries	D 42-a
CAPITAL GOODS		
see also CONSTRUCTION EQUIPMENT		
MACHINE TOOLS		
MACHINERY		
PRODUCER GOODS		
% change in output	E European countries & USSR	U 16-a
Exports by value in $m & % growth rates	Main countries	U 38-a
Imports by value in $m	Asian, Far East & Australasian countries	U 45-a
investment goods by value in UA	AASM countries	E 41-a
ex EEC area by value in UA	AASM countries	E 41-a
Production - index nos	ECE countries	U 42-m
CAPITAL GOODS BY KIND		
Exports by NIMEXE classes by value in $m	All countries	E 20-a
SITC classes by value in $m	All countries	U 50-a U 59-a
Imports by NIMEXE classes by value in $m	All countries	E 20-a
SITC classes by value in $m	All countries	U 50-a U 59-a

Capital inflow   see   OVERSEAS INVESTMENT INCOME
                       REMITTANCES
                       TRANSFER PAYMENTS

Capital investment   see   INVESTMENT

Capital issues   see   SHARES & SECURITIES

Capital movements   see   INVESTMENT

Capital outflow   see   INVESTMENT, PRIVATE OVERSEAS
                        INVESTMENT, PUBLIC OVERSEAS
                        REMITTANCES
                        TRANSFER PAYMENTS

CAPITAL OUTPUT RATIOS

Gross & net increment ratios	E European countries	U 16-a

Capital subscription payments   see   DEVELOPMENT AID

Capital transfers   see   TRANSFER PAYMENTS

Capital yields tax   see   TAXATION
                       CORPORATION TAX

Capsicums   see   SPICES & ESSENCES

CAPSTAN LATHES

% growth in imports & exports (incl turret type)	EEC countries	B 20-a
Imports & exports (incl turret type) by value in £m	EEC countries	B 20-a

Car accessories   see   AUTOMOTIVE ACCESSORIES

Car industry   see   MOTOR VEHICLES INDUSTRY

Caravans   see   TRAILERS

Carbides, sintered   see   SINTERED CARBIDES

	Territorial coverage	Title codes

Carbon bisulphide   see   CHEMICAL PRODUCTS

CARBON BLACK
    see also   GRAPHITE

Consumption: tonnage	USA	N 1-a
Exports by destination: tonnage	Main countries	U 2-a
Imports & exports: tonnage	European countries, Japan & USA	U 25-a
Production (excl graphite): tonnage	All countries	U 22-a
tonnage	European countries, Japan & USA	U 25-a
	Main countries	N 1-a
Stocks held at producers' premises: tonnage	USA	N 1-a
Wholesale prices ex plant in cents per lb	USA	N 1-a
World production: tonnage	Main countries	N 1-a

Carbon compounds   see   CHEMICALS, ORGANIC

Carbon disulphide   see   CHEMICAL PRODUCTS

CARBON MONOXIDE

Consumption for organic synthesis: tonnage	OECD countries	D 5-a
tonnage	OECD countries	D 5-a
Production: tonnage from coal derivatives	OECD countries	D 5-a
natural gas	OECD countries	D 5-a
oil natural gas	OECD countries	D 5-a

Carbon steels   see   CRUDE STEEL, CARBON

Carborundum   see   ABRASIVES, ARTIFICIAL

Carcasses   see   CATTLE CARCASSES

Cardamons   see   SPICES & ESSENCES

Cardboard   see   PAPER & PAPERBOARD

Cargo   see   DRY CARGO

Cargo co-efficients   see   AIR TRANSPORT

Cargo freight   see   AIR FREIGHT
        INLAND WATERWAYS
        KIEL CANAL
        MAIL FREIGHT
        PANAMA CANAL
        RAIL FREIGHT
        ROAD TRANSPORT
        SEABORNE FREIGHT

Cargo planes   see   AIRCRAFT

CARGO SHIPS
    see also   BULK CARRIERS
                 SHIPS & BOATS
                 TRAMP SHIPPING

% of total EEC-registered vessels: tonnage	EEC countries	R 5-a	
Age distribution of world merchant fleets	World regions	U 37-a	
Bunker capacity for coal: tonnage	Country of flag	S 16-a	
for diesel oil: tonnage	Country of flag	S 16-a	
for fuel oil: tonnage	Country of flag	S 16-a	
Cargo fleets by age groups & loading capacity: tonnage	EEC countries	E 43-a	
Construction completed: tonnage	World regions	U 37-a	
Conversion tonnage & sales of ships abroad	EEC countries	E 43-a	
Deliveries of new merchant ships: no & tonnage	Worldwide	S 15-a	
Exports of general cargo carriers: no & tonnage	OECD countries	D 9-a	
Freight rates: tramp time charter - index nos	Worldwide	U 37-a	
tramp voyage charter - index nos		U 37-a	
Hold capacities & refrigerated space in cu ft	Country of flag	S 16-a	
No & loading capacity by size classifications: tonnage	EEC countries	E 43-a	
growth from 1938: tonnage	EEC countries	E 43-a	
tonnage acquisitions of new & second-hand vessels	Country of flag	U 37-a	
afloat: general cargo ships	Country of flag	S 2-a	
over 10,000 dwt	Country of flag	S 22-a2	
afloat (total)	EEC countries	E 43-a	
arriving & departing at or from main ports	EEC countries	E 43-a	
broken up for scrap	Country of flag	S 16-m	
bulk carriers & tankers afloat	OAS member countries	N 15-a	
completed	Country of build	S 3-q	
dry-cargo vessels afloat	OAS member countries	N 15-a	
laid up by size classes	UK & Worldwide	S 23-m	
by year of construction	Worldwide	S 23-m	S 16-a
for lack of employment	Country of flag	S 16-m	S 17-m
		S 23-m	
	Worldwide	S 17-m	S 15-a
merchant ships launched	Country of build	S 3-q	S 1-a
vessels afloat by flag	Worldwide	S 16-a	
multi-decker fixtures by kind of cargo	Worldwide	S 17-m	
on order but not started	All countries	S 3-q	

	Territorial coverage	Title codes
CARGO SHIPS, continued		
No & tonnage on order by size for Norwegian companies	Norway	S 15-a
on order	Country of build	D 28-a
owned by each shipping company	Finland	S 16-a
reefers in fleet	Norway	S 15-a
refrigerated cargo vessels afloat	OAS member countries	N 15-a
refrigerated ships launched	Poland	S 16-a
roll-on roll-off vessels afloat	Norway	S 15-a
sailing ships: historical table of vessels registered from 1788	Main European countries	Z 1-a
steamships: historical table of vessels registered from 1814	Main European countries	Z 1-a
time charter commitments by charterer	Worldwide	S 17-m
under construction	All countries	S 3-q
under construction by engine hp	EEC countries	E 43-a
No by engine hp, capacity tonnage & year of build	EEC countries	E 43-a
No entered & cleared ports	ECAFE countries	U 32-m
No, tonnage & hp using inland waterways	EEC countries	E 43-a
Ocean freight rates for dry cargo vessels on time charter - index nos	Worldwide	D 28-m
Passenger accommodation available on vessels	Country of flag	S 16-a
Prices ex shipyards: closed-deck type per ton	Worldwide	S 16-a2
open-deck type per ton	Worldwide	S 16-a2
Sales of named Norwegian vessels by value in $m	Buying country	S 15-a
of named vessels: tonnage, age, speed & price in $m	Worldwide	S 17-m
Seaborne freight carried in ton-miles	UK	S 16-a
Tonnage afloat as % tonnage of world fleets		U 37-a
general cargo vessels & as % world fleets	Worldwide	D 28-a
Tonnage afloat	Country of flag	R 5-a
broken up for scrap	Worldwide	D 28-a
contracted for building	Worldwide	S 15-a
dry cargo ships broken up for scrap by hp groups	EEC countries	E 43-a
dry cargo ships broken up for scrap	Worldwide	S 15-a
laid up for lack of employment	Country of flag	D 28-a
launched during period	Main countries	E 3-a
under construction at end-yr	Worldwide	R 5-a
	Main countries	E 3-a R 5-a
Trip & time shipments by kind of cargo: tonnage	Worldwide	S 17-m
CARGO SHIPS, SECOND-HAND		
Bulk carriers sold by value in $m (average)	Worldwide	S 15-a
Dry cargo ships sold by value in $m (average)	Worldwide	S 15-a
Exports: no & tonnage as scrap	Norway	S 15-a
Vessels by size, age & value in $m (average)	Worldwide	S 16-a
CARGO SHIPS BY AGE		
Tonnage by year of build	Worldwide	S 22-a
CARGO SHIPS BY FLAG		
Tonnage of vessels over 10,000 dwt	Country of flag	S 22-a2
CARGO SHIPS BY TYPE		
No & tonnage afloat	OAS member countries	N 15-a
under construction or completed	Poland	S 16-q
Sales tonnage, age, speed, price, buyer & seller	Worldwide	S 17-m
Cargo traffic see KIEL CANAL		
PANAMA CANAL		
SEABORNE FREIGHT		
CAROBS		
Export prices in drachma	Greece	A 9-a
CARPET MANUFACTURING INDUSTRY		
Capital expenditure in £m	UK	B 29-a
Gross output by value in $m	OECD countries	D 46-a
Investment in $m	OECD countries	D 46-a
Labour force employed projected to 1977	UK	B 29-a
no of salaried staff employed	OECD countries	D 46-a
wage earners employed	OECD countries	D 46-a
Production - index nos	OECD countries	D 46-a
Usage of artificial yarns: tonnage	OECD countries	D 46-a
cotton waste yarn: tonnage	OECD countries	D 46-a
cotton yarn: tonnage	OECD countries	D 46-a
flax & tow yarn: tonnage	OECD countries	D 46-a
jute yarn: tonnage	OECD countries	D 46-a
man-made yarns: tonnage	OECD countries	D 46-a
manila hemp yarn: tonnage	OECD countries	D 46-a
sisal yarn: tonnage	OECD countries	D 46-a
soft hemp & tow: tonnage	OECD countries	D 46-a
synthetic yarns: tonnage	OECD countries	D 46-a
wool yarn: tonnage	OECD countries	D 46-a
worsted yarn: tonnage	OECD countries	D 46-a

	Territorial coverage	Title codes
CARPETS		
see also FLOOR COVERING		
Consumption of textile fibres by carpet industry: tonnage	Main countries	K 4-a
of wool by kind by carpet industry: tonnage	Main countries	K 6-a
Deliveries by manufacturers - index nos	UK	B 29-a
Demand projected to 1977 in million lbs	UK	B 29
Exports (incl rugs) by value in local currency	Afghanistan	U 32-m
tufted & woven carpets projected to 1977 in lbs	UK	B 29
Imports & exports & trade balance in million sq yds	UK	B 29-a
tufted & woven carpets projected to 1977 in lbs	UK	B 29
Production: tufted & woven carpets projected to 1977 in lbs	UK	B 29
volume by type (incl rugs)	All countries	U 22-a
volume in m² (incl tufted)	OECD countries	D 46-a
made of cotton	OECD countries	D 46-a
made of man-made fibres	OECD countries	D 46-a
made of wool	OECD countries	D 46-a
CARPETS, HAND-MADE		
Exports by value in local currency	Iran	U 32-m
CARPETS, WOOLLEN		
Production by volume	EEC countries	E 28-q E 27-a
Carriers, wet or dry see BULK CARRIERS		
CARROTS		
Area harvested, production tonnage & yield per ha	All countries	A 9-a
under crop (incl turnips for animal feed) in ha	EEC countries	E 12-a
Crop yield (incl turnips for animal feed) in 100 kg per ha	EEC countries	E 12-a
Production: tonnage (incl turnips for animal feed)	EEC countries	E 12-a
tonnage	Czechoslovakia, E Germany & Poland	U 20-a
Cars see PASSENGER CARS		
Cars, second-hand see PASSENGER CARS, SECOND-HAND		
Cartons, paper see PACKING CONTAINERS		
Casein, hardened see PLASTICS		
CASEIN		
% of output exported	Australia, Canada, France & New Zealand	B 4-a
% of skim milk production used in making casein	EEC countries	B 3-a
Consumption: tonnage	Denmark, France, W Germany & UK	B 3-a
Expenditure on production of casein from milk powder under EEC budget	EEC area	B 3-a
Export prices	New Zealand	A 9-a
Exports by destination of rennet & lactic casein: tonnage	New Zealand	B 12-m
tonnage	Argentine, Australia & New Zealand	B 4-a
	Argentine, Australia, France & New Zealand	B 12-a
(incl casein derivatives): tonnage	EEC countries	B 3-a
tonnage	Main countries	B 4-a B 12-a
Import prices ex New Zealand & Poland in £ per ton cif	UK	B 4-m B 12-m
Imports by source lactic casein: tonnage	Main countries	B 12-a
rennet: tonnage	Main countries	B 12-a
caseinates & derivatives: tonnage	Main countries	B 12-a
tonnage	Italy, Japan, UK & USA	B 4-a
(incl casein derivatives): tonnage	EEC countries	B 3-a
tonnage	Main countries	B 4-a B 12-a
Production: tonnage	EEC countries	B 3-a
	Main countries	B 4-a
CASH FLOW		
see also SALES BY VALUE		
Motor vehicle industry in £m	UK	B 28
projected to 1977 in £m	UK	B 28
CASHEW KERNELS		
Exports from Mozambique, Kenya & Tanzania: tonnage	E African countries	P 4-m
tonnage	Main countries	P 4-m
Import prices by grade in £ per ton c & f	UK	P 4-m
Imports of raw cashew seeds: tonnage	India	P 4-m
tonnage	Main countries	P 4-m
CASHEW NUTSHELL OIL		
Exports: tonnage	Brazil, India & Mozambique	B 19-a
Cassa del Mezzogiorno (Fund for Development of S Italy) see DEVELOPMENT PLANS		

	Territorial coverage	Title codes

CASSAVA
    see also   SAGO & TAPIOCA

Area harvested, production tonnage & yield per ha	All countries	A 9-a
under crop in ha	OAS member countries	N 13-a
Consumption of manioc in production of animal feed: tonnage	EEC countries	P 5-a
Import prices in $ per ton	France	A 9-a
Production tonnage, area under crop & yield per ha	Latin American countries	J 5-a
tonnage	AASM countries	E 41-a
	Asian & Far East countries	U 32-a
	Latin American countries	U 40-a
	OAS member countries	N 13-a
Wholesale prices in $ per ton	Brazil	A 9-a
Yield in kg per ha	OAS member countries	N 13-a

Cassia   see   CINNAMON & CASSIA

Cast-iron   see   IRON CASTINGS

Cast-iron pipes   see   PIPES, CAST-IRON

Cast-iron tubes & fittings   see   PIPES, CAST-IRON

Casting plants, steel   see   STEEL FOUNDRIES

CASTINGS
    see also   CRUDE STEEL
                    DIE CASTINGS
                    IRON CASTINGS
                    SAND CASTINGS
                    STEEL CASTINGS

Consumption of magnesium in production of die castings: tonnage	USA	T 4-a
mould castings: tonnage	USA	T 4-a
sand castings: tonnage	USA	T 4-a
Exports by destination: tonnage	EEC countries	E 5-q
Imports by source: tonnage	EEC countries	E 5-q
Production: iron & steel foundries: tonnage	Main countries	C 2-a

CASTINGS, ALUMINIUM

Production tonnage & value in £m	UK	B 25-a
Sales of die castings: tonnage	USA	J 6-a
high-pressure die castings: tonnage	UK	C 30-a
low-pressure gravity castings: tonnage	UK	C 30-a
permanent mould castings: tonnage	USA	J 6-a
sand castings: tonnage	UK	C 30-a
	USA	J 6-a
Sales: tonnage	OECD countries	D 21-a
World production: tonnage	Main countries	T 4-a

CASTINGS, BRASS

Production: tonnage	Italy	C 12-a

CASTINGS, BRONZE

Production: tonnage	Italy	C 12-a

CASTINGS, COPPER-ALLOY

Consumption of zinc in production of copper-alloy castings: tonnage	France & Italy	T 4-a

CASTINGS, COPPER

Production: tonnage & value in £m	UK	B 25-a

CASTINGS, FERROUS
    see also   IRON CASTINGS
                    STEEL CASTINGS

Consumption by building industry: tonnage	France, W Germany & UK	B 25-a
collieries: tonnage	France, W Germany & UK	B 25-a
engineering industry: tonnage	France, W Germany & UK	B 25-a
railways: tonnage	France, W Germany & UK	B 25-a
rolling mills: tonnage	France, W Germany & UK	B 25-a
vehicles industry: tonnage	France, W Germany & UK	B 25-a

CASTINGS, LEAD

Consumption of lead in production of castings: tonnage	USA	T 4-a

CASTINGS, MAGNESIUM

Production: tonnage & value in £m	UK	B 25-a
Sales of magnesium anodes: tonnage	USA	J 6-a
die castings: tonnage	USA	J 6-a
permanent mould castings: tonnage	USA	J 6-a
sand castings: tonnage	USA	J 6-a

CASTINGS, ZINC

Production: tonnage & value in £m	UK	B 25-a

	Territorial coverage	Title codes	
CASTOR BEANS			
Import prices in $ per ton	European countries	A 9-a	
Production: tonnage	S American countries	U 40-a	
Wholesale prices in $ per ton	Brazil & India	A 9-a	
World production: tonnage		B 2-a	
CASTOR OIL			
Exports by destination: tonnage	Brazil & India	B 19-a	
tonnage & value in $m	Main countries	B 2-a	
tonnage	Main producing countries	B 18-q	B 19-q
Import prices ex Brazil in $ per ton cif	European countries	R 2-m	
in £ per ton cif	UK	B 2-a	
Imports by source: tonnage	UK	B 19-a	
Production: tonnage (& world total)	All countries	B 18-a	
estimates for ensuing yr	World regions	P 1-a	
	Commonwealth & world totals	B 19-a	
tonnage	Brazil, Japan, UK & USA	P 1-a	
	Main countries	B 19-a	
Wholesale prices ex tanks in cents per lb at New York market	USA	R 2-m	
in $ per ton	USA	A 9-a	
World production: tonnage		A 4-a	A 5-a
		N 10-a	
CASTOR SEED			
Crop tonnage & world total (estim)	All countries	P 1-a	
estimates for ensuing yr	World regions	P 1-a	
Export prices in $ per ton cif	Sudan	A 9-a	
Exports by destination: tonnage	Tanzania & Thailand	B 19-a	
Exports: tonnage & value in $m	Main countries	B 2-a	
tonnage	Main countries	B 18-q	B 19-a
Import prices ex E Africa in £ per ton cif	UK	R 2-m	
	European countries	B 19-q	
Imports by source: tonnage	EEC countries	B 19-a	
tonnage	Main countries	B 19-a	
Producer prices received in $ per ton	Uganda	A 9-a	
Production: tonnage	Main countries	B 19-a	

Casual day labourers   see   SEASONAL WORKERS

Casualties at sea   see   ACCIDENTS, MARITIME

CATALYSTS

Consumption of cobalt in production of catalysts in lbs	USA	T 4-a
mercury in production of catalysts in flasks	USA	T 4-a
silver in production of catalysts in oz	USA	T 4-a

Catering, public   see   RESTAURANT MEALS

CATHODES, BRASS

Consumption of copper in production of brass cathodes: tonnage	USA	T 4-a

CATHODES, COPPER

Consumption of copper in production of copper cathodes: tonnage	USA	T 4-a	
Production: tonnage	USA	J 6-m	
Wholesale prices (3 mths forward) in £ per ton	UK	C 12-m	T 4-m
electrolytic quality in yen per kg	Japan	T 4-w	

CATHODES, NICKEL

Wholesale prices ex refinery in cents per lb	USA	R 2-m
in lire per kg at Milan market	Italy	C 12-m
in $ per lb on New York market	USA	C 12-m

CATTLE

        see also   CALVES
                      LIVESTOCK

% changes in producer prices	W European countries	U 30-a
% sale for direct human consumption or processing	ECE countries	U 34-a
% usage for market sales or consumption by producers	ECE countries	U 34-a
Auction prices: fat cattle (average)	Main countries	B 11-a
live beef cattle (all grades)	W European countries	U 30-a
	EEC countries	E 34-m
steers, cows & calves in local currency	EEC countries	C 9-m
Dairy herds by size groups as % total population	EEC countries	B 3-a
Distribution for market sales	Czechoslovakia, Hungary & Poland	U 34-a
for own farm consumption	Czechoslovakia, Hungary & Poland	U 34-a
Exports by destination: fat cattle by volume	Main countries	B 12-m
live cattle by volume	Denmark, Eire, France & UK	B 11-a
by value as % value on total exports	Main countries	B 11-a
live cattle by volume	Main countries	B 11-a
Feed requirements for beef production per kg projected to 1985	Main countries	P 5-a
Government expenditure on price guarantees in £m	UK	P 5-a
Gross output by value (incl calves) at current prices in $	ECE countries	U 34-a
Imports by source (incl calves) by volume	Main countries	B 12-m
live cattle by volume	EEC countries	B 11-a

	Territorial coverage	Title codes
CATTLE, continued		
Inter-EEC imports & exports: tonnage	EEC countries	B 12-a
No of dairy cows (Dec census data)	EEC countries	B 3-a
per herd (Dec census data)	EEC countries	B 3-a
of dairy herds (Dec census data)	EEC countries	B 3-a
of heifers over 1 yr old per herd (census data)	EEC countries	B 3-a
Nutrient requirements for dairy cows per lb of dry diet		P 5
Population & cows as % total cattle population	Main countries	E 3-a
Population: beef cattle by areas	EEC countries	E 38-a
beef cattle in million head	Main countries	B 11-a
cattle & breeding cows projected to 1978	OECD countries	D 15-a
cattle & no per 100 ha of usable land	EEC countries	E 1-a
cattle (all kinds) & of cows	OECD countries	D 1-a
cows (census data)	Main countries	C 9-a
dairy cows & heifers	Australia, Canada, UK & USA	B 11-a
historical tables from 1816	Main European countries	Z 1-a
Population by age: milk cows, heifers, bulls & oxen	EEC countries	E 1-a
in 1,000 head	AASM countries	E 41-a
in million head (census data)	Main countries	C 9-a
in million head	All countries	A 9-a U 43-a
Prices paid as state purchases for slaughter	OAS member countries	N 13-a
Producer prices beef cattle for slaughter	Poland	U 30-a
	All countries	A 9-a
Production costs per ton on collective farms	E European countries excl USSR	U 30-a
Production: tonnage	USSR	U 34-a
by value in £m	Czechoslovakia, Hungary & Poland	U 34-a
Production value as % gross output (incl crops)	EEC countries	B 1-a
Production volume: dairy cows	E European countries	U 34-a
all cattle	Main countries	B 3-a
Reference prices in £ per live cwt	Latin American countries	J 5-a
Slaughter weight in kg per head (average)	EEC countries	C 9-m
Slaughterings: volume & % change	OAS member countries	N 14-a
volume	EEC countries	C 9-q
	All countries	A 9-a
	Main countries	B 11-a
volume (incl calves)	Argentina, Australia & USA	C 9-m
volume of beef cattle, imports, exports & supply	EEC countries	E 1-a
tonnage (carcase wt)	Main countries	B 12-m
Wholesale prices: beef cattle (live wt)	Main countries	A 9-a
bullocks & steers per cwt	Main countries	B 12-m
dairy cattle per head in £ equiv	EEC countries	B 3-a
fat cattle by kind per cwt	Main countries	B 12-m
fat cattle (live wt) - index nos	EEC countries	B 3-a
cattle for slaughter - index nos (unit value basis)	W European countries	U 30-a
in £ per ton (equiv live wt)	EEC countries	B 3-a
in local currency per 100 kg (live wt)	EEC countries	B 3-a
CATTLE BY BREED		
% of dairy livestock population: Anglers for milk	W Germany	B 3-a
Ayrshires for milk	UK	B 3-a
Charolais (all purpose)	France	B 3-a
German breeds (all purpose)	EEC countries	B 3-a
Guernseys for milk	UK	B 3-a
Herefords for meat	UK	B 3-a
Jerseys for milk	UK	B 3-a
Limousins for meat	France	B 3-a
local Belgian breeds (all purpose)	Belgium	B 3-a
local breeds of Friesian (all purpose)	EEC countries	B 3-a
local Danish breeds (all purpose)	Denmark	B 3-a
Schwarzbunt for meat	EEC countries	B 3-a
Shorthorns (all purpose)	UK	B 3-a
Simmental breeds (all purpose)	EEC countries	B 3-a
Whitehead Groningen (all purpose)	Netherland	B 3-a
% of dairy herds by main purpose breeds & breeds meat & milk	EEC countries	B 3-a
CATTLE BY KIND		
Population in 1,000 head	Main countries	R 5-a
cows & bulls: under & over 1 yr age	EEC countries	E 1-a
(end-yr census data)	E European countries & USSR	U 16-a
Sales by volume: bulls, bullocks & steers	Argentine	B 12-m
calves, cows & heifers	Argentine	B 12-m
CATTLE CARCASSES		
% contribution to export earnings	Botswana	E 45-a
Cattle hides see HIDES		
CAULIFLOWERS		
see also VEGETABLES, FRESH		
Intervention prices per kg	EEC area	U 20-m
Production: tonnage by areas	EEC countries	E 38-a
tonnage	European countries	U 20-a
Sales (wholesale): tonnage	Netherlands	U 20-a
Wholesale prices per kg	EEC countries	U 20-m

	Territorial coverage	Title codes	
CAUSTIC SODA			
Consumption: tonnage	OAS member countries	N 17-a	
Exports by destination: tonnage	Main countries	U 2-a	
tonnage	ECE countries	U 15-a	
	European countries, Japan & USA	U 25-a	
	OECD countries	D 5-a	
Imports: tonnage	ECE countries	U 15-a	
	European countries, Japan & USA	U 25-a	
	OECD countries	D 5-a	
Production: tonnage	African countries	U 44-a	
	All countries	U 27-m	U 22-a
		U 43-a	
	E European countries & USSR	U 16-a	
	ECE countries	U 15-a	
	EEC countries	E 26-m	
	European countries, Japan & USA	U 25-a	
	Main countries	E 3-a	R 5-a
	OAS member countries	N 14-a	
	OECD countries	D 5-a	
Production – index nos	OECD countries	D 5-a	

Ceiling & floor prices   see   INTERNATIONAL TIN AGREEMENT

Celestite   see   STRONTIUM

Cellulose derivatives   see   PLASTICS

Cellulose, regenerated   see   PLASTICS

CELLULOSE
       see also   PAINTS & VARNISHES

Consumption: tonnage	OAS member countries	N 17-a	
Production: regenerated cellulose: tonnage	All countries	U 22-a	

Cellulosic fabrics   see   WOVEN CELLULOSIC FABRICS

Cellulosic fibre yarn   see   MAN-MADE FIBRE YARN
                                 RAYON YARN

CELLULOSIC FIBRES
       see also   MAN-MADE FIBRES
                     NON-CELLULOSIC FIBRES
                     RAYON YARN

% of total EEC area production	EEC countries	R 5-a	
Consumption by end-use in production of clothing	EEC countries	K 4-a	
by mills: tonnage	All countries	A 6-a	
in production of carpets: tonnage	EEC countries	K 4-a	
of pneumatic tyres: tonnage	EEC countries	K 4-a	
by spindles: tonnage	W European countries	K 2-q	
of rayon & acetate fibres: tonnage	OAS member countries	N 17-a	
tonnage	European countries, Canada, Japan & USA	D 27-a	
Exports: artificial staple fibres: tonnage	Main countries	U 26-a	
Exports as % of production	European countries, Canada, Japan & USA	D 27-a	
by destination: tonnage	Main countries	K 4-a	
rayon acetate staple: tonnage	Main countries	B 10-a	
staple & tow: tonnage	Main countries	K 4-a	
synthetic staple: tonnage	Main countries	K 4-a	U 26-a
tonnage	All countries	A 6-a	
	OECD countries	D 46-a	
Imports: artificial staple fibres: tonnage	Main countries	U 26-a	
as % of production	European countries, Canada, Japan & USA	D 27-a	
by source of rayon fibre: tonnage	Main countries	B 10-a	
tonnage	Main countries	K 4-a	
of staple & tow: tonnage	Main countries	K 4-a	
synthetic staple: tonnage	Main countries	K 4-a	U 26-a
tonnage	All countries	A 6-a	
	OECD countries	D 46-a	
Plant capacity: tonnage	European countries, Canada, Japan & USA	D 27-a	
Production: artificial staple: tonnage	Main countries	U 26-a	
continuous filaments: tonnage	All countries	U 22-a	
	European countries, Canada, Japan & USA	D 27-a	
(incl filaments): tonnage	Main countries	R 5-a	
rayon & acetate fibres: tonnage	OAS member countries	N 14-a	
rayon acetate staple: tonnage	Main countries	K 1-q	B 10-a
		D 27-a	J 7-a
		K 4-a	U 26-a
rayon acetate thread: tonnage	OAS member countries	N 14-a	
rayon staple & yarn: tonnage	All countries	B 10-a	E 3-a
staple & tow: tonnage	All countries	U 22-a	
viscose fibres: tonnage	Main countries	K 4-a	
tonnage	All countries	A 6-a	K 4-a
	OECD countries	D 46-a	R 5-a
Usage of acetate fibre by textile industry: tonnage	OECD countries	D 46-a	
in spinning mills: tonnage	OECD countries	D 46-a	
in spinning of artificial yarn: tonnage	World regions	K 5-a	

	Territorial coverage	Title codes	
CELLULOSIC FIBRES, continued			
Usage: viscose fibre by textile industry: tonnage	OECD countries	D 46-a	
in spinning mills	OECD countries	D 46-a	
Wholesale prices by kind in local currency	Italy, Japan & UK	A 9-a	
World consumption: rayon staple fibre in lbs million		B 10-a	
in tonnage & kg per capita		A 6-a	
tonnage projected to 1980		B 29	
World production: rayon staple fibre in million lbs		B 10-a	

Cellulosic paints   see   PAINTS & VARNISHES, CELLULOSIC

Cellulosic waste   see   FIBRES, CELLULOSIC WASTE

CEMENT
    see also   CLINKER
                  LIMESTONE

	Territorial coverage	Title codes	
% contribution to export earnings	Bahamas	E 45-a	
% change in consumption	Main countries	D 4-a	
% of production consumed domestically	OECD countries	D 4-a	
% of total EEC area production	EEC countries	R 5-a	
Consumption (in bags) as % of own production	OECD countries	D 4-a	
(in bulk) as % of own production	OECD countries	D 4-a	
per capita in kg	ECE countries	U 15-a	
	European countries & USA	U 5-a	
	OECD countries	D 4-a	
tonnage	European countries & USA	U 5-a	
	OAS member countries	N 17-a	
	OECD countries	D 4-a	
	USA	N 1-a	
Deliveries ex mills of portland & masonry cement: tonnage	USA	N 1-a	
Exports by destination areas: tonnage	OECD countries	D 4-a	
by CST classes: tonnage & value in $m	Main countries	D 2-q	
by SITC classes by value in $m	OECD countries	D 3-a2	
tonnage & value in $m	EEC countries	E 48-a	
NIMEXE classes: tonnage & value in $m	All countries	E 20-a	
SITC classes: tonnage & value in $m	All countries	U 50-a	U 59-a
sea, inland waterways, road & rail: tonnage	European countries	U 8-a	
Exports: tonnage & value in $m	Bahamas	E 45-a	
tonnage	European countries & USA	U 5-a	
unit value in $ per ton	OAS member countries	N 15-a	
Imports by NIMEXE classes: tonnage & value in $m	All countries	E 20-a	
SITC classes: tonnage & value in $m	All countries	U 50-a	U 59-a
sea, inland waterways, road & rail: tonnage	European countries	U 8-a	
source by CST classes: tonnage & value in $m	EEC countries	E 21-a	
SITC classes by value in $m	Main countries	D 2-q	
SITC classes: tonnage & value in $m	OECD countries	D 3-a2	
ex world regions: tonnage	OECD countries	D 4-a	
tonnage	European countries	U 5-a	
Producer prices (type 425) in lire per sack	Italy	R 2-m	
Production capacity: tonnage	Main countries	N 1-a	
	OECD countries	D 4-a	
in Europe as % of world cement output	European area	D 4-a	
incl world total: historical table from 1913: tonnage	Main countries & world economic areas	C 4-a	
incl world total: tonnage	All countries	R 5-a	
	OECD countries	R 5-a	
by areas: tonnage	EEC countries	E 38-a	
by kind: tonnage	EEC countries	E 28-q	E 27-a
natural, masonry & portland: tonnage	All countries	B 15-a	
for building construction: tonnage	All countries	U 43-a	
tonnage	AASM countries	E 41-a	
	African countries	U 44-a	
	All countries	U 27-m	U 22-a
	Asian & Far East countries	U 32-q	
	E European countries & USSR	U 16-a	
	ECAFE countries	U 32-q	
	EEC countries	E 26-m	
	European countries & USA	U 5-a	
	Latin American countries	J 5-a	U 40-a
	Main countries	E 3-a	N 1-a
	OAS member countries	N 14-a	
	OECD countries	D 4-a	
Production - index nos	OECD countries	D 4-a	
Stocks at mills: tonnage	USA	N 1-a	
Wholesale prices in local currency per ton	OAS member countries	N 17-a	
in $ per ton	USA	N 1-a	
of portland cement (in sacks) in $ per ton	USA	R 2-m	
to building industry - index nos	OAS member countries	N 14-a	
- index nos	Austria, Canada, Italy & Switzerland	A 13-a	
	European countries & USA	U 5-a	
	OECD countries	D 4-a	
World production: tonnage of hydraulic cement		N 4-a	
tonnage (all kinds)		N 1-a	

CEMENT & PLASTER INDUSTRY
    see also   BUILDING MATERIALS INDUSTRY

	Territorial coverage	Title codes
Costs for salaried staff per mth	EEC countries	E 11-a
IDA loans approved in $m	OAS member countries	N 16-a

	Territorial coverage	Title codes	
CEMENT & PLASTER INDUSTRY, continued			
Investment in buildings in local currency	EEC countries	E 40-a	
machinery in local currency	EEC countries	E 40-a	
Labour costs by kind of employer as % of total costs	EEC countries	E 8-a	
by status of employees in local currency	EEC countries	E 8-a	
per hr: all employees	EEC countries	E 2-a	E 11-a
wage earners	EEC countries	E 11-a	
Labour force employed	OECD countries	D 4-a	
Labour force employed: administrative & clerical staff	OECD countries	D 4-a	
Labour force employed: production workers	OECD countries	D 4-a	
salaried staff	EEC countries	E 11-a	
wage earners & salaried staff	EEC countries	E 8-a	
wage earners	EEC countries	E 11-a	
No of new grinding mills installed by capacity: tonnage	OECD countries	D 4-a	
of new kilns installed by type	OECD countries	D 4-a	
by capacity: tonnage	OECD countries	D 4-a	
of hrs worked per wk by area	EEC countries	E 25-a	E 26-a
per wk	Main countries	R 3-a	
per yr	EEC countries	E 8-a	
salaried staff per mth	EEC countries	E 11-a	
wage earners per wk	EEC countries	E 11-a	
Wage rates per hr in local currency	EEC countries	E 25-a2	
by sex in local currency	Main countries	R 3-m	
CENTRAL BANKS			
see also BUDGET ACCOUNTS			
% re-discount rates	OAS member countries	N 16-a	
Assets by type (home, foreign, government & private) in $m	EEC countries	E 26-m	
cash deposits, loans & transfers in $m	EEC countries	E 4-a	
debts as payment balances component in $m	OECD countries	D 12-a	
loans & net claims in $m	All countries	F 1-a	
Claims (net) on government treasury in $m	Asian, Far East & Australasian countries	U 45-a	
on discount houses in $m	All countries	F 5-m	F 6-q
Foreign assets & foreign liabilities in $m	All countries	F 5-m	F 6-q
Liabilities & assets in $m	All countries	F 5-m	F 6-q
home & foreign governments in $m	Asian, Far East & Australasian countries	U 45-a	
private sector & bank deposits in $m	EEC countries	E 26-m	
to US government agencies in $m	EEC countries	E 26-m	
Reserves: gold & foreign exchange holdings in $m	All countries	F 1-a	
	EEC countries	E 4-a	

Central government debt   see   PUBLIC DEBT

Central government financing   see   BUDGET ACCOUNTS

Central heating   see   DWELLINGS

CENTRALISED STATE INVESTMENT

Amortisation allowances in $m	E European countries	U 16-a
Budgetary allocations in $m	E European countries	U 16-a
Capital formation in $m	E European countries & USSR	U 16-a
Long-term bank credits in $m	E European countries	U 16-a

CENTRE LATHES

see also LATHES, AUTOMATIC

Deliveries (domestic) by value in $m	EEC countries	B 31-a
Exports as % of production (value basis)	EEC countries	B 31-a
Imports & exports (incl multi-tool lathes) & % growth rates	EEC countries	B 20-a
as % of consumption (value basis)	EEC countries	B 31-a
Production by value in $m	EEC countries	B 31-a

Centrifuges   see   PUMPS

Ceramic products   see   EARTHENWARE PRODUCTS

CERAMICS INDUSTRY

Costs for salaried staff per mth	EEC countries	E 11-a
Investment in buildings in local currency	EEC countries	E 40-a
land purchase in local currency	EEC countries	E 40-a
machinery in local currency	EEC countries	E 40-a
Labour costs by kind as % of total costs	EEC countries	E 8-a
by status of employees in local currency	EEC countries	E 8-a
per hr: all employees in local currency	EEC countries	E 11-a
wage earners in local currency	EEC countries	E 11-a
Labour force employed: no of salaried staff	EEC countries	E 11-a
wage earners	EEC countries	E 11-a
& salaried staff	EEC countries	E 8-a
No of hrs worked per yr by labour force	EEC countries	E 8-a
salaried staff	EEC countries	E 11-a
wage earners	EEC countries	E 11-a

	Territorial coverage	Title codes

CEREAL PREPARATIONS
    % changes in retail sales   E European countries & USSR   U 16-a
    Consumption per capita by income levels   USA   C 27-a
                           in kg   E European countries   U 16-a
    Exports by value in $m   W European countries   U 33-a
    Imports by value in $m   W European countries   U 33-a
    Income elasticity of demand - index nos   USA   C 27-a
    Maize consumption in production of breakfast cereals: tonnage   UK   B 8-a
    Retail prices by kind of cereal in local currency   OAS member countries   N 17-a
    Wholesale prices by kind of cereal in local currency   OAS member countries   N 17-a

CEREALS
        see also   BREAD GRAINS
                         CEREAL PREPARATIONS
                         MILLING OFFALS
                         STATE PROCUREMENT

    As source of fat protein & calorie intake per capita   OAS member countries   N 17-a
    A.I.D. feedgrain sales under food aid programs by value in $m   All countries   M 1-a
    Area harvested, production tonnage & yield per ha   All countries   A 9-a
            under crop (all grains) in ha   EEC countries   E 12-a
                               in ha   OAS member countries   N 13-a
                                        OECD countries   D 1-a
            under feedgrains: maize & sorghum in ha   USA   A 12-a
    Availability & home production as % of supply   All countries   U 43-a
    Commonwealth share in production of grain: tonnage & as % world
        total   B 8-a
    Consumption tonnage & consumption per capita per day   OECD countries   D 14-a
            of all kinds of grain as seed: tonnage   OECD countries   D 1-a
            as % of total animal feed   Main European countries, Japan & USA   A 12-a
            as animal feed projected to 1978: tonnage   UK   P 5-a
            as animal feed: tonnage   EEC countries   E 3-a
                                         Main countries   A 12-a   C 27-a
            bread grains as animal feed: tonnage   OECD countries   D 1-a
            cereals (imported) as animal feed: tonnage   OECD countries   D 1-a
                   (locally-grown) as animal feed: tonnage   OECD countries   D 1-a
            coarse grains as animal feed: tonnage   World regions   C 27-a
                          as human food: tonnage   World regions   C 27-a
                          (excl barley) as animal feed: tonnage   UK   B 7-a
            coarse grains: tonnage   World regions   C 27-a
            cost to private sector at current prices   EEC countries, Japan & Spain   A 12-a
            feedgrains, maize & sorghum: tonnage   EEC countries   E 32-a
            for industrial processing & as seed: tonnage   USA   A 12-a
            in production of animal feed: tonnage   EEC countries   E 3-a
            on farms: for own use: tonnage   EEC countries   P 5-a
            per capita (all kinds) in kg per yr   USSR   C 27-a
                                    W European countries   P 5-a
                                    Canada, European countries, USA & USSR   E 44-a
                          as flour in kg per yr   OECD countries   D 1-a
                          in grammes per day   India   C 27-a
            requirements of coarse grains (excl barley): tonnage   UK   B 7-a
            wheat & rye as animal feed: tonnage   OECD countries   D 1-a
                          as seed: tonnage   OECD countries   D 1-a
    Crop yield: feedgrains, maize & sorghum in kg per ha   USA   A 12-a
            in 100 kg per ha   EEC countries   E 12-a
            in quintals per ha   E European countries & USSR   U 16-a
    Expenditure on price guarantees under EEC budget in £m   B 3-a
    Export prices: coarse grains in $ per ton   Canada & USA   U 35-a
    Export prices - index nos   Worldwide   U 54-a
                     - index nos (weighted average of sub-groups)   Worldwide   U 29-q
    Exports by sea, inland waterways, road & rail: tonnage   European countries   U 8-a
            value in $m   W European countries   U 33-a
            to E European bloc in $m   E European countries   U 20-a
            of coarse grains: tonnage   All countries   A 17-a
                            by value in $ Developing countries   U 11-a
            (incl cereal preparations) by value in $ OECD countries   D 1-a
                          to EEC & non-EEC area by value
                                               in $m   EEC countries   E 24-a
            tonnage: historical tables from 1750   Main European countries   Z 1-a
            tonnage   Asian & Far East countries   U 32-q
                                   E European countries & USSR   U 16-a
    Feed characteristics of barley: % content of protein & lysine   A 12-a
                                  barley: energy in calories per kg   A 12-a
                                  maize: % content of protein & lysine   A 12-a
                                  maize: energy in calories per kg   A 12-a
                                  oats: % content of protein & lysine   A 12-a
                                  oats: energy in calories per kg   A 12-a
                                  sorghum: % content of protein & lysine   A 12-a
                                  sorghum: energy in calories per kg   A 12-a
                                  wheat: % content of protein & lysine   A 12-a
    Food aid: budget expenditure on cereals in £m   EEC area   B 3-a
    Freight: imports by cargo source: tonnage   Main countries   D 28-a
    Freight rates for cereals shipped to India from Australia &
                                           N America per ton   C 29-m
                    to Japan from Australia,
                               Argentine & USA per ton   C 29-m

	Territorial coverage	Title codes

CEREALS, continued

Item	Territorial coverage	Title codes
Freight rates for cereals shipped to Rotterdam from Argentine, Australia & USA per ton		C 29-m
Freight rates for cereals shipped to UK from Argentine, Australia, Canada & USA per ton		C 29-m
Imports & exports of coarse grains: tonnage	E European countries	U 35-a
Imports as % of consumption of coarse grains	World regions	C 27-a
by sea, inland waterways, road & rail: tonnage	European countries	U 8-a
by value from E Europe in $m	W European countries	U 20-a
in $m	W European countries	U 33-a
in local currency	Asian & Far East countries	U 32-a
coarse grains: tonnage	All countries	A 17-a
	EEC countries, Israel, Japan & Spain	A 12-a
(incl cereal preparations) by value in $	OECD countries	D 1-a
from EEC & non-EEC area by value in $	EEC countries	E 24-a
tonnage: historical tables from 1750	Main European countries	Z 1-a
tonnage	E European countries & USSR	U 16-a
Industrial consumption in distilling & malting: tonnage	UK	C 27-a
in production of food preparations: tonnage	EEC countries	E 44-a
Ocean freight rates (main routes: single voyage) in £ & $ per ton	Worldwide	S 16-a
Production by value at current prices	EEC countries	E 44-a
Production by value: coarse grains as % of value of gross output of cereals	E European countries	U 34-a
Production costs: grains (excl maize) per ton	USSR	U 34-a
Production: flour (other than from wheat): tonnage	All countries	U 22-a
Production, imports, exports, stocks & consumption: tonnage	EEC countries	E 44-a
Production: meal & groats (from all cereals): tonnage	All countries	U 22-a
Production, stocks, imports, exports & domestic consumption: tonnage	EEC countries	E 3-a
Production, stocks, industrial usage & usage as fodder & seed: tonnage	OECD countries	D 14-a
Production & consumption forecast for ensuing yr: tonnage	Main countries	A 1
(all kinds) incl world total: tonnage	Main countries	C 4-a
(all kinds): tonnage	E European countries & USSR incl Ukraine	U 16-a
	OECD countries	D 1-a
coarse grains: tonnage	EEC countries, Japan & Spain	A 12-a
	European countries	U 35-a
	Czechoslovakia, Hungary & Poland	U 34-a
feedgrains, maize & sorghum: tonnage	USA	A 12-a
(less usage as feed & seed): tonnage	OECD countries	D 1-a
mixed grains: tonnage	European countries	U 35-a
tonnage	Asian, Far East & Australasian countries	U 45-a
	E European countries & USSR	C 27-a
	EEC countries	E 12-a
	OAS member countries	N 13-a
Sales for human consumption: tonnage	USSR	C 27-a
of marketable grain to state agencies: tonnage	USSR	C 27-a
on collective farm markets: tonnage	USSR	C 27-a
Shipment by cargo vessels (trip & period charter): tonnage	Worldwide	S 17-m
grain tankers (trip & period charter): tonnage	Worldwide	S 17-m
Shipments through Kiel Canal eastwards: tonnage		D 28-a
westwards: tonnage		D 28-a
through Panama Canal westwards: tonnage		D 28-a
Shipping charterings: bulk carrier fixtures by loading zones: tonnage	Worldwide	S 17-m
by loading zones: tonnage	Worldwide	S 17-m
cargo ship fixtures by loading zones: tonnage	Worldwide	S 17-m
by size of vessels: tonnage	Worldwide	S 17-m
multi-decker fixtures loading by zones: tonnage	Worldwide	S 17-m
State procurement: tonnage	E European countries & USSR incl Ukraine	U 16-a
Stocks of coarse grains: tonnage at end-yr	Main countries	A 11-a
on farms: coarse grains (excl barley): tonnage	UK	B 7-a
tonnage	EEC countries	E 44-a
Supply & production: coarse grains (excl barley): tonnage	UK	B 7-a
Supply, production, consumption imports & exports: tonnage	EEC countries	B 1-a
Supply (net) per capita per day in kg	All countries	U 43-a
Trade balance & net imports per capita in kg	All countries	A 1
World estimate of seaborne grain trade: tonnage		D 28-a
exports: coarse grains by value in $m		A 5-a
market prices - index nos		U 23-a
production of coarse grains: tonnage	World regions	U 35-a
supply of coarse grains: tonnage	All countries	U 35-a
trade in coarse grains: tonnage	World regions	U 35-a

CEREALS BY KIND

Item	Territorial coverage	Title codes	
% composition of gross output at current prices	ECE countries	U 34-a	
% for sale, farm consumption or processing	ECE countries	U 34-a	
% sold for direct human consumption	ECE countries	U 34-a	
for export (unprocessed)	ECE countries	U 34-a	
for industrial processing	ECE countries	U 34-a	
Area under crops in ha	All countries	C 16-a	
	EEC countries	B 1-a	E 3-a
		E 44-a	
in ha: historical tables	Main European countries	Z 1-a	
Basic price structure for cereals by kind	EEC area	B 8-a	

		Territorial coverage	Title codes	
CEREALS BY KIND, continued				
Consumption as animal feed: tonnage		Worldwide	C 27-a	
	for industrial processing	World regions	C 27-a	
	per capita in kg	EEC countries	B 1-a	E 44-a
	tonnage	OAS member countries	N 17-a	
Crop yields in cwt per acre		Main countries	B 8-a	
Deliveries by farmers: tonnage		Main countries	B 7-a	
Distribution for market sales: tonnage		E European countries	U 34-a	
	own farm consumption: tonnage	E European countries	U 34-a	
	production of processed foods: tonnage	E European countries	U 34-a	
EEC levy on cereals imported from non-EEC area per ton			B 7-m	
EEC: threshold prices per ton			B 7-m	
Exports by destination by CST classes: tonnage & value in $m		EEC countries	E 48-a	
	SITC classes: tonnage & value in $m	OECD countries	D 3-a2	
	SITC classes by value in $m	Main countries	D 2-q	
	NIMEXE classes: tonnage & value in $m	All countries	E 20-a	
	SITC classes: tonnage & value in $m	All countries	U 50-a	U 59-a
	tonnage (in detail)	World regions	A 11-a	
	tonnage	Australia, Canada, European countries & USA	B 8-a	
Feed characteristics: energy-protein ratios		Worldwide	A 12-a	
Guaranteed prices for wheat per cwt		UK	B 8-a	
Imports by NIMEXE classes: tonnage & value in $m		All countries	E 20-a	
port of entry: tonnage		UK	B 7-m	
SITC classes: tonnage & value in $m		All countries	U 50-a	U 59-a
source by CST classes: tonnage & value in $m		EEC countries	E 21-a	
SITC classes by value in $m		Main countries	D 2-q	
SITC classes: tonnage & value in $m		OECD countries	D 3-a2	
source: tonnage		EEC area	B 8-a	
tonnage		Canada, European countries, USA & USSR	A 11-a	
		Main countries	B 8-a	
Income elasticity of demand: rural areas		India	C 27-a	
	urban areas	India	C 27-a	
Increments (cumulative) to threshold prices		EEC countries	B 8-m	
Prices paid as state purchases		Poland	U 30-a	
Producer prices		Main countries	B 8-a	
		E European countries & USSR	U 30-a	
Producer prices – index nos		EEC countries	E 44-a	
Production: tonnage by areas		EEC countries	E 38-a	
	(in detail)	World regions	A 11-a	
		Asian & Far East countries	U 32-a	
		E European countries	C 27-a	
		Canada, European countries, USA & USSR	E 44-a	
		Latin American countries	J 5-a	U 40-a
		Main countries	B 7-a	E 3-a
		World regions	B 8-a	
Proportion of harvest exported		Main countries	B 8-a	
Requirements & supplies for animal feed: tonnage		UK	B 7-a	
	for human consumption: tonnage	UK	B 7-a	
Self-sufficiency ratios		EEC countries	B 1-a	E 3-a
Stocks at wholesalers' premises: tonnage		EEC countries	E 12-m	
on farms (end-month): tonnage		EEC countries	E 12-m	
(end-season): tonnage		Main countries	B 7-m	
Supply, output & net imports: tonnage		Main countries	B 8-a	
Supply of wheat & coarse grains: tonnage		E European countries	C 27-a	
Target price: wheat in £ per cwt		UK	B 8-a	
Wholesale prices in local currency		OAS member countries	N 17-a	
World demand per capita projected to 1985			A 1	
exports: unit value in $ per ton			A 11-a	
market prices (incl rice) in $ per 100 kg			E 34-m	
– index nos			G 1-a	

Cerium chloride   see   RARE EARTH MINERALS

CESIUM

Production: cesium compounds: tonnage	USA	N 1-a	
Wholesale prices: cesium metal in $ per ton	USA	N 1-a	

CESIUM ORE

Import prices: pollucite concentrates per ton	European countries	T 4-m	
Production: pollucite: tonnage	Canada	N 1-a	
Reserves (estim): tonnage	Canada, Namibia & Rhodesia	N 1-a	
Wholesale prices of pollucite in $ per ton	USA	N 1-a	

CHALK

Production: natural calcium carbonate: tonnage	All countries	U 22-a

Chamois   see   LEATHER

CHARCOAL

Exports of charcoal (incl fuel wood): tonnage	All countries	A 23-a

Charolais   see   CATTLE BY BREED

Charter flights   see   AIR PASSENGER TRAFFIC

Charter rates   see   FREIGHT RATES

	Territorial coverage	Title codes	
CHARTERINGS			
see also AIRCRAFT			
TANKERS			
No, tonnage & release dates for period commitments	Worldwide	S 17-q	
No & tonnage: carrier fixtures on time charter	Worldwide	S 17-m	
trip charter	Worldwide	S 17-m	
oil tanker fixtures by route & name of vessel	Worldwide	S 17-m	
ships chartered by kind of cargo	Japan	S 17-m	
tanker fixtures by charter in mths	Worldwide	S 17-m	
charterer	Worldwide	S 17-m	
routes & by charterer	Worldwide	S 17-m	
of aircraft by type under charter to airline companies	Worldwide	S 11-a	
ships trip-chartered by loading & unloading zones	Worldwide	S 17-m	
tanker fixtures & cargo: tonnage (clean single voyage)	Worldwide	S 17-m	
(dirty single voyage)	Worldwide	S 17-m	
time charter fixtures by size of vessel - index nos	Worldwide	S 23-q	
CHASSIS, AUTOMOTIVE			
Exports by destination (all types): no & value	European countries	V 1-a	
Chattels insurance see PROPERTY DAMAGE OR LOSS			
Cheddar see CHEESE BY VARIETY			
CHEESE			
see also COTTAGE CHEESE			
% changes in producer prices for gouda (over 12 mths)	Belgium & Netherlands	E 34-m	
in retail sales	France & W Germany	E 34-m	
in wholesale prices (over 12 mths)	E European countries & USSR	U 16-a	
% of output exported	Main countries	B 4-a	
% of production from dairy co-operatives	EEC countries	B 3-a	
% of skim milk production used in making cheese	EEC countries	B 3-a	
% share of world imports & world exports	Main countries	B 1-a	
Commonwealth share of UK imports: tonnage	UK	B 4-a	
Consumption (incl farmhouse cheese): tonnage	EEC countries	B 3-a	
tonnage	EEC countries	E 44-a	
	EEC area	B 4-a	
of milk in cheese factories in gallons	Main countries	B 4-a	
tonnage	EEC countries	E 44-a	
	Main countries	B 12-m	
per capita in kg per yr	OECD countries	D 1-a	
	E European countries & USSR	U 16-a	
	EEC countries	B 1-a	B 3-a
		E 44-a	
tonnage & consumption per capita in lbs per yr	Main European countries	U 35-a	
projected to 1978	Main countries	B 4-a	
tonnage	OECD countries	D 15-a	
Expenditure on storage of surpluses in £m	OAS member countries	N 17-a	
Export availability & import needs projected to 1978	EEC countries	B 3-a	
prices - index nos (weighted average main sources)	OECD countries	D 15-a	
in local currency		U 29-q	
Exports by destination: tonnage	Australia, Eire, Netherlands & New Zealand	A 9-a	
	Main countries	B 12-m	B 4-a
EEC destinations: tonnage	EEC countries	B 3-a	
value & as % of exports of farm products	W European countries	U 20-a	
in $m	W European countries	U 33-a	
to E European bloc by value in $m	W European countries	U 20-a	
(incl curd) by value in $	New Zealand	U 32-m	
tonnage & EEC area % share of world exports	EEC area	B 3-a	
tonnage	European countries	U 35-q	
	Main countries	B 4-a	
Imports by source: tonnage	Main countries	B 12-m	
	UK	B 4-a	
by value & as % of imports of farm products	W European countries	U 20-a	
from E European bloc by value in $m	W European countries	U 20-a	
by value in $m	W European countries	U 33-a	
from EEC sources: tonnage	EEC countries	B 3-a	
tonnage & EEC area % share of world imports	EEC area	B 3-a	
tonnage	Main countries	B 4-a	
Inter-EEC imports & exports: tonnage	EEC countries	B 3-a	B 12-a
Intervention prices fixed by EEC commission	EEC area	E 44-a	
Net trade: tonnage	EEC countries	B 4-a	
Price paid to factory for export per lb	New Zealand	B 4-a	
Prices in EEC area as %of world market prices		E 44-a	
Producer prices in £ per cwt	EEC countries	B 1-a	
gouda in local currency per 100 kg	Belgium, Italy & Netherlands	E 34-m	
in local currency per kg	Denmark, Sweden & Switzerland	D 1-a	
	All countries	A 9-a	
Production, imports, exports, stocks & consumption: tonnage	EEC countries	E 44-a	
Production per cheese factory per yr: tonnage (average)	EEC countries	E 44-a	
Production, stocks & consumption per capita per day in kg	EEC countries	B 3-a	
Production, supply, trade, consumption & stocks: tonnage	OECD countries	D 14-a	
Production: tonnage by kind of milk used in production of cheese	EEC countries	B 3-a	
(excl processed cheese)	All countries	A 9-a	
(incl farm & cottage cheese)	All countries	U 22-a	
	OECD countries	D 1-a	
	EEC countries	B 3-a	

75

	Territorial coverage	Title codes	
CHEESE, continued			
Production: tonnage projected to 1978	OECD countries	D 15-a	
tonnage	African countries	U 44-a	
	European countries	U 35-a	
	EEC countries	E 28-q	B 1-a
		E 27-a	
	Canada, European countries, Japan, USA & USSR	E 44-a	
	Latin American countries	J 5-a	
	Main countries	A 5-a	B 4-a
		E 3-a	U 43-a
	OAS member countries	N 14-a	
Purchase price by commodity credit corporation in cents per lb	USA	B 4-a	
Retail prices (comparative) in $ per kg	EEC countries	Z 3-a	
Self-sufficiency ratios	EEC countries	B 1-a	E 3-a
		E 44-a	
Stocks at beginning & end-yr: tonnage	EEC countries	B 3-a	
at end-month: tonnage	Main countries	B 12-m	
	UK	U 35-m	
(incl other milk products): tonnage	EEC countries	E 44-a	
tonnage	Main European countries	U 35-a	
Subsidy paid for private storage in EEC area in £ per ton	EEC area	B 3-a	
Supply, production, consumption & trade: tonnage	EEC countries	B 1-a	B 4-a
Surplus of production over requirements projected to 1978	OECD countries	D 15-a	
Threshold price of Cheddar cheese in £ per cwt	EEC countries	B 1-a	
Voluntary restraints on deliveries of Cheddar by source: tonnage	UK	B 4-a	
Wholesale prices (annual average)	Main countries	B 4-a	
by kind in £ per cwt on London market	UK	B 12-m	
ex dairies in $	Main European countries	U 35-q	
of home-produced Cheddar in £ per cwt	UK	B 4-m	
imported cheese ex New Zealand & Netherlands in £ per cwt	UK	B 4-a	
cheese (45% fat) in local currency per 100 kg	France & W Germany	E 34-a	
white ex New Zealand in £ per 56 lbs	UK	U 20-q	
in local currency	Argentine, Canada, France, UK & USA	A 9-a	
World exports of cheese: unit value in $ per ton		A 11-a	
World market prices: Cheddar ex New Zealand in £ per 100 kg on London market		E 34-m	
cheese ex Denmark in £ per 100 kg on London market		E 34-m	
CHEESE BY VARIETY			
Import quotas in lbs	USA	B 4-a	
Imports of processed blue-veined cheddar: tonnage	UK	B 12-m	
Production: Amsterdam: tonnage	Netherlands	B 3-a	
Blue-vein: tonnage	France & UK	B 3-a	
Caerphilly, Cheshire & Lancashire: tonnage	UK	B 3-a	
Camembert & Emmental: tonnage	France & W Germany	B 3-a	
Cheddar: tonnage	Belgium, Eire, Netherlands & UK	B 3-a	
Danablu, Danbo, Esrom, Havarti & Samso: tonnage	Denmark	B 3-a	
Edam: tonnage	France, W Germany & Netherlands	B 3-a	
Edelpilz & Tilsit: tonnage	W Germany	B 3-a	
Gorgonzola, Grana, Italico, Parmesan & Provolone: tonnage	Italy	B 3-a	
Gouda: tonnage	Belgium & Netherlands	B 3-a	
Gruyere: tonnage	France	B 3-a	
St Paulin: tonnage	Belgium & France	B 3-a	
Retail prices in local currency	OAS member countries	N 17-a	
Subsidies by zone per 100 kg	EEC area	B 4-a	
Wholesale prices in £ per ton equiv	Main countries	B 12-m	
local currency	OAS member countries	N 17-a	
CHEESE FACTORIES			
No in operation by size (based on production): over 1000 tons per yr	EEC countries	B 3-a	
up to 1000 tons per yr	EEC countries	B 3-a	
200 tons per yr	EEC countries	B 3-a	

Chemical carriers (shipping)   see   BULK CARRIERS

Chemical elements   see   ELEMENTS

Chemical fibres   see   MAN-MADE FIBRES

Chemical fibres industry   see   MAN-MADE FIBRES INDUSTRY

CHEMICAL INDUSTRY

see also   METALLURGY
PETRO-CHEMICAL INDUSTRY

% contribution to gross national product	Canada, European countries, Japan & USA	U 38-a	
% growth in output (incl coal & oil)	Main countries	U 38	
% increase in cost of plant & equipment	UK	B 21-a	
gross output	European countries, Japan & USA	U 25-a	
material costs	UK	B 21-a	
production costs by kind	UK	B 21-a	
wages & salary costs	UK	B 21-a	
% share of electricity as energy source	European countries	U 16-a	
industrial production (value basis)	Main countries	U 38-a	
oil as energy source	W European countries	U 16-a	

CHEMICAL INDUSTRY, continued

	Territorial coverage	Title codes	
% share of total capital investment	E European countries	U 16-a	
Assets of corporations as % of sales turnover	USA	J 2-a	
Capital formation by areas in $m	EEC countries	E 38-a	
by sector in £m	UK	B 21-a	
in $m	European countries, Japan & USA	U 25-a	
Consumption of aluminium: tonnage	Main countries	U 21-a	
coal & agglomerates: tonnage	EEC countries, Japan & USA	C 12-a	
in production of coal tar: tonnage	EEC countries	E 14-a	
& patent fuels: tonnage	OECD countries	D 5-a	
coke oven gas in coal equiv: tonnage	OECD countries	D 5-a	
& coke: tonnage	EEC countries	E 14-a	
coke: tonnage	OECD countries	D 5-a	
crude petroleum: tonnage	EEC countries	E 14-a	
	EEC countries	E 14-a	
diesel oil: tonnage	Japan	D 5-a	
electricity by areas in kWh	EEC countries	E 14-a	
in kWh	EEC countries	E 38-a	
	USA	U 1-a	
in coal equiv: tonnage	OECD countries	D 5-a	D 8-a
energy by kind	EEC countries	E 14-a	
fuel oil: tonnage	OECD countries	D 5-a	
lignite & briquettes: tonnage	EEC countries	E 14-a	
manufactured gas in m³	EEC countries	E 14-a	
	OECD countries	D 5-a	
materials for production of alcohol: tonnage	European countries & USA	U 3-a	
natural gas in coal equiv: tonnage	OECD countries	D 5-a	
in m³	EEC countries	E 14-a	
natural phosphates: tonnage	OECD countries	D 5-a	
oil for production of distillates: tonnage	European countries, Japan & USA	U 25-a	
of natural gas: tonnage	OECD countries	D 5-a	
petroleum products by kind: tonnage	OECD countries	D 5-a	
products: tonnage	OECD countries	D 31-a	
	EEC countries	E 16-q	E 14-a
		E 15-a	
salt by kind & brine: tonnage	OECD countries	D 5-a	
salt: tonnage	European countries, Japan & USA	U 25-a	
steel castings: tonnage	UK	B 25-a	
Costs for salaried staff per mth	EEC countries	E 11-a	
Depreciation of corporate assets as % of sales turnover	USA	J 2-a	
Earnings (average) in local currency per hr	All countries	L 4-a	
of corporations as % of sales turnover	USA	J 2-a	
by areas per hr	EEC countries	E 38-a	
sex in local currency per hr	Main countries	R 3-a	
Electricity consumption as % of supply	W European countries	U 16-a	
in kWh	All countries	C 23-a	
Employment by areas	EEC countries	E 38-a	
Employment: no of operatives	European countries, Japan & USA	U 25-a	
salaried personnel	European countries, Japan & USA	U 25-a	
- index nos	All countries	L 4-a	
Frequency of accidents at work	EEC countries	E 2-a	
Gross output by value in $m	Main countries	U 21-a	U 25-a
Investment as % of capital formation in manufacturing industry	Main countries	U 25-a	
in total industry	Main countries	U 25-a	
	OECD countries	D 5-a	
as % of value added in production	OECD countries	D 5-a	
by sector in £m	UK	B 21-a	
in buildings in local currency	EEC countries	E 40-a	
land purchase in local currency	EEC countries	E 40-a	
machinery in local currency	EEC countries	E 40-a	
$m	Main European countries	B 30-a	
	OECD countries	D 5-a	
Labour costs by kind as % of total costs	EEC countries	E 8-a	
by status of employees in local currency	EEC countries	E 8-a	
in DMm	W Germany	H 3-a	
per hr	EEC countries	E 11-a	
basic chemicals industry per hr	EEC countries	E 2-a	
areas per hr	EEC countries	E 38-a	
wage earners per hr in chemical industry	EEC countries	E 11-a	
Labour force employed	Main countries	U 21-a	
(incl oil, coal & rubber industries)	OECD countries	D 23-a	
no of salaried staff	EEC countries	E 11-a	
staff & operatives	EEC countries	E 2-a	E 8-a
	European countries, Japan & USA	U 25-a	
	OECD countries	D 5-a	
no of wage earners	EEC countries	E 11-a	
No of hrs worked by area per wk	All countries	E 25-a	
labour force per yr	EEC countries	E 8-a	
laboratory assistants in chemical industry	All countries	L 1-a	
per wk	Main countries	R 3-a	
	All countries	L 4-a	
	OAS member countries	N 18-a	
salaried staff per yr	EEC countries	E 11-a	
wage earners per yr	EEC countries	E 11-a	
No of establishments (chemical product manufacturers)	African countries	U 44-a	
times inventory turned by corporations	USA	J 2-a	
Production as % general world activity		U 38	
by value in Lit	EEC countries	C 6-a	

77

	Territorial coverage	Title codes

CHEMICAL INDUSTRY, continued

Production by value in Lit by sectors of chemical industry	Italy	C 6-a
Production - index nos	Asian & Far East countries	U 32-q
	ECE countries	U 42-m
	EEC countries	E 26-m E 28-q
		E 27-a
	European countries, Japan & USA	U 38-a
	Latin American countries	J 5-a
	Main countries	R 5-a
	OAS member countries	N 14-a
	OECD countries	D 5-a
	USA	J 2-a
Profits of corporations as % of turnover	All countries	L 1-a
Salaries (monthly) of laboratory assistants	W Germany	H 3-a
Turnover of chemical industry in DMm	European area, Japan & USA	D 5-a
in $m	OECD countries	D 5-a
Usage of acetylene for synthesis: tonnage	OECD countries	D 5-a
aliphatics for synthesis: tonnage	OECD countries	D 5-a
aromatics for synthesis: tonnage	OECD countries	D 5-a
benzene for synthesis: tonnage	OECD countries	D 5-a
butylene for synthesis: tonnage	OECD countries	D 5-a
carbon monoxide for synthesis: tonnage	OECD countries	D 5-a
chemicals for synthesis: tonnage	OECD countries	D 5-a
cyclalkene for synthesis: tonnage	OECD countries	D 5-a
ethyl alcohol for synthesis: tonnage	OECD countries	D 5-a
ethylene for synthesis: tonnage	OECD countries	D 5-a
methane for synthesis: tonnage	OECD countries	D 5-a
naphthalene for synthesis: tonnage	OECD countries	D 5-a
organic chemicals for synthesis: tonnage	OECD countries	D 5-a
platinum & palladium for all purposes in oz	USA	J 6-q
propylene for synthesis: tonnage	OECD countries	D 5-a
toluene for synthesis: tonnage	OECD countries	D 5-a
xylenes for synthesis: tonnage	OECD countries	D 5-a
Value added (at factor cost) in $m	Main countries	U 25-a
in manufacture in $m	OECD countries	D 5-a
per capita employed in $	OECD countries	D 5-a
Value of output: chemical compounds in £m	European countries	U 25-a
chemical fertilisers in £m	UK	B 21-a
dyestuffs pigments in £m	UK	B 21-a
inorganic chemicals in £m	UK	B 21-a
organic chemicals in £m	UK	B 21-a
paints in £m	UK	B 21-a
pharmaceuticals in £m	UK	B 21-a
soap & detergents in £m	UK	B 21-a
synthetic resins in £m	UK	B 21-a
synthetic rubber in £m	UK	B 21-a
toilet preparations in £m	UK	B 21-a
Wage & salary costs	Main countries	U 21-a
Wage rates: acids & salts sector in local currency	OAS member countries	N 17-a
in local currency per hr (average)	EEC countries	E 25-a2
in basic chemicals sector per hr	OAS member countries	N 17-a
by sex per hr in local currency	Main countries	R 3-m
- index nos	Main countries	R 3-a
in local currency	Main countries	C 7-a
per hr in DM	W Germany	H 3-a
per hr: skilled workers by sex in local currency	Main countries	R 4-q
unskilled workers by sex in local currency	Main countries	R 4-q
soaps & detergents sector in local currency	OAS member countries	N 17-a
vegetable fats & margarine sector in local currency	OAS member countries	N 17-a

CHEMICAL INDUSTRY BY SECTOR

% share of turnover	Main countries	U 25-a
Concentration ratios	Main countries	U 25-a
Gross & net output & as % total in £m	UK	B 21-a
No of operating companies	USA	U 25-a

CHEMICAL PRODUCTS

    see also   CHEMICALS, INORGANIC
                  CHEMICALS, ORGANIC
                  DYESTUFFS, SYNTHETIC
                  FERTILISERS
                  MAN-MADE FIBRES
                  PAINTS & VARNISHES
                  PHARMACEUTICAL PRODUCTS
                  PLASTICS
                  SOAP
                  SYNTHETIC RUBBER
                  TOILET PREPARATIONS

% change in exports by destination (value basis)	EEC countries	E 23-a
imports by source (value basis)	EEC countries	E 23-a
exports of fertilisers	Main countries	U 25-a
inorganic chemicals	Main countries	U 25-a
man-made fibres	Main countries	U 25-a
organic chemicals	Main countries	U 25-a
pharmaceuticals	Main countries	U 25-a
plastics	Main countries	U 25-a
synthetic rubber	Main countries	U 25-a

CHEMICAL PRODUCTS, continued	Territorial coverage	Title codes

	Territorial coverage	Title codes
% changes in imports of fertilisers	Main countries	U 25-a
inorganic chemicals	Main countries	U 25-a
man-made fibres	Main countries	U 25-a
organic chemicals	Main countries	U 25-a
pharmaceuticals	Main countries	U 25-a
plastics	Main countries	U 25-a
synthetic rubber	Main countries	U 25-a
in trade in chemical products	Japan & world regions	U 25-a
% consumption trend projected to 1977	UK	B 21-a
% export trend projected to 1977	UK	B 21-a
% import trend projected to 1977	UK	B 21-a
% increase in employment projected to 1977	UK	B 21-a
imports	European countries, Canada, Japan & USA	D 5-a
net output projected to 1977	UK	B 21-a
output of chemicals projected to 1977	EEC countries	
per capita projected to 1977	UK	B 21-a
projected to 1977	UK	B 21-a
Calcium carbide as source of acetylene	Main countries	U 26-a
Coastal shipping: tonnage	EEC countries	E 43-a
Consumption by value in £m	UK	B 21-a
in $m	E European countries	U 25-a
per capita in $	European countries, Japan & USA	U 25-a
of zinc in production of zinc oxide: tonnage	European countries, Japan & USA	U 25-a
Excise duties rates charged: acetic acid	USA	J 6-a
benzole	EEC countries	E 31-a
Exports of chemical products as % of total exports	EEC countries	E 31-a
Exports by destination: aluminium oxide: tonnage	World economic areas	D 5-a
destination areas by value in $m	Main countries	U 2-a
by value in UA	World regions	U 25-a
in $m	EEC countries	E 23-a
calcium carbide: tonnage	Main countries	U 2-a
glycerine by value in $	Main countries	U 2-a
heterocyclic compounds by value in $	Main countries	U 2-a
by value in $m	Main countries	U 2-a
nitrogenous compounds by value in $	USSR	U 25-a
tonnage	Main countries	U 2-a
regions of origin by value in $	OECD countries	D 5-a
value in $m	EEC countries	E 38-a
to non-EEC area by value in UA	Main countries & world regions	U 23-a
of calcium carbide: tonnage	EEC countries	E 24-a
	Main countries	U 25-a
	OECD countries	D 5-a
nitrogenous fertilisers: tonnage	Main countries	B 15-a
phenol: tonnage	European countries, Japan & USA	U 26-a
zinc oxide: tonnage	OECD countries	D 5-a
Exports - index nos (volume & value basis)	OECD countries	D 16-q
Gross value of output of major oil companies in $m	Worldwide	C 3-a
Imports by source by value in UA	EEC countries	E 23-a
tonnage	OECD countries	D 5-a
value ex EEC area in UA	African, Caribbean countries & Pacific Is	E 45-a
ex non-EEC area in UA	EEC countries	E 24-a
in $m	African, Caribbean countries & Pacific Is	E 45-a
in $m & as % of total imports	Main countries	U 25-a
of calcium carbide: tonnage	Main countries	U 25-a
	OECD countries	D 5-a
nitrogenous fertilisers: tonnage	Main countries	B 15-a
phenol: tonnage	European countries, Japan & USA	U 26-a
zinc oxide: tonnage	OECD countries	D 5-a
Imports - index nos (volume & value basis)	OECD countries	D 16-q
Inter-EEC exports by value in UA	EEC countries	E 22-m E 24-a
imports by value in UA	EEC countries	E 22-m E 24-a
Inter-OECD exports by value in $m	OECD countries	D 5-a
imports by value in $m	OECD countries	D 5-a
Inter-regional trade by value in $m projected to 1980	World regions	U 25-a
Intra-European trade by source: tonnage	OECD countries	D 5-a
Lead consumption in manufacture of chemical production: tonnage	European countries & USA	C 12-a
Production of calcium carbide - index nos	OECD countries	D 5-a
capacity: acetaldehyde: tonnage	European countries	U 26-a
formaldehyde: tonnage	European countries	U 26-a
maleic anhydride: tonnage	European countries	U 26-a
phthalic anhydride: tonnage	European countries	U 26-a
Production: acetaldehyde: tonnage	All countries	U 22-a
	Main countries	U 26-a
aluminium oxide: tonnage	All countries	C 12-a H 2-a
benzene: tonnage	All countries	B 15-a U 22-a
butyl alcohol: tonnage	All countries	U 22-a
calcium carbide: tonnage	All countries	U 22-a
	Main countries	E 3-a R 5-a
		U 25-a
	OECD countries	D 5-a
carbon bisulphide: tonnage	All countries	U 22-a
crude benzole: tonnage	All countries	B 15-a
ethylene oxide: tonnage	All countries	U 22-a
ethylene: tonnage	All countries	U 22-a
formaldehyde: tonnage	Main countries	U 26-a
glycerine: tonnage	All countries	U 22-a
maleic anhydride: tonnage	Main countries	U 26-a

	Territorial coverage	Title codes	
CHEMICAL PRODUCTS, continued			
Production tonnage: methyl alcohol	All countries	U 22-a	
napthalene	All countries	B 15-a	U 22-a
phthalic anhydride	All countries	U 22-a	U 26-a
	OECD countries	D 5-a	
propylene	All countries	U 22-a	
pure phenol	All countries	U 22-a	
	European countries, Japan & USA	U 26-a	
toluene	All countries	B 15-a	U 22-a
xylenes	All countries	B 15-a	
zinc oxide from scrap	USA	T 4-a	
zinc oxide	Main countries	H 2-a	
	OECD countries	D 5-a	
	UK	T 4-a	
Production - index nos (quantum basis)	S American countries	U 40-a	
	African countries	U 44-a	
Retail prices - index nos	EEC countries	E 26-m	
Usage of bauxite in production of chemicals: tonnage	USA	T 4-a	
cobalt by chemical industry in lbs	USA	T 4-a	
magnesium in production of chemicals: tonnage	USA	T 4-a	
tin in production of chemicals: tonnage	European countries & USA	C 12-a	
	UK & USA	J 6-a	
zinc in production of chemicals: tonnage	France & Italy	T 4-a	
of zinc oxides: tonnage	Main countries	T 4-a	
Wholesale prices: zinc oxide in £ per ton	UK	T 4-m	
- index nos	EEC countries	E 26-m	
	OECD countries	D 5-a	
CHEMICAL PRODUCTS BY KIND			
Exports by destination by CST classes by value in $m	EEC countries	E 48-a	
by SITC classes by value in $m	Main countries	D 2-q	
tonnage & value in $m	OECD countries	D 3-a2	
tonnage & value in $m	All countries	U 12-a	
NIMEXE classes by value in $m	All countries	E 20-a	
SITC classes by value in $m	All countries	U 50-a	U 59-a
to EEC & non-EEC areas by value in $m	EEC countries	E 24-a	
tonnage	OECD countries	D 5-a	
by value (in detail) in Lit	Italy	C 6-a	
Imports as % of all chemical imports (value basis)	Main countries	U 25-a	
by NIMEXE classes by value in $m	All countries	E 20-a	
SITC classes by value in $m	All countries	U 50-a	U 59-a
source by CST classes by value in $m	EEC countries	E 21-a	
by SITC classes by value in $m	Main countries	D 2-q	
tonnage & value in $m	OECD countries	D 3-a2	
tonnage & value in $m	All countries	U 12-a	
ex EEC & non-EEC area by value in $m	EEC countries	E 24-a	
into USA by value in $m	OECD countries	D 5-a	
tonnage	OECD countries	D 5-a	
by value (in detail) in Lit	Italy	C 6-a	
Production: tonnage	EEC countries	E 28-q	E 27-a
Wholesale prices in local currency	OAS member countries	N 17-a	
Chemical pulp see WOOD PULP, CHEMICAL			
CHEMICALS			
% share of EEC area imports	Developing countries	U 52-a	
Consumption by value in $m	EEC countries, Japan, UK & USA	U 23-a	
of tin in production of chemical oxides: tonnage	UK & USA	C 20-m	
Exports as % of domestic consumption	EEC countries, Japan, UK & USA	U 23-a	
by kind by value in Lit (in detail)	Italy	C 6-a	
sea, inland waterways, road & rail: tonnage	European countries	U 8-a	
value in $m	World regions	U 52-a	
	Asian & Far East areas	U 32-a	
	Australia, Hong Kong, India, Japan & S Korea	U 32-m	
in Lit	Main countries	C 6-a	
to Communist area in $m	Developing countries	U 52-a	
Imports as % of domestic consumption	EEC countries, Japan, UK & USA	U 23-a	
by sea, inland waterways, road & rail: tonnage	European countries	U 8-a	
by value in Lit	Main countries	C 6-a	
in $m	Developing countries	U 52-a	
in $m ex developing countries	EEC countries	U 52-a	
in local currency	ECAFE countries	U 32-m	
Production (incl oil derivatives) - index nos	Italy	C 6-a	
oil coal derivatives - index nos	OECD countries	D 19-m	D 20-m
Production - index nos	India, Japan, Philippines & S Korea	U 32-q	
Rail freight (inland & abroad) of basic chemicals: tonnage	EEC countries	E 43-a	
Seaborne freight of basic chemicals: tonnage	EEC countries	E 43-a	
Shipments through Panama Canal westwards: tonnage		D 28-a	
Wholesale prices - index nos	Thailand	U 32-m	
CHEMICALS BY KIND			
Imports by value in Lit	Italy	C 6-a	
Imports & exports by country by rail: tonnage	EEC countries	E 43-a	
road: tonnage	EEC countries	E 43-a	
sea: tonnage	EEC countries	E 43-a	
Production: tonnage (in detail)	Italy	C 6-a	
Road transport over frontiers: tonnage	EEC countries	E 43-a	

	Territorial coverage	Title codes

CHEMICALS, INORGANIC

% changes in imports (value basis)	Main countries	U 25-a
Exports by destination of epoxyesters: tonnage	Main countries	U 2-a
esters & derivatives by value in $m	Main countries	U 2-a
oxides & halogen salts by value in $m	Main countries	U 2-a
Gross & net value of output in £m	UK	B 21-a
Imports by value in $m & as % all chemicals imported	Main countries	U 25-a
Plant investment & capital expenditure in £m	UK	B 21-a
Production – index nos	OECD countries	D 5-a

CHEMICALS, INORGANIC BY KIND

Exports by destination by value in $m	Main countries	U 2-a
tonnage & value in $m	All countries	U 12-a
Imports by source: tonnage & value in $m	All countries	U 12-a

CHEMICALS, ORGANIC
    see also   CHEMICAL PRODUCTS

% change in exports (value basis)	Main countries	U 25-a
imports (value basis)	Main countries	U 25-a
Consumption for synthesis: tonnage	OECD countries	D 5-a
primary chemicals: tonnage	OECD countries	D 5-a
tonnage	OECD countries	D 5-a
Exports by destination: aldehydes by value in $	Main countries	U 2-a
epoxy derivatives: tonnage	Main countries	U 2-a
phenols by value in $	Main countries	U 2-a
phenols: tonnage	Main European countries	U 2-a
styrene: tonnage	Main European countries	U 2-a
Exports: tonnage	OECD countries	D 5-a
Gross & net value of output in £m	UK	B 21-a
Imports by value in $ & as % of all chemical imports	Main countries	U 25-a
Imports: tonnage	OECD countries	D 5-a
Plant investment & capital expenditure in £m	UK	B 21-a
Production capacity: ethylene oxide: tonnage	European countries	U 26-a
tonnage	OECD countries	D 5-a
Production: acetaldehyde: tonnage	OECD countries	D 5-a
acrylonitrile: tonnage	OECD countries	D 5-a
anthracene: tonnage	W Germany	D 5-a
basic chemicals: tonnage	All countries	U 43-a
chemical glycerine: tonnage	OECD countries	D 5-a
cyclohexane: tonnage	OECD countries	D 5-a
dichloreothane: tonnage	OECD countries	D 5-a
distilled phenol: tonnage	OECD countries	D 5-a
ethylene oxide: tonnage	Main countries	U 26-a
	OECD countries	D 5-a
from coal: tonnage	OECD countries	D 5-a
from natural gas: tonnage	OECD countries	D 5-a
methanol: tonnage	W Germany & Japan	D 5-a
phenol: tonnage	OECD countries	D 5-a
pyridine: tonnage	W Germany	D 5-a
styrene: tonnage	OECD countries	D 5-a
sulphite alcohol: tonnage	Finland	D 5-a
vinyl chloride: tonnage	OECD countries	D 5-a

CHEMICALS, ORGANIC BY KIND

Exports by destination by value in $m	Main countries	U 2-a
tonnage & value in $m	All countries	U 12-a
Imports by source: tonnage & value in $m	All countries	U 12-a
Production: tonnage	OECD countries	D 5-a

Chemicals, zinc-based   see   ZINC COMPOUNDS

CHEMISTRY

No of students enrolled on university courses in chemistry	OAS member countries	N 19-a

Chemists   see   PHARMACISTS

Cherries   see   FRUIT, FRESH

Cheshire   see   CHEESE BY VARIETY

CHESTNUTS

Production & consumption: tonnage	Austria, Belgium & Spain	D 14-a

Chewing tobacco   see   TOBACCO

Chianti   see   WINE

CHICK PEAS

Area harvested, production tonnage & yield per ha	All countries	A 9-a
Area under crop in ha	OAS member countries	N 13-a
Crop yield in kg per ha	OAS member countries	N 13-a
Export prices	Chile, Netherlands & Sudan	A 9-a
Producer prices in Esc per 100 kg	Portugal	D 1-a
local currency	Peru	A 9-a

	Territorial coverage	Title codes
CHICK PEAS, continued		
Production: tonnage of dried chick peas	African countries	U 44-a
Production: tonnage	OAS member countries	N 13-a
	Argentine, Chile, Peru & Mexico	U 40-a
Wholesale prices in local currency	Ethiopia, India, Pakistan & Spain	A 9-a

Chicken eggs   see   EGGS, HEN

Chickens   see   POULTRY

Children's wear   see   CLOTHING

Chillies   see   SPICES & ESSENCES

CHINA CLAY
    see also   BENTONITE

	Territorial coverage	Title codes	
Imports & exports by source & destination: tonnage	All countries	B 15-a	
Production: ball clay: tonnage	USA	N 1-a	
common clay: tonnage	USA	N 1-a	
fire clay: tonnage	USA	N 1-a	
kaolin: tonnage	USA	N 1-a	
tonnage	All countries	B 15-a	U 22-a

China ware   see   EARTHENWARE PRODUCTS

China ware industry   see   CERAMICS INDUSTRY

Chipboard   see   PARTICLE & CHIPBOARD

Chlordane   see   INSECTICIDES

CHLORINE

	Territorial coverage	Title codes	
Exports by destination: tonnage	Main countries	U 2-a	
Exports: tonnage	European countries, Japan & USA	U 25-a	
	OECD countries	D 5-a	
Imports: tonnage	European countries, Japan & USA	U 25-a	
	OECD countries	D 5-a	
Production: tonnage	EEC countries	E 26-m	E 28-q
		E 27-a	
	European countries, Japan & USA	U 25-a	
	Main countries	E 3-a	R 5-a
		U 22-a	
	OECD countries	D 5-a	
- index nos	OECD countries	D 5-a	

Chocolate confectionery   see   CONFECTIONERY

Chocolate crumb   see   MILK PRODUCTS

CHOCOLATE PRODUCTS
    see also   CONFECTIONERY

	Territorial coverage	Title codes
Exports: tonnage	Main countries	A 3-m
Imports: tonnage	Main countries	A 3-m
Production of chocolate confectionery: tonnage	All countries	A 3-q
of powder & drinking chocolate: tonnage	All countries	A 3-m
Retail prices: chocolate bars per kg	Main countries	A 3-q

Cholera   see   DISEASES, CONTAGIOUS

CHROME ORE

	Territorial coverage	Title codes	
Consumption: tonnage	OAS member countries	N 17-a	
Export prices - index nos (weighted average)	Worldwide	U 29-q	
Exports total & to EEC area: tonnage & value in UA	Madagascar	E 41-a	
Import prices by grade in $ per ton cif on London market	UK	C 12-m	
ex USSR in $ per ton cif European ports	European countries	T 4-m	
friable chromite concentrate ex Turkey per ton	Main countries	T 4-m	
Imports by source: tonnage	Main countries	T 4-a	
& exports by source & destination: tonnage	All countries	B 15-a	
Production: tonnage	Main countries	C 12-a	N 1-a
		R 5-a	
	USA	J 6-a	
metallurgical chromite: tonnage	Philippines	T 4-a	
refractory chromite: tonnage	Philippines	T 4-a	
tonnage	All countries	B 15-a	
	OAS member countries	N 14-a	
	USA	N 1-a	
Stocks at consumers' premises: tonnage	Main countries	T 4-a	
World export trade: tonnage	All countries	C 12-a	
production: tonnage	Main countries	C 30-a	N 1-a
		N 4-a	T 4-a
reserves: tonnage (estim)	Main countries	N 1-a	

	Territorial coverage	Title codes	
CHROME ORE BY KIND			
Consumption of chemical chromite: tonnage	USA	T 4-a	
metallurgical chromite: tonnage	USA	T 4-a	
refractory chromite: tonnage	USA	T 4-a	
Stocks of chromite: tonnage	USA	T 4-a	
Chromite see CHROME ORE			
CHROMIUM			
see also FERRO-CHROMIUM			
Consumption of imported metal: tonnage	USA	N 1-a	
Export prices of electrolytic chromium in cents per lb fob	USA	T 4-m	
Exports by destination of chrome metal: tonnage	France & UK	T 4-a	
Imports by source: chrome ore & alloys by grade: tonnage	Italy	C 12-a	
tonnage	Sweden & USA	T 4-a	
Production tonnage based on metal content of ore	All countries	B 15-a	U 22-a
of chromic oxide	All countries	U 43-a	
Wholesale prices: chemical grade in $ per ton of ore	USA	N 1-a	
metallic chromium in £ per lb	UK	C 12-m	
metallic chromium in pence per lb	UK	T 4-m	
metallurgical grade in $ per lb	USA	N 1-a	
Chrysotile see ASBESTOS			
Cigarette filter fibre see FILTRATION TOW			
CIGARETTE PAPER			
Production: tonnage	All countries	U 22-a	
CIGARETTE-MAKING INDUSTRY			
Wage rates in local currency	OAS member countries	N 17-a	
CIGARETTES			
Consumption: volume per adult per yr	Main countries	B 16-a	
volume of plain cigarettes	UK	B 13-a	
of tipped cigarettes	UK	B 13-a	
Consumption by volume	OAS member countries	N 17-a	
weight in lbs million	Main countries	B 16-a	
in lbs per yr per adult	Main countries	B 16-a	
Exports by destination in lbs million	UK	B 13-a	B 17-a
Imports by source in lbs million	UK	B 17-a	
Production: tonnage	AASM countries	E 41-a	
by volume incl world total	All countries	R 5-a	U 22-a
		U 43-a	
by volume	African countries	U 44-a	
	EEC countries	E 26-m	E 28-q
		E 27-a	
	Latin American countries	J 5-a	
	Main countries	E 3-a	
	OAS member countries	N 14-a	
Retail prices per pack in local currency	OAS member countries	N 17-a	
in $	EEC countries	Z 3-a	
CIGARETTES, HAND-ROLLED			
Consumption: light tobacco in lbs million	Main countries	B 16-a	
Consumption volume per adult per yr (estim)	Main countries	B 16-a	
CIGARS			
Consumption by volume in million	Main countries	B 16-a	
	OAS member countries	N 17-a	
by weight in lbs million	UK	B 13-a	
	Main countries	B 16-a	
of cigarillos by volume	Main countries	B 16-a	
by weight in lbs million	Main countries	B 16-a	
Imports by source in lbs	UK	B 17-a	
Production by volume: all sizes of cigars & cheroots	All countries	U 22-a	
(incl cigarillos)	Main countries	E 3-a	R 5-a
	African countries	U 44-a	
Production by volume	All countries	U 43-a	
	EEC countries	E 28-q	E 27-a
	OAS member countries	N 14-a	
Cinder, volcanic see PUMICE			
Cine cameras see PHOTOGRAPHIC APPARATUS			
Cinema screen advertising see ADVERTISING BY MEDIA			
CINEMAS			
Attendance per person per yr (average)	All countries	U 62-a	
	OAS member countries	N 19-a	
Costs of admission in local currency	OAS member countries	N 17-a	
No of cinemas in use, seat capacity & attendance	EEC countries	E 38-a	
	OAS member countries	N 19-a	

		Territorial coverage	Title codes
CINEMAS, continued			
	No of cinemas in use & seat capacity per 1000 attendances	All countries	U 43-a
	cinemas in use & seat capacity	Asian, Far East & Australasian countries	U 45-a
	by size of films shown & attendance	Latin American countries	J 5-a
	cinemas in use, seat capacity & seats per 1000 population	All countries	U 62-a
	mobile cinemas in use	All countries	U 62-a

Cinematographic films   see   FILMS

Cinematographic materials   see   PHOTOGRAPHIC MATERIALS

Cinnamon & cassia   see   SPICES & ESSENCES

Circuit breakers   see   SWITCHGEAR, ELECTRIC

Circulation   see   MONEY SUPPLY
               NEWSPAPERS

Cirrhosis   see   DISEASES

CITRUS FRUITS

	Territorial coverage	Title codes	
% contribution to export earnings	Swaziland	E 45-a	
Area under citrus orchards in ha: historical table from 1860	Main European countries	Z 1-a	
in ha	Italy	D 38-a	
Consumption & demand projected to 1975: tonnage	World regions	A 1	
(incl tropical fruits): tonnage	OECD countries	D 37-a	
lemons & grapefruit for processing: tonnage	All countries	A 7-a	
oranges & mandarins: tonnage	OECD countries	D 37-a	
tangerines for processing	All countries	A 7-a	
per capita in kg	EEC countries	B 1-a	E 44-a
		U 20-a	
tonnage	EEC countries	E 44-a	
Export availability projected to 1975	Main countries	B 2-a	
Exports by value in $m	World regions	A 1	
	Main countries	B 2-a	
of lemons & limes in $m	W European countries	U 33-a	
oranges & tangerines in $m	Main countries	B 2-a	
of grapefruit: tonnage	Main countries	B 2-a	
(incl conserves & fruit juices): tonnage	EEC countries	E 44-a	
of lemons & grapefruit: unit value in $ per ton	W European countries	U 20-a	
limes: tonnage	Main countries	B 2-a	
of oranges & tangerines: tonnage	Main countries	B 2-a	
unit value in $ per ton	W European countries	U 20-a	
of oranges: unit value in $ per ton	W European countries	U 20-a	
tonnage: historical tables from 1850	Italy & Spain	Z 1-a	
tonnage	World regions	A 11-a	
Import prices: oranges	France & W Germany	A 9-a	
Imports by value in $m	W European countries	U 33-a	
(incl conserves & fruit juices): tonnage	EEC countries	E 44-a	
of lemons & grapefruit: unit value in $ per ton	W European countries	U 20-a	
of oranges, lemons & tangerines: tonnage	USSR	U 20-a	
& tangerines: unit value in $ per ton	W European countries	U 20-a	
of oranges: tonnage	Main countries	B 6-a	
unit value in $ per ton	Main W European countries	U 20-a	
tonnage	Canada, European countries, USA & USSR	A 11-a	
Prices paid by processing plants in $ per ton	All countries	A 7-a	
Producers' sales for export: tonnage	Israel	B 6-a	
industrial use: tonnage	Israel	B 6-a	
local consumption: tonnage	Israel	B 6-a	
Production by value at current prices	EEC countries	E 44-a	
by areas: tonnage	EEC countries	E 38-a	
consumption & industrial usage: tonnage	OECD countries	D 14-a	
grapefruit: tonnage	Main countries	B 2-a	
	OAS member countries	N 13-a	
historical tables: tonnage	Main European countries	Z 1-a	
lemons & limes: tonnage	EEC countries	B 1-a	
	Main countries	B 2-a	
lemons: tonnage	Italy	U 20-a	
	OAS member countries	N 13-a	
oranges, lemons & grapefruit: tonnage	All countries	A 9-a	
oranges & mandarins: tonnage	EEC countries	B 1-a	
tangerines: tonnage	Italy	U 20-a	
	Main countries	B 2-a	
oranges: tonnage	OAS member countries	N 13-a	
tonnage	France & Italy	E 44-a	
	Latin American countries	J 5-a	
	OECD countries	D 1-a	
Retail prices (comparative) of oranges in cents per kg	EEC countries	Z 3-a	
Sales in local markets: tonnage	S Africa	B 6-a	
Self-sufficiency ratios	EEC countries	B 1-a	E 3-a
		E 44-a	
World demand per capita per year projected to 1985		A 1	

CITRUS FRUITS, CANNED

	Territorial coverage	Title codes
Exports of grapefruit: tonnage	All countries	A 7-a
oranges: tonnage	Cyprus, Israel & Japan	A 7-a

	Territorial coverage	Title codes	
CITRUS FRUITS BY KIND			
Area under crop in ha	Israel & Lebanon	B 6-a	
Export prices in cents per 15 kg	S Africa	B 6-a	
in local currency	Main countries	A 9-a	
Exports: tonnage	All countries	B 5-a	
Import prices in £ per cwt	UK	B 2-a	B 6-a
Imports by source of grapefruit: tonnage	OECD countries	D 37-a	
lemons: tonnage	OECD countries	D 37-a	
mandarins & clementines: tonnage	OECD countries	D 37-a	
oranges: tonnage	OECD countries	D 37-a	
tonnage	UK	B 6-m	
Intervention prices per kg	EEC area	U 20-m	
Producer prices in lire per 100 kg	Italy	U 20-a	
in $	All countries	A 9-a	
Production: tonnage & value in local currency	W Indies & Caribbean countries	T 6-a	
Production tonnage (in detail)	World regions	A 11-a	
lemons & limes: tonnage	European countries	U 20-a	
oranges: tonnage	European countries	U 20-a	
	African countries	U 44-a	
tonnage	Main countries	A 5-a	B 5-a
		B 6-a	
Retail prices in local currency	OAS member countries	N 17-a	
Sales for processing: tonnage	S Africa	B 6-a	
Usage for industrial processing: tonnage	USA	B 6-a	
Wholesale prices for processing	All countries	A 7-a	
in £ per pack	UK	B 6-m	
in local currency per kg	OAS member countries	N 17-a	
	Main countries	A 9-a	
in $ per kg	EEC countries	U 20-m	
World export trade: tonnage	Main countries	A 5-a	
World production: tonnage		U 11-a	

Civil aircraft   see   AIRCRAFT, PISTON-ENGINED
AIRCRAFT, ROTARY-WING
AIRCRAFT, TURBO-JET
AIRCRAFT, TURBO-PROP

CIVIL AVIATION

see also   AIR PASSENGER TRAFFIC
AIR TRAFFIC

	Territorial coverage	Title codes
Aircraft movement at specific airports	Worldwide	S 9-a
no of domestic flights by airport	Worldwide	S 9-a
of international flights by airport	Worldwide	S 9-a
Distances flown & freight & mail carried: tonnage	All countries	U 43-a
No of aircraft departures: domestic flights by airport	Worldwide	S 9-m
international flights by airport	Worldwide	S 9-m
scheduled flights by airport	Worldwide	S 9-m
unscheduled flights by airport	Worldwide	S 9-m
aircraft in use	Asian, Far East & Australasian countries	U 45-a
aircraft landings: domestic flights by airport	Worldwide	S 9-m
international flights by airport	Worldwide	S 9-m
scheduled flights by airport	Worldwide	S 9-m
unscheduled flights by airport	Worldwide	S 9-m
aircraft used by specific airlines	Worldwide	S 11-a
hrs & distances flown	Latin American countries	J 5-a
hrs flown	Asian, Far East & Australasian countries	U 45-a
passenger-km flown	ECAFE area	U 32-m
passengers carried on scheduled services	Latin American countries	J 5-a
passengers carried	All countries	U 43-a
personnel employed by airlines	Worldwide	S 11-a
	Asian, Far East & Australasian countries	U 45-a

Civil aviation costs   see   OPERATING COSTS, AIRLINE

Civil engineering   see   BUILDING CONSTRUCTION

CIVIL EXPENDITURE

see also   DEFENCE EXPENDITURE

	Territorial coverage	Title codes
As % of gross national product (annual averages to 1969)	OECD countries	D 11-a
total government expenditure	All countries	M 6-a
Cost of pay & allowances of armed forces	EEC countries	E 32-a
Road building & highway maintenance costs in $m	All countries	S 13-a

Civil research   see   RESEARCH & DEVELOPMENT

Civil servants   see   CIVIL SERVICE
PUBLIC EMPLOYEES

CIVIL SERVICE

	Territorial coverage	Title codes
Government expenditure on wages & salaries in local currency	African countries	U 44-a
No of employees of each government ministry	OAS member countries	N 20-a
Salary received per public employee for each ministry (average)	OAS member countries	N 20-a
Salary costs for public employees for each ministry	OAS member countries	N 20-a
Wages of unskilled workers in government employment – index nos	Sri Lanka	U 32-m

Civilian employment   see   EMPLOYMENT

	Territorial coverage	Title codes	
Civilian labour force see LABOUR FORCE			
POPULATION, ECONOMICALLY-ACTIVE			
Clams see CRUSTACEANS & MOLLUSCS			
Clay see CHINA CLAY			
CLEANING & POLISHING PREPARATIONS			
Exports by destination in $	Main countries	U 2-a	
Retail prices in $	EEC countries	Z 3-a	
CLEARING BANKS			
see also BANK CLEARINGS			
Advances, investments & deposits in $m	All countries	F 5-m	F 6-q
Liquid assets & restricted deposits in $m	All countries	F 5-m	F 6-q
No of cheques et al cleared through banks	All countries	F 5-m	F 6-q
CLERICAL WORKERS			
% growth rates of employment by sex	ECAFE countries	U 17	
No employed by sex	All countries	L 4-a	
of technical employees in iron & steel industry	OECD countries	D 22-a	
clerical workers unemployed	All countries	L 4-a	
Climate see RAINFALL			
TEMPERATURE			
Clinics see HEALTH CENTRES & CLINICS			
CLINKER			
see also CEMENT			
Exports by destination: tonnage	OECD countries	D 4-a	
Imports by source: tonnage	OECD countries	D 4-a	
CLOCKS & WATCHES			
% adults buying watches (by price ranges) in £	W European countries	Z 3	
% changes in retail sales of watches	E European countries	U 16-a	
Exports (incl parts & movements) by value in $	OECD countries	D 9-a	
Production by volume: wrist & pocket watches	All countries	U 22-a	
by volume	EEC countries	E 28-q	E 27-a
Sales demand for watches per 1000 population	E European countries	U 16-a	
Value added in manufacture in $m	OECD countries	D 9-a	
Cloth, cotton see WOVEN COTTON FABRICS			
Cloth, rayon see WOVEN RAYON			
CLOTH, RUBBERISED			
Consumption of rubber in production	Japan	C 18-a	
CLOTHING			
see also OUTERWEAR			
OVERCOATS & RAINCOATS			
RAYON PIECE GOODS			
STOCKINGS & TIGHTS			
UNDERWEAR			
% growth rates in consumption, 1955-1969	OECD countries	D 11	
% of males buying made-to-measure suits by kind of shop	W European countries	Z 3	
suits by price ranges in £	W European countries	Z 3	
% males normally wearing made-to-measure suits by social classes	W European countries	Z 3	
ready-to-wear suits by social classes	W European countries	Z 3	
% contribution to export earnings	Mauritius	E 45-a	
% share of EEC imports (value basis) ex developing countries		U 52-a	
Consumer expenditure as % of total consumer expenditure	UK	B 22-a	B 29-a
on clothing in £m	UK	B 22-a	
projected to 1977 in £m	UK	B 22	B 29
Consumer expenditure - index nos	Main countries	K 4-a	
	OECD countries	D 46-a	
Consumption cost at manufacturers' prices in $m	EEC countries	B 22-a	
clothes & shoes as % total outlay	EEC countries	E 2-a	
in $m		U 23-a	
private sector in local currency	EEC countries	E 32-a	
	AASM countries	E 41-a	
	OAS member countries	N 16-a	
of wool in production of children's wear in kg	Main countries	K 6-a	
jackets & coats in kg	Main countries	K 6-a	
kimonos in kg	Japan	K 6-a	
men's wear in kg	Main countries	K 6-a	
socks in kg	Main countries	K 6-a	
suits & trousers in kg	Main countries	K 6-a	
sweaters & skirts in kg	Main countries	K 6-a	
women's wear in kg	Main countries	K 6-a	
Expenditure as factor in cost of living - index nos	OAS member countries	N 17-a	
Exports by value as % of domestic consumption	EEC countries, Japan, UK & USA	U 23-a	
manufacturers' sales	EEC countries	B 22-a	

	Territorial coverage	Title codes	
CLOTHING, continued			
Exports by value: clothes of cellulosic fibre	All countries	A 6-a	
of non-cellulosic fibre	All countries	A 6-a	
in local currency	Hong Kong & S Korea	U 32-m	
to EEC & non-EEC area in $m	EEC countries	E 24-a	
Exports (incl accessories): tonnage	OECD countries	D 46-a	
Imports as % of domestic consumption	EEC countries, Japan, UK & USA	U 23-a	
by source by value in $m	EEC countries	U 52-a	
value as % of manufactuers' sales	EEC countries	B 22-a	
in $m	Developing countries	U 52-a	
	Main countries	G 1-a	
of clothes made of cellulosic fibre	All countries	A 6-a	
of non-cellulosic fibre	All countries	A 6-a	
ex EEC & non-EEC areas by value in $m	EEC countries	E 24-a	
(incl accessories): tonnage	OECD countries	D 46-a	
of textiles by value in $	Asian, Far East & Australasian countries	U 32-m	
Production : rayon piece goods: tonnage	Main countries	K 1-a	
by volume: blazers, jackets & shirts by kind	EEC countries	K 4-a	
blouses	All countries	U 22-a	
coats & dresses	All countries	U 22-a	
foundation garments by kind of materials used	EEC countries	K 4-a	
jackets (for males)	All countries	U 22-a	
knitted outerwear & underwear	OECD countries	D 46-a	
nightwear by kind of material used	EEC countries	K 4-a	
skirts, dresses & suits	EEC countries	K 4-a	
skirts & slacks	All countries	U 22-a	
suits	All countries	U 22-a	
swimwear by kind of material used	EEC countries	K 4-a	
trousers & costumes	EEC countries	K 4-a	
trousers (for males)	All countries	U 22-a	
Production - index nos (quantum basis)	S American countries	U 40-a	
Retail prices (comparative) men's shirts in $	EEC countries	Z 3-a	
slacks in $	EEC countries	Z 3-a	
suits in $	EEC countries	Z 3-a	
(incl footwear) - index nos	UK	B 22-a	
- index nos	AASM countries	E 41-a	
	African countries	U 44-a	
	All countries	L 4-a	
	EEC countries	E 26-m	
Sales turnover of manufacturers (at current prices) in £m	UK	B 22-a	
corsets & gloves in £m	UK	B 22-a	
dresses & lingerie in £m	UK	B 22-a	
hats & caps in £m	UK	B 22-a	
infantwear in £m	UK	B 22-a	
shirts & underwear in £m	UK	B 22-a	
tailored outerwear for females in £m	UK	B 22-a	
for males in £m	UK	B 22-a	
women's wear in multiple stores by value in £m	UK	B 22-a	
independent stores by value in £m	UK	B 22-a	
men's wear in independent stores by value in £m	UK	B 22-a	
multiple stores by value in £m	UK	B 22-a	
Sales (wholesale): weatherproof outerwear by value in £m	UK	B 22-a	
CLOTHING, READY-MADE			
% changes in retail sales	E European countries	U 16-a	
% of males buying from mail order houses	W European countries	Z 3	
in departmental stores	W European countries	Z 3	
independent tailor shops	W European countries	Z 3	
men's outfitters	W European countries	Z 3	
multiple tailor shops	W European countries	Z 3	
wearing ready-made suits by social classes	W European countries	Z 3	
Consumption per capita (volume basis)	E European countries	U 16-a	
Deliveries by manufacturers - index nos	UK	B 29-a	
Demand projected to 1977 in lbs million	UK	B 29	
Exports by destination by value in £m	UK	B 29-a	
Imports as % of domestic consumption	UK	B 29-a	
by source by value in £m	UK	B 29-a	
Imports, exports & trade balance in £	UK	B 29-a	
Production by kind for males & females	EEC countries	E 28-q	E 27-a
Wholesale prices - index nos	UK	B 22-a	
CLOTHING BY KIND			
Exports by destination by CST classes: tonnage & value in $	EEC countries	E 48-a	
SITC classes by value in $	Main countries	D 2-q	
SITC classes: tonnage & value in $	OECD countries	D 3-a2	
NIMEXE classes by value in $	All countries	E 20-a	
SITC classes by value in $	All countries	U 50-a	U 59-a
value in £m	UK	B 22-a	
Imports by NIMEXE classes by value in $	All countries	E 20-a	
SITC classes by value in $	All countries	U 50-a	U 59-a
source by CST classes: tonnage & value in $	EEC countries	E 21-a	
SITC classes by value in $	Main countries	D 2-q	
SITC classes: tonnage & value in $	OECD countries	E 3-a2	
value in £m	UK	B 22-a	
Net output & net output per capita in £	UK	B 22-a	
Production by volume	EEC countries	K 4-a	

	Territorial coverage	Title codes
CLOTHING BY KIND, continued		
Retail prices: boy's clothing in local currency	OAS member countries	N 17-a
girl's clothing in local currency	OAS member countries	N 17-a
men's clothing in local currency	OAS member countries	N 17-a
women's clothing in local currency	OAS member countries	N 17-a
Sales turnover of co-operatives in £m	UK	B 29-a
independent stores in £m	UK	B 29-a
multiple stores in £m	UK	B 29-a
Wholesale prices in local currency	OAS member countries	N 17-a
CLOTHING INDUSTRY		
see also TEXTILE INDUSTRY		
% contribution to gross national product	European countries, Canada, Japan & USA	U 38-a
% share of total industrial production (value basis)	European countries, Japan & USA	U 38-a
Capital investment in £m	UK	B 22-a
Electricity consumption in kWh	All countries	C 23-a
Employment – index nos	UK	B 22-a
Gross output by value in $m	OECD countries	D 46-a
Investment in buildings in local currency	EEC countries	E 40-a
land purchase in local currency	EEC countries	E 40-a
machinery in local currency	EEC countries	E 40-a
in $m	OECD countries	D 46-a
Labour costs as % of total costs	EEC countries	E 8-a
by status of employees in local currency	EEC countries	E 8-a
per hr (comparative)	EEC countries	B 29-a
Labour force employed as % of total employment – index nos	UK	B 22-a
projected to 1977	UK	B 29-a
no of salaried staff	EEC countries	E 11-a
	OECD countries	D 46-a
wage earners	EEC countries	E 11-a
	OECD countries	D 46-a
sales & distribution staff	UK	B 22-a
wage earners & salaried staff	EEC countries	E 8-a
(all occupations)	UK	B 22-a
Labour productivity: costs per man-hr	EEC countries	B 29-a
– index nos	UK	B 22-a
Net output & output per capita in £	UK	B 22-a
No of hrs worked per wk by region (average)	EEC countries	E 25-a
per wk	Main countries	R 3-a
	OAS member countries	N 18-a
per yr	EEC countries	E 8-a
– index nos	UK	B 22-a
establishments in operation (incl leather industry)	African countries	U 44-a
Production as % of world industrial activity		U 38
by value per capita in $	EEC countries	B 22-a
Production – index nos (volume basis)	UK	B 22-a
	OECD countries	D 46-a
Sales turnover in $m	EEC countries	B 22-a
per employee in $	EEC countries	B 22-a
Wage rates by sex – index nos	UK	B 22-a
per hr by sex in local currency	EEC countries	E 25-a2
	Main countries	R 3-m
by sex: skilled workers	Main countries	R 4-q
unskilled workers	Main countries	R 4-q
by sex	Main countries	C 7-a
per hr: cutters, sewers & tailors	OAS member countries	N 17-a
CLOTHING INDUSTRY BY SECTOR		
Capital investment in £m	UK	B 22-a
Cost structure: income as % of costs	UK	B 22-a
overheads as % of costs	UK	B 22-a
purchases as % of costs	UK	B 22-a
wages bill as % of costs	UK	B 22-a
Gross output by value in £m	UK	B 22-a
Labour force employed by sex	UK	B 22-a
Material purchases in £m	UK	B 22-a
Net output by value in £m	UK	B 22-a
per employee in £	UK	B 22-a
No of weeks material held in stock	UK	B 22-a
Turnover by manufacturers in £m	UK	B 22-a
projected to 1977 in £m	UK	B 22-a
Work in progress by value in £m	UK	B 22-a
CLOVER		
Area under crop in ha	EEC countries	E 12-a
Crop yield in 100 kg per ha	EEC countries	E 12-a
Production: tonnage	EEC countries	E 12-a
Cloves see VANILLA & CLOVES		
CO-OPERATIVE FARMS		
see also COLLECTIVE FARMS		
Investment for production & marketing in $m	E European countries	U 34-a

	Territorial coverage	Title codes	
CO-OPERATIVE SOCIETIES			
Labour force employed on clothing sales	UK	B 22-a	
Membership of agricultural co-operatives	OAS member countries	N 18-a	
consumer co-operatives	OAS member countries	N 18-a	
fishing co-operatives	OAS member countries	N 18-a	
housing co-operatives	OAS member countries	N 18-a	
savings & loan co-operatives	OAS member countries	N 18-a	
No of agricultural co-operatives	Asian, Far East & Australasian countries	U 45-a	
co-operatives by kind	OAS member countries	N 18-a	
consumer co-operatives	OAS member countries	N 18-a	
fishing co-operatives	OAS member countries	N 18-a	
housing co-operatives	OAS member countries	N 18-a	
savings & loan co-operatives	OAS member countries	N 18-a	
Retail trade turnover of co-operatives - index nos	EEC countries	E 26-m	
CO-OPERATIVE SOCIETIES, AGRICULTURAL			
No of societies & membership	OAS member countries	N 18-a	
CO-OPERATIVE SOCIETIES, CONSUMER			
No of societies & membership	OAS member countries	N 18-a	
self-service stores operated	W European countries	Z 2-a	
CO-OPERATIVE SOCIETIES, HOUSING			
No of societies & membership	OAS member countries	N 18-a	
CO-OPERATIVE SOCIETIES, RETAIL			
% share of total sales of clothing	UK	B 22-a	
non-food items	EEC countries	B 29-a	
Sales of clothing by kind by value in £m	UK	B 29-a	

Co-operatives   see   COLLECTIVE FARMS
                              CO-OPERATIVE FARMS
                              DAIRY CO-OPERATIVES
                              HOUSING, STATE-FINANCED

Co-operatives, credit   see   CREDIT UNIONS

Coaches   see   BUSES & COACHES

COAL
       see also   ANTHRACITE
                       COKING COAL
                       COAL BY-PRODUCTS
                       LIGNITE

	Territorial coverage	Title codes	
% change in production & consumption	E European countries & USSR	U 16-a	
% of EEC area bituminous coal production	EEC countries	R 5-a	
% share of energy supply sources	Main countries	U 16-a	
Availability (domestic): tonnage	European countries	U 31-q	
Changes in stocks held by industrial consumers: tonnage	E European countries & USSR	U 4-a	
(indigenous & imported): tonnage	EEC countries	E 14-a	
Consumption: anthracite & lignite: tonnage	Spain	U 10-a	
	Main countries	N 2-a	
at coking plants: tonnage	Belgium	U 10-a	
	European countries	U 31-q	
	UK	U 10-a	
	USA	N 1-a	
mines: tonnage	Belgium	U 10-a	
power stations for electricity production: tonnage	EEC countries	E 16-m	E 15-a
	UK	U 10-a	
power stations, gasworks & coke ovens: tonnage	EEC countries	E 16-q	E 15-a
power stations: tonnage	Belgium	U 10-a	
	USA	N 1-a	
	European countries	U 31-q	
bituminous coal & lignite: tonnage	OAS member countries	N 17-a	
brown coal for thermal processing purposes: tonnage	Main countries	N 2-a	
in briquetting plants: tonnage	Main countries	N 2-a	
public electricity undertakings: tonnage	Main countries	N 2-a	
by chemical industry (incl patent fuel plants): tonnage	OECD countries	D 5-a	
tonnage	EEC countries	E 14-a	
colliery power stations: tonnage	Belgium	U 10-a	
conversion industry: tonnage	UK	U 10-a	
gasworks: tonnage	UK	U 10-a	
households & small consumers: tonnage	European countries	U 31-q	
industry: tonnage	EEC countries	E 14-a	
	Belgium	U 10-a	
	European countries	U 31-q	
iron & steel industry: tonnage	France	U 10-a	
	EEC countries	E 14-a	
	UK	T 2-m	
kind in thermal power stations: tonnage	OECD countries	D 8-a	
non-ferrous metals industry: tonnage	EEC countries	E 14-a	
patent fuel plants: tonnage	Belgium	U 10-a	
	OECD countries	D 44-a	
power stations: tonnage	UK	U 10-a	
railways & coastal shipping: tonnage	OECD countries	D 44-a	
railways: tonnage	Belgium & France	U 10-a	
transport undertakings: tonnage	UK	U 10-a	

COAL, continued

	Territorial coverage	Title codes	
Consumption (domestic & industrial): tonnage	OECD countries	D 44-a	
by domestic sector: tonnage	European countries	U 10-a	
	Italy	H 4-a	
anthracite: tonnage	UK	U 10-a	
house coal: tonnage	UK	U 10-a	
for industrial use: tonnage	UK	U 10-a	
patent fuels production & for briquetting: tonnage	EEC countries	E 16-q	E 15-a
transformation by product: tonnage	OECD countries	D 44-a	
transformation into energy: tonnage	EEC countries	E 16-q	E 15-a
hard coal & brown coal: tonnage	European countries	U 10-a	
by industrial sector: tonnage	Turkey	U 10-a	
public electricity plants: tonnage	European countries	U 1-a	
steelworks: tonnage	EEC area	U 6-a	U 7-a
	Main countries	H 3-a	
in coke ovens: tonnage	EEC countries	E 14-a	
electricity generating plants: tonnage	EEC countries	E 14-a	
gasworks to produce town gas: tonnage	OECD countries	D 44-a	
gasworks: tonnage	EEC countries	E 14-a	
in petroleum equiv tonnage	Latin American countries	U 18-a	
in production of briquettes: tonnage	EEC countries	E 14-a	
of manufactured gas: tonnage	European countries & USA	U 3-a	
in thermo-electric generating plants: tonnage	OECD countries	D 44-a	
(incl briquettes) in foundries: tonnage	EEC countries	E 29-a	
in steel industry: tonnage	EEC countries	E 29-a	
(incl lignite) by industry: tonnage	Main countries	N 2-a	
iron & steel industry: tonnage	Main countries	N 2-a	
manufactured gas plants: tonnage	Main countries	N 2-a	
patent fuel plants: tonnage	Main countries	N 2-a	
public sector: tonnage	Main countries	N 2-a	
public utilities: tonnage	Main countries	N 2-a	
state railways: tonnage	Main countries	N 2-a	
for domestic heating: tonnage	Main countries	N 2-a	
tonnage	Main countries	E 3-a	
(incl other solid fuels): tonnage	EEC countries	E 14-a	
(industrial) by areas: tonnage	EEC countries	E 38-a	
Consumption as allowances to miners: tonnage	Belgium	U 10-a	
at collieries: tonnage	UK	U 10-a	
in petroleum equiv: tonnage	EEC area	E 7-a	
tonnage	Denmark, Eire, Norway & UK	E 7-a	
	EEC area	E 7-a	
	EEC countries	E 16-q	E 14-a
		E 15-a	
	Main countries	N 5-a	
	UK	U 10-m	
Deliveries: hard coal by consuming sector: tonnage	European countries	U 10-a	
Deliveries made to private householders: tonnage	European countries	U 10-a	
received at coke ovens: tonnage	European countries	U 10-a	
thermal power stations: tonnage	European countries	U 10-a	
by industrial undertakings: tonnage	European countries	U 10-a	
to EEC area: tonnage	EEC countries	E 14-a	
to EEC area & other exports: tonnage	EEC countries	E 16-q	E 15-a
Export prices - index nos (weighted average)		U 29-q	U 54-q
Exports by destination of hard coal: tonnage	Main countries	U 10-a	
tonnage	EEC countries	E 5-q	
by value to non-EEC area in $	EEC countries	E 29-a	
to E European area: tonnage	E European countries & USSR	U 16-a	
to non-EEC area: tonnage	EEC countries	E 14-a	
historical tables from 1827: tonnage	Main European countries	Z 1-a	
tonnage	Asian & Far East countries	U 32-q	
	European countries	U 31-q	
	India & S Korea	U 32-m	
Extraction potential by coalfield: tonnage	EEC countries	E 46-a	
Freight by cargo source: tonnage	Main countries	D 28-a	
Import prices in S Kr per ton cif	Sweden	U 10-a	
Imports & exports: tonnage	EEC countries	E 16-q	E 15-a
	European countries, USA & USSR	U 4-a	
by source of bituminous coal: tonnage & value in $	Main countries	N 2-a	
of hard coal: tonnage	EEC countries	E 5-q	
by value ex non-EEC area in $	EEC area	E 29-a	
ex E European area: tonnage	E European countries & USSR	U 16-a	
non-EEC area: tonnage	EEC countries	E 14-a	
(net) & as % of consumption	E European countries & USSR	U 16-a	
	ECE countries	U 16-a	
historical tables from 1827: tonnage	Main European countries	Z 1-a	
tonnage	European countries	U 31-q	
Inter-EEC trade by value in $ & as % of EEC trade	EEC countries	E 29-a	
of world trade	EEC countries	E 30-q	
Ocean freight rates: main routes (single voyage) in £ or $	Worldwide	S 16-a	
Prices at pit-head of house coal (50-80mm) in Fr per ton	France	R 2-m	
(Ruhr mines) in DM per ton	W Germany	R 2-m	
Production: bituminous coal & lignite in tons per man-day	USA	N 1-a	
by kind: tonnage	Spain	U 10-a	
Production, imports, exports, consumption & stocks: tonnage	OECD countries	D 44-a	
Production & estimated reserves: tonnage	All countries	U 43-a	
(incl world total): tonnage	Main countries	R 5-a	

90

	Territorial coverage	Title codes	
COAL, continued			
Production: all grades (incl lignite): tonnage	All countries	B 15-a	
bituminous coal & lignite: tonnage	Main countries	N 1-a	
bituminous coal (incl world total): tonnage	Main countries	R 5-a	
by coal-producing areas: tonnage	EEC countries	E 16-q	E 15-a
kind of anthracite & coking coal: tonnage	EEC countries	E 16-m	E 15-a
regions: tonnage	Main countries	N 2-a	
hard coal by areas: tonnage	EEC countries	E 38-a	
by size of mines: tonnage	EEC countries	E 15-a	
hard coal: tonnage	All countries	U 22-a	
	ECE countries	U 15-a	
	European countries, USA & USSR	U 10-a	
	European countries	U 31-q	
high volatile coking & gas coals: tonnage	EEC countries	E 16-m	E 15-a
historical tables from 1815: tonnage	Main European countries	Z 1-a	
(incl hard coal & lignite): tonnage	E European countries & USSR	U 16-a	
(incl derivatives): tonnage	EEC countries	E 14-a	
(incl lignite & world total): tonnage	All countries	C 4-a	U 55-a
	Main countries	E 3-a	
in petroleum equivalent: tonnage	Latin American countries	U 18-a	
recovered slurry: tonnage	European countries	U 31-q	
tonnage	African countries	U 39-a	U 44-a
	Asian & Far East countries	U 32-q	
	ECAFE countries	U 32-q	
	EEC countries	E 26-m	E 16-q
		E 28-q	E 3-a
		E 15-a	E 27-a
	European countries, USA & USSR	U 4-a	
	Latin American countries	J 5-a	
	Main countries	U 27-m	N 2-a
		N 5-a	U 55-a
	OAS member countries	N 14-a	
	S American countries	U 40-a	
	Zaire	E 41-a	
Rate & amount of levies by grade per ton	EEC countries	E 15-a	
Receipts (incl briquettes) at steelworks: tonnage	EEC area	E 29-a	
Reserves: tonnage (estim)	African countries	U 39-a	
Resources, changes in stocks & recoveries: tonnage	EEC countries	E 16-q	E 15-a
Resources ex indigenous production & imports: tonnage	EEC countries	E 14-a	
Retail prices in local currency	OAS member countries	N 17-a	
Seaborne movement by source: tonnage	Main countries	D 28-a	
tonnage	Worldwide	D 28-a	
Shipment (on trip & period charter): tonnage	Worldwide	S 17-m	
Shipments through Kiel Canal: eastwards (incl coke): tonnage		D 28-a	
westwards (incl coke): tonnage		D 28-a	
through Panama Canal westwards: tonnage		D 28-a	
Stocks at collieries: tonnage	EEC countries	E 26-m	
collieries by kind & grade (end-yr): tonnage	Belgium	U 10-a	
by kind (end-yr): tonnage	Spain	U 10-a	
changes in inventory held: tonnage	European countries	U 31-q	
of hard coal at collieries: tonnage	EEC countries	E 16-m	E 15-a
	European countries	U 10-a	
	UK	U 10-a	
Supply of deep-mined & opencast coal: tonnage	EEC countries	E 16-q	E 15-a
from EEC area production & imports: tonnage	Worldwide	U 37-m	
Tramp shipping freight rates - index nos	USA	N 1-a	
Wholesale prices: bituminous & lignite at mines in $ per ton	Italy	R 2-m	
coal ex Poland in lire per ton (on wagons)			
per ton	Canada, W Germany, Italy & USA	U 27-m	
World production: tonnage of bituminous coal & lignite		N 1-a	N 4-a
hard coal		E 15-a	
resources of bituminous coal & lignite: tonnage		N 1-a	

Coal & Steel Community (EEC)   see   ECSC

Coal briquettes   see   HARD COAL BRIQUETTES

COAL BY-PRODUCTS

  see also   TAR

As source of benzene production: tonnage	European countries, Japan & USA	U 26-a	
toluene production: tonnage	European countries, Japan & USA	U 26-a	
xylene production: tonnage	European countries, Japan & USA	U 26-a	
Coal consumption in production of coal tar	OECD countries	D 5-a	
Consumption of creosote & pitch by steel industry: tonnage	UK	T 2-q	
pitch by steel industry: tonnage	EEC countries	E 29-a	
tar & pitch by steel industry: tonnage	ECE countries	U 6-a	U 7-a
	Main countries	H 3-a	
Exports by destination: tar by value in $	Main countries	U 2-a	
Production: by kind: tonnage	All countries	B 15-a	
creosote oil: tonnage	All countries	B 15-a	
cresylic acid: tonnage	All countries	B 15-a	
	UK	D 5-a	
crude tar: tonnage	All countries	B 15-a	
natural phenol: tonnage	All countries	B 15-a	
pitch: tonnage	All countries	B 15-a	
toluol: tonnage	All countries	B 15-a	
tonnage	EEC countries	E 14-a	

	Territorial coverage	Title codes

Coal mines   see   COLLIERIES

COAL MINING
    see also   BRIQUETTING PLANTS
                   COKE OVENS

% absenteeism in collieries due to accidents	EEC countries	E 33-a
holidays	EEC countries	E 33-a
illness	EEC countries	E 33-a
% absenteeism in collieries	EEC countries	E 33-a
% changes in output per man-shift	European countries	U 10-a
% rate of increase in output per man-yr	European countries	U 10-a
Capital formation in $m	Main countries	U 21-a
by regions in UA million	EEC countries	E 46-a
Consumption of iron castings for colliery permanent way: tonnage	UK	B 25-a
Costs: salaried staff per mth in local currency	EEC countries	E 11-a
Electricity consumption from own production in kWh	All countries	C 23-a
public supply in kWh	All countries	C 23-a
Employment - index nos	EEC countries	E 26-m
Fatality rates for colliery accidents	All countries	L 4-a
Gross output by value in $m	Main countries	U 21-a
Investment by regions in UA million	EEC countries	E 46-a
Labour costs in collieries in DMm	W Germany	H 3-a
per hr (incl staff salaries) in local currency	EEC countries	E 2-a E 11-a
per hr: wage earners in local currency	EEC countries	E 11-a
Labour force employed	EEC countries	E 33-a
	Main countries	U 21-a
Labour force employed: no of foreign workers	EEC countries	E 33-a
salaried staff	EEC countries	E 11-a
wage earners	EEC countries	E 11-a
No & % by nationality of foreign workers employed in mines	EEC countries	E 15-a
of face, underground & auxiliary workers employed in mines	EEC countries	E 16-m E 15-a
hrs worked per wk	Main countries	R 3-a
per yr: salaried staff	EEC countries	E 11-a
wage earners	EEC countries	E 11-a
underground workers employed	EEC countries	E 16-q E 15-a
	European countries	U 10-a
	Main countries	E 3-a
workers & salaried staff employed	EEC countries	E 2-a
employed by age groups	EEC countries	E 33-a
officials employed at collieries	EEC countries	E 16-m E 15-a
Production; hard coal per man-shift: tonnage	EEC countries	E 16-m E 15-a
per worker per man-shift: tonnage	Main countries	E 3-a
- index nos	ECE countries	U 42-m
Turnover of collieries in DMm	W Germany	H 3-a
Wage rates per hr by sex in local currency	Main countries	R 3-m
per hr in DM	W Germany	H 3-a
Wages & salary costs in collieries	Main countries	U 21-a

Coal stocks   see   COLLIERY STOCKS

Coal tar   see   CHEMICAL PRODUCTS
                     COAL BY-PRODUCTS
                     HARD COAL BRIQUETTES

Coarse grains   see   BARLEY
                          CEREALS
                          OATS
                          MAIZE
                          MILLET
                          SORGHUM

COASTAL SHIPPING

Building materials: tonnage	EEC countries	E 43-a
Chemical products: tonnage	EEC countries	E 43-a
Fertilisers: tonnage	EEC countries	E 43-a
Food & agricultural products: tonnage	EEC countries	E 43-a
Freight tonnage by flags of vessels	EEC countries	E 43-a
Goods loaded & unloaded: tonnage at specific ports	Worldwide	U 43-a
Incoming & outgoing cargoes: tonnage	Main ports of EEC countries	E 43-a
Iron & steel products: tonnage	EEC countries	E 43-a
Machinery: tonnage	EEC countries	E 43-a
Metal ores: tonnage	EEC countries	E 43-a
Oil products: tonnage	EEC countries	E 43-a
Petroleum products: tonnage	EEC countries	E 16-q E 15-a
Solid fuels: tonnage	EEC countries	E 43-a

Coats   see   CLOTHING

COBALT

% consumed by aircraft industry	USA	N 1-a
ceramics & glass industry	USA	N 1-a
chemical industry	USA	N 1-a
electrical industry	USA	N 1-a
machinery production industry	USA	N 1-a
paint industry	USA	N 1-a
% contribution to export earnings	Zambia	E 45-a

	Territorial coverage	Title codes
COBALT, continued		
Consumption in production of alloy steels in lbs	USA	T 4-a
carbon steels in lbs	USA	T 4-a
cast iron in lbs	USA	T 4-a
catalysts in lbs	USA	T 4-a
ceramics in lbs	USA	T 4-a
chemical products in lbs	USA	T 4-a
cobalt powder products in lbs	USA	T 4-a
electric steels in lbs	USA	T 4-a
ferro-alloys: tonnage	UK	T 4-a
glass decolourisers in lbs	USA	T 4-a
pigments in lbs	USA	T 4-a
sintered carbides in lbs	USA	T 4-a
stainless steels in lbs	USA	T 4-a
tool steels in lbs	USA	T 4-a
welding rods in lbs	USA	T 4-a
Consumption: tonnage	USA	N 1-a
Export prices: metal shot in $ per lb (in drums) cif	USA ports	T 4-m
Exports by destination: tonnage	Main countries	T 4-a
tonnage & value in $m	Zambia	E 45-a
Government stockpile & sales: tonnage	USA	N 1-a
Import price (contract) delivered in £ per kg cif	UK	C 12-m
(free market) delivered in £ per kg cif	UK	C 12-m
Imports by source: cobalt (unwrought & refined): tonnage	Italy	C 12-a
tonnage	Main countries	T 4-a
Imports & exports by source & destination: tonnage	Main countries	B 15-a
Producer price in $ per lb on New York metal market	USA	C 12-m
Production in lbs	Canada, Morocco, USA, Zaire & Zambia	J 6-a
tonnage based on metal content of ore	All countries	B 15-a U 22-a
	Zaire	E 41-a
	Main countries	N 1-a
Stocks held at consumers' premises: tonnage	USA	N 1-a
Wholesale prices in $ per lb	USA	N 1-a
(contract) in £ per lb	UK	T 4-m
World production: tonnage	Reporting countries only	C 30-a
	Worldwide excl USA	N 4-a
	All countries	C 12-a T 4-a
COBALT ORE		
Production: tonnage	African countries	U 44-a
World production: tonnage based on metal content of ore	Main countries	C 12-a N 1-a
COBALT POWDER PRODUCTS		
Consumption in lbs	USA	T 4-a
Coca cola see SOFT DRINKS		
Coca leaf see DRUGS & MEDICINES		
COCAINE		
Consumption in kg & per million population	All countries	U 46-a
Exports by destination (incl other opium alkaloids) by value in $	Main countries	U 2-a
in kg	Main countries	U 46-a
of coca leaves for cocaine production in kg	Bolivia & Peru	U 46-a
Illicit traffic seizures in kg	All countries	U 46-a
Production from coca leaves in kg	All countries	U 46-a
Usage (industrial) for production of medical preparations for export in kg	All countries	U 46-a
of coca leaves for production of cocaine in kg	All countries	U 46-a
World requirements in kg (estim)		U 19-a
Cockles & crabs see CRUSTACEANS & MOLLUSCS		
Cockpit personnel see AIRCRAFT PERSONNEL		
COCOA		
% contribution to export earnings	African, Caribbean countries & Pacific Is	E 45-a
Consumption in raw bean equivalent tonnage	All countries	B 13-a
per capita in kg per yr	OECD countries	D 1-a
in lb per yr	Main countries	B 13-a
tonnage	OAS member countries	N 17-a
Excise duties: rates charged	EEC countries	E 31-a
Export prices - index nos (weighted average main sources)	Worldwide	U 29-q U 54-q
Exports by destination of raw cocoa: tonnage	Main producing countries	B 18-q
value & as % of value of total exports of goods	All countries	B 13-a
in local currency	Main countries	B 13-a
tonnage	Main countries	A 5-a B 13-a
Import prices: fermented ghana (main crop) in £ per ton	UK	P 2-m
Imports: tonnage	Main countries	B 18-q B 13-a
Prices (spot) ex warehouse by quality in London & New York per ton	UK & USA	B 18-a
Producer prices in local currency	Cameroon, Ghana, Ivory Coast & Nigeria	P 2-a
Production tonnage & Commonwealth exports as % of world total		B 13-a
tonnage (incl world total)	All countries	P 1-a R 5-a
raw cocoa: tonnage	Main countries	B 13-a B 18-a
Stocks of raw cocoa: tonnage	USA	B 18-m

	Territorial coverage	Title codes	
COCOA, continued			
Turnover on London terminal market: tonnage & no lots	UK	P 2-m	
on New York terminal market: tonnage & no lots	USA	P 2-m	
Wholesale prices: Brazilian & Ghana cocoa in cents per lb	USA	P 1-m	
on London terminal market in £ per ton	UK	P 2-m	
(spot) ex warehouse in £ per ton	UK	P 2-m	
in cents per lb	USA	P 2-m	
(spot) Ghana in cents per lb (average)	USA	B 13-a	
in local currency	France, UK & USA	U 27-m	
World exports by value (incl cocoa products) in $	World regions	A 5-a	
production (net crop after loss): tonnage since 1946	Worldwide	P 2-a	
production, grindings & stock changes: tonnage	Main countries	U 11-a	
tonnage	Main countries	A 5-a	B 13-a
COCOA BEANS			
Area under crop in ha	OAS member countries	N 13-a	
Availability: historical table since 1946: tonnage	Worldwide	P 2-a	
tonnage	Worldwide	P 3-a	
Crop: tonnage	Worldwide	P 3-a	
Export prices ex Accra & Bahia in cents per lb at New York	USA	R 2-m	
Ghana in £ per ton on London market	UK	R 2-m	
– index nos	S American countries	U 40-q	
in local currency	Brazil, Ghana & Western Samoa	A 9-a	
Exports by destination by CST classes: tonnage & value in $	EEC countries	E 48-a	
SITC classes by value in $	Main countries	D 2-q	
SITC classes: tonnage & value in $	OECD countries	D 3-a2	
tonnage	All countries	A 3-m	
NIMEXE classes: tonnage & value in $	All countries	E 20-a	
SITC classes: tonnage & value in $	All countries	U 50-a	U 59-a
value in $m	Main countries	A 3-a	
in local currency	Developing countries	U 11-a	
	Papua New Guinea	U 32-m	
to EEC area: tonnage & by value in UA	AASM countries	E 41-a	
in $m	Main countries	B 2-a	
	African, Caribbean countries & Pacific Is	E 45-a	
tonnage (incl world total)	All countries	A 3-a	
tonnage	Producing countries	P 3-a	
	Main exporting countries	A 3-m	
unit value in $ per kg	OAS member countries	N 15-a	
	Main countries	A 3-m	
Grindings: raw cocoa as % of world grindings: tonnage	Main countries	P 2-a	
tonnage (incl world total)	All countries	A 3-a	A 5-a
		B 13-a	P 3-a
historical table since 1946	Main countries	P 2-a	
historical table	All countries	A 3-a	
tonnage	All countries	P 3-a	
	Main importing countries	A 3-a	
	Main countries	P 2-q	B 2-a
		P 1-a	
	Producing countries	A 3-a	
	W Germany, Netherland, UK & USA	B 18-q	
Import prices: % changes over previous yr	W Germany	E 34-m	
in DM per kg cif, Hamburg	W Germany	E 34-m	
(spot) ex Ghana on London market in $ per ton	UK	B 2-a	
cif in local currency	France, Spain & European ports	A 9-a	
Imports by NIMEXE classes: tonnage & value in $	All countries	E 20-a	
SITC classes: tonnage & value in $	All countries	U 50-a	U 59-a
source by CST classes: tonnage & value in $	EEC countries	E 21-a	
SITC classes by value in $	Main countries	D 2-q	
SITC classes: tonnage & value in $	OECD countries	D 3-a2	
historical table from 1947: tonnage	UK	P 2-a	
unit value in local currency per kg	Main countries	A 3-a	
tonnage	Main countries	A 3-m	P 3-a
Producer prices in £ per ton	Ghana, Ivory Coast & Nigeria	P 3-a	
$ per ton	Ghana & Nigeria	B 2-a	
local currency	Cameroon, Guatemala & Peru	A 9-a	
Production forecast for ensuing yr: tonnage	World regions	A 1	
Production: tonnage	All countries	P 3-a	
tonnage & area under crop in ha	Latin American countries	J 5-a	
tonnage (incl world total)	Main countries	B 2-a	
tonnage, area under crop & yield in ha	All countries	A 9-a	
tonnage: historical table	All countries	A 3-a	
tonnage, imports, exports & supply	EEC countries	B 1-a	
tonnage, stocks & consumption per capita	OECD countries	D 14-a	
tonnage	AASM countries	E 41-a	
	Ivory Coast, Cameroon, Gabon, Togo & Zaire	E 41-a	
	Latin American countries	U 40-a	
	OAS member countries	N 13-a	
	World regions	U 43-a	
Re-export trade: tonnage	Main countries	A 3-a	
Stocks as % of world grindings	Worldwide	P 3-a	
(end-year): tonnage	Main countries	B 13-a	
in terms of months supply	Worldwide	P 3-a	
tonnage	Worldwide	P 3-a	
Supply & demand position: tonnage	Worldwide	P 3-a	
Wholesale prices: % change over previous yr	EEC countries	E 34-m	
by grade on London & New York markets	UK & USA	B 13-m	

	Territorial coverage	Title codes	
COCOA BEANS, continued			
Wholesale prices in local currency per kg	EEC countries	E 34-m	
	OAS member countries	N 17-a	
	Brazil, Ecuador, Netherlands & USA	A 9-a	
London futures in £ per ton	UK	A 3-m	
New York futures in cents per lb	USA	A 3-m	
(spot) ex Brazil on New York market in cents per lb	USA	A 3-m	
Ghana on London Market in £ per ton	UK	A 3-m	
Ghana on New York market in cents per lb	USA	A 3-m	P 3-a
Ivory Coast at Le Havre in Fr per kg	France	A 3-m	
World consumption: tonnage	Main countries	B 2-a	
export trade: tonnage	All exporting countries	A 3-a	
grindings: tonnage	Worldwide	B 13-a	
imports: tonnage	World economic areas	P 3-a	
market prices in cents per lb fob US ports	USA	P 3-a	
(ex Martinique) in Fr per kg	France	E 41-a	
production per capita population in lbs	Worldwide	P 2-a	
tonnage	All countries	P 2-a	
	Worldwide	A 3-a	P 3-a
stock changes: tonnage	Worldwide	B 2-a	
stocks (end-yr): tonnage	Worldwide	G 1-a	
COCOA BUTTER			
% contribution to export earnings	Cameroon & Ivory Coast	E 45-a	
Exports by main destinations: tonnage	Main countries	A 3-a	
tonnage & value in $m	African, Caribbean countries & Pacific Is	E 45-a	
tonnage	Main countries	A 3-m	B 13-a
		B 18-a	P 3-a
Imports & exports: historical table from 1947: tonnage	UK	P 2-a	
by main sources: tonnage	Main countries	A 3-a	
tonnage	Main countries	A 3-m	B 13-a
		P 3-a	
Production: tonnage	All countries	U 22-a	
	EEC countries	E 28-q	E 27-a
Wholesale prices (high & low) since 1938 in £ per ton	UK	P 2-a	
in £ per ton	UK	P 3-a	
COCOA PASTE			
Exports: tonnage	Main countries	A 3-m	B 13-a
Imports: tonnage	Main countries	A 3-m	B 13-a
COCOA POWDER			
Consumption in production of cocoa products: tonnage	World regions	A 1-a	
Exports (incl cocoa paste): tonnage	Main countries	B 18-a	
tonnage	Main countries	A 3-m	B 13-a
		P 3-a	
Imports (incl cocoa paste): tonnage	Main countries	B 18-a	
tonnage	Main countries	B 13-a	P 3-a
Production tonnage & grindings projected to 1985	Main countries	A 1	
tonnage	All countries	U 22-a	
	EEC countries	E 28-q	E 27-a
Retail prices in local currency per kg	Main countries	A 3-q	
COCOA PRODUCTS			
see also COCOA BUTTER			
COCOA PASTE			
COCOA POWDER			
Exports by value in $m	Main countries	A 3-a	
Cocoa, raw see COCOA BEANS			
Coconut cake see OILCAKE & MEAL			
COCONUT OIL			
see also COPRA OIL			
Export prices of crude coconut oil (in drums) in $ per picul	Singapore	U 32-m	
fob in local currency	Main producing countries	A 4-m	
in cents per lb fob	USA	A 4-m	R 2-m
in Rs per ton fob	Sri Lanka	U 32-m	
- index nos (weighted average)	Worldwide	U 29-q	
in local currency per kg	Main countries	A 9-a	
Exports by destination: tonnage	Malaysia, Netherlands, Sri Lanka & Singapore	B 19-a	
by value in local currency	Fiji, Papua & Sri Lanka	U 32-m	
to European area & to USA: tonnage	Philippines	A 4-a	B 19-a
tonnage (incl world total)	All countries	A 4-a	
tonnage	Main countries	B 19-a	
	Primary producing countries	B 18-q	
	W Malaysia	U 32-m	
	Papua New Guinea	U 32-m	
unit value in $ per ton		A 4-m	
Freight rates (in bulk) to Europe ex Fiji & Philippines per ton			
Import prices (in bulk) in £ per ton, cif	UK	P 1-a	

	Territorial coverage	Title codes	
COCONUT OIL, continued			
Import prices ex Malaysia in £ per ton cif	UK	A 4-m	
Philippines in fl per kg cif	Netherlands	R 2-m	
Sri Lanka in £ per ton cif	UK	A 4-m	
	European ports	A 9-a	B 19-a
	UK	R 2-m	
Imports: tonnage	Main countries	A 4-a	B 19-a
		P 1-a	
Production tonnage for ensuing yr (estim)	World regions	P 1-a	
	Main countries	P 1-a	
tonnage	Japan, Malaysia & Philippines	U 32-q	
	Main European countries	P 1-a	
	Main countries	B 19-a	
Retail prices in local currency	OAS member countries	N 17-a	
Stocks at end-yr: tonnage	USA	B 19-a	
Supply & mill production: tonnage	USA	B 19-a	
Usage in production of confectionery & ice cream: tonnage	Norway	A 4-a	
cooking fats: tonnage	UK & USA	B 19-a	
	Main countries	A 4-a	
detergents: tonnage	Japan	A 4-a	B 19-a
edible products: tonnage	Main countries	A 4-a	
fatty acids: tonnage	USA	B 19-a	
	Japan & USA	A 4-a	
inedible products: tonnage	Japan & USA	A 4-a	
margarine & cooking fats: tonnage	Main countries	A 4-a	
margarine: tonnage	Main countries	A 4-a	B 19-a
	USA	B 19-a	
paints & varnishes: tonnage	USA	A 4-a	
soap & detergents: tonnage	Main countries	A 4-a	
soap: tonnage	UK & USA	B 19-a	
Wholesale prices at Bombay in Rs per 100 kg	India	A 4-m	
at Manila in Pesos per kg	Philippines	U 32-m	
in cents per lb	Philippines	A 4-m	
cents per lb (Pacific Coast)	UK	B 2-a	
£ per ton	USA	P 1-m	
local currency	India, Philippines & USA	A 9-a	
	European countries, UK & USA	U 27-m	
World & Commonwealth production: tonnages		B 19-a	
World production: tonnage forecast for ensuing yr		A 1	
tonnage		A 4-a	A 5-a
		N 10-a	
COCONUTS			
see also COIR FIBRE			
COPRA			
% contribution to export earnings	Tonga	E 45-a	
Export prices in $	Philippines	A 9-a	
Exports by value in $m	Philippines	U 32-m	
tonnage & value in $m	Tanzania	E 45-a	
Production, supply, consumption & trade: tonnage	EEC countries	B 1-a	
Production: tonnage	All countries	A 9-a	
by volume	Latin American countries	J 5-a	
COCONUTS, DESICCATED			
Export prices in Rs per lb	Sri Lanka	A 4-m	
Exports by value in local currency	Tonga	U 32-m	
to W European area & USA: tonnage	Philippines	A 4-a	
Cod (& similar fish species) see STOCKFISH			
CODEINE			
Consumption in kg & in kg per million population	All countries	U 46-a	
Exports by destination in kg	Main countries	U 46-a	
Usage (industrial) for production of preparations for export in kg	All countries	U 46-a	
World requirements in kg (estim)		U 19-a	
Coefficients of demand see INDUSTRY			
MACHINERY			
Coefficients of mobility see POPULATION MOVEMENT			
COFFEE			
see also INSTANT COFFEE			
INTERNATIONAL COFFEE AGREEMENT			
ROASTED COFFEE INDUSTRY			
% changes in retail sales	E European countries & USSR	U 16-a	
% contribution to export earnings	African, Caribbean countries & Pacific Is	E 45-a	
% population (over 15 yrs age) who drink coffee	W European countries	J 1-a	
Area harvested, production tonnage & yield per ha	All countries	A 9-a	
Consumption & demand projections by 1975		A 1	
Consumption: no of cups per person per day (estim)	European countries	J 1-a	
at home or at work per day (estim)	USA	J 1-a	
bean, instant or decaffeinated per day(estim)	USA	J 1-a	
by age groups & by sex per day (estim)	USA	J 1-a	
in restaurants or cafes per day (estim)	USA	J 1-a	

	Territorial coverage	Title codes	
COFFEE, continued			
Consumption (domestic): roasted coffee in lbs per yr	USA	J 1-a	
in green bean equiv in bags	Main countries	B 13-a	
households in lbs & as % total consumption	USA	J 1-a	
institutions in lbs & as % total consumption	USA	J 1-a	
restaurants or cafes in lbs & as % total consumption	USA	J 1-a	
work-places in lbs & as % total consumption	USA	J 1-a	
terms of cups per person per day (estim)	USA	J 1-a	
(industrial) for production of flavours & extracts: tonnage	USA	J 1-a	
per capita in decagrams	E European countries & USSR	U 16-a	
in lbs per yr	Main countries	B 13-a	
of regular coffee in lbs retail weight per yr	USA	J 1-a	
tonnage & per capita in kg per yr	Main countries	U 43-a	
tonnage (total)	Producing countries	A 5-a	
	Main countries	B 2-a	
	OAS member countries	N 17-a	
Contract price of robusta grades on London terminal market in pence per lb	UK	J 1-m	
Excise duties: rates charged	EEC countries	E 31-a	
Export availability projected to ensuing yr: tonnage	World regions	A 1	
prices by grade in cents per lb cif (average)	Main producing countries	B 2-a	
- index nos (weighted average main sources)	Worldwide	U 29-q	U 54-q
	S American countries	U 40-a	
in local currency	Main countries	A 9-a	
quota shortfalls under International Coffee Agreement	ICA member countries	J 1-a	
quotas under International Coffee Agreement in bags	ICA member countries	A 5-a	B 18-a
		J 1-a	
Exports as % of total world coffee exports	Main countries	J 1-a	
by destination by CST classes: by tonnage & value in $	EEC countries	E 48-a	
SITC classes by value in $	Main countries	D 2-q	
SITC classes: tonnage & value in $	OECD countries	D 3-a2	
in bags	Main countries	J 1-a	
grade: unit value in $ per ton fob	Main countries	A 5-a	
NIMEXE classes: tonnage & value in $	All countries	E 20-a	
SITC classes: tonnage & value in $	All countries	U 50-a	U 59-a
value & as % value of all exports	All producing countries	J 1-a	
in $	Developing countries	U 11-a	
tonnage & value in $m	Main countries	B 2-a	
	African, Caribbean countries & Pacific Is	E 45-a	
tonnage	Asia & Far East area	U 32-q	
unit value in $ per kg	OAS member countries	N 15-a	
Extraction rates: lbs of instant coffee per lb of coffee beans	USA	J 1-a	
Household purchases in lbs per yr	Canada & USA	J 1-a	
Import prices in local currency per kg	France, W Germany & UK	A 9-a	
Imports by NIMEXE classes: tonnage & value in $	All countries	E 20-a	
SITC classes: tonnage & value in $	All countries	U 50-a	U 59-a
source by CST classes: tonnage & value in $	EEC countries	E 21-a	
SITC classes by value in $	Main countries	D 2-q	
SITC classes: tonnage & value in $	OECD countries	D 3-a2	
Indicator prices under International Coffee Agreement by grade in cents per lb	ICA member countries	B 18-m	
Prices of London terminal market futures on London terminal market in £ per ton	UK	B 18	
Producer prices in local currency	All countries	A 9-a	
Production: tonnage & area under coffee crop in ha	Latin American countries	J 5-a	
(incl world total)	Main countries	B 2-a	R 5-a
& exports of Commonwealth countries as % of total		B 13-a	
Production, supply, consumption & trade: tonnage	EEC countries	B 1-a	
tonnage	AASM countries	E 41-a	
	Latin American countries	U 40-a	
Retail prices (bag & vacuum-packed coffee) in cents per lb	USA	J 1-m	
(comparative) of pure roasted coffee in $ per kg	EEC countries	Z 3-a	
Stocks held by producers: tonnage	Brazil	A 5-a	
at end-June: tonnage	Brazil & USA	B 2-a	
end-month: tonnage	EEC countries & USA	B 13-m	
tonnage	USA	A 5-a	
at end of crop yr: tonnage	Brazil & USA	A 11-a	
Tonnage of regular, instant & processed coffee manufactured	Canada	J 1-a	
Wholesale prices: roasted beans in 1 lb vacuum cans	USA	J 1-m	
(spot) by source in cents per lb	USA	J 1-m	
	Brazil, Colombia, Indonesia, Mexico & USA	A 9-a	
in local currency	El Salvador & France	U 27-m	
World carry-over stocks & stock distribution: tonnage	Worldwide	J 1-a	
supplies exports & stocks: tonnage		U 11-a	
demand per capita projected to 1985		A 1	
consumption in bags per yr		J 1-a	
exports by value in $m		A 5-a	M 4-a
		G 1-a	
market prices - index nos		M 4-a	
of coffee ex Uganda in cents per lb on New York market	USA	E 41-a	
stocks (end-yr): tonnage		G 1-a	
supply position, stock carry-over, production & consumption: tonnage		B 13-a	

COFFEE, GREEN

	Territorial coverage	Title codes	
Export prices by grade in cents per lb fob	USA	R 2-m	
robusta ex Uganda in £ per kg	UK	R 2-m	
santos prime ex Brazil in £ per kg	UK	R 2-m	
Exports by destination in bags	Main countries	B 18-q	B 13-a
	Latin American countries	J 1-a	
value as % of total exports	Main countries	B 13-a	
in local currency	All countries	B 13-a	
	Indonesia	U 32-m	
home-produced coffee in bags	Main countries	B 13-a	
tonnage	India, Indonesia, Laos & Papua New Guinea	U 32-m	
Import prices in $ per bag & cents per lb	USA	J 1-m	
in $ per lb	Canada	J 1-a	
Imports by source & customs districts: tonnage	USA	J 1-m	
in bags	Canada	J 1-a	
by value in cents per lb	USA	J 1-m	
into European area: tonnage	Main exporting countries	J 1-a	
into USA: tonnage	All exporting countries	J 1-m	
in bags	Main importing countries	B 18-q	B 13-a
Prices (at auction) in EA Shs per 50 kg	Kenya	B 18	
(spot) by grade in cents per lb on New York market	USA	B 13-m	B 18-m
Production in bags (incl world total): tonnage	All countries	B 13-a	
raw coffee: tonnage	Main countries	A 5-a	
	World regions	U 43-a	
Roastings for instant coffee preparation in bags	USA	J 1-a	
regular coffee in bags	USA	J 1-a	
Stocks held by roasters, dealers & importers: tonnage	USA	J 1-a	
(end-month) in bags	W Germany & USA	B 18-m	
in bags	ICA member countries	B 18-q	
World export trade in bags	World regions of origin	J 1-a	
market price per 100 kg cif at N sea ports	European countries	E 34-m	
production in bags	World regions	J 1-a	

Coffee, raw   see   COFFEE, GREEN

Coffee, roasted   see   COFFEE BEANS

Coffee, soluble   see   INSTANT COFFEE

COFFEE BEANS

see also   COFFEE, GREEN
              ROASTED COFFEE INDUSTRY

	Territorial coverage	Title codes	
Area under crop in ha	OAS member countries	N 13-a	
Exports (total) & to EEC area: tonnage & value in UA	AASM countries	E 41-a	
by value in local currency	Singapore & Papua New Guinea	U 32-m	
coffee (roasted) in bags	Main countries	B 13-a	
Import prices (average) in $ per lb	Canada	J 1-a	
Imports by source: roasted beans: tonnage	Main countries	J 1-a	
Processing (domestic) & availability: tonnage	USA	J 1-a	
Production: roasted beans in lbs	Canada	J 1-a	
tonnage	OAS member countries	N 13-a	
Wholesale prices in local currency	OAS member countries	N 17-a	

COFFEE BY KIND

	Territorial coverage	Title codes	
Export quotas under International Coffee Agreement in bags	ICA member countries	J 1-a	
Exports (incl world total) in bags	All countries	J 1-a	
Production (incl world totals) in bags	All countries	J 1-a	
Retail prices in local currency	OAS member countries	N 17-a	
of instant coffee in cents per lb	USA	J 1-m	
of regular coffee in cents per lb	USA	J 1-m	
Wholesale prices in cents per lb (average)	USA	J 1-m	
coffee ex Brazil & Colombia in cents per lb	USA	A 5-a	
mild arabicas grade in cents per lb	USA	A 5-a	
robustas grade in cents per lb	USA	A 5-a	
(spot) in cents per lb	USA	J 1-m	A 5-a
World exports in bags	Main countries	U 11-a	
market prices: arabica ex Brazil in Fr per kg	France	E 41-a	
robusta ex Angola in Fr per kg	France	E 41-a	

Coffee plantations   see   PLANTATIONS, COFFEE

Coffee powder   see   INSTANT COFFEE

COINAGE

	Territorial coverage	Title codes	
Consumption of silver for minting coins in troy oz million	All countries	J 6-a	
	USA	N 1-a	T 4-a

COIR FIBRE

	Territorial coverage	Title codes	
Consumption (incl jute) in production of floor covering	EEC countries	K 4-a	
Exports of bristle fibre: tonnage & value in local currency	Sri Lanka	A 5-a	B 10-a
of mattress fibre: tonnage & value in local currency	Sri Lanka	A 5-a	B 10-a
(incl manufactures): tonnage	Main countries	B 10-a	
Wholesale prices: bristle fibre in Rs per cwt	Sri Lanka	B 10-m	
mattress fibre in Rs per cwt	Sri Lanka	B 10-m	

	Territorial coverage	Title codes	
COIR MANUFACTURES			
Exports of cordage & ropes manufactured of coir yarn in cwt	India	B 10-a	
of floor rugs to UK & USSR in cwt	India	B 10-a	
COIR YARN			
Exports by destination: tonnage	India	B 10-a	
tonnage & value (incl coir products)	India	A 5-a	
Wholesale prices: anjengo yarn in Rs per cwt	India	B 10-m	
COKE			
Availability of coke-oven coke: tonnage	European countries	U 31-q	
from EEC area production & from imports: tonnage	EEC countries	E 16-q	E 15-a
Changes in stocks (indigenous & imported): tonnage	EEC countries	E 14-a	
Consumption as additive per ton of pig iron	EEC countries	E 29-a	
at power stations for electricity production: tonnage	EEC countries	E 16-q	E 15-a
power stations, gasworks & coke ovens: tonnage	EEC countries	E 16-q	E 15-a
by chemical industry of coke oven & gas coke: tonnage	OECD countries	D 5-a	
chemical industry: tonnage	EEC countries	E 14-a	
households of coke-oven coke: tonnage	European countries	U 31-q	
households: tonnage	EEC countries	E 14-a	
	Turkey	U 10-a	
industrial sector: tonnage	Turkey	U 10-a	
iron & steel industry of coke-oven coke: tonnage	European countries	U 31-q	
iron & steel industry of coke-oven coke (incl breeze): tonnage	UK	T 2-m	
iron & steel industry: tonnage	ECE countries	U 6-a	U 7-a
	EEC countries	E 14-a	E 29-a
	Main countries	H 3-a	
	OECD countries	D 22-a	D 44-a
kind of usage in steel industry: tonnage	EEC countries	E 30-q	
railways of coke-oven coke: tonnage	Main countries	N 2-a	
of coke-oven coke: tonnage	European countries, USSR & USA	U 49-a	
in thermal power stations: tonnage	Main countries	N 2-a	
for production of brown coal briquettes: tonnage	ECE countries	U 6-a	U 7-a
	Main countries	H 3-a	
of manufactured gas: tonnage	European countries & USA	U 3-a	
of pig iron: tonnage	Main countries	T 1-a	
transformation into energy: tonnage	EEC countries	E 16-q	E 15-a
in blast furnaces of coke-oven coke: tonnage	EEC area	E 16-q	E 14-a
		E 15-a	E 29-a
		U 6-a	U 7-a
	Main countries	H 3-a	
	ECE countries	U 6-a	U 7-a
	Main countries	H 3-a	T 1-a
		U 49-a	
in electric furnaces: tonnage	ECE countries	U 6-a	U 7-a
	Main countries	H 3-a	
kg per ton of pig iron produced	EEC countries	E 29-a	
of sinter & pig iron produced	EEC countries	E 30-q	
of sinter produced	EEC countries	E 29-a	
refineries: tonnage	EEC countries	E 14-a	
sinter plants: tonnage	EEC countries	E 29-a	
steel foundries: tonnage	EEC area	E 29-a	
(industrial) by areas: tonnage	EEC countries	E 38-a	
of metallurgical coke: tonnage	OAS member countries	N 17-a	
coke from petroleum refineries: tonnage	Main countries	C 14-a	
tonnage	European countries, USA & USSR	U 4-a	
	Main countries	N 5-a	
Deliveries of hard coke to industry, commerce & households: tonnage	EEC countries	E 16-m	E 15-a
Exports by destination: tonnage	EEC countries	E 5-q	
	Main countries	U 10-a	
of coke-oven coke by world regions: tonnage	OECD countries	D 22-a	
tonnage	European countries	U 31-q	
to non-EEC area: tonnage	EEC countries	E 14-a	
tonnage	ECE countries, Japan & USA	U 7-m	U 6-a
	Main countries	H 3-a	
	W Germany	C 5-m	
Import prices in S Kr per ton cif	Sweden	U 10-a	
Imports by source: tonnage	EEC countries	E 5-q	
of coke-oven coke from world areas: tonnage	OECD countries	D 22-a	
tonnage	European countries	U 31-q	
& exports: tonnage	EEC countries	E 16-q	E 15-a
from non-EEC area: tonnage	EEC countries	E 14-a	
tonnage	ECE countries, Japan & USA	U 7-m	U 6-a
	Main countries	H 3-a	N 2-a
	W Germany	C 5-m	
Inter-EEC deliveries: tonnage	EEC countries	E 16-q	E 14-a
		E 15-a	
Prices of imported local blast-furnace coke - index nos	OECD countries	D 22-a	
Production: as distillate from oil refining: tonnage	All countries	U 22-a	
by coal distillation in coke ovens: tonnage	All countries	U 43-a	
kind & process: tonnage	All countries	B 15-a	
	European countries, USA & USSR	U 4-a	
process & size in coke ovens: tonnage	EEC countries	E 29-a	
type of hard coke or gas coke: tonnage	EEC countries	E 16-q	E 15-a
coke-oven coke by process: tonnage	EEC countries	E 30-q	
Production tonnage, imports & exports of coke-oven coke	OECD countries	D 44-a	
in coal equivalent	EEC countries	E 16-q	E 15-a

	Territorial coverage	Title codes	
COKE, continued			
Production in coke ovens & gasworks: tonnage	Main countries	E 3-a	
in coke ovens: tonnage	African countries	U 44-a	
	ECE area, Japan & USA	U 6-a	U 7-a
	ECE countries	U 15-a	
	EEC area	E 46-a	
	EEC countries	E 26-m	E 28-q
		E 27-a	
	European countries, USA & USSR	U 10-a	
	European countries	U 31-q	
	Main countries	H 3-a	R 5-a
		U 22-a	U 55-a
	OECD countries	D 22-a	
gasworks: tonnage	All countries	U 22-a	
of metallurgical coke: tonnage	OAS member countries	N 14-a	
petroleum coke: tonnage	African countries	U 44-a	
potential of independent coking plants: tonnage	EEC countries	E 46-a	
mine-owned coking plants: tonnage	EEC countries	E 46-a	
steelworks coking plants: tonnage	EEC countries	E 46-a	
tonnage	All countries	N 5-a	
	EEC countries	E 14-a	
	European countries	C 5-m	
Receipts (incl powder) at steelworks: tonnage	EEC area	E 29-a	
Resources & changes in stocks by producers & importers: tonnage	EEC countries	E 16-q	E 15-a
ex indigenous production & imports: tonnage	EEC countries	E 14-a	
Stocks at coke ovens at end-Dec: tonnage	European countries	U 10-a	
at iron & steel works: tonnage	European countries	U 10-a	
at producers' plants: tonnage	European countries	U 31-q	
Supply ex coke ovens, production & trade: tonnage	ECE area	U 49-a	
Transformation of coke-oven coke to blast furnace gas	OECD countries	D 44-a	
Wholesale prices ex coke ovens (40-70 mm) in lire per ton	Italy	R 2-m	
(60-90 mm) in Fr per ton	France	R 2-m	
in $ per ton	USA	R 2-m	
in local currency	OAS member countries	N 17-a	
ex Ruhr area (40-90 mm) in DM per ton	W Germany	R 2-m	
World production: tonnage of coke-oven coke	All countries	E 15-a	
of metallurgical coke	Worldwide	N 4-a	
COKE BREEZE			
Consumption in production of agglomerates: tonnage	ECE countries	U 7-q	U 6-a
	Main countries	H 3-a	
sinter: tonnage	UK	T 2-q	
COKE BY-PRODUCTS			
Production: tonnage	EEC countries	E 14-a	
COKE OVEN GAS			
Average calorific value	European countries & USA	U 3-a	
Changes in stocks in coal equiv tonnage	EEC countries	E 14-a	
Consumption as primary energy source: tonnage	European countries	U 10-a	
by chemical industry in coal equiv tonnage	EEC countries	E 14-a	
industry in coal equiv tonnage	EEC countries	E 14-a	
iron & steel industry in coal equiv tonnage	EEC countries	E 14-a	E 29-a
non-ferrous metals industry in coal equiv tonnage	EEC countries	E 14-a	
non-metallic minerals industry in coal equiv tonnage	EEC countries	E 14-a	
steel industry in m³	ECE countries	U 6-a	U 7-a
	Main countries	H 3-a	
in coal equiv tonnage	EEC countries	E 29-a	
Consumption for industrial purposes in coal equiv tonnage	EEC countries	E 16-q	E 15-a
power & energy production in coal equiv tonnage	EEC countries	E 16-q	E 15-a
in electricity generation in coal equiv tonnage	EEC countries	E 14-a	
Open-hearth furnaces in m³	ECE countries	U 6-a	U 7-a
Consumption: tonnage	Main countries	H 3-a	
Deliveries in coal equiv tonnage	European countries, USA & USSR	U 4-a	
Distribution losses in calorific value	EEC countries	E 46-a	
Exports by destination in calorific value	EEC countries	E 16-q	E 15-a
to non-EEC area in coal equiv tonnage	European countries & USA	U 3-a	
Imports by source in calorific value	EEC countries	E 14-a	
Inter-EEC deliveries in coal equiv tonnage	European countries & USA	U 3-a	
Production & consumption in m³	EEC countries	E 14-a	
	All countries	U 55-a	
in calorific value	EEC countries	E 16-q	E 15-a
	European countries & USSR	U 4-a	
	Main countries	E 3-a	
coal equiv tonnage	EEC countries	E 14-a	
	European countries & USSR	U 4-a	
Resources ex indigenous production in coal equiv tonnage	EEC countries	E 14-a	
COKE OVENS			
Capacity of coking plants in tonnage per yr by areas	EEC countries	E 38-a	
Capital expenditure by regions in UA million	EEC countries	E 46-a	
Coal input & coke output ratios by kind of coal	EEC countries	E 46-a	
Consumption of bituminous coal & lignite: tonnage	USA	N 1-a	
blast furnace gas for heating ovens in m³	EEC countries	E 46-a	
coal & agglomerates: tonnage	EEC countries	E 14-a	
coal in ovens to produce coke: tonnage	OECD countries	D 44-a	

	Territorial coverage	Title codes
COKE OVENS, continued		
Consumption of coke-oven gas for heating ovens in m³	EEC countries	E 46-a
electricity in kWh in coking plants	European countries & USA	U 1-a
manufactured gas in coking plants in m³	USA	U 3-a
producer gas in calorific value	EEC area	E 46-a
Costs for salaried staff per mth in local currency	EEC countries	E 11-a
Deliveries of coke-oven gas to industry in calorific value	EEC countries	E 46-a
Gas output in kcal per ton of charged coal	EEC countries	E 46-a
Investment in buildings in local currency	EEC countries	E 40-a
machinery in local currency	EEC countries	E 40-a
steelworks-owned plants in UA million	EEC countries	E 46-a
(incl at collieries & in steel industry)	EEC countries	E 15-a
Labour costs as % of total costs in coking plants	EEC countries	E 8-a
by status of employee in local currency	EEC countries	E 8-a
per hr: all employees in local currency	EEC countries	E 11-a
wage earners in local currency	EEC countries	E 11-a
Labour force employed	EEC area	E 29-a
no of salaried staff	EEC countries	E 11-a
wage earners	EEC countries	E 11-a
wage earners & salaried staff	EEC countries	E 8-a
List of existing plants by capacity & production: tonnage	EEC countries	E 15-a
No of hrs worked per yr	EEC countries	E 8-a
per yr by salaried staff	EEC countries	E 11-a
wage earners	EEC countries	E 11-a
COKING COAL		
Consumption in coke ovens: tonnage	USA	N 1-a
Imports for iron & steel industry use: tonnage	OECD countries	D 22-a
Coking plants see COKE OVENS		
Cold storage plants see REFRIGERATING EQUIPMENT, INDUSTRIAL		
COLD-ROLLED STRIP		
see also HOOP & STRIP, STEEL		
HOT-ROLLED STRIP		
Deliveries to user industries: tonnage	ECE countries	U 7-q U 6-a
	Main countries	H 3-a
Exports by destination: tonnage	EEC countries	E 5-q
	Main countries	T 4-a
tonnage & % share	Main countries	U 49-a
Imports by source: tonnage	EEC countries	E 5-q
	Main countries	T 4-a
of coated steel strip: tonnage	Main countries	T 1-a
electrical steel strip: tonnage	Main countries	T 1-a
high carbon steel strip: tonnage	Main countries	T 1-a
stainless steel strip: tonnage	Main countries	T 1-a
Production capacity: tonnage	Main countries	U 57-a
hoop & strip: tonnage	All countries	U 22-a
tonnage	ECE countries	U 7-m U 6-a
	EEC countries	E 28-q E 27-a
		E 29-a
	Main countries	H 3-a T 4-a
	OECD countries	D 22-a
Wholesale prices in $ per ton	Main countries	U 57-a
Colemanite see BORON		
COLLECTIVE FARMS		
Capital investment on construction in roubles	USSR	U 16-a
machinery in roubles	USSR	U 16-a
state farms in roubles	USSR	U 16-a
Direct invesment in roubles	USSR	U 16-a
Irrigated areas used for fruit production in ha	Bulgaria	U 20-a
vegetable production in ha	Bulgaria	U 20-a
Labour force employed by socio-economic groups	USSR	C 28-(irr)
Prices paid for animal feeding stuffs in $	E European countries	U 30-a
Production costs for farm products by kind in $	USSR	U 34-a
COLLEGES, ENGINEERING		
No of students enrolled	EEC countries	E 2-a
COLLEGES, PROFESSIONAL		
No of students enrolled	EEC countries	E 2-a
COLLEGES, TECHNICAL		
% of enrolment studying agricultural subjects	ECAFE countries	U 17
education	ECAFE countries	U 17
engineering	ECAFE countries	U 17
fine arts	ECAFE countries	U 17
humanities	ECAFE countries	U 17
law	ECAFE countries	U 17
medicine	ECAFE countries	U 17
natural sciences	ECAFE countries	U 17
social sciences	ECAFE countries	U 17

	Territorial coverage	Title code
COLLEGES, TECHNICAL continued		
Enrolment by type of course as % total enrolment	ECAFE countries	U 17-a
No of students (full or part-time)	EEC countries	E 2-a
COLLEGES, VOCATIONAL		
Expenditure per pupil – index nos	All countries	U 62-a
No of student teachers enrolled	African countries	U 44-a
students enrolled by sex	AASM countries	E 41-a
	Main countries	R 5-a
	African countries	U 44-a
students enrolled (incl teacher trainees)	AASM countries	E 41-a
teachers employed in training colleges	African countries	U 44-a
	AASM countries	E 41-a
Student-teacher ratios	AASM countries	E 41-a
COLLIERIES		
% absenteeism by causes in coal mining	EEC countries	E 33-a
Coal output per mine by district per day: tonnage	EEC countries	E 15-a
Consumption of electric power in coal mines in kWh	All countries	C 23-a
	OECD countries	D 8-a D
Fatality rates applying to coal mine accidents	All countries	L 4-a
Investment in buildings (incl patent fuel industry) in local currency	EEC countries	E 40-a
machinery by districts in local currency	EEC countries	E 15-a
land purchase (incl patent fuel industry) in local currency	EEC countries	E 40-a
machinery (incl patent fuel industry) in local currency	EEC countries	E 40-a
Labour costs as % of total operating costs	EEC countries	E 8-a
by status of employees in local currency	EEC countries	E 8-a
Labour force: no of coal-face workers employed	European countries	U 31-q
underground workers employed	EEC countries	E 15-a
wage earners & salaried staff employed	EEC countries	E 8-a
workers & officials employed by area	EEC countries	E 38-a
List of coal mining enterprises & outputs: tonnage	EEC countries	E 15-a
Loss of coal tonnage due to labour disputes	EEC countries	E 15-a
No of hrs worked per wk at coal-face by area	EEC countries	E 25-a
at pit-head by area	EEC countries	E 25-a
per yr	EEC countries	E 8-a
of mines in operation	Main countries	E 3-a
opencast coal mines	European countries	U 10-a
underground coal mines	European countries	U 10-a
producing hard coal by areas	EEC countries	E 38-a
experiencing short-time working	EEC countries	E 15-a
No of surface, underground workers & apprentices employed	EEC countries	E 3-a
of working days (& tonnage) lost through strikes	EEC countries	E 15-a
Output per man-shift: tonnage	European countries	U 31-q U 1
Stocks of coal at pit-head by grade: tonnage	EEC countries	E 15-a
Supply of electricity to coal mines in kWh	European countries & USA	U 1-a
Wage rates: coal mining industry in local currency	OAS member countries	N 17-a
coal-face workers in local currency per hr	EEC countries	E 25-a2
	Main countries	R 4-a
pit-head workers in local currency per hr	EEC countries	E 25-a2
	Main countries	R 4-a
Columbite see TANTALUM & NIOBIUM		
COLUMBITE CONCENTRATES		
see also COLUMBIUM POWDERS		
FERRO-COLUMBIUM		
Disposals ex govt stockpile: tonnage	USA	N 1-a
Government stockpile: tonnage	USA	N 1-a
Import prices by kind per ton	European countries	T 4-m
Production: tonnage of pyrochlore concentrates	Brazil	T 4-a
tonnage	Main countries	N 1-a
Wholesale prices in $ per lb	USA	N 1-a
World production: tonnage	Main countries	N 1-a
World reserves: tonnage (estim)	Main countries	N 1-a
COLUMBIUM ORE		
Contract prices for columbite in cents per lb	USA	T 4-m
pyrochlore in cents per lb	USA	T 4-m
Imports by source (incl columbite concentrates): tonnage	Main countries	T 4-a
Production: columbite & tantalite: tonnage	Main countries	T 4-a
columbite: tonnage	Malaysia	T 4-a
tantalite: tonnage	Main countries	T 4-a
Wholesale prices of tantalite in $ per lb	USA	N 1-a
World production: tonnage by kind	Main countries	T 4-a
incl tantalum	Non-Communist countries only	C 30-a
COLUMBIUM POWDERS		
Government stockpile of columbium carbide: tonnage	USA	N 1-a
columbium oxide: tonnage	USA	N 1-a
COLUMBIUM-TANTALUM CONCENTRATES		
Production in lbs	USA	J 6-a
World production in lbs	Non-Communist countries only	N 4-a

	Territorial coverage	Title codes	
Colza see RAPESEED			
Combined carriers see BULK CARRIERS			
COMBINED HARVESTER-THRESHERS			
see also THRESHING MACHINES			
Exports by destination: tonnage & value in $m	All countries	U 12-a	
Imports by source: tonnage & value in $m	All countries	U 12-a	
No in use & no per 100 ha of cereal crops	EEC countries	E 3-a	
& no per 100 ha	EEC countries	E 44-a	
(incl world total)	Main countries	R 5-a	
No in use	All countries	A 9-a	U 43-a
	Asian, Far East & Australasian countries	U 45-a	
	EEC countries	B 1-a	
	UK	V 1-q	
No of new registrations	UK	V 1-q	
Production by volume	All countries	U 22-a	U 38-a
	EEC countries	E 28-q	E 27-a
Combines see COMBINED HARVESTER-THRESHERS			
COMMERCE & FINANCE			
see also BANKING & INSURANCE			
COMMERCIAL BANKS			
RETAIL TRADE			
WHOLESALE TRADE			
% changes in implicit price deflator	Developing countries	D 25-a	
% contribution to gross national product: historical table from 1800	Main European countries	Z 1-a	
to national income	Developing countries	D 25-a	
% growth rates in gross product	Developing countries	D 25-a	
Contribution to gross domestic product in local currency	Latin American countries	U 18-a	
Gross product as component in gross domestic product	Developing countries	D 25-a	
Incidence of labour disputes	Main countries	R 3-a	
Labour force employed by sex: historical table 1750-1969	Main European countries	Z 1-a	
wholesale & retail trade	OAS member countries	N 18	
No of employees involved in strikes	Main countries	R 3-a	
of working days lost through strikes	Main countries	R 3-a	
Commercial bank profits see PROFITS			
COMMERCIAL BANKS			
see also BANK ADVANCES			
BANK DEPOSITS			
CREDIT			
% overdraft rates charged to borrowers	OECD countries	D 12-a	
Assets & indebtedness (short-term long-term) in local currency	EEC countries	E 26-q	E 4-a
	OECD countries	D 12-a	
as factor in balance of payments in local currency	African countries	U 44-a	
Change in net external short-term position in local currency	EEC countries	E 26-q	
Deposits: historical table in local currency from 1848	Main European countries	Z 1-a	
Details of loans, securities, credits, deposits & bonds of			
banking system	OECD countries	D 12-a	
Liabilities & foreign position (net) in $m	OECD countries	D 26-q	
as component in balance of payments	African countries	U 44-a	
Loans to private sector in $m	Asian, Far East & Australasian countries	U 45-a	
Name of largest British banks & % change in deposits held	UK	H 1	
& net trading profit in £m	UK	H 1	
& volume of deposits held in £m	UK	H 1	
Canadian banks & % change in deposits held	Canada	H 1	
& net trading profit in $m	Canada	H 1	
& volume of deposits held in $m	Canada	H 1	
French banks & % change in deposits held in Frs million	France	H 1	
& net trading profit in Frs million	France	H 1	
& volume of deposits in Frs million	France	H 1	
W German banks & % change in deposits held in DM million	W Germany	H 1	
& net trading profits in DM million	W Germany	H 1	
& volume of deposits held in DM million	W Germany	H 1	
Italian banks & % change in deposits held in lire million	Italy	H 1	
& net trading profit in lire million	Italy	H 1	
& volume of deposits held in lire million	Italy	H 1	
Japanese banks & % change in deposits held in yen million	Japan	H 1	
& labour force employed	Japan	H 1	
& volume of deposits held in yen million	Japan	H 1	
Swiss banks & % change in deposits held	Switzerland	H 1	
& net trading profits in FrS million	Switzerland	H 1	
& volume of deposits held in FrS million	Switzerland	H 1	
US banks & % change in deposits held	USA	H 1	
& labour force employed	USA	H 1	
& net trading profit in $m	USA	H 1	
& volume of deposits held in $m	USA	H 1	

	Territorial coverage	Title codes
COMMERCIAL BANKS, continued		
Name of world's largest banks & % change in deposits held		H 1
labour force employed		H 1
location of head office		H 1
volume of deposits held in FrS million		H 1
Net foreign external liabilities of banking system	OECD countries	D 26-q
Commercial market rates see EXCHANGE RATES		
COMMERCIAL UNDERTAKINGS		
Contribution to gross domestic product at factor cost in $	African countries	U 44-a
Details of world's 100 largest commercial enterprises		H 1
Direct taxation paid in local currency	AASM countries	E 41-a
Distributed income in local currency	AASM countries	E 41-a
Gross sales income in local currency	AASM countries	E 41-a
Labour force employed by sex (census data)	African countries	U 44-a
Loan advances from banks in local currency	OAS member countries	N 16-a
Name of largest Canadian firms & % change in turnover	Canada	H 1
labour force employed	Canada	H 1
net trading profits in $m	Canada	H 1
turnover in $m	Canada	H 1
Swiss firms & % change in turnover	Switzerland	H 1
labour force employed	Switzerland	H 1
turnover in FrS million	Switzerland	H 1
US corporations & % change in turnover	USA	H 1
labour force employed	USA	H 1
net trading profit in $m	USA	H 1
turnover in $m	USA	H 1
Savings effected in local currency	AASM countries	E 41-a
COMMERCIAL VEHICLES		
see also TRAILERS		
% exports by destination areas (value basis)	UK	B 28-a
% increase in demand projected to 1977	UK	B 28
exports projected to 1977	UK	B 28
imports projected to 1977	UK	B 28
% of total EEC production (volume basis)	EEC countries	R 5-a
% of world export trade	Main countries	B 28
production (volume basis)	Main countries	B 28
% share of each manufacturer	All countries	V 4-a
main markets (value basis)	UK	V 1-a
Assembly by model by overseas subsidiaries by volume	Main countries	V 2-a
volume by laden wt	All countries	V 1-a
from imported assemblies & parts	All countries	U 43-a V 1-a
Consumption (domestic) or sales by volume	Latin American countries	U 38-a
Demand by wt classes projected to 1977 by volume	UK	B 28
projections (incl buses) by volume	E African countries	U 38-a
Distances run (incl articulated vehicles) in km (estim)	EEC countries	E 43-a
per yr in km (estim)	Main countries	S 24-a
by size & type (estim)	EEC countries	E 43-a
Exports by destination: no, value in $, & gross wt	USA	V 1-a
of assembled vehicles: no & value in $m	USA	V 1-a
diesel-driven vehicles: no & value in $m	USA	V 1-a
petrol-driven vehicles: no & value in $m	USA	V 1-a
unassembled vehicles: no & value in $m	USA	V 1-a
no & value	Canada & Japan	V 1-a
	UK	V 1-a
	W European countries	V 1-a
4x2 rigid trucks by volume	UK	V 1-a
4x4 rigid trucks by volume	UK	V 1-a
buses by volume	UK	V 1-a
by CST classes: tonnage & value in $m	EEC countries	E 48-a
SITC classes by value in $m	Main countries	D 2-q
tonnage & value in $m	OECD countries	D 3-a2
volume	All countries	V 1-a
car-derived vans by volume	UK	V 1-a
chassis: no & value in £m	UK	V 1-a
no, gross wt & value in £m	UK	V 1-a
& value of trucks in £m	UK	V 1-a
in £m	UK	V 1-a
special purpose vehicles by volume	UK	V 1-a
tractive units by volume	UK	V 1-a
by value in DM	W Germany	H 3-a
volume	UK	V 1-a
	USSR	V 1-a
tonnage & value in $m	All countries	U 12-a
by NIMEXE classes by volume & by value in $m	All countries	E 20-a
SITC classes by volume & by value in $m	All countries	U 50-a U 59-a
value: historical table in £m	UK	B 28-a V 1-a
value - index nos	UK	V 1-m
volume: goods vehicles	All countries	S 24-a
all commercial vehicles	All countries	V 4-a
Exports: chassis only by volume	All countries	V 4-a
complete & chassis only by value in £m	UK	B 28-a
historical table by volume	All countries	V 1-a
(incl buses) by value in $m	All countries	U 38-a
new trucks & buses by volume	All countries	V 3-a

COMMERCIAL VEHICLES, continued | Territorial coverage | Title codes
Exports: spares for trucks dumpers by value in £m	UK	V 1-a
Exports to USA (chassis only) by volume	All countries	V 4-a
(complete) by volume	Main countries	V 4-a
Forward sales forecasts by volume	Main countries	V 4-a
Future market absorption rate (estim)	Main countries	V 4-a
Imports by NIMEXE classes by volume & value in $m	All countries	E 20-a
SITC classes by volume & value in $m	All countries	U 50-a U 59-a
source: no & value in £m	UK	V 1-a
value in £m	All countries	U 12-a
in $m	UK	B 28-a
volume	All countries	U 38-a
from USA by volume	Latin American region	U 38-a
(incl vehicle chassis) by volume	Main countries	V 4-a
No of new registrations of commercial vehicles	Main countries	V 4-a
by type of road licence issued	European countries & USA	U 47-a
No of current licences in force by areas	EEC countries	E 43-a
goods vehicles crossing frontiers	UK	V 1-q
in use (end-yr)	European countries	U 8-a
heavy lorries in use	Main countries	S 24-a
in use & projected usage by 1980	Main countries	R 5-a
% rate of increase	E African countries	U 38-a
by areas	ECE countries	U 15-a
type & load capacity	EEC countries	E 38-a
	EEC countries	E 43-a
type	European countries	U 8-a
historical tables from 1906	AASM countries	E 41-a
(or registered)	Main European countries	Z 1-a
per 1000 population	Main countries	E 3-a U 43-a
(incl world total)	Main countries	R 5-a
No in use	World regions	N 8-a
	African countries	U 44-a
	Asian, Far East & Australasian countries	U 45-a
	EEC countries	E 43-a
	European countries & USA	U 47-a
	Main countries	V 1-a
	OECD countries	R 5-a
	UK	V 1-a
	W Indies & Caribbean countries	T 6-a
No of km run by commercial vehicles (estim)	European countries & USA	U 47-a
licenced by unladen wt classes	UK	V 1-q
by unladen wt classes & age	UK	V 1-a
locally-assembled by kind	Main countries	V 2-a
locally-assembled	Main countries	V 2-a
of new registrations	All countries	S 24-a
produced for export	All countries	U 49-a
for home sale	All countries	U 49-a
(or assembled)	OAS member countries	N 14-a
registered & in use	All countries	V 4-a
for use on public roads	OAS member countries	N 15-a
road freight firms by size	EEC countries	E 43-a
trucks & buses in use	All countries	S 13-a V 3-a
Production assembly volume	Main countries	E 3-a
volume & % exports	Main countries	V 1-a
all types	OECD countries	R 5-a
articulated trucks	Main countries	V 1-a
by gross weight classes	UK	V 1-m
by kind of fuel	All countries	V 4-a
	Main countries	V 4-a
by load capacity	All countries	V 4-a
by make	All countries	V 1-a
by manufacturers	All countries	V 4-a
by wt classes	All countries	V 4-a
goods vehicles	All countries	S 24-a
historical table from 1907	European countries	Z 1-a
	UK	V 1-a
(incl articulated)	All countries	U 38-a
(incl buses)	Latin American countries	U 38-a
lorries & light vans	All countries	U 22-a
lorries	E European countries	U 16-a
panel vans	All countries	V 1-a
rigid trucks	All countries	V 1-a
utility vans	All countries	V 1-a
	African countries	U 44-a
volume	All countries	U 27-m C 2-a
		N 8-a R 5-a
		U 43-a
	EEC countries	E 26-m E 28-q
		E 27-a
	OECD countries	D 26-m
Registrations (new): all types	Latin American countries	J 5-a
	Main countries	U 27-q
diesel-driven vehicles	Main countries	V 4-a
(incl world total)	All countries	N 8-a
(new) by area	UK	V 1-a
laden wt classes	Eire	V 1-a
make (home-produced)	UK	V 1-a
(imported)	UK	V 1-a
model	Main countries	V 4-a

105

E

	Territorial coverage	Title codes
COMMERCIAL VEHICLES, continued		
Registrations (new) by unladen wt classes	UK	V 1-q
	N Ireland	V 1-q
delivery vans	UK	V 1-a
goods vehicles	Main countries	B 28-a
projected to 1977	W European areas	B 28
works trucks	N Ireland	V 1-q
Registrations (new) - index nos	Main countries	V 1-a
all classes	UK	V 1-a
petrol-driven	Main countries	V 4-a
trucks & buses	World regions	V 3-a
Retail sales volume by model	Main countries	V 4-a
Tax receipts by government in local currency	Main countries	S 24-a
Taxes on transportation in local currency	Main countries	S 24-a
Traffic volume in million vehicle-km	Main countries	S 24-a
World assembly: volume from imported parts		V 4-a
World export trade (incl buses) by value in $m		U 38-a
World production by volume		V 1-a
COMMERCIAL VEHICLES, ARTICULATED		
Production by volume	Main countries	V 1-a
No of new registrations	UK	V 1-a
COMMERCIAL VEHICLES, SECOND-HAND		
Exports by destination: no & value in £m	UK	V 1-a
by volume	USA	V 1-a
	W European countries	V 1-a
COMMERCIAL VEHICLES BY KIND		
Exports by destination by volume	UK	V 1-a
no & value in £m	UK	V 1-a
Production by volume	All countries	V 1-a
COMMERCIAL VEHICLES BY MAKE		
Production by overseas companies by volume	Main countries	V 2-a
volume	All countries	V 3-a
COMMERCIAL VEHICLES INDUSTRY		
No of hrs worked per week	Main countries	R 3-m
Wage rates per hr by sex	Main countries	R 3-m
COMMODITIES		
see also PRIMARY COMMODITIES		
RAW MATERIALS		
% changes in world output of main products	Worldwide	U 54-a
Consumption: tonnage	Asian, Far East & Australasian countries	U 45-a
Food supplies: self-sufficiency ratios	All countries	U 43-a
Main export goods as % of world trade (tonnage basis)	Latin American countries	J 5-a
Production of main export goods: tonnage	Latin American countries	U 18-a
	ECE countries	U 42-m
World market prices: main trading goods in local currency	Main countries	R 5-a
World production: tonnage covered by International Commodity Agreements	Worldwide	U 11-a
COMMODITIES, AGRICULTURAL		
see also TROPICAL PRODUCTS		
% share of world exports	Main countries	B 1-a
imports	Main countries	B 1-a
% usage by purpose	ECE countries	U 34-a
Export prices - index nos	Worldwide	U 33-q
Exports as % imports (value basis)	W European countries	U 20-a
(tonnage basis)	W European countries	U 20-a
of farm products as % of total exports	OECD countries	D 1-a
by areas of destination by value in $m	OECD countries	D 1-a
destination by value in $m	EEC countries	E 44-a
	W European countries	U 33-a
regions of origin: tonnage	EEC countries	E 38-a
value in $m	OECD countries	D 1-a
	W European countries	U 20-a U 33-a
ex EEC area by value shipped to E Europe & USSR in $m	World regions	A 5-a
W European area by value shipped to E Europe & USSR in $m	EEC area	U 33-a
Exports - index nos (value basis)	W European area	U 20-a
Farm prices & wholesale prices in local currency	World regions	A 11-a
Freight by kind of farm products: tonnage	All countries	A 9-a
Imports & exports by kind of farm products: tonnage	EEC countries	E 43-a
of farm products as % total	All countries	A 14-a
	EEC countries	E 44-a
of farm products as % of total imports	OECD countries	D 1-a
	W European countries	U 20-a
by areas of source by value in $m	OECD countries	D 1-a
source by value in $m	EEC countries	E 44-a
	W European countries	U 20-a U 33-a
	OECD countries	D 1-a

		Territorial coverage	Title codes	
COMMODITIES, AGRICULTURAL continued				
Imports ex E European Bloc by value in $m		EEC countries	U 33-a	
into W European area by value in $m		E European supplying countries	U 20-a	
Imports - index nos (value basis)		World regions	A 11-a	A 14-a
Inter-EEC exports as % total exports		EEC countries	U 20-a	
imports as % total imports		EEC countries	U 20-a	
by value in $m		EEC countries	U 33-a	
Main crops: tonnage & value in local currency		Caribbean countries	T 6-a	
Sales by value in local currency		OECD countries	D 37-a	
Self-sufficiency ratios		EEC countries	B 1-a	
Trade by product groups: tonnage		All countries	A 14-a	
Wholesale prices - index nos		OAS member countries	N 17-a	
		Thailand	U 32-m	
World market prices (non-food items) - index nos		Worldwide	U 23-a	
COMMODITIES, AGRICULTURAL BY KIND				
Exports ex EEC area by value in $		E European countries	U 33-a	
tonnage		World regions	A 11-a	
Imports & exports by value in $m		EEC countries	E 44-a	
tonnage		World regions	A 11-a	
Production: tonnage		World regions	A 11-a	
World exports: unit value in $m		World regions	A 11-a	

Commodity agreements   see   INTERNATIONAL COFFEE AGREEMENT
                                       INTERNATIONAL SUGAR AGREEMENT
                                       INTERNATIONAL TIN AGREEMENT
                                       INTERNATIONAL WHEAT AGREEMENT

COMMODITY CREDIT CORPORATION			
Purchase price of butter in cents per lb		USA	B 4-a
Cheddar cheese in cents per lb		USA	B 4-a
milk powder in cents per lb		USA	B 4-a
Rice purchases (as price supports): tonnage		USA	B 14-a
Wheat & flour credits: tonnage		USA	C 16-a

Common Agricultural Policy (C.A.P.)   see   EEC BUDGET
                                                  IMPORT LEVIES
                                                  INTERVENTION PRICES
                                                  PRICE SUPPORTS
                                                  SUBSIDIES, AGRICULTURAL
                                                  TARGET PRICES

Common stocks & shares   see   SHARES, COMMON

Commonwealth bonds   see   GOVERNMENT BONDS, COMMONWEALTH

Communications   see   LETTER MAIL
                             MAIL FREIGHT
                             RADIO COMMUNICATIONS
                             TELEGRAPH SERVICE
                             TELEPHONE EXCHANGES
                             TELEPHONE SERVICE
                             TELEX SERVICE

Communications equipment   see   ELECTRONIC EQUIPMENT
                                                 TELECOMMUNICATIONS EQUIPMENT

COMMUNITY INVESTMENT FUNDS			
% scale contributions to FEOGA	EEC area	B 8-a	
Contributions & reimbursements	EEC area	B 1-a	
Disbursements by purpose	EEC area	E 38-a	
under CECA	EEC area	E 38-a	
FEOGA	EEC area	B 1-a	E 38-a
FEOGA credits & debits	EEC area	B 1-a	
expenditure budget	EEC area	B 1-a	
Iron & steel industry by sector: receipts from CIF	EEC area	E 29-a	

Community price controls   see   INTERVENTION PRICES

COMMUNITY SERVICES

         see also   BUSES & COACHES
                     HOSPITALS
                     LIBRARIES, PUBLIC
                     MEDICAL PERSONNEL
                     PUBLIC HEALTH
                     PUBLIC TRANSPORT
                     PUBLIC UTILITIES
                     SOCIAL SERVICES

Contribution to gross domestic product in local currency	Latin American countries	U 18-a

Companies   see   INDUSTRIAL COMPANIES
                     PRIVATE COMPANIES

Company finance   see   ASSETS & LIABILITIES
                             BALANCE SHEETS
                             FINANCIAL RATIOS, CORPORATE

	Territorial coverage	Title codes	
Company profits see PROFITS			
COMPENSATION PAYMENTS			
see also BALANCE OF PAYMENTS			
As component in balance of payments in $m	OAS member countries	N 16-a	
	All countries	F 1-a	
Components, electronic see ELECTRONIC COMPONENTS			
Compound feed see FEEDING STUFFS, MIXED			
Compound growth rates see GROSS NATIONAL PRODUCT			
COMPRESSORS			
Production by volume: compressors & air pumps	EEC countries	E 28-q	E 27-a
motor-driven air compressor	All countries	U 22-a	
by volume	European countries, Japan, UK & USA	U 38-a	
Computer & components industry see DATA-PROCESSING			
EQUIPMENT INDUSTRY			
ELECTRONICS INDUSTRY			
COMPUTER SCIENCE			
see also RESEARCH & DEVELOPMENT			
Public expenditure (incl automation) in $m	EEC countries	E 36-a	
on research in $m	EEC countries	E 39-a	
Computers see ELECTRONIC COMPUTERS			
CONCERTS			
Attendance at musical concerts held in public	OAS member countries	N 19-a	
No of musical concerts held in public	OAS member countries	N 19-a	
CONCRETE, READY-MIXED			
Production in m³	Netherlands & UK	U 5-a	
CONCRETE MIXERS			
Production by volume of mixers for use on site	All countries	U 22-a	U 38-a
CONCRETE PRODUCTS			
see also BUILDING MATERIALS			
Production: tonnage for use of building industry	All countries	U 22-a	
Concrete reinforcing rounds see REINFORCING RODS, STEEL			
Condensation products see PLASTICS			
CONDENSED & EVAPORATED MILK			
see also MILK POWDER			
% of output exported	Main countries	B 4-a	
% of production by dairy co-operatives	EEC countries	B 3-a	
% of skim milk used in production of condensed milk	EEC countries	B 3-a	
Consumption: fresh milk in production of condensed milk	Main countries	B 4-a	
per capita in kg	EEC countries	B 1-a	B 3-a
		E 44-a	
	Main countries	B 4-a	
tonnage	EEC countries	B 3-a	
	OAS member countries	N 17-a	
Export prices in local currency	Netherlands & UK	A 9-a	
subsidies by zone	EEC area	B 4-a	
Exports by destination: tonnage	Main countries	B 12-m	B 4-a
tonnage	EEC countries	B 3-a	
	Main countries	B 4-a	
of unsweetened milk: tonnage	EEC countries	B 3-a	
Import quotas in lbs	USA	B 4-a	
Imports & exports: tonnage	EEC countries	B 12-a	
by source: tonnage	Main countries	B 12-m	B 4-a
	EEC countries	B 3-a	
of unsweetened milk by source: tonnage	EEC countries	B 3-a	
Net trade: tonnage	EEC countries	B 4-a	
Production: tonnage & consumption	OECD countries	D 14-a	
& trade	EEC countries	E 44-a	
by kind	Main countries	B 4-a	
of skim milk	EEC countries	B 3-a	
whole milk	EEC countries	B 3-a	
tonnage	All countries	A 9-a	U 22-a
	European countries	U 35-a	
	EEC countries	E 28-q	B 1-a
		B 3-a	E 27-a
	Main countries	A 5-a	
	OAS member countries	N 14-a	
	Main countries (total)	B 4-a	

CONDENSED & EVAPORATED MILK,   continued

	Territorial coverage	Title codes
Retail prices in local currency	OAS member countries	N 17-a
Stocks: tonnage	EEC countries	E 44-a
Supply, production, consumption & trade: tonnage	EEC countries	B 1-a
Threshold prices in £ per cwt	EEC countries	B 1-a
Wholesale prices in local currency	OAS member countries	N 17-a
	Main countries	A 9-a

Condenser film   see   MICA PRODUCTS

Condensers   see   BOILERHOUSE PLANT
        ELECTRONIC COMPONENTS

CONDUCTORS, ELECTRICAL

Production in aluminium: tonnage	Japan & W Germany	T 4-a

Conduits   see   TUBES, STEEL

CONFECTIONERY

  see also   CHOCOLATE PRODUCTS

Consumption per capita in oz per wk	UK	P 2-a
Production (incl chocolates): tonnage	All countries	U 22-a
chocolates & confectionery: tonnage	All countries	A 3-q
Ratio of sales of chocolate to sugar confectionery	UK	P 2-a
Sales of chocolate & sugar confectionery: tonnage	UK	P 2-a
Wholesale prices of chocolate – index nos	UK	P 2-a

CONFECTIONERY BY KIND

Consumption expenditure in £m	UK	P 2-a	
Production: tonnage	EEC countries	E 28-q	E 27-a

Confectionery industry   see   BAKING & CONFECTIONERY
              INDUSTRY

Coniferous forests   see   FORESTS, CONIFEROUS
           TIMBER, CONIFEROUS

Conifers   see   TIMBER, CONIFEROUS

Consolidated fund   see   BUDGET ACCOUNTS

Construction   see   BUILDING CONSTRUCTION

Construction board   see   PAPER & PAPERBOARD

CONSTRUCTION EQUIPMENT

  see also   BULLDOZERS
       COMPRESSORS
       CONCRETE MIXERS
       DUMPERS & DUMP TRUCKS
       EXCAVATING MACHINES
       GRADERS & LEVELLERS
       SCRAPERS
       TRENCH DIGGERS

% share of world exports	UK	B 27-a
Exports by value in $m	All countries	U 38-a
Imports by value in $m	All countries	U 38-a
No of current licences: mobile cranes	UK	V 1-q
trench diggers	UK	V 1-q
registrations: trench diggers	N Ireland	V 1-q
Production volume by kind	All countries	U 38-a
World export trade by value in $m	Worldwide	U 38-a

Construction industry   see   BUILDING INDUSTRY
            STEEL FABRICATION INDUSTRY

Construction materials industry   see   BUILDING MATERIALS
                   INDUSTRY

Consumer co-operatives   see   CO-OPERATIVE SOCIETIES,
                 CONSUMER

Consumer credit   see   INSTALMENT CREDIT

Consumer durables   see   DOMESTIC EQUIPMENT

Consumer expenditure   see   HOUSEHOLD BUDGETS
             PRIVATE EXPENDITURE

CONSUMER GOODS

  see also   CAPITAL GOODS
       DISTRIBUTION OUTLETS
       FOOD
       PRODUCER GOODS

	Territorial coverage	Title codes
CONSUMER GOODS, continued		
% change in output	E European countries & USSR	U 16-a
Expenditure (private) in local currency	OAS member countries	N 16-a
Exports by value in $m & % growth rates	Main countries	U 38-a
Imports by value in $m	Asian, Far East & Australasian countries	U 45-a
Imports: coal & fuels by value in UA	AASM countries	E 41-a
ex EEC area by value in UA	AASM countries	E 41-a
foodstuffs by value in UA	AASM countries	E 41-a
ex EEC area by value in UA	AASM countries	E 41-a
household durables by value in UA	AASM countries	E 41-a
ex EEC area by value in UA	AASM countries	E 41-a
household goods by value in UA	AASM countries	E 41-a
ex EEC area by value in UA	AASM countries	E 41-a
(incl food) by value in $m	Asian & Far East area	U 32-q
Production: electronic equipment in £m	UK	B 24-a
of consumer durables - index nos	ECE countries	U 42-m
non-durables - index nos	ECE countries	U 42-m
	Japan & S Korea	U 32-m
Wholesale prices - index nos	OAS member countries	N 17-a
CONSUMER GOODS BY KIND		
% changes in retail sales	E European countries	U 16-a
Exports by NIMEXE classes by value in $m	All countries	E 20-a
SITC classes by value in $m	All countries	U 50-a U 59-a
Imports by NIMEXE classes by value in $m	All countries	E 20-a
SITC classes by value in $m	All countries	U 50-a U 59-a
Retail prices (comparative) in $	EEC countries	Z 3-a

Consumer goods industries   see   ALCOHOLIC DRINKS INDUSTRY
BAKING & CONFECTIONERY INDUSTRY
CARPET MANUFACTURING INDUSTRY
CLOTHING INDUSTRY
DOMESTIC EQUIPMENT INDUSTRY
ELECTRIC SUPPLY INDUSTRY
ENGINEERING INDUSTRY, ELECTRICAL
FOOD, DRINK & TOBACCO INDUSTRIES
FOOD PROCESSING INDUSTRY
FOOTWEAR INDUSTRY
GAS SUPPLY INDUSTRY
KNITTING MILLS
LEATHER GOODS INDUSTRY
PHARMACEUTICAL INDUSTRY
PRINTING & PUBLISHING
PUBLIC UTILITIES
RETAIL TRADE
SERVICE INDUSTRIES
TEXTILE INDUSTRY
TOBACCO INDUSTRY
WATER SUPPLY INDUSTRY
WOODWORKING INDUSTRY

Consumer prices   see   RETAIL PRICES

CONSUMPTION
see also   PRIVATE CONSUMPTION
PUBLIC CONSUMPTION
CONSUMPTION, INDUSTRIAL

	Territorial coverage	Title codes
As component in national accounts in local currency	AASM countries	E 41-a
In $m (at 1960 prices)	Latin American region	U 18-a
% change in demand	W European countries, Canada & USA	U 16-a
% of domestic primary energy sources by kind	Italy	H 4-a
% of petroleum products produced	Latin American countries	U 18-a
Aluminium (primary) - index nos	EEC countries & USA	C 12-a
tonnage	Main countries	B 2-a
Availability of fibres by kind: tonnage	All countries	A 6-a
Aviation fuel: tonnage	Main countries	C 14-a
Bananas: tonnage	Main countries	B 2-a
Bitumen: tonnage	Main countries	C 14-a
Butane & propane: tonnage	Main countries	C 14-a
Calfskins: tonnage	Main countries	B 2-a
Casein: tonnage	Denmark, France, W Germany & UK	B 3-a
Cattle hides: tonnage	Main countries	B 2-a
Cement as % of world production	OECD countries	D 4-a
tonnage	European countries	U 5-a
Cereals in production of animal feed: tonnage	EEC countries	P 5-a
Cigarettes by volume per adult per yr	Main countries	B 16-a
(hand-rolled) in lbs million	Main countries	B 16-a
per adult per yr	Main countries	B 16-a
in lbs million per yr	Main countries	B 16-a
Cigarillos by volume & by wt in lbs million	Main countries	B 16-a
in lbs million per yr	Main countries	B 16-a
Cigars in lbs million per yr	Main countries	B 16-a
Citrus fruits by kind: tonnage	Main countries	B 2-a

	Territorial coverage	Title codes	
CONSUMPTION, continued			
Coal & agglomerates: tonnage	EEC countries	E 14-a	
other solid fuels: tonnage	EEC countries	E 14-a	
by households & small users: tonnage	European countries	U 31-q	
industrial sector: tonnage	France	U 10-a	
Coal, coke, diesel & fuel oil: tonnage	European countries	U 31-q	
for household heating: tonnage	Sweden	U 10-a	
(incl lignite): tonnage	Main countries	N 2-a	
tonnage	Main countries	H 4-a	
Cocoa: tonnage	Denmark, Eire, Norway & UK	E 7-a	
Coffee (roasted) in 60kg bags	Main countries	B 2-a	
in lbs	Worldwide	J 1-a	
tonnage	USA	J 1-a	
Coke: tonnage	Main countries	B 2-a	
Condensed milk: tonnage	EEC countries	E 14-a	
Copper (refined): tonnage	EEC countries	B 3-a	
scrap: tonnage	Main countries	B 2-a	
Cotton by grade in bales	UK & USA	T 4-a	
by origin in bales	Main countries	K 1-m	
Crude petroleum in coal equiv tonnage	Main countries	K 1-m	
	Eire, Norway & UK	E 7-a	
Deliveries (domestic) of cement in bags & as % of production	EEC countries	E 14-a	
in bulk & as % of production	OECD countries	D 4-a	
Diesel oil: tonnage	OECD countries	D 4-a	
Electric power in coal equiv tonnage	Main countries	C 14-a	S 24-a
as % all energy used	EEC countries	E 14-a	
Electricity by agriculture & forestry in kWh	Main countries	H 4-a	
as % of total supply	All countries	C 23-a	
by households by areas in kWh	W European countries	U 16-a	
households in kWh	EEC countries	E 38-a	
in coal equiv tonnage	All countries	C 23-a	
	EEC area	E 7-a	E 14-a
from public supply in kWh	Eire, Norway & UK	E 7-a	
in kWh	All countries	C 23-a	
	EEC countries	E 16-q	E 15-a
	European countries & USA	U 1-a	
for public lighting in kWh	OECD countries	D 8-a	
railways, trams & buses in kWh	All countries	C 23-a	
Energy (all kind) in calorific value	All countries	C 23-a	
per capita in kg of coal equiv	Main countries	H 4-a	
resources: tonnage in coal equiv	OECD countries	R 5-a	
& dependence on foreign supply	EEC countries	E 14-a	
Fish & meat meal in production of animal feed: tonnage	EEC countries	E 26-q	
Fresh apples: tonnage	EEC countries	P 5-a	
peaches: tonnage	OECD countries	D 29-a	
pears: tonnage	OECD countries	D 29-a	
Fuel oil: tonnage	OECD countries	D 29-a	
Fuels (liquid) in coal equiv tonnage	Main countries	C 14-a	
& energy sources by kind	EEC area	E 7-a	
tonnage	Italy	H 4-a	
Glutenfeed in production of animal feed: tonnage	EEC area	E 7-a	
Heat in coal equiv tonnage	EEC countries	P 5-a	
by households & small consumers in coal equiv tonnage	EEC area	E 7-a	
Jute & allied fibres: tonnage	European countries	U 31-q	
bags & sacks: tonnage	Main countries	B 2-a	
Kerosene & jet fuel: tonnage	W European countries	C 22-a	
Lignite & briquettes: tonnage	Main countries	C 14-a	
brown coal: tonnage	EEC countries	E 14-a	
tonnage	EEC countries	E 14-a	
Lubricating oils: tonnage	Denmark	E 7-a	
Man-made fibres by kind: tonnage	Main countries	C 14-a	
Manioc in production of animal feed: tonnage	European countries, Japan & USA	D 27-a	
Manufactured gas in coal equiv tonnage	EEC countries	P 5-a	
in m³	EEC area	E 7-a	
Meat: tonnage & per capita by kind	European countries & USA	U 3-a	
Milk powder & skim: tonnage	EEC countries	E 1-a	
(whole): tonnage	EEC countries	B 3-a	
products in production of animal feed: tonnage	EEC countries	B 3-a	
Milling offals in production of animal feed: tonnage	EEC countries	P 5-a	
Molasses in production of animal feed: tonnage	EEC countries	P 5-a	
Motor spirit: tonnage	EEC countries	P 5-a	
Natural gas as % of all energy consumed	Main countries	C 14-a	S 24-a
in coal equiv tonnage	Main countries	H 4-a	
	UK	E 7-a	
	EEC area	E 7-a	
in m³	Main countries	H 4-a	
in coal equiv tonnage	EEC countries	E 14-a	
liquids by kind: tonnage	Main countries	C 14-a	
No of consumers of domestic gas	European countries & USA	U 3-a	
Oils & fats in production of animal feed: tonnage	EEC countries	P 5-a	
Patent fuels by canal barges: tonnage	Main countries	N 2-a	
households: tonnage	Main countries	N 2-a	
state railways: tonnage	Main countries	N 2-a	
Pepper: tonnage	Main countries	B 2-a	
Petroleum as % of all energy used	Main countries	H 4-a	
products by kind: tonnage	Main countries	C 14-a	
	OECD countries	D 31-a	
	EEC countries	E 14-a	
tonnage	Main countries	H 4-a	

	Territorial coverage	Title codes	
CONSUMPTION, continued			
Pipe tobacco in lbs million	Main countries	B 16-a	
Primary energy sources by kind: tonnage	EEC countries	E 14-a	
Rice as animal feed: tonnage	Main countries	A 19-a	B 14-a
for human food: tonnage	Main countries	A 19-a	B 14-a
for seed: tonnage	Main countries	B 14-a	
tonnage	Main countries	B 2-a	B 8-a
Rubber: tonnage	Main producing countries	C 18-a	
Sisal & hemp: tonnage	Main countries	B 2-a	
Snuff in lbs million	Main countries	B 16-a	
Solid fuels as % of all energy consumed	Main countries	H 4-a	
by kind: tonnage	Main countries	N 2-a	
Steel tubes & fittings: tonnage	Developing countries	U 57-a	
Sugar (non-centrifugal): tonnage	Main countries	A 20-a	
(raw centrifugal): tonnage	All countries	A 20-a	C 25-a
tonnage	International Sugar Agreement countries & EEC area	C 19-m	
	Main countries	B 2-a	
Tea: tonnage	Main countries	B 2-a	C 1-a
Tobacco goods per adult per yr in lbs	Main countries	B 16-a	
products by kind: tonnage	Main countries	B 17-a	
Tobacco: tonnage	W European countries, UK & USA	B 2-a	
Tomatoes: tonnage	OECD countries	D 29-a	
Value of resources used in $m	E European countries & USSR	U 16-a	
Wheat (hard): tonnage	Main countries	C 29-a	
(home-grown) as animal feed: tonnage	UK	P 5-a	
for flour milling: tonnage	UK	P 5-a	
in processing plants: tonnage	UK	P 5-a	
tonnage	Main countries	C 29-a	
Whey powder: tonnage	EEC countries	B 3-a	
Whisky by volume in proof gallons	UK	Z 6-a	
	Worldwide	A 16-a	Z 6-a
Whisky – index nos	UK	Z 6-a	
White spirit: tonnage	Main countries	C 14-a	
Wood pulp by kind: tonnage	OECD countries	D 40-a	
CONSUMPTION, INDUSTRIAL			
Of primary energy products by area	EEC countries	E 38-a	
% growth in machine tools usage by type	EEC countries	B 20-a	
% increase in machine tools requirements projected to 1985	EEC countries	B 20-a	
% of milk supply consumed in processing	Main countries	B 4-a	
Aluminium by building industry: tonnage	Main countries	T 4-a	
engineering industry: tonnage	Main countries	T 4-a	
iron & steel industry: tonnage	Main countries	T 4-a	
metal industries: tonnage	Main countries	T 4-a	
packaging industry: tonnage	Main countries	T 4-a	
Aluminium (primary) by use: tonnage	Main countries	T 4-a	
tonnage	USA	N 1-a	
Ammonia: tonnage	USA	N 1-a	
Anthracite & coal: tonnage	USA	N 1-a	
Antimony for production of ammunition: tonnage	USA	T 4-a	
batteries: tonnage	UK	T 4-a	
bearings: tonnage	UK & USA	T 4-a	
cable coverings: tonnage	USA	T 4-a	
oxides: tonnage	UK	T 4-a	
sulphides: tonnage	UK	T 4-a	
type metal: tonnage	USA	T 4-a	
Antimony metal by use: tonnage	UK & USA	T 4-a	
(primary & secondary): tonnage	USA	N 1-a	
Apples for processing: tonnage	OECD countries	D 29-a	
Artificial fibre for production of yarn: tonnage	World regions	K 5-a	
Asbestos: tonnage	USA	N 1-a	
Barite (ground or crushed): tonnage	USA	N 1-a	
Barley for distilling: tonnage	UK	C 27-a	
food preparations: tonnage	EEC countries	E 44-a	
malting: tonnage	UK	C 27-a	
milling & malting: tonnage	Main countries	B 8-a	
processing: tonnage	World regions	C 27-a	
Bauxite for production of abrasives: tonnage	USA	T 4-a	
alumina: tonnage	USA	T 4-a	
chemicals: tonnage	USA	T 4-a	
refractories: tonnage	USA	T 4-a	
tonnage	USA	N 1-a	
Beryllium: tonnage	USA	N 1-a	
Bismuth for production of alloys: tonnage	USA	T 4-a	
metal additives: tonnage	USA	T 4-a	
pharmaceuticals: tonnage	USA	T 4-a	
Bismuth: tonnage	USA	N 1-a	
Bituminous coal at coking plants: tonnage	USA	N 1-a	
power stations: tonnage	USA	N 1-a	
Blast furnace gas in coal equiv tonnage	EEC countries	E 14-a	
Boring machines for metalwork by value in $m	EEC countries	B 31-a	
Bromide: tonnage	USA	N 1-a	
Brown coal at thermal power plants: tonnage	European countries	U 31-q	
Cadmium for production of alloys: tonnage	UK	T 4-a	
plating anodes: tonnage	UK	T 4-a	
plating salts: tonnage	UK	T 4-a	
solder: tonnage	UK	T 4-a	

	Territorial coverage	Title codes	
CONSUMPTION, INDUSTRIAL continued			
Cadmium: tonnage	USA	N 1-a	
Carbon black: tonnage	USA	N 1-a	
Cellulosic fibres in spindles: tonnage	W European countries	K 2-q	
filament: tonnage	Main countries	D 27-a	
staple fibres: tonnage	Main countries	D 27-a	
Cement: tonnage	USA	N 1-a	
Cereals for food preparations: tonnage	EEC countries	E 3-a	E 44-a
	World regions	C 27-a	
for distilling & malting: tonnage	UK	C 27-a	
Chromium metal (imported): tonnage	USA	N 1-a	
Coal & agglomerates: tonnage	EEC area	E 7-a	
at coke oven plants: tonnage	European countries	U 31-q	
thermal power plants: tonnage	European countries	U 31-q	
by areas: tonnage	EEC countries	E 38-a	
iron & steel industry: tonnage	Main countries	N 2-a	
	UK	T 2-m	
manufactured gas plants: tonnage	Main countries	N 2-a	
patent fuel plants: tonnage	Main countries	N 2-a	
public utilities: tonnage	Main countries	N 2-a	
state railway systems: tonnage	Main countries	N 2-a	
thermal power stations: tonnage	Main countries	N 2-a	
in briquetting plants: tonnage	Main countries	N 2-a	
tonnage	France	U 10-a	
	Main countries	N 2-a	
Cobalt in production of alloy steels in lbs	USA	T 4-a	
carbon steels in lbs	USA	T 4-a	
cast iron in lbs	USA	T 4-a	
catalysts in lbs	USA	T 4-a	
ceramics in lbs	USA	T 4-a	
chemical products: tonnage	USA	T 4-a	
cobalt powder products in lbs	USA	T 4-a	
electric steels: tonnage	USA	T 4-a	
glass decolourisers in lbs	USA	T 4-a	
pigments in lbs	USA	T 4-a	
sintered carbides in lbs	USA	T 4-a	
stainless steels: tonnage	USA	T 4-a	
tool steels in lbs	USA	T 4-a	
welding rods in lbs	USA	T 4-a	
Cobalt: tonnage	USA	N 1-a	
Coffee for production of flavours & extracts: tonnage	USA	J 1-a	
Coke & coke breeze by iron & steel industry: tonnage	UK	T 2-m	
Coke by areas: tonnage	EEC countries	E 38-a	
in patent fuel plants: tonnage	Main countries	N 2-a	
by state railway system: tonnage	Main countries	N 2-a	
thermal power stations: tonnage	Main countries	N 2-a	
(from petroleum refineries): tonnage	Main countries	C 14-a	
Coke-oven gas in coal equiv tonnage	EEC countries	E 14-a	
Coke-oven coke by iron & steel industry: tonnage	European countries	U 31-q	
Copper by brass mills: tonnage	USA	T 4-a	
by wire mills: tonnage	USA	T 4-a	
for production of cathodes: tonnage	USA	T 4-a	
of slabs & billets: tonnage	USA	T 4-a	
wire bars: tonnage	USA	T 4-a	
(refined): tonnage	All countries	T 4-a	
	USA	N 1-a	
Cotton (raw): historical table from 1750: tonnage	Main European countries	Z 1-a	
Crude steel per capita in kg	OECD countries	R 5-a	
Crustaceans & molluscs for meal & oil extracts: tonnage	Main countries	A 5-a	
Deliveries: metal-cutting machine tools	USA	J 2-a	
metal-forming machine tools	USA	J 2-a	
Diatomite: tonnage	USA	N 1-a	
Drilling machines (for metal) by value in $m	EEC countries	B 31-a	
Electricity & heat in coal equiv tonnage	EEC countries	E 7-a	
Electricity by building industry in kWh	EEC countries	E 38-a	
	All countries	C 23-a	
area in coal equiv tonnage	EEC countries	E 38-a	
steel industry in gWh	UK	T 2-m	
chemical industry in kWh	All countries	C 23-a	
	EEC countries	E 38-a	
coal & lignite mining in kWh	All countries	C 23-a	
coal derivatives industry in kWh	All countries	C 23-a	
engineering industry in kWh	All countries	C 23-a	
food, drink & tobacco industry in kWh	EEC countries	E 38-a	
	All countries	C 23-a	
iron & steel industry in kWh	All countries	C 23-a	
leather goods industry in kWh	All countries	C 23-a	
manufacturing industry in kWh	All countries	C 23-a	
metal industries in kWh	EEC countries	E 38-a	
mining & quarrying in kWh	All countries	C 23-a	
	EEC countries	E 38-a	
natural gas industry in kWh	All countries	C 23-a	
non-ferrous metals industry in kWh	All countries	C 23-a	
paper & board industry in kWh	All countries	C 23-a	
	EEC countries	E 38-a	
paper & printing industry in kWh	EEC countries	E 38-a	
petroleum industry & refineries in kWh	All countries	C 23-a	
printing & publishing in kWh	All countries	C 23-a	
public works in kWh	All countries	C 23-a	

	Territorial coverage	Title codes
CONSUMPTION, INDUSTRIAL continued		
Electricity by rubber processing industry in kWh	All countries	C 23-a
shipbuilding & repairing in kWh	All countries	C 23-a
textile & clothing industry in kWh	All countries	C 23-a
textile industry in kWh	EEC countries	E 38-a
transport services in kWh	All countries	C 23-a
wood-working industry in kWh	All countries	C 23-a
Feldspar in ceramics & glass industry: tonnage	USA	N 1-a
Ferrous scrap: tonnage	USA	N 1-a
Fibres by kind in production of belting: tonnage	EEC countries	K 4-a
of tyres: tonnage	EEC countries	K 4-a
for carpets: tonnage	All countries	K 4-a
production of knitted wear: tonnage	Main countries	K 4-a
weaving: tonnage	All countries	K 4-a
Fish for food preparations: tonnage	EEC countries	E 44-a
Fluorspar (acid grade): tonnage	USA	N 1-a
(ceramics grade): tonnage	USA	N 1-a
(metallurgical grade): tonnage	USA	N 1-a
Fruit by kind for non-food purposes: tonnage	OECD countries	D 29-a
for food processing: tonnage	OECD countries	D 29-a
Garnet (as abrasive): tonnage	USA	N 1-a
Gas by areas in m³	EEC countries	E 38-a
by iron & steel industry in therms million	UK	T 2-m
Gear production machines by value in $m	EEC countries	B 31-a
Germanium in lbs	USA	N 1-a
Gold in troy oz	USA	N 1-a
Grinding machines for metal by value in $m	EEC countries	B 31-a
Gypsum (crude): tonnage	USA	N 1-a
Hafnium crystal bars: tonnage	USA	N 1-a
Helium (as high-purity gas) in cu ft	USA	N 1-a
Ilmenite concentrates: tonnage	USA	N 1-a
Iron & steel - index nos	EEC countries	E 30-q
Iron castings: tonnage	UK	B 25-a
Iron ore: tonnage	USA	N 1-a
Kyanite: tonnage	USA	N 1-a
Lathes (automatic) by value in $m	EEC countries	B 31-a
(non-automatic) by value in $m	EEC countries	B 31-a
Lead by end-use: tonnage	UK	C 30-m
tonnage	USA	N 1-a
Lignite & briquettes: tonnage	EEC area	E 7-a
Lignite by areas: tonnage	EEC countries	E 38-a
Lime & quicklime: tonnage	USA	N 1-a
Liquid fuels by iron & steel industry: tonnage	UK	T 2-m
Machine tools by kind by value in $m	EEC countries	B 31-a
value projected to 1985 in $m	EEC countries	B 20-a
Magnesium metal: tonnage	USA	N 1-a
Maize for brewing, malting & distilling: tonnage	UK	B 8-a
distilling: tonnage	UK	C 27-a
food preparations: tonnage	EEC countries	E 44-a
	UK	B 8-a
	World regions	C 27-a
production of starch & breakfast cereals: tonnage	UK	B 8-a
glucose: tonnage	UK	C 27-a
Manganese: tonnage	USA	N 1-a
Manufactured gas in coal equiv tonnage	EEC area	E 7-a
in m³	European countries & USA	U 3-a
Mercury in 76 lb flasks	USA	N 1-a
Metals (basic) by end-use: tonnage	USA	J 3-a
Mica (natural sheet): tonnage	USA	N 1-a
Milk for butter production: tonnage	Main countries	B 4-a
cheese production: tonnage	Main countries	B 12-m B 4-a
condensed milk production: tonnage	Main countries	B 4-a
ice cream production: tonnage	USA	B 4-a
milk powder production: tonnage	Main countries	B 4-a
Milling machines for metal by value in $m	EEC countries	B 31-a
Minerals by kind by end-use: tonnage	USA	J 3-a
Natural gas by industrial sectors in m³	Italy	H 4-a
in coal equiv tonnage	EEC countries	E 7-a
Natural rubber: tonnage	Main countries	C 18-q B 2-a
Nickel by end-use: tonnage	UK	C 30-m
Nitrogen (elemental & fixed): tonnage	USA	N 1-a
Non-cellulosic fibres in spindles: tonnage	W European countries	K 2-q
filaments: tonnage	Main countries	D 27-a
staple fibres: tonnage	Main countries	D 27-a
Oats for food preparations: tonnage	EEC countries	E 44-a
Oxygen: tonnage	USA	N 1-a
Patent fuels by iron & steel industry: tonnage	Main countries	N 2-a
Peaches for processing: tonnage	OECD countries	D 29-a
Pears for processing: tonnage	OECD countries	D 29-a
Perlite: tonnage	USA	N 1-a
Petroleum products by area: tonnage	EEC countries	E 38-a
by kind: tonnage	OECD countries	D 31-a
in coal equiv tonnage	EEC countries	E 7-a E 14-a
Phosphate rock: tonnage	USA	N 1-a
Pig iron: tonnage	USA	N 1-a
Platinum group metals: tonnage	USA	N 1-a
Potatoes for food preparations: tonnage	EEC countries	E 44-a
Presses for metal by value in $m	EEC countries	B 31-a
Primary energy in coal equiv tonnage	EEC area	E 7-a

	Territorial coverage	Title codes
CONSUMPTION, INDUSTRIAL continued		
Primary energy sources by kind: tonnage	EEC countries	E 14-a
Pumice & volcanic cinder: tonnage	USA	N 1-a
Quartz crystal (natural): tonnage	USA	N 1-a
Rare earth minerals: tonnage	USA	N 1-a
Raw cotton in spindles: tonnage	W European countries	K 2-q
yarn spinning process: tonnage	World regions	K 5-a
Raw materials consumed by industry by value in $m	OAS countries	N 14-a
Rhenium metal: tonnage	USA	N 1-a
Rice for food processing: tonnage	EEC countries	E 44-a
	Main countries	A 19-a B 8-a
		B 14-a
	UK	B 8-a
Rubber in production of aircraft tyres: tonnage	France	C 18-a
automotive tyres: tonnage	Main countries	C 18-a
belting: tonnage	France & Japan	C 18-a
cables: tonnage	France & Japan	C 18-a
footwear: tonnage	Canada & Japan	C 18-a
hose & tubing: tonnage	France & Japan	C 18-a
inner tubes for tyres: tonnage	France	C 18-a
rubberised cloth: tonnage	Japan	C 18-a
soles & heels for footwear: tonnage	France	C 18-a
sponge rubber: tonnage	France	C 18-a
sports goods: tonnage	France	C 18-a
surgical products: tonnage	France	C 18-a
Rutile concentrates: tonnage	USA	N 1-a
Rye for food processing: tonnage	EEC countries	E 44-a
	Main countries	B 8-a
Scandium for lamp production: tonnage	USA	N 1-a
Selenium: tonnage	USA	N 1-a
Silver (incl art work) in million oz	Main countries	T 4-a
for coinage in million oz	USA	N 1-a
in million oz	USA	N 1-a
Soda ash: tonnage	USA	N 1-a
Sodium sulphate: tonnage	USA	N 1-a
Steel castings: tonnage	UK	B 25-a
Strontium minerals: tonnage	USA	N 1-a
Sugar beet for alcohol distillation: tonnage	EEC countries	E 44-a
for sugar production: tonnage	EEC countries	E 44-a
Synthetic fibre for production of yarn: tonnage	World regions	K 5-a
rubber: tonnage	Main countries	C 18-q
Tantalum: tonnage	USA	N 1-a
Tellurium in lbs	USA	N 1-a
Thorium: tonnage	USA	N 1-a
Tin by end-use: tonnage	UK	C 30-m
(primary & secondary): tonnage	USA	N 1-a
Titanium minerals: tonnage	USA	N 1-a
Tomatoes for processing: tonnage	OECD countries	D 36-a
Tungsten metal: tonnage	USA	N 1-a
Vanadium products in lbs	USA	N 1-a
Wheat for food processing: tonnage	EEC countries	E 44-a
	UK	B 8-a
	World regions	C 27-a
for malting: tonnage	UK	C 27-a
for starch & glucose production: tonnage	UK	C 27-a
Wine for further processing: tonnage	EEC countries	E 44-a
Wool at carding stage: tonnage	Main countries	B 10-a
for production of clothing: tonnage	Main countries	K 6-a
Zinc slabs: tonnage	USA	N 1-a
slabs by end-use: tonnage	UK	C 30-m
CONSUMPTION BY PURPOSE		
Barley as animal feed: tonnage	UK	B 8-a
for seed: tonnage	UK	B 8-a
human food: tonnage	UK	B 8-a
industrial usage: tonnage	UK	B 8-a
Maize as animal feed: tonnage	UK	B 8-a
for human food: tonnage	UK	B 8-a
industrial usage: tonnage	UK	B 8-a
Oats as animal feed: tonnage	UK	B 8-a
for seed: tonnage	UK	B 8-a
human food: tonnage	UK	B 8-a
Rice for human food: tonnage	UK	B 8-a
industrial usage: tonnage	UK	B 8-a
Rye as animal feed: tonnage	UK	B 8-a
for human food: tonnage	UK	B 8-a
Wheat as animal feed: tonnage	UK	B 8-a
for seed: tonnage	UK	B 8-a
human food: tonnage	UK	B 8-a
industrial usage: tonnage	UK	B 8-a

Consumption goods   see   CONSUMER GOODS

CONSUMPTION PER CAPITA		
% calorie intake per day from meat	ECE countries	U 15-a
Animal fats & fish oils in kg per yr	EEC countries	E 44-a
	E European countries & USSR	U 16-a

CONSUMPTION PER CAPITA, continued

Item	Territorial coverage	Title codes	
Apples (fresh) in kg per yr	EEC countries	U 20-a	
	OECD countries	D 33-a	
	Main European countries & Australia	D 38-a	
(processed) in kg per yr	OECD countries	D 33-a	
	Australia	D 38-a	
Artificial fibres in kg per yr	Main countries	A 6-a	
Bacon & ham in lbs per yr	UK	B 12-a	
in lbs per year	UK	B 11-a	
Barley in kg per yr	EEC countries	B 1-a	
	OECD countries	D 14-a	
Beef & veal in kg per yr	OECD countries	D 1-a	
	EEC countries	B 1-a	
	European countries	U 36-a	
	Main countries	B 11-a	
in lbs per yr	UK	B 12-a	
Beef in kg per yr	EEC countries	E 1-a	
	OECD countries	D 14-a	
Beer in kg per yr	OECD countries	D 1-a	D 14-a
litres per yr	E European countries & USSR	U 16-a	
Bread grains (as flour) in kg per yr	OECD countries	D 1-a	
in kg per yr	OECD countries	D 14-a	
Bread products in kg per yr	USSR	C 27-a	
Butter in kg per yr	OECD countries	D 1-a	D 14-a
	European countries	U 35-a	
	E European countries & USSR	U 16-a	
	EEC countries	B 1-a	B 3-a
	Main countries	B 19-a	
	UK	B 12-a	B 19-a
Calorie intake per day (average)	ECE countries	U 15-a	
	OECD countries	D 1-a	
Canned apricots in kg per yr	Main countries	A 7-a	
fish in kg per yr	OECD countries	D 14-a	
meat in lbs per yr	Main countries	B 11-a	
	UK	B 12-a	
peaches in kg per yr	Main countries	A 7-a	
pineapples in kg per yr	Main countries	A 8-a	
soups in kg per yr	OECD countries	D 14-a	
tomato products in kg per yr	Main countries	A 7-a	
Carcase meat in lbs per yr	Main countries	B 11-a	
Cattle hides & calf skins in kg per yr	World regions	A 18-a	
Cement in kg per yr	ECE countries	U 15-a	
	European countries	U 5-a	
	OECD countries	D 4-a	
Cereal products in kg per yr	E European countries & USSR	U 16-a	
Cereals by income levels – index nos	USA	C 27-a	
kind in kg per yr	EEC countries	E 44-a	
(excl rice) as flour in kg per yr	OECD countries	D 1-a	
in kg per yr	OECD countries	D 14-a	
	W European countries	P 5-a	
	E European countries & USSR	U 16-a	
Cheese in kg per yr	EEC countries	B 1-a	B 3-a
	European countries	U 35-a	
	OECD countries	D 1-a	
	Main countries	B 4-a	
lbs per yr	UK	B 12-a	
Chemical fibres in kg per yr	Main countries	U 26-a	
products by value in $ per yr	European countries, Japan & USA	U 25-a	
	E European countries	U 25-a	
Cigarettes in lbs per yr	Main countries	B 16-a	
(hand-rolled) by volume per yr	Main countries	B 16-a	
Citrus fruits in kg per yr	EEC countries	B 1-a	E 44-a
		U 20-a	
	Spain & UK	U 20-a	
Cocoa in kg per yr	OECD countries	D 1-a	D 14-a
lbs per yr	Main countries	B 13-a	
Coffee beans in lbs per yr	USA	J 1-a	
Coffee by population 10 yrs of age & over in lbs per yr	USA	J 1-a	
in decagrams per yr	USSR	U 16-a	
lbs per yr	Main countries	B 13-a	
	All countries	U 43-a	
Condensed milk in kg per yr	EEC countries	B 1-a	B 3-a
		E 44-a	
in lbs per yr	Main countries	B 4-a	
(sweetened) in lbs per yr	UK	B 12-a	
(unsweetened) in lbs per yr	UK	B 12-a	
Confectionery made of chocolate in oz per wk	UK	P 2-a	
Cotton (raw) in lbs per yr	Worldwide	B 10-a	
kg per yr	Main countries	A 1-a	A 6-a
		U 26-a	
Cotton fabrics in m per yr	E European countries & USSR	U 16-a	
Cream (40% fat content) in lbs per yr	UK	B 12-a	
whole milk equiv in kg per yr	EEC countries	B 3-a	
	Main countries	B 4-a	
Crude steel in kg per yr	EEC countries, UK & USA	E 29-a	
	All countries	U 43-a	
	Arab countries	T 4-a	
	Main countries	T 4-a	U 49-a
	OECD countries	D 22-a	R 5-a

	Territorial coverage	Title codes	
CONSUMPTION PER CAPITA, continued			
Crustaceans & molluscs in kg per yr	OECD countries	D 14-a	
Dairy products by income levels in lbs per yr	USA	C 27-a	
by kind in kg per yr	OECD countries	D 14-a	
Dried fruit in kg per yr	OECD countries	D 14-a	
herrings in kg per yr	OECD countries	D 14-a	
& smoked fish in kg per yr	OECD countries	D 14-a	
Durable goods per 1000 population per yr	E European countries	U 16-a	
Edible offal in kg per yr	OECD countries	D 14-a	
in lbs per yr	Main countries	B 11-a	
	UK	B 12-a	
oils & fats in lbs per yr	UK	B 12-a	B 19-a
Eggs by volume per yr (estim)	Main countries	B 4-a	
by volume per yr	E European countries & USSR	U 16-a	
in kg per yr	EEC countries	B 1-a	E 44-a
	OECD countries	D 14-a	
	W European countries	P 5-a	
Energy in kg coal equiv per yr	Worldwide	C 14-a	
	OECD countries	R 5-a	
	Developing world regions	U 23-a	
in kg oil equiv per yr	World regions	U 18-a	
Farm products - index nos	World regions	A 11-a	
Fat content of butter in kg	OECD countries	D 1-a	
Fats & oils in kg per yr	OECD countries	D 1-a	
(incl butter) in kg per yr	W European countries	P 5-a	
Fertilisers in kg per yr	All countries	A 2-a	
Fibreboard in kg per yr	Main countries	A 25-a	
Fish & fish products in kg per yr	E European countries	U 16-a	
Fish in kg per yr	EEC countries	E 44-a	
by kind: fresh dried & canned in kg per yr	OECD countries	D 14-a	
roes in kg per yr	OECD countries	D 14-a	
Flax in kg per yr	Main countries	A 6-a	
Food by income levels - index nos	USA	C 27-a	
products & beverages in kg per yr	E European countries	U 16-a	
& grains by kind in kg per yr	OECD countries	D 14-a	
- index nos	World regions	A 11-a	
Footwear in pairs per yr	E European countries & USSR	U 16-a	
of leather in pairs per yr	OECD countries	D 18-a	
plastic materials in pairs per yr	OECD countries	D 18-a	
textile materials in pairs per yr	OECD countries	D 18-a	
Fresh fruit by income levels in lbs per yr	USA	C 27-a	
by kind in lbs per yr	UK	B 6-a	
in kg per yr	OECD countries	D 1-a	D 14-a
in kg	E European countries & USSR	U 16-a	
	EEC countries	E 44-a	U 20-a
	Main E European countries	U 20-a	
	Switzerland, Spain & UK	U 20-a	
Fruit (fresh & processed) in kg per yr	EEC countries	U 20-a	
in lbs per yr	UK	B 5-a	
juices (citrus) in kg per yr	Main countries	A 7-a	
in kg per yr	OECD countries	D 14-a	
preparations in kg per yr	UK	U 20-a	
Glucose in kg per yr	OECD countries	D 14-a	
Goat meat in kg per yr	OECD countries	D 14-a	
Grapes (for table) in kg per yr	EEC countries	U 20-a	
Groundnuts in kg per yr	OECD countries	D 14-a	
Honey in kg per yr	OECD countries	D 14-a	
Horse meat in kg per yr	OECD countries	D 14-a	
Ice cream in kg per yr	EEC countries	B 3-a	
	OECD countries	D 14-a	
Instant coffee in lbs per yr	USA	J 1-a	
oz per wk	UK	B 18-a	
Jowar & gram by income groups by value in Rs per mth	India	C 27-a	
Lamb & mutton in kg per yr	EEC countries	B 1-a	E 1-a
		E 44-a	
	OECD countries	D 14-a	
	UK	B 12-a	
	Main countries	B 11-a	
Lard & cooking fats in lbs per yr	UK	B 12-a	B 19-a
in kg per yr	OECD countries	D 14-a	
Maize in kg per yr	EEC countries	B 1-a	
	OECD countries	D 14-a	
Man-made fibres (excl rayon) in lbs per yr	Worldwide	B 10-a	
in kg per yr	Main countries	A 6-a	
Margarine in kg per yr	OECD countries	D 1-a	
	European countries	U 35-a	
	EEC countries	B 1-a	E 44-a
	OECD countries	D 14-a	
	Main countries	B 4-a	B 19-a
lbs per yr	UK	B 12-a	B 19-a
Meat & edible offal in kg per yr	OECD countries	D 1-a	
Meat by income levels - index nos	USA	C 27-a	
kind in kg per yr	EEC countries	E 1-a	
lbs per yr	UK	B 12-a	
in kg per yr	E European countries & USSR	U 16-a	
	W European countries	P 5-a	
Meat products in kg per yr	E European countries & USSR	U 16-a	

	Territorial coverage	Title codes	
CONSUMPTION PER CAPITA, continued			
Milk (fermented) & yogurt in kg per yr	EEC countries	B 3-a	
(fresh) in gallons per yr	Main countries	B 4-a	
kg per yr	EEC countries	B 3-a	
	OECD countries	D 14-a	
	W European countries	P 5-a	
litres per yr	E European countries & USSR	U 16-a	
(fresh incl cream) in gallons per yr	USA	B 4-a	
powder in kg per yr	EEC countries	E 44-a	
	OECD countries	D 14-a	
lbs per yr	UK	B 12-a	
(skimmed) in kg per yr	EEC countries	B 1-a	B 3-a
(whole) in kg per yr	EEC countries	B 3-a	
(skimmed & buttermilk) in gallons per yr	Main countries	B 4-a	
in kg per yr	EEC countries	B 3-a	
(skimmed & dried) in lbs per yr	UK	B 12-a	
(skimmed) in kg per yr	OECD countries	D 14-a	
Natural fibres in kg per yr	Main countries	A 6-a	
Natural rubber in lbs per yr	Main countries	B 13-a	
	All countries	U 43-a	
Newsprint in kg per yr	All countries	U 62-a	
	World economic areas	D 32-a	
lbs per yr	USA	J 7-a	
Oats in kg per yr	EEC countries	B 1-a	
	OECD countries	D 14-a	
Olive oil in kg per yr	OECD countries	D 14-a	
Paints & varnishes in kg per yr	OECD countries	D 5-a	
Paper & board (cultural) in kg per yr	Main countries	D 32-a	
(industrial) in kg per yr	Main countries	D 32-a	
paperboard in lbs per yr	USA	J 7-a	
Particle board in m³ per yr	Main countries	A 25-a	
Peaches (fresh) in kg per yr	EEC countries	U 20-a	
	OECD countries	D 35-a	
(processed) in kg per yr	OECD countries	D 35-a	
Pears (fresh) in kg per yr	EEC countries	U 20-a	
	OECD countries	D 34-a	
(processed) in kg per yr	OECD countries	D 34-a	
Peas & beans by income levels in lbs per yr	USA	C 27-a	
Pig-meat in kg per yr	OECD countries	D 1-a	
lbs per yr	Main countries	B 11-a	
Plastics in kg per yr	European countries, Japan & USA	U 26-a	
	OECD countries	D 5-a	
Plywood & blockboard in m³ per yr	All countries	A 25-a	
Polymerisation products in kg per yr	OECD countries	D 5-a	
Pork in kg per yr	European countries & USSR	U 36-a	
	EEC countries	B 1-a	E 1-a
		E 44-a	
	OECD countries	D 14-a	
lbs per yr	UK	B 11-a	B 12-a
Potato flour in kg per yr	OECD countries	D 14-a	
Potatoes in kg per yr	OECD countries	D 1-a	D 14-a
	E European countries & USSR	U 16-a	
	EEC countries	B 1-a	E 44-a
	W European countries	P 5-a	
	UK	B 12-a	
Poultry & game in lbs per yr	OECD countries	D 1-a	
meat in kg per yr	European countries	U 36-a	
	EEC countries	B 1-a	
	OECD countries	D 14-a	
lbs per yr	Main countries	B 11-a	B 12-a
	UK	B 12-a	
Primary energy in coal equiv per yr	Norway, Eire & UK	E 7-a	
Printing & writing paper in kg per yr	All countries	U 62-a	
Protein of animal origin in grammes per day	OECD countries	D 1-a	
in grammes per day	ECE countries	U 15-a	
	OECD countries	D 1-a	
of vegetable origin in grammes per day	OECD countries	D 1-a	
Rabbit meat in kg per yr	OECD countries	D 14-a	
Rayon & acetate fibres in lbs per yr	Worldwide	B 10-a	
Ready-made clothing in pieces per yr	E European countries	U 16-a	
Rice (husked) in kg per yr	OECD countries	D 1-a	D 14-a
	Main countries	A 19-a	
in kg per yr	EEC countries	B 1-a	
by income levels by value in Rs per mth	India	C 27-a	
Rye in kg per yr	EEC countries	B 1-a	
	OECD countries	D 14-a	
Sausages in kg per yr	W Germany	U 36-a	
Sawn hardwood in m³ per yr	Main countries	A 25-a	
softwood in m³ per yr	Main countries	A 24-a	
Sheepskins & goatskins in kg per yr	World regions	A 18-a	
Silk (raw) in kg per yr	Main countries	A 6-a	
Slippers & house shoes in pairs per yr	OECD countries	D 18-a	
Soybeans in kg per yr	OECD countries	D 14-a	
Steel products - index nos	Main countries	U 57-a	
Sugar in kg per yr	E European countries & USSR	U 16-a	
	EEC countries	E 44-a	
lbs per yr	Main countries	B 13-a	

	Territorial coverage	Title codes	
CONSUMPTION PER CAPITA, continued			
Sugar (non-centrifugal) in kg per yr	Main countries	A 20-a	
(raw centrifugal) in kg per yr	Main countries	A 20-a	F 25-a
(refined) in kg per yr	All countries	U 43-a	
	OECD countries	D 1-a	
	EEC countries	E 44-a	
	W European countries	P 5-a	
Synthetic fibres in kg per yr	Main countries	A 6-a	
Synthetic rubber in lbs per yr	Main countries	B 13-a	
Syrup in kg per yr	All countries	U 43-a	
Tea in decagrams per yr	OECD countries	D 14-a	
	E European countries & USSR	U 16-a	
in kg per yr	Main countries	C 1-a	U 43-a
in lbs per yr	Main countries	B 13-a	
Textile fibres by kind in kg per yr	Main countries	U 26-a	
Textiles by kind in m per yr	E European countries & USSR	U 16-a	
Tomato juice in kg per yr	Canada & USA	A 7-a	
	USA	D 36-a	
Tomato ketchup in kg per yr	USA	D 36-a	
Tomato pulp & puree in kg per yr	USA	D 36-a	
Tomato sauce & paste in kg per yr	USA	D 36-a	
Tomatoes (fresh) in kg per yr	EEC countries	U 20-a	
	Main countries	A 7-a	
	UK	U 20-a	
	USA	D 36-a	
(processed) in kg per yr	Main countries	A 7-a	
Veal in kg per yr	OECD countries	D 14-a	
Vegetable & animal oils & fats in kg per yr	OECD countries	D 14-a	
	E European countries	U 16-a	
Vegetable oils & fats in kg per yr	EEC countries	B 1-a	
Vegetables in kg per yr	Switzerland & UK	U 20-a	
	W European countries	P 5-a	
by income levels in lbs per yr	USA	C 27-a	
(canned) in kg per yr	OECD countries	D 14-a	
	Switzerland & UK	U 20-a	
(fresh) in kg per yr	E European countries & USSR	U 16-a	
	EEC countries	B 1-a	E 44-a
	Main E European countries	U 20-a	
	OECD countries	D 14-a	
	Spain, Switzerland & UK	U 20-a	
(fresh & canned) in kg per yr	EEC countries	U 20-a	
	OECD countries	D 1-a	
(frozen) in kg per yr	OECD countries	D 14-a	
Vegetables, fruit & meat by kind in kg per yr	OECD countries	D 14-a	
Water (from public supply) in litres per yr	Main countries	W 2-a	
Wheat (as human food) in kg per yr	Main countries	C 27-a	
	World regions	C 27-a	
Wheat flour in lbs per yr	Main countries	B 8-a	
Wheat in kg per yr	EEC countries	B 1-a	E 44-a
	OECD countries	D 14-a	
by income levels by value in Rs per mth	India	C 27-a	
Wine in kg per yr	OECD countries	D 1-a	
in litres per yr	E European countries & USSR	U 16-a	
	EEC countries	B 1-a	E 44-a
Wool in kg per yr	Main countries	A 6-a	U 26-a
in lbs per yr	Worldwide	B 10-a	
Woollen fabrics in m per yr	E European countries & USSR	U 16-a	

Contagious diseases   see   DISEASES, CONTAGIOUS

CONTAINER SHIPS

Capacity (in 20 ft equiv) by route	Worldwide	U 37-a
Construction: tonnage completed	World regions	U 37-a
Deliveries of new vessels	Netherlands	S 16-a
No & gross tonnage afloat	Countries of registration	S 16-a
No built & size in T.E.U.	Countries of build	S 16-a
built by each manufacturer & size in T.E.U.	Worldwide	S 16-a
of operators & no of ships: tonnage by route	Worldwide	U 37-a
of sailings per wk by route & yr of inauguration	Worldwide	U 37-a
& tonnage afloat by flag	Worldwide	S 2-a
Prices ex shipyards by tonnage sizes in £m	Worldwide	S 16-a2
Tonnage afloat & % change	Worldwide	D 28-a
as % of tonnage of all vessels afloat	Worldwide	U 37-a

CONTAINERS

see also   TANKS & VATS

Production volume over 1 m³ in size	All countries	U 22-a

CONTAINERS, RAIL

No in use by ownership (state-owned & private)	European countries	U 8-a
in use	ECE countries	U 15-a
of containers forwarded by size	European countries	U 8-a
owned or used by railways	European countries	U 8-a
Production of aluminium dry freight containers by size	UK	V 1-a
of aluminium refrigerated containers by size	UK	V 1-a
of steel dry freight by size	UK	V 1-a
of steel refrigerated by size	UK	V 1-a
Tonnage of goods carried by rail in containers	European countries	U 8-a

	Territorial coverage	Title codes

Contingency funds   see   DEVELOPMENT AID

Continuous steel casting plants   see   STEEL FOUNDRIES

CONTRACTOR'S PLANT & EQUIPMENT
    see also   FORK LIFT TRUCKS
                MECHANICAL HANDLING EQUIPMENT

Exports by value in $m	OECD countries	D 9-a

Contractors, farm   see   AGRICULTURAL CONTRACTORS
                             FARM SERVICES

CONTROL INSTRUMENTATION, ELECTRONIC

Deliveries by kind by value in £m	UK	C 24-a

CONTROL INSTRUMENTATION, NUCLEONIC
    see also   NUCLEAR REACTOR CONTROL DEVICES
                  RADIATION DETECTION EQUIPMENT

Deliveries by kind by value in £m	UK	C 24-a

CONTROL INSTRUMENTATION

Deliveries of machine tool controls by value in £	UK	C 24-a
non-electrical equipment by value in £	UK	C 24-a
process control systems by value in £	UK	C 24-a
Demand domestic by value in £	UK	C 24-a
Usage of mercury in production of instrumentation in flasks	USA	T 4-a

Controlled market rates   see   EXCHANGE RATES

CONVALESCENT HOMES

No of beds available (incl in sanatoria)	OECD countries	D 47-a

CONVENIENCE FOODS

% of households using frozen fish or meat	W European countries	Z 3
frozen vegetables in packs	W European countries	Z 3
instant potatoes	W European countries	Z 3
soup (packaged or cubes)	W European countries	Z 3
soup (tinned)	W European countries	Z 3

Converters, oxygen-blown   see   CRUDE STEEL

Convertible stocks   see   STOCKS, CONVERTIBLE

CONVEYOR BELTS, RUBBER

Production: tonnage	EEC countries	E 28-q	E 27-a

Cookers & stoves   see   OVENS, DOMESTIC

COOKING FATS
    see also   LARD
                VEGETABLE OILS

Production & consumption by kind per capita in kg	OECD countries	D 14-a
Production: compound fats: tonnage	Main countries	A 4-a
shortening: tonnage	Main countries	B 19-a
Usage of coconut oil in production of cooking fats: tonnage	USA	B 19-a
cottonseed oil in production of cooking fats: tonnage	USA	B 19-a
soybean oil in production of cooking fats: tonnage	USA	B 19-a
cooking oils: tonnage	USA	B 19-a
vegetable oils by kind as ingredients in production of cooking fats: tonnage	Main countries	A 4-a

Cooking oil   see   CORN OIL
                    VEGETABLE OILS

Cooling equipment, industrial   see   HEATING & COOLING
                                           EQUIPMENT, INDUSTRIAL

COPPER

% contribution to export earnings	Uganda & Zambia	E 45-a	
% of EEC area production of refined copper	EEC countries	R 5-a	
Consumption in brass mills: tonnage	USA	C 12-a	T 4-a
copper foundries: tonnage	USA	C 12-a	
copper powder plants: tonnage	USA	C 12-a	
production of bars & sections: tonnage	UK	J 6-a	
brass castings: tonnage	European countries	C 12-a	
brass products: tonnage	European countries	C 12-a	
bronze castings: tonnage	European countries	C 12-a	
castings: tonnage	OECD countries	D 21-a	
copper ingots: tonnage	USA	C 12-a	
copper salts: tonnage	OECD countries	D 21-a	
	W Germany	C 12-a	
copper sulphate: tonnage	UK	J 6-a	
semi-finished products: tonnage	European countries	C 12-a	
	OECD countries	D 21-a	

	Territorial coverage	Title codes	
COPPER, continued			
Consumption in production of sheets, plate & strips: tonnage	UK	J 6-a	
tubes: tonnage	UK	J 6-a	
wire rods: tonnage	UK	J 6-a	
Consumption in wire mills: tonnage	USA	C 12-a	T 4-a
Consumption of primary metal: tonnage	All countries	H 2-a	
Consumption of refined copper & copper scrap: tonnage	UK	C 30-m	
refined copper for semis production: tonnage	UK	C 30-m	
tonnage: historical table	World regions	C 12-a	
tonnage	All countries	C 30-m	
	EEC countries	C 12-a	
	Main countries	B 2-a	
	OAS member countries	N 17-a	
	OECD countries	D 21-q	
	USA	N 1-a	
	World regions	C 12-a	
	Brazil, Chile, Mexico & Peru	U 18-a	
Disposals ex US government stockpile: tonnage	USA	U 11-a	
Export prices - index nos (weighted average main sources)	Worldwide	U 29-q	
	S American countries	U 40-q	
Exports by destination of refined copper: tonnage	Main countries	T 4-a	
refined & unrefined copper: tonnage	Main countries	H 2-a	
by value in $m	Chile, Congo Rep, Peru & Zambia	U 11-a	
of copper concentrates by value in $	Philippines	U 32-m	
tonnage	Asian & Far East areas	U 32-q	
	Philippines	U 32-m	
refined copper by value in $m	Developing countries	U 11-a	
tonnage	All countries	C 30-m	
unwrought metal: tonnage	Canada, Chile, Congo Rep, & USA	B 2-a	
tonnage & by value in $m	Uganda, Zambia & Zaire	E 45-a	
Import prices ex USA shipped to European area in cents per lb cif	European countries	C 12-m	
Imports & exports by source or destination: tonnage	Main countries	B 15-a	
Imports by kind: tonnage	USA	J 6-a	
source of refined copper: tonnage	Main countries	T 4-a	
of refined & unrefined copper: tonnage	Main countries	H 2-a	
of refined copper: tonnage	Main countries	C 30-m	
Plant capacity for copper refining by company: tonnage	Worldwide	C 12-a	
Producer prices for export in cents per lb fob	USA	C 12-m	
Production of electrolytic copper & compounds by usage: tonnage	Main countries	H 2-a	
recovered from scrap material: tonnage	USA	H 2-a	
at mines extracted from domestic ores: tonnage	Main countries	J 6-a	
at smelter plants: tonnage	All countries	C 30-m	J 6-a
based on metal content of ore: tonnage	All countries	C 30-m	U 27-m
		B 15-a	C 4-a
		C 12-a	H 2-a
		R 5-a	U 22-a
		U 43-a	
	Latin American countries	J 5-a	U 40-a
	Main countries	B 2-a	E 3-a
	All countries	U 22-a	
of blister & unrefined copper: tonnage	Worldwide	T 4-a	
by individual mining companies: tonnage	Japan & S Korea	U 53-a	
from tungsten-copper ore: tonnage	USA	J 6-a	
historical table from 1897: tonnage	USA	N 1-a	
primary & secondary copper: tonnage	World regions	C 12-a	
refined copper: historical table: tonnage	All countries	C 30-m	
refined copper: tonnage	EEC countries	C 12-a	
	Main countries	E 3-a	
	OECD countries	D 21-q	R 5-a
	World regions	C 12-a	
	Brazil, Chile, Mexico & Peru	U 18-a	
refined & unwrought copper: tonnage	All countries	U 22-a	
semi-manufactured copper products: tonnage	EEC countries	E 26-m	E 28-q
		E 27-a	
tonnage	Bolivia, Chile, Mexico & Peru	U 18-a	
	OAS member countries	N 14-a	
Refining capacity by company: tonnage per yr	All countries	J 6-a	
Smelter production from ore & concentrates: tonnage	All countries	U 27-m	U 43-a
Smelter production, trade & changes in stocks: tonnage	Main countries	H 2-a	
Stocks of blister copper: tonnage	Main countries	C 30-m	
copper concentrates: tonnage	Main countries	C 30-m	
refined copper at producers' plant: tonnage	USA	N 1-a	
tonnage	Main countries	C 30-m	C 12-a
	USA	T 4-a	
Wholesale price of refined copper in cents per lb	USA	N 1-a	
electrolytic copper in local currency	Belgium, Canada & UK	U 27-m	
home-refined copper on New York market in cents per lb	USA	J 6-m	
ingot bars & wire bars in $ per ton	USA	U 27-m	
wire bars in lire per kg	Italy	C 12-m	
Wholesale prices on London Metal Exchange in £ per ton	UK	J 6-a	
World consumption of metallic copper: tonnage: historical table	Worldwide	C 12-a	
refined copper: tonnage	Worldwide	C 30-a	
	Main countries	J 6-a	U 11-a
	All countries	T 4-a	
World export trade by value in $bn	Worldwide	M 4-a	
World market prices in £ per ton (average): historical table from 1875		T 4-a	
cents per lb (in London & New York)	UK & USA	U 18-a	
World market prices - index nos		M 4-a	

	Territorial coverage	Title codes
COPPER, continued		
World production of smeltered & refined copper: tonnage	Worldwide	C 30-a
refined metal: tonnage	All countries	C 12-a N 4-a
		T 4-a

COPPER, BLISTER

	Territorial coverage	Title codes
Exports by destination: tonnage	Main countries	T 4-a
	Australia	H 2-a
(incl refined copper) by destination: tonnage	OECD countries	D 21-q
tonnage	All countries	C 30-m
	Main countries	C 12-a
	Zambia	B 2-a
total & to EEC area: tonnage & value in UA	Zaire	E 41-a
Imports by source (incl refined copper): tonnage	OECD countries	D 21-q
tonnage	Main countries	H 2-a T 4-a
tonnage	Main countries	C 30-m C 12-a
Imports of unrefined copper (in pigs): tonnage	UK	J 6-a
Production: tonnage	USA	J 6-a
	Brazil, Chile, Mexico & Peru	U 18-a
Stocks at smelter plants & refineries: tonnage	USA	J 6-a
in process of refining: tonnage	USA	J 6-a
transit to refineries: tonnage	USA	J 6-a
tonnage	Main countries	C 30-m C 12-a
World production: tonnage	All countries	C 12-a T 4-a

COPPER, ELECTROLYTIC

	Territorial coverage	Title codes
Export prices in A$ per ton fob	Australia	T 4-w
in cents per lb fob	USA	T 4-m
Exports by destination: tonnage	Chile, UK & Zaire	H 2-a
(incl fire-refined copper): tonnage	UK	J 6-a
	Main countries	H 2-a
tonnage	Zambia	B 2-a
Imports by source: tonnage	UK	T 4-a
(incl fire-refined copper): tonnage	Main countries	H 2-a
tonnage	UK	J 6-a
Price quotations for wire bars & cathodes in £	UK	H 2-m
Producer prices for copper bars per ton	W Germany, UK & USA	H 2-m
Production: refined electrolytic metal: tonnage	All countries	U 27-m U 43-a
Re-exports: tonnage	UK	J 6-a
Stocks at London Metal Exchange warehouses: tonnage	UK	C 12-a J 6-a
Wholesale prices in FrB per ton	Belgium	T 4-w
in cents per lb	Canada	J 6-m
World prices in £ per ton		E 41-a

COPPER, REFINED

	Territorial coverage	Title codes
Consumption by kind of usage: tonnage	Main countries	H 2-a
primary & secondary copper: tonnage	All countries	J 6-a
tonnage	Japan	H 2-a
Deliveries to fabricators (home & export): tonnage	USA	J 6-m
Exports by destination: tonnage	Main countries	H 2-a
	USA	J 6-a
(in ingot or bar form): tonnage	USA	J 6-a
Imports by source: tonnage	Main countries	H 2-a
of fire-refined copper: tonnage	UK	J 6-a
Production: tonnage from scrap	USA	J 6-a
tonnage	All countries	J 6-a R 5-a
	USA	J 6-m
Stocks of fire-refined copper at London Metal Exchange		
warehouses: tonnage	UK	J 6-a
Stocks held by industry (end-period): tonnage	USA	J 6-m
other users (end-period): tonnage	USA	J 6-m

COPPER, SEMI-FINISHED

    see also   BARS RODS SECTIONS, COPPER
                  PLATES SHEETS, COPPER

	Territorial coverage	Title codes
World production of copper semi-manufactured products: tonnage		C 30-m

COPPER, UNREFINED

	Territorial coverage	Title codes
Exports by destination: tonnage	Main countries	H 2-a
Imports by source: tonnage	Main countries	H 2-a
Production: tonnage of primary & secondary metal	USA	J 6-m
World consumption: tonnage	Main countries	J 6-a

Copper alloy castings   see   CASTINGS, COPPER ALLOY

Copper alloy ingots   see   INGOTS, COPPER ALLOY

COPPER ALLOY PRODUCTS, SEMI-FINISHED

	Territorial coverage	Title codes
Exports by destination: tonnage	Main countries	T 4-a
tonnage	Main countries	C 30-m
Imports by source: tonnage	Main countries	T 4-a
tonnage	Main countries	C 30-m
Production: tonnage	Main countries	C 30-m T 4-a
Wholesale prices by kind	Main countries	T 4-w

	Territorial coverage	Title codes

COPPER ALLOY SCRAP
    see also BRASS SCRAP
                  GUNMETAL SCRAP

Wholesale prices of brass scrap by kind	Main countries	T 4-w

COPPER ALLOYS
    see also BRASS
                  BRAZING METALS
                  BRONZE
                  COPPER ALLOY PRODUCTS, SEMI-FINISHED
                  GILDING METAL
                  GUNMETAL
                  INGOTS, BERYLLIUM-COPPER ALLOY
                  INGOTS, COPPER ALLOY
                  INGOTS, CUPRO-NICKEL
                  INGOTS, NICKEL-SILVER
                  INGOTS, PHOSPHOR-BRONZE
                  PLATES & SHEETS, COPPER ALLOY
                  RODS BARS SECTIONS, COPPER ALLOY
                  TUBES, COPPER ALLOY
                  WIRE, COPPER ALLOY

Exports by destination: tonnage	Main countries	H 2-a	T 4-a
by kind: tonnage	USA	T 4-a	
Imports by source: tonnage	Main countries	H 2-a	T 4-a
Production: brass: tonnage	France & Italy	C 12-a	
bronze: tonnage	France & Italy	C 12-a	
copper alloy manufactures: tonnage	Sweden	H 2-a	
tonnage	European countries, Japan & USA	C 12-a	
	Main countries	H 2-a	
Stocks held at smelters & brass mills: tonnage	USA	T 4-a	
World production of copper alloy semi-manufactures: tonnage		C 30-m	

Copper cathodes   see   CATHODES, COPPER

COPPER FOIL
    see also ALUMINIUM FOIL
                  LEAD FOIL
                  TIN FOIL

Exports by destination: tonnage	Japan	T 4-a
Imports by source (incl alloy foil): tonnage	USA	J 6-a

Copper ingots   see   INGOTS, COPPER

COPPER ORE

% contribution to export earnings	Mauritania & Zambia	E 45-a	
% share of estimated world reserves	Latin American countries	U 18-a	
Export prices - index nos (weighted average)	Worldwide	U 29-q	
Exports based on metal content of ore: tonnage	USA	J 6-a	
by destination (incl concentrates): tonnage	Main countries	H 2-a	T 4-a
	OECD countries	D 21-q	
by value in $m	Developing countries	U 11-a	
(incl concentrates) total & to EEC area: tonnage	AASM countries	E 41-a	
tonnage & by value in UA	AASM countries	E 41-a	
(incl concentrates): tonnage	All countries	C 30-m	
(incl residues): tonnage & value in $m	Zambia	E 45-a	
Imports & exports by source & destination: tonnage	All countries	B 15-a	
Imports based on metal content: tonnage	USA	J 6-a	
by source: tonnage	Main countries	H 2-a	
source (incl concentrates): tonnage	OECD countries	D 21-q	
of concentrates based on metal content: tonnage	USA	J 6-a	
(incl concentrates): tonnage	All countries	C 30-m	
Production: tonnage based on metal content of ore	All countries	J 6-a	U 11-a
by leading mining companies: tonnage	Main countries	J 6-a	
historical table from 1750: tonnage	Main European countries	Z 1-a	
(incl concentrates): tonnage	Chile & Mexico	U 18-a	
	OECD countries	D 21-q	
	African countries	U 44-a	
	Congo Republic & Zaire	E 41-a	
	Italy	C 12-a	
tonnage	Main countries	N 1-a	
	Australia & Zambia	C 12-a	
Stocks of concentrates: tonnage	Main countries	T 4-a	
World export trade: tonnage	Worldwide	N 4-a	
production: tonnage	Main countries	N 1-a	T 4-a
reserves: tonnage (estim)	Main countries	N 1-a	

COPPER POWDER

Exports by destination: tonnage	Japan	T 4-a
Imports by source: tonnage	USA	T 4-a

COPPER PRODUCTS, SEMI-FINISHED

Consumption by uses: tonnage	USA	H 2-a
of copper in production of semis: tonnage	OECD countries	D 21-a
Exports by destination: tonnage	France	T 4-a
tonnage	Main countries	C 30-m

	Territorial coverage	Title codes
COPPER PRODUCTS, SEMI-FINISHED continued		
Imports: tonnage	Austria & France	T 4-a
	Main countries	C 30-m
Production: for electrical goods industries: tonnage	All countries	H 2-a
by kind: tonnage	Italy	C 12-a
of castings: tonnage	All countries	H 2-a
tonnage	All countries	C 30-m
	Belgium	T 4-a
Stocks by kind: tonnage	UK	C 12-a
Wholesale prices: copper sheets in lire per kg	Italy	C 12-m
tubes in lire per kg	Italy	C 12-m
wire in lire per kg	Italy	C 12-m
COPPER PRODUCTS, SEMI-FINISHED BY KIND		
Exports: tonnage	Main countries	T 4-a
	UK	J 6-a
Imports by source: tonnage	USA	J 6-a
tonnage	Main countries	T 4-a
Production: tonnage	Main countries	C 30-m
Wholesale prices in local currency per ton	Main countries	T 4-m
COPPER SCRAP		
Consumption at brass mills: tonnage	USA	T 4-a
at foundries & chemical plants: tonnage	USA	T 4-a
by copper smelters: tonnage	USA	T 4-a
primary copper producers: tonnage	USA	T 4-a
(incl alloys) in brass mills: tonnage	USA	C 12-a
foundries: tonnage	USA	C 12-a
(incl alloys) in production of copper ingots: tonnage	USA	C 12-a
copper powder plants: tonnage	USA	C 12-a
(incl alloy scrap): tonnage	Japan	H 2-a
	UK	T 4-a
tonnage	Main countries	H 2-a
Exports by destination: tonnage	Main countries	T 4-a
	USA	J 6-a
Imports by source: tonnage	Main countries	T 4-a
tonnage	USA	J 6-a
Stocks at smelters & brass mills: tonnage	USA	T 4-a
Wholesale prices by grade in lire per kg	Italy	C 12-m
of heavy scrap in cents per lb	USA	J 6-m
in local currency per kg	Main countries	T 4-w
paid by domestic refiners of copper in $ per lb	USA	U 27-m
Copper strip see STRIP IN COIL, COPPER		
COPPER SULPHATE		
Consumption of copper in production of copper sulphate: tonnage	UK	J 6-a
Export prices in 50 kg bags in £ per ton fob	UK	T 4-w
Production: tonnage (& % copper content)	USA	J 6-a
tonnage	All countries	U 22-a
Copper wire see WIRE, COPPER		
Copper wire bars see WIRE BARS, COPPER		
COPRA CAKE		
Export prices (20% protein) at Los Angeles in $ per ton fob	USA	A 4-m
in local currency per ton	Netherlands	A 9-a
Exports (incl copra meal): tonnage	Main countries	A 4-a
tonnage & value in $m	Main countries	B 2-a
Freight rates to Europe & to USA ex Philippines in $ per ton		A 4-m
Import prices (ex Philippines) at N Sea ports in DM per ton cif	European countries	A 4-m
World market prices (incl meal) - index nos		A 4-m
in Fr per ton (based Madagascar)	France	E 41-a
Copra oil see COCONUT OIL		
COPRA		
% contribution to export earnings	Tonga & W Samoa	E 45-a
Crop tonnage (incl world total)	All countries	P 1-a
Crop tonnage for ensuing year (estim)	World regions	P 1-a
Export prices ex Colombo in Rs per candy	Sri Lanka	A 4-m
Honiara in A$ per ton cif	British Solomon Is	A 4-m
Manila in pesos per 100 kg cif	Philippines	A 4-m
in $ per ton cif	Philippines	B 19-a
Papeete in Frs per ton cif	French Polynesia	A 4-m
Port Luganville in local currency	New Hebrides	A 4-m
Tawau in M$ per ton cif	Sabah	A 4-m
in $ per 100 lbs cif	Philippines	U 17-m
A$ per ton cif	Papua New Guinea	A 4-m
Rs per lb cif	Sri Lanka	U 32-m
unit value in $ per 100 lbs	Indonesia	U 32-m
- index nos (weighted average main sources)		U 29-q
in local currency	Ghana, Philippines & W Samoa	A 9-a
Exports by destination: tonnage	Main countries	B 18-a
	Papua New Guinea	B 19-a

	Territorial coverage	Title codes	
COPRA, continued			
Exports (incl cake) by value in local currency	Malaysia, Papua New Guinea, Tonga & W Samoa	U 32-m	
shipped to EEC areas: tonnage & value in UA	AASM countries	E 41-a	
to W European area & to USA: tonnage	Philippines	A 4-a	B 19-a
tonnage & value in $m	Main countries	B 2-a	
	Tonga & W Samoa	E 45-a	
tonnage	British Solomon Is, Cook Is, Fiji & Indonesia	U 32-m	
	Main countries	A 4-a	B 19-a
	Primary producing countries	B 18-q	
Freight rates from producers to ports of main buyers in bags		A 4-m	
in bulk		A 4-m	
Import prices ex Papua & Philippines in £ per ton cif	UK	U 32-m	
Philippines in £ per ton cif	UK	B 19-q	
in $ per kg cif	UK	R 2-m	
in $ per ton cif	European countries	A 4-m	
	Pacific Coast of USA	A 4-m	
New Hebrides in Frs per kg cif Marseilles	France	R 2-m	
Singapore & Straits in £ per ton	UK	P 1-a	
Straits & Borneo in £ per ton cif	UK	P 1-m	
in $ per ton	European countries & USA	A 9-a	
Imports in oil conversion equiv tonnage	UK	P 1-a	
by source: tonnage	EEC countries	B 19-a	
tonnage	France, W Germany & Japan	B 19-a	
for production of animal feed: tonnage	UK	P 5-a	
tonnage	Main countries	A 4-a	B 19-a
Producer prices in F$ per ton	Fiji	A 4-m	
Production (incl world total): tonnage	All countries	A 4-a	B 2-a
		B 18-a	
on estates: tonnage	W Malaysia	B 19-a	
smallholdings: tonnage	W Malaysia	B 19-a	
tonnage	AASM countries	E 41-a	
	Asian & Far East countries	U 32-a	
	Latin American countries	J 5-a	
	Main countries	B 19-a	
Wholesale prices on London market in £ per ton	UK	B 2-a	
of rescada grade in $ per kg	Philippines	U 32-m	
in local currency	India, Indonesia & Singapore	A 9-a	
	European countries	U 27-m	
World market prices (based ex Philippines) in $ per ton in USA		E 41-a	
in £ per 100kg at N Sea ports		E 34-m	

Cordage see ROPES CORDAGE & TWINE

Cordage fibres see HEMP
JUTE

Corfam see LEATHER SUBSTITUTE

Coriander seed see SPICES & ESSENCES

CORK

Exports: tonnage: historical table from 1873	Portugal	Z 1-a	
Production tonnage & exports of raw cork	All countries	A 23-a	

Corn see MAIZE

CORN FLOUR

Retail prices in local currency	OAS member countries	N 17-a	
Wholesale prices in local currency	OAS member countries	N 17-a	

CORN OIL

Export prices of raw corn oil ex tanks in cents per lb fob at New York	USA	R 2-m	
Exports: tonnage	Belgium, France & Netherlands	B 19-a	
Imports: tonnage	Belgium, Canada, France & USA	B 19-a	
Production for ensuing year: tonnage (estim)	World regions	P 1-a	
Usage in production of cooking fats: tonnage	USA	B 19-a	
margarine & cooking fats: tonnage	USA	A 4-a	
margarine: tonnage	USA	B 19-a	
Wholesale prices of refined corn oil in cents per lb at New York	USA	R 2-m	
World production: tonnage		A 4-a	N 10-a

Corned beef see CANNED MEAT

Cornflakes see CEREAL PREPARATIONS

Corporate bond yields see INTEREST RATES

Corporate earnings see BALANCE SHEETS
EARNINGS, CORPORATE
PROFITS, CORPORATE
REVENUE, CORPORATE
SALES BY VALUE

Corporate finance ratios see FINANCIAL RATIOS, CORPORATE

	Territorial coverage	Title codes
Corporate overseas investment see INVESTMENT, CORPORATE OVERSEAS		
Corporate profits see PROFITS, CORPORATE		
CORPORATE SAVINGS		
As component of national income in local currency	OAS member countries	N 16-a
Corporate transfer payments see TRANSFER PAYMENTS, CORPORATE		
Corporation stocks see MUNICIPAL BONDS		
CORPORATION TAX		
As % of gross national product & of total revenue	OECD countries	D 11 D 42-a
of total revenue from taxation	Main countries	E 3-a
As component of national income in local currency	OAS member countries	N 16-a
% contribution to government income	Main countries	R 5-a
Basis of assessment & rates of taxation levied on corporations	EEC countries	E 31-a
Receipts from taxes levied on corporations in local currency	EEC countries	E 42-a
Corporations see INDUSTRIAL COMPANIES PUBLIC CORPORATIONS		
Corrosion-resistant steel see ALLOY STEEL		
Corrugated sheets see GALVANISED SHEETS		
Corsets see UNDERWEAR, FEMALE		
Corundum see ABRASIVES		
Cosmetics & bath salts see TOILET PREPARATIONS		
Cost of industrial materials see MATERIAL COSTS		
COST OF LIVING		
By kind of personal expenditure – index nos	Main countries	R 5-a
% changes (mainly excl rents)	Main countries	R 1-m
% changes	Latin American countries	U 18-a
Clothing cost element – index nos	OAS member countries	N 17-a
Comparisons based on gold parities	Main countries	R 1-m
Food element – index nos	OAS member countries	N 17-a
Housing cost element – index nos	OAS member countries	N 17-a
Index nos (incl 12 month % increases)	Main countries	R 2-m
(on changed bases from 1820)	Main European countries	Z 1-a
Index nos	All countries	M 6-a
	Australia, N European countries & USA	C 2-a
	Czechoslovakia, E Germany & Poland	U 16-a
	Main countries	A 9-a
	OAS member countries	N 17-a
	OECD countries	R 5-a
International comparison of % changes	Main countries	R 1-m
(on DM basis)	Main countries	R 5-a
Retail price index nos for most large cities (see no 2, 8)	Worldwide	U 27-m
Costs in agriculture see ELECTRICITY FARM COSTS FEEDING STUFFS FERTILISERS MAINTENANCE & REPAIRS PESTICIDES		
Costs in industry see DISTRIBUTION COSTS LABOUR COSTS MATERIAL COSTS SOCIAL CHARGES WAGES		
Costs of airline operations see OPERATING COSTS, AIRLINE		
COTTAGE CHEESE		
Production & consumption in kg	Greece, Portugal & USA	D 14-a
COTTON		
Area under crop & yield per ha	Main countries	A 1-a
in acres & ha	All countries	K 1-a
acres (incl world total)	All countries	B 10-a
acres	Main countries	B 19-a
ha & harvested tonnage	All countries	R 5-a
ha: historical tables	Main European countries	Z 1-a
ha	World regions	U 11-a
Consumption by end-use in clothing production: tonnage	EEC countries	K 4-a
end-use	Japan, USA & W European countries	A 1-a
grade in bales	Main countries	K 1-m
source of raw cotton imports in lbs million	UK	B 10-a
in lbs million	All countries	B 10-a
production of carpets: tonnage	EEC countries & USA	K 4-a

		Territorial coverage	Title codes	
COTTON, continued				
Consumption in spinning & weaving mills: tonnage		All countries	A 6-a	
	in spinning mills: tonnage	Main countries	U 43-a	
	per capita in kg	Main countries	A 1-a	U 26-a
	tonnage	OAS member countries	N 17-a	
Crop harvest of raw cotton in bales		USA	P 1-a	
Crop yields in kg per ha		World economic areas	U 11-a	
	lbs per acre & kg per ha	All countries	K 1-a	
	lbs per acre	Main countries	B 10-a	
	quintals per ha	E European countries & USSR	U 16-a	
Demand by end-use projected to 1975: tonnage		Main countries	A 1	
Dependence on cotton as % of export earnings		African, Caribbean countries & Pacific Is	E 45-a	
Export prices ex USA & Brazil in cents per lb fob		Brazil & USA	B 10-a	
	- index nos (weighted average main sources)	Worldwide	U 29-q	
	in local currency	Main countries	A 9-a	
Exports by destination in bales		USA	P 1-a	
		Main Commonwealth countries	B 10-a	
	in million lbs	Main countries	B 10-a	
	tonnage & value in $m	African, Caribbean countries & Pacific Is	E 45-a	
	(incl world total)	Main countries	A 5-a	
Import prices in pence per lb		UK	A 9-a	
Imports by source in lbs million		Main countries	B 10-a	
	ex British Commonwealth countries in million lbs	EEC countries	B 10-a	
	in bales & tonnage (incl world total)	All countries	K 1-a	
Producer prices in local currency		Guatemala, Peru, Uganda & USA	A 9-a	
Production by staple length in lbs million		India, Egypt, Pakistan & USA	B 10-a	
	costs of unginned cotton on collective farms	USSR	U 34-a	
	(incl world total): tonnage	Main countries	A 5-a	B 2-a
	cleaned cotton & historical table of world total output from 1909: tonnage	Main countries	C 4-a	
	lint & fibre: tonnage	Main countries	U 43-a	
Stocks at mills at ports & in transit: tonnage		OECD countries	D 46-a	
	in million lbs (incl world total)	All countries	B 10-a	
Wholesale prices: American cotton - index nos		UK	B 10-m	
	American middling grade in pence per lb	UK	B 10-m	
	Sudan lambert grade in pence per lb	UK	B 10-m	
	in local currency	Brazil, Egypt, Mexico, Pakistan & USA	U 27-m	
		Main countries	A 9-a	
World consumption in million lbs & % usage as apparel fibre		Worldwide	B 10-a	
	tonnage & consumption per capita in kg	Worldwide	A 6-a	
	tonnage projected to 1980	Worldwide	B 29	
	exports by value in $bn	Worldwide	M 4-a	
	unit value in $ per ton	World regions	A 5-a	
	market prices (based ex India) in cents per lb at UK ports		A 11-a	
			E 41-a	
	- index nos		G 1-a	M 4-a
	production in bales	All countries	P 1-a	
	in million lbs	All countries	B 10-a	
	stocks (end-yr): tonnage	Worldwide	G 1-a	
	in million lbs	Worldwide	B 10-a	
	(incl E European area & USSR) in bales	Worldwide	P 1-a	
	supply, production & stocks (carry-over) in bales	Worldwide	P 1-a	
	production, stocks & consumption in bales & tonnage	Worldwide	K 1-a	
COTTON, RAW				
Consumption by origin of raw cotton: tonnage		Main countries	K 1-m	
	by textile industry: tonnage	OECD countries	D 46-a	
	in bales & tonnage	All countries	K 1-a	
	spinning mills: tonnage	OECD countries	D 46-a	
		W European countries	K 2-q	
		World regions	K 5-a	
	textile mills in million lbs	UK	B 29-a	
	(industrial) since 1750: tonnage	Main European countries	Z 1-a	
	tonnage	Main countries	K 4-a	
	tonnage (incl world total)	Main countries	B 2-a	
	tonnage	OAS member countries	N 17-a	
	in million bales & tonnage	Worldwide	K 1-a	
Export earnings in $m		Main countries	A 5-a	
Export prices by grade in local currency per kg		Main countries	A 5-a	
	in $ per 100 lbs	Pakistan	U 17-m	
Exports by destination in bales		Main countries	K 1-m	
	value in $m	W European countries	U 33-a	
		Developing countries	U 11-a	
		Afghanistan & Pakistan	U 32-m	
	tonnage & value in $m	Main countries	B 2-a	
	tonnage	Afghanistan, India, Iran & Pakistan	U 32-m	
		Asian & Far East area	U 32-q	
Import prices by quality in cents per lb cif		UK	U 11-a	
	raw cotton ex Turkey in DM per kg	W Germany	R 2-m	
	ex N Brazil in DM per kg	W Germany	R 2-m	
Imports by value in $m		W European countries	U 33-a	
	in local currency	Hong Kong	U 32-m	
	ex USA & elsewhere: tonnage	OECD countries	D 46-a	
	by source in bales	Main countries	K 1-m	
Production by staple length bales in bales & tonnage		All countries	K 1-a	
	tonnage for textile industry	OECD countries	D 46-a	
	historical tables	Main European countries	Z 1-a	

127

	Territorial coverage	Title codes
COTTON, RAW continued		
Production: tonnage	E European countries & USSR	U 16-a
	Main countries	K 4-a
	OECD countries	D 46-a
	World economic areas	U 11-a
in million bales & tonnage	Worldwide	K 1-a
Stocks (end-July): tonnage	Main countries	B 2-a
(end-period) in bales	Main countries	K 1-m
		A 5-a
held by net importing & exporting countries: tonnage		
of raw cotton in bales & tonnage	Worldwide	K 1-a
Supply, production, consumption & trade: tonnage	EEC countries	B 1-a
Supply, stocks, ginnings & imports in bales	All countries	K 1-a
Wholesale prices in cents per lb	Brazil, Pakistan & USA	B 2-a
in Rs per lb	India & Pakistan	U 32-m
middling upland grade in cents per lb	USA	R 2-m
strict middling grade in cents per lb	UK	R 2-m
World exports: tonnage & value in $m	World regions	U 11-a
tonnage	Worldwide	A 5-a
production in million lbs & % produced by Commonwealth countries		B 10-a
tonnage	Main countries	B 2-a K 4-a
	World regions	U 11-a
World stocks as % of world consumption		U 11-a
COTTON BY KIND		
Export prices in cents per lb	All countries	K 1-m
Export prices – index nos	S American countries	U 40-q
Ginnings by grades of cotton in bales	USA	K 1-a
Stocks (end-period) held by consuming firms: tonnage	USA	K 1-m
in public storage: tonnage	USA	K 1-m
Cotton cloth or fabrics see WOVEN COTTON FABRICS		
Cotton industry see TEXTILE INDUSTRY, COTTON		
COTTON LINT		
Area under cotton crop in ha	OAS member countries	N 13-a
Exports total & to EEC area: tonnage & value in UA	AASM countries	E 41-a
Production tonnage & yield per 100 ha	Latin American countries	J 5-a
short fibre cotton: tonnage	All countries	U 22-a
tonnage	AASM countries	E 41-a
	African countries	U 44-a
	All countries	A 9-a
	Asia & Far East countries	U 32-a
	Latin American countries	U 40-a
	OAS member countries	N 13-a
	OECD countries	D 1-a
Wholesale prices by quality in local currency	OAS member countries	N 17-a
COTTON PIECE GOODS		
see also RAYON PIECE GOODS		
Exports by value in $m	Developing countries	A 5-a
Production: tonnage	Main countries	K 1-q
Wholesale prices of cotton cloth in Rs per metre	India	U 32-m
shirting in yen per yard	Japan	U 32-m
COTTON WASTE YARN		
Consumption in looms: tonnage	W European countries	K 2-q
COTTON WASTE		
Consumption by textile industry: tonnage	OECD countries	D 46-a
in spinning mills: tonnage	OECD countries	D 46-a
COTTON YARN		
% of total EEC area production	EEC countries	R 5-a
Consumption in knitting mills: tonnage	OECD countries	D 46-a
in production of clothing by kind: tonnage	EEC countries	K 4-a
of household textiles: tonnage	EEC countries	K 4-a
textile looms: tonnage	W European countries	K 2-q
(incl waste) in weaving industry: tonnage	OECD countries	D 46-a
of raw cotton in spinning of yarn: tonnage	World regions	K 5-a
tonnage	OAS member countries	N 17-a
Deliveries to textile industry – index nos	UK	B 29-a
Exports (incl fabrics) by value in Rs	India	U 32-m
through port of Karachi: tonnage	India	S 16-a
tonnage	Hong Kong & Japan	U 32-m
	OECD countries	D 46-a
Imports as % of domestic consumption	UK	B 29-a
Imports, exports & trade balance in lbs	UK	B 29-a
tonnage	Main countries	K 1-q
	OECD countries	D 46-a
Production: by areas: tonnage	EEC countries	E 38-a
historical table since 1912: tonnage	Main countries	C 4-a
since 1923: tonnage	Main countries	Z 1-a
(incl mixtures): tonnage	OECD countries	R 5-a

	Territorial coverage	Title codes	
COTTON YARN, continued			
Production (incl thread): tonnage	OAS member countries	N 14-a	
mixed & pure spun cotton yarn: tonnage	All countries	U 22-a	
pure spun cotton yarn: tonnage	All countries	U 43-a	
tonnage	African countries	U 44-a	
	All countries	K 1-q	
	Asian & Far East countries	U 32-q	
	Central African Republic, Ivory Coast & Senegal	E 41-a	
	ECAFE countries	U 32-q	
	EEC countries	E 26-m	E 28-q
		E 27-a	
	Latin American countries	J 5-a	
	Main countries	U 27-m	E 3-a
		R 5-a	
	OECD countries	D 46-a	
	W European countries	K 2-q	
Wholesale prices in $ per ton	France, Italy, Japan & USA	U 27-m	
COTTONSEED			
Acreage subsidy in £ per ton	EEC area	B 1-a	
Area under crop in ha	OAS member countries	N 13-a	
& production: tonnage	All countries	A 9-a	
Consumption as seed: tonnage	USA	B 19-a	
for oil crushing: tonnage	USA	B 19-a	
Crop tonnage (incl world total)	All countries	P 1-a	
Export prices in local currency per ton	Sudan	A 9-a	
Exports by destination: tonnage	Nicaragua, Nigeria & Sudan	B 19-a	
	Main countries	B 18-a	
tonnage & value in $m	Main countries	B 2-a	
tonnage	Main exporting countries	B 19-a	
	Main producing countries	B 18-q	
Harvest estimates for ensuing crop yr: tonnage	Main world regions	P 1-a	
Import prices ex Nigeria in £ per ton cif	UK	B 19-q	
Imports for production of animal feed: tonnage	UK	P 5-a	
in vegetable oil equiv tonnage	EEC countries	P 5-a	
tonnage & oil conversion equiv	UK	P 1-a	
tonnage	Importing countries	B 19-a	
Producer prices in local currency per ton	Egypt, Kenya & USA	A 9-a	
Production: tonnage (world total)	All countries	B 2-a	B 18-a
tonnage & yield per 100 ha	Latin American countries	J 5-a	
tonnage	African countries	U 44-a	
	Brazil, Egypt, India & USA	P 1-a	
	Latin American countries	U 40-a	
	Main countries	B 19-a	
	OAS member countries	N 13-a	
Stocks (initial & end-yr): tonnage	USA	B 19-a	
Wholesale prices ex Nigeria in £ per ton on London market	UK	B 2-a	
in Rs per ton	India	A 9-a	
COTTONSEED MEAL			
Export prices of meal & cake in local currency	Brazil & Uganda	A 9-a	
Exports: tonnage & value in $m	Main countries	B 2-a	
Import prices in £ per ton cif	UK	R 2-m	A 9-a
Imports as animal feed: tonnage	UK	P 5-a	
Prices paid by farmers as animal feed in $ per ton	W European countries	U 30-a	
	USA	U 30-a	
Wholesale prices ex Pakistan in £ per ton	UK	B 2-a	
in $ per ton	USA	A 9-a	
COTTONSEED OIL			
Export prices in cents per lb fob	USA	B 19-a	
in local currency	Sudan	A 9-a	
- index nos (weighted average main sources)		U 29-q	
Exports: tonnage & value in $m	Main countries	B 2-a	
	Main countries	B 18-q	B 19-a
tonnage	Main countries	B 19-a	
Import prices: semi-refined cottonseed oil in £ per ton cif per ton	UK	A 9-a	
	European countries	P 1-a	
Imports: crude & refined cottonseed oil: tonnage	Main countries	B 19-a	
tonnage	Main countries	P 1-a	
Production: crude cottonseed oil in lbs	USA	B 19-a	
crude & refined cottonseed oil: tonnage	All countries	U 22-a	
estimated for ensuing yr: tonnage	World regions	P 1-a	
tonnage	Brazil, Egypt, Japan, UK & USA	P 1-a	
	Main countries	B 19-a	
	USA	B 19-a	
Retail prices in local currency	OAS member countries	N 17-a	
Stocks (initial & end-yr): tonnage	USA	B 19-a	
Usage for production of cooking fats: tonnage	UK & USA	A 4-a	B 19-a
frying fats: tonnage	USA	B 19-a	
margarine: tonnage	Main countries	A 4-a	B 19-a
Wholesale prices ex Sudan in £ per ton on London Market	UK	B 2-a	
raw cottonseed oil in cents per lb on New York Market	USA	R 2-m	
refined cottonseed oil in £ per ton (ex mills)	UK	R 2-m	
(spot) in cents per lb on New York Market	USA	P 1-m	A 9-a
		B 19-a	
World & British Commonwealth production: tonnage		A 1	
World production forecast for ensuing yr: tonnage		A 4-a	N 10-a
tonnage			

	Territorial coverage	Title codes

COUNCIL OF EUROPE
    Budget: allocations from EEC funds in £m — EEC area — B 3-a
            costs for administration of Council of Europe — EEC area — B 1-a

County councils   see   REGIONAL AUTHORITIES

COURT OF JUSTICE
    Budget: allocations from EEC funds in £m — EEC area — B 3-a
            costs for administration of Court of Justice — EEC area — B 1-a

Courtelle   see   MAN-MADE FIBRES
              NON-CELLULOSIC FIBRES

COURTS OF LAW
    No of civil cases tried & completed — OAS member countries — N 20-a
        commercial cases contested & completed — OAS member countries — N 20-a
        minor criminal cases tried — OAS member countries — N 20-a
        serious criminal cases tried — OAS member countries — N 20-a
        offenders before court proving illiterate — OAS member countries — N 20-a
            sentenced for indictable crimes — OAS member countries — N 20-a

Cow & bull hides   see   HIDES

Cows   see   LIVESTOCK

Cows' milk   see   MILK, FRESH

Crabs   see   CRUSTACEANS & MOLLUSCS

Craft industries   see   ART & CRAFT INDUSTRIES

CRAFTSMEN & PROCESS WORKERS
    see also   PRODUCTION WORKERS

    As % of total employed population — EEC countries — E 33-a
    No employed by sex — All countries — L 4-a
            iron & steel industry — W Germany — H 3-a
                    — OECD countries — D 22-a
    No of process workers unemployed — All countries — L 4-a
    Wages per hr in wood panel industry in local currency — European countries — A 26-a

Cranes & hoists   see   MECHANICAL HANDLING EQUIPMENT

CRANES, FLOATING
    Deliveries of new vessels — Netherlands — S 16-a

Cranes, mobile   see   SERVICE VEHICLES

Crawlers   see   TRACTORS, TRACK-LAYING

Cream   see   MILK PRODUCTS

CREAMERIES
    see also   BUTTER
              CHEESE FACTORIES
              DAIRIES

    No of butter creameries in operation — EEC countries — B 3-a
    No producing over 1000 tons of butter per yr — EEC countries — B 3-a
              to 1000 tons of butter per yr — EEC countries — B 3-a
              to 250 tons of butter per yr — EEC countries — B 3-a
    Size structure based on output of butter per yr — EEC countries — B 3-a

CREDIT
    see also   BANK ADVANCES
              DOMESTIC DEBT
              DRAWING RIGHTS (IMF)
              INSTALMENT CREDIT
              PRIVATE BORROWING
              STAND-BY CREDITS (IMF)
              TRADE CREDITS

    Domestic & hire purchase credit position in $m — ECE countries — U 42-m
        credit outstanding (incl retail trade credit) in $m — OECD countries — D 26-q
    New credit granted by finance houses in $m — OECD countries — D 26-q

CREDIT, INTERNATIONAL
    Credits from European Development Fund cancelled in $m — OECD countries — D 10-a
                    granted in $m — OECD countries — D 10-a
                    repaid in $m — OECD countries — D 10-a
        from International Monetary Fund taken up in $m — All countries — F 5-m   F 6-q
        US aid institutions in $m — Recipient countries — R 5-a
    Status of European Development Fund credits granted in $m — OECD countries — D 10-a
    Tranche positions in International Monetary Fund — All countries — F 5-m   F 6-q

Credit, personal   see   PRIVATE BORROWING

Credit co-operatives   see   CREDIT UNIONS

	Territorial coverage	Title codes

CREDIT FINANCE
    see also   INSTALMENT CREDIT

% of employed persons engaged in credit finance	EEC countries	E 33-a
Grants by private organisations in $m	European countries	R 5-a
New instalment credit granted in $m	OECD countries	D 26-q
No of persons employed by sex & status by areas in credit business	EEC countries	E 38-a
hrs worked per wk (incl insurance business) by sex	EEC countries	E 18-a
wage & salary earners (incl insurance business) by sex	EEC countries	E 18-a

Credit institutions   see   BANK ADVANCES
                                    COMMERCIAL BANKS
                                    CREDIT FINANCE
                                    CREDIT UNIONS
                                    INSTALMENT CREDIT

Credit insurance   see   EXPORT CREDIT INSURANCE

Credit sales   see   INSTALMENT CREDIT

CREDIT UNIONS

Deposits & savings in $m	OAS member countries	N 18-a
Loans outstanding in $m	OAS member countries	N 18-a
No of credit co-operatives in operation & membership	OAS member countries	N 18-a
Shares issued by value in $m	OAS member countries	N 18-a

Creosote   see   COAL BY-PRODUCTS

Crepe rubber   see   LATEX CREPE

Cresylic acid   see   COAL BY-PRODUCTS

Crime   see   CRIMINAL OFFENCES

CRIMINAL OFFENCES
    see also   COURTS OF LAW
                     JUVENILE DELINQUENCY

No of arrests made per 1000 population	OAS member countries	N 20-a
reported cases of arson	OAS member countries	N 20-a
assault & wounding	OAS member countries	N 20-a
forgery & fraud	OAS member countries	N 20-a
homicide	OAS member countries	N 20-a
larceny & robbery	OAS member countries	N 20-a
narcotics traffic	OAS member countries	N 20-a
sexual offences	OAS member countries	N 20-a
No reported by kind to police	OAS member countries	N 20-a

CRIMINAL OFFENDERS

No arrested by type of offence or crime	OAS member countries	N 20-a
brought before courts of law by age groups	OAS member countries	N 20-a
committed to penal institutions	OAS member countries	N 20-a
in court acquitted	OAS member countries	N 20-a
by marital status	OAS member countries	N 20-a
occupation	OAS member countries	N 20-a
residential location (rural & urban)	OAS member countries	N 20-a
sentence imposed	OAS member countries	N 20-a
sex	OAS member countries	N 20-a

Crocheted textiles   see   KNITTED FABRICS

Crocidolite   see   ASBESTOS

CROP YIELDS

Apples in kg per tree	OECD countries	D 29-a	D 33-a
tons per ha	OECD countries	D 29-a	
Barley in cwt per acre	Main countries	B 8-a	
kg per ha	EEC countries	B 1-a	E 44-a
	Main countries	R 5-a	
	OAS member countries	N 13-a	
	OECD countries	D 1-a	
quintals per ha	E European countries & USSR incl Ukraine	U 16-a	
tons per ha	All countries	C 16-a	
Cassava in kg per ha	OAS member countries	N 13-a	
Cauliflowers in tons per ha: open field & under glass	OECD countries	D 37-a	
Cereals & main farm crops in kg per ha	All countries	A 9-a	
Cereals (all kinds) in quintals per ha	E European countries & USSR	U 16-a	
by kind in kg per ha	EEC countries	E 44-a	
	Latin American countries	J 5-a	
in tons per ha	All countries	C 16-a	
Cereals, root crops & lucerne in kg per ha	EEC countries	E 3-a	
Chick peas in kg per ha	OAS member countries	N 13-a	
Cotton in lbs per acre & kg per ha	All countries	K 1-a	
lbs per acre	Main countries	B 10-a	
quintals per ha	E European countries & USSR incl Ukraine	U 16-a	
Cucumbers in tons per ha: open field & under glass	OECD countries	D 37-a	
Dried broad beans in kg per ha	OAS member countries	N 13-a	
Dry beans in kg per ha	OAS member countries	N 13-a	

CROP YIELDS, continued

Item	Territorial coverage	Title codes	
Dry peas in kg per ha	OAS member countries	N 13-a	
Feedgrains: maize & sorghum in kg per ha	USA	A 12-a	
Figs per tree (average) in kg	Turkey	D 37-a	
Flax in kg per ha	EEC countries	E 44-a	
Fodder beet, turnips & swedes in kg per ha	EEC countries	B 1-a	
Fruit in quintals per ha	E European countries & USSR	U 16-a	
Groundnuts in kg per ha	OAS member countries	N 13-a	
Hazelnuts in kg per tree (average)	Turkey	D 37-a	
Hemp in kg per ha	EEC countries	E 44-a	
Hops in kg per ha	EEC countries	B 1-a	E 44-a
Lentils in kg per ha	OAS member countries	N 13-a	
Linseed in kg per ha	OAS member countries	N 13-a	
Lucerne in kg per ha	EEC countries	B 1-a	E 44-a
Maize in cwt per acre	Main countries	B 8-a	
kg per ha	EEC countries	B 1-a	E 44-a
	Main countries	R 5-a	
	OAS member countries	N 13-a	
	OECD countries	D 1-a	
quintals per ha	E European countries & USSR	U 16-a	
tons per ha	All countries	C 16-a	
Oats in cwt per acre	Main countries	B 8-a	
kg per ha	EEC countries	B 1-a	E 44-a
	Main countries	R 5-a	
	OAS member countries	N 13-a	
	OECD countries	D 1-a	
quintals per ha	E European countries & USSR	U 16-a	
tons per ha	Australia	C 16-a	
Oilseeds in quintals per ha	E European countries & USSR incl Ukraine	U 16-a	
Onions in kg per ha	OAS member countries	N 13-a	
tons per ha	OECD countries	D 37-a	
Opium (from poppies) in kg per ha	Main countries	U 46-a	
Paddy rice in kg per ha	Burma	A 10-a	
	OAS member countries	N 13-a	
	OECD countries	D 1-a	
Passion fruit: tonnage per acre	Australia & Hawaii	A 8-a	
Peaches in kg per tree (average)	OECD countries	D 29-a	
tons per ha	OECD countries	D 29-a	D 35-a
Pears in kg per tree (average)	OECD countries	D 29-a	
tons per ha	OECD countries	D 29-a	D 34-a
Peas & beans in kg per ha	EEC countries	E 44-a	
Plant seeds (for oil extraction) in kg per ha	EEC countries	E 44-a	
Potatoes in kg per ha	EEC countries	B 1-a	E 44-a
	Main countries	R 5-a	
	OAS member countries	N 13-a	
	OECD countries	D 1-a	
quintals per ha	E European countries & USSR incl Ukraine	U 16-a	
Rice in cwt per acre (milled equiv)	Main countries	B 8-a	
	All countries	B 14-a	
in kg per ha	EEC countries	B 1-a	E 44-a
	Main countries	R 5-a	
Root crops & tubers by kind in kg per ha	EEC countries	E 44-a	
	OAS member countries	N 13-a	
(for feeding stuffs) in kg per ha	EEC countries	E 44-a	
Rye in cwt per acre	Main countries	B 8-a	
kg per ha	EEC countries	B 1-a	E 44-a
	Main countries	R 5-a	
	OAS member countries	N 13-a	
	OECD countries	D 1-a	
quintals per ha	E European countries & USSR	U 16-a	
Sesame seed in kg per ha	OAS member countries	N 13-a	
Sorghum & millet in tons per ha	All countries	C 16-a	
Soybeans in kg per ha	OAS member countries	N 13-a	
Sugar beet in kg per ha	EEC countries	B 1-a	E 44-a
	OECD countries	D 1-a	
quintals per ha	E European countries & USSR	U 16-a	
cane in kg per ha	OAS member countries	N 13-a	
tons per acre	India	B 13-a	
Sunflower seed in kg per ha	OAS member countries	N 13-a	
Sweet potatoes in kg per ha	OAS member countries	N 13-a	
Tea in kg per ha by district	India	P 6-a	
Tobacco (flue & fired-cured types) per acre	Main countries	B 13-a	
in kg per ha	EEC countries	E 44-a	
	OAS member countries	N 13-a	
lbs per acre by region	USA	B 17-a	
lbs per acre	Main countries	B 13-a	
quintals per ha	E European countries & USSR incl Ukraine	U 16-a	
suitable for cigar production in lbs per acre	Canada & USA	B 13-a	
Tomatoes in kg per ha	OAS member countries	N 13-a	
open field crop in tons per ha	OECD countries	D 29-a	D 36-a
		D 37-a	
under glass in tons per ha	OECD countries	D 36-a	D 37-a
Vegetables (all kinds) in kg per ha	EEC countries	E 44-a	
in quintals per ha	E European countries & USSR	U 16-a	
Wheat in bushels per acre & in kg per ha	All countries	C 29-a	
cwt per acre	Main countries	B 8-a	
kg per ha by kind (soft & hard)	EEC countries	E 44-a	
kg per ha	EEC countries	E 44-a	
	Main countries	R 5-a	
	OAS member countries	N 13-a	

	Territorial coverage	Title codes
CROP YIELDS, continued		
Wheat in quintals per ha	All countries	C 16-a
	E European countries & USSR	U 16-a
	World regions	C 16-a
in tons per ha	All countries	C 16-a
(incl spelt) in kg per ha	OECD countries	D 1-a
(soft for home consumption) in kg per ha	EEC countries	B 1-a
Wine by volume per ha of vineyards	EEC countries	E 44-a

CROPS

see also   STATE PROCUREMENT (COMMUNIST COUNTRIES)
          TROPICAL PRODUCTS

	Territorial coverage	Title codes
Area under principal crops in ha	Asian, Far East & Australasian countries	U 45-a
Change in stocks as % output (at current prices)	ECE countries	U 34-a
Output: changes in value at market prices - index nos	ECE countries	U 34-a
Production as % contribution to gross farm output	E European countries	U 34-a
- index nos (value basis)	E European countries	U 34-a
by value in local currency	Czechoslovakia & USSR	U 34-a
of main farm crops: tonnage	Asian, Far East & Australasian countries	U 45-a
Stocks: changes as % gross output	Czechoslovakia, Hungary & Poland	U 34-a
World production of main crops & primary products by region	Worldwide	A 9-a

Crops, industrial   see   COCOA BEANS
                        GROUNDNUTS
                            OILSEEDS
                            SUGAR BEET
                            SUGAR CANE
                            TOBACCO

Crude birth rates   see   BIRTH RATES

Crude death rates   see   DEATH RATES

Crude oil   see   CRUDE PETROLEUM

CRUDE OIL PIPELINES

see also   NATURAL GAS PIPELINES
          REFINED OIL PIPELINES

	Territorial coverage	Title codes	
Diameter of each pipeline in inches	OPEC countries	C 3-a	
Labour force employed on pipelines	EEC countries	E 43-a	
Length, diameter, capacity & location of pipelines	EEC countries	E 43-a	
Length in km & diameter of pipelines	Worldwide	C 14-a	
in km	Canada, European countries, USA & USSR	C 14-a	
Location by oil company ownership	Main countries	H 4	
Location, length in km & diameter in inches	Worldwide	H 4	
No of pumping stations working on pipelines	EEC countries	E 43-a	
Route, name of operator & length in miles	OPEC countries	C 3-a	
Throughput: capacity tonnage & dimensions	EEC countries	E 15-a	
tonnage in each pipeline	EEC countries	E 43-a	

CRUDE PETROLEUM

see also   OIL REFINERIES

	Territorial coverage	Title codes	
& products loaded & unloaded by ship: tonnage	All countries	U 43-a	
As % of all energy sources consumed	Main countries	H 4-a	
% change in export earnings	Main oil exporting countries	U 11-a	
in daily production rate	OPEC countries	C 3-a	
% distribution of known reserves	World regions	C 14-a	
% growth rate in refining capacity	Latin American countries	U 18-a	
% impact of price increase on industrial costs	European countries	U 16-a	
% industrial cost increases expected due to price changes	Worldwide	U 16-a	
% contribution to export earnings	Congo Rep, Gabon, Nigeria & Trinidad	E 45-a	
% of world production accounted for by individual companies	Worldwide	H 4-a	
% world freight tonnage shipped	World regions	U 37-a	
Availability, production & imports: tonnage	Main countries	C 14-a	
Consumption at refineries: tonnage	EEC countries	B 30-a	
by chemical industry: tonnage	EEC countries	E 14-a	
organic chemical industry: tonnage	OPEC countries	D 5-a	
for refining: tonnage	EEC countries	E 14-a	
of imported oil by source: tonnage	Main countries	H 4-a	
in coal equiv tonnage	EEC countries	E 16-q	E 7-a
		E 14-a	E 15-a
	Main countries	E 3-a	
	Denmark, Eire, Norway & UK	E 7-a	
	OAS member countries	N 17-a	
litres	European countries & USA	U 3-a	
production of gas	EEC countries	E 16-q	E 15-a
refineries: tonnage	Italy	H 4-a	
	Main countries	H 4-a	
	OECD countries	D 44-a	
Demand (domestic) in 42 gallon barrels	USA	N 1-a	
Export prices at main ports in $ per barrel	Main countries	H 4-a	
in $ per barrel fob Kharg Is	Iran	U 32-m	
in $ per barrel fob	Colombia & Venezuela	U 18-a	
- index nos (weighted average)	Worldwide	U 29-q	
	S American countries	U 40-q	
Exports by destination in barrels per day	OPEC countries	C 3-a	

	Territorial coverage	Title codes	
CRUDE PETROLEUM, continued			
Exports by destination: tonnage	World regions	U 55-a	
tonnage & value in $	All countries	U 12-a	
by value in $m	African, Caribbean countries & Pacific Is	E 45-a	
in coal equiv tonnage	European countries & USA	U 4-a	
in m³	Latin American countries	U 18-a	
in order of importance of sources in barrels per yr	Main countries	C 14-a	
to E European area: tonnage	E European countries	U 16-a	
tonnage: historical tables from 1864	Main European countries	Z 1-a	
tonnage	Asian & Far East area	U 32-q	
	Iran	U 32-m	
	World regions	T 3-a	
(total) & to EEC area: tonnage & by value	Congo Rep & Gabon	E 41-a	
unit value in cents per barrel	Main countries	U 18-a	
in M$ per ton	Sarawak	U 32-m	
in $ per ton	OAS member countries	N 15-a	
Freight arrivals by source: tonnage	EEC countries	E 43-a	
despatch: tonnage by destination	EEC countries	E 43-a	
rates (general purpose rates)	Worldwide	E 14-m	
for medium & large tankers	Worldwide	E 14-m	
spot	Worldwide	E 14-m	
Import prices in lire per ton fob	Italy	H 4-a	
$ per barrel	Argentine & Brazil	U 18-a	
Imports & exports by source & destination: tonnage	All countries	B 15-a	
in coal equiv tonnage	EEC countries	E 16-q	E 15-a
throughput in refineries: tonnage	EEC countries	E 26-m	
as % of domestic supply	Main countries	H 4-a	
by source: tonnage	EEC countries	C 14-a	
	Italy	H 4-a	
tonnage & value in $m	All countries	U 12-a	
value in local currency	Australia & India	U 32-m	
ex world oil-producing regions: tonnage	EEC countries	E 16-a	E 15-a
crude oil feedstocks: tonnage	World regions	D 31-a	
	OECD countries	D 39-q	
ex E European area: tonnage	E European countries & USSR	U 16-a	
non-EEC area: tonnage	EEC countries	E 14-a	
in barrels per day (incl world total)	All countries	C 3-a	
coal equiv tonnage	European countries & USA	U 4-a	
by volume in m³	Latin American countries	U 18-a	
countries in order of importance in barrels	Main countries	C 14-a	
into world regions	World regions	D 31-a	
(net): tonnage	ECE countries	U 15-a	
historical tables from 1856: tonnage	Main European countries	Z 1-a	
tonnage	Main countries	E 3-a	
	World regions	T 3-a	
Inland transportation: tonnage	EEC countries	E 43-a	
Inter-regional imports & exports: tonnage	Main countries	D 28-a	
oil movements by source: tonnage		D 28-a	
No of barrels processed by main oil companies per day	Worldwide	C 3-a	
wells drilled & no proving dry	All countries	C 14-a	
Price change impact on private consumption	European countries	U 16-a	
on public consumption	European countries	U 16-a	
increases expected by components of demand	Worldwide	U 16-a	
Prices posted for Arabian light crude oil in $ per barrel	Worldwide	U 16-q	
at ports in $ per barrel fob	Worldwide	C 3-a	
Production & specific gravities by grade	All countries	U 27-m	
(planned) in barrels million per day	OPEC countries	U 16-q	
by value at wells in $ per barrel	USA	N 1-a	
volume in m³	Latin American countries	U 18-a	
	OAS member countries	N 14-a	
	World regions	U 18-a	
	S American countries & Trinidad	U 40-a	
daily average of no of barrels produced	OPEC countries	C 3-a	
Production, imports, exports & consumption: tonnage	OECD countries	D 44-a	
& supply: tonnage	All countries	U 55-a	
in barrels per day by OPEC companies	Worldwide	C 3-a	
by main oil companies	Worldwide	C 3-a	
& tonnage per day	All countries	C 21-a	
per day	OPEC countries	U 16-q	C 3-a
	All countries	C 3-a	N 5-a
coal equiv tonnage	All countries	U 55-a	
	Main countries	E 3-a	
	EEC countries	E 16-q	E 15-a
Latin America as % of world total		U 18-a	
Production, reserves & specific gravity	World petroleum areas	U 43-a	
& imports: tonnage	EEC countries	E 16-q	E 15-a
(incl world total): historical table from 1913: tonnage	All countries	C 4-a	
(incl world total): tonnage	Main countries	E 14-a	
by areas: tonnage	EEC countries	E 38-a	
fields & regions: tonnage	EEC countries	E 15-a	
individual large companies: tonnage	Worldwide	H 4-a	
historical table from 1857: tonnage	Main European countries	Z 1-a	
from 1860: tonnage	All countries	C 14-a	
imports & supply: tonnage	OECD countries	D 39-q	D 31-a
trade & consumption: tonnage	Italy	H 4-a	
(incl natural gas liquids): tonnage	All countries	T 3-a	
(incl shale oil): tonnage	ECE countries	U 15-a	

	Territorial coverage	Title codes	
CRUDE PETROLEUM, continued			
Production: tonnage	AASM countries	E 41-a	
	African countries	U 39-a	U 44-a
	All countries	B 15-a	U 22-a
	Asian & Far East countries	U 32-q	
	Congo Rep & Gabon	E 41-a	
	ECAFE countries	U 32-q	
	EEC countries	E 28-q	E 27-a
	European countries, USA & USSR	U 4-a	
	Latin American countries	J 5-a	U 18-a
	Main countries	E 3-a	R 5-a
	OECD countries	D 39-q	
	Developing countries	U 57-q	
Production - index nos	Oil-producing countries	F 5-m	F 6-q
Refinery intake, output, imports, exports & disposal: tonnage	OECD countries	D 39-q	D 31-a
throughput: tonnage	EEC countries	E 16-q	E 15-a
Refining capacity & degree of utilisation	EEC countries	E 15-a	
in m³ per day	Latin American countries	U 18-a	
in use: tonnage	EEC countries	E 14-a	
Reserves: tonnage (estim)	African countries	U 39-a	
	Main countries	E 3-a	
	Latin American countries	U 18-a	
(known) in m³ million	World regions	U 18-a	
Resources & changes in stocks: tonnage	EEC countries	E 16-q	E 15-a
ex indigenous production & imports: tonnage	EEC countries	E 14-a	
	W European countries	S 16-a	
Sales in barrels per day by main oil companies	Worldwide	C 3-a	
Seaborne freight as % of total world freight tonnage		U 37-a	
tonnage (estim)	Worldwide	D 28-a	
Share of exports by value in $m	OPEC countries	C 3-a	
Shipments by destination areas: tonnage	Main countries	H 4-a	
through Panama Canal: tonnage		D 28-a	
Stocks held at refineries: tonnage	W European countries	S 16-a	
in million barrels	USA	N 1-a	
Supply & disposal of feedstocks & components: tonnage	OECD countries	D 39-q	D 31-a
Supply: tonnage by source	EEC area	E 14-a	
tonnage	OECD countries	D 39-q	
Tax reference prices in $ per barrel fob at ports	Worldwide	C 3-a	
Throughput & capacity of oil pipelines: tonnage	EEC countries	E 15-a	
Volume of crude oil refined in m³ million	Latin American countries	U 18-a	
World consumption at refineries: tonnage	Worldwide	B 30-a	
exports by value in $bn		M 4-a	
prices (incl petroleum products) - index nos		G 1-a	
in $ per barrel ex Texas fields	USA	R 2-m	
fob Algerian ports		R 2-m	
Iranian ports		R 2-m	
Iraqi ports		R 2-m	
Kuwait		R 2-m	
Libyan ports		R 2-m	
Nigerian ports		R 2-m	
Saudi-Arabia		R 2-m	
Venezuelan ports		R 2-m	
production in barrels million	All countries	N 1-a	N 4-a
in coal equiv tonnage	All countries	C 14-a	E 15-a
proven reserves in barrels million	Worldwide	C 14-a	
	All countries	N 1-a	
	World regions	T 3-a	
	Main countries	E 14-a	
tonnage	World regions	C 13-a	C 21-a
		T 3-a	
refining capacity in barrels per day	Worldwide	C 3-a	
tonnage	World regions	C 14-a	
CRUDE PETROLEUM INDUSTRY			
Capital formation in $m	Main countries	U 21-a	
Gross output by value in $m	Main countries	U 21-a	
Labour force employed	Main countries	U 21-a	
Wages & salary costs	Main countries	U 21-a	

Crude petroleum reserves   see   WORLD PETROLEUM RESERVES

Crude rubber   see   LATEX
                     NATURAL RUBBER

CRUDE STEEL

see also   INGOTS, STEEL
           WROUGHT STEEL

	Territorial coverage	Title codes	
% of EEC area production	EEC countries	E 29-a	R 5-a
% of production by process	Main countries	U 57-a	
for ingots or steel castings	EEC countries	E 29-a	
of ingots by process	EEC countries	E 30-a	
% of total investment channelled into steel production	OECD countries	D 22-a	
Bessemer quality as % of total production	Main countries	U 57-a	
Consumption duplexed in electric furnaces: tonnage	ECE countries	U 7-q	U 6-a
	Main countries	H 3-a	
in open-hearth furnaces: tonnage	ECE countries	U 7-q	U 6-a
	Main countries	H 3-a	

135

	Territorial coverage	Title codes	
CRUDE STEEL, continued			
Consumption for production of steel products: tonnage	EEC countries	E 29-a	
of ferrous scrap in steel furnaces: tonnage	Main countries	T 4-a	
per capita in kg	EEC countries & USA	E 29-a	
	Main countries	T 4-a	U 49-a
	OECD countries	D 22-a	R 5-a
& consumption per capita: tonnage	EEC countries	E 30-q	E 29-a
	Main countries	U 43-a	
for processing – index nos (wt basis)	EEC countries	E 30-q	
in steelworks: tonnage	OAS member countries	N 17-a	
historical table from 1925: tonnage	EEC countries & USA	E 29-a	
tonnage	Arab countries	T 4-a	
	ECE countries	U 15-a	
	Main countries	U 49-a	
	OECD countries	D 22-a	
	S E Asian countries	T 4-a	
	World regions	T 4-a	
Deliveries for conversion to castings: tonnage	ECE countries	U 7-q	U 6-a
	Main countries	H 3-a	
domestic re-rolling: tonnage	EEC countries	E 29-a	
export: tonnage	ECE countries	U 7-q	U 6-a
	Main countries	H 3-a	
production of forgings & stampings	ECE countries	U 7-q	U 6-a
	Main countries	H 3-a	
sale in non-EEC area: tonnage	EEC countries	E 29-a	
sale in EEC area: tonnage	EEC countries	E 29-a	
Electric quality as % of total production	Main countries	U 57-a	
Exports by destination: tonnage	ECE countries	U 48-a	
	EEC countries	E 5-q	
	Main countries	T 4-a	
tonnage	ECE countries	U 15-a	
	European countries, Japan & USA	C 5-m	
Imports & exports by source & destination: tonnage	All countries	B 15-a	
by source: tonnage	EEC countries	E 5-q	
	Main countries	T 4-a	
(incl semis): tonnage	European countries, Japan & USA	C 5-m	
tonnage	UK	T 2-m	
Inter-EEC deliveries: ingots & semis: tonnage	EEC countries	E 30-m	
imports & exports as % of world trade	EEC countries	E 30-q	
Investment in steel production in $ per ton	OECD countries	D 22-a	
New orders for domestic re-rolling: tonnage	EEC countries	E 29-a	
for export sale outside EEC area: tonnage	EEC countries	E 29-a	
for shipment within EEC area: tonnage	EEC countries	E 29-a	
New orders received: tonnage & index nos	EEC countries	E 30-m	
Open-hearth quality as % of total production	Main countries	U 57-a	
Oxygen-blown converter quality as % of total production	Main countries	U 57-a	
Prices (less tax but incl rebates) at main centres	EEC countries	E 30-a2	
Production capacity projected to 1976: tonnage	OECD countries	D 22-a	
in existing plants: tonnage	EEC countries	E 30-a	
Bessemer process: tonnage	Main countries	U 57-a	
Electric process: tonnage	Main countries	U 57-a	
Open-hearth process: tonnage	Main countries	U 57-a	
Oxygen-blown converters: tonnage	Main countries	U 57-a	
historical table from 1937: tonnage	Main countries	U 57-a	
Thomas process: tonnage	Main countries	U 57-a	
Production of liquid steel for castings as % of total production	EEC countries	E 29-a	
of liquid steel for castings: tonnage	W Germany	C 5-m	
Production potential of basic Bessemer steel: tonnage	EEC countries	E 46-a	
Bottom-blown steel: tonnage	EEC countries	E 46-a	
L.D. & Kaldo steel: tonnage	EEC countries	E 46-a	
Open-hearth steel: tonnage	EEC countries	E 46-a	
requirements projected to 1977: tonnage	UK	B 25-a	
Production (actual) & production capacity: tonnage	All countries	U 49-a	
as % of existing capacity: tonnage	EEC countries	E 30-a	
as % of world steel production: tonnage	All countries	E 29-a	
Bessemer steel for casting: tonnage	EEC countries	E 29-a	
Bessemer steel: tonnage	All countries	T 4-a	
	ECE countries	U 7-m	U 6-a
	EEC countries	E 29-a	
	Main countries	H 3-a	
by 25 largest steel companies: tonnage	Worldwide	T 4-a	
kind & process: tonnage	EEC countries	E 30-m	
phosphoric content: tonnage	EEC countries	E 30-m	
process for production of castings: tonnage	EEC countries	E 30-q	E 29-a
producing regions: tonnage	EEC countries	E 30-q	E 29-a
		E 38-a	
Electric quality for production of castings: tonnage	EEC countries	E 29-a	
Electric quality: tonnage	All countries	T 4-a	
	EEC countries	E 29-a	
for production of steel castings: tonnage	EEC countries	E 29-a	
historical table from 1860: tonnage	Main European countries	Z 1-a	
from 1913: tonnage	All countries	C 4-a	
in Thomas converters: tonnage	EEC countries	E 29-a	
(incl steel for castings): tonnage	Main countries	C 5-m	
ingots & as % of world production: tonnage	EEC countries	E 30-m	
castings: tonnage	All countries	U 27-m	B 15-a
		U 43-a	
	Latin American countries	U 40-a	
	USA	N 1-a	

	Territorial coverage	Title codes	
CRUDE STEEL, continued			
Production: ingots & steel for production of castings: tonnage	EEC countries	E 30-q	
	Asian & Far East countries	U 32-q	
ingots: tonnage	Australia, India, Japan & S Korea	U 32-q	
Kaldo steel: tonnage	UK	U 7-m	H 3-a
		U 6-a	
L.D. steel: tonnage	ECE countries	U 7-m	U 6-a
	Main countries	H 3-a	
liquid steel for castings: tonnage	All countries	U 22-a	
	EEC countries	E 29-a	
	Main countries	T 4-a	
non-phosphoric grade: tonnage	EEC countries	E 29-a	
of each iron & steel company: tonnage	W Germany	H 3-a	
Open-hearth steel: tonnage	All countries	T 4-a	
	ECE area	U 7-m	U 6-a
	Main countries	H 3-a	
Oxygen-blown steel: tonnage	All countries	T 4-a	
	ECE area	U 7-m	U 6-a
	EEC countries	E 29-a	
	Main countries	H 3-a	
phosphoric grade: tonnage	EEC countries	E 29-a	
Rotor steel: tonnage	UK	U 7-m	H 3-a
		U 6-a	
Siemens Martin steel: tonnage	EEC countries	E 29-a	
for production of castings: tonnage	EEC countries	E 29-a	
historical table from 1913: tonnage	World regions	C 4-a	
special quality steels: tonnage	Main countries	E 29-a	
Thomas, Martin, Bessemer & Electric qualities: tonnage	EEC countries	E 30-m	
Thomas steel by grade: tonnage	EEC area	E 29-a	
Thomas steel: tonnage	ECE countries	U 7-m	U 6-a
	EEC countries	E 29-a	
	Main countries	H 3-a	
by US Steel Corporation & as % of total production: tonnage	US	J 3-a	
tonnage	African countries	U 44-a	
	E European countries & USSR	U 16-a	
	ECE countries, Japan & USA	U 6-a	U 7-a
	ECE countries	U 15-a	
	EEC countries	E 26-m	E 28-q
		E 3-a	E 27-a
	Main countries	C 2-a	E 3-a
		H 3-a	R 5-a
		T 4-a	
	OAS member countries	N 14-a	
	OECD countries	D 26-m	D 22-a
		R 5-a	
	UK	T 2-m	
	World regions	D 22-a	U 57-a
Productivity per worker per yr - index nos	OECD countries	D 22-a	
Rates of output for ingots & raw steel per day: tonnage	EEC countries	E 30-q	
Thomas quality as % of total production	Main countries	U 57-a	
World production & world production capacity: tonnage		U 49-a	
Bessemer steel for ingots & castings: tonnage		T 1-a	
Electric steel for ingots & castings: tonnage		T 1-a	
historical table from 1870: tonnage		E 29-a	
Open-hearth steel for ingots & castings: tonnage		T 1-a	
Oxygen-blown steel for ingots & castings: tonnage		T 1-a	
steel ingots & castings (all qualities): tonnage		N 4-a	
tonnage	All countries	N 1-a	T 4-a
CRUDE STEEL, BESSEMER			
Production: acid Bessemer quality: tonnage	OECD countries	D 22-a	
basic Bessemer quality: tonnage	OECD countries	D 22-a	
(all grades): tonnage	All countries	B 15-a	
CRUDE STEEL, CARBON			
Consumption of cobalt in carbon quality steel production in lbs	USA	T 4-a	
Production: tonnage	All countries	T 4-a	
CRUDE STEEL, ELECTRIC			
see also ALLOY STEEL			
TOOL STEEL			
Consumption of cobalt in Electric quality steel production in lbs	USA	T 4-a	
Production: historical table from 1925: tonnage	EEC countries	E 29-a	
tonnage	All countries	B 15-a	T 4-a
	OECD countries	D 22-a	
CRUDE STEEL, OPEN-HEARTH			
Production: tonnage	All countries	B 15-a	
	OECD countries	D 22-a	
Crude steel, special quality see ALLOY STEEL			

	Territorial coverage	Title codes	
CRUDE STEEL BY PROCESS			
Production capacity: tonnage	Main countries	U 57-a	
& as % of world total	EEC area	E 29-a	
	OECD countries	D 22-a	
for production of castings as % of world total	EEC area	E 29-a	
Production: tonnage	All countries	H 3-a	T 1-a
		T 4-a	
	ECE countries	U 7-m	U 6-a
World production: tonnage	All countries	T 1-a	

Crushed stone   see   BUILDING MATERIALS

CRUSTACEAN PRODUCTS
    see also   MOLLUSC PRODUCTS

% contribution to export earnings	Guyana	E 45-a	
Imports & exports: tonnage & value in $m	All countries	A 21-a	
Production tonnage: lobsters et al	Main countries	A 21-a	

CRUSTACEAN PRODUCTS, CANNED BY KIND

Exports: tonnage	All countries	A 21-a	
Production: tonnage	Main countries	A 21-a	

CRUSTACEANS & MOLLUSCS
    see also   CRUSTACEAN PRODUCTS

% of catch marketed fresh	Worldwide	A 5-a	
used for canning	Worldwide	A 5-a	
for freezing & curing	Worldwide	A 5-a	
for meal production & oil extraction	Worldwide	A 5-a	
Catch: tonnage & value: crustaceans in $	OAS member countries	N 13-a	
molluscs in $	OAS member countries	N 13-a	
tonnage	All countries	A 22-a	
Consumption for industrial processing	OECD countries	D 14-a	
per capita in kg per yr	OECD countries	D 14-a	
Exports of shellfish: tonnage & value in $m	OECD countries	D 43-a	
Imports & exports: tonnage & value in $m	All countries	A 21-a	
shellfish: tonnage & value in $m	OECD countries	D 43-a	
tonnage	World regions	A 11-a	
Landings of cockels & crabs: tonnage & value in £	UK	D 43-a	
lobsters, prawns & shrimps: tonnage	OECD countries	D 43-a	
mussels & clams: tonnage	OECD countries	D 43-a	
oysters, scallops & abalone: tonnage	OECD countries	D 43-a	
squid, cuttlefish & octopus: tonnage	OECD countries	D 43-a	
Production: tonnage	OAS member countries	N 14-a	
	World regions	A 11-a	
		A 21-a	
World catch, imports & exports by kind: tonnage			
tonnage	All countries	A 5-a	
usage for meal production & oil extraction as % catch		A 5-a	

CRUSTACEANS & MOLLUSCS BY KIND

Catch: tonnage	All countries	A 22-a	
Exports: tonnage & value in $	All countries	A 21-a	
tonnage	World regions	A 11-a	
Production: tonnage	Main countries	A 21-a	

CRUSTACEANS & MOLLUSCS, CANNED

Consumption per capita in kg per yr	OECD countries	D 14-a	

CRUSTACEANS & MOLLUSCS, FRESHWATER

Catch: tonnage	All countries	A 22-a	

CRYOLITE
    see also   BAUXITE

Production & exports: tonnage	Greenland	B 15-a	

Crystallised or candied fruit   see   FRUIT, CRYSTALLISED OR CANDIED

CUCUMBERS & GHERKINS

Area harvested, production tonnage & yield per ha	All countries	A 9-a	
Production: tonnage (under glass)	UK	U 20-a	
tonnage	Main E European countries	U 20-a	

CULTIVATING MACHINES
    see also   GARDEN TRACTORS
                 MOTOR CULTIVATORS

Exports by value in $m	Main countries	U 38-a	
Imports by value in $m	All countries	U 38-a	
Production by volume (all kinds)	All countries	U 22-a	U 38-a

Cumin seed   see   SPICES & ESSENCES

Cupro-nickel tubes   see   TUBES, COPPER ALLOY

	Territorial coverage	Title codes

Cured fish products   see   FISH, DRIED OR SMOKED

Currants   see   RAISINS & CURRANTS

Currency   see   MONEY SUPPLY

Currency buying & selling rates   see   EXCHANGE RATES

CURRY POWDER
    see also   SPICES & ESSENCES

Exports in lbs & value in Rs	India	B 13-a
by destination in lbs	India & Singapore	B 13-a
Imports in lbs	Main countries	B 13-a

Curtains & drapery   see   HOUSEHOLD TEXTILES

Customs duties   see   IMPORT DUTIES

CUTLERY

Exports: tonnage	OECD countries	D 9-a
Production of knives, forks & spoons in kg	Zaire	E 41-a

Cyanamide   see   FERTILISERS, NITROGENOUS

CYCLES & MOPEDS

% changes in retail sales of bicycles	E European countries	U 16-a	
Exports of bicycles by value in $m	All countries	U 38-a	
by destination by CST classes: tonnage & value in $	EEC countries	E 48-a	
by SITC classes by value in $	Main countries	D 2-q	
tonnage & value in $	OECD countries	D 3-a2	
by value in $	Main countries	U 9-a	
volume	OECD countries	D 9-a	
of mopeds ex home production by volume	All countries	S 24-a	
Imports by source by CST classes: tonnage & value in $	EEC countries	E 21-a	
by SITC classes by value in $	Main countries	D 2-q	
tonnage & value in $	OECD countries	D 3-a2	
value in $m	All countries	U 38-a	
New registrations of mopeds	European countries & USA	U 47-a	
No of km run (estim)	European countries & USA	U 47-a	
of mopeds in use (at end-yr)	Main countries	S 24-a	
	European countries & USA	U 47-a	
Production by volume: bicycles	AASM countries	E 41-a	
	All countries	U 38-a	
mopeds & scooters	All countries	U 38-a	
mopeds	All countries	S 24-a	
volume	All countries	U 22-a	
	EEC countries	E 26-m	E 28-q
		E 27-a	
Sales demand for bicycles per 1000 population			
Value added in manufacture	E European countries	U 16-a	
World export trade: bicycles by value in $m	OECD countries	D 9-a	
		U 38-a	

Cyclic hydrocarbons   see   HYDROCARBONS, AROMATIC

Cyclo-hexane   see   CHEMICALS, ORGANIC

D.A.C. (Development Assistance Committee)   see   DEVELOPMENT AID

DDT   see   INSECTICIDES

Dacron   see   POLYESTER

Daily newspapers   see   NEWSPAPERS, DAILY

DAIRIES
    see also   CHEESE FACTORIES
                CREAMERIES
                DAIRY CO-OPERATIVES

Costs for salaried staff per month	EEC countries	E 11-a
Intake of liquid milk per dairy: tonnage	EEC countries	B 3-a
Labour costs as % of total costs	EEC countries	E 8-a
by status of employees in local currency	EEC countries	E 8-a
for all employees per hr	EEC countries	E 11-a
wage earners per hr	EEC countries	E 11-a
Labour force employed: no of salaried staff	EEC countries	E 11-a
wage earners & salaried staff	EEC countries	E 8-a
wage earners	EEC countries	E 11-a
No of hrs worked by labour force per yr	EEC countries	E 8-a
salaried staff per yr	EEC countries	E 11-a
wage earners per yr	EEC countries	E 11-a
No in operation (incl milk collection centres)	EEC countries	B 3-a

	Territorial coverage	Title codes	
DAIRIES BY SIZE			
Based on milk intake from 10-30 million litres	EEC countries	B 3-a	
less than 10 million litres	EEC countries	B 3-a	
over 30 million litres	EEC countries	B 3-a	
DAIRY CO-OPERATIVES			
No of members	EEC countries	B 3-a	
organisations in operation	EEC countries	B 3-a	
Dairy cows see CATTLE			
LIVESTOCK			
DAIRY EQUIPMENT			
see also MILKING MACHINES			
Exports by destination & value in $m	Main countries	U 9-a	
value in $m	Main countries	U 38-a	
Imports by value in $m	Main countries	U 38-a	
World export trade by value in $m		U 38-a	
Dairy herds see CATTLE			
LIVESTOCK			
DAIRY PRODUCTS			
see also BUTTER			
CHEESE			
MILK			
As source of fat protein & calorie intake in grammes	OAS member countries	N 17-a	
A.I.D. sales under food aid programs in $	Recipient countries	M 1-a	
Consumption cost of milk, cheese & eggs	EEC countries	E 32-a	
Consumption per capita in kg per yr by income levels	USA	C 27-a	
Export prices - index nos (weighted average)	Worldwide	U 29-q	U 54-q
in local currency	Asian, Far East & Australasian countries	U 45-a	
Exports by destination areas by value in local currency	Australasian countries	B 4-a	
value in local currency	Main countries	B 4-a	
(incl eggs) by value in $	OECD countries	D 1-a	
to EEC & non-EEC area by value in $m	EEC countries	E 24-a	
tonnage	Australia & New Zealand	U 32-m	
Imports of fresh & canned cream & yoghurt	UK	B 12-m	
ex EEC & non-EEC area by value in $m	EEC countries	E 24-a	
(incl eggs) by value in $	OECD countries	D 1-a	
Production & consumption projected to 1985: tonnage	Worldwide	A 1	
Retail prices of eggs in local currency	OAS member countries	N 17-a	
milk, butter & cheese - index nos	EEC countries	E 26-m	
milk products in local currency	OAS member countries	N 17-a	
- index nos	EEC countries	E 44-a	
World market prices - index nos		U 30-a	
DAIRY PRODUCTS BY KIND			
% changes in retail sales	E European countries	U 16-a	
% of output exported	Main countries	B 4-a	
Commonwealth share of UK import trade: tonnage		B 4-a	
Consumption: tonnage	OAS member countries	N 17-a	
Export subsidies per 100 kg	EEC area	B 4-a	
Exports by destination by CST classes: tonnage & value in $	EEC countries	E 48-a	
	Main countries	D 2-q	
SITC classes: tonnage & value in $	OECD countries	D 3-a2	
NIMEXE classes: tonnage & value in $	All countries	E 20-a	
SITC classes: tonnage & value in $	All countries	U 50-a	U 59-a
tonnage (in detail)	World regions	A 11-a	
Import duties (in detail)	Main countries	B 4-a	
quotas in lbs per yr	USA	B 4-a	
Imports by NIMEXE classes: tonnage & value in $	All countries	E 20-a	
SITC classes: tonnage & value in $	All countries	U 50-a	U 59-a
source by CST classes: tonnage & value in $	EEC countries	E 21-a	
	Main countries	D 2-q	
SITC classes by value in $	OECD countries	D 3-a2	
tonnage & value in $	World regions	A 11-a	
tonnage	EEC countries	B 4-a	
Net trade: tonnage	All countries	A 9-a	
Producer prices received	World regions	A 11-a	
Production: tonnage (in detail)	OECD countries	D 14-a	
Production, stocks & consumption: tonnage	EEC countries	B 4-a	
supply & trade: tonnage	Main countries	E 3-a	
Production: tonnage	Canada, European countries, USA & USSR	E 44-a	
Self-sufficiency ratios	EEC countries	E 3-a	
Wholesale prices in local currency	OAS member countries	N 17-a	
World exports: unit value in $ per ton		A 11-a	
World trade: tonnage	European & developing countries	A 1-a	

Damage to property see PROPERTY DAMAGE OR LOSS

Danablu & Danbo see CHEESE BY VARIETY

Danube see INLAND WATERWAYS

Darning wool see HOME SEWING

	Territorial coverage	Title codes

DATA-PROCESSING EQUIPMENT INDUSTRY
    see also   ELECTRONICS INDUSTRY

Labour costs	EEC countries	E 11-a
Labour costs: salaried staff per month	EEC countries	E 11-a
wage earners per week	EEC countries	E 11-a
No of hrs worked: salaried staff per month	EEC countries	E 11-a
wage earners per week	EEC countries	E 11-a
salaried staff employed	EEC countries	E 11-a
wage earners employed	EEC countries	E 11-a

DATES & FIGS
    see also   FRUIT, DRIED

Export prices in local currency	Greece, Iraq & Tunisia	A 9-a
Exports of dates: tonnage & value in $m	Main countries	U 11-a
unit value in $ per ton	Main countries	U 11-a
Producer prices received for figs in lire	Italy	A 9-a
Production: dates: tonnage	Main countries	A 5-a
figs (fresh & dried): tonnage	Turkey	D 37-a
figs: tonnage	OAS member countries	N 13-a
(incl prunes): tonnage	All countries	B 5-a
Production, supply, consumption & trade: tonnage	EEC countries	B 1-a
tonnage	African countries	U 44-a
	All countries	A 9-a
Wholesale prices in local currency	Turkey & USA	A 9-a

DEATH BENEFITS

Cost to National Health Service	All countries	L 2-a
No of pensions paid to surviving spouses	OAS member countries	N 18-a

DEATH DUTIES

Government revenue from death duties	EEC countries	E 42-a

DEATH RATES

From suicide per 100,000 population	OAS member countries	N 20-a
Per 1000 population: historical table, 1750-1969	Main European countries	Z 1-a
infants under 1 yr by regions	OAS member countries	N 12-a
aged 1 to 4 yrs	Developed countries	M 4-a
	Developing countries	M 4-a
by areas	EEC countries	E 38-a
(in 5-yr periods)	Main countries	R 5
world average (excl USSR)	Worldwide	R 5
Per 1000 population	All countries	W 1-q
	E European countries	N 6-a
	ECAFE countries	U 32-q
	ECE countries	U 15-a
	EEC countries	E 2-a
	Latin American countries	J 5-a U 40-a
	Main countries	U 27-m
	OECD countries	D 23-a
No of deaths (urban & rural) & rate per 1000 population	All countries	U 14-a

DEATH RATES BY AGE

No of deaths by sex, by cause & type of disease	All countries	U 14-a

DEATHS
    see also   INFANT MORTALITY

Infant mortality by sex in rural areas	OAS member countries	N 12-a
urban areas	OAS member countries	N 12-a
(under 1 yr age)	OAS member countries	N 12-a
No of deaths & rate per 1000 population	EEC countries	E 33-a
	Main countries	R 5-a
by age & rate per 1000 population	Asian, Far East & Australasian countries	U 45-a
& sex	Latin American countries	J 5-a
	OAS member countries	N 12-a
sex by regions	OAS member countries	N 12-a
in rural areas	OAS member countries	N 12-a
urban areas	OAS member countries	N 12-a
& death rates per 1000 population	All countries	U 28-a
(with annual totals)	EEC countries	E 26-m
historical tables	EEC countries	E 2-a
due to aircraft accidents on scheduled services	Worldwide	S 21-a
road accidents by age groups	European countries	U 47-a
from earliest records to 1969	Main European countries	Z 1-a

DEATHS, FOETAL

No of deaths & rates per 1000 live births	OAS member countries	N 12-a
	All countries	U 14-a

DEATHS BY CAUSE
    see also   ACCIDENTS
                   DEATHS IN CHILDBIRTH
                   SUICIDE

	Territorial coverage	Title codes

DEATHS BY CAUSE, continued

	Territorial coverage	Title codes
Global mortality from infectious diseases	Main countries	W 1-a
No by diseases: infants 1-4 yrs of age	OAS member countries	N 12-a
under 1 yr of age	OAS member countries	N 12-a
main diseases & as % total deaths	OAS member countries	N 12-a
of deaths of children under 5 yrs of age	Latin American countries	J 5-a
in road accidents per 1000 population	All countries	W 1-a
resulting from cirrhosis	All countries	W 2-a
homicide & war operations	All countries	W 2-m
pneumonia & bronchitis	All countries	W 2-a
road vehicle accidents	All countries	W 2-m
senility	All countries	W 2-m
suicide & self-inflicted injury	All countries	W 2-a
tuberculosis	All countries	W 2-a
by disease	Asian, Far East & Australasian countries	U 45-a
	OECD countries	R 5-a
of infants 1-4 yrs of age by disease	OAS member countries	N 12-a
under 1 yr by disease	OAS member countries	N 12-a
Rates per 1000 population by cause	Latin American countries	J 5-a
	Main countries	W 1-m
100,000 population: cerebro-vascular diseases	All countries	W 2-m
cirrhosis	All countries	W 2-a
heart diseases	All countries	W 2-m
homicide	All countries	W 2-m
hypertensive diseases	All countries	W 2-m
pneumonia & bronchitis	All countries	W 2-a
rheumatic fever	All countries	W 2-m
road vehicle accidents	All countries	W 2-m
senility	All countries	W 2-m
suicide & self-inflicted injury	All countries	W 2-m
tuberculosis	All countries	W 2-a

DEATHS BY SUICIDE

	Territorial coverage	Title codes
No of deaths resulting from strangulation	OAS member countries	N 20-a
from use of firearms	OAS member countries	N 20-a
poison	OAS member countries	N 20-a

DEATHS IN CHILDBIRTH

	Territorial coverage	Title codes
No of fatalities & no per 1000 live births	OAS member countries	N 12-a

Deaths in industrial accidents   see   FATALITIES

Deaths in road accidents   see   ACCIDENTS, ROAD

Debt   see   DOMESTIC DEBT
             FOREIGN DEBT
             PUBLIC DEBT

Debt amortisation   see   DEBT SERVICING

Debt interest   see   DEBT SERVICING

Debt repayments   see   DEBT SERVICING
                         DOMESTIC DEBT
                         FOREIGN DEBT
                         GOVERNMENT EXPENDITURE
                         PUBLIC DEBT

DEBT SERVICING

	Territorial coverage	Title codes	
As factor in national income & expenditure in local currency	OAS member countries	N 16-a	
Amortisation as payment balances component	Latin American countries	U 18-a	
Amortisation costs on loans received	World regions	M 3-a	
Government expenditure on interest payments in local currency	African countries	U 44-a	
	OAS member countries	N 16-a	
Interest payments as % of government expenditure	Main countries	R 5-a	
made in $m	World regions	M 3-a	M 4-a
by municipal authorities on loans in $m	OAS member countries	N 16-a	
on debts as % of export income	Developing countries	M 3-a	
debts by kind (projected) in $m	Worldwide	M 3-a	
European Development Fund loans in UA	AASM countries	E 41-a	
foreign loans in $m	Main countries	D 7-a	
Provincial government interest payments on loans in $m	OAS member countries	N 16-a	
Public expenditure on debt servicing in local currency	Caribbean countries & W Indies	T 6-a	

Deciduous forests   see   FORESTS, NON-CONIFEROUS
                           TIMBER, DECIDUOUS
                           TIMBER, TROPICAL

Deck officers & deckhands   see   MERCHANT SEAMEN

Deep-sea fishing trawlers   see   TRAWLERS

	Territorial coverage	Title codes

DEFENCE EXPENDITURE
    see also   ARMED FORCES
                CIVIL EXPENDITURE

As % of gross national product (annual averages to 1969)	OECD countries	D 11
by world regions	Main countries	N 9-a
projected to ensuing yr	OECD countries	D 11
of government expenditure	Main countries	R 5-a
	All countries	M 6-a
of gross domestic product	All countries	M 6-a
By governments in local currency	Asian, Far East & Australasian countries	U 45-a
	Latin American countries	J 5-a
Compared with cost of education	Main countries	N 9-a
foreign aid	Main countries	N 9-a
public health	Main countries	N 9-a
In $bn	Developed countries (as total)	N 9-a
	Developing countries (as total)	N 9-a
In $m	Main countries	N 9-a
Per capita in $	Developed countries (as total)	N 9-a
	Developing countries (as total)	N 9-a
	NATO member countries	N 9-a
	Warsaw Pact member countries	N 9-a
Cost within budget accounts in $m	Main countries	U 43-a
Research & development costs of governments on defence equipment	EEC countries	E 36-a

Deferred capital shares   see   SHARES, COMMON

DEFICIENCY PAYMENTS
    see also   INTERVENTION PRICES
                PRICE SUPPORTS

On unsold cereals & seed off farm	UK	U 34-a
Cost to Exchequer in £	UK	B 8-a
Subsidy per cwt of barley, oats & wheat	UK	B 8-a

Deflator, implicit   see   GROSS DOMESTIC PRODUCT
                                GROSS NATIONAL PRODUCT
                                INFLATION

Degrees   see   UNIVERSITY DEGREES

DELIVERIES
    see also   NEW ORDERS

% growth in sales of machine tools by type	EEC countries	B 20-a
Gas turbines by size in MW	European countries, Japan & USA	D 45-a
Hydraulic generators by size in MW	European countries, Japan & USA	D 45-a
Hydraulic & steam turbines by size in MW	European countries, Japan & USA	D 45-a
Ingots & semi-manufactured steel to non-EEC area: tonnage	EEC countries	E 30-m
Iron & steel products & index nos	EEC countries	E 30-m
Milk (liquid) by consuming sector	EEC countries	B 3-a
Nuclear reactors by size in MWe	European countries, Japan & USA	D 45-a
Power transformers by size in MVa	European countries, Japan & USA	D 45-a
Steam boilers by size in ton-hr capacity	European countries & USA	D 45-a
Thermal generators by size in MW	European countries, Japan & USA	D 45-a

Delivery statistics see under name of product

Demand   see   CONSUMER GOODS
                    CONSUMPTION PER CAPITA
                    DURABLE GOODS
                    RETAIL TRADE

Demand deposit rates (banking)   see   INTEREST RATES

Demand deposits   see   MONEY SUPPLY

Demand elasticity   see   INCOME ELASTICITY OF DEMAND

Demand forecasts   see   PROJECTIONS, INDUSTRIAL

Dental preparations & dentifrice   see   TOILET PREPARATIONS

DENTISTRY

No of students enrolled on university courses	OAS member countries	N 19-a
Usage of platinum & palladium in manufacture of false teeth in oz	USA	J 6-a

Dentists   see   MEDICAL PERSONNEL

DEOXIDISERS

Usage of magnesium in production of deoxidisers: tonnage	USA	T 4-a

Départements (France)   see   REGIONAL AUTHORITIES

Departmental stores   see   MULTIPLE STORES

Deposit bank savings   see   INVESTMENT, PERSONAL

	Territorial coverage	Title codes

Deposit rates (banking)   see   INTEREST RATES

Deposits   see   BANK DEPOSITS
                 MONEY SUPPLY
                 NATIONAL SAVINGS

DEPRECIATION
   see also   CAPITAL FORMATION
              FINANCIAL RATIOS, CORPORATE

As % of fixed capital formation in agriculture	ECE countries	U 34-a
As component in assessment of net domestic product in $m	OAS member countries	N 16-a
gross capital formation	Latin American countries	J 5-a
net product of agriculture in £m	EEC countries	B 1-a
On assets as % of sales turnover: chemical manufacturing corporations	USA	J 2-a
engineering corporations	USA	J 2-a
machine tool corporations	USA	J 2-a
manufacturing corporations	USA	J 2-a
motor vehicle corporations	USA	J 2-a
Amortisation of assets in agricultural sector	EEC countries	E 44-a
forestry sector	EEC countries	E 44-a
Provision made by specific oil companies in $m	Worldwide	C 3-a

DEPRECIATION ALLOWANCES

As % of farm capital formation	E European countries	U 34-a
gross farm output	E European countries	U 34-a
	ECE countries	U 34-a
gross farm product	E European countries	U 34-a
At current values in $m	ECE countries	U 34-a
Granted in agriculture as component of gross domestic product	EEC countries	E 32-a
agriculture in $m	E European countries	U 34-a
Changes in agriculture in $m	ECE countries	U 34-a
Farm machinery as % of depreciation allowances	ECE countries	U 34-a

DETERGENTS

Consumption of vegetable oils by kind in production of detergents: tonnage	Main countries	A 4-a
Production: detergent powder: tonnage	OECD countries	D 5-a
(incl washing powder): tonnage	All countries	U 22-a
tonnage	OAS member countries	N 14-a
Retail prices (comparative) per 430 grammes	EEC countries	Z 3-a
in local currency	OAS member countries	N 17-a

DETERGENTS, LIQUID

Production: tonnage	OECD countries	D 5-a

DETERGENTS, SYNTHETIC
   see also   SCOURING POWDER

Imports by value in $m	European countries, Japan & USA	U 26-a
Production by value in $m	European countries, Japan & USA	U 26-a
	Communist countries	U 26-a
tonnage by kind	OECD countries	D 5-a
tonnage	All countries	A 4-a
	Main countries	B 19-a
unit value in $ per ton	OECD countries	D 5-a

Devaluation   see   EXCHANGE RATES

DEVELOPMENT AID
   see also   A.I.D.
              IBRD
              IDA
              IDB
              IFC
              BILATERAL AID
              EUROPEAN DEVELOPMENT FUND
              EUROPEAN INVESTMENT BANK
              EXPORT CREDITS
              FOOD AID
              MULTILATERAL AID
              TECHNICAL ASSISTANCE
              WORLD BANK

By private organisations through development banks in $m	European countries	R 5-a
By purpose of commitments as % of total aid	Main countries	D 7-a
A.I.D. fund for agriculture in $m	Recipient countries	M 1-a
business promotion in $m	Recipient countries	M 1-a
education in $m	Recipient countries	M 1-a
health in $m	Recipient countries	M 1-a
industry in $m	Recipient countries	M 1-a
public administration in $m	Recipient countries	M 1-a
social welfare in $m	Recipient countries	M 1-a
transportation in $m	Recipient countries	M 1-a

	Territorial coverage	Title codes
DEVELOPMENT AID, continued		
Received in $m	Recipient countries	D 7-a
% element of grants in aid received	Developing countries	M 3-a
loans in aid received	Developing countries	M 3-a
% of total loaned or granted as debt relief	Main countries	D 7-a
as technical assistance	Main countries	D 7-a
appropriated for agricultural projects	Main countries	D 7-a
capital projects	Main countries	D 7-a
energy projects	Main countries	D 7-a
industrial projects	Main countries	D 7-a
social infrastructure improvements	Main countries	D 7-a
transportation projects	Main countries	D 7-a
to finance current expenditure	Main countries	D 7-a
current imports (in general)	Main countries	D 7-a
food imports	Main countries	D 7-a
A.I.D. commitments by appropriation categories in $m	Recipient countries	M 1-a
expenditure as contingency funds in $m	Recipient countries	M 1-a
loans in $m	Recipient countries	M 1-a
supporting assistance in $m	Recipient countries	M 1-a
technical assistance in $m	Recipient countries	M 1-a
by category by project in $m	Recipient countries	M 1-a
for administration improvements in $m	Recipient countries	M 1-a
loans administered by other agencies in $m	Recipient countries	M 1-a
for "Alliance for Progress" program	Recipient countries	M 1-a
as contingency funds in $m	Recipient countries	M 1-a
for development projects in $m	Recipient countries	M 1-a
supporting assistance in $m	Recipient countries	M 1-a
loans granted by purpose in $m	OAS member countries	N 16-a
supporting assistance appropriations in $m	Recipient countries	M 1-a
technical assistance appropriations in $m	Recipient countries	M 1-a
Administrative expenses in $m	Main countries	D 7-a
Assistance grants & loan commitments: terms	DAC member countries	U 43-a
Bilateral capital commitments in $m	E European countries & China	U 43-a
Bilateral flows by country of source in $m	African recipient countries	U 44-a
(net) by kind in $m	African recipient countries	U 44-a
official grants in $m	African recipient countries	U 44-a
loans in $m	African recipient countries	U 44-a
Bilateral loans as % of total overseas aid	Worldwide	M 4-a
in $m	Worldwide	M 3-a
receipts by income groups	Recipient countries	D 7-a
Capital subscription payments to International Development Agency in $m	OECD countries	D 13-a
Commitments to Communist & non-Communist countries in $m	China	D 13-a
by China (to date) in $m	Recipient countries	D 13-a
Congressional overseas aid appropriations in $m	USA	D 13-a
Contributions to bodies administering multilateral aid in $m	OECD countries	D 13-a
Credits granted by European Development Fund in UA	OECD countries	D 10-a
US organisations in $m	Recipient countries	R 5-a
Disbursements as grants in $m	World regions	M 3-a
loans in $m	World regions	M 3-a
by major recipients in $m	OECD countries	D 13-a
(net) by kind in $m	Developed countries	U 43-a
of International Development Agency in $m	Worldwide	M 3-a
US loans in $m	Main recipient countries	D 13-a
World Bank in $m	Worldwide	M 3-a
official & private in $m	Worldwide	M 3-a
	Finland & New Zealand	D 13-a
to other Communist countries in $m	China	D 13-a
Distribution of USSR aid in $m	USSR	D 13-a
European Development Fund: aid by project (in detail) in UA	African, Asian & S American countries	D 13-a
to diversify production in UA	Recipient countries	E 19-a
improve infrastructure	Recipient countries	E 19-a
European Development Fund: technical assistance costs for co-operation projects (in detail) in UA	Recipient countries	E 19-a
Eximbank loans in $m	OAS recipient countries	N 16-a
	Recipient countries	D 13-a
Expenditure on foreign aid planned to 1977 in £m	UK	D 13-a
Flow as % of gross national product	Main countries	D 7-a
	OECD countries	D 13-a
of Overseas Development Agency Fund as % of gross national product	Donating countries	M 4-a
of resources by kind in $m	Donating countries	U 43-a
in $m	World regions	M 3-a
(public & private) as % of gross national product	Donating countries	M 4-a
Flow target of EEC commission as % of gross national product	Donating EEC countries	M 4-a
of UN as % of gross national product	Donating countries	M 4-a
Food aid shipments of surplus crops by value in $	OAS member countries	N 16-a
Government receipts from foreign loans in local currency	African countries	U 44-a
overseas grants in local currency	African countries	U 44-a
Grants & multilateral contributions in $m	Worldwide	M 3-a
Grants as % of gross domestic product	Main countries	D 7-a
total overseas aid	Worldwide	M 4-a
received in $m	Developing countries	M 4-a
to multilateral institutions in $m	OECD countries	D 13-a
IBRD loans granted by purpose in $m	OAS recipient countries	N 16-a

	Territorial coverage	Title codes
DEVELOPMENT AID, continued		
International Development Association: loans granted by purpose in $m	OAS recipient countries	N 16-a
International Development Bank: loans granted by purpose in $m	OAS recipient countries	N 16-a
International Finance Corporation: capital subscriptions by source in $m	Worldwide	M 2-a
commitments as % of total aid	World regions	M 2-a
by type of business assisted in $m	Worldwide	M 2-a
income (net) & reserves against losses in $m		M 2-a
investment projects (in detail) by company in $m	Worldwide	M 2-a
loan & equity investments in $m	All countries	M 2-a
project costs in $m	Worldwide	M 2-a
Interest payments received on overseas loans in $m	Main countries	D 7-a
Loans & grants from overseas in $m	Latin American countries	J 5-a
(interest-free) granted in $m	China	D 13-a
by OECD countries in $m	Recipient countries	D 13-a
Maturity periods stipulated for loans	OECD countries	D 13-a
Multilateral aid as % of total overseas aid	Worldwide	M 4-a
flows (net) in $m	African recipient countries	U 44-a
Net flow: disbursements in $m	Main countries	D 7-a
of aid from African Development Bank in $m	Worldwide	M 4-a
as % of gross national product	Donating countries	U 23-a
	Main donating countries	D 7-a
of aid from Asian Development Bank in $m	Worldwide	M 4-a
European Development Fund in $m	Worldwide	M 4-a
Inter-American Development Bank in $m	Worldwide	M 4-a
International Development Association in $m	Worldwide	M 4-a
from International Finance Corporation in $m	Worldwide	M 4-a
World Bank in $m	Worldwide	M 4-a
of official aid	Main countries	D 7-a
private capital in $m	Main countries	D 7-a
	OECD countries	D 13-a
of aid under United Nations Development Projects in $m	Worldwide	M 4-a
financial resources in $m	Recipient developing world regions	U 23-a
Net receipts of aid per capita in $	Recipient countries	D 7-a
No of loans granted by Eximbank	Recipient countries	D 13-a
projects by kind (completed & planned)	China	D 13-a
Official aid granted in $m	DAC countries	U 23-a
as % of total overseas aid	Worldwide	M 4-a
development assistance (ODA) in $m	Worldwide	M 3-a
loans as % of total overseas aid	Worldwide	M 4-a
Private capital contributions in $m	Main donating countries	U 43-a
investment overseas development aid in $m	Worldwide	M 3-a
loans as % of total overseas aid	Worldwide	M 4-a
Status of agency for international development loans (specific projects) in $m	Worldwide	M 1-a
of European Development Fund credits granted in $m	OECD countries	D 10-a
Technical assistance through US organisations in $m	Recipient countries	R 5-a
Terms of loan commitments & interest rates charged	EEC countries	D 13-a
maturity periods	China	D 13-a
World bank loans & credits approved for specific projects in $m	Worldwide	M 3-a
DEVELOPMENT AID PER CAPITA		
In $ per yr	Developing countries	U 52-a
Grants as % of gross national product	Main countries	D 7-a
Net transfers as % of gross national product	Main countries	D 7-a
Total flows as % of gross national product	Main countries	D 7-a
DEVELOPMENT AID, OFFICIAL FLOW		
see also DEVELOPMENT AID, PUBLIC FLOW		
INVESTMENT, PUBLIC OVERSEAS		
As % of total overseas aid	Worldwide	M 4-a
Through development banks in $m	European countries	R 5-a
Assistance in $m	Worldwide	M 3-a
Bilateral aid in $m	Developing world regions	U 23-a
Credits in $m	European countries	R 5-a
Disbursements by Eximbank in $m	Worldwide	D 13-a
by kind in $m	OECD countries	D 13-a
Grants in $m	European countries	R 5-a
Loans (bilateral) in $m	Developing countries	M 4-a
(multilateral) in $m	Developing countries	M 4-a U 23-a
DEVELOPMENT AID, PRIVATE FLOW		
see also INVESTMENT, PRIVATE OVERSEAS		
As % of gross national product	Main countries	D 7-a
total overseas aid	Worldwide	M 4-a
Assistance in $m	Worldwide	M 3-a
Bilateral aid in $m	Developing world regions	U 23-a
Capital projects (long-term) in $m	European countries	R 5-a
Direct investment by individual companies in $m	OECD countries	D 13-a
in $m	Developing world regions	U 23-a
Disbursements by kind in $m	OECD countries	D 13-a
Export credits (guaranteed) in $m	Main countries	D 7-a
	OECD countries	D 13-a

	Territorial coverage	Title codes
DEVELOPMENT AID, PRIVATE FLOW continued		
Grants of voluntary agencies in $m	OECD countries	D 13-a
	Main countries	D 7-a
Loans to developing countries in $m	Worldwide	M 4-a
Multilateral aid in $m	Developing world regions	U 23-a
Net direct investment in $m	Main countries	D 7-a
New investment by individual companies in $m	OECD countries	D 13-a
Portfolio investments in $m	Main countries	D 7-a
	OECD countries	D 13-a
DEVELOPMENT AID, PUBLIC FLOW		
To multilateral agencies in $m	Main countries	D 7-a
Bilateral assistance in $m	Main countries	D 7-a
Capital subscriptions in $m	Main countries	D 7-a
Concessional loans in $m	Main countries	D 7-a
Export credits in $m	Main countries	D 7-a
Food aid in $m	Main countries	D 7-a
Grants to UN agencies in $m	Main countries	D 7-a
New loans in $m	Main countries	D 7-a
Official commitments in $m	Main countries	D 7-a
Technical assistance in $m	Main countries	D 7-a
DEVELOPMENT PLANS		
see also GOVERNMENT EXPENDITURE		
RESEARCH & DEVELOPMENT		
% of foreign component in costs of development	All countries	A 11-a
% increases planned: cereal production	All countries	A 11-a
employment	All countries	A 11-a
export income	All countries	A 11-a
farm income	All countries	A 11-a
farm labour employed	All countries	A 11-a
farm output	All countries	A 11-a
livestock production	E European countries	U 16-a
	E European countries	U 16-a
Investment by sector in $m	Small African countries	U 39-a
Mezzogiorno funds: farm improvements in million Lit	Italy	D 38-a
fruit tree planting in million Lit	Italy	D 38-a
general infrastructure improvements in million Lit	Italy	D 38-a
handicraft industries development in million Lit	Italy	D 38-a
industrial expansion in million Lit	Italy	D 38-a
tourism expansion in million Lit	Italy	D 38-a
Planned & relationship in expansion of crops & animal husbandry	E European countries	U 16-a
Public investment from local resources	All countries	A 11-a

Dextromoramide   see   SYNTHETIC NARCOTICS

Diabetes   see   DISEASES

DIAMONDS		
% contribution to export earnings	Botswana & Sierra Leone	E 45-a
Exports by value in $m	African, Caribbean countries & Pacific Is	E 45-a
(total) & to EEC area in carats & by value in UA	AASM countries	E 41-a
Imports & exports by source & destination in carats	Main countries	B 15-a
Production of gem stones (uncut) & industrial stones in carats	All countries	U 43-a
(unpolished)	All countries	B 15-a U 22-a
in carats	AASM countries	E 41-a
of synthetic stones in carats	USA	B 15-a
Sales through Central Diamond Corporation by value in $m	USA	B 15-a
World production of gems in carats		N 4-a
DIAMONDS, INDUSTRIAL		
% contribution to export earnings	Liberia	E 45-a
Consumption: tonnage	USA	N 1-a
Exports by value in $	Liberia	E 45-a
Government stockpile by kind: tonnage	USA	N 1-a
Import prices in $ per carat cif	USA	N 1-a
Production of rough uncut stones: tonnage	All countries	U 22-a
World production in carats		N 4-a
tonnage	Main countries	N 1-a
reserves: tonnage (estim)		N 1-a
DIATOMACEOUS EARTH		
% usage for filtration purposes: tonnage	USA	N 1-a
insulation purposes: tonnage	USA	N 1-a
in production of industrial fillers: tonnage	USA	N 1-a
Consumption of diatomite: tonnage	USA	N 1-a
Imports & exports by source & destination: tonnage	Main countries	B 15-a
Production: tonnage	Main countries	B 15-a
World production: tonnage of diatomite		N 4-a

Diatomite   see   DIATOMACEOUS EARTH

Dichloroethane   see   CHEMICALS, ORGANIC

	Territorial coverage	Title codes	
DIE-CASTINGS			
Consumption of zinc in production of die-castings: tonnage	USA	J 6-a	
Sales of aluminium die castings: tonnage	USA	J 6-a	
magnesium die castings: tonnage	USA	J 6-a	
DIE-CASTING ALLOYS			
Consumption of zinc in production of die-cast alloys	UK	J 6-a	
die-castings	Main countries	T 4-a	

Dieldrin   see   INSECTICIDES

Diesel engines   see   ENGINES, DIESEL

	Territorial coverage	Title codes	
DIESEL OIL			
% consumption of world supply	Latin American countries	U 18-a	
% of total EEC area production	EEC countries	R 5-a	
% tax element in retail prices	Main countries	S 24-a	
	W European countries	C 14-a	
Consumption by chemical industry: tonnage	EEC countries	E 14-a	
end-user sectors & transport: tonnage	OECD countries	D 31-a	
industry (in general): tonnage	EEC countries	E 14-a	
iron & steel industry: tonnage	EEC area	U 6-a	U 7-a
	EEC countries	E 14-a	
	Main countries	H 3-a	
	OECD countries	D 44-a	
motor vehicles: tonnage	European countries	U 8-a	
non-ferrous metals industry: tonnage	EEC countries	E 14-a	
non-metallic mineral industry: tonnage	EEC countries	E 14-a	
rail transportation: tonnage	EEC countries	E 14-a	
road transportation: tonnage	EEC countries	E 14-a	
transportation (in general): tonnage	EEC countries	E 14-a	
in litres	OAS member countries	N 17-a	
of gas oil in m³	AASM countries	E 41-a	
tonnage	Main countries	C 14-a	S 24-a
total & from own refineries: tonnage	Italy	H 4-a	
Deliveries for household consumption: tonnage	EEC countries	E 16-m	E 15-a
own consumption, exports & bunkers: tonnage	OECD countries	D 39-q	D 31-a
Export prices at main ports in cents per gallon fob	Worldwide	H 4-a	
by grade in local currency	All countries	R 2-m	
Import prices per m³ in S Kr cif	Sweden	U 10-a	
Imports by source: tonnage	OECD countries	D 31-a	
& exports by source & destination: tonnage	Main countries	B 15-a	
tonnage	Main countries	C 14-a	
Price increases affected for bunker oil in $	World ports	S 16-q	
Prices posted at specific ports in cents per gallon fob	Worldwide	C 3-a	
Production & consumption: tonnage	OECD countries	D 44-a	
tonnage (incl world total): tonnage	OECD countries	R 5-a	
tonnage	EEC countries	E 26-m	E 28-q
		E 27-a	
	European countries, USA & USSR	U 4-a	
	Main countries	B 15-a	E 3-a
	S American countries & Mexico	U 40-a	
volume in m³	OECD countries	D 39-q	D 31-a
Refinery output, imports & supply: tonnage	Main countries	S 24-a	
Retail prices in cents per litre	W Germany	E 34-m	
in DM per 100 litres	W European countries	C 14-a	
in local currency per litre	Main countries	S 24-a	
Taxes levied on motor fuel in local currency	OAS member countries	N 17-a	
Wholesale prices in local currency			

Diesel-driven locomotives   see   LOCOMOTIVES, DIESEL

	Territorial coverage	Title codes	
DIETETIC FOODS			
Production & consumption of canned baby foods: tonnage	OECD countries	D 14-a	
tonnage	EEC countries	E 28-q	E 27-a

Diggers   see   CONSTRUCTION EQUIPMENT

Dihydrocodeine & dionine   see   OPIUM ALKALOIDS

Diphenoxylate   see   SYNTHETIC NARCOTICS

Diphtheria   see   DISEASES, INFECTIOUS

	Territorial coverage	Title codes
DIPLOMAS & CERTIFICATES		
No gained by sex of students	All countries	U 62-a

Direct costs   see   LABOUR COSTS

Direct investment   see   DEVELOPMENT AID, PRIVATE FLOW

Direct purchases   see   COMMODITY CREDIT CORPORATION
                               INVENTORIES
                               PRICE SUPPORTS

Direct selling margins   see   SALES MARGINS, DIRECT SALES

Direct taxation   see   TAXATION, DIRECT

	Territorial coverage	Title codes

Disablement benefits   see   INJURY & DISABLEMENT BENEFITS

Disaster relief   see   FOOD AID

Disasters   see   NATURAL DISASTERS

Disc brake assemblies   see   REPLACEMENT PARTS

DISCOUNT HOUSES
    see also   TREASURY BILLS

Claims by central monetary institutions	All countries	F 5-m F 6-q

DISCOUNT RATES
    see also   INTEREST RATES
                RE-DISCOUNT RATES

Of central banks: % per annum & validity periods	Main countries	R 5-a
% interest rates charged by banking system	All countries	F 5-m F 6-q
	Asian, Far East & Australasian countries	U 45-a
Central banks: changes in % rates per annum (see no 9)	All countries	U 27-a U 43-a
Official % discount rates of central banks	EEC countries	E 26-m
	Main countries	E 3-a
	OECD countries	D 12-a

Discounts for cash sales   see   SALES DISCOUNTS FOR CASH

DISEASES
    see also   DEATHS BY CAUSE
                LEPROSY
                RABIES
                VENEREAL DISEASES

Death rates per 100,000 population by kind of disease	All countries	W 2-m
from notifiable diseases	Latin American countries	J 5-a
abortion	All countries	W 2-m
cancer	All countries	W 2-m
cerebro-vascular diseases	All countries	W 2-m
diabetes	All countries	W 2-m
enteritis	All countries	W 2-m
heart diseases	All countries	W 2-m
hypertensive diseases	All countries	W 2-m
pregnancy & childbirth	All countries	W 2-m
rheumatic fever	All countries	W 2-m
tuberculosis	All countries	W 2-m
No of deaths by diseases (in detail)	OAS member countries	N 12-a
from cerebro-vascular diseases	All countries	W 2-m
cirrhosis	All countries	W 2-a
heart diseases	All countries	W 2-m
hypertensive diseases	All countries	W 2-m
pneumonia & bronchitis	All countries	W 2-a

DISEASES, CONTAGIOUS

No of reported cases: cholera	All countries	W 2-m
plague	All countries	W 2-m
smallpox	All countries	W 2-m
yellow fever	All countries	W 2-m
	OAS member countries	N 18-a
vaccinations given against smallpox	OAS member countries	N 18-a
against yellow fever	OAS member countries	N 18-a

DISEASES, INDUSTRIAL

No of benefits paid out for disabilities	OAS member countries	N 18-a
to victims	OAS member countries	N 18-a
to widows for fatalaties	OAS member countries	N 18-a
deaths from lung diseases in foundrymen	UK	B 25-a

DISEASES, INFECTIOUS

No of reported cases by kind	Main countries	W 1-m
of diphtheria	All countries	W 2-m
dysentery	All countries	W 2-m
encephalitis	All countries	W 2-m
hepatitis	All countries	W 2-m
influenza	All countries	R 2-m
measles	All countries	W 2-m
meningitis	All countries	W 2-m
poliomyelitis	All countries	W 2-m
scarlet fever	All countries	W 2-m
typhoid fever	All countries	W 2-m
	OAS member countries	N 18-a
whooping cough	All countries	W 2-m

DISINFECTANTS
    see also   FUMIGANTS
                INSECTICIDES

	Territorial coverage	Title codes

DISINFECTANTS, continued

% contribution to export earnings	Rwanda	E 45-a
Consumption of fungicides & fumigants: tonnage	All countries	A 9-a
Production (incl insect & fungicides): tonnage	All countries	U 22-a
Usage of mercury in production of fungicides in flasks	USA	T 4-a

Disposable income   see   NATIONAL INCOME

Dissolving pulp   see   WOOD PULP, DISSOLVING

Distillates   see   FUEL OIL
               PETROLEUM PRODUCTS

DISTILLATION CAPACITY

    see also   CRUDE PETROLEUM
                     PETROLEUM REFINERIES

Petroleum refineries: tonnage	Main countries	E 3-a
World crude oil refining capacity: tonnage		H 4-a U 43-a

Distilled spirits   see   BEVERAGES, ALCOHOLIC

DISTILLING & MALTING

    see also   BREWING INDUSTRY
                     MALT

Barley consumption for malting: tonnage	Main countries	B 8-a
Industrial usage of barley: tonnage	UK	C 27-a
maize: tonnage	UK	C 27-a
wheat: tonnage	UK	C 27-a
Investment in buildings in local currency	EEC countries	E 40-a
machinery in local currency	EEC countries	E 40-a
Maize consumption: tonnage	UK	B 8-a

DISTRIBUTION COSTS

% gross retail margins: men's wear shops	UK	B 22-a
women's wear shops	UK	B 22-a
Banana industry: export handling costs	Main countries	A 15-a
freight insurance	Main countries	A 15-a
import duties: rates charged on bananas	Main countries	A 15-a
retailer's % margins	Main countries	A 15-a
ripener's % margins	Main countries	A 15-a
Freight & insurance charged in world trade	Main countries	F 2-a

DISTRIBUTION OUTLETS

% male & female clothing sales by co-operative societies	UK	B 22-a
general shops	UK	B 22-a
independent stores	UK	B 22-a
mail order houses	UK	B 22-a
multiples stores	UK	B 22-a

DIVERSIFICATION, INDUSTRIAL

Use of European Development Fund credits for diversification in UA	AASM countries	E 41-a

Dividend tax   see   TAXATION

DIVIDENDS

Declared by largest European industrial companies		F 9-a
Income (incl interest) as component in national income	OAS member countries	N 16-a
Receipts from taxes on dividends & interest	EEC countries	E 42-a
Taxes levied: rates & basis of assessment	EEC countries	E 31-a

DIVORCE RATES

Per 1000 population	Asian, Far East & Australasian countries	U 45-a
	OAS member countries	N 12-a
No of divorces & rate per 1000 population	All countries	U 14
	Latin American countries	J 5-a

DIVORCES

No of divorces legalised by size of family	OAS member countries	N 12-a

DO-IT-YOURSELF

% of householders mainly carrying out own carpentry	W European countries	Z 3
electrical work	W European countries	Z 3
painting & redecoration (incl wall-papering)	W European countries	Z 3
plumbing	W European countries	Z 3
gardening work by social classes	W European countries	Z 3
D.I.Y. work by social classes	W European countries	Z 3
mainly doing own dress-making	W European countries	Z 3
making own knitted garments	W European countries	Z 3

	Territorial coverage	Title codes
Doctors see MEDICAL PERSONNEL		
Dog licence taxes see LICENCE FEES		
DOLLAR PREMIUMS		
Discounts or premiums in US dollars (3 months)	EEC countries	E 26-m
DOLOMITE		
see also MAGNESITE		
Imports & exports by source & destination: tonnage	Main countries	B 15-a
Production: tonnage of crude calcined dolomite	All countries	B 15-a
Domestic cleaning materials see CLEANING & POLISHING MATERIALS		
Domestic consumption see CONSUMPTION		
DOMESTIC DEBT		
Claims on government ministries, in local currency	African countries	U 44-a
All countries	F 5-m F 6-q
on private sector in local currency	African countries	U 44-a
All countries	F 5-m F 6-q
Government expenditure on debt repayments in local currency	African countries	U 44-a
Public internal debt (short & long-term) in $m	EEC countries	E 26-m
Domestic deliveries see DELIVERIES		
DOMESTIC EQUIPMENT		
see also DRYING MACHINES, ELECTRIC		
ELECTRIC COOKERS		
ELECTRIC IRONS		
ELECTRIC KETTLES		
HEATING APPLIANCES, ELECTRIC		
OVENS, DOMESTIC		
REFRIGERATORS, DOMESTIC		
SEWING MACHINES		
VACUUM CLEANERS		
WASHING MACHINES		
% increase in demand projected to 1977	UK	B 23
% of households owning air conditioning equipment	W European countries	Z 3
deep freezers	W European countries	Z 3
dish washing machines	W European countries	Z 3
electric food mixers	W European countries	Z 3
electric irons	W European countries	Z 3
electric toasters	W European countries	Z 3
refrigerators	W European countries	Z 3
spin-driers	W European countries	Z 3
tumbler driers	W European countries	Z 3
vacuum cleaners	W European countries	Z 3
washing machines	W European countries	Z 3
water softeners	W European countries	Z 3
% share of world export trade (value basis)	Main countries	B 23-a
% of world exports to developed countries (value basis)		U 38-a
developing countries (value basis)		U 38-a
Expenditure on furniture et al as % of total household outlay	EEC countries	E 2-a
Exports by destination: electrical apparatus by value in $m	Main countries	U 9-a
by value in $m	Main countries	U 9-a
Exports of cookers & heaters by value in $	OECD countries	D 9-a
electrical apparatus by value in $m	Main countries	U 38-a
non-electric equipment by value in $m	Main countries	U 38-a
Exports - index nos (volume & value basis)	OECD countries	D 16-q
Imports of durable goods by value in UA	AASM countries	E 41-a
electrical apparatus by value in $	All countries	U 38-a
non-durable goods ex EEC area by value in UA	AASM countries	E 41-a
non-electrical goods by value in $	All countries	U 38-a
Imports - index nos (volume & value basis)	OECD countries	D 16-q
Private expenditure on household equipment in UA	AASM countries	E 41-a
Receipts of steel supplies by domestic equipment manufacturing industries: tonnage	OECD countries	D 22-a
Retail prices (comparative): electric irons in $	EEC countries	Z 3-a
light bulbs in cents	EEC countries	Z 3-a
records for reproduction equipment in $	EEC countries	Z 3-a
refrigerators in $	EEC countries	Z 3-a
tape recorders in $	EEC countries	Z 3-a
transistor radios in $	EEC countries	Z 3-a
vacuum cleaners in $	EEC countries	Z 3-a
washing machines in $	EEC countries	Z 3-a
Sales of electrical apparatus by value in $	Central African countries	U 38
Use of plastics for production of domestic equipment as % of total usage	European countries	U 26-a
Value added in manufacture in $m	OECD countries	D 9-a
World export trade: home electrical goods by value in $m		U 38-a

	Territorial coverage	Title codes	
DOMESTIC EQUIPMENT BY KIND			
% of households owning specific kinds of machines & equipment	W European countries	Z 3	
Exports by destination by CST classes by value	EEC countries	E 48-a	
by SITC classes by value in $	OECD countries	D 3-a2	
destination: tonnage & value in $	Main countries	D 2-q	
	All countries	U 12-a	
NIMEXE classes by volume	All countries	E 20-a	
SITC classes by volume	All countries	U 50-a	U 59-a
Imports by NIMEXE classes by volume	All countries	E 20-a	
SITC classes by volume	All countries	U 50-a	U 59-a
source by CST classes by value	EEC countries	E 21-a	
SITC classes by value in $	Main countries	D 2-q	
tonnage & value in $	OECD countries	D 3-a2	
tonnage & value in $	All countries	U 12-a	
Retail prices (comparative) in $	EEC countries	Z 3-a	
DOMESTIC EQUIPMENT INDUSTRIES			
International Development Agency loans in $	OAS member countries	N 16-a	
Receipts of aluminium products for fabrication: tonnage	OECD countries	D 21-a	
Usage of brass mill products: tonnage	USA	J 6-a	
copper rods & wire: tonnage	USA	J 6-a	
sheets: tonnage	USA	J 6-a	
tubes: tonnage	USA	J 6-a	

Domestic expenditure   see   HOUSEHOLD BUDGETS

Domestic furnishings   see   HOUSEHOLD TEXTILES

Domestic lighting & heating   see   LIGHTING & HEATING, DOMESTIC

Domestic ovens or cookers   see   OVENS, DOMESTIC

Domestic service   see   SERVICES, DOMESTIC

	Territorial coverage	Title codes	
DONKEYS			
Population	France, Italy & Netherlands	E 1-a	
DRAWING RIGHTS			
see also INTERNATIONAL MONETARY FUND			
Allocations as payment balances component in $m	All member countries	F 1-a	
in International Monetary Fund in $	OAS member countries	N 16-a	
Availability of International Monetary Fund credits in $m	Main countries	E 3-a	
Changes in reserve position in International Monetary Fund in $	OECD countries	D 10-a	
Drawings on International Monetary Fund as payment balances component in $	Latin American countries	U 18-a	
Equivalent in terms of International Monetary Fund's currency holdings in $m		F 4-a	
Holdings & reserve position in International Monetary Fund in $m	EEC countries	E 26-m	
Position in International Monetary Fund: holdings, drawings & balances in $	All member countries	F 5-m	F 6-q
Special reserves available for members of International Monetary Fund in $		D 26-m	
Summary of transactions: money received & used in $m		F 4-a	
Transfers of drawing rights to acquire currencies		F 4-a	

Drawn wire   see   WIRE, STEEL

	Territorial coverage	Title codes
DREDGERS		
Deliveries of new dredgers by kind: volume	Netherlands	S 16-a

Dresses   see   CLOTHING

Dried fruit   see   FRUIT, DRIED

Dried vegetables   see   DRY BEANS, DRY PEAS VEGETABLES, DRIED

	Territorial coverage	Title codes
DRILLING MACHINES		
see also MACHINE TOOLS		
Consumption by value by supply area in $m	EEC countries	B 31-a
Deliveries by industrial sector by value in $m	USA	J 2-a
(domestic) by value in $m	EEC countries	B 31-a
Exports as % of production (value basis)	EEC countries	B 31-a
by destination of metal-drilling machines by value in £m	UK	B 31-a
volume & value in $m	USA	J 2-a
Imports as % of consumption (value basis)	EEC countries	B 31-a
by source of metal-drilling machines by value in £m	UK	B 31-a
volume & value in $m	USA	J 2-a
Inter-EEC trade by value in $m & % growth rates	EEC countries	B 20-a
Production of automatic numerically-controlled type by volume	EEC countries	B 20-a
by value in $m	EEC countries	B 31-a
Production, imports, exports & home sales in $m	EEC countries	B 20-a
by volume: metal-drilling machines	EEC countries	B 31-a
Sales by type by volume & value in $m	USA	J 2-a

	Territorial coverage	Title codes

Drilling rigs   see   OIL EXPLORATION

Drink   see   FOOD, DRINK & TOBACCO
              BEVERAGES, ALCOHOLIC

Drinks, alcoholic   see   BEVERAGES, ALCOHOLIC

Dripping   see   BEEF FATS

Driving licences   see   VEHICLE DRIVING LICENCES

Drug industry   see   PHARMACEUTICAL INDUSTRY

DRUGS & MEDICINES
    see also   COCAINE
                       CODEINE
                       HEROIN
                       HYGIENE REQUISITES
                       MORPHINE
                       OPIUM
                       PETHIDINE
                       SYNTHETIC NARCOTICS

	Territorial coverage	Title codes
Consumption by name of drug per million population in kg	All countries	U 46-a
of coca leaves in production of cocaine in kg	Peru	U 46-a
Consumption cost: private sector	EEC countries	E 32-a
Consumption: cannabis resin in kg	India & Pakistan	U 46-a
coca leaves for chewing in kg	Peru	U 46-a
cocaine in kg	All countries	U 46-a
codeine in kg	All countries	U 46-a
dextromoramide in kg	All countries	U 46-a
ethylmorphine in kg	All countries	U 46-a
methadone in kg	All countries	U 46-a
morphine in kg	All countries	U 46-a
pethidine in kg	All countries	U 46-a
Exports by destination: coca leaf in kg	Bolivia & Peru	U 46-a
cocaine in kg	All countries	U 46-a
codeine in kg	All countries	U 46-a
ethylmorphine in kg	All countries	U 46-a
medicinal products by value in $	Main countries	U 2-a
methadone in kg	Switzerland & UK	U 46-a
morphine in kg	All countries	U 46-a
opium in kg	All countries	U 46-a
poppy straw in kg	All countries	U 46-a
poppy straw & concentrates in kg	All countries	U 46-a
of coca leaf for production of cocaine in kg	Bolivia & Peru	U 46-a
medicinal ingredients by value in $m	Main countries	U 26-a
Illicit traffic seizures: cannabis resin in kg	All countries	U 46-a
coca leaves in kg	All countries	U 46-a
cocaine in kg	All countries	U 46-a
heroin in kg	All countries	U 46-a
morphine in kg	All countries	U 46-a
opium in kg	All countries	U 46-a
Imports of coca leaves (for chewing) in kg	Bolivia	U 46-a
medicinal ingredients by value in $m	Main countries	U 26-a
No of doses consumed per 1000 population per yr	Main countries	U 46-a
Production: coca leaves in kg	Bolivia & Peru	U 46-a
in kg	India & Pakistan	U 46-a
medical products by value in $m	Communist countries	U 26-a
medicinal ingredients by value in $m	Main countries	U 26-a
methadone intermediates in kg	Netherlands	U 46-a
opium alkaloids in kg	All countries	U 46-a
synthetic narcotics in kg	All countries	U 46-a
Requirements for manufacture & for export in kg	Main countries	U 19-a
special stocks in kg	Main countries	U 19-a
of narcotic drugs in kg	Main countries	U 19-a
Usage of morphine in production of codeine in kg	All countries	U 46-a
ethylmorphine in kg	All countries	U 46-a
pholcodine in kg	All countries	U 46-a
World requirements by kinds of narcotics in kg		U 19-a

DRY BEANS
    see also   CAROBS

	Territorial coverage	Title codes
Area harvested in ha, production tonnage & yield per ha	All countries	A 9-a
under crop in ha	OAS member countries	N 13-a
Consumption: tonnage	OAS member countries	N 17-a
Crop yield in kg per ha	OAS member countries	N 13-a
Export prices (incl broad beans) in local currency per ton	Main countries	A 9-a
Import prices in £ per ton cif	UK	A 9-a
Producer prices of broad beans in local currency per ton	Cyprus, Egypt & Italy	A 9-a
in local currency	All countries	A 9-a
Production tonnage & yield per 100 ha	Latin American countries	J 5-a
	OAS member countries	N 13-a
Wholesale prices in local currency	India, Italy & Mexico	A 9-a

	Territorial coverage	Title codes
DRY CARGO		
% of world freight tonnage shipped	World regions	U 37-a
Loaded & unloaded by seaborne shipping: tonnage	All countries	U 43-a
Seaborne freight as % total world freight tonnage		U 37-a

Dry-cargo freight rates   see   OCEAN FREIGHT RATES

Dry-cargo ships   see   CARGO SHIPS

	Territorial coverage	Title codes
DRY PEAS		
Area under crop in ha	OAS member countries	N 13-a
Consumption: tonnage	OAS member countries	N 17-a
Crop yield in kg per ha	OAS member countries	N 13-a
Export prices in local currency	Australia, Madagascar & Netherlands	A 9-a
Producer prices in local currency	Uganda & USA	A 9-a
Production: tonnage	OAS member countries	N 13-a
Supply, production, consumption & trade: tonnage	EEC countries	B 1-a
Wholesale prices in local currency	Ethiopia & India	A 9-a

Dry whey   see   MILK POWDER

	Territorial coverage	Title codes	
DRYING MACHINES, DOMESTIC			
Production by volume	All countries	U 22-a	U 38-a

Ducks   see   POULTRY

	Territorial coverage	Title codes
DUMPERS & DUMP TRUCKS		
Exports by destination: no & value in £m	UK	V 1-a
Imports by source: no & value in £m	UK	V 1-a
Production by capacity in cu yards	UK	V 1-q
DURABLE GOODS		
see also DOMESTIC EQUIPMENT		
% growth rates in consumption, 1955-1969	OECD countries	D 11
Consumption cost to private sector in $m	EEC countries	E 32-a
Demand per 1000 population: bicycles	E European countries & USSR	U 16-a
furniture	E European countries & USSR	U 16-a
motor cars	E European countries & USSR	U 16-a
motor cycles & scooters	E European countries & USSR	U 16-a
radio sets	E European countries & USSR	U 16-a
refrigerators	E European countries	U 16-a
sewing machines	E European countries	U 16-a
television sets	E European countries	U 16-a
vacuum cleaners (domestic)	E European countries	U 16-a
washing machines (domestic)	E European countries	U 16-a
watches	E European countries & USSR	U 16-a
Expenditure (private) on durable goods in local currency	OAS member countries	N 16-a
Imports by value in UA	AASM countries	E 41-a
ex EEC area by value in UA	AASM countries	E 41-a
Retail prices of domestic equipment - index nos	EEC countries	E 26-m
- index nos	Mexico	U 18-a
Sales - index nos (value basis)	OECD countries	D 26-m

Durum wheat   see   WHEAT, HARD

Duties   see   DEATH DUTIES
              EXCISE TAX
              EXPORT DUTIES
              IMPORT DUTIES
              LICENCE FEES
              MOTOR VEHICLE DUTIES
              STAMP DUTIES

	Territorial coverage	Title codes
DWELLINGS		
see also BUILDING CONSTRUCTION		
% built by co-operative societies	E European countries & USSR	U 16-a
by private enterprise with state credit	E European countries & USSR	U 16-a
by state enterprises	E European countries & USSR	U 16-a
% change in cost of residential building	All countries	U 13-a
% of households owning or buying second homes	W European countries	Z 3
% of new building financed by housing associations	European countries	U 5-a
housing co-operatives	European countries	U 5-a
municipal authorities	European countries	U 5-a
private bodies	European countries & USA	U 5-a
private persons	European countries & USA	U 5-a
public authorities	European countries	U 5-a
semi-public bodies	European countries	U 5-a
state co-operatives	European countries	U 5-a
with installed fixed bath facilities	European countries	U 5-a
central heating	European countries	U 5-a
piped water facilities	European countries	U 5-a
% of dwellings & flats with bathrooms	EEC countries	E 2-a
% of existing dwellings by year of construction	W European countries	Z 3
% of dwellings or flats owned by occupiers but mortgage repayments outstanding	W European countries	Z 3
by social classes	W Euorpean countries	Z 3

	Territorial coverage	Title codes
DWELLINGS, continued		
% of dwellings or flats owned by occupiers & mortgages paid off	W European countries	Z 3
with installed bath (or shower)	W European countries	Z 3
central heating	W European countries	Z 3
electric lighting	All countries	U 13-a
flush toilet	All countries	U 13-a
piped water	All countries	U 13-a
	Developing countries	U 23-a
piped cold water	W European countries	Z 3
piped hot water	W European countries	Z 3
private garden	W European countries	Z 3
telephone	W European countries	Z 3
% of dwellings overcrowded (3 or more persons per room)	All countries	U 13-a
owner-occupied & % rented	EEC countries	E 2-a
Building construction as assets in capital formation & as % of gross national product	All countries	U 13-a
in $m	EEC countries	E 32-a
by value as % of capital formation	Main countries	E 3-a
Density of population: no of persons per room	All countries	U 13-a
Floor area authorised by building permits in m²	ECAFE countries	U 32-q
Housing space constructed in million m²	E European countries	U 16-a
Labour costs of house construction - index nos	European countries	U 5-a
Material costs of house construction - index nos	European countries	U 5-a
New building construction completed: all types of dwellings	Main countries	U 58-a
floor space per dwelling in m³ (average)	European countries	U 5-a
no of multi-dwelling buildings	Main countries	U 58-a
one or two dwelling buildings	Main countries	U 58-a
dwellings & no of rooms (total)	European countries	U 5-a
	Main countries	E 3-a
completions	European countries, Canada, USA & USSR	A 24-a
no of permits issued & no dwellings built	EEC countries	E 26-m
by areas	EEC countries	E 38-a
No of new buildings (residential) completed	Main countries	U 43-a
& no built per 1000 population	ECE countries	U 15-a
	EEC countries	E 2-a
constructed by private enterprise	Main countries	U 58-a
state or local government authorities	Main countries	U 58-a
No built: conventional dwelling houses	All countries	U 13-a
	E European countries & USSR	U 16-a
	Main countries	R 5-a
conventional dwelling houses (incl flats)	ECAFE countries	U 32-q
per 1000 population	All countries	U 13-a
	Main countries	E 3-a
100,000 population	E European countries	U 16-a
No of existing stock & % change	European countries	U 5-a
	EEC countries	E 2-a
	ECE countries	U 15-a
available per 1000 population	European countries	U 5-a
	All countries	U 13-a
100 households	OECD countries	D 47-a
houses available for tourist letting	All countries	U 13-a
living quarters available (excl housing units)	All countries	U 13-a
: hotel rooming houses	All countries	U 13-a
: institutions & camps	European countries & USA	U 5-a
houses located in rural areas as % of total stock	European countries & USA	U 5-a
in urban areas as % of total stock	All countries	U 13-a
needed & needs for replacement	OAS member countries	N 18-a
occupied by kind of tenure: rural areas	OAS member countries	N 18-a
urban areas	OAS member countries	N 18-a
by tenants in urban & rural areas	All countries	U 13-a
unoccupied (incl vacancy ratios)	OAS member countries	N 18-a
housing units: buildings not fitted for human use	OAS member countries	N 18-a
by no of occupants per room	OAS member countries	N 18-a
by no of rooms: rural areas	OAS member countries	N 18-a
urban areas	OAS member countries	N 18-a
conventional dwellings	OAS member countries	N 18-a
improvised marginal dwellings	OAS member countries	N 18-a
mobile homes	OAS member countries	N 18-a
temporary rustic houses	OAS member countries	N 18-a
with electric lighting	OAS member countries	N 18-a
fixed bath or shower	OAS member countries	N 18-a
lamps (oil-burning) for lighting	OAS member countries	N 18-a
mains disposal of sewerage	OAS member countries	N 18-a
outside sources of water: rural areas	OAS member countries	N 18-a
urban areas	OAS member countries	N 18-a
piped water (urban & rural areas)	OAS member countries	N 18-a
toilets (flush) rural areas	OAS member countries	N 18-a
urban areas	OAS member countries	N 18-a
(other than flush): rural areas	OAS member countries	N 18-a
urban areas	OAS member countries	N 18-a
without electric lighting installation	OAS member countries	N 18-a
fixed baths or showers	OAS member countries	N 18-a
mains disposal of sewerage	OAS member countries	N 18-a
owner-occupied in urban & rural areas	European countries	U 5-a
per 1000 population in rural areas	European countries	U 5-a
urban areas	European countries	U 5-a
per 1000 population	European countries & USA	U 5-a

	Territorial coverage	Title codes
DWELLINGS, continued		
No of new dwellings under construction & floor areas in m²	EEC countries	E 28-q E 27-a
& no completed	ECE countries	U 42-q
	EEC area	E 13-m
with piped water & toilets	Asian, Far East & Australasian countries	U 45-a
persons in occupation per housing unit: children by sex	OAS member countries	N 18-a
guests by sex	OAS member countries	N 18-a
heads of households	OAS member countries	N 18-a
relatives by sex	OAS member countries	N 18-a
servants by sex	OAS member countries	N 18-a
spouses of house-holders	OAS member countries	N 18-a
per room in existing dwellings	EEC countries	E 2-a
rented apartments available for tourist letting	OECD countries	D 47-a
restored or converted dwellings	Main countries	U 58-a
room units available per 1000 population	ECE countries	U 15-a
in existing dwellings	ECE countries	U 15-a
new dwellings per 1000 population	ECE countries	U 15-a
new dwellings	Main countries	U 58-a
per 1000 population	European countries	U 5-a
Ownership as component in capital formation	EEC countries	E 32-a
gross domestic product (at factor cost) in local currency	African countries	U 44-a
Tender value of new building construction in $m	Main countries	U 58-a
DWELLINGS BY AGE		
% constructed before or after 1945	EEC countries	E 2-a
% of houses with 1, 2 or more storeys	W European countries	Z 3
DWELLINGS BY SIZE		
In m² of floor area	Main countries	R 5-a
% constructed for one or two families	Main countries	R 5-a
for several families	Main countries	R 5-a
% of dwellings comprising one room only	All countries	U 13-a
New construction: no of rooms per dwelling (average)	European countries	U 5-a
volume by no of rooms	European countries	U 5-a
No of dwellings built by type of investor	All countries	U 13-a
by private enterprise	All countries	U 13-a
by public enterprise	All countries	U 13-a
in m² (average)	E European countries & USSR	U 16-a
of occupied dwellings in urban & rural areas	All countries	U 13-a
of households & kinds of facilities installed in dwellings	Latin American countries	J 5-a
of persons per room in urban & rural areas	All countries	U 13-a
of rooms per dwelling (average)	All countries	U 13-a
DWELLINGS BY TYPE OF CONSTRUCTION		
No of adobe houses	OAS member countries	N 18-a
of dwellings built of asbestos sheets	OAS member countries	N 18-a
bricks	OAS member countries	N 18-a
cement	OAS member countries	N 18-a
clay tiles	OAS member countries	N 18-a
metal sheets	OAS member countries	N 18-a
straw & daub	OAS member countries	N 18-a
timber	OAS member countries	N 18-a
% constructed by type of building materials	European countries	U 5-a
of assembled frames	European countries	U 5-a
cast concrete in situ	Hungary & Italy	U 5-a
concrete blocks	European countries	U 5-a
medium-sized panels	European countries	U 5-a
monolithic frames	Czechoslovakia	U 5-a
re-inforced concrete	European countries	U 5-a
room-sized panels	E European countries & Netherlands	U 5-a
steel frames	Netherlands, Portugal & UK	U 5-a
stone & bricks	European countries	U 5-a
sun-dried bricks	Turkey	U 5-a
timber & wood frames	European countries	U 5-a
traditional mixed materials	European countries	U 5-a
Dwellings, pre-fabricated see HOUSING, PRE-FABRICATED		
Dyeing extracts see DYESTUFFS, SYNTHETIC		
DYESTUFFS		
Exports by destination: tonnage & value in $m	OECD countries	D 5-a
Imports by source: tonnage & value in $m	OECD countries	D 5-a
Production: tonnage & value in $m	OECD countries	D 5-a
tonnage	OECD area	D 5-a
DYESTUFFS, SYNTHETIC		
Exports by destination by value in $	Main countries	U 2-a
synthetic dyeing extracts by value in $	Main countries	U 2-a
tanning extracts by value in $	Main countries	U 2-a
Plant investment (incl pigments production) in £m	UK	B 21-a
Production by value (gross & net) in £m	UK	B 21-a
tonnage	All countries	U 22-a

Dynamo steel   see   STEEL SHEETS, MAGNETIC

Dysentery   see   DISEASES, INFECTIOUS

	Territorial coverage	Title codes

E.C.S.C. (EUROPEAN COAL & STEEL COMMUNITY)

	Territorial coverage	Title codes
Export price per ton fixed for chequer plates	EEC countries	T 4-a
heavy plates over 8 mm	EEC countries	T 4-a
hot-rolled steel coil	EEC countries	T 4-a
strip	EEC countries	T 4-a
medium plates 3-8 mm	EEC countries	T 4-a
reinforcing steel rounds	EEC countries	T 4-a
sections, universal beams & wide-flange beams	EEC countries	T 4-a
sheets (galvanised)	EEC countries	T 4-a
steel coil (cold-rolled)	EEC countries	T 4-a
(galvanised)	EEC countries	T 4-a
merchant bars	EEC countries	T 4-a
tube strip	EEC countries	T 4-a
wire rods	EEC countries	T 4-a
universal plates	EEC countries	T 4-a
wire (black annealed)	EEC countries	T 4-a
(bright steel)	EEC countries	T 4-a
(galvanised)	EEC countries	T 4-a
Prices fixed for export per ton: steel products by kind	EEC countries	T 4-a
pig iron (hematite by grade) per ton	EEC countries	T 4-a
(phosphoric by grade) per ton	EEC countries	T 4-a

E.D.F.   see   EUROPEAN DEVELOPMENT FUND

EEC BUDGET

	Territorial coverage	Title codes
% of total budgetary contributions	EEC countries	B 3-a
Allocations to court of justice in £m	EEC countries	B 3-a
European Commission in £m	EEC countries	B 3-a
European Council in £m	EEC countries	B 3-a
European Parliament in £m	EEC countries	B 3-a
Appropriations for ensuing yrs in £m	EEC countries	B 3-a
Contributions from member countries in £m	EEC countries	B 3-a
Expenditure in £m	EEC countries	B 3-a
on agricultural price guarantees in £m	EEC countries	B 3-a
aid to fruit & vegetable growers in £m	EEC countries	B 3-a
export refunds in £m	EEC countries	B 3-a
food aid: supply of butter in £m	EEC countries	B 3-a
of skim powder in £m	EEC countries	B 3-a
intervention activity on food products in £m	EEC countries	B 3-a
on milk in £m	EEC countries	B 3-a
monetary compensation to farmers in £m	EEC countries	B 3-a
priority area development in £m	EEC countries	B 3-a
skim milk aid for animal feed in £m	EEC countries	B 3-a
for casein production in £m	EEC countries	B 3-a
slaughtering premiums for cows in £m	EEC countries	B 3-a
storage of cheese in £m	EEC countries	B 3-a
of milk powder in £m	EEC countries	B 3-a
of surplus butter in £m	EEC countries	B 3-a
structural farm improvements in £m	EEC countries	B 3-a

EARNINGS

see also   WAGES

	Territorial coverage	Title codes
% change in gross nominal wage income	E European countries	U 16-a
real wages (after price changes)	E European countries	U 16-a
in industry per hr	European countries & USA	U 16-q
wages per hr (in cash terms)	European countries, Canada & USA	U 16-q
(in real terms)	European countries, Canada & USA	U 16-q
% increase in earnings per man-hr: manufacturing industry	Main countries	B 27-a
% of households by social classes & by income levels	W European countries	Z 3
Abattoir workers per hr - index nos	EEC countries	E 25-a
Aircraft & parts industry per wk & per hr in $	USA	J 2-a
per hr by sex - index nos	EEC countries	E 25-a
Alcoholic drinks industry per hr - index nos	EEC countries	E 25-a
Briquetting industry per hr - index nos	EEC countries	E 25-a
Building & manufacturing industries per hr in $	ECE countries	U 42-m
industry per hr in local currency	EEC countries	E 3-a
by areas in local currency	EEC countries	E 38-a
- index nos	EEC countries	E 25-a
wages & salaries in $	Main countries	U 58-a
Building materials industry per hr - index nos	EEC countries	E 25-a
Carpet industry as % all manufacturing industry	UK	B 29-a
Cement industry per hr - index nos	EEC countries	E 25-a
Ceramics industry per hr by sex - index nos	EEC countries	E 25-a
Chemical industry per hr by areas	EEC countries	E 38-a
by sex - index nos	EEC countries	E 25-a
Clothing industry by sector: females in £ per wk	UK	B 22-a
males in £ per wk	UK	B 22-a
per hr by sex - index nos	EEC countries	E 25-a

	Territorial coverage	Title codes
EARNINGS, continued		
Collieries per hr: coal-face workers – index nos	EEC countries	E 25-a
pit-head workers – index nos	EEC countries	E 25-a
Confectionery & baking industry per hr – index nos	EEC countries	E 25-a
Cotton industry per hr by sex – index nos	EEC countries	E 25-a
Cotton spinning sector as % all manufacturing industry	UK	B 29-a
Cotton weaving sector as % all manufacturing industry	UK	B 29-a
Dairy industry per hr by sex – index nos	EEC countries	E 25-a
Durable goods industry per wk & per hr in $	USA	J 2-a
Electrical engineering industry per hr in FrS	Main countries	C 2-a
per hr – index nos	EEC countries	E 25-a
Engineering industry: skilled workers (excl overtime) in £ per wk	UK	B 28-a
(incl overtime) in £ per wk	UK	B 28-a
Farm machinery industry per hr by sex – index nos	EEC countries	E 25-a
Food, drink & tobacco industry per hr by areas in local currency	EEC countries	E 38-a
Food processing industry per hr by sex – index nos	EEC countries	E 25-a
Footwear industry per hr by sex – index nos	EEC countries	E 25-a
Foundries (iron & steel) by sex – index nos	EEC countries	E 25-a
per hr in FrS	Main countries	C 2-a
Furniture industry per hr by sex – index nos	EEC countries	E 25-a
Glass industry per hr by sex – index-nos	EEC countries	E 25-a
Hosiery & knitted goods industry as % all manufacturing	UK	B 29-a
Industrial workers per hr by sex – index nos	EEC countries	E 25-a
Instrument engineering industry per hr – index nos	EEC countries	E 25-a
Instruments (incl watch industry) per hr in FrS	Main countries	C 2-a
Iron & steel industry per hr by sex – index nos	EEC countries	E 25-a
per hr in local currency	Main countries	C 2-a
	EEC countries	E 30-m
Iron ore mines per hr: surface workers in local currency	EEC countries	E 29-a
underground workers in local currency	EEC countries	E 29-a
Knitting mills per hr by sex – index nos	EEC countries	E 25-a
Leather goods industry per hr by sex – index nos	EEC countries	E 25-a
Machine tools industry per hr by sex – index nos	EEC countries	E 25-a
(male) – index nos	EEC countries	B 31-a
Machinery industry (non-electrical) per wk & per hr in $	USA	J 2-a
Male workers (skilled & unskilled) in piastres	S Vietnam	U 32-m
Man-made fibre industry per hr by sex – index nos	EEC countries	E 25-a
as % of all manufacturing industry	UK	B 29-a
Manufacturing industry by sex (incl bonuses) per hr in $	Main countries	U 27-m
per hr by sex – index nos	EEC countries	E 25-a
by sex in local currency	All countries	U 43-a
Mechanical engineering industry per hr in local currency	Main countries	C 2-a
per hr – index nos	EEC countries	E 25-a
Metal ore mining per hr by areas in local currency	EEC countries	E 38-a
products industry per hr by areas in local currency	EEC countries	E 38-a
by sex – index nos	EEC countries	E 25-a
in FrS	Main countries	C 2-a
Metal-cutting machinery industry per wk & per hr in $	USA	J 2-a
Metal-working machinery industry per wk & per hr in $	USA	J 2-a
Mining & quarrying by kind per hr (average) in local currency	EEC countries	E 3-a
per hr – index nos	EEC countries	E 25-a
Motor vehicles industry: skilled workers (excl overtime) in £ wk	UK	B 28-a
(incl overtime) in £ wk	UK	B 28-a
per hr by sex – index nos	EEC countries	E 25-a
in local currency	Main countries	C 2-a
wk & per hr (average) in $	USA	J 2-a
Non-ferrous metals industry by sex – index nos	EEC countries	E 25-a
Non-metallic mineral mining industry per hr – index nos	EEC countries	E 25-a
per hr by areas in local currency	EEC countries	E 38-a
Office machinery industry per hr – index nos	EEC countries	E 25-a
Oil & natural gas industry per hr – index nos	EEC countries	E 25-a
Ore mining industry per hr – index nos	EEC countries	E 25-a
Paper & board industry per hr by sex – index nos	EEC countries	E 25-a
printing industry per hr by areas in local currency	EEC countries	E 38-a
Plastics industry per hr by sex – index nos	EEC countries	E 25-a
Printing & publishing industry per hr – index nos	EEC countries	E 25-a
Rubber estate workers & tappers in M$	Malaysia	U 32-m
products manufacturing industry per hr – index nos	EEC countries	E 25-a
Salaried staff: all industries: main occupations by sex – index nos	EEC countries	E 25-a
all industries: main occupations per mth	All countries	L 1-a
briquetting industry by sex – index nos	EEC countries	E 25-a
building industry by sex – index nos	EEC countries	E 25-a
chemical industry by sex – index nos	EEC countries	E 25-a
clothing & footwear industry – index nos	EEC countries	E 25-a
coke ovens by sex – index nos	EEC countries	E 25-a
electrical engineering industry – index nos	EEC countries	E 25-a
food, drink & tobacco industry – index nos	EEC countries	E 25-a
furniture industry by sex – index nos	EEC countries	E 25-a
instruments industry by sex – index nos	EEC countries	E 25-a
leather goods industry by sex – index nos	EEC countries	E 25-a
man-made fibre industry by sex – index nos	EEC countries	E 25-a
manufacturing industry by sex – index nos	EEC countries	E 25-a
mechanical engineering industry – index nos	EEC countries	E 25-a
metals fabrication industry by sex – index nos	EEC countries	E 25-a
mining & quarrying by sex – index nos	EEC countries	E 25-a
motor vehicles industry – index nos	EEC countries	E 25-a
non-metallic minerals industry – index nos	EEC countries	E 25-a

	Territorial coverage	Title codes
EARNINGS, continued		
Salaried staff: office machinery industry – index nos	EEC countries	E 25-a
oil & gas industry by sex – index nos	EEC countries	E 25-a
oil refineries by sex – index nos	EEC countries	E 25-a
ore mining industry by sex – index nos	EEC countries	E 25-a
paper & board industry by sex – index nos	EEC countries	E 25-a
rubber & plastics industry – index nos	EEC countries	E 25-a
textile industry by sex – index nos	EEC countries	E 25-a
transport equipment manufacturing industry – index nos	EEC countries	E 25-a
wood-working industry by sex – index nos	EEC countries	E 25-a
Shipbuilding industry per hr by sex – index nos	EEC countries	E 25-a
per hr in local currency	Main countries	C 2-a
Structural steel industry per hr – index nos	EEC countries	E 25-a
Tanning industry per hr by sex – index nos	EEC countries	E 25-a
Textile & leather industry per hr by areas in local currency	EEC countries	E 38-a
finishing industry as % of all manufacturing industry	UK	B 29-a
industry by sector as % of all manufacturing industry	UK	B 29-a
female earnings as % of male earnings	EEC countries	B 29
per hr by sex – index nos	EEC countries	E 25-a
per hr: males & females in local currency	EEC countries	B 29
Tobacco industry per hr by sex – index nos	EEC countries	E 25-a
Transport equipment industry per hr – index nos	EEC countries	E 25-a
Wage incomes in local currency per mth (average)	E European countries	U 16-a
rate differentials: manufacturing industry – index nos	Main countries	B 28-a
motor vehicles industry by sex in local currency	EEC countries	B 28-a
– index nos	Main countries	B 28-a
Woollen textile industry as % of manufacturing industry	UK	B 29-a
per hr by sex – index nos	EEC countries	E 25-a
(Hourly gross) by sex – index nos	EEC countries	E 3-a
By industrial sectors by sex in local currency	EEC countries	E 25-a2
per hr (average)	All countries	L 4-a
	EEC countries	E 3-a
per hr by areas	EEC countries	E 38-a
Casual daily industrial labour – index nos	Main countries	R 3-a
Full-time monthly-paid industrial employees – index nos	Main countries	R 3-a
weekly-paid industrial employees – index nos	Main countries	R 3-a
Industrial labour force by sex, age groups & degree of skill – index nos	EEC countries	E 2-a
Industrial labour force: earnings (average) – index nos	All countries	F 5-m F 6-q
Per capita per yr in $	Main countries	M 4-a
Per hr in local currency	Main countries	C 7-a
Per wk by industrial sectors	Main countries	R 3-a
Manufacturing industry (average) – index nos	OECD countries	D 26-m
	All countries	L 4-a
EARNINGS, CORPORATE		
Chemical industry as % of sales turnover	USA	J 2-a
Engineering industry as % of sales turnover	USA	J 2-a
Machine tools industry as % of sales turnover	USA	J 2-a
Manufacturing industry as % of sales turnover	USA	J 2-a
Motor vehicles industry as % of sales turnover	USA	J 2-a

Earnings from exports   see   EXPORT EARNINGS

Earnings from overseas   see   REMITTANCES

Earnings of companies   see   BALANCE SHEETS
                                 CASH FLOW
                                 PROFITS
                                 REVENUE
                                 SALES BY VALUE

EARTHENWARE PRODUCTS		
Consumption of cobalt in production of ceramics	USA	T 4-a
Production by kind: tonnage	EEC countries	E 28-q E 27-a

Earthenware products industry   see   CERAMICS INDUSTRY

Earthmoving equipment   see   EXCAVATING MACHINES

Economic growth   see   GROSS DOMESTIC PRODUCT (G.D.P.)

ECONOMIC INDICATORS, BASIC

       see also   BALANCE OF PAYMENTS
                     CAPITAL FORMATION
                     EMPLOYMENT
                     GROSS DOMESTIC PRODUCT (G.D.P.)
                     GROSS DOMESTIC PRODUCT PER CAPITA
                     GOVERNMENT EXPENDITURE
                     INDUSTRIAL PRODUCTION
                     INTEREST RATES
                     MONEY SUPPLY
                     PRIVATE EXPENDITURE
                     RETAIL PRICES
                     TRADE BALANCES
                     UNEMPLOYMENT

	Territorial coverage	Title codes

ECONOMIC INDICATORS, BASIC   continued
    By country — ECAFE countries — U 17-a
    Key statistics on gross national product & trade — EEC countries — E 13-a
                                          Japan — U 17-q

ECONOMIC PLANNING
    see also   AGRICULTURE
                       CAPITAL INVESTMENT
                       CREDIT
                       DEVELOPMENT PLANS
                       EMPLOYMENT
                       FARM COSTS
                       FARM INCOME
                       GOVERNMENT EXPENDITURE
                       INVESTMENT
                       LABOUR COSTS
                       LABOUR PRODUCTIVITY
                       MANPOWER
                       PLANT CAPACITY
                       PRIVATE CONSUMPTION
                       PUBLIC CONSUMPTION
                       PUBLIC FINANCE
                       RESEARCH & DEVELOPMENT

    Planned % increase in crop production — E European countries — U 16-a
                      employment — E European countries — U 16-a
                      farm output — E European countries — U 16-a
                      industrial output — E European countries — U 16-a
                      livestock rearing — E European countries — U 16-a
                      output per man — E European countries — U 16-a
    State procurement: bread grains: tonnage — E European countries — U 16-a
                      cereals: tonnage — E European countries — U 16-a
                      hen eggs: tonnage — E European countries — U 16-a
                      meat: tonnage — E European countries — U 16-a
                      milk: tonnage — E European countries — U 16-a
                      potatoes: tonnage — E European countries & USSR — U 16-a
                      sugar beet: tonnage — E European countries & USSR — U 16-a
                      sunflower seed: tonnage — E European countries — U 16-a

ECONOMICS
        see also   SOCIAL SCIENCES
    No of students enrolled on university courses in economic subjects — OAS member countries — N 19-a

Edam & Edelpilz   see   CHEESE BY VARIETY

Edible offal   see   OFFAL, EDIBLE

EDIBLE OILS
    see also   CORN OIL
                       COTTONSEED OIL
                       GROUNDNUT OIL
                       OLIVE OIL
                       RAPESEED OIL
                       SESAME SEED OIL
                       SOYBEAN OIL

    Consumption by kind: tonnage — OAS member countries — N 17-a
    Wholesale prices in local currency — OAS member countries — N 17-a

EDUCATION
    see also   ADULT EDUCATION
                       SCHOOL ATTENDANCES
                       TEACHER TRAINING

    % allocation of gross national product to education & manpower — OECD countries — D 11
    % attendance rate by age in full-time education — EEC countries — E 3-a
    % enrolment of school-age population in schools — World regions — M 4-a
                  in primary & secondary education — Main countries — U 23-a
    % of government expenditure on salaries, goods & services — OECD countries — D 11
    % of adults by age when their full-time education ceased — W European countries — Z 3
    % of females at school in urban & rural areas — ECAFE countries — U 17
                leaving school at 15 yrs of age by social classes — W European countries — Z 3
    % of males leaving school at 15 yrs of age by social classes — W European countries — Z 3
    % of public expenditure allocated to education — Main countries — R 5-a
    % of students enrolled studying education — ECAFE countries — U 17
    A.I.D. grants to extend educational facilities in $ — All countries — M 1-a
    Age limits & duration of compulsory education in yrs — All countries — U 62
    Budgetary expenditure in local currency — OAS member countries — N 19-a
    Capital expenditure as % of gross national product — All countries — U 62-a
                  as % of total budget — All countries — U 62-a
    Cost to private sector in $m — EEC countries — E 32-a
    Costs (recurrent) per capita student in $ — ECAFE countries — U 17
    Development aid authorisation for education in $ — Recipient countries — M 1-a
    Enrolment in private schools as % total enrolment — ECAFE countries — U 17-a
    Expenditure at cost & as % total domestic outlay — EEC countries — E 2-a
                by levels of instruction — All countries — U 62-a
                per pupil - index nos — All countries — U 62-a
                public & private as % of gross national product — OECD countries — D 11

	Territorial coverage	Title codes
EDUCATION, continued		
IBRD loans approved in $m	OAS member countries	N 16-a
IDA loans approved in $m	OAS member countries	N 16-a
IDB loans approved in $m	OAS member countries	N 16-a
Medians of educational attainment by age	All countries	U 62-a
No of full & part-time research staff in educational methods	All countries	U 62-a
full-time students as % of total population	EEC countries	E 3-a
higher education institutions in use	OAS member countries	N 19-a
hrs of educational radio broadcasts	All countries	U 62-a
television programs	All countries	U 62-a
professors & lecturers employed by kind of college	OAS member countries	N 19-a
pupils & students (full-time) & % change in enrolment	EEC countries	E 26-a
enrolled by grade in schools	Continents	U 62
enrolled by grade of school: historical table from 1841	Main European countries	Z 1-a
enrolled by grade - index nos	World regions	U 62-a
over 15 yrs of age by grade & level of attainment	All countries	U 14-a
& students & no of schools & universities in use	EEC countries	E 3-a
students enrolled on university courses	OAS member countries	N 19-a
teachers employed by grade of school: historical table from 1830	Main European countries	Z 1-a
employed by grade	African countries	U 44-a
universities, faculties & colleges in use	OAS member countries	N 19-a
university degrees awarded in educational subjects	All countries	U 62-a
students studying educational subjects	All countries	U 62-a
Population of school age by age groups	ECAFE region	U 17-a
Public expenditure as % of total budget	Latin American countries	J 5-a
	ECAFE countries	U 17-a
as % of gross national product	Main ECAFE countries	U 17-a
	All countries	M 6-a
on education in local currency	OAS member countries	N 16-a N 19-a
	Latin American countries	J 5-a
	Caribbean countries & W Indies	T 6-a
on education by grade as % of total expenditure	ECAFE countries	U 17-a
on kindergarten schools in $m	All countries	U 62-a
on schools by type	All countries	U 62-a
Pupil-teacher ratios in junior schools	ECAFE countries	U 17-a
in secondary schools	ECAFE countries	U 17-a
School enrolment ratios by grade & sex	All countries	U 62-a
Teacher's salaries as % of expenditure on education	All countries	U 62-a
World bank loans & credits for educational improvements in $m	Worldwide	M 3-a
EDUCATION, HIGHER		
see also TEACHER TRAINING		
UNIVERSITIES		
Expenditure on research & development in $m	All countries	U 62-a
Government research & development expenditure in local currency	EEC countries	E 36-a
No of establishments in use by type	Latin American countries	J 5-a
students enrolled by sex & % females	All countries	U 62-a
by sex	Latin American countries	J 5-a
teachers employed by academic status	Latin American countries	J 5-a
by sex & % females	All countries	U 62-a
by sex	Latin American countries	J 5-a
in private schools by sex	Latin American countries	J 5-a
Public expenditure per student in $	All countries	U 62-a
Education, preparatory see KINDERGARTEN		
EDUCATION, PRIMARY		
% of school enrolment in primary education	All countries	M 6-a
No of primary schools established of all schools	All countries	U 62-a
pupils in primary schools per 100,000 population	ECE countries	U 15-a
pupils & teachers & pupil-teacher ratios	EEC countries	E 3-a
schools by type in urban & rural areas	Latin American countries	J 5-a
pupils enrolled by grade	Latin American countries	J 5-a
by sex	Latin American countries	J 5-a
Pupil-teacher ratios in primary education	All countries	U 62-a
EDUCATION, PRIVATE		
% of all pupils enrolled in primary education	All countries	U 62-a
EDUCATION, SECONDARY		
% of school enrolment in secondary education	All countries	M 6-a
No of certificates awarded & index nos	EEC countries	E 3-a
pupils by sex & % female	All countries	U 62-a
in secondary education per 100,000 population	ECE countries	U 15-a
schools (public & private)	Latin American countries	J 5-a
students enrolled by age	All countries	U 62-a
by grade	Latin American countries	J 5-a
EDUCATION, VOCATIONAL		
see also TEACHER TRAINING		
Age limits applied to students & course durations	All countries	U 62-a
No of students enrolled & % female	All countries	U 62-a
Public expenditure per pupil in $	All countries	U 62-a

	Territorial coverage	Title codes
EDUCATIONAL INSTITUTIONS		
see also SCHOOLS		
By type & sex of students	All countries	U 43-a
No of teachers & no of students enrolled	Continents	U 43-a
teachers employed by sex	All countries	U 43-a
Eels see FISH, FRESHWATER		
Efficiency see LABOUR PRODUCTIVITY		
EGG PRODUCTS		
Exports by destination: tonnage	Main countries	B 12-m
tonnage	Main countries	B 4-a
Imports by source: tonnage	Main countries	B 12-m
	W Germany & UK	B 4-a
of egg yolks (frozen & dried): tonnage	Main countries	B 4-a
Egg yolks, frozen or dried see EGG PRODUCTS		
Egg-laying hens see POULTRY		
EGGPLANTS (Aubergines)		
Area harvested, production tonnage & yield per ha	All countries	A 9-a
EGGS, HEN		
see also STATE PROCUREMENT (Communist countries)		
As source of fat protein & calorie intake per capita	OAS member countries	N 17-a
% changes in producer prices	EEC countries	E 34-m
	W European countries	U 30-a
in retail sales	E European countries	U 16-a
% sale for direct human consumption or export	ECE countries	U 34-a
% share of world import & export trade	Main countries	B 1-a
% usage for sale, farm consumption or processing	ECE countries	U 34-a
Consumption by quantity	OAS member countries	N 17-a
tonnage	EEC countries	E 44-a
per capita by volume per yr	Main countries	B 4-a
by volume	E European countries & USSR	U 16-a
	European countries, Canada, Japan & USA	E 44-a
in kg per yr	W European countries	P 5-a
	EEC countries	B 1-a
	Main countries	E 3-a
Distribution for market sales	Czechoslovakia, Hungary & Poland	U 34-a
own farm use	Czechoslovakia, Hungary & Poland	U 34-a
Export prices - index nos (weighted average main sources)		U 29-q
Export prices in local currency	Australia, Israel, Netherlands & Poland	A 9-a
Exports by destination by volume	EEC countries	E 47-m
tonnage	EEC countries	E 47-m
	Main countries	B 12-m
	Belgium, Denmark, Netherlands & Poland	B 4-a
value & as % of exports of farm products	W European countries	U 20-a
in $m	W European countries	U 33-a
to E European area in $m	W European countries	U 20-a
volume: historical table from 1861	Denmark	Z 1-a
in million doz	Main countries	B 4-a
Government expenditure on price guarantees in £m	UK	P 5-a
Import prices of eggs ex Holland & Belgium in DM	W Germany	U 30-a
Imports by source by volume	EEC countries	E 47-m
	Main countries	B 12-m
tonnage	EEC countries	E 47-m
	W Germany, Italy, Switzerland & UK	B 4-a
value & as % of imports of farm products	W European countries	U 20-a
ex E European area in $m	W European countries	U 20-a
in $m	W European countries	U 33-a
Inter-EEC shipments of eggs (in shell) by volume & tonnage	EEC countries	E 47-m
Prices in EEC area as % of world market prices		E 44-a
Producer prices in local currency	W European countries	U 30-a
	All countries	A 9-a
	E European countries excl USSR	U 30-a
	EEC countries	E 34-m E 44-a
in local currency per ton & by volume	OECD countries	D 1-a
in pence per doz	EEC countries	B 1-a
received from wholesalers in $	W European countries	U 30-a
per 100 kg in local currency	W European countries	E 35-a
per doz in $	USA	E 35-a
per kg	Denmark & Netherlands	R 2-m
Producer prices - index nos	EEC countries	E 44-a
Production by value as % of gross output (incl crops)	E European countries	U 34-a
in local currency	EEC countries	E 44-a
& consumption projected to 1985	World regions	A 1
costs per ton on collective farms	USSR	U 34-a
by volume per hen per year (average)	EEC countries	E 44-a
imports, exports & consumption: tonnage	EEC countries	E 44-a
(incl eggs for hatching): tonnage	OECD countries	D 1-a
stocks & consumption per capita per yr: tonnage	OECD countries	D 14-a
	Czechoslovakia, Hungary & Poland	U 34-a
	EEC countries	B 1-a
tonnage	Canada, European countries, Japan, USA & USSR	E 44-a

	Territorial coverage	Title codes	
EGGS, HEN continued			
Production: tonnage	Latin American countries	U 40-a	
	Main countries	E 3-a	
by volume	Main countries	A 9-a	B 4-a
		U 43-a	
	OAS member countries	N 13-a	
	EEC countries	E 44-a	
	E European countries & USSR (incl Ukraine)	U 16-a	
	Latin American countries	J 5-a	
Ratio of prices of eggs to feed prices for hens	W European countries	U 30-a	
Retail prices (comparative) of one egg in cents	EEC countries	Z 3-a	
in local currency	OAS member countries	N 17-a	
Self-sufficiency ratios	EEC countries	B 1-a	E 44-a
Sluice-gate prices: egg yolks (liquid, dried or frozen) in local currency	EEC countries	B 4-a	
eggs in shell (dried or preserved) in local currency	EEC countries	B 4-a	
eggs in shell in pence per doz	EEC countries	B 1-a	
eggs in shell per kg	EEC area	B 4-a	
State procurement by volume	E European countries & USSR incl Ukraine	U 16-a	
Usage of chicken eggs for hatching purposes by volume	EEC countries	E 44-a	
Wholesale prices: grade A4 eggs delivered Hamburg in DM per 100	W Germany	B 4-a	
home-produced eggs by size in £ per 10 doz	UK	B 4-a	
of eggs shipped ex Denmark in £ per 10 doz	UK	B 4-a	
in local currency	Main countries	A 9-a	
	OAS member countries	N 17-a	
World demand per capita per yr projected to 1985		A 1	
market prices per one thousand (based ex Denmark)		E 34-m	

Elasticity of demand   see   INCOME ELASTICITY OF DEMAND

ELASTOMERS
    see also   NATURAL RUBBER
                  RUBBER
                  SYNTHETIC RUBBER

World demand projected to 1980: tonnage		U 26-a	

Electric appliances, domestic   see   DOMESTIC EQUIPMENT

Electric bulbs for cars   see   REPLACEMENT PARTS

Electric cables   see   INSULATED WIRE & CABLES

ELECTRIC COOKERS
    see also   OVENS, DOMESTIC

Production by volume of domestic cookers	EEC countries	E 28-q	E 27-a

Electric energy   see   ELECTRICITY

Electric energy, nuclear   see   NUCLEAR ENERGY

Electric energy, thermal   see   ELECTRICITY

Electric equipment for cars   see   REPLACEMENT PARTS

Electric furnace alloys   see   FERRO-ALLOYS

Electric furnaces   see   FURNACES, ELECTRIC

ELECTRIC IRONS

% of households owning electric irons	W European countries	Z 3	
Production by volume	EEC countries	E 28-q	E 27-a
Retail prices (comparative) in $	EEC countries	Z 3-a	

Electric lamps   see   LAMPS, INCANDESCENT

ELECTRIC MOTORS

Production of fractional hp motors by value in $	All countries	U 38-a	
in kW	All countries	U 38-a	
by volume	All countries	U 22-a	U 38-a
over 1hp in kW	All countries	U 38-a	
by volume over 1hp rating	All countries	U 22-a	U 38-a

ELECTRIC POWER EQUIPMENT
    see also   GAS TURBINES
                  GENERATORS
                  HYDRAULIC TURBINES
                  POWER GENERATING EQUIPMENT
                  STEAM TURBINES
                  SWITCHGEAR, ELECTRIC
                  TRANSFORMERS

% share of world exports	Main countries	T 7-a	
% of world exports shipped to developed countries		U 38-a	
developing countries		U 38-a	

	Territorial coverage	Title codes
ELECTRIC POWER EQUIPMENT, continued		
Consumption: tonnage	Central African countries	U 38
Exports by destination by value in $m	Main countries	U 9-a
type	OECD countries	D 9-a
value in $m	All countries	U 38-a
Exports of steam turbines in MW	W European countries	T 7-a
Imports by value in $m	All countries	U 38-a
Investment by iron & steel industry in power equipment in local currency	EEC countries	E 29-a
Length of cables in km & high-voltage grid installations in use	EEC countries	E 15-a
Production: steam turbines in MW	European countries	T 7-a
Steam turbines as % of world exports (value basis)	W European countries	T 7-a

Electric power plant manufacturing industry see POWER EQUIPMENT INDUSTRY

Electric power plants see POWER STATIONS

Electric razors see RAZORS, ELECTRIC

Electric space heaters see HEATING APPLIANCES, ELECTRIC

Electric steel see CRUDE STEEL, ELECTRIC

	Territorial coverage	Title codes
ELECTRIC SUPPLY INDUSTRY		
Consumption of coal & agglomerates: tonnage	EEC countries	E 14-a
coke oven gas in m³	EEC countries	E 14-a
electric power in kWh	EEC countries	E 14-a
lignite & briquettes: tonnage	EEC countries	E 14-a
natural gas in m³	EEC countries	E 14-a
petroleum products: tonnage	EEC countries	E 14-a
Investment needs projected by type in $m	OECD countries	D 8-a

Electric switchgear see SWITCHGEAR, ELECTRIC

Electric-driven locomotives see LOCOMOTIVES, ELECTRIC

Electrical appliances see APPLIANCES, ELECTRICAL

Electrical conductors see CONDUCTORS, ELECTRICAL

Electrical domestic equipment see DOMESTIC EQUIPMENT

Electrical engineering see ENGINEERING INDUSTRY, ELECTRICAL

	Territorial coverage	Title codes
ELECTRICAL EQUIPMENT, AUTOMOTIVE		
Exports by value in $m	All countries	U 38-a
Imports by value in $m	All countries	U 38-a
World export trade by value in $m		U 38-a

Electrical machinery see MACHINERY, ELECTRICAL

Electrical measuring instruments see MEASURING APPARATUS, ELECTRICAL

Electrical power equipment see POWER GENERATING EQUIPMENT

	Territorial coverage	Title codes	
ELECTRICITY			
see also HYDROELECTRICITY			
POWER STATIONS			
As % of all energy sources consumed	Main countries	H 4-a	
% change in gross output (incl heating)	E European countries	U 16-a	
% consumption by domestic sector	EEC area	E 7-a	
industrial sectors	EEC area	E 7-a	
iron & steel industry	EEC area	E 7-a	
transportation industry	EEC area	E 7-a	
% generation in hydroelectric power stations	All countries	H 4-a	
nuclear power stations	All countries	H 4-a	
thermal power stations	All countries	H 4-a	
% growth rate in electricity generation	Latin American countries	U 18-a	
% of EEC area power generation	EEC countries	R 5-a	
% of generation from primary sources	ECE countries	U 16-a	
secondary sources	ECE countries	U 16-a	
% of supply used by chemical industry	W European countries	U 16-a	
domestic consumers	W European countries	U 16-a	
iron & steel industry	W European countries	U 16-a	
transport services	W European countries	U 16-a	
% of population not receiving public power supply	Latin American countries	U 18-a	
Amount of electricity absorbed by storage pumping in kWh	EEC countries	E 16-m	E 15-a
Availability for domestic consumption in kWh	EEC countries	E 16-m	E 15-a
Calorific value of electricity compared with refined petroleum fuels		C 21	
Consumption & usage per capita in kWh	European countries	U 1-a	
& net imports in kWh	Main countries	E 3-a	
as % of total energy usage	ECE area	U 10-a	

ELECTRICITY, continued

	Territorial coverage	Title codes	
Consumption by agriculture & forestry in kWh	European countries	U 1-a	
	OECD countries	D 8-a	
	All countries	C 23-a	
building industry by areas in kWh	EEC countries	E 38-a	
in kWh	All countries	C 23-a	
chemical industry by areas in kWh	EEC countries	E 38-a	
in coal equiv tonnage	EEC countries	E 14-a	
in kWh	All countries	C 23-a	
	OECD countries	D 5-a	
coal & lignite mining in kWh	All countries	C 23-a	
coal derivatives industry in kWh	All countries	C 23-a	
electrical machinery industry in kWh	All countries	C 23-a	
energy industry itself by areas in kWh	EEC countries	E 38-a	
engineering industry in kWh	All countries	C 23-a	
food, drink & tobacco industry in kWh	EEC countries	E 38-a	
	All countries	C 23-a	
households by areas in kWh	EEC countries	E 38-a	
in GWh	Latin American countries	U 18-a	
in kWh	EEC countries	E 26-m	E 16-q
		E 15-a	
	OECD countries	D 8-a	D 44-a
	All countries	C 23-a	
	European countries	U 1-a	
industrial sectors in kWh	EEC countries	E 15-a	
	Main countries	U 21-a	
industry & transportation	EEC countries	E 16-q	E 15-a
by area in kWh	EEC countries	E 38-a	
in calorific value	Main countries	H 4-a	
coal equiv tonnage	EEC countries	E 14-a	
per capita in kWh	EEC countries	E 15-a	
	Main countries	E 3-a	
in kWh	OECD countries	D 8-a	
iron & steel industry in GWh	UK	T 2-m	
in kWh	All countries	C 23-a	
	EEC countries	E 14-a	E 29-a
	OECD countries	D 22-a	
in calorific value	Main countries	H 4-a	
leather goods & footwear industry in kWh	All countries	C 23-a	
manufacturing industry (all sectors) in kWh	All countries	C 23-a	
metal industries by areas in kWh	EEC countries	E 38-a	
mining & quarrying by areas in kWh	EEC countries	E 38-a	
in GWh	Latin American countries	U 18-a	
in kWh	All countries	C 23-a	
non-ferrous metals industry in kWh	All countries	C 23-a	
	EEC countries	E 14-a	
non-metallic minerals industry in kWh	EEC countries	E 14-a	
paper & board industry in kWh	All countries	C 23-a	
printing industry by areas in kWh	EEC countries	E 38-a	
petroleum & natural gas industry in kWh	All countries	C 23-a	
refineries in kWh	All countries	C 23-a	
pottery, lime, cement & glass industries in kWh	All countries	C 23-a	
printing & publishing industry in kWh	All countries	C 23-a	
public works activities in kWh	All countries	C 23-a	
railways, trams & buses in kWh	All countries	C 23-a	
road transport industry in calorific value	Main countries	H 4-a	
rubber goods manufacturing industry in kWh	All countries	C 23-a	
shipbuilding & repairing industry in kWh	All countries	C 23-a	
steel foundries in kWh	EEC area	E 29-a	
	EEC countries	E 30-q	
steelworks (for heating) in kWh	ECE countries	U 6-a	U 7-a
	Main countries	H 3-a	
textile & clothing industries in kWh	All countries	C 23-a	
industries by areas in kWh	EEC countries	E 38-a	
transport services & communications in kWh	EEC countries	E 38-a	
in kWh	All countries	C 23-a	
equipment manufacturing industry in kWh	All countries	C 23-a	
transportation in calorific value	Main countries	H 4-a	
in coal equiv tonnage	EEC countries	E 14-a	
wood-working & furniture industries in kWh	All countries	C 23-a	
Consumption cost: private sector in local currency	EEC countries	E 32-a	
Consumption ex public supply stations in kWh	All countries	C 23-a	
for public lighting in kWh	All countries	C 23-a	
for water storage pumping in kWh	All countries	C 23-a	
from own generation by industry in kWh	All countries	C 23-a	
in coal equiv tonnage	All countries	U 55-a	
	EEC countries	E 16-q	E 15-a
	EEC area	E 7-a	
	Main countries	E 3-a	
	Eire, Norway & UK	E 7-a	
	European countries, USA & USSR	U 4-a	
in kWh	EEC countries	E 16-q	E 15-a
	Italy	H 4-a	
	Main countries	H 4-a	
	OAS member countries	N 17-a	
	Caribbean countries & W Indies	T 6-a	
in power generation plants in kWh	EEC countries	E 14-a	
in pumped storage generators in kWh	All countries	C 23-a	

ELECTRICITY, continued

	Territorial coverage	Title codes	
Consumption of imported power in kWh	All countries	C 23-a	
of primary power in coal equiv tonnage	EEC countries	E 14-a	
per capita in kWh	Caribbean countries & W Indies	T 6-a	
Costs of electricity & other fuels as % of value of farm output	All countries	U 55-a	
& lubricants on farms	Hungary & Poland	U 34-a	
Costs (incl fuels) as % of farm expenses	Hungary & Poland	U 34-a	
	ECE countries	U 34-a	
as % of value of gross farm output	Hungary & Poland	U 34-a	
on farm in $	ECE countries	U 34-a	
Deliveries to EEC area & for export in kWh	ECE countries	U 34-a	
	EEC countries	E 16-q	E 15-a
in coal equiv tonnage	EEC countries	E 14-a	
Demand (maximum permissable) & load utilisation in kWh	OECD countries	D 8-a	
by kind of user projected to 1976 in kWh	OECD countries	D 8-a	
Distribution losses in network in kW	EEC countries	E 16-q	E 15-a
	OECD countries	D 44-a	
Expenditure on electric power by industrial sectors in $	OAS member countries	N 14-a	
Exports in kWh	All countries	C 23-a	
	ECE countries	U 15-a	
Exports & power exchange within OECD area in kWh	OECD countries	D 8-a	
to EEC & non-EEC areas by value in $m	EEC countries	E 24-a	
in coal equiv tonnage	EEC countries	E 14-a	
Farm expenditure (incl fuel) as % of operating costs	ECE countries	U 34-a	
on fuels & power - index nos	ECE countries	U 34-a	
Fuels (gaseous) as % of electricity generation media	ECE countries	U 16-a	
(liquid) as % of electricity generation media	ECE countries	U 16-a	
(solid) as % of electricity generation media	ECE countries	U 16-a	
Generating capacity by type of plant in kWh	OECD countries	D 8-a	
	EEC countries	E 38-a	
projected to 1976 in kWh	OECD countries	D 8-a	
Generation by kind of plant in kWh	African countries	U 44-a	
power stations: hydroelectric in kWh	All countries	C 23-a	
	African countries	U 44-a	
	OAS member countries	N 14-a	
nuclear in kWh	All countries	C 23-a	H 4-a
		R 5-a	
thermal in kWh	UK	U 10-a	
thermal from coal in kWh	All countries	C 23-a	
from lignite in kWh	All countries	C 23-a	
from liquid fuels in kWh	All countries	C 23-a	
public utilities & industrial plants in kWh	EEC countries	E 16-m	
sources of primary energy in kWh	EEC countries	E 16-q	E 3-a
		E 15-a	
steelworks in kWh	ECE area	U 6-a	U 7-a
	Main countries	H 3-a	
thermal means in kWh	EEC countries	E 16-m	E 15-a
	African countries	U 44-a	
	European countries, USA & USSR	U 4-a	
type of plant: hydroelectric, nuclear & thermal in kWh	EEC countries	E 16-q	E 15-a
hydroelectric & nuclear in kWh	European countries & USSR	U 4-a	
	All countries	U 55-a	
by areas in kWh	EEC countries	E 38-a	
in kWh	All countries	C 23-a	U 55-a
	EEC countries	E 26-m	E 28-q
		E 27-a	
	European countries & USA	U 1-a	
	Main countries	E 3-a	
	OECD countries	D 8-a	
world economic areas: historical table from 1913 in kWh		C 4-a	
for household & industrial use in kWh	All countries	U 27-m	U 43-a
Generation, imports, exports & consumption in kWh	OECD countries	D 44-a	
in coal equiv tonnage	EEC countries	E 16-q	E 14-a
		E 15-a	
kWh & index nos	Worldwide	U 27-q	
kWh (incl world total)	All countries	R 5-a	
historical table from 1927	All countries	C 4-a	
kWh	All countries	U 22-a	
kWh: historical tables from 1900	Main European countries	Z 1-a	
public utilities in kWh	Latin American countries	U 18-a	
self-suppliers in kWh	Latin American countries	U 18-a	
kWh	AASM countries	E 41-a	
	African countries	U 39-a	U 44-a
	All countries	C 23-a	
	Asian, Far East & Australasian countries	U 45-a	
	Asian & Far East countries	U 32-q	
	E European countries & USSR	U 16-a	
	ECAFE countries	U 32-q	
	ECE countries	U 15-a	
	Latin American countries	J 5-a	
	Main countries	E 3-a	
kWh per $ of gross national product	Latin American countries	U 18-a	
privately-owned plants in kWh	OAS member countries	N 14-a	
publicly-owned plants in kWh	OAS member countries	N 14-a	

	Territorial coverage	Title codes	
ELECTRICITY, continued			
Generation: nuclear energy by reactor type in kWh	Worldwide	H 4-a	
public supply & industrial producers in kWh	EEC countries	E 15-a	
Generation – index nos	Latin American countries	J 5-a	
	OAS member countries	N 14-a	
Heat & steam produced in power generation	European countries & USA	U 4-a	
Hydro-producibility coefficients	EEC countries	E 16-m	E 15-a
Imports & exports by European sources & destinations in kWh	European countries	U 1-a	
in coal equiv tonnage	EEC countries	E 16-m	E 16-q
		E 15-a	
ex EEC & non-EEC areas by value in $m	European countries & USA	U 1-a	
ex non-EEC area in coal equiv tonnage	EEC countries	E 24-a	
in coal equiv tonnage	EEC countries	E 14-a	
	EEC area	E 7-a	
in kWh	EEC countries	E 14-a	
	All countries	C 23-a	
(net) as % of consumption	ECE countries	U 15-a	
	E European countries & USSR	U 16-a	
Installed generating capacity in kW	Asian, Far East & Australasian countries	U 45-a	
	AASM countries	E 41-a	
	Latin American countries	J 5-a	
	African countries	U 44-a	
(incl hydroelectric) in kW	All countries	U 43-a	U 55-a
(maximum by type) in kW	European countries & USA	U 1-a	
	Asian, Far East & Australasian countries	U 45-a	
	OECD countries	D 8-a	
per capita	All countries	U 55-a	
by type in kW	All countries	C 23-a	
	African countries	U 39-a	
Investment in public supply installations in $m	EEC countries	E 15-a	
in plant & public supply grids in $m	EEC countries	E 15-a	
Labour force employed & wages & salaries costs in electricity generation	African countries	U 39-a	
Losses in distribution & transport in kW	European countries & USA	U 1-a	
No of dwellings with electric lighting installed	Asian, Far East & Australasian countries	U 45-a	
Nuclear production of electricity as % of world energy generation	All countries	H 4-a	
Plant capacity of power stations: hydroelectric in kW	All countries	C 23-a	
nuclear in kW	All countries	C 23-a	
thermal by type in kW	All countries	C 23-a	
Resources ex indigenous production & imports in kWh	EEC countries	E 14-a	
Supply for consumption for public & home lighting in kWh	All countries	C 23-a	
for transport purposes in kWh	All countries	C 23-a	
in industrial boilers in kWh	All countries	C 23-a	
ex EEC area production & imports in kWh	EEC countries	E 16-q	E 15-a
to agriculture & forestry in kWh	All countries	C 23-a	
chemical industry in kWh	All countries	C 23-a	
coal mines in kWh	All countries	C 23-a	
coke oven plants in kWh	European countries & USA	U 1-a	
commercial undertakings in kWh	All countries	C 23-a	
energy-producing industry in kWh	European countries & USA	U 1-a	
hard coal briquetting plants in kWh	European countries	U 1-a	
metal industries in kWh	All countries	C 23-a	
mining industries in kWh	All countries	C 23-a	
patent fuel plants in kWh	USA	U 1-a	
petroleum refineries in kWh	USA	U 1-a	
public utilities in kWh	All countries	C 23-a	
steel industry in kWh	All countries	C 23-a	
	EEC area	E 29-a	
transport services in kWh	All countries	C 23-a	
World consumption in coal equiv tonnage		C 14-a	
electric energy generation in kWh		E 15-a	
production in coal equiv tonnage		C 14-a	

Electricity meters   see   METERS, ELECTRICITY SUPPLY

Electricity supply industry   see   ELECTRIC SUPPLY INDUSTRY
PUBLIC UTILITIES

Electricity transmission lines   see   POWER TRANSMISSION LINES

Electro-magnetic appliances   see   APPLIANCES, ELECTRO-MAGNETIC

Electro-mechanical hand tools   see   POWER TOOLS

ELECTRO-MEDICAL APPARATUS
see also   MEDICAL EQUIPMENT

% of world exports shipped to developed countries		U 38-a	
to developing countries		U 38-a	
Deliveries by value in £m	UK	C 24-a	
Exports by value in $m & % growth rates	Main countries	U 38-a	

Electro-plating anodes   see   ANODES

Electro-zinc sheets   see   GALVANISED SHEETS

Electrolysis   see   AMMONIA, SYNTHETIC

	Territorial coverage	Title codes

Electrolytic copper bars   see   WIRE BARS, COPPER

Electrolytic tinplate   see   TINPLATE, ELECTROLYTIC

Electron accelerators   see   ACCELERATORS, ELECTRON & PROTON

ELECTRONIC CALCULATORS, DESK-TYPE

Production by volume	All countries	U 38-a

ELECTRONIC COMPONENTS

see also   ELECTRONIC COMPUTERS
ELECTRONIC EQUIPMENT
ELECTRONIC TUBES, DOMESTIC
ELECTRONIC TUBES, INDUSTRIAL
ELECTRONIC VALVES
TRANSISTORS

Exports by value in $m	Main countries	U 38-a
Home sales by value: capacitors in £m	UK	B 24-a
connectors in £m	UK	B 24-a
record player mechanisms in £m	UK	B 24-a
relays in £m	UK	B 24-a
resistors in £m	UK	B 24-a
semi-conductors in £m	UK	B 24-a
television tubes in £m	UK	B 24-a
World export trade: condensers by value in $m		U 38-a

ELECTRONIC COMPUTERS

% market share projected to 1977	European countries	B 24
% market share	European countries	B 24
Domestic sales projected to 1977 by value in £m	UK	B, 24-a
Exports by value projected to 1977 by value in £m	UK	B 24-a
in $m	OECD countries	D 9-a
Imports by value projected to 1977 by value in £m	UK	B 24-a
Prices (current) & 1977 estimate in £m	UK	B 24-a
Production by value (current) & 1977 estimate in £m	UK	B 24-a
projected to 1977 in £m	UK	B 24-a
Size of market by value in £m	European countries	B 24

ELECTRONIC EQUIPMENT

Deliveries of telemetry equipment by value in £	UK	C 24-a
Demand (domestic) by value in £	UK	C 24-a
	European countries	B 24
	W Germany & UK	B 24
Exports: analytical instruments by value in £m	UK	B 24-a
broadcasting equipment by value in £m	UK	B 24-a
communications equipment by value in £m	UK	B 24-a
computers & related equipment by value in £m	UK	B 24-a
control equipment by value in £m	UK	B 24-a
domestic electronic equipment by value in £m	UK	B 24-a
electronic components by value in £m	UK	B 24-a
instrument & control products by value in £	UK	B 24-a
radar & navigation aids by value in £m	UK	B 24-a
radio communications equipment by value in £m	UK	B 24-a
telecommunications equipment by value in £m	UK	B 24-a
test instruments by value in £m	UK	B 24-a
by value in $m & growth rates	Main countries	U 38-a
in £m	UK	B 24-a
Home sales: broadcasting equipment by value in £m	UK	B 24-a
communications equipment by value in £m	UK	B 24-a
computers & related equipment by value in £m	UK	B 24-a
domestic electronic equipment by value in £m	UK	B 24-a
electronic components by value in £m	UK	B 24-a
instruments & control products by value in £m	UK	B 24-a
radar & navigation aids by value in £m	UK	B 24-a
radio communications equipment by value in £m	UK	B 24-a
telecommunications equipment by value in £m	UK	B 24-a
Imports: broadcasting equipment by value in £m	UK	B 24-a
communications equipment by value in £m	UK	B 24-a
computers & related equipment by value in £m	UK	B 24-a
domestic electronic equipment by value in £m	UK	B 24-a
electronic components by value in £m	UK	B 24-a
instrument & control products by value in £m	UK	B 24-a
radar & navigation aids by value in £m	UK	B 24-a
radio communications equipment in £m	UK	B 24-a
telecommunications equipment in £m	UK	B 24-a
Production by value: analytical instruments in £m	UK	B 24-a
communications equipment in £m	UK	B 24-a
computers & related equipment in £m	UK	B 24-a
domestic electronic equipment in £m	UK	B 24-a
electronic components in £	UK	B 24-a
instrument & control products in £m	UK	B 24-a
measuring test instruments in £m	UK	B 24-a
process & control equipment in £m	UK	B 24-a
telecommunications equipment in £m	UK	B 24-a

	Territorial coverage	Title codes
ELECTRONIC EQUIPMENT BY KIND		
% market share of sales (value basis)	European countries	B 24
Deliveries by value in £	UK	C 24-a
Exports by destination: tonnage & value in $	All countries	U 12-a
Imports by source: tonnage & value in $	All countries	U 12-a
Size of market by value in £m	European countries	B 24
ELECTRONIC TUBES		
Exports (incl components) by value in $	OECD countries	D 9-a
Production by volume for television receivers	All countries	U 22-a
	EEC countries	E 28-q E 27-a
	European countries, Canada, Japan & USA	U 38-a
ELECTRONIC VALVES		
see also TRANSISTORS		
Exports by destination by value in $	Main countries	U 9-a
(incl tubes) by value in $m	All countries	U 38-a
Imports by value in $m	All countries	U 38-a
Production by volume: valves & tubes	EEC countries	E 28-q E 27-a
World export trade (incl tubes) by value in $m		U 38-a
ELECTRONICS INDUSTRY		
see also DATA-PROCESSING EQUIPMENT INDUSTRY		
ENGINEERING INDUSTRY, ELECTRICAL		
Employment as % of total manufacturing employment	UK	B 24-a
by sector & as % of total employment	UK	B 24-a
Gross value of output in £m	UK	B 24-a
Investment in buildings in local currency	EEC countries	E 40-a
in machinery in local currency	EEC countries	E 40-a
Labour force employed: communications equipment industry	UK	B 24-a
computer & components industry	UK	B 24-a
instruments & control equipment industry	UK	B 24-a
telecommunications equipment industry	UK	B 24-a
Production by value: communications equipment in £m	UK	B 24-a
computers & related equipments components in £m	UK	B 24-a
consumer goods & components in £m	UK	B 24-a
instrument engineering products in £m	UK	B 24-a
telecommunications equipment in £m	UK	B 24-a
ELEMENTS		
Symbols, atomic numbers & atomic weights of all metals		J 6-a
Symbols, atomic weights, melting points (centigrade) & year of discovery		J 3-a
Emeralds see GEM STONES		
Emergency assistance grants see A.I.D.		
Emergency food consignments see FOOD AID		
Emergency relief see BILATERAL AID		
FOOD AID		
Emery powder see ABRASIVES, NATURAL		
EMIGRATION		
Movement by decades: historical table from 1850-1960	European countries	Z 1
Emmental see CHEESE BY VARIETY		
EMPLOYMENT		
see also CIVIL SERVICE		
LABOUR FORCE		
SELF-EMPLOYED PERSONS		
YOUTH EMPLOYMENT		
By branch of activity at end-yr	EEC countries	E 33-a
in agriculture by sex & status by areas	EEC countries	E 38-a
in industry by areas	EEC countries	E 38-a
% of active population 14-24 yrs employed in industry, agriculture & service industries	EEC countries	E 2-a
over 60 yrs employed in agriculture	EEC countries	E 2-a
in industry	EEC countries	E 2-a
service industries	EEC countries	E 2-a
% change in labour force employed in basic metals industries	World regions	U 38
in chemical, oil, coal & rubber industries	World regions	U 38
& of output compared by industrial sectors	Main countries	C 2-a
available during each decade	EEC countries	E 37
employed (total)	Main European countries & USA	U 16-a
employed in manufacturing industry	Main European countries & USA	U 16-a
	World regions	U 38

169

G

EMPLOYMENT, continued

	Territorial coverage	Title codes	
% change in labour force employed in metal & engineering industries	World regions	U 38	
mining, manufacturing industry & public utilities	World regions	U 38	
public utilities (electricity & gas)	World regions	U 38	
% growth expectancy assumed in development plans	All countries	A 11-a	
% growth rates of labour force (over decades)	ECAFE countries	U 17-a	
% growth rates: no of female salaried staff employed	ECAFE countries	U 17	
no of salaried staff employed	ECAFE countries	U 17	
working population in agriculture	ECAFE countries	U 17-a	
industry	ECAFE countries	U 17-a	
service industries	ECAFE countries	U 17-a	
compared with population growth projected to 1980	OECD countries	D 11	
no of persons in paid employment	EEC countries	E 13-a	
in employment to 1968	Main countries	D 17	
% increase in no of working population	E European countries & USSR	U 16-a	
% increase in no of working population projected for ensuing yr	ECAFE countries	U 17-a	
% of labour force employed in industrial occupations	Main countries	M 4-a	
industry projected to 1980	Main countries	D 17-a	
service industries projected to 1980	Main countries	D 17-a	
% of population employed in agriculture	EEC countries	B 3-a	E 13-a
	Main countries	M 4-a	
agriculture projected to 1980	Main countries	D 17-a	
industry	EEC countries	E 13-a	
industry: no of wage & salary earners	EEC countries	E 8-a	
service industries	EEC countries	E 13-a	
% of employed females having two jobs	EEC countries	E 33-a	
% of employed persons having two jobs	EEC countries	E 33-a	
working in agriculture	EEC countries	E 33-a	
building construction	EEC countries	E 33-a	
commerce & sales promotion	EEC countries	E 33-a	
credit & insurance	EEC countries	E 33-a	
gas, electricity & water supply undertakings	EEC countries	E 33-a	
general administration	EEC countries	E 33-a	
manufacturing industry	EEC countries	E 33-a	
mining & quarrying	EEC countries	E 33-a	
service industries	EEC countries	E 33-a	
transport services	EEC countries	E 33-a	
% of heads of households by kind of occupation	W European countries	Z 3	
by social groups	W European countries	Z 3	
serving in armed forces	W European countries	Z 3	
working as employees	W European countries	Z 3	
as employers	W European countries	Z 3	
as manual workers	W European countries	Z 3	
full-time	W European countries	Z 3	
in commerce	W European countries	Z 3	
farming	W European countries	Z 3	
industry	W European countries	Z 3	
the professions	W European countries	Z 3	
public administration	W European countries	Z 3	
working part-time	W European countries	Z 3	
% of married women working in agriculture	EEC countries	E 2-a	
in industry	EEC countries	E 2-a	
in service industries	EEC countries	E 2-a	
% of population from 14-24 yrs of age in employment	EEC countries	E 2-a	
% rate of change: manufacturing industry (compounded)	Main countries	N 7-a	
non-farm employment (compounded)	Main countries	N 7-a	
% share of total labour force by regions	EEC countries	E 37-a	
General level (seasonally adjusted) – index nos	All countries	F 5-m	F 6-q
Index nos of non-agricultural employment	Main countries	N 7-a	
Index nos	All countries	L 1-a	L 4-a
	OAS member countries	N 18-a	
Planned % growth rates in labour force to 1980	Greece	D 17	
Planned % increase in industrial labour force	E European countries	U 16-a	
Private sector as % of economically-active population	AASM countries	E 41-a	
Public sector as % of economically-active population	AASM countries	E 41-a	
Transfer increase rates to agriculture	ECAFE countries	U 17-a	
industry	ECAFE countries	U 17-a	
service industries	ECAFE countries	U 17-a	
Wage & salary earners as % of total population	OECD countries	D 23-a	
Abattoirs: no of wage earners & salaried staff employed	EEC countries	E 8-a	E 11-a
Aerospace equipment industry: no of wage earners & salaried staff employed	EEC countries	E 8-a	
Agricultural labour force as % of total employment	EEC countries	B 3-a	
Agriculture & forestry: no of administrative personnel employed	AASM countries	E 41-a	
labourers employed	AASM countries	E 41-a	
managerial staff employed	AASM countries	E 41-a	
salaried staff employed	AASM countries	E 41-a	
wage earners employed	AASM countries	E 41-a	
as % of total civilian labour force	OECD countries	D 24-q	D 1-a
by sex	Main OECD countries	D 24-q	
– index nos	OAS member countries	N 18-a	
Aircraft production industry: no of wage & salary-earners employed	EEC countries	E 11-a	
Airline staff by occupation by airline company (end-yr)	Worldwide	S 21-a	
	IATA membership countries	S 21-a	

	Territorial coverage	Title codes	
EMPLOYMENT, continued			
Alcoholic drinks industry: no of wage & salary-earners employed	EEC countries	E 11-a	
All occupations (excl agriculture & industry) as % total	OECD countries	D 24-q	
Baking & confectionery industry: no of wage earners & salaried staff employed	EEC countries	E 8-a	
Briquetting plants: no of earners & salaried staff employed	EEC countries	E 8-a	E 11-a
Building & construction industries	Main countries	R 5-a	
Building construction - index nos	All countries	L 4-a	
by areas	European countries & USA	U 5-a	
no of persons employed	EEC countries	E 38-a	
	Main countries	U 58-a	
	ECE countries	U 15-a	
of wage earners & salaried staff employed	EEC countries	E 8-a	E 11-a
	OAS member countries	N 18-a	
Building materials industry: no of wage earners & salaried staff employed	EEC countries	E 8-a	E 11-a
Carpet & rugs manufacturing industry	OECD countries	D 46-a	
Cement industry: no of administrative & clerical employees	OECD countries	D 4-a	
wage earners & salaried staff employed	EEC countries	E 8-a	E 11-a
production workers employed	OECD countries	D 4-a	
Ceramics industry: no of earners & salaried staff employed	EEC countries	E 8-a	E 11-a
Change in employment in mechanical engineering industry projected to 1977	UK	B 27	
Chemical industry: no of salaried staff employed	European countries, Japan & USA	U 25-a	
wage earners & salaried staff employed	EEC countries	E 8-a	E 11-a
wage-earning operatives employed	Main countries	U 25-a	
administrative staff & operatives employed	OECD countries	D 5-a	
Chemical industry by areas	EEC countries	E 38-a	
Chemical industry	European countries, Japan & USA	U 25-a	
Civil engineering industry: no of wage earners & salaried staff employed	EEC countries	E 11-a	
Civilian employment as % of total population	OECD countries	D 23-a	
in industry & agriculture	OECD countries	D 23-a	
(total) & index nos	OECD countries	D 23-a	
Clothing & footwear industry: no of wage earners & salaried staff employed	EEC countries	E 11-a	
Clothing industry: no of wage earners & salaried staff employed	EEC countries	E 8-a	
by sector	UK	B 22-a	
Clothing industry - index nos	UK	B 22-a	
Clothing industry	OECD countries	D 46-a	
	UK	B 22-a	
Coal mining industry: no of wage earners & salaried staff employed	EEC countries	E 8-a	E 11-a
foreign migrant workers as % total employed	EEC countries	E 33-a	
foreign migrant workers employed	EEC countries	E 33-a	
workers employed (average)	EEC countries	E 33-a	
total labour force employed	EEC countries	E 33-a	
Coke oven plants: no of wage earners & salaried staff employed	EEC countries	E 8-a	E 11-a
Confectionery industry: no of wage earners & salaried staff employed	EEC countries	E 11-a	
Cotton industry: no of wage earners & salaried staff employed	EEC countries	E 8-a	E 11-a
Dairy industry: no of wage earners & salaried staff employed	EEC countries	E 8-a	E 11-a
Data-processing machinery industry: no of wage earners & salaried staff employed	EEC countries	E 11-a	
Drinks industry: no of wage earners & salaried staff employed	EEC countries	E 8-a	
Electrical engineering industry: no of production workers employed	Main countries	C 2-a	
salaried staff employed	Main countries	C 2-a	
labour force projected to 1977	UK	B 23	
no of wage earners & salaried staff employed	EEC countries	E 8-a	E 11-a
Energy production industries: no of wage earners & salaried staff employed	EEC countries	E 8-a	
labour force employed by areas	EEC countries	E 38-a	
Farm machinery industry: no of wage earners & salaried staff employed	EEC countries	E 8-a	E 11-a
Food, drink & tobacco industry: no of wage earners & salaried staff employed	EEC countries	E 8-a	E 11-a
labour force by areas	EEC countries	E 38-a	
Foundries (iron & steel): no of production workers employed	Main countries	C 2-a	
salaried staff employed	Main countries	C 2-a	
wage earners & salaried staff employed	EEC countries	E 8-a	
Furniture industry: no of wage earners & salaried staff employed	EEC countries	E 8-a	E 11-a
	W European countries	C 8-a	
Glass industry: no of wage earners & salaried staff employed	EEC countries	E 8-a	E 11-a
Hotel industry: no of employees per room	World regions	Z 5-a	
Iron & steel foundries: no of wage earners & salaried staff employed	EEC countries	E 11-a	
Iron & steel industry: no of wage earners & salaried staff employed	EEC countries	E 8-a	E 11-a
by sector: labour force employed	W Germany	H 3-a	
occupation	EEC countries	E 30-m	
no of apprentices employed	W Germany	H 3-a	
process workers employed	W Germany	H 3-a	
	Main countries	C 2-a	
salaried staff employed	Main countries	C 2-a	
	W Germany	H 3-a	
skilled workers employed	W Germany	H 3-a	
unskilled workers employed	W Germany	H 3-a	
wage earners employed	W Germany	H 3-a	

EMPLOYMENT, continued

	Territorial coverage	Title codes	
Iron ore mining: no of foreign migrant workers as % of total labour force	EEC countries	E 33-a	
no of foreign migrant workers employed	EEC countries	E 33-a	
no of wage earners & salaried staff employed	EEC countries	E 8-a	E 11-a
labour force employed in open-cast mines & % total	EEC countries	E 29-a	
labour force employed	EEC countries	E 33-a	
labour force employed in underground mines & % total	EEC countries	E 29-a	
Iron-working industry: no of wage earners & salaried staff employed	EEC countries	E 8-a	
Jute products industry: labour force employed by sex	W European countries	C 22-a	
Knitting mills: no of wage earners & salaried staff employed	EEC countries	E 8-a	E 11-a
Labour force employed & civilian labour force by sex	Main OECD countries	D 24-q	
by each iron & steel company	W Germany	H 3-a	
areas	EEC countries	E 37-a	
age groups: iron & steel industry	EEC countries	E 29-a	
iron ore mining	EEC countries	E 29-a	
broad sectors of activity	EEC countries	E 2-a	
	OECD countries	D 23-a	
industrial sectors	All countries	L 4-a	
kind in public water supply undertakings	All countries	W 2-a	
sex & % married	OECD countries	D 23-a	
(total)	Main countries	R 5-a	
historical table from 1950	EEC countries	E 37-a	
in agriculture & % change	EEC countries	E 26-a	
agriculture & forestry	Japan & Philippines	U 32-q	
	OECD countries	D 1-a	
banking & insurance	EEC countries	E 33-a	
building construction	Far East countries	U 32-q	
building construction - index nos	EEC countries	E 26-m	
coal mining industry	India	U 32-q	
coal mining industry - index nos	EEC countries	E 26-m	
commercial occupations	Australasian & Far East countries	U 32-q	
cotton mills	India	U 32-q	
electricity, water & gas undertakings	EEC countries	E 33-a	
electronics industry	UK	B 24-a	
farming, forestry & fishing	ECE countries	U 15-a	
	EEC countries	E 33-a	
farming services by region	EEC countries	E 3-a	
government service	India	U 32-q	
industrial occupations	ECE countries	U 15-a	
	Main countries	U 21-a	
	Australasian & Far East countries	U 32-q	
iron & steel foundries (at mid-yr)	UK	B 25-a	
iron & steel industry - index nos	EEC countries	E 26-m	
manufacturing industries	Australasian & Far East countries	U 32-q	
	EEC countries	E 33-a	
manufacturing industries - index nos	EEC countries	E 26-m	
mining & quarrying	EEC countries	E 33-a	
	Japan, S Korea, Philippines & Thailand	U 32-q	
paper & printing industry by areas	EEC countries	E 38-a	
public administration	India & New Zealand	U 32-q	
public utilities	EEC countries	E 33-a	
service industries	Australasian & Far East countries	U 32-q	
	ECE countries	U 15-a	
service industries & % change	EEC countries	E 26-a	
social services & service industries	EEC countries	E 33-a	
tin mining industry	Malaysia	U 32-q	
transport & warehousing	Australasian & Far East countries	U 32-q	
	EEC countries	E 33-a	
wholesale & retail trade	EEC countries	E 33-a	
(incl military personnel)	EEC countries	E 33-a	
by local authorities	India	U 32-q	
by public utilities	Australasian & Far East countries	U 32-q	
total & index nos	OECD countries	D 23-a	
no unemployed	ECAFE countries	U 17-a	
Labour force employed	EEC countries	E 13-a	
	OECD countries	D 26-m	
Leather goods industry: no of wage earners & salaried staff employed	EEC countries	E 8-a	E 11-a
Leather industry: no of wage earners & salaried staff employed	EEC countries	E 8-a	
Machine tools industry: no of wage earners & salaried staff employed	EEC countries	E 8-a	E 11-a
labour force employed	UK	B 26-a	
	USA	J 2-a	
Man-made fibres industry: no of wage earners & salaried staff employed	EEC countries	E 8-a	E 11-a
Manual labour force employed by kind of occupation in motor vehicle industry	UK	B 28-a	
Manufacturing industry by sector as % of total employment	Main industries	U 38-a	
no of wage earners & salaried staff employed	EEC countries	E 8-a	E 11-a
employees by age groups & sex	UK	B 28-a	
- index nos	All countries	L 1-m	L 4-a
		U 43-a	
	Main countries	U 27-m	
	OAS member countries	N 18-a	
	UK	B 28-a	
	OECD countries	D 26-m	

172

EMPLOYMENT, continued   Territorial coverage   Title codes

Subject	Territorial coverage	Title codes	
Marine engineering industry: no of wage earners & salaried staff employed	EEC countries	E 11-a	
Mechanical engineering industry: no of production workers employed	Main countries	C 2-a	
salaried staff employed	Main countries	C 2-a	
wage earners & salaried staff employed	EEC countries	E 8-a	E 11-a
Metal industries: no of wage earners & salaried staff employed	EEC countries	E 8-a	
Metal ore mining: labour force employed by areas	EEC countries	E 38-a	
no of wage earners & salaried staff employed	EEC countries	E 11-a	
Metal products industry: no of wage earners & salaried staff employed	EEC countries	E 11-a	
labour force employed by areas	EEC countries	E 38-a	
Metals industry: no of wage earners & salaried staff employed	EEC countries	E 11-a	
Mining & manufacturing industries: labour force employed	ECE countries	U 42-m	
Mining & quarrying - index nos	All countries	L 4-a	
	OAS member countries	N 18-a	
no of labourers employed	AASM countries	E 41-a	
managerial employees	AASM countries	E 41-a	
wage earners & salaried staff employed	EEC countries	E 11-a	
salaried staff employed	AASM countries	E 41-a	
wage earners employed	AASM countries	E 41-a	
Motor vehicles industry: no of production workers employed	Main countries	C 2-a	
salaried staff employed	Main countries	C 2-a	
wage earners & salaried staff employed	EEC countries	E 8-a	E 11-a
labour force employed by age groups & sex	UK	B 28-a	
- index nos	UK	B 28-a	
No of administrative & managerial employees: private sector	AASM countries	E 41-a	
public sector	AASM countries	E 41-a	
& local government employees	EEC countries	E 2-a	
aircraft personnel employed by category by airline	Worldwide	S 11-a	
applicants applying for employment through advertising	EEC countries	E 33-a	
government agencies	EEC countries	E 33-a	
personal connections	EEC countries	E 33-a	
private agencies	EEC countries	E 33-a	
economically-active population	ECE countries	U 15-a	
economically-active population & % change	EEC countries	E 26-a	
employees in commercial occupations	All countries	L 4-a	
family helpers employed in family businesses	EEC countries	E 18-a	
farm occupations	EEC countries	E 18-a	
service industries	EEC countries	E 18-a	
females employed as % of female population over 14 yrs	EEC countries	E 2-a	
fishermen employed: deep-sea & coastal (full & part-time)	OECD countries	D 43-a	
foreign migrant workers employed: iron & steel industry	EEC countries	E 29-a	
iron ore mining	EEC countries	E 29-a	
labourers employed in private sector	AASM countries	E 41-a	
public sector	AASM countries	E 41-a	
married women employed in agriculture	EEC countries	E 3-a	
manufacturing industries	EEC countries	E 3-a	
service industries	EEC countries	E 3-a	
merchant seamen employed by occupation	Worldwide	D 28-a	
persons employed in farming occupations	EEC countries	E 18-a	
	Panama & Venezuela	T 6-a	
industrial occupations	EEC countries	E 18-a	
	Panama & Venezuela	T 6-a	
service industries	EEC countries	E 18-a	
	Panama & Venezuela	T 6-a	
employed in more than one occupation	EEC countries	E 18-a	
wholly in one occupation	EEC countries	E 18-a	
employed in family businesses	EEC countries	E 18-a	
occasionally employed by areas	EEC countries	E 18-a	
as % total labour force	EEC countries	E 2-a	
seeking work by areas	EEC countries	E 18-a	
with two occupations as % of those with one	EEC countries	E 2-a	
working part-time	EEC countries	E 18-a	
salaried employees in private sector	AASM countries	E 41-a	
public sector	AASM countries	E 41-a	
school-leavers entering textile industry as % total	UK	B 29-a	
self-employed persons engaged in farming	EEC countries	E 18-a	
industry	EEC countries	E 18-a	
services	EEC countries	E 18-a	
semi-skilled workers employed in motor vehicles industry projected to 1977	UK	B 28	
skilled workers employed in motor vehicles industry projected to 1977	UK	B 28	
unskilled workers employed in motor vehicles industry projected to 1977	UK	B 28	
vacancies filled by government employment agencies	EEC countries	E 2-m	E 33-a
wage earners & salaried staff engaged in farming	EEC countries	E 18-a	
industry	EEC countries	E 18-a	
services	EEC countries	E 18-a	
employed: non-ferrous metals industry	EEC countries	E 8-a	E 11-a
non-metallic mineral industry	EEC countries	E 8-a	
wage earners employed in private sector	AASM countries	E 41-a	
public sector	AASM countries	E 41-a	

	Territorial coverage	Title codes	
EMPLOYMENT, continued			
No of wage earners (nationals & foreigners) employed in iron ore mines	EEC countries	E 29-a	
employed in steel industry	EEC countries	E 29-a	
of working married women as % of total no of married women	EEC countries	E 2-a	
Non-agricultural occupations - index nos	Main countries	U 27-m	
Non-metallic mineral mining: labour force by areas	EEC countries	E 11-a	E 38-a
Nuclear fuels industry: no of wage earners & salaried staff employed	EEC countries	E 8-a	E 11-a
Office machinery industry: no of wage earners & salaried staff employed	EEC countries	E 8-a	
Oil refining industry: no of wage earners & salaried staff employed	EEC countries	E 11-a	
Ore mining industry: no of wage earners & salaried staff employed	EEC countries	E 8-a	
Paper & board industry: no of wage earners & salaried staff employed	EEC countries	E 8-a	E 11-a
Petroleum industry: no of wage earners & salaried staff employed	EEC countries	E 11-a	
Petroleum refineries: no of wage earners & salaried staff employed	EEC countries	E 8-a	
Plastics industry: no of wage earners & salaried staff employed	EEC countries	E 8-a	E 11-a
Printing & publishing: no of wage earners & salaried staff employed	EEC countries	E 8-a	E 11-a
Public utilities: no of wage earners & salaried staff employed	EEC countries	E 8-a	E 11-a
Public utilities - index nos	OAS member countries	N 18-a	
Rubber products industry: no of wage earners & salaried staff employed	EEC countries	E 8-a	E 11-a
Scientific instruments industry: no of wage earners & salaried staff employed	EEC countries	E 8-a	E 11-a
Service industries & commerce: no of managerial staff employed	AASM countries	E 41-a	
salaried staff employed	AASM countries	E 41-a	
unskilled workers employed	AASM countries	E 41-a	
wage earners employed	AASM countries	E 41-a	
Shipbuilding industry: no of wage earners & salaried staff employed	EEC countries	E 8-a	E 11-a
labour force employed	W Germany	S 16-m	
no of production workers employed	Main countries	C 2-a	
no of salaried staff employed	Main countries	C 2-a	
Spinning weaving & finishing industry: labour force employed	OECD countries	D 46-a	
Tanneries & leather dressing industry: labour force employed by kind	EEC countries	E 8-a	
Textile & leather dressing industry: labour force employed by area	EEC countries	E 38-a	
Tanning industry: no of wage & salaried staff employed	EEC countries	E 11-a	
Textile industry: no of wage earners & salaried staff employed	EEC countries	E 8-a	E 11-a
labour force employed	OECD countries	D 46-a	
Textiles & clothing industry: labour force by sector projected to 1977	UK	B 29-a	
Timber & sawmill industry: no of wage earners & salaried staff employed	EEC countries	E 8-a	E 11-a
Tin mining industry: labour force employed	Malaysia, Nigeria & Thailand	C 20-m	
Tobacco industry: no of wage earners & salaried staff employed	EEC countries	E 8-a	E 11-a
Tourist industry: labour force employed by sex	OECD countries	D 47-a	
Transport & communications industry - index nos	All countries	L 4-a	
Transport & communications - index nos	OAS member countries	N 18-a	
Transport equipment manufacturing industry: no of wage earners & salaried staff employed	EEC countries	E 8-a	
Transport services: no of labourers employed	AASM countries	E 41-a	
managerial staff employed	AASM countries	E 41-a	
salaried staff employed	AASM countries	E 41-a	
wage earners employed	AASM countries	E 41-a	
Vehicles assembly industry: no of wage earners & salaried staff employed	EEC countries	E 11-a	
Water supply industry: no of wage earners & salaried staff employed	EEC countries	E 8-a	E 11-a
Wholesale & retail trade: labour force employed	Main countries	U 43-a	
Woollen textile industry: no of wage earners & salaried staff employed	EEC countries	E 8-a	E 11-a
EMPLOYMENT, INDUSTRIAL			
All sectors (incl service industries by age & sex)	UK	B 28-a	
As % of total labour force	OECD countries	D 24-q	
By main sectors - index nos	All countries	L 4-a	
	World regions	U 43-a	
By sector - index nos	OAS member countries	N 18-a	
Including non-farming occupations - index nos	All countries	L 1-m	L 4-a
% of economically-active population: over 60 yrs of age employed	EEC countries	E 2-a	
14-24 yrs of age employed	EEC countries	E 2-a	
% of economically-active married women employed	EEC countries	E 2-a	
% share of industrial employment: basic metals industries	Main countries	U 38-a	
chemical, oil & coal industry	Main countries	U 38-a	
engineering industry	Main countries	U 38-a	
food, drink & tobacco industry	Main countries	U 38-a	
non-metallic mineral industry	Main countries	U 38-a	
paper & printing industry	Main countries	U 38-a	
textile industry	Main countries	U 38-a	
wood working industry	Main countries	U 38-a	
Civilian labour force employed (in detail)	OECD countries	D 9-a	D 23-a
Index nos	Asian, Far East & Australasian countries	U 45-a	
	Developed areas & world regions	U 23-a	
Labour force employed by sectors	OAS member countries	N 14-a	
no of wage & salary earners	EEC countries	E 32-a	
salaried staff	Main countries	R 5-a	
wage earners	Main countries	R 5-a	
by sex in industry	Main OECD countries	D 24-q	

	Territorial coverage	Title codes
EMPLOYMENT, INDUSTRIAL continued		
No of apprentices in iron & steel industry	EEC countries	E 29-a
persons employed & % change	EEC countries	E 26-a
by industrial sectors	Main countries	U 21-a
by sex & status by areas	EEC countries	E 38-a
salaried staff employed in industry	EEC countries	E 8-a
wage earners employed in industry	EEC countries	E 8-a
process workers entering steel industry	EEC countries	E 29-a
leaving steel industry	EEC countries	E 29-a
employed in roasted coffee industry	USA	J 1-a
EMPLOYMENT, PART-TIME		
Textile industry: females as % of female employment	UK	B 29-a
no of females employed by sector	UK	B 29-a
EMPLOYMENT BY AGE		
% age distribution: all employees	EEC countries	E 2-a
female employees	EEC countries	E 2-a
of labour force employed in industry	EEC countries	E 2-a
in service industries	EEC countries	E 2-a
Textile industry by sector: females under 18 yrs	UK	B 29-a
males under 18 yrs	UK	B 29-a
EMPLOYMENT BY REGION		
Labour employed in agriculture as % of total regional employment	EEC countries	E 2-a
building industry as % of total regional employment	EEC countries	E 2-a
manufacturing industry as % of total regional employment	EEC countries	E 2-a
service industries as % of total regional employment	EEC countries	E 2-a
transport industry as % of total regional employment	EEC countries	E 2-a
motor vehicles industry by sex by region	UK	B 28-a
projected to 1977 by region	UK	B 28
textile & clothing industry by sector by region	UK	B 29-a
EMPLOYMENT BY SEX		
By industrial sector (at census dates)	OAS member countries	N 18
by areas	EEC countries	E 38-a
% of active population by 5 yr age groups	EEC countries	E 2-a
Labour force employed - index nos	Main OECD countries	D 24-q
No of civilians in employment	Main OECD countries	D 24-q
economically-active males & females	EEC countries	E 33-a
employees by economic groups	All countries	C 28-a
Textile industry by sector: females as % of total labour force	UK	B 29-a
no of wage earners & salaried staff employed	OECD countries	D 46-a
Wool textile industry	Main countries	K 6-a

Emulsions & distempers   see   PAINTS, WATER

Enamel & distemper   see   PAINTS & VARNISHES

Encephalitis   see   DISEASES, INFECTIOUS

Endives   see   VEGETABLES, FRESH

ENDOWMENTS

Amounts paid out by insurance companies in local currency	OAS member countries	N 16-a

Endrin   see   INSECTICIDES

ENERGY

see also   ELECTRIC ENERGY
NUCLEAR ENERGY

	Territorial coverage	Title codes
% consumption by domestic sector	EEC area	E 7-a
industrial sector	EEC area	E 7-a
iron & steel industry	EEC area	E 7-a
road transport services	EEC area	E 7-a
sectors	EEC area	E 7-a
transportation services	EEC area	E 7-a
% growth of primary energy sources by kind	E European countries & USSR	U 16-a
% growth rate of consumption of energy (all kinds)	World regions	U 18-a
of consumption per capita	World regions	U 18-a
Availability in coal equiv tonnage & per capita	All countries	U 55-a
Black oils as % of total primary energy use	ECE areas	U 10-a
Consumption (all kinds) in coal equiv tonnage	Latin American countries	J 5-a
by industry, transport & households	EEC countries	E 26-q
kind in coal equiv tonnage	Non-Communist countries	C 13-a
source: coke oven gas in coal equiv tonnage	European countries	U 10-a
firewood & peat in coal equiv tonnage	European countries	U 10-a
hard brown coal: tonnage	European countries	U 10-a
hydroelectricity in coal equiv tonnage	European countries	U 10-a

	Territorial coverage	Title codes	
ENERGY, continued			
Consumption by source: methane gas in coal equiv tonnage	European countries	U 10-a	
mineral oils in coal equiv tonnage	European countries	U 10-a	
natural gas in coal equiv tonnage	European countries	U 10-a	
nuclear energy coal equiv tonnage	European countries	U 10-a	
kind of primary sources: coal, oil & gas	EEC countries	E 16-q	E 15-a
	European countries & USSR	U 4-a	
type of user industry & households: tonnage	EEC countries	E 16-q	E 15-a
of electricity (domestic & industrial) in kWh	EEC countries	E 15-a	
electricity by energy industry itself in kWh	EEC countries	E 38-a	
in agriculture by value in $	EEC countries	E 44-a	
coal equiv tonnage	African countries	U 39-a	
	ECE countries	U 15-a	
	EEC countries	E 16-q	E 15-a
	Main countries	E 3-a	
petroleum equiv tonnage	World regions	U 18-a	
forestry by value in $	EEC countries	E 44-a	
of nuclear & hydroelectric energy	ECE countries	U 15-a	
energy (incl electricity) at steelworks	EEC countries	E 30-q	
gas in energy production in m³	European countries & USA	U 3-a	
Consumption per capita in coal equiv tonnage	Denmark, Eire, Norway & UK	E 7-a	
	Main countries	E 3-a	
in coal equiv in kg	OECD countries	R 5-a	
	World regions	U 18-a	
	Developing world regions	U 23-a	
of primary energy in coal equiv tonnage	EEC countries	E 7-a	
	Main countries	U 10-a	
	ECE regions	U 10-a	
products by industry	EEC countries	E 38-a	
sources as % of domestic usage	EEC countries	E 3-a	
by kind: tonnage	Main countries	N 2-a	
Exports of electrical power by regions of origin in kWh	EEC countries	E 38-a	
Fixed capital investment in energy production in $m	EEC countries	E 38-a	
Fuels (solid) as % of total primary energy usage	ECE countries	U 10-a	
Funds for development of energy resources as aid from European Development Fund	EEC countries	D 13-a	
Household budget expenses for lighting & heating in local currency	AASM countries	E 41-a	
Imports & exports of energy in coal equiv tonnage	All countries	U 55-a	
Imports as % of consumption	E European countries	U 16-a	
in coal equiv tonnage	E European countries	U 16-a	
(net) as % of total domestic energy consumption	EEC countries	E 3-a	
excl bunkers: tonnage	EEC countries	E 26-q	
Natural gas as % of total primary energy use	ECE areas	U 10-a	
Overall balance of resources, production & consumption	European countries & USA	U 4-a	
	EEC countries	E 16-q	E 15-a
Production & consumption of energy sources by kind	OECD countries	D 44-a	
in coal equiv tonnage	All countries	U 43-a	
by type of fuel (incl nuclear & hydroelectric)	World regions	U 43-a	
Production, consumption, imports & exports by kind	World regions	U 55-a	
in coal equiv tonnage	African countries	U 39-a	
	Latin American countries	J 5-a	
(incl bunkers) in coal equiv tonnage	All countries	U 55-a	
of nuclear & hydroelectric energy in million kWh	ECE countries	U 15-a	
derivatives: coke, gas & oil products	EEC countries	E 16-q	E 15-a
	ECE countries	U 15-a	
primary energy in coal equiv tonnage	EEC countries	E 26-q	
	Main countries	E 3-a	
	EEC countries	E 3-a	
primary energy sources & trade	European countries & USSR	U 4-a	
primary energy sources: coal & gas	Main countries	E 3-a	
primary energy sources, imports, exports & usage	EEC countries	E 16-q	E 15-a
coke, gas & oil derivatives in coal equiv tonnage	European countries & USA	U 4-a	
hydroelectricity in kWh	African countries	U 39-a	
Requirements of energy (all kinds) in coal equiv tonnage	EEC area	E 7-a	
fuels (all kinds): tonnage	EEC countries	E 14-a	
Resources, indigenous consumption, supply & stocks: tonnage	EEC countries	E 14-a	
Supply of fuels (all kinds) from imports: tonnage	EEC countries	E 14-a	
own resources: tonnage	EEC countries	E 14-a	
stock: tonnage	EEC countries	E 14-a	
Transformation at power stations, gas & coking plants & oil refineries	EEC countries	E 16-q	E 15-a
	European countries & USSR	U 4-a	
World consumption by energy source in coal equiv tonnage		N 5-a	

Energy, hydroelectric   see   HYDROELECTRICITY

Energy, nuclear   see   NUCLEAR ENERGY

ENERGY BY KIND

	Territorial coverage	Title codes	
Consumption by chemical industry	OECD countries	D 5-a	
steel industry	ECE countries	U 6-a	U 7-a
	Main countries	H 3-a	
in coal equiv tonnage	EEC countries	E 14-a	
World production in million tons coal equiv		C 14-a	

                                                                    Territorial coverage   Title codes

ENERGY INDUSTRIES
    see also   BLAST FURNACE GAS
                COAL MINING
                COKE OVENS
                COLLIERIES
                ELECTRIC SUPPLY INDUSTRY
                ENERGY SOURCES, PRIMARY
                HYDROELECTRICITY
                MANUFACTURED GAS
                NATURAL GAS
                NUCLEAR FUEL INDUSTRY
                PETROLEUM INDUSTRY
                PETROLEUM REFINERIES
                POWER STATIONS
                REFINERY GAS

    Labour costs by status of employee in local currency   EEC countries   E 8-a
    Labour force employed: wage earners & salaried staff   EEC countries   E 8-a
    No of hrs worked by labour force per yr   EEC countries   E 8-a
    Structure of labour costs as % of total costs   EEC countries   E 8-a

ENERGY SOURCES, PRIMARY
    see also   COAL
                CRUDE PETROLEUM
                NATURAL GAS

    Consumption by value in $m   Main countries   U 23-a
    Exports as % of consumption   Main countries   U 23-a
    Imports as % of consumption   Main countries   U 23-a
    Production by kind: tonnage   EEC countries   E 14-a

ENERGY SOURCES, PRIMARY BY KIND

    Consumption in coal equiv tonnage   EEC area   E 7-a
             coke ovens: tonnage   Italy   H 4-a
             factories: tonnage   Italy   H 4-a
             power stations: tonnage   Italy   H 4-a
             refineries: tonnage   Italy   H 4-a
             (total): tonnage   EEC countries   E 14-a
    Costs to steel industry in DM per ton   W Germany   H 3-a
    Deliveries within EEC area: tonnage   EEC countries   E 14-a
    Exports to non-EEC area: tonnage   EEC countries   E 14-a
    Imports of solid fuels & gas in coal equiv tonnage   Italy   H 4-a
            tonnage   EEC countries   E 14-a
    Industrial consumption: tonnage   EEC countries   E 14-a
                                                                   Italy   H 4-a
    Labour force employed in processing industry   Italy   H 4-a
    Production of natural gas in m³   Italy   H 4-a
            of solid fuels: tonnage   All countries   H 4-a
            tonnage   EEC countries   E 14-a
    Resources available: tonnage   Italy   H 4-a
            (indigenous): tonnage   EEC countries   E 14-a
    Stock changes: tonnage   EEC countries   E 14-a
    Supply: tonnage   EEC countries   E 14-a
    Volume processed & refined   EEC countries   E 14-a

Engine room officers   see   MERCHANT SEAMEN

Engine spares   see   REPLACEMENT PARTS

ENGINEERING

    % of students enrolled studying engineering science   ECAFE countries   U 17
    No of engineering students at university   All countries   U 62-a
            full & part-time research workers in engineering field All countries   U 62-a
            students enrolled abroad by country of origin   All countries   U 64-a
            university degrees obtained in engineering subjects   All countries   U 62-a

ENGINEERING INDUSTRY

    % change in output by product   E European countries & USSR U 16-a
    % contribution to gross national product   European countries, Japan & USA U 38-a
    % growth in output (5 yr period)   Main countries   U 38
    % production increase projected to 1977   UK   B 26
    % share of industrial production   Main countries   U 38-a
            of total capital investment   E European countries   U 16-a
    Assets of corporations as % of liabilities   USA   J 2-a
    Capital formation projected to 1980   N African countries   U 38
    Consumption of electricity in kWh   All countries   C 23-a
                                                                   European countries & USA   U 1-a
                                                                   OECD countries   D 8-a
            of primary aluminium: tonnage   Main countries   T 4-a
    Depreciation of corporate assets as % of sales turnover   USA   J 2-a
    Earnings (average) in local currency   All countries   L 4-a
            of engineering corporations as % of sales turnover   USA   J 2-a
            skilled workers in £ per wk   UK   B 28-a
    Employment in machinery industry   All countries   L 4-a
    Frequency of industrial accidents   EEC countries   E 2-a
    Gross output - index nos   Main countries   U 38
    Investment in buildings in local currency   EEC countries   E 40-a

	Territorial coverage	Title codes	
ENGINEERING INDUSTRY, continued			
Investment in land purchase in local currency	EEC countries	E 40-a	
in machinery in local currency	EEC countries	E 40-a	
Labour costs - index nos	Main countries	B 27-a	
Labour force employed (incl metal products industries)	OECD countries	D 23-a	
Labour force employed	EEC countries	E 2-a	
No of apprentices in machine tools industry	UK	B 26-a	
hrs worked as overtime per wk	USA	J 2-a	
per wk	All countries	L 4-a	
times inventory turned by engineering corporations	USA	J 2-a	
working days lost per employee	UK	B 29-a	
Production in engineering as % of general world activity		U 38	
Profits of corporations as % of sales turnover	USA	J 2-a	
Receipts of steel for processing: tonnage	OECD countries	D 22-a	
Wage rates per hr by sex	Main countries	C 7-a	
ENGINEERING INDUSTRY, ELECTRICAL			
see also ELECTRONICS INDUSTRY			
% change in output & labour force employed	Main countries	C 2-a	
in output per man	UK	B 23	
% production increase projected	UK	B 26	
% usage of machine tool park	EEC countries	B 20-a	
Consumption of aluminium: tonnage	EEC countries	C 12-a	
electricity in kWh	EEC countries	E 14-a	
	European countries	U 1-a	
	OECD countries	D 8-a	
iron castings: tonnage	UK	B 25-a	
steel castings: tonnage	UK	B 25-a	
Costs of staff salaries per mth in $	EEC countries	E 11-a	
Earnings per yr (average) in local currency	All countries	L 4-a	
female workers per wk in local currency	Main countries	C 2-a	
per hr by sex in local currency	Main countries	R 3-a	
per hr in FrS	Main countries	C 2-a	
piece rate per hr in local currency	Main countries	C 2-a	
semi-skilled workers per hr in local currency	Main countries	C 2-a	
skilled workers per hr in local currency	Main countries	C 2-a	
time rate per hr in local currency	Main countries	C 2-a	
unskilled workers per hr in local currency	Main countries	C 2-a	
Electricity consumption in kWh	All countries	C 23-a	
Frequency of industrial accidents	EEC countries	E 2-a	
International Development Agency loans approved in $	OAS member countries	N 16-a	
Investment in buildings in $	EEC countries	E 40-a	
land in $	EEC countries	E 40-a	
machinery in $	EEC countries	E 40-a	
per employee in £	Main countries	B 23-a	
Labour costs as % of total costs	EEC countries	E 8-a	
Labour costs: female workers per hr in local currency	Main countries	C 2-a	
in DM million	W Germany	H 3-a	
local currency	EEC countries	E 8-a	E 11-a
per hr in FrS	Main countries	C 2-a	
semi-skilled workers in local currency	Main countries	C 2-a	
skilled workers in local currency	Main countries	C 2-a	
unskilled workers in local currency	Main countries	C 2-a	
wage earners in local currency	EEC countries	E 11-a	
Labour force employed by occupation	Main countries	C 2-a	
status	EEC countries	E 8-a	
projected to 1977	UK	B 23-a	
no of production workers	Main countries	C 2-a	
no of salaried staff	EEC countries	E 11-a	
	Main countries	C 2-a	
Labour force employed	EEC countries	E 2-a	
No of hrs worked per wk	Main countries	R 3-m	
	EEC countries	E 25-a	
	All countries	L 4-a	
	OAS member countries	N 18-a	
per yr	EEC countries	E 8-a	E 11-a
per mth: salaried staff	EEC countries	E 11-a	
No of machine tools in use	USA	J 2-a	
Production by value in FrS	Main countries	C 2-a	
of components by value in £	UK	B 24-a	
consumer goods by value in £	UK	B 24-a	
Production - index nos	Main countries	R 5-a	
Receipts of aluminium: tonnage	OECD countries	D 21-a	
Usage of copper: tonnage	Main countries	H 2-a	
of platinum & palladium in oz	USA	J 6-a	
Wage rates: electricians in local currency	OAS member countries	N 17-a	
per hr in local currency	EEC countries	E 25-a2	
by sex in local currency	Main countries	R 3-m	
in DM	W Germany	H 3-a	
in FrS	Main countries	C 2-a	
skilled workers in local currency	Main countries	R 4-q	
unskilled workers in local currency	Main countries	R 4-q	
Wage rates per hr - index nos	EEC countries	E 26-a2	
Wages by sex - index nos	Main countries	R 3-a	

Engineering industry, marine   see   SHIPBUILDING

	Territorial coverage	Title codes	
ENGINEERING INDUSTRY, MECHANICAL			
% change in output & labour force employed	Main countries	C 2-a	
% production increase projected	UK	B 26	
projected to 1977 by value in £m	UK	B 27	
% usage of machine tool park	EEC countries	B 20-a	
Capital investment per capita in $	Main countries	B 27-a	
in $	Main countries	B 27-a	
Consumption of aluminium: tonnage	EEC countries	C 12-a	
of iron castings: tonnage	UK	B 25-a	
of steel castings: tonnage	UK	B 25-a	
Contribution to gross domestic product projected to 1985	EEC countries	B 20-a	
Costs for salaried staff per mth in $	EEC countries	E 11-a	
Domestic demand for mechanical engineering products in £m	UK	B 27-a	
Earnings: female workers per wk in local currency	Main countries	C 2-a	
per hr in local currency	Main countries	C 2-a	
in FrS	Main countries	C 2-a	
piece rate per hr in local currency	Main countries	C 2-a	
semi-skilled workers per hr in local currency	Main countries	C 2-a	
skilled workers per hr in local currency	Main countries	C 2-a	
time rates per hr in local currency	Main countries	C 2-a	
unskilled workers per hr in local currency	Main countries	C 2-a	
Electricity consumption in kWh	All countries	C 23-a	
Investment in buildings in local currency	EEC countries	E 40-a	
land purchase in local currency	EEC countries	E 40-a	
machinery in local currency	EEC countries	E 40-a	
Labour costs: all employees in local currency	EEC countries	E 11-a	
as % of total costs	EEC countries	E 8-a	
female workers per hr in local currency	Main countries	C 2-a	
in DM million	W Germany	H 3-a	
in local currency	EEC countries	E 8-a	
per hr in FrS	Main countries	C 2-a	
semi-skilled workers in local currency	Main countries	C 2-a	
skilled workers in local currency	Main countries	C 2-a	
unskilled workers in local currency	Main countries	C 2-a	
wage earners in local currency	EEC countries	E 11-a	
Labour force employed by occupation	Main countries	C 2-a	
by status	EEC countries	E 8-a	
no of production workers	Main countries	C 2-a	
salaried staff	Main countries	C 2-a	
	EEC countries	E 11-a	
No of industrial accidents & fatalities	UK	B 25-a	
of hrs worked per wk: all employees	Main countries	R 3-m	
	EEC countries	E 8-a	E 25-a
wage earners	EEC countries	E 11-a	
	OAS member countries	N 18-a	
per mth: salaried staff	EEC countries	E 11-a	
Production by value in FrS	Main countries	C 2-a	
Receipts of aluminium: tonnage	OECD countries	D 21-a	
Wage rates per hr: assembly workers	OAS member countries	N 17-a	
in local currency	EEC countries	E 25-a2	
locomotive shops per hr	UK	R 4-a	
truck builders per hr	UK	R 4-a	
per hr in DM	W Germany	H 3-a	
in local currency	Main countries	R 3-m	C 2-a
– index nos	EEC countries	E 26-a2	
ENGINEERING PRODUCTS			
% growth rates in output	Developing countries	U 38-a	
% share of EEC area imports (value basis)	Developing countries	U 52-a	
Availability per capita in $	African countries	U 38-a	
Consumption: tonnage	Central African countries	U 38-a	
Exports as % of world total exports (value basis)	All countries	U 38-a	
by commodity structure by value in $	Main countries	U 38-a	
destination by value in $	Main countries	U 9-a	
value in $m	All countries	U 38-a	
to world regions by value in $m	World regions	U 38-a	
tonnage & value in $m (in detail)	OECD countries	D 9-a	
Imports by value in $m	Developing countries	U 52-a	
	All countries	U 38-a	
into EEC area ex developing countries by value in $		U 52-a	
Value added in manufacture	OECD countries	D 9-a	
World exports by value in $m		U 38-a	

ENGINEERING PRODUCTS, ELECTRICAL

see also   DOMESTIC EQUIPMENT
ELECTRIC IRONS
ELECTRIC MOTORS
ELECTRIC POWER EQUIPMENT
ELECTRIC RAZORS
ELECTRICAL EQUIPMENT, AUTOMOTIVE
ELECTRONIC COMPUTERS
ELECTRONIC EQUIPMENT
INSULATED WIRE & CABLES
MACHINERY, ELECTRICAL
OVENS, DOMESTIC
POWER TOOLS
REFRIGERATING EQUIPMENT

	Territorial coverage	Title codes

ENGINEERING PRODUCTS, ELECTRICAL   continued
    see also   TELECOMMUNICATIONS EQUIPMENT
                 TELEVISION RECEIVERS

World exports trade by kind by value in $		U 38-a
% demand increase projected to 1977	UK	B 23

ENGINEERING PRODUCTS, MECHANICAL
    see also   AIR CONDITIONING MACHINERY
                 AIRCRAFT ENGINES
                 BEARINGS
                 BOILERS
                 BULLDOZERS
                 CALCULATING MACHINES
                 COMPRESSORS
                 CONSTRUCTION EQUIPMENT
                 ENGINES, DIESEL
                 ENGINES, INDUSTRIAL
                 ENGINES, INTERNAL COMBUSTION
                 EXCAVATING MACHINERY
                 FOOD PROCESSING MACHINES
                 FORESTRY EQUIPMENT
                 FURNACES, INDUSTRIAL
                 GAS TURBINES
                 GLASS-WORKING MACHINERY
                 GRADERS & LEVELLERS
                 INDUSTRIAL PLANT & STEELWORK
                 LOCOMOTIVES
                 MACHINE TOOLS
                 MACHINERY, AGRICULTURAL
                 MARINE ENGINES
                 MECHANICAL HANDLING EQUIPMENT
                 METAL-WORKING MACHINES
                 MILITARY EQUIPMENT
                 MILKING MACHINES
                 MINERAL PROCESSING MACHINERY
                 MINING MACHINERY
                 OFFICE MACHINERY
                 PACKAGING MACHINERY
                 PAPER & PULP MACHINES
                 PRINTING MACHINERY
                 PUMPS
                 REFRIGERATING EQUIPMENT
                 ROLLING STOCK
                 SCRAPERS
                 SEWING MACHINES
                 STEAM TURBINES
                 STEEL RE-ROLLING PLANTS
                 TEXTILE MACHINERY
                 TRACTORS, AGRICULTURAL
                 TRANSPORT EQUIPMENT
                 WEIGHING MACHINERY
                 WOODWORKING MACHINERY

% exports by destination	Main countries	B 27-a
% growth in production capacity	African countries	U 38-a
% growth rate in output	UK	B 27-a
% share of exports (value basis)	UK	B 27-a
% share of exports (value basis) to European countries	UK	B 27-a
of world trade by product	UK	B 27-a
Deliveries by value in $m	Main countries	B 27-a
Demand (domestic) by value in £m	UK	B 27-a
past & projected by value in £m	UK	B 27
Exports by value in £m	UK	B 27-a
projected to 1977 in £m	UK	B 27
unit value per ton	Main countries	B 27-a
Imports by value in £m	UK	B 27-a
projected to 1977 in £m	UK	B 27
unit value per ton	Main countries	B 27-a
Output for domestic consumption projected to 1977	UK	B 27
Production requirements projected to 1977	UK	B 27
Sales per employee in $	Main countries	B 27-a

ENGINEERING PRODUCTS BY KIND

Exports by destination: tonnage & value in $m	All countries	U 12-a
by value in $m & % growth rates	Main countries	U 38-a
- index nos	Main countries	U 38-a
Imports by source: tonnage & value in $m	All countries	U 12-a
World exports by value in $m		U 38-a
by destination regions by value in $m		U 38-a

ENGINEERS

No (incl scientists) engaged in research work	All countries	U 62-a

Engines, aircraft   see   AIRCRAFT ENGINES

ENGINES, AUXILIARY

Production by value in million yen	Japan	S 16-a

	Territorial coverage	Title codes	
ENGINES, DIESEL			
Production by value in million yen	Japan	S 16-a	
ENGINES, INDUSTRIAL			
Exports by destination by value in £m	UK	V 1-a	
Imports of industrial engines up to 200 hp by source & value in £	UK	V 1-a	
Production (incl turbines) as % of machine production	Main countries	U 38-a	
by volume: historical tables	UK	V 1-a	

ENGINES, INTERNAL COMBUSTION
    see also   AIRCRAFT ENGINES
                  ENGINES, INDUSTRIAL
                  ENGINES, MARINE

	Territorial coverage	Title codes	
% share of world exports (value basis)	UK	B 27-a	
Exports: no & value by destination	UK	V 1-a	
Imports by value in $m	Indonesia	U 32-m	
	All countries	U 38-a	
Production by hp classes	All countries	U 38-a	
volume	All countries	U 38-a	
volume & hp	All countries	U 22-a	
	EEC countries	E 28-q	E 27-a

ENGINES, OUTBOARD			
Production by value in million yen	Japan	S 16-a	

Engines, railway   see   LOCOMOTIVES

ENGINES, STEAM
       see also   LOCOMOTIVES, STEAM

	Territorial coverage	Title codes	
Exports by destination by value in $m	Main countries	U 9-a	
Imports by value in $m	All countries	U 38-a	

ENGINES BY KIND			
Exports by destination by CST classes: tonnage & value in $	EEC countries	E 48-a	
by SITC classes by value in $	Main countries	D 2-q	
tonnage & value in $	OECD countries	D 3-a2	
tonnage & value in $	All countries	U 12-a	
NIMEXE classes: volume & value in $	All countries	E 20-a	
SITC classes: volume & value in $	All countries	U 50-a	U 59-a
Imports by NIMEXE classes: volume & value in $	All countries	E 20-a	
SITC classes: volume & value in $	All countries	U 50-a	U 59-a
source by CST classes: tonnage & value in $	EEC countries	E 21-a	
SITC classes: value in $	Main countries	D 2-q	
tonnage & value in $	OECD countries	D 3-a2	
tonnage & value in $	All countries	U 12-a	

Enteritis   see   DISEASES

ENTERTAINMENT & RECREATION			
Expenditure (private) in local currency	OAS member countries	N 16-a	
	EEC countries	E 32-a	
No of hrs of television broadcast time	All countries	U 62-a	
of radio programs broadcast	All countries	U 62-a	

Entertainment taxes   see   TAXATION

Environmental problems   see   RESEARCH & DEVELOPMENT

Epoxides   see   CHEMICALS, ORGANIC

Epoxyalcohols   see   CHEMICALS, ORGANIC

Epoxyesters   see   CHEMICALS, INORGANIC

Epoxyphenols   see   CHEMICALS, ORGANIC

Equalisation of burdens levies   see   LEVIES

Equipment, domestic   see   DOMESTIC EQUIPMENT

Equipment, military   see   MILITARY EQUIPMENT

Equities   see   INDUSTRIAL SHARES
                        SHARES, COMMON

ESPARTO GRASS			
Consumption in production of wood pulp: tonnage	OECD countries	D 40-a	

Esrom   see   CHEESE BY VARIETY

Essences   see   SPICES & ESSENCES
                       VANILLA & CLOVES

	Territorial coverage	Title codes
ESSENTIAL OILS		
Exports by destination by value in $	Main countries	U 2-a
Estate companies see REAL ESTATE COMPANIES		
Estate taxes see TAXATION		
Esters & derivatives see CHEMICALS, INORGANIC		
ETHNIC GROUPS		
Amerind population by area (estim)	Latin American countries	J 5-a
No of hrs of radio broadcasts for minorities	All countries	U 62-a
of television broadcasts for minorities	All countries	U 62-a
Population by tribes	All countries	U 14
ETHYL ALCOHOL		
see also CHEMICAL PRODUCTS		
Consumption for organic synthesis: tonnage	OECD countries	D 5-a
of materials for production by chemical industry: tonnage	OECD countries	D 5-a
tonnage	OAS member countries	N 17-a
	OECD countries	D 5-a
Excise duties: % rates charged	EEC countries	E 31-a
Exports by destination by value in $	Main countries	U 2-a
tonnage	European countries, Japan & USA	U 26-a
Imports: tonnage	European countries, Japan & USA	U 26-a
Production: tonnage from oil & natural gas & total production	OECD countries	D 5-a
tonnage	European countries, Japan & USA	U 26-a
by volume (100% spirit)	All countries	U 22-a
ETHYLENE		
see also CHEMICAL PRODUCTS		
HYDROCARBONS, ALIPHATIC		
Consumption for organic synthesis: tonnage	OECD countries	D 5-a
tonnage	OECD countries	D 5-a
Production from coal, oil & natural gas: tonnage	OECD countries	D 5-a
tonnage	ECE countries	U 15-a
	European countries, Japan & USA	U 26-a
Refining capacity in tons per yr	EEC countries	B 30-a
Ethylene oxide see CHEMICALS, ORGANIC		
Ethylmorphine see DRUGS & MEDICINES		
EURODOLLAR RATES		
% interest rates payable on Eurodollars	All countries	F 5-m F 6-q
European Agricultural Guidance & Guarantee Fund (F.E.O.G.A.) see COMMUNITY INVESTMENT FUNDS		
European Coal & Steel Community see E.C.S.C.		
EUROPEAN COMMISSION		
see also COUNCIL OF EUROPE		
COURT OF JUSTICE		
EUROPEAN DEVELOPMENT FUND		
EUROPEAN INVESTMENT BANK		
EUROPEAN PARLIAMENT		
Budget allocations from EEC funds in £m	EEC area	B 3-a
EEC community: budget costs in £m		B 1-a
European council see COUNCIL OF EUROPE		
EUROPEAN DEVELOPMENT FUND		
see also CREDIT, INTERNATIONAL		
DEVELOPMENT AID		
INTEREST RATES		
% interest rates charged on loans	OECD countries	D 10-a
Administration costs in UA		E 19-a
Aid by project (in detail) in UA		E 19-a
by purpose in UA	Recipient countries	E 19-a
disbursements, grants & loans in UA		D 13-a
Appropriations from Fund for economic planning in UA	AASM countries	E 41-a
for social projects in UA	AASM countries	E 41-a
Assets (liquid) gold holdings & holdings of US $ by Fund		D 10-a
Called-up capital in $m from member countries	OECD countries	D 10-a
Capital as % of contributions	OECD countries	D 10-a
of the Fund in $m	OECD countries	D 10-a
Commitments by type of capital project in UA	Worldwide	D 13-a
Contributions by EEC community in $m	EEC countries	D 13-a
Credit drawing periods	OECD countries	D 10-a
Credits granted in $m	OECD countries	D 10-a
Development aid appropriations in UA	Donating countries	E 19-a

	Territorial coverage	Title codes
EUROPEAN DEVELOPMENT FUND, continued		
Disbursements by kind in UA	Donating countries	E 19-a
of aid in UA	Recipient countries	D 13-a
Expenditure on capital projects in UA	AASM countries	E 41-a
diversification projects in UA	AASM countries	E 41-a
emergency aid in UA	AASM countries	E 41-a
interest payments in UA	AASM countries	E 41-a
price supports in UA	AASM countries	E 41-a
sales promotion projects in UA	AASM countries	E 41-a
special projects in UA	AASM countries	E 41-a
technical aid in UA	AASM countries	E 41-a
Expenditure (total) in UA	AASM countries	E 41-a
Liabilities of European Development Fund in $m		D 10-a
Loans (long-term) granted by European Development Fund in $m		D 10-a
No of projects aided in UA	Developing countries	E 19-a
Obligations of contracting parties in $m	Donating countries	D 10-a
Payments made to Fund in $m	Donating countries	D 10-a
Price stabilisation aid granted by product in UA	Worldwide	E 19-a
Service charges on unused credit in UA	OECD countries	D 10-a
Uncalled capital in $m	OECD countries	D 10-a
EUROPEAN INVESTMENT BANK		
see also COMMUNITY INVESTMENT FUNDS		
DEVELOPMENT AID		
Disbursements by areas	EEC countries	E 38-a
Loans granted for development projects by European Investment Bank		D 13-a
European Monetary Agreement see EUROPEAN DEVELOPMENT FUND		
EUROPEAN PARLIAMENT		
see also EUROPEAN COMMISSION		
Budget allocations from EEC funds in £m		B 3-a
Budgeted expenditure on upkeep of the European Parliament in £m		B 1-a
Evaporated milk see CONDENSED & EVAPORATED MILK		
Evening schools see COLLEGES, TECHNICAL		
Ewes see SHEEP		
Ex factory prices see PRODUCER PRICES		
EXCAVATING MACHINES		
Production by volume	All countries	U 22-a
	Canada, European countries, Japan & USA	U 38-a
Exchange Certificates selling rates see EXCHANGE RATES		
EXCHANGE RATES		
see also EURODOLLAR RATES		
PAR VALUES		
Against US dollars & EEC units of account	Main countries	E 22-m
at end-yr	OPEC countries	C 3-a
historical table from 1937 (average)	Main countries	C 4-a
	All countries	L 4-a
	Latin American countries	J 5-a
	Main ECAFE countries	U 17-a
	Asian, Far East & Australasian countries	U 45-a
% change: spot value of sterling against main currencies		C 9-q
% changes against US dollars of main currencies		U 16-a U 54-a
		U 62-a
% relationship of principal currencies to purchasing power parities	Main countries	C 2-a
Buying rates against US dollars at end-yr	OAS member countries	N 16-a
Commission selling rate against US dollars at end-yr	OAS member countries	N 16-a
Comparisons of world currencies based on gold parities & par values		R 1-m
Controlled market rates of exchange (average)	All countries	M 8-a
Currency buying rates (average)	All countries	M 8-a
selling rates (average)	All countries	M 8-a
Export rate for coffee against US dollars at end-yr	OAS member countries	N 16-a
goods against US dollars at end-yr	OAS member countries	N 16-a
petroleum against US dollars at end-yr	OAS member countries	N 16-a
Export rates of exchange (average) for all currencies		M 8-a
Financial markets' selling rates (average) for all currencies		M 8-a
Financial markets' rate against US dollars at end-yr	OAS member countries	N 16-a
Forward (90 days) buying rate for main European currencies		D 26-q
Forward rates of exchange against US dollars at end-yr	OAS member countries	N 16-a
Free buying rates of exchange against US dollars at end-yr	OAS member countries	N 16-a
at bazaars (average)	All countries	M 8-a
(average) of all currencies		M 8-a
for banking system (average)	All countries	M 8-a
Imports rate of exchange (average) for all currencies		M 8-a
Local currency units per US dollars	African countries	U 44-a
Mid-point rates against US dollars	All countries	U 27-a U 43-a

	Territorial coverage	Title codes
EXCHANGE RATES, continued		
Movements & annual averages of exchange rate fluctuations	Worldwide	M 8-a
No of DM per one unit of main overseas currencies		R 1-m
Non-commercial transactions rates of exchange for all currencies		M 8-a
Official buying rate against US dollars at end-yr	OAS member countries	N 16-a
of exchange of all currencies (average)		M 8-a
certificate buying rates of all currencies (average)		M 8-a
selling rate against US dollars at end-yr	OAS member countries	N 16-a
	All countries	M 8-a
Parity & official rates against US dollars	All countries	M 6-a
Parity rates (average)	All countries	M 8-a
(based on tourist currency values)	Main countries	R 5-a
Selling rates against US dollars at end-yr	OAS member countries	N 16-a
for exchange certificates	All countries	M 8-a
Spot & forward rates against US dollars	All countries	F 5-m F 6-q
Tourist rates of exchange (average)	All countries	M 8-a
Transfer buying rates (average)	All countries	M 8-a
selling rates (average)	All countries	M 8-a
EXCISE TAX		
As element in retail prices of bunkers	Main countries	C 3-a
kerosene	Main countries	C 3-a
lubricating oil	Main countries	C 3-a
motor spirit	Main countries	C 3-a
Government revenue from excise duties in local currency	African countries	U 44-a
	EEC countries	E 42-a
	OECD countries	D 42-a
Government revenue: historical tables from 1750 in local currency	Main European countries	Z 1-a
Rates charged & basis of assessment:-		
acetic acid (vinegar)	EEC countries	E 31-a
bananas	EEC countries	E 31-a
beer & wines	EEC countries	E 31-a
benzole	EEC countries	E 31-a
beverages	EEC countries	E 31-a
cocoa	EEC countries	E 31-a
coffee	EEC countries	E 31-a
electric lamp bulbs	EEC countries	E 31-a
ethyl alcohol	EEC countries	E 31-a
gas & electricity	EEC countries	E 31-a
gramophone records	EEC countries	E 31-a
liquefied petroleum gases	EEC countries	E 31-a
manufactured tobacco	EEC countries	E 31-a
margarine	EEC countries	E 31-a
matches	EEC countries	E 31-a
mineral oils	EEC countries	E 31-a
motor vehicles	Main countries	S 24-a
playing cards	EEC countries	E 31-a
salt	EEC countries	E 31-a
sugar & sweeteners	EEC countries	E 31-a
table waters	EEC countries	E 31-a
tea	EEC countries	E 31-a
vegetable & animal oils	EEC countries	E 31-a
yarns & woven materials	EEC countries	E 31-a
EXCURSIONS		
see also TOURISM		
No of land excursions taken by short-term visitors	OECD countries	D 47-a
of shore excursions taken by short-term visitors	OECD countries	D 47-a
EXPECTATION OF LIFE		
At birth by sex in yrs	Developing world regions	U 23-a
At specific ages by sex in yrs	All countries	U 14-a
	Latin American countries	J 5-a
	Main countries	W 1-a
	OAS member countries	N 12-a
every ten years by sex	EEC countries	E 2-a
Life expectancy at 1 yr of age in yrs	Main countries	W 2-a
at 65 yrs of age in yrs	Main countries	W 2-a
at birth in yrs	Main countries	W 2-a
Male workers by yr 2000 (estim) in yrs	World regions	L 3
EXPENDITURE		
see also BUDGET ACCOUNTS		
CIVIL EXPENDITURE		
DEFENCE EXPENDITURE		
GOVERNMENT EXPENDITURE		
OPERATING EXPENSES		
PRIVATE EXPENDITURE		
SOCIAL FUNDS		
% changes in consumer expenditure	Main countries	D 17-a
government expenditure	Main countries	D 17-a
machinery & equipment purchase	Main countries	D 17-a
main components of gross domestic product	Main countries	D 17-a
non-residential construction	Main countries	D 17-a
residential construction	Main countries	D 17-a

	Territorial coverage	Title codes

EXPENDITURE, continued
    Capital transfers from rest of world in local currency — African countries — U 44-a
    Disbursements on external transactions in local currency — African countries — U 44-a
    Industrial companies on general consumption goods by value in $ — OAS member countries — N 14-a
        on raw materials by value in $ — OAS member countries — N 14-a
    Industrial costs on salaried personnel in $ — OAS member countries — N 14-a
    Manufacturing industry on consumption goods in $ — OAS member countries — N 14-a
    Surpluses on external transactions in local currency — African countries — U 44-a

EXPENDITURE, ADMINISTRATIVE
    Budget costs of Council of Europe in £m — B 1-a
                Court of Justice in £m — B 1-a
                European Parliament in £m — B 1-a
    Budgeted running expenses in £m — EEC Institutions — B 1-a

Expenditure, capital   see   INVESTMENT

Expenditure, domestic   see   HOUSEHOLD BUDGETS

EXPENDITURE, MUNICIPAL
    Cost of goods & services in local currency — OAS member countries — N 16-a
    Interest on public debt in local currency — OAS member countries — N 16-a
    Transfers to individuals in local currency — OAS member countries — N 16-a
              to provincial treasuries in local currency — OAS member countries — N 16-a

Expenditure, private   see   PRIVATE EXPENDITURE

EXPENDITURE, PROVINCIAL
    see also   SOCIAL FUNDS
                SOCIAL SERVICES
    Cost of goods & services in local currency — OAS member countries — N 16-a
    Interest payments on debts in local currency — OAS member countries — N 16-a
    Subsidy payments in local currency — OAS member countries — N 16-a
    Transfers to individuals in local currency — OAS member countries — N 16-a
              to municipal treasuries in local currency — OAS member countries — N 16-a

Expenditure, social welfare   see   SOCIAL FUNDS
                                    SOCIAL SERVICES

Exploration   see   OIL EXPLORATION

EXPLOSIVES
    see also   PYROTECHNIC PRODUCTS
    Exports (incl pyrotechnics) by destination by value in $ — Main countries — U 2-a
            to EEC & non-EEC area by value in $m — EEC countries — E 24-a
    Imports ex EEC & non-EEC area by value in $m — EEC countries — E 24-a
                                  EEC countries — E 28-q   E 27-a
    Production: tonnage — Zaire — E 41-a

EXPORT CREDITS
    As % of total financial flow — Developing areas — U 23-a
    As factor in exchange receipts — Developing areas — U 23-a
    Net change in guaranteed private credits — Main countries — D 7-a
        credits covered by export-import bank in $m — — D 13-a
        guaranteed private credits in $m — European countries — R 5-a
                                     — Main countries — D 7-a
                public credits in $m — Main countries — D 7-a
    Private credits to overseas importers — Developing countries — M 3-a
    Receipts of guaranteed credits — Recipient countries — D 13-a
    Wheat & flour: guaranteed insurance credits — Canada — B 8-a

EXPORT-DUTIES
    EEC levies on rice imports from non-EEC area — — B 14-m
    Government receipts in local currency — African countries — U 44-a
                         in $m — Latin American countries — J 5-a
    Receipts as factor in budget accounts — Main countries — U 43-a
    Tea duties levied at Colombo in Rs per lb — Sri Lanka — B 13-m

EXPORT EARNINGS
    From rest of world in local currency — OAS member countries — N 16-a
    % change in export values of crude oil — Main countries — U 11-a
                             farm products — Developing countries — U 11-a
                           food products — Developing countries — U 11-a
                           manufactured goods — Israel & S Korea — U 11-a
                           metallic minerals — Bolivia — U 11-a
                           tropical foods — Developing countries — U 11-a
    % earnings from alcoholic drinks — Bahamas & Jamaica — E 45-a
                   aluminium — Cameroon & Sierra Leone — E 45-a
                   asbestos — Swaziland — E 45-a
                   bananas — Jamaica, Tonga & W Samoa — E 45-a
                   bauxite — Guyana & Jamaica — E 45-a
                   beef — Chad Rep — E 45-a
                   cattle carcasses — Botswana — E 45-a
                   cattle hides — Botswana & Rwanda Burundi — E 45-a

	Territorial coverage	Title codes
EXPORT EARNINGS, continued		
% earnings from cement	Bahamas	E 45-a
citrus fruits	Swaziland	E 45-a
clothing	Mauritius	E 45-a
cocoa butter	Cameroon & Ivory Coast	E 45-a
cocoa	African, Caribbean countries & Pacific Is	E 45-a
coconuts	Tonga	E 45-a
coffee	African, Caribbean countries & Pacific Is	E 45-a
copper ore	Mauritania & Zambia	E 45-a
copper (unrefined)	Uganda & Zambia	E 45-a
copra	Tonga & W Samoa	E 45-a
cotton	African, Caribbean countries & Pacific Is	E 45-a
crude petroleum	African, Caribbean countries & Pacific Is	E 45-a
crustacean products	Guyana	E 45-a
diamonds	Botswana & Sierra Leone	E 45-a
disinfectants	Rwanda	E 45-a
dried fish	Gambia, Mali & Mauritania	E 45-a
dried vegetables	Kenya	E 45-a
electrical appliances	Barbados	E 45-a
fertilisers	Trinidad & Tobago	E 45-a
frozen fish	Mauritania	E 45-a
fuel oil	Kenya	E 45-a
goatskins	Ethiopia & Somalia	E 45-a
groundnut oil	African, Caribbean countries & Pacific Is	E 45-a
groundnuts	African, Caribbean countries & Pacific Is	E 45-a
hemp fibre	Tanzania	E 45-a
hormones	Bahamas	E 45-a
industrial diamonds	Liberia	E 45-a
iron ore	African, Caribbean countries & Pacific Is	E 45-a
lead	Zambia	E 45-a
livestock	Somali Republic & Upper Volta	E 45-a
manganese ore	Botswana	E 45-a
meat preparations	Kenya & Madagascar	E 45-a
metallic cobalt	Zambia	E 45-a
molasses	Mauritius	E 45-a
natural gums	Chad & Senegal	E 45-a
natural rubber	Liberia	E 45-a
non-ferrous metal ores	Niger	E 45-a
oilcake	Benin, Gambia & Sudan	E 45-a
oilseeds by kind	African, Caribbean countries & Pacific Is	E 45-a
palm kernels	Nigeria & Sierra Leone	E 45-a
palm oil	Benin & Zaire	E 45-a
petroleum products	Chad & Senegal	E 45-a
phosphates	Senegal & Togo	E 45-a
plywood	Gabon	E 45-a
potash fertilisers	Congo Republic	E 45-a
precious stones & pearls	Mauritius	E 45-a
pulp wood	Bahamas	E 45-a
rice	Guyana & Madagascar	E 45-a
sawn hardwood	Cameroons & Ivory Coast	E 45-a
sheep	Ethiopia, Somali Republic & Upper Volta	E 45-a
sheepskins	Somali Republic	E 45-a
spices	Madagascar & Tanzania	E 45-a
sugar	Barbados, Fiji & Jamaica	E 45-a
tea	Malawi, Mauritius & Uganda	E 45-a
timber (hardwood)	Central African Republic & Ivory Coast	E 45-a
tin ore	Rwanda	E 45-a
tobacco	Malawi	E 45-a
uranium ore	Gabon	E 45-a
vegetables (prepared)	Malawi & Ethiopia	E 45-a
wood pulp	Swaziland	E 45-a
wool & mohair	Lesotho	E 45-a
woven woollen fabrics	Fiji	E 45-a
zinc concentrates	Zambia	E 45-a
EXPORT LEVIES (EEC)		
On beef in EEC trade in pence per lb		C 9
EXPORT PRICES		
By commodity markets - index nos (see no 3, 6, 9 & 12)	Worldwide	U 27-q
Of main export products in local currency	Latin American countries	J 5-a
Abaca in $ per 100 lbs	Philippines	U 17-m
& raw hemp in pesos fob Manila	Philippines	U 32-m
Acrylic Orlon fibre (4.5 denier) in cents per lb fob	USA	R 2-m
Agricultural non-food products - index nos	Worldwide	U 23-a
Agricultural products, fruits & seeds in local currency fob	Main countries	A 9-a
Agricultural raw materials by kind - index nos	Latin American countries	U 18-a
Aluminium (primary in cents) per lb fob	Canada	R 2-m
Antimony ore (lump sulphide) in $ per ton fob	European countries	T 4-w
Aviation fuel in cents per gallon fob at specific ports	Worldwide	C 3-a
Bananas (minimum shipside price per box) in local currency	Main countries	A 15-a
Barley (by grade) as fodder in local currency	Canada & USA	R 2-m
(for milling, malting & animal feed) in £ per ton	Main countries	B 8-a
in $ per ton fob	Canada & USA	C 16-m
Beryllium-copper alloy ingots in $ per lb fob	USA	T 4-m
Bismuth metal in $ per lb fob at ports	USA	T 4-m
Bunker C fuel oil at main world ports in cents per gallon	Worldwide	C 3-a H 4-a
Butter ex dairy in local currency per kg	Denmark & Netherlands	R 2-m

EXPORT PRICES, continued

Item	Territorial coverage	Title codes	
Canned apricots (ex Australia & S Africa shipped to UK) in $		A 7-a	
Canned peaches (ex Australia & S Africa shipped to UK) in $		A 7-a	
Cereals, feedstuffs & vegetable oils in local currency	Main countries	A 9-a	
Cereals - index nos	Worldwide	U 23-a	
Chromium (electrolytic) in cents per lb fob	USA	T 4-m	
Citrus fruits by kind in cents per 15 kg	S Africa	B 6-a	
Coarse grains by kind in $ per ton	Canada & USA	C 16-a	U 35-a
Cobalt metal shot in $ per lb (in drums)	USA	T 4-m	
Cocoa beans (ex Accra & Bahia) in cents per lb at New York	USA	R 2-m	
(ex Ghana) in £ per ton on London market	UK	R 2-m	
Coconut oil (crude in drums) in $ per pical	Singapore	U 32-m	
(delivered wharf Colombo) in Rs per ton	Sri Lanka	A 4-m	
in cents per lb fob at New York	USA	A 4-m	
M$ per picul fob Singapore		A 4-m	
F$ per ton at Suva	Fiji	A 4-m	
cents per lb fob	USA	R 2-m	
Rs per ton fob	Sri Lanka	U 32-m	
Coffee (Santos no 4) ex Brazil in cents per lb	Brazil	B 2-a	
Coffee, cocoa & tea - index nos	Worldwide	U 23-a	
Coffee (Mams) ex Colombia in cents per lb	Colombia	B 2-a	
(high-grown) ex El Salvador in cents per lb	El Salvador	B 2-a	
(raw by grade) in cents per lb fob at New York	USA	R 2-m	
(raw Robusta) ex Uganda in £ per kg fob on London market	UK	R 2-m	
(raw Santos Prime) in £ per kg fob	Brazil	B 2-a	
(washed clean beans) in cents per lb fob	Uganda	B 2-a	
Cold-rolled steel sheets in FrB per ton fob	EEC countries	U 49-m	
Copper (electrolytic) in A$ per ton fob	Australia	T 4-w	
in cents per lb fob	USA	T 4-m	
Copper sulphate (in 50 kg bags) in £ per ton fob	UK	T 4-w	
Copra cake & meal (20% protein) at Los Angeles in £ per ton	USA	A 4-m	
Copra ex Philippines in $ per ton cif at ports	European countries	B 19-a	
in local currency per ton fob at main ports	Worldwide	A 4-m	
in Rs per lb fob	Sri Lanka	U 32-m	
in $ per 100 lbs fob	Philippines	U 17-m	
unit values in $ per 100 lbs	Indonesia	U 32-m	
Corn oil (raw ex tanks) in cents per lb fob at New York	USA	R 2-m	
Cotton raw ex Sao Paulo in pence per lb (incl export tax)	Brazil	B 10-m	
ex USA: spot prices (average) in cents per lb	USA	B 10-m	
Cotton (raw by grade) in local currency per kg	Main countries	A 5-a	
Cotton raw (quote 3 months shipment) in local currency	All countries	K 1-m	
in Rs per 100 lbs fob	Pakistan	U 17-m	
Cottonseed oil in cents per lb fob	USA	B 19-a	
Crude petroleum (at Kharg Is) in $ per barrel fob	Iran	U 32-m	
(at main ports) in $ per barrel	Main countries	H 4-a	
in M$ per ton	Sarawak	U 32-m	
(at specific ports) in $ per barrel fob	Worldwide	C 3-q	
in cents per gallon	Worldwide	C 3-a	
in $ per barrel	Colombia & Venezuela	U 18-a	
Diesel oil (at main world ports) in cents per gallon fob	Worldwide	H 4-a	
by grade in local currency	All countries	R 2-m	
Ferrous scrap in $ per ton fob	EEC countries	E 29-a	
Finished steel products by kind in $ per ton	OECD countries	D 22-a	
Fish oil in cents per lb fob	USA	R 2-m	
Food & beverages by kind - index nos	Latin American countries	U 18-a	
Food products - index nos	Worldwide	U 23-a	
Fuel oil in cents per gallon fob (at specific ports)	Worldwide	C 3-a	
Fuels - index nos	Worldwide	U 23-a	
Galvanised sheets (17-20 gauge) in $ per ton fob	Belgium	R 2-m	
Hardwood logs & lumber in $ per 1000 ft fob	Philippines	U 32-m	
Heavy sections of Bessemer steel in $ per 100 lbs fob	USA	R 2-m	
of Thomas steel in $ per ton fob	Belgium	R 2-m	
Heavy steel sections in FrB per ton fob	EEC countries	U 49-m	
Ilmenite concentrates in $ per ton fob	USA	N 1-a	
Iron ore by grade in $ per ton cif	Main countries	U 56-a	
Jute in £ per ton fob	Bangladesh & Thailand	A 5-a	
in $ per ton fob	Pakistan	U 17-m	
Kerosene in cents per gallon fob (at specific ports)	Worldwide	C 3-a	
Lard in cents per lb fob	USA	R 2-m	
Lead pigs (refined) in A$ per ton fob	Australia	R 2-m	
Main commodities of S American origin - index nos		U 40-q	
- index nos	Main countries	F 5-m	F 6-q
		U 54-m	
Maize ex Argentine, S Africa & Thailand in £ per ton		B 8-m	
(by grade) in cents per 56 lbs fob	USA	B 8-m	R 2-m
in $ per ton fob Gulf ports	USA	C 16-m	
Major primary export commodities in $ per unit wt	ECAFE countries	U 17-a	
Manganese (electrolytic metal) in cents per lb fob	USA	T 4-m	
Manganese ingots in cents per lb fob Texas ports	USA	R 2-m	
Manufactured goods (unit value basis) - index nos	Worldwide	U 29-q	
Metal ores & minerals - index nos	Worldwide	U 23-a	
Metals by kind- index nos	Latin American countries	U 18-a	
Motor spirit (80 octane) in cents per gallon fob	Iran	R 2-m	
(90 octane) in cents per gallon fob	Iran	R 2-m	
(92 octane) in $ per ton fob	Netherlands	R 2-m	
(98 octane) in cents per gallon fob	Iran	R 2-m	
in cents per gallon fob at main world ports		C 3-a	H 4-a

	Territorial coverage	Title codes	
EXPORT PRICES, continued			
Natural rubber (by grade) in local currency fob	Singapore	C 17-m	
Natural rubber: unit value in bahts per kg	Indonesia & Singapore	U 17-m	U 32-m
Nickel in cents per lb fob (ex warehouse)	Thailand	U 32-m	
Nickel sheets (cold-rolled) in cents per lb fob	Canada	T 4-m	
Non-ferrous base metals - index nos (weighted average)	USA	T 4-m	
Non-ferrous metals by kind in local currency	Worldwide	U 29-q	
Non-ferrous metals by kind - index nos	Main countries	T 4	
Nylon staple fibre (1.5 denier) in cents per lb fob	Worldwide	G 1-a	
Oats by quality as animal feed in $ per ton	USA	R 2-m	
in local currency per ton	Canada & USA	C 16-m	R 2-m
Oils, oilseeds & fats - index nos	Main countries	B 8-a	
Olive oil (edible) in £ per ton fob	Worldwide	G 1-a	U 23-a
Palladium in $ per troy oz fob (ex refinery)	Spain	B 19-a	
Palm oil in $ per picul fob	USA	T 4-w	
Petroleum products: unit value in $ per barrel	Singapore	U 32-m	
in $ per barrel fob	Indonesia	U 32-m	
Petroleum products - index nos	Venezuela	U 18-a	
Plates (heavy hot-rolled steel) in $ per 100 lbs fob	Latin America	U 18-a	
(heavy Thomas steel over 4.75 mm) in FrB per ton	USA	R 2-m	
Platinum in $ per troy oz fob	Belgium	R 2-m	
Polyester "Dacron" fibre in cents per lb fob	USA	T 4-w	
Polyester terylene fibre in pence per lb fob	USA	R 2-m	
Primary commodities - index nos (weighted average)	UK	R 2-m	
Regulus metal at Laredo in cents per lb fob	Worldwide	U 29-q	
Rice (broken) in £ per ton: historical table 1921-1964	USA	T 4-m	
(by grade ex warehouse) in cents per lb fob	Thailand	A 19-a	
in £ per ton fob	USA	R 2-m	
by kind (under bilateral contracts) - index nos	Thailand	B 14-m	
in £ per ton fob	Worldwide	A 19-a	
in £ per ton	Burma	B 8-m	
in $BWI per ton	Burma, China & Thailand	A 19-a	
(private trade) - index nos	Guyana	A 19-a	
by quality in local currency per ton	Worldwide	A 19-a	
(husked) in £ per ton: historical table, 1951-1964	Thailand & USA	B 8-a	
in $ per 100 lbs fob	Thailand	A 19-a	
in $ per ton fob	Burma & Thailand	U 17-m	
(parboiled): historical table from 1955-1964 in £ per ton	Taiwan	A 19-a	
(white): historical table from 1921-1964 in £ per ton	Thailand	A 19-a	
(whole): historical table from 1921-1964 in £ per ton	Thailand	A 19-a	
Rye (main N American grades) in cents per bushel fob	USA	B 8-a	
(normal grade) in cents per 56 lbs cif Winnipeg	Canada	R 2-m	
in $ per ton fob at E Coast ports	Canada	C 16-m	
Sawn softwood in £ per m³ fob	Finland	A 24-a	
forward sales in local currency per m³	Scandinavian countries & USSR	A 24-a	
Silicon in cents per lb fob	USA	T 4-m	
Silk (raw 20-22 denier) in yen per kg fob shipped Yokohama	Japan	R 2-m	
Sorghum in $ per ton fob at Galveston	USA	C 16-m	
Soybean oil (raw) in cents per lb fob at Decatur	USA	B 19-m	
in cents per lb fob at New York	USA	R 2-m	
Soybeans in cents per bushel fob at Chicago	USA	B 19-m	
Steel bars (hot-rolled) in $ per 100 lbs fob	USA	R 2-m	
merchant bars in FrB per ton fob	EEC countries	U 49-m	
products by kind per ton: prices fixed by European Coal & Steel Community	EEC countries	T 4	
sheets (cold-rolled) in $ per ton	Belgium	R 2-m	
(hot-rolled) in $ per 100 lbs	USA	R 2-m	
Sugar (granulated) in £ per ton fob	UK	R 2-m	
in $ per 100 lbs fob	Philippines	U 17-m	
(raw centrifugal) in cents per lb: historical table from 1900	USA	A 20-a	
in cents per lb shipped to UK	USA	C 25-a	
under International Sugar Agreement in cents per lb fob	Caribbean countries	U 20-q	
Tea (at auction) in Rs per lb for export	India & Sri Lanka	U 32-m	
(average all grades at Colombo & Calcutta) in Rs per kg	India & Sri Lanka	A 5-a	
in $ per 100 lbs fob	Sri Lanka	U 17-m	
Textile raw materials - index nos	Worldwide	U 23-a	
Thorium ore (ex Australia) in $ per ton	European countries	T 4-m	
Tin in M$ per 100 lbs	Singapore	U 17-m	
Unit value of motor fuel in $ per barrel	Venezuela	C 3-a	
propane in $ per barrel	Venezuela	C 3-a	
petroleum exports in cents per barrel	Main countries	U 18-a	
sawn logs & veneer in M$ per ton	Sabah	U 32-m	
teak in local currency	Burma & Thailand	U 32-m	
Wheat (at Gulf, Atlantic & Pacific ports) in $ per ton fob	USA	C 29-m	
by grade (by port areas) in $ per ton	Canada	C 29-m	
ex Australia, N America & Argentine in £ per ton fob			
in $ per ton fob	Main countries	B 8-m	
in $ per bushel fob	Main countries	C 29-m	
ex Australia, Canada, Argentine & USA in £ per ton fob		C 16-m	
in $ per bushel fob	Main countries	B 7-m	
(hard) in $ per ton fob	Argentine, Canada & USA	C 16-m	U 11-a
(hard red) in $ per 60 lbs at Gulf ports	USA	C 29-m	U 35-a
	Argentine	U 20-q	U 33-q
(hard winter grade) in $ per 60 lbs fob	USA	U 33-m	
		U 33-m	

	Territorial coverage	Title codes	
EXPORT PRICES, continued			
Wheat in cents per 60 lbs fob	Australia	U 32-m	
(soft by grade) in local currency per ton	Canada & USA	R 2-m	U 30-q
(soft standard quality) in $ per ton fob	EEC countries	C 29-m	
Wheat flour by grade in $ per ton fob	Australia, Canada & USA	C 16-m	
Wire bars (electrolytic copper) in cents per lb fob	USA	R 2-m	
Wire rod (Bessemer steel) in $ per 100 lbs fob	USA	R 2-m	
(Thomas steel 5.5 mm) in $ per ton fob	Belgium	R 2-m	
Wood pulp (bleached & unbleached) in DM per 100 kg	Sweden	R 2-m	
Wool (greasy raw): unit value in Rs per lb fob	Pakistan	U 32-m	
Wool - index nos	Worldwide	U 23-a	
Zinc in $A per ton fob	Australia	T 4-m	
(prime western grade) in cents per lb fob	Canada	R 2-m	
sheets in cents per lb fob	USA	T 4-m	
EXPORT PROMOTION			
see also SALES PROMOTION			
Use of European Development Fund credits for export projects in UA	AASM countries	E 41-a	
EXPORT QUOTAS			
see also IMPORT QUOTAS			
INTERNATIONAL COFFEE AGREEMENT			
Coffee: basic quotas (under International Coffee Agreement) in bags	Member countries	B 18-a	J 1-a
Sugar by recipient countries: tonnage	USA	C 25-a	
(under Commonwealth Sugar Agreement): tonnage	Commonwealth countries	C 25-a	
(under International Sugar Agreement): tonnage	Member countries	B 13-a	
Tea (black) proposed by FAO: tonnage	All countries	C 1-a	
quotas agreed internationally: tonnage	All countries	B 13-a	
Export rates of exchange see EXCHANGE RATES			
EXPORT RESTITUTION PAYMENTS			
On pig-meat in £ per ton		C 9-m	
EXPORT SUBSIDIES			
Butter & butterfat by zone per 100 kg	EEC area	B 4-a	
Cereals by kind per ton	EEC area	B 8-a	
Cheese by kind by zone per 100 kg	EEC area	B 4-a	
Dairy products by kind per 100 kg	EEC area	B 4-a	
Milk (evaporated) by zone per 100 kg	EEC area	B 4-a	
Milk powder by zone per 100 kg	EEC area	B 4-a	
Rates in £ per cwt for beef (fresh & chilled)	EEC area	B 11-a	
beef (frozen)	EEC area	B 11-a	
bovine fats	EEC area	B 11-a	
live cattle	EEC area	B 11-a	
meat preparations	EEC area	B 11-a	
rice by quality	EEC area	B 14-m	
veal (fresh & chilled)	EEC area	B 11-a	
Rye, barley, oats, maize & rice per ton	EEC area	B 8-a	
Wheat flour & rye flour per ton	EEC area	B 8-a	
EXPORT TRADE			
see also Appendix 1			
AIR FREIGHT EXPORTS			
INLAND WATERWAYS EXPORTS			
MARKET SHARE			
RAIL FREIGHT EXPORTS			
RE-EXPORT TRADE			
ROAD FREIGHT EXPORTS			
SEABORNE FREIGHT			
TRADE BALANCES			
TRANSIT TRADE			
As % of gross national product projected to 1975	OECD countries	D 11	
of gross domestic product	Main countries	E 3-a	
As factor in foreign exchange income	Developing world regions	U 23-a	
By destination by CST classes: tonnage & value in $m	EEC countries	E 48-a	
by SITC classes: tonnage & value in $m	OECD countries	D 3-a2	
by value in $m	All countries	U 12-a	
& % of total world trade	Main countries	E 3-a	
all products by value in $m	Main countries	D 16-m	
by product (in detail): tonnage & value in $	All countries	U 12-a	
by value in $m	Asian & Far East countries	U 32-q	
historical table by value in local currency	Main European countries	Z 1-a	
by value in UA	AASM countries	E 41-a	
in $m	African, Caribbean countries & Pacific Is	E 45-a	
By main products - index nos (quantum basis)	OAS member countries	N 15-a	
(value basis)	OAS member countries	N 15-a	
	Main countries	F 5-m	F 6-q
by value by world regions	EEC countries	E 38-a	
unit value in $	OAS member countries	N 15-a	
By NIMEXE classes by value in $	All countries	E 20-a	
By product groups by value & as % total exports	Main countries	E 3-a	
in $m	Main countries	E 24-a	
ex world regions - index nos		U 43-a	
- index nos (see No 3, 6, 9, 12)		U 27-q	

	Territorial coverage	Title codes	
EXPORT TRADE, continued			
By SITC classes by destination by value in $m	Main countries	D 2-q	
by value in $m	All countries	U 50-a	U 59-a
By value by areas of destination in $m	ECAFE countries	U 32-m	
		U 23-a	
category of exporting country in $m	African, Caribbean countries & Pacific Is	E 45-a	
product groups by destination in UA	Caribbean countries & W Indies	T 6-a	
in local currency	African, Caribbean countries & Pacific Is	E 45-a	
to EEC area in UA	EEC countries	E 24-a	
world regions: historical table	Asian, Far East & Australasian countries	U 45-a	
world regions of supply in $m	Main countries	B 11-a	
cattle as % of total exports	Main European countries	B 27-a	
engineering products: unit value per ton	All countries	F 2-a	
ex Communist countries in $m		E 24-a	
Africa from 1958 in UA to EEC area in UA		E 24-a	
Central & S American countries to EEC area in UA		E 24-a	
E European area from 1958 to EEC area in UA		E 24-a	
EFTA area from 1958 to EEC area in UA		E 24-a	
USA from 1958 to EEC area in UA		E 24-a	
W Asian area from 1958 to EEC area in UA		E 24-a	
in DM million	Main countries	R 5-a	
	W European countries	R 5-a	
	Main European countries	Z 1-a	
local currency: historical table from 1796	World excl W European Bloc	R 5-a	
	ECAFE area	U 32-m	
local currency	African countries	U 44-a	
	All countries	F 5-m	F 6-q
UA	AASM countries	E 41-a	
	EEC countries	E 23-a	
$m & % change	E European countries & USSR	U 16-a	
$m (monthly averages)	OECD countries	D 26-q	
(seasonally-adjusted)	Main countries	U 16-q	
$m by level of gross national product per capita	Worldwide	U 23-a	
by world regions	African, Caribbean countries & Pacific Is	E 45-a	
$m: historical table from 1927	Main countries	C 4-a	
$m to EEC area	Non-EEC area countries	E 24-a	
$m	African, Caribbean countries & Pacific Is	E 45-a	
	Asian & Far East area	U 32-q	
	Asian, Far East & Australasian countries	U 45-a	
	China	F 3-m	
	Developing countries	U 23-a	
	E European countries	F 3-m	
	ECAFE countries	U 17-a	
	ECE countries	U 42-a	
	Latin American countries	U 40-a	
	Main countries	F 3-m	E 24-a
	Main non-EEC area countries	E 24-a	
	Main oil-exporting countries	U 23-a	
	OECD countries	D 16-m	
	Worldwide	F 2-a	
	OECD countries	R 5-a	
per capita in DM	All countries	M 6-a	
in $	AASM countries	E 41-a	
shipped to EEC area by value in UA	OECD countries	D 16-m	
economic groups of countries by value in $m	OECD countries	D 16-m	
OECD area countries by value in $m	OECD countries	D 16-m	
world regions in $m	Developing countries	U 52-a	
Communist countries in $m		E 26-m	
Intra & extra EEC area trade by commodity groups by value in $		R 5-a	
Of developed countries by destination areas by value in DM		R 5-a	
developing countries by destination areas by value in DM		E 3-a	
EEC area countries to non-EEC area destinations - index nos		E 3-a	
by value in $	EEC countries	E 22-m	
in UA	EEC countries	E 22-q	
to world regions in UA	Main countries	E 24-a	
On value basis - index nos	Worldwide	R 5-a	
	EEC countries	E 24-a	
volume basis - index nos	African, Caribbean countries & Pacific Is	E 45-a	
Shipments to EEC area by value in UA	OECD countries	R 5-a	
Communist countries by value in DM million	OECD countries	R 5-a	
developed countries by value in DM million	All countries	F 2-a	
in $m	OECD countries	R 5-a	
developing countries by value in DM million	All countries	F 2-a	
in $m	Main countries	E 22-q	
EEC area by value in $m	African countries	U 44-a	
main trading partners by value in local currency	Main countries	G 1-a	
Unit value of all products - index nos	OAS member countries	N 15-a	
of main products in $	Main countries	B 8-a	
% cereals by kind	ECE countries	U 15-a	
% changes & index nos (quantum basis)	Main countries	G 1-a	
based on unit values	Japan	G 1-a	
value of goods & services	African countries	G 1-a	
value	Australia & New Zealand	G 1-a	
	Centrally-planned economies	U 18-a	
	Communist Bloc	G 1-a	
	Developed countries	U 18-a	
	Developing countries	U 18-a	
	Inter-Communist area	U 18-a	
	Latin American countries	G 1-a	
	Latin American region	U 18-a	

	Territorial coverage	Title codes	
EXPORT TRADE, continued			
% changes based on value	Main countries incl China	U 18-a	
	Main European countries, Japan & USA	G 1-a	
	Middle East countries	G 1-a	
	S Africa	G 1-a	
	S E Asian countries	G 1-a	
	World regions	U 18-a	
	Developed countries	U 18-a	
	Developing countries	U 18-a	
	Latin American region	U 18-a	
on volume	Main countries	U 18-a	
	Main European countries, Japan & USA	G 1-a	
	World regions	U 18-a	
	EEC countries	E 23-a	
by destination (over previous yr)		U 18-a	
EEC area exports with rest of the world (value basis)		U 54-a	
ex main trading areas (quantum & value bases)	Developing countries	A 1-a	
farm products by kind	Main countries	U 25-a	
fertilisers	Main countries	U 25-a	
inorganic chemicals	Main countries	U 25-a	
man-made fibres	Main countries	U 25-a	
organic chemicals	Main countries	U 25-a	
pharmaceuticals	Main countries	U 25-a	
plastics	Main countries	U 25-a	
synthetic rubber	Main countries	U 25-a	
in inter-E European trade	Main countries	U 16-a	
% composition of trade by product groups	E European countries	U 16-a	
% dependence on one (or few) products for export earnings	African, Caribbean countries & Pacific Is	E 45-a	
% distribution of meat trade by destination	Australia & New Zealand	B 11-a	
% of gross national product spent on export of goods & services	ECE countries	U 15-a	
% growth in exports projected for chemicals	UK	B 21	
machine tools	UK	B 26	
% growth rates (based on value)	Latin American countries	U 18-a	
	Developing countries	U 23-a	
	Main oil-exporting countries	U 23-a	
of exports between developing countries & Communist areas		U 23-a	
by level of gross national product per capita		U 23-a	
by SITC classes between developed world regions		U 23-a	
of exports compared with growth of industrial output (on volume & value bases)	Main countries	D 17-a	
of goods & services (value basis)	Main countries	D 17-a	
	All countries	M 6-a	
% growth in exports projected to 1980 per 1% change in gross national product	OECD countries	D 11	
% increase in commercial vehicle exports projected to 1977	UK	B 28	
motor vehicle exports projected to 1977	UK	B 28	
passenger car exports projected to 1977	UK	B 28	
% market share in battery export trade	Main countries	B 23-a	
domestic appliances export trade	Main countries	B 23-a	
electric lamp export trade	Main countries	B 23-a	
electric machinery export trade	Main countries	B 23-a	
insulated cables export trade	Main countries	B 23-a	
% of inter-EEC exports in agricultural products		U 33-a	
% of groups of export products by value freighted by air	USA	D 28-a	
shipped by sea	USA	D 28-a	
by weight freighted by air	USA	D 28-a	
shipped by sea	USA	D 28-a	
% of steam boiler exports by destination (value basis)	UK	B 30-a	
% of total exports shipped to EEC area (value basis)	Main countries	E 3-a	
% share of exports of boilerhouse plant by kind (value basis)	EEC countries	B 30-a	
farm products	Main countries	A 11-a	
steam boilers by kind	EEC countries	B 30-a	
by destination (based on value)	African, Caribbean countries & Pacific Is	E 45-a	
by product (based on value)	African, Caribbean countries & Pacific Is	E 45-a	
Commodities by CST classes by destination: tonnage & value in $m	EEC countries	E 48-a	
NIMEXE classes: tonnage & value in $m	All countries	E 20-a	
SITC classes by destination by value in $m	Main countries	D 2-q	
	OECD countries	D 3-a2	
	All countries	U 50-a	U 59-a
Commodity structure as % of world trade (all products)		U 23-a	
of exports (value basis)	OAS member countries	N 15-a	
by value in local currency	African countries	U 44-a	
in $m	Latin American countries	J 5-a	U 18-a
Despatches by destination & product by rail	EEC countries	E 43-a	
by road	EEC countries	E 43-a	
by sea	EEC countries	E 43-a	
Goods & services: % volume changes	EEC countries	E 13-a	
as % of gross domestic product	All countries	U 60-a	
	Developing countries	D 25-a	
of net material product	All countries	U 60-a	
component of gross domestic product in local currency	Main countries	R 5-a	
	African countries	U 44-a	
	Developing countries	D 25-a	
by value & % changes	EEC countries	E 26-a	
	African countries	U 44-a	
- index nos	EEC countries	E 26-a	
Goods loaded at ports: tonnage	EEC countries	E 26-m	
Index nos (quantum & unit value bases)	All countries	U 27-m	
(quantum basis)	All countries	F 5-m	F 6-q

191

		Territorial coverage	Title codes	
EXPORT TRADE, continued				
Index nos (quantum basis)		Asian & Far East regions	U 32-q	
		Developed countries	M 4-a	U 23-a
		Developing countries	M 4-a	U 23-a
		ECAFE area	U 32-m	
(unit value basis)		Asian & Far East regions	U 32-q	
		African countries	U 44-a	
		ECAFE countries	U 32-m	
		World regions	U 23-a	
(value basis)		Developing countries	U 23-a	
		W European Bloc	R 5-a	
		African countries	U 44-a	
		Developed countries	M 4-a	
		Developing countries	M 4-a	
(volume basis)		EEC countries	E 22-m	
Unit prices - index nos		Main countries	E 24-a	
		Developed countries	U 18-a	
		Developing countries	U 18-a	
		Main countries	U 18-a	
		World regions	U 18-a	
Unit value (all products) - index nos		EEC countries	E 24-a	
EXPORT TRADE, INTER-EEC				
By value in UA		EEC countries	E 22-m	
% changes (based on value)			U 18-a	
(based on volume)			U 18-a	
Agricultural products: tonnage			E 43-a	
Beef & veal: tonnage			B 12-a	
Building materials: tonnage			E 43-a	
Butter: tonnage			B 12-a	
Cheese: tonnage			B 12-a	
Chemical products by value in UA			E 22-m	
tonnage			E 43-a	
Coal by value & as % total trade			E 29-a	
Condensed milk: tonnage			B 12-a	
Ferrous scrap by value & as % total trade			E 29-a	
Fertilisers: tonnage			E 43-a	
Food, drink & tobacco by value in UA			E 22-m	
Fuels by value in UA			E 22-m	
Lamb & mutton: tonnage			B 12-a	
Live cattle by volume			B 12-a	
pigs by volume			B 12-a	
sheep by volume			B 12-a	
Machinery & transport equipment by value in UA			E 22-m	
Machinery: tonnage			E 43-a	
Manufactured goods by value in UA			E 22-a	
Metal ores: tonnage			E 43-a	
Milk powder (whole & skimmed): tonnage			B 12-a	
Minerals by value & as % total trade			E 29-a	
Petroleum products: tonnage			E 43-a	
Pig iron by value & as % total trade			E 29-a	
Pig meat: tonnage			B 12-a	
Raw materials by value in UA			E 22-m	
Solid fuels: tonnage			E 43-a	
Steel products by value & as % total trade			E 30-q	E 29-a
tonnage			E 43-a	
Unit prices - index nos			U 18-a	
EXPORT TRADE, INTER-LATIN AMERICAN				
Exports of Andean group by value in $m			U 18-a	
by country in $m			U 18-a	
of CACM group by value in $m			U 18-a	
CARIFTA group by value in $m			U 18-a	
LAFTA group by value in $m			U 18-a	
EXPORT TRADE BY PRODUCT (& DESTINATION) see APPENDIX 1				
EXPORT-IMPORT BANK (EXIMBANK)				
Loans & disbursements in $m		USA	F 1-a	
Loans granted to energy & power industries in $m		Latin American countries	U 18-a	

Export/import ratios   see   TERMS OF TRADE

Expropriation of holdings   see   AGRARIAN REFORM

External debt   see   FOREIGN DEBT

External financing   see   BALANCE OF PAYMENTS

External investment income   see   OVERSEAS INVESTMENT INCOME

External liabilities   see   COMMERCIAL BANKS
                                GOVERNMENT BORROWING

External trade   see   FOREIGN TRADE

External transactions   see   EXPORT EARNINGS
                                TRANSFER PAYMENTS

	Territorial coverage	Title codes

Extruded products   see   ALUMINIUM PRODUCTS, SEMI-FINISHED
TUBES, SEAMLESS
WIRE

F.E.O.G.A. (European Agricultural Guidance & Guarantee Fund)
      see   COMMUNITY INVESTMENT FUNDS

Fabricated materials   see   MANUFACTURED GOODS
SEMI-MANUFACTURED PRODUCTS

Fabrication industry, steel   see   STEEL FABRICATION INDUSTRY

FABRICS
      see also   KNITTED FABRICS
WOVEN CELLULOSIC FABRICS
WOVEN CELLULOSIC SPUN YARN FABRICS
WOVEN COTTON FABRICS
WOVEN JUTE FABRICS
WOVEN LINEN FABRICS
WOVEN NON-CELLULOSIC FABRICS
WOVEN NON-CELLULOSIC SPUN YARN FABRICS
WOVEN RAYON FABRICS
WOVEN SILK FABRICS
WOVEN WOOLLEN FABRICS
WOVEN WORSTED FABRICS

	Territorial coverage	Title codes
Demand for furnishing textiles projected to 1977 in million lbs	UK	B 29
Exports: woven materials by kind projected to 1977 in lbs	UK	B 29
by destination by value in £m	UK	B 29-a
woven textiles (all kinds): tonnage	OECD countries	D 46-a
Imports: woven materials by kind projected to 1977 in lbs	UK	B 29
by source by value in £m	UK	B 29-a
woven textiles (all kinds): tonnage	OECD countries	D 46-a
Production: woven textiles projected to 1977 in lbs	UK	B 29
standard woven textile fabrics: tonnage	OECD countries	D 46-a
Projected demand: textile end-products by kind in lbs	UK	B 29
Retail prices of woven materials by kind in local currency	OAS member countries	N 17-a
Wholesale prices - index nos	OAS member countries	N 17-a

Facilities, domestic   see   HOUSING BY FACILITY

Factory selling prices   see   PRODUCER PRICES

Factory ships   see   TRAWLERS
WHALE OIL FACTORY SHIPS
WHALING OPERATIONS
WORLD FISHING FLEETS

FAMILY ALLOWANCES

	Territorial coverage	Title codes
As % of gross national product	OECD countries	D 11
of total social expenditure	All countries	L 2-a
Per child under 15 yrs of age - index nos	EEC countries	E 6-a
Administrative costs in $m	All countries	L 2-a
Cash benefits of recipients in local currency	All countries	L 2-a
Cost to national funds in $m	All countries	L 2-a
Expenditure in local currency	EEC countries	E 6-a
No of children qualifying for benefits	All countries	L 2-a
	OAS member countries	N 18-a
of families receiving benefits	OAS member countries	N 18-a
	All countries	L 2-a
of short-term cash benefits paid out	OAS member countries	N 18-a
Payments as % of expenditure on social welfare	EEC countries	E 6-a
from social security funds	EEC countries	E 3-a
per child under 15 yrs of age in FrsB	EEC countries	E 6-a

FAMILY PLANNING

	Territorial coverage	Title codes
Loans approved by world bank to extend advice clinics in $	OAS member countries	N 16-a

Fan belts   see   REPLACEMENT PARTS

FANCY GOODS
      see also   GOATSKINS
SHEEPSKINS

	Territorial coverage	Title codes
% of light leather products used in production of gloves & garments	USA	A 18-a
Consumption of goatskins & sheepskins in production of fancy goods	France	B 9-a

Fares   see   INTERNATIONAL FARE PAYMENTS
PUBLIC TRANSPORT

Farinaceous products   see   MACARONI & SPAGHETTI
SAGO & TAPIOCA
SEMOLINA

	Territorial coverage	Title codes
Farm accidents see ACCIDENTS, FARM		
Farm buildings see BUILDING CONSTRUCTION, AGRICULTURAL		
Farm co-operatives see CO-OPERATIVE FARMS		
CO-OPERATIVE SOCIETIES, AGRICULTURAL		
DAIRY CO-OPERATIVES		

FARM COSTS

	Territorial coverage	Title codes
% change in prices of fertilisers by kind (over previous yr)	EEC countries	E 34-m
% composition of farm operating expenditure	ECE countries	U 34-a
Components of farm operating expenditure	Hungary & Poland	U 34-a
Compound feed for cows in £ per ton (equiv)	ECE countries	U 34-a
	EEC countries	B 3-a
in local currency per 100 kg	EEC countries	B 3-a
Depreciation allowances as % of gross output	ECE countries	U 34-a
Expenditure by kind as % of value of farm output	ECE countries	U 15-a
on animal feed in local currency	Hungary & Poland	U 34-a
animal feed - index nos	ECE countries	U 34-a
fertilisers in local currency	Hungary & Poland	U 34-a
fuel, electricity & lubricants in local currency	Hungary & Poland	U 34-a
fuel & electricity - index nos	ECE countries	U 34-a
livestock management - index nos	ECE countries	U 34-a
maintenance & repairs in local currency	Hungary & Poland	U 34-a
	ECE countries	U 34-a
pesticides in local currency	Hungary & Poland	U 34-a
purchase of seeds - index nos	ECE countries	U 34-a
Fertiliser prices paid - index nos	All countries	A 2-a
(ammonium nitrate) per 50 kg bag in local currency	EEC countries	E 34-m
(ammonium sulphate 21% N) per 50 kg bag in local currency	EEC countries	E 34-m
basic slag per 100 kg in local currency	EEC countries	E 34-m
calcium cyanamide per 50 kg bag in local currency	EEC countries	E 34-m
calcium nitrate per 50 kg bag in local currency	EEC countries	E 34-m
nitrogenous fertilisers by kind in 50 kg bags in local currency	EEC countries	E 34-m
potassium chloride per 50 kg bag in local currency	EEC countries	E 34-m
potassium sulphate per 50 kg bag in local currency	EEC countries	E 34-m
sodium nitrate (16% N) per 50 kg bag in local currency	EEC countries	E 34-m
Gross farm product as % of gross output	ECE countries	U 34-a
Net product at factor cost as % of gross output	ECE countries	U 34-a
Operating expenses by kind as % of gross farm output	ECE countries	U 15-a U 34-a
at current prices in $	ECE countries	U 34-a
in local currency	E European countries	U 34-a
changes - index nos	ECE countries	U 34-a
Prices paid by farmers - index nos	ECAFE area	U 32-m
	OECD countries	D 1-a
Production costs on collective farms: cattle	USSR	U 34-a
cereals	USSR	U 34-a
cotton	USSR	U 34-a
eggs	USSR	U 34-a
milk	USSR	U 34-a
pigs	USSR	U 34-a
potatoes	USSR	U 34-a
sheep	USSR	U 34-a
sugar beet	USSR	U 34-a
wool	USSR	U 34-a
Soybean meal for livestock in £ per ton (equiv)	EEC countries	B 3-a
in local currency per 100 kg	EEC countries	B 3-a
Superphosphate prices per 50 kg bag in local currency	EEC countries	E 34-m

Farm efficiency see LABOUR PRODUCTIVITY, AGRICULTURAL		
Farm expropriation see AGRARIAN REFORM		
Farm implements see CULTIVATING MACHINES		
IMPLEMENTS, MULTI-PURPOSE FARM		
MACHINERY, AGRICULTURAL		
MOTOR CULTIVATORS		
PLOUGHS		
SEEDERS & PLANTERS		

FARM INCOME

	Territorial coverage	Title codes
% change in income from agriculture	E European countries	U 16-a
% composition of income (after payment of wages)	ECE countries	U 34-a
% growth expectancy embodied in agricultural development plans	All countries	A 11-a
Distribution to debt servicing as % of net value of product	Poland	U 34-a
private income as % of net value of product	Poland	U 34-a
taxation as % of net value of product	Poland	U 34-a
wages as % of net value of product	Poland	U 34-a
Interest received on debts as % of total farm income	ECE countries	U 34-a
Labour & management income as % of total income	ECE countries	U 34-a
Net income from agricultural activity in £m	EEC countries	B 1-a

Farm infra-structure   see   AGRICULTURE

Farm inputs   see   AGRICULTURAL INPUTS

	Territorial coverage	Title codes

Farm investment   see   INVESTMENT, AGRICULTURAL

Farm labourers   see   FARM WORKERS, UNSKILLED

Farm machinery   see   COMBINED HARVESTER-THRESHERS
　　　　　　　　　　　CULTIVATING MACHINES
　　　　　　　　　　　DAIRY EQUIPMENT
　　　　　　　　　　　IMPLEMENTS, MULTI-PURPOSE
　　　　　　　　　　　MACHINERY, AGRICULTURAL
　　　　　　　　　　　MILKING MACHINES
　　　　　　　　　　　MOTOR CULTIVATORS
　　　　　　　　　　　PLOUGHS
　　　　　　　　　　　SEEDERS & PLANTERS
　　　　　　　　　　　TRACTORS, AGRICULTURAL

Farm machinery hire   see   FARM SERVICES

FARM MACHINERY INDUSTRY

	Territorial coverage	Title codes
Costs for salaried staff per mth	EEC countries	E 11-a
Investment in buildings in local currency	EEC countries	E 40-a
on land purchase in local currency	EEC countries	E 40-a
on machinery in local currency	EEC countries	E 40-a
Labour costs as % of total farm expenditure	EEC countries	E 8-a
by status of employees in local currency	EEC countries	E 8-a
per hr: all employees in local currency	EEC countries	E 11-a
wage earners in local currency	EEC countries	E 11-a
Labour force employed: no of salaried staff	EEC countries	E 11-a
wage earners	EEC countries	E 11-a
no of wage earners & salaried staff	EEC countries	E 8-a
wheeled tractor industry	UK	B 28-a
No of hrs worked by labour force per yr	EEC countries	E 8-a
per week	Main countries	R 3-m
wk by region	EEC countries	E 25-a
yr: salaried staff	EEC countries	E 11-a
wage earners	EEC countries	E 11-a
Wage rates per hr in local currency	EEC countries	E 25-a2
by sex in local currency	Main countries	R 3-m

Farm output   see   AGRICULTURAL PRODUCTION

Farm price review   see   PRICE SUPPORTS

FARM PRICES

　　see also   FARM COSTS
　　　　　　　 PRODUCER PRICES

	Territorial coverage	Title codes
Received by producers - index nos	Main countries	A 9-a
% change in fresh milk prices over previous yr	EEC countries	E 34-m
in prices received by farmers	W European countries	U 30-a
in prices received by product	W European countries	U 30-a
% price changes: barley & maize for animal feed	W European countries	U 30-a
compound feed for broilers	W European countries	U 30-a
oilcake for animal feed	W European countries	U 30-a
compound feed for calves, cows, hens & pigs	W European countries	U 30-a
Barley prices: % change over previous yr	EEC countries	E 34-m
as animal feed per 100 kg in local currency	European countries	E 35-a
for malting & for animal feed in £ per ton	UK	B 7-m
in local currency per kg	EEC countries	E 34-m
	W European countries	E 35-a
Cereals by kind: prices paid to farmers	All countries	B 8-a
Eggs per 100 kg in local currency	W European countries	E 35-a
per doz in $	USA	E 35-a
Fertiliser prices received - index nos	All countries	A 2-a
by kind & subsidies paid in $	E European countries	U 30-a
Maize prices: % change over previous yr	France & Italy	E 34-m
per kg in local currency	France & Italy	E 34-m
per 100 kg in local currency	Austria, France, Greece & Italy	E 35-a
Milk (fresh) per 100 kg in local currency	EEC countries	E 34-m
per 100 kg fat content in local currency	W European countries	E 35-a
Minimum prices: fresh fruit by kind in R per ton	S Africa, Union of	B 6-a
Oats prices: % change over previous yr	EEC countries	E 34-m
for milling & for animal feed in £ per ton	UK	B 7-m
in local currency per kg	EEC countries	E 34-m
	W European countries	E 35-a
Oilcakes as ratio of prices received for milk	W European countries	U 30-a
Potatoes: % change over previous yr	EEC countries	E 34-m
in local currency per kg	EEC countries	E 34-m
	W European countries	E 35-a
	W European countries	U 30-a
Prices paid for fertilisers - index nos	OECD countries	D 1-a
Producer prices received for animal products - index nos	OECD countries	D 1-a
crop products - index nos	Australia & Far East countries	U 32-m
Receipts by farmers - index nos	France & Italy	E 34-m
Rice: % change over previous yr	France & Italy	E 34-m
in local currency per kg	Main countries	A 19-a
per unit wt: historical table from 1900-1964 in local currency	W European countries	E 35-a
Rye per 100 kg in local currency	W European countries	U 30-a
Significant % changes in prices of main farm products	W European countries	E 35-a
Sugar beet per 100 kg in local currency		

	Territorial coverage	Title codes
ARM PRICES, continued		
Wheat (hard): % change over previous yr	France & Italy	E 34-m
in local currency per kg	France & Italy	E 34-m
(hard & soft) & for animal feed in £ per ton	UK	B 7-m
(soft): % change over previous yr	EEC countries	E 34-m
in local currency per kg	EEC countries	E 34-m
	W European countries	E 35-a

FARM PRODUCTIVITY
    Planned % growth rates — Greece, Iberia & Turkey — D 17

Farm products   see   COMMODITIES, AGRICULTURAL

FARM SERVICES
    Tractor & machinery hire & transport costs — W Germany — U 34-a

Farm sizes   see   AGRICULTURAL HOLDINGS

Farm subsidies   see   SUBSIDIES, AGRICULTURAL

FARM TENURE
    see also   AGRICULTURAL HOLDINGS
    No & area of agricultural holdings by kind of tenure — Latin American countries — J 5-a

FARM TRACTION
    Power in use (mechanised & animal) in traction units — EEC countries — E 44-a
        (mechanised) in hp — EEC countries — E 44-a

Farm tractors   see   TRACTORS, AGRICULTURAL

FARM WAGES

	Territorial coverage	Title codes
% change in wages paid for hired farm labour per wk	W European countries	U 30-a
cowmen per wk	W European countries	U 30-a
tractor drivers per wk	W European countries	U 30-a
Basic wage rates for cowmen, tractor drivers & labourers per wk	EEC countries	B 1-a
cattle minders (hourly & daily rates) in local currency	OAS member countries	N 17-a
Composition of wages for hired labour: cash or kind	ECE countries	U 34-a
General labourers (hourly & daily) in local currency	OAS member countries	N 17-a
Labour cost (incl social charges): cowmen	E European countries	U 30-a
labourers	E European countries	U 30-a
	All countries	L 4-a
Milking staff (hourly & daily) in local currency	OAS member countries	N 17-a
Wage rates per day for agricultural workers in local currency	Fiji & Japan	U 32-m
by sex - index nos	W European countries	U 30-a
in $ & in local currency	Main countries	A 9-a
per hr by age of worker by area	Eire	R 4-q
by farm occupation in local currency	Main countries	R 4-a
by farm occupation by sex in local currency	OAS member countries	N 17-a

FARM WORKERS
    see also   SEASONAL WORKERS
                  TRACTOR DRIVERS

	Territorial coverage	Title codes
As % of total employed population	EEC countries	E 33-a
% growth expectancy embodied in development plans	All countries	A 11-a
Hired labour employed in agriculture - index nos	ECE countries	U 34-a
Hired labour: input as % of total farm labour	ECE countries	U 34-a
Incomes of wage earners in agriculture	EEC countries	E 44-a
No employed by sex by areas (incl family helpers) in agriculture	EEC countries	E 38-a
	All countries	L 4-a
No of labourers employed in agriculture	AASM countries	E 41-a
farm workers unemployed	All countries	L 4-a
Wage rates per hr by province in lire	Italy	R 4-a
Wage rates per hr: cow-hands by sex	Main countries	R 4-a
farm hands	Main countries	R 4-a
fodder supervisors	Main countries	R 4-a
horse-plough workers	Main countries	R 4-a
milkers & milkmaids	Main countries	R 4-a
shepherds	Main countries	R 4-a
tractor drivers	Main countries	R 4-a
Wages costs for hired labour as % of net farm product	ECE countries	U 34-a
- index nos	ECE countries	U 34-a
Wages per day (normal wage conditions) in $	Canada & USA	R 4-q
(with free board & housing) in $	Canada & USA	R 4-q

Farming   see   AGRICULTURE
                   COLLECTIVE FARMS
                   CO-OPERATIVE FARMS
                   LIVESTOCK FARMING

Fat content   see   MILK

	Territorial coverage	Title codes

FATALITIES
    see also   ACCIDENTS, AIRCRAFT
                    ACCIDENTS, FARM
                    ACCIDENTS, INDUSTRIAL
                    ACCIDENTS, MARITIME
                    ACCIDENTS, ROAD
                    DEATHS
                    INFANT MORTALITY

	Territorial coverage	Title codes
No per 10,000 employees in industrial accidents	W Germany	H 3-a
resulting from accidents in iron foundries	UK	B 25-a
manufacturing industry	UK	B 25-a
mechanical engineering industry	UK	B 25-a
metal industries	UK	B 25-a
lung diseases: iron foundry staff	UK	B 25-a
steel foundry staff	UK	B 25-a
road accidents	OAS member countries	N 12-a

FATALITY RATES
    see also   ACCIDENTS
                    DEATH RATES

	Territorial coverage	Title codes
Accident deaths of employees: on railways & in mining industry	All countries	L 4-a
No of air passenger-km per passenger fatality	Worldwide	S 21-a
of aircraft passenger fatalities per 100 million passenger-km flown	Worldwide	S 21-a
per 100 million km flown by aircraft	Worldwide	S 21-a
per 100 million miles flown by aircraft	Worldwide	S 21-a
per 100,000 aircraft-hrs flown	Worldwide	S 21-a
Steel industry per million man-hrs worked	EEC countries	E 3-a

FATS & OILS
    see also   ANIMAL FATS & OILS
                    BEEF FATS
                    ESSENTIAL OILS
                    FATTY OILS
                    FISH OILS & FATS
                    VEGETABLE OILS
                    WHALE OIL

	Territorial coverage	Title codes	
As source of fat protein & calorie intake per capita	OAS member countries	N 17-a	
A.I.D. sales under food aid programs in $	Recipient countries	M 1-a	
Consignments as emergency food aid in $	Recipient countries	M 1-a	
Consumption of animal & fish oils & fats: tonnage	EEC countries	E 44-a	
per capita: animal & fish oils & fats in kg	EEC countries	E 44-a	
projected to 1985 in kg	World regions	A 1	
in kg per yr	Main countries	E 3-a	
	OECD countries	D 1-a	
	W European countries	P 5-a	
	UK	B 19-a	
in lbs per yr	Canada, European countries, Japan & USA	E 44-a	
tonnage	OAS member countries	N 17-a	
Export prices (incl oilseeds by kind) - index nos	Worldwide	G 1-a	
Export prices - index nos (weighted average)	Worldwide	U 29-q	U 54-q
Exports (all kinds) - index nos (quantum & value bases)	OECD countries	D 16-q	
(incl oilseeds) by value in $	OECD countries	D 1-a	
Imports (all kinds) - index nos (quantum & value bases)	OECD countries	D 16-q	
(incl oilseeds) by value in $	OECD countries	D 1-a	
Production, imports, exports & consumption: tonnage	EEC countries	E 44-a	
Self-sufficiency ratios	All countries	U 43-a	
	EEC countries	E 44-a	
Supply (net) per capita in kg per day	All countries	U 43-a	
World exports by value in $m	World regions	A 5-a	
World supply (all kinds): incl Commonwealth supplies: tonnage	Worldwide	B 19-a	

FATS & OILS BY KIND

	Territorial coverage	Title codes	
Exports by destination by CST classes: tonnage & value in $	EEC countries	E 48-a	
by SITC classes by value in $	Main countries	D 2-q	
: tonnage & value in $	OECD countries	D 3-a2	
tonnage & value in $	All countries	U 12-a	
NIMEXE classes: tonnage & value in $	All countries	E 20-a	
SITC classes: tonnage & value in $	All countries	U 50-a	U 59-a
Imports by NIMEXE classes: tonnage & value in $	All countries	E 20-a	
SITC classes: tonnage & value in $	All countries	U 50-a	U 59-a
source by CST classes: tonnage & value in $	EEC countries	E 21-a	
by SITC classes by value in $	Main countries	D 2-q	
: tonnage & value in $	OECD countries	D 3-a2	
tonnage & value in $	All countries	U 12-a	
Production: tonnage (incl world total)	All countries	A 4-a	
World market prices: all fats & oils - index nos		A 5-a	
edible & soap fats - index nos		A 5-a	
marine oils - index nos		A 5-a	
soft & hard oils - index nos		A 5-a	
technical oils - index nos		A 5-a	
World production forecast to 1975: tonnage		A 1	
tonnage		A 5-a	

	Territorial coverage	Title codes

Fatstock   see   CALVES
                        CATTLE
                        PIGS

FATTY ACIDS

Consumption in production of detergents: tonnage	Japan	B 19-a
(incl oleine) in production of soap: tonnage	UK	B 19-a
of coconut oil in production of fatty acids: tonnage	USA	B 19-a

FATTY OILS

Consumption in production of soap: tonnage	Japan & Netherlands	A 4-a

Feathers   see   BIRD'S FEATHERS

Federal expenditure   see   GOVERNMENT EXPENDITURE

Feed characteristics   see   CEREALS
                                  NUTRITION
                                  PROTEIN

Feed concentrates   see   FEEDING STUFFS

Feed-heaters & economisers   see   BOILERHOUSE PLANT

Feedgrains   see   CEREALS
                          MAIZE
                          SORGHUM

FEEDING STUFFS

       see also   ALFALFA MEAL
                       COTTONSEED MEAL
                       GROUNDNUT CAKE
                       LINSEED CAKE
                       LUCERNE
                       OILCAKE & MEAL
                       PALM KERNEL CAKE
                       RAPESEED CAKE
                       SOYBEAN MEAL

	Territorial coverage	Title codes	
% of skim milk production used as animal feed	EEC countries	B 3-a	
Arable land under green fodder crops in ha	EEC countries	E 3-a	
Changes in stocks of animal feed on farms	ECE countries	U 34-a	
Consumption as animal feed: tonnage	Main countries	C 29-a	
	EEC countries	E 44-a	
barley as animal feed: tonnage	Main countries	C 27-a	
	UK	B 7-a	B 8-a
	EEC countries	E 44-a	
bread grains: wheat & rye as animal feed: tonnage	OECD countries	D 1-a	
cereals as animal feed	EEC countries	E 3-a	
	Main countries	A 12-a	C 27-a
	OECD countries	D 1-a	
by kind as animal feed: tonnage	OECD countries	D 14-a	
	Worldwide	C 27-a	
(imported) as animal feed: tonnage	OECD countries	D 1-a	
(locally-grown) as animal feed: tonnage	OECD countries	D 1-a	
coarse grains as animal feed: tonnage	UK	B 7-a	
feed concentrate: tonnage	European countries & Japan	A 12-a	
fish meal as animal feed: tonnage	EEC countries	E 44-a	
maize as animal feed: tonnage	Main countries	C 27-a	
	UK	B 8-a	
	EEC countries	E 44-a	
oats as animal feed: tonnage	Main countries	C 27-a	
	UK	B 8-a	
	EEC countries	E 44-a	
	Main countries	B 8-a	
potatoes as animal feed: tonnage	EEC countries	E 44-a	
	OECD countries	D 1-a	
refined sugar as animal feed: tonnage	EEC countries	E 44-a	
rice as animal feed: tonnage	EEC countries	E 44-a	
	Main countries	B 8-a	B 14-a
rye as animal feed: tonnage	Main countries	C 27-a	
	UK	B 8-a	
	EEC countries	E 44-a	
	Main countries	B 8-a	
sorghum as animal feed: tonnage	Main countries	A 12-a	
sugar beet as animal feed: tonnage	EEC countries	E 44-a	
by value of feeding stuffs used in livestock farming	EEC countries	E 44-a	
of vegetables as animal feed: tonnage	EEC countries	E 44-a	
wheat as animal feed: tonnage	Canada & USA	B 7-a	
	Main countries	C 27-a	
	UK	B 8-a	
wheat & rye (imported) as animal feed: tonnage	OECD countries	D 1-a	
(locally-grown) as animal feed: tonnage	OECD countries	D 1-a	
Costs of animal feed as % of farm operating expenses	Hungary & Poland	U 34-a	
gross value of farm output	ECE countries	U 34-a	
value of output of livestock products	ECE countries	U 34-a	
animal feed as factor in farm operating expenditure - index nos	ECE countries	U 34-a	

	Territorial coverage	Title codes
FEEDING STUFFS, continued		
Costs of animal feed as factor in farm operating expenditure in $	Hungary & Poland	U 34-a
	ECE countries	U 34-a
of animal feed to farmers - index nos	EEC countries	E 44-a
EEC subsidy: skim milk (liquid) for animal feed in pence per gallon		B 3-a
skim milk powder for animal feed in £ per ton		B 3-a
Expenditure on imported animal feed - index nos	ECE countries	U 34-a
seeds & livestock as % of value of farm output	ECE countries	U 15-a
Exports by value in $m	OECD countries	D 1-a
	W European countries	U 33-a
by value - index nos	World regions	A 11-a
to EEC & non-EEC areas by value in $m	EEC countries	E 24-a
Farm costs as % of total operating expenses	ECE countries	U 34-a
of value of gross output	Hungary & Poland	U 34-a
for domestically-produced animal feed	ECE countries	U 34-a
imported animal feed	ECE countries	U 34-a
inter-farm handling of feed	ECE countries	U 34-a
re-purchase of by-products	ECE countries	U 34-a
re-purchase of processed feed	ECE countries	U 34-a
fattening compounds for pigs - index nos	W Germany	C 9-m
IDA loans for projects to increase production of animal feed	Recipient OAS member countries	N 16-a
Import prices of continental wheat for feed in £ per ton	UK	B 7-m
Imports by value in $m	OECD countries	D 1-a
	W European countries	U 33-a
by value - index nos	World regions	A 11-a
ex EEC & non-EEC areas by value in $	EEC countries	E 24-a
tonnage	World regions	A 11-a
Price ratios of feed per quintal compared with pigs (live wt)	W European countries	U 30-a
Prices (ex-mill) of weaner compound for pigs in DM per ton	W Germany	C 9-m
Prices paid by farmers for feed barley	W European countries	U 30-a
feed maize	W European countries	U 30-a
wheat, barley & oats as animal feed ex farm	UK	B 7-m
Production from fish & animal origin: tonnage	All countries	U 43-a
Production: balancers for calf feed: tonnage	UK	P 5-a
pig feed: tonnage	UK	P 5-a
poultry feed: tonnage	UK	P 5-a
compound feed for broilers: tonnage	UK	P 5-a
cattle: tonnage	EEC countries	P 5-a
lambs: tonnage	UK	P 5-a
livestock: tonnage	EEC countries	P 5-a
pigs: tonnage	EEC countries	P 5-a
poultry: tonnage	EEC countries	P 5-a
turkeys feed: tonnage	UK	P 5-a
concentrates for cattle: tonnage	UK	P 5-a
pigs: tonnage	UK	P 5-a
poultry: tonnage	UK	P 5-a
flake maize for animal feed: tonnage	UK	P 5-a
for broilers: tonnage	Canada, Japan & USA	P 5-a
cattle: tonnage	Canada, Japan & USA	P 5-a
dairy herds: tonnage	Canada, Japan & USA	P 5-a
pigs: tonnage	Canada, Japan & USA	P 5-a
poultry: tonnage	Canada, Japan & USA	P 5-a
turkeys: tonnage	Canada, Japan & USA	P 5-a
molassed compounds for feed: tonnage	UK	P 5-a
prepared animal feed: tonnage	All countries	U 22-a
starters for calves: tonnage	UK	P 5-a
starters for pigs: tonnage	UK	P 5-a
Ratio of prices of feed to poultry meat prices	W European countries	U 30-a
Requirements of feed per kg of beef & veal production projected for 1985		P 5-a
cow milk production projected for 1985		P 5-a
pork production projected for 1985		P 5-a
poultry meat production projected for 1985		P 5-a
Stocks at farms, purchases & usage tonnage	Hungary & Poland	U 34-a
World exports: unit value in $ per ton		A 11-a
World market prices: cassava meal per 100 kg		E 34-m
fish meal ex Peru per 100 kg		E 34-m
groundnut cake per 100 kg		E 34-m
soybean meal per 100 kg		E 34-m
FEEDING STUFFS, MIXED		
% protein content by type used in W Europe		U 30-a
Imports of compound feed for animals: tonnage	UK	P 5-a
Prices paid by farmers in £ per ton	EEC countries	B 3-a
in local currency per 100 kg	EEC countries	B 3-a
of mixed feed paid by farmers for broilers	W European countries	U 30-a
calves	W European countries	U 30-a
chickens	W European countries	U 30-a
dairy cows	W European countries	U 30-a
pigs	W European countries	U 30-a
Production: compound feed: tonnage	EEC countries	B 3-a P 5-a
	European countries & Japan	A 12-a

	Territorial coverage	Title codes	
FEEDING STUFFS BY KIND			
Exports by destination by CST classes: tonnage & value in $	EEC countries	E 48-a	
SITC classes: tonnage & value in $	OECD countries	D 3-a2	
SITC classes by value in $	Main countries	D 2-q	
NIMEXE classes: tonnage & value in $	All countries	E 20-a	
SITC classes: tonnage & value in $	All countries	U 50-a	U 59-a
Import prices at European & UK ports per ton		P 1-m	
Imports by NIMEXE classes: tonnage & value in $	All countries	E 20-a	
SITC classes: tonnage & value in $	All countries	U 50-a	U 59-a
source by CST classes: tonnage & value in $	EEC countries	E 21-a	
by SITC classes: tonnage & value in $	OECD countries	D 3-a2	
by SITC classes by value in $	Main countries	D 2-q	
Prices paid by co-operative farms in $ per ton	E European countries	U 30-a	
farmers in $ per ton	USA	U 30-a	
in local currency per 100 kg	EEC countries	B 3-a	
FEEDSTOCKS			
see also PETROLEUM REFINERIES			
Imports for processing in oil refineries: tonnage	European countries	D 31-a	
Imports: oil feedstocks by source: tonnage	OECD countries	D 31-a	
Production tonnage, oil refinery output & deliveries	OECD countries	D 31-a	
FELDSPAR			
Imports & exports by source & destination: tonnage	Main countries	B 15-a	
Production: tonnage	All countries	B 15-a	
Stocks at producers' plant: tonnage	USA	N 1-a	
Usage (industrial) in glass ceramics & enamel industry: tonnage	USA	N 1-a	
Wholesale prices in $ per ton	USA	N 1-a	
World production: tonnage	Main countries	N 1-a	N 4-a
World reserves: tonnage (estim)	Main countries	N 1-a	
FELT			
Consumption of wool for production of felts in kg	Main countries	K 6-a	
Production: bitumen felt: tonnage	Yugoslavia	U 5-a	
Fenugreek seed see SPICES & ESSENCES			
Ferries see PASSENGER FERRIES			
FERRO-ALLOYS			
see also PIG IRON			
Consumption of alloying elements: tonnage	UK	T 4-a	
in steel foundries: tonnage	EEC area	E 29-a	
Exports by destination in kg	EEC countries	E 5-q	
tonnage	Belgium, Italy, Japan, Sweden & USA	T 2-m	
	E Germany & USSR	T 1-a	
	EEC countries, Japan & USA	U 7-m	U 6-a
	Main countries	H 3-a	
Government stockpile of silico-manganese: tonnage	USA	N 1-a	
Imports (all kinds): tonnage	Main countries	T 1-a	
by source: tonnage	EEC countries	E 5-q	
Imports & exports by source & destination: tonnage	All countries	B 15-a	
Imports of silico-manganese by source: tonnage	UK	T 4-a	
tonnage	ECE countries, Japan & USA	U 7-m	U 6-a
	Main countries	H 3-a	
Production: electric furnace alloys: tonnage	ECE countries	U 7-m	U 6-a
	Main countries	H 3-a	
in blast furnaces: tonnage	UK	T 4-a	
in electric furnaces: tonnage	Main countries	T 4-a	
(incl pig iron): tonnage	OECD countries	D 22-a	
(incl spiegeleisen): tonnage	EEC countries	E 30-m	
silico-manganese: tonnage	USA	T 4-a	
tonnage	All countries	U 22-a	
	Canada	T 4-a	
FERRO-ALLOYS BY KIND			
Imports by source: tonnage	Main countries	T 4-a	
tonnage	Main countries	T 1-a	
Production: tonnage	All countries	B 15-a	
	Italy	C 12-a	
	Main countries	T 4-a	
FERRO-BORON			
Wholesale prices in £ per kg	UK	T 4-m	
Ferro-cerium see RARE EARTH MINERALS			
FERRO-CHROMIUM			
Consumption by grade: tonnage	UK	T 4-a	
exothermic alloy: tonnage	UK	T 4-a	
Exports by destination: tonnage	France	T 4-a	
	Main countries	T 4-a	
Imports by source: tonnage	Main countries	T 4-a	
tonnage	Main countries	T 1-a	

	Territorial coverage	Title codes	
FERRO-CHROMIUM, continued			
Production: tonnage	Norway, Sweden & USA	T 4-a	
tonnage by kind	Italy	C 12-a	
Wholesale prices by grade in £ per ton	UK	T 4-m	
Wholesale prices in local currency per kg	France & Japan	T 4-m	
FERRO-COLUMBIUM			
Exports: tonnage	UK	T 4-a	
Wholesale prices in £ per lb of metal content	UK	T 4-m	
FERRO-MANGANESE			
Consumption for Converter steel production: tonnage	ECE countries	U 7-q	U 6-a
	Main countries	H 3-a	
Electric steel production: tonnage	ECE countries	U 7-q	U 6-a
	EEC area	E 29-a	
	Main countries	H 3-a	
Open-hearth steel production: tonnage	ECE countries	U 7-q	U 6-a
	Main countries	H 3-a	
Siemens-Martin steel production: tonnage	EEC countries	E 29-a	
Thomas steel production: tonnage	EEC countries	E 29-a	
in foundries: tonnage	EEC area	E 29-a	
in furnaces & steelworks: tonnage	EEC countries	E 30-q	
of spiegeleisen by steel process: tonnage	EEC countries	E 29-a	
in foundries: tonnage	EEC countries	E 29-a	
in steelworks: tonnage	ECE countries	U 7-q	U 6-a
	Main countries	H 3-a	
of spiegeleisen: tonnage	UK	T 4-a	
at steel foundries: tonnage	EEC countries	E 30-q	
in foundries & steelworks: tonnage	EEC countries	E 30-q	
Deliveries (domestic) of spiegeleisen: tonnage	EEC countries	E 29-a	
to EEC area: tonnage	EEC countries	E 29-a	
Exports by destination: tonnage	EEC countries	E 5-q	E 29-a
	Main countries	T 4-a	
tonnage & value in $m	All countries	U 12-a	
of spiegeleisen: tonnage	ECE countries	U 7-m	U 6-a
	Main countries	H 3-a	
tonnage	Main countries	B 15-a	
Government stockpile: tonnage	USA	N 1-a	
Imports by destination: tonnage	Main countries	B 15-a	
	EEC countries	E 5-q	E 29-a
	Main countries	T 4-a	
by source: tonnage & value in $m	All countries	U 12-a	
from EEC area: tonnage	EEC countries	E 29-a	
of spiegeleisen: tonnage	ECE countries	U 7-m	U 6-a
	Main countries	H 3-a	
tonnage	Italy	C 12-a	
	Main countries	T 1-a	
Prices in £ per ton	UK	R 2-m	
in Frs per ton	France	R 2-m	
(less tax) incl spiegeleisen in local currency per ton	EEC countries	E 30-a2	
Production (incl spiegeleisen): tonnage	France	C 5-m	
based on metal content of ore: tonnage	Italy	C 12-a	
ore at mines: tonnage	Italy	C 12-a	
spiegeleisen: tonnage	All countries	B 15-a	
	EEC countries	E 29-a	
tonnage	All countries	U 22-a	
	Main countries	T 4-a	
Wholesale prices of ferro-manganese in local currency per ton	Main countries	T 4-w	
spiegeleisen in $ per ton	EEC countries	E 29-a2	
in local currency per ton	Main countries	T 4-w	
FERRO-MOLYBDENUM			
see also MOLYBDENUM COMPOUNDS			
Exports: tonnage	France, W Germany & UK	T 4-a	
Imports: tonnage	Italy	C 12-a	
	Main countries	T 1-a	T 4-a
Production: tonnage	Italy	C 12-a	
	OAS member countries	N 14-a	
	Sweden	T 4-a	
Wholesale prices of climax lump in $ per lb	USA	C 12-m	
in £ per lb	UK	T 4-w	
in £ per ton	UK	C 12-m	
in yen per kg	Japan	T 4-w	
FERRO-NICKEL			
Exports by destination: tonnage	France & UK	T 4-a	
tonnage	W Germany	T 4-a	
Imports by source: tonnage	Main countries	T 4-a	
tonnage	Belgium, Japan & USA	T 4-a	
	Main countries	T 1-a	
Wholesale prices in local currency per kg	France & Japan	T 4-m	
FERRO-NIOBIUM			
Consumption: tonnage	UK	T 4-a	

	Territorial coverage	Title codes	
FERRO-PHOSPHORUS			
Consumption: tonnage	UK	T 4-a	
Production: tonnage	USA	T 4-a	
FERRO-SILICON			
Consumption by grade: tonnage	UK	T 4-a	
Exports by destination: tonnage	Main countries	T 4-a	
Imports by source: tonnage	Main countries	T 4-a	
tonnage	Main countries	T 1-a	
Production: tonnage of metallic silicon	Italy	C 12-a	
of silicon compounds by kind	Italy	C 12-a	
Production: tonnage	India, Norway, Sweden & USA	T 4-a	
Wholesale prices by grade in £ per ton	UK	T 4-m	
in cents per lb	USA	N 1-a	
local currency per ton	France & Japan	T 4-m	
$ per ton (on New York market)	USA	C 12-m	
FERRO-TITANIUM			
Exports: tonnage	France & UK	T 4-a	
Imports: tonnage	Main countries	T 1-a	
	W Germany, Italy, Japan & Sweden	T 4-a	
Production: tonnage	Italy	C 12-a	
Wholesale prices in £ per ton	UK	T 4-m	
by grade in £ per ton	UK	C 12-m	
FERRO-TUNGSTEN			
Exports: tonnage	France & UK	T 4-a	
Imports: tonnage	Main countries	T 1-a	T 4-a
Production: tonnage	Sweden	T 4-a	
Wholesale prices in £ per kg of metal content	UK	C 12-m	
cents per lb	USA	C 12-m	
local currency per ton	Japan & UK	T 4-w	
FERRO-VANADIUM			
Exports: tonnage	France & UK	T 4-a	
Government stockpile in lbs	USA	N 1-a	
Imports & exports by source & destination: tonnage	All countries	R 15-a	
tonnage	Main countries	T 4-a	
Production: tonnage	Italy	C 12-a	
	Sweden	T 4-a	
Wholesale prices in local currency per ton	Japan & USA	T 4-w	
FERROUS SCRAP			
Consumption for steel production: tonnage	UK	T 2-m	
	EEC countries	E 30-q	E 29-a
for production of converter steel: tonnage	ECE countries	U 7-q	U 6-a
	Main countries	H 3-a	
of Electric steel: tonnage	ECE countries	U 7-q	U 6-a
	Main countries	H 3-a	
of Open-hearth steel: tonnage	ECE countries	U 7-q	U 6-a
	Main countries	H 3-a	
in blast furnaces: tonnage	Main countries	T 1-a	T 4-a
converters at steelworks: tonnage	Main countries	T 4-a	
Electric steel production: tonnage	EEC area	E 29-a	
	Main countries	T 4-a	
iron & steel foundries: tonnage	EEC area	E 29-a	
iron & steel industry by process: tonnage	EEC countries	E 29-a	
iron foundries: tonnage	ECE countries	U 7-q	U 6-a
	EEC countries	E 29-a	
	Main countries	H 3-a	
iron production: tonnage	Main countries	U 49-a	
kg per ton of steel produced by process	EEC countries	E 30-q	
L.D. steelworks: tonnage	Main countries	T 4-a	
Open-hearth steelworks: tonnage	Main countries	T 4-a	
production of ferro-manganese: tonnage	Main countries	T 4-a	
of foundry iron: tonnage	Main countries	T 4-a	
of pig iron: tonnage	Main countries	T 4-a	
re-rolling plants: tonnage	ECE countries	U 7-q	U 6-a
	Main countries	H 3-a	
Siemens steel production: tonnage	EEC area	E 29-a	
steel foundries: tonnage	EEC area	E 29-a	
steel rolling mills: tonnage	EEC area	E 29-a	
Thomas steel production: tonnage	EEC area	E 29-a	
(industrial): tonnage	USA	N 1-a	
per ton of Electric steel produced in kg	EEC countries	E 29-a	
of foundry steel produced in kg	EEC countries	E 29-a	
of pig iron produced in kg	EEC countries	E 29-a	
of Siemens steel produced in kg	EEC countries	E 29-a	
of Thomas steel produced in kg	EEC countries	E 29-a	
tonnage at steel foundries	EEC countries	E 30-q	
by domestic users	EEC countries	E 30-m	
tonnage	UK	T 2-m	
Deliveries by dealers for export: tonnage	EEC countries	E 29-a	
home & export: tonnage	EEC countries	E 30-m	
of process scrap: tonnage	ECE countries	U 6-a	U 7-a
	Main countries	H 3-a	

FERROUS SCRAP, continued

	Territorial coverage	Title codes	
Deliveries by dealers of railway materials scrap: tonnage	ECE countries	U 6-a	U 7-a
	Main countries	H 3-a	
of ship-breaking scrap: tonnage	ECE countries	U 6-a	U 7-a
	Main countries	H 3-a	
to EEC area domestic consumers: tonnage	EEC countries	E 29-a	
of foundry scrap to EEC area: tonnage	EEC countries	E 29-a	
of galvanised scrap to EEC area: tonnage	EEC countries	E 29-a	
Export prices in $ per ton fob	EEC countries	E 5-q	
Exports by destination: tonnage	EEC area & World regions	E 29-a	
	Main countries	T 4-a	
by value to non-EEC area in local currency	EEC countries	E 29-a	
tonnage	Australia, Canada, France, W Germany & USA	T 2-m	
	ECE countries, Japan & USA	U 7-m	U 6-a
	Main countries	H 3-a	
Import prices in $ per ton cif	EEC countries	E 29-a	
Imports by source: tonnage	EEC countries	E 5-q	E 29-a
	Main countries	T 1-a	T 4-a
by value ex non-EEC area into EEC area in local currency	EEC countries	E 29-a	
Imports & exports by source & destination: tonnage	All countries	B 15-a	
ex non-EEC area: tonnage	EEC countries	E 29-a	
tonnage	ECE countries, Japan & USA	U 7-m	U 6-a
	Japan	T 4-a	
	Main countries	H 3-a	
of used steel rails: tonnage	Main countries	T 1-a	
Inter-EEC imports & exports as % of world trade (value basis)	EEC countries	E 30-q	E 29-a
Prices (less tax) loaded for in local currency	EEC countries & USA	E 30-m	
of domestic scrap in $ per ton	OECD countries	D 22-a	
Production by iron & steel industry: tonnage	EEC countries	E 29-a	
home scrap: tonnage	USA	N 1-a	
purchased scrap: tonnage	USA	N 1-a	
tonnage	All countries	N 5-a	
Receipts of foundry scrap ex EEC area: tonnage	EEC countries	E 29-a	
of galvanised steel ex EEC area: tonnage	EEC countries	E 29-a	
Sales by collieries: tonnage	ECE countries	U 6-a	U 7-a
	Main countries	H 3-a	
dealers to iron foundries: tonnage	ECE countries	U 6-a	U 7-a
	Main countries	H 3-a	
to other consumers: tonnage	ECE countries	U 6-a	U 7-a
	Main countries	H 3-a	
to steelworks: tonnage	ECE countries	U 6-a	U 7-a
	Main countries	H 3-a	
iron & steel industry to dealers: tonnage	EEC countries	E 29-a	
railways of old rails: tonnage	ECE countries	U 6-a	U 7-a
	Main countries	H 3-a	
railways of scrap other than rails: tonnage	ECE countries	U 6-a	U 7-a
	Main countries	H 3-a	
Shipments of scrap by cargo vessels on trip & period charter: tonnage	Worldwide	S 17-m	
Stocks at blast furnaces & sinter plants: tonnage	UK	T 4-a	
iron foundries: tonnage	UK	T 4-a	
steelworks & foundries: tonnage	UK	T 4-a	
consumers' premises: tonnage	USA	N 1-a	
Supply arising from iron & steel production: tonnage	Japan & UK	T 4-a	
iron castings production: tonnage	Japan & UK	T 4-a	
rolling mills & other sources: tonnage	ECE countries	U 6-a	U 7-a
	Main countries	H 3-a	
in steel rerolling plants: tonnage	Japan & UK	T 4-a	
(domestic) & consumption: tonnage	ECE area	U 49-a	
available on domestic market: tonnage	EEC countries	E 29-a	
Wholesale prices of scrap (for steel-making): tonnage	Japan, UK & USA	U 27-m	
heavy steel scrap per ton in local currency	Main countries	R 2-m	
in $ per ton	EEC countries & USA	E 29-m	

FERROUS SCRAP BY KIND

	Territorial coverage	Title codes
Consumption: tonnage	USA	J 3-a
Merchant's selling prices per ton in local currency	Main countries	T 4-w
Wholesale prices in $ per ton	USA	J 3-a

Fertiliser raw materials   see   PHOSPHATE ROCK
                                   SULPHUR
                                   SULPHURIC ACID

Fertiliser, animal   see   MANURE

FERTILISERS

see also   FISH MEAL
            NUTRIENT CONTENT
            POTASH SALTS
            UREA

	Territorial coverage	Title codes
% changes in exports	European countries, Japan & USA	U 25-a
in imports	European countries, Japan & USA	U 25-a
% contribution to export earnings	Trinidad & Tobago	E 45-a
% of total world production: tonnage	World regions	A 2-a
Availability for use in agriculture: tonnage	USSR	U 16-a
in kg per ha of arable land	USSR	U 16-a
Coastal shipping of fertilisers: tonnage	EEC countries	E 43-a

FERTILISERS, continued	Territorial coverage	Title codes
Consumption (all kinds): tonnage	All countries	A 2-a
of ammonium nitrate: tonnage	All countries	A 2-a
ammonium phosphate: tonnage	All countries	A 2-a
ammonium sulphate: tonnage	All countries	A 2-a
calcium cyanamide: tonnage	All countries	A 2-a
calcium nitrate: tonnage	All countries	A 2-a
nitrogenous & phosphate fertilisers: tonnage	Latin American countries	J 5-a
nitrogenous fertilisers (all kinds): tonnage	Main countries	U 43-a
sodium nitrate: tonnage	All countries	A 2-a
urea: tonnage	All countries	A 2-a
Consumption per hectare of agricultural land	All countries	A 2-a
of arable land	All countries	A 2-a
projected to 1980: tonnage	World regions	A 2-a
Costs for fertilisers as % of farm operating expenses	Hungary & Poland	U 34-a
value of gross farm output	ECE countries	U 34-a
to farmers: chemical fertilisers - index nos	EEC countries	E 44-a
Export prices - index nos	Worldwide	U 54-q
Exports of ammonium nitrate: tonnage	All countries	A 2-a
phosphate: tonnage	All countries	A 2-a
sulphate: tonnage	All countries	A 2-a
by sea, inland waterways, road & rail: tonnage	European countries	U 8-a
of calcium cyanamide: tonnage	All countries	A 2-a
calcium nitrate: tonnage	All countries	A 2-a
sodium nitrate: tonnage	All countries	A 2-a
urea: tonnage	All countries	A 2-a
to EEC & non-EEC areas by value in $m	EEC countries	E 24-a
tonnage & value in $m	Trinidad & Tobago	E 45-a
Farm costs: ammonium nitrate per 50 kg bag in local currency	EEC countries	E 34-m
ammonium sulphate per 50 kg bag in local currency	EEC countries	E 34-m
as % of total operating expenses	ECE countries	U 34-a
of value gross output	Hungary & Poland	U 34-a
basic slag per 100 kg in local currency	EEC countries	E 34-m
calcium cyanamide per 50 kg bag in local currency	EEC countries	E 34-m
calcium nitrate per 50 kg bag in local currency	EEC countries	E 34-m
(incl fuel & maintenance) as % of value of farm output	ECE countries	U 15-a
potassium chloride per 50 kg bag	EEC countries	E 34-m
potassium sulphate per 50 kg bag	EEC countries	E 34-m
sodium nitrate (16% nitrogen) per 50 kg bag	EEC countries	E 34-m
superphosphates per 50 kg bag in local currency	EEC countries	E 34-m
Farm expenditure as % of gross agricultural output	ECE countries	U 34-a
as % of total operating costs	ECE countries	U 34-a
IDA loans for promoting increased fertiliser production in $	OAS member countries	N 16-a
Imports of ammonium nitrate: tonnage	All countries	A 2-a
ammonium phosphate: tonnage	All countries	A 2-a
ammonium sulphate: tonnage	All countries	A 2-a
by sea, inland waterways, road & rail: tonnage	European countries	U 8-a
by value in $m	Indonesia	U 32-m
by value in $m as % of value of imports of all chemical products	Main countries	U 25-a
of calcium cyanamide: tonnage	All countries	A 2-a
calcium nitrate: tonnage	All countries	A 2-a
Imports & exports by country by kind of fertilisers by rail: tonnage	EEC countries	E 43-a
by road: tonnage	EEC countries	E 43-a
by sea: tonnage	EEC countries	E 43-a
of fertilisers by value in $	All countries	A 14-a
Imports ex EEC & non-EEC areas by value in $m	EEC countries	E 24-a
of sodium nitrate: tonnage	All countries	A 2-a
of urea: tonnage	All countries	A 2-a
Investment in chemical fertiliser plants in £m	UK	B 21-a
Plant capacity tonnage: new factories for fertiliser production	All countries	A 2-a
Prices paid by farmers: ammonium sulphate in $ per ton	W European countries	U 30-a
basic slag in $ per ton	W European countries	U 30-a
calcium cyanamide in $ per ton	W European countries	U 30-a
Prices: fertilisers by kind - index nos	W European countries	U 30-a
Production: ammonium nitrate: tonnage	All countries	A 2-a
ammonium phosphate: tonnage	All countries	A 2-a
ammonium sulphate: tonnage	All countries	A 2-a B 15-a
	Asian countries & Australia	U 32-q
	OECD countries	D 5-a
basic slag: tonnage	All countries	U 22-a
	Main countries	B 15-a
calcium cyanamide: tonnage	All countries	A 2-a
calcium nitrate: tonnage	All countries	A 2-a
complex fertilisers: tonnage	OECD countries	D 5-a
mineral fertilisers: tonnage	E European countries	U 16-a
phosphoric acid: tonnage	OECD countries	D 5-a
sodium nitrate: tonnage	All countries	A 2-a
superphosphates: tonnage	OECD countries	D 5-a
urea: tonnage	All countries	A 2-a
of chemical fertilisers by value in £m	UK	B 21-a
Rail freight tonnage (inland & abroad) of natural & chemical fertilisers	EEC countries	E 43-a
Seaborne freight tonnage of natural & chemical fertilisers	EEC countries	E 43-a
Shipment of fertilisers by cargo vessels on trip & period charter: tonnage	Worldwide	S 17-m
through Kiel Canal eastwards: tonnage		D 28-a
Subsidies: country listing by % range of subsidy payments		A 2-a

	Territorial coverage	Title codes
FERTILISERS, continued		
Tramp shipping: freight rates - index nos		U 37-m
Wholesale prices of ammonium nitrate in $ per ton	Main countries	A 9-a
ammonium sulphate in $ per ton	Main countries	A 9-a
basic slag in $ per ton	France, W Germany & USA	A 9-a
sodium nitrate in $ per ton	USA	A 9-a
FERTILISERS, MANUFACTURED		
% of total EEC area production	EEC countries	R 5-a
Exports by destination by value in $	Main countries	U 2-a
Imports & exports by value in $	All countries	A 14-a
Production based on nitrogen content: tonnage	OECD countries	R 5-a
tonnage	Main countries	R 5-a
FERTILISERS, MIXED		
Prices paid of ground rock in A.Sch per ton	Austria	U 30-a
potassic slag in Frs per ton	France	U 30-a
ternary in Frs per ton	France	U 30-a
vollkorn (green & red) in A.Sch per ton	Austria	U 30-a
(by nutrient content) in $ per ton	USA	U 30-a
FERTILISERS, NITROGENOUS		
Consumption in kg per ha	All countries	A 2-a
	EEC countries	B 1-a
tonnage	All countries	T 5-a
	ECE countries	U 15-a
	EEC countries	B 1-a E 44-a
	OAS member countries	N 17-a
	OECD countries	D 1-a
Exports by destination: tonnage	Main countries	U 2-a
tonnage	OECD countries	D 5-a
Imports by source: tonnage	All countries	B 15-a
tonnage	OECD countries	D 5-a
Prices paid by farmers for ammonium nitrate in $ per ton	Main countries	B 15-a
calcium nitrate in $ per ton	W European countries	U 30-a
sodium nitrate in $ per ton	W European countries	U 30-a
by farmers in $ per ton	W European countries	U 30-a
collective farms in $ per ton	USA	U 30-a
per kg of plant nutrient in $	E European countries	U 30-a
Production from calcium cyanamide: tonnage	W European countries	U 30-a
recovered ammonia: tonnage	OECD countries	D 5-a
synthetic ammonia: tonnage	OECD countries	D 5-a
urea: tonnage	OECD countries	D 5-a
tonnage	OECD countries	D 5-a
	African countries	U 44-a
	All countries	A 9-a T 5-a
		U 22-a U 43-a
	ECE countries	U 15-a
	EEC countries	E 26-m
	Main countries	E 3-a
	OAS member countries	N 14-a
Sales (domestic) for use in agriculture: tonnage	Main countries	R 5-a
World consumption: tonnage		T 5-a
	World regions	A 2-a
World production: % change (wt basis)	World regions	A 2-a
tonnage		N 4-a T 5-a
FERTILISERS, NITROGENOUS BY KIND		
% increase in prices	EEC countries	E 34-m
Price per bag to farmers in local currency	EEC countries	E 34-m
Production: tonnage	All countries	A 2-a B 15-a
	Italy	C 6-a
FERTILISERS, PHOSPHATE		
see also BASIC SLAG		
SUPERPHOSPHATES		
% change in prices of basic slag	EEC countries	E 34-m
Consumption of basic slag: tonnage	All countries	A 2-a
by kind: tonnage	All countries	A 2-a
in kg per ha	All countries	A 2-a
	EEC countries	B 1-a
of superphosphates: tonnage	All countries	A 2-a
tonnage	EEC countries	B 1-a
	All countries	T 5-a
	Main countries	U 43-a
	ECE countries	U 15-a
	EEC countries	E 44-a
	OAS member countries	N 17-a
	OECD countries	D 1-a
Exports of basic slag: tonnage	All countries	A 2-a
by destination: tonnage	Main countries	U 2-a
of superphosphates: tonnage	All countries	A 2-a
tonnage by kind of phosphate fertiliser	All countries	A 2-a
Imports of basic slag: tonnage	OECD countries	D 5-a
	All countries	A 2-a
of superphosphates: tonnage	All countries	A 2-a

	Territorial coverage	Title codes
FERTILISERS, PHOSPHATE continued		
Prices paid by farmers in $ per ton	USA	U 30-a
collective farms in $ per ton	E European countries	U 30-a
per kg of plant nutrient in $	W European countries	U 30-a
Production of basic slag: tonnage	All countries	A 2-a
Production by kind: tonnage	All countries	A 2-a
of superphosphates: tonnage	OECD countries	D 5-a
basic slag: tonnage	OECD countries	D 5-a
complex fertilisers: tonnage	EEC countries	E 29-a
furnace slag: tonnage	OECD countries	D 5-a
superphosphates: tonnage	All countries	A 9-a T 5-a
tonnage	ECE countries	U 15-a
	Main countries	E 3-a
	OAS member countries	N 14-a
Sales (domestic) for use in agriculture: tonnage	Main countries	R 5-a
World consumption: tonnage	Worldwide	T 5-a
production: tonnage & % change	World regions	A 2-a
tonnage	World regions	A 2-a
	Worldwide	T 5-a
FERTILISERS, PHOSPHATE BY KIND		
Exports: tonnage	Main countries	B 15-a
	OECD countries	D 5-a
Imports: tonnage	All countries	A 2-a
	Main countries	B 15-a
	OECD countries	D 5-a
Production: tonnage	Italy	C 6-a
	OECD countries	D 5-a
FERTILISERS, POTASH		
% change in prices to farmers per bag	EEC countries	E 34-m
% contribution to export earnings	Congo Rep	E 45-a
Consumption of crude potash salts: tonnage	All countries	A 2-a
in kg per ha	All countries	A 2-a
	EEC countries	B 1-a
of potassium muriate	All countries	A 2-a
potassium sulphate	All countries	A 2-a
potash fertilisers: tonnage	EEC countries	B 1-a
	All countries	T 5-a
	ECE countries	U 15-a
	EEC countries	E 44-a
	Main countries	U 43-a
	OAS member countries	N 17-a
	OECD countries	D 1-a
Exports by destination: tonnage	Main countries	U 2-a
of crude potassium salts: tonnage	All countries	A 2-a
potassium muriate	All countries	A 2-a
potassium sulphate	All countries	A 2-a
tonnage & value in $m	Congo Rep	E 45-a
Imports of crude potassium salts: tonnage	All countries	A 2-a
potassium muriate: tonnage	All countries	A 2-a
potassium sulphate: tonnage	All countries	A 2-a
Prices of potassium chloride in $ per ton	All countries	U 30-a
potassium muriate in $ per ton	All countries	U 30-a
potassium sulphate in $ per ton	All countries	U 30-a
Prices paid by farmers in $ per ton	USA	U 30-a
by collective farms in $ per ton	E European countries	U 30-a
per kg of plant nutrient in $	W European countries	U 30-a
Production tonnage: complex potash fertilisers	OECD countries	D 5-a
crude potash salts	All countries	A 2-a
	OECD countries	D 5-a
potassium muriate	All countries	A 2-a
	OECD countries	D 5-a
potassium sulphate	All countries	A 2-a
tonnage	All countries	A 9-a T 5-a
	ECE countries	U 15-a
	Main countries	E 3-a
	OAS member countries	N 14-a
Sales domestic for use in agriculture: tonnage	Main countries	R 5-a
Wholesale prices: potash muriate in $ per ton	France & USA	A 9-a
potash sulphate in $ per ton	W Germany	A 9-a
World consumption: tonnage & % change	World regions	A 2-a
tonnage	Worldwide	T 5-a
production: tonnage & % change	World regions	A 2-a
tonnage	Worldwide	T 5-a
FERTILISERS, POTASH BY KIND		
Consumption: tonnage	All countries	A 2-a
Exports: tonnage	All countries	A 2-a
Imports: tonnage	All countries	A 2-a
Production: tonnage	All countries	A 2-a
	Italy	C 6-a
	OECD countries	D 5-a

	Territorial coverage	Title codes	

FERTILISERS BY KIND

% change in farm costs over previous yr	EEC countries	E 34-m	
Consumption of chemical fertilisers: tonnage	EEC countries	E 3-a	E 44-a
on farms in kg per ha	EEC countries	E 3-a	
tonnage (in detail)	All countries	A 2-a	
tonnage	ECE countries	U 15-a	
Exports by destination by CST classes: tonnage & value in $	EEC countries	E 48-a	
SITC classes: tonnage & value in $	OECD countries	D 3-a2	
by value in $	Main countries	D 2-q	
by value in $	Main countries	U 2-a	
NIMEXE classes: tonnage & value in $	All countries	E 20-a	
SITC classes: tonnage & value in $	All countries	U 50-a	U 59-a
Imports by NIMEXE classes: tonnage & value in $	All countries	E 20-a	
SITC classes: tonnage & value in $	All countries	U 50-a	U 59-a
source by CST classes: tonnage & value in $	EEC countries	E 21-a	
SITC classes by value in $	Main countries	D 2-q	
tonnage & value in $	OECD countries	D 3-a2	
Prices paid & subsidies granted in $	E European countries	U 30-a	
for fertilisers by farmers in $	Main countries	A 9-a	
Production: tonnage	Latin American countries	J 5-a	
	All countries	U 22-a	
	ECE countries	U 15-a	
	EEC countries	E 28-q	E 27-a
Road freight over frontiers: tonnage	EEC countries	E 43-a	
Sales (domestic) for use in agriculture: tonnage	Main countries	R 5-a	
World consumption tonnage & % change	World regions	A 2-a	
production: tonnage & % change	World regions	A 2-a	
trade: tonnage & % change	World regions	A 2-a	

Fertility rates   see   VITAL STATISTICS

FIBREBOARD

    see also   MANUFACTURED TIMBER PRODUCTS
                PARTICLE & CHIPBOARD

Consumption of hardboard: tonnage	Main countries	A 26-a
insulation board: tonnage	Main countries	A 26-a
per capita in kg	Main countries	A 25-a
of raw materials in production of fibreboard: tonnage	All countries	A 26-a
Exports by destination: tonnage	European countries	A 13-q
of construction board: tonnage	OECD countries	D 41-q
tonnage (incl world total)	All countries	A 5-a
	Main countries	A 25-a
Imports by source: tonnage	European countries	A 13-q
of construction board: tonnage	OECD countries	D 41-q
tonnage	Main countries	A 25-a
unit value in £ per ton: hardboard	UK	A 25-m
insulation board	UK	A 25-m
Imports - index nos (value basis)	W Germany	A 25-m
No of fibreboard manufacturing plants in operation	Main countries	A 25-a
Production & requirement forecast by volume in m³	European countries	A 24-a
Production capacity by process (wet or dry): tonnage	All countries	A 26-a
tonnage of compressed board	All countries	A 26-a
non-compressed board	All countries	A 26-a
Production, consumption, imports & exports: tonnage	Main countries	A 25-a
Production: tonnage (incl world total)	All countries	A 5-a
tonnage: construction board	OECD countries	D 41-q
hardboard	All countries	A 25-a
insulation board	All countries	A 25-a
tonnage	Canada, European countries, USA & USSR	A 13-q
volume in m³	ECE countries	U 15-a

FIBREBOARD, COMPRESSED

Consumption - index nos	European area	A 24-a
Production: tonnage	Canada, European countries, USA & USSR	A 13-q

FIBREBOARD, NON-COMPRESSED

Consumption - index nos	European area	A 24-a
Production: tonnage	Canada, European countries, USA & USSR	A 13-q

FIBRES

    see also   CELLULOSIC FIBRES
                COIR FIBRE
                COTTON
                FLAX
                HARD FIBRES
                HEMP
                JUTE
                MAN-MADE FIBRES
                NON-CELLULOSIC FIBRES
                POLYESTER
                SILK, RAW
                WOOL, GREASY RAW

Availability of man-made fibres for domestic use: tonnage	All countries	A 6-a
of natural fibres for domestic use: tonnage	All countries	A 6-a
Consumption (at carding stage) by textile industry: tonnage	Main countries	B 10-a

	Territorial coverage	Title codes
FIBRES, continued		
Consumption of main textile fibres by kind in lbs	UK	B 10-a
Production tonnage: artificial & synthetic fibres	E European countries & USSR	U 16-a
Production, supply, imports & exports: tonnage	EEC countries	B 1-a
Wholesale prices (incl fibre products) - index nos	S Korea	U 32-m
World consumption per capita: cotton, wool & man-made fibres in kg		B 10-a

Fibres, acrylic   see   MAN-MADE FIBRES

FIBRES, CELLULOSIC WASTE

Exports by destination: tonnage	Main countries	K 4-a
Imports by source: tonnage	Main countries	K 4-a

FIBRES, SYNTHETIC WASTE

Exports by destination: tonnage	Main countries	K 4-a
Imports by source: tonnage	Main countries	K 4-a

FIBRES BY KIND

% increases in consumption projected to 1980	Main countries	B 29-a
Consumption by mills: tonnage	World regions	A 6-a
by clothing industry for interlinings	EEC countries	K 4-a
as wadding	EEC countries	K 4-a
for medical & sanitary usage: tonnage	EEC countries	K 4-a
for industrial use as cleaning cloths: tonnage	EEC countries	K 4-a
tonnage	European countries, Japan & USA	B 29-a
Exports: tonnage	All countries	A 6-a
Imports ex British Commonwealth area: tonnage	EEC countries, Japan, USA & USSR	B 10-a
tonnage	All countries	A 6-a
Production of acrylics as % of total fibre production	European countries, Japan & USA	D 27-a
of polyamides as % of total fibre production	European countries, Japan & USA	D 27-a
of polyesters as % of total fibre production	European countries, Japan & USA	D 27-a
tonnage (in detail)	World regions	A 11-a
Wholesale prices - index nos	UK	B 10-m
World consumption: apparel fibres in million lbs		B 10-a
World production: industrial fibres in million lbs		B 10-a

Fibrosis   see   DISEASES, INDUSTRIAL

Fibrous pulp (non-wood based)   see   PULP, FIBROUS NON-WOOD

FIBROUS WASTE

Consumption of rags in production of wood pulp	OECD countries	D 40-a

Fields of study   see   AGRICULTURE
                      EDUCATION
                      ENGINEERING
                      FINE ARTS
                      HUMANITIES
                      LAW
                      MEDICAL SCIENCE
                      NATURAL SCIENCES
                      SOCIAL SCIENCES

Figs   see   DATES & FIGS

Filament   see   MAN-MADE FIBRES
                NON-CELLULOSIC FIBRES

File machines   see   MACHINE TOOLS
                        SAW & FILE MACHINES

Film   see   PHOTOGRAPHIC FILM

FILMS

No of cinematographic films approved by censor & length in m.	All countries	U 62-a
approved by censor	OAS member countries	N 19-a
completed by length in m.	All countries	U 62-a
produced by length in ft	OAS member countries	N 19-a
released for public showing	OAS member countries	N 19-a
released & commercially first-time shown	All countries	U 62-a
produced by length (incl co-productions)	All countries	U 43-a

FILTRATION TOW

    see also   FLAX TOW

Production: tonnage of acetate for production of cigarette filter	Main countries	U 43-a
	OECD countries	D 46-a

Finance houses   see   CREDIT FINANCE
                        INSTALMENT CREDIT

Finance markets' selling rates   see   EXCHANGE RATES

Territorial coverage   Title codes

Finance, external   see   BALANCE OF PAYMENTS
BILATERAL AID
CENTRALISED STATE INVESTMENT
COMMUNITY INVESTMENT FUNDS
CORPORATE TRANSFER PAYMENTS
CREDIT, INTERNATIONAL
DEVELOPMENT AID
DRAWING RIGHTS (I.M.F.)
EURODOLLAR RATES
EXCHANGE RATES
EXPORT CREDITS
EXPORT EARNINGS
FOREIGN ASSETS
FOREIGN BANKS
FOREIGN DEBT
FOREIGN EXCHANGE
FOREIGN LOANS
INVESTMENT, CORPORATE OVERSEAS
INVESTMENT, PRIVATE OVERSEAS
INVESTMENT, PUBLIC OVERSEAS
INVISIBLE TRADE
MULTILATERAL AID
OVERSEAS INVESTMENT INCOME
PAR VALUES
REMITTANCES
STAND-BY CREDITS
TRADE CREDITS
TRANSFER PAYMENTS

Finance, internal   see   ASSETS & LIABILITIES
BALANCE SHEETS
BANK ADVANCES
BANK CLEARINGS
BANK DEPOSITS
BANK INVESTMENTS
BANK PROFITS
BANK RATE
BANKING & INSURANCE
BUDGET ACCOUNTS
CAPITAL ACCUMULATION
CAPITAL FORMATION
CAPITAL GAINS
CAPITAL INVESTMENT
CASH FLOW
CENTRAL BANKS
CLEARING BANKS
COMMERCE & FINANCE
COMMERCIAL BANKS
CORPORATE SAVINGS
CORPORATION TAX
CREDIT FINANCE
DEBT SERVICING
DEFENCE EXPENDITURE
DEPRECIATION
DISCOUNT RATES
DISTRIBUTION COSTS
DOMESTIC DEBT
EXPENDITURE, MUNICIPAL
FINANCIAL RATIOS, CORPORATE
GOLD HOLDINGS
GOVERNMENT BONDS
GOVERNMENT BORROWING
GOVERNMENT EXPENDITURE
GOVERNMENT SAVINGS
INCOME TAX
INDUSTRIAL SHARES
INSTALMENT CREDIT
INTEREST RATES
LABOUR COSTS
LOSSES, COMMERCIAL
MATERIAL COSTS
MINIMUM LENDING RATE
MONEY SUPPLY
MONOPOLY PROFITS
MUNICIPAL BONDS
NATIONAL ACCOUNTS
NATIONAL SAVINGS
PRICE SUPPORTS
PRIVATE BONDS
PRIVATE BORROWING
PROFITS
PROFITS TAX
PROPERTY INCOME
PUBLIC DEBT
PUBLIC FINANCE
PUBLIC LOANS
RESERVES
REVENUE
SHARES & SECURITIES
SHARE CAPITAL   continued

	Territorial coverage	Title codes

continued
Finance, internal   see   SHARES, COMMON
                            SHARES, PREFERENCE
                            SOCIAL FUNDS
                            STOCK EXCHANGE
                            SUBSIDIES
                            TAXATION
                            TAXATION, DIRECT
                            TAXATION, INDIRECT

Financial assistance, overseas   see   DEVELOPMENT AID

Financial flows   see   INVESTMENT, PRIVATE OVERSEAS
                          INVESTMENT, PUBLIC OVERSEAS

Financial institutions   see   BANKING & INSURANCE
                                 CREDIT FINANCE

Financial planning   see   BUDGET ACCOUNTS

FINANCIAL RATIOS, CORPORATE

Assets as % of liabilities by industrial sector	USA	J 2-a
Depreciation as % of sales by industrial sector	USA	J 2-a
Earnings as % of sales by industrial sector	USA	J 2-a
No of times inventory turned by industrial sector	USA	J 2-a
Profit as % of turnover by industrial sector	USA	J 2-a

Financing, external   see   BALANCE OF PAYMENTS

Financing, internal   see   BUDGET ACCOUNTS

FINE ARTS

% of students enrolled studying fine arts	ECAFE countries	U 17
No of new book titles covering artistic subjects	All countries	U 62-a
published on fine arts	OAS member countries	N 19-a
book translations published on fine arts	OAS member countries	N 19-a
university degrees granted in fine arts	All countries	U 62-a
students of fine arts enrolled abroad by country of origin	All countries	U 64-a
students enrolled in faculty of architecture	OAS member countries	N 19-a
on university courses in artistic subjects	OAS member countries	N 19-a
	All countries	U 62-a

FINISHED GOODS
    see also   WORK IN PROGRESS

Engineering products held in stock awaiting sale by value	OECD countries	D 9-a
Stocks in hand by value in $m	OAS member countries	N 14-a
Wholesale prices - index nos	ECAFE countries	U 32-m
	OAS member countries	N 17-a

Finished rolled steel products   see   STEEL PRODUCTS

Fire & ball clay   see   CHINA CLAY

Fire engines   see   SERVICE VEHICLES

Fire extinguishers   see   METAL PRODUCTS

Fire insurance taxes   see   TAXATION

Fireclay goods   see   EARTHENWARE PRODUCTS

FIRES

Claims paid out by insurance companies in local currency	OAS member countries	N 16-a
No of casualties in fires & value of houses destroyed in $	Asian, Far East countries & Australasia	U 45-a

Fireworks   see   PYROTECHNIC PRODUCTS

FISH, DRIED OR SMOKED

% contribution to export earnings	Gambia, Mali & Mauritania	E 45-a
% of total catch cured	OECD countries	D 43-a
Exports: tonnage & value in $m	African, Caribbean countries & Pacific Is	E 45-a
	OECD countries	D 43-a
Imports & exports: tonnage & value in $m	Main countries	A 21-a
Imports: tonnage & value in $m	OECD countries	D 43-a
Production tonnage & consumption per capita in kg	OECD countries	D 14-a
tonnage	Main countries	A 21-a
	OAS member countries	N 14-a
Retail prices by kind in local currency	OAS member countries	N 17-a
World production, imports & exports by kind: tonnage		A 21-a

FISH, FRESH OR CHILLED

% of EEC total fish catch	EEC countries	R 5-a
% of catch sold as fresh fish as human food	OECD countries	D 43-a
Catch: tonnage & value in $ of aquatic plants	OAS member countries	N 13-a
cod, hake & haddock	OAS member countries	N 13-a
crustaceans	OAS member countries	N 13-a

	Territorial coverage	Title codes
FISH, FRESH OR CHILLED continued		
Catch: tonnage & value in $ of herrings, sardines & anchovies	OAS member countries	N 13-a
mackerel, bonito & tuna	OAS member countries	N 13-a
molluscs	OAS member countries	N 13-a
mullet, jack & sea bass	OAS member countries	N 13-a
plaice, sole & flounder	OAS member countries	N 13-a
salmon & trout	OAS member countries	N 13-a
skate & shark-fish	OAS member countries	N 13-a
Catch, imports, exports & consumption: tonnage	EEC countries	E 44-a
Catch: tonnage (all species)	Main countries	R 5-a
	African countries	U 44-a
Consumption cost to private sector in local currency	EEC countries	E 32-a
Consumption (all kinds): tonnage	EEC countries	E 44-a
fresh & salted fish: tonnage	OAS member countries	N 17-a
fresh, frozen, cured, canned & reduced: tonnage	All countries	A 21-a
per capita in kg per yr	EEC countries	E 44-a
Export prices – index nos (weighted average main sources)	Worldwide	U 29-q
Exports by value in $m	OECD countries	D 43-a
(incl preparations) in $m	ECAFE area	U 32-m
tonnage (incl dried fish)	Asian & Far East countries	U 32-q
tonnage: historical table from 1830	Norway	Z 1-a
tonnage	ECAFE countries	U 32-m
Imports by value in $m	OECD countries	D 43-a
Imports & exports: tonnage & by value in $	All countries	A 21-a
Landings (all kinds): sea, inshore & inland waterways: tonnage	Main countries	R 5-a
tonnage & value in local currency	OECD countries	D 43-a
cod, haddock & plaice by value in £ per ton (average)	UK	D 43-a
pelagic species: herrings & sprats by value in $	OECD countries	D 43-a
tonnage: historical tables from 1860	Main European countries	Z 1-a
tonnage & value in local currency: edible shark	Australia	D 43-a
mackerel	OECD countries	D 43-a
mullet, flathead & marwong	Australia	D 43-a
plaice, sole & halibut	OECD countries	D 43-a
skate & turbot	OECD countries	D 43-a
snoek & snapper fish	Australia	D 43-a
tonnage	Bulgaria, E Germany, Poland & USSR	U 16-a
Nominal catch of aquatic animals by kind: tonnage	All countries	A 22-a
by oceans: tonnage	All countries	A 22-a
of fish by species: tonnage & value	All countries	A 22-a
sea & inland waters: tonnage	All countries	U 43-a
tonnage & value in $	Latin American countries	J 5-a
tonnage	AASM countries	E 41-a
	Caribbean countries & W Indies	T 6-a
by species (in detail): tonnage	World regions	A 22-a
Producer prices received: fresh & frozen fish	Canada & UK	A 9-a
Production by kind, imports & exports: tonnage	Worldwide	A 21-a
by value for food in $ per ton	OECD countries	D 43-a
for industrial processing in $ per ton	OECD countries	D 43-a
Production, stocks & consumption: tonnage	OECD countries	D 14-a
tonnage for food & for industrial use	OECD countries	D 43-a
tonnage	Main countries	A 21-a
Retail prices (comparative) in $ per kg	EEC countries	Z 3-a
Sales for human consumption by kind: demersal & pelagic	UK	D 43-a
Self-sufficiency ratios	EEC countries	E 44-a
Usage for canning: tonnage	OAS member countries	N 13-a
chilling, freezing, canning & curing: tonnage	OECD countries	D 43-a
curing: tonnage	OAS member countries	N 13-a
freezing, canning & curing: tonnage	Latin American countries	J 5-a
freezing: tonnage	OAS member countries	N 13-a
industrial processing: tonnage	OAS member countries	N 13-a
reduction to fishmeal: tonnage	OECD countries	D 43-a
sale as canned products: tonnage	OECD countries	D 43-a
fresh food: tonnage	OAS member countries	N 13-a
fresh, chilled or frozen: tonnage	OECD countries	D 43-a
salted, smoked or dried: tonnage	OECD countries	D 43-a
Wholesale prices by quality in $	USA	A 9-a
World consumption by kind of use: % sold fresh, frozen or canned: tonnage		A 21-a
for oils extraction & fish meal production: tonnage		A 21-a
World demand per capita projected to 1985 in kg per yr		A 1
World market prices – index nos		G 1-a
World nominal catch by classes & species (in detail): tonnage		A 22-a
by main fishing zones: tonnage		A 22-a
for food & industrial use: tonnage		A 21-a
of fish: tonnage	All countries	A 22-a
FISH, FRESHWATER		
Nominal catches by areas & species in detail: tonnage	Worldwide	A 22-a
eels: tonnage	Netherlands	D 43-a
tonnage & value in $	OAS member countries	N 13-a
tonnage	All countries	A 22-a
FISH & FISH PRODUCTS		
% changes in retail sales	E European countries & USSR	U 16-a
As source of fat protein & calorie intake per capita in grammes	OAS member countries	N 17-a
Consumption per capita in kg	E European countries	U 16-a

	Territorial coverage	Title codes
FISH & FISH PRODUCTS, continued		
Exports by kind: tonnage & value in $	Main countries	A 21-a
of local specialities: tonnage	All countries	A 21-a
tonnage (dried or salted fish)	Main countries	A 21-a
tonnage & value in $	Main countries	A 5-a
tonnage (tinned fish by kind)	All countries	A 21-a
Imports & exports: tonnage & value in $	All countries	A 21-a
Production tonnage: dried or salted fish	Main countries	A 21-a
local specialities	All countries	A 21-a
smoked fish products	Main countries	A 21-a
tinned fish products by kind	Main countries	A 21-a
smoked & frozen fish by kind	All countries	A 21-a
tonnage	All countries	A 21-a
	OAS member countries	N 14-a
Retail prices by kind in local currency	OAS member countries	N 17-a
Wholesale prices by kind in local currency	OAS member countries	N 17-a
World exports by value in $	World regions	A 5-a
FISH & FISH PRODUCTS, FROZEN		
% of export earnings	Mauritania	E 45-a
Exports by kind: tonnage	Main countries	A 21-a
by value in $	OECD countries	D 1-a
by value: processed fish in local currency	Brit Solomon Is & Japan	U 32-m
to EEC & non-EEC areas in $	EEC countries	E 24-a
tonnage & value in $	Mauritania	E 45-a
	OECD countries	D 43-a
Imports by value in $	OECD countries	D 1-a
Imports & exports in $	All countries	A 21-a
ex EEC & non-EEC areas: tonnage	EEC countries	E 24-a
tonnage & value in $	OECD countries	D 43-a
Production: tonnage by kind	Main countries	A 21-a
tonnage	All countries	U 22-a
FISH BY KIND		
see also CANNED FISH		
CRUSTACEANS & MOLLUSCS		
FISH FILLETS		
FISH FINGERS		
FISH MEAL		
FISH OFFAL		
FISH ROES		
HERRINGS		
SALMON		
SALTED FISH		
SARDINES & ANCHOVIES		
SEALS		
STURGEON		
STOCKFISH		
TUNA FISH		
Catch by species: tonnage & value in local currency	OECD countries	D 43-a
in $	OAS member countries	N 13-a
tonnage (in detail)	World regions	A 11-a
tonnage	Asian, Far East & Australasian countries	U 45-a
Exports: tonnage & value in local currency	OECD countries	D 43-a
tonnage (in detail)	World regions	A 11-a
Imports by source: tonnage & value in $m	UK	D 43-a
Imports & exports: tonnage & value in $m	Main countries	A 21-a
Imports: tonnage & value in local currency	OECD countries	D 43-a
tonnage	Main countries	A 11-a
Retail prices in local currency	OAS member countries	N 17-a
Sales for industrial reduction to fish meal: tonnage	UK	D 43-a
of shellfish for human consumption: tonnage	UK	D 43-a
World exports: unit value in $ per ton		A 11-a
FISH FACTORY SHIPS		
Deliveries new vessels	Netherlands	S 16-a
No & tonnage by size classes by flag	Worldwide	S 2-a
FISH FILLETS		
Exports fresh or chilled: tonnage	Main countries	A 21-a
Production fresh, chilled & frozen by kind: tonnage & value in $	Main countries	A 21-a
FISH FINGERS		
Imports from Norway & Denmark: tonnage & value in £	UK	D 43-a
Production: tonnage	Canada & USA	A 21-a
FISH MEAL		
see also WHALE BY-PRODUCTS		
% of fish catch reduced to fish meal	OECD countries	D 43-a
Consumption (incl meat meal) in production of animal feed: tonnage	EEC countries	P 5-a
Export prices - index nos	S American countries	U 40-q
Exports by value in $m	W European countries	U 33-a
crustacean meal by kind: tonnage	All countries	A 21-a
meal solubles of oily white fish: tonnage	All countries	A 21-a

	Territorial coverage	Title codes
FISH MEAL, continued		
Exports: tonnage & value in local currency & in $m	OECD countries	D 43-a
tonnage	Main countries	P 5-a
Import prices ex Peru or Chile in Fl per kg	Netherlands	R 2-m
ex Hamburg (under contract) in $	USA	R 2-m
Imports by value in $m	W European countries	U 33-a
Imports & exports (incl solubles): tonnage	All countries	A 21-a
(incl meat meal) as animal feed: tonnage	UK	P 5-a
by source: tonnage	UK	P 5-a
tonnage & value in local currency & in $m	OECD countries	D 43-a
tonnage	Main countries	P 5-a
Production: animal feed of aquatic origin: tonnage	OAS member countries	N 14-a
feeding stuffs: tonnage	Main countries	A 21-a
fertilisers of aquatic origin: tonnage	OAS member countries	N 14-a
from crustaceans & molluscs: tonnage	All countries	A 21-a
from oily & white fish: tonnage	All countries	A 21-a
(incl solubles): tonnage	Main countries	A 5-a
Production, supply, imports & exports: tonnage	EEC countries	B 1-a
whale meal & solubles: tonnage	All countries	A 21-a
tonnage	African countries	U 44-a
	Main countries	D 43-a P 5-a
Shipments through Panama Canal eastwards: tonnage		D 28-a
Wholesale prices in $ per ton	USA	A 9-a
World exports of meals of whale & aquatic animal origin: tonnage		A 21-a
World market prices: fish meal ex Peru as animal feed per 100 kg		E 34-m
World production of animal feed of aquatic origin: tonnage		A 21-a
FISH OILS & FATS		
see also WHALE OIL		
Export prices in cents per lb fob	USA	R 2-m A 9-a
Exports of fish body oils: tonnage	Main countries	B 19-a
(incl marine mammal oil): tonnage	Main countries	P 1-a
tonnage & by value in local currency	OECD countries	D 43-a
Import prices: fish oil by source per ton	W European countries	B 19-a
Imports & exports: tonnage & by value in $	All countries	A 21-a
Imports: fish body oils: tonnage	Main countries	B 19-a
tonnage & value in local currency	OECD countries	D 43-a
Production: (incl liver oils) in barrels: tonnage	Japan	P 1-a
by kind: tonnage	All countries	A 21-a
of fish body oils: tonnage	Main countries	B 19-a
tonnage	All countries	U 22-a
	OAS member countries	N 14-a
Self-sufficiency ratios	EEC countries	E 3-a E 44-a
Supply, production, consumption imports & exports: tonnage	EEC countries	B 1-a
Usage production of margarine: tonnage	Japan, Norway & UK	A 4-a
of soap & detergents: tonnage	Norway	A 4-a
World market prices: marine oils - index nos		A 5-a
World production (excl fish liver oil): tonnage		A 4-a
of oils & fats aquatic animal origin: tonnage		A 21-a
by kind: tonnage		N 10-a
(incl fish liver oil): tonnage		N 10-a
tonnage		A 5-a
World supply: tonnage		B 19-a
FISH OILS & FATS BY KIND		
Exports by destination by CST classes: tonnage	EEC countries	E 48-a
by SITC classes by value in $	Main countries	D 2-q
tonnage & value in $	OECD countries	D 3-a2
NIMEXE classes: tonnage & value in $	All countries	E 20-a
SITC classes: tonnage & value in $	All countries	U 50-a U 59-a
tonnage & value in $	All countries	A 21-a
Imports by NIMEXE classes: tonnage & value in $	All countries	E 20-a
SITC classes: tonnage & value in $	All countries	U 50-a U 59-a
source by CST classes: tonnage	EEC countries	E 21-a
by SITC classes by value in $	Main countries	D 2-q
tonnage & value in $	OECD classes	D 3-a2
Production: tonnage	Main countries	A 21-a
FISH PROCESSING INDUSTRY		
Wage rates per hr by sex	Main countries	R 3-m
per hr: females	Austria	R 4-a
FISH ROES		
Consumption tonnage & per capita in kg	Greece	D 14-a
FISHERIES RESEARCH SHIPS		
Deliveries of new vessels	Netherlands	S 16-a
Fishery products see FISH & FISH PRODUCTS		
FISHING INDUSTRY		
Financial aid received for trawler construction in $	Belgium	D 43-a
premiums for recruitment of labour in $	Belgium	D 43-a
sales promotion subsidies in $	Belgium	D 43-a
scrapping premiums in $	Belgium	D 43-a
to improve gear & equipment in $	Belgium	D 43-a

		Territorial coverage	Title codes	

FISHING INDUSTRY, continued
    IBRD loans approved in $ OAS member countries   N 16-a
    Petroleum products: consumption by fishing fleets   EEC countries   E 16-q   E 15-a
    Value of output & production: tonnage   W Germany   D 43-a

Fishing taxes   see   LICENCE FEES

Fishing vessels   see   TRAWLERS
                                 WORLD-FISHING FLEETS

Fishplates & soleplates   see   RAILS & TRACK-LAYING MATERIAL

Fittings for pipes   see   PIPES, CAST-IRON
                            TUBES

Fixed asset formation   see   CAPITAL FORMATION

Fixed assets   see   BUILDING CONSTRUCTION
                        CAPITAL FORMATION
                        INVESTMENT
                        LAND & PROPERTY
                        MACHINERY

Fixed capital formation   see   CAPITAL FORMATION

Fixed prices   see   PRICE SUPPORTS

Flat product mills   see   STEEL RE-ROLLING PLANTS

Flats   see   DWELLINGS

Flavouring materials   see   ESSENTIAL OILS

FLAX
    Acreage subsidy in £ per ton   EEC countries   B 1-a
    Area harvested, production tonnage & yield in kg per ha   All countries   A 9-a
    Area under crop in acres   All countries   B 10-a
                    in ha   EEC countries   B 1-a   E 12-a
                                                                                              E 44-a
    Consumption by linen industry: historical table from 1760   Main European countries   Z 1-a
              by spinning mills: tonnage   All countries   A 6-a
              of scutched flax by textile industry: tonnage   OECD countries   D 46-a
                              in spinning mills: tonnage   OECD countries   D 46-a
                        tonnage   OAS member countries   N 17-a
    Export prices - index nos (weighted average main sources)   Worldwide   U 29-q
              in local currency per ton   Belgium & Netherlands   A 9-a
    Exports by destination: tonnage   Benelux countries, France & USSR   B 10-a
                              tonnage   Main countries   B 10-a
    Import prices ex Belgium & USSR in £ per ton   UK   B 10-m
                in £ per ton   UK   A 9-a
    Imports by source: flax fibre & tow: tonnage   EEC area   B 10-a
    Imports: flax fibre & tow: tonnage   Main countries   B 10-a
              tonnage & oil conversion equiv   UK   P 1-a
    Production: tonnage & historical table showing % change from 1909   Main countries   C 4-a
              flax fibre: tonnage   OECD countries   D 1-a
              New Zealand-type flax: tonnage   Argentine & Brazil   U 40-a
              scutched flax for textile industry: tonnage   All countries   B 10-a
                                     tonnage   OECD countries   D 46-a
    Wholesale prices ex Belgium - index nos   EEC countries   E 12-a   E 44-a
              in local currency per ton   UK   B 10-m
    World consumption: tonnage & consumption per capita in kg   France & UK   U 27-m
    World production in million lbs & % share of British Commonwealth
                                                                  countries   Worldwide   A 6-a
                          tonnage   B 10-a
    Yield in 100 kg per ha   K 4-a
          in form of flax straw per ha   EEC countries   E 12-a
                                      EEC countries   E 44-a

Flax cake   see   OILCAKE & MEAL

Flax seed   see   LINSEED

FLAX TOW
    Consumption by textile industry: tonnage   OECD countries   D 46-a
                           in spinning mills: tonnage   OECD countries   D 46-a
    Production: tonnage from scutching plants   OECD countries   D 46-a

FLAX YARN
        see also   HEMP YARN
                        LINEN YARN

    Consumption in knitting mills: tonnage   OECD countries   D 46-a
    Consumption (incl tow) by weaving industry: tonnage   OECD countries   D 46-a
    Production: tonnage by spinning industry   OECD countries   D 46-a
              tonnage of flax, ramie & hemp yarn   All countries   U 22-a
              tonnage   Mauritius   E 41-a

Floating rates   see   EXCHANGE RATES

	Territorial coverage	Title codes

Floor areas   see   DWELLINGS

FLOOR COVERINGS
    see also   CARPETS
               MATS & MATTING, COIR

Consumption of jute, sisal & coir in production of floor coverings: tonnage	EEC countries	K 4-a
Demand for linoleum projected to 1977 in lbs	UK	B 29
Production by volume (incl linoleum)	All countries	U 22-a
Usage of linseed oil in linoleum production	USA	B 19-a

Floor tiles   see   BUILDING MATERIALS

Flooring (hardwood, softwood or vitreous)   see   BUILDING MATERIALS

Flounder   see   FISH

Flour   see   POTATO FLOUR
             RYE FLOUR
             WHEAT FLOUR

FLOUR MILLING INDUSTRY
    see also   ANIMAL FEED MILLS

IDA loans for improving output in $m	OAS member countries	N 16-a
Investment in buildings in local currency	EEC countries	E 40-a
land purchase in local currency	EEC countries	E 40-a
machinery in local currency	EEC countries	E 40-a

Flow measurement gauges   see   MEASURING APPARATUS

FLUORESCENT TUBES

Production by volume	All countries	U 22-a
	Canada, European countries, Japan & USA	U 38-a

FLUORSPAR

% usage in production of industrial chemicals	USA	N 1-a
in steel fluxing process	USA	N 1-a
Consumption of acid grade fluorspar: tonnage	USA	N 1-a
of metallurgical & ceramic grades: tonnage	USA	N 1-a
Government stockpile by grade: tonnage	USA	N 1-a
Imports & exports by source & destination: tonnage	Main countries	B 15-a
Production: tonnage	All countries	B 15-a
	Main countries	N 1-a
by value (at mine) in $ per ton	USA	N 1-a
Stocks at consumers' premises: tonnage	USA	N 1-a
at mines: tonnage (estim)	USA	N 1-a
World production: tonnage	Main countries	N 1-a N 4-a
World reserves: tonnage (estim)	Main countries	N 1-a

Fluting paper   see   WRAPPING PAPER

Flying accidents   see   ACCIDENTS, AIRCRAFT

Foamed rubber   see   LATEX FOAM
                   SPONGE RUBBER

Fodder   see   BARLEY
             FEEDING STUFFS
             HAY
             OATS

Fodder barley   see   BARLEY

FODDER BEET

Area under crop in ha	EEC countries	E 12-a
Production: tonnage	EEC countries	B 1-a E 12-a
Yield in 100 kg per ha	EEC countries	E 12-a
(incl turnips & swedes) in kg per ha	EEC countries	B 1-a

FODDER CROPS, GREEN
    see also   FEEDING STUFFS
                 HAY
                 LUCERNE

Area under crop in ha	EEC countries	E 12-a
Production: tonnage	EEC countries	E 12-a
Yield in 100 kg per ha	EEC countries	E 12-a

Fodder oats   see   OATS

Foetal deaths   see   DEATHS, FOETAL

Foil   see   ALUMINIUM FOIL
           COPPER FOIL
           LEAD FOIL
           TIN FOIL

	Territorial coverage	Title codes

Fonds Européen de Développement   see   EUROPEAN DEVELOPMENT FUND

Fonium   see   SORGHUM

FOOD
    see also   CONVENIENCE FOODS
                DIETETIC FOODS
                FROZEN MEALS, PREPARED
                RETAIL FOOD PRICES, COMPARATIVE
                SELF-SERVICE STORES

	Territorial coverage	Title codes
% calorie intake per capita in meat consumed per day	ECE countries	U 15-a
% change in retail prices	W European countries, Canada, Japan & USA	U 16-q
	Greece, Portugal, Spain & Turkey	U 16-a
% changes in retail sales of food products	E European countries & USSR	U 16-a
% growth rates in consumption of food from 1955-1969	OECD countries	D 11-a
% of households using biscuits (packaged)	W European countries	Z 3
coffee (ground or beans)	W European countries	Z 3
crispbread	W European countries	Z 3
fruit (tinned)	W European countries	Z 3
instant coffee	W European countries	Z 3
instant potatoes	W European countries	Z 3
olive oil or corn oil	W European countries	Z 3
soup (packaged or cubes)	W European countries	Z 3
soup (tinned)	W European countries	Z 3
sugarless sweeteners (saccharin)	W European countries	Z 3
tea or tea bags	W European countries	Z 3
vegetables (frozen in packs)	W European countries	Z 3
yoghurt	W European countries	Z 3
% of exports to world destination areas (based on value)	W European countries	U 20-a
% of imports by world source areas (based on value)	W European countries	U 20-a
% share of world imports & world exports	Main countries	B 1-a
Calorie consumption per capita per yr	World regions	C 27-a
per day	All countries	M 6-a
	Developing countries	U 23-a
	ECE countries	U 15-a
Calorific value of food consumed per capita	Main countries	E 3-a
Coastal & seaborne freight: tonnage by kind of food	EEC countries	E 43-a
of farm products	EEC countries	E 43-a
Coefficients of income elasticity of demand	Main countries	A 1
Consignments (as emergency aid) of food by value in $	Recipient countries	M 1-a
Consumption cost to private sector	EEC countries	E 32-a
of main food items: tonnage	EEC countries	E 44-a
of food products - index nos (value basis)	EEC countries	E 44-a
per capita: main foodstuffs in kg	EEC countries	E 44-a
by kind in kg	EEC countries	B 1-a
urban & rural areas by income levels	USA	C 27-a
Earnings from sales in international hotels per room in $	Worldwide	Z 5-a
tourist hotels per room in $	Worldwide	Z 5-a
Expenditure on food & drink (at cost) & as % of total outlay	EEC countries	E 2-a
Export prices - index nos (weighted average main sources)	Worldwide	U 29-q
Exports by sea, inland waters, road, rail & air	European countries	U 8-a
by value by world destination areas in $m	W European countries	U 20-a
in $m	W European countries	U 33-a
in local currency	Australasian countries, India, Japan, S Korea & Singapore	U 32-m
Exports - index nos (quantum basis)	Asian & Far East area	U 32-q
(value basis)	World regions	A 11-a
(unit value basis)	Asian & Far East area	U 32-q
Household budget expenses in local currency	AASM countries	E 41-a
on food & soft drinks in local currency	OAS member countries	N 16-a
Imports - index nos (quantum & value basis)	World regions	A 14-a
Imports & exports as % of total agricultural trade	W European countries	U 20-a
by product groups by value in $m	European countries	U 33-a
sea, inland waters, road, rail & air: tonnage	European countries	U 8-a
value by world source areas in $m	W European countries	U 20-a
ex EEC area in UA	African, Caribbean countries & Pacific Is	E 45-a
in $m	African, Caribbean countries & Pacific Is	E 45-a
in local currency	Asian, Far East & Australasian countries	U 32-m
- index nos	World regions	A 11-a
Imports & exports by kind of food by rail: tonnage	EEC countries	E 43-a
by road: tonnage	EEC countries	E 43-a
by sea: tonnage	EEC countries	E 43-a
(incl other consumables) by value in $	Asian & Far East areas	U 32-a
Income elasticity of demand - index nos	USA	C 27-a
No of calories, proteins & fats contained in each kind of food product		D 14-a
Producer prices of main food products - index nos	EEC countries	E 44-a
Production & production per capita - index nos	Latin American countries	U 40-a
	African countries	U 44-a
	Asian & Far East countries	U 32-a
by value in local currency	OECD countries	D 37-a
per capita - index nos	All countries	A 9-a
	ECAFE countries	U 17-a
	Latin American countries	J 5-a
	Main countries	R 5-a
	World regions	U 23-a U 43-a

	Territorial coverage	Title codes
FOOD, continued		
Production - index nos		
	All countries	A 9-a
	Australia, India, Korea & Philippines	U 32-q
	Developed countries	A 11-a
	Developing countries	A 11-a
	Latin American countries	J 5-a
	Main countries	R 5-a
	OAS member countries	N 13-a
	World regions	A 1-a A 11-a
		U 23-a
Rail freight (inland & shipment over frontiers): tonnage	EEC countries	E 43-a
Retail price changes as factor in cost of living	European countries & USA	U 16-q
in cost of living - index nos	OAS member countries	N 17-a
Retail prices (comparative) apples in cents per kg	EEC countries	Z 3-a
bacon (smoked slices) in $ per kg	EEC countries	Z 3-a
beef (boned sirloin) in $ per kg	EEC countries	Z 3-a
butter in $ per kg	EEC countries	Z 3-a
cabbage in cents per kg	EEC countries	Z 3-a
cheese in $ per kg	EEC countries	Z 3-a
coffee (pure roasted) in $ per kg	EEC countries	Z 3-a
cooking salt in cents per kg	EEC countries	Z 3-a
fish (fresh) in $ per kg	EEC countries	Z 3-a
lamb (leg) in $ per kg	EEC countries	Z 3-a
margarine in $ per kg	EEC countries	Z 3-a
milk (whole fresh) in cents per litre	EEC countries	Z 3-a
one chickens egg in cents	EEC countries	Z 3-a
oranges in cents per kg	EEC countries	Z 3-a
pork (loin chops) in $ per kg	EEC countries	Z 3-a
potatoes in cents per kg	EEC countries	Z 3-a
sugar (granulated) in cents per kg	EEC countries	Z 3-a
tea in $ per kg	EEC countries	Z 3-a
white bread in cents per kg	EEC countries	Z 3-a
white wheat flour in cents per kg	EEC countries	Z 3-a
Retail prices of meat & fish - index nos	EEC countries	E 44-a
Retail prices - index nos	AASM countries	E 41-a
	African countries	U 44-a
	Asian, Far East & Australasian countries	U 45-a
	E European countries & USSR	U 16-a
	Main countries	A 9-a
Retail trade turnover of multiple stores in local currency	EEC countries	E 26-m
Self-sufficiency ratios: main food items	EEC countries	E 44-a
Shipments of refrigerated food through Panama Canal		
eastwards: tonnage		D 28-a
Wholesale prices - index nos	ECAFE countries	U 32-m
	OAS member countries	N 17-a
World demand per capita projected to 1985 in kg per yr		A 1
World export trade by SITC classes in $m	World regions	U 23-a
World market prices - index nos		U 23-a
FOOD BY KIND		
Consumption in grammes per person per day	Main countries	R 5-a
per capita: cereals by income levels	USA	C 27-a
dairy products by income levels	USA	C 27-a
food products per day	Main countries	A 1
fruit (fresh) by income levels	USA	C 27-a
meat by income levels	USA	C 27-a
pulses by income levels	USA	C 27-a
vegetables by income levels	USA	C 27-a
tonnage	OAS member countries	N 17-a
Export prices - index nos	Latin American countries	U 18-a
Exports (incl animal products) by destination: tonnage & value in $	All countries	U 12-a
to EEC & non-EEC areas by value in $m	EEC countries	E 24-a
Imports from EEC & non-EEC areas by value in $m	EEC countries	E 24-a
(incl animal products) by source: tonnage & value in $	All countries	U 12-a
Nutritional content of food by kind: calories, protein & fat		A 1
Retail prices in local currency (in detail)	OAS member countries	N 17-a
Road transport of food by kind over frontiers: tonnage	EEC countries	E 43-a
World market prices - index nos		G 1-a
FOOD AID		
see also DEVELOPMENT AID		
% share of aid contributions by product	EEC countries	D 13-a
A.I.D. sales agreements repayable in foreign currencies & in US $		M 1-a
Assistance in form of shipment of surplus crops by value in $	OAS member countries	N 16-a
Bilateral aid: emergency food & relief grants in $m	OECD countries	D 13-a
Budgeted expenditure by EEC Commission on food aid		B 1-a
Commodities shipped as emergency supplies:-		
corn meal by value in $	Recipient countries	M 1-a
dried milk by value in $	Recipient countries	M 1-a
fats & oils by value in $	Recipient countries	M 1-a
food products by value in $	Recipient countries	M 1-a
grain & sorghum by value in $	Recipient countries	M 1-a
maize by value in $	Recipient countries	M 1-a
rolled oats by value in $	Recipient countries	M 1-a
wheat & wheat flour by value in $	Recipient countries	M 1-a
Commodity composition of emergency aid & as % of total food aid	USA	D 13-a
Cost of emergency assistance: disaster relief in $	All countries	M 1-a
refugee relief in $	All countries	M 1-a

	Territorial coverage	Title codes
FOOD AID, continued		
Donations of agricultural commodity surpluses by value in $	Recipient countries	M 1-a
by major recipients under US schemes in $	USA	D 13-a
type of programme of aid & welfare in $	USA	D 13-a
voluntary agencies for relief in $	USA	D 13-a
of food products: EEC expenditure & appropriations	EEC countries	B 3-a
govt-sponsored wheat & wheat flour in $	USA	B 8-a
	Participating countries	C 16-a
soybean oil (on govt to govt basis): tonnage	USA	B 19-a
through voluntary agencies: tonnage	USA	B 19-a
under World Food Programme in $	USA	D 13-a
wheat & flour: tonnage	Australia, Canada, EEC countries & USA	C 16-a
	Australia & Canada	B 8-a
wheat under GATT sponsorship: tonnage	GATT member countries	B 8-a
Emergency assistance by commodity by value in $	Recipient countries	M 1-a
Expenditure & appropriations on butter oil in £m	EEC countries	B 3-a
cereals in £m	EEC countries	B 3-a
skim powder in £m	EEC countries	B 3-a
Expenditure on supply of surplus butter in £m	EEC countries	B 3-a
milk powder in £m	EEC countries	B 3-a
Exports of soybean oil under A.I.D. Relief Program: tonnage	USA	B 19-a
ex USA: tonnage	Recipient countries	B 18-q
Government to government donations in $	OECD countries	D 13-a
Public disbursements in $m	Main countries	D 7-a
Shipments under EEC Action Program: tonnage	Recipient countries	B 7-a
National Action Program: tonnage	Recipient countries	B 7-a
FOOD, DRINK & TOBACCO		
% change in export earnings	Developing countries	U 11-a
in exports by destination	EEC countries	E 23-a
in imports by source	EEC countries	E 23-a
% share of EEC area imports	Developing countries	U 52-a
Consumption by value in $m	Main countries	U 23-a
Exports as % of consumption	Main countries	U 23-a
by destination by value in UA	EEC countries	E 23-a
by regions of origin within EEC area by value in local currency		
by value in $m	Main countries	E 38-a
	Main countries	E 24-a
(incl farm raw materials) by value in $	Asian & Far East areas	U 32-a
to non-EEC area by value in UA	ECE countries	U 15-a
	EEC countries	E 24-a
Exports - index nos (quantum & value bases)	OECD countries	D 16-q
Imports as % of consumption	Main countries	U 23-a
by source by value in UA	EEC countries	E 23-a
value & as % of total imports	ECE countries	U 15-a
value ex EEC area in UA	African, Caribbean countries & Pacific Is	E 45-a
value in $m	African, Caribbean countries & Pacific Is	E 45-a
in UA	AASM countries	E 41-a
	Developing countries	U 52-a
	Main countries	E 24-a
ex EEC area by value in UA	AASM countries	E 41-a
non-EEC area by value in UA	EEC countries	E 24-a
developing countries by value in $m	EEC area	U 52-a
in local currency	ECAFE countries	U 32-m
Imports - index nos (quantum & value bases)	OECD countries	D 16-q
Inter-EEC exports by value in UA	EEC countries	E 22-m E 24-a
imports by value in UA	EEC countries	E 22-m E 24-a
Labour costs of production per hr	EEC countries	E 2-a
	African countries	U 44-a
Production - index nos	EEC countries	E 44-a
	OECD countries	D 19-m D 20-m
FOOD, DRINK & TOBACCO INDUSTRIES		
see also ALCOHOLIC DRINKS INDUSTRY		
BAKING & CONFECTIONERY INDUSTRY		
TOBACCO INDUSTRY		
% contribution to gross domestic product	Main countries	U 38-a
% share of capital investment	E European countries	U 16-a
industrial production	Main countries	U 38-a
Capital formation in $m	EEC countries	E 38-a
	Main countries	U 21-a
Consumption of electricity in kWh	EEC countries	E 38-a
	All countries	C 23-a
	European countries	U 1-a
	OECD countries	D 8-a
of gas in m³	European countries & USA	U 3-a
Costs for salaried staff per month in local currency	EEC countries	E 11-a
Earnings per hr in local currency	All countries	L 4-a
per hr by areas in local currency	EEC countries	E 38-a
Employment by areas	EEC countries	E 38-a
(total)	EEC countries	E 2-a
Employment - index nos	All countries	L 4-a
Gross output by value in $m	Main countries	U 21-a
Labour costs as % of total costs	EEC countries	E 8-a
by status of employees in local currency	EEC countries	E 8-a
per hr: wage earners	EEC countries	E 11-a
per hr	EEC countries	E 11-a E 38-a

	Territorial coverage	Title codes	
FOOD, DRINK & TOBACCO INDUSTRIES continued			
Labour force employed by status	EEC countries	E 8-a	E 11-a
Labour force employed	OECD countries	D 23-a	
	Main countries	U 21-a	
No of hrs worked per wk	Main countries	R 3-m	
per wk by areas	EEC countries	E 25-a	
per yr	EEC countries	E 8-a	
salaried staff per mth	EEC countries	E 11-a	
wage earners per wk	EEC countries	E 11-a	
	All countries	L 4-a	
No of industrial accidents reported	EEC countries	E 2-a	
No of establishments in operation	African countries	U 44-a	
Production as % of world activity		U 38	
	Australia	U 32-q	
Production – index nos	EEC countries	E 28-q	E 27-a
	Far East countries	U 32-q	
	Latin American countries	J 5-a	
	Main countries	R 5-a	
	OAS member countries	N 14-a	
Wage rates per hr in local currency	EEC countries	E 25-a2	
by grade in local currency	Main countries	R 4-q	
by sex in local currency	Main countries	R 3-m	C 7-a
Wages & salary costs in $	Main countries	U 21-a	

Food for Peace Programs   see   DEVELOPMENT AID

Food prices   see   RETAIL FOOD PRICES, COMPARATIVE

FOOD PROCESSING INDUSTRY

	Territorial coverage	Title codes
IDA loans for improving output in $	OAS member countries	N 16-a
Investment in buildings by sector of industry in local currency	EEC countries	E 40-a
land by sector of industry in local currency	EEC countries	E 40-a
machinery by sector of industry in local currency	EEC countries	E 40-a
No of hrs worked per wk	OAS member countries	N 18-a
Wage rates: bakery industry in local currency	OAS member countries	N 17-a
by sector in local currency	OAS member countries	N 17-a
canned meat industry in local currency	OAS member countries	N 17-a
grain milling industry in local currency	OAS member countries	N 17-a
Wages costs per hr by sex	Main countries	C 7-a

FOOD PROCESSING MACHINERY

	Territorial coverage	Title codes
% share of world exports held (value basis)	UK	B 27-a
Imports by value in $m	All countries	U 38-a
Exports by destination by value in $m	Main countries	U 9-a
by value in $m	Main countries	U 38-a
	OECD countries	D 9-a
Imports by value in $m	All countries	U 38-a
World export trade by value in $m		U 38-a

FOOD SUPPLY

	Territorial coverage	Title codes
By kind per capita per day	All countries	U 43-a
	Asian, Far East & Australasian countries	U 45-a
By kind: self-sufficiency ratios	All countries	U 43-a
Calorific value of supply per capita	All countries	U 43-a
Protein content of per capita supply	All countries	U 43-a

Foodboard (folding box-board)   see   PAPER & PAPERBOARD

Foods, canned for infants   see   DIETETIC FOODS

Football matches   see   SPORTS

FOOTWEAR

see also   LEATHER INDUSTRY
SOLES FOR FOOTWEAR

	Territorial coverage	Title codes
% changes in retail sales		U 16-a
Consumer outlay as % of total private expenditure		A 18-a
Consumption cost of private sector		E 32-a
Consumption of footwear made of textile materials in pairs		D 18-a
of slippers & house-shoes in pairs		D 18-a
per capita: footwear made of textile materials		D 18-a
footwear in pairs		U 16-a
slippers in pairs		D 18-a
Exports by destination of footwear made of plastic materials by value in $	OECD countries	D 18-a
made of textile materials by value in $	OECD countries	D 18-a
made of textile materials in pairs	OECD countries	D 18-a
of slippers in pairs	OECD countries	D 18-a
by value in $	OECD countries	D 18-a
Exports to EEC & non-EEC area by value in $m	EEC countries	E 24-a
to non-OECD area of footwear made of plastic materials in pairs	non-OECD countries	D 18-a
of footwear made of textile materials in pairs	non-OECD countries	D 18-a
of slippers in pairs	non-OECD countries	D 18-a

	Territorial coverage	Title codes	
FOOTWEAR, continued			
Imports by source: footwear made of plastic materials in pairs	OECD countries	D 18-a	
textile materials in pairs	OECD countries	D 18-a	
plastic materials by value in $	OECD countries	D 18-a	
textile materials by value in $	OECD countries	D 18-a	
textile materials in pairs	OECD countries	D 18-a	
slippers by value in $	OECD countries	D 18-a	
slippers in pairs	OECD countries	D 18-a	
ex EEC & non-EEC areas by value in $m	EEC countries	E 24-a	
Labour costs of production per hr: shoe industry	EEC countries	E 2-a	
Production by kind: boots, shoes & slippers in pairs	EEC countries	E 28-q	E 27-a
Production costs: upper leather for men's shoes in $	USA	A 18-a	
Production of footwear in million pairs	AASM countries	E 41-a	
	E European countries & USSR	U 16-a	
made of plastic materials in pairs	OECD countries	D 18-a	
of textile materials in pairs	OECD countries	D 18-a	
Production: slippers & house-shoes in pairs	OECD countries	D 18-a	
	EEC countries	K 4-a	
Retail prices (comparative): man's shoes in $	EEC countries	Z 3-a	
woman's shoes in $	EEC countries	Z 3-a	
Retail prices - index nos	EEC countries	E 26-m	
FOOTWEAR, LEATHER			
see also SOLES FOR FOOTWEAR			
% of production using leather soles	Main countries	D 18-a	
Consumption in million pairs	Main countries	A 18-a	
	OECD countries	D 18-a	
Exports by destination by value in $	OECD countries	D 18-a	
in million pairs	OECD countries	D 18-a	
in million pairs	Developed & E European countries	A 18-a	
to non-OECD area in million pairs	non-OECD countries	D 18-a	
Imports by source by value in $	OECD countries	D 18-a	
in million pairs	OECD countries	D 18-a	
in million pairs	Developed & E European countries	A 18-a	
Per capita availability in pairs	Main countries	A 18-a	
Production in million pairs	Main countries	A 18-a	
	OAS member countries	N 14-a	
leather uppers & linings: tonnage	Main countries	A 18-a	
volume by kind in pairs	All countries	U 22-a	
volume for children in pairs	OECD countries	D 18-a	
men in pairs	OECD countries	D 18-a	
women in pairs	OECD countries	D 18-a	
World exports of footwear with leather uppers by value in $m		A 18-a	
FOOTWEAR, RUBBER			
Consumption of rubber in production of rubber footwear: tonnage	Canada & Japan	C 18-a	
per capita in pairs	OECD countries	D 18-a	
in million pairs	OECD countries	D 18-a	
Exports by destination by value in $	OECD countries	D 18-a	
by volume in million pairs	OECD countries	D 18-a	
Exports by volume to non-OECD area in pairs	OECD countries	D 18-a	
Imports by source by value in $	OECD countries	D 18-a	
by volume in million pairs	OECD countries	D 18-a	
Production: tonnage (incl soles & heels of rubber)	EEC countries	E 28-q	E 27-a
volume in million pairs	OECD countries	D 18-a	
	All countries	U 22-a	
FOOTWEAR BY KIND			
Exports by destination by CST classes: tonnage & value in $	EEC countries	E 48-a	
SITC classes by value in $	Main countries	D 2-q	
SITC classes: tonnage & value in $	OECD countries	D 3-a2	
Imports by source by CST classes: tonnage & value in $	EEC countries	E 21-a	
SITC classes by value in $	Main countries	D 2-q	
SITC classes: tonnage & value in $	OECD countries	D 3-a2	
Retail prices: shoes for boys in local currency	OAS member countries	N 17-a	
girls in local currency	OAS member countries	N 17-a	
men in local currency	OAS member countries	N 17-a	
women in local currency	OAS member countries	N 17-a	
Wholesale prices in local currency	OAS member countries	N 17-a	
FOOTWEAR INDUSTRY			
see also LEATHER GOODS INDUSTRY			
Investment in buildings in local currency	EEC countries	E 40-a	
land purchase in local currency	EEC countries	E 40-a	
machinery in local currency	EEC countries	E 40-a	
Labour force employed (total) & no of operatives	Main countries	U 21-a	
No of hrs worked per wk by region	EEC countries	E 25-a	
per wk	Main countries	R 3-m	
Wage rates (average) in local currency per hr by sex	EEC countries	E 25-a2	
in local currency	OAS member countries	N 17-a	
by grade of employee per day in Esc	Portugal	R 4-q	
grade per hr in A.Sch	Austria	R 4-a	
sex per hr in local currency	Main countries	R 3-m	C 7-a

Footwear materials, non-permeable   see   LEATHER SUBSTITUTE

	Territorial coverage	Title codes

FOOTWEAR UPPERS, LEATHER
    Consumption in sq ft   OECD countries   D 18-a
    Exports by destination in sq ft   OECD countries   D 18-a
                  by value in $ OECD countries   D 18-a
    Exports ex OECD area to non-OECD area in sq ft   non-OECD countries   D 18-a
    Imports by source in sq ft   OECD countries   D 18-a
                by value in $ OECD countries   D 18-a
        ex non-OECD area in sq ft   OECD countries   D 18-a
    Production in sq ft   OECD countries   D 18-a

Forecast trends   see   PROJECTIONS, INDUSTRIAL

Foreign aid   see   DEVELOPMENT AID

FOREIGN ASSETS
    (Net) in local currency   African countries   U 44-a
    Overseas assets (net) or deficits   All countries   F 5-m   F 6-q

Foreign balances   see   BALANCE OF PAYMENTS

FOREIGN BANKS
    Advances, investments & value of bills discounted   All countries   F 5-m   F 6-q
    Deposits of foreign currencies   All countries   F 5-m   F 6-q
            of non-residents' funds   All countries   F 5-m   F 6-q

Foreign bonds   see   GOVERNMENT BONDS, FOREIGN

Foreign credits   see   CREDIT, INTERNATIONAL

FOREIGN DEBT
    External public debt by type of creditor in $m   M 3-a
                    by kind of liability in $m   Developing countries   M 3-a
                    in local currency   African countries   U 44-a
                    in $m   EEC countries   E 26-m
                          USA   U 16-a
                          World regions   M 4-a

FOREIGN EXCHANGE
        see also   GOLD HOLDINGS
    Holdings as component in payment balances   All countries   F 1-a
            of banking system in $m   Main countries   R 5-a
                central banks in $ OAS member countries   N 16-a
          OECD countries   D 26-m
    Allocation of special drawing rights in $m   Developing countries   U 23-a
    Capital flows (official) in $m   Developing countries   U 23-a
                (private) in $m   Developing countries   U 23-a
    Changes in reserves in £m   OECD countries   D 10-a
          Developing countries   U 23-a
    Costs of debt servicing in $m   Developing countries   U 23-a
        of imports in $m cif   Developing countries   U 23-a
        of transfer payments   Developing countries   U 23-a
    Export credits guaranteed in $m   Developing countries   U 23-a
    Monetary reserves as % of value of imports cif   ECE countries   U 15-a
    Receipts & disbursements by use in $m   Developing world regions   U 23-a
            from export trade in $m   Developing countries   U 23-a
            from services in $m   Developing countries   U 23-a
    Reserves held by Central Banks in $m   Main countries   U 43-a
    Transfer payments received in $m   Developing countries   U 23-a
    Travel allowances granted per journey in local currency   OECD countries   D 47-a
                      per person in local currency   OECD countries   D 47-a

Foreign investment   see   INVESTMENT, CORPORATE OVERSEAS
                                  INVESTMENT, PRIVATE OVERSEAS
                                  INVESTMENT, PUBLIC OVERSEAS
                                  OVERSEAS INVESTMENT INCOME
                                  TRANSFER PAYMENTS

Foreign liabilities   see   BALANCE OF PAYMENTS
                            FOREIGN DEBT

FOREIGN LOANS
    As component in balance of payments   All countries   F 1-a
    % of loan element in aid commitments   Main countries   D 7-a
    Construction & sewage disposal projects: loans in $ All countries   W 2-a
                & water supply projects: loans in $ All countries   W 2-a
    Credits from IBRD, IFC & IDB in $m   Recipient countries   F 1-a
    Disbursements & grants (net) in $m   Recipient countries   U 23-a
                by government agencies in $m   All countries   F 1-a
    Drawings on trade credits & bank loans in $m   All countries   F 1-a
    Electric power industry: loans from A.I.D. in $m   Latin American countries   U 18-a
                              EXIMBANK in $m   Latin American countries   U 18-a
                              IBRD in $m   Latin American countries   U 18-a
                              IDB in $m   Latin American countries   U 18-a
    Government receipts in local currency   African countries   U 44-a
    Grants as % of total aid commitments   Main countries   D 7-a

	Territorial coverage	Title codes
FOREIGN LOANS, continued		
Loans & grants: net value as % of value of exports	Recipient countries	U 23-a
of imports	Recipient countries	U 23-a
received in $m	ECAFE countries	U 17
Loans (long-term) from export-import bank in $m	Recipient countries	F 1-a
from international banks in $m	Recipient countries	F 1-a
Official bilateral loans granted in $m	Recipient countries	M 4-a
Official multilateral loans granted in $m	Recipient countries	M 4-a
Private loans granted in $m	Recipient countries	M 4-a
Public disbursements in $m	Main countries	D 7-a
Terms of commitment: % interest rates	World regions	M 3-a
maturity in yrs	World regions	M 3-a
Terms parameters: % interest rates	Main countries	D 7-a
maturity in yrs	Main countries	D 7-a
repayment grace periods in yrs	Main countries	D 7-a
FOREIGN MIGRANT WORKERS		
No employed in iron & steel industry (total)	EEC countries	E 29-a
by nationality	EEC countries	E 29-a
in iron ore mining (total)	EEC countries	E 29-a
by nationality	EEC countries	E 29-a
as % of total labour force in collieries	EEC countries	E 33-a
in coalmining	EEC countries	E 15-a E 33-a
in iron ore mining	EEC countries	E 33-a
in steel industry as % of total employment	EEC countries	E 30-a
in steel industry by nationality	EEC countries	E 30-a

Foreign students   see   STUDENTS, FOREIGN

FOREIGN TRADE
    see also   EXPORT TRADE
                IMPORT TRADE
                INVISIBLE TRADE
                RE-EXPORT TRADE
                TERMS OF TRADE
                WORLD TRADE

	Territorial coverage	Title codes
As balance of payments factor component: historical table from 1816	Main European countries	Z 1-a
By commodity classes & regions: historical table by value from 1953 in $m	Worldwide	C 4-a
By countries by value (see no 6 or 7)	USSR	U 27-a
By main areas: planned % change	E European countries & USSR	U 54-a
By main commodity groups by value in $m	Asian, Far East & Australasian countries	U 45-a
By value: imports & exports by world regions in $m	All countries	U 27-q
in DM million	Non-Communist countries	R 5-a
imports & exports - index nos	Worldwide	R 5-a
By volume: imports & exports - index nos	Worldwide	R 5-a
In DM million	Europe excl EEC area	R 5-a
% change in exports of agricultural products & non-fuel minerals	Developing countries	G 1-a
imports & exports of fuels	Developing countries	G 1-a
imports & exports of all goods (value basis)	Main countries	G 1-a
imports of manufactured goods	E European countries	U 16-a
% growth rates in international trade as component of gross national product	Developing countries	G 1-a
compared with change in gross domestic product	All countries	U 60-a
% share of imports & exports of EEC area of world trade	Main countries	D 17-a
	AASM countries	E 41-a
Countries listed by degree of change in value of international trade	All countries	U 54-a
Exports (all products) on world basis in $m	S American countries	F 2-a
Goods & services as factor in gross domestic product	S American countries	U 41-a
Goods & services - index nos	World economic areas	U 60-a
Imports (all products) on world basis in $m	All countries	F 2-a
Imports & exports by value in $m	Asian, Far East & Australasian countries	U 45-a
	Latin American countries	J 5-a
of goods & services as component in gross national product	EEC countries	E 32-a
per capita in $	ECE countries	U 15-a
Index nos (quantum basis)	Asian, Far East & Australasian countries	U 45-a
(unit value basis)	Asian, Far East & Australasian countries	U 45-a
Inter-African trade by products by value in $	African countries	U 39-a
Inter-EEC trade by value in $m	EEC countries	E 3-a
Inter-regional trade by value in $m	Latin American countries	J 5-a
	LAFTA countries	J 5-a
Invisible trade in $m	ECE countries	U 15-a
Petroleum crude & products (incl bunkers): tonnage	UK	T 3-a
FORESTRY EQUIPMENT		
Cost of maintenance & repair in local currency	EEC countries	E 44-a

	Territorial coverage	Title codes

FORESTRY PRODUCTS BY KIND
    see also   BAMBOO
                    CORK, RAW
                    GUMS GLUES SOLUTIONS
                    NATURAL GUMS
                    NATURAL WAX
                    NEWSPRINT
                    OILSEEDS
                    PAPER & PAPERBOARD
                    RAILWAY SLEEPERS
                    TANNING BARK
                    TIMBER
                    VEGETABLE OILS
                    VENEER SHEETS
                    WOOD PULP

	Territorial coverage	Title codes
Exports: tonnage (in detail)	World regions	A 11-a
Imports: tonnage	World regions	A 11-a
Production, imports & exports: tonnage	All countries	A 23-a
Production by value in $	EEC countries	E 44-a
tonnage	Austria, France, Spain & USA	U 34-a
Production: (in detail)	World regions	A 11-a
World exports: unit value in $ per ton		A 11-a

FORESTRY UNDERTAKINGS

Consumption of materials in forestry	Czechoslovakia & E Germany	U 34-a
Electricity consumption from own production in kWh	All countries	C 23-a
from public supply in kWh	All countries	C 23-a
Loan advances from banking system in local currency	OAS member countries	N 16-a
Timber felling: soft & hardwoods in m³	Caribbean countries & W Indies	T 6-a

FORESTS
    see also   LAND UTILISATION

% of afforested areas under conifers	All countries	A 16-a
under trees other than conifers	All countries	A 16-a
Area afforested as % of total land area	All countries	A 16-a
	World regions	A 16
by grades of timber density in ha	All countries	A 16-a
(coniferous) by density 50-150 m³ per ha	All countries	A 16-a
over 150 m³ per ha	All countries	A 16-a
up to 50 m³ per ha	All countries	A 16-a
felled & unreplanted in ha	All countries	A 16-a
(non-coniferous) by density 50-150 m³ per ha	All countries	A 16-a
up to 50 m³ per ha	All countries	A 16-a
of permanent reserves as % of total forest land	All countries	A 16-a
of forest land in ha	All countries	A 16-a
per capita of population in ha	All countries	A 16-a
planted with conifers & per capita in ha	World regions	J 7-a
presently exploited for timber in ha	All countries	A 16-a
unproductive or brush in ha million	World regions	A 16
	All countries	A 16-a
protected against felling in ha million	World regions	A 16
afforested (total) in ha	All countries	A 16-a
under conifers in ha	All countries	A 16-a
trees other than conifers in ha	All countries	A 16-a
Productive afforested area as % of total forest land	Continents	J 7-a
Wooded & afforested area in ha	Latin American countries	J 5-a
	Main countries	E 3-a

FORESTS BY KIND

Area covered by conifers in ha	World regions	A 16
by mixed trees in ha	World regions	A 16
by trees other than conifers in ha	World regions	A 16
of high forest or of coppice in ha	All countries	A 16-a

FORESTS BY OWNERSHIP

Area: management-controlled in ha	All countries	A 16-a
owned by farmers in ha	All countries	A 16-a
by industry in ha	All countries	A 16-a
privately-owned in ha	World regions	A 16
	All countries	A 16-a
publicly-owned in ha	World regions	A 16
	All countries	A 16-a
state-owned in ha	All countries	A 16-a

FORGING BARS, ALUMINIUM

Despatches: tonnage	UK	C 30-a
Exports by destination: tonnage	Main countries	T 4-a
Production: tonnage	W Germany	T 4-a
Wholesale prices in Frs per kg	France	T 4-q

FORGING BILLETS, TITANIUM

Sales in lbs	USA	J 6-a

	Territorial coverage	Title codes	
FORGINGS & PRESSINGS			
see also PRESSINGS & STAMPINGS			
Production: tonnage by kind	EEC countries	E 28-q	E 27-a
Sales by end-use by value in $	USA	J 3	
Sales to agricultural machinery industry by value in $	USA	J 3-a	
aircraft industry by value in $	USA	J 3-a	
automotive industry by value in $	USA	J 3-a	
engine & turbine industry by value in $	USA	J 3-a	
machinery & metalwork industry by value in $	USA	J 3-a	
motorcycle & bicycle industry by value in $	USA	J 3-a	
nuclear power industry by value in $	USA	J 3-a	
petrochemicals industry by value in $	USA	J 3-a	
pumps & compressor industry by value in $	USA	J 3-a	
railway companies by value in $	USA	J 3-a	
refrigeration industry by value in $	USA	J 3-a	
FORGINGS & PRESSINGS, ALUMINIUM			
Consumption: tonnage	UK & USA	T 4-a	
Production: tonnage	Main countries	T 4-a	
Sales despatches: tonnage	OECD countries	D 21-a	
	UK	C 30-a	
	USA	J 6-a	
FORGINGS & PRESSINGS, STEEL			
Crude steel production for forgings: tonnage	EEC countries	E 29-a	
Deliveries to user industries: tonnage	ECE countries	U 7-q	U 6-a
	Main countries	H 3-a	
Exports by destination: tonnage	EEC area	E 5-q	
	EEC countries	E 29-a	
	Main countries	T 4-a	
tonnage	ECE countries	U 7-m	U 6-a
	Main countries	H 3-a	
Imports by source: tonnage	EEC countries	E 5-q	E 29-a
	Main countries	T 4-a	
iron & steel forgings & pressings: tonnage	Main countries	T 1-a	
tonnage	ECE countries	U 7-m	U 6-a
	Main countries	H 3-a	
Inter-EEC area deliveries: tonnage	EEC countries	E 29-a	
Production: tonnage	All countries	U 22-a	
	ECE countries	U 7-m	U 6-a
	EEC countries	E 30-q	E 29-a
	Main countries	H 3-a	T 4-a
FORK LIFT TRUCKS			
Exports by destination: no & value in £m	UK	V 1-a	
Production by load capacity in lbs & by type	UK	V 1-a	
by volume	All countries	U 22-a	
	EEC countries	E 28-q	E 27-a

Formaldehyde   see CHEMICAL PRODUCTS

Forward estimates   see PROJECTIONS

Forward rates of exchange (90 days)   see EXCHANGE RATES

Foundation garments   see CLOTHING
                                                UNDERWEAR

FOUNDRIES
      see also IRON FOUNDRIES

% change in output compared with % change in labour employed	Main countries	C 2-a	
Costs for salaried staff per month	EEC countries	E 11-a	
Earnings per hr in FrS	Main countries	C 2-a	
(piece rates): female workers in FrS per hr	Main countries	C 2-a	
in FrS per hr	Main countries	C 2-a	
semi-skilled workers in FrS per hr	Main countries	C 2-a	
skilled workers in FrS per hr	Main countries	C 2-a	
unskilled workers in FrS per hr	Main countries	C 2-a	
(time rate) per hr in FrS	Main countries	C 2-a	
Labour costs as % of total costs	EEC countries	E 8-a	
by status of employees in local currency	EEC countries	E 8-a	
in steel foundries in DM million	W Germany	H 3-a	
per hr: all employees	EEC countries	E 11-a	
female workers in FrS	Main countries	C 2-a	
per hr in foundries in FrS	Main countries	C 2-a	
in local currency	EEC countries	E 2-a	
semi-skilled workers in FrS	Main countries	C 2-a	
skilled workers in FrS	Main countries	C 2-a	
unskilled workers in FrS	Main countries	C 2-a	
wage earners in local currency	EEC countries	E 11-a	
Labour force employed by occupation	Main countries	C 2-a	
no of salaried staff	EEC countries	E 11-a	
wage earners & slaried staff	EEC countries	E 8-a	
wage earners	EEC countries	E 11-a	
production workers	Main countries	C 2-a	
salaried staff	Main countries	C 2-a	

	Territorial coverage	Title codes
FOUNDRIES, continued		
No of hrs worked per wk by region	EEC countries	E 25-a
per yr	EEC countries	E 8-a
per yr by salaried staff	EEC countries	E 11-a
by wage earners	EEC countries	E 11-a
Production: aluminium castings: tonnage & value in £	UK	B 25-a
copper-based castings: tonnage & value in £	UK	B 25-a
iron castings: tonnage & value in £	UK	B 25-a
magnesium castings: tonnage & value in £	UK	B 25-a
steel castings: tonnage & value in £	UK	B 25-a
zinc-based castings: tonnage & value in £	UK	B 25-a
Sales turnover in steel foundry products in DM million	W Germany	H 3-a
Wage rates per hr in local currency	EEC countries	E 25-a2
in FrS	Main countries	C 2-a
FOUNDRY IRON		
see also PIG IRON		
Basic domestic prices for pig iron in $A per ton	Australia	T 4-m
Deliveries (domestic): non-phosphoric foundry iron: tonnage	EEC countries	E 29-a
phosphoric foundry iron: tonnage	EEC countries	E 29-a
for export to non-EEC area: tonnage	EEC countries	E 29-a
to EEC area: tonnage	EEC countries	E 29-a
Exports by destination: tonnage	EEC countries	E 5-q E 29-a
	OECD countries	D 22-a
Imports by source: tonnage	EEC countries	E 5-q E 29-a
	OECD countries	D 22-a
Production: by grade: tonnage	EEC countries	E 29-a
of non-phosphoric foundry iron: tonnage	EEC area	E 29-a
of phosphoric foundry iron: tonnage	EEC area	E 29-a
Receipts from EEC area: tonnage	EEC countries	E 29-a
Wholesale prices in $ per ton	EEC countries	E 29-a2

Fractional hp motors   see   ELECTRIC MOTORS, FRACTIONAL HP

Free buying rates (bazaars)   see   EXCHANGE RATES

Free buying rates (of banking system)   see   EXCHANGE RATES

Freight & insurance charges   see   DISTRIBUTION COSTS

Freight carriage by canals   see   INLAND WATERWAYS - FREIGHT TRANSPORT

Freight carriage by rail   see   RAIL FREIGHT

Freight carriage by road   see   ROAD TRANSPORT

Freight income   see   BALANCE OF PAYMENTS   INVISIBLE TRADE

	Territorial coverage	Title codes
FREIGHT RATES		
see also OCEAN FREIGHT RATES		
RAIL FREIGHT RATES		
Coconut oil in bulk to Europe ex Fiji & Philippines		A 4-m
Copra cake to Europe & USA (in bags) ex Philippines		A 4-m
(in bulk) ex Philippines		A 4-m
Copra (in bags) from producers to ports of main buyers		A 4-m
(in bulk) from producers to ports of main buyers		A 4-m
Crude petroleum: general purpose rates	Worldwide	E 14-m
medium large tanker rates	Worldwide	E 14-m
spot rates	Worldwide	E 14-m
Grain to India from Australia & N America		C 29-m
Japan from Australia, Argentine & N America		C 29-m
Rotterdam from Argentine, Australia & N America		C 29-m
UK from Argentine, Australia & N America		C 29-m
Tanker rates on AFRA world scale by tonnage		E 16-m E 15-a
on single dirty mullion scale by area		E 16-m E 15-a
FREIGHT TRANSPORT		
see also AIR FREIGHT		
MAIL FREIGHT		
RAIL FREIGHT		
ROAD TRANSPORT		
SEABORNE FREIGHT		
% by rail, road & water (based on tons-km)	European countries	U 8-a
Expenditure on transportation by specific oil companies in $m	Worldwide	C 3-a
Exports by rail, road, sea & air: tonnage	European countries	U 8-a
of goods by type: rail, road, sea & air: tonnage	European countries	U 8-a
Imports by rail, road, sea & air: tonnage	European countries	U 8-a
of goods by type: rail, road, sea & air: tonnage	European countries	U 8-a
Inland waterways: freight carried in million tons	Main countries	S 24-a
Inter-EEC freight by rail, road or sea: tonnage	EEC countries	E 3-a
Labour costs & social charges for transport drivers	EEC countries	E 10-a
wages per hr for transport drivers	EEC countries	E 10-a
wages per mth for salaried staff	EEC countries	E 10-a

	Territorial coverage	Title codes

Freight wagons, rail   see   ROLLING STOCK

Freighters   see   CARGO SHIPS

French chalk   see   TALC

Fresh fruit   see   FRUIT, FRESH

Fresh vegetables   see   VEGETABLES, FRESH

Frozen fish   see   FISH & FISH PRODUCTS, FROZEN

Frozen fruit & vegetables   see   FRUIT, FROZEN
                                                              VEGETABLES, FROZEN

FROZEN MEALS, PREPARED

Production by kind: tonnage	UK	B 12-a
tonnage	All countries	U 22-a

FRUIT, CRYSTALLISED OR CANDIED

Imports by source: tonnage	UK	B 6-m
Production: tonnage	OECD countries	D 37-a

FRUIT, DRIED

    see also   DATES & FIGS
                PRUNES
                RAISINS & CURRANTS

Consumption of apples for drying purposes: tonnage	Australia	D 33-a
of imported dried fruit: tonnage	OECD countries	D 37-a
Exports by value in $m	W European countries	U 33-a
tonnage & value in $	EEC area	U 20-a
	W European area	U 20-a
Imports by value in $m	W European countries	U 33-a
by source: currants, raisins & sultanas: tonnage	UK	B 6-m
tonnage & value in $	EEC area	U 20-a
	W European area	U 20-a
tonnage	Main OECD countries	B 6-a
Production: dried peaches: tonnage	S Africa	D 35-a
dried pears: tonnage	Argentine & Australia	D 34-a
figs, prunes & dates: tonnage	All countries	B 5-a
Production tonnage, stocks & consumption per capita in kg	OECD countries	D 14-a
tonnage	All countries	U 22-a

FRUIT, DRIED BY KIND

Exports by destination: tonnage	Australia	B 6-a
tonnage	All countries	B 5-a
	Main countries	A 5-a
Imports by source: tonnage	UK	B 6-m
tonnage	All countries	B 5-a
Production: tonnage	Australia	B 6-a
	Main countries	A 5-a

FRUIT, FRESH

    see also   CITRUS FRUITS
                TROPICAL FRUITS

% changes in retail sales	E European countries & USSR	U 16-a	
% of production of apples processed	OECD countries	D 33-a	
peaches processed	OECD countries	D 35-a	
pears processed	OECD countries	D 34-a	
% usage of apple crop for canning purposes	Japan	D 33-a	
fruit juice production	Japan	D 33-a	
jam production	Japan	D 33-a	
processing	OECD countries	D 37-a	
of pear crop for consumption as fresh food	OECD countries	D 37-a	
for processing	OECD countries	D 37-a	
Area (irrigated & non-irrigated) under fruit crop in ha	Romania	U 20-a	
of orchards in ha	EEC countries	E 3-a	E 44-a
	OAS member countries	N 13-a	
for production of apples in ha	OECD countries	D 29-a	
of peaches in ha	OECD countries	D 29-a	
of pears in ha	OECD countries	D 29-a	
under strawberry crop in ha	Bulgaria & E Germany	U 20-a	
Consumption tonnage & consumption per capita in kg	OECD countries	D 14-a	
Consumption & sales of apples (dessert): tonnage	OECD countries	D 37-a	
of apples for processing: tonnage	OECD countries	D 29-a	
of peaches for processing: tonnage	OECD countries	D 29-a	
of pears for processing: tonnage	OECD countries	D 29-a	
(industrial) in production of food preparations: tonnage	EEC countries	E 44-a	
of apples (as fresh food): tonnage	OECD countries	D 33-a	
for processing in bushels	Australia	D 38-a	
for processing: tonnage	OECD countries	D 37-a	
tonnage	OECD countries	D 29-a	
of home-produced fruit: tonnage	OAS member countries	N 17-a	
of peaches (as fresh food): tonnage	OECD countries	D 37-a	
for canning: tonnage	OECD countries	D 35-a	
for compotes: tonnage	Italy	D 35-a	

FRUIT, FRESH   continued

	Territorial coverage	Title codes	
Consumption of peaches for drying: tonnage	W Germany & USA	D 35-a	
frozen products: tonnage	Italy	D 35-a	
jam production: tonnage	Main OECD countries	D 35-a	
puree: tonnage	Italy	D 35-a	
tonnage	OECD countries	D 29-a	
	OAS member countries	N 17-a	
of pears (as fresh food): tonnage	OECD countries	D 34-a	D 37-a
canning: tonnage	Main OECD countries	D 34-a	
fruit pulp: tonnage	Netherlands	D 34-a	
juice extraction: tonnage	Netherlands	D 34-a	
processing: tonnage	OECD countries	D 37-a	
syrup production: tonnage	Netherlands	D 34-a	
tonnage	OECD countries	D 29-a	
	OAS member countries	N 17-a	
of strawberries: tonnage	OAS member countries	N 17-a	
per capita by income levels in lbs per yr	USA	C 27-a	
per capita in kg per yr: apples	Australia	D 38-a	
	EEC countries	U 20-a	
	OECD countries	D 33-a	
peaches	EEC countries	U 20-a	
	OECD countries	D 35-a	
pears	EEC countries	U 20-a	
	OECD countries	D 1-a	D 34-a
table grapes	EEC countries	U 20-a	
	E European countries & USSR	U 16-a	
in kg per yr	EEC countries	B 1-a	E 44-a
		U 20-a	
Crop yields in quintals per ha	Main E European countries	U 20-a	
Export prices - index nos (weighted average)	E European countries & USSR	U 16-a	
Exports by destination: apples in bushels	Worldwide	U 29-q	
apples: tonnage	Australia	D 38-a	
peaches: tonnage	Main OECD countries	D 33-a	
tonnage	Main OECD countries	D 35-a	
sea, inland waterways, road, rail & air: tonnage	Bulgaria	U 20-a	
value & as % of exports of farm products	European countries	U 8-a	
value in $m	W European countries	U 20-a	
(incl dried fruit): tonnage	W European countries	U 33-a	
(incl nuts) by value in $	Asian & Far East countries	U 32-q	
of apples by kind to UK in bushels	ECAFE countries	U 32-m	
tonnage	Australia	B 6-a	
unit value in $ per ton	OECD countries	D 33-a	
peaches: tonnage	W European countries	U 20-a	
pears by destination: tonnage	OECD countries	D 35-a	
tonnage	OECD countries	D 34-a	
tonnage	OECD countries	D 34-a	
Imports as % of consumption	Main E European countries	U 20-a	
by sea, inland waterways, road, rail & air: tonnage	OECD countries	D 37-a	
source of apples: tonnage	European countries	U 8-a	
of peaches: tonnage	OECD countries	D 33-a	
of apples by value in $m	OECD countries	D 35-a	
apples: tonnage	W European countries	U 33-a	
	USSR	U 20-a	
unit value in $ per ton	OECD countries	D 33-a	
bananas: tonnage	W European countries	U 20-a	
lemons: tonnage	USSR	U 20-a	
oranges: tonnage	USSR	U 20-a	
peaches: tonnage	USSR	U 20-a	
pears: tonnage	OECD countries	D 35-a	
table grapes: tonnage	OECD countries	D 34-a	
tangerines: tonnage	USSR	U 20-a	
temperate fruit: tonnage & value in local currency	USSR	U 20-a	
tropical fruits: tonnage & value in local currency	OECD countries	D 37-a	
tonnage	OECD countries	D 37-a	
Income elasticity of demand	Main E European countries	U 20-a	
Market losses of apples: tonnage	USA	C 27-a	
peaches: tonnage	OECD countries	D 29-a	
pears: tonnage	OECD countries	D 29-a	
No of applications received for bonuses by orchard areas	OECD countries	D 29-a	
for apple production	EEC countries	U 20-a	
Pear crop by variety in million cartons	EEC countries	U 20-a	
Producer prices received for apples in local currency per ton	Australia	B 6-a	
for fruit by kind	OECD countries	D 1-a	
Production as % of all food (based on value)	All countries	A 9-a	
as % of consumption	OECD countries	D 37-a	
by value in £m	OECD countries	D 37-a	
in local currency	EEC countries	B 1-a	
in $m	OECD countries	D 37-a	
Production, industrial usage & stocks: tonnage	EEC countries	E 44-a	
Production of apples by variety in million cartons	OECD countries	D 14-a	
in bushels	Australia	B 6-a	
apples & pears in bushels	Australia	D 38-a	
pears in bushels	Australia	B 6-a	
tonnage by kind of fruit	Australia	D 38-a	
(all fruit excl citrus)	Greece & Turkey	D 35-a	
(all kinds)	OECD countries	D 1-a	
	Main E European countries	U 20-a	
	E European countries & USSR	U 16-a	
	OECD countries	D 37-a	

FRUIT, FRESH   continued

	Territorial coverage	Title codes
Production: apples by variety: tonnage	OECD countries	D 33-a
apples, pears & peaches: tonnage	W European countries	U 20-a
apples & pears: tonnage	EEC countries	B 1-a
apples (processed): tonnage	OECD countries	D 33-a
apples: tonnage	European countries	U 20-a
	OAS member countries	N 13-a
	OECD countries	D 33-a
apricots: tonnage	African countries	U 44-a
	European countries	U 20-a
cherries: tonnage	Main E European countries	U 20-a
	OAS member countries	N 13-a
commercially-grown apples: tonnage	OECD countries	D 29-a
cherries: tonnage	OECD countries	D 37-a
peaches: tonnage	OECD countries	D 29-a
pears: tonnage	OECD countries	D 29-a D 37-a
plums: tonnage	OECD countries	D 37-a
strawberries: tonnage	OECD countries	D 37-a
historical tables: tonnage	Main European countries	Z 1-a
imports, exports & consumption: tonnage	EEC countries	E 44-a
lemons & limes: tonnage	European countries	U 20-a
melons & cantaloups: tonnage	African countries	U 44-a
oranges & tangerines: tonnage	European countries	U 20-a
oranges, tangerines & lemons: tonnage	W European countries	U 20-a
peaches & nectarines: tonnage	African countries	U 44-a
peaches by province: tonnage	Italy	D 38-a
peaches (processed): tonnage	OECD countries	D 35-a
peaches (fresh): tonnage	European countries	U 20-a
	OAS member countries	N 13-a
	OECD countries	D 35-a
pears by region & by variety: tonnage	Main OECD countries	D 34-a
pears (processed): tonnage	OECD countries	D 34-a
pears (fresh): tonnage	African countries	U 44-a
	European countries	U 20-a
	OAS member countries	N 13-a
	OECD countries	D 34-a D 37-a
plums & prunes: tonnage	European countries	U 20-a
plums, grapes & apricots: tonnage	W European countries	U 20-a
plums: tonnage	African countries	U 44-a
	OAS member countries	N 13-a
	European countries	U 20-a
strawberries: tonnage	European countries	U 20-a
table grapes: tonnage	W European countries	U 20-a
tomatoes: tonnage	EEC countries	Z 3-a
Retail prices (comparative) of apples (eating) per kg	OECD countries	D 37-a
Sales by value in local currency	Netherlands	U 20-a
tonnage of strawberries grown in open fields	Netherlands	U 20-a
grown under glass tonnage	OECD countries	D 37-a
Sales value as % of sales of all agricultural products	OECD countries	D 37-a
Self-sufficiency ratios	EEC countries	B 1-a E 3-a
		E 44-a
Wholesale prices: apples (home-grown) by kind in pence per lb	UK	B 6-m
apples (imported) by kind in pence per lb	UK	B 6-m
apricots for canning in local currency	All countries	A 7-a
peaches for canning in local currency	All countries	A 7-a
World export trade: peaches (fresh): tonnage	World regions	D 35-a
pears (fresh): tonnage	World regions	D 34-a
World market prices - index nos		G 1-a
World production of peaches: tonnage	World regions	D 35-a
of pears: tonnage	World regions	D 34-a

FRUIT, FRESH BY KIND

	Territorial coverage	Title codes
% of harvest industrially processed	UK	B 5-a
Area under crop (incl fruit in shell) in ha	Italy	D 38-a
Canning intake: tonnage by variety	S Africa	B 6-a
Consumption for industrial processing: tonnage	Main countries	B 5-a
per capita in lbs	UK	B 6-a
tonnage	EEC countries	E 44-a
Export prices in local currency	USA	B 6-a
Exports by destination: tonnage	Main countries	A 9-a
tonnage & value in $	World regions	B 5-a
tonnage	EEC area	U 20-a
	All countries	B 5-a
	ECAFE countries	U 32-m
unit value in $ per ton	Main countries	B 6-a
Harvested tonnage & supply of fruit by kind	Main W European countries	U 20-a
of apples	Main countries	B 5-a
peaches	OECD countries	D 29-a
pears	OECD countries	D 29-a
Import prices in £ per cwt	OECD countries	D 29-a
Imports by source of apples for cider: tonnage	UK	B 6-a
apricots: tonnage	OECD countries	D 37-a
cherries: tonnage	OECD countries	D 37-a
currants: tonnage	OECD countries	D 37-a
fruit berries: tonnage	OECD countries	D 37-a
grapes for table: tonnage	OECD countries	D 37-a
melons: tonnage	OECD countries	D 37-a
peaches: tonnage	OECD countries	D 37-a

	Territorial coverage	Title codes	
FRUIT, FRESH BY KIND continued			
Imports by source of pears for perry: tonnage	OECD countries	D 37-a	
plums: tonnage	OECD countries	D 37-a	
stone fruits: tonnage	OECD countries	D 37-a	
strawberries: tonnage	OECD countries	D 37-a	
tonnage (all fruits)	Czechoslovakia & Poland	U 20-a	
	UK	B 6-a	
(net) of apples: tonnage	OECD countries	D 29-a	
peaches: tonnage	OECD countries	D 29-a	
pears: tonnage	OECD countries	D 29-a	
tonnage & value in $	EEC area	U 20-a	
	W European area	U 20-a	
tonnage	Canada, European countries, USA & USSR	A 11-a	
	Main countries	B 6-a	
unit value in $ per ton	Main W European countries	U 20-a	
Producer prices (minimum) in R per ton	S Africa	B 6-a	
in $ per 100 kg	EEC countries	U 20-a	
Production by volume & value in local currency	Caribbean countries & W Indies	T 6-a	
Production, imports, exports & consumption	EEC countries	E 44-a	
Production: tonnage by areas	EEC countries	E 38-a	
tonnage produced by commercial growers	Canada	B 6-a	
tonnage (in detail)	World regions	A 11-a	
tonnage	EEC countries	E 44-a	
	All countries	A 9-a	
	Main countries	B 5-a	
	OAS member countries	N 13-a	
	OECD countries	D 37-a	
	W European countries	U 20-a	
Production, imports, exports & consumption: tonnage	OECD countries	D 29-a	
Retail prices in local currency	OAS member countries	N 17-a	
Sales in local markets: tonnage	S Africa	B 6-a	
Stock changes: fruit held in cold storage: tonnage	Australia & USA	D 29-a	
Supply for home consumption: tonnage	UK	B 5-a	
Supply, production, consumption & trade: tonnage	EEC countries	B 1-a	
Wholesale prices by source in pence per lb	UK	B 6-w	B 5-m
in local currency per kg	OAS member countries	N 17-a	
in $ per kg	EEC countries	D 38-a	
in local currency	Main countries	A 9-a	
World exports: unit value in $ per ton		A 11-a	
FRUIT, FROZEN			
Consumption: tonnage	OAS member countries	N 17-a	
Production: tonnage	All countries	B 5-a	U 22-a
FRUIT, FROZEN BY KIND			
Exports by destination: tonnage	OECD countries	B 6-a	
Imports by source with & without sugar content: tonnage	UK	B 6-m	
tonnage	OECD countries	B 6-a	
Production: tonnage	Canada & USA	B 5-a	
FRUIT, PROCESSED			
see also FRUIT, DRIED			
FRUIT, FROZEN			
FRUIT JUICES			
FRUIT PREPARATIONS			
Consumption of apple preparations: tonnage	OECD countries	D 33-a	
apples for canning: tonnage	Australia	D 33-a	
for juice & cider: tonnage	Australia	D 33-a	
pear preparations: tonnage	OECD countries	D 34-a	
per capita of apple preparations in kg per yr	OECD countries	D 33-a	
of apples in kg per yr	Australia	D 38-a	
of peaches (canned) in kg per yr	OECD countries	D 35-a	
of plums in production of spirits: tonnage	Yugoslavia	D 37-a	
Exports by destination: peaches (canned): tonnage	Main OECD countries	D 35-a	
pears (processed): tonnage	Main OECD countries	D 34-a	
of apples (processed): tonnage	Main OECD countries	D 33-a	
peaches (canned): tonnage	Main OECD countries	D 35-a	
pears (canned & dried): tonnage	Argentine	D 34-a	
pears (processed): tonnage	Main OECD countries	D 34-a	
Imports by source: peaches (canned): tonnage	Main OECD countries	D 35-a	
pears (processed): tonnage	Main OECD countries	D 34-a	
of apples (processed): tonnage	Main OECD countries	D 33-a	
peaches (canned): tonnage	Main OECD countries	D 35-a	
pears (processed): tonnage	Main OECD countries	D 34-a	
Production: candied peel: tonnage	W Germany	D 37-a	
fruit (canned & bottled): tonnage	OECD countries	D 37-a	
(candied): tonnage	OECD countries	D 37-a	
preserves & jam: tonnage	OECD countries	D 37-a	
syrup: tonnage	OECD countries	D 37-a	
FRUIT & VEGETABLES			
see also CANNED & BOTTLED FRUIT			
CANNED VEGETABLES			
CITRUS FRUITS			
% used on farm for sale or processing: tonnage	ECE countries	U 34-a	
Distribution for food processing: tonnage	E European countries	U 34-a	

	Territorial coverage	Title codes
FRUIT & VEGETABLES, continued		
Distribution for market sales: tonnage	E European countries	U 34-a
for own farm consumption: tonnage	E European countries	U 34-a
Expenditure on EEC area price supports in £m	E European countries	B 3-a
Exports by destination: tonnage	OECD countries	D 37-a
value in $m	OECD countries	D 1-a
	W European countries	U 33-a
value shipped to E Europe in $m	W European countries	U 20-a
to EEC & non-EEC areas by value in $m	EEC countries	E 24-a
unit value in $ per ton	W European countries	U 20-a
Gross output as % of all crops (value basis)	ECE countries	U 34-a
Imports by source: tonnage	OECD countries	D 37-a
by value ex E Europe Bloc by value in $m	W European countries	U 20-a
in $m	OECD countries	D 1-a
	W European countries	U 33-a
ex EEC & non-EEC areas by value in $m	EEC countries	E 24-a
unit value in $ per ton	W European countries	U 20-a
Production by value in billion Lit	Italy	D 38-a
tonnage of fruit (all kinds)	EEC countries	U 20-a
of vegetables (all kinds)	EEC countries	U 20-a
tonnage	Czechoslovakia, Hungary & Poland	U 34-a
value as % of gross output	E European countries	U 34-a
Retail prices - index nos	EEC countries	E 26-m
FRUIT & VEGETABLES, PROCESSED		
Production of deep-frozen products: tonnage	OECD countries	D 37-a
of juices in litres	OECD countries	D 37-a
of preserves: tonnage	OECD countries	D 37-a
FRUIT & VEGETABLES BY KIND		
Consumption per capita in kg	OECD countries	D 37-a
tonnage	OECD countries	D 37-a
Exports by CST classes by destination: tonnage & value in $	EEC countries	E 48-a
SITC classes by value in $	Main countries	D 2-q
tonnage & value in $	All countries	U 50-a U 59-a
	OECD countries	D 3-a2
NIMEXE classes: tonnage & value in $	All countries	E 20-a
Imports by CST classes by source: tonnage & value in $	EEC countries	E 21-a
NIMEXE classes: tonnage & value in $	All countries	E 20-a
SITC classes: tonnage & value in $	All countries	U 50-a U 59-a
source by SITC classes by value in $	Main countries	D 2-q
tonnage & value in $	OECD countries	D 3-a2
Production: tonnage	Main countries	B 6-a
	OECD countries	D 37-a
FRUIT JUICES		
Consumption tonnage & consumption per capita in kg	OECD countries	D 14-a
Consumption: canned fruit juices: tonnage	OAS member countries	N 17-a
Exports of lemon juice: tonnage	Italy	A 5-a
of orange juice: tonnage	Brazil, Israel & USA	A 5-a
tonnage & value of fruit juices in $	EEC countries	U 20-a
tonnage & value in $	W European area	U 20-a
tonnage	Main countries	B 5-a
Import prices: passion fruit juice in $ cif	UK & USA	A 8-a
Imports: citrus fruit juices by kind by source in gallons	UK	B 6-m
pineapple juice: tonnage	Main countries	A 8-a
tonnage & value in $	EEC area	U 20-a
	W European area	U 20-a
Production & stocks: frozen & canned fruit juice in litres	OECD countries	D 14-a
Production: concentrated fruit juice: tonnage	All countries	U 22-a
passion fruit juice: tonnage	Australia & Hawaii	A 8-a
volume in litres	OECD countries	D 37-a
in gallons	All countries	B 5-a
Retail prices: orange concentrate in 6 oz cans in cents	USA	A 5-a
orange juice in 20 oz cans in $	Canada	A 5-a
(unsweetened) in DM per litre	W Germany	A 5-a
FRUIT JUICES, CITRUS		
Consumption per capita in kg	Main countries	A 7-a
Customs duties: rates charged	Main countries	A 7-a
Exports of grapefruit juice: tonnage	All countries	A 7-a
lemon juice: tonnage	All countries	A 7-a
orange juice by destination: tonnage	All countries	A 7-a
orange juice: tonnage	All countries	A 7-a
Import prices: canned grapefruit juice in $	European countries	A 7-m
orange juice in $	European countries	A 7-m
Imports of grapefruit juice: tonnage	Main countries	A 7-a
lemon juice: tonnage	Main countries	A 7-a
orange juice: tonnage	Main countries	A 7-a
Internal taxes on consumption in local currency	All countries	A 7-a
Production by volume: concentrated citrus juices	USA	B 5-a
frozen packs	USA	B 5-a
heat-processed citrus juices	USA	B 5-a
Quantitative import restrictions applied on citrus juices	All countries	A 7-a

	Territorial coverage	Title codes
FRUIT JUICES BY KIND		
Exports in gallons	Main countries	B 5-a
of canned fruit juices by value in local currency	Cook Is	U 32-m
Imports in gallons	Main OECD countries	B 6-a
(incl citrus) in gallons	UK	B 5-a
Production: apple & pear juice in litres	OECD countries	D 37-a
stone fruit juices in litres	OECD countries	D 37-a
grape juice in litres	OECD countries	D 37-a
orange juice in litres	OECD countries	D 37-a
Retail prices in local currency	OAS member countries	N 17-a
FRUIT PREPARATIONS		
see also FRUIT JUICES		
Apricots (processed): tonnage	All countries	A 7-a
Exports: tonnage & value in $	EEC area	U 20-a
	W European area	U 20-a
Imports: preserved fruit by kind by source: tonnage	UK	B 6-m
tonnage & value in $	EEC area	U 20-a
	W European area	U 20-a
Peaches (canned, dried & frozen): tonnage	USA	A 7-a
(processed): tonnage	All countries	A 7-a
Production by kind: tonnage	Israel	B 6-a
FRUIT TREES		
Area of apple orchards in production in ha	OECD countries	D 33-a
not in production in ha	OECD countries	D 33-a
orchards in ha (all fruit trees)	Main E European countries	U 20-a
	Netherlands	U 20-a
orchards in ha: apple trees	Netherlands	U 20-a
cherry trees	Netherlands	U 20-a
pear trees	Netherlands	U 20-a
plum trees	Netherlands	U 20-a
peach trees in production in ha	OECD countries	D 35-a
not in production in ha	OECD countries	D 35-a
pear trees in production in ha	OECD countries	D 34-a
not in production in ha	OECD countries	D 34-a
under fruit (incl strawberries) in ha	EEC countries	B 1-a
Bonus applications: no received for planting: apple trees	EEC countries	U 20-a
peach trees	EEC countries	U 20-a
pear trees	EEC countries	U 20-a
Changes in areas of orchards by kind of tree in ha	UK	U 20-a
No of trees in production by kind: apple in million	OECD countries	D 37-a
apricot in million	OECD countries	D 37-a
cherry in million	OECD countries	D 37-a
greengage in million	OECD countries	D 37-a
peach in million	OECD countries	D 37-a
pear in million	OECD countries	D 37-a
plum in million	OECD countries	D 37-a
apple trees in commercial production	OECD countries	D 29-a
	Hungary	D 33-a
	S Africa & New Zealand	D 33-a
not in production	S Africa & New Zealand	D 33-a
fruit trees (all kinds)	Czechoslovakia & Poland	U 20-a
peach trees in commercial production	OECD countries	D 29-a
	S Africa	D 35-a
not in production	S Africa	D 35-a
pear trees in commercial production	OECD countries	D 29-a
	S Africa	D 34-a
not in production	S Africa	D 34-a
Plantings financed by development funds for Mezzogiorno	Italy	D 38-a
Yield of apples in tons per ha	OECD countries	D 33-a
peaches in tons per ha	OECD countries	D 35-a
pears in tons per ha	OECD countries	D 34-a
FRUIT TREES BY AGE		
% of apple trees by age groups (census data)	Italy	D 33-a
Production: apples by age of trees: tonnage	OECD countries	D 33-a
peaches by age of trees: tonnage	OECD countries	D 35-a
pears by age of trees: tonnage	OECD countries	D 34-a
FRUIT TREES BY KIND		
No of apple trees	European countries	U 20-a
apricot trees	European countries	U 20-a
cherry trees	European countries	U 20-a
peach trees	European countries	U 20-a
pear trees	European countries	U 20-a
plum trees	European countries	U 20-a
trees & acreage of orchards planted	Main countries	B 5-a

Fuel distillates   see   FUEL OIL, DISTILLATE
                           TAR

FUEL OIL

see also   BUNKERS
           PETROLEUM PRODUCTS

		Territorial coverage	Title codes	
FUEL OIL, continued				
% consumption of world supply		Latin American countries	U 18-a	
% growth in demand		World regions & Japan	G 1-a	
% contribution to export earnings		Kenya	E 45-a	
% yields in refining of crude oil		W European countries & USA	C 21-a	
Consumption as % of total primary energy used		ECE areas	U 10-a	
	by chemical industry: tonnage	EEC countries	E 14-a	
	industry: tonnage	EEC countries	E 14-a	
	iron & steel industry: tonnage	EEC countries	E 14-a	
	non-ferrous metals industry: tonnage	EEC countries	E 14-a	
	non-metallic mineral industry: tonnage	EEC countries	E 14-a	
	power stations in electricity production: tonnage	UK	U 10-a	
	steel industry (incl diesel oil): tonnage	EEC countries	E 29-a	
	steel industry: tonnage	ECE countries	U 6-a	U 7-a
	of distillates in barrels per day	Main countries	H 3-a	
	of heavy fuel oil in litres	World regions	C 3-a	
	in agriculture & in fishing industry: tonnage	OAS member countries	N 17-a	
		EEC countries	E 14-a	
	in m³	AASM countries	E 41-a	
	in open-hearth furnaces: tonnage	ECE countries	U 6-a	U 7-a
		Main countries	H 3-a	
	of residual & distillate oils in litres	OAS member countries	N 17-a	
	residual oils by industrial end-users: tonnage	OECD countries	D 31-a	
	in barrels	World regions	C 3-a	
	tonnage	Main countries	C 14-a	
	(total) & from own refineries: tonnage	Italy	H 4-a	
Deliveries for domestic consumption: tonnage		EEC countries	E 16-m	E 15-a
	residual oils for home consumption: tonnage	OECD countries	D 39-q	D 31-a
Demand (domestic) incl distillates: tonnage		Main countries	C 21-a	
Import prices in S Kr per m³ cif		Sweden	U 10-a	
Imports & exports by source & destination: tonnage		Main countries	B 15-a	
Imports, exports, consumption & consumption per capita in kg		All countries	U 55-a	
Imports by source of residual oil: tonnage		OECD countries	D 31-a	
	tonnage	Main countries	C 14-a	
Price increases: oil for bunkers in $		World regions	S 16-q	
Prices posted at specific ports in cents per gallon fob		Worldwide	C 3-a	
Production of distillates in barrels per day		OPEC countries	C 3-a	
	in m³	OAS member countries	N 14-a	
	in barrels	All countries	N 5-a	
	in coal equiv tonnage	EEC countries	E 16-q	E 15-a
	of residual fuel oils in barrels per day	OPEC countries	C 3-a	
	in m³	OAS member countries	N 14-a	
	distillate & residual oils: tonnage	AASM countries	E 41-a	
		All countries	U 55-a	
	distillates: tonnage	African countries	U 44-a	
		All countries	U 22-a	
	residual fuel oil: tonnage	African countries	U 44-a	
		EEC countries	E 28-q	E 27-a
		Main countries	E 3-a	
	tonnage	African countries	U 39-a	U 44-a
		EEC countries	E 26-m	
		Latin American countries	J 5-a	
		Main countries	B 15-a	R 5-a
		S American countries & Mexico	U 40-a	
Refinery output & consumption: tonnage		OECD countries	D 31-a	
	of residual oil: imports & supply: tonnage	OECD countries	D 39-q	D 31-a
Retail prices (bunker C) in cents per gallon		Main countries	U 18-a	
	by grade - index nos	EEC countries	E 17-q	
	in major cities by grade in local currency	EEC countries	E 17-q	
	tractor fuels in local currency per 100 litres	EEC countries	E 34-m	
World market prices - index nos		EEC countries	U 23-a	

FUEL OIL, DISTILLATE
    see also   FUEL OIL

Production: tonnage		All countries	U 43-a
tonnage (see No 1, 4, 7, 10)		World regions	U 27-q

FUEL OIL, RESIDUAL
    see also   FUEL OIL

Production: hydrocarbon mixtures: tonnage		All countries	U 22-a

Fuel tax   see   MOTOR FUEL TAX

Fuel wood   see   TIMBER

FUELS
    see also   MINERAL FUELS

% changes in exports	EEC countries	E 23-a
in imports by source	EEC countries	E 23-a
Consumption cost to private sector	EEC countries	E 32-a
Exports by destination by value in UA	EEC countries	E 23-a
value in $m	Main countries	E 24-a
to non-EEC area in UA	EEC countries	E 24-a
Imports by source by value in UA	EEC countries	E 23-a
value ex EEC area in UA	African, Caribbean countries & Pacific Is	E 45-a
ex non-EEC area in UA	EEC countries	E 24-a
in $m	African, Caribbean countries & Pacific Is	E 45-a
	Main countries	E 24-a

	Territorial coverage	Title codes	
FUELS, continued			
Inter-EEC exports by value in UA	EEC countries	E 22-m	E 24-a
imports by value in UA	EEC countries	E 22-m	E 24-a
Retail prices: fuel & light – index nos	All countries	L 4-a	
(incl domestic lighting) – index nos	AASM countries	E 41-a	
FUELS, GASEOUS			
see also BLAST FURNACE GAS			
COKE OVEN GAS			
GAS, MANUFACTURED			
METHANE			
NATURAL GAS			
% share as source of electricity generation	ECE countries	U 16-a	
Exports in coal equiv tonnage	ECE countries	U 15-a	
Imports in coal equiv tonnage	ECE countries	U 15-a	
Production & consumption by kind in coal equiv tonnage	European countries incl USSR	U 4-a	
Production by kind in million cu ft	All countries	N 5-a	
FUELS, LIQUID			
see also AVIATION FUEL			
CRUDE PETROLEUM			
DIESEL OIL			
FUEL OIL			
KEROSENE			
MOTOR SPIRIT			
NAPHTHA			
NATURAL GAS LIQUIDS			
% share as source of electricity generation	ECE countries	U 16-a	
Consumption by households in coal equiv tonnage	EEC countries	E 7-a	
by iron & steel industry: tonnage	EEC countries	E 30-a	
	UK	T 2-m	
by kind by iron & steel industry: tonnage	UK	T 2-q	
by public electricity plants: tonnage	European countries	U 1-a	
Consumption cost to private sector in local currency	EEC countries	E 32-a	
Consumption in coal equiv tonnage	ECE countries	U 15-a	
	EEC countries	E 7-a	E 14-a
in thermal power stations: tonnage	OECD countries	D 8-a	
refined fuels per capita	All countries	U 55-a	
Deliveries to non-EEC area: tonnage	EEC countries	E 14-a	
Exports in coal equiv tonnage	EEC area	E 7-a	
	EEC countries	E 14-a	
Imports in coal equiv tonnage	EEC area	E 7-a	
	EEC countries	E 14-a	
Production by kind, consumption & trade: tonnage	European countries & USA	U 4-a	
Production by kind in barrels	All countries	N 5-a	
Production, trade, consumption & stocks: tonnage	All countries	U 55-a	
World consumption in million tons coal equiv		C 14-a	
FUELS, PATENT			
Availability: tonnage	European countries	U 31-q	
Consumption by households: tonnage	Main countries	N 2-a	
	OECD countries	D 44-a	
internal navigation barges: tonnage	Main countries	N 2-a	
iron & steel industry: tonnage	Main countries	N 2-a	
railways: tonnage	Main countries	N 2-a	
	OECD countries	D 44-a	
of coal in production of patent fuels	OECD countries	D 44-a	
coke in production of patent fuels	ECE countries	U 6-a	U 7-a
	Main countries	H 3-a	
tonnage	European countries, USA & USSR	U 4-a	
Exports by destination: tonnage	Main countries	N 2-a	
tonnage	European countries	U 31-q	
Imports: tonnage	European countries	U 31-q	
Investment by patent fuel plants by district in local currency	EEC countries	E 15-a	
Production, imports & deliveries to households: tonnage	EEC countries	E 15-a	
Production, imports, exports & consumption: tonnage	OECD countries	D 44-a	
Production: tonnage	European countries, USA & USSR	U 4-a	
FUELS, SOLID			
see also COAL			
COKE			
FUELS, PATENT			
HARD COAL BRIQUETTES			
LIGNITE			
PEAT			
PEAT BRIQUETTES			
% share as source of electricity generation	ECE countries	U 16-a	
Coastal freight shipping: tonnage	EEC countries	E 43-a	
Consumption by households: tonnage	EEC area	E 7-a	
Consumption cost to private sector	EEC countries	E 32-a	
Consumption: tonnage	EEC countries	E 7-a	E 14-a
	ECE countries	U 15-a	
in production of manufactured gas: tonnage	European countries & USA	U 3-a	
(incl coke) in steel industry: tonnage	EEC countries	E 30-q	
per capita: tonnage	All countries	U 55-a	

	Territorial coverage	Title codes
FUELS, SOLID continued		
Exports by sea, inland waterways, road & rail: tonnage	European countries	U 8-a
ex world regions by destination: tonnage	All countries	U 55-a
tonnage	ECE countries	U 15-a
Imports & exports by country by kind of fuel by rail: tonnage	EEC countries	E 43-a
by road: tonnage	EEC countries	E 43-a
by sea: tonnage	EEC countries	E 43-a
Imports by sea, inland waterways, road & rail: tonnage	European countries	U 8-a
tonnage	EEC countries	E 7-a E 14-a
	ECE countries	U 15-a
Inter-EEC deliveries: tonnage	EEC countries	E 14-a
Production, trade, consumption & stocks: tonnage	All countries	U 55-a
Receipts by type of fuel at steelworks: tonnage	EEC countries	E 30-q
World consumption: tonnage		C 14-a
World movement between regions: tonnage	World regions	U 55-a
FUELS, SOLID BY KIND		
Consumption by state industry	E European countries	U 10-a
Exports by destination by SITC classes: tonnage & value in $	OECD countries	D 3-a2
by CST classes: tonnage & value in $	EEC countries	E 48-a
by SITC classes by value in $	Main countries	D 2-q
NIMEXE classes: tonnage & value in $	All countries	E 20-a
SITC classes: tonnage & value in $	All countries	U 50-a U 59-a
Freight consigned (inland & overseas): tonnage	EEC countries	E 43-a
Imports by NIMEXE classes: tonnage & value in $	All countries	E 20-a
SITC classes: tonnage & value in $	All countries	U 50-a U 59-a
source by CST classes: tonnage & value in $	EEC countries	E 21-a
by SITC classes by value in $	Main countries	D 2-q
: tonnage & value in $	OECD countries	D 3-a2
	Main countries	N 2-a
tonnage	Italy	H 4-a
Production, consumption, imports & exports: tonnage	European countries & USSR	U 4-a
Production: tonnage	All countries	N 5-a
	Italy	H 4-a
Road transport over frontiers: tonnage	EEC countries	E 43-a
FUELS BY KIND		
Consumption in thermal power stations: tonnage	OECD countries	D 8-a
of solid liquid in coal equiv tonnage	All countries	U 55-a
Exports to EEC & non-EEC areas by value in $m	EEC countries	E 24-a
Imports ex EEC & non-EEC areas by value in $m	EEC countries	E 24-a
FULLER'S EARTH		
see also BENTONITE		
Production: tonnage	All countries	B 15-a
	USA	N 1-a
FUMIGANTS		
Consumption in agriculture: tonnage	All countries	A 9-a
Fuming operations see ZINC FUMING		
Fungicides see DISINFECTANTS		
FUR MANUFACTURING INDUSTRY		
Investment in buildings in local currency	EEC countries	E 40-a
in land purchase in local currency	EEC countries	E 40-a
in machinery in local currency	EEC countries	E 40-a
Fur skins see HIDES		
Furnace gas see BLAST FURNACE GAS		
FURNACE SLAG		
see also FERTILISERS, PHOSPHATE		
% change in prices to farmers as fertiliser	EEC countries	E 34-m
Consumption in production of sinter: tonnage	UK	T 2-q
tonnage	All countries	A 2-a
Exports: tonnage	All countries	A 2-a
Farm costs per 100 kg as farm fertiliser	EEC countries	E 34-m
Imports: tonnage	All countries	A 2-a
Production: furnace by-products & slag: tonnage	EEC countries	E 30-q
tonnage	All countries	A 2-a
	EEC countries	E 29-a
FURNACES, ELECTRIC		
Consumption of coke in electric steel production: tonnage	ECE countries	U 6-a U 7-a
	Main countries	H 3-a
Exports by destination by value in $	Main countries	U 9-a
value in $m	All countries	U 38-a
Imports by value in $m	All countries	U 38-a
Investment for electric steel production by regions	EEC countries	E 46-a
Labour force employed	EEC countries	E 29-a
No of electric furnaces built & no in operation	EEC countries	E 30-q E 29-a

	Territorial coverage	Title codes
FURNACES, ELECTRIC continued		
Production capacity: tonnage	EEC countries	E 29-a
Production: no of furnaces built	All countries	U 22-a
	European countries & Japan	U 38-a
Production potential of electric steel: tonnage	EEC countries	E 46-a
Production: tonnage of electric steel over last decade	EEC countries	E 29-a
World export trade in $m		U 38-a
FURNACES, INDUSTRIAL		
Exports by destination by value in $m	Main countries	U 9-a
	All countries	U 38-a
Imports by value in $m	All countries	U 38-a
World export trade by value in $m		U 38-a
FURNACES, STEEL		
Consumption: fuel oil in open-hearth steel furnaces	ECE countries	U 6-a U 7-a
	Main countries	H 3-a
iron ore: tonnage	Main countries	T 1-a
pig iron: tonnage	Main countries	T 1-a
Industrial furnaces (incl equipment) in use	OECD countries	D 9-a
Investment in new equipment financed by EEC funds	EEC countries	E 29-a
in new equipment in $m	Main countries	U 49-a
Investment programs projected by steel industry	EEC countries	E 30-a2
Labour force employed by type of furnace	EEC countries	E 29-a
No of conventional types of steel furnace in operation in use	EEC countries	E 29-a
of electric arc types in operation	EEC countries	E 29-a
of furnaces in operation by type	EEC countries	E 30-q
of furnaces in operation	EEC countries	H 3-a
of Siemens Martin built & no in operation	EEC countries	E 30-q E 29-a
of Thomas converters built & no in operation	EEC countries	E 29-a
Production capacity: Bessemer quality steel: tonnage	EEC countries	E 29-a
Siemens Martin steel: tonnage	EEC countries	E 29-a
Thomas converters: tonnage	EEC countries	E 29-a
steel in Thomas converters: tonnage	EEC countries	E 29-a

Furnishing textiles   see   FABRICS

Furnishings   see   FURNITURE
                     HOUSEHOLD TEXTILES

FURNITURE

      see also   TIMBER PRODUCTS

	Territorial coverage	Title codes
% changes in retail sales	E European countries & USSR	U 16-a
% of credit sales to total sales	W European countries	C 8-a
% sales distribution direct to customers	W European countries	C 8-a
through retailers	W European countries	C 8-a
through wholesalers direct	W European countries	C 8-a
% sales margins of retailers (reckoned on wholesale prices)	W European countries	C 8-a
of wholesalers (reckoned on factory prices)	W European countries	C 8-a
Consumption cost to private sector in $m	EEC countries	E 32-a
Demand per capita by value in £	W European countries	C 8-a
Exports by destination (incl timber products) by CST classes: tonnage & value in $	EEC countries	E 48-a
by SITC classes by value in $	Main countries	D 2-q
	OECD countries	D 3-a2
by value in £	W European countries	C 8-a
by value to EEC countries in £	W European countries	C 8-a
to EFTA countries in £	W European countries	C 8-a
to Third Markets in £	W European countries	C 8-a
(incl timber products) by NIMEXE classes by value in $	All countries	E 20-a
by SITC classes by value in $	All countries	U 50-a U 59-a
Imports & exports: kitchen furniture by value in £	W European countries	C 8-a
metal furniture by value in £	W European countries	C 8-a
office furniture by value in £	W European countries	C 8-a
shopfittings by value in £	W European countries	C 8-a
tables by value in £	W European countries	C 8-a
upholstered furniture by value in £	W European countries	C 8-a
wooden chairframes by value in £	W European countries	C 8-a
Imports by source by SITC classes by value in $	Main countries	D 2-q
tonnage & value in $	OECD countries	D 3-a2
by value in £	W European countries	C 8-a
(incl timber products) by CST classes: tonnage & value in $	EEC countries	E 21-a
by value in £	W European countries	C 8-a
Imports: chairs, bedding & parts by value in £	W European countries	C 8-a
ex EEC area by value in £	W European countries	C 8-a
ex E European countries by value in £	W European countries	C 8-a
ex EFTA countries by value in £	W European countries	C 8-a
(incl timber products) by NIMEXE classes by value in $	All countries	E 20-a
by SITC classes by value in $	All countries	U 50-a U 59-a
Labour costs in wooden furniture industry	EEC countries	E 2-a
No of hours worked per week: furniture industry	All countries	L 4-a
Private expenditure (incl domestic equipment)	AASM countries	E 41-a
Production by value by size of firms in local currency	W European countries	C 8-a
of metal furniture: tonnage	EEC countries	E 28-q E 27-a
Sales demand per 1000 population by value in $	E European countries & USSR	U 16-a
Use of plastics in furniture industry as % of total usage of plastics	European countries	U 26-a

	Territorial coverage	Title codes

FURNITURE INDUSTRY
    see also   WOOD-WORKING INDUSTRY

Capital formation in $m	Main countries	U 21-a
Earnings of employees (average)	All countries	L 4-a
Employment - index nos	All countries	L 4-a
Gross output by value in $m	Main countries	U 21-a
Labour force employed	EEC countries	E 2-a
	Main countries	U 21-a
Wages & salary costs in $	Main countries	U 21-a

GDP (GROSS DOMESTIC PRODUCT)
    see also   INDUSTRIAL INPUTS
                    NATIONAL INCOME
                    NET MATERIAL PRODUCT

And per capita at current values & by areas	EEC countries	E 32-a	E 38-a
At constant prices in local currency & % growth rates	ECE countries	U 15-a	
	Latin American countries	J 5-a	
	Main countries	R 5-a	
At current values in DM mrd	W Germany	H 3-a	
in $m	All countries	U 60-a	
	EEC countries	E 32-a	
	Main countries	U 43-a	
	OECD countries	D 30-a	
	Main African countries	U 44-a	
	Developing countries	D 25-a	
in local currency	Main countries	R 5-a	
in local currency by areas	EEC countries	E 38-a	
in total & per capita	All countries	U 43-a	
index nos	EEC countries	E 44-a	
per capita economically-active population by industrial origin	EEC countries	E 32-a	
per capita total population in $	EEC countries	E 44-a	
At factor cost by industry in $m	EEC countries	E 32-a	
in local currency & index nos	Czechoslovakia & Poland	U 34-a	
in $m	OECD countries	D 26-m	
	Developing countries	D 25-a	
projected to 1980 in $m	Main countries	D 17-a	
By administrative regions in local currency	EEC countries	E 37-a	
By industrial origin: % share & % growth rates	Singapore	U 17-a	
as % of gross domestic product	All countries	M 6-a	
at factor cost in local currency	OAS member countries	N 16-a	
in $m	All countries	U 23-a	
	S American countries	U 41-a	
By industrial origin - index nos	Country groups	U 43-a	
	World economic areas	U 60-a	
By kind of activity as % of total gross domestic product	AASM countries	E 41-a	
at factor cost in local currency	OAS member countries	N 16-a	
in local currency	AASM countries	E 41-a	
	Main African countries	U 44-a	
	Latin American countries	U 18-a	
	Main countries	U 27-a	
	All countries	U 60-a	
	OECD countries	D 30-a	
	EEC countries	E 32-a	
	S American countries	U 41-a	
	Developing countries	D 25-a	
By kind of activity: farming, industry & services	EEC countries	E 44-a	
product of administration	Developing countries	D 25-a	
agriculture	Developing countries	D 25-a	
building construction	Developing countries	D 25-a	
finance & real estate	Developing countries	D 25-a	
housing	Developing countries	D 25-a	
manufacturing	Developing countries	D 25-a	
mining & quarrying	Developing countries	D 25-a	
public utilities	Developing countries	D 25-a	
service industries	Developing countries	D 25-a	
trade & commerce	Developing countries	D 25-a	
transport industry	Developing countries	D 25-a	
By type of expenditure - index nos	Country groups	U 43-a	
	World economic areas	U 60-a	
in local currency	OAS member countries	N 16-a	
in $m	Main countries	U 27-a	
	S American countries	U 41-a	
% distribution	All countries	U 43-a	
In local currency & per capita	AASM countries	E 41-a	
In local currency	OAS member countries	N 14-a	
In $bn	Asian & Far East areas	U 32-a	
In $bn & gross product per capita - index nos	Latin American countries	J 5-a	
Of agriculture & food industries in local currency	AASM countries	E 41-a	
agriculture, forestry & fishing (at constant values)	ECE countries	U 15-a	
agriculture in $m & as % of total gross product	Main countries	A 11-a	
agriculture per capita in $	Main countries	A 11-a	

	Territorial coverage	Title codes	
GDP, continued			
Of banking, insurance & real estate in local currency	OAS member countries	N 16-a	
building construction in local currency	OAS member countries	N 16-a	
energy industries in local currency	AASM countries	E 41-a	
industry (incl mining & public utilities) in $m	ECE countries	U 15-a	
manufacturing industry in $m	ECE countries	U 15-a	
in local currency	OAS member countries	N 16-a	
mining & quarrying in local currency	OAS member countries	N 16-a	
ownership of dwellings in local currency	OAS member countries	N 16-a	
public administration & defence in local currency	OAS member countries	N 16-a	
public utility undertakings in local currency	OAS member countries	N 16-a	
raw materials industries in local currency	AASM countries	E 41-a	
service industries in $m	ECE countries	U 15-a	
transport industries & warehousing in local currency	OAS member countries	N 16-a	
wholesale & retail trade in local currency	OAS member countries	N 16-a	
Per capita (at 1968 prices) projected to 1980 in $m	Main countries	D 17-a	
at constant prices in local currency	Main countries	R 5-a	
at current prices in $m	All countries	U 60-a	
	OECD countries	D 30-a	
	Latin American countries	J 5-a	
by administrative areas	EEC countries	E 37-a	E 38-a
economically-active population at current values	EEC countries	E 26-a	E 32-a
economically-active population - index nos	EEC countries	E 26-a	
in local currency & % rate of change	ECE countries	U 15-a	
in $m	Asian & Far East areas	U 32-a	
projected to 1985	All countries	A 1	
% change (volume basis)	EEC area	E 13-a	
% growth rates	All countries	U 23-a	
% real estate of economic growth	Developing countries	M 3-a	
Per capita - index nos	World economic areas	U 60-a	
% change in gross domestic product	All countries	U 13-a	
	Developed countries	U 54-a	
	Developing countries	U 54-a	
	E European countries & USSR	U 54-a	
	W European countries, Canada & USA	U 16-a	
implicit price deflator by sector	Developed countries	D 25-a	
implicit price deflator	All countries	M 6-a	
	European countries & USA	U 16-a	
	Greece, Portugal, Spain & Turkey	U 16-a	
by type of expenditure	Main countries	D 17-a	N 7-a
major components of gross domestic product	Developed countries	D 25-a	
resources (i.e. gross product plus imports)	Main countries	U 54-a	
% contribution by agriculture, industry & services	W European countries	U 16-a	
	EEC countries	E 44-a	
agriculture	Main countries	E 3-a	
	EEC area	E 13-a	
	AASM countries	E 41-a	
kind of economic activity	OECD countries	D 1-a	
manufacturing industry	Main countries	U 43-a	
	EEC area	E 13-a	
manufacturing industry by sector	OAS member countries	N 14-a	
	Main countries	U 38-a	
	AASM countries	E 41-a	
service industries	EEC area	E 13-a	
	AASM countries	E 41-a	
type of expenditure	Main countries	U 43-a	
mechanical engineering industry projected to 1985	EEC countries	B 20-a	
% decrease in gross domestic product associated with 1% rise in unemployment	Main countries	D 17	
% growth rate of gross product: agriculture	Latin American countries	U 18-a	
agriculture, forestry & fishing	ECE countries	U 15-a	
building construction	Latin American countries	U 18-a	
commerce, finance & defence	Latin American countries	U 18-a	
industry, mining & public utility undertakings	ECE countries	U 15-a	
manufacturing industry	Latin American countries	U 18-a	
	ECE countries	U 15-a	
mining & quarrying	Latin American countries	U 18-a	
public services	Latin American countries	U 18-a	
service industries	ECE countries	U 15-a	
& % growth rate per capita	All countries	M 6-a	
	AASM countries	E 41-a	
at constant prices	Main countries	U 43-a	U 60-a
at factor cost: projected to 1985	All countries	A 1	
at factor cost	Latin American countries	U 18-a	
by administrative areas	EEC countries (excl Netherlands)	E 38-a	
by kind of economic activity	All countries	U 60-a	
	Latin American countries	J 5-a	U 18-a
by kind of expenditure	All countries	U 60-a	
in real terms (based on current values)	All countries	U 23-a	
	EEC countries	E 13-a	
planned in development programs	Small African countries	U 39	
% growth rates (over 5 yr periods)	Main countries	U 38	
per capita (at constant prices)	All countries	U 60-a	
(projected to 1985)	All countries	A 1	
projected by economic sectors	Small African countries	U 39-a	
projected to 1977 & gross product in £m	UK	B 28	
projected	Canada, European countries, Japan & USA	D 10-a2	
% growth rates	AASM countries	E 41-a	
	Developed countries	C 9-a	

	Territorial coverage	Title codes
GDP, continued		
% rate of inflation	Canada, European countries, Japan & USA	D 10-a2
% real rate of economic growth	Developing countries	M 3-a
% share of gross domestic product by regions	EEC countries	E 37-a
Capital investment as component in gross domestic product in local currency	Main countries	R 5-a
Compensation of employees as component in costs	Developing countries	D 25-a
Consumption expenditure by sector (at constant prices) in local currency	African countries	U 44-a
Contribution of agriculture in local currency	African countries	U 44-a
	Latin American countries	U 18-a
building construction in local currency	African countries	U 44-a
	Latin American countries	U 18-a
commercial activity in local currency	Latin American countries	U 18-a
community services in local currency	Latin American countries	U 18-a
domestic services in local currency	African countries	U 44-a
electricity, water & gas industries in local currency	African countries	U 44-a
financial services & banking in local currency	Latin American countries	U 18-a
industrial activity in local currency	African countries	U 44-a
in $ by sectors	S American countries	U 41-a
manufacturing industry in local currency	Latin American countries	U 18-a
mining & quarrying in local currency	African countries	U 44-a
	Latin American countries	U 18-a
ownership of dwellings in local currency	African countries	U 44-a
public administration in local currency	African countries	U 44-a
public utility undertakings in local currency	African countries	U 44-a
	Latin American countries	U 18-a
transport & communications in local currency	African countries	U 44-a
	Latin American countries	U 18-a
wholesale & retail trade in local currency	African countries	U 44-a
Cost of consumption of fixed capital in local currency	African countries	U 44-a
Cost structure: indirect taxes less subsidies in local currency	African countries	U 44-a
wages & salaries of employees in local currency	African countries	U 44-a
Expenditure on social welfare as % of gross domestic product (at purchasers' values) in $m	EEC countries	E 6-a
	Asian, Far East & Australasian countries	U 45-a
Exports of goods & services as component of gross domestic product	Developing countries	D 25-a
Historical tables from 1850 in local currency	Main European countries	Z 1-a
Implicit price deflator for exports of goods & services	Main countries	D 17-a
for flows of aid – index nos	Main countries	D 7-a
of aid	Main countries	D 7-a
of food aid	Main countries	D 7-a
of resources	Main countries	D 7-a
of technical aid	Main countries	D 7-a
Implicit price deflator	Main industrial countries	D 17-a
Implicit price deflator – index nos	Main countries	N 7-a
Imports: goods & services as component of gross domestic product	All countries	D 25-a
Incomes & capital financing by kind	Developing countries	D 25-a
Income & remittances from abroad as component of gross domestic product	Developed countries	D 25-a
Index nos	Canada, European countries, Japan & USA	U 38
Indirect taxation: receipts as component of gross domestic product	Developing countries	D 25-a
Investment (public & private) allocated for research as % of gross domestic product	EEC countries	E 36-a
Private consumption as component of gross domestic product in local currency	Main countries	R 5-a
Public consumption as component of gross domestic product in local currency	Main countries	R 5-a
Subsidies as component of gross domestic product in local currency	Developing countries	D 25-a
GNP (GROSS NATIONAL PRODUCT)		
% gross product per capita in $m	All countries	U 23-a
index nos	All countries	U 60-a
At current values & index nos (volume basis)	Main countries	E 3-a
& per capita incl % growth rates	EEC countries	E 32-a
in local currency	All countries	L 2-a
	Developing countries	D 25-a
in $m & % growth rates	EEC countries	E 26-a
in $m	Main countries	M 4-a
	OPEC member countries	C 3-a
At factor cost in $m	All countries	M 6-a
	EEC countries	E 32-a
By components of income & expenditure as % of gross national product	OECD countries	D 11-a
By industrial origin in local currency	Main countries	R 5-a
By kind of expenditure in $	S American countries	U 41-a
of receipts & of income transfers	Main countries	E 3-a
In agriculture as % of gross national product in 1970	All countries	L 3
In local currency at 1958 prices	Main countries	N 7-a
at current prices	Main countries	N 7-a R 5-a
Per capita at constant prices – index nos	OAS member countries	N 16-a
historical tables from 1899 in $	Main countries	M 4-a
index nos	EEC countries	E 26-a
in $	Developed world regions	M 4-a
	Developing world regions	M 4-a
	Main countries	M 4-a
	EEC countries	E 26-a
Per capita in $	Developing countries (exceeding 1m population)	U 23-a

GNP, continued   Territorial coverage   Title codes

   Per capita: % growth rates & gross national product at current
                                                                values in $m   All countries   M 5-a
                                                                                      Main countries   M 4-a
                by country groups & by income levels   Main countries   U 23-a
   % allocation of national resources by purpose or function   OECD countries   D 11
   % changes in expenditure on private consumption   Japan   G 1-a
                foreign balances held   USA   G 1-a2
                gross output by main sectors   E European countries & USSR   U 16-a
                        of agriculture   E European countries & USSR   U 16-a
                        of building construction industry   E European countries & USSR   U 16-a
                        of industry   E European countries & USSR   U 16-a
                gross national product per capita economically-active
                                                  population   E European countries & USSR   U 16-a
                implicit price deflator   Main countries   G 1-a
                inventories in $bn   USA   G 1-a2
                main demand components of gross national product in $bn   USA   G 1-a2
                non-residential investment in $bn   USA   G 1-a2
                private consumption in $bn   USA   G 1-a2
                public expenditure in $bn   Japan   G 1-a
      (on previous yr)   Main countries   G 1-a
   % contribution by agriculture: historical table from 1800 Main European countries   Z 1-a
                          basic metals industry   Canada, European countries, Japan & USA   U 38-a
                          chemical, oil, coal & rubber industries Main countries   U 38-a
                          clothing industry   Canada, European countries, Japan & USA   U 38-a
                          commercial & finance sectors: historical table
                                          from 1800   Main European countries   Z 1-a
                          construction industry: historical table from 1800   Main European countries   Z 1-a
                          engineering industries   Canada, European countries, Japan & USA   U 38-a
                          food, drink & tobacco industries   Canada, European countries, Japan & USA   U 38-a
                          industrial activity: historical table from 1800   Main European countries   Z 1-a
                          non-metallic mineral industries   Main countries   U 38-a
                          paper, printing & publishing industries   Main countries   U 38-a
                          textile industry   Canada, European countries, Japan & USA   U 38-a
                          transportation services: historical table from 1850   Main European countries   Z 1-a
                          wood-working & furniture manufacturing industries   Main countries   U 38-a
   % of gross national product disbursed as development grants
                                                overseas   Main countries   D 7-a
                          disbursed as net aid & transfers
                                                overseas   Main countries   D 7-a
                              as official foreign aid   Main countries   D 7-a
                              as total flow of development
                                        aid overseas   Main countries   D 7-a
   % expenditure on imports: goods & services   ECE countries   U 15-a
   % growth rates at constant prices   Main ECAFE countries   U 17
        by kind of expenditure (at constant prices)   OECD countries   D 11-a
            (compound)   Developing countries   D 25-a
        in real gross national product   Developing countries   D 25-a
        of major components of expenditure   OECD countries   D 11-a
        over last decade (average)   Main countries   E 3-a
        per capita (compound)   Developing countries   D 25-a
        per capita economically-active population (over
                                          decades)   Main countries   E 3-a
   % increase in gross national product & of fixed assets   E European countries   U 16-a
   % of expenditure on consumption & on investment   OECD countries   D 11
   % of gross national product spent on advertising   Main countries   Z 4-a
   % rate of change (compounded) at 1958 prices   Main countries   N 7-a
Capital expenditure on education as % of gross national product   All countries   U 62-a
Capital formation as % of total expenditure   ECE countries   U 15-a
Capital inflow (net) as component of gross national product   Developing countries   D 25-a
Chemical industry: gross output at factor cost in $m   European countries   U 25-a
                                                                      Japan, UK & USA   U 25-a
Development aid: flow of private & government funds as % of
  gross national product   OECD countries   D 13-a
Disposable income in local currency   Developing countries   D 25-a
Expenditure (before adjustment for terms of trade) in $m   OAS member countries   N 16-a
     by kind as % of gross national product (at current values)   ECE countries   U 15-a
     by kind   Main countries   E 3-a
     on gross fixed capital formation in $ All countries   U 23-a
                                                in local currency   OAS member countries   N 16-a
        imports of goods & services in local currency   OAS member countries   N 16-a
        inventory accumulation in local currency   OAS member countries   N 16-a
                                                in $m   All countries   U 23-a
        private consumption in local currency   OAS member countries   N 16-a
                                              in $m   All countries   U 23
        public consumption in local currency   OAS member countries   N 16-a
                                             in $m   All countries   U 23-a
Export income projected to 1980 as % change in gross national
  product   OECD countries   D 11
Goods & services: cost as % of total expenditure   ECE countries   U 15-a
Growth in building projected to 1980 as % change in gross national
                                                               product   OECD countries   D 11
       exports projected to 1980 as % change in gross national
                                                              product   OECD countries   D 11
       imports projected to 1980 as % change in gross national
                                                              product   OECD countries   D 11
Growth rate parameters & projections of gross national product   ECAFE countries   U 17
Historical tables from 1850 in local currency   Main European countries   Z 1-a

	Territorial coverage	Title codes	
GNP, continued			
Imports: costs projected to 1980 as % change in gross national product	OECD countries	D 11	
Index nos (volume basis)	EEC countries	E 26-a	
Industry: gross output at factor cost in $m	E European countries	U 25-a	
Investment projected to 1980 as % change in gross national product	OECD countries	D 11	
Invisible payments as % of gross national product	Main countries	M 9-a	
Invisible receipts as % of gross national product	Main countries	M 9-a	
Main components of national income in local currency	OAS member countries	N 16-a	
Manufacturing industry: gross output (at factor cost) in $m	E European countries	U 25-a	
National accounts: items as components of gross national product	All countries	F 5-m	F 6-q
National product per capita at factor cost	All countries	M 6-a	
Private consumption as % of total expenditure	ECE countries	U 15-a	
projected to 1980 as % change in gross national product	OECD countries	D 11	
Proportion of gross national product spent on defence	OECD countries	D 11	
on education	OECD countries	D 11	
on family allowances, old age pensions & sickness benefits	OECD countries	D 11	
on health services	OECD countries	D 11	
housing & community amenities	OECD countries	D 11	
public transport services	OECD countries	D 11	
social & welfare services	OECD countries	D 11	
unemployment benefits	OECD countries	D 11	
Public consumption expenditure as % of total expenditure	ECE countries	U 15-a	
projected to 1980 as % change in gross national product	OECD countries	D 11	
Ratio of marginal stocks to output projected to 1980	OECD countries	D 11	
Savings as component of gross national product in local currency	Developing countries	D 25-a	
Transfers (net) from abroad as component of gross national product in local currency	Developing countries	D 25-a	
GALLIUM			
Wholesale prices in $ per kg	USA	N 1-a	
GALVANISATION			
Lead consumption in galvanising process: tonnage	USA	J 6-a	T 4-a
Zinc consumption in coating of fencing & netting	USA	C 12-a	
steel plates	European countries	C 12-a	
steel sheets	European countries, Japan & USA	C 12-a	
steel strip	European countries, Japan & USA	C 12-a	
steel tubes	European countries & USA	C 12-a	
steel wire	European countries & USA	C 12-a	
tanks & containers	USA	C 12-a	
in galvanising process: tonnage	UK	J 6-a	
	European countries & Japan	C 12-a	
	Main countries	T 4-a	

Galvanised sheets   see   SHEETS, GALVANISED

Game   see   POULTRY

GARDEN TRACTORS

see also   MOTOR CULTIVATORS

No in use	All countries	A 9-a	
Production (incl mechanised cultivators) by volume	All countries	U 22-a	
GARLIC			
Area harvested in ha, & production & yield per ha	All countries	A 9-a	
GARNET			
Consumption (as abrasive) & used in glass & optical industries: tonnage	USA	N 1-a	
in wood-working furniture industries: tonnage	USA	N 1-a	
tonnage	USA	N 1-a	
Production: tonnage	Main countries	N 1-a	
Wholesale prices (abrasive grade) in $ per ton	USA	N 1-a	
World production: tonnage at mines	Main countries	N 1-a	

GAS

see also   MANUFACTURED GAS
NATURAL GAS

Consumption (all kinds) for industrial purposes	OECD countries	D 44-a	
in coke ovens & oil refineries in m³	OECD countries	D 44-a	
thermo-electric plants in m³	OECD countries	D 44-a	
Production, imports, exports, consumption & stocks of gas by kind in m³	OECD countries	D 44-a	
Production volume: natural & manufactured gas in m³	OECD countries	D 44-a	

	Territorial coverage	Title codes

GAS MAINS NETWORKS
    see also   NATURAL GAS PIPELINES

Length of transmission mains in use in km	EEC countries	E 15-a
	European countries & USA	U 3-a
Loans approved by IBRD for gas pipelines construction in $	OAS member countries	N 16-a

Gas meters   see   METERS, GAS SUPPLY

Gas oil   see   DIESEL OIL

GAS SUPPLY INDUSTRY
    see also   PUBLIC UTILITIES

Investment in buildings in local currency	EEC countries	E 40-a
in land purchase in local currency	EEC countries	E 40-a
in machinery & equipment in local currency	EEC countries	E 40-a

GAS TURBINES
    see also   POWER GENERATING EQUIPMENT
                STEAM TURBINES

Capacity installed by kind of plant in MW	OECD countries	D 45-a
in electric power stations in MW	EEC countries	E 15-a
new equipment in MW	OECD countries	D 45-a
Deliveries of gas turbines by size in MW	European countries, Japan & USA	D 45-a
Exports as % of production	European countries, Japan & USA	D 45-a
by destination by value in $m	Main countries	U 9-a
by value in $m	All countries	U 38-a
Imports by value in $m	All countries	U 38-a
New orders & orders on hand by value in $m	European countries, Japan & USA	D 45-a
No in service (& location) using liquid fuels	OECD countries	D 45-a
natural gas	OECD countries	D 45-a
virgin naphtha	OECD countries	D 45-a
Production volume in MW	W European countries, Japan & USA	D 45-a
	All countries	U 22-a
World export trade by value in $m		U 38-a

Gaseous fuels   see   FUELS, GASEOUS

Gasolene   see   MOTOR SPIRIT

GASWORKS
    see also   PUBLIC UTILITIES

Consumption of coal in manufactured gas production: tonnage	EEC countries	E 14-a
of natural gas in manufactured gas production: tonnage	EEC countries	E 14-a
of petroleum products in manufactured gas production: tonnage	EEC countries	E 14-a

Gasworks gas   see   MANUFACTURED GAS

GEAR PRODUCTION MACHINES
    see also   MACHINE TOOLS

Deliveries by industrial sector by value in $m	USA	J 2-a
Exports by volume & value in $m	USA	J 2-a
Imports by volume & value in $m	USA	J 2-a
Inter-EEC trade by value in $m & % growth rate		B 20-a
Production, trade & home sales by value in $m	EEC countries	B 20-a
Sales by type by volume & value in $m	USA	J 2-a

Geese   see   POULTRY

GEM STONES

% contribution to export earnings: pearls & precious stones	Mauritius	E 45-a
Consumption by value in $m	USA	N 1-a
World production at mines by value in $m	Main countries	N 1-a

Generating capacity   see   POWER STATIONS

Generating equipment   see   POWER GENERATING EQUIPMENT

GENERATORS
    see also   POWER GENERATING EQUIPMENT

Deliveries as steam turbine auxiliaries in MV	W European countries, Japan & USA	D 45-a
Exports by destination: steam turbine generators in MV	Japan	T 7-a
Imports by source: steam turbine generators by make	USA	T 7-a
No installed by type & size in MV	W Germany	T 7-a
Power generators installed in MW	Canada & USA	T 7-a
Production as turbine auxiliaries by type	All countries	U 22-a
Production: steam turbine generators by volume	All countries	T 7-a
World production: steam turbine generators in MW		T 7-a

	Territorial coverage	Title codes
GENERATORS, HYDRAULIC		
see also HYDRAULIC TURBINE GENERATORS		
Deliveries by size in MW	W European countries, Japan & USA	D 45-a
Exports as % of production	W European countries, Japan & USA	D 45-a
New orders & orders in hand in MW	W European countries, Japan & USA	D 45-a
Production in MW	W European countries, Japan & USA	D 45-a
GENERATORS, HYDROELECTRIC		
see also WATER WHEELS		
Exports by destination in MW	Japan	T 7-a
in MW	W European countries, Japan & USA	T 7-a
No installed & size in MW	Main countries	T 7-a
	USA & W Germany	T 7-a
Production in MW	W European countries, Japan & USA	T 7-a
GENERATORS, NUCLEAR		
No installed & size in MW	W Germany	T 7-a
GENERATORS, PUMPED STORAGE		
Consumption of electricity in kWh	All countries	C 23-a
Exports to USA by make	Japan	T 7-a
No installed & size in MW	Canada, USA & W Germany	T 7-a
domestically by size in MW	Japan	T 7-a
GENERATORS, STEAM		
No of turbine generators installed & size in MW	Main countries	T 7-a
GENERATORS, THERMAL		
see also STEAM TURBINES		
Deliveries by size in MW	W European countries, Japan & USA	D 45-a
Exports as % of production	W European countries, Japan & USA	D 45-a
New orders & orders in hand in MW	W European countries, Japan & USA	D 45-a
No installed by make in MW	W Germany	T 7-a
in MW	USA	T 7-a
Production in MW	W European countries, Japan & USA	D 45-a
Geography see HISTORY & GEOGRAPHY		
GERMANIUM		
Consumption in lbs	USA	N 1-a
Exports by destination: unwrought & refined: tonnage	Italy	C 12-a
Import prices: refined metal in £ per kg (duty-paid)	UK	C 12-m
Imports by source: unwrought & refined metal: tonnage	Italy	C 12-a
Production based on content of ore in lbs	Main countries	T 4-a
in kg	Austria, Japan, USA & Zaire	B 15-a
	Zaire	E 41-a
Wholesale prices in cents per gramme	USA	N 1-a
in $ per kg (New York dealers)	USA	C 12-m
World production (based on metal content of ore) in lbs		T 4-a
tonnage at mines	Main countries	N 1-a
GERMANIUM DI-OXIDE		
Import prices in £ per kg (duty-paid)	UK	C 12-m
Wholesale prices in $ per kg (at New York dealers)	USA	C 12-m
Gift tax see TAXATION		
GILDING METAL		
Production: ingots & billets: tonnage	UK	C 30-m
Gilt-edged stocks see GOVERNMENT BONDS		
GOVERNMENT BONDS, COMMONWEALTH		
GOVERNMENT BONDS, FOREIGN		
Gilts see PIGS		
GINGER		
see also SPICES & ESSENCES		
Exports by destination: dried ginger in cwt	India, Nigeria & Sierra Leone	B 13-a
	Main countries	B 18-q
dried ginger in cwt	All countries	B 13-a
Import prices by source of product in £ per ton on London market	UK	B 18-m
Imports by source: dried ginger in cwt	Main countries	B 18-q B 13-a
Re-exports: dried ginger in cwt	Singapore	B 13-a
Wholesale prices: ginger by kind on London market in £ per ton	UK	B 13-a
Girders, steel see HEAVY SECTIONS, STEEL		
GLASS & GLASS PRODUCTS		
Exports by destination by SITC classes: tonnage & value in $	OECD countries	D 3-a2
by value in $	Main countries	D 2-q
by CST classes: tonnage & value in $	EEC countries	E 48-a

	Territorial coverage	Title codes	
GLASS & GLASS PRODUCTS, continued			
Exports by NIMEXE classes by value in $	All countries	E 20-a	
SITC classes by value in $	All countries	U 50-a	U 59-a
Imports by NIMEXE classes by value in $	All countries	E 20-a	
SITC classes by value in $	All countries	U 50-a	U 59-a
source by CST classes: tonnage & value in $	EEC countries	E 21-a	
by SITC classes: tonnage & value in $	OECD countries	D 3-a2	
by value in $	Main countries	D 2-q	
Production: tonnage	EEC countries	E 28-q	E 27-a
drawn & blown glass: tonnage	All countries	U 22-a	
laminated glass in m²	All countries	U 22-a	
plate glass in m²	European countries	U 5-a	
sheet glass in m²	European countries	U 5-a	
	S American countries	U 40-a	
Wholesale prices: window glass to building industry – index nos	OAS member countries	N 14-a	
Wholesale prices – index nos	European countries & USA	U 5-a	

Glass bottles   see   BOTTLES & CONTAINERS, GLASS

GLASS INDUSTRY

see also   BUILDING MATERIALS INDUSTRY

	Territorial coverage	Title codes	
Consumption of electricity in kWh (incl ceramics industry)	EEC countries	E 15-a	
	OECD countries	D 8-a	
of petroleum products by kind: tonnage	OECD countries	D 31-a	
platinum & palladium in oz	USA	J 6-a	
silver in production of mirrors in troy oz	USA	T 4-a	
Costs of production: wages costs in $	Main countries	U 21-a	
for salaried staff per mth	EEC countries	E 11-a	
Investment: capital formation in $m	Main countries	U 21-a	
in buildings in local currency	EEC countries	E 40-a	
in land purchase in local currency	EEC countries	E 40-a	
in machinery in local currency	EEC countries	E 40-a	
Labour costs as % of total costs	EEC countries	E 8-a	
by status of employees in local currency	EEC countries	E 8-a	
per hr (all employees)	EEC countries	E 2-a	E 11-a
per hr: wage earners	EEC countries	E 11-a	
Labour force employed: salaried staff	EEC countries	E 11-a	
(total)	EEC countries	E 8-a	
	Main countries	U 21-a	
wage earners	EEC countries	E 11-a	
No of hrs worked per wk	Main countries	R 3-m	
per wk by region & by sex	EEC countries	E 25-a	
per yr: salaried staff	EEC countries	E 11-a	
wage earners	EEC countries	E 11-a	
all employees	EEC countries	E 8-a	
Value of output of glass industry in $m	Main countries	U 21-a	
Wage rates per hr by grade of employee in A Sch	Austria	R 4-a	
by sex in local currency	EEC countries	E 25-a2	
	Main countries	R 3-m	

Glass sheets   see   GLASS & GLASS PRODUCTS

Glass windscreens   see   REPLACEMENT PARTS

GLASS-WORKING MACHINERY

	Territorial coverage	Title codes
Exports by destination by value in $m	Main countries	U 9-a
by value in $m	All countries	U 38-a
Imports by value in $m	OECD countries	D 9-a
	All countries	U 38-a
World export trade by value in $m		U 38-a

Glassine   see   PAPER, GREASE-PROOF

GLOVES

see also   FANCY GOODS

	Territorial coverage	Title codes
Consumption of sheep, lamb & goatskins in production of gloves: tonnage	Main European countries	B 9-a
Wholesale sales (by manufacturers) by value in £m	UK	B 22-a

GLUCOSE

	Territorial coverage	Title codes
Consumption & consumption per capita per day	OECD countries	D 14-a
(industrial): maize in production of glucose & starch: tonnage	UK	C 27-a
wheat in production of glucose & starch: tonnage	UK	C 27-a
Production: tonnage & consumption in production of food products	OECD countries	D 14-a

Glues   see   GUMS, GLUES & SOLUTIONS

Glutenfeed   see   OILCAKE & MEAL

Glycerine   see   CHEMICAL PRODUCTS

Glycerine, synthetic   see   CHEMICALS, ORGANIC

	Territorial coverage	Title codes	
GOAT MEAT			
Production: tonnage & consumption per capita per yr in kg	Greece & Spain	D 14-a	
Production: tonnage	OAS member countries	N 14-a	
Wholesale prices in local currency	OAS member countries	N 17-a	
Goat, sheep & buffalo milk see MILK			
GOATS			
Nos slaughtered	All countries	A 9-a	
Population: no of head over & under 1 yr of age	EEC countries	E 1-a	
	AASM countries	E 41-a	
no of head	African countries	U 44-a	
	All countries	A 9-a	
	OAS member countries	N 13-a	
	OECD countries	D 1-a	
World total: no of head	Main countries	R 5-a	
GOATS, ANGORA			
see also MOHAIR			
Population in million head	Lesotho, S Africa, Turkey & USA	B 10-a	K 6-a
GOATSKINS			
see also LEATHER, SHEEP & GOATSKIN			
% consumption (incl kidskins) for footwear linings	USA	A 18-a	
for footwear uppers	USA	A 18-a	
% contribution to export earnings	Ethiopia & Somali Rep	E 45-a	
Consumption for production of leather products: tonnage	Spain, USA & W Germany	B 9-a	
tonnage (dry wt)	OECD countries	D 18-a	
Exports by destination: tonnage	OECD countries	D 18-a	
(incl kidskins): tonnage (dry wt)	Main countries	A 18-a	B 9-m
tonnage & value in $m	Ethiopia	E 45-a	
	World regions	A 5-a	
	OECD countries in Europe	D 18-a	
Imports by source: tonnage & value in $	OECD countries	D 18-a	
ex non-OECD countries: tonnage (dry wt)	OECD countries	D 18 a	
(incl kidskins): tonnage (dry wt)	Main countries	A 18-a	B 9-m
Intra-European trade: tonnage	European economic areas	D 18-a	
Production for manufacture of fancy goods & clothing	Main countries	B 9-a	
gloves	Main countries	B 9-a	
shoe uppers & linings	France	B 9-a	
tonnage (dry wt)	OECD countries	D 18-a	
tonnage of hides (untanned)	OAS member countries	N 14-a	
of skins by volume as % of goat population	Main countries	A 18-a	
volume	World regions	A 5-a	
Wholesale prices: raw skins in Rs per 100 pieces	India	U 32-m	
World production by volume	All countries	A 18-a	
GOLD			
see also BULLION			
Buying price in Lire per gramme at Milan Gold Market	Italy	C 12-m	
in $ per troy oz (from main dealers)	USA	C 12-m	
Consumption (industrial) in troy oz	USA	N 1-a	
Exports (based on metal content of ore) in troy oz	All countries	B 15-a	
by destination: refined metal in troy oz	Main countries	T 4-a	
Imports (based on metal content of ore) in troy oz	All countries	B 15-a	
by source: refined metal in troy oz	Main countries	T 4-a	
Production (based on metal content of ore) in kg	All countries	U 43-a	
	Latin American countries	U 40-a	
in troy oz	USA	J 6-a	
	All countries	B 15-a	
tonnage	All countries	U 22-a	
	Latin American countries	J 5-a	
by large mining cos in troy oz	Main countries	J 6-a	
refined metal in kg	AASM countries	E 41-a	
	All countries (excl USSR)	R 5-a	T 4-a
	OAS member countries	N 14-a	
by regions in troy oz	USA	J 6-a	
Selling price of gold in $ per troy oz: "initial" quotation	UK	C 12-m	
in $ per troy oz	All countries	F 5-m	F 6-q
	USA	N 1-a	
by US Treasury in $ per troy oz	USA	T 4-m	
Stocks held by industry, dealers & refiners in million troy oz	USA	N 1-a	
Wholesale prices: industrial gold bars in pence per troy oz	UK	R 2-m	
World price (based on London market) in £ per troy oz	UK	T 4-m	
World production (based on metal content of ore mined) in kg		T 4-a	
in troy oz		N 4-a	
	All countries	J 6-a	
refined metal: tonnage		C 12-a	C 30-a
GOLD HOLDINGS			
see also FOREIGN EXCHANGE			
As component in balance of payments	All countries	F 1-a	
Foreign exchange assets incl gold at end-period in $m	Far East countries	U 32-q	

	Territorial coverage	Title codes	
GOLD HOLDINGS, continued			
Central bank reserves in $m	Main countries	R 5-a	U 43-a
	OECD countries	D 26-m	
	OAS member countries	N 16-a	
Changes in central bank reserves in $m	OECD countries	D 10-a	
Federal bank reserves in $bn	USA	U 16-a	
Of US Treasury in $bn	USA	N 1-a	
GOLD ORE			
Content of metallic gold in grammes per ton	Italy	C 12-a	
Exports (incl bullion & coin) by value in $	USA	J 6-a	
Imports (incl bullion & coin) by value in $	USA	J 6-a	
Production: tonnage (at mines)	Italy	C 12-a	
World production (at mines) in troy oz		N 1-a	
World reserves in million troy oz (estimated)	Main countries	N 1-a	

Gold reserves   see   GOLD HOLDINGS

Goods   see   CONSUMER GOODS
                MANUFACTURED GOODS
                PRODUCER GOODS

Goods traffic   see   AIR FREIGHT
                        RAIL FREIGHT
                        ROAD TRANSPORT
                        SEABORNE FREIGHT

Goods wagons, rail   see   ROLLING STOCK

Goods, manufactured   see   MANUFACTURED GOODS
                                  PRODUCER GOODS

Gorgonzola & Gouda   see   CHEESE BY VARIETY

GOVERNMENT ASSISTANCE

    see also   ADVISORY SERVICES, OFFICIAL
                        SUBSIDIES

	Territorial coverage	Title codes
Advisory services: costs in agriculture in $	ECE countries	U 34-a
Cost of farm infra-structure improvements in $	ECE countries	U 34-a
Fishing industry: aid to improve equipment in $	OECD countries	D 43-a
aid for trawler building in $	OECD countries	D 43-a
recruiting premiums in FrB	Belgium	D 43-a
sales promotion purposes in FrB	Belgium	D 43-a
Grants for marketing improvements of farm products in $	ECE countries	U 34-a
research education in agricultural methods in $	ECE countries	U 34-a
social allowances for farm community in $	ECE countries	U 34-a

Government Bond yields   see   INTEREST RATES

GOVERNMENT BONDS

    see also   MUNICIPAL BONDS
                      PRIVATE BONDS
                      TREASURY BILLS

	Territorial coverage	Title codes	
% interest rates & yield per annum	Main countries	M 7	
% yield (current) per annum or at maturity	Main countries	U 43-a	
by kind of securities per annum	OECD countries	D 12-a	
on fixed-interest securities per annum	EEC countries	E 26-m	
on long-term bonds per annum	Main countries	U 27-m	
	OECD countries	D 26-q	
on short & long-term bonds per annum	All countries	F 5-m	F 6-q
Borrowings (by bond issue) to finance World Bank operations in local currency	Worldwide	M 3-a	
Income from bonds as component of payment balances	All countries	F 1-a	
Market valuations: quoted treasury bonds	OAS member countries	N 16-a	
Nominal & market valuations of bonds in £m	UK	F 8-q	
Transactions: purchases of foreign securities in $m	OAS member countries	N 16-a	
US securities in $m	OAS member countries	N 16-a	

GOVERNMENT BONDS, COMMONWEALTH

	Territorial coverage	Title codes
Market valuation in £m	UK	F 8-q

GOVERNMENT BONDS, FOREIGN

	Territorial coverage	Title codes
% yield per annum on new issues	European countries & USA	M 3-q
Nominal & market valuation in £m	UK	F 8-q

GOVERNMENT BORROWING

    see also   GOVERNMENT BONDS
                    PUBLIC DEBT
                    TREASURY BILLS

	Territorial coverage	Title codes	
External claims on central banks in $m	All countries	F 5-m	F 6-q
Loans by kind (short & long-term) in $m	All countries	F 5-m	F 6-q
from counterpart funds in $m	All countries	F 5-m	F 6-q
Overseas debts in foreign currencies in $m	All countries	F 5-m	F 6-q

Government debt   see   PUBLIC DEBT

GOVERNMENT EXPENDITURE
    see also   PUBLIC FINANCE

	Territorial coverage	Title codes	
As % of gross domestic product in $m	ECAFE countries	U 17	
	EEC area	E 13-a	
	OECD countries	D 11-a	
of gross national product at market prices	EEC countries	E 13-a	
of research appropriations in $m	All countries	U 62-a	
As component of gross domestic product in local currency	Main countries	R 5-a	
At constant prices in local currency	ECE countries	U 15-a	
	OPEC member countries	C 3-a	
By project as % of gross national product	EEC countries	E 39-a	
per capita in $	EEC countries	E 39-a	
By purpose in $m	Asian, Far East & Australasian countries	U 45-a	
By type & purpose in $m	Main countries	U 43-a	
as % of total expenditure	All countries	M 6-a	
of disbursement in $m	OECD countries	D 30-a	
in local currency	Caribbean countries & W Indies	T 6-a	
Historical tables from 1750 in local currency	Main European countries	Z 1-a	
In local currency	Main countries	R 5-a	
	OECD countries	R 5-a	
In $m	Latin American countries	U 18-a	
On agriculture as % of total capital formation	ECE countries	U 34-a	
On education as % of gross national product	Main ECAFE countries	U 17-a	
as % of total expenditure	ECAFE countries	U 17-a	
by grade of school as % of total expenditure	ECAFE countries	U 17-a	
per capita in $	ECAFE area	U 17-a	
Per pupil by kind of school in $	All countries	U 62-a	
% change in public investment	Japan	G 1-a	
	Main European countries	U 16-a	
% growth rates of specific components of public expenditure	OECD countries	D 11-a	
% of public expenditure by sector or purpose	Main countries	R 5-a	
on agriculture	Main countries	R 5-a	
debt servicing & interest payments on loans	Main countries	R 5-a	
defence commitments	Main countries	R 5-a	
education services	Main countries	R 5-a	
health & defence commitments	OECD countries	D 11	
social & welfare services	Main countries	R 5-a	
transportation services	Main countries	R 5-a	
% rate of increase (on previous yr)	EEC countries	E 13-a	
% share from central government resources	All countries	M 6-a	
Agricultural subsidies in local currency	OAS member countries	N 16-a	
Allocation of resources by use in $m	OECD countries	D 11	
Amortisation payments in $m	Latin American countries	U 18-a	
Applied research & development expenditure in $m	All countries	U 62-a	
Bilateral research costs as % of total expenditure	EEC countries	E 39-a	
in $	EEC countries	E 39-a	
Budget accounts (current) in Fr CFA mrd	AASM countries	E 41-a	
Budgeted salary costs of Civil Service	OAS member countries	N 20-a	
Capital expenditure by purpose in local currency	African countries	U 44-a	
grants for agricultural improvements	ECE countries	U 34-a	
in local currency	OAS member countries	N 16-a	
in $m	Main Latin American countries	U 18-a	
Components of public expenditure as % of gross domestic product	OECD countries	D 11-a	
Cost of family allowances in $m	Main Latin American countries	U 18-a	
imported goods & services in local currency	OAS member countries	N 16-a	
Debt servicing costs in local currency	African countries	U 44-a	
in $m	Main Latin American countries	U 18-a	
Defence budgets in local currency	OAS member countries	N 16-a	
Deficits & surpluses on revenue in $m	All countries	F 5-m	F 6-q
European Development Fund aid by purpose in UA	AASM countries	E 41-a	
for capital projects in UA	AASM countries	E 41-a	
debt servicing in UA	AASM countries	E 41-a	
diversification of economic effort in UA	AASM countries	E 41-a	
export promotion purposes in UA	AASM countries	E 41-a	
price supports for commodities in UA	AASM countries	E 41-a	
special infrastructure projects in UA	AASM countries	E 41-a	
technical assistance in UA	AASM countries	E 41-a	
Education: actual expenditure (& budget) in local currency	OAS member countries	N 19-a	
by kind of outlay in $m	All countries	U 62-a	
costs in local currency	OAS member countries	N 16-a	
in $m	Latin American countries	J 5-a	
per pupil in $	All countries	U 62-a	
Fixed capital consumption in local currency	OAS member countries	N 16-a	
Fixed capital formation in local currency	African countries	U 44-a	
Fundamental research & development costs in $m	All countries	U 62-a	
General administration costs in local currency	OAS member countries	N 16-a	
Goods (imported) & cost of services in local currency	African countries	U 44-a	
Health services costs in local currency	Main countries	W 2-a	
costs per capita in local currency	Main countries	W 1-a	W 2-a
Interest payments on public debt in local currency	OAS member countries	N 16-a	
in $m	Latin American countries	U 18-a	
national debt in local currency	African countries	U 44-a	

	Territorial coverage	Title codes
GOVERNMENT EXPENDITURE, continued		
Loan repayments (domestic) in local currency	African countries	U 44-a
(overseas) in local currency	African countries	U 44-a
Medical pollution & noise research expenditure in $m	EEC countries	E 36-a
Multilateral research: costs as % of total expenditure	EEC countries	E 39-a
cost of projects in $	EEC countries	E 36-a E 39-a
New road construction expenditure in local currency	Main countries	S 24-a
Nuclear research: costs for civil purposes in $m	EEC countries	E 36-a
Oceanographic & meteorological research in $m	EEC countries	E 36-a
Pay & allowances of armed forces in $m	EEC countries	E 32-a
Price guarantees: costs for cereals by kind in £m	UK	P 5-a
livestock by kind in £m	UK	P 5-a
milk in £m	UK	P 5-a
Projects financed by public funds: analysis (in detail)	EEC countries	E 39-a
Public health costs in local currency	OAS member countries	N 16-a
in $m	Latin American countries	J 5-a
Public investment as % of gross national product	OECD countries	D 11
Public investment expenditure in $m	Latin American countries	U 18-a
Public works: expenditure in local currency	OAS member countries	N 16-a
Purchase of imported goods & services in $m	Main Latin American countries	U 18-a
Research & development expenditure by objectives in $m	EEC countries	E 39-a
Research & development: civil grants in $m	EEC countries	E 36-a
Research expenditure as % of gross national product	EEC countries	E 39-a
as % of public expenditure	EEC countries	E 39-a
civil projects in $	EEC countries	E 39-a
per capita in $	EEC countries	E 39-a
Research funds allocated by objective in $m	EEC countries	E 36-a
Research grants & credits given to firms in $m	EEC countries	E 36-a
Research (industrial) for social purposes in $	EEC countries	E 36-a
Research expenditure on agricultural productivity & technology in $m	EEC countries	E 39-a
atmospheric pollution in $	EEC countries	E 39-a
automation techniques in $	EEC countries	E 39-a
computer science & techniques in $	EEC countries	E 39-a
environmental problems in $	EEC countries	E 36-a E 39-a
exploration of space & satellite launching systems in $	EEC countries	E 36-a E 39-a
health promotion projects in $	EEC countries	E 39-a
industrial productivity problems in $	EEC countries	E 39-a
military & defence projects in $	EEC countries	E 36-a
nuclear power development in $	EEC countries	E 39-a
promotion of scientific knowledge in $	EEC countries	E 39-a
social science projects in $m	EEC countries	E 39-a
per capita in $	EEC countries	E 39-a
Research projects: cost analysis in $	EEC countries	E 39-a
Road building & maintenance: expenditure in local currency	All countries	S 13-a
Road maintenance & improvements: expenditure in local currency	Main countries	S 24-a
Servicing costs of loans granted for road improvements in local currency	Main countries	S 24-a
Social security: costs of benefits in $	All countries	L 2-a
	EEC countries	E 32-a
Social services: costs in local currency	OAS member countries	N 16-a
Subsidy payments in local currency	OAS member countries	N 16-a
Transfer payments from Exchequer to local authorities in $	EEC countries	E 32-a
private sector in $	Latin American countries	U 18-a
	OAS member countries	N 16-a
provincial authorities in $	OAS member countries	N 16-a
public sector in $	Latin American countries	U 18-a
Treasury disbursements in local currency	EEC countries	E 26-m
Wages & salaries: Civil Service in local currency	African countries	U 44-a
in $m	Latin American countries	U 18-a

Government income   see   REVENUE

Government investment   see   GOVERNMENT EXPENDITURE

Government price supports   see   PRICE SUPPORTS

GOVERNMENT SAVINGS		
Savings as % of current government revenue	All countries	M 6-a
disposable income	All countries	U 60-a
gross national product	ECAFE countries	U 17
as financing media in capital formation in $m	EEC countries	E 32-a
(incl corporative) as % of total savings	Latin American countries	J 5-a
central government & local authorities in $m	OECD countries	D 12-a
excess of government income over expenditure in local currency	AASM countries	E 41-a

Government securities   see   GOVERNMENT BONDS

Government stockpiles   see   STOCKPILES, GOVERNMENT

Government workers   see   CIVIL SERVICE

GRADERS & LEVELLERS		
see also BULLDOZERS		
Production by volume	All countries	U 22-a
	Canada, European countries, Japan & USA	U 38-a

	Territorial coverage	Title codes
GRADUATES		
see also DIPLOMAS & CERTIFICATES		
No by field of study at universities	All countries	U 62-a
of degrees gained by class (first or higher degrees)	All countries	U 62-a
post-graduate by field of study	All countries	U 62-a
of students graduating from medical schools	Latin American countries	J 5-a
from universities by sex & by field of study	OAS member countries	N 19-a
GRADUATES BY SEX		
No of degrees gained in agricultural subjects	All countries	U 62-a
education	All countries	U 62-a
engineering	All countries	U 62-a
fine arts	All countries	U 62-a
humanities	All countries	U 62-a
jurisprudence	All countries	U 62-a
medical science	All countries	U 62-a
natural sciences	All countries	U 62-a
social sciences	All countries	U 62-a
GRAIN		
Supply by kind from production as % of requirements	EEC countries	E 44-a
Tramp shipping freight rates - index nos	Worldwide	U 37-m
World market prices - index nos		U 30-a
Grain crops see BREAD GRAINS		
CEREALS		
Grain milling industry see FLOUR MILLING INDUSTRY		
GRAMOPHONE RECORDS		
Excise duties: rates charged	EEC countries	E 31-a
Production volume	All countries	U 22-a
Retail prices (comparative) in $ per disc	EEC countries	Z 3-a
Gramophones see SOUND REPRODUCERS		
Grana see CHEESE BY VARIETY		
GRANITE		
Production: tonnage of building stone	All countries	U 22-a
Grants & loans see DEVELOPMENT AID		
Grapefruit see CITRUS FRUITS		
Grapefruit juice see FRUIT JUICES, CITRUS		
GRAPES		
Area planned for growing table grapes by 1985 in ha	E European countries	U 20-a
under grape vines in ha	OAS member countries	N 13-a
in acres	All countries	B 5-a
Export prices in drachma	Greece	A 9-a
Exports by value in $m	W European countries	U 33-a
table grapes: unit value in $ per ton	W European countries	U 20-a
Imports by value in $m	W European countries	U 33-a
table grapes: unit value in $ per ton	W European countries	U 20-a
Production: tonnage & value in dinars	Yugoslavia	D 37-a
for table or for wine-making: tonnage	All countries	A 9-a B 5-a
	Czechoslovakia	U 34-a
grapes other than for wine-making: tonnage	European countries	U 20-a
	World regions	A 5-a
Production, supply, consumption & trade: tonnage	EEC countries	B 1-a
tonnage	OAS member countries	N 13-a
GRAPHITE		
see also CARBON BLACK		
Consumption: tonnage (estimated)	USA	N 1-a
Government stockpile by kinds of natural graphite: tonnage	USA	N 1-a
Imports & exports by source & destination: tonnage	Main countries	B 15-a
Production tonnage: natural black lead	All countries	B 15-a U 22-a
	Main countries	N 1-a
	Madagascar	E 41-a
World production: natural black lead: tonnage	World (excl USA)	N 4-a
	Main countries	N 1-a

Grass see HAY

Grass, area under see LAND UTILISATION

Gravel & crushed stone see BUILDING MATERIALS

Grease-proof paper see PAPER, GREASE-PROOF

Green fodder crops see FODDER CROPS, GREEN

Territorial coverage | Title codes

Green peppers see VEGETABLES, GREEN

Green Plan for Agriculture (Italy) see DEVELOPMENT PLANS

Green vegetables see VEGETABLES, GREEN

GRINDING MACHINES
    see also MACHINE TOOLS

	Territorial coverage	Title codes
Consumption by supply areas by value in $m	EEC countries	B 31-a
Deliveries by industrial sector by value in $m	USA	J 2-a
(domestic) by value in $m	EEC countries	B 31-a
Exports as % of production (value basis)	EEC countries	B 31-a
by volume & value in $m	USA	J 2-a
Imports as % of consumption (value basis)	EEC countries	B 31-a
by volume & value in $m	USA	J 2-a
Inter-EEC trade by value in $m & % growth rates		B 20-a
Production by value in $m	EEC countries	B 31-a
Production, imports, exports & home sales by value in $m	EEC countries	B 20-a
Sales by type of machine by volume & value in $m	USA	J 2-a

Grinding mills see CEMENT & PLASTER INDUSTRY
                      PLANT CAPACITY

Grindings see COCOA BEANS
               COFFEE BEANS

Gross domestic investment see INVESTMENT

Gross domestic product see GDP (page 236)

Gross fixed capital formation see CAPITAL FORMATION

Gross national product & gross output see GNP (page 238)

GROSS REPRODUCTION RATES

	Territorial coverage	Title codes
Reproduction rates projected to 1990	E European countries	N 6
(current)	Asian, Far East & Australasian countries	U 45-a

Ground rock see FERTILISERS, MIXED

GROUNDNUT CAKE

	Territorial coverage	Title codes	
Export prices in local currency	Brazil & Netherlands	A 9-a	
Exports: tonnage & value in $m	Main countries	B 2-a	
Import prices in £ per ton	UK	R 2-m	A 9-a
Imports (as animal feeding stuffs): tonnage	UK	P 5-a	
Prices paid by farmers (as animal feeding stuffs) in $ per ton	W European countries	U 30-a	
Production: tonnage	France & W Germany	N 10-a	
Wholesale prices (ex factory) in Frs per kg	France	R 2-m	A 9-a
(ex Nigeria) in £ per ton	UK	B 2-a	
World market prices in $ per 100 kg		E 34-m	
(based ex Nigeria) in £ per ton		E 41-a	

GROUNDNUT OIL

	Territorial coverage	Title codes	
% change in producer prices (over previous yr)	Belgium	E 34-m	
in wholesale prices (over previous yr)	EEC countries	E 34-m	
% contribution to export earnings	Fiji, Gambia, Mali & Niger	E 45-a	
Consumption in production of cooking fats: tonnage	UK & USA	B 19-a	
of margarine: tonnage	Main countries	B 19-a	
	Portugal & UK	A 4-a	
tonnage	OAS member countries	N 17-a	
Export prices - index nos (weighted average)	Worldwide	U 29-q	
in local currency	Netherlands & UK	A 9-a	
Exports by destination: tonnage	Argentina, Gambia, Nigeria & Senegal	B 19-a	
	Main countries	B 18-a	
tonnage & value in $m	Mali	E 45-a	
	Main countries	B 2-a	
tonnage	Main countries	B 18-q	B 19-a
		P 1-a	
(total) & to EEC area: tonnage & value in UA	AASM countries	E 41-a	
Import prices: crude groundnut oil in £ per ton	UK	P 1-a	
ex Nigeria in £ per ton	UK	P 1-m	
ex Nigeria & Gambia in £ per ton	UK	R 2-m	
ex W Africa in £ per ton	UK	B 19-m	
Import prices in local currency	W European countries	A 9-a	
Imports by source: tonnage (shelled groundnut equiv)	UK	B 19-a	
tonnage (of oil)	UK	B 19-a	
tonnage	Main countries	B 19-a	P 1-a
Producer prices ex factory in FrB per 100 litres	Belgium	E 34-m	
Production: crude & refined groundnut oil: tonnage	All countries	U 22-a	
for ensuing yr: tonnage (estim)	World regions & Main countries	P 1-a	
tonnage	AASM countries	E 41-a	
	Main countries	B 19-a	
	W Germany	N 10-a	
	OAS member countries	N 17-a	
Retail prices in local currency per ton	UK	B 2-a	
Wholesale prices (ex Nigeria) in £ per ton	EEC countries	E 34-m	
in local currency per litre			

	Territorial coverage	Title codes	
GROUNDNUT OIL, continued			
Wholesale prices: raw groundnut oil (ex tanks) in cents per lb	USA	R 2-m	
in Rs per quintal	India	U 32-m	
in local currency	France, India & USA	A 9-a	
	European countries	U 27-m	
World & Commonwealth production: tonnage		B 19-a	
World market prices per 100 kg	W European ports	E 34-m	
World production: tonnage for ensuing yrs (estim)		A 1	
tonnage		A 5-a	N 10-a
GROUNDNUTS			
% contribution to export earnings	Gambia, Malawi, Mali, Nigeria & Sudan	E 45-a	
Area harvested in ha, production tonnage & yield per ha	All countries	A 9-a	
under crop in acres	Main countries	B 18-a	B 19-a
in ha	OAS member countries	N 13-a	
Consumption (as seed): tonnage	India, Nigeria & USA	B 19-a	
(for edible use): tonnage	India, Nigeria & USA	B 19-a	
(for oil crushing): tonnage	India, Nigeria & USA	B 19-a	
tonnage & per capita in kg per day	OECD countries	D 14-a	
Crop tonnage & estimated world total tonnage	All countries	P 1-a	
Export prices - index nos (weighted average)	Worldwide	U 29-q	
Export prices in $ per ton	Brazil, Malawi, Sudan & Zambia	A 9-a	
Exports as % of total exports (value basis)	Main countries	B 19-a	
by destination: tonnage	Gambia, Nigeria, Senegal & Sudan	B 19-a	
	Main countries	B 18-a	
(incl groundnut oil) by value in £m	Gambia & Nigeria	B 19-a	
in Fr CFA	Nigeria & Senegal	B 19-a	
tonnage	Main countries	B 18-q	
	Thailand	U 32-m	
tonnage & value in $m	Main countries	B 2-a	
	African, Caribbean countries & Pacific Is	E 45-a	
tonnage (unshelled equiv)	Main countries	B 19-a	
total & to EEC area: tonnage & value in UA	AASM countries	E 41-a	
Harvest estimates for ensuing crop yr: tonnage	World regions	P 1-a	
Import prices (ex Nigeria) in £ per ton	UK	B 19-m	
in local currency per ton	W European ports	P 1-m	A 9-a
(shelled) ex Nigeria in £ per ton	UK	P 1-a	
Imports by source: tonnage	EEC countries	P 5-a	
for production of animal feeding stuffs: tonnage	UK	P 5-a	
in vegetable oil equivalent tonnage	UK	P 1-a	
	EEC countries	P 5-a	
tonnage (shelled equiv)	Main countries	B 19-a	
New crop: tonnage	India, Nigeria & USA	B 19-a	
Producer prices in local currency per ton	OECD countries	D 1-a	
in $ per ton	All countries	A 9-a	
Production: tonnage (incl world total)	Main countries	B 2-a	
Production, stocks & industrial usage for food processing: tonnage	OECD countries	D 14-a	
tonnage	AASM countries	E 41-a	
	All countries	B 18-a	B 19-a
		P 1-a	U 43-a
	Asian & Far East countries	U 32-a	
	Latin American countries	U 40-a	
	OAS member countries	N 13-a	
Stocks (initial & end-yr): tonnage	Nigeria & USA	B 19-a	
Wholesale prices (ex Nigeria) in £ per ton	UK	B 2-a	
in local currency per ton	OAS member countries	N 17-a	
	India & Indonesia	A 9-a	
in $ per ton	USA	U 27-m	
Yield in kg per ha	OAS member countries	N 13-a	
GROUNDNUTS, SHELLED			
Import prices ex Ghana & Nigeria in £ per ton	UK	R 2-m	
Imports by source: tonnage	EEC countries	B 19-a	
in oil equivalent tonnage	UK	P 1-a	
Wholesale prices in Rs per quintal	India	U 32-m	
World market prices in $ per 100 kg	W European ports	E 34-m	
(based ex Nigeria) in £ per ton		E 41-a	

Gruyère see CHEESE BY VARIETY

Guano see NATURAL NITRATES
NITRATE
PHOSPHATIC GUANO

Guaranteed prices see INTERVENTION PRICES
PRICE SUPPORTS

Guava see TROPICAL FRUITS

Guernseys see CATTLE BY BREED

Guide prices see INTERVENTION PRICES

Guillotine shears see MACHINE TOOLS

Guinea fowls see POULTRY

	Territorial coverage	Title codes	
GUM ARABIC			
Production: tonnage	Mauritania	E 41-a	
GUMS, GLUES & SOLUTIONS			
see also NATURAL GUMS			
Exports by destination: glues by value in $	Main countries	U 2-a	
GUMS, GLUES & SOLUTIONS, RUBBER			
Production: tonnage	EEC countries	E 28-q	E 27-a
GUNMETAL SCRAP			
Wholesale prices in £ per ton	UK	T 4-w	
Gypsum see BUILDING MATERIALS			
Hackney cabs see TAXI CABS			
HAFNIUM			
Consumption of crystal bar: tonnage	USA	N 1-a	
Production: tonnage of crystal bar	USA	N 1-a	
Wholesale prices: crystal bar in $ per lb	USA	N 1-a	
Halogen salts see CHEMICALS, INORGANIC			
Halogenated acids see ACIDS, ORGANIC			
HAM			
see also BACON			
Export prices in $ per ton	Poland	A 9-a	
Exports by destination: prepared or cooked ham: tonnage	EEC countries	E 47-m	
Imports by source: prepared or cooked ham: tonnage	EEC countries	E 47-m	
Inter-EEC shipments: prepared or cooked ham: tonnage	EEC countries	E 47-m	
Production: tonnage (incl gammon)	UK	B 12-a	
Retail prices by kind in local currency	OAS member countries	N 17-a	
Hand drills see POWER TOOLS			
HAND KNITTING			
Consumption: domestic knitting wool	Main countries	K 6-a	
Demand: domestic yarn projected to 1977 in lbs million	UK	B 29	
HAND TOOLS			
Exports of tools, cutting blades & sintered tips by value in $	OECD countries	D 9-a	
Hard coal see COAL			
HARD COAL BRIQUETTES			
see also PEAT BRIQUETTES			
Availability: domestic brown coal briquettes: tonnage	European countries	U 31-q	
Changes in stocks at producers' plants: tonnage	EEC countries	E 16-q	E 15-a
Consumption (industrial): tonnage	Main countries	N 2-a	
	OECD countries	D 44-a	
by households: tonnage	EEC countries	E 16-q	E 15-a
	Main countries	N 2-a	
	Turkey	U 10-a	
industry & transport services: tonnage	EEC countries	E 16-q	E 15-a
steel industry: tonnage	EEC countries	E 30-a	
transport industry: tonnage	Turkey	U 10-a	
of coal in production of briquettes: tonnage	EEC countries	E 14-a	
of lignite in production of briquettes: tonnage	OECD countries	D 44-a	
	EEC countries	E 14-a	
tonnage	European countries, USA & USSR	U 4-a	
Deliveries to EEC & non-EEC areas: tonnage	EEC countries	E 16-q	E 15-a
Exports by destination: tonnage	EEC countries	E 5-q	
	Czechoslovakia & E Germany	U 10-a	
tonnage	European countries	U 31-q	
Imports by source: tonnage	EEC countries	E 5-q	
tonnage	EEC countries	E 16-q	E 15-a
	European countries	U 31-q	
Production potential by region: tonnage	EEC countries	E 46-a	
Production, imports & exports: tonnage	OECD countries	D 44-a	
Production: lignite briquettes: tonnage	EEC countries	E 16-q	E 15-a
solid fuels: tonnage	All countries	U 22-a	
	EEC countries	E 28-q	E 27-a
tonnage	European countries, USA & USSR	U 4-a	
	Main countries	E 3-a	N 2-a
		N 5-a	
Rate & amount of levies payable per ton	EEC countries	E 15-a	
Supply ex EEC area, production & imports: tonnage	EEC countries	E 16-q	E 15-a
World production of fuel briquettes: tonnage		N 4-a	

	Territorial coverage	Title codes

HARD FIBRES
    see also   ABACA
                  HEMP

Area under sisal, abaca & henequen in acres	All countries	B 10-a
Consumption & stocks: abaca, sisal & tow: tonnage	UK	B 10-a
tonnage	Main producing countries	B 10-a
Exports as % of total exports (value basis)	All countries	B 10-a
by destination: tonnage	Main countries	B 10-a
sisal, abaca & henequen: tonnage	All countries	B 10-a
Imports: sisal, abaca & henequen: tonnage	Main countries	B 10-a
Production: abaca, henequen & sisal: tonnage	All countries	B 2-a
abaca: tonnage	Main countries	U 11-a
henequen: tonnage	Mexico	U 11-a
sisal: tonnage	Main countries	U 11-a
Stocks held in strategic stockpile: tonnage	USA	B 10-a
tonnage	Main producing countries	B 10-a
Supply (incl US strategic stockpile releases): tonnage	Worldwide	B 10-a
World exports by value in $m	World regions	A 5-a

Hard oils   see   COPRA OIL
                    PALM KERNEL OIL
                    PALM OIL

Hard spirits   see   ALCOHOLIC DRINKS

Hardboard   see   FIBREBOARD
                    MANUFACTURED TIMBER PRODUCTS

HARDENED PROTEINS
    see also   PLASTICS

Exports (in unworked form): tonnage	Main countries	U 26-a
Imports (in unworked form): tonnage	Main countries	U 26-a
Production: tonnage	European countries, Japan & USA	U 26-a

Hardness testing machines   see   SCIENTIFIC INSTRUMENTS

HARDWARE

Exports: nails, screws, nuts & bolts, etc: tonnage	OECD countries	D 9-a
Production: nails, screws, nuts, bolts & rivets: tonnage	All countries	U 22-a

HARDWOOD LOGS

Exports by destination by volume in m³	Canada, European countries, USA & USSR	A 13-q
by value in $	Malaysia, Papua New Guinea, Sabah & Solomon Is	U 32-m
by volume in m³	Main European countries & USA	A 25-a2
Exports: oak, beech & tropical woods by volume in m³	European countries	A 25-a
Fellings for industrial use by volume in m³	AASM countries	E 41-a
by volume in m³	AASM countries	E 41-a
Import prices in £ per m³	UK	A 25-a
Imports by source by volume in m³	European countries	A 13-q
by volume in m³	European countries	A 25-a

HARDWOOD, SAWN
    see also   TIMBER, TROPICAL

% contribution to export earnings	Cameroun & Ivory Coast	E 45-a
Consumption in Europe (excl USSR) - index nos		A 24-a
Consumption - index nos	European region	A 24-a
per capita by volume in m³	Main countries	A 25-a
Export prices: logs & veneer in M$ per ton	Sabah	U 32-m
Exports: beech, oak & tropical woods by volume in m³	European countries	A 25-a
by destination by volume in m³	Canada, European countries & USA	A 13-q
by volume in m³	Canada, European countries & USA	A 25-a
logs & lumber: unit value in $	Philippines	U 32-m
teak by value in local currency	Burma	U 32-m
unit value in local currency	Burma & Thailand	U 32-m
tonnage & value in $m	Ivory Coast & Ghana	E 45-a
Fellings by volume in m³	Main countries	R 5-a
Import prices in £ per m³	UK	A 25-a
beech, birch & oak in £ per m³	UK	A 25-a
keruing & sipo in £ per m³	UK	A 25-a
mahogany & obeche in £ per m³	UK	A 25-a
ramin & teak in £ per m³	UK	A 25-a
Imports by source by volume in m³	EEC countries	A 25-a
	European countries	A 13-q
by volume in m³	Main countries	A 25-a
Production & European requirements: forecast volume in m³		A 24-a
Production: broad-leaved logs by volume in m³	All countries	A 5-a
Production, consumption, imports & exports in m³	Canada, European countries & USA	A 25-a
Production (for industrial use) by volume in m³	AASM countries	E 41-a
(for industrial use or as fuel) by volume in m³	World regions	J 7-a
by volume in m³	AASM countries	E 41-a
	Canada, European countries, USA & USSR	A 13-q
	Main countries	A 24-a A 25-a
Stocks by volume in m³	Canada, Main European countries & USA	A 25-a
Wholesale prices: mahogany in local currency per m³	OAS member countries	N 17-a
oak boards in lire per m³	Italy	R 2-m
roundwood - index nos	European countries	A 26-a

	Territorial coverage	Title codes

Harvesters   see   COMBINED HARVESTER-THRESHERS

Hats   see   MILLINERY

HAULAGE INDUSTRY
   No of hrs worked per wk — Main countries — R 3-m
   Wage rates per hr by sex in local currency — Main countries — R 3-m

Haulage vehicles   see   COMMERCIAL VEHICLES
                                   TRAILERS

Havarti   see   CHEESE BY VARIETY

HAY
   Crop yield in 100 kg per ha — EEC countries — E 12-a
   Imports (incl fodder) as animal feed: tonnage — UK — P 5-a
   Producer prices in local currency per ton — OECD countries — D 1-a
   Production (incl green crops & lucerne): tonnage — EEC countries — P 5-a
                tonnage — EEC countries — E 12-a

HAZELNUTS
   Exports: tonnage (in shell) — Italy, Spain, Turkey & USA — P 4-m
             (unshelled) — Italy, Spain, Turkey & USA — P 4-m
   Import prices ex Turkey in £ per ton fob — UK — P 4-m
   Imports: tonnage — Main countries — P 4-m
   Production: tonnage of world crop (unshelled) — All countries — P 4-a

HEALTH
   see also   MENTAL WELFARE
                  PUBLIC HEALTH

   % of government expenditure on wages, goods & services in
     Health Service — OECD countries — D 11
   Cost to private sector (incl personal care & medicine) — EEC countries — E 32-a

Health & welfare benefits   see   SICKNESS BENEFITS

HEALTH CENTRES & CLINICS
   No of consultations given & no per 1000 population — AASM countries — E 41-a
                                                   — OAS member countries — N 18-a
      of centres in use — AASM countries — E 41-a
                       — African countries — U 44-a
                       — OAS member countries — N 18-a
      of out-patient clinics in use — OAS member countries — N 18-a
      of persons using the service — OAS member countries — N 18-a

Health insurance   see   NATIONAL HEALTH INSURANCE

Health service hospitals   see   HOSPITALS, NATIONAL

HEARSES
   No in use — Main countries — V 4-a

Heat units   see   CALORIFIC VALUE

HEATING & COOLING EQUIPMENT, INDUSTRIAL
   Imports by value in $m — All countries — U 38-a

HEATING APPLIANCES, ELECTRIC
   Production: volume: space heaters — All countries — U 38-a
                  volume — EEC countries — E 28-q   E 27-a

Heavy oil products   see   PETROLEUM PRODUCTS

HEAVY SECTIONS, STEEL
   see also   LIGHT SECTIONS, STEEL
                  STRUCTURAL STEEL PRODUCTS

   Basic domestic prices per ton — OECD countries — D 22-a
   Consumption: tonnage — EEC countries — E 29-a
                      — OECD countries — D 22-a
   Deliveries by dealers: tonnage — EEC countries — E 29-a
          (home & export): tonnage — OECD countries — D 22-a
          to EEC area: tonnage — EEC countries — E 29-a
          to user industries: tonnage — ECE countries — U 7-q   U 6-a
                           — Main countries — H 3-a
          tonnage — EEC countries — E 30-m
   Export prices: Bessemer quality in $ per 100 lbs fob — USA — R 2-m
               Thomas quality in $ per ton fob — Belgium — R 2-m
               in FrB per ton fob — EEC countries — U 49-m
               in $ per ton fob — OECD countries — D 22-a
   Exports by destination: tonnage — EEC area — E 5-q
                             — EEC countries — E 29-a
                             — Main countries — T 4-a
          tonnage & % share of world total — Main countries — U 49-a

	Territorial coverage	Title codes	

HEAVY SECTIONS, STEEL
    Exports: tonnage   ECE countries   U 7-m   U 6-a

	Territorial coverage	Title codes	
HEAVY SECTIONS, STEEL			
Exports: tonnage	ECE countries	U 7-m	U 6-a
	Main countries	H 3-a	
Imports by source: tonnage	EEC countries	E 5-a	E 29-a
tonnage	Main countries	T 4-a	
	ECE countries	U 7-m	U 6-a
Inter-EEC trade: steel rails: tonnage	Main countries	H 3-a	
Prices (net less tax) at main centres in local currency	EEC countries	E 29-a	
Production capacity: tonnage	EEC countries	E 30-a	
Production: tonnage (incl girders)	Main countries	U 57-a	
profiles & rails: tonnage	EEC countries	E 30-m	E 29-a
rails: tonnage	Latin American countries	U 40-a	
tonnage	Main countries	T 4-a	
	All countries	T 1-a	U 22-a
	ECE countries	U 7-m	U 6-a
	Main countries	H 3-a	T 4-a
	OAS member countries	N 14-a	
	OECD countries	D 22-a	
Receipts by dealers: tonnage	EEC countries	E 29-a	
ex EEC area: tonnage	EEC countries	E 29-a	
Wholesale prices in $ per ton	Main countries	U 49-m	U 57-a
Heifers see LIVESTOCK			
Helicopters see AIRCRAFT, ROTARY-WING			
HELIUM			
Consumption: high-purity gas by volume in cu ft	USA	N 1-a	
Production by volume in cu ft	USA	B 15-a	
extracted from natural gas by volume in cu ft	USA	N 1-a	
high-purity gas for sale by volume in cu ft	USA	N 1-a	
World production by volume in cu ft	Main countries	N 1-a	
HEMP			
see also ABACA			
BURLAP			
% contribution to export earnings from sisal	Tanzania	E 45-a	
Acreage subsidy on hemp in £ per ton	EEC countries	B 1-a	
Area harvested, production tonnage & yield per ha	All countries	A 9-a	
under crop: hard fibres, sisal & abaca in acres	All countries	B 10-a	
hemp (all kinds) in ha	EEC countries	E 12-a	E 44-a
Consumption: sisal & hemp: tonnage	Main countries	B 2-a	
sisal & manila hemp by spinning mills: tonnage	OECD countries	D 46-a	
by textile industry: tonnage	OECD countries	D 46-a	
Disposals of sisal ex US strategic stockpile: tonnage	USA	U 11-a	
Export prices of sisal - index nos (weighted average)	Worldwide	U 29-q	
of hemp in local currency per ton	Brazil, India, Kenya & Madagascar	A 9-a	
Exports by destination: tonnage	Kenya & Tanzania	B 10-a	
Exports: raw hemp: tonnage	Asian & Far East areas	U 32-q	
	India, Sabah & Philippines	U 32-m	
sisal, abaca & henequen: tonnage	Main countries	A 5-a	
sisal & henequen: tonnage	Brazil & Tanzania	U 11-a	
sisal, henequen, true hemp & sunn hemp: tonnage	All countries	B 10-a	
sisal: tonnage & value in $m	Tanzania	E 45-a	
total & to EEC area: tonnage & value in UA	AASM countries	E 41-a	
unit value in cents per kg	Main countries	U 11-a	
Import prices: E African sisal in £ per ton cif	UK	B 10-m	B 2-a
sisal ex N Africa in Frs per kg cif	France	R 2-m	
in £ per ton cif	UK	R 2-m	
in $ per ton cif	UK & USA	A 9-a	
Imports (ex British Commonwealth countries): tonnage	EEC countries	B 10-a	
sisal & henequen: tonnage	Main countries	A 5-a	
Production & projected output by 1975: tonnage	Main countries	A 1	
Production: abaca, henequen & sisal: tonnage	All countries	A 5-a	B 2-a
hemp fibre: tonnage	OECD countries	D 1-a	
henequen & sisal: tonnage	Main countries	U 11-a	
sisal: tonnage	AASM countries	E 41-a	
tonnage	Brazil, Dominican Republic, Haiti & Venezuela	U 40-a	
	EEC countries	E 12-a	E 44-a
	OECD countries	D 46-a	
Stocks: hard fibres (held in strategic stockpile): tonnage	USA	B 10-a	
sisal (at end-yr): tonnage	Main countries	B 2-a	
Wholesale prices: sisal ex E Africa - index nos	UK	B 10-m	
in local currency per ton	Italy, Philippines & UK	U 27-m	
World exports of sisal & hemp: tonnage & value in $m	Main countries	B 2-a	
unit value of hemp in $ per ton	Worldwide	A 11-a	
World market prices: sisal ex E Africa in £ per ton	UK	E 41-a	
World production of hemp in lbs million & % produced in			
Commonwealth countries			
sisal, manila hemp & henequen: tonnage	All countries	B 10-a	
Yield in kg per ha	EEC countries	E 12-a	E 44-a
HEMP SEED			
Exports: tonnage	Turkey & Yugoslavia	B 19-a	
Imports: tonnage	Main countries	B 19-a	

	Territorial coverage	Title codes

HEMP YARN
    see also   LINEN YARN
    Consumption by knitting mills: tonnage   OECD countries   D 46-a
          (incl tow) by weaving industry: tonnage   OECD countries   D 46-a
          manila hemp yarn by weaving industry: tonnage   OECD countries   D 46-a
          sisal yarn by weaving industry: tonnage   OECD countries   D 46-a
    Production by spinning industry: tonnage   OECD countries   D 46-a
          hemp, ramie & flax yarn: tonnage   All countries   U 22-a
          manila hemp & sisal yarn: tonnage   OECD countries   D 46-a
          tonnage   EEC countries   E 28-q   E 27-a

Henequen   see   HEMP

Hens   see   POULTRY

Hepatitis   see   DISEASES, INFECTIOUS

HERBS, MEDICINAL
    Exports: plants for medicine & scents by value in $ Laos   U 32-m

Herefords   see   CATTLE BY BREED

HEROIN
    Illicit traffic seizures in kg   All countries   U 46-a
    World requirements in kg (estim)   U 19-a

HERRINGS
    Catch by kind: tonnage   All countries   A 22-a
          tonnage & value in local currency   OECD countries   D 43-a
          in $ (incl sardines)   OAS member countries   N 13-a

HERRINGS, DRIED OR SALTED
    Consumption: tonnage & per capita in kg   Greece   D 14-a
    Exports by kind: tonnage & value in $ Main countries   A 21-a
    Production: tonnage   Main countries   A 21-a

HERRINGS, FRESH OR CHILLED
    Exports: tonnage & value in $ Main countries   A 21-a

HERRINGS, FROZEN
    Exports by kind: tonnage & value in $ Main countries   A 21-a
    Production: tonnage   Main countries   A 21-a

HERRINGS, SMOKED
    Exports by kind: tonnage & value in $ Main countries   A 21-a
    Production: tonnage   Main countries   A 21-a

HERRINGS, TINNED
    Exports by kind: tonnage & value in $ All countries   A 21-a
    Production: tonnage   Main countries   A 21-a

Hessian   see   JUTE MANUFACTURES

Hessian cloth   see   BURLAP

Hide leather   see   LEATHER

HIDES
    see also   CALFSKINS
                      GOATSKINS
                      HORSEHIDES
                      LEATHER INDUSTRY
                      PIGSKINS
                      SHEEPSKINS
                      TANNERIES
    % contribution to export earnings   Botswana, Chad & Rwanda Burundi   E 45-a
    Consumption of calfskins: tonnage   Main countries   B 2-a
          cattle hides & calfskins: tonnage   World regions   A 18-a
          tonnage   Main countries   B 2-a
          hides & skins by purpose: tonnage   Main countries   B 9-a
          sheep & goatskins: tonnage   World regions   A 18-a
          tonnage (salted wt)   OECD countries   D 18-a
    Demand for cattle & calfskins projected to 1985: tonnage   Worldwide   A 18-a
          for sheep & goatskins projected to 1985: tonnage   Worldwide   A 18-a
          per capita projected to 1985: tonnage   World regions   A 18-a
    Export prices: cattle hides (heavy wt) in cents per lb at Chicago   USA   R 2-m
                  cattle hides, sheep & goatskins in cents per lb   Main countries   A 9-a
                  hides & fur skins - index nos (weighted average)   Worldwide   U 29-q
                  light cow hides in cents per lb fob at Chicago   USA   R 2-m
    Export prices - index nos   S American countries   U 40-q
    Exports by destination: dry-cured hides: tonnage   Main countries   B 9-m
                  (incl skins) by CST classes: tonnage & value
                                                          in $ EEC countries   E 48-a

	Territorial coverage	Title codes
HIDES, continued		
Exports by destination (incl skins) by SITC classes by value in $	Main countries	D 2-q
tonnage & value in $	OECD countries	D 3-a2
wet-cured hides: tonnage	Main countries	B 9-m
tonnage	OECD countries	D 18-a
Exports by value in $m	W European countries	U 33-a
Exports: calfskins: tonnage	European OECD countries	D 18-a
cattle hides by value in $m	Main countries	B 2-a
cattle hides (incl buffalo): tonnage	Main countries	B 2-a
tonnage	All countries	A 18-a
	European OECD countries	D 18-a
goatskins: tonnage	Main countries	B 9-m B 2-a
(incl raw skins): tonnage	European OECD countries	D 18-a
by NIMEXE classes by value in $	Asian & Far East countries	U 32-q
by SITC classes by value in $	All countries	E 20-a
by value in $	All countries	U 50-a U 59-a
sheep & lamb skins: tonnage	Afghanistan	U 32-m
sheepskins: tonnage	Main countries	B 2-a
to EEC & non-EEC areas by value in $m	European OECD countries	D 18-a
tonnage & value in $m	EEC countries	E 24-a
tonnage	Burundi	E 45-a
Import prices: dried cattle hides (18-22 lbs) in pence per lb	India, Iran, Laos, Pakistan & Thailand	U 32-m
Imports by source by value in $	UK	R 2-m A 9-a
(incl skins) by CST classes: tonnage & value in $	OECD countries	D 18-a
by SITC classes by value in $	EEC countries	E 21-a
tonnage & value in $	Main countries	D 2-q
	OECD countries	D 3-a2
tonnage	OECD countries	D 18-a
by value in $m	W European countries	U 33-a
ex EEC & non-EEC areas by value in $m	EEC countries	E 24-a
ex non-OECD countries: tonnage (salted wt)	OECD countries	D 18-a
(incl skins) by NIMEXE classes: tonnage & value in $	All countries	E 20-a
by SITC classes: tonnage & value in $	All countries	U 50-a U 59-a
Intra-European trade: tonnage	European economic areas	D 18-a
Production as % of livestock population	All countries	A 18-a
by volume: hides & skins by kind	All countries	A 18-a
	World regions	A 5-a
tonnage: cattle & buffalo hides	Main countries	B 2-a
cattle & calfskins projected to 1985	Worldwide	A 18-a
cattle hides, calf & buffalo skins	All countries	A 18-a
cattle hides (salted wt)	OECD countries	D 18-a
	AASM countries	E 41-a
goatskins (untanned)	OAS member countries	N 14-a
pigskins (untanned)	OAS member countries	N 14-a
raw hides of cattle, horses & buffaloes	OAS member countries	N 14-a
raw hides (untanned)	All countries	A 9-a
	All countries	U 22-a
sheep & goatskins	Main countries	B 2-a
sheepskins & as % of sheep population	All countries	A 18-a
sheepskins (untanned)	OAS member countries	N 14-a
Supply (domestic) of calfskins, cattle hides & horsehides	France	B 9-a
Utilisation: cattle & buffalo hides: tonnage	Main countries	A 18-a
Weight of hides produced in kg per ton of meat produced	European countries & USA	A 18-a
Wholesale prices: cattle hides & calfskins	Main countries	A 9-a
cow, bull & oxhides – index nos	OECD countries	D 18-a
hides (net salted) in Rs per piece	Pakistan	U 32-m
ox hides in pence per kg	UK	B 2-a
raw goat skins in Rs per 100 skins	India	U 32-m
raw sheep skins in Rs per 100 pieces	Pakistan	U 32-m
in local currency	OAS member countries	N 17-a
	S Africa & UK	U 27-a
(by thickness) by kind of hide in local currency	France, UK & USA	B 9-m
World exports (incl skins) by value in $m	World regions	A 5-a
World market prices (incl skins) – index nos	Worldwide	G 1-a
World production: cattle & buffalo hides by volume	All countries	A 18-a

High schools   see   COLLEGES

High-pressure conduits   see   TUBES, STEEL

High-speed steel   see   ALLOY STEEL

Highways   see   ROADS

Hire purchase   see   INSTALMENT CREDIT

Hired labour   see   FARM WORKERS
                               LABOUR FORCE

Hired machinery   see   FARM SERVICES

HISTORY & GEOGRAPHY
    No of new book titles published on these subjects   All countries   U 62-a
                                                                                           OAS member countries   N 19-a

Hoes, tractor-drawn   see   CULTIVATING MACHINES

	Territorial coverage	Title codes	
Hogs see PIGS			
Holdings see AGRICULTURAL HOLDINGS			
LAND UTILISATION			
PLANTATIONS			
HOLIDAY CAMPS			
No of beds available in holiday centres	OECD countries	D 47-a	
HOLIDAY TRIPS			
see also EXCURSIONS			
TOURISM			
No of holiday-makers & cruise travellers	OECD countries	D 47-a	
nights spent abroad by holiday-makers	OECD countries	D 47-a	
HOLIDAYS			
% of adults taking package holidays by age & social classes	W European countries	Z 3	
vacations (away from home) by social classes	W European countries	Z 3	
in specific countries	W European countries	Z 3	
overseas by social classes	W European countries	Z 3	
travelling on vacation by air by social classes	W European countries	Z 3	
HOLIDAYS, INDUSTRIAL			
Entitlement of wage earners in engineering industry	EEC countries	B 28-a	
No of paid annual holidays in days	EEC countries	B 29	
HOLLOW-WARE			
Receipts of steel for fabrication by industrial sectors	OECD countries	D 22-a	
Home deliveries & home sales see DELIVERIES, DOMESTIC			
HOME SEWING			
Consumption (domestic) of mending wool	Main countries	K 6-a	
HOMICIDE			
Death rates by homicide per 100,000 population	All countries	W 2-m	
No of deaths by homicide & no of war casualties	Main countries	W 1-a	
HONEY			
Consumption: tonnage	OAS member countries	N 17-a	
Production & consumption: tonnage & consumption per capita per day	OECD countries	D 14-a	
Production: tonnage	All countries	A 9-a	
Retail prices in local currency	OAS member countries	N 13-a	
Wholesale prices in local currency	OAS member countries	N 17-a	
	OAS member countries	N 17-a	
Hoop & strip, steel see COLD-ROLLED STRIP			
HOT-ROLLED STRIP			
HOPS			
Area harvested, production tonnage & yield per ha	All countries	A 9-a	
under crop in ha	EEC countries	B 1-a	E 12-a
		E 44-a	
Producer prices in £ per 100 kg	UK	D 1-a	
Production by value (at current prices) in local currency	EEC countries	E 44-a	
tonnage by administrative areas	EEC countries	E 38-a	
tonnage	EEC countries	B 1-a	E 12-a
		E 44-a	
Yield in kg per ha	EEC countries	B 1-a	E 12-a
		E 44-a	
Horizontal borer-millers & milling machines see MACHINE TOOLS			
HORMONES			
% contribution to export earnings	Bahamas	E 45-a	
Exports by destination by value in $	Main countries	U 2-a	
by value in $m	Bahamas	E 45-a	
HORSE MEAT			
Imports - index nos (volume basis)	European area	U 36-a	
Production: tonnage & human consumption per capita in kg	OECD countries	D 14-a	
by administrative areas: tonnage	EEC countries	E 38-a	
(incl mule & ass meat): tonnage	OECD countries	D 1-a	
slaughtered animals: tonnage	All countries	A 9-a	
Horse-racing see SPORTS			
HORSEHIDES			
see also FOOTWEAR UPPERS, LEATHER			
Exports by destination: tonnage	OECD countries	D 18-a	
Imports by source: tonnage & value in $	OECD countries	D 18-a	

		Territorial coverage	Title codes
HORSEHIDES, continued			
	Production: tonnage (salted wt)	OECD countries	D 18-a
	Supply (domestic), imports & exports: tonnage	France	B 9-a
HORSES			
	Nos reared	Latin American countries	J 5-a
	Nos slaughtered	All countries	A 9-a
	Population & no per 100 ha of usable land	EEC countries	E 1-a
	by administrative areas	EEC countries	E 38-a
	by age groups	EEC countries	E 1-a
	historical tables from 1816	Main European countries	Z 1-a
	in 1000 head (incl world total)	Main countries	R 5-a
	(incl donkeys) in million head	African countries	U 44-a
	Population	AASM countries	E 41-a
		All countries	A 9-a U 43-a
		OAS member countries	N 13-a
		OECD countries	D 1-a
HORTICULTURAL AREAS			
	Area under glass (& heated) in ha	France	U 20-a
	for cucumbers, fruit, tomatoes & vegetables in ha	UK	U 20-a
	in ha	France	U 20-a
HORTICULTURE			
	see also FRUIT TREES		
	% of output controlled by growers' associations	EEC countries	U 20-a
	Market garden cultivation: tomatoes in ha	OECD countries	D 36-a
	tomatoes: production: tonnage	OECD countries	D 36-a
	yield per ha	OECD countries	D 36-a
	No of growers' associations operating & no of members	EEC countries	U 20-a
	Production (under glass) of cauliflowers, cucumbers, kohlrabi, lettuce & tomatoes: tonnage	OECD countries	D 37-a
HOSE & TUBING, RUBBER			
	Consumption of rubber in production of hose & tubing: tonnage	France & Japan	C 18-a
Hosiery see STOCKINGS & TIGHTS			
HOSPITAL PERSONNEL			
	see also MEDICAL PERSONNEL		
	No employed by occupation	Asian, Far East & Australasian countries	U 45-a
	No of laboratory & x-ray technicians employed	Latin American countries	J 5-a
	nurses employed	African countries	U 44-a
	physicians & doctors employed	African countries	U 44-a
HOSPITALS			
	see also HEALTH CENTRES & CLINICS		
	MATERNITY HOSPITALS		
	PUBLIC HEALTH		
	No of admissions per auxiliary nurse (on staff)	Main countries	W 1-a
	physician (on staff)	Main countries	W 1-a
	qualified nurse (on staff)	Main countries	W 1-a
	beds available & no per 1000 population by areas	EEC countries	E 38-a
	per 100,000 population	Main countries	E 3-a
	in general hospitals	OAS member countries	N 18-a
	mental hospitals	OAS member countries	N 18-a
	sanatoria	OAS member countries	N 18-a
	specialist hospitals	OAS member countries	N 18-a
	beds available, no of patient admissions & patient-days	All countries	W 1-a
	per 1000 population in capital city	OAS member countries	N 18-a
	in rest of country	OAS member countries	N 18-a
	1000 population	OAS member countries	N 18-a
	auxiliary nurse (on staff)	Main countries	W 1-a
	physician (on staff)	Main countries	W 1-a
	qualified nurse (on staff)	Main countries	W 1-a
	hospitals built, no of beds available & population per bed	All countries	U 43-a
	& no of beds available	Asian, Far East & Australasian countries	U 45-a
	(general) in use	OAS member countries	N 18-a
	(specialist) in use	OAS member countries	N 18-a
	in use, no of beds available & no of beds per 10,000 population	Main countries	R 5-a
	in use & no of beds available	AASM countries	E 41-a
	maternity hospitals in use	African countries	U 44-a
	medical staff employed by occupation	AASM countries	E 41-a
	occupied beds in hospitals (daily average)	African countries	U 44-a
	physicians, nurses & auxiliary staff employed	Main countries	W 1-a
	staff by occupation & population per physician	Main countries	W 1-a
	Population per available hospital bed	All countries	U 43-a
		AASM countries	E 41-a
HOSPITALS, GENERAL			
	Length of stay: infectious disease cases: no of days (average)	OAS member countries	N 18-a
	maternity cases: no of days (average)	OAS member countries	N 18-a
	patients: no of days (average)	OAS member countries	N 18-a
	No of beds available	OAS member countries	N 18-a

	Territorial coverage	Title codes	
HOSPITALS, MENTAL			
see also INSTITUTIONS			
No of beds available	OAS member countries	N 18-a	
HOSPITALS, SPECIALIST			
No of beds available (incl sanatoria)	OAS member countries	N 18-a	
for child patients	Main countries	R 5-a	
internal disease cases	Main countries	R 5-a	
neurological cases	Main countries	R 5-a	
surgical cases	Main countries	R 5-a	
tuberculosis cases	Main countries	R 5-a	
in maternity hospitals	Main countries	R 5-a	
HOSPITALS BY KIND			
No of general, maternity & specialist hospitals in use	Latin American countries	J 5-a	
government-controlled & private hospitals in use	Main countries	W 1-a	
medical personnel employed by occupation	Main countries	W 1-a	
Hostels see YOUTH HOSTELS			
HOT-ROLLED STRIP			
see also COLD-ROLLED STRIP			
HOOP & STRIP, STEEL			
Consumption: tonnage	EEC countries	E 29-a	
	OECD countries	D 22-a	
Deliveries (home & export): tonnage	OECD countries	D 22-a	
to EEC area: tonnage	EEC countries	E 29-a	
to user industries: tonnage	ECE countries	U 7-q	U 6-a
	Main countries	H 3-a	
Export prices in $ per ton	OECD countries	D 22-a	
Exports by destination: tonnage	EEC countries	E 5-q	E 29-a
	Main countries	T 4-a	
tonnage	E European countries & USSR	T 1-a	
	ECE countries, Japan & USA	U 7-m	U 6-a
	Main countries	H 3-a	
Imports by quality: tonnage	Main countries	T 1-a	
by source: tonnage	EEC countries	E 5-q	E 29-a
	Main countries	T 4-a	
high carbon steel strip: tonnage	Main countries	T 1-a	
stainless steel strip: tonnage	Main countries	T 1-a	
tonnage	ECE countries, Japan & USA	U 7-m	U 6-a
	Main countries	H 3-a	
Inter-EEC trade: tonnage & value in $	EEC countries	E 29-a	
Prices (net less tax) at main centres in local currency	EEC countries	E 30-a	
Production: hoop & strip: tonnage	All countries	T 1-a	U 22-a
	EEC countries	E 30-m	E 29-a
(incl strip for tubes): tonnage	OECD countries	D 22-a	
tonnage	Main countries	T 4-a	
	OAS member countries	N 14-a	
Receipts at steel processing plants: tonnage	EEC countries	E 29-a	
ex EEC area: tonnage	EEC countries	E 29-a	
HOTELS			
see also BOARDING HOUSES			
INNS			
MOTELS			
% increase in charges	OECD countries & Yugoslavia	D 47-a	
% rate of occupancy (on annual basis)	OECD countries & Yugoslavia	D 47-a	
% rate of occupancy	OECD countries & Yugoslavia	D 47-m	
Investment in new hotel buildings & costs of modernisation in $	OECD countries	D 47-a	
No of beds available by areas	EEC countries	E 38-a	
as result of new hotel building	OECD countries	D 47-a	
for visitors & for tourists	OECD countries	D 47-a	
hotels built, extended & modernised	OECD countries & Yugoslavia	D 47-a	
tourist-nights spent by nationals & foreigners by areas	EEC countries	E 38-a	
HOTELS, INTERNATIONAL			
% deviation from average income in cities	World regions	Z 5-a	
in holiday resorts	World regions	Z 5-a	
% of earnings arising from beverage sales	World regions	Z 5-a	
businessmen (expense accounts)	World regions	Z 5-a	
conference participants	World regions	Z 5-a	
food sales	World regions	Z 5-a	
government officials	World regions	Z 5-a	
home nationals	World regions	Z 5-a	
overseas visitors	World regions	Z 5-a	
room occupancy	World regions	Z 5-a	
sales	World regions	Z 5-a	
store rentals	World regions	Z 5-a	
tourist expenditure	World regions	Z 5-a	
% of expenditure on administration	World regions	Z 5-a	
beverage purchases	World regions	Z 5-a	
depreciation on equipment	World regions	Z 5-a	
food purchases	World regions	Z 5-a	

	Territorial coverage	Title codes
HOTELS, INTERNATIONAL continued		
% of expenditure on heat, light & power used	World regions	Z 5-a
rent	World regions	Z 5-a
repairs & maintenance charges	World regions	Z 5-a
staff wages & salaries	World regions	Z 5-a
% of guests by nationality	World regions	Z 5-a
% of reservation agents' commissions	World regions	Z 5-a
% profit ratios to room sales	Worldwide	Z 5-a
% registrations by direct approach	World regions	Z 5-a
through reservation agents	World regions	Z 5-a
travel agents	World regions	Z 5-a
% sales of beverages by room service	World regions	Z 5-a
in banquetting rooms	World regions	Z 5-a
bars	World regions	Z 5-a
coffee rooms	World regions	Z 5-a
dining rooms	World regions	Z 5-a
hotel-controlled night clubs	World regions	Z 5-a
of food by room service	World regions	Z 5-a
in banquetting rooms	World regions	Z 5-a
coffee rooms	World regions	Z 5-a
dining rooms	World regions	Z 5-a
hotel-controlled night clubs	World regions	Z 5-a
Administration costs by kind per room in $	World regions	Z 5-a
Advance registrations as % of total registrations	World regions	Z 5-a
Advertising costs per room in $	World regions	Z 5-a
Earnings from beverage sales per room in $	World regions	Z 5-a
from food sales per room in $	World regions	Z 5-a
from room occupancy per room in $	World regions	Z 5-a
of hotels per employee in $	World regions	Z 5-a
Food bills per guest for each meal (average) in $	World regions	Z 5-a
Heating & lighting costs per room in $	World regions	Z 5-a
Length of stay of guests in days (average)	World regions	Z 5-a
No of guests per room	World regions	Z 5-a
of staff & employees per room	World regions	Z 5-a
No of times room rate was earned	World regions	Z 5-a
Profit (before tax) as % of costs	Worldwide	Z 5-a
(gross) per room per yr in $	Worldwide	Z 5-a
Ratio of hotel assets to liabilities	World regions	Z 5-a
of beverages to food sales by meal	World regions	Z 5-a
Repair costs & maintenance charges per room in $	World regions	Z 5-a
Room occupancy charges in $ per day (average)	World regions	Z 5-a
Room usage: occupancy as % of no of rooms available	World regions	Z 5-a
Sales of beverages by room service per guest in $	World regions	Z 5-a
in bars per seat per yr in $	World regions	Z 5-a
of food by room service per guest in $	World regions	Z 5-a
in dining rooms per seat per yr in $	World regions	Z 5-a
Staff wages as % of total sales income	World regions	Z 5-a
cost per room in $	World regions	Z 5-a
Stocks: beverages by value in $	World regions	Z 5-a
food by value in $	World regions	Z 5-a
Supplies of saleable items by value in $	World regions	Z 5-a
HOTELS, INTERNATIONAL BY AGE		
% deviation from average income per room	World regions	Z 5-a
Administrative costs per room in $	World regions	Z 5-a
Advertising costs per room in $	World regions	Z 5-a
Beverage & food sales: earnings per room	World regions	Z 5-a
Earnings & expenses per room in $	World regions	Z 5-a
Heating & lighting: costs per room in $	World regions	Z 5-a
Operating profit per room in $	World regions	Z 5-a
Repair & maintenance charges per room in $	World regions	Z 5-a
HOTELS, INTERNATIONAL BY LOCATION		
Earnings in cities per room in $	World regions	Z 5-a
in holiday resorts per room in $	World regions	Z 5-a
Expenses in cities per room in $	World regions	Z 5-a
in holiday resorts per room in $	World regions	Z 5-a
Operating profit in cities per room in $	World regions	Z 5-a
in holiday resorts per room in $	World regions	Z 5-a
HOTELS, INTERNATIONAL BY SIZE		
% deviation from average income per room	World regions	Z 5-a
Administrative costs per room in $	World regions	Z 5-a
Advertising costs per room in $	World regions	Z 5-a
Beverage & food sales: earnings per room in $	World regions	Z 5-a
Earnings & expenses per room in $	World regions	Z 5-a
Heating & lighting costs per room in $	World regions	Z 5-a
Operating profit per room in $	World regions	Z 5-a
Repair & maintenance charges per room in $	World regions	Z 5-a
HOTELS, TOURIST		
Costs for advertising per room in $	World regions	Z 5-a
food & beverages per room in $	World regions	Z 5-a
heating & lighting per room in $	World regions	Z 5-a
repairs & maintenance per room in $	World regions	Z 5-a
Earnings per room by source of income in $	World regions	Z 5-a
Expenses per room by kind in $	World regions	Z 5-a
Operating profit per room in $	World regions	Z 5-a

	Territorial coverage	Title codes
HOURS OF WORK		
see also ABSENTEEISM		
LOST WORKING DAYS		
SHORT-TIME WORKING		
By branch of economic activity per wk	EEC countries	E 18-a
By industrial sectors per employee per wk	EEC countries	E 2-a
as second occupation per wk	EEC countries	E 18-a
per yr	EEC countries	E 2-a
By industry by sex per wk	EEC countries	E 33-a
per wk (average)	EEC countries	E 25-a2
per wk (in detail)	Main countries	R 3-m R 5-a
manual workers	OECD countries	D 9-a
non-agricultural sector	EEC countries	E 3-a
per wk	All countries	L 1-m
	All countries	L 4-a
	Asian, Far East & Australasian countries	U 45-a
per wk: wage earners (all occupations)	Main countries	U 27-m
per yr (average)	EEC countries	E 8-a
(in detail)	EEC countries	E 11-a
	Peru, Trinidad & USA	N 18-a
salaried staff per yr (in detail)	EEC countries	E 11-a
wage earners per yr (in detail)	EEC countries	E 11-a
% change in no of man-hrs worked	Main European countries & USA	U 16-a
Index nos	Main countries	L 4-a
Abattoirs & meat preparation industry per wk	EEC countries	E 25-a2
Aerospace equipment manufacturing industry per wk	EEC countries	E 25-a2
Agriculture by sex per wk	EEC countries	E 2-a E 18-a
		E 33-a
Aircraft industry per wk	EEC countries	E 25-a2
Alcoholic drinks industry per wk	EEC countries	E 25-a2
Assurance companies per yr	EEC countries	E 9-a
Banking institutions per yr	EEC countries	E 9-a
Basic metals industries per wk	OAS member countries	N 18-a
Building industry (incl civil engineering) per wk	EEC countries	E 25-a2
by sex per wk	EEC countries	E 18-a E 33-a
per wk	All countries	L 4-a
	EEC countries	E 26-a2
	OAS member countries	N 18-a
Building materials & refractories industry per wk	EEC countries	E 25-a2
Cement manufacturing industry per wk	EEC countries	E 25-a2
Ceramics industry per wk	EEC countries	E 25-a2
Chemical industry per wk	EEC countries	E 25-a2
	All countries	L 4-a
	OAS member countries	N 18-a
	EEC countries	E 25-a2
Clothing industry per wk	OECD countries	D 46-a
Clothing industry - index nos	UK	B 22-a
Coal mining industry per wk	EEC countries	E 25-a2
Coking plants & ovens per wk	EEC countries	E 25-a2
Commercial & marketing occupations by sex per wk	EEC countries	E 33-a
Confectionery & baking industry per wk	EEC countries	E 25-a2
Cotton textile industry per wk	EEC countries	E 25-a2
looms per yr in operation	W European countries	K 2-a
spindles per yr in operation	W European countries	K 2-a
Credit & insurance companies by sex per wk	EEC countries	E 18-a
Dairying industry per wk	EEC countries	E 25-a2
Durable goods industry: overtime worked per wk (average) in hrs	USA	J 2-a
Electrical engineering industry per wk	All countries	L 4-a
	EEC countries	E 25-a2
Engineering industry (electrical) per wk	OAS member countries	N 18-a
(mechanical) per wk	OAS member countries	N 18-a
overtime worked per wk (average) in hrs	USA	J 2-a
Farm machinery & tractor manufacturing industry per wk	EEC countries	E 25-a2
Food, drink & tobacco industry per wk	All countries	L 4-a
	OAS member countries	N 18-a
Food processing industry (excl sugar refineries) per wk	EEC countries	E 25-a2
Footwear manufacturing industry per wk	EEC countries	E 25-a2
Foundries (iron & steel) per wk	EEC countries	E 25-a2
Furniture manufacturing industry per wk by sex	W European countries	C 8-a
per wk	EEC countries	E 25-a2
Glass & glassware manufacturing industry per wk	All countries	L 4-a
Instrument engineering industry per wk	EEC countries	E 25-a2
Iron & steel industry in man-hrs	EEC countries	E 25-a2
per wk	EEC countries	E 29-a
per wk by sex	EEC countries	E 25-a2
no of man-hrs worked per wk	W Germany	H 3-a
Iron ore mining (at face & underground) per wk	EEC countries	E 30-m
per wk	EEC countries	E 30-m
per shift	EEC countries	E 25-a2
Knitting mills per wk	EEC countries	E 29-a
Leather & leather goods manufacturing industry per wk	EEC countries	E 25-a2
	EEC countries	E 25-a2
	OAS member countries	N 18-a
	All countries	L 4-a
Local government employees by sex per wk	EEC countries	E 18-a
Machine tools & parts industry per wk	EEC countries	E 25-a2
by sector per wk	USA	J 2-a
Machine tools industry: overtime worked per wk (average) in hrs	USA	J 2-a

261

	Territorial coverage	Title codes	
HOURS OF WORK, continued			
Man-made fibres industry per wk	EEC countries	E 25-a2	
Manufacturing industry: no of hrs of overtime worked per wk (average)	USA	J 2-a	
no of hrs worked per employee	Main countries	U 43-a	
per wk	All countries	L 1-m	L 4-a
	EEC countries	E 25-a2	E 26-a2
per wk by sex	EEC countries	E 33-a	
Mechanical engineering industry per wk	All countries	L 4-a	
	EEC countries	E 25-a2	
Metal fabricating & processing industry per wk	EEC countries	E 25-a2	
	All countries	L 4-a	
	OAS member countries	N 18-a	
Mineral oil refining industry per wk	EEC countries	E 25-a2	
Mining & manufacturing industries per wk	ECE countries	U 42-m	
Mining & quarrying per wk by sex	EEC countries	E 18-a	
per wk	All countries	L 4-a	
	EEC countries	E 25-a2	
	OAS member countries	N 18-a	
Motor vehicle industry: engine production plants per wk	EEC countries	E 25-a2	
per wk	EEC countries	E 25-a2	
Non-ferrous metals industry per wk	EEC countries	E 25-a2	
Non-metallic minerals industry per wk	EEC countries	E 25-a2	
	OAS member countries	N 18-a	
Non-metallic mining industry per wk	All countries	L 4-a	
Office machinery manufacturing industry per wk	EEC countries	E 25-a2	
Ore mining & quarrying per wk	EEC countries	E 25-a2	
Paper & board manufacturing industry per wk	EEC countries	E 25-a2	
	All countries	L 4-a	
Petroleum & coal products industries per wk	OAS member countries	N 18-a	
Petroleum & natural gas industries per wk	EEC countries	E 25-a2	
Plastics industry per wk	EEC countries	E 25-a2	
Printing & publishing per wk	All countries	L 4-a	
	EEC countries	E 25-a2	
	OAS member countries	N 18-a	
Public utilities by sex per wk	EEC countries	E 18-a	
Refineries (of mineral oils) per wk	EEC countries	E 25-a2	
Retail trade (by kind of goods sold) per yr	EEC countries	E 9-a	
by sex per wk	EEC countries	E 18-a	
Rubber processing industry per wk	EEC countries	E 25-a2	
Rubber products manufacturing industry per wk	All countries	L 4-a	
	OAS member countries	N 18-a	
Scientific instruments manufacturing industry per wk	OAS member countries	N 18-a	
Self-employed persons (all activities) per wk	EEC countries	E 18-a	
engaged in farming per wk	EEC countries	E 18-a	
in service industries per wk	EEC countries	E 18-a	
Service industries employees by sex per wk	EEC countries	E 33-a	
Shipbuilding, repairing & marine engineering industry per wk	EEC countries	E 25-a2	
Solid fuels briquetting industry per wk	EEC countries	E 25-a2	
Structural steel industry per wk	EEC countries	E 25-a2	
Tanning & leather-dressing industry per wk	EEC countries	E 25-a2	
Textile & clothing manufacturing industries per wk	OAS member countries	N 18-a	
	All countries	L 4-a	
	EEC countries	B 29	E 25-a2
	OECD countries	D 46-a	
Timber & sawmill industry per wk	EEC countries	E 25-a2	
Timber, wood products & furniture manufacturing industry per wk	OAS member countries	N 18-a	
Tobacco processing industry per wk	EEC countries	E 25-a2	
Transport equipment manufacturing industry per wk	EEC countries	E 25-a2	
	All countries	L 4-a	
	OAS member countries	N 18-a	
Transport service industries per wk	All countries	L 4-a	
Wood-working industry per wk	All countries	L 4-a	
Woollen textile manufacturing industry per wk	EEC countries	E 25-a2	
HOUSEHOLD BUDGETS			
see also PRIVATE CONSUMPTION			
% of expenditure by kind by clerical workers	EEC countries	Z 3-a	
by manual workers	EEC countries	Z 3-a	
on clothing & footwear	EEC countries	Z 3-a	
education & entertainment	EEC countries	Z 3-a	
food, drink & tobacco	EEC countries	Z 3-a	
footwear	Main countries	A 18-a	
furnishing & domestic appliances	EEC countries	Z 3-a	
medicine, sanitary products & toiletries	EEC countries	Z 3-a	
rent, fuel & light	All countries	U 13-a	
	EEC countries	Z 3-a	
social security levies & local taxes	EEC countries	Z 3-a	
transport services	EEC countries	Z 3-a	
Expenditure by items in local currency	EEC countries	E 2-a	
on alcoholic drinks in local currency	OAS member countries	N 16-a	
charcoal in local currency	OAS member countries	N 17-a	
chemical products in local currency	AASM countries	E 41-a	
clothing & personal items in local currency	OAS member countries	N 16-a	
	AASM countries	E 41-a	
electricity & gas in local currency	AASM countries	E 41-a	
energy needs in local currency	AASM countries	E 41-a	
food & beverages in local currency	OAS member countries	N 16-a	
	AASM countries	E 41-a	

	Territorial coverage	Title codes
HOUSEHOLD BUDGETS, continued		
Expenditure on fuel & lighting in local currency	OAS member countries	N 16-a
furniture & household goods in local currency	OAS member countries	N 16-a
	AASM countries	E 41-a
gas in local currency	OAS member countries	N 17-a
lighting & water supply	OAS member countries	N 17-a
personal health & hygiene in local currency	OAS member countries	N 16-a
private consumption in local currency	AASM countries	E 41-a
materials in local currency	AASM countries	E 41-a
recreation & entertainment in local currency	OAS member countries	N 16-a
	AASM countries	E 41-a
rent by kind of accomodation in local currency	OAS member countries	N 17-a
rent, water charges & local taxes in local currency	OAS member countries	N 16-a
rent in local currency	AASM countries	E 41-a
services in local currency	AASM countries	E 41-a
	OAS member countries	N 16-a
specific items as % of total expenditure	EEC countries	E 2-a
textile products in local currency	AASM countries	E 41-a
tobacco goods in local currency	OAS member countries	N 16-a
transport services in local currency	OAS member countries	N 16-a
	AASM countries	E 41-a
water supply in local currency	AASM countries	E 41-a
Expenditure - total domestic costs (all outgoings)	OAS member countries	N 17-a

Household employees   see   SERVICES, DOMESTIC

Household expenditure   see   HOUSEHOLD BUDGETS

Household soap   see   SOAP, HOUSEHOLD

	Territorial coverage	Title codes
HOUSEHOLD TEXTILES		
Production volume: bedspreads & quilts	EEC countries	K 4-a
by kind of material: blankets	EEC countries	K 4-a
curtains	EEC countries	K 4-a
sheets	EEC countries	K 4-a
towels	EEC countries	K 4-a
Production: mattresses by volume	Zaire	E 41-a
upholstery by kind	EEC countries	K 4-a
Retail prices by kind of textiles in local currency	OAS member countries	N 17-a
blankets & bedspreads in local currency	OAS member countries	N 17-a
mattresses in local currency	OAS member countries	N 17-a
sheets & pillowcases in local currency	OAS member countries	N 17-a
tablecloths & towels in local currency	OAS member countries	N 17-a

	Territorial coverage	Title codes
HOUSEHOLDS		
% growth rates: no of householders projected to 1985	All countries	U 13-a
% housewives using specific domestic cleaning products	W European countries	Z 3
washing products	W European countries	Z 3
% of households by no of persons	W European countries	Z 3
by social classes & by income brackets	W European countries	Z 3
in lower & higher income brackets	W European countries	Z 3
with bank or giro accounts by social classes	W European countries	Z 3
credit cards or instalment commitments	W European countries	Z 3
deposit bank savings accounts	W European countries	Z 3
fixed-interest securities as investments	W European countries	Z 3
government savings bonds as investments	W European countries	Z 3
Post Office savings accounts	W European countries	Z 3
premium or lottery bonds as investments	W European countries	Z 3
shares in industrial companies as investments	W European countries	Z 3
in property companies as investments	W European countries	Z 3
tax-free savings accounts	W European countries	Z 3
unit trust shares as investments	W European countries	Z 3
% of housewives by age groups	W European countries	Z 3
working full or part-time by age groups	W European countries	Z 3
% owning labour-saving domestic equipment by kind	W European countries	Z 3
% usage of electricity as source of domestic energy	W European countries	U 16-a
oil as source of domestic energy	W European countries	U 16-a
other fuels as source of domestic energy	W European countries	U 16-a
Electricity consumption as % of total supply	W European countries	U 16-a
from public supply in kWh	All countries	C 23-a
domestic consumption in kWh	European countries & USA	U 1-a
	OECD countries	D 8-a
No of housing units by tenure (owner-occupied or rented)	All countries	U 13-a
children per household by social classes	W European countries	Z 3
domestic gas consumers	European countries & USA	U 3-a
households projected (5 yearly periods) to 1985	All countries	U 13-a
owner-occupiers & no of tenants	Asian, Far East & Australasian countries	U 45-a
persons accommodated per housing unit	OAS member countries	N 18-a
per household	All countries	U 14
per household by social classes	W European countries	Z 3
projected to 1985	World regions	U 13-a
urban & rural	All countries	U 13-a
privately-owned households by no of persons	Main countries	E 3-a
privately-owned households	EEC countries	E 2-a

	Territorial coverage	Title codes
HOUSEWIVES		
No of females permanently economically-inactive	EEC countries	E 18-a

	Territorial coverage	Title codes
HOUSING		
see also BUILDING CONSTRUCTION, RESIDENTIAL DWELLINGS		
% allocation of gross national product to procuring new houses	OECD countries	D 11
% changes in implicit price deflator for housing	Developing countries	D 25-a
% growth rates: contribution of housing to gross national product	Developing countries	D 25-a
% of dwellings provided with piped water facility	Developing countries	U 23-a
% of gross national product allocated to new housing construction	OECD countries	D 11-a
A.I.D. grants to improve housing standards in $	Recipient countries	M 1-a
Availability of living quarters by kind as % of total	All countries	U 13-a
Capital formation in housing as % of total capital formation	European countries & USA	U 5-a
of total construction	European countries & USA	U 5-a
of gross national product	European countries & USA	U 5-a
	All countries	U 43-a
Construction of dwellings: % contribution to national income	Developing countries	D 25-a
as component of gross national product in local currency	Developing countries	D 25-a
no of dwellings built per 1000 population	All countries	U 13-a
Costs of housing as element in cost of living - index nos	OAS member countries	N 17-a
Disbursement under CECA Programs for workers' housing construction	EEC countries	E 38-a
Expenditure on housing as % of total capital investment	E European countries & USSR	U 16-a
Facilities by type: piped water & toilets installed	All countries	U 43-a
Floor area of new dwellings in m²	Main countries	U 58-a
Future requirements of new dwellings (estim)	All countries	U 13-a
Institutional & camp accommodation as % of all housing units	All countries	U 13-a
Membership of housing co-operative societies	OAS member countries	N 18-a
No of dwellings & no of persons per household	All countries	U 43-a
available per 1000 population	ECE countries	U 15-a
constructed by local authorities	Main countries	U 58-a
by private enterprise	Main countries	R 5-a U 58-a
per 1000 population	All countries	U 43-a
new construction by type	Main countries	U 58-a
owner-occupied or rented	All countries	U 43-a
restored or converted	Main countries	U 58-a
of housing co-operative societies in operation	OAS member countries	N 18-a
living quarters available: hotels & rooming houses	All countries	U 13-a
permits issued for construction of new dwellings	Main countries	U 58-a
persons living in rented rural accommodation	All countries	U 13-a
urban accommodation	All countries	U 13-a
rooms in new dwellings completed	Main countries	U 58-a
Public & private expenditure on housing as % of gross national product	OECD countries	D 11
Rooming house accommodation as % of all living quarters	All countries	U 13-a
Size & density of occupation: over-crowding	All countries	U 43-a
World bank loans & credits for urbanisation projects in $m	Worldwide	M 3-a
HOUSING, PRE-FABRICATED		
As % of new construction	European countries	U 5-a
HOUSING, STATE-FINANCED		
As % of new building by public authorities	European countries	U 5-a
by semi-public bodies	European countries	U 5-a
by state co-operatives	European countries	U 5-a
HOUSING, TEMPORARY		
No of improvised housing units as % of total stock of houses	All countries	U 13-a
of living quarters improvised within camps	All countries	U 13-a
HOUSING BY FACILITY		
No of dwellings with installed baths & showers: rural areas	All countries	U 13-a
urban areas	All countries	U 13-a
with electricity: rural areas	All countries	U 13-a
urban areas	All countries	U 13-a
kitchens: rural areas	All countries	U 13-a
urban areas	All countries	U 13-a
without baths & showers: rural areas	All countries	U 13-a
urban areas	All countries	U 13-a
electricity: rural areas	All countries	U 13-a
urban areas	All countries	U 13-a
kitchens: rural areas	All countries	U 13-a
urban areas	All countries	U 13-a

Housing co-operatives   see   CO-OPERATIVE SOCIETIES, HOUSING

HUMANITIES

% of students enrolled on courses in humanities	ECAFE countries	U 17
No of students enrolled on university courses in humanities	OAS member countries	N 19-a

Hunting taxes   see   LICENCE FEES

Husked peanuts   see   GROUNDNUTS, SHELLED

Hydraulic alternators   see   ALTERNATORS, HYDRAULIC

Hydraulic generators   see   GENERATORS, HYDRAULIC

	Territorial coverage	Title codes	
HYDRAULIC TURBINE GENERATORS			
Power of generators produced in kW	All countries	U 38-a	
Production volume	All countries	U 38-a	
HYDRAULIC TURBINES			
Deliveries in MW	European countries, Japan & USA	D 45-a	
Exports as % of production	European countries, Japan & USA	D 45-a	
in MV	European countries, Japan & USA	D 45-a	
New orders & orders in hand in MV	European countries, Japan & USA	D 45-a	
Production in kW	All countries	U 38-a	
in MW	W European countries, Japan & USA	D 45-a	
volume	All countries	U 22-a	U 38-a

Hydrocarbon oils   see   MOTOR SPIRIT

HYDROCARBONS
      see also   NATURAL GAS
                      PETROLEUM PRODUCTS

	Territorial coverage	Title codes
% share of consumption of commercial energy	Latin American countries	U 18-a
Exports by destination: tonnage	Main countries	U 2-a
by kind by destination by value in $	Main countries	U 2-a
Production: crude mineral fuels: tonnage	Main countries	H 4-a
Reserves of crude mineral fuels: tonnage	Main countries	H 4-a
World known reserves of hydrocarbon fuels: tonnage		H 4-a

HYDROCARBONS, ALIPHATIC
      see also   ACETYLENE
                      BUTYLENE
                      ETHYLENE
                      METHANE
                      PROPYLENE

	Territorial coverage	Title codes
As source of acetylene production: tonnage	Main countries	U 26-a
Consumption for purposes of chemical synthesis: tonnage	OECD countries	D 5-a
tonnage	OECD countries	D 5-a
Production from coal derivatives: tonnage	OECD countries	D 5-a
from natural gas: tonnage	OECD countries	D 5-a

HYDROCARBONS, AROMATIC
      see also   BENZENE
                      TOLUENE
                      XYLENE

	Territorial coverage	Title codes
Consumption for purposes of organic synthesis: tonnage	OECD countries	D 5-a
tonnage	OECD countries	D 5-a
Production from coal derivatives: tonnage	OECD countries	D 5-a
from oil & natural gas: tonnage	OECD countries	D 5-a

HYDROCHLORIC ACID

	Territorial coverage	Title codes	
Consumption: tonnage	OAS member countries	N 17-a	
Production: tonnage	All countries	R 5-a	U 22-a
		U 43-a	
	EEC countries	E 28-q	E 27-a
	OAS member countries	N 14-a	

Hydrocodone   see   SYNTHETIC NARCOTICS

Hydroelectric generators   see   GENERATORS, HYDROELECTRIC

Hydroelectric power   see   POWER STATIONS, HYDROELECTRIC

HYDROELECTRICITY
      see also   POWER STATIONS, HYDROELECTRIC

	Territorial coverage	Title codes	
% change in output & consumption	E European countries	U 16-a	
% share in consumption of energy	Latin American countries	U 18-a	
Consumption as primary energy source	European countries	U 10-a	
in coal equiv tonnage	Main countries	N 2-a	
UK	UK	U 10-m	
Generation in kWh	All countries	C 23-a	
	European countries, USA & USSR	U 4-a	
	EEC countries	E 16-m	E 15-a
Plant capacity of storage reservoirs in kW	All countries	C 23-a	
Plant regenerating capacity in kW	All countries	C 23-a	
Production in kWh	African countries	U 44-a	
in petroleum equiv tonnage	Latin American countries	U 18-a	
known potential in GWh	Latin American countries	U 18-a	

Hydrogen peroxide   see   CHEMICAL PRODUCTS

HYGIENE REQUISITES

	Territorial coverage	Title codes
Expenditure (at cost) & as % of total outlay	EEC countries	E 2-a
Production: phytosanitary products by value in $	OECD countries	D 5-a

Hypermarkets   see   SELF-SERVICE STORES

Hyperphosphates   see   SUPERPHOSPHATES

	Territorial coverage	Title codes
IATA (International Air Transport Association) see AIR PASSENGER TRAFFIC		
IBRD (International Bank for Reconstruction & Development)		
Loans approved for agriculture in $	OAS member countries	N 16-a
air pollution control in $	OAS member countries	N 16-a
airport construction in $	OAS member countries	N 16-a
communications improvements in $	OAS member countries	N 16-a
education in $	OAS member countries	N 16-a
electric power installations in $	OAS member countries	N 16-a
	Latin American countries	U 18-a
family planning clinics in $	OAS member countries	N 16-a
fishing development in $	OAS member countries	N 16-a
gas pipeline construction in $	OAS member countries	N 16-a
industrial development in $	OAS member countries	N 16-a
irrigation purposes in $	OAS member countries	N 16-a
mining development in $	OAS member countries	N 16-a
port development in $	OAS member countries	N 16-a
railway re-construction in $	OAS member countries	N 16-a
road construction in $	OAS member countries	N 16-a
steel industry development in $	OAS member countries	N 16-a
tourism expansion in $	OAS member countries	N 16-a
water & sewage disposal projects in $	OAS member countries	N 16-a
Loans granted by purpose in $	OAS member countries	N 16-a
Subscribed capital & member's voting power in IBRD	OAS member countries	N 16-a
I. C. A. see INTERNATIONAL COFFEE AGREEMENT		
IDA (International Development Association)		
Credits in $m	Recipient countries	M 3-a
Disbursements as development aid in $m	Worldwide	M 3-a
Loans approved for aircraft repair plants in $	OAS member countries	N 16-a
automotive assembly industry in $	OAS member countries	N 16-a
building construction projects in $	OAS member countries	N 16-a
building materials industries in $	OAS member countries	N 16-a
cement industry in $	OAS member countries	N 16-a
concrete (pre-mixed) industry in $	OAS member countries	N 16-a
construction equipment industry in $	OAS member countries	N 16-a
domestic appliances manufacturing industry in $	OAS member countries	N 16-a
education in $	OAS member countries	N 16-a
electric power installation in $	OAS member countries	N 16-a
electrical engineering projects	OAS member countries	N 16-a
fertiliser production projects in $	OAS member countries	N 16-a
fibreboard manufacturing industry in $	OAS member countries	N 16-a
financing of infrastructure projects in $	OAS member countries	N 16-a
flour milling industry in $	OAS member countries	N 16-a
food-processing industry in $	OAS member countries	N 16-a
furniture manufacturing industry in $	OAS member countries	N 16-a
industrial equipment manufacturing industry in $	OAS member countries	N 16-a
iron & steel industry in $	OAS member countries	N 16-a
leather industry in $	OAS member countries	N 16-a
livestock & animal feed production in $	OAS member countries	N 16-a
livestock-rearing projects in $	OAS member countries	N 16-a
mining & quarrying in $	OAS member countries	N 16-a
petrochemicals manufacturing industry in $	OAS member countries	N 16-a
printing & publishing industry in $	OAS member countries	N 16-a
pulp & paper manufacturing industry in $	OAS member countries	N 16-a
road improvements in $	OAS member countries	N 16-a
storage & warehousing facilities in $	OAS member countries	N 16-a
textile manufacturing industries in $	OAS member countries	N 16-a
tourism development in $	OAS member countries	N 16-a
water supply facilities in $	OAS member countries	N 16-a
Loans granted by purpose in $	OAS member countries	N 16-a
Net flow of development aid from IDA as % of total overseas aid	Worldwide	M 4-a
Projects approved by IDA & credits granted in $m	Worldwide	M 3-a
Subscribed capital of IDA & member's voting power	OAS member countries	N 16-a
IDB (Inter-American Development Bank)		
Loans approved by purpose in $	OAS member countries	N 16-a
for agriculture in $	OAS member countries	N 16-a
education in $	OAS member countries	N 16-a
electric power installations in $	OAS member countries	N 16-a
	Latin American countries	U 18-a
housing development in $	OAS member countries	N 16-a
industrial development in $	OAS member countries	N 16-a
mining development in $	OAS member countries	N 16-a
telephones & communications installations in $	OAS member countries	N 16-a
water & sewage systems in $	OAS member countries	N 16-a
Net flow of IDB development aid as % of total overseas aid	Worldwide	M 4-a
Subscribed capital of IDB & member's voting power	OAS member countries	N 16-a
IFC (International Finance Corporation) see also DEVELOPMENT AID		
Net flow of development aid as % of total overseas aid	Worldwide	M 4-a

	Territorial coverage	Title codes	
IMF (International Monetary Fund)			
see also DRAWING RIGHTS			
STAND-BY CREDITS			
Drawing rights (at end-yr) in UA	Member countries	R 5-a	
Drawings: gold or credit tranches in $m	All countries	F 1-a	
credits taken up in UA	Member countries	R 5-a	
Holdings in specific currencies & drawing rights equivalents	Member countries	F 4-a	
Members' positions in drawing rights outstanding	Member countries	F 5-m	F 6-q
	EEC countries	E 4-a	
fund quotas	Member countries	F 5-m	F 6-q
stand-by credits	Member countries	F 5-m	F 6-q
use of IMF credits	Member countries	F 5-m	F 6-q
Participant's obligations to provide currencies for the fund	Member countries	F 4-a	
Quotas, gold subscriptions & total funds in $m	Main countries	E 3-a	
Receipts & payments (incl summary of financial transactions) of IMF	Worldwide	F 4-q	
Reserve positions in IMF & use of fund credits	Main countries	E 3-a	
as payment balances component	All countries	F 1-a	
Resources used in specific currencies (incl repurchases)	Worldwide	F 4-q	
Special drawing rights outstanding	Asian, Far East & Australasian countries	U 45-a	
Transfers of special drawing rights for purposes of currency acquisition	Worldwide	F 4-q	
ICE CREAM			
Consumption of fresh milk in production of ice cream in gallons	USA	B 4-a	
per capita: dairy ice cream in kg per yr	EEC countries	B 3-a	
Import quotas in lbs	USA	B 4-a	
Production & consumption per capita in lbs	USA	D 14-a	
volume	All countries	U 22-a	
	EEC countries	E 28-q	E 27-a
ILLEGITIMACY			
see also LIVE BIRTHS			
No of illegitimate births & as % of total live births	OAS member countries	N 12-a	
Illicit traffic see DRUGS & MEDICINES			
ILLIPE NUTS			
Exports: tonnage	Indonesia & Sarawak	B 19-a	
Imports: tonnage	Netherlands & UK	B 19-a	
ILLITERACY			
see also LITERACY			
% rate of adult illiteracy (by decade)	All countries	U 62	
adults by sex (census data)	ECAFE countries	U 17	
% success rates in overcoming illiteracy in special schools by sex	All countries	U 62-a	
No of adults illiterate	All countries	U 62-a	
	OAS member countries	N 19-a	
illiterates over 15 yrs by sex	OAS member countries	N 19-a	
offenders before courts proving illiterate	OAS member countries	N 20-a	
illiterate pupils enrolled at special schools	All countries	U 62-a	
Ilmenite see TITANIUM MINERALS			
IMMIGRATION			
No of immigrants: historical table from 1815-1969	Main European countries	Z 1-a	
Implements, agricultural see FARM MACHINERY			
IMPLEMENTS, MULTI-PURPOSE FARM			
MACHINERY, AGRICULTURAL			
IMPLEMENTS, MULTI-PURPOSE FARM			
No of single-axle implements in use	Main countries	R 5-a	
Implicit deflator see EXPORT PRICES			
GDP			
IMPORT DUTIES			
see also IMPORT LEVIES (EEC)			
% contribution to government income	Main countries	R 5-a	
Government revenue from vehicle imports in local currency	Main countries	S 24-a	
	OAS member countries	N 16-a	
	Latin American countries	J 5-a	
Receipts as component of budget accounts in $m	Main countries	U 43-a	
Revenue from import duties in local currency	EEC countries	E 42-a	
historical tables from 1750 in local currency	Main European countries	Z 1-a	
in local currency	Asian, Far East & Australasian countries	U 45-a	
	OECD countries	D 42-a	
IMPORT LEVIES			
EEC area levy on beef & veal (fresh or frozen) in $ per 100 kg		B 11-a	
live cattle & calves in $ per 100 kg		B 11-a	
live pigs in $ per 100 kg		B 11-a	
pig-meat by kind in $ per 100 kg		B 11-a	

	Territorial coverage	Title codes
IMPORT LEVIES, continued		
EEC area levy on pig-meat in £ per ton		C 9-m
sugar (raw & refined) in $ per 100 kg		B 13-m
eggs in pence per 4 doz		B 1-a
in $ per kg		B 12-m B 4-a
egg yolks (liquid frozen & dried) in $ per kg		B 4-a
eggs (fresh, preserved & dried) in $ per kg		B 4-a
poultry by kind in $ per kg		B 11-a
pigs (for pig-meat) in £ per score		B 1-a
barley ex non-EEC area in $ per ton		B 7-m
maize ex non-EEC area in $ per ton		B 7-m
millet ex non-EEC area in $ per ton		B 7-m
oats ex non-EEC area in $ per ton		B 7-m
rye flour ex non-EEC area in $ per ton		B 7-m
rye ex non-EEC area in $ per ton		B 7-m
sorghum ex non-EEC area in $ per ton		B 7-m
wheat flour ex non-EEC area in $ per ton		B 7-m
IMPORT PRICES		
Abaca (manilla grade 2) ex Phillipines in £ per ton cif	UK	B 2-a
(non davao 2S) in Frs per kg cif (tax-paid)	France	R 2-m
(non davao G) in £ per ton cif	UK	R 2-m
Agricultural products in local currency	Main countries	A 9-a
Almonds by grade in £ per ton c & f	UK	P 4-m
Aluminium (primary) ex Canada in cents per lb cif	European ports	R 2-m
Antimony-lead alloy in £ per ton cif	UK	C 12-m
Bananas ex Jamaica on London market in £ per 21 lb box	UK	B 2-a
in $ per ton cif France, W Germany, UK & USA		A 5-a
Barley ex Argentine, S Africa & USA in £ per ton cif	UK	B 8-m
ex USA in $ per ton cif	N Sea ports	C 16-m U 35-a
for animal feed: spot quotations in £ per ton cif	UK	B 7-m
Beef (chilled) ex Argentine in pence per kg cif	UK	U 33-q
Beryllium ore (cobbed lump) in $ per ton cif	European ports	T 4-m
Brazil nuts (medium kernels) in £ per ton cif	UK	P 4-m
Butter ex Denmark, Australia & New Zealand in £ per ton cif	UK	R 2-m
(salted) ex N Zealand in £ per 112 lbs cif	UK	U 33-q
Cadmium ingots in $ per lb cif	UK	C 12-m
Cadmium metal: free market price in £ per lb	UK	T 4-m
(in sticks) in £ per lb cif	UK	T 4-m
in $ per lb cif	UK	C 12-m
Caesium ore (pollucite concentrates) in local currency per ton cif	European countries	T 4-m
Canned fruit (in syrup) by kind in £ per cwt cif	UK	B 6-a
Casein ex N Zealand & Poland in £ per ton cif	UK	B 12-m B 4-a
Cashew kernels by grade in £ per ton c & f	UK	P 4-m
Castor oil ex Brazil in £ per ton cif	UK	B 19-q
in cents per lb at New York	USA	B 19-q
in $ per ton cif	European ports	B 19-q
in $ per ton cif at Rotterdam	Netherlands	R 2-m
in £ per ton cif	UK	B 2-a
Castor seed ex E Africa in £ per ton cif	UK	R 2-m
	European ports	B 19-q
Cattle & calves: regulated market prices in £	EEC countries	B 11-a
Cattle hides (dried of 18-22 lbs wt) in pence per lb	UK	R 2-m
Chrome ore by grade in $ per ton cif	UK	C 12-m
ex USSR in $ per ton cif	European countries	T 4-m
ex Turkey: (friable concentrate) in local currency per ton	Main countries	T 4-m
Cinnamon bark & cassia ex Seychelles & China in £ per ton cif	UK	B 18-m
Citrus fruits by kind in £ per cwt cif	UK	B 6-a
Cloves ex Zanzibar & Madagascar in £ per ton cif	UK	B 18-m
Coal & coke in S Kr per ton cif	Sweden	U 10-a
Coarse grains by kind ex USA in $ per ton cif	North Sea ports	C 16-m
ex Argentina & USA in $ per ton cif	European ports	U 35-a
Cobalt: contract price (delivered) in £ per kg cif	UK	C 12-m
free market price (delivered) in £ per kg cif	UK	C 12-m
Cocoa beans at Hamburg in DM per kg cif	W Germany	E 34-m
(spot price) ex Ghana on London market in $ per ton cif	UK	B 2-a
(spot price ex Ghana & 3 mths forward) in $ per ton cif	UK & USA	A 5-a
Cocoa (fermented) ex Ghana in £ per ton cif	UK	P 2-m
Coconut oil ex Philippines in Fl per kg cif	Netherlands	R 2-m
ex Sri Lanka in £ per ton cif	UK	R 2-m B 19-q
	European ports	B 19-a
(in bulk) in £ per ton cif	UK	P 1-a
ex Malaysia in £ per ton cif	UK	A 4-m
ex Sri Lanka in £ per ton cif	UK	A 4-m
Coffee beans (green) & instant coffee in cents per lb cif	Canada	J 1-a
in $ per bag & in cents per lb cif	USA	J 1-m
Copper ex USA in cents per lb cif	European countries	C 12-m
Copra in local currency per ton cif	European & USA ports	A 4-m
ex New Hebrides in Frs per kg cif at Marseilles	France	R 2-m
Papua & Philippines in $ per ton cif	UK	U 32-m
Philippines in £ per ton cif	UK	B 19-q
in $ per kg cif	UK	R 2-m
Straits & Borneo in £ per ton cif	UK	P 1-m
Straits in £ per ton cif	UK	P 1-a
Cotton (raw) by quality in cents per lb cif	UK	U 11-a
ex Izmir (Turkey) & N Brazil in DM per kg cif at Bremen	W Germany	R 2-m

IMPORT PRICES, continued | Territorial coverage | Title codes

Cottonseed meal in £ per ton cif	UK	R 2-m
ex Nigeria in £ per ton cif	UK	B 19-q
oil (semi-refined) in £ per ton cif	UK	B 19-q
Crude petroleum in Lit per ton cif	Italy	H 4-a
in $ per barrel cif	European ports	U 16-q
	Argentine & Brazil	U 18-a
Diesel & fuel oil in S Kr per ton cif	Sweden	U 10-a
Feeding stuffs by kind in local currency per ton cif	UK & European ports	P 1-m
Ferrous scrap in $ per ton cif	EEC countries	E 29-a
Fish meal ex Peru or Chile in Fl per kg cif	Netherlands	R 2-m
(under contract) ex Hamburg in $ per ton cif	USA	R 2-m
Fish oil ex Peru, Denmark & Iceland in £ per ton cif	W European countries	B 19-a
Flax ex Belgium & USSR in £ per ton cif	UK	B 10-m
Fruit (fresh) by kind in £ per cwt cif	UK	B 6-a
Germanium di-oxide in £ per kg cif (duty-paid)	UK	C 12-m
(refined) in £ per kg cif (duty-paid)	UK	C 12-m
Ginger (by source of product) in £ per ton cif	UK	B 18-m
Grapefruit ex Israel in £ per 85 lb box	UK	B 2-a
ex S Africa in £ per 68 lb box	UK	B 2-a
Grapefruit juice (canned) in $ cif	European ports	A 7-m
Groundnut cake in £ per ton cif	UK	R 2-m
Groundnut oil (crude) in £ per ton cif	UK	P 1-a
ex Nigeria in £ per ton cif	UK	P 1-m
ex Nigeria & Gambia in £ per ton cif	UK	R 2-m
ex W Africa in £ per ton cif	UK	B 19-m B 19-q
Groundnuts ex Nigeria in £ per ton cif	UK	B 19-m B 19-q
in local currency per ton cif	European ports	P 1-m
(shelled) ex Nigeria in £ per ton cif	UK	P 1-a
ex Nigeria & Ghana in £ per ton cif	UK	R 2-m
Hardwood logs in £ per m³ cif	UK	A 25-a
Hazelnuts ex Turkey in £ per ton fob UK port	UK	P 4-m
Ilmenite concentrates ex Australia in $A per ton cif	European countries	T 4-m
Iron ore (from major sources) in $ per ton cif	EEC countries	E 29-a
Jute (at Dundee) in £ per ton cif (monthly or annual averages)	UK	B 10
(on London market) in £ per ton cif	UK	B 2-a
(raw fibre) ex Bangladesh in £ per ton cif	UK	U 32-m
Lamb (frozen) ex N Zealand in pence per lb cif	UK	U 33-q
Lard (prime steam) ex USA in £ per ton cif	UK	R 2-m
Latex crepe in £ per kg cif	UK & European ports	C 17-m
(liquid) in £ per kg cif	UK & European ports	C 17-m
Lead ore (incl concentrates) in $ per ton cif	European countries	T 4-m
Lemons ex Italy in £ per 80 lb box	UK	B 2-a
Linseed ex Canada in £ per ton cif	UK	R 2-m B 19-q
		B 19-a P 1-a
	European ports	P 1-m
Linseed oil ex Argentina in £ per ton cif	UK	B 19-q B 19-a
in £ per ton cif	UK	R 2-m B 2-a
Magnesium ingots in £ per ton cif	UK	C 12-m
Maize by quality in local currency cif	European ports	R 2-m
spot quotations in £ per ton cif	UK	B 7-m
ex Argentine in $ per ton cif	N Sea ports	C 16-m
Argentine, S Africa & USA in £ per ton	UK	B 8-m
Argentine & USA in $ per ton	N Sea ports	U 35-a
USA in $ per ton cif	N Sea ports	A 12-a
	UK	U 20-q U 33-q
Manganese ore (ex major sources) in $ per ton cif	EEC countries	E 29-a
in cents per ton cif	European countries & USA	T 4-m
Mercury in £ per flask (of 76 lbs) cif	UK	C 12-m
in $ per flask (of 34.5 kg) cif	European ports	T 4-m
(of 76 lbs) cif	N Sea ports	R 2-m
Natural rubber in £ per ton cif	UK	U 32-m
by grade in local currency per ton cif	N Sea ports	C 17-m
Nickel (refined metal) in $ per lb cif	UK	R 2-m
Non-ferrous metals by kind in local currency cif	Main countries	T 4
Nuts by kind & quality in £ per ton c & f	UK	P 4-m
Oats ex Argentine in $ per ton cif	N Sea ports	U 35-a
(for animal feed) ex Australia & Canada in £ per ton cif	UK	B 8-a
Oilcake & meal by kind in local currency per ton cif	UK & European ports	P 1-m
Oilseeds by kind in £ per ton cif	W European countries	B 18-m
Olive oil ex Spain (in barrels) in £ per ton cif	UK	R 2-m
in $ per ton cif	USA	R 2-m
Orange juice (canned) in $ cif	European ports	A 7-m
Oranges ex Israel in £ per 88 lb box cif	UK	B 2-a
ex Morocco in Fr per kg for	France	A 5-m
ex Spain in £ per 68 lb box cif	UK	B 2-a
Palm kernel oil (crude) in £ per ton cif	UK	P 1-a
ex W Africa in £ per ton cif	UK	B 19-q
	European ports	B 19-m B 2-a
Palm kernels ex Nigeria in £ per ton cif	UK	P 1-m R 2-m
		B 19-q
	European ports	B 19-m
Palm oil ex Malaysia in £ per ton cif	European ports	B 19-m
	UK	B 19-q P 1-a
Pepper by kind (at London & New York markets) in local currency per ton		B 18-m
in £ per ton cif	UK	B 13-m
ex Malabar & Sarawak in £ per ton cif	UK	B 2-a
ex Malabar (on New York market) in cents per lb cif	USA	B 13-m

	Territorial coverage	Title codes	
IMPORT PRICES, continued			
Pineapples (canned in slices or pieces) in $ per ton cif	Main countries	A 8-a	
Rapeseed ex Canada in £ per ton cif	UK	B 19-q	
	W European ports	B 19-a	
Rapeseed oil in £ per ton cif	W European ports	B 19-a	
	UK	B 19-a	
Regulus metal in £ per ton cif	UK	C 12-m	T 4-m
Rice by grade in local currency per kg cif	N Sea ports	R 2-m	
ex Thailand & USA in £ per ton cif	UK	B 2-a	
in £ per ton c & f	UK & N Sea ports	B 14-m	
Rutile concentrates ex Australia in $A per ton cif	European countries	T 4-m	
Rye ex USA in $ per ton cif	N Sea ports	C 16-m	U 35-a
Sawn hardwood in £ per m³ cif	UK	A 25-a	
beech, birch & oak in £ per m³ cif	UK	A 25-a	
keruing & sipo in £ per m³ cif	UK	A 25-a	
mahogany & obeche in £ per m³ cif	UK	A 25-a	
ramin & teak in £ per m³ cif	UK	A 25-a	
Sesame seed ex Sudan in £ per ton cif	European ports	B 19-q	
Silk raw (20-22 denier) in $ per lb cif	USA	R 2-m	
Sisal ex E Africa in £ per ton cif	European ports	B 10-m	
	UK	B 2-a	
ex N Africa in $ per ton cif	UK	R 2-m	
in Fr per kg cif	France	R 2-m	
Softwood: white & red deal battens in £ per m³ cif	UK	R 2-m	
Sorghum ex USA in $ per ton cif	European ports	C 16-m	A 12-a
		U 35-a	
spot quotations by quality in $ per ton cif	UK	B 7-m	
Soybean oil (ex tank at Rotterdam) in £ per ton cif	UK	B 19-m	B 19-q
(under contract) in $ per ton cif	UK	R 2-m	
Soybeans (American yellow) in £ per ton cif	UK	B 19-m	P 1-a
		B 19-q	P 1-a
Spices & essences by kind in £ per cwt cif	UK	B 18-m	
Sugar ex Caribbean area in local currency per lb cif (at London & New York)	UK & USA	R 2-m	
(in bulk) in £ per ton cif	UK	B 2-a	
(raw centrifugal) in £ per ton cif	UK	C 25-a	
in £ per cwt: historical table from 1900	UK	A 20-a	
Sunflower seed oil (ex tank at Rotterdam) in £ per ton cif	UK	B 19-q	
in $ per ton cif	UK	B 19-b	
in Fl per kg cif (at Rotterdam)	Netherlands	R 2-m	
(under contract) in £ per ton cif	UK	R 2-m	
Tantalum ore in $ per lb cif	European ports	T 4-m	
Tin in £ per ton cif	European ports	C 20-m	
(on London & New York markets) in £ per ton cif	UK & USA	B 2-a	
ore by grade in £ per ton cif	European countries	T 4-m	
Tung oil ex S America in $ per ton cif	UK	B 19-m	
Tungsten concentrates in £ per ton cif	UK	U 53-m	
in $ per ton cif	USA	U 53-m	
Tungsten ore in $ per ton cif (based on metal content)	UK	U 11-a	
Vanadium pentoxide in $ per kg cif	N Sea ports	T 4-m	
Vegetable oils by kind in £ per ton cif	W European countries	B 18-m	
Walnuts ex France & India in £ per ton cif	UK	P 4-m	
Wheat by grade in £ per ton cif	UK	B 8-m	
in $ per ton cif (at Antwerp & Rotterdam)	Belgium & Netherlands	C 16-m	
spot quotations in £ per ton cif	UK	B 7-m	
ex Canada & USA (at Rotterdam) in $ per ton cif	Netherlands	U 35-a	
USA by grade in $ per ton c & f	Japan	C 16-m	
flour ex Canada & Australia in £ per ton cif	UK	R 2-m	
(hard) ex main sources in $ per ton cif (at Rotterdam)	Netherlands	C 29-m	
ex USA in $ per ton c & f	Japan	C 29-m	
in £ per ton cif	UK	C 29-m	
in $ per 100 kg cif (average)	W European countries	U 30-a	
in $ per ton cif (at Rotterdam)	Netherlands	C 29-m	
in $ per ton c & f by grade & source	Japan	C 16-m	
in $ per ton cif by grade & source	UK	C 16-m	
	European countries	C 16-m	
(soft) by grade in local currency per ton cif	N Sea ports	R 2-m	
(spring) ex Canada in DM per ton cif	European ports	U 33-a	
Wine (common red) ex France in DM (free border)	W Germany	A 5-a	
Wood pulp (bleached & unbleached) in Lit per 100 kg cif	Italy	R 2-m	
Wool (merino crossbred) ex N Zealand & Australia in £ per ton cif	UK	B 10-m	
(raw) ex Australia & N Zealand (clean basis) in £ per ton cif	UK	A 5-a	
Zinc ore sulphide in $ per ton cif	European countries	T 4-w	
Zirconium sand in £ per ton cif	European countries	T 4-m	

IMPORT QUOTAS

see also   EXPORT QUOTAS
                 SUPPLY QUOTAS

Butter quotas authorised by supplying country in lbs	UK	B 4-a
Cheese (cheddar & processed blue) by kind in lbs	USA	B 4-a
Dairy products (incl cheese) by kind in lbs	USA	B 4-a
Milk products: butter, cream, skim & ice cream in lbs	USA	B 4-a
Sugar: quota-exempt imports by source: tonnage	USA	C 19-m

Import rates of exchange   see   EXCHANGE RATES

IMPORT SUBSIDIES

Beef in EEC trade in pence per lb	EEC countries	C 9

	Territorial coverage	Title codes	
IMPORT TRADE see also Appendix 2			
SEABORNE FREIGHT			
TRADE BALANCES			
As % of gross product	Latin American region	U 18-a	
By areas of origin by value in $m & as % of world total	Main countries	E 3-a	
broad product groups by value & as % of world total	Main countries	E 3-a	
category of importing country by value in $m		U 23-a	
commodity groups by value in $m	Main countries	E 24-a	
commodity groups: EEC & non-EEC area countries	EEC countries	E 26-m	
CST classes by source: tonnage & value in $	EEC countries	E 21-a	
farm products ex E European countries by value in $m	EEC countries	U 33-a	
groups of manufactured products by value in $m	Developing countries	U 52-a	
main groups of products ex EEC area by value in UA	AASM countries	E 41-a	
world basis by value in UA	AASM countries	E 41-a	
main ports: tonnage & value	Caribbean countries	T 6-a	
NIMEXE classes by value in $	All countries	E 20-a	
product by source by SITC classes by value in $m (in detail)	All countries	U 12-a	
quantity & value in local currency	African countries	U 44-a	
SITC classes by source by value in $m	All countries	U 12-a	
	Main countries	D 2-q	
tonnage & value in $m	OECD countries	D 3-a2	
by value in $	All countries	U 50-a	U 59-a
	Asian & Far East areas	U 32-a	
By source & by product groups by rail transport	EEC countries	E 43-a	
by road transport	EEC countries	E 43-a	
by sea freight	EEC countries	E 43-a	
all products by value in $	Main countries	D 16-m	
	ECAFE countries	U 32-m	
By value by source in UA	African, Caribbean countries & Pacific Is	E 45-a	
	AASM countries	E 41-a	
historical table in local currency	EEC countries	E 23-a	
ex world regions: historical table in UA	Main countries	Z 1-a	
African countries from 1958 in UA	EEC countries	E 24-a	
Central & S American countries from 1958 in UA	EEC countries	E 24-a	
Communist countries in DM million	EEC countries	E 24-a	
developed countries in DM million	OECD countries	R 5-a	
in $m	OECD countries	R 5-a	
developing countries in DM million	All countries	F 2-a	
in $m	OECD countries	R 5-a	
E European countries from 1958 in UA	All countries	F 2-a	
EFTA countries from 1958 in UA	EEC countries	E 24-a	
Far East countries from 1958 in UA	EEC countries	E 24-a	
USA from 1958 in UA	EEC countries	E 24-a	
W Asian countries from 1958 in UA	EEC countries	E 24-a	
EEC area in $m	Main non-EEC countries	E 24-a	
	Main countries	E 22-q	
in UA	AASM countries	E 41-a	
economic groups of countries in $m	OECD countries	D 16-m	
OECD area in $m	OECD countries	D 16-m	
world regions in $m	OECD countries	D 16-m	
historical tables from 1796 in local currency	Main European countries	Z 1-a	
from 1927 in $m	Main countries	C 4-a	
in DM million	Main countries	R 5-a	
local currency	W Indies & Caribbean countries	T 6-a	
	African countries	U 44-a	
$m (& % change)	European countries & USSR	U 16-a	
$m (incl monthly averages)	OECD countries	D 16-q	
$m (seasonally adjusted)	Main countries	U 16-q	
$m (by level of gross national product per capita of population)		U 23-a	
$m	African, Caribbean countries & Pacific Is	E 45-a	
	All countries	F 5-m	F 6-q
	Asian & Far East regions	U 32-q	
	Asian, Far East & Australasian countries	U 45-a	
	China	F 3-m	
	Developing countries with over 1m population	U 23-a	
	Developing countries	U 23-a	
	E European countries	F 3-m	
	ECE countries	U 42-m	
	ECAFE countries	U 17-a	
	ECAFE area	U 32-m	
	Latin American countries	U 40-a	
	Main non-EEC area countries	E 24-a	
	Main countries	F 3-m	E 24-a
	Main oil-exporting countries	U 23-a	
	OECD countries	D 16-m	
	OPEC countries	C 3-a	
	AASM countries	E 41-a	
in UA (ex all sources)	AASM countries	E 45-a	
(ex EEC area)		R 5-a	
into W European Bloc - index nos	OECD countries	R 5-a	
per capita in DM	All countries	M 6-a	
in $		R 5-a	
world basis - index nos	Asian, Far East & Australasian countries	U 45-a	
By world areas of origin		E 45-a	
world economic regions by value in $ per capita of population	All countries	F 2-a	
Consigned to Communist countries by value in $m	World regions	R 5-a	
developed countries by value in DM million	World regions	R 5-a	
developing countries by value in DM million			

	Territorial coverage	Title codes	
IMPORT TRADE, continued			
Consigned to EEC area ex non-EEC countries by value in $m	EEC countries	E 22-m	E 3-a
- index nos	EEC countries	E 3-a	
ex world economic areas by value in UA	EEC countries	E 22-q	
In goods & services as % of gross national product	All countries	M 6-a	
In steel products between EEC member countries as % of world imports		E 30-q	
On value basis - index nos	Main countries	E 24-a	
volume basis - index nos	EEC countries	E 24-a	
world basis (all products) by value in $m	All countries	F 2-a	
% change & index nos (quantum basis)	World regions	U 23-a	
(quantum & value basis)	ECE countries	U 15-a	
by source	World regions	U 54-a	
farm products by kind	EEC countries	E 23-a	
imports (total) & ex E European countries	Developed countries	A 1	
in implicit price deflator for imports	E European countries	U 16-a	
in imports (total)	Developing countries	D 25-a	
	African countries	G 1-a	
	Asian countries	G 1-a	
	Australasian countries	G 1-a	
	Communist Bloc countries	G 1-a	
	Latin American countries	G 1-a	
	Middle East countries	G 1-a	
	S Africa	G 1-a	
in imports of fertilisers	Main countries	U 25-a	
goods & services	Japan	G 1-a	
inorganic chemicals	Main countries	U 25-a	
man-made fibres	Main countries	U 25-a	
organic chemicals	Main countries	U 25-a	
pharmaceutical products	Main countries	U 25-a	
plastics	Main countries	U 25-a	
synthetic rubber	Main countries	G 1-a	
in unit value of total imports	Main European countries, Japan & USA	G 1-a	
on value basis	Main European countries, Japan & USA	G 1-a	
on volume basis	ECE countries	U 15-a	
% of gross national product spent on import of goods & services	Developing countries	U 23-a	
% growth rates (based on import values)	Main oil exporting countries	U 23-a	
(based on level of gross national product per capita)	Main countries	U 23-a	
(based on value)	Latin American countries	U 18-a	
	World regions	U 23-a	
by value projected to 1980	OECD countries	D 11	
goods & services (value basis)	All countries	M 6-a	
machine tools by type by source	EEC countries	B 20-a	
machine tools by type	EEC countries	B 20-a	
(on volume & value bases)	Main countries	D 17-a	
% import penetration: clothing (weatherproof)	UK	B 22-a	
corsets & gloves	UK	B 22-a	
dresses & lingerie	UK	B 22-a	
infantwear	UK	B 22-a	
millinery & caps	UK	B 22-a	
shirts, overalls & underwear	UK	B 22-a	
tailored outerwear (for females)	UK	B 22-a	
(for males)	UK	B 22-a	
% import trend of chemicals projected to 1977	UK	B 21	
machine tools projected to 1977	UK	B 26	
% increase in motor vehicle imports projected to 1977	UK	B 28	
% of imports: circuit breakers & switchgear by source	Main countries	T 7-a	
power transformers by source	Main countries	T 7-a	
% of inter-EEC imports: agricultural products (value basis)	EEC countries	U 33-a	
% of machine tools consigned ex EEC area (value basis)	EEC countries	B 20-a	
% share: farm products of total imports (value basis)	Main countries	A 11-a	
steam boilers by source	Main countries	B 30-a	
Index nos (quantum & unit value bases)	All countries	U 27-m	
(quantum basis)	All countries	F 5-m	F 6-q
	Asian & Far East areas	U 32-q	
	ECAFE area	U 32-m	
	EEC countries	E 22-m	
	Main countries	E 24-a	
	OAS member countries	N 15-a	
	African countries	U 44-a	
	Asian & Far East areas	U 32-q	
(unit value basis)	EEC countries	E 22-m	E 24-a
	ECAFE countries	U 32-m	
	Main countries	G 1-a	
	World regions	U 23-a	
	African countries	U 44-a	
(value basis)	Developing world regions	U 23-a	
	EEC countries	E 26-m	
	OAS member countries	N 15-a	
IMPORT TRADE, INTER-EEC			
By value in UA	EEC countries	E 22-m	
Chemical products by value in UA	EEC countries	E 22-m	
Food, drink & tobacco by value in UA	EEC countries	E 22-m	
Fuels by value in UA	EEC countries	E 22-m	
Machinery & transport equipment by value in UA	EEC countries	E 22-m	
Manufactured goods by value in UA	EEC countries	E 22-a	
Raw materials by value in UA	EEC countries	E 22-m	

	Territorial coverage	Title codes

IMPORT TRADE BY PRODUCT (& SOURCE)   see   APPENDIX 2

Impurity standards, metallic   see   QUALITY STANDARDS, METAL

Incandescent lamps   see   LAMPS, INCANDESCENT

Income   see   EARNINGS
              NATIONAL INCOME
              PERSONAL INCOME
              WAGES

Income elasticity of demand   see   CEREAL PREPARATIONS
                                              FOOD
                                              MEAT
                                              RICE
                                              WHEAT

Income from abroad   see   OVERSEAS INVESTMENT INCOME
                              REMITTANCES
                              TRANSFER PAYMENTS

Income from freight insurance   see   INVISIBLE TRADE

Income from goods & services   see   BALANCE OF PAYMENTS

Income from overseas visitors   see   INVISIBLE TRADE

Income from services   see   INVISIBLE TRADE

Income from tourism   see   BALANCE OF PAYMENTS

INCOME TAX

	Territorial coverage	Title codes
As % of gross national product and of revenue	OECD countries	D 42-a
of gross national product to 1969	OECD countries	D 11
of tax revenue	OECD countries	D 11
Basis of assessment & rates of tax	EEC countries	E 31-a
Direct taxation levied on income in $m	OECD countries	D 30-a
Levied on individuals as % of tax receipts	Main countries	E 3-a
Revenue as component of budget accounts in $	Main countries	U 43-a
from income & wealth taxes in $m	Asian, Far East & Australasian countries	U 45-a
	EEC countries	E 42-a

Income, agricultural   see   FARM INCOME

Independent retailers   see   RETAILERS, INDEPENDENT

INDEPENDENT STORES

    see also   MULTIPLE STORES

% market share: non-food items	EEC countries	B 29-a
% of clothing sales marketed by independent stores	UK	B 22-a
Labour force: retail clothing sales	UK	B 22-a
Sales: clothing by kind by value in £m	UK	B 29-a

Indices   see   INDEX NOS   (APPENDIX 3)

Indirect taxation   see   TAXATION, INDIRECT

INDIUM

    see also   INGOTS, INDIUM

% of consumption in production of electronic components & instruments	USA	N 1-a
Production in troy oz	Main countries	N 1-a
Wholesale prices: metal bars in pence per troy oz	UK	T 4-m
in $ per troy oz	USA	N 1-a
World production (at smelters) in troy oz	Main countries	N 1-a
World reserves in troy oz (estim)	Main countries	N 1-a

Industrial accidents   see   ACCIDENTS, INDUSTRIAL

INDUSTRIAL COMPANIES

    see also   BALANCE SHEETS
                  DIVIDENDS
                  INDUSTRIAL SHARES
                  PRIVATE COMPANIES
                  PROFITS
                  SHARE CAPITAL
                  SHARES & SECURITIES
                  STOCK EXCHANGE
                  YIELDS

% change in turnover (5 yr averages)	European countries	F 9-a
Consumption expenditure in $	OAS member countries	N 14-a
Details of world's 100 largest corporations	Worldwide	H 1
Equity valuation of largest foreign companies		F 8-q
of largest UK companies		F 8-q
Loan advances to industrial enterprises by banks in local currency	OAS member countries	N 16-a

	Territorial coverage	Title codes
INDUSTRIAL COMPANIES, continued		
Names of largest British companies & % change in turnover		H 1
fields of activity		H 1
labour force employed		H 1
turnover in £m		H 1
Canadian companies & % change in turnover		H 1
fields of activity		H 1
labour force employed		H 1
turnover in $m		H 1
French companies & % change in turnover		H 1
fields of activity		H 1
labour force employed		H 1
turnover in Frs million		H 1
German companies & % change in turnover		H 1
fields of activity		H 1
labour force employed		H 1
turnover in DM million		H 1
Italian companies & % change in turnover		H 1
fields of activity		H 1
labour force employed		H 1
turnover in Lit million		H 1
Japanese companies & % change in turnover		H 1
fields of activity		H 1
labour force employed		H 1
turnover in Yen million		H 1
Swiss companies & % change in turnover		H 1
fields of activity		H 1
labour force employed		H 1
turnover in FrS million		H 1
US corporations & % change in turnover		H 1
fields of activity		H 1
labour force employed		H 1
net trading profit in $m		H 1
turnover in $m		H 1
of world's largest corporations & % change in turnover		H 1
fields of activity		H 1
country of ownership		H 1
labour force employed		H 1
turnover in FrS million		H 1
No of industrial enterprises in operation	OAS member countries	N 14-a
Production of industrial enterprises by value in $	OAS member countries	N 14-a
Raw materials consumed by industrial enterprises by value in $	OAS member countries	N 14-a
Share capital (nominal value) of major European companies in $m		F 9-a

Industrial consumption   see   CONSUMPTION, INDUSTRIAL

Industrial costs   see   DISTRIBUTION COSTS
                            LABOUR COSTS
                            SOCIAL CHARGES
                            WAGES

Industrial disputes   see   STRIKES & LOCK-OUTS

Industrial diversification   see   DIVERSIFICATION, INDUSTRIAL

Industrial efficiency   see   LABOUR PRODUCTIVITY, INDUSTRIAL

Industrial employment   see   EMPLOYMENT, INDUSTRIAL

Industrial engines   see   ENGINES, INDUSTRIAL

Industrial forecasts   see   PROJECTIONS, INDUSTRIAL

Industrial furnaces   see   FURNACES, INDUSTRIAL

Industrial heating & cooling equipment   see   HEATING & COOLING
                                                                        EQUIPMENT, INDUSTRIAL

	Territorial coverage	Title codes
INDUSTRIAL INPUTS		
As % total industrial output	Main countries	D 17-a
% growth rates of labour & capital inputs	Main countries	D 17-a

Industrial investment   see   INVESTMENT

Industrial prices   see   PRICES, INDUSTRIAL

INDUSTRIAL PRODUCTION

      see also   MANUFACTURING INDUSTRY
                         PRODUCTION

	Territorial coverage	Title codes	
As % of gross domestic product	All countries	U 60-a	
By ISIC groups - index nos	All countries	U 27-m	
By main products by value in local currency	Caribbean countries & W Indies	T 6-a	
by value in $	Asian, Far East & Australasian countries	U 45-a	
By sectors - index nos (see no 2, 5, 8, 11)	Main countries	U 27-q	
index nos	Latin American countries	J 5-a	
	Main countries	U 21-a	U 43-a
	OECD countries	D 26-m	
	Senegal & Zaire	E 41-a	

	Territorial coverage	Title codes	
INDUSTRIAL PRODUCTION, continued			
By sectors - index nos (see no 3)	USSR	U 27-a	
Excl building - index nos	EEC countries	E 26-m	
% changes as component of gross national product	All countries	U 60-a	
in output by industrial sectors	Groups of countries	U 54-q	
(value basis)	E European countries & USSR	U 16-a	
	Main countries	G 1-a	
	Centrally-planned economies	U 18-a	
	Developed countries	U 18-a	
	Developing countries	U 18-a	
(on previous quarter)	EEC countries	E 13-q	
% contribution to gross domestic product	AASM countries	E 41-a	
	All countries	U 23-a	
	S European countries	U 16-a	
% growth rates (actual)	Developed countries	U 54-a	
	Developing countries	U 54-a	
	E European countries & USSR	U 54-a	
(compounded)	Main countries	N 7-a	
(over 5 yr periods)	Main countries	U 38	
(planned)	E European countries & USSR	U 54-a	
% share contributed by basic metals industries	Main countries	U 38-a	
chemical industries	European countries, Japan & USA	U 38-a	
clothing industries	European countries, Japan & USA	U 38-a	
engineering industries	Main countries	U 38-a	
food, drink & tobacco industries	Main countries	U 38-a	
non-metallic mineral industry	Main countries	U 38-a	
paper & printing industries	Main countries	U 38-a	
textile industries	European countries, Japan & USA	U 38-a	
wood-working industry	Main countries	U 38-a	
% structure by manufacturing sector	Main countries	U 38-a	
Chemicals production - index nos	African countries	U 44-a	
Clothing & footwear production - index nos	OECD countries	D 46-a	
Food, drink & tobacco production - index nos	African countries	U 44-a	
Gross manufacturing output by value in $m	All countries	U 43-a	
	Asian, Far East & Australasian countries	U 45-a	
	E European countries	U 25-a	
Gross manufacturing output - index nos	Far East countries	U 32-q	
Gross output of industry by sectors - index nos	OAS member countries	N 14-a	
Index nos: historical table of production from 1801	Main European countries	Z 1-a	
(incl world index no)	Main countries	C 4-a	
(seasonally adjusted)	All countries	F 5-m	F 6-q
	European countries	U 16-a	
of industrial production	African countries	U 44-a	
	Asian & Far East countries	U 32-q	
	Asian, Far East & Australasian countries	U 45-a	
	Developed areas & world regions	U 23-a	
	Canada, European countries, Japan & USA	U 49-a	
	ECE countries	U 42-m	
	EEC area	E 13-m	
	EEC countries	E 28-q	E 27-a
		E 44-a	
	Main countries	E 3-a	N 7-a
		R 5-a	U 38-a
	OECD countries	D 19-m	D 20-m
		D 26-m	
	World economic areas	U 60-a	
	World regions	U 43-a	
Manufactured products by kind - index nos	Worldwide	U 43-a	
Manufactured products - index nos	African countries	U 44-a	
	Asian countries	U 32-q	
	UK	B 28-a	
Mining & quarrying - index nos	African countries	U 44-a	
Motor vehicles - index nos	UK	B 28-a	
Public utilities - index nos	African countries	U 44-a	
Textiles - index nos	African countries	U 44-a	
Value added (at factor cost) in $m	Main countries	U 25-a	
INDUSTRIAL PRODUCTIVITY			
see also LABOUR PRODUCTIVITY			
% growth rates planned	Greece, Portugal, Spain & Turkey	D 17	
Of manufacturing enterprises - index nos	Main countries	J 2-a	
Public expenditure on research into productivity problems in $m	EEC countries	E 39-a	
Industrial sales see SALES, INDUSTRIAL			
INDUSTRIAL SHARES			
see also SHARES, COMMON			
SHARES, PREFERENCE			
% equity held by governments in oil companies	OPEC member countries	C 3-a	
by oil companies in their own enterprises	OPEC member countries	C 3-a	
% yields, dividends & earnings	OECD countries	D 12-a	
% yields per annum: stocks & securities	Main countries	E 3-a	
Bank holdings: securities & bonds in $m	OECD countries	D 12-a	
Equity values by kinds of investment in $m	OECD countries	D 12-a	
new issues (incl bonds) in $m	OECD countries	D 12-a	
nominal & market values of shares in £m	UK	F 8-q	
Market prices & % yields (high & low)	Main companies (worldwide)	F 9-a	
	EEC countries	E 26-m	

	Territorial coverage	Title codes	
INDUSTRIAL SHARES, continued			
Market prices (daily average) – index nos	Main countries	C 4-a	
Market prices – index nos	Worldwide	R 5-a	
	All countries	F 5-m	F 6-q
	ECE countries	U 42-m	
	EEC countries	E 26-m	
	Main countries	U 27-m	E 3-a
		U 43-a	
	OECD countries	D 26-q	
Price-earnings ratios per share unit	Main European companies	F 9-a	
Sales value of industrial shares on stock exchanges in local currency	OAS member countries	N 16-a	
Transactions on stock exchanges in foreign shares in $m	OAS member countries	N 16-a	
in US industrial shares in $m	OAS member countries	N 16-a	

Industrial soap   see   SOAP, INDUSTRIAL

Industrial trucks   see   WORKS' TRUCKS

Industrial workers   see   CRAFTSMEN & PROCESS WORKERS

INDUSTRY
        see also   SERVICE INDUSTRIES

	Territorial coverage	Title codes	
% of consumption by kind of energy sources	Main countries	H 4-a	
% contribution to gross national product: historical table from 1800	Main European countries	Z 1-a	
% growth in output per capita projected to 1980	Main countries	D 17-a	
of industrial labour force employed	ECAFE countries	U 17-a	
% growth rates in planned output	Greece, Portugal, Spain & Turkey	D 17	
% of total labour force engaged in industry projected to 1980	Main countries	D 17-a	
% share of capital invested in industry	E European countries & USSR	U 16-a	
A.I.D. grants to promote industrial & mining activity in $m	Recipient countries	M 1-a	
Capital formation in $m	Main countries	U 25-a	
Consumption of electric power by industry in calorific value	Main countries	H 4-a	
natural gas by industry in calorific value	Main countries	H 4-a	
petroleum products by industry in calorific value	Main countries	H 4-a	
Contribution of industrial activity to gross domestic product in local currency	African countries	U 44-a	
Coefficients of demand: machinery by sector	Main countries	U 38-a	
Development aid authorisations in $	All recipient countries	M 1-a	
Earnings in specific main industries (average)	All countries	L 4-a	
Employers' direct & indirect costs per employee	Main countries	R 3-m	
Employment by sector: wage earners & labourers	OAS member countries	N 14-a	
Expenditure on electric energy by sector in $	OAS member countries	N 14-a	
fuel & oils by sector in $	OAS member countries	N 14-a	
machinery by sector as % total investment	Main countries	U 38-a	
packaging & warehousing in $	OAS member countries	N 14-a	
raw materials by sector in $	OAS member countries	N 14-a	
Funds available for industrial development from European Development Fund in $		D 13-a	
Government financing: research into new industrial techniques in $m	EEC countries	E 36-a	
Gross output by value by industrial sector in $m	Main countries	U 21-a	
IBRD loans approved for industrial projects in $m	OAS member countries	N 16-a	
Labour costs per hr by kind of goods produced	EEC countries	E 2-a	
Labour force employed as % of total employment	OECD countries	D 24-q	
by age & sex	UK	B 28-a	
by age, sex & degree of skill	EEC countries	E 2-a	
by sex (census data)	OAS member countries	N 18	
by sex	OECD countries	D 24-q	
– index nos	Main OECD countries	D 24-q	
(total)	EEC countries	E 18-a	
in manufacturing industry: 14-24 yrs of age	EEC countries	E 3-a	
over 60 yrs of age	EEC countries	E 3-a	
in manufacturing industry – index nos	Main countries	U 27-m	
Labour productivity – index nos	Main countries	L 4-a	
No of employees in industry involved in strike action	UK	B 28-a	
of enterprises by kind in operation	Main countries	U 21-a	
in operation	Main countries	R 5-a	
family helpers as % of total employment in business enterprises	EEC countries	E 18-a	
hrs worked by wage earners by sex	EEC countries	E 33-a	
per wk by sex (average)	EEC countries	E 2-a	E 33-a
stoppages of work due to labour disputes	UK	B 28-a	
working days lost per 1000 workers as result of strikes	UK	B 28-a	
as result of labour disputes	UK	B 28-a	
self-employed persons as % of total labour force employed	EEC countries	E 18-a	
wage & salary earners employed as % of total labour force	EEC countries	E 18-a	
Production per hr: metal industry – index nos	W Germany	H 3-a	
Stocks of finished goods held by industrial users by value in $m	OAS member countries	N 14-a	
of raw materials held by industrial users by value in $m	OAS member countries	N 14-a	
Unemployment as % of total economically-active population	Main OECD countries	D 24-q	
Wage rates per hr by sex in local currency (average)	Main countries	R 3-m	
in DM (average)	W Germany	H 3-a	
Work in progress by value in $m	OAS member countries	N 14-a	
World bank loans & credits granted for industrial expansion in $m	Worldwide	M 3-a	

INFANT MORTALITY

	Territorial coverage	Title codes
No of deaths & death rate per 1000 live births	All countries	U 28-a
by age (in days) & rate per 1000 live births	All countries	U 14

	Territorial coverage	Title codes

INFANT MORTALITY, continued

No of deaths under 1 yr of age by regions	OAS member countries	N 12-a
under 1 yr of age	Asian, Far East & Australasian countries	U 45-a
	EEC countries	E 26-m
under 1 yr of age & rate per 1000 live births	All countries	U 14-a
per 1000 live births: foetal & perinatal deaths	Latin American countries	J 5-a
historical table from 1750-1969	Main European countries	Z 1-a
per 1000 live births	All countries	W 1-q
	Main developed countries	M 4-a
	Main developing countries	M 4-a
per 1000 live births: infants under 1 yr of age	ECE countries	U 15-a
	EEC countries	E 2-a
	Latin American countries	J 5-a
	OAS member countries	N 12-a
per 100 live births by area	EEC countries	E 38-a

Infant schools   see KINDERGARTEN

Infectious diseases   see DISEASES, INFECTIOUS

INFLATION

    see also PURCHASING POWER PARITIES

% change in consumer prices (general level)	European countries & USA	U 16-q
in retail food prices	European countries & USA	U 16-q
% gross national product deflator rate	Main European countries, Canada, Japan & USA	D 10-a2
Countries listed by % degrees of price inflation	Main countries	U 54-a
Food prices as component in general price increases	Main countries	U 16-q
Fuel prices as component in general price increases	Main countries	U 16-q
Price deflators for flows of development aid	Main countries	D 7-a
Purchasing power (internal) of pound sterling - index nos	UK	T 4-a

Influenza   see DISEASES, INFECTIOUS

Ingots for tubes   see BLANKS FOR TUBES

INGOTS, ALLOY STEEL

    see also CRUDE STEEL, ELECTRIC
                INGOTS, STAINLESS STEEL

Exports by destination: tonnage	Main countries	T 4-a
by quality: tonnage	Main countries	T 4-a
Imports by source by quality: tonnage	Main countries	T 4-a
Production by quality: tonnage	UK	T 4-a
tonnage	Main countries	T 4-a

INGOTS, ALUMINIUM

Consumption: tonnage	Canada	J 6-a
Contract prices ex Canada in £ per ton	UK	R 2-m
Exports (incl alloy ingots): tonnage	USA	J 6-a
(incl notch bars): tonnage	UK	C 30-a
Imports (incl alloy ingots): tonnage	USA	J 6-a
(incl notch bars): tonnage	UK	C 30-a
Plant production capacity by company: tonnage	USA	J 6-a
Production: virgin secondary aluminium ingots: tonnage	UK	C 30-a
tonnage	Canada	J 6-a
Wholesale prices in £ per ton on London Metal Exchange	UK	R 2-m
in cents per lb (ex works)	USA	R 2-m N 1-a
World prices: foundry grade aluminium ingots (based on UK prices in £ per ton)		E 41-a
World production of unalloyed aluminium ingots: tonnage		N 4-a

INGOTS, BERYLLIUM-COPPER ALLOY

Export prices in $ per lb	USA	T 4-m
Wholesale prices in £ per lb	UK	T 4-m

INGOTS, BRASS

    see also BRASS PRODUCTS, SEMI-FINISHED

Deliveries (incl bronze) to user industries: tonnage	USA	J 6-m
Production for castings: tonnage	UK	C 30-m
for fabrication in extrusion plants: tonnage	UK	C 30-m
in rolling mills: tonnage	UK	C 30-m
Wholesale prices by grade in £ per ton	UK	T 4-w
in local currency per kg	Main countries	T 4-w

INGOTS, BRONZE

Wholesale prices by grade in Lit per kg	Italy	C 12-m

Ingots, carbon steel   see CRUDE STEEL, CARBON

INGOTS, COPPER ALLOY

Production: brass strip ingots: tonnage	UK	C 30-m
by kind & by quality: tonnage	UK	C 30-m
cupro-nickel ingots for remelting: tonnage	UK	C 30-m
ferro-copper ingots: tonnage	UK	C 30-m
manganese-copper ingots: tonnage	UK	C 30-m

	Territorial coverage	Title codes	
INGOTS, COPPER-ALLOY continued			
Production: phosphor-copper ingots: tonnage	UK	C 30-m	
silicon-copper ingots: tonnage	UK	C 30-m	
Production: tonnage	UK	T 4-a	
INGOTS, COPPER			
Imports by source: tonnage	Netherlands	T 4-a	
Ingots, electric see CRUDE STEEL, ELECTRIC			
INGOTS, GUNMETAL			
Wholesale prices by grade in £ per ton	UK	T 4-w	
INGOTS, INDIUM			
Wholesale prices in $ per troy oz	USA	T 4-a	
INGOTS, MAGNESIUM			
Plant production capacity by company & process: tonnage	USA	J 6-a	
Wholesale prices: electrolytic magnesium ingots in £ per ton	UK	T 4-w	
pig magnesium ingots in cents per lb	USA	T 4-w	
INGOTS, MANGANESE			
Export prices in cents per lb fob Texas	USA	R 2-m	
Wholesale prices: sandcasting alloy in £ per ton	UK	T 4-m	
INGOTS, NICKEL-SILVER			
Production: tonnage (for remelting)	UK	C 30-m	
INGOTS, PHOSPHOR-BRONZE			
Production: tonnage (for remelting)	UK	C 30-m	
Wholesale prices in £ per ton	UK	T 4-w	
INGOTS, STAINLESS STEEL			
Exports by destination: tonnage	Main countries	T 4-a	
Imports by source: tonnage	Main countries	T 4-a	
tonnage	Main countries	T 1-a	
Production: tonnage	Main countries	T 4-a	
INGOTS, STEEL			
see also CRUDE STEEL, CARBON			
INGOTS FOR TUBES			
Deliveries by destination: tonnage	EEC area & world regions	E 29-a	
(domestic): tonnage	EEC countries	E 29-a	
(overseas) by destination: tonnage	EEC countries	E 29-a	
to EEC area: tonnage	EEC countries	E 29-a	
Exports by destination: tonnage & value in $	EEC countries	E 5-q	
tonnage	EEC countries	E 29-a	
	Main countries	T 4-a	
shipped to non-EEC area: tonnage	EEC area	E 3-a	
(incl semis): tonnage	European countries, Japan & USA	C 5-m	
	ECE countries	U 7-m	U 6-a
	Main countries	H 3-a	
tonnage & % share of world exports	Main countries	U 49-a	
Imports by quality: tonnage	All countries	T 1-a	
by source: tonnage	EEC countries	E 5-q	E 29-a
	Main countries	T 4-a	
(incl semis): tonnage	ECE countries	U 7-m	U 6-a
	Main countries	H 3-a	
of non-alloy steel ingots: tonnage	Main countries	T 1-a	
Production by process: tonnage	All countries	T 4-a	
	EEC area	E 29-a	
Production, consumption & stocks: tonnage	EEC countries	E 3-a	
Production potential: all qualities by regions: tonnage	EEC countries	E 46-a	
basic Bessemer quality: tonnage	EEC countries	E 46-a	
bottom-blown steel ingots: tonnage	EEC countries	E 46-a	
electric quality: tonnage	EEC countries	E 46-a	
L.D. & Kaldo steel quality: tonnage	EEC countries	E 46-a	
open-hearth steel ingots: tonnage	EEC countries	E 46-a	
Production by quality: tonnage	All countries	T 1-a	T 4-a
	EEC countries	E 29-a	
Electric steel: historical table from 1925: tonnage	EEC countries	E 29-a	
tonnage	European countries & USA	C 5-m	
ingots (for tube production): tonnage	All countries	U 22-a	
(incl steel for castings): tonnage	Main countries	C 5-m	
liquid steel for castings: tonnage	Main countries	C 5-m	
oxygen steel ingots: tonnage	European countries	C 5-m	
Siemens steel ingots: historical table from 1925: tonnage	EEC countries	E 29-a	
special steels (for castings): tonnage	EEC countries	E 29-a	
tonnage	EEC countries	E 29-a	
Thomas quality steel ingots: historical table from 1925:			
tonnage	EEC countries	E 29-a	
tonnage	European countries & USA	C 5-m	
	ECE countries, Japan & USA	U 6-a	U 7-a
	Main countries	H 3-a	
	OAS member countries	N 14-a	

	Territorial coverage	Title codes
INGOTS, STEEL continued		
Receipts of steel ingots at re-rolling plants: tonnage	EEC area	E 29-a
ex steelworks located in EEC area: tonnage	EEC countries	E 29-a
Stocks: tonnage & % change	EEC countries	E 29-a
World production: tonnage of crude steel		N 4-a
(incl castings by process)		T 1-a
(incl castings)		C 30-a
INGOTS, TIN		
Wholesale prices in Lit per kg at Milan	Italy	C 12-m
INGOTS, TITANIUM		
Production (incl alloys): tonnage	USA	J 6-a
INGOTS, ZINC		
Exports (incl bars) by destination: tonnage	Zambia	T 4-a
Wholesale prices in £ per ton on London Metal Exchange	UK	R 2-m
Wholesale prices: electrolytic zinc ingots in lire per kg at Milan	Italy	C 12-m
primary ingots in lire per kg at Milan	Italy	C 12-m
Inheritance taxes see TAXATION		
Injuries at work see ACCIDENTS, INDUSTRIAL		
Injuries in air crashes see ACCIDENTS, AIRCRAFT		
Injuries in road accidents see ACCIDENTS, ROAD		
INJURY & DISABLEMENT BENEFITS		
Expenditure by insurance companies in $m	OAS member countries	N 16-a
on benefits in local currency	EEC countries	E 6-a
Health Service costs in $m	All countries	L 2-a
No of benefits paid out	OAS member countries	N 18-a
Payments & % of total expenditure paid out on welfare benefits	EEC countries	E 6-a
Inland freight see FREIGHT TRANSPORT		
INLAND WATERWAYS		
Cargo loaded & unloaded: tonnage	AASM countries	E 41-a
as inland freight: tonnage	Main countries	R 5-a
as overseas freight: tonnage	Main countries	R 5-a
loaded & unloaded in transit: tonnage	European countries	U 8-a
unloaded as inland freight: tonnage	Main countries	R 5-a
overseas freight: tonnage	Main countries	R 5-a
(incl domestic freight): tonnage	EEC countries	E 43-a
Exports: agricultural products by kind: tonnage	European countries	U 8-a
building materials (incl timber): tonnage	European countries	U 8-a
cereals: tonnage	European countries	U 8-a
chemical products: tonnage	European countries	U 8-a
fertilisers: tonnage	European countries	U 8-a
machinery: tonnage	European countries	U 8-a
metal ores: tonnage	European countries	U 8-a
oil products: tonnage	European countries	U 8-a
solid fuels: tonnage	European countries	U 8-a
Freight carried by range of distances: tonnage	European countries	U 8-a
by type of craft in ton-km	European countries	U 8-a
historical table from 1835: tonnage	European countries	Z 1-a
in ton-km million	Main countries	E 3-a S 24-a
international transit: tonnage	Main countries	R 5-a
on barges by type: tonnage	European countries	U 8-a
on tankers by type: tonnage	European countries	U 8-a
over frontiers on river Danube: tonnage		U 8-a
on river Rhine: tonnage		U 8-a
tonnage	EEC countries	E 26-m
	Main countries	S 24-a
Imports & exports (incl transit): tonnage	European countries	U 8-a
Imports: agricultural products by kind: tonnage	European countries	U 8-a
building materials & timber: tonnage	European countries	U 8-a
cereals: tonnage	European countries	U 8-a
chemical products: tonnage	European countries	U 8-a
fertilisers: tonnage	European countries	U 8-a
machinery: tonnage	European countries	U 8-a
metal ores: tonnage	European countries	U 8-a
oil products: tonnage	European countries	U 8-a
solid fuels: tonnage	European countries	U 8-a
Inter-EEC transit freight: tonnage	EEC countries	E 43-a
Navigable length of canals in km & depth in m		R 5
of canals, rivers & lakes in km	EEC countries	E 43-a
	European countries	U 8-a
in km suitable for craft by capacity: tonnage	European countries	U 8-a
inland waterways in use in km	Main countries	E 3-a
No & tonnage of barges in use on inland waterways	Main countries	R 5-a
of bulk carriers in use on inland waterways	Main countries	R 5-a
of cargo boats in use on inland waterways	Main countries	E 3-a R 5-a
No of motor vessels & tankers in use on inland waterways	EEC countries	E 43-a
Traffic density by class of inland waterways in ton-km	EEC countries	E 43-a
in ton-km	ECE countries	U 15-a
Traffic volume in ton-km	ECE countries	U 15-a

	Territorial coverage	Title codes
INNER TUBES, RUBBER		
see also TYRES		
Consumption: natural rubber for production of tubes: tonnage	UK	C 18-a
rubber by kind for production of tubes: tonnage	Canada & France	C 18-a
synthetic rubber for production of tubes: tonnage	UK	C 18-a
Exports by destination: no & value in £m for tractors	UK	V 1-a
for trucks	UK	V 1-a
no & value in £m	UK	V 1-a
Imports by source: no & value in £m for cars	UK	V 1-a
for tractors	UK	V 1-a
for commercial vehicles	UK	V 1-a
Production by volume for all vehicles	OAS member countries	N 14-a
	All countries	U 22-a
	UK	V 1-q
for cars	UK	V 1-q
for commercial vehicles	UK	V 1-q
historical tables	UK	V 1-q
Sales volume by kind (as original equipment)	UK	C 18-a
(as replacements)	UK	C 18-a
(on government account)	UK	C 18-a
INNS		
see also HOTELS		
No of beds available in inns for visitors & tourists	OECD countries	D 47-a
Inorganic chemicals see CHEMICALS, INORGANIC		
INSECTICIDES		
see also DISINFECTANTS		
Consumption by kind in agriculture: tonnage	All countries	A 9-a
Export prices: pyrethrum extract in local currency per ton cif	Kenya	A 9-a
Exports (incl fungicides & disinfectants) by value in $	Main countries	U 2-a
Insemination see ARTIFICIAL INSEMINATION		
INSTALMENT CREDIT		
see also CREDIT FINANCE		
FINANCE HOUSES		
As % of turnover: retail clothing trade	UK	B 22-a
% of furniture sold on credit terms	W European countries	C 8-a
Motor vehicles: hire purchase debt in £m	UK	V 1-a
INSTANT COFFEE		
Consumption as % of total consumption of coffee	European countries	J 1-a
in bags & lbs	European countries	J 1-a
in terms of cups per person per day (estim)	USA	J 1-a
per capita in lbs per yr	USA	J 1-a
in oz per wk	UK	B 18-a
roasted coffee in production of instant coffee: tonnage	USA	J 1-a
Exports by destination in bags	Main countries	B 13-a
soluble coffee in bags	Brazil	B 18-m
Household purchases in lbs & as % of all coffee sales	USA	J 1-a
Import prices in $ per lb	Canada	J 1-a
Imports by source in bags	UK & USA	B 18-m
	European countries	J 1-a
Production (domestic) imports & supplies: tonnage	Canada	J 1-a
Share as % of all kinds of coffee consumed	W European countries	J 1-a
Wholesale prices in cents per 6oz jar	USA	J 1-m
in local currency	OAS member countries	N 17-a
Instant potatoes see CONVENIENCE FOODS		
INSTANT TEA		
Exports by destination in kg	India, Uganda & UK	C 1-a
in lbs	India, Sri Lanka, Uganda & UK	B 13-a
Imports by source in kg	UK	C 1-a
Production in kg	India & Uganda	C 1-a
in lbs	India, Sri Lanka & Uganda	B 13-a
INSTITUTIONS		
see also HOSPITALS, MENTAL		
No of living quarters available in institutions (all kinds)	All countries	U 13-a
Instrument & control engineering see ELECTRONIC EQUIPMENT		
SCIENTIFIC INSTRUMENTS INDUSTRY		
Instrument industry see MUSICAL INSTRUMENTS INDUSTRY		
SCIENTIFIC INSTRUMENTS INDUSTRY		
Instruments see MUSICAL INSTRUMENTS		
SCIENTIFIC INSTRUMENTS		
Instruments, analytical see ELECTRONIC EQUIPMENT		

	Territorial coverage	Title codes	
INSULATED WIRE & CABLES			
% increase in demand projected to 1977	UK	B 23	
% share of world export trade	Main countries	B 23-a	
Consumption of lead in production of cables: tonnage	European countries & USA	C 12-a	
of rubber in production of cables: tonnage	France & Japan	C 18-a	
Demand projected to 1980 by value in $m	E African countries	U 38	
Exports by value in $m	All countries	U 38-a	
Imports by value in $m	All countries	U 38-a	
Production: tonnage	All countries	U 22-a	U 38-a
value in $m	All countries	U 38-a	
World export trade by value in $m		U 38-a	

Insulation board   see   FIBREBOARD

INSURANCE

        see also   EXPORT CREDIT INSURANCE
                       LIFE INSURANCE
                       NATIONAL HEALTH INSURANCE
                       UNEMPLOYMENT INSURANCE

	Territorial coverage	Title codes
% of households holding insurance policies by kind of risk	W European countries	Z 3
No of persons insured by kind of risk	OAS member countries	N 18-a
INSURANCE CLAIMS		
Amounts paid out against business losses in local currency	OAS member countries	N 16-a
disability risks in local currency	OAS member countries	N 16-a
disturbance & riots in local currency	OAS member countries	N 16-a
fire insurance risks in local currency	OAS member countries	N 16-a
health policies in local currency	OAS member countries	N 16-a
life insurance policies in local currency	OAS member countries	N 16-a
marine insurance policies in local currency	OAS member countries	N 16-a
professional risks in local currency	OAS member countries	N 16-a
as annuity payments in local currency	OAS member countries	N 16-a
as mature endowments in local currency	OAS member countries	N 16-a
for air travel accidents in local currency	OAS member countries	N 16-a
motor vehicle accidents in local currency	OAS member countries	N 16-a
personal accidents in local currency	OAS member countries	N 16-a
property damage in local currency	OAS member countries	N 16-a
robbery & theft in local currency	OAS member countries	N 16-a
traffic accidents in local currency	OAS member countries	N 16-a
INSURANCE PREMIUMS		
Amounts charged: accidents at work in local currency	OAS member countries	N 16-a
air travel risks in local currency	OAS member countries	N 16-a
business losses in local currency	OAS member countries	N 16-a
cargo & marine policies in local currency	OAS member countries	N 16-a
disturbance & riots risks in local currency	OAS member countries	N 16-a
earthquake & cyclone risks in local currency	OAS member countries	N 16-a
fire risks to property in local currency	OAS member countries	N 16-a
goods & chattels: fire & theft in local currency	OAS member countries	N 16-a
health insurance in local currency	OAS member countries	N 16-a
life insurance in local currency	OAS member countries	N 16-a
motor vehicles insurance in local currency	OAS member countries	N 16-a
personal accidents in local currency	OAS member countries	N 16-a
public liability insurance in local currency	OAS member countries	N 16-a
real estate insurance in local currency	OAS member countries	N 16-a
traffic accidents in local currency	OAS member countries	N 16-a
Premiums collected by type of risk in local currency	OAS member countries	N 16-a

Insurance taxes   see   TAXATION

Inter-American Development Bank   see   IDB

INTER-EEC TRADE

	Territorial coverage	Title codes	
% changes in visible trade (volume basis)		E 13-a	
Bacon & lard: tonnage	EEC countries	E 47-m	
Boring machine tools by value in $m & % growth rate	EEC countries	B 20-a	
Drilling machine tools by value in $m & % growth rate	EEC countries	B 20-a	
Eggs (in shell) by volume & tonnage	EEC countries	E 47-m	
Exports by value in UA	EEC countries	E 22-m	E 24-a
chemical products by value in UA	EEC countries	E 24-a	
farm products as % of total inter-EEC trade	EEC countries	U 20-a	
food, drink & tobacco by value in UA	EEC countries	E 24-a	
fuels (all kinds) by value in UA	EEC countries	E 24-a	
machinery & transport equipment by value in UA	EEC countries	E 24-a	
raw materials by value in UA	EEC countries	E 24-a	
Forging presses by value in $m & % growth rate	EEC countries	B 20-a	
Fruit (fresh) by value in $m	EEC countries	U 20-a	
Gear production machines by value in $m & % growth rate	EEC countries	B 20-a	
Grinding machine tools by value in $m & % growth rate	EEC countries	B 20-a	
Ham (cooked or prepared): tonnage	EEC countries	E 47-m	
Historical table (on value basis) in UA	EEC countries	E 24-a	
Imports by value in UA	EEC countries	E 22-m	E 24-a
chemical products by value in UA	EEC countries	E 24-a	
iron & steel products: tonnage	EEC countries	E 3-a	
Imports & exports by value in UA	EEC countries	E 22-q	
farm products as % of total inter-EEC trade	EEC countries	U 20-a	
food, drink & tobacco by value in UA	EEC countries	E 24-a	

	Territorial coverage	Title codes
INTER-EEC TRADE, continued		
Imports: fuels (all kinds) by value in UA	EEC countries	E 24-a
machinery & transport equipment by value in UA	EEC countries	E 24-a
raw materials by value in UA	EEC countries	E 24-a
Live pigs for slaughter by volume	EEC countries	E 47-m
Milling machine tools by value in $m & % growth rate	EEC countries	B 20-a
Pig-meat (chilled or frozen): tonnage	EEC countries	E 47-m
(salted or dried): tonnage	EEC countries	E 47-m
Potatoes: tonnage & value in $	EEC countries	U 20-a
Poultry meat & chickens: tonnage	EEC countries	E 47-m
Pressed pork: tonnage	EEC countries	E 47-m
Sausages: tonnage	EEC countries	E 47-m
Tomatoes: tonnage & value in $	EEC countries	U 20-a
Turning machine tools by value in $m & % growth rate	EEC countries	B 20-a
Vegetable preparations: tonnage & value in $	EEC countries	U 20-a
Vegetables (dried): tonnage & value in $	EEC countries	U 20-a
(fresh) by value in $m	EEC countries	U 20-a

Inter-regional migration   see   MIGRATION, INTER-REGIONAL

Interest payments   see   DEBT SERVICING

INTEREST RATES

    see also   BANK RATE
               DISCOUNT RATES
               MINIMUM LENDING RATE

Weighted averages per annum	Main countries	M 7-a
% bankers acceptance rates	Main countries	M 7-a
% change in long-term lending rates per annum	EEC countries	E 13-a
in short-term lending rates per annum	EEC countries	E 13-a
% day-to-day money rates	Main countries	E 3-a
% deposit rates on Euro-currency market	OECD countries	D 12-a
per annum	Canada, European countries, Japan & USA	M 7-q
	Main countries	M 7
% discount rates & bond rates per annum	Asian, Far East & Australasian countries	U 45-a
(official) per annum	Main countries	M 7
% minimum lending rates enforced by Central Banks	OECD countries	D 26-q
% paid on overdrafts & mortgages per annum	OECD countries	D 12-a
to lenders by savings banks & building societies per annum	OECD countries	D 12-a
% prime rates charged for unsecured credit per annum	Main countries	M 7
% rate structures (comparative) per annum	Canada, European countries, Japan & USA	M 7-q
% rates charged for bank loans per annum	Canada, European countries, Japan & USA	M 7-q
on bills of exchange per annum	Main countries	M 7
Central Bank securities per annum	EEC countries & USA	E 3-a
development loans & grants per annum	OECD countries	D 13-a
European Development Fund credits per annum	OECD countries	D 10-a
Treasury Bills per annum	Main countries	M 7
% saving deposits rates per annum	Main countries	M 7
% term bank deposit rates per annum	EEC countries	E 26-m
% time deposit rates per annum	Main countries	M 7
% yields on corporate securities per annum	Main countries	M 7
on government bonds per annum	Main countries	M 7

Intermediate goods   see   SEMI-MANUFACTURED PRODUCTS

Internal combustion engines   see   ENGINES, INTERNAL
                                                     COMBUSTION

Internal financing   see   BUDGET ACCOUNTS

Internal public debt   see   DOMESTIC DEBT

INTERNAL TRADE

    see also   RETAIL TRADE
               WHOLESALE TRADE

% growth rates as component in gross national product	All countries	U 60-a
Contribution to gross domestic product in $m	S American countries	U 41-a
Income distribution (at factor cost) in $m	S American countries	U 41-a
Index nos	World economic areas	U 60-a
Indirect taxes levied on retail & wholesale trade in $m	S American countries	U 41-a
No of persons employed by sex & status by areas	EEC countries	E 38-a
shops, hotels & restaurants	EEC countries	E 2-a
wholesale & retail trade	OECD countries	D 23-a
No of persons employed	Asian, Far East & Australasian countries	U 45-a
Sales turnover of wholesale & retail trade in $m	Asian, Far East & Australasian countries	U 45-a
Wage & salary costs in wholesale & retail trade in $m	Asian, Far East & Australasian countries	U 45-a
Wholesale & retail trade as % of gross domestic product	All countries	U 60-a

International Bank for Reconstruction & Development   see   IBRD

International bond issues   see   GOVERNMENT BONDS, FOREIGN

INTERNATIONAL COFFEE AGREEMENT

Export quotas for coffee in bags	Member countries	A 5-a
Indicator prices for coffee by grade per lb	Member countries	B 13-m B 18-m
		B 13-a

	Territorial coverage	Title codes	
INTERNATIONAL COFFEE AGREEMENT, continued			
Production quotas: tonnage	Member countries	J 1-a	
by grade in million bags	Member countries	B 13-a	B 18-a
(effective) by grades & areas: tonnage	Member countries	B 13-a	
Shipments of coffee under quota agreements by grade: tonnage	Member countries	B 13-a	

International credit   see   CREDIT, INTERNATIONAL
                               DRAWING RIGHTS
                               IMF

International Development Association   see   IDA

International development organisations
        see   A.I.D.
               AFRICAN DEVELOPMENT BANK
               ASIAN DEVELOPMENT BANK
               EXPORT-IMPORT BANK (EXIMBANK)
               IBRD
               IDA
               IDB
               IFC
               UNDP
               WORLD BANK

INTERNATIONAL FARE PAYMENTS			
Receipts & expenditure in $m	OECD countries	D 47-a	

International Finance Corporation   see   IFC

International financial institutions   see   DEVELOPMENT AID
                                                 IMF

INTERNATIONAL LIQUIDITY
       see also   CREDIT, INTERNATIONAL
                       DRAWING RIGHTS
                       FOREIGN EXCHANGE
                       GOLD HOLDINGS
                       IMF
                       RESERVES

As % of imports	ECAFE countries	U 17-a	
In $m	African countries	U 44-a	
	ECE countries	U 42-m	
Changes (net) in $m	Main country groups	U 54-a	
INTERNATIONAL LOANS			
A.I.D. commitments as % of total foreign loans	Recipient countries	M 1-a	
by purpose in $m	All countries	M 1-a	
loans & grants in $m	All countries	M 1-a	
Granted to electric power generation industry in $m	Latin American countries	U 18-a	
Long-term debt amortization	All countries	M 6-a	

International Monetary Fund   see   IMF

International reserves   see   RESERVES

INTERNATIONAL SUGAR AGREEMENT			
Export prices of sugar under ISA in cents per lb fob	Member countries	U 33-q	
Export quotas under ISA & shortfalls against quotas: tonnage	Member countries	B 13-a	
Exports (net) to free markets: tonnage	Member countries	B 13-a	
(free market): tonnage	All countries	B 13-a	
Prices fixed under ISA in cents per lb	Member countries	B 13-m	B 13-a
	Caribbean countries	U 20-q	
INTERNATIONAL TIN AGREEMENT			
Ceiling & floor prices under ITA in £ per ton	Member countries	C 20	

International trade   see   FOREIGN TRADE
                             INVISIBLE TRADE

INTERNATIONAL WHEAT AGREEMENT			
Exports: tonnage	Member countries	B 7-a	C 29-a
Prices under IWA (minimum & maximum) in $ per bushel	Member countries	B 8-a	
Sales (normal) between members outside IWA: tonnage	Member countries	B 8-a	C 29-a
(special) between members: tonnage	Member countries	B 7-a	C 29-a

Intervention costs (community farming)   see   EEC BUDGET

INTERVENTION PRICES
       see also   IMPORT LEVIES
                       TARGET PRICES

As fixed by Commission	EEC area	E 44-a	
Barley & rye by sales centres in £ per ton	EEC countries	B 8-a	
Beef cattle: guide prices in £ per cwt	EEC countries	B 1-a	
Butter (82% fat) in £ per ton	Denmark, Eire & UK	B 3-a	
per 100 kg	EEC countries	B 3-a	

	Territorial coverage	Title codes	
INTERVENTION PRICES, continued			
Butter: Intervention & threshold prices in £ per cwt	EEC countries	B 1-a	
in £ per 100kg	EEC countries	B 12-m	B 4-a
Calves: guide prices in £ per cwt	EEC countries	B 1-a	
Cauliflowers in $ per kg	EEC area	U 20-m	
Cereals: cumulative price increments	EEC area	B 8-a	
by kind in £ per ton	EEC countries	B 8-a	
Cheese by kind in £ per 100kg	EEC area	B 4-a	
Citrus fruits by kind in $ per kg	EEC area	U 20-m	
Expenditure by product on Common Agricultural Policy (CAP) in £m	EEC area	B 1-a	
FEOGA expenditure on Common Agricultural Policy in £m	EEC area	B 1-a	
Fresh fruits: apples, pears & lemons in $ per kg	EEC area	U 20-m	
oranges in $ per kg	EEC area	U 20-m	
peaches in $ per kg	EEC area	U 20-m	
table grapes in $ per kg	EEC area	U 20-m	
tangerines in $ per kg	EEC area	U 20-m	
Lactose in £ per 100kg	EEC area	B 4-a	
Maize: Intervention & threshold price in £ per ton	EEC area	B 1-a	
Milk: condensed & evaporated in £ per 100kg	EEC area	B 4-a	
Milk per 100kg	EEC countries	B 3-a	
Milk powder in £ per 100kg	EEC area	B 4-a	
(skimmed) in £ per cwt	EEC area	B 1-a	
Milk products by kind in £ per 100kg	EEC area	B 4-a	
Olive oil: Intervention & target price in £ per ton	EEC area	B 18-a	
threshold price in £ per ton	EEC area	B 1-a	
in UA per ton	EEC area	B 19-a	
Rapeseed & colza in £ per cwt	EEC area	B 1-a	
Rapeseed: target price in £ per ton	EEC area	B 18-a	
in UA per ton	EEC area	B 19-a	
Rice: Intervention & threshold price in £ per ton	EEC area	B 1-a	
Rye: Intervention & threshold price in £ per ton	EEC area	B 1-a	
Skim milk powder in £ per ton	EEC area	B 3-a	
Sugar (raw & refined) in £ per 100kg	EEC area	B 13-a	
Sunflower seed in £ per cwt	EEC area	B 1-a	
Intervention & target price in £ per ton	EEC area	B 18-a	
in UA per ton	EEC area	B 19-a	
Tomatoes in $ per kg	EEC area	U 20-m	
Threshold price: barley in £ per ton	EEC area	B 7-m	B 1-a
durum wheat in £ per ton	EEC area	B 7-m	
maize in £ per ton	EEC area	B 7-m	
millet in £ per ton	EEC area	B 7-m	
oats in £ per ton	EEC area	B 7-m	
rye flour in £ per ton	EEC area	B 7-m	
rye in £ per ton	EEC area	B 7-m	
soft wheat in £ per ton	EEC area	B 7-m	
sorghum in £ per ton	EEC area	B 7-m	
wheat flour in £ per ton	EEC area	B 7-m	
Wheat (durum): Intervention & threshold price in £ per ton	EEC area	B 1-a	
sole derived price per ton	France & Italy	B 7-m	
(soft & durum) in £ per ton by areas	EEC countries	B 8-a	
in £ per ton	EEC countries	B 7-m	
(soft): Intervention & threshold price per ton	EEC area	U 33-m	B 1-a
Wine by quality per hectolitre	EEC area	A 5-a	
INVENTORIES			
see also STEEL STOCKHOLDERS			
STOCKPILES, GOVERNMENT			
WORLD STOCKS & SUPPLY (Appendix 4)			
Held by industrial sectors by value in $	OAS member countries	N 14-a	
wholesale & retail traders by value in $m	All countries	U 43-a	
Investment in materials for stock accumulation in $bn	OECD countries	D 30-a	
Stockpiling: expenditure as % of gross national product	USA	G 1-a2	
No of times inventory was turned: chemical manufacturing	All countries	U 23-a	
corporations (value basis)	USA	J 2-a	
engineering corporations (value basis)	USA	J 2-a	
machine tool manufacturing corporations (value basis)	USA	J 2-a	
manufacturing corporations (value basis)	USA	J 2-a	
motor vehicle manufacturing corporations (value basis)	USA	J 2-a	
% changes in stocks as component of gross domestic product	African countries	U 44-a	
in wood pulp stocks held at paper & pulp mills	OECD countries	D 40-a	
Retail trade: stocks of goods - index nos	OECD countries	D 26-m	
INVENTORIES BY PRODUCT			
Aluminium: stocks: tonnage	EEC countries, Japan & USA	C 12-a	
Ammonia: stocks held at producers' plants: tonnage	USA	N 1-a	
Anthracite: stocks held at coking plants: tonnage	USA	N 1-a	
at electric power stations	USA	N 1-a	
by retail trade: tonnage	USA	N 1-a	
Antimony metal: stocks: tonnage	USA	T 4-a	
Asbestos: stocks held by user industries: tonnage	USA	N 1-a	
Barley: stocks (end-season): tonnage	Main countries	B 7-a	B 8-a
on farms & at wholesalers' premises: tonnage	EEC countries	E 12-m	
on farms & left unsold: tonnage	UK	B 7-a	

INVENTORIES BY PRODUCT, continued

	Territorial coverage	Title codes	
Basic metals: stocks by kind at end-period: tonnage	USA	J 3-a	
Bauxite: stocks (excl government stockpile): tonnage	USA	B 2-a	
Beef, pork & lamb: stocks: tonnage & % change	France & W Germany	E 1-a	
Beryllium: stocks held at consumers' premises: tonnage	USA	N 1-a	
Bismuth: stocks held at consumers' & dealers' premises: tonnage	USA	N 1-a	
Blister copper: stocks: tonnage	Main countries	C 12-a	
Butter: stocks held at creameries at end-period: tonnage	Eire	B 12-m	
end-Aug & Dec: tonnage	EEC countries	B 3-a	
end-Jan & July: tonnage	Main countries	B 4-a2	
end-mth: tonnage	Main countries	B 12-m	
end-yr: tonnage	Main countries	A 11-a	
Butter, milk & cheese stocks: tonnage	EEC countries	E 44-a	
	Main W European countries	U 35-q	
Cadmium: stocks held at producers' & dealers' premises: tonnage	USA	N 1-a	
(excl strategic stockpile): tonnage	USA	T 4-a	
Carbon black: stocks held at producers' premises: tonnage	USA	N 1-a	
Cement: stocks held at mills: tonnage	USA	N 1-a	
Cereals: stocks by kind: tonnage & % change	OECD countries	D 14-a	
stocks: coarse grains: tonnage	Main countries	A 11-a	
tonnage	EEC countries	E 44-a	
Changes in stocks of materials & goods by value in $m	All countries	F 5-m	F 6-q
in animal feed stocks held on farms: tonnage	ECE countries	U 34-a	
blast furnace gas stocks in coal equiv tonnage	EEC countries	E 14-a	
butter stocks: tonnage	EEC countries	E 44-a	
cheese stocks: tonnage	EEC countries	E 44-a	
cocoa beans stocks: tonnage	Worldwide	B 2-a	
coke oven gas stocks in coal equiv tonnage	EEC countries	E 14-a	
condensed & evaporated milk stocks: tonnage	EEC countries	E 44-a	
crops & animal stocks as % of production	E European countries	U 34-a	
domestic stocks (all fuels): tonnage	EEC countries	E 14-a	
egg stocks: tonnage	EEC countries	E 44-a	
fish stocks: tonnage	EEC countries	E 44-a	
full cream milk stocks: tonnage	EEC countries	E 44-a	
imported coal stocks: tonnage	EEC countries	E 14-a	
coke stocks: tonnage	EEC countries	E 14-a	
lignite stocks: tonnage	EEC countries	E 14-a	
indigenous coal stocks: tonnage	EEC countries	E 14-a	
coke stocks: tonnage	EEC countries	E 14-a	
lignite stocks: tonnage	EEC countries	E 14-a	
iron ore & steel ingot stocks: tonnage	EEC countries	E 3-a	
lamb & mutton stocks: tonnage	EEC countries	E 44-a	
manufacturing raw materials stocks: tonnage	OECD countries	D 26-m	
margarine stocks: tonnage	EEC countries	E 44-a	
meat stocks: tonnage	EEC countries	E 44-a	
milk powder & dried milk: stocks	EEC countries	E 44-a	
natural gas stocks in coal equiv tonnage	EEC countries	E 14-a	
petroleum products stocks: tonnage	EEC countries	E 14-a	
pork stocks: tonnage	EEC countries	E 44-a	
poultry stocks: tonnage	EEC countries	E 44-a	
refined sugar stocks: tonnage	EEC countries	E 3-a	
skim milk stocks: tonnage	EEC countries	E 44-a	
solid fuel stocks: tonnage	All countries	U 55-a	
in stocks by value as % of gross domestic product	Main countries	E 3-a	
as component in capital formation in $m	Latin American countries	J 5-a	
	AASM countries	E 41-a	
as component in gross domestic product in local currency	Main countries	R 5-a	
as component in gross domestic product in $m	S American countries	U 41-a	
(at market prices) as % of gross national product	OECD countries	D 11	
projected to 1980 as % change in gross national product	OECD countries	D 11	
in vegetable & animal fish oils stocks: tonnage	EEC countries	E 44-a	
in wheat & cereal stocks: tonnage	EEC countries	E 3-a	
Cheese: stocks (beginning & end-yr): tonnage	EEC countries	B 3-a	
(end-period): tonnage	Main countries	B 12-m	
Chrome ore: stocks held at consumers' premises: tonnage	USA	N 1-a	
by kind: tonnage	USA	T 4-a	
Coarse grains by kind: carry-over stocks at end-mth: tonnage	Main countries	C 16-m	
Cobalt metal: stocks held at consumers' premises: tonnage	USA	N 1-a	
Cocoa beans: stocks (end-yr): tonnage	Main countries	B 13-a	
Coconut oil: stocks (end-yr): tonnage	USA	B 19-a	
Coffee (green): stocks at end-period: tonnage	W Germany & USA	B 18-m	
stocks held by dealers & importers: tonnage	USA	J 1-a	
Coffee stocks: carry-over in 60kg bags	Worldwide	J 1-a	
(end-yr): tonnage	Main countries	A 11-a	
(end-mth) incl world total: tonnage	EEC area & USA	B 13-m	
held by producers: tonnage	Brazil	A 5-a	
tonnage	Brazil & USA	B 2-a	
Coke: stocks at coke ovens: tonnage	European countries	U 10-a	
Coke-oven coke: stocks held at producers' plants: tonnage	European countries	U 31-q	
Copper alloy: stocks held at smelters & brass mills: tonnage	USA	T 4-a	
Copper blister: stocks in transit to refineries: tonnage	USA	J 6-a	
held at refineries: tonnage	USA	J 6-a	
smelter plants: tonnage	USA	J 6-a	
tonnage	Main countries	C 30-m	
Copper concentrates: stocks: tonnage	Australia & Zambia	C 12-a	
	Main countries	C 30-m	

INVENTORIES BY PRODUCT, continued

Product	Territorial coverage	Title codes	
Copper (electrolytic): stocks held at London Metal Exchange warehouses: tonnage	UK	C 12-a	J 6-a
(fire-refined): stocks held at London Metal Exchange warehouses: tonnage	UK	J 6-a	
Copper products (semi-finished): stocks: tonnage	UK	C 12-a	
(refined): stocks held at producers' plants: tonnage	USA	N 1-a	
held by industrial users: tonnage	USA	J 6-m	
held by other users: tonnage	USA	J 6-m	
tonnage	Main countries	C 30-m	C 12-a
Copper scrap: stocks held at smelters & brass mills: tonnage	USA	T 4-a	
Copper: stocks (end-yr): tonnage	Main countries	B 2-a	
(refined metal): tonnage	USA	T 4-a	
Cotton by kind: stocks (end-period) held by consumers: tonnage	USA	K 1-m	
in public storage: tonnage	USA	K 1-m	
(raw): stocks held at end-July: tonnage	Main countries	B 2-a	
held by importers & exporters: tonnage	Worldwide	A 5-a	
held at end-August in bales & tons	All countries	K 1-a	
held at mills, ports & in transit: tonnage	OECD countries	D 46-a	
(end-period) in bales	Main countries	K 1-m	
in bales	Worldwide (incl Communist countries)	P 1-a	
in lbs million (estim)	Worldwide	B 10-a	
world & USA stocks in bales & tons		K 1-a	
Cotton yarn (incl cloth): stocks: tonnage	Main countries	K 1-q	
Cottonseed oil: stocks (initial & end-yr): tonnage	USA	B 19-a	
Cottonseed: stocks (initial & end-yr): tonnage	USA	B 19-a	
Crude petroleum: stocks (in 42 gallon barrels)	USA	N 1-a	
Feldspar: stocks held at producers' plants: tonnage	USA	N 1-a	
Ferrous scrap: stocks held at iron & steelworks: tonnage	UK	T 4-a	
Finished steel products: stocks held at consumers' premises: tonnage	UK	T 2-q	
Fluorspar stocks held at consumers' premises: tonnage	USA	N 1-a	
at mines: tonnage (estim)	USA	N 1-a	
Fruit & meat: stocks by kind: tonnage & as % change	OECD countries	D 14-a	
Fruit (fresh): stocks by kind: tonnage	Australia & USA	D 29-a	
Groundnuts: stocks (initial & end-yr): tonnage	Nigeria & USA	B 19-a	
Gypsum (crude): stocks held at producers' premises: tonnage	USA	N 1-a	
Hard coal: stocks at pithead: tonnage	European countries	U 10-a	
(end-period): tonnage	European countries	U 31-q	
Hard fibre: stocks held in US government stockpile: tonnage	USA	B 10-a	
tonnage	Producing countries	B 10-a	
Hardwood (sawn): stocks by volume in m³	Canada, European countries & USA	A 25-q	
Ilmenite: stocks held at mines & users' premises: tonnage	USA	N 1-a	
Iron ore: stocks held at mines & consumers' plants: tonnage	USA	N 1-a	
	EEC countries	E 30-m	E 29-a
Jute stocks (incl allied fibres): tonnage	Main countries	A 5-a	
(end-season): tonnage	India & Pakistan	B 2-a	B 10-a
Lard: stocks: tonnage	USA	P 1-m	
Latex: stocks: tonnage	Main consuming countries	C 18-m	
Lead scrap: stocks held at smelters & refineries: tonnage	USA	T 4-a	
Lead: stocks held at London Metal Exchange warehouses: tonnage	USA	J 6-a	
consumers' & producers' premises: tonnage	Main countries	C 12-a	
consumers' premises: tonnage	UK	J 6-a	
producers' & users' premises: tonnage	USA	N 1-a	
home-refined metal: tonnage	UK	J 6-a	
imported virgin metal: tonnage	UK	J 6-a	
in ore & matte form held at smelters' plants: tonnage	USA	J 6-a	
refined metal: tonnage	European countries & USA	U 24-m	
Linseed: stocks (initial & end-yr): tonnage	Canada & USA	B 19-a	
Magnesium metal stocks: tonnage	USA	N 1-a	
Maize (for seed): stocks held on farms & at wholesalers' premises: tonnage	EEC countries	E 12-m	
stocks (end-season): tonnage	Main exporting countries	B 7-a	
	Main producing countries	B 8-a	
Manganese ore: stocks (end-period): tonnage	USA	T 4-a	
(untreated) stocks at end-period: tonnage	EEC countries	E 29-a	
Main kinds of manufactured goods by value in $m	E European countries & USSR	U 16-a	
Meat: stocks (frozen in storage): tonnage	UK	B 12-w	
Metallic tin: stocks in transit: tonnage	Country of destination	C 20-m	
Mica sheet: stocks held at consumers' premises: tonnage	USA	N 1-a	
Milk powder (skim): stocks: tonnage	EEC countries	B 3-a	
Minerals by kind (end-period) stocks: tonnage	USA	J 3-a	
Molybdenum concentrates: stocks held at mines in lbs	USA	N 1-a	
Narcotic drug requirements for stock in kg	Main countries	U 19-a	
Natural nitrates: stocks held at producers' premises: tonnage	USA	N 1-a	
Natural rubber: stocks: afloat & in transit: tonnage	Worldwide	B 2-a	
afloat: tonnage	IRSG member countries	C 18-m	
held by consuming countries: tonnage		C 18-m	B 2-a
held by producing countries: tonnage		C 18-m	B 2-a
tonnage	Main countries	B 13-a	
tonnage	Worldwide	C 17-m	
Nickel metal: stocks held at consumers' premises: tonnage	USA	T 4-a	
Nitrogen (elemental): stocks held at producers' plants: tonnage	USA	N 1-a	
(fixed): stocks held at producers' plants: tonnage	USA	N 1-a	
Oats: stocks (end-season): tonnage	Main countries	B 7-a	B 8-a
held on farms & at wholesalers' premises: tonnage	EEC countries	E 12-m	
Palm kernels: stocks (end-yr): tonnage	Indonesia & Malaysia	B 19-a	
Palm oil: stocks (end-yr): tonnage	Indonesia & Malaysia	B 19-a	
Pepper: stocks (end-period) held in London warehouses in cwt	UK	B 13-m	
(end-yr): black & white pepper held in London warehouses in cwt	UK	B 2-a	

INVENTORIES BY PRODUCT, continued

	Territorial coverage	Title codes	
Phosphate rock: stocks held at producers' plants: tonnage	USA	N 1-a	
Pig iron: stocks: tonnage	USA	N 1-a	
Platinum-group metals: stocks held by dealers & at refineries in oz	USA	N 1-a	
Potash: stocks held at producers' plants: tonnage	USA	N 1-a	
Potatoes: stocks held at wholesalers' premises: tonnage	UK	E 12-m	
tonnage	W Germany	E 44-a	
Pumice & volcanic cinder: stocks: tonnage	USA	N 1-a	
Quartz crystals: stocks held at users' premises in lbs	USA	N 1-a	
Rare earth oxide: stocks held at users' plants in lbs	USA	N 1-a	
Raw materials & fuels: stocks held by industry: tonnage	OECD countries	D 9-a	
& semi-processed goods: stocks held by industry by value in $m	ECE countries	U 42-q	
Reclaimed rubber: stocks: tonnage	Main countries	C 18-m	
Rice (carry-over stocks) in milled equiv tonnage	Main countries	A 10-a	
stocks held at wholesalers' premises: tonnage	EEC countries	E 12-m	
(end-yr): tonnage	EEC countries	E 44-a	
	India, Japan, Taiwan & USA	B 2-a	
	Main countries	A 11-a	
Rye: stocks (end-season): tonnage	Main countries	B 7-a	B 8-a
held on farms & at wholesalers' premises: tonnage	EEC countries	E 12-m	
Silicon: stocks held at producers' & consumers' plants: tonnage	USA	N 1-a	
Silk (raw): stocks in lbs	France, Italy, Japan, UK & USA	B 10-a	
Sisal & hemp (end-yr): stocks: tonnage	Main countries	B 2-a	
Skim milk powder: public stocks (end-period): tonnage	EEC countries	U 35-a	
Softwood (sawn) stocks in m³ (end-period)	European countries	A 24-a2	
Sorghum: stocks held at wholesalers' premises: tonnage	EEC countries	E 12-m	
(end-season): tonnage	Argentine & USA	B 7-a	
Soybeans: stocks (initial & end-yr): tonnage	USA	B 19-a	
Steel ingots; semis & finished steel products: stocks: tonnage	EEC countries	E 30-q	
stocks: tonnage	EEC countries	E 29-a	
Steel plates: stocks held by industry by sector: tonnage	UK	T 2-q	
Steel (finished) products: stocks: tonnage	EEC countries	E 29-a	
(semi-finished): stocks: tonnage	EEC countries	E 29-a	
Steel sheets: stocks held by industry by sector: tonnage	UK	T 2-q	
Sugar (raw centrifugal): stocks (end-period): tonnage	Main countries	B 13-a	C 25-a
(refined): stocks: tonnage	EEC countries	E 44-a	
stocks (at end of selected month): tonnage	Main countries	A 20-a	
(end crop-yr): tonnage	Main countries	A 11-a	
& world carry-over: tonnage	Worldwide	A 5-a	
	Producing & importing countries	C 19-a	
	Main countries	B 2-a	
Sulphur: stocks held at producers' plants: tonnage	USA	N 1-a	
Synthetic rubber: stocks (end-yr): tonnage	Main countries	C 18-m	B 2-a
		B 13-a	
	World regions	C 18-m	
Tea: stocks entered for customs clearance: tonnage	UK	C 11-m	
(excl primary wholesaler stocks): tonnage	UK	C 1-m	
held at public & private warehouses: tonnage	India	C 1-q	
at warehouses: tonnage	Ceylon & Bangladesh	C 1-a	
by primary wholesalers: tonnage	UK	C 1-q	C 11-q
in bonded warehouses: tonnage	UK	C 11-m	P 6-m
in lbs	Bangladesh, India, Sri Lanka & UK	B 13-q	
tonnage	Ceylon, India, Pakistan & UK	B 2-a	
Tin concentrates: stocks in transit: tonnage	Country of destination	C 20-m	
Tin metal: stocks held at consumers' premises: tonnage	UK	T 4-a	
held at London Metal Exchange warehouses: tonnage	UK	T 4-a	
held by importers or jobbers: tonnage	USA	T 4-a	
in internal transit: tonnage	USA	T 4-a	
(primary & secondary): tonnage	Worldwide	T 4-a	
Tin pigs: stocks held at processing plants: tonnage	USA	T 4-a	
Tin (refined): stocks held at consumers' premises: tonnage	UK & USA	J 6-a	
held at dealers' & consumers' plants: tonnage	USA	N 1-a	
held at London Metal Exchange warehouses: tonnage	UK	J 6-a	
held at London Metal Exchange warehouses: daily	UK	C 20	
(incl ore & concentrates): tonnage	UK	C 30-q	
in concentrates in transit: tonnage	Worldwide	T 4-a	
in concentrates: tonnage	Worldwide	T 4-a	
in processing stage held at plants: tonnage	USA	T 4-a	
tonnage	Main countries	B 2-a	
Tinplate: stocks held by industry by sector: tonnage	UK	T 2-q	
Titanium metal: stocks held by industry: tonnage	USA	N 1-a	
Tobacco (fire-cured): stocks at end-period in lbs	UK	B 17-a	
(flue-cured): stocks at end-period in lbs	UK	B 17-a	
stocks (all kinds): tonnage	Greece, Canada & UK	A 5-a	
by kind (home-grown & foreign) in lbs	USA	B 13-a	
stocks held by co-operative stabilisation corporation: tonnage	USA	B 17-m	
stocks by kind: tonnage	USA	A 5-a	
in lbs million	Puerto Rico & USA	B 17-m	
(unmanufactured): stocks in lbs	Canada & UK	B 13-a	
	Main countries	B 17-a	
Tung oil: stocks (initial & end-yr): tonnage	USA	B 19-a	
Tungsten ore: stocks held at consumers' premises: tonnage	Main countries	U 53-q	
at producers' premises: tonnage	Main countries	U 53-a	
Tungsten: stocks held at producers' & users' premises: tonnage	USA	N 1-a	

	Territorial coverage	Title codes	
INVENTORIES BY PRODUCT, continued			
Wheat & flour: stocks (opening & closing): tonnage	Main countries	C 16-a	
(hard): stocks (at beginning of crop yr): tonnage	Main countries	C 29-a	
stocks (at beginning of crop yr): tonnage	Main countries	C 29-a	
(carry-over at end crop yr): tonnage	Main countries	A 11-a	B 7-a
		B 8-a	C 29-a
on farms & at wholesalers premises: tonnage	EEC countries	E 12-m	
on farms left unsold: tonnage	UK	B 7-a	P 5-a
tonnage	EEC countries	E 44-a	
Wine: stocks by volume in litres	EEC countries	E 44-a	
Wire bars (of refined copper): stocks held at users premises: tonnage	UK	J 6-a	
Wood pulp: stocks held at pulp & paper mills: tonnage	OECD countries	D 41-q	
stocks (by kind) held at pulp & paper mills: tonnage	OECD countries	D 41-q	
Wool, cotton, silk, jute & hard fibres stocks: tonnage	Worldwide	B 10-a	
Wool (greasy raw): stocks (commercial) in kg	Main countries	K 6-a	
	EEC countries, Japan & USA	A 5-a	
stocks: tonnage	Producing countries	A 5-a	
World stocks: raw sugar: tonnage (at end-yr)	Main countries	C 25-a	
World sugar stocks: tonnage		B 13-a	
Woven woollen fabrics: stocks in kg	Main countries	K 6-a	
Zinc slabs: stocks held at consumers' premises: tonnage	UK	J 6-a	T 4-a
in London Metal Exchange warehouses: tonnage	UK	C 30-m	J 6-a
Zinc: stocks held at producers' & users' plants: tonnage	USA	N 1-a	
at smelters' plants: tonnage	USA	J 6-a	T 4-a
(end-period): tonnage	Main countries	U 24-m	

Inventory times turned   see   FINANCIAL RATIOS, CORPORATE INVENTORIES

INVESTMENT

       see also   BANK INVESTMENTS
                 CENTRALISED STATE INVESTMENT
                 GOVERNMENT EXPENDITURE
                 OVERSEAS INVESTMENT INCOME

	Territorial coverage	Title codes	
As % of gross domestic product (as forecast in economic plans)	Small African countries	U 39-irr	
of gross national product (at current prices)	ECAFE countries	U 17-a	
As component in balance of payments in $m	OAS member countries	N 16-a	
	All countries	F 1-a	
	Latin American countries	U 18-a	
By foreign banks in $m	All countries	F 5-m	F 6-q
By governments as embodied in economic plans in $m	All countries	A 11-a	
on research in agricultural & industrial improvements in $m	EEC countries	E 36-a	
on research in advanced technology in $m	EEC countries	E 36-a	
By kinds of financial agencies in $m	OECD countries	D 12-a	
By sectors in economic plans in $m	Small African countries	U 39	
(Direct) by US corporations in $m	World regions	D 17-a	
by US government in manufacturing industry in $m	OAS member countries	N 16-a	
mining in $m	OAS member countries	N 16-a	
petroleum industry in $m	OAS member countries	N 16-a	
public utilities in $m	OAS member countries	N 16-a	
on collective farms in roubles million	USSR	U 16-a	
In farm machinery per person employed on farms in $	ECE countries	U 34-a	
materials: inventory accumulation by value in $bn	USA	G 1-a2	
plant & machinery in local currency	Main countries	R 5-a	
On capital projects with European Development Fund aid in UA	AASM countries	E 41-a	
machinery as % of total investment	Main countries	U 38-a	
purchase of farm machinery in roubles	USSR	U 16-a	
road building projects & maintenance in $m	All countries	S 13-a	
(Private) in local currency	Latin American countries	U 18-a	
Projected to 1980 as % of gross national product	OECD countries	D 11	
Projections embodied in economic plans	Small African countries	U 39-irr	
(Public) in local currency	Latin American countries	U 18-a	
% change as share of gross domestic product to 1969	OECD countries	D 11	
in fixed assets per capita in $	European countries	U 16-a	
in gross private domestic fixed investment in $	Japan	G 1-a	
% of gross national product spent on building machinery & construction equipment	OECD countries	D 11	
% growth rates: capital investment to 1975 & 1980	OECD countries	D 11	
gross domestic capital investment	All countries	M 6-a	
% increase in costs of plant & equipment for chemical industry	UK	B 21-a	
% real rate of growth of investment	Main Developed countries	M 3-a	
Building construction: % share of investment in dwellings	Developing countries	U 57-a	
in office buildings	Developing countries	U 57-a	
in other construction works	Developing countries	U 57-a	
investment as % of gross national product	OECD countries	D 11	
on farms in roubles	USSR	U 16-a	
Buildings: investment by baking & confectionery industry in local currency	EEC countries	E 40-a	
brewing industry in local currency	EEC countries	E 40-a	
building industry in local currency	EEC countries	E 40-a	
building materials manufacturing industry in local currency	EEC countries	E 40-a	
cement & plaster manufacturing industry in local currency	EEC countries	E 40-a	
ceramics manufacturing industry in local currency	EEC countries	E 40-a	

		Territorial coverage	Title codes
INVESTMENT, continued			
Buildings: investment by	chemical industry in local currency	EEC countries	E 40-a
	clothing manufacturing industry in local currency	EEC countries	E 40-a
	coalmining & patent fuel manufacturing industry in local currency	EEC countries	E 40-a
	coke ovens in local currency	EEC countries	E 40-a
	cotton textile manufacturing industry in local currency	EEC countries	E 40-a
	distilleries & malting industry in local currency	EEC countries	E 40-a
	electrical engineering industry in local currency	EEC countries	E 40-a
	electronics industry in local currency	EEC countries	E 40-a
	engineering industries in local currency	EEC countries	E 40-a
	farm machinery manufacturing industry in local currency	EEC countries	E 40-a
	flour milling industry in local currency	EEC countries	E 40-a
	food processing industry in local currency	EEC countries	E 40-a
	footwear manufacturing industry in local currency	EEC countries	E 40-a
	fur manufacturing industry in local currency	EEC countries	E 40-a
	gas supply industry in local currency	EEC countries	E 40-a
	glass manufacturing industry in local currency	EEC countries	E 40-a
	industrial enterprises in local currency	EEC countries	E 40-a
	iron & steel industry by sector in local currency	EEC countries	E 40-a
	jewellery manufacturing industry in local currency	EEC countries	E 40-a
	jute product manufacturing industry in local currency	EEC countries	E 40-a
	knitting mills in local currency	EEC countries	E 40-a
	leather goods manufacturing industry in local currency	EEC countries	E 40-a
	leather tanneries in local currency	EEC countries	E 40-a
	lignite & briquetting plants in local currency	EEC countries	E 40-a
	locomotive & rolling stock manufacturing industry in local currency	EEC countries	E 40-a
	machine tools manufacturing industry in local currency	EEC countries	E 40-a
	man-made fibres manufacturing industry in local currency	EEC countries	E 40-a
	manufacturing industry (in general) in local currency	EEC countries	E 40-a
	marine engineering industry & shipyards in local currency	EEC countries	E 40-a
	mechanical engineering industry in local currency	EEC countries	E 40-a
	metals fabrication industry in local currency	EEC countries	E 40-a
	motor cycle manufacturing industry in local currency	EEC countries	E 40-a
	musical instruments manufacturing industry in local currency	EEC countries	E 40-a
	non-ferrous metals industry in local currency	EEC countries	E 40-a
	non-metallic mineral industry in local currency	EEC countries	E 40-a
	office machinery manufacturing industry in local currency	EEC countries	E 40-a
	optical instruments manufacturing industry in local currency	EEC countries	E 40-a
	ore mining industry in local currency	EEC countries	E 40-a
	paper & board manufacturing industry in local currency	EEC countries	E 40-a
	petroleum & natural gas industries in local currency	EEC countries	E 40-a
	petroleum refineries in local currency	EEC countries	E 40-a
	plastics manufacturing industry in local currency	EEC countries	E 40-a
	power stations in local currency	EEC countries	E 40-a
	printing & publishing industry in local currency	EEC countries	E 40-a
	public utilities in local currency	EEC countries	E 40-a
	rubber processing industry in local currency	EEC countries	E 40-a
	silk industry in local currency	EEC countries	E 40-a
	sugar refining industry in local currency	EEC countries	E 40-a
	textile machinery manufacturing industry in local currency	EEC countries	E 40-a
	timber & sawmill industry in local currency	EEC countries	E 40-a
	toys & sports goods manufacturing industries in local currency	EEC countries	E 40-a
	watch-making industry in local currency	EEC countries	E 40-a
	wire & cable manufacturing industry in local currency	EEC countries	E 40-a
	wood-working industry in local currency	EEC countries	E 40-a
	woollen textile manufacturing industry in local currency	EEC countries	E 40-a

	Territorial coverage	Title codes
INVESTMENT, continued		
Capital expenditure budget in FrCFA mrd	AASM countries	E 41-a
on education in $m	All countries	U 62-a
Capital investment by kind (short & long-term) in $m	All countries	F 5-m F 6-
agriculture in roubles million	USSR	U 16-a
aircraft industry: plant & equipment in $m	USA	J 2-a
American companies share of investment in petroleum industry	Latin American countries	U 18-a
ancillary equipment for steelworks in $m	EEC countries	E 29-a
basic Bessemer steelworks by regions in UA	EEC countries	E 46-a
battery & accumulator industry in £m	UK	B 23-a
bilateral & multilateral portfolios as overseas development aid in $	OECD countries	D 13-a
blast furnaces & coke ovens in $m	Main countries	U 49-a
in UA by regions	EEC countries	E 46-a
bottom-blown & other types of steel plants in UA	EEC countries	E 46-a
briquetting plants in UA million by regions	EEC countries	E 46-a
building construction industry in local currency	EEC countries	E 38-a
chemical industry by areas in local currency	EEC countries	E 38-a
clothing manufacturing industry in £m	UK	B 22-a
co-operative farms in $m	E European countries	U 34-a
computer industry: projections by 1977 in £m	UK	B 24-a
electrical engineering industry per employee in £	Main countries	B 23-a
electronic components industry in £m	UK	B 24-a
electronic consumer goods manufacturing industry in £m	UK	B 24-a
energy production installations by area in local currency	EEC countries	E 38-a
engineering industries by sector in $m	OECD countries	D 9-a
farm machinery industry in $m	ECE countries	U 34-a
farm machinery industry - index nos	ECE countries	U 34-a
food, drink & tobacco industry in local currency	EEC countries	E 38-a
machine tools manufacturing industry in $m	USA	J 2-a
machinery manufacturing as % of gross national product	OECD countries	D 11
metals fabrication industry by areas in local currency	EEC countries	E 38-a
mining & quarrying by areas in local currency	EEC countries	E 38-a
non-metallic mineral by areas in local currency	EEC countries	E 38-a
public electricity supply undertakings in $	EEC countries	E 15-a
roasted coffee industry in $m	USA	J 1-a
state & collective farms in roubles	USSR	U 16-a
	E European countries	U 34-a
textile manufacturing industry by areas in local currency	EEC countries	E 38-a
Capital transfers: % gross accumulation	All countries	U 60-a
(net) received by source in $m	OECD countries	D 30-a
	Asian, Far East & Australasian countries	U 45-a
Carpet & rug manufacturing industry in $m	OECD countries	D 46-a
in £m	UK	B 29-a
Chemical industry as % of manufacturing industry investment	Main countries	U 25-a
total industrial investment	Main countries	U 25-a
	OECD countries	D 5-a
value added in production	OECD countries	D 5-a
by sector in £m	UK	B 21-a
in $m	Main European countries	B 30-a
projected capital expenditure in £m	UK	B 21
in Lit million	EEC countries	C 6-a
planned increase by area in Lire	Italy	C 6-a
Clothing manufacturing industry in $m	OECD countries	D 46-a
in £m	UK	B 29-a
on land for factory buildings in £m	UK	B 22-a
new buildings in £m	UK	B 22-a
plant & machinery in £m	UK	B 22-a
vehicles in £m	UK	B 22-a
Coal industry by regions in UA	EEC countries	E 46-a
Coke ovens by regions in UA	EEC countries	E 46-a
in $m	EEC countries	E 29-a
(steelworks-owned) in UA	EEC countries	E 46-a
Construction of rural sewage disposal systems in $m	All countries	W 2-a
water supply projects in $m	All countries	W 2-a
urban sewage disposal systems in $m	All countries	W 2-a
water supply projects in $m	All countries	W 2-a
Cost of investment embodied in economic plans: foreign component	All countries	A 11-a
Direct investment, assets & liabilities in $m	EEC countries	E 4-a
Disbursements under CECA programs	EEC countries	E 38-a
Domestic deposits with finance companies in $m	All countries	F 5-m F 6-q
Domestic electrical appliances industry in £m	UK	B 23-a
Durable goods industry: plant & equipment in $m	USA	J 2-a
Electric furnace steelworks by regions in UA	EEC countries	E 46-a
in $m	EEC countries	E 29-a
Electric lamp manufacturing industry in £m	UK	B 23-a
Electrical machinery, plant & equipment manufacturing industry in $m	USA	J 2-a
Electricity supply industry: investment needs in $	OECD countries	D 8-a
Electrical engineering industry: plant & equipment in $m	USA	J 2-a
by sector in £m	UK	B 23-a
Gross domestic investment in local currency & in $m	Latin American countries	U 18-a
Gross marginal capital output ratios	All countries	M 6-a

VESTMENT, continued

	Territorial coverage	Title codes
Growth in corporative expenditure projected to 1980 as % of gross national product	OECD countries	D 11
public expenditure projected to 1980 as % of gross national product	OECD countries	D 11
investment projected to 1980 as % change in gross national product	OECD countries	D 11
Hot wide steel strip mills by regions in UA	EEC countries	E 46-a
Income from overseas: long-term capital in $m	Japan	G 1-a
short-term capital in $m	Japan	G 1-a
Industrial plant & equipment in $m	USA	J 2-a
Installation of power generating plants in $m	Latin American countries	U 18-a
Insulated wire & cables manufacturing industry in £m	UK	B 23-a
Iron & steel foundries in $m	France, W Germany & UK	B 25-a
Iron & steel industry & ore mining projects in $	EEC countries	E 29-a
by regions in UA	EEC countries	E 46-a
by sectors in $ & as % total iron & steel investment	OECD countries	D 22-a
in $ per ton of output	OECD countries	D 22-a
in $m	EEC countries	E 29-a
	Main countries	U 49-a
per ton of crude steel produced	EEC countries	E 29-a
per ton of iron ore produced	EEC countries	E 29-a
since 1952 in £m	UK	U 57-a
in $m	ECSC countries	U 57-a
value of projects planned in $	EEC countries	E 30-a2 E 29-a
Iron foundries: land & buildings in £m	UK	B 25-a
plant & machinery in £m	UK	B 25-a
vehicles in £	UK	B 25-a
Iron ore mining in $m	EEC countries	E 29-a
Jute products manufacturing industry in £m	UK	B 29-a
Knitting mills in $m	OECD countries	D 46-a
Knitwear & hosiery manufacturing industry in £m	UK	B 29-a
L.D. & Kaldo steel plants by regions in UA	EEC countries	E 46-a
Land purchase: baking & confectionery industry in local currency	EEC countries	E 40-a
building industry in local currency	EEC countries	E 40-a
building materials industry in local currency	EEC countries	E 40-a
ceramics industry in local currency	EEC countries	E 40-a
chemical industry in local currency	EEC countries	E 40-a
clothing manufacturing industry in local currency	EEC countries	E 40-a
coalmining & patent fuel production in local currency	EEC countries	E 40-a
cotton textile manufacturing industry in local currency	EEC countries	E 40-a
electrical engineering industry in local currency	EEC countries	E 40-a
engineering industries in local currency	EEC countries	E 40-a
farm machinery manufacturing industry in local currency	EEC countries	E 40-a
flour milling industry in local currency	EEC countries	E 40-a
food processing industry in local currency	EEC countries	E 40-a
footwear manufacturing industry in local currency	EEC countries	E 40-a
fur manufacturing industry in local currency	EEC countries	E 40-a
gas supply industry in local currency	EEC countries	E 40-a
glass manufacturing industry in local currency	EEC countries	E 40-a
industrial enterprises in local currency	EEC countries	E 40-a
iron & steel industry by sector in local currency	EEC countries	E 40-a
jewellery manufacturing industry in local currency	EEC countries	E 40-a
knitting mills in local currency	EEC countries	E 40-a
leather goods manufacturing industry in local currency	EEC countries	E 40-a
leather tanneries in local currency	EEC countries	E 40-a
lignite & briquetting plants in local currency	EEC countries	E 40-a
machine tools manufacturing industry in local currency	EEC countries	E 40-a
manufacturing industry (in general) in local currency	EEC countries	E 40-a
mechanical engineering industry in local currency	EEC countries	E 40-a
metals fabrication industry in local currency	EEC countries	E 40-a
musical instruments manufacturing industry in local currency	EEC countries	E 40-a
non-ferrous metals industry in local currency	EEC countries	E 40-a
non-metallic mineral industry in local currency	EEC countries	E 40-a
office machinery manufacturing industry in local currency	EEC countries	E 40-a
optical instruments manufacturing industry in local currency	EEC countries	E 40-a
ore mining industry in local currency	EEC countries	E 40-a
paper & board manufacturing industry in local currency	EEC countries	E 40-a
petroleum & natural gas industries in local currency	EEC countries	E 40-a
petroleum refineries in local currency	EEC countries	E 40-a
plastics manufacturing industry in local currency	EEC countries	E 40-a
power stations in local currency	EEC countries	E 40-a
printing & publishing industry in local currency	EEC countries	E 40-a
public utilities in local currency	EEC countries	E 40-a
rubber processing industry in local currency	EEC countries	E 40-a
silk industry in local currency	EEC countries	E 40-a
sugar refining industry in local currency	EEC countries	E 40-a
textile machinery manufacturing industry in local currency	EEC countries	E 40-a
timber & sawmill industry in local currency	EEC countries	E 40-a
toys & sports goods manufacturing industries in local currency	EEC countries	E 40-a

INVESTMENT, continued   Territorial coverage   Title codes

  Land purchase: watch-making industry in local currency   EEC countries   E 40-a
        wire & cable manufacturing industry in local
                  currency   EEC countries   E 40-a
      wood-working industry in local currency   EEC countries   E 40-a
      woollen textile manufacturing industry in local
                  currency   EEC countries   E 40-a
 Life insurance funds invested on deposit in $m   All countries   F 5-m   F 6-q
 Liquefied gas processing industry in $m   Latin American countries   U 18-a
 Loans advanced by acceptance houses in $m   All countries   F 5-m   F 6-q
 Machine tools in mechanical engineering industry per employee in $ EEC countries   B 20-a
 Machinery & equipment in local currency   Latin American countries   U 18-a
 Machinery: baking & confectionery industry in local currency   EEC countries   E 40-a
    brewing industry in local currency   EEC countries   E 40-a
    building industry in local currency   EEC countries   E 40-a
    building materials manufacturing industry in local
                currency   EEC countries   E 40-a
    cement & plaster manufacturing industry in local
                currency   EEC countries   E 40-a
    ceramics manufacturing industry in local currency   EEC countries   E 40-a
    chemical industry in local currency   EEC countries   E 40-a
    clothing manufacturing industry in local currency   EEC countries   E 40-a
    coalmining & patent fuel production in local currency   EEC countries   E 40-a
    coke oven plants in local currency   EEC countries   E 40-a
    cotton textile manufacturing industry in local currency   EEC countries   E 40-a
    distilleries & malting industry in local currency   EEC countries   E 40-a
    electrical engineering industry in local currency   EEC countries   E 40-a
    electronics industry in local currency   EEC countries   E 40-a
    engineering industries in local currency   EEC countries   E 40-a
    farm machinery manufacturing industry in local currency   EEC countries   E 40-a
    flour milling industry in local currency   EEC countries   E 40-a
    food processing industry in local currency   EEC countries   E 40-a
    footwear manufacturing industry in local currency   EEC countries   E 40-a
    fur manufacturing industry in local currency   EEC countries   E 40-a
    gas supply industry in local currency   EEC countries   E 40-a
    glass manufacturing industry in local currency   EEC countries   E 40-a
    industrial enterprises in local currency   EEC countries   E 40-a
    industrial plant & equipment in $m   USA   J 2-a
    iron & steel industry by sector in local currency   EEC countries   E 40-a
    jewellery manufacturing industry in local currency   EEC countries   E 40-a
    jute product manufacturing industry   EEC countries   E 40-a
    knitting mills in local currency   EEC countries   E 40-a
    leather goods manufacturing industry in local currency   EEC countries   E 40-a
    leather tanneries in local currency   EEC countries   E 40-a
    lignite & briquetting plants in local currency   EEC countries   E 40-a
    locomotive & rolling stock manufacturing industry in
                local currency   EEC countries   E 40-a
    machine tools manufacturing industry in local currency   EEC countries   E 40-a
    man-made fibres manufacturing industry in local currency   EEC countries   E 40-a
    manufacturing industry (in general) in local currency   EEC countries   E 40-a
    marine engineering industry & shipyards in local currency   EEC countries   E 40-a
    mechanical engineering industry in local currency   EEC countries   E 40-a
    metals fabrication industry in local currency   EEC countries   E 40-a
    motor cycle manufacturing industry in local currency   EEC countries   E 40-a
    musical instruments manufacturing industry in local
                currency   EEC countries   E 40-a
    non-ferrous metals industry in local currency   EEC countries   E 40-a
    non-metallic mineral industry in local currency   EEC countries   E 40-a
    office machinery manufacturing industry in local currency   EEC countries   E 40-a
    optical instruments manufacturing industry in local
                currency   EEC countries   E 40-a
    ore mining industry in local currency   EEC countries   E 40-a
    paper & board manufacturing industry in local currency   EEC countries   E 40-a
    petroleum & natural gas industries in local currency   EEC countries   E 40-a
    petroleum refineries in local currency   EEC countries   E 40-a
    plastics manufacturing industry in local currency   EEC countries   E 40-a
    power stations in local currency   EEC countries   E 40-a
    printing & publishing industry in local currency   EEC countries   E 40-a
    public utilities in local currency   EEC countries   E 40-a
    rubber processing industry in local currency   EEC countries   E 40-a
    silk industry in local currency   EEC countries   E 40-a
    sugar refining industry in local currency   EEC countries   E 40-a
    textile machinery manufacturing industry in local
                currency   EEC countries   E 40-a
    timber & sawmill industry in local currency   EEC countries   E 40-a
    toys & sports goods manufacturing industries in local
                currency   EEC countries   E 40-a
    watch-making industry in local currency   EEC countries   E 40-a
    wire & cable manufacturing industry in local currency   EEC countries   E 40-a
    wood-working industry in local currency   EEC countries   E 40-a
    woollen textile manufacturing industry in local currency   EEC countries   E 40-a
 Man-made fibres manufacturing industry in £m   UK   B 29-a
              in $m   OECD countries   D 5-a
 Manufacturing industry: plant & equipment in $m   USA   J 2-a
 Mechanical engineering industry in $m   Main countries   B 27-a
             per employee in $ Main countries   B 27-a
 Metal products industry: plant & equipment in $m   USA   J 2-a
 Motor vehicles industry: plant & equipment in $m   USA   J 2-a
 Natural gas industry in $m   Latin American region   U 18-a

	Territorial coverage	Title codes
INVESTMENT, continued		
Net capital expenditure as % of output: carpet manufacturing industry	UK	B 29-a
clothing manufacturing industry	UK	B 29-a
jute products manufacturing industry	UK	B 29-a
knitwear & hosiery manufacturing industries	UK	B 29-a
man-made fibre manufacturing industry	UK	B 29-a
spinning & weaving in textile industry	UK	B 29-a
textile processing industry	UK	B 29-a
woollen & worsted manufacturing industry	UK	B 29-a
Non-residential construction projects in $bn	USA	G 1-a2
Oil marketing expenditure in $m	Venezuela	U 18-a
Oil pipelines construction in $m	Venezuela	U 18-a
Oil prospecting in $m	Venezuela	U 18-a
Oil refinery construction in $m	Venezuela	U 18-a
Oil tankers: purchases in $m	Venezuela	U 18-a
Petroleum & natural gas industry in $m	Venezuela	U 18-a
Petroleum industry (by American companies) in $m	Latin American countries	U 18-a
Power generating plants in steelworks by regions	EEC countries	E 29-a E 46-a
Public & private financing of research as % of total investment in economic plans in $m	EEC countries	E 36-a
Re-rolling mills for producing steel blooms & flats by regions in UA	Small African countries	U 39-irr
steel slabs & sections by regions in UA	EEC countries	E 46-a
in $m	EEC countries	E 46-a
	EEC countries	E 29-a
Savings as % of gross capital accumulation	All countries	U 60-a
Section re-rolling mills by regions in UA	EEC countries	E 46-a
Services for steelworks by regions in UA	EEC countries	E 46-a
Spinning & weaving of cotton fibre in £m	UK	B 29-a
of man-made fibres in £m	UK	B 29-a
Spinning, weaving & textile finishing in $m	OECD countries	D 46-a
Steel foundries: continuous casting plants by regions in UA	EEC countries	E 46-a
land & buildings in £m	UK	B 25-a
plant & machinery in £m	UK	B 25-a
vehicles: purchases in £	UK	B 25-a
Steel furnaces (for crude steel production) in $m	Main countries	U 49-a
	EEC countries	E 29-a
Steel re-rolling plants by type by regions in UA	EEC countries	E 46-a
Steel rolling (incl re-rolling mills) in $m	Main countries	U 49-a
Steelworks (all types) by regions in UA	EEC countries	E 46-a
(open-hearth) by regions in UA	EEC countries	E 46-a
(Siemens) in $m	EEC countries	E 29-a
(Thomas) in $m	EEC countries	E 29-a
Textile industry in $	OECD countries	D 46-a
	UK	B 29-a
Wool & worsted weaving industry in £m	UK	B 29-a

Investment goods   see   CAPITAL GOODS
                             PRODUCER GOODS

Investment income   see   INVISIBLE TRADE
                             OVERSEAS INVESTMENT INCOME

INVESTMENT, AGRICULTURAL		
Outlay on buildings (agricultural) in roubles million	USSR	U 16-a
collective farms in roubles million	USSR	U 16-a
farm machinery in roubles million	USSR	U 16-a
state farms in roubles million	USSR	U 16-a
Total farm investment in roubles million	USSR	U 16-a
INVESTMENT, CORPORATE OVERSEAS		
By all enterprises in $bn	USA	J 2-a
By US corporations in $m	Worldwide	R 5-a
By manufacturing industry: investment of US corporations in $m	Main countries	J 2-a R 5-a
Mining, quarrying & smelting: investment by US corporations in $m	Main countries	J 2-a R 5-a
Petroleum extraction: investment by US corporations in $m	Main countries	J 2-a R 5-a
Private direct investment of capital in $m		R 5-a
INVESTMENT, DOMESTIC		
As % of gross domestic product	All countries	M 6-a
By sector of industry in $m	All countries	M 6-a
By type of asset in $m	All countries	M 6-a
Expenditure in public & private sectors in $m	All countries	M 6-a
% changes in investment planned	E European countries & USSR	U 54-a
Investment expenditure in $m	EEC countries	E 4-a
INVESTMENT, PERSONAL		
% of households holding deposit bank savings	W European countries	Z 3
fixed-interest securities	W European countries	Z 3
government savings bonds	W European countries	Z 3
Post Office savings	W European countries	Z 3
shares of industrial companies	W European countries	Z 3
of property companies	W European countries	Z 3

	Territorial coverage	Title codes	
INVESTMENT, PERSONAL continued			
% of households holding shares of unit trusts	W European countries	Z 3	
tax-free savings accounts	W European countries	Z 3	
INVESTMENT, PRIVATE			
In research & development & as % of gross domestic product	EEC countries	E 36-a	
% change private investment in manufacturing industry	Main European countries	U 16-a	
Expenditure as % of gross national product	OECD countries	D 11	
INVESTMENT, PRIVATE OVERSEAS			
As development aid in $m	Main countries	D 7-a	
Bilateral flow in $m	Developing regions	U 23-a	
Capital outflow (long-term) in $m	USA	U 16-a	
Capital transfers in $m	EEC countries	E 4-a	
Cash flow as % of private foreign investment	Developing regions	U 23-a	
as development aid in $m	Main countries	D 7-a	
Direct investment funds: inflow in $m	ECE countries	U 15-a	
outflow in $m	ECE countries	U 15-a	
in $m	All countries	M 6-a	
Exchange receipts in $m	Developing regions	U 23-a	
Income as component of payment balances in $m	OAS member countries	N 16-a	
	All countries	F 5-m	F 6-q
Income, debits & credits in $m	All countries	F 1-a	
Multilateral flow in $m	Developing regions	U 23-a	
Net flow (long-term) in $m	ECE countries	U 15-a	
Portfolio investments: bilateral in $m	Worldwide	M 3-a	
multilateral in $m	Worldwide	M 3-a	
Private development assistance in $m	Worldwide	M 3-a	
INVESTMENT, PUBLIC			
In research & development & as % of gross domestic product	EEC countries	E 36-a	
Needs to 1976 for electricity supply programs in $	OECD countries	D 8-a	
No of houses built by local authorities	All countries	U 13-a	
INVESTMENT, PUBLIC OVERSEAS			
As % of gross national product	Developed countries	U 23-a	
Bilateral flow in $m	Developing regions	U 23-a	
Capital outflow (long-term) in $m	USA	U 16-a	
Cash flow as % of public foreign investment	Developing regions	U 23-a	
as development aid in $m	Main countries	D 7-a	
Exchange receipts in $m	Developing regions	U 23-a	
Long-term capital flow in $m	All countries	F 5-m	F 6-q
Multilateral flow in $m	Developing regions	U 23-a	
Net flow (long-term) in $m	ECE countries	U 15-a	
Official development assistance in $m	Worldwide	M 3-a	
US government: direct investment in $m	OAS member countries	N 16-a	
INVISIBLE TRADE			
see also OVERSEAS INVESTMENT INCOME			
% dependence on invisible income	Main countries	M 9-a	
% growth rates: investment income	Main countries	M 9-a	
investment payments abroad	Main countries	M 9-a	
payments for transport services	Main countries	M 9-a	
for travel purposes	Main countries	M 9-a	
payments - index nos	Main countries	M 9-a	
receipts from transport services	Main countries	M 9-a	
from travellers & tourism	Main countries	Z 9-a	
receipts	Main countries	M 9-a	
receipts - index nos	Main countries	M 9-a	
% share: world investment: income	Main countries	M 9-a	
payments	Main countries	M 9-a	
world payments for transport services	Main countries	M 9-a	
for travel abroad & tourism	Main countries	M 9-a	
(for all invisibles)	Main countries	M 9-a	
world receipts from transport services	Main countries	M 9-a	
from abroad & tourism	Main countries	M 9-a	
Balance of payments: invisibles in local currency from 1816	Main European countries	Z 1-a	
Balances (net) by source of invisible income in $m	Main countries	M 9-a	
of total invisible income in $m	Main countries	M 9-a	
Balances on trade & transfers in $m	Main countries	M 9-a	
Donations abroad: official in $m	Worldwide	M 9-a	
private in $m	Worldwide	M 9-a	
Foreign exchange income in $m	Developing countries	U 23-a	
Freight & insurance transactions in local currency	African countries	U 44-a	
Government transfer payments in $m	Worldwide	M 9-a	
Income from agents' fees abroad in $m	Main countries	F 1-a	
brokerage commissions in $m	All countries	F 1-a	
film rentals in $m	All countries	F 1-a	
patent fees in $m	All countries	F 1-a	
royalties & copyrights in $m	Main countries	F 1-a	
workers' foreign earnings remitted in $m	All countries	F 1-a	
(net) from freight insurance in $m	All countries	F 1-a	
payments in $m	All countries	F 1-a	
tourist expenditure in $m	All countries	F 1-a	
Investment transfers abroad in $m	Worldwide	M 9-a	

	Territorial coverage	Title codes
INVISIBLE TRADE, continued		
Payments in $m & % growth rates	Main countries	M 9-a
Payments & receipts in $m	OAS member countries	N 16-a
as % of world total	Main countries	M 9-a
balances on freight in $m	All countries	F 5-m F 6-q
by nationals on foreign travel in $m	Main countries	M 9-a
by travellers overseas & holiday-makers in $m	Main countries	M 9-a
investments overseas in $m	Main countries	M 9-a
services provided by foreigners in $m	Worldwide	M 9-a
	Main countries	M 9-a
transport services in $m	Main countries	M 9-a
	Worldwide	M 9-a
on invisibles in $m	Main countries	M 9-a
as % of gross national product	Main countries	M 9-a
as % of total payments	Main countries	M 9-a
per capita for services received by kind	Main countries	M 9-a
Receipts & payments by source in $m	Main countries	M 9-a
for services in $m	All countries	M 6-a
as % of gross national product	Main countries	M 9-a
total receipts	Main countries	M 9-a
total world invisible income	Worldwide	M 9-a
	Main countries	M 9-a
from investments overseas in $m	Main countries	M 9-a
services provided in $m	Main countries	M 9-a
transport services in $m	Main countries	M 9-a
travellers overseas & tourism in $m	Main countries	M 9-a
in $m	Main countries	M 9-a
per capita by source of invisible income in $	Main countries	M 9-a
Surpluses & deficits on invisibles in $m	ECE countries	U 15-a
World income from overseas visitors as % of invisible income		M 9-a
World investment income as % of invisible income		M 9-a
World receipts from foreign travel income in $m		M 9-a
investment income in $m		M 9-a
invisible income in $m		M 9-a
transport services in $m		M 9-a
World transport service income as % of invisible income		M 9-a
IODINE		
% of consumption in production of animal feeding stuffs	USA	N 1-a
catalysts	USA	N 1-a
disinfectants	USA	N 1-a
pharmaceutical products	USA	N 1-a
Government strategic stockpile of iodine in lbs	USA	N 1-a
Imports & exports by source & destination: tonnage	Main countries	B 15-a
Production in lbs	Chile, Japan & USA	N 1-a
tonnage	Chile, Indonesia & Japan	B 15-a
Wholesale prices of crude iodine in $ per lb	USA	N 1-a
of resublimed iodine in $ per lb	USA	N 1-a
World production (at mines) in lbs		N 1-a
Iridium see PLATINUM, REFINED		
Iron see METALLIC IRON		
IRON CASTINGS		
SPONGE IRON		
WROUGHT IRON, ROLLED		
IRON & STEEL COMMUNITY		
see also COMMUNITY INVESTMENT FUNDS		
Investment funds by industrial sector in $m	EEC countries	E 29-a
IRON & STEEL COMPANIES		
Capital structure by company in DM million	W Germany	H 3-a
Labour force employed by company at end-yr	W Germany	H 3-a
Production: crude steel by company by process: tonnage	W Germany	H 3-a
Re-rolling program by company by product: tonnage	W Germany	H 3-a
Turnover by company in DM million	W Germany	H 3-a
IRON & STEEL INDUSTRY		
see also BLAST FURNACES		
FURNACES, STEEL		
IRON FOUNDRIES		
IRON-WORKING INDUSTRY		
METAL INDUSTRIES		
METAL PRODUCTS INDUSTRIES		
STEEL FABRICATION INDUSTRY		
STEEL FOUNDRIES		
STEEL RE-ROLLING PLANTS		
STEELWORKS		
% change in output & of labour force employed	Main countries	C 2-a
% consumption by kind of energy sources	Main countries	H 4-a
% share of use of electricity as energy source	W European countries	U 16-a
oil as energy source	W European countries	U 16-a
electricity consumption	EEC area	E 7-a
energy consumption	EEC area	E 7-a
Capital formation in steel industry in $m	Main countries	U 21-a

IRON & STEEL INDUSTRY, continued

	Territorial coverage	Title codes	
Coke consumption: tonnage	Main countries	H 3-a	
Consumption: blast furnace gas by volume in m³	EEC countries	E 14-a	E 29-a
coal (incl agglomerates): tonnage	EEC countries	E 14-a	
tonnage	EEC area	E 29-a	
	OECD countries	D 44-a	
	UK	T 2-m	
coal-tar: tonnage	EEC area	E 29-a	
coke & coke breeze: tonnage	UK	T 2-m	
coke oven gas in coal equiv tonnage	EEC countries	E 14-a	
by volume in m³	EEC countries	E 16-q	E 15-a
		E 29-a	
coke: tonnage	ECE countries	U 6-a	U 7-a
	EEC countries	E 14-a	
	EEC area	E 29-a	
diesel oil: tonnage	EEC countries	E 14-a	
	OECD countries	D 44-a	
electricity as % of total supply	W European countries	U 16-a	
in calorific value	Main countries	H 4-a	
in coal equiv tonnage	EEC countries	E 14-a	
in GWh	UK	T 2-m	
in kWh	All countries	C 23-a	
	EEC countries	E 29-a	
	OECD countries	D 8-a	D 22-a
	European countries & USA	U 1-a	
from own production in kWh	All countries	C 23-a	
from public supply in kWh	All countries	C 23-a	
energy sources by kind: tonnage	OECD countries	D 44-a	
ferrous scrap: tonnage	UK	T 2-m	
fuel oil: tonnage	EEC countries	E 14-a	
gas in therms million	UK	T 2-m	
gas oils: tonnage	OECD countries	D 22-a	
lignite (incl briquettes): tonnage	EEC countries	E 14-a	
tonnage	EEC area	E 29-a	
liquid fuels: tonnage	UK	T 2-m	
manufactured gas in m³	European countries & USA	U 3-a	
metallic iron: tonnage	UK	T 2-m	
natural gas in coal equiv tonnage	EEC countries	E 14-a	
in calorific value	Main countries	H 4-a	
petroleum products in calorific value	Main countries	H 4-a	
tonnage	EEC countries	E 16-q	E 14-a
		E 15-a	
primary aluminium: tonnage	OECD countries	D 31-a	
steel castings: tonnage	Main countries	T 4-a	
steel (for further processing): tonnage	UK	B 25-a	
Earnings per hr in FrS	EEC countries	E 30-q	
Earnings: piece rate: female workers per hr in FrS	Main countries	C 2-a	
per hr in FrS	Main countries	C 2-a	
semi-skilled workers per hr in FrS	Main countries	C 2-a	
skilled workers per hr in FrS	Main countries	C 2-a	
unskilled workers per hr in FrS	Main countries	C 2-a	
time rate: female workers per hr in FrS	Main countries	C 2-a	
per hr in FrS	Main countries	C 2-a	
semi-skilled workers per hr in FrS	Main countries	C 2-a	
skilled workers per hr in FrS	Main countries	C 2-a	
unskilled workers per hr in FrS	Main countries	C 2-a	
Employment: no of foreign workers in steel industry	EEC countries	E 29-a	
Employment - index nos	EEC countries	E 26-m	
Gross output of steel industry by value in $m	Main countries	U 21-a	
Historical table: investment from 1952 in £m	UK	U 57-a	
in $m	ECSC countries	U 57-a	
IBRD loans approved for steel industry in $m	OAS member countries	N 16-a	
IDA loans approved for raising steel output in $m	OAS member countries	N 16-a	
Imports: coke oven coke for steel industry: tonnage	OECD countries	D 22-a	
coking coal for steel industry: tonnage	OECD countries	D 22-a	
Income (net) of US steel corporation in $m	USA	J 3-q	
Investment in steel industry as % of total investment	EEC countries	E 29-a	
by sector in $m	OECD countries	D 22-a	
in $m	Main countries	U 49-a	
by sector in buildings, land & machinery in local currency	EEC countries	E 40-a	
in coke ovens in $	EEC countries	E 15-a	
plant & equipment (projected) in $m	EEC countries	E 30-a2	
$ per ton of steel produced	OECD countries	D 22-a	
$m	EEC countries	E 29-a	
ancillary equipment in $	EEC countries	E 29-a	
furnaces by type in $m	EEC countries	E 29-a	
power equipment in $m	EEC countries	E 29-a	
re-rolling mills in $m	EEC countries	E 29-a	
rolling mills in $m	EEC countries	E 29-a	
per ton of crude steel produced	EEC countries	E 29-a	
iron ore extracted	EEC countries	E 29-a	
Labour costs as % of total costs in steel industry	EEC countries	E 8-a	
by sector in DM million	W Germany	H 3-a	
by status of employees in local currency	EEC countries	E 8-a	
female workers per hr in local currency	Main countries	C 2-a	
(incl staff) per hr in local currency	EEC countries	E 2-a	
per hr in FrB	EEC countries	E 29-a	
per hr in FrS	Main countries	C 2-a	

	Territorial coverage	Title codes	
IRON & STEEL INDUSTRY, continued			
Labour costs: semi-skilled workers per hr in local currency	Main countries	C 2-a	
skilled workers per hr in local currency	Main countries	C 2-a	
unskilled workers per hr in local currency	Main countries	C 2-a	
Labour force employed & % foreign workers	EEC countries	E 29-a	
(incl salaried staff)	EEC countries	E 2-a	E 29-a
by age groups	EEC countries	E 29-a	
nationality	EEC countries	E 29-a	
sex	EEC area	E 29-a	
status	Main countries	C 2-a	
in steel industry	France	C 5-m	
	W Germany	H 3-a	
no of administrative employees	Main countries	U 21-a	
auxiliary workers	EEC area	E 29-a	
foreign workers as % of total	EEC countries	E 29-a	
production workers	EEC countries	E 30-a	
salaried staff	Main countries	C 2-a	
wage earners & salaried staff	Main countries	C 2-a	
workers entering steel industry	EEC countries	E 8-a	
leaving steel industry	EEC countries	E 29-a	
	EEC countries	E 29-a	
New orders received by product: tonnage	EEC countries	E 30-m	
No of days work lost per accident	EEC countries	E 2-a	
through accidents	EEC countries	E 3-a	
of hrs worked per wk	Main countries	R 3-m	
	W Germany	H 3-a	
per wk by region	EEC countries	E 25-a	
per yr	EEC countries	E 8-a	
of man-hrs worked	EEC countries	E 29-a	
of non-fatal accidents reported by kind	EEC countries	E 2-a	
by process	EEC countries	E 2-a	
by size of firm	EEC countries	E 2-a	
Output per man-yr - index nos	UK	T 2-q	
Receipts: aluminium: tonnage	OECD countries	D 21-a	
blast furnace gas in m³	EEC countries	E 29-a	
coal: tonnage	EEC area	E 29-a	
coke (incl powder): tonnage	EEC countries	E 29-a	
ferrous scrap: tonnage	ECE countries	U 6-a	U 7-a
	Main countries	H 3-a	
lignite: tonnage	EEC area	E 29-a	
solid fuels: tonnage	EEC area	E 29-a	
Sales turnover by sector in DM million	W Germany	H 3-a	
Wage rates per hr by sex in DM	W Germany	H 3-a	
in local currency	Main countries	R 3-m	C 7-a
in local currency	EEC countries	E 25-a2	E 29-a
	Main countries	C 2-a	
Wage rates per hr - index nos	EEC countries	E 26-a2	
Wages & salary costs in $	Main countries	U 21-a	

Iron & steel merchants   see   STEEL STOCKHOLDERS

IRON & STEEL PRODUCTS

see also   ENGINEERING PRODUCTS
FOUNDRY IRON

% share of EEC area imports	Developing countries	U 52-a	
Exports by destination: tonnage	UK	T 2-m	
by value in $m	Asian & Far East areas	U 32-a	
	World regions	U 23-a	
to EEC & non-EEC areas by value in $m	EEC countries	E 24-a	
Import duties: rates in % ad val	USA	J 3	
Imports by source: tonnage	EEC countries	E 3-a	
by value in $m	Developing countries	U 52-a	
ex EEC & non-EEC areas by value in $m	EEC countries	E 24-a	
into EEC area by value in $m	Developing countries	U 52-a	
Producer prices - index nos	W Germany	H 3-a	
Production - index nos	OECD countries	D 19-m	D 20-m
Shipments by cargo ship (trip period charter): tonnage	Worldwide	S 17-m	
through Panama Canal: tonnage		D 28-a	

IRON & STEEL PRODUCTS BY KIND

Exports by destination by SITC classes: tonnage & value in $m	OECD countries	D 3-a2	
CST classes: tonnage & value in $m	EEC countries	E 48-a	
SITC classes by value in $m	Main countries	D 2-q	
tonnage	EEC area	E 5-q	
tonnage & value in $m	All countries	U 12-a	
by NIMEXE classes by value in $m	All countries	E 20-a	
SITC classes by value in $m	All countries	U 50-a	U 59-a
tonnage	Main countries	T 2-m	
Imports by NIMEXE classes by value in $	All countries	E 20-a	
SITC classes by value in $	All countries	U 50-a	U 59-a
source by CST classes: tonnage & value in $m	EEC countries	E 21-a	
SITC classes by value in $m	Main countries	D 2-q	
:tonnage & value in $m	OECD countries	D 3-a2	
by source: tonnage	EEC area	E 5-q	
tonnage & value in $m	All countries	U 12-a	

Iron & steel scrap   see   FERROUS SCRAP

297

	Territorial coverage	Title codes	
IRON CASTINGS			
see also FOUNDRY IRON			
Consumption by building industry: tonnage	UK	B 25-a	
coal mining industry: tonnage	UK	B 25-a	
domestic goods manufacturing industry: tonnage	UK	B 25-a	
electrical engineering industry: tonnage	UK	B 25-a	
industrial sector: tonnage	UK	B 25-a	
machine tools manufacturing industry: tonnage	UK	B 25-a	
mechanical engineering industry: tonnage	UK	B 25-a	
motor vehicles manufacturing industry: tonnage	UK	B 25-a	
pipes & fittings manufacturing industry: tonnage	UK	B 25-a	
shipbuilding & repair industry: tonnage	UK	B 25-a	
tractor manufacturing industry: tonnage	UK	B 25-a	
Consumption: cobalt in production of iron castings in lbs	USA	T 4-a	
nickel in production of iron castings: tonnage	USA	J 6-a	
Consumption in production of ingot moulds & plates: tonnage	UK	B 25-a	
railway permanent way: tonnage	UK	B 25-a	
tunnel segments: tonnage	UK	B 25-a	
Deliveries to consuming industries: tonnage	UK	B 25-a	
Demand & required production projected to 1977: tonnage	UK	B 25-a	
Despatches (ex ironworks): tonnage	USA	N 1-a	
Exports as % of home production (wt basis)	UK	B 25-a	
by destination: tonnage	EEC countries	E 5-q	
Fuel & power costs in castings production in £ per ton	UK	B 25-a	
Imports by source: tonnage	EEC countries	E 5-q	
Price (on production value basis) in £ per ton	UK	B 25-a	
Production by grade: tonnage & value in £m	UK	B 25-a	
grey castings: tonnage & value in £m	UK	B 25-a	
malleable castings: tonnage & value in £m	UK	B 25-a	
spheroidal graphite castings: tonnage & value in £m	UK	B 25-a	
tonnage & value in £m	France, W Germany & UK	B 25-a	
tonnage	ECE countries, Japan & USA	U 6-a	U 7-a
	EEC countries	E 30-q	E 29-a
	Main countries	H 3-a	
Profit & depreciation: iron foundries in £ per ton	UK	B 25-a	
Raw materials: costs: iron foundries in £ per ton	UK	B 25-a	
Sales value: iron castings in £ per ton	UK	B 25-a	
per ton in local currency	France, W Germany & UK	B 25-a	
Wages & salary costs: iron foundries in £ per ton	UK	B 25-a	
World production: tonnage	Main countries	B 25-a	T 4-a
IRON FOUNDRIES			
As source of ferrous scrap for steel industry: tonnage	ECE countries	U 6-a	U 7-a
	Main countries	H 3-a	
Consumption of castings: tonnage	UK	B 25-a	
Investment as % of value of output of iron castings	France, W Germany & UK	B 25-a	
Labour force employed	France, W Germany & UK	B 25-a	
No of accidents reported & no of resulting fatalities	UK	B 25-a	
fatalities resulting from lung diseases contracted in foundries	UK	B 25-a	
hrs worked per wk	Main countries	R 3-m	
in operation & net closures during yr	UK	B 25-a	
by size of labour force employed	UK	B 25-a	
by volume of output	UK	B 25-a	
(total)	France, W Germany & UK	B 25-a	
Productivity in tons of castings per man-yr	France, W Germany & UK	B 25-a	
Purchases of ferrous scrap for foundries from dealers: tonnage	ECE countries	U 6-a	U 7-a
	Main countries	H 3-a	
Receipts of ferrous scrap by foundries: tonnage	ECE area	U 6-a	U 7-a
	Main countries	H 3-a	
Wage rates per hr in iron foundries by sex in local currency	Main countries	R 3-m	
Iron foundry products see IRON CASTINGS			
IRON ORE			
% chemical content of iron, sulphur & phosphorus	Main countries	U 51	
% content of trace elements by grade of ore	Main countries	U 56	
% contribution to export earnings: iron ore	African, Caribbean countries & Pacific Is	E 45-a	
% iron content of ore mined	World regions	U 56-a	
of shipments	Main countries	U 56-a	
% of EEC area production (based on metal content of ore)	EEC countries	R 5-a	
% share of estimated world reserves	Latin American area	U 18-a	
world production	All countries	E 29-a	
Consumption: foreign iron ore in sinter plants: tonnage	EEC countries	E 29-a	
in steel furnaces: tonnage	EEC countries	E 29-a	
home-mined iron ore in sinter plants: tonnage	EEC countries	E 29-a	
in steel furnaces: tonnage	EEC countries	E 29-a	
home-mined & imported iron ore: tonnage	UK	T 2-m	
imported ore ex EEC area in sinter plants	EEC countries	E 29-a	
in steel furnaces	EEC countries	E 29-a	
in agglomeration plants: tonnage	Main countries	U 56-a	
blast furnaces: tonnage	EEC countries	E 29-a	
	Main countries	T 1-a	U 56-a
production of agglomerates: tonnage	ECE countries	U 7-q	U 6-a
	Main countries	H 3-a	
of sinter: tonnage	EEC countries	E 29-a	
	UK	T 2-q	
steel furnaces: tonnage	EEC countries	E 30-q	E 29-a
	Main countries	T 1-a	U 56-a

	Territorial coverage	Title codes	
IRON ORE, continued			
Consumption: (incl concentrates): tonnage	ECE countries	U 7-q	U 6-a
	Main countries	H 3-a	
of agglomerates & sinter pellets: tonnage	ECE area	U 7-q	U 6-a
	Main countries	H 3-a	
tonnage	Main countries	N 5-a	U 49-a
	USA	N 1-a	
Deliveries (ex mines) for export shipment: tonnage	All countries & world regions	U 56-a	
to domestic consumers & for export: tonnage	EEC countries	E 29-a	
to EEC area: tonnage	EEC countries	E 30-m	
for smelting in non-EEC area: tonnage	EEC countries	E 29-a	
Export prices by grade of ore in $ per ton cif	EEC countries	E 29-a	
Export prices - index nos (weighted average main sources)	Main countries	U 56-a	
	Worldwide	U 29-q	
Exports by destination: tonnage	S American countries	U 40-a	
	EEC countries	E 5-q	E 29-a
regions of destination: tonnage	All countries	U 56-a	
sea, inland waterways, road & rail: tonnage	European countries	U 8-a	
value in $m	Developing countries	U 11-a	
to world regions of destination: tonnage	OECD countries	D 22-a	
(incl concentrates) by value in Rs	India	U 32-m	
tonnage	Asian & Far East areas	U 32-q	
	ECE countries	U 7-m	U 6-a
	Main countries	H 3-a	
(incl manganiferous ores): tonnage	All countries	B 15-a	
to non-EEC area: tonnage	EEC area	E 29-a	
tonnage & value in $m	African, Caribbean countries & Pacific Is	E 45-a	
historical tables from 1850	Main European countries	Z 1-a	
tonnage	Australia, Canada, France, W Germany, Sweden & USA	T 2-m	
	European countries	C 5-m	
	Hong Kong, India, Malaysia & S Korea	U 32-m	
	World regions	U 56-a	
	AASM countries	E 41-a	
total & to EEC area: tonnage & value in UA	Main countries	U 11-a	U 56-a
unit value in $ per ton	Developed countries	U 11-a	
Import demand (based on iron content): tonnage	EEC countries	E 29-a	
Import prices (ex major suppliers) per ton cif	EEC countries	E 29-a	
Import prices - index nos	Canada, European countries & Japan	D 22-a	
Import requirements projected to 1980: tonnage	All countries	U 56	
Imports, exports & home deliveries within EEC area: tonnage	EEC countries	E 30-m	
Imports & exports by source & destination: tonnage	Main countries	B 15-a	
Imports by sea, inland waterways, road & rail: tonnage	European countries	U 8-a	
by source: tonnage & % iron content (average)	W Germany, Japan & UK	U 56-a	
tonnage	EEC countries	E 5-q	E 29-a
	Main countries	D 28-a	T 1-a
		U 49-a	
by world regions of source: tonnage	OECD countries	D 22-a	
	Main countries	U 56-a	
ex non-EEC area: tonnage	EEC area	E 29-a	
historical tables from 1847: tonnage	Main European countries	Z 1-a	
(incl concentrates): tonnage	ECE countries	U 7-m	U 6-a
	Main countries	H 3-a	
(incl manganiferous ore): tonnage	All countries	B 15-a	
tonnage	W Germany	C 5-m	
Inter-EEC imports & exports as % of world trade in iron ore	EEC countries	E 30-q	
International trade flows: forecasts by source: tonnage	Main consuming countries	U 56	
Potential resources & probable world reserves: tonnage		U 51	
by type of ore & as % of total resources	World regions	U 51	
Prices (51.5% iron) ex US mines in $ per ton	USA	E 41-a	
Lake Superior ore in $ per ton	USA	N 1-a	
ore pellets in cents per ton of metallic iron content	USA	N 1-a	
Production: tonnage & % metallic iron content	Main countries	E 3-a	
agglomerates & sinter pellets: tonnage	ECE countries	U 7-m	U 6-a
	Main countries	H 3-a	
(based on metal content of ore): tonnage	ECE area, Japan & USA	U 6-a	U 7-a
	All countries	R 5-a	U 22-a
	Latin American countries	U 40-a	
	Main countries	H 3-a	U 43-a
	OECD countries	D 22-a	R 5-a
	AASM countries	E 41-a	
by grade: tonnage	Main countries	B 15-a	
region: tonnage	EEC countries	E 30-m	E 29-a
		E 38-a	
from open-cast mines: tonnage	EEC area	E 29-a	
underground mines: tonnage	EEC area	E 29-a	
historical table from 1822: tonnage	Main European countries	Z 1-a	
imports & exports: tonnage	Main countries	U 49-a	
(incl agglomerates): tonnage	W Germany	C 5-m	
(incl manganiferous ores): tonnage	All countries	B 15-a	
(incl world total): tonnage	All countries	E 29-a	
ore less than 42% metallic iron content: tonnage	EEC area	U 7-m	U 6-a
	Main countries	H 3-a	
over 42% metallic iron content	EEC area	U 7-m	U 6-a
	Main countries	H 3-a	
ore & metallic iron extracted: tonnage	EEC area	E 29-a	
ore & pellets: tonnage	All countries	U 56-a	
ore agglomerates: tonnage	All countries	U 56-a	
pellets: tonnage	Latin American countries	U 18-a	
projected to 1980: tonnage	All countries	U 56	

	Territorial coverage	Title codes	
IRON ORE, continued			
Production: sinter: tonnage	Latin American countries	U 18-a	
Production, supply, imports & exports: tonnage	Main countries	U 56-a	
unprocessed ore	Latin American countries	U 18-a	
tonnage	African countries	U 44-a	
	All countries	T 2-m	N 5-a
		T 1-a	U 56-a
	Asian & Far East countries	U 32-q	
	ECAFE countries	U 32-q	
	EEC countries	E 26-m	E 30-m
		E 28-q	E 27-a
	Canada, EEC countries, Sweden, USA & USSR	E 30-m	
	Main countries	N 1-a	
	Mauritania	E 41-a	
	OAS member countries	N 14-a	
tonnage (with % metallic iron content)	All countries	U 27-m	
Receipts from EEC area: tonnage	EEC area	E 29-a	
Requirement forecasts: tonnage	World regions	U 56-a	
Resources by type of deposit & location: tonnage	World regions	U 51	
bedded residual iron ore: tonnage	World regions	U 51	
of mineral in ore mined: tonnage	World regions	U 51	
Seaborne freight by destination in ton-km	All exporting countries	U 56-a	
tonnage (estim)	Worldwide	D 28-a	
Shipments (as ore concentrates): tonnage	ECE area, Japan & USA	U 7-m	U 6-a
	Main countries	H 3-a	
(as mined ore): tonnage	ECE area, Japan & USA	U 7-m	U 6-a
	Main countries	H 3-a	
by cargo vessels by source of cargo: tonnage	EEC area, Japan & USA	D 28-a	
(trip & period charter): tonnage	Worldwide	S 17-m	
through Panama Canal eastwards: tonnage		D 28-a	
Stocks at mines & metal extracted: tonnage	EEC area	E 29-a	
mines, docks & consumers' plant: tonnage	USA	N 1-a	
mines: tonnage	EEC countries	E 30-m	
Supply, production, stocks & imports (net): tonnage	EEC countries	E 3-a	
Tramp shipping freight rates for iron ore – index nos		U 37-m	
Transport costs (mines to ports) in $ per ton	Main countries	U 56	
Transport distances (mines to ports) in km	Main countries	U 56	
Wholesale prices per ton in local currency	France, Sweden & USA	U 27-m	
World exports: tonnage & as % of world output		U 56-a	
World market prices – index nos		G 1-a	
World production (based on metallic iron content): tonnage	World regions	U 11-a	
	Worldwide	U 56-a	
		U 51	
historical table from 1850: tonnage	Worldwide	C 30-a	N 4-a
tonnage	All countries	T 1-a	T 4-a
	Main countries	N 1-a	
	World regions	U 49-a	U 56-a
	All countries	U 56-a	
World reserves of iron ore by kind: tonnage		N 1-a	
by value (at current prices) in $m			
tonnage & % of metallic iron content	World regions	U 56-a	
tonnage	All countries	N 1-a	
Iron ore carriers see BULK CARRIERS			
IRON ORE MINING			
see also ORE MINING INDUSTRY			
Absenteeism from work (by reasons given)	EEC countries	E 29-a	
Costs for salaried staff per mth in local currency	EEC countries	E 11-a	
Earnings per hr: surface workers in local currency	EEC countries	E 29-a	
underground workers in local currency	EEC countries	E 29-a	
Investment funds granted for new projects in $	EEC countries	E 29-a	
in $m	EEC countries	E 29-a	
plans projected in $m	EEC area	E 30-a2	
Labour costs as % of total costs	EEC countries	E 8-a	
by status of employee in local currency	EEC countries	E 8-a	
in DM million	W Germany	H 3-a	
per hr (all employees) in local currency	EEC countries	E 11-a	
in FrB	EEC countries	E 29-a	
(incl staff salaries) in local currency	EEC countries	E 2-a	
wage earners in local currency	EEC countries	E 11-a	
Labour force employed & % of foreign workers	EEC countries	E 29-a	
by age groups: open-cast mines	EEC countries	E 29-a	
underground mines	EEC countries	E 29-a	
nationality	EEC countries	E 29-a	
occupation: open-cast mines	EEC countries	E 29-a	
deep mines	EEC countries	E 29-a	
no of salaried staff	EEC countries	E 11-a	
wage earners	EEC countries	E 11-a	
(total)	EEC countries	E 2-a	E 8-a
		E 33-a	
no of foreign workers as % of total labour force	EEC countries	E 33-a	
no of foreign workers employed	EEC countries	E 33-a	
No of hrs worked per wk by region	EEC countries	E 25-a	
per yr: salaried staff	EEC countries	E 11-a	
wage earners	EEC countries	E 11-a	
per yr	EEC countries	E 8-a	
Output per man-shift: deep mining: tonnage	EEC countries	E 29-a	
opencast mining: tonnage	EEC countries	E 29-a	

	Territorial coverage	Title codes
IRON ORE MINING, continued		
Wage rates per hr in DM	W Germany	H 3-a
in local currency	EEC countries	E 25-a2
	OAS member countries	N 17-a
IRON OXIDE		
see also PIGMENTS, MINERAL		
Exports: tonnage	OECD countries	D 5-a
Imports: tonnage	OECD countries	D 5-a
Production: tonnage	OECD countries	D 5-a
Iron pipes see PIPES, CAST-IRON		
IRON PRODUCTS		
see also IRON CASTINGS		
PIG IRON		
PIPES, CAST-IRON		
SPONGE IRON		
WROUGHT IRON, ROLLED		
Imports by kind: tonnage	Main countries	T 1-a
iron shot & wire pellets: tonnage	Main countries	T 1-a
Wholesale prices for building industry - index nos	Switzerland	U 5-a
IRON PYRITES		
Exports by destination: tonnage	EEC countries	E 5-q E 29-a
to non-EEC area: tonnage	EEC countries	E 29-a
Imports & exports: burnt pyrites: tonnage	All countries	B 15-a
by source: tonnage	EEC countries	E 5-q E 29-a
ex non-EEC area: tonnage	EEC area	E 29-a
Production: tonnage (incl world total)	All countries	R 5-a
unroasted pyrites: tonnage	All countries	U 22-a
Receipts ex EEC area: tonnage	EEC area	E 29-a
IRON-WORKING INDUSTRY		
Labour costs as % of total costs	EEC countries	E 8-a
by status of employee in local currency	EEC countries	E 8-a
Labour force employed: no of wage earners & salaried staff	EEC countries	E 8-a
No of hrs worked per wk	Main countries	R 3-m
per yr	EEC countries	E 8-a
Wage rates per hr per yr by sex in local currency	Main countries	R 3-m
Irons see ELECTRIC IRONS		
IRRIGATION		
Area irrigated for fruit production on collectives in ha	Bulgaria	U 20-a
on state farms in ha	Bulgaria	U 20-a
for vegetable production on collectives in ha	Bulgaria	U 20-a
on state farms in ha	Bulgaria	U 20-a
in ha	All countries	A 9-a
of irrigated arable land in ha	Asian, Far East & Australasian countries	U 45-a
IBRD loans approved for irrigation projects in $m	OAS member countries	N 16-a
Italico see CHEESE BY VARIETY		
Jails see PENAL INSTITUTIONS		
JAM & MARMALADE		
Production: jam (bottled) by kind: tonnage	Japan	B 6-a
(canned) by kind: tonnage	Japan	B 6-a
tonnage	All countries	U 22-a
	EEC countries	E 28-q E 27-a
	OECD countries	D 37-a
Jeeps see MOTOR VEHICLES		
Jerseys see CATTLE BY BREED		
Jet aircraft see AIRCRAFT, TURBO-JET		
Jet fuel see KEROSENE		
Jet-engined planes see AIRCRAFT, TURBO-JET		
JEWELLERY INDUSTRY		
Consumption of platinum & palladium in oz	USA	J 6-a
of silver in oz	USA	T 4-a
Investment in buildings in local currency	EEC countries	E 40-a
land purchase in local currency	EEC countries	E 40-a
machinery in local currency	EEC countries	E 40-a
No of hrs worked per wk	Main countries	R 3-m
Wage rates per hr by sex	Main countries	R 3-m

	Territorial coverage	Title codes
Joists, steel see HEAVY SECTIONS, STEEL		
Jowar see SORGHUM		
Jurisprudence see LAW		
JUTE		
see also BURLAP		
Area harvested, production tonnage & yield per ha	All countries	A 9-a
under jute & Kenaf crop & yield per ha	India & Pakistan	A 1
jute crop in acres	Main countries	B 10-a
Kenaf crop in acres	Spain, S Vietnam & Thailand	B 10-a
Mesta crop in acres	India & Pakistan	B 10-a
Urena & Punga crop in acres	Zaire	B 10-a
Consumption & demand projections to 1975: tonnage	Main countries	A 1
by textile industry: tonnage	OECD countries	D 46-a
spinning mills: tonnage	India & Pakistan	B 10-a
	OECD countries	D 46-a
(incl allied fibres): tonnage	Main countries	B 2-a
(incl coir & sisal) in production of floor coverings: tonnage	EEC countries	K 4-a
Export prices in £ per ton fob	Bangladesh & Thailand	A 5-a
Dundee Daisy grade in Rs per 400 lbs	India	R 2-m
in local currency per ton	Bangladesh & Brazil	A 9-a
in $ per ton	Pakistan	U 17-m
Export prices - index nos (weighted average main sources)		U 29-q
Exports as % of value of total exports	India & Pakistan	B 10-a
by destination: tonnage	Pakistan & Thailand	B 10-a
by value: raw jute in Rs per ton	Pakistan	U 32-m
(incl allied fibres) by value in $m	Developing countries	U 11-a
tonnage	Asian & Far East areas	U 32-q
	India, Pakistan & Thailand	U 32-m
	Main countries	A 5-a
tonnage & by value in $m	Pakistan & Thailand	B 2-a
Import prices in £ per ton cif at Dundee (incl annual averages)	UK	B 10
on London market	UK	B 2-a
raw jute fibre (ex Bangladesh) in £ per ton cif	UK	R 2-m U 32-m
in £ per ton cif	UK	A 9-a
Imports as % of world import trade (value basis)	W European countries	C 22-a
by source: raw jute & allied fibres: tonnage	W European countries	C 22-a
(ex British Commonwealth countries): tonnage	EEC countries	B 10-a
tonnage	Main countries	B 10-a
Production (incl allied fibres) & world total: tonnage	Main countries	A 5-a B 2-a
	Asian & Far East countries	U 32-a
Kenaf: tonnage	Iran, Spain, S Vietnam & Thailand	B 10-a
Malva & Guaxima: tonnage	Brazil	B 10-a
Mesta: tonnage	India & Pakistan	B 10-a
Urena & Punga: tonnage	Zaire	B 10-a
tonnage	Main countries	B 10-a
Stocks: raw jute (at end-season): tonnage	India & Pakistan	B 10-a
(incl allied fibres): tonnage	India & Pakistan	B 2-a
	Main countries	A 5-a
tonnage	India & Pakistan	B 10-a
Wholesale prices: raw jute in Rs per 180kg at Calcutta	India	U 32-m
in local currency	Bangladesh, India, UK & USA	U 27-m
World exports (incl allied fibres) by value in $m	India & USA	A 9-a
unit value in $ per ton	World regions	A 5-a
World production in million lbs & % share held by Commonwealth countries	Worldwide	A 11-a
		B 10-a
raw jute & allied fibres (incl Kenaf): tonnage		K 4-a U 11-a
	All countries	C 22-a
World stocks of jute (at end-yr): tonnage		G 1-a
JUTE MANUFACTURES		
see also WOVEN JUTE FABRICS		
Consumption of jute bags & sacks: tonnage	W European countries	C 22-a
of jute goods: tonnage	All countries	B 10-a
Exports: jute bags & sacks by value in $	Pakistan	U 32-m
by destination: jute bags (new): tonnage	W European countries	C 22-a
jute cloth: tonnage	W European countries	C 22-a
tonnage	W European countries	C 22-a
by value in $m	India & Pakistan	B 10-a
	Bangladesh & India	A 5-a
Imports by source: jute bags (new): tonnage	W European countries	C 22-a
jute cloth: tonnage	W European countries	C 22-a
(ex Commonwealth countries) by value in £	EEC countries	B 10-a
jute bags & sacks (new): tonnage	W European countries	C 22-a
cloth: tonnage	W European countries	C 22-a
piece goods & sacks: tonnage	UK	B 10-a
Production: hessian: tonnage	India & Pakistan	B 10-a
jute bags & sacks: tonnage	W European countries	C 22-a
cloth: tonnage	Main countries	B 10-a
sacking material: tonnage	India & Pakistan	B 10-a
tonnage	Asian & Far East countries	U 32-q
	ECAFE countries	U 32-q
	Bangladesh, European countries & India	A 5-a
Stocks: hessian sacking: tonnage	India & Pakistan	B 10-a

	Territorial coverage	Title codes	
JUTE MANUFACTURES, continued			
Wholesale prices: burlap in Rs per 100 metres	India	U 32-m	
hessian in Rs per 100 metres	India & Pakistan	B 10-a	
jute bags in Rs per 100 bags	India	U 32-m	
jute yarn in pence per lb	UK	B 10-a	
sacking twills in Rs per 100 metres	India & Pakistan	B 10-a	
World production: all jute products: tonnage	Main countries	B 10-a	C 22-a
JUTE MANUFACTURES BY KIND			
Exports by destination by CST classes by value in $	EEC countries	E 48-a	
by SITC classes by value in $	Main countries	D 2-q	
tonnage & value in $	OECD countries	D 3-a2	
NIMEXE classes by value in $	All countries	E 20-a	
SITC classes by value in $	All countries	U 50-a	U 59-a
Imports by NIMEXE classes by value in $	All countries	E 20-a	
SITC classes by value in $	All countries	U 50-a	U 59-a
source by CST classes by value in $	EEC countries	E 21-a	
by SITC classes by value in $	Main countries	D 2-q	
tonnage & value in $	OECD countries	D 3-a2	
JUTE PRODUCTS INDUSTRY			
Capital expenditure in £m	UK	B 29-a	
Investment in buildings in local currency	EEC countries	E 40-a	
in machinery in local currency	EEC countries	E 40-a	
Labour force employed by sex	W European countries	C 22-a	
No of firms in operation by size of labour force employed	W European countries	C 22-a	
spinning & weaving mills	W European countries	C 22-a	
JUTE YARN			
Consumption by weaving industry: tonnage	OECD countries	D 46-a	
tonnage	W European countries	C 22-a	
Exports by destination: tonnage	W European countries	C 22-a	
(incl fabrics) by value in Rs	India & Pakistan	U 32-m	
tonnage	W European countries	C 22-a	
Imports & exports (incl trade balance) in jute yarn: tonnage	W European countries	C 22-a	
Imports by source: tonnage	W European countries	C 22-a	
tonnage	Main countries	B 10-a	
	W European countries	C 22-a	
Production: tonnage	OECD countries	D 46-a	
	All countries	U 22-a	
	EEC countries	E 28-q	E 27-a
	W European countries	C 22-a	
JUVENILE DELINQUENCY			
see also CRIMINAL OFFENCES			
No of cases by age of offender	OAS member countries	N 20-a	
kind of offence	OAS member countries	N 20-a	
sex of offender	OAS member countries	N 20-a	
dismissed	OAS member countries	N 20-a	
heard in courts of law	OAS member countries	N 20-a	
involving illiterate offenders	OAS member countries	N 20-a	
leading to convictions	OAS member countries	N 20-a	

Kaldo steel   see   CRUDE STEEL

Kaldo steel plants   see   STEELWORKS

Kale   see   VEGETABLES, GREEN

Kaolin   see   CHINA CLAY

KAPOK SEED			
Exports: tonnage	Cambodia, Indonesia & Thailand	B 19-a	
Imports: tonnage	Japan	B 19-a	

Kardiseed   see   SAFFLOWER SEED

Kenaf   see   JUTE

KEROSENE

see also   AVIATION FUEL
                   WHITE SPIRIT

% consumption of world supply	Latin American countries	U 18-a	
Consumption for domestic heating: tonnage	OECD countries	D 31-a	
in barrels per day	World regions	C 3-a	
in m³	AASM countries	E 41-a	
in litres (as jet fuel)	OAS member countries	N 17-a	
in litres	OAS member countries	N 17-a	
(incl jet fuel): tonnage	Main countries	C 14-a	
Deliveries, consumption & supply of jet fuel: tonnage	OECD countries	D 31-a	
Deliveries for domestic consumption & exports: tonnage	OECD countries	D 39-q	
tonnage	EEC countries	E 16-m	E 15-a

	Territorial coverage	Title codes	
KEROSENE, continued			
Imports & exports by source & destination: tonnage	Main countries	B 15-a	
Imports by source: kerosene-type jet fuel: tonnage	OECD countries	D 31-a	
tonnage	OECD countries	D 31-a	
Prices posted at specific ports in cents per gallon fob	Worldwide	C 3-a	
Production in barrels per day	OPEC member countries	C 3-a	
in barrels	All countries	N 5-a	
Production: jet fuel by volume in m³	OAS member countries	N 14-a	
tonnage	African countries	U 44-a	
Production & consumption: tonnage	OECD countries	D 44-a	
Production, trade & consumption: tonnage	All countries	U 55-a	
tonnage	African countries	U 39-a	U 44-a
	All countries	U 22-a	U 43-a
	EEC countries	E 28-q	E 27-a
	European countries, USA & USSR	U 4-a	
	Latin American countries	J 5-a	
	Main countries	U 27-q	B 15-a
		E 3-a	
	OECD countries	D 44-a	
Refinery output & consumption: tonnage	Cuba, Mexico & S American countries	U 40-a	
Refinery output, imports & supply: jet fuel: tonnage	OECD countries	D 31-a	
Retail prices of kerosene in cents per gallon	OECD countries	D 39-q	
in local currency	Main countries	U 18-a	
Wholesale prices in local currency	OAS member countries	N 17-a	
Wholesale prices - index nos	OAS member countries	N 17-a	
	Nepal	U 32-m	

Kerosene, household   see   PARAFFIN

Keruing   see   HARDWOOD, SAWN

Ketchup   see   TOMATO PRODUCTS

KETTLES			
Production: electric kettles by volume	EEC countries	E 28-q	E 27-a

Key indicators   see   ECONOMIC INDICATORS, BASIC

Kid for glove-making   see   LEATHER

Kidskins   see   GOATSKINS

KIEL CANAL		
Cargo traffic westwards: all cargo: tonnage		D 28-a
coal & coke: tonnage		D 28-a
general cargo: tonnage		D 28-a
grain: tonnage		D 28-a
metallic ores: tonnage		D 28-a
mineral oils: tonnage		D 28-a
timber: tonnage		D 28-a
wood pulp: tonnage		D 28-a
Traffic (by commodity groups) in both directions: tonnage		D 28-a
Transit goods traffic carried on foreign ships (eastbound): tonnage		S 16-m
(westbound): tonnage		S 16-m
German ships (eastbound): tonnage		S 16-m
(westbound): tonnage		S 16-m

Kieselguhr   see   DIATOMACEOUS EARTH

Kilns   see   CEMENT & PLASTER INDUSTRY
                 PLANT CAPACITY

KIMONOS		
Consumption of wool for kimono production in kg	Japan	K 6-a

KINDERGARTEN		
No of kindergarten in use (public & private)	OAS member countries	N 19-a
kindergarten in use, no of pupils enrolled & % private	All countries	U 62-a
pupils enrolled by sex	OAS member countries	N 19-a
pupils (or places available) in kindergarten	EEC countries	E 2-a
teachers employed by sex & % female	All countries	U 62-a
	OAS member countries	N 19-a
Public expenditure on nursery education in $m	All countries	U 62-a
per pupil in $	All countries	U 62-a

Kips   see   CALFSKINS

Kitchen equipment   see   DOMESTIC EQUIPMENT

KNITTED FABRICS		
Deliveries to textile industry - index nos	UK	B 29-a
Exports: cellulosic fabrics: tonnage	All countries	A 6-a
garments & lace projected to 1977 in lbs	UK	B 29
(incl crocheted fabrics): tonnage	OECD countries	D 46-a
non-cellulosic fabrics: tonnage	All countries	A 6-a
Imports & exports (incl trade balance) in sq yds	UK	B 29-a
Imports as % of domestic consumption	UK	B 29-a

	Territorial coverage	Title codes	
KNITTED FABRICS, continued			
Imports: cellulosic fabrics: tonnage	All countries	A 6-a	
(incl crocheted fabrics): tonnage	OECD countries	D 46-a	
non-cellulosic fabrics: tonnage	All countries	A 6-a	
Production by volume in m²	OECD countries	D 46-a	
KNITTED GOODS			
Deliveries (incl hosiery) – index nos	UK	B 29-a	
Demand (domestic) projected to 1977 in lbs million	UK	B 29	
Import forecast: garments & lace projected to 1977 in lbs	UK	B 29	
Imports & exports (incl trade balance): knitted goods & hosiery	UK	B 29-a	
Imports (incl hosiery) as % of domestic consumption	UK	B 29-a	
Production: knitted goods (made of weft-knitted fabrics) by volume & value in $	OECD countries	D 46-a	
knitted goods by value in $	OECD countries	D 46-a	
garments & lace projected to 1977 in lbs	UK	B 29	
knitted & crocheted goods in kg	All countries	U 22-a	
knitted goods made of man-made fabrics by volume & value in $	OECD countries	D 46-a	
made of pure cotton fabrics by volume & value in $	OECD countries	D 46-a	
warp-knitted fabrics by volume & value in $	OECD countries	D 46-a	
outerwear & underwear by volume	EEC countries	E 28-q	E 27-a

Knitting   see   HAND KNITTING

Knitting machines   see   TEXTILE MACHINERY

KNITTING MILLS
    see also   TEXTILE INDUSTRY

	Territorial coverage	Title codes
Capital expenditure in £m	UK	B 29-a
Consumption in knitting mills of acetate yarn: tonnage	OECD countries	D 46-a
acrylic yarn: tonnage	OECD countries	D 46-a
cotton yarn (incl waste): tonnage	OECD countries	D 46-a
flax & tow: tonnage	OECD countries	D 46-a
man-made fibre, artificial & synthetic yarns: tonnage	OECD countries	D 46-a
polyamide & polyester yarns: tonnage	OECD countries	D 46-a
silk yarn (incl thrown silk): tonnage	OECD countries	D 46-a
soft hemp & tow: tonnage	OECD countries	D 46-a
wool & worsted yarns: tonnage	OECD countries	D 46-a
yarn (all kinds): tonnage	OECD countries	D 46-a
Costs for salaried staff in knitting mills per mth in local currency	EEC countries	E 11-a
Gross output by value in $	OECD countries	D 46-a
Investment by knitting industry in buildings in local currency	EEC countries	E 40-a
land purchase in local currency	EEC countries	E 40-a
machinery in local currency	EEC countries	E 40-a
in $m	OECD countries	D 46-a
Labour costs in knitting mills as % of total costs	EEC countries	E 8-a
by status of employees in local currency	EEC countries	E 8-a
per hr (all employees) in local currency	EEC countries	E 11-a
(wage earners) in local currency	EEC countries	E 11-a
Labour force employed: no of salaried staff	EEC countries	E 11-a
	OECD countries	D 46-a
wage earners	EEC countries	E 11-a
	OECD countries	D 46-a
wage earners & salaried staff	EEC countries	E 8-a
Labour force in knitting mills projected to 1977	UK	B 29-a
No of hrs worked per yr: salaried staff	EEC countries	E 11-a
wage earners	EEC countries	E 11-a
(all employees)	EEC countries	E 8-a
Production – index nos	OECD countries	D 46-a

Knitting wool   see   HAND-KNITTING YARN

Knives, forks & spoons   see   CUTLERY

Kraft paper   see   WRAPPING PAPER

Kraftliners   see   WRAPPING PAPER

KYANITE
    see also   SILLIMANITE

	Territorial coverage	Title codes	
% of consumption in boilers & furnaces (as refractories)	USA	N 1-a	
glass-making industry	USA	N 1-a	
processing of ferrous metals	USA	N 1-a	
non-ferrous metals	USA	N 1-a	
Consumption: tonnage	USA	N 1-a	
Government strategic stockpile & sales: tonnage	USA	N 1-a	
Imports & exports by source & destination: tonnage	All countries	B 15-a	
Production: tonnage	India, S Africa, USA & USSR	B 15-a	N 1-a
World production: tonnage	Main countries	N 1-a	
World reserves: tonnage (estim)	Main countries	N 1-a	

	Territorial coverage	Title codes
L.D. steel see CRUDE STEEL		
L.D. steel plants see STEELWORKS		
L.P.G. (Liquefied petroleum gas) see NATURAL GAS LIQUIDS		
Laboratory equipment see SCIENTIFIC INSTRUMENTS		
Laboratory technicians see HOSPITAL PERSONNEL		

LABOUR COSTS
    see also   DISTRIBUTION COSTS
                 LABOUR RATIOS
                 SOCIAL CHARGES
                 WAGES

	Territorial coverage	Title codes	
By industrial sector for salaries in $	OAS member countries	N 14-a	
by status of employee in local currency	EEC countries	E 8-a	
By kind for monthly-paid staff per mth in local currency	Main countries	R 3-a	
for weekly-paid employees per hr in local currency	Main countries	R 3-a	
Employers' direct costs per employee per mth	Main countries	R 3-m	
per process worker per hr	Main countries	R 3-m	
indirect costs per employee per mth	Main countries	R 3-m	
per process worker per hr	Main countries	R 3-m	
In agriculture: wages & social charges per hr in $	E European countries	U 30-a	
	W European countries	U 30-a	
In industry as % of total industrial costs	EEC countries	E 8-a	
per hr by areas in local currency	EEC countries	E 38-a	
(incl staff salaries) in local currency	EEC countries	E 2-a	
per unit of gross value added	EEC countries	E 13-a	
social charges as % of total costs	EEC countries	E 11-a	
wages & salaries as % of total costs	EEC countries	E 11-a	
In manufacturing industry per unit of output - index nos	Main countries	B 28-a	
as % of total costs	EEC countries	E 8-a	
in local currency per hr	EEC countries	E 11-a	
index nos	Main countries	B 27-a	
	Main countries	C 7-a	
per unit of output - index nos	Main countries	B 23-a	
salaried staff per mth	EEC countries	E 3-a	
wage bill in local currency	EEC countries	E 11-a	
Manual workers employed in mining, building & industry	EEC countries	E 3-a	
Staff wages: international hotels per room in $	World regions	Z 5-a	
tourist hotels per room in $	World regions	Z 5-a	
% changes in manufacturing industry from 1967-72	France, W Germany & UK	B 28	
in wage costs per unit in building industry	E European countries	U 16-a	
in industry	E European countries	U 16-a	
% of costs by kind: salaried staff	EEC countries	E 11-a	
wage earners	EEC countries	E 11-a	

LABOUR COSTS BY INDUSTRY

	Territorial coverage	Title codes	
Abattoirs as % of total costs	EEC countries	E 8-a	
costs per hr in local currency	EEC countries	E 11-a	
Aerospace equipment industry as % of total costs	EEC countries	E 8-a	
Aircraft industry per hr in local currency	EEC countries	E 11-a	
Alcoholic drinks industry per hr in local currency	EEC countries	E 11-a	
Assurance companies per mth in local currency	EEC countries	E 9-a	
Baking & confectionery industry as % of total costs	EEC countries	E 8-a	
per hr in local currency	EEC countries	E 11-a	
Banking & insurance companies per salary-earner per mth in local currency	EEC countries	E 3-a	E 9-a
Beverages industry by sex per hr	Main countries	C 7-a	
as % of total costs	EEC countries	E 8-a	
Boot & shoe manufacturing industry by sex per hr	Main countries	C 7-a	
Briquetting plants per hr in local currency	EEC countries	E 11-a	
Building industry as % of total costs	EEC countries	E 8-a	
per hr by sex	Main countries	C 7-a	
by areas in local currency	EEC countries	E 38-a	
in local currency	EEC countries	E 11-a	
salaried staff per mth in local currency	EEC countries	E 3-a	
Building industry - index nos	European countries & USA	U 5-a	
Building materials industry as % of total costs	EEC countries	E 8-a	
per hr by sex	Main countries	C 7-a	
per hr in local currency	EEC countries	E 11-a	
Cement & plaster industry per hr in local currency	EEC countries	E 11-a	
as % of total costs	EEC countries	E 8-a	
Ceramics industry as % of total costs	EEC countries	E 8-a	
per hr in local currency	EEC countries	E 11-a	
Chemical industry as % of total costs	EEC countries	E 8-a	
per hr by sex	Main countries	C 7-a	
per hr in local currency by area	EEC countries	E 38-a	
per hr in local currency	EEC countries	E 11-a	
wages & salaries in DM million	W Germany	H 3-a	
Clothing manufacturing industry as % of total costs	EEC countries	E 8-a	
costs (comparative) per hr in £	EEC countries	B 29-a	
Coal mining industry: wages & salaries in DM million	W Germany	H 3-a	
as % of total costs	EEC countries	E 8-a	
per hr in local currency	EEC countries	E 11-a	
Coke oven plants as % of total costs	EEC countries	E 8-a	
per hr in local currency	EEC countries	E 11-a	

LABOUR COSTS BY INDUSTRY, continued

	Territorial coverage	Title codes	
Cotton textile manufacturing industry as % total costs	EEC countries	E 8-a	
per hr in local currency	EEC countries	E 11-a	
Dairying industry as % of total costs	EEC countries	E 8-a	
per hr in local currency	EEC countries	E 11-a	
Data-processing equipment industry per hr in local currency	EEC countries	E 11-a	
Electrical engineering industry as % of total costs	EEC countries	E 8-a	
per hr in local currency	EEC countries	E 11-a	
wages & salaries in DM million	W Germany	H 3-a	
wages rates per hr in FrS	Main countries	C 2-a	
Energy production industry as % of total costs	EEC countries	E 8-a	
per hr by area in local currency	EEC countries	E 38-a	
Engineering industries per hr by sex	Main countries	C 7-a	
index nos	Main countries	B 27-a	
Farm machinery manufacturing industry as % of total costs	EEC countries	E 8-a	
per hr in local currency	EEC countries	E 11-a	
Farm wage bill as % of net product (at factor cost)	ECE countries	U 34-a	
Food, drink & tobacco industries as % of total costs	EEC countries	E 8-a	
per hr in local currency	EEC countries	E 11-a	E 38-a
Food processing industry per hr	Main countries	C 7-a	
Foundries (iron & steel) as % of total costs	EEC countries	E 8-a	
per hr in local currency	EEC countries	E 11-a	
per hr in FrS	Main countries	C 2-a	
Furniture manufacturing industry as % of total costs	EEC countries	E 8-a	
per hr in local currency	EEC countries	E 11-a	
Glass manufacturing industry as % of total costs	EEC countries	E 8-a	
per hr in local currency	EEC countries	E 11-a	
Goods transport: social charges per hr in local currency	EEC countries	E 10-a	
wage rates per hr in local currency	EEC countries	E 10-a	
Housing construction - index nos	European countries & USA	U 5-a	
Instruments manufacturing industry: wage rates per hr in FrS	Main countries	C 2-a	
Iron & steel industry as % of total costs	EEC countries	E 8-a	
by sector: wages & salaries in DM	W Germany	H 3-a	
earnings per hr in local currency	Main countries	C 2-a	
per hr by sex	Main countries	C 7-a	
per hr in FrB	EEC countries	E 29-a	
salaried staff in DM million	W Germany	H 3-a	
wage earners in DM million	W Germany	H 3-a	
wage rates per hr in local currency	Main countries	C 2-a	
Iron ore mining as % of total costs	EEC countries	E 8-a	
per hr in local currency	EEC countries	E 11-a	
per hr in FrB	EEC countries	E 29-a	
wages & salaries in DM million	W Germany	H 3-a	
Iron-working industry as % of total costs	EEC countries	E 8-a	
Knitting mills as % of total costs	EEC countries	E 8-a	
per hr in local currency	EEC countries	E 11-a	
Leather goods manufacturing industry as % of total costs	EEC countries	E 8-a	
per hr in local currency	EEC countries	E 11-a	
Leather industry as % of total costs	EEC countries	E 8-a	
per hr by sex	Main countries	C 7-a	
Machine tools manufacturing industry as % of total costs	EEC countries	E 8-a	
in $m	USA	J 2-a	
per hr in local currency & % increase	EEC countries	B 20-a	
hr in local currency	EEC countries	E 11-a	
man-hr in $	EEC countries	B 31-a	
unit of output in $	EEC countries	B 31-a	
unit of output - index nos	EEC countries	B 20-a	
production workers in $m	USA	J 2-a	
wages & salaries in DM million	W Germany	H 3-a	
Man-made fibres industry as % of total costs	EEC countries	E 8-a	
per hr in local currency	EEC countries	E 11-a	
Mechanical engineering industry as % of total costs	EEC countries	E 8-a	
earnings per hr in local currency	Main countries	C 2-a	
	EEC countries	E 11-a	
wage rates per hr in local currency	Main countries	C 2-a	
wages & salaries in DM million	W Germany	H 3-a	
Metal industries as % of total costs	EEC countries	E 8-a	
per hr in local currency	EEC countries	E 11-a	
wages & salaries in DM million	W Germany	H 3-a	
Metal ore mining per hr by areas in local currency	EEC countries	E 38-a	
Metal products manufacturing industries per hr in local currency	EEC countries	E 11-a	E 38-a
wage rates per hr in FrS	Main countries	C 2-a	
Mining & quarrying per hr by sex	Main countries	C 7-a	
per hr in local currency	EEC countries	E 11-a	
salaried staff per mth in local currency	EEC countries	E 3-a	
wage bill in local currency	EEC countries	E 11-a	
Motor vehicles industry as % of total costs	EEC countries	E 8-a	
differentials in wages costs by sex	EEC countries	B 28-a	
earnings per hr in local currency	Main countries	C 2-a	
	EEC countries	E 11-a	
wage rates per hr in local currency	Main countries	C 2-a	
wages & social levies as % of total costs	EEC countries	B 28-a	
salaries in DM million	W Germany	H 3-a	
Non-ferrous metals industry as % of total costs	EEC countries	E 8-a	
per hr in local currency	EEC countries	E 11-a	
wages & salaries in DM million	W Germany	H 3-a	
Non-metallic mineral industry as % of total costs	EEC countries	E 8-a	
per hr in local currency	EEC countries	E 38-a	

	Territorial coverage	Title codes
LABOUR COSTS BY INDUSTRY, continued		
Nuclear fuel industry as % of total costs	EEC countries	E 8-a
per hr in local currency	EEC countries	E 11-a
Office machinery industry as % of total costs	EEC countries	E 8-a
Ore mining industry as % of total costs	EEC countries	E 8-a
per hr in local currency	EEC countries	E 11-a
Paper & board industry as % of total costs	EEC countries	E 8-a
per hr in local currency	EEC countries	E 11-a
Paper & printing industry per hr in local currency	EEC countries	E 38-a
Paper & pulp industry per hr by sex	Main countries	C 7-a
Passenger transport: salaried staff per mth in local currency	EEC countries	E 10-a
social charges per hr in local currency	EEC countries	E 10-a
wages per hr in local currency	EEC countries	E 10-a
Petroleum refineries as % of total costs	EEC countries	E 8-a
per hr in local currency	EEC countries	E 11-a
Plastics industry as % of total costs	EEC countries	E 8-a
per hr in local currency	EEC countries	E 11-a
Printing & publishing as % of total costs	EEC countries	E 8-a
per hr by sex	Main countries	C 7-a
per hr in local currency	EEC countries	E 11-a
Public utilities as % of total costs	EEC countries	E 8-a
per hr in local currency	EEC countries	E 11-a
Ready-made clothing industry per hr by sex	Main countries	C 7-a
Retail distribution outlets: shops by type in local currency	EEC countries	E 3-a
Retail trade in clothing per mth in local currency	EEC countries	E 9-a
cosmetics per mth in local currency	EEC countries	E 9-a
domestic equipment per mth in local currency	EEC countries	E 9-a
foodstuffs per mth in local currency	EEC countries	E 9-a
house furnishings per mth in local currency	EEC countries	E 9-a
leather goods per mth in local currency	EEC countries	E 9-a
of newsagents & bookshops per mth in local currency	EEC countries	E 9-a
pharmacists per mth in local currency	EEC countries	E 9-a
Retail trade (in general) per mth in local currency	EEC countries	E 9-a
Road vehicle manufacturing industry per hr by sex	Main countries	C 7-a
Roasted coffee industry per man-hr in $	USA	J 1-a
per worker in $	USA	J 1-a
Rubber processing industry as % of total costs	EEC countries	E 8-a
per hr by sex	Main countries	C 7-a
in local currency	EEC countries	E 11-a
Scientific instruments manufacturing industry as % of total costs	EEC countries	E 8-a
Shipbuilding & repair industry as % of total costs	EEC countries	E 8-a
earnings per hr in local currency	Main countries	C 2-a
per hr by sex	Main countries	C 7-a
in local currency	EEC countries	E 11-a
wage rates per hr in local currency	Main countries	C 2-a
Steel fabrication industry: wages & salaries in DM million	W Germany	H 3-a
Steel foundries: wages & salaries in DM million	W Germany	H 3-a
Tanneries & leather dressing industry as % of total costs	EEC countries	E 8-a
per hr in local currency	EEC countries	E 11-a
Textile (incl leather industry) per hr in local currency	EEC countries	E 38-a
Textile manufacturing industry as % of total costs	EEC countries	E 8-a
per hr by sex	Main countries	C 7-a
in pence	EEC countries	B 29
Timber & sawmill industry as % of total costs	EEC countries	E 8-a
per hr by sex	Main countries	C 7-a
in local currency	EEC countries	E 11-a
Tobacco processing industry as % of total costs	EEC countries	E 8-a
per hr in local currency	EEC countries	E 11-a
Transport drivers: social charges in local currency	EEC countries	E 10-a
Transport equipment manufacturing industry as % of total costs	EEC countries	E 8-a
Transport services by size: salaried staff per mth in local currency	EEC countries	E 10-a
wage earners per hr in local currency	EEC countries	E 10-a
social charges per hr in local currency	EEC countries	E 10-a
wage earners per hr in local currency	EEC countries	E 10-a
Wages costs: hired farm labour as % of net product of agriculture	ECE countries	U 34-a
hired farm labour - index nos	ECE countries	U 34-a
Water supply industry as % of total costs	EEC countries	E 8-a
Wood-working machinery manufacturing industry per hr in local currency	EEC countries	E 11-a
Woollen textile manufacturing industry as % of total costs	EEC countries	E 8-a
per hr in local currency	EEC countries	E 11-a

Labour disputes   see   STRIKES & LOCK-OUTS

LABOUR FORCE

 see also   APPRENTICESHIP
      CLERICAL WORKERS
      CRAFTSMEN & PROCESS WORKERS
      FARM WORKERS
      FOREIGN MIGRANT WORKERS
      MANPOWER
      MERCHANT SEAMEN
      POPULATION, ECONOMICALLY-ACTIVE
      SALARIED STAFF
      WAGE EARNERS

% by age groups: semi-skilled industrial workers	EEC countries	E 2-a
% earnings of women compared with men by age groups (semi-skilled occupations)	EEC countries	E 2-a

	Territorial coverage	Title codes	
LABOUR FORCE, continued			
% by age groups & sex: skilled industrial workers	EEC countries	E 2-a	
% of earnings of women compared with men by age groups (skilled occupations)	EEC countries	E 2-a	
% by age groups & sex: unskilled industrial workers	EEC countries	E 2-a	
% of earnings of women compared with men by age groups (unskilled occupations)	EEC countries	E 2-a	
% employed by regions	EEC area	E 37-a	
in agricultural occupations	Main countries	M 4-a	
industry (by qualifications)	EEC countries	E 2-a	
industry, farming & service industries	Main countries	E 3-a	
manufacturing occupations	Main countries	M 4-a	
% growth rates in economically-active population	ECAFE countries	U 17-a	
in employment: manufacturing industry (compounded)	Main countries	N 7-a	
over decades	ECAFE countries	U 17	
projected to yr 2000	World regions	L 3	
no of workers employed in agriculture	ECAFE countries	U 17-a	
industry	ECAFE countries	U 17-a	
service industries	ECAFE countries	U 17-a	
% of economically-active population unemployed	European countries & USA	U 16-a	
% of employed persons helping in family businesses	EEC countries	E 18-a	
in agricultural occupations	EEC countries	B 3-a	
of self-employed status	EEC countries	E 18-a	
% of female population employed in industry	USSR	C 28-irr	
% of married women employed in agriculture	EEC countries	E 2-a	E 3-a
industry	EEC countries	E 2-a	
manufacturing industry	EEC countries	E 3-a	
service industries	EEC countries	E 2-a	E 3-a
% of persons (14-24 yrs of age) employed in agriculture	EEC countries	E 3-a	
manufacturing industry	EEC countries	E 3-a	
service industries	EEC countries	E 3-a	
(over 60 yrs of age) employed in agriculture	EEC countries	E 3-a	
manufacturing industry	EEC countries	E 3-a	
service industries	EEC countries	E 3-a	
% of economically-inactive population by areas	EEC countries	E 38-a	
% of population (15 to 65 yrs of age) by sex	OECD countries	D 23-a	
% of total population by areas	EEC countries	E 38-a	
% of unemployed labour being over 60 yrs of age	EEC countries	E 2-a	
Employed by age by industry (incl service industries) by sex	UK	B 28-a	
by sex (census data)	USSR	C 28	
% breakdown (all occupations)	EEC countries	E 18-a	
farm workers	EEC countries	E 18-a	
industrial employees by sex	EEC countries	E 2-a	
% of population (14-24 yrs) employed in agriculture	EEC countries	E 2-a	
in industry	EEC countries	E 2-a	
in service industries	EEC countries	E 2-a	
out of work	EEC countries	E 2-a	
over 60 yrs employed in agriculture	EEC countries	E 2-a	
in industry	EEC countries	E 2-a	
in service industries	EEC countries	E 2-a	
by 100 largest US industrial corporations		H 1	
10 largest British industrial companies		H 1	
French industrial companies		H 1	
Italian industrial companies		H 1	
20 largest Canadian commercial firms		H 1	
industrial companies		H 1	
German commercial firms		H 1	
Swiss commercial firms		H 1	
Swiss transport companies		H 1	
25 largest Japanese industrial companies		H 1	
30 largest Japanese banks		H 1	
US commercial banks		H 1	
firms		H 1	
public utility undertakings		H 1	
transport companies		H 1	
administrative regions	EEC countries	E 37-a	
grade: private sector	AASM countries	E 41-a	
public sector	AASM countries	E 41-a	
largest US airline companies		H 1	
sex - index nos	Main OECD countries	D 24-q	
sex	Main OECD countries	D 24-q	
socio-economic categories	USSR	C 28-irr	
specific IATA airlines		S 21-a	
iron & steel companies	W Germany	H 3-a	
world's 100 largest banking corporations		H 1	
100 largest companies		H 1	
industrial sector as % of total employment	All countries	M 6-a	
by sex	EEC countries	E 18-a	
kind: carpet & rug manufacturing industry: salaried staff	OECD countries	D 46-a	
wage earners	OECD countries	D 46-a	
cement industry	OECD countries	D 4-a	
chemical industry: administrative & staff	OECD countries	D 5-a	
employers	OECD countries	D 46-a	
clothing industry: salaried staff	OECD countries	D 46-a	
wage earners	OECD countries	D 46-a	
iron foundries: no of clerical staff employed	UK	B 25-a	
managerial grades employed	UK	B 25-a	

	Territorial coverage	Title codes
LABOUR FORCE, continued		
Employed by kind: iron foundries: no of operators employed	UK	B 25-a
no of skilled employees, technicians & technologists employed	UK	B 25-a
knitting industry: no of salaried staff employed	OECD countries	D 46-a
wage earners employed	OECD countries	D 46-a
man-made fibres industry: no of staff employed	OECD countries	D 5-a
spinning & weaving: no of salaried staff employed	OECD countries	D 46-a
wage earners employed	OECD countries	D 46-a
steel foundries: no of clerical staff employed	UK	B 25-a
managerial grades employed	UK	B 25-a
operators employed	UK	B 25-a
skilled employees, technicians & technologists employed	UK	B 25-a
steel industry: no of process & clerical workers employed	OECD countries	D 22-a
textile industry: no of salaried staff employed	OECD countries	D 46-a
wage earners employed	OECD countries	D 46-a
occupational groups by sex (census data)	OAS member countries	N 18
increase projected	ECAFE countries	U 17-a
occupational status: employers & employed	Main countries	E 3-a
sex & age: projected to yr 2000	Worldwide	L 3
sex: % of economically-active population (5-yr age groups)	EEC countries	E 2-a E 3-a
sex: % employment of men & women projected to 1977	UK	B 28
% qualified, semi-skilled or unskilled	EEC countries	E 2-a
administrative & executive staff	OAS member countries	N 18-a
armed forces personnel	OAS member countries	N 18-a
artisans & skilled workers	OAS member countries	N 18-a
commercial undertakings (census data)	African countries	U 44-a
farmers, timber fellers & fishermen	OAS member countries	N 18-a
iron & steel industry: salaried staff	EEC countries	E 29-a
miners & quarrymen	OAS member countries	N 18-a
miners & quarrymen (census data)	African countries	U 44-a
office workers	OAS member countries	N 18-a
professional & technical staff	OAS member countries	N 18-a
public utility undertakings (census data)	African countries	U 44-a
sales personnel	OAS member countries	N 18-a
service industries (census data)	African countries	U 44-a
service industries	OAS member countries	N 18-a
textile industry: wage earners & salaried staff	OECD countries	D 46-a
tourist industry	OECD countries	D 47-a
transport service employees (census data)	African countries	U 44-a
	OAS member countries	N 18-a
in agriculture: no of workers 60 yrs of age & over	EEC countries	E 44-a
agriculture & industry	OECD countries	D 23-a
agriculture as % of total labour force	EEC countries	B 3-a
by kinds of occupation - index nos	E European countries	U 34-a
by sex (census data)	OAS member countries	N 18
	Main OECD countries	D 24-q
agriculture & forestry by kind of occupation	AASM countries	E 41-a
agriculture, forestry & fishing: historical table 1750-1969	Main European countries	Z 1-a
	OECD countries	D 23-a
owners of farms & farm workers by sex	EEC countries	E 44-a
projected to yr 2000	Worldwide	L 3
	World regions	A 11-a
tenants, farm owners & labourers	EEC countries	E 3-a
index nos	OECD countries	D 24-q D 1-a
agriculture	EEC countries	B 3-a
agriculture (census data)	African countries	U 44-a
coal mining industry	EEC countries	E 33-a
iron & steel industry	EEC countries	E 29-a
iron ore mining industry	EEC countries	E 33-a
in open-cast mines	EEC countries	E 29-a
in underground mines	EEC countries	E 29-a
industry by sector by status	Main countries	C 28-irr
by sex (census data)	OAS member countries	N 18
	Main OECD countries	D 24-q
no of wage earners & salaried staff	EEC countries	E 8-a
industry - index nos	OECD countries	D 24-q
manufacturing industry by sex: historical table 1750-1969	Main countries	Z 1-a
by sex	UK	B 28-a
manufacturing industry - index nos	UK	B 28-a
manufacturing industry	EEC countries	E 8-a
	OECD countries	D 23-a
motor vehicles manufacturing industry by sex	UK	B 28-a
over 14 yrs by age groups by areas	EEC countries	E 38-a
Active population as % of total population	OECD countries	D 23-a
by sex as % of total population	EEC countries	E 2-a
Age of male workers by yr 2000 (estim)	World regions	L 3
Aid grants to promote higher labour standards in $	All countries	M 1-a
Civilian labour force by sex	OECD countries	D 23-a
(total) & index nos	OECD countries	D 23-a
Comparative labour inputs: industry & agriculture - index nos	ECE countries	U 34-a
Economically-active population & nos unemployed	ECAFE countries	U 17-a
by sex	OAS member countries	N 18

	Territorial coverage	Title codes	
LABOUR FORCE, continued			
Employed, unemployed population & armed forces as % of total labour force	OECD countries	D 23-a	
Employment increase: chemical industry projected to 1977	UK	B 21	
mechanical engineering industry projected to 1977	UK	B 27	
motor vehicles manufacturing industry projected to 1977	UK	B 28	
Entry into labour market by males to yr 2000 (estim)	World regions	L 3	
Farm labour input – index nos	ECE countries	U 34-a	
Females as % of total working population	All countries	M 6-a	
Labour input in agriculture – index nos	ECE countries	U 34-a	
No of industrial fatalities: male labour to yr 2000 (estim)	World regions	L 3	
dependants per 1000 workers by area in yr 2000 (estim)	World regions	L 3	
economically-active females as % of population over 14 yrs	EEC countries	E 2-a	
population & index nos	OECD countries	D 23-a	
population employed & % change	EEC countries	E 26-a	
employees & nos unemployed by areas	EEC countries	E 38-a	
by categories	Asian, Far East & Australasian countries	U 45-a	
by industrial sectors	All countries	L 4-a	
	OAS member countries	N 14-a	
historical table from 1960	EEC countries	E 37-a	
in farming occupations	EEC countries	E 18-a	
in industrial occupations	EEC countries	E 18-a	
in industry (excl building)	ECE countries	U 15-a	
family helpers by occupational groups	Main countries	R 5-a	
farm workers as % of employed population	All countries	L 3	
foreign migrant workers employed in coalmining	EEC countries	E 15-a	
machine tool firms in operation by size of labour force	EEC countries	B 20-a	
salaried employees by industrial sectors	EEC countries	E 11-a	
	Main countries	R 5-a	
yrs of working life during period 1970-2000 (estim)	Worldwide	L 3	
scientists, technicians & engineers	All countries	U 43-a	
wage earners employed in industrial occupations	Main countries	R 5-a	
	EEC countries	E 11-a	
	OAS member countries	N 14-a	
workers, employers & unpaid helpers	Main countries	E 3-a	
Planned % increase in industrial employment	E European countries	U 16-a	
Population pyramids by age & sex to yr 2000 (estim)	World regions	L 3	
Transfer increase rate to farming	Main ECAFE countries	U 17-a	
industry	Main ECAFE countries	U 17-a	
service industries	Main ECAFE countries	U 17-a	
Trend of average age to yr 2000	World regions	L 3	
Wage & salary earners as % of economically-active population	EEC countries	E 18-a	
Working population as % of total population	All countries	M 6-a	
projected to yr 2000	World regions	L 3	
LABOUR FORCE BY INDUSTRY			
Abattoirs: no of wage earners & salaried staff	EEC countries	E 8-a	
Aerospace equipment industry: no of wage earners & salaried staff	EEC countries	E 8-a	
Agriculture: no employed by sex	EEC countries	E 18-a	
Aircraft industry: no of wage earners & salaried staff	EEC countries	E 11-a	
Airline companies (by category of staff) by specific airline companies of IATA membership	Worldwide	S 11-a	
		S 21-a	
Alcoholic drinks industry: no of wage earners & salaried staff	EEC countries	E 11-a	
Baking & confectionery industry: no of wage earners & salaried staff	EEC countries	E 8-a	
Briquetting plants: labour wages as % of total costs	EEC countries	E 8-a	
no of wage earners & salaried staff	EEC countries	E 8-a	E 11-a
Building & construction industries	Main countries	R 5-a	
Building industry (census data)	OAS member countries	N 18	
by sex: historical table 1750-1969	Main European countries	Z 1-a	
no of wage earners & salaried staff	EEC countries	E 8-a	E 11-a
no of employees by sex	EEC countries	E 18-a	
Building materials manufacturing industry: no of wage earners & salaried staff	EEC countries	E 8-a	E 11-a
Cement industry: no of wage earners & salaried staff	EEC countries	E 8-a	E 11-a
Ceramics industry: no of wage earners & salaried staff	EEC countries	E 8-a	E 11-a
Chemical industry: no of wage earners & salaried staff	EEC countries	E 8-a	E 11-a
	European countries, Japan & USA	U 25-a	
Civil engineering industry: no of wage earners & salaried staff	EEC countries	E 11-a	
Clothing (incl footwear) industry: no of wage earners & salaried staff	EEC countries	E 11-a	
Clothing manufacturing industry: no of wage earners & salaried staff	EEC countries	E 8-a	
by sector: nos employed	UK	B 22-a	
Coal mining industry: no of face & underground workers	EEC countries	E 16-m	E 15-a
foreign workers as % of total	EEC countries	E 33-a	
foreign workers	EEC countries	E 33-a	
workers	EEC countries	E 33-a	
underground workers	EEC countries	E 16-q	E 15-a
wage earners & salaried staff	EEC countries	E 8-a	E 11-a
Coke oven plants: no of wage earners & salaried staff	EEC countries	E 8-a	E 11-a
Commerce & finance: no by sex: historical table 1750-1969	Main European countries	Z 1-a	
Commerce (incl service industries) by grade of employees	AASM countries	E 41-a	
Confectionery industry: no of wage earners & salaried staff	EEC countries	E 11-a	
Cotton textile manufacturing industry: no of wage earners & salaried staff	EEC countries	E 8-a	E 11-a
Credit & insurance companies: no employed by sex	EEC countries	E 18-a	
Crude oil pipelines projects: no employed	EEC countries	E 43-a	

LABOUR FORCE BY INDUSTRY, continued

	Territorial coverage	Title codes	
Dairying industry: no of wage earners & salaried staff	EEC countries	E 8-a	E 11-a
Data-processing machinery manufacturing industry: no of wage earners & salaried staff	EEC countries	E 11-a	
Drinks manufacturing industry: no of wage earners & salaried staff	EEC countries	E 8-a	
Electrical engineering industry: no of wage earners & salaried staff	EEC countries	E 11-a	
no of production workers	Main countries	C 2-a	
no of salaried staff	Main countries	C 2-a	
no of employees projected to 1977	UK	B 23	
no of wage earners & salaried staff	EEC countries	E 8-a	
Electronic equipment manufacturing industry by 1977	UK	B 24-a	
Energy production industries: no of wage earners & salaried staff	EEC countries	E 8-a	
Farm machinery manufacturing industry: no of wage earners & salaried staff	EEC countries	E 8-a	E 11-a
Fishing industry (deep-sea & coastal): nos employed	OECD countries	D 43-a	
Food, drink & tobacco industries: no of wage earners & salaried staff	EEC countries	E 8-a	E 11-a
Foundries (iron & steel): no of production workers	Main countries	C 2-a	
no of salaried staff	Main countries	C 2-a	
no of wage earners & salaried staff	EEC countries	E 8-a	E 11-a
Furniture manufacturing industry: no of wage earners & salaried staff	EEC countries	E 8-a	E 11-a
	W European countries	C 8-a	
Glass manufacturing industry: no of wage earners & salaried staff	EEC countries	E 8-a	E 11-a
Hotel industry: no of employees per guest room	World regions	Z 5-a	
Industries processing primary energy sources	Italy	H 4-a	
Instrument manufacturing industry: no of wage earners & salaried staff	EEC countries	E 11-a	
Insurance, finance & real estate companies: nos employed	OECD countries	D 23-a	
Iron & steel industry: no of wage earners & salaried staff	EEC countries	E 11-a	
% of foreign workers to total labour force	EEC countries	E 29-a	E 30-a
no of apprentices	EEC countries	E 29-a	
employees by occupation & sex	EEC countries	E 30-m	
employees	EEC countries	E 29-a	
	OECD countries	D 22-a	
production workers	Main countries	C 2-a	
salaried staff	Main countries	C 2-a	
wage earners & salaried staff	EEC countries	E 8-a	
Iron ore mining: no of wage earners by occupation	EEC countries	E 30-m	
% of foreign workers to total labour force	EEC countries	E 29-a	E 33-a
no of apprentices	EEC area	E 29-a	
foreign workers	EEC countries	E 33-a	
salaried staff	EEC area	E 29-a	
employees (total)	EEC countries	E 8-a	E 29-a
		E 33-a	
wage earners & salaried staff	EEC countries	E 11-a	
open-cast mines as % of total labour force	EEC countries	E 29-a	
underground mines as % of total labour force	EEC countries	E 29-a	
Iron-working industry: no of wage earners & salaried staff	EEC countries	E 8-a	
Jute products industry: no of employees by sex	W European countries	C 22-a	
Knitting mills: no of wage earners & salaried staff	EEC countries	E 8-a	E 11-a
Leather goods manufacturing industry: no of wage earners & salaried staff	EEC countries	E 8-a	E 11-a
Leather manufacturing industry: no of wage earners & salaried staff	EEC countries	E 8-a	
Local government services: no of employees by sex	EEC countries	E 18-a	
Machine tools manufacturing industry: no of wage earners & salaried staff	EEC countries	E 11-a	
by sector: no of production workers	USA	J 2-a	
by sector: no of employees	USA	J 2-a	
no of employees	UK	B 26-a	
	USA	J 2-a	
wage earners & salaried staff	EEC countries	E 8-a	
Man-made fibres industry: no of wage earners & salaried staff	EEC countries	E 8-a	E 11-a
	All countries	K 4-a	
Manganese ore mines: no of employees	Italy	E 30-m	
	EEC countries	E 29-a	
Manufacturing industry: no of employees by sex	EEC countries	E 11-a	E 18-a
Marine engineering industry: no of wage earners & salaried staff	EEC countries	E 11-a	
Mechanical engineering industry: no of wage earners & salaried staff	EEC countries	E 11-a	
production workers	Main countries	C 2-a	
salaried staff	Main countries	C 2-a	
wage earners & salaried staff	EEC countries	E 8-a	
Metal fabricating industries: no of wage earners & salaried staff	EEC countries	E 8-a	E 11-a
Metal ores extraction industry: no of wage earners & salaried staff	EEC countries	E 11-a	
Metal producing & fabricating industries: no of employees	W Germany	H 3-a	
Metal products manufacturing industry: no of wage earners & salaried staff	EEC countries	E 11-a	
Mining & quarrying: no of employees by occupation	AASM countries	E 41-a	
occupation by sex: historical table 1750-1969	Main European countries	Z 1-a	
sex	EEC countries	E 18-a	
wage earners & salaried staff	EEC countries	E 11-a	
	OECD countries	D 23-a	
Motor vehicles manufacturing industry: no of direct manual workers	UK	B 28-a	
indirect manual workers	UK	B 28-a	
production workers	Main countries	C 2-a	

	Territorial coverage	Title codes	
LABOUR FORCE BY INDUSTRY, continued			
Motor vehicles manufacturing industry: no of salaried staff	Main countries	C 2-a	
no of skilled workers by kind as % total labour force	UK	B 28	
no of wage earners & salaried staff	EEC countries	E 8-a	E 11-a
no of employees - index nos	UK	B 28-a	
National airlines: no of employees by occupation	EEC countries	E 43-a	
Non-ferrous metals industry: no of employees	EEC countries	E 8-a	
no of wage earners & salaried staff	EEC countries	E 11-a	
Non-metallic mineral industry: no of wage earners & salaried staff	EEC countries	E 8-a	E 11-a
Nuclear fuel industry: no of wage earners & salaried staff	EEC countries	E 8-a	E 11-a
Office machinery manufacturing industry: no of wage earners & salaried staff	EEC countries	E 8-a	
Oil refineries: no of wage earners & salaried staff	EEC countries	E 11-a	
Ore mining industry: no of wage earners & salaried staff	EEC countries	E 8-a	
Paper & board manufacturing industry: no of wage earners & salaried staff	EEC countries	E 8-a	E 11-a
Petroleum refineries: no of wage earners & salaried staff	EEC countries	E 8-a	E 11-a
Plastics manufacturing industry: no of wage earners & salaried staff	EEC countries	E 8-a	E 11-a
Printing & publishing industry: no of wage earners & salaried staff	EEC countries	E 8-a	E 11-a
Public administration by sex (census data)	OAS member countries	N 18	
Public utilities (census data)	OAS member countries	N 18	
no of employees	OECD countries	D 23-a	
no of employees by sex	EEC countries	E 18-a	
no of wage earners & salaried staff	EEC countries	E 8-a	E 11-a
Railways: no of employees by kind of administrative responsibility	EEC countries	E 43-a	
no of employees	European countries	U 8-a	
Retail trade (incl catering): no of employees by sex	EEC countries	E 18-a	
by areas	EEC countries	E 38-a	
Roasted coffee industry: no of production workers	USA	J 1-a	
Rubber processing industry: no of wage earners & salaried staff	EEC countries	E 8-a	E 11-a
Sales distribution (clothing): no of employees	UK	B 22-a	
Scientific instruments manufacturing industry: no of wage earners & salaried staff	EEC countries	E 8-a	E 11-a
Service industries by sector: no of employees by sex	EEC countries	E 18-a	
by sex (census data)	OAS member countries	N 18	
historical table 1750-1969	Main European countries	Z 1-a	
Shipbuilding & repairing industry: no of wage earners & salaried staff	EEC countries	E 8-a	E 11-a
no of employees	W Germany	S 16-m	
no of production workers	Main countries	C 2-a	
no of salaried staff	Main countries	C 2-a	
Slaughter houses: no of wage earners & salaried staff	EEC countries	E 11-a	
Social welfare community & personal services: no of employees	OECD countries	D 23-a	
Social services by sex (census data)	OAS member countries	N 18	
Spinning & weaving industries (incl finishing): no of employees	OECD countries	D 46-a	
Tanneries & leather dressing industries: no of employees by occupation	EEC countries	E 8-a	E 11-a
Television & sound reproduction equipment industry: no of employees	UK	B 24-a	
Textile industries: no of wage earners & salaried staff	EEC countries	E 8-a	E 11-a
no of employees	OECD countries	D 46-a	
Timber & sawmill industry: no of wage earners & salaried staff	EEC countries	E 8-a	E 11-a
Tin mining industry: no of employees	Malaya, Nigeria & Thailand	C 20-m	
Tobacco processing industry: no of wage earners & salaried staff	EEC countries	E 8-a	E 11-a
Transport & communications: no of employees by sex	EEC countries	E 18-a	
Transport, communications & storage: no of employees	OECD countries	D 23-a	
Transport equipment manufacturing industry: no of wage earners & salaried staff	EEC countries	E 8-a	
no of employees by sex (census data)	OAS member countries	N 18	
Transport services: no of employees by occupation	AASM countries	E 41-a	
by sex: historical table 1750-1969	Main European countries	Z 1-a	
Vehicles assembly industry: no of wage earners & salaried staff	EEC countries	E 11-a	
Water supply industry: no of wage earners & salaried staff	EEC countries	E 8-a	E 11-a
Water supply undertakings: no of employees	All countries	W 2-a	
Wholesale & retail trade (incl catering & hotels): no of employees	OECD countries	D 23-a	
Wholesale trade: no of employees by areas	EEC countries	E 38-a	
Woollen textile industry: no of wage earners & salaried staff	EEC countries	E 8-a	E 11-a

Labour input   see   HOURS OF WORK

LABOUR PRODUCTIVITY

	Territorial coverage	Title codes
In agriculture: gross output per worker	ECE countries	U 34-a
gross product per worker	ECE countries	U 34-a
In industry - index nos	All countries	L 4-a
In industry: value added per employee in $	UK & USA	U 52-a
In main industries - index nos	World regions	U 43-a
In manufacturing industry - index nos	All countries	L 4-a
Index nos	All countries	L 4-a
% change in building construction	E European countries	U 16-a
in labour force employed & output	Main countries	C 2-a
in output per employee	E European countries	U 16-a
per man-hr	Main European countries	U 16-a
planned	E European countries & USSR	U 54-a
(actual)	E European countries & USSR	U 54-a
% growth rates per capita projected to 1980	OECD countries	D 11

	Territorial coverage	Title codes
LABOUR PRODUCTIVITY BY INDUSTRY		
Carpet industry: planned % increase by 1977	UK	B 29
Chemical industry: value added per capita	Main countries	U 25-a
Clothing industry: output per capita in $	EEC countries	B 22-a
costs per man-hr in £	EEC countries	B 29-a
planned % increase by 1977	UK	B 29
index nos	UK	B 22-a
Cotton spinning industry: planned % increase by 1977	UK	B 29
Cotton textiles weaving industry: planned % increase by 1977	UK	B 29
Hosiery & knitwear industry: planned % increase by 1977	UK	B 29
Iron foundries in tons per man-year	France, W Germany & UK	B 25-a
Jute industry: planned % increase by 1977	UK	B 29
Machine tools industry – index nos	EEC countries	B 31-a
Man-made fibres industry: planned % increase by 1977	UK	B 29
Manufacturing industry – index nos	UK	B 28-a
Motor vehicles industry – index nos	UK	B 28-a
Steel foundries in tons per man-yr	France, W Germany & UK	B 25-a
Steel industry per man-yr – index nos	UK	T 2-q
Wool textile industry: planned % increase by 1977	UK	B 29
Wool weaving industry: planned % increase by 1977	UK	B 29
LABOUR RATIOS		
Machine tools industry: no of productive workers as % of total labour force	USA	J 2-a
earnings per employee in $	USA	J 2-a
man-hrs of work performed by value in $	USA	J 2-a
value added per employee in $m	USA	J 2-a
per man-hr in $	USA	J 2-a
wages costs as % of value added in $	USA	J 2-a

Labourers   see   FARM WORKERS, UNSKILLED
                      MANUAL WORKERS

Lace   see   KNITTED FABRICS

Laid-up tonnage   see   BULK CARRIERS
                           CARGO SHIPS
                           PASSENGER VESSELS
                           TANKERS
                           WORLD FLEETS

Lakes   see   INLAND WATERWAYS
                 ST LAWRENCE SEAWAY

	Territorial coverage	Title codes
LAMB & MUTTON		
% share of world import & export trade	Main countries	B 1-a
Availability for consumption: tonnage	Main countries	B 11-a
Consumption per capita in kg per yr	EEC countries	B 1-a
in lbs per yr	UK	B 12-a
tonnage & per capita in kg per yr	Main countries	B 11-a
tonnage	EEC countries	E 1-a
	EEC countries	E 44-a
	OAS member countries	N 17-a
Export prices in $ per 100 lbs	New Zealand	U 32-m
Export prices – index nos (weighted average main sources)	Worldwide	U 29-q
in $ per ton	Australia & New Zealand	A 9-a
Exports by destination: tonnage	Australia, Argentine & New Zealand	B 11-a
	Main countries	B 12-m
by value as % of total exports	Main countries	B 11-a
in $m	W European countries	U 33-a
tonnage	European countries	U 36-a
	EEC countries	E 1-a
	Main countries	B 11-a
Import prices: frozen lamb ex N Zealand in pence per lb	UK	U 33-q
Imports & exports: dried or salted lamb & mutton: tonnage	EEC countries	E 1-a
Imports by source: chilled or frozen lamb: tonnage	UK	B 11-a
fresh, chilled or frozen mutton: tonnage	UK	B 11-a
tonnage	France, Greece, Japan & USA	B 11-a
by value in $m	Main European countries	U 33-a
tonnage	European countries	U 36-a
	EEC countries	E 1-a
Inter-EEC area imports & exports: tonnage	Main countries	B 11-a
Production for export: tonnage	EEC countries	B 12-a
Production, imports, exports & domestic supply: tonnage	Main countries	B 12-a
(incl goat-meat): tonnage	EEC countries	E 1-a
	AASM countries	E 41-a
	European countries	U 36-a
	EEC countries	B 1-a
	OECD countries	D 1-a
by areas: tonnage	EEC countries	E 38-a
Production, stocks: tonnage & consumption per capita in kg	OECD countries	D 14-a
tonnage (estim)	Main countries	B 11-a
Production, supply, consumption & trade: tonnage	EEC countries	B 1-a
tonnage	African countries	U 44-a
	All countries	A 9-a U 22-a
	EEC countries	C 9-q
	Canada, European countries, USA & USSR	E 44-a
	Latin American countries	U 40-a
	OAS member countries	N 14-a

	Territorial coverage	Title codes
LAMB & MUTTON, continued		
Retail prices (comparative): leg of lamb per kg	EEC countries	Z 3-a
in local currency	OAS member countries	N 17-a
Self-sufficiency ratios	EEC countries	B 1-a
Stocks & % change (on previous yr)	France & W Germany	E 1-a
Stocks (imported frozen) held in cold storage: tonnage	UK	B 12-w
Wholesale prices by quality in £ per ton	Main countries	B 12-w
in local currency per ton	OAS member countries	N 17-a
carcasses ex N Zealand in pence per lb	UK	U 20-q
English & N Zealand lamb – index nos	UK	B 11-q
fat live lambs in £	Australia, Canada, New Zealand & USA	B 11-a
lamb (English & N Zealand) at Smithfield market		
in pence per lb	UK	B 11-m
lamb in pence per lb (incl subsidy)	UK	B 12-m
in local currency	Australia, Canada & USA	B 12-m
World exports by value in $m	Australia, France, Uruguay & USA	A 9-a
World production: tonnage	World regions	A 5-a
	World regions	A 5-a
Lambs see SHEEP		
Lambskins see SHEEPSKINS		
LAMPS, INCANDESCENT		
see also FLUORESCENT TUBES		
% excise duties: rates charged	EEC countries	E 31-a
% increase in demand projected to 1977	UK	B 23
% share of world trade (value basis)	Main countries	B 23-a
Exports by destination by value in $m	Main countries	U 9-a
electric lamp bulbs by value in $m	Main countries	U 38-a
Imports: electric lamp bulbs by value in $m	All countries	U 38-a
Production: electric lamp bulbs by kind by volume	EEC countries	E 28-q E 27-a
by volume in million	All countries	U 22-a U 38-a
Retail prices (comparative): electric lamp bulbs in $	EEC countries	Z 3-a
World export trade: electric lamp bulbs in $m		U 38-a
Lancashire see CHEESE BY VARIETY		
LAND & PROPERTY		
Investment: baking & confectionery industry in local currency	EEC countries	E 40-a
building industry in local currency	EEC countries	E 40-a
building materials manufacturing industry in local currency	EEC countries	E 40-a
ceramics manufacturing industry in local currency	EEC countries	E 40-a
chemical industry in local currency	EEC countries	E 40-a
clothing manufacturing industry in local currency	EEC countries	E 40-a
coal mining industry in local currency	EEC countries	E 40-a
cotton textile manufacturing industry in local currency	EEC countries	E 40-a
electrical engineering industry in local currency	EEC countries	E 40-a
engineering industries in local currency	EEC countries	E 40-a
farm machinery manufacturing industry in local currency	EEC countries	E 40-a
flour milling industry in local currency	EEC countries	E 40-a
food processing industry in local currency	EEC countries	E 40-a
footwear manufacturing industry in local currency	EEC countries	E 40-a
fur manufacturing industry in local currency	EEC countries	E 40-a
gas supply industry in local currency	EEC countries	E 40-a
glass manufacturing industry in local currency	EEC countries	E 40-a
industrial enterprises in local currency	EEC countries	E 40-a
iron & steel industry by sector in local currency	EEC countries	E 40-a
jewellery manufacturing industry in local currency	EEC countries	E 40-a
knitting mills in local currency	EEC countries	E 40-a
leather goods manufacturing industry in local currency	EEC countries	E 40-a
leather tanneries in local currency	EEC countries	E 40-a
lignite mines & briquetting industries in local currency	EEC countries	E 40-a
machine tools industry in local currency	EEC countries	E 40-a
manufacturing industry in local currency	EEC countries	E 40-a
mechanical engineering industry in local currency	EEC countries	E 40-a
metals industry in local currency	EEC countries	E 40-a
musical instruments manufacturing industry in local currency	EEC countries	E 40-a
non-ferrous metals industry in local currency	EEC countries	E 40-a
non-metallic mineral industry in local currency	EEC countries	E 40-a
office machinery manufacturing industry in local currency	EEC countries	E 40-a
optical instruments manufacturing industry in local currency	EEC countries	E 40-a
ore mining industry in local currency	EEC countries	E 40-a
paper & board manufacturing industry in local currency	EEC countries	E 40-a
petroleum & natural gas industries in local currency	EEC countries	E 40-a
petroleum refineries in local currency	EEC countries	E 40-a
plastics manufacturing industry in local currency	EEC countries	E 40-a
power stations in local currency	EEC countries	E 40-a
printing & publishing industry in local currency	EEC countries	E 40-a
public utilities in local currency	EEC countries	E 40-a
rubber processing industry in local currency	EEC countries	E 40-a
silk industry in local currency	EEC countries	E 40-a
sugar refining industry in local currency	EEC countries	E 40-a
textile machinery manufacturing industry in local currency	EEC countries	E 40-a

	Territorial coverage	Title codes
LAND & PROPERTY, continued		
Investment: timber & sawmill industry in local currency	EEC countries	E 40-a
toys & sports goods manufacturing industries in local currency	EEC countries	E 40-a
watch-making industry in local currency	EEC countries	E 40-a
wire & cable manufacturing industry in local currency	EEC countries	E 40-a
wood-working industry in local currency	EEC countries	E 40-a
woollen textile manufacturing industry in local currency	EEC countries	E 40-a
LAND AREA		
& area used for agricultural purposes in ha	EEC countries	E 44-a
& population density	Asian, Far East & Australasian countries	U 45-a
By administrative regions in sq km	OAS member countries	N 11-a
	EEC countries	E 37-a
By major political divisions in sq km	Latin American countries	J 5-a
In ha	All countries	A 9-a
In sq km	All countries & world regions	U 23
	All countries	U 62
	Main countries & continents	M 4-a
	OAS member countries	N 12-a
	EEC countries	E 13-a
	Main countries	R 5
(incl inland waterways) in sq km	OPEC countries	C 3-a
Of capital cities & population (census data)	All countries	R 5
Of the earth in sq km million		R 5
% of EEC land area	EEC countries	R 5-a
Afforested area in ha and as % of total land area	EEC countries	B 1-a
Agricultural area in ha as % of total land area	EEC countries	B 1-a
in m² per inhabitant	EEC countries	E 44-a
Proportion under crops or pasture	Latin American countries	J 5-a
Total area of land & of water in ha	All countries	A 16-a
Land distribution see AGRICULTURAL HOLDINGS		
Land improvements see AGRICULTURE DEVELOPMENT PLANS		
LAND TAXES		
Basis of assessment & rates of tax	EEC countries	E 31-a
Incidence of land taxes levied on farmers	ECE countries	U 34-a
Revenue accruing from taxation on land values in local currency	EEC countries	E 42-a
	Asian, Far East & Australasian countries	U 45-a
Revenue: historical tables from 1750 in local currency	Main European countries	Z 1-a
LAND UTILISATION		
see also HORTICULTURAL AREAS		
% arable & meadows under permanent grass	EEC countries	E 3-a
% area used for farming & forestry	EEC countries	E 44-a
% changes in area of farmland exploited	EEC countries	E 44-a
% distribution by form of farm tenure	OAS member countries	N 13-a
% growth rate of areas harvested	Developing countries	A 11-a
% of farm land under specific crops (in detail)	EEC countries	E 3-a
Afforested area as % of total area by regions	EEC countries	E 38-a
of total land area	World regions	A 16
exploited in ha	All countries	A 16-a
felled & unreplanted in ha	All countries	A 16-a
in ha	All countries	A 16-a
	Continents	J 7-a
	Main countries	R 5-a
productive as % of total land area	World regions	J 7-a
protected in ha	World regions	A 16
stocked with conifer trees in ha	World regions	J 7-a
unproductive brush-land in ha	All countries	A 16-a
	World regions	A 16-a
Agricultural land (actual or potential) in ha	All countries	A 16-a
as % of total land area	Main countries	E 3-a
in ha (incl world total)	Main countries	R 5-a
in ha	E European countries & USSR	U 16-a
	Main countries	R 5-a
Arable land & pasture as % of agricultural land	Main countries	E 3-a
by regions in ha	EEC countries	E 38-a
as % of usable land by areas	EEC countries	E 38-a
in ha	Developing countries	A 11-a
	E European countries & USSR	U 16-a
	EEC countries	B 1-a
	Main countries	R 5-a
	OECD countries	D 1-a
pasture & forest land in ha	Asian, Far East & Australasian countries	U 45-a
per capita in ha	Developing countries	U 52-a
	Main countries	A 11-a
per farmer in ha	OAS member countries	N 13-a
under specific crops in ha	EEC countries	E 3-a
used for horticulture in ha	EEC countries	E 44-a
Area by type of usage & forests in ha	Latin American countries	J 5-a
of exploited farm land in ha	OECD countries	D 1-a
	OAS member countries	N 13-a
(irrigated) under fruit crops in ha	Romania	U 20-a
paddy rice crop in ha	All countries	A 19-a

LAND UTILISATION, continued

	Territorial coverage	Title codes	
Area (irrigated) under vegetable crops in ha	Romania	U 20-a	
(non-irrigated) under fruit crops in ha	Romania	U 20-a	
under vegetable crops in ha	Romania	U 20-a	
planned for vineyards by 1985 in ha	E European countries	U 20-a	
under banana crop in ha	OAS member countries	N 13-a	
barley crop in acres	Main countries	B 8-a	
in ha: historical table	Main countries	Z 1-a	
in ha	EEC countries	E 12-a	E 44-a
	Main countries	R 5-a	
	OAS member countries	N 13-a	
	OECD countries	D 1-a	
bean crop in ha	OAS member countries	N 13-a	
bread grains (excl wheat & rye) in ha	OECD countries	D 1-a	
broad bean crop in ha	OAS member countries	N 13-a	
buckwheat crop in ha: historical table	Main European countries	Z 1-a	
cassava crop in ha	OAS member countries	N 13-a	
cereal crops by kind in ha	EEC countries	B 1-a	
in ha	E European countries	U 16-a	
	OAS member countries	N 13-a	
	OECD countries	D 1-a	
chick pea crop in ha	OAS member countries	N 13-a	
citrus crops in ha: historical table	Main European countries	Z 1-a	
cocoa bean crop in ha	Main countries	R 5-a	
	OAS member countries	N 13-a	
coconuts (on estates) in acres	Malaysia	B 19-a	
(on smallholdings)	Malaysia	B 19-a	
coffee bean crop in ha	Main countries	R 5-a	
	OAS member countries	N 13-a	
cotton crop in acres	Main countries	B 19-a	
in ha: historical table	Main European countries	Z 1-a	
in ha	Main countries	R 5-a	
	OAS member countries	N 13-a	
cottonseed crop in ha	OAS member countries	N 13-a	
flax crop in ha	EEC countries	B 1-a	E 12-a
grass, arable land & forests in ha	All countries	A 9-a	
grass in ha	EEC countries	E 12-a	
groundnuts in acres	Main countries	B 19-a	
in ha	OAS member countries	N 13-a	
hops in ha	EEC countries	B 1-a	E 12-a
lentils crop in ha	OAS member countries	N 13-a	
linseed crop in acres	Main countries	B 19-a	
in ha	OAS member countries	N 13-a	
maize crop in acres	Main countries	B 8-a	
in ha: historical table	Main European countries	Z 1-a	
in ha	EEC countries	E 12-a	E 44-a
	Main countries	R 5-a	
	OAS member countries	N 13-a	
	OECD countries	D 1-a	
meadow land for grazing: natural pasture in ha	EEC countries	E 12-a	
	OECD countries	D 1-a	
	OAS member countries	N 13-a	
oats crop in acres	Main countries	B 8-a	
in ha: historical table	Main European countries	Z 1-a	
in ha	EEC countries	E 12-a	E 44-a
	Main countries	R 5-a	
	OAS member countries	N 13-a	
	OECD countries	D 1-a	
oil palms in acres	Indonesia & Malaysia	B 19-a	
oilseed crops in ha	EEC countries	B 1-a	
olive trees in ha: historical table	Main European countries	Z 1-a	
in ha	EEC countries	B 1-a	
onion crop in ha	OAS member countries	N 13-a	
paddy rice crop (by method of planting) in ha	All countries	A 19-a	
in ha	All countries	A 19-a	
	OAS member countries	N 13-a	
peas in ha	OAS member countries	N 13-a	
permanent crops by area in ha	EEC countries	E 38-a	
in ha	EEC countries	B 1-a	
	OECD countries	D 1-a	
permanent grass & pasture in ha	EEC countries	B 1-a	E 3-a
		E 12-a	
	OAS member countries	N 13-a	
	Main countries	R 5-a	
	EEC countries	E 12-a	
poppy crop (for opium production) in ha	Main countries	U 46-a	
potato crop: historical table in ha	Main European countries	Z 1-a	
in ha	EEC countries	B 1-a	E 12-a
		E 44-a	
	Main countries	R 5-a	
	OAS member countries	N 13-a	
	OECD countries	D 1-a	
rapeseed crop in acres	Main countries	B 19-a	
rice crop (upland) in ha	All countries	A 19-a	
in acres	Main countries	B 8-a	
in ha	EEC countries	B 1-a	E 12-a
		E 44-a	
	Main countries	R 5-a	
	OECD countries	D 1-a	

	Territorial coverage	Title codes	
LAND UTILISATION, continued			
Area under root crops (incl tubers) by kind in ha	OAS member countries	N 13-a	
rubber trees in ha	All countries	R 5-a	
(on estates) in ha	All countries	C 18-a	
(on smallholdings) in ha	All countries	C 18-a	
rye crop: historical table in ha	Main European countries	Z 1-a	
in acres	Main countries	B 8-a	
in ha	EEC countries	E 12-a	E 44-a
	Main countries	R 5-a	
	OAS member countries	N 13-a	
	OECD countries	D 1-a	
safflower seeds in acres	Australia	N 10-a	
sesame seed crop in acres	Main countries	B 19-a	
in ha	OAS member countries	N 13-a	
soybean crop in acres	Main countries	B 19-a	
in ha	Main countries	R 5-a	
	OAS member countries	N 13-a	
specific main crops (in detail) in ha	EEC countries	E 44-a	
sugar beet crop (5 yr averages) in ha	All countries	A 20-a	
historical table	Main European countries	Z 1-a	
in ha	EEC countries	B 1-a	E 12-a
		E 44-a	
	Main countries	R 5-a	
	OECD countries	D 1-a	
sugar cane crop: historical table in ha	Main European countries	Z 1-a	
(5 yr averages) in ha	All countries	A 20-a	
in ha	Main countries	R 5-a	
	OAS member countries	N 13-a	
sunflower crop in acres	Main countries	B 19-a	
in ha	Australia & France	N 10-a	
	OAS member countries	N 13-a	
sweet potato crop in ha	OAS member countries	N 13-a	
tea crop in ha	Producing world regions	P 6-a	
	Main countries	R 5-a	
temporary grass & pasture in ha	EEC countries	B 1-a	
tobacco crop: historical table in ha	Main European countries	Z 1-a	
in ha	EEC countries	B 1-a	E 12-a
	Main countries	R 5-a	
	OAS member countries	N 13-a	
tomato crop (open fields) in ha	OECD countries	D 29-a	D 36-a
(under glass) in ha	OECD countries	D 36-a	
in ha	OAS member countries	N 13-a	
turnip & rape crop in ha	Finland	N 10-a	
vegetable crops by kind in acres	UK	B 6-a	
in ha	E European countries	U 20-a	
	EEC countries	E 12-a	
vineyards: historical table in ha	Main European countries	Z 1-a	
in ha	EEC countries	B 1-a	
	OAS member countries	N 13-a	
wheat crop in acres	Main countries	B 8-a	
historical table in ha	Main European countries	Z 1-a	
in ha	E European countries & USSR	U 16-a	
	EEC countries	E 12-a	
	Main countries	R 5-a	
	OAS member countries	N 13-a	
	OECD countries	D 1-a	
(soft & hard) in ha	EEC countries	E 44-a	
woodland by areas in ha	EEC countries	E 38-a	
Area used as permanent pasture in ha	EEC countries	E 44-a	
for double cropping of rice in ha	All countries	A 19-a	
Crop yield of hay from grassland in tons per ha	EEC countries	E 12-a	
Cultivated area as % of total land area by regions	EEC countries	E 38-a	
under fruit, olives & vines in ha	EEC countries	E 3-a	
Distribution of land per inhabitant in ha	OAS member countries	N 13-a	
Holdings producing rubber in acres	Sri Lanka	B 13-a	
Mountainous & wooded areas in ha	OAS member countries	N 13-a	
No of rubber plantations in operation by size	Sri Lanka	B 13-a	
Orchards by kind in ha	Netherlands	U 20-a	
for apple production in ha	OECD countries	D 29-a	D 33-a
for peach production in ha	OECD countries	D 29-a	D 35-a
for pear production by region in ha	Main countries	D 34-a	
in ha	OECD countries	D 29-a	
Orchards: historical table in ha	Main European countries	Z 1-a	
in ha	Bulgaria, Hungary, Romania & USSR	U 20-a	
	EEC countries	E 44-a	
Production of hay: tonnage	EEC countries	E 12-a	

Landing & handling charges see DISTRIBUTION COSTS

LANGUAGES
    see also PHILOLOGY

% of adults able to read a specific foreign language	W European countries	Z 3	
to speak a specific foreign language	W European countries	Z 3	
to speak two or more foreign languages	W European countries	Z 3	

Lanthanide see RARE EARTH MINERALS

Lapilli see ABRASIVES, NATURAL

	Territorial coverage	Title codes

LARD
    see also   ANIMAL FATS & OILS
                 COOKING FATS

Consumption per capita in lbs per yr	UK	B 12-a B 19-a
in production of cooking fats: tonnage	UK & USA	B 19-a
of margarine & cooking fats: tonnage	Japan, UK & USA	A 4-a
of margarine: tonnage	UK	B 19-a
tonnage	OAS member countries	N 17-a
Export prices in cents per lb	USA	R 2-m
	Netherlands	A 9-a
Import prices (American prime steam quality) in £ per ton cif	UK	R 2-m
in DM per ton	W Germany	A 9-a
Imports (incl margarine & shortening): tonnage	Main countries	P 1-a
Production for ensuing yr: tonnage (estim)	World regions	P 1-a
(incl pork fat): tonnage	USA	P 1-a
rendered pig fat: tonnage	All countries	A 9-a U 22-a
Production, stocks & consumption per capita per day	OECD countries	D 14-a
Production, supply, consumption, imports & exports: tonnage	EEC countries	B 1-a
tonnage	OAS member countries	N 14-a
Retail prices: lard by kind in local currency	OAS member countries	N 17-a
Stocks: tonnage (end month)	USA	P 1-m
Wholesale prices in local currency	OAS member countries	N 17-a
prime steam lard (on Chicago market) in cents per lb	USA	P 1-m
in £ per ton	UK	U 27-m
in $ per ton	USA	A 9-a
World market prices - index nos		A 4-m
World market prices: lard ex USA in £ per 100 kg		E 34-m
World production: forecast by 1975: tonnage		A 1
tonnage		A 4-a A 5-a
		N 10-a
World supply: tonnage		B 19-a

Large enterprises   see   AIRLINE COMPANIES
                                COMMERCIAL BANKS
                                COMMERCIAL UNDERTAKINGS
                                INDUSTRIAL COMPANIES
                                PUBLIC UTILITIES
                                TRANSPORT UNDERTAKINGS

LATEX
    see also   RUBBER

Consumption (incl crude rubber): tonnage	Malaysia & Singapore	C 18-m
tonnage	Main countries	C 18-m
Exports (incl crude rubber) by destination: tonnage	Main countries	C 18-m
Import prices: liquid latex in £ per ton cif	European ports & UK	C 17-m
Imports: tonnage	Main countries	C 18-m
Production: natural latex: tonnage	Brazil & India	C 18-m
Stocks: tonnage	Main consuming countries	C 18-m

LATEX CREPE

Import prices in pence per kg cif	European ports & UK	C 17-m

LATEX FOAM

Consumption of rubber in production of cellular latex foams: tonnage	UK	C 18-a

LATHES

Deliveries (all types) by industrial sector by value in $m	USA	J 2-a
Exports by destination by value in £m	UK	B 31-a
(excl turret type) by volume & value in $m	USA	J 2-a
Imports & exports by type by value in $m & % growth rates	EEC countries	B 20-a
by source by value in £m	UK	B 31-a
(excl turret type) by volume & value in $m	USA	J 2-a
Production volume (all types)	France, W Germany, Italy & UK	B 31-a
	Main countries	R 5-a

LATHES, AUTOMATIC
    see also   CENTRE LATHES

Consumption by supply area by value in $m	EEC countries	B 31-a
by value in $m	EEC countries	B 31-a
Deliveries (domestic) by value in $m	EEC countries	B 31-a
Exports as % of production (value basis)	EEC countries	B 31-a
Imports & exports by value in $m & % growth rates	EEC countries	B 20-a
numerically-controlled lathes by type by value in $m	UK	B 20-a
Imports as % of consumption (value basis)	EEC countries	B 31-a
Production: multi-spindle lathes by value in $m	EEC countries	B 31-a
numerically-controlled type by volume	EEC countries	B 20-a
single spindle type by value in $m	EEC countries	B 31-a
Sales by type by volume & value in $m	USA	J 2-a

Lathes, capstan & turret   see   CAPSTAN LATHES

	Territorial coverage	Title codes	
LATHES, NON-AUTOMATIC			
Consumption by supply area by value in $m	EEC countries	B 31-a	
by value in $m	EEC countries	B 31-a	
Imports & exports by type by value in $m	UK	B 20-a	
Production by value in $m	EEC countries	B 31-a	
Sales by volume & value by type in $m	USA	J 2-a	
LATHES, VERTICAL BORING			
Imports & exports by value in $m & % growth rates	EEC countries	B 20-a	
Sales by volume & value in $m	USA	J 2-a	

Latices, synthetic   see   SYNTHETIC RUBBER

Launchings   see   MERCHANT SHIPPING FLEETS

Lauric acid oils   see   BABASSU OIL
                              COCONUT OIL
                              PALM KERNEL OIL

Lava sand   see   ABRASIVES, NATURAL

LAW

% of students enrolled studying jurisprudence	ECAFE countries	U 17	
No of students enrolled abroad by origin studying jurisprudence	All countries	U 64-a	
on university courses in jurisprudence	OAS member countries	N 19-a	
	All countries	U 62-a	
of university degrees gained in jurisprudence	All countries	U 62-a	

Laying hens   see   POULTRY

LEAD
    see also   INGOTS, LEAD

	Territorial coverage	Title codes	
% contribution to export earnings	Zambia	E 45-a	
Consumption by chemical industry: tonnage	OECD countries	D 21-a	
by end-use & principal trades: tonnage	Main countries	H 2-a	
(incl production of lead products): tonnage	UK & USA	J 6-a	
of refined lead: tonnage	Main countries	T 4-a	
tonnage	Italy	C 12-a	
by industry: tonnage	USA	J 6-a	
for production of accumulators: tonnage	OECD countries	D 21-a	
alloys: tonnage	Main countries	T 4-a	
ammunition & shot: tonnage	UK & USA	J 6-a	T 4-a
	All countries	C 30-q	
anti-friction bearings: tonnage	All countries	C 30-q	
anti-friction metals: tonnage	France & Italy	C 12-a	
anti-knock compounds: tonnage	All countries	C 30-q	
	UK & USA	T 4-a	
	France & Italy	C 12-a	
antimonial lead: tonnage	Canada	T 4-a	
battery grids & oxides: tonnage	UK & USA	J 6-a	
battery oxides: tonnage	UK & USA	T 4-a	
bearing metals: tonnage	All countries	C 30-q	
	USA	J 6-a	T 4-a
brass & bronze: tonnage	USA	J 6-a	T 4-a
cable coverings: tonnage	Main countries	T 4-a	
	UK & USA	J 6-a	
	All countries	C 30-q	
calking metal: tonnage	USA	J 6-a	T 4-a
chemicals: tonnage	France, Italy & USA	C 12-a	
	USA	J 6-a	
collapsible tubes: tonnage	USA	J 6-a	
	W Germany, France & USA	T 4-a	
colours & paint pigments: tonnage	USA	J 6-a	
electric cables: tonnage	Italy	C 12-a	
	OECD countries	D 21-a	
lead alloys: tonnage	France, Italy & W Germany	C 12-a	
	OECD countries	D 21-a	
	UK	J 6-a	
lead castings: tonnage	W Germany & USA	T 4-a	
lead compounds: tonnage	All countries	C 30-q	
lead foil (incl collapsible tubes): tonnage	UK	J 6-a	
	All countries	C 30-q	
	France, UK & USA	T 4-a	
	USA	J 6-a	
lead oxides: tonnage	France, Italy & USA	C 12-a	
lead shot: tonnage	Main countries	T 4-a	
lead tubing: tonnage	All countries	C 30-q	
litharge: tonnage	USA	J 6-a	
pigments, paints & chemicals: tonnage	Main countries	T 4-a	
	All countries	C 30-q	
pigments by kind: tonnage	USA	J 6-a	
pipes & sheets: tonnage	Main countries	T 4-a	
	All countries	C 30-q	
pipes & fittings: tonnage	UK & USA	J 6-a	
red & white lead: tonnage	USA	J 6-a	
red lead & litharge: tonnage	USA	T 4-a	
	All countries	C 30-q	

	Territorial coverage	Title codes	
LEAD, continued			
Consumption for production of semi-finished lead products: tonnage	OECD countries	D 21-a	
solder: tonnage	Italy	C 12-a	
	France, Italy, UK & USA	C 12-a	
	All countries	C 30-q	
storage batteries: tonnage	UK & USA	J 6-a	T 4-a
	All countries	C 30-q	
	Main countries	T 4-a	
	Italy	C 12-a	
terne metal: tonnage	USA	J 6-a	T 4-a
tetraethyl lead: tonnage	UK & USA	J 6-a	
type metal (incl anti-friction (metals): tonnage	Main countries	T 4-a	
type metal: tonnage	France, Italy & USA	C 12-a	
	USA	J 6-a	
weights & ballast: tonnage	USA	J 6-a	T 4-a
white lead: tonnage	UK & USA	J 6-a	T 4-a
	All countries	C 30-q	
imported refined lead & lead from scrap: tonnage	UK	C 30-m	
in annealing processes: tonnage	USA	J 6-a	T 4-a
in galvanising processes: tonnage	USA	J 6-a	T 4-a
in lead plating processes: tonnage	USA	J 6-a	
primary metal: tonnage	All countries	J 6-a	
refined & remelted lead: tonnage	UK	C 30-m	
refined lead: historical table: tonnage	World regions	C 12-a	
tonnage	All countries	C 30-m	
	Argentine, Brazil, Mexico & Peru	U 18-a	
	EEC countries	C 12-a	
	OAS member countries	N 17-a	
	OECD countries	D 21-q	
	World regions	C 12-a	
	USA	N 1-a	
Deliveries to domestic user industries: tonnage	USA	J 6-m	
Disposals ex US strategic stockpile: tonnage		U 11-a	
Export prices: refined pig lead in $A per ton fob	Australia	R 2-m	
Export prices - index nos (weighted average main sources)	Worldwide	U 29-q	
	S American countries	U 40-q	
Exports by destination: lead pigs & bars: tonnage	USA	J 6-a	
lead pigs by kind: tonnage	Main countries	H 2-a	
refined lead (incl lead bullion): tonnage	UK	C 30-m	
based on content of ore: tonnage	All countries	T 4-a	
lead by value in $m	Developing countries	U 11-a	
refined lead: tonnage	All countries	C 12-a	
soft & antimonial lead: tonnage	All countries	C 30	
tonnage & by value in $m	Zambia	E 45-a	
Imports & exports by source & destination: tonnage	All countries	B 15-a	
by source: bullion & refined lead: tonnage	Main countries	U 24-a	
pig lead & bars: tonnage	USA	J 6-a	
refined lead (incl lead bullion): tonnage	UK	C 30-m	
tonnage	All countries	T 4-a	
pig lead by kind (incl scrap): tonnage	All countries	H 2-a	
refined lead: tonnage	All countries	C 12-a	
	UK	C 30-m	
soft & antimonial lead: tonnage	Main countries	C 30-m	
Producer prices: lead (in cable form) in DM per ton	W Germany	H 2-m	
refined pig lead in $ per ton	W Germany, UK & USA	H 2-m	
Production capacity by individual companies: tonnage	Worldwide	C 12-a	
Production based on metal content of ore: tonnage	Latin American countries	J 5-a	U 18-a
	All countries	C 30-m	U 27-m
		B 15-a	C 12-a
		H 2-a	R 5-a
		T 4-a	U 22-a
		U 43-a	
	Main countries	E 3-a	
by individual mining companies: tonnage	Worldwide	J 6-a	
by individual smelters & refineries: tonnage	Worldwide	J 6-a	
from domestic lead ore: tonnage	USA	J 6-a	
foreign lead ore by source: tonnage	USA	J 6-a	
ores & concentrates: tonnage	All countries	U 43-a	
historical table from 1897: tonnage	USA	J 6-a	
primary & secondary metal: tonnage	All countries	B 15-a	
	USA	N 1-a	
refined lead extracted from imported bullion: tonnage	UK	C 30-m	
from indigenous scrap: tonnage	UK	C 30-m	
historical table: tonnage	World regions	C 12-a	
(primary & secondary): tonnage	USA	J 6-a	
tonnage	African countries	U 44-a	
	All countries	C 30-m	C 12-a
		R 5-a	T 4-a
	Argentine, Mexico & Peru	U 18-a	
	EEC countries	C 12-a	
	Latin American countries	U 18-a	U 40-a
	Main countries	E 3-a	
	OECD countries	D 21-q	R 5-a
	OAS member countries	N 14-a	
	World regions	C 12-a	
	USA	N 1-a	
secondary lead: tonnage	EEC countries	E 28-q	E 27-a
semi-manufactured lead products: tonnage	All countries	U 22-a	
unwrought lead: tonnage			

	Territorial coverage	Title codes	
LEAD, continued			
Refining & smelting capacity by individual companies: tonnage	Worldwide	C 12-a	
Sales turnover: lead on London Metal Exchange in £m	UK	C 12-m	
Smelter production: tonnage	All countries	J 6-a	
Stocks at consumers' premises & producers' plants: tonnage	Main countries	C 12-a	
	USA	N 1-a	
in antimonial lead form: tonnage	USA	J 6-a	
tonnage	UK	C 30-m	J 6-a
at lead market dealers' warehouses: tonnage	UK	C 30-m	
at London Metal Exchange warehouses: tonnage	UK	J 6-a	
at refineries & smelting plants in antimonial lead form: tonnage	USA	J 6-a	
at refineries, at ports & in transit: tonnage	UK	C 30-m	
in base bullion form: tonnage	USA	J 6-a	
in refined pig lead form: tonnage	USA	J 6-a	
in refined soft lead form (at consumers' premises): tonnage	USA	J 6-a	
home-refined lead: tonnage	UK	J 6-a	
imported virgin lead: tonnage	UK	J 6-a	
Wholesale prices (at London Metal Exchange) in £ per ton (3 mths forward)	UK	C 12-m	T 4-m
in £ per ton	UK	C 12-m	J 6-m
		U 11-a	
in £ per ton (daily & monthly)	UK	U 24	
(at overseas metal markets) in $ per ton		U 24-a	
(at New York & St Louis markets) in cents per lb	USA	J 6-m	
(at New York market) in cents per lb (daily & monthly)	USA	C 12-m	U 24
by grade in cents per lb	Canada & USA	R 2-m	
historical table from 1875: tonnage	UK	T 4-a	
in cents per lb (annual averages)	USA	N 1-a	
in local currency per ton	Canada, UK & USA	U 27-m	
lead ingots in lire per kg	Italy	C 12-m	
pig lead in local currency per lb (or ton)	Main countries	J 6-m	
refined lead (at London Metal Exchange) in £ per ton	UK	R 2-m	
spot price (& 3 mths forward) in £ per ton	UK	U 24-m	
virgin soft lead in local currency per ton	Main countries	T 4-w	
World consumption: historical table: tonnage		C 12-a	U 11-a
refined lead: tonnage	Worldwide	C 30-a	
	All countries	C 12-a	T 4-a
tonnage	All countries	J 6-a	
World exports: refined lead: tonnage	Main countries	T 4-a	
World market prices: historical table from 1875 in £ per ton		T 4-a	
in cents per lb (based on London & New York markets)		U 18-a	
World production: mined & refined lead: tonnage		C 30-a	
refined lead: tonnage	All countries	T 4-a	N 4-a
tonnage		C 12-a	
		T 4-a	U 11-a
	All countries	C 12-a	
	Main countries	N 1-a	
World reserves: tonnage (estim)	Main countries	N 1-a	
Lead, natural black see GRAPHITE			
LEAD, REFINED			
Consumption by main user industries: tonnage	Main countries	H 2-a	
tonnage	All countries	U 24-m	
Exports (incl bullion): tonnage	Main countries	U 24-m	
Imports (incl bullion): tonnage	Main countries	U 24-m	
Production, imports, exports & consumption: tonnage	Main countries	H 2-a	
Production: tonnage	All countries	U 24-m	
	EEC countries	R 5-a	
Stocks held by producers (end-period): tonnage	Worldwide	U 24-a	
LEAD ALLOYS			
Lead consumption in manufacture of lead alloys: tonnage	European countries	C 12-a	
	Main countries	T 4-a	
Production (incl semis & castings): tonnage	Main countries	H 2-a	
Stocks held at consumers' premises: tonnage	USA	J 6-a	
Lead arsenate see INSECTICIDES			
LEAD BULLION			
Exports (incl refined lead) by destination: tonnage	OECD countries	D 21-q	
(incl re-exports): tonnage	UK	C 30-m	
Imports by source (incl refined lead): tonnage	OECD countries	D 21-q	
tonnage	USA	J 6-a	
tonnage	UK	C 30-m	
Production, imports, exports & stocks: tonnage	Main countries	H 2-a	
tonnage	UK	C 30-m	
Lead castings see CASTINGS, LEAD			
LEAD FOIL			
see also ALUMINIUM FOIL			
COPPER FOIL			
TIN FOIL			

	Territorial coverage	Title codes

LEAD FOIL, continued
    Consumption of lead in production of foil: tonnage France, UK & USA T 4-a
          USA J 6-a

LEAD ORE
    % share of estimated world reserves Latin American area U 18-a
    Export prices - index nos (weighted average main sources)   U 29-q
    Exports by destination (incl concentrates): tonnage Italy C 12-a
      OECD countries D 21-q
      Developing countries U 11-a
        by value in $m Main countries U 24-m
        (incl concentrates): tonnage European countries T 4-m
    Import prices (incl concentrates) in $ per ton Main countries B 15-a
    Imports & exports by source & destination: tonnage Main countries H 2-a
        by source by kind: tonnage Italy C 12-a
            (incl concentrates): tonnage OECD countries D 21-q
      UK C 30-m
      USA J 6-a
        (incl concentrates): tonnage Main countries U 24-m
    Production by region: tonnage USA J 6-a
        historical table from 1845: tonnage Main European countries Z 1-a
        (incl concentrates): tonnage Argentine, Mexico & Peru U 18-a
      OECD countries D 21-q
      USA T 4-a
        (incl zinc ore): tonnage Madagascar E 41-a
        tonnage African countries U 44-a
      All countries J 6-a
      EEC countries E 28-q   E 27-a
      OAS member countries N 14-a
    Receipts of lead ore (incl scrap) at smelter plants: tonnage USA J 6-m
    Stocks (incl matte) at smelting plants: tonnage USA J 6-a
    World production: tonnage   U 11-a

LEAD OXIDE
    Wholesale price: dry red oxide in $ per ton USA T 4-w

Lead pigments   see   PIGMENTS, MINERAL

Lead products   see   BATTERIES & ACCUMULATORS
                          INSULATED WIRE & CABLES
                          LEAD ALLOYS

LEAD PRODUCTS, SEMI-FINISHED
    Exports: foil & powders: tonnage UK C 30-m
        lead oxides: tonnage UK C 30-m
        red & orange lead: tonnage UK C 30-m
        rods, wire sheets, strip, tubes & pipes: tonnage UK C 30-m
    Wholesale prices by kind in local currency Main countries T 4-w
        pipes in local currency Japan & UK T 4-w
        sheets in lire per ton Italy C 12-m
        tubes in lire per ton Italy T 4-w   C 12-m

LEAD RESIDUES
    Wholesale prices: lead ashes (for metal refining) in £ per ton UK T 4-w

LEAD SCRAP
    Consumption by purpose: tonnage USA T 4-a
        in production of antimonial lead: tonnage USA T 4-a
        babbitt metal: tonnage USA T 4-a
        battery plates: tonnage USA T 4-a
        cable covering: tonnage USA T 4-a
        dross & residues: tonnage USA T 4-a
        soft lead: tonnage USA T 4-a
        solder: tonnage USA T 4-a
        type metal: tonnage USA T 4-a
        (incl remelted lead): tonnage UK T 4-a
    Exports by destination: tonnage Main countries T 4-a
    Imports by source: tonnage Main countries T 4-a
        (incl lead alloy scrap): tonnage UK C 30-m
    Production by kind (as antimonial lead): tonnage USA T 4-a
        (as secondary recovery): tonnage USA T 4-a
    Stocks held at smelters & refineries: tonnage USA T 4-a
    Wholesale prices: car battery lead scrap & plates in lire per kg Italy C 12-m
        in £ per ton UK T 4-w
        in £ per ton UK T 4-w
        in cents per lb USA J 6-m
        in local currency per ton Main countries T 4-w
        soft lead scrap in lire per kg Italy C 12-m

Lead sheets   see   LEAD PRODUCTS, SEMI-FINISHED

Lead tubes & pipes   see   LEAD PRODUCTS, SEMI-FINISHED

LEATHER
    % share (incl footwear) of EEC area exports Developing countries U 52-a
    Exports by value in $m Main countries A 18-a
      Argentine, Brazil, India & Pakistan A 5-a

	Territorial coverage	Title codes
LEATHER, continued		
Exports (incl leather goods) by value in $	India	U 32-m
rough-tanned & finished leather: tonnage	Main countries	A 5-a
Imports (incl footwear) by value in $	Developing countries	U 52-a
into EEC area ex developing countries by value in $		U 52-a
Production from chrome-tanned hides: tonnage	Main countries	B 9-a
from hides by type: tonnage	Netherlands	B 9-a
from vegetable-tanned hides: tonnage	Main countries	B 9-a
leather for manufacture of footwear uppers: tonnage	OECD countries	D 18-a
of shoe soles & repairs: tonnage	Netherlands	B 9-a
light & heavy hides & skins: tonnage	All countries	U 22-a
volume by kind	EEC countries	E 27-a
for chamois leather production	W Germany	B 9-a
gloves production	W Germany	B 9-a
harness leather production	W Germany	B 9-a
protective clothing production	W Germany	B 9-a
Wholesale prices: box calf & sides - index nos	OECD countries	D 18-q
kid for glove-making - index nos	OECD countries	D 18-q
roll butts - index nos	OECD countries	D 18-q
World exports: leather made from hides & skins by value in $m		A 18-a
LEATHER, HEAVY		
% of production used by footwear industry	Main countries	A 18-a
for manufacture of footwear soles	All countries	A 18-a
Consumption: tonnage	Developed countries incl USSR	A 18-a
Exports: tonnage	Main countries	A 18-a
Imports: tonnage	Main countries	A 18-a
Production: tonnage	All countries	A 18-a
LEATHER, LIGHT		
% of production used by footwear industry	Main countries	A 18-a
for manufacture of footwear uppers	All countries	A 18-a
% of usage of hides in production of footwear linings	USA	A 18-a
footwear uppers	USA	A 18-a
garments & gloves	USA	A 18-a
luggage	USA	A 18-a
upholstery	USA	A 18-a
Consumption: tonnage	Developed countries incl USSR	A 18-a
Exports: cattle & calf leather: tonnage	Main countries	A 18-a
Imports: cattle & calf leather: tonnage	Main countries	A 18-a
Production: cattle & calf leather by volume in sq ft	Main countries	A 18-a
tonnage	Main countries	A 18-a
uppers & linings for footwear: tonnage	All countries	A 18-a
LEATHER, SHEEP & GOATSKIN		
Consumption by volume in sq ft	OECD countries	D 18-a
tonnage	Developed countries incl USSR	A 18-a
Exports by destination by volume in sq ft	OECD countries	D 18-a
by value in $	OECD countries	D 18-a
ex OECD area shipped to non-OECD countries by volume in sq ft		D 18-a
tonnage	Main countries	A 18-a
Imports by source by value in $	OECD countries	D 18-a
by volume in sq ft	OECD countries	D 18-a
ex non-OECD countries by volume in sq ft	OECD countries	D 18-a
tonnage	Main countries	A 18-a
Production by volume in sq ft	All countries	A 18-a
	OECD countries	D 18-a
LEATHER BY KIND		
Exports by destination: tonnage	Main countries	B 9-m
Imports by source: tonnage	Main countries	B 9-m
Production (by purpose) for footwear: tonnage	All countries	B 9-a
heavy & light grades: tonnage	Main countries	B 9-a
tonnage	EEC countries	E 28-q
Wholesale prices - index nos	OECD countries	D 18-a
Leather footwear see FOOTWEAR, LEATHER		
LEATHER GOODS INDUSTRY		
see also FOOTWEAR INDUSTRY		
Costs for salaried staff in local currency per mth	EEC countries	E 11-a
Electricity consumption (incl footwear industry) in kWh	All countries	C 23-a
Investment in buildings in local currency	EEC countries	E 40-a
in land purchase in local currency	EEC countries	E 40-a
in machinery in local currency	EEC countries	E 40-a
Labour costs as % of total costs	EEC countries	E 8-a
by status of employees in local currency	EEC countries	E 8-a
per hr in local currency (all employees)	EEC countries	E 11-a
(wage earners)	EEC countries	E 11-a
Labour force employed: no of salaried staff	EEC countries	E 11-a
wage earners & salaried staff	EEC countries	E 8-a
wage earners	EEC countries	E 11-a
No of hrs worked per wk by region	EEC countries	E 25-a
per wk	OAS member countries	N 18-a

	Territorial coverage	Title codes
LEATHER GOODS INDUSTRY, continued		
No of hrs worked per yr: salaried staff	EEC countries	E 11-a
wage earners	EEC countries	E 11-a
per yr	EEC countries	E 8-a
Wage rates in local currency per hr	EEC countries	E 25-a2
	OAS member countries	N 17-a
LEATHER INDUSTRY		
see also TANNERIES		
TANNING BARK		
Earnings in local currency	All countries	L 4-a
Employment - index nos	All countries	L 4-a
Frequency of accidents at work	EEC countries	E 2-a
IDA loans granted for improving leather output in $	OAS member countries	N 16-a
Labour costs as % of total costs	EEC countries	E 8-a
by status of employees in local currency	EEC countries	E 8-a
(incl leather goods industry) per hr	EEC countries	E 2-a
Labour force employed: no of wage earners & salaried staff	EEC countries	E 8-a
Labour force employed	EEC countries	E 2-a
	Main countries	U 21-a
No of hrs worked per wk	All countries	L 4-a
	Main countries	R 3-m
per yr	EEC countries	E 8-a
Production - index nos (quantum basis)	S American countries	U 40-a
	EEC countries	E 26-m E 28-q
		E 27-a
Wage rates in local currency per hr by sex	Main countries	C 7-a
(incl footwear) by sex	Main countries	R 3-m
skilled workers by sex	Main countries	R 4-q
unskilled workers by sex	Main countries	R 4-q
LEATHER PRODUCTS BY KIND		
see also FOOTWEAR, LEATHER		
Exports by destination by SITC classes by value in $	Main countries	D 2-q
	OECD countries	D 3-a2
by CST classes by value in $	EEC countries	E 48-a
by NIMEXE classes by value in $	All countries	E 20-a
SITC classes by value in $	All countries	U 50-a U 59-a
Imports by NIMEXE classes by value in $	All countries	E 20-a
SITC classes by value in $	All countries	U 50-a U 59-a
by source by CST classes by value in $	EEC countries	E 21-a
SITC classes by value in $	Main countries	D 2-q
tonnage & value in $	OECD countries	D 3-a2
Production: tonnage	Zaire	E 41-a
LEATHER SUBSTITUTE		
Production capacity by make	Main countries	A 18-a
Wholesale prices: Corfam per sq ft	USA	A 18-a
poromerics per sq ft	W Germany & UK	A 18-a
LEATHERCLOTH		
Production volume	EEC countries	E 28-q E 27-a
LEISURE EQUIPMENT		
% of households owning 3 cars or more	W European countries	Z 3
a boat	W European countries	Z 3
a caravan	W European countries	Z 3
cameras by kind	W European countries	Z 3
ciné cameras	W European countries	Z 3
electric drills	W European countries	Z 3
film projectors	W European countries	Z 3
hair-dryers (electric)	W European countries	Z 3
lawn mowers (powered)	W European countries	Z 3
one or two cars	W European countries	Z 3
record players	W European countries	Z 3
sewing machines (electric)	W European countries	Z 3
tape recorders	W European countries	Z 3
television sets (colour)	W European countries	Z 3
television sets	W European countries	Z 3
transistor radios	W European countries	Z 3

Leisure pursuits   see   RECREATION

Lemon juice   see   FRUIT JUICES, CITRUS

Lemons & limes   see   CITRUS FRUITS

LENSES & FRAMES
see also   OPTICAL INSTRUMENTS

Deliveries of lenses & prisms by value in £	UK	C 24-a

	Territorial coverage	Title codes

LENTILS

Area harvested, production tonnage & yield per ha under crop in ha	All countries	A 9-a
	France & Italy	E 12-a
	OAS member countries	N 13-a
Crop yield in 100 kg per ha	France & Italy	E 12-a
in kg per ha	OAS member countries	N 13-a
Export prices in local currency per ton	Chile & Madagascar	A 9-a
Producer prices received in local currency per ton	Peru	A 9-a
Production tonnage & area under crop in ha	Turkey	D 37-a
tonnage	African countries	U 44-a
	Argentine, Chile, Ecuador, Peru & Mexico	U 40-a
	France & Italy	E 12-a
	OAS member countries	N 13-a
Wholesale prices in Rs per ton	India & Pakistan	A 9-a

Lepidolite   see   LITHIUM MINERALS

LEPROSY

No of cases under active examination	OAS member countries	N 18-a
of registered cases of leprosy	OAS member countries	N 18-a

LETTER MAIL

No of letters carried (domestic & overseas) in million	Main countries	R 5-a
	Asia, Far East & Australasian countries	U 45-a
(domestic) in million	African countries	U 44-a
	OAS member countries	N 15-a
(overseas) in million	OAS member countries	N 15-a
carried in million	OAS member countries	N 15-a
received from abroad in million	African countries	U 44-a
sent abroad in million	African countries	U 44-a
Volume of unregistered mail: historical table from 1830	Main European countries	Z 1-a

Lettuce   see   VEGETABLES, GREEN

Leucoxene   see   TITANIUM MINERALS

LEVIES

    see also   IMPORT LEVIES
                  SOCIAL SECURITY LEVIES
                  TOLLS

% rates for equalisation of burdens	EEC countries	E 31-a
for sewage disposal levies	EEC countries	E 31-a

Liabilities   see   ASSETS & LIABILITIES
                          BALANCE SHEETS

Liabilities, foreign   see   BALANCE OF PAYMENTS
                                     FOREIGN DEBT

LIBRARIES, NATIONAL

% of expenditure on new books	All countries	U 62-a
on staff salaries	All countries	U 62-a
Length of shelving in use in metres	All countries	U 62-a
No of additions to stock of volumes	All countries	U 62-a
librarians & staff employed	All countries	U 62-a
libraries & no of volumes stocked	All countries	U 62-a
	OAS member countries	N 19-a
registered borrowers	All countries	U 62-a
volumes loaned out	All countries	U 62-a

LIBRARIES, PUBLIC

% of expenditure on new book acquisitions	All countries	U 62-a
on staff salaries	All countries	U 62-a
Length of shelving in use in metres	All countries	U 62-a
No of libraries & no of volumes stocked	Latin American countries	J 5-a
additions to stock of volumes	All countries	U 62-a
librarians & staff employed	All countries	U 62-a
libraries & no of volumes stocked	All countries	U 62-a
	OAS member countries	N 19-a
registered borrowers	All countries	U 62-a
volumes loaned out	All countries	U 62-a

LIBRARIES, SPECIALIST

Length of shelving in use in metres	All countries	U 62-a
No of libraries & no of volumes stocked	All countries	U 62-a
	OAS member countries	N 19-a

LIBRARIES, UNIVERSITY

% of expenditure on new book acquisitions	All countries	U 62-a
on staff salaries	All countries	U 62-a
Length of shelving in use in metres	All countries	U 62-a
No of additions to stock of volumes	All countries	U 62-a
librarians & staff employed	All countries	U 62-a
libraries & no of volumes stocked	All countries	U 62-a
	OAS member countries	N 19-a

	Territorial coverage	Title codes	
LIBRARIES, UNIVERSITY continued			
No of registered borrowers	All countries	U 62-a	
volumes loaned out	All countries	U 62-a	
LICENCE FEES			
see also VEHICLE DRIVING LICENCES			
% rates charged: alcohol sales (incl basis of assessment)	EEC countries	E 31-a	
dog licence fees	EEC countries	E 31-a	
fishing & hunting taxes	EEC countries	E 31-a	
Life expectancy see EXPECTATION OF LIFE			
LIFE INSURANCE			
Annuities paid out by insurance companies in local currency	OAS member countries	N 16-a	
Claims on public & on private sector in $m	All countries	F 5-m	F 6-q
paid out by insurance companies in local currency	OAS member countries	N 16-a	
Foreign assets of insurance companies in $m	Main countries	F 5-m	F 6-q
Funds invested by insurance companies in $m	All countries	F 5-m	F 6-q
No of life insurance policies outstanding & value in $	Asian, Far East & Australasian countries	U 45-a	
Premiums paid to insurance companies in local currency	OAS member countries	N 16-a	
Lifting machinery see MECHANICAL HANDLING EQUIPMENT			
Light bulbs see LAMPS, INCANDESCENT			
LIGHT SECTIONS, ALUMINIUM			
Consumption: tonnage	UK	T 4-a	
Despatches: tonnage	UK	C 30-a	
Imports by source: tonnage	Main countries	T 4-a	
Production: tonnage	Main countries	T 4-a	
LIGHT SECTIONS, STEEL			
Deliveries to user industries: tonnage	ECE countries	U 7-q	U 6-a
	Main countries	H 3-a	
Exports: angles & shapes: tonnage	E European countries	T 1-a	
by destination: tonnage	Main countries	T 4-a	
tonnage	ECE countries	U 7-m	U 6-a
	European countries, Japan & USA	C 5-m	
	Main countries	H 3-a	
Imports alloy steel sections: tonnage	Main countries	T 1-a	
by grade: tonnage	Main countries	T 1-a	
by source: tonnage	Main countries	T 4-a	
free-cutting steel: tonnage	Main countries	T 1-a	
high-carbon steel: tonnage	Main countries	T 1-a	
tonnage	ECE countries	U 7-m	U 6-a
	European countries, Japan & USA	C 5-m	
	Main countries	H 3-a	
Production capacity: tonnage	Main countries	U 57-a	
Production: tonnage	All countries	T 1-a	
	ECE countries	U 7-m	U 6-a
	Main countries	H 3-a	T 4-a
	OAS member countries	N 14-a	
Wholesale prices in local currency per ton	Latin American countries	U 57-a	
LIGHTING & HEATING, DOMESTIC			
see also PUBLIC LIGHTING			
Consumption of electricity in kWh	All countries	C 23-a	
of gas & fuel oils	OECD countries	D 31-a	
Expenditure in local currency	AASM countries	E 41-a	
LIGNITE			
see also HARD COAL BRIQUETTES			
Availability & changes in stocks: tonnage	EEC countries	E 16-q	E 15-a
(domestic) of brown coal: tonnage	European countries	U 31-q	
ex indigenous production & imports: tonnage	EEC countries	E 16-q	E 14-a
		E 15-a	
Changes in stocks (indigenous & imported): tonnage	EEC countries	E 14-a	
Consumption at electric power-generating stations: tonnage	EEC countries	E 16-m	E 15-a
at power stations & for briquetting	EEC countries	E 16-q	E 15-a
brown coal at thermal power plants: tonnage	European countries	U 31-q	
by industry: tonnage	European countries	U 31-q	
by industrial sector: tonnage	Turkey	U 10-a	
	OECD countries	D 44-a	
by public electricity supply plants: tonnage	European countries	U 1-a	
for transformation into energy: tonnage	EEC countries	E 16-q	E 15-a
in electricity generation plants: tonnage	EEC countries	E 14-a	
in production of brown coal briquettes: tonnage	EEC countries	E 14-a	
	OECD countries	D 44-a	
of manufactured gas: tonnage	European countries & USA	U 3-a	
of patent fuels: tonnage	EEC countries	E 16-q	E 15-a
in steel foundries: tonnage	EEC area	E 29-a	
in thermal electric power stations: tonnage	OECD countries	D 8-a	
(incl briquettes) by steelworks: tonnage	EEC countries	E 29-a	
(incl brown coal) by steelworks: tonnage	ECE countries	U 6-a	U 7-a
	Main countries	H 3-a	

	Territorial coverage	Title codes	
LIGNITE, continued			
Consumption (industrial) by areas: tonnage	EEC countries	E 38-a	
in petroleum equiv tonnage	EEC area	E 7-a	
tonnage	Denmark	E 7-a	
	EEC area	E 7-a	
	EEC countries	E 16-q	E 14-a
		E 15-a	
	European countries, USA & USSR	U 4-a	
	Italy	H 4-a	
	Main countries	N 2-a	
Deliveries to EEC area & exports: tonnage	EEC countries	E 16-q	E 15-a
to EEC countries: tonnage	EEC countries	E 14-a	
Exports: brown coal: tonnage	European countries	U 31-q	U 10-a
by destination: tonnage	EEC countries	E 5-q	
to non-EEC area: tonnage	EEC countries	E 14-a	
Imports & exports: tonnage	EEC countries	E 16-q	E 15-a
by source: brown coal: tonnage	EEC countries	E 5-q	
brown coal: tonnage	European countries	U 31-q	
ex non-EEC area: tonnage	EEC countries	E 14-a	
Production & reserves (estim): tonnage	All countries	U 43-a	
(incl world total): tonnage	All countries	C 4-a	
brown coal: historical table from 1837: tonnage	Main European countries	Z 1-a	
tonnage	ECE countries	U 15-a	
	EEC countries	E 26-m	
	European countries	U 31-q	
	Main countries	R 5-a	
by areas: tonnage	EEC countries	E 38-a	
Production, imports, exports, consumption & stocks: tonnage	OECD countries	D 44-a	
(incl briquettes): tonnage	EEC countries	E 14-a	
tonnage	All countries	U 22-a	
	EEC countries	E 16-m	E 28-q
		E 27-a	
	European countries, USA & USSR	U 4-a	
	Main countries	U 27-m	E 3-a
Receipts (incl briquettes) at steelworks: tonnage	EEC countries	E 29-a	
World production: tonnage	Worldwide	N 4-a	
	All countries	E 15-a	
LIGNITE BY-PRODUCTS			
Production: tonnage	EEC countries	E 14-a	
LIME & QUICKLIME			
see also BUILDING MATERIALS			
% usage in building construction industry	USA	N 1-a	
in production of alkali compounds & refractories	USA	N 1-a	
of steel products	USA	N 1-a	
in water purification processes	USA	N 1-a	
Consumption: tonnage	USA	N 1-a	
Prices (ex plant) in $ per ton	USA	N 1-a	
Production: tonnage of lime	Zaire	E 41-a	
	Main countries	N 1-a	
Wholesale prices - index nos	OAS member countries	N 14-a	
Lime phosphate see PHOSPHATE OF LIME			
LIMESTONE			
Production: calcareous rocks: tonnage	All countries	U 22-a	
limestone flux: tonnage	All countries	U 22-a	
tonnage	W Germany	U 5-a	
Limousin see CATTLE BY BREED			
Linen see WOVEN LINEN FABRICS			
LINEN INDUSTRY			
Input: flax & hemp: historical table from 1760: tonnage	Main European countries	Z 1-a	
Linen piece goods see WOVEN LINEN FABRICS			
LINEN YARN			
Production: historical table from 1796: tonnage	W Germany	Z 1-a	
Linerboard see PAPER & PAPERBOARD			
Liners see PASSENGER VESSELS			
Liners (kraft) see WRAPPING PAPER			
Lingerie see UNDERWEAR, FEMALE			
Linguistics see PHILOLOGY			
Linings & uppers see LEATHER, LIGHT			
Linoleum see FLOOR COVERING			

LINSEED

	Territorial coverage	Title codes	
Area harvested, production tonnage & yield per ha	All countries	A 9-a	
under crop in acres	Main countries	B 18-a	B 19-a
in ha	EEC countries	E 12-a	
	OAS member countries	N 13-a	
Consumption for oil crushing & for seed: tonnage	Canada & USA	B 19-a	
tonnage	Canada & USA	B 19-a	
Crop: (incl world total): tonnage	Main countries	B 18-a	
	All countries	P 1-a	
yield in 100 kg per ha	EEC countries	E 12-a	
in kg per ha	OAS member countries	N 13-a	
Export prices - index nos (weighted average main sources)	Worldwide	U 29-q	
Exports by destination: tonnage	Canada	B 19-a	
	World regions	B 2-a	
tonnage & by value in $m	Main countries	B 18-q	B 19-a
Harvest: ensuing crop yr: tonnage (estim)	Main world regions	P 1-a	
Import prices ex Canada in £ per ton at European ports		P 1-m	
UK ports		R 2-m	B 19-q
		A 9-a	B 19-a
Imports by source: tonnage	EEC countries	B 19-a	
for production of animal feed: tonnage	UK	P 5-a	
in oil conversion equiv tonnage	UK	P 1-a	
tonnage	Main countries	B 19-a	
Producer prices in $ per ton	Argentine, Uruguay & USA	A 9-a	
Production (incl world total): tonnage	All countries	B 18-a	
	African countries	U 44-a	
	EEC countries	E 12-a	
	Main countries	B 19-a	
tonnage	OAS member countries	N 13-a	
	Argentine, Brazil, Chile, Uruguay & Mexico	U 40-a	
Stocks (initial & end-yr): tonnage	Canada & USA	B 19-a	
Supply (new crop): tonnage	Canada & USA	B 19-a	
Wholesale prices in cents per 56 lbs	Canada & USA	N 10-m	R 2-m
in $ per ton	Canada, India & USA	A 9-a	
	European countries	U 27-m	
World production: tonnage		B 2-a	

LINSEED CAKE

Export prices in local currency fob	Netherlands	A 9-a	
Exports: tonnage & by value in $m	World regions	B 2-a	
Import prices in £ per ton fob	UK	A 9-a	
Imports (as animal feed): tonnage	UK	P 5-a	
Prices paid by farmers (as animal feed)	W European countries	U 30-a	
Production: tonnage	W Germany	N 10-a	
Wholesale prices (ex store) in lire per 100 kg at Milan	Italy	R 2-m	
in £ per ton	UK	P 1-a	
in cents per lb	Canada	N 10-m	

LINSEED OIL

Bonded stocks held at Rotterdam: tonnage	Netherlands	N 10-w	
Consumption for production of linoleum & oilcloth: tonnage	USA	B 19-a	
paints & varnishes: tonnage	USA	B 19-a	
printing ink & fatty acids: tonnage	USA	B 19-a	
resins: tonnage	USA	B 19-a	
tonnage	USA	B 19-a	
Export prices - index nos (weighted average main sources)	Worldwide	U 29-q	
	S American countries	U 40-q	
in local currency	Netherlands & UK	A 9-a	
Exports by destination: tonnage	Argentine, Uruguay & USA	B 19-a	
tonnage & by value in $m	World regions	B 2-a	
tonnage	Main countries	B 19-a	P 1-a
	Primary producing countries	B 18-q	
Import prices in £ per ton cif	UK	R 2-m	B 2-a
ex Argentine in £ per ton cif	UK	B 19-a	
in $ per ton	UK	A 9-a	
Imports by source: tonnage	Main European countries	B 19-a	
tonnage	Main countries	B 19-a	P 1-a
Production for current yr: tonnage (partly estim)	Main countries	P 1-a	
for ensuing yr: tonnage (estim)	World regions	P 1-a	
tonnage	Main countries	B 19-a	
	USA	B 19-a	
	W Germany	N 10-a	
Stocks (initial & end-yr): tonnage	USA	B 19-a	
Wholesale prices in cents per lb	Canada	N 10-m	
	India & USA	A 9-a	
raw linseed oil (ex tanks) in cents per lb at New York	USA	R 2-m	
in local currency	European countries	U 27-m	
World & Commonwealth production: tonnage		B 19-a	
World production: tonnage		A 4-a	A 5-a
		N 10-a	

Liquefied gas carriers (shipping)   see   BULK CARRIERS

Liquefied petroleum gas   see   NATURAL GAS LIQUIDS

Liquid detergents   see   DETERGENTS, LIQUID

	Territorial coverage	Title codes
Liquid fuels see FUELS, LIQUID		
Liquid steel (for castings or forgings) see CRUDE STEEL		
Liquidity see INTERNATIONAL LIQUIDITY		

LITERACY
    see also   ILLITERACY

Of population (over 15 yrs of age) by age groups & sex	Latin American countries	J 5-a
% adult literacy rates: population (over 15 yrs of age)	All countries	M 6-a
	Developing countries	M 4-a
	Main countries	U 23-a
urban & rural population by sex	Latin American countries	J 5-a
No of foreign pupils enrolled at special schools	All countries	U 62-a
of language teachers employed at special schools	All countries	U 62-a
of successful special school students	All countries	U 62-a

LITERATURE

No of new book titles published on literary subjects	All countries	U 62-a
	OAS member countries	N 19-a

LITHARGE
    see also   LEAD

Consumption of lead in production of red lead & litharge: tonnage	USA	T 4-a
Exports: tonnage	USA	J 6-a
Imports: tonnage	USA	J 6-a
Production: tonnage	Main countries	H 2-a

LITHIUM MINERALS

Imports & exports by source & destination: tonnage	Main countries	B 15-a	
Imports: tonnage	Main countries	T 4-a	
Production: amblygonite: tonnage	Brazil	T 4-a	
lepidolite: tonnage	Mozambique & Portugal	T 4-a	
petalite: tonnage	Australia	T 4-a	
by kind: tonnage	All countries	B 15-a	T 4-a
tonnage	Main countries	N 1-a	
Reserves: tonnage (estim)	Canada, China, African countries & USA	N 1-a	
Wholesale prices in $ per ton	USA	N 1-a	
World production: tonnage	Main countries	N 1-a	

LITHOPONE
    see also   PAINTS & VARNISHES
               PIGMENTS, MINERAL

Exports: tonnage	OECD countries	D 5-a
Imports & exports by source & destination: tonnage	All countries	B 15-a
tonnage	Main countries	H 2-a
Imports: tonnage	OECD countries	D 5-a
Production: tonnage	OECD countries	D 5-a
	France, W Germany, Italy & USSR	H 2-a

Live animals   see   LIVESTOCK

LIVE BIRTHS

No by age of mother & sex of child	All countries	U 14-a
age of mother	Asian, Far East & Australasian countries	U 45-a
	Canada, Latin American countries & USA	J 5-a
age of mother & of father	OAS member countries	N 12-a
sex by regions	OAS member countries	N 12-a
in rural areas	OAS member countries	N 12-a
in urban areas	OAS member countries	N 12-a
sex	OAS member countries	N 12-a
of illegitimate births & as % of total births	OAS member countries	N 12-a
births registered: historical tables	EEC countries	E 2-a
(with annual totals)	EEC countries	E 26-m
from earliest records	Main European countries	Z 1-a
births registered	Asian, Far East & Australasian countries	U 45-a
	Latin American countries	U 40-a
births registered per 1000 population	ECAFE countries	U 32-q
	ECE countries	U 15-a
	EEC countries	E 33-a
	Main countries	R 5-a

Liver oils, fish   see   FISH OILS & FATS

LIVESTOCK
    see also   CATTLE

% of dairy herds by breed & main purpose: meat or milk	EEC countries	B 3-a
% of EEC area livestock population	EEC countries	R 5-a
% contribution to export earnings	Upper Volta & Somalia	E 45-a
% price changes: animal feed grains	W European countries	U 30-a
% share of world import & export trade	Main countries	B 1-a
Cattle (incl breeding-cow population) projected to 1978	OECD countries	D 15-a
produced for slaughter – index nos (unit value basis)	W European countries	U 30-a
population (census data)	Main countries	C 9-a

LIVESTOCK, continued	Territorial coverage	Title codes
Changes in livestock population as % of output of livestock	ECE countries	U 34-a
Consumption per capita: beef cattle in kg	EEC countries	E 44-a
Cow population (census data)	Main countries	C 9-a
Expenditure on livestock maintenance as % of value of total farm output	ECE countries	U 34-a
Exports as % of exports of farm products (value basis)	W European countries	U 20-a
by value in $m	W European countries	U 33-a
live cattle & calves by volume	European countries	U 36-a
live cattle - index nos (quantum & value bases)	Netherlands & W Germany	C 9-m
live pigs by destination by volume	OECD countries	D 16-q
shipped to EEC & non-EEC areas by value in UA	EEC countries	E 47-m
tonnage & value in $m	EEC countries	E 24-a
Feed requirements per cow per kg of milk produced by 1985 (estim)	Mali, Somalia & Upper Volta	E 45-a
Guide prices: beef cattle in £ per cwt	Main countries	P 5-a
calves in £ per cwt	EEC countries	B 1-a
Imports as % of imports of farm products (value basis)	EEC countries	B 1-a
in local currency	W European countries	U 20-a
shipped ex EEC & non-EEC areas by value in UA	Hong Kong	U 32-m
live cattle by source	EEC countries	E 24-a
by value in $m	EEC countries	B 11-a
live cattle & calves by volume	European countries	U 33-a
live cattle - index nos (quantum & value bases)	European countries	U 36-a
Inter-EEC shipments: live pigs by volume	OECD countries	D 16-q
No of agricultural holdings by size of dairy herds	EEC countries	E 47-m
Population of livestock & no per ha of land area in use	EEC countries	B 1-a
(all kinds) in 1000 head (incl world total)	EEC countries	E 44-a
(all kinds)	Main countries	R 5-a
by kind & no per 100 ha	European countries & USSR	U 36-a
as % of total livestock	EEC countries	E 1-a
of beef cattle as % of total livestock	EEC countries	E 3-a
by regions	EEC countries	E 44-a
cattle & horses: historical table from 1816	EEC countries	E 38-a
cattle (all kinds)	Main European countries	Z 1-a
cattle, pigs, sheep & horses	OECD countries	D 1-a
cattle, pigs & sheep	All countries	U 43-a
	Developed countries	C 27-a
	Developing countries	C 27-a
	Main countries	E 3-a
	Worldwide (excl Communist countries)	C 27-a
cattle, sheep & goats	Main countries	A 18-a
cows - index nos	Main countries	B 4-a
cows	European countries	U 35-a
	OECD countries	D 1-a
dairy & beef cows, calves, bulls & heifers	EEC countries	B 1-a
dairy cows (census data)	Main countries	A 5-a
dairy cows & heifers in milk	Main countries	B 4-a
goats	OECD countries	D 1-a
horses	OECD countries	D 1-a
milking cows (incl milk yield per cow in litres)	EEC countries	E 44-a
mules & asses	OECD countries	D 1-a
mules, asses & reindeer: historical table	Main European countries	Z 1-a
pigs, sheep & goats: historical table from 1816	Main European countries	Z 1-a
pigs	OECD countries	D 1-a
poultry (all kinds)	OECD countries	D 1-a
poultry: historical table from 1816	Main European countries	Z 1-a
sheep	OECD countries	D 1-a
sows (for breeding)	OECD countries	D 1-a
Producer prices: beef cattle (at auction)	European countries	U 36-q
in cents per kg	Main countries	A 5-q
in local currency per 100 kg	W European countries	E 35-a
in $ per 100 lbs	USA	E 35-a
bullocks in local currency per kg	Eire	D 1-a
cows (for slaughter) in local currency per kg	OECD countries	D 1-a
heifers in local currency per head or kg	OECD countries	D 1-a
in £ per cwt	EEC countries	B 1-a
quality cattle (for slaughter) in local currency	EEC countries	E 44-a
steers (for slaughter) in local currency	OECD countries	D 1-a
Production as % of gross farm output (at market prices)	ECE countries	U 34-a
by value in local currency	Czechoslovakia & USSR	U 34-a
Production, imports, exports & consumption: beef cattle	EEC countries	E 44-a
Production - index nos (constant value basis)	E European countries	U 34-a
(value basis)	ECE countries	U 34-a
(volume basis)	EEC countries	E 44-a
	Latin American countries	U 40-a
Sizes of dairy herds & no of dairy farms	EEC countries	B 1-a
Slaughterings (incl average carcase weight in kg)	EEC countries	E 44-a
cattle (all types)	European countries	U 36-q
cattle, sheep, calves & lambs	Main countries	B 9-m
cattle, sheep, pigs & goats	OAS member countries	N 14-a
cattle, sheep & pigs	Main countries	B 12-m
Stocks: changes in livestock ownership as % of gross output	E European countries	U 34-a
Wholesale prices: fat cattle in £ per ton	Main countries	B 12-m
oxen & heifers in D Kr per kg	Denmark	R 2-m
young cows in D Kr per kg	Denmark	R 2-m

	Territorial coverage	Title codes	
LIVESTOCK BY KIND			
Dead wt per head in kg (average)	OAS member countries	N 14-a	
Exports by destination by CST classes: tonnage & value in $m	EEC countries	E 48-a	
SITC classes by value in $	Main countries	D 2-q	
tonnage & value in $m	OECD countries	D 3-a2	
by volume	Main countries	B 12-m	
NIMEXE classes by value in $m	All countries	E 20-a	
SITC classes by value in $m	All countries	U 50-a	U 59-a
Imports by NIMEXE classes by value in $	All countries	E 20-a	
SITC classes by value in $	All countries	U 50-a	U 59-a
source by CST classes: tonnage & value in $m	EEC countries	E 21-a	
SITC classes by value in $m	Main countries	D 2-q	
tonnage & value in $m	OECD countries	D 3-a2	
Imports: tonnage	Canada, European countries, USA & USSR	A 11-a	
Population: cattle, pigs, sheep & goats	AASM countries	E 41-a	
horses, mules, asses & camels	AASM countries	E 41-a	
in million head (census data)	E European countries	U 16-a	
	African countries	U 44-a	
	Main countries	C 9-a	
	OAS member countries	N 13-a	
on state farms & collectives in million head	USSR	B 12-a	
Producer prices - index nos	EEC countries	E 44-a	
Production: value in £m	EEC countries	B 1-a	
volume	Asian, Far East & Australasian countries	U 45-a	
Wholesale prices in local currency	OAS member countries	N 17-a	
World exports: unit value in $ per ton		A 11-a	
LIVESTOCK FARMING			
Capital formation in local currency	OAS member countries	N 16-a	
IDA loans: livestock rearing projects in $	OAS member countries	N 16-a	
Loan advances (from commercial banks) in local currency	OAS member countries	N 16-a	
LIVESTOCK PRODUCTS			
see also AQUATIC ANIMAL PRODUCTS			
EGGS, HEN			
HIDES			
MEAT			
MILK			
STATE PROCUREMENT (COMMUNIST COUNTRIES)			
WOOL			
Consumption per capita (by income levels)	USA	C 27-a	
Government expenditure: price guarantees in £m	UK	P 5-a	
Gross output by kind by value in $m	EEC countries	U 34-a	
by value in $m	EEC countries	E 44-a	
Production as % of gross farm output	E European countries	U 34-a	
by kind: tonnage	Asian, Far East & Australasian countries	U 45-a	
(less feed & cattle) - index nos	OECD countries	D 1-a	
Production - index nos	OECD countries	D 1-a	
Self-sufficiency ratios	EEC countries	E 3-a	
Wholesale prices - index nos	OAS member countries	N 17-a	
	EEC countries	E 26-m	

Livestock slaughtering premiums   see   EEC BUDGET

Living standards   see   GDP PER CAPITA
                               HOUSEHOLD BUDGETS
                               PRIVATE CONSUMPTION
                               PRIVATE EXPENDITURE

Load factors   see   AIR PASSENGER TRAFFIC

Loading capacity of holds   see   CARGO SHIPS

Loan rates (banking)   see   INTEREST RATES

Loan stocks   see   GOVERNMENT BONDS
                        MUNICIPAL BONDS
                        PRIVATE BONDS
                        SHARES & SECURITIES

Loans   see   BANK ADVANCES
              FOREIGN LOANS
              PRIVATE BORROWING
              PUBLIC LOANS

Loans & grants, bilateral   see   BILATERAL AID

Loans & grants, multilateral   see   MULTILATERAL AID

Loans, interest-free   see   DEVELOPMENT AID

Lobsters, shrimps & prawns   see   CRUSTACEANS & MOLLUSCS

	Territorial coverage	Title codes

LOCAL AUTHORITIES
    see also   REGIONAL AUTHORITIES

Debt position in local currency	Main countries	R 5-a
Expenditure on highway research in local currency	Main countries	S 24-a
new road construction in local currency	Main countries	S 24-a
road maintenance in local currency	Main countries	S 24-a
Income transfers from central government in local currency	EEC countries	E 32-a
Labour force employed in local government	India	U 32-q
Loan advances (from commercial banks) in local currency	OAS member countries	N 16-a
(from acceptance houses) in $	All countries	F 5-m F 6-q
Receipts & expenditure of municipalities in local currency	Main countries	R 5-a
Revenue by source in local currency	EEC countries	E 42-a

LOCAL GOVERNMENT SERVICES

Labour force employed by local authorities by sex	EEC countries	E 18-a
No of hrs worked per wk by municipal employees by sex	EEC countries	E 18-a

Lock-outs   see   STRIKES & LOCK-OUTS

Locks & fittings   see   METAL PRODUCTS

LOCOMOTIVE & ROLLING STOCK INDUSTRY

Investment in buildings in local currency	EEC countries	E 40-a
machinery in local currency	EEC countries	E 40-a
No of hrs worked per wk	Main countries	R 3-m
Wage rates per hr by sex in local currency	Main countries	R 3-m

Locomotive wheels & axles   see   WHEELS TYRES AXLES, STEEL

LOCOMOTIVES
    see also   RAILWAY TRAINS
                ROLLING STOCK

Exports by type by volume	OECD countries	D 9-a
No in use by traction power	Developing countries	U 57-a
by type: steam, diesel & electric traction	S American countries	U 40-a
	EEC countries	E 43-a
	European countries	U 8-a
	African countries	U 44-a
(all types)	Main countries	R 5-a
Production by volume: diesel & electric locomotives	E European countries	U 16-a
	EEC countries	E 28-q E 27-a
World exports: steam locomotives by value in $m		U 38-a

LOCOMOTIVES, DIESEL

Production by volume & engine hp	All countries	U 22-a U 38-a

LOCOMOTIVES, ELECTRIC

Exports by destination by value in $	Main countries	U 9-a
value in $m	All countries	U 38-a
Imports by value in $m	All countries	U 38-a
Production by volume & engine hp	All countries	U 22-a U 38-a
World export trade by value in $m		U 38-a

LOCOMOTIVES, STEAM

Exports by destination by value in $m	Main countries	U 9-a
value in $m	All countries	U 38-a
Imports by value in $m	All countries	U 38-a
World export trade by value in $m		U 38-a

Lodgings   see   DWELLINGS
                    HOUSING

Logs   see   HARDWOOD LOGS
            SOFTWOOD LOGS
            TIMBER

Looms   see   TEXTILE MACHINERY

Lorries   see   COMMERCIAL VEHICLES

Loss at sea   see   ACCIDENTS, MARITIME

LOSSES, COMMERCIAL

Claims paid out by insurance companies in local currency	OAS member countries	N 16-a

LOST WORKING DAYS
    see also   SHORT-TIME WORKING

Motor vehicle industry: % due to absence (authorised)	UK	B 28-a
(unauthorised)	UK	B 28-a
certified sickness	UK	B 28-a
lay-off (by management)	UK	B 28-a
strikes (external)	UK	B 28-a
(internal)	UK	B 28-a
waiting time	UK	B 28-a

	Territorial coverage	Title codes

Lotions & medicinal creams   see   MEDICAMENTS

Lotteries   see   STATE LOTTERIES

Lottery taxes   see   TAXATION

LUBRICATING OIL
    Consumption in litres   OAS member countries   N 17-a
              tonnage   Main countries   C 14-a
                  (total) & from own plants: tonnage   Italy   H 4-a
    Deliveries for home consumption & export: tonnage   OECD countries   D 31-a
    Imports & exports by source & destination: tonnage   All countries   B 15-a
    Imports by source: tonnage   OECD countries   D 31-a
              (incl greases): tonnage   Main countries   C 14-a
    Production by volume in m³   OAS member countries   N 14-a
                        EEC countries   E 28-q   E 27-a
              (incl greases): tonnage   All countries   U 22-a   U 43-a
              tonnage   Latin American countries   J 5-a
                    Main countries   B 15-a
    Refinery output, imports & supply: tonnage   OECD countries   D 31-a
    Retail prices in cents per gallon   Main countries   C 3-a
              local currency   OAS member countries   N 17-a
    Tax receipts by government levied on vehicle lubricants   Main countries   S 24-a
    Wholesale prices in local currency   OAS member countries   N 17-a

LUCERNE
    Area under crop in ha   EEC countries   E 12-a
    Production (incl grass for hay): tonnage   EEC countries   P 5-a
              tonnage   EEC countries   B 1-a   E 12-a
    Yield (as green animal fodder) in kg per ha   EEC countries   B 1-a   E 3-a
             E 12-a   E 44-a

LUGGAGE, LEATHER
    % consumption of light leather hides in production of luggage   USA   A 18-a

Lumber   see   TIMBER

Lump sulphide   see   ANTIMONY ORE

Lunacy   see   MENTAL WELFARE

Lutetium   see   RARE EARTH MINERALS

Lysine   see   PROTEIN

MACARONI & SPAGHETTI
    Production: tonnage   EEC countries   E 28-q   E 27-a
          All countries   U 22-a
    Retail prices in local currency   OAS member countries   N 17-a

Mace   see   SPICES & ESSENCES

Machine operatives   see   PRODUCTION WORKERS

MACHINE TOOLS
    see also   BORING MACHINES
                 CAPSTAN LATHES
                 CENTRE LATHES, MULTI-SPINDLE
                 CENTRE LATHES, SINGLE-SPINDLE
                 DRILLING MACHINES
                 GEAR PRODUCTION MACHINES
                 GRINDING MACHINES
                 LATHES, AUTOMATIC
                 LATHES, NON-AUTOMATIC
                 LATHES, VERTICAL BORING
                 MILLING MACHINES
                 MILLING MACHINES, HORIZONTAL

                 PRESSES, HYDRAULIC
                 PRESSES, MECHANICAL
                 PUNCH & SHEARING MACHINES
                 SAW & FILE MACHINES
                 THREAD & TAP MACHINES
                 TRANSFER MACHINES
                 TURNING MACHINES

    % change: consumption projected to 1977   UK   B 26
               export growth projected to 1977   UK   B 26
               home deliveries projected to 1977   UK   B 26
               imports projected to 1977   UK   B 26
               output (value basis) projected to 1977   UK   B 26
               sales by type of machine tool   EEC countries   B 31-a
    % increase in consumption (value basis)   EEC countries   B 20-a
              in production: all types (value basis)   EEC countries   B 20-a

	Territorial coverage	Title codes
MACHINE TOOLS, continued		
Consumption: by value in £m	EEC countries	B 20-a
in $m	EEC countries	B 31-a
	Main countries	J 2-a
boring machines by supply area by value in $m	EEC countries	B 31-a
by value in $m	EEC countries	B 31-a
drilling machines by supply area by value in $m	EEC countries	B 31-a
by value in $m	EEC countries	B 31-a
gear production machines by supply area by value in $m	EEC countries	B 31-a
value in $m	EEC countries	B 31-a
grinding machines by supply area by value in $m	EEC countries	B 31-a
by value in $m	EEC countries	B 31-a
increase projected to 1985 by value in $	EEC countries	B 20-a
presses by supply area by value in $m	EEC countries	B 31-a
by value in $m	EEC countries	B 31-a
projected to 1985 by value in $m	EEC countries	B 20-a
Deliveries by volume & value in $m	USA	J 2-a
(domestic): boring machines by value in $m	EEC countries	B 31-a
centre lathes by value in $m	EEC countries	B 31-a
drilling machines by value in $m	EEC countries	B 31-a
gear production machines by value in $m	EEC countries	B 31-a
grinding machines by value in $m	EEC countries	B 31-a
guillotine shears by value in $m	EEC countries	B 31-a
lathes (automatic) by value in $m	EEC countries	B 31-a
(multi-spindle) by value in $m	EEC countries	B 31-a
(single spindle) by value in $m	EEC countries	B 31-a
milling machines by value in $m	EEC countries	B 31-a
press brakes by value in $m	EEC countries	B 31-a
presses (hydraulic) by value in $m	EEC countries	B 31-a
(mechanical) by value in $m	EEC countries	B 31-a
punch & shearing machines by value in $m	EEC countries	B 31-a
metal-cutting type (for export) by value in $m	USA	J 2-a
metal-cutting type (for home market) by value in $m	USA	J 2-a
metal-forming type (for export) by value in $m	USA	J 2-a
metal-forming type (for home market) by value in $m	USA	J 2-a
Exports (all types) by value in £m	EEC countries	B 20-a
as % of production (value basis)	EEC countries	B 31-a
by destination: boring machines by value in £m	UK	B 31-a
drilling machines by value in £m	UK	B 31-a
horizontal borer-millers by value in $m	EEC countries	B 20-a
lathes (all types) by value in £m	UK	B 31-a
machining centres by value in £m	UK	B 31-a
milling machines by value in £m	UK	B 31-a
by value in £m	EEC countries	B 20-a
in $m	EEC countries	B 31-a
by world regions by value in £m	Main countries	U 9-a
by value in £m	EEC countries	B 20-a
in £m	UK	B 20-a
	ECE countries	U 15-a
in $m	EEC countries	B 31-a
	Main countries	U 38-a
shipped to EEC area by value in £m	UK	B 31-a
to EFTA area by value in £m	UK	B 31-a
Imports as % of consumption (value basis)	EEC countries	B 20-a B 31-a
	Main countries	J 2-a
by source: boring machines by volume	UK	B 31-a
by value in £m	EEC countries	B 20-a
in $m	EEC countries	B 31-a
drilling machines by value in £m	UK	B 31-a
lathes (all types) by value in £m	UK	B 31-a
machining centres by value in £m	UK	B 31-a
metal-cutting machine tools by value in $m	USA	J 2-a
	EEC countries	B 31-a
metal-forming machine tools by value in $m	USA	J 2-a
metal-working machine tools by value in $m	EEC countries	B 31-a
milling machines by value in £m	UK	B 31-a
ex EEC & EFTA areas by value in £m	UK	B 20-a
EEC countries by value in £m	UK	B 31-a
EFTA countries by value in £m	UK	B 31-a
by value in £m	EEC countries	B 20-a
in $m	EEC countries	B 31-a
	All countries	U 38-a
Investment: mechanical engineering industry per employee in $	EEC countries	B 20-a
Labour costs of production per hr	EEC countries	E 2-a
New orders & deliveries: metal-cutting machine tools by value in $	USA	J 3-m
metal-forming machine tools by value in $	USA	J 3-m
New orders: metal-cutting machine tools (for domestic market) by value in $m	USA	J 2-a
(for export) by value in $m	USA	J 2-a
metal-forming machine tools (for export) by value in $m	USA	J 2-a
(for home market) by value in $m	USA	J 2-a
No in storage (i.e. surplus to current industrial needs)	USA	J 2-a
in use (total) & no of imported machine tools in use	EEC countries	B 31-a
by 5 yr age groups	Italy & UK	B 20-a
by kind	Main S American countries & USA	U 38-a

	Territorial coverage	Title codes
MACHINE TOOLS, continued		
No in use in electrical engineering plants	USA	J 2-a
metal furniture-making factories	USA	J 2-a
metal-working industry (for cutting)	USA	J 2-a
(for forming)	USA	J 2-a
non-metal-working industries (for cutting)	USA	J 2-a
(for forming)	USA	J 2-a
ordnance factories	USA	J 2-a
plants for metal products fabrication	USA	J 2-a
precision instruments industry	USA	J 2-a
transport equipment manufacturing plants	USA	J 2-a
Prices - index nos	W Germany, Italy & UK	B 31-a
Production (all types) by value in £m	EEC countries	B 20-a
by value (all types) in $m	EEC countries	B 31-a
automatic lathes (multi-spindle) in $m	EEC countries	B 31-a
(single spindle) in $m	EEC countries	B 31-a
boring machines in $m	EEC countries	B 31-a
centre lathes in $m	EEC countries	B 31-a
drilling machines in $m	EEC countries	B 31-a
gear production machines in $m	EEC countries	B 31-a
grinding machines in $m	EEC countries	B 31-a
guillotine shears in $m	EEC countries	B 31-a
lathes (non-automatic) in $m	EEC countries	B 31-a
milling machines in $m	EEC countries	B 31-a
press brakes in $m	EEC countries	B 31-a
presses (hydraulic) in $m	EEC countries	B 31-a
(mechanical) in $m	EEC countries	B 31-a
punch & shearing machines in $m	EEC countries	B 31-a
sawing & cutting machines in $m	W Germany	B 31-a
section-forming machines in $m	UK	B 31-a
transfer machines in $m	EEC countries	B 31-a
wire-working machines in $m	UK	B 31-a
by volume by type	EEC countries	E 28-q E 27-a
by volume: drilling machines	EEC countries	B 31-a
horizontal borer-millers	EEC countries	B 31-a
lathes (all types)	EEC countries	B 31-a
machines for contouring control	EEC countries	B 31-a
machines for metal-cutting	E European countries	U 16-a
machines for position control	EEC countries	B 31-a
machining centres	EEC countries	B 31-a
milling machines	EEC countries	B 31-a
Value added in manufacture in $m	OECD countries	D 9-a
Wholesale prices: metal-cutting type - index nos	USA	J 2-a
metal-forming type - index nos	USA	J 2-a
MACHINE TOOLS, AUTOMATIC		
% of consumption by aerospace industry	EEC countries	B 20-a
electrical engineering industry	EEC countries	B 20-a
instrument engineering industry	EEC countries	B 20-a
mechanical engineering industry	EEC countries	B 20-a
motor vehicle manufacturing industry	EEC countries	B 20-a
shipbuilding & repairing industry	EEC countries	B 20-a
% share of imports ex EEC area	EEC countries	B 20-a
Exports by destination by volume	EEC countries	B 20-a
by volume & value in $m	EEC countries	B 20-a
Imports by source by type by value in £m	UK	B 20-a
by type by volume	EEC countries	B 20-a
No in use & no imported	France, W Germany & UK	B 20-a
by region & by function	USA	J 2-a
(multi-purpose type)	USA	J 2-a
in use	France, W Germany & UK	B 20-a
of numerically-controlled type in use by industrial sector	USA	J 2-a
Production by type by volume	EEC countries	B 20-a
Production: contouring control type by volume	EEC countries	B 20-a
numerically-controlled types as % of total	EEC countries	B 20-a
by volume & value in $m	EEC countries	B 20-a
position control type	EEC countries	B 20-a
Sales: numerically-controlled type: no & value in $m	USA	J 2-a
Machine tools, numerically-controlled see MACHINE TOOLS, AUTOMATIC		
MACHINE TOOLS BY TYPE		
% growth in domestic sales	EEC countries	B 20-a
in import & export trade	EEC countries	B 20-a
production	EEC countries	B 20-a
Deliveries (domestic market) by value in $m	EEC countries	B 20-a
Exports as % of production (value basis)	EEC countries	B 31-a
by destination by CST classes: tonnage & value in $m	EEC countries	E 48-a
SITC classes: tonnage & value in $m	OECD countries	D 3-a2
value in $m	Main countries	D 2-q
tonnage & value in $m	All countries	U 12-a
by NIMEXE classes: volume & value in $m	All countries	E 20-a
SITC classes by volume & value in $m	All countries	U 50-a U 59-a
by value in $m	EEC countries	B 20-a
shipped ex EEC area (in detail) by value in $m	EEC countries	J 2-a
Imports as % of consumption (value basis)	EEC countries	B 31-a

	Territorial coverage	Title codes	
MACHINE TOOLS BY TYPE, continued			
Imports by NIMEXE classes by volume & value in $m	All countries	E 20-a	
SITC classes by volume & value in $m	All countries	U 50-a	U 59-a
by source by CST classes: tonnage & value in $m	EEC countries	E 21-a	
SITC classes by value in $m	Main countries	D 2-q	
tonnage & value in $m	OECD countries	D 3-a2	
by value in £m	EEC countries	B 20-a	
tonnage & value in $m	All countries	U 12-a	
by value in $m	EEC countries	B 20-a	J 2-a
No in use by age (in detail)	USA	J 2-a	
region for boring, drilling, milling & turning	USA	J 2-a	
(multi-purpose type)	USA	J 2-a	
Production by value in $m	EEC countries	B 20-a	
volume & value in $m	EEC countries	B 31-a	
Relative competitiveness with EEC firms: assessment	Main countries	J 2-a	
Sales (under military contract) by value in $m	UK	B 31-a	
	USA	J 2-a	
MACHINE TOOLS INDUSTRY			
% distribution by size of labour force employed	EEC countries	B 20-a	
% increases in output per man employed	EEC countries	B 31-a	
% usage of machine tool park	EEC countries	B 20-a	
Assets of machine tool corporations as % of liabilities	USA	J 2-a	
Capital expenditure: buildings in $m	USA	J 2-a	
machinery & equipment in $m	USA	J 2-a	
Consumption: iron castings: tonnage	UK	B 25-a	
steel castings: tonnage	UK	B 25-a	
Cost of materials used in $m	USA	J 2-a	
Costs: salaried staff per mth	EEC countries	E 11-a	
Deliveries: metal-working machine tools by value in $m	USA	J 2-m	
Depreciation of corporate assets as % of liabilities	USA	J 2-a	
Earnings of corporations as % of sales turnover	USA	J 2-a	
per employee in $ per yr (average)	USA	J 2-a	
per hr by sex	Main countries	R 3-a	
per hr per man employed - index nos	EEC countries	B 31-a	
Income (net) as % of assets (after tax)	USA	J 2-a	
as % of sales turnover	USA	J 2-a	
Investment in buildings in local currency	EEC countries	E 40-a	
land purchase in local currency	EEC countries	E 40-a	
machinery in local currency	EEC countries	E 40-a	
Labour costs as % of total costs	EEC countries	E 8-a	
by status of employees in local currency	EEC countries	E 8-a	
in DM million	W Germany	H 3-a	
in local currency per hr (all employees)	EEC countries	E 11-a	
(wage earners)	EEC countries	E 11-a	
per man-hr in $	EEC countries	B 31-a	
per unit of output in $	EEC countries	B 31-a	
Labour force employed: metal-cutting sector	USA	J 2-a	
metal-forming sector	USA	J 2-a	
no of production workers	USA	J 2-a	
salaried staff	EEC countries	E 11-a	
wage earners	EEC countries	E 11-a	
Labour force employed in machine tool industry	EEC countries	E 8-a	
	USA	J 2-a	
Materials used in machine tool production by kind: tonnage	USA	J 2-a	
New orders received: metal-working machine tools by value in $m	USA	J 2-m	
No of firms in operation by size of labour force employed	EEC countries	B 20-a	
with labour force of over 20 employees	USA	J 2-a	
of hrs worked (as overtime) per wk	USA	J 2-a	
per wk	Main countries	R 3-m	
per wk by region	EEC countries	E 25-a	
per wk by sector of industry	USA	J 2-a	
per yr (all employees)	EEC countries	E 8-a	
salaried staff	EEC countries	E 11-a	
wage earners	EEC countries	E 11-a	
of man-hrs of work performed per yr	USA	J 2-a	
of manufacturing firms in operation	EEC countries	B 20-a	
of numerically-controlled types of tools	EEC countries	B 20-a	
of times inventory turned by corporations	USA	J 2-a	
of production workers as % of total labour force employed	USA	J 2-a	
Orders on hand: metal-working machine tools by value in $m	USA	J 2-m	
Production - index nos	Main countries	R 5-a	
Profits of machine tool corporations as % of sales turnover	USA	J 2-a	
Turnover: home & export sales by value in $m	USA	J 2-a	
in DM million	W Germany	H 3-a	
in $m	USA	J 2-a	
Value added in manufacture of machine tools in $m	USA	J 2-a	
per employee per yr & per man-hr	USA	J 2-a	
Wage rates by sex - index nos	Main countries	R 3-a	
in local currency per hr	EEC countries	E 25-a2	
in DM per hr	W Germany	H 3-a	
per hr by sex	Main countries	R 3-m	
skilled workers by sex in local currency	Main countries	R 4-q	
unskilled workers by sex in local currency	Main countries	R 4-q	
Wages costs as % of value added in manufacture	USA	J 2-a	

MACHINERY

	Territorial coverage	Title codes	
% change: exports (incl transport equipment) by destination	EEC countries	E 23-a	
imports (incl transport equipment) by source	EEC countries	E 23-a	
% growth rates: investment in machinery & equipment	Developing countries	D 25-a	
projected to 1980	OECD countries	D 11	
output of machinery	Developing countries	U 38-a	
% of production by type	Canada, European countries, Japan & USA	U 38-a	
As % of total fixed capital investment	All countries	M 6-a	
As component in capital formation by industrial sector	Main countries	U 21-a	
By kind: exports by destination by CST classes: tonnage & value in $	EEC countries	E 48-a	
SITC classes by value in $	Main countries	D 2-q	
tonnage & value in $	OECD countries	D 3-a2	
tonnage & value in $	All countries	U 12-a	
(incl transport equipment) by value in $m	ECE countries	U 15-a	
special purpose equipment by value in $	OECD countries	D 9-a	
freight: imports & exports by rail: tonnage	EEC countries	E 43-a	
by road: tonnage	EEC countries	E 43-a	
by sea: tonnage	EEC countries	E 43-a	
imports by source by CST classes: tonnage & value in $	EEC countries	E 21-a	
SITC classes by value in $	Main countries	D 2-q	
tonnage & value in $	OECD countries	D 3-a2	
tonnage & value in $	All countries	U 12-a	
production by volume by purpose of machine	EEC countries	E 28-q	E 27-a
Coastal seaborne freight: machinery by kind: tonnage	EEC countries	E 43-a	
Coefficients of demand by industrial sector	Main countries	U 38-a	
Consumption by value in $m	Main Latin American countries	U 38-a	
Equipment & plant as assets in capital formation in local currency	EEC countries	E 32-a	
Expenditure: % changes in implicit deflator	Developed countries	D 25-a	
as % of gross domestic product	Developing countries	D 25-a	
on capital equipment in $m by industry	USA	J 2-a	
in $m	Developing countries	D 25-a	
Exports by destination (incl transport equipment) by value in $m	EEC countries	E 23-a	
by value in $m	Main countries	U 9-a	
sea, inland waterways, road, rail & air: tonnage	European countries	U 8-a	
value in $m	Main countries	E 24-a	
	Australia, Hong Kong & Japan	U 32-m	
Exports (excl electrical machinery) by value in $m	ECE countries	U 15-a	
(incl transport equipment) by value in $m	World regions	U 23-a	
to non-EEC area by value in UA	EEC countries	E 24-a	
by value in $	Asian & Far East countries	U 32-a	
non-electrical machines by value in $m	Main countries	U 38-a	
shipped ex developed countries by value in $m	World regions	U 52-a	
to Communist area by value in $m	Developing countries	U 52-a	
to EEC & non-EEC areas by value in $m	EEC countries	E 24-a	
Exports - index nos (quantum & value bases)	OECD countries	D 16-q	
Imports by sea, inland waterways, road, rail & air: tonnage	European countries	U 8-a	
Imports by source (incl transport equipment) by value in $m	EEC countries	E 23-a	
value in $m	Main countries	E 24-a	
	All countries	U 38-a	
	Main Latin American countries	U 38-a	
	African, Caribbean countries & Pacific Is	E 45-a	
in local currency	ECAFE countries	U 32-m	
ex EEC & non-EEC areas by value in $m	EEC countries	E 24-a	
ex EEC area by value in UA	African, Caribbean countries & Pacific Is	E 45-a	
Imports (incl accessories) by value in UA	AASM countries	E 41-a	
ex EEC area by value in UA	AASM countries	E 41-a	
(incl transport equipment) ex non-EEC area by value in UA	EEC countries	E 24-a	
Imports - index nos (quantum & value basis)	OECD countries	D 16-q	
Inter-EEC exports (incl transport equipment) by value in UA	EEC countries	E 22-m	E 24-a
imports (incl transport equipment) by value in UA	EEC countries	E 22-m	E 24-a
Investment by baking & confectionery industry in local currency	EEC countries	E 40-a	
brewing industry in local currency	EEC countries	E 40-a	
building industry in local currency	EEC countries	E 40-a	
building materials manufacturing industry in local currency	EEC countries	E 40-a	
cement & plaster manufacturing industry in local currency	EEC countries	E 40-a	
ceramics manufacturing industry in local currency	EEC countries	E 40-a	
chemical industry in local currency	EEC countries	E 40-a	
clothing manufacturing industry in local currency	EEC countries	E 40-a	
coal mining industry in local currency	EEC countries	E 40-a	
cotton textile manufacturing industry in local currency	EEC countries	E 40-a	
distilleries & malting industry in local currency	EEC countries	E 40-a	
electrical engineering industry in local currency	EEC countries	E 40-a	
electronics industry in local currency	EEC countries	E 40-a	
engineering industries (all products) in local currency	EEC countries	E 40-a	
farm machinery manufacturing industry in local currency	EEC countries	E 40-a	
flour milling industry in local currency	EEC countries	E 40-a	
food processing industry in local currency	EEC countries	E 40-a	
footwear manufacturing industry in local currency	EEC countries	E 40-a	
fur manufacturing industry in local currency	EEC countries	E 40-a	
gas supply industry in local currency	EEC countries	E 40-a	
glass manufacturing industry in local currency	EEC countries	E 40-a	
industrial enterprises (all kinds) in local currency	EEC countries	E 40-a	
iron & steel industry by sector in local currency	EEC countries	E 40-a	
jewellery manufacturing industry in local currency	EEC countries	E 40-a	
jute product manufacturing industry in local currency	EEC countries	E 40-a	

	Territorial coverage	Title codes

MACHINERY, continued
    Investment by knitting mills in local currency   EEC countries   E 40-a
        leather goods manufacturing industry in local currency   EEC countries   E 40-a
        leather tanneries in local currency   EEC countries   E 40-a
        lignite mines (incl Briquetting industry) in local currency   EEC countries   E 40-a
        locomotive & rolling stock manufacturing industry in local currency   EEC countries   E 40-a
        machine tools manufacturing industry in local currency   EEC countries   E 40-a
        man-made fibres manufacturing industry in local currency   EEC countries   E 40-a
        manufacturing industry (all products) in local currency   EEC countries   E 40-a
        marine engineering industry in local currency   EEC countries   E 40-a
        mechanical engineering industry in local currency   EEC countries   E 40-a
        metals fabrication industry in local currency   EEC countries   E 40-a
        motor cycle manufacturing industry in local currency   EEC countries   E 40-a
        musical instruments manufacturing industry in local currency   EEC countries   E 40-a
        non-ferrous metals industry in local currency   EEC countries   E 40-a
        non-metallic mineral industry in local currency   EEC countries   E 40-a
        office machinery manufacturing industry in local currency   EEC countries   E 40-a
        optical instruments manufacturing industry in local currency   EEC countries   E 40-a
        ore mining industry in local currency   EEC countries   E 40-a
        paper & board manufacturing industry in local currency   EEC countries   E 40-a
        petroleum & natural gas industries in local currency   EEC countries   E 40-a
        petroleum refineries in local currency   EEC countries   E 40-a
        plastics manufacturing industry in local currency   EEC countries   E 40-a
        power stations in local currency   EEC countries   E 40-a
        printing & publishing industry in local currency   EEC countries   E 40-a
        public utilities (all undertakings) in local currency   EEC countries   E 40-a
        rubber processing industry in local currency   EEC countries   E 40-a
        shipyards, shipbuilding & repairing industries in local currency   EEC countries   E 40-a
        silk processing industry in local currency   EEC countries   E 40-a
        sugar refining industry in local currency   EEC countries   E 40-a
        textile machinery manufacturing industry in local currency   EEC countries   E 40-a
        timber & sawmill industry in local currency   EEC countries   E 40-a
        toys & sports goods manufacturing industries in local currency   EEC countries   E 40-a
        watch-making industry in local currency   EEC countries   E 40-a
        wire & cable manufacturing industries in local currency   EEC countries   E 40-a
        wood-working industry in local currency   EEC countries   E 40-a
        woollen textile manufacturing industry in local currency   EEC countries   E 40-a
    coke ovens in local currency   EEC countries   E 40-a
    machinery & equipment as % expenditure of gross national product   OECD countries   D 11
Production: machinery as % of total industrial production   Developing countries   U 38-a
    non-electrical machinery - index nos   OECD countries   D 19-m   D 20-m
        projected by value in $m to 1980   N African countries   U 38
Production - index nos (quantum basis)   S American countries   U 40-a
Purchase of machinery as % share in capital formation   Developing countries   U 38-a
Rail freight: machinery by kind (inland & abroad): tonnage   EEC countries   E 43-a
Road transport: machinery by kind over frontiers: tonnage   EEC countries   E 43-a
Shipments of machinery through Panama Canal westwards: tonnage   D 28-a

MACHINERY, AGRICULTURAL
    see also   COMBINED HARVESTER-THRESHERS
                  CULTIVATING MACHINES
                  DAIRY EQUIPMENT
                  MILKING MACHINES
                  PLOUGHS
                  SEEDERS & PLANTERS
                  THRESHING MACHINES

%share of world exports   UK   B 27-a
        exports shipped to developed countries   All countries   U 38-a
            developing countries   All countries   U 38-a
Capital formation: farm equipment   E European countries   U 34-a
Capital investment - index nos   ECE countries   U 34-a
Consumption: tonnage   Central African countries   U 38
Cost of equipment maintenance (incl buildings)   EEC countries   E 44-a
Cost to farmers - index nos   EEC countries   E 44-a
Deliveries (ex works): combined harvester-threshers   USSR   U 16-a
        farm tractors   USSR   U 16-a
Depreciation allowances as % of total allowances   ECE countries   U 34-a
Exports by destination by CST classes by value in $ EEC countries   E 48-a
        by kind: tonnage & value in $m   All countries   U 12-a
        by SITC classes by value in $ Main countries   D 2-q
            tonnage & value in $m   OECD countries   D 3-a2
        tonnage & value in $m   All countries   U 12-a

	Territorial coverage	Title codes	
MACHINERY, AGRICULTURAL continued			
Exports by NIMEXE classes: volume & value in $m	All countries	E 20-a	
SITC classes: volume & value in $m	All countries	U 50-a	U 59-a
by value in $m	Main countries	U 38-a	
Exports: farm equipment by value in $	OECD countries	D 9-a	
Fixed assets on farms (at cost) in $m	E European countries	U 34-a	
Gross capital formation in $m	ECE countries	U 34-a	
Imports by NIMEXE classes: volume & value in $m	All countries	E 20-a	
SITC classes: volume & value in $m	All countries	U 50-a	U 59-a
Imports by source by CST classes: tonnage & value in $m	EEC countries	E 21-a	
kind: tonnage & value in $m	All countries	U 12-a	
SITC classes by value in $m	Main countries	D 2-q	
tonnage & value in $m	OECD countries	D 3-a2	
Imports by source: tonnage & value in $m	All countries	U 12-a	
value in $m	All countries	U 38-a	
Labour costs of production & tractor costs (comparative)	EEC countries	E 2-a	
No of current licences in force: diggers	UK	V 1-q	
mowers	UK	V 1-q	
agricultural machines by kind in use	EEC countries	E 3-a	
	OAS member countries	N 13-a	
combine harvesters in use	USSR	U 16-a	
farm tractors in use	OAS member countries	N 13-a	
	USSR	U 16-a	
single-axle farm implements in use	Main countries	R 5-a	
Production as % of total machinery production (value basis)	Main countries	U 38-a	
by volume by kind	All countries	U 22-a	U 38-a
Registrations: new diggers	N Ireland & UK	V 1-q	
new mowers	N Ireland	V 1-q	
Retail prices: farm implements by kind	Main countries	A 9-a	
Value added in manufacture of farm machinery in $m	OECD countries	D 9-a	
World exports by value in $m		U 38-a	
MACHINERY, ELECTRICAL			
see also ELECTRIC MOTORS			
ELECTRIC POWER EQUIPMENT			
FURNACES, ELECTRIC			
HYDRAULIC TURBINE GENERATORS			
METERS, ELECTRICITY SUPPLY			
STEAM TURBINE GENERATORS			
SWITCHGEAR, ELECTRIC			
TRANSFORMERS			
% demand increase projected to 1977	UK	B 23	
% growth rates in output	Developing countries	U 38-a	
% share of world exports	Main countries	B 23-a	
Consumption by value in $m	Main Latin American countries	U 38-a	
Exports by destination by value in $m	Main countries	U 9-a	
type by value in $m	OECD countries	D 9-a	
value in $m	ECE countries	U 15-a	
	Main countries	U 38-a	
shipped to EEC & non-EEC areas by value in $	EEC countries	E 24-a	
Growth in production capacity: tonnage	African countries	U 38-a	
Imports by value in local currency	Iran	U 32-m	
in $m	All countries	U 38-a	
	Main Latin American countries	U 38-a	
ex EEC & non-EEC areas by value in $m	EEC countries	E 24-a	
Labour costs of production per hr in local currency	EEC countries	E 2-a	
Production as % of world output	Developing countries	U 38-a	
- index nos (quantum basis)	S American countries	U 40-a	
Receipts: steel supplies by electrical machinery industry: tonnage	OECD countries	D 22-a	
Value added in manufacture of electrical machines in $m	OECD countries	D 9-a	
World exports: power machinery by value in $m		U 38-a	
MACHINERY, ELECTRICAL BY TYPE			
Exports by destination by CST classes by value in $	EEC countries	E 48-a	
SITC classes: tonnage & value in $	OECD countries	D 3-a2	
by value in $	Main countries	D 2-q	
tonnage & value in $m	All countries	U 12-a	
NIMEXE classes: volume & value in $m	All countries	E 20-a	
SITC classes: volume & value in $m	All countries	U 50-a	U 59-a
Imports by NIMEXE classes: volume & value in $m	All countries	E 20-a	
SITC classes: volume & value in $m	All countries	U 50-a	U 59-a
source by CST classes by value in $m	EEC countries	E 21-a	
SITC classes by value in $m	Main countries	D 2-q	
tonnage & value in $m	OECD countries	D 3-a2	
tonnage & value in $m	All countries	U 12-a	
Production by volume	All countries	U 38-a	
MACHINERY, MARINE			
Exports by destination by value in million yen	Japan	S 16-a	
Production by kind by value in million yen	Japan	S 16-a	

Machinery hire, agricultural   see   FARM SERVICES

Machinery industry   see   ENGINEERING INDUSTRY

Machining centres   see   MACHINE TOOLS

	Territorial coverage	Title codes	
Mackerel see FISH			
Mackintoshes see OUTERWEAR, WEATHERPROOF			
Made-up clothing see CLOTHING, READY-MADE			

MAGNESITE
    see also   DOLOMITE

	Territorial coverage	Title codes	
Imports & exports by source & destination: tonnage	Main countries	B 15-a	
Production: crude magnesite: tonnage	All countries	B 15-a	U 22-a
		U 43-a	
World production: tonnage		N 4-a	
World reserves: tonnage (estim)	Main countries	N 1-a	

MAGNESIUM
    see also   INGOTS, MAGNESIUM

	Territorial coverage	Title codes	
% consumption in production of castings	USA	N 1-a	
chemicals	USA	N 1-a	
Consumption in production of aluminium alloys: tonnage	USA	T 4-a	
chemical products & deoxidisers: tonnage	USA	T 4-a	
die & mould castings: tonnage	USA	T 4-a	
reducing agents: tonnage	USA	T 4-a	
rods & extrusions: tonnage	USA	T 4-a	
sand castings: tonnage	USA	T 4-a	
zinc alloys: tonnage	USA	T 4-a	
Consumption: magnesium (metallic): tonnage	USA	N 1-a	
(non-metallic): tonnage	USA	N 1-a	
primary magnesium metal in ingot equiv tonnage	USA	J 6-a	
Exports by destination: tonnage	Main countries	T 4-a	
unwrought metallic magnesium: tonnage	Italy	C 12-a	
Exports: magnesium (metallic): tonnage	All countries	B 15-a	
Government strategic stockpile: tonnage	USA	N 1-a	
Import prices: magnesium ingots in £ per ton cif	UK	C 12-m	
Imports by source: unwrought magnesium (metallic): tonnage	Italy	C 12-a	
	Main countries	T 4-a	
Producer prices: magnesium ingots in cents per lb	USA	C 12-m	
	UK & USA	H 2-a	
Production: magnesium (metallic): tonnage	USA	N 1-a	
(non-metallic): tonnage	USA	N 1-a	
primary & secondary metal: tonnage	USA	J 6-a	N 1-a
tonnage	All countries	B 15-a	
	OAS member countries	N 14-a	
Stocks: magnesium (metallic): tonnage	USA	N 1-a	
Wholesale prices in cents per lb	USA	N 1-a	
in Frs per kg	France	T 4-m	
in lire per kg (ex works)	Italy	T 4-w	
magnesium ingots in lire per kg	Italy	C 12-m	
World production (based on metal content of ore): tonnage	Worldwide	C 12-a	C 30-a
		N 4-a	
tonnage	All countries	J 6-a	N 1-a
		T 4-a	

Magnesium bars & rounds   see   MAGNESIUM PRODUCTS, SEMI-FINISHED

Magnesium carbonate   see   MAGNESITE

Magnesium castings   see   CASTINGS, MAGNESIUM

Magnesium ore   see   MAGNESITE

MAGNESIUM POWDER

	Territorial coverage	Title codes
Wholesale prices in £ per ton	UK	T 4-m

MAGNESIUM PRODUCTS, SEMI-FINISHED

	Territorial coverage	Title codes
Sales: wrought magnesium products: tonnage	USA	J 6-a
Wholesale prices: magnesium products by kind in local currency	Main countries	T 4-m

Magnesium sheets & plates   see   MAGNESIUM PRODUCTS, SEMI-FINISHED

Magnetic steel   see   STEEL SHEETS, MAGNETIC

Magnetos   see   REPLACEMENT PARTS

Mahogany   see   HARDWOOD, SAWN

Mail   see   AIR MAIL
    LETTER MAIL
    MAIL FREIGHT

MAIL FREIGHT

	Territorial coverage	Title codes
Carried on domestic IATA flights: tonnage	Worldwide	S 21-a
on international IATA flights: tonnage	Worldwide	S 21-a
Domestic & foreign mail sent & received: tonnage	All countries	U 43-a

	Territorial coverage	Title codes

MAIL FREIGHT, continued
    Postal freight carried by air transport   EEC countries   E 43-a
    Revenue of IATA airline companies from mail freight in $m   Worldwide   S 21-a

MAIL ORDER HOUSES
    % of clothing sales covered by mail order companies   UK   B 22-a

MAINTENANCE & REPAIRS
    Carried out by building industry by value in $ Main countries   U 58-a
    Costs of maintenance of farm equipment as % farm expenses   Hungary & Poland   U 34-a
        in local currency   Hungary & Poland   U 34-a
             ECE countries   U 34-a
        as % value of farm output   Hungary & Poland   U 34-a
    as item in farm operating expenses in $ ECE countries   U 34-a
    of maintenance & repairs of iron ore carriers by size   Worldwide   U 56-a
    per room in international hotels in $ World regions   Z 5-a
        in tourist hotels in $ World regions   Z 5-a

Maintenance staff, aircraft   see   AIRCRAFT PERSONNEL

MAIZE
        see also   CORN OIL
                     POP CORN
    % changes in prices received by farmers   France & Italy   E 34-m
         W European countries   U 30-a
    % of maize harvest exported   Main countries   B 8-a
    Area harvested, production tonnage & yield per ha   All countries   A 9-a
        under crop (for fodder) in ha   EEC countries   E 12-a
                (for seed) in ha   EEC countries   E 12-a
        in acres   Main countries   B 8-a
        in ha & harvest: tonnage   Main countries   R 5-a
        in ha: historical table from 1815   Main European countries   Z 1-a
        in ha   EEC countries   B 1-a   E 44-a
             OAS member countries   N 13-a
             OECD countries   D 1-a
    Consignments of maize imported as emergency food aid by value
        in $ Recipient countries   M 1-a
    Consumption as animal feed: tonnage   EEC countries   E 44-a
         UK   B 8-a
        as human food: tonnage   UK   B 8-a
        (industrial) for processing: tonnage   UK   B 8-a
         World regions   C 27-a
            for brewing, malting & distilling: tonnage   UK   B 8-a
            for production of starch & breakfast
                  cereals: tonnage   UK   B 8-a
                  starch & glucose: tonnage   UK   C 27-a
            for spirit distillation: tonnage   UK   C 27-a
        per capita in kg   EEC countries   B 1-a   E 44-a
        tonnage & consumption per capita per day   OECD countries   D 14-a
        tonnage   EEC countries   E 44-a
         OAS member countries   N 17-a
    Crop estimates (for ensuing yr): tonnage   Main countries   P 1-a
    Crop yield (for fodder) in 100 kg per ha   EEC countries   E 12-a
        (for seed) in 100 kg per ha   EEC countries   E 12-a
        in cwt per acre   Main countries   B 8-a
            kg per ha   EEC countries   B 1-a   E 3-a
         Main countries   R 5-a
         OAS member countries   N 13-a
         OECD countries   D 1-a
        in quintals per ha   E European countries & USSR incl Ukraine   U 16-a
    Deliveries by farmers: tonnage   Main countries   B 7-a
    EEC levy on imported maize ex non-EEC sources in local currency
        per ton   EEC countries   B 7-m
    Export prices by grade in cents per 56 lbs fob at ports   USA   R 2-m
        in $ per ton fob Gulf ports   USA   C 16-m   U 35-a
    Export prices - index nos (weighted average main sources)   U 29-q   U 54-a
         S American countries   U 40-q
        in local currency per ton   Main countries   A 9-a
    Export subsidies in £ per ton   EEC countries   B 8-a
    Exports by destination: tonnage   China, E European countries & USSR   A 17-a
         European countries   U 35-a
         Main countries   A 17-a   B 8-a
        by value & as % of exports of agricultural products   W European countries   U 20-a
            as % of total exports   Main countries   B 8-a
            in local currency   Burma & Thailand   U 32-m
            in $m   W European countries   U 33-a
        tonnage (incl world total)   Main countries   C 16-a
        tonnage   All countries   A 17-a
         Burma & Thailand   U 32-m
         European countries   U 35-a
         Main countries   B 7-m   P 5-a
    Feed price ratios per quintal: pigs (live wt)   W European countries   U 30-a
    Harvest (for seed) during crop year: tonnage   EEC countries   E 12-a
    Import prices by grade in £ per ton cif   UK   B 7-m
            in local currency cif   European countries   R 2-m
        (ex Argentine) in $ per ton cif   European countries   U 35-a
         USA   U 30-a

	Territorial coverage	Title codes	
MAIZE, continued			
Import prices (ex Argentine, S Africa & USA) in £ per ton cif	UK	B 8-m	
(ex USA) in $ per ton cif	UK	U 20-q	U 33-q
		A 9-a	
in $ per 100 kg cif	W European countries	U 30-a	
Imports by port of entry: tonnage	UK	B 7-m	P 5-a2
by source (incl maize meal & flour): tonnage	UK	P 5-a	
tonnage	EEC area	B 8-a	
into USSR: tonnage	All countries	A 17-a	
	Main countries	B 8-a	
by value in $m & as % of imports of agricultural products	W European countries	U 20-a	
in $m	W European countries	U 33-a	
(for production of animal feed): tonnage	UK	P 5-a	
shipped into E European countries, USSR & China: tonnage	Non-Communist countries	A 17-a	
tonnage	All countries	A 17-a	
	Japan & W European countries	B 8-a	
Intervention price fixed for maize	EEC area	E 44-a	
Prices: EEC area as % of world market prices		E 44-a	
Prices paid by farmers (as animal feed)	European countries	U 30-a	
Producer prices in local currency per 100 kg	Main W European countries	E 35-a	
per kg	France & Italy	E 34-m	
per ton	OECD countries	D 1-a	
in $ per bushel	USA	E 35-a	
(prime quality feed maize) in $ per kg	W European countries	U 30-a	
in $ per ton	All countries	A 9-a	
	France & Italy	E 44-a	
Production, stocks, industrial usage & consumption as fodder & seed: tonnage	OECD countries	D 14-a	
Production: tonnage & value of output in £m	EEC countries	B 1-a	
Production & yield in tonnage per 100 ha	Latin American countries	J 5-a	
by regions: tonnage	EEC countries	E 38-a	
Production, consumption & trade: tonnage	EEC countries	B 1-a	
Production for animal feed: tonnage	EEC countries	E 12-a	
for seed: tonnage	EEC countries	E 12-m	E 12-a
historical table: tonnage	Main European countries	Z 1-a	
tonnage	AASM countries	E 41-a	
	African countries	U 44-a	
	All countries	U 43-a	
	Asian & Far East countries	U 32-a	
	European countries	U 35-a	
	E European countries & USSR incl Ukraine	U 16-a	
	EEC countries	E 44-a	
	Canada, European countries, Japan, USA & USSR	E 44-a	
	Latin American countries	U 40-a	
	Main countries	B 7-a	B 8-a
		E 3-a	P 5-a
	OAS member countries	N 13-a	
	OECD countries	D 1-a	
Retail prices by grade in local currency	OAS member countries	N 17-a	
Sales (ex farm): maize for seed: tonnage	EEC countries	E 12-m	
Self-sufficiency ratios	EEC countries	B 1-a	
Stocks (carry-over at end-season) held on farms: tonnage	Main countries	B 7-a	
tonnage	Argentine, S Africa & USA	B 8-a	
	Main countries	B 7-a	C 16-a
for seed on farms (end-month): tonnage	EEC countries	E 12-m	
held for sale as seed (at wholesalers' premises): tonnage	EEC countries	E 12-m	
Supply & disposal of maize by purpose: tonnage	Main countries	B 8-a	
Target, intervention & threshold prices in £ per cwt	EEC countries	B 1-a	
Value of maize production (at current prices) in $	EEC countries	E 44-a	
Wholesale prices: % change over previous yr	EEC countries	E 34-m	
in cents per bushel (on Chicago market)	USA	P 1-m	
in local currency per kg	EEC countries	E 34-m	
	OAS member countries	N 17-a	
in $ per ton	Main countries	A 9-a	
	Netherlands, UK & USA	U 27-m	
World production: tonnage		C 16-a	

Maize cake   see   OILCAKE & MEAL

Maize oil   see   CORN OIL

Makori   see   HARDWOOD LOGS

Malathion   see   INSECTICIDES

MALT
    Production: roasted barley: tonnage   All countries   U 22-a

Malting   see   DISTILLING & MALTING

Malva & guaxima   see   JUTE

Man-hours worked   see   HOURS OF WORK
                             LABOUR RATIOS

Man-made fibre fabrics   see   WOVEN CELLULOSIC FABRICS
                                   WOVEN NON-CELLULOSIC FABRICS

	Territorial coverage	Title codes	
MAN-MADE FIBRE TOPS			
Production (first combing): tonnage	OECD countries	D 46-a	
MAN-MADE FIBRE YARN			
Consumption in production of clothing	EEC countries	K 4-a	
household textiles	EEC countries	K 4-a	
in knitting mills: tonnage	OECD countries	D 46-a	
synthetic yarn: tonnage	Main countries	K 4-a	
Exports by destination in million lbs	UK	B 10-a	
tonnage	Main countries	K 4-a	
cellulosic spun yarn: tonnage	Main countries	K 4-a	
spun yarn: tonnage	Main countries	K 4-a	
synthetic yarn: tonnage	Main countries	K 4-a	
tonnage (all kinds)	Main countries	K 4-a	
Imports & exports in lbs	UK	B 29-a	
as % of domestic consumption	UK	B 29-a	
by source: tonnage	Main countries	K 4-a	
cellulosic spun yarn: tonnage	Main countries	K 4-a	
spun yarn: tonnage	Main countries	K 4-a	
synthetic yarn: tonnage	Main countries	K 4-a	
tonnage (all kinds)	Main countries	K 4-a	
Production by kind: tonnage	European countries, Japan & USA	K 4-a	
acetate yarn: tonnage	OECD countries	D 46-a	
acrylic yarn: tonnage	OECD countries	D 46-a	
artificial yarn: tonnage	W European countries	K 2-q	
cellulosic yarn: tonnage	All countries	K 4-a	
	OECD countries	D 46-a	
non-cellulosic yarn: tonnage	OECD countries	D 46-a	
polyamide yarn: tonnage	OECD countries	D 46-a	
polyester yarn: tonnage	OECD countries	D 46-a	
synthetic yarn: tonnage	Main countries	K 4-a	U 26-a
	W European countries	K 2-q	
viscose yarn: tonnage	OECD countries	D 46-a	
World production: synthetic & cellulosic fibre yarns: tonnage		K 4-a	
MAN-MADE FIBRES			
see also CELLULOSIC FIBRES			
NON-CELLULOSIC FIBRES			
POLYESTER			
% changes in exports (value basis)	European countries, Japan & USA	U 25-a	
in imports (value basis)	European countries, Japan & USA	U 25-a	
% of total EEC area production	EEC countries	R 5-a	
% of utilisation of plant capacity for production of acrylics	European countries, Japan & USA	D 27-a	
polyamides	European countries, Japan & USA	D 27-a	
polyester fibres	European countries, Japan & USA	D 27-a	
Consumption: textile mills in million lbs	UK	B 29-a	
by end-usage: tonnage	EEC countries	K 4-a	
in clothing production by kind: tonnage	EEC countries	K 4-a	
in household textiles production: tonnage	EEC countries	K 4-a	
polyamide fibre for production of textiles: tonnage	EEC countries	K 4-a	
of floor coverings:			
tonnage	EEC countries	K 4-a	
of clothing: tonnage	EEC countries	K 4-a	
polyester fibre for production of textiles: tonnage	EEC countries	K 4-a	
polyester yarn for production of clothing: tonnage	EEC countries	K 4-a	
in kg	Main countries	K 6-a	
tonnage	Main countries	K 4-a	
	OAS member countries	N 17-a	
per capita: chemical fibres in kg	Main countries	U 26-a	
Deliveries: man-made staple to textile industry - index nos	UK	B 29-a	
Export prices: acrylic "Orlon" (4.5 denier) in $	USA	R 2-m	
Exports by destination: cellulosic & non-cellulosic fibres in lbs	UK	B 10-a	
synthetic fibre: tonnage	All countries	K 4-a	
yarn & staple in lbs	UK & USA	B 10-a	
in lbs million	UK	B 10-a	
for spinning by value in $	Main countries	U 2-a	
rayon staple & waste in lbs	UK	B 19-a	
cellulosic filament as % of production	Main countries	D 27-a	
cellulosic staple as % of production	Main countries	D 27-a	
non-cellulosic filament as % of production	Main countries	D 27-a	
spun yarn (cellulosic): tonnage	All countries	A 6-a	
(non-cellulosic): tonnage	All countries	A 6-a	
Imports as % of domestic consumption	UK	B 29-a	
by source: synthetic staple: tonnage	All countries	K 4-a	
by value in $m & as % of all chemical products imported	Main countries	U 25-a	
cellulosic filament as % of production	Main countries	D 27-a	
cellulosic staple as % of production	Main countries	D 27-a	
Imports & exports (incl trade balance) in lbs	UK	B 29-a	
filament yarn & rayon acetate in lbs	UK	B 10-a	
non-cellulosic filament & staple as % of production	Main countries	D 27-a	
spun yarn (cellulosic): tonnage	All countries	A 6-a	
(non-cellulosic): tonnage	All countries	A 6-a	
Labour costs of production per hr	EEC countries	E 2-a	
Prices: polyester in US cents per lb	UK	K 1-q	
rayon staple in US cents per lb	UK	K 1-q	
Production: acetate fibres: tonnage	Canada, European countries, Japan & USA	D 27-a	
	OECD countries	D 46-a	

	Territorial coverage	Title codes	
MAN-MADE FIBRES, continued			
Production: acrylic fibres as % of total man-made fibres	European countries, Japan & USA	D 27-a	
in lbs million	Main countries	B 10-a	
tonnage	OECD countries	D 46-a	
acrylic staple: tonnage	European countries, Japan & USA	D 27-a	
cellulosic fibres: tonnage	All countries	K 4-a	
	OECD countries	D 46-a	R 5-a
cellulosic yarn in lbs million	Main countries	E 3-a	
forecast to 1977 in lbs million	UK	B 29	
staple in lbs million	UK	B 29	
yarn in lbs million	UK	B 29	
Production: historical table from 1910: tonnage	Main European countries	Z 1-a	
in kg	Main countries	K 6-a	
man-made fibres (incl filaments): tonnage	Main countries	R 5-a	
man-made fibre waste: tonnage	OECD countries	D 46-a	
non-cellulosic yarn in lbs million	Main countries	E 3-a	
nylon in lbs million	Main countries	B 10-a	
piece goods made of synthetic fibres in lbs million	USA	K 1-q	
polyamides as % of total man-made fibres	European countries, Japan & USA	D 27-a	
polyamide fibres: tonnage	OECD countries	D 46-a	
polyamide filament & staple: tonnage	European countries, Japan & USA	D 27-a	
	Japan & USA	K 4-a	
polyester fibres: tonnage	European countries, Japan & USA	K 4-a	
	OECD countries	D 46-a	
polyester in lbs million	Main countries	B 10-a	
as % of total man-made fibres	European countries, Japan & USA	D 27-a	
polyester filament: tonnage	Japan	D 27-a	
polyester staple: tonnage	European countries, Japan & USA	D 27-a	
rayon & acetate staple in lbs million	Main countries	K 1-q	
yarn in lbs million	All countries	B 10-a	J 7-a
rayon: tonnage	Canada, European countries, Japan & USA	D 27-a	
staple yarn in lbs million	All countries	U 22-a	
synthetic fibres (all kinds): tonnage	All countries	K 4-a	
viscose fibres: tonnage	OECD countries	D 46-a	
Supply: rayon acetate yarn & staple: tonnage	All countries	B 10-a	
Wholesale prices: "Courtelle" in pence per kg	UK	R 2-m	
Wholesale prices - index nos	OECD countries	D 5-a	
World consumption: non-cellulosic fibres in lbs million		B 10-a	
World production: acrylic yarn & staple in lbs million		B 10-a	
non-cellulosic fibres in lbs million		B 10-a	
non-cellulosic yarn & staple in lbs million		B 10-a	
polyamide yarn & staple in lbs million		B 10-a	
polyester yarn & staple in lbs million		B 10-a	
synthetic & cellulosic fibres: tonnage		K 4-a	
MAN-MADE FIBRES BY KIND			
Consumption by textile industry: tonnage	OECD countries	D 46-a	
(domestic): tonnage	European countries, Japan & USA	D 27-a	
in spinning mills: tonnage	OECD countries	D 46-a	
Exports by destination by CST classes: tonnage & value in $	EEC countries	E 48-a	
SITC classes by value in $	Main countries	D 2-q	
tonnage & value in $	OECD countries	D 3-a2	
by NIMEXE classes by value in $	All countries	E 20-a	
SITC classes by value in $	All countries	U 50-a	U 59-a
Exports: filament & staple: tonnage	Canada, European countries, Japan & USA	D 27-a	
Imports by NIMEXE classes by value in $	All countries	E 20-a	
SITC classes by value in $	All countries	U 50-a	U 59-a
by source by CST classes: tonnage & value in $	EEC countries	E 21-a	
SITC classes by value in $	Main countries	D 2-q	
tonnage & value in $	OECD countries	D 3-a2	
Plant capacity: tonnage	Canada, European countries, Japan & USA	D 27-a	
Production: staple & filaments: tonnage	Main countries	D 27-a	
tonnage	OAS member countries	N 14-a	
MAN-MADE FIBRES INDUSTRY			
% projected productivity increase by 1977	UK	B 29	
Costs: salaried staff per month	EEC countries	E 11-a	
Investment in buildings in local currency	EEC countries	E 40-a	
machinery in local currency	EEC countries	E 40-a	
(total) in $m	OECD countries	D 5-a	
Labour costs as % of total costs	EEC countries	E 8-a	
by status of employees	EEC countries	E 8-a	
per hr in local currency (all employees)	EEC countries	E 11-a	
(wage earners)	EEC countries	E 11-a	
Labour force employed: projection to 1977	UK	B 29-a	
by occupational status	OECD countries	D 5-a	
no of salaried staff	EEC countries	E 11-a	
wage earners	EEC countries	E 11-a	
(all employees)	EEC countries	E 8-a	
	All countries	K 4-a	
No of hrs worked per wk	Main countries	R 3-m	
	EEC countries	E 25-a	
per yr (all employees)	EEC countries	E 8-a	
salaried staff	EEC countries	E 11-a	
wage earners	EEC countries	E 11-a	
Production - index nos	OECD countries	D 5-a	
Turnover in $m	OECD countries	D 5-a	
Value added in manufacture in $m	OECD countries	D 5-a	

	Territorial coverage	Title codes	
MAN-MADE FIBRES INDUSTRY, continued			
Wage rates per hr by grade in lire	Italy	R 4-a	
by sex in local currency	Main countries	R 3-m	
in local currency	EEC countries	E 25-a2	
MANGANESE			
see also FERRO-MANGANESE			
Consumption: blast furnaces: tonnage	EEC countries	E 29-a	
sinter plants: tonnage	EEC countries	E 29-a	
steelworks: tonnage	EEC countries	E 29-a	
(industrial): tonnage	USA	N 1-a	
Export prices: electrolytic metallic manganese in cents per lb	USA	T 4-m	
Exports by destination: metallic manganese: tonnage	S Africa & USA	T 4-a	
Government strategic stockpile: electrolytic metallic manganese: tonnage	USA	N 1-a	
synthetic dioxide of manganese: tonnage	USA	N 1-a	
Imports by source: metallic manganese: tonnage	UK	T 4-a	
Production (based on metal content of ore): tonnage	All countries	B 15-a	R 5-a
		U 22-a	U 43-a
	Latin American countries	J 5-a	U 40-a
treated metallic manganese: tonnage	EEC countries	E 29-a	
Wholesale prices: electrolytic metallic manganese in £ per ton	UK	C 12-m	
in lire per kg	Italy	C 12-m	T 4-m
(normal grade) metallic manganese in cents per lb	USA	C 12-m	
Manganese ingots see INGOTS, MANGANESE			
MANGANESE MINES			
Labour force employed (at end-period)	EEC area	E 29-a	
Production manganese ore (raw): tonnage	EEC countries	E 29-a	
metallic manganese: tonnage	EEC countries	E 29-a	
Stocks: manganese ore held at mines (at end-period)	EEC area	E 29-a	
MANGANESE ORE			
% contribution to export earnings	Botswana	E 45-a	
% share of world reserves (estim)	Latin American countries	U 18-a	
Consumption in steelworks & blast furnaces: tonnage	UK	T 4-a	
tonnage	ECE countries, Japan & USA	U 7-q	U 6-a
	Japan & USA	T 4-a	
	Main countries	H 3-a	
	OAS member countries	N 17-a	
Deliveries for smelting in non-EEC area: tonnage	EEC countries	E 29-a	
Export prices - index nos (weighted average main sources)		U 29-q	
Exports (based on metal content of ore): tonnage	Main countries	U 11-a	
by destination: tonnage	EEC countries	E 5-q	E 29-a
	Main countries	T 4-a	
by value in $m	Developing countries	U 11-a	
	Main countries	U 11-a	
(incl concentrates): tonnage	Asian & Far East countries	U 32-q	
shipped to non-EEC area: tonnage	EEC countries	E 29-a	
tonnage & value in $m	Gabon	E 45-a	
tonnage	ECE countries, Japan & USA	U 7-m	U 6-a
	India, Iran, Philippines & Thailand	U 32-m	
	Main countries	H 3-a	
total & to EEC area: tonnage & value in UA	AASM countries	E 41-a	
Government strategic stockpile: chemical ore: tonnage	USA	N 1-a	
metallurgical ore: tonnage	USA	N 1-a	
natural ore: tonnage	USA	N 1-a	
Import prices in cents per ton cif	European countries & USA	T 4-m	
(ex major suppliers) in local currency	EEC countries	E 29-a	
Import prices - index nos	EEC countries	E 29-a	
Imports & exports by source & destination: tonnage	Main countries	B 15-a	
Imports by source: tonnage	EEC countries	E 5-q	E 29-a
	Italy	C 12-a	
	Main countries	T 4-a	
shipped ex non-EEC area: tonnage	EEC area	E 29-a	
tonnage	ECE countries, Japan & USA	U 7-m	U 6-a
	Main countries	H 3-a	
Prices: manganese ore in $ per ton	W Germany	C 5-m	
Production (based on metal content of ore): tonnage	USA	N 1-a	
manganese ore: tonnage	AASM countries	E 41-a	
	USA	J 6-a	
manganese ore over 35% metal content: tonnage	USA	J 6-a	
tonnage	African countries	U 44-a	
	All countries	B 15-a	H 3-a
		T 1-a	
	ECE countries & Japan	U 7-m	U 6-a
	EEC countries	E 29-a	
	Italy	E 30-m	
	OAS member countries	N 14-a	
Receipts ex EEC area: tonnage	EEC area	E 29-a	
Stocks held at mines: tonnage	Italy	E 30-m	
(end-period): tonnage	USA	T 4-a	
World prices: high grade manganese ore in local currency per ton		E 41-a	
World production: tonnage	Worldwide	C 30-a	N 4-a
		U 11-a	

	Territorial coverage	Title codes	
MANGANESE ORE, continued			
World production: tonnage	All countries	C 12-a	T 1-a
		T 4-a	
	Main countries	N 1-a	
World reserves: tonnage (estim)	Main countries	N 1-a	
MANGOES			
Production: tonnage	All countries	A 9-a	

Manila hemp   see   ABACA

Manioc   see   CASSAVA

Manpower   see   LABOUR FORCE

MANUAL WORKERS
    see also   WAGE EARNERS

	Territorial coverage	Title codes	
Labour costs per hr by industrial sector in local currency	EEC countries	E 3-a	
in construction industry in local currency	EEC countries	E 3-a	
manufacturing industry in local currency	EEC countries	E 3-a	
mining & quarrying in local currency	EEC countries	E 3-a	
public utility undertakings in local currency	EEC countries	E 3-a	
No employed: agriculture & forestry	AASM countries	E 41-a	
mining & quarrying	AASM countries	E 41-a	
private sector	AASM countries	E 41-a	
public sector	AASM countries	E 41-a	
service industries & commercial enterprises	AASM countries	E 41-a	
transport service industries	AASM countries	E 41-a	

Manufactured fertilisers   see   FERTILISERS, MANUFACTURED

MANUFACTURED GAS
    see also   BLAST FURNACE GAS
                CALORIFIC VALUE
                COKE OVEN GAS
                REFINERY GAS
                NATURAL GAS

	Territorial coverage	Title codes	
% change in output & consumption	E European countries	U 16-a	
Calorific value (average)	European countries & USA	U 3-a	
compared with petroleum fuels		C 21	
Changes in stocks by volume in m^3	European countries & USA	U 3-a	
Consumption (as raw material) by volume in m^3	European countries & USA	U 3-a	
at power stations & gasworks by volume in m^3	EEC countries	E 16-q	E 15-a
by chemical industry by volume in m^3	OECD countries	D 5-a	
industry & road transport undertakings by volume in m^3	EEC countries	E 16-q	E 15-a
iron & steel industry in therms million	UK	T 2-m	
steel foundries by volume in m^3	EEC countries	E 29-a	
type of use by volume in m^3	European countries & USA	U 3-a	
of user by volume in m^3	European countries & USA	U 3-a	
cost: private sector in local currency	EEC countries	E 32-a	
(domestic) by volume in m^3	EEC countries	E 16-q	E 15-a
in dwellings by volume in m^3	European countries & USA	U 3-a	
for energy production by volume in m^3	European countries & USA	U 3-a	
in coke ovens by volume in m^3	European countries & USA	U 3-a	
electricity generation by volume in m^3	EEC countries	E 16-q	E 15-a
in electricity supply plants by volume in m^3	European countries	U 1-a	
in steel foundries by volume in m^3	EEC countries	E 30-q	
in thermal power stations by volume in m^3	OECD countries	D 8-a	
(industrial) by area by volume in m^3	EEC countries	E 38-a	
by sector by volume in m^3	European countries & USA	U 3-a	
in m^3	European countries, USA & USSR	U 4-a	
Deliveries: domestic consumption by volume in m^3	EEC countries	E 16-q	E 15-a
to EEC countries by volume in m^3	EEC countries	E 16-q	E 15-a
Distribution losses in calorific value	EEC countries	E 16-q	E 15-a
Exports by destination in calorific value	European countries & USA	U 3-a	
to E European Bloc by volume in m^3	E European countries & USSR	U 16-a	
Imports by source in calorific value	European countries & USA	U 3-a	
ex E European Bloc by volume in m^3	E European countries & USSR	U 16-a	
in coal equiv tonnage	EEC area	E 7-a	
Losses in transport & distribution by volume in m^3	European countries & USA	U 3-a	
No of household consumers	European countries & USA	U 3-a	
Overall balance: conversion & supply	European countries & USA	U 3-a	
Prices to consumers for domestic use in local currency	EEC countries	E 15-a	
Production at gasworks & coke ovens by volume in m^3	All countries	U 27-m	U 43-a
by volume in m^3	All countries	U 22-a	
	OAS member countries	N 14-a	
by areas by volume in m^3	EEC countries	E 38-a	
by volume in m^3	African countries	U 44-a	
Production & consumption by volume in m^3	All countries	U 55-a	
Production, imports & exports by volume in m^3	European countries & USA	U 3-a	
in calorific value	European countries & USSR	U 4-a	
	EEC countries	E 16-q	E 15-a
in coke ovens by volume in m^3	All countries	R 5-a	U 22-a
	OAS member countries	N 14-a	
in m^3	All countries	R 5-a	
	EEC countries	E 28-q	E 27-a

	Territorial coverage	Title codes	
MANUFACTURED GAS, continued			
Production in gasworks by volume in m³	All countries	R 5-a	
in public gas undertakings by volume in m³	OECD countries	D 31-a	
in oil refineries by volume in m³	OAS member countries	N 14-a	
(incl blast furnace gas) by volume in m³	EEC countries	E 26-m	
Resources & changes in stocks by volume in m³	EEC countries	E 16-q	E 15-a
Supply at gasworks & coke ovens by volume in m³	European countries & USA	U 3-a	
available for electricity production by volume in m³	European countries & USA	U 3-a	
(ex EEC production) & imports by volume in m³	EEC countries	E 16-q	E 15-a
for production of goods by volume in m³	European countries & USA	U 3-a	
MANUFACTURED GOODS			
see also PRIMARY COMMODITIES			
PRODUCER GOODS			
As % of value of all goods entering international trade	Worldwide	U 23-a	
% change in export earnings	Israel & S Korea	U 11-a	
in exports (by destination)	EEC countries	E 23-a	
in imports (by source)	EEC countries	E 23-a	
in wholesale prices	Main countries	G 1-a	
% share of EEC area imports	Developing countries	U 52-a	
Consumption by value in $m	Main countries	U 23-a	
Export prices - index nos (unit value basis)		U 29-q	
Exports by destination by value in UA	EEC countries	E 23-a	
in $m	Main countries	E 24-a	
	World regions	U 23-a	
ex developed countries by value in $m	World regions	U 52-a	
Exports - index nos (quantum & value bases)	OECD countries	D 16-q	
per capita in $	Developing countries	U 52-a	
shipped to Communist area by value in $m	Developing countries	U 52-a	
to non-EEC area by value in UA	EEC countries	E 24-a	
US share by SITC classes by value in $m	Main countries	N 3-a	
Imports as % of domestic consumption	EEC countries, Japan & USA	U 23-a	
by source by value in UA	EEC countries	E 23-a	
ex EEC area by value in UA	African, Caribbean countries & Pacific Is	E 45-a	
ex non-EEC area by value in UA	EEC countries	E 24-a	
in $m	African, Caribbean countries & Pacific Is	E 45-a	
	Developing countries	U 52-a	
	Main countries	E 24-a	
into EEC area by value in $m	Developing countries	U 52-a	
Imports - index nos (quantum & value bases)	OECD countries	D 16-q	
Inter-EEC imports & exports by value in UA	EEC countries	E 22-m	E 24-a
Producer prices - index nos	W Germany	H 3-a	
Terms of trade in manufactured products - index nos	Worldwide	U 23-a	
Wholesale prices - index nos	India & Pakistan	U 32-m	
	OAS member countries	N 17-a	
World exports as % of world exports (all products)	Developed countries	M 4-a	
	Developing countries	M 4-a	
by value in $bn	Developed countries	M 4-a	
	Developing countries	M 4-a	
exports - index nos (quantum & unit value bases)		U 23-a	
market prices - index nos		G 1-a	
production - index nos (quantum basis)		U 23-a	
MANUFACTURED GOODS BY KIND			
Exports by destination by CST classes by value in $m	OECD countries	D 3-a2	
SITC classes by value in $m	EEC countries	E 48-a	
tonnage & value in $m	Main countries	D 2-q	
tonnage & value in $m	All countries	U 12-a	
value in $m	Main countries	N 3-a	
by NIMEXE classes by value in $m	All countries	E 20-a	
SITC classes by value in $m	All countries	U 50-a	U 59-a
shipped to EEC & non-EEC areas by value in $m	EEC countries	E 24-a	
Imports by NIMEXE classes by value in $m	All countries	E 20-a	
SITC classes by value in $m	All countries	U 50-a	U 59-a
by source by CST classes: tonnage & value in $m	EEC countries	E 21-a	
SITC classes by value in $m	Main countries	D 2-q	
tonnage & value in $m	OECD countries	D 3-a2	
tonnage & value in $m	All countries	U 12-a	
ex EEC & non-EEC areas by value in $m	EEC countries	E 24-a	
Manufactured metal goods see METAL PRODUCTS			
MANUFACTURED TEXTILE PRODUCTS			
see also CLOTHING			
% change in production (incl clothing)	Main countries	G 1-a	
% share of EEC area imports	Developing countries	U 52-a	
Exports by value in $m	OECD countries	D 46-a	
ex developed countries by value in $m	World regions	U 52-a	
forecast to 1977 in lbs	UK	B 29	
(incl clothing) by value in $m	Main countries	G 1-a	
shipped to Communist area by value in $	Developing countries	U 52-a	
via Karachi: tonnage	India	S 16-a	
Imports by value in $m	Developing countries	U 52-a	
	OECD countries	D 46-a	
shipped ex developing countries by value in $m	EEC countries	U 52-a	
forecast to 1977 in lbs	UK	B 29	
(incl clothing) by value in $m	Main countries	G 1-a	

	Territorial coverage	Title codes

MANUFACTURED TEXTILE PRODUCTS, continued
    Private expenditure on clothing in local currency — AASM countries — E 41-a
    Production: forecasts by kind of products in lbs — UK — B 29-a

MANUFACTURED TIMBER PRODUCTS
    see also   FIBREBOARD
                  NEWSPRINT
                  PAPER & PAPERBOARD
                  PARTICLE & CHIPBOARD
                  PRINTING PAPER
                  PLYWOOD & BLOCKBOARD
                  VENEER SHEETS
                  WOOD-BASED PANELS
                  WOOD PULP

    Consumption by value in $ — Main world regions — U 23-a
    Exports as % of domestic consumption — Main world regions — U 23-a
        by kind: tonnage — World regions — A 11-a
            fibreboard: tonnage — All countries — A 23-a
            plywood: tonnage — All countries — A 23-a
    Imports as % of domestic consumption — Main world regions — U 23-a
        fibreboard: tonnage — All countries — A 23-a
        plywood: tonnage — All countries — A 23-a
    Production by kind: tonnage — World regions — A 11-a
            chipboard: tonnage — All countries — U 22-a
            fibreboard: tonnage — All countries — A 23-a   U 22-a
            hardboard: tonnage — OECD countries — D 40-a
            plywood: tonnage — All countries — A 23-a   U 22-a
            timber products by kind — EEC countries — E 28-q   E 27-a
            veneer: tonnage — All countries — U 22-a

Manufactured timber products industry   see   WOOD-WORKING
                                                          INDUSTRY

MANUFACTURING INDUSTRY
    As % of world industrial activity (5 yr periods) — — U 38
    By sector: % of expenditure allocated to machinery purchase — Main countries — U 38-a
            employment as % of total labour force — Main countries — U 38-a
            inventories by value in $m — OAS member countries — N 14-a
            labour force employed — All countries — C 28-a
            no of hrs worked per wk — OAS member countries — N 18-a
            production - index nos — Far East countries — U 32-q
                                 S American countries — U 40-a
            production by value in $m — Asian, Far East & Australasian countries — U 45-a
    % change as component of gross national product — All countries — U 60-a
    % change: cash earnings of manufacturing enterprises — European countries & USA — U 16-q
            employment in manufacturing industry — Main European countries & USA — U 16-a
            implicit deflator — Developed countries — D 25-a
            labour costs — France, W Germany & UK — B 28-a
            output (volume basis) — Main European countries — U 16-a
            output: main manufactured goods — Latin American countries — U 18-a
            output per employee — European countries — U 16-a
    % contribution to gross domestic product — All countries — U 23-a   U 60-a
                                 — OAS member countries — N 14-a
            to national income — Developing countries — D 25-a
    % growth rate: output — All countries — M 6-a
                         — Main ECAFE countries — U 17-a
                         — Canada, W European countries, Japan & USA — G 1-a
    % increase: earnings per man-hr — Main countries — B 27-a
    % of consumption: petroleum products — Latin American countries — U 18-a
    % of labour force employed by region in manufacturing industry — EEC countries — E 33-a
    % rate of change: employment (compounded) — Main countries — N 7-a
                    in gross product of manufacturing industry — Latin American countries — U 18-a
    % real growth rates — Developing countries — M 3-a
    % share of industrial production (incl mining) — Main countries — U 38-a
    Assets of manufacturing corporations as % of liabilities — USA — J 2-a
    Capital formation in local currency — OAS member countries — N 16-a
                      in $m — Main countries — U 25-a
    Coefficient of demand: machinery in manufacturing industry — Main countries — U 38-a
    Consumption expenditure in $m — OAS member countries — N 14-a
    Contribution to gross domestic product in local currency — African countries — U 44-a
                      in $m — EEC countries — E 32-a
                             — Latin American countries — U 18-a
                             — S American countries — U 41-a
    Corporate investment: US manufacturing corporations abroad in $m — Main countries — R 5-a
    Costs: salaried staff per mth — EEC countries — E 11-a
    Depreciation: corporate assets as % of sales turnover — USA — J 2-a
    Direct labour costs per hr in local currency — EEC countries — E 11-a
    Direct investment: US government in manufacturing industry in $m — OAS member countries — N 16-a
    Earnings: US manufacturing as % of sales turnover — USA — J 2-a
    Electricity generation from own plant in kWh — All countries — C 23-a
            usage from public supply in kWh — All countries — C 23-a
    Employment as % of total economically-active population by region — EEC countries — E 2-a
            by status by area — EEC countries — E 38-a
            (yr-end) in manufacturing industry — EEC countries — E 33-a
                                           — All countries — L 1-m   L 4-a
    Employment - index nos — EEC countries — E 26-m
                         — OAS member countries — N 18-a

	Territorial coverage	Title codes	
MANUFACTURING INDUSTRY, continued			
Fatality rates for accidents in manufacturing industry	All countries	L 4-a	
Gross earnings per hr by kind of product manufactured	EEC countries	E 3-a	
Gross fixed capital formation in $m	EEC countries	E 32-a	
Gross output (at factor cost) in $m	E European countries	U 25-a	
	All countries	U 43-a	
Gross product: manufacturing industry as component of gross domestic product in $	Developed countries	D 25-a	
Gross product: manufacturing industry in local currency	OAS member countries	N 14-a	N 16-a
Incidence of strikes (or lock-outs) in manufacturing industry	Main countries	R 3-a	
Investment by manufacturing: buildings in local currency	EEC countries	E 40-a	
land purchase in local currency	EEC countries	E 40-a	
machinery in local currency	EEC countries	E 40-a	
Labour costs as % of total manufacturing costs	EEC countries	E 8-a	
by status of employees in local currency	EEC countries	E 8-a	
(in detail): staff per mth	Main countries	R 3-a	
workers per wk	Main countries	R 3-a	
manual workers per hr	EEC countries	E 3-a	
per hr (incl staff)	EEC countries	E 2-a	E 11-a
wage earners	EEC countries	E 11-a	
Labour costs – index nos	Main countries	B 27-a	
Labour force employed (census data)	OAS member countries	N 18	
by occupation	OECD countries	D 23-a	
sex & age	UK	B 28-a	
sex	EEC countries	E 18-a	
status of employees	Main countries	C 28-a	
no of salaried staff	EEC countries	E 11-a	
wage earners	EEC countries	E 11-a	
(total)	Asian, Far East & Australasian countries	U 32-q	
	EEC countries	E 8-a	
	OECD countries	D 26-m	
Labour productivity – index nos	Main countries	L 4-a	
Loan advances to manufacturing industry (from banks) in local currency	OAS member countries	N 16-a	
No of accidents reported & no of resulting fatalities	UK	B 25-a	
employees involved in strikes	Main countries	R 3-a	
former workers currently unemployed	All countries	L 4-a	
hrs of overtime worked per wk (average)	USA	J 2-a	
hrs worked per wk by sex	EEC countries	E 33-a	
by area & by sex	EEC countries	E 25-a	
per wk	All countries	L 1-m	
	EEC countries	E 26-a2	
	Main countries	R 3-m	
	OAS member countries	N 18-a	
per yr: salaried staff	EEC countries	E 11-a	
wage earners	EEC countries	E 11-a	
(all employees)	EEC countries	E 2-a	E 8-a
of manufacturing establishments in operation	African countries	U 44-a	
	OAS member countries	N 14-a	
salaried staff employed as % of total labour force	EEC countries	E 2-a	
times inventory was turned by manufacturing corporations	USA	J 2-a	
wage & salary earners employed by region	EEC countries	E 18-a	
working days lost in manufacturing industry through strikes	Main countries	R 3-a	
Output & employment – index nos	UK	B 28-a	
Output per man-hr – index nos	Main countries	B 23-a	
projected to 1980 by value in $m	N African countries	U 38	
Plant capacity: utilisation – index nos	USA	J 2-a	
Production (excl food & tobacco) – index nos	EEC countries	E 26-a	
Production – index nos (quantum basis)	S American countries	U 40-a	
	African countries	U 44-a	
	Australasian countries	U 32-q	
	EEC countries	E 28-q	E 27-a
	Latin American countries	J 5-a	
	OECD countries	D 19-m	D 20-m
	World regions	U 60-a	
Productivity – index nos	Main countries	J 2-a	
	UK	B 28-a	
Profits of manufacturing corporations as % of sales turnover	USA	J 2-a	
Receipts of steel products for fabrication: tonnage	OECD countries	D 22-a	
Value added (at factor cost) in manufacturing in $m	Main countries	U 25-a	
	OECD countries	D 9-a	
Wage costs per unit of manufactured output	Main countries	B 27-a	
Wage rates: hourly, daily & weekly in local currency	OAS member countries	N 17-a	
per hr in local currency	EEC countries	E 25-a2	
	All countries	L 1-m	L 4-a
in local currency by sex	Main countries	R 3-m	C 7-a
per hr (gross) – index nos	EEC countries	E 26-a2	
basic contract rates in local currency	OAS member countries	N 17-a	
index nos	Main countries	C 4-a	
skilled workers by sex	Main countries	R 4-q	
unskilled workers by sex	Main countries	R 4-q	
Wages costs per hr in FrS	Main countries	C 7-a	
per unit of output – index nos	Main countries	B 23-a	
MANURE			
Usage in farming: animal fertiliser by value in $m	EEC countries	E 44-a	

	Territorial coverage	Title codes	
MAPLE SUGAR			
Production & consumption: tonnage & per capita in kg per yr	OECD countries	D 14-a	
MARBLE			
Production (incl travertines) by volume	All countries	U 22-a	
MARGARINE			
% change: wholesale prices	France & Italy	E 34-m	
producer prices	Belgium & W Germany	E 34-m	
Consumption: coconut oil in production of margarine: tonnage	USA	B 19-a	
cottonseed oil in production of margarine: tonnage	USA	B 19-a	
soybean oil in production of margarine: tonnage	USA	B 19-a	
vegetable oils by kind in production of margarine	Main countries	A 4-a	
per capita in kg per yr	European countries	U 35-a	
	EEC countries	B 1-a	
	OECD countries	D 1-a	
	Main countries	B 19-a	
in lbs per yr	UK	B 12-a	B 19-a
tonnage & per capita in kg per yr	EEC countries	E 44-a	
in lbs per yr	Main countries	B 4-a	
tonnage	Main countries	B 12-a	
Excise duties: rates charged	OAS member countries	N 17-a	
Exports by destination: tonnage	EEC countries	E 31-a	
tonnage	Main countries	B 12-a	
Imports by source: tonnage	Main countries	B 4-a	
tonnage	Main countries	B 12-a	
	Main countries	B 4-a	
Producer prices per 100 kg in local currency	Belgium & W Germany	E 34-m	
Production: edible oils & vanaspati: tonnage	India	U 32-q	
Production, imports, exports & consumption of margarine: tonnage	EEC countries	E 44-a	
(incl prepared cooking fats): tonnage	All countries	U 22-a	
(incl vanaspati): tonnage	Main countries	B 12-a	
Production, stocks & consumption per capita in kg per yr	OECD countries	D 14-a	
Production, supply, consumption & trade: tonnage	EEC countries	B 1-a	
tonnage	African countries	U 44-a	
	All countries	B 19-a	U 43-a
	EEC countries	E 26-m	E 28-q
		E 27-a	
	Main countries (incl E European)	A 4-a	B 4-a
		P 1-a	R 5-a
	OAS member countries	N 14-a	
	Zaire	E 41-a	
Retail prices (comparative) in $ per kg	EEC countries	Z 3-a	
in local currency	OAS member countries	N 17-a	
in pence per lb (equiv)	Main countries	B 12-q	
Self-sufficiency ratios	EEC countries	E 44-a	
Wholesale prices in local currency	OAS member countries	N 17-a	
in $ per ton	Canada, Main European countries & USA	A 9-a	
oilseeds used in margarine production in £ per ton	UK	B 12-m	
per 100 kg	France & Italy	E 34-m	

Margins (wholesale & retail)   see   DISTRIBUTION COSTS: SALES MARGINS

Marine boilers   see   BOILERS, MARINE

Marine engineering industry   see   SHIPBUILDING

MARINE ENGINES

Exports by destination up to 200 hp by value in £	UK	V 1-a	
Imports by source up to 200 hp by value in £	UK	V 1-a	

Marine oils   see   FISH OILS & FATS
                           WHALE OIL

Maritime disasters   see   ACCIDENTS, MARITIME

Maritime transport   see   CONTAINER TRAFFIC
                            OCEAN PASSENGER TRAFFIC
                            SEABORNE SHIPPING

Market gardens   see   HORTICULTURE

Market pulp   see   WOOD PULP

MARKET SHARE

% share of world trade: boilerhouse plant	Main European countries	B 30-a	
steam boilers	Main European countries	B 30-a	
% US share of world exports: manufactured goods (by SITC classes)		N 3-a	

Market valuations   see   STOCK EXCHANGE

MARKETING

Expenditure on sales promotion by specific major oil companies in $m	Worldwide	C 3-a	

Marmalade   see   JAM & MARMALADE

	Territorial coverage	Title codes

MARRIAGE RATES
    see also   DIVORCE RATES

Per 1000 population: historical table 1750-1969	Main European countries	Z 1-a
by areas	EEC countries	E 38-a
Per 1000 population	EEC countries	E 2-a
	Main countries	U 27-m
	OAS member countries	N 12-a

MARRIAGES

No registered: historical table	EEC countries	E 2-a
	Main European countries	Z 1-a
& rate per 1000 population	All countries	U 14-a
	EEC countries	E 33-a
	Latin American countries	J 5-a
	Main countries	R 5-a
(with annual total)	EEC countries	E 26-m
by age groups	OAS member countries	N 12-a
by age of bride & groom	All countries	U 14-a
by regions	OAS member countries	N 12-a
No registered	Asian, Far East & Australasian countries	U 45-a

Married working women   see   EMPLOYMENT

MASTICS
    see also   PAINTS & VARNISHES

Exports: tonnage & value in $	OECD countries	D 5-a
Imports: tonnage & value in $	OECD countries	D 5-a
Production by value in $ per ton	OECD countries	D 5-a
tonnage	OECD countries	D 5-a

MATCHES

Excise duties: rates charged	EEC countries	E 31-a	
Production: volume	EEC countries	E 28-q	E 27-a
Retail prices in local currency	OAS member countries	N 17-a	
Wholesale prices in local currency	OAS member countries	N 17-a	

Maté   see   YERBA MATE

MATERIAL COSTS
    see also   DISTRIBUTION COSTS
                  LABOUR COSTS
                  SOCIAL CHARGES
                  WAGES

% increase in material costs of the chemical industry	UK	B 21-a
Brimstone (in production of sulphuric acid)	Main countries	U 25-a
Building industry - index nos	European countries & USA	U 5-a
Gypsum (in production of sulphuric acid) in $	Main countries	U 25-a
Housing construction - index nos	European countries & USA	U 5-a
Machine tools industry in $m	USA	J 2-a
Pyrites (in production of sulphuric acid) in $	Main countries	U 25-a

MATERNITY BENEFITS

Cost to National Health Service in $	All countries	L 2-a
Expenditure in local currency	EEC countries	E 6-a
Payments made as % of expenditure: social welfare	EEC countries	E 6-a

MATERNITY HOSPITALS

No in use	AASM countries	E 41-a
of consultations	AASM countries	E 41-a
post-natal consultations	AASM countries	E 41-a

MATS & MATTING

Consumption: acrylic yarn in production of mats: tonnage	EEC countries	K 4-a
cellulosic fibres in production of mats: tonnage	EEC countries	K 4-a
coir fibre in production of matting: tonnage	EEC countries	K 4-a
cotton yarn in production of mats: tonnage	EEC countries	K 4-a
polyamide fibre in production of mats: tonnage	EEC countries	K 4-a
yarn in production of mats: tonnage	EEC countries	K 4-a
polyester fibre in production of mats: tonnage	EEC countries	K 4-a
yarn in production of mats: tonnage	EEC countries	K 4-a
polyolefin fibre in production of mats: tonnage	EEC countries	K 4-a
yarn in production of mats: tonnage	EEC countries	K 4-a
synthetic fibres in production of mats: tonnage	EEC countries	K 4-a
wool in production of mats: tonnage	EEC countries	K 4-a
Exports by destination: mats made of coir fibre: tonnage	India	B 10-a

Mattress fibre   see   COIR FIBRE

Mattresses   see   HOUSEHOLD TEXTILES

Means of payment   see   MONEY SUPPLY

Measles   see   DISEASES, INFECTIOUS

	Territorial coverage	Title codes

MEASURING APPARATUS
see also WEIGHING MACHINERY

Deliveries: precision balances by value in £m	UK	C 24-a
measuring equipment (electrical) by value in £m	UK	C 24-a
(electronic) by value in £m	UK	C 24-a
(nucleonic) by value in £m	UK	C 24-a
radiation detection apparatus by value in £m	UK	C 24-a
radioactive devices by value in £m	UK	C 24-a
thermometers (liquid) by value in £	UK	C 24-a
Demand (domestic) by value in £	UK	C 24-a
Exports by value in $m	All countries	U 38-a
measuring equipment by value in $m & % growth rates	Main countries	U 38-a
Imports by value in $m	All countries	U 38-a
World exports by value in $m		U 38-a

MEAT
see also CANNED MEAT
GOAT MEAT
HORSE MEAT
OFFAL, EDIBLE
POULTRY MEAT
RABBIT MEAT
REINDEER MEAT
STATE PROCUREMENT (Communist countries)

% changes in volume of retail sales	E European countries incl USSR	U 16-a	
% of daily calorie intake obtained from meat consumption	ECE countries	U 15-a	
% of human calorie intake obtained from meat consumption	World regions	C 27-a	
% of production by member countries of EEC area	EEC countries	R 5-a	
Availability (incl home output as % of supply)	All countries	U 43-a	
Budget cost: price supports for meat (incl poultry)	EEC area	B 3-a	
Consumption cost: private sector (at current values)	EEC countries	E 32-a	
per capita by income levels in lbs per yr	USA	C 27-a	
carcase meat in lbs per yr	Main countries	B 11-a	
in kg per yr	Main countries	E 3-a	
	E European countries incl USSR	U 16-a	
	EEC countries	E 44-a	
	Canada, European countries, Japan, USA & USSR	E 44-a	
	W European countries	P 5-a	
	OECD countries	D 1-a	
		U 29-q	U 54-q
Export prices - index nos (weighted average of sub-groups) in local currency	Asian, Far East & Australasian countries	U 45-a	
Exports: beef, veal & lamb: tonnage	Argentine & Australasian countries	C 9-m	
beef: tonnage & value in $m	Chad & Madagascar	E 45-a	
historical table from 1831: tonnage	Denmark & Eire	Z 1-a	
by value & as % of exports of farm products	W European countries	U 20-a	
& as % of total exports	E African & Australasian countries	B 11-a	
(incl live animals) to E European area by value in $	W European countries	U 20-a	
in $m	Australasian countries	U 32-m	
(incl live animals & meat preparations) in $m	OECD countries	D 1-a	
(incl meat products) in £m	Main countries	B 11-a	
tonnage	Australia & New Zealand	U 32-m	
Imports & exports: tonnage	EEC countries	E 1-a	
Imports by value & as % of imports of farm products	W European countries	U 20-a	
(incl live animals) ex E European area in $	W European countries	U 20-a	
(incl live animals & meat preparations) in $	OECD countries	D 1-a	
tonnage	Main countries	A 11-a	
Income elasticity of demand for meat - index nos	USA	C 27-a	
Inter-EEC imports & exports: tonnage	EEC countries	E 1-a	
Production by value (at current prices) in local currency	EEC countries	E 44-a	
Production & consumption projected to 1985: tonnage	Main countries	A 1	
Production: beef, pork, lamb, mutton & goat-meat: tonnage	OAS member countries	N 14-a	
beef, veal, lamb, mutton & pork: tonnage	All countries	A 9-a	U 43-a
beef, veal & pork: tonnage	EEC countries	E 26-m	
by kind (incl offal): tonnage	Main countries	E 3-a	
Production, consumption, imports, exports & supply: tonnage	EEC countries	B 1-a	
historical table from 1903: tonnage	Main European countries	Z 1-a	
imports, exports, consumption & stocks: tonnage	EEC countries	E 44-a	
imports, exports & domestic supply: tonnage	EEC countries	E 1-a	
(incl edible offal): tonnage	OECD countries	D 1-a	
tonnage	African countries	U 44-a	
	E European countries & USSR (incl Ukraine)	U 16-a	
	Latin American countries	J 5-a	
	Main countries	R 5-a	
Retail prices: beef, veal & pig-meat - index nos	EEC countries	C 9-m	
meat - index nos	EEC countries	E 26-m	
Self-sufficiency ratios	EEC countries	E 44-a	
State procurement: tonnage	E European countries & USSR (incl Ukraine)	U 16-a	
Supply (net) per capita per day	All countries	U 43-a	
Wholesale prices: beef, veal & pig-meat - index nos	EEC countries	C 9-m	
World market prices - index nos		U 30-a	

MEAT, DRIED OR SALTED

Imports & exports: tonnage	EEC countries	E 1-a
Inter-EEC imports & exports: tonnage	EEC countries	E 1-a
Retail prices by kind of meat in local currency	OAS member countries	N 17-a
Wholesale prices by kind of meat in local currency	OAS member countries	N 17-a

	Territorial coverage	Title codes
MEAT BY KIND		
% distribution of exports by destination	Australia & New Zealand	B 11-a
% share of Commonwealth imports (incl offal)	UK	B 11-a
Consumption per capita in lbs per yr	UK	B 12-a
tonnage & consumption per capita in kg	OECD countries	D 14-a
tonnage	OAS member countries	N 17-a
Exports by destination: tonnage	Main countries	B 12-m
by value in $m	W European countries	U 33-a
Imports: live animals by value in $m	European countries	U 33-a
Per capita annual world demand projected to 1985		A 1
Production: beef, veal & pig-meat: tonnage	EEC countries	C 9-m
by areas: tonnage	EEC countries	E 38-a
from indigenous livestock: tonnage	AASM countries	E 41-a
tonnage	All countries	U 22-a
	EEC countries	E 1-a
	Canada, European countries, USA & USSR	E 44-a
Production - index nos	Main countries	B 12-a
Stocks held by producers: tonnage	Main countries	B 11-a
imported & frozen meat (incl offal): tonnage	Main countries	B 12-m
World exports: tonnage	UK	B 12-w
unit value in $ per ton		B 11-a
World production: beef, lamb, pork & poultry: tonnage		A 11-a
		A 5-a

Meat meals, prepared   see   FROZEN MEALS, PREPARED

	Territorial coverage	Title codes
MEAT PREPARATIONS		
see also CANNED MEAT		
SAUSAGES		
% changes in volume of retail sales	E European countries (incl USSR)	U 16-a
% contribution to export earnings	Kenya & Madagascar	E 45-a
Consumption per capita in kg	E European countries	U 16-a
Exports by destination: canned meat: tonnage	Main countries	B 12-m
by value in $m	European countries	U 33-a
tonnage & value in $m	Kenya	E 45-a
Imports by source: canned meat: tonnage	Main countries	B 12-m
by value in $m	European countries	U 33-a
Production: canned meat by kind: tonnage	UK	B 12-a
from beef & pork: tonnage	Madagascar	E 41-a
tongues & slicing meat: tonnage	UK	B 12-a
Retail prices by kind in local currency	OAS member countries	N 17-a
Wholesale prices by kind of prepared meats in local currency	OAS member countries	N 17-a

Mechanical cultivators   see   GARDEN TRACTORS

Mechanical engineering   see   ENGINEERING INDUSTRY, MECHANICAL

	Territorial coverage	Title codes	
MECHANICAL HANDLING EQUIPMENT			
see also CONTRACTORS PLANT & EQUIPMENT			
FORK LIFT TRUCKS			
% share of world exports (value basis)	UK	B 27-a	
Exports by destination by value in $	Main countries	U 9-a	
NIMEXE classes by value in $m	All countries	E 20-a	
SITC classes by value in $m	All countries	U 50-a	U 59-a
type & by value in $m	OECD countries	D 9-a	
value in $m	Main countries	U 38-a	
Imports by NIMEXE classes by value in $m	All countries	E 20-a	
SITC classes by value in $m	All countries	U 50-a	U 59-a
value in $m	All countries	U 38-a	
Production: fork-lift trucks by volume	All countries	U 22-a	
by value in $	EEC countries	E 28-q	E 27-a
World exports by value in $m		U 38-a	

Mechanical pulp   see   WOOD PULP, MECHANICAL

Mechanisation, agricultural   see   FARM TRACTION
                                          FARM TRACTORS
                                          MACHINERY, AGRICULTURAL

	Territorial coverage	Title codes
MEDICAL EQUIPMENT		
see also ELECTRO-MEDICAL APPARATUS		
Exports by destination by value in $m	Main countries	U 9-a
by value in $m	All countries	U 38-a
Imports by value in $m	All countries	U 38-a

Medical facilities   see   HEALTH CENTRES & CLINICS
                                HOSPITALS
                                MATERNITY HOSPITALS
                                MENTAL WELFARE
                                PUBLIC HEALTH

	Territorial coverage	Title codes

MEDICAL PERSONNEL
    see also   HOSPITAL PERSONNEL
                   PHARMACISTS
                   SCHOOLS, MEDICAL

	Territorial coverage	Title codes
No of dentists in practice or employed in hospitals	African countries	U 44-a
in practice	AASM countries	E 41-a
	Main countries	R 5-a
	OAS member countries	N 18-a
doctors & dentists in practice (incl ratio)	Latin American countries	J 5-a
doctors, dentists & pharmacists in practice	EEC countries	E 38-a
doctors & pharmacists in practice	Main countries	E 3-a
doctors & physicians in practice	AASM countries	E 41-a
	Main countries	R 5-a
	OAS member countries	N 18-a
doctors in practice or employed in hospitals	African countries	U 44-a
per 100,000 population	Main countries	R 5-a
graduate nurses: no employed in hospitals	OAS member countries	N 18-a
hospital physicians & nurses: no employed	All countries	W 1-a
medical workers (all occupations): no employed	Main countries	R 5-a
midwives (incl hospital midwives): no employed	African countries	U 44-a
	AASM countries	E 41-a
	Main countries	R 5-a
nurses & doctors: no employed or in practice	Asian, Far East & Australasian countries	U 45-a
nursing auxiliaries: no employed in hospitals	OAS member countries	N 18-a
	AASM countries	E 41-a
pharmacists: no employed	AASM countries	E 41-a
veterinary surgeons: no in practice	Main countries	R 5-a
Population per doctor & per dentist	ECE countries	U 15-a
per doctor	Asian, Far East & Australasian countries	U 45-a
	Developing countries	U 23-a
	Main countries	R 5-a
	OAS member countries	N 18-a

Medical research   see   RESEARCH & DEVELOPMENT

Medical research apparatus   see   ELECTRO-MEDICAL APPARATUS

Medical schools   see   SCHOOLS, MEDICAL

MEDICAL SCIENCE

% of students enrolled studying medicine	ECAFE countries	U 17
No of full & part-time research staff engaged in medicine	All countries	U 62-a
medical students enrolled at universities	All countries	U 62-a
enrolled abroad by origin	All countries	U 64-a
university degrees gained in medicine	All countries	U 62-a

Medical services   see   HOSPITALS
                            VETERINARY MEDICINE

MEDICAMENTS

Exports by destination by value in $	Main countries	U 2-a

Medicinal herbs & plants   see   HERBS, MEDICINAL

Medicines   see   ANTIBIOTICS
                     COCAINE
                     DRUGS & MEDICINES
                     HORMONES
                     MEDICAMENTS
                     OPIUM ALKALOIDS
                     PHARMACEUTICAL PRODUCTS
                     VITAMINS

MELONS

Area under melon crop by kind in acres	USA	B 6-a
& yield per ha (incl production): tonnage	All countries	A 9-a
Imports by source: tonnage	OECD countries	D 37-a
water melons: tonnage	Poland	U 20-a
Production: melons & water melons: tonnage	African countries	U 44-a

Men's wear   see   CLOTHING

Mending wool   see   HOME SEWING

Meningitis   see   DISEASES, INFECTIOUS

Mental health   see   MENTAL WELFARE

Mental institutions   see   HOSPITALS, MENTAL

MENTAL WELFARE

Sickness benefits paid out as % of gross national product	OECD countries	D 11-a

	Territorial coverage	Title codes	
MERCHANT BARS, STEEL			
Basic domestic prices in local currency per ton	OECD countries	D 22-a	
Consumption: tonnage	EEC countries	E 29-a	
Deliveries by dealers: tonnage	EEC countries	E 29-a	
to EEC area: tonnage	EEC countries	E 29-a	
Export prices in FrB per ton fob	EEC countries	U 49-m	
in $ per 100 lbs fob	USA	R 2-m	
in $ per ton fob	OECD countries	D 22-a	
Exports by destination: tonnage	EEC countries	E 29-a	
	EEC area	E 5-q	
	Main countries	T 4-a	
Exports: hot-rolled bars: tonnage	E European countries	T 1-a	
tonnage	European countries, Japan & USA	C 5-m	
Imports: alloy steel by quality: tonnage	Main countries	T 1-a	
by source: tonnage	EEC countries	E 5-q	E 29-a
	Main countries	T 4-a	
free-cutting steel by quality: tonnage	Main countries	T 1-a	
high-carbon steel by quality: tonnage	Main countries	T 1-a	
high-speed steel by quality: tonnage	Main countries	T 1-a	
reinforcement bars by quality: tonnage	Main countries	T 1-a	
stainless steel bars by quality: tonnage	Main countries	T 1-a	
tonnage	European countries, Japan & USA	C 5-m	
Inter-EEC trade: tonnage & value in $	EEC countries	E 29-a	
Production: tonnage	All countries	T 1-a	
	European countries	C 5-m	
	EEC countries	E 29-a	
	Main countries	T 4-a	
Receipts by dealers: tonnage	EEC countries	E 29-a	
ex EEC area: tonnage	EEC countries	E 29-a	
Wholesale prices in $ per ton	Main countries	U 49-m	U 57-a
MERCHANT SEAMEN			
No employed by nationality & by flag	Worldwide	D 28-a	
by occupation & by flag	Worldwide	D 28-a	
catering staff & pursers by flag	Worldwide	D 28-a	
deck officers, deckhands & ratings by flag	Worldwide	D 28-a	
engine-room officers by flag	Worldwide	D 28-a	

Merchant shipping fleet in reserve (US)   see   Appendix 4: WORLD MARITIME FLEETS

MERCHANT SHIPPING FLEETS

    see also   BULK CARRIERS
                CARGO SHIPS
                TRAMP SHIPPING
                Appendix 4: WORLD MARITIME FLEETS

	Territorial coverage	Title codes	
Launchings: no by type	Country of build	S 1-a	
tonnage of new construction as % of total afloat	All countries	S 1-a	
New construction	Country of build	S 3-q	S 2-a
	Worldwide	D 28-a	
New construction: no by type	All countries	S 2-a	
no & tonnage by flag	All countries	S 2-a	
by type	Worldwide	S 2-a	
no & tonnage: motorships	Worldwide	S 2-a	
steamships	Worldwide	S 2-a	
tonnage on order	All countries	D 28-a	
No afloat by size & kind	Country of build	S 1-a	
by type of engine	All countries	S 2-a	
in course of construction by size	All countries	S 3-q	
of motorships & tonnage afloat by flag		S 2-a	
(diesel engine propelled) afloat	Worldwide	S 2-a	
(diesel-electric propelled) afloat	Worldwide	S 2-a	
ordered by size (but not started)	All countries	S 3-q	
of steamships & tonnage afloat by flag	Worldwide	S 2-a	
(by type of propulsion) afloat	Worldwide	S 2-a	
(turbine engine propelled) afloat	Worldwide	S 2-a	
(turbo-electric propelled) afloat	Worldwide	S 2-a	
(using reciprocating engines) afloat	Worldwide	S 2-a	
No & tonnage afloat by flag & by size	Worldwide	S 2-a	
flag & by age	Countries of registration	S 2-a	
type & by age	Countries of registration	S 2-a	
type & by flag	Countries of registration	S 2-a	
new ocean-going vessels	World regions	U 37-a	
of vessels (& tonnage) afloat: historical table from 1904	Worldwide	S 2-a	
by country of registration	Latin American countries	J 5-a	
	OAS member countries	N 15-a	
laid up by flag	Worldwide	S 23-m	D 28-a
Tonnage afloat by flag: historical table from 1913	Worldwide	C 4-a	
flag	Developing countries	U 37-a	
	E European countries & USSR	D 28-a	
	Asian, Far East & Australasian countries	U 45-a	
flags of convenience		D 28-a	
type	Latin American countries	U 40-a	
type: tankers & bulk carriers	Countries of registration	U 43-a	

	Territorial coverage	Title codes

MERCHANT VESSELS
    see also CARGO SHIPS

	Territorial coverage	Title codes
No & tonnage afloat	Countries of registration	S 16-a
launched (excl tankers)	All countries	U 38-a
(all vessels)	All countries	U 22-a
No launched by type: steam or motor-driven	Worldwide	U 38-a
Tonnage launched by type: steam or motor-driven	Worldwide	U 38-a
Tonnage launched	All countries	U 43-a
	Main countries	E 3-a
under construction	Main countries	E 3-a

MERCURY

	Territorial coverage	Title codes
% consumption in electrolysis of chlorine & caustic soda	USA	N 1-a
in production of control instrumentation	USA	N 1-a
electrical apparatus	USA	N 1-a
special mercuric paints	USA	N 1-a
Consumption in electrolysis of chlorine & caustic soda	USA	T 4-a
in experimental laboratories in flasks (of 76 lbs)	USA	T 4-a
in manufacture of catalysts in flasks (of 76 lbs)	USA	T 4-a
control instrumentation in flasks (of 76 lbs)	USA	T 4-a
dental preparations in flasks (of 76 lbs)	USA	T 4-a
electrical apparatus in flasks (of 76 lbs)	USA	T 4-a
fungicides in flasks (of 76 lbs)	USA	T 4-a
paper & pulp in flasks (of 76 lbs)	USA	T 4-a
pharmaceutical products in flasks (of 76 lbs)	USA	T 4-a
special paints in flasks (of 76 lbs)	USA	T 4-a
in flasks (of 76 lbs)	USA	N 1-a
Exports by destination in flasks (of 76 lbs)	Spain & Mexico	T 4-a
tonnage	Italy	C 12-a
Government strategic stockpile in flasks (of 76 lbs)	USA	N 1-a
Import prices in £ per flask (of 76 lbs) cif	UK	C 12-m
in $ per flask (of 34.5 kg) cif	European countries	T 4-m
(of 76 lbs) cif	European countries	R 2-m
Imports & exports by source & destination in flasks (of 76 lbs)	Main countries	B 15-a
by source in flasks (of 76 lbs)	Main countries	T 4-a
tonnage	Italy	C 12-a
Producer prices in $ per flask (of 76 lbs)	UK & USA	H 2-a
Production (based on metal content of ore): tonnage	All countries	U 22-a U 43-a
in flasks (of 76 lbs)	USA	J 6-a
in kg	OAS member countries	N 14-a
in lbs & kg	All countries	B 15-a
secondary mercury in flasks (of 76 lbs)	USA	N 1-a
tonnage	Chile, Mexico & Peru	U 40-a
Wholesale prices in lire per flask (of 76 lbs)	Italy	C 12-m R 2-m
in $ per flask (of 76 lbs) at London Metal Exchange	UK	N 1-a
(duty paid) at New York	USA	C 12-m R 2-m
		T 4-m N 1-a
World production in flasks (of 76 lbs)		N 1-a N 4-a
		T 4-a
tonnage	Worldwide	C 30-a
	All countries	C 12-a
World reserves (known) in flasks (of 76 lbs)	Main countries	N 1-a

MERCURY COMPOUNDS

	Territorial coverage	Title codes
Consumption (as fungicide): tonnage	All countries	A 9-a

MERCURY ORE

	Territorial coverage	Title codes
Production: historical tables: tonnage	Italy	C 12-a

Mesta   see   JUTE

Metal bending & folding machines   see   MACHINE TOOLS

Metal cans   see   CANS, METAL

Metal castings industries   see   FOUNDRIES

Metal cutting machine tools   see   MACHINE TOOLS
                                        METAL-WORKING MACHINES

Metal impurity standards   see   QUALITY STANDARDS

METAL INDUSTRIES
    see also   IRON & STEEL INDUSTRY
                   NON-FERROUS METALS INDUSTRY

	Territorial coverage	Title codes
% contribution to gross national product	Canada, European countries, Japan & USA	U 38-a
% share of industrial production	Main countries	U 38-a
of total capital investment	E European countries	U 16-a
Capital investment by areas in local currency	EEC countries	E 38-a
projected to 1980 in $m	N African countries	U 38

	Territorial coverage	Title codes	
METAL INDUSTRIES, continued			
Consumption: aluminium (primary): tonnage	Main countries	T 4-a	
tonnage	EEC countries, Japan & USA	C 12-a	
electric power by areas in kWh	EEC countries	E 38-a	
in kWh	All countries	C 23-a	
gas (in metals production) by volume in m³	European countries & USA	U 3-a	
sulphuric acid: tonnage	OECD countries	D 5-a	
Costs: salaried staff per mth in local currency	EEC countries	E 11-a	
Earnings per hr by areas in local currency	EEC countries	E 38-a	
by sex in local currency	Main countries	R 3-a	
in local currency	All countries	L 4-a	
Employment - index nos	All countries	L 4-a	
Frequency of accidents at work in metal fabricating industries	EEC countries	E 2-a	
Investment in buildings in local currency	EEC countries	E 40-a	
land purchase in local currency	EEC countries	E 40-a	
machinery in local currency	EEC countries	E 40-a	
Labour costs as % of total costs in metal production	EEC countries	E 8-a	
by status of employees in local currency	EEC countries	E 8-a	
per hr (all employees) in local currency	EEC countries	E 11-a	
by areas in local currency	EEC countries	E 38-a	
wage earners in local currency	EEC countries	E 11-a	
Labour force employed: basic metals industry	OECD countries	D 23-a	
by areas	EEC countries	E 11-a	
no of salaried staff	EEC countries	E 11-a	
wage earners	EEC countries	E 11-a	
Labour force employed (total)	EEC countries	E 2-a	E 8-a
No of accidents reported & no of resulting fatalities	UK	B 25-a	
of hrs worked per wk	All countries	L 4-a	
	Main countries	R 3-m	
per wk by region	EEC countries	E 25-a	
per yr: all employees	EEC countries	E 8-a	
salaried staff	EEC countries	E 11-a	
wage earners	EEC countries	E 11-a	
of establishments for metal production in operation	African countries	U 44-a	
Production in metals industries as % of world industrial activity		U 38	
basic metals - index nos	Far East countries	U 32-q	
metal products - index nos	Far East countries	U 32-q	
Production - index nos	EEC countries	E 28-q	E 27-a
	Latin American countries	J 5-a	
	OAS member countries	N 14-a	
Receipts: aluminium products: tonnage	OECD countries	D 21-a	
Wage rates: castors & rollers per hr in local currency	OAS member countries	N 17-a	
per hr in local currency	EEC countries	E 25-a2	
by sex in local currency	Main countries	R 3-m	
skilled workers by sex in local currency	Main countries	R 4-q	
unskilled workers by sex in local currency	Main countries	R 4-q	
Wage rates - index nos	Main countries	R 3-a	

Metal mining   see   IRON ORE MINING
                          MANGANESE MINES
                          ORE MINING INDUSTRY

METAL ORES

         see also   BAUXITE
                     CHROME ORE
                     COPPER ORE
                     IRON ORE
                     LEAD ORE
                     MANGANESE ORE
                     NICKEL ORE
                     PLATINUM ORE
                     TIN ORE
                     TUNGSTEN ORE
                     ZINC ORE

	Territorial coverage	Title codes	
% contribution of non-ferrous ores to export earnings	Niger	E 45-a	
Capital formation in ore mining industry in $m	Main countries	U 21-a	
Coastal shipping: tonnage	EEC countries	E 43-a	
Export prices: metallic ores - index nos	Worldwide	U 29-q	U 54-q
Exports: non-ferrous ores by sea, road & rail: tonnage	European countries	U 8-a	
% contribution of non-ferrous ores to export earnings	Niger	E 45-a	
Capital formation in ore mining industry in $m	Main countries	U 21-a	
Coastal shipping: tonnage	EEC countries	E 43-a	
Export prices: metallic ores - index nos	Worldwide	U 29-q	U 54-q
non-ferrous metal ores - index nos	Worldwide	U 29-q	
Exports: non-ferrous ores by sea, road & rail: tonnage	European countries	U 8-a	
by regions of origin by value in $	EEC countries	E 38-a	
(incl crude minerals) by value in $ & as % of total exports	ECE countries	U 15-a	
tonnage & value in $m: non-ferrous ores	Niger	E 45-a	
Imports & exports: iron ore by rail, road & sea: tonnage	EEC countries	E 43-a	
by road, rail & sea: tonnage	European countries	U 8-a	
(incl scrap) by value in local currency	Japan	U 32-m	
(incl crude minerals) by value in $ & as % of total imports	ECE countries	U 15-a	
Labour force employed: ore mining	Main countries	U 21-a	
Ocean freight rates (main routes single voyage)	Worldwide	S 16-a	
Producer prices by kind of ores (at end-June)	W Germany & UK	H 2-a	
Production by kind: historical table from 1750: tonnage	Main European countries	Z 1-a	
tonnage	All countries	N 5-a	
Rail freight: iron ore (incl waste): inland & abroad: tonnage	EEC countries	E 43-a	
Road transport (over frontiers) by kinds of ore: tonnage	EEC countries	E 43-a	
Seaborne freight by kinds of ore (incl waste): tonnage	EEC countries	E 43-a	

	Territorial coverage	Title codes	
METAL ORES, continued			
Shipments through Kiel Canal: eastwards & westwards: tonnage		D 28-a	
Panama Canal: eastwards: tonnage		D 28-a	
Wages & salary costs: ore mining industry in $	Main countries	U 21-a	
World market prices: non-ferrous ores - index nos		G 1-a	
metallic ores - index nos		U 23-a	
METAL PRODUCTS			
Consumption by value in $m	Main Latin American countries	U 38-a	
tonnage	Central African countries	U 38-a	
Exports by areas by value in local currency	EEC countries	E 38-a	
by sea, inland waters, road & rail: tonnage	European countries	U 8-a	
machinery & transport equipment by value in $	ECE countries	U 15-a	
Growth in production capacity: tonnage	African countries	U 38-a	
Imports by sea, inland waters, road & rail: tonnage	European countries	U 8-a	
machinery & transport equipment by value in $	ECE countries	U 15-a	
Production as % of total industrial output	Developing countries	U 38-a	
metal furniture by volume	Zaire	E 41-a	
projected to 1980 by value in $m	N African countries	U 38	
Production - index nos	Australia & Philippines	U 32-q	
	OECD countries	D 19-m	D 20-m
Retail prices - index nos	EEC countries	E 26-m	
Road transport of metal goods over frontiers: tonnage	EEC countries	E 43-a	
Wholesale prices - index nos	EEC countries	E 26-m	
	Japan & S Korea	U 32-m	
METAL PRODUCTS BY KIND			
Exports (incl tools) by destination by CST classes by value in $	EEC countries	E 48-a	
NIMEXE classes by value in $	All countries	E 20-a	
SITC classes by value in $	Main countries	D 2-q	
	OECD countries	D 3-a2	
	All countries	U 50-a	U 59-a
Imports & exports by source & destination by road, rail & sea: tonnage	EEC countries	E 43-a	
by source by SITC classes: tonnage & value in $	OECD countries	D 3-a2	
by value in $	Main countries	D 2-q	
(incl tools) by NIMEXE classes by value in $	All countries	E 20-a	
SITC classes by value in $	All countries	U 50-a	U 59-a
source by CST classes by value in $	EEC countries	E 21-a	
Production: tonnage	EEC countries	E 28-q	E 27-a
Rail & seaborne freight (inland & abroad): tonnage	EEC countries	E 43-a	
METAL PRODUCTS INDUSTRIES			
% share of total capital investment	E European countries & USSR	U 16-a	
Capital formation in $m	Main countries	U 21-a	
Costs: salaried staff per mth in local currency	EEC countries	E 11-a	
Earnings: female workers per hr in FrS	Main countries	C 2-a	
per hr in FrS	Main countries	C 2-a	
per hr piece rates in FrS	Main countries	C 2-a	
semi-skilled workers per hr in FrS	Main countries	C 2-a	
skilled workers per hr in FrS	Main countries	C 2-a	
time rates per hr in FrS	Main countries	C 2-a	
unskilled workers per hr in FrS	Main countries	C 2-a	
Gross output of metals industries by value in $m	Main countries	U 21-a	
Labour costs: female workers per hr in FrS	Main countries	C 2-a	
per hr in local currency	EEC countries	E 2-a	E 11-a
in DM million	W Germany	H 3-a	
in FrS	Main countries	C 2-a	
semi-skilled workers in FrS	Main countries	C 2-a	
skilled workers in FrS	Main countries	C 2-a	
unskilled workers in FrS	Main countries	C 2-a	
wage earners in local currency	EEC countries	E 11-a	
Labour force employed: no of salaried staff	EEC countries	E 11-a	
of wage earners	EEC countries	E 11-a	
No of hrs worked per wk	OAS member countries	N 18-a	
per wk by region	EEC countries	E 25-a	
salaried staff	EEC countries	E 11-a	
wage earners	EEC countries	E 11-a	
machine tools in use for cutting metals	USA	J 2-a	
for forming metals	USA	J 2-a	
establishments producing metal goods in operation	African countries	U 44-a	
operatives employed in metal fabricating industries	Main countries	U 21-a	
Production - index nos	Main countries	R 5-a	
Receipts: steel for fabrication: tonnage	OECD countries	D 22-a	
Turnover in metal products industry by sector in DM million	W Germany	H 3-a	
Wage rates per hr in DM	W Germany	H 3-a	
in local currency	EEC countries	E 25-a2	
in FrS	Main countries	C 2-a	
Wages & salary costs in $	Main countries	U 21-a	

Metal scrap   see   SCRAP, METALLIC

Metal section-forming machines   see   MACHINE TOOLS

	Territorial coverage	Title codes	

METAL-WORKING MACHINES
    see also   MACHINE TOOLS

% of world exports shipped to developed countries		U 38-a	
to developing countries		U 38-a	
Exports by destination by value in $	Main countries	U 9-a	
by kind by value in $	OECD countries	D 9-a	
by value in $m	Main countries	U 38-a	
Imports by value in $m	All countries	U 38-a	
No in use by kind	Main S American countries & USA	U 38-a	
Consumption: tonnage	Central African countries	U 38	
Exports: machine tools by value in $m	ECE countries	U 15-a	
Production as % of total machinery production	Main countries	U 38-a	
by volume	E European countries, USSR & USA	U 38-a	
World export trade by value in $m		U 38-a	

METALLIC IRON
    see also   IRON ORE

Consumption (for steel production): tonnage	UK	T 2-m	
Production (based on content of ore): tonnage	All countries	C 4-a	
Smelter production by areas: tonnage	EEC countries	E 29-a	

Metals, anti-friction   see   ANTI-FRICTION METALS

METALS, BASIC
    see also   NON-FERROUS METALS

% share of world production of metals (in detail)	All countries	N 4-a	
Consumption by value in $m	EEC countries, Japan & USA	U 23-a	
Export prices – index nos	Latin American countries	U 18-a	
Exports as % of consumption	EEC countries, Japan & USA	U 23-a	
by sea, inland waters, road, rail & air: tonnage	European countries	U 8-a	
by value in $m	Australia, Hong Kong, India & Japan	U 32-m	
Imports as % of consumption	EEC countries, Japan & USA	U 23-a	
by sea, inland waters, road, rail & air: tonnage	European countries	U 8-a	
by value in $m	Asian, Far East & Australasian countries	U 32-m	
Production – index nos (quantum basis)	S American countries	U 40-a	
	OECD countries	D 19-m	D 20-m
Symbols, atomic numbers & atomic weights for all elements		J 6-a	

METALS, BASIC BY KIND

Consumption by end-use: tonnage	USA	J 3-a	
tonnage	Main countries	N 5-a	
Exports by destination by CST classes: tonnage & value in $	EEC countries	E 48-a	
SITC classes by value in $	Main countries	D 2-q	
tonnage & value in $	OECD countries	D 3-a2	
by NIMEXE classes: tonnage & value in $	All countries	E 20-a	
SITC classes: tonnage & value in $	All countries	U 50-a	U 59-a
Import duties: rates in % ad val	USA	J 3-a	
Imports by NIMEXE classes: tonnage & value in $	All countries	E 20-a	
SITC classes: tonnage & value in $	All countries	U 50-a	U 59-a
Imports by source by CST classes: tonnage & value in $	EEC countries	E 21-a	
SITC classes by value in $	Main countries	D 2-q	
tonnage & value in $	OECD countries	D 3-a2	
Production: tonnage	All countries	N 5-a	
	USA	J 3-a	
	Zaire	E 41-a	
Stocks held (end-period): tonnage	USA	J 3	
Wholesale prices in cents per lb or $ per ton	USA	J 3-a	
in local currency per ton	OAS member countries	N 17-a	
World production: tonnage	Main countries	J 3-a	

Meteorological instruments   see   SCIENTIFIC INSTRUMENTS

Meteorological research   see   RESEARCH & DEVELOPMENT

METERS, ELECTRICITY SUPPLY

Production by volume	All countries	U 22-a	U 38-a

METERS, WATER SUPPLY

Deliveries by value in £	UK	C 24-a	

Methadone   see   DRUGS & MEDICINES
                              SYNTHETIC NARCOTICS

METHANE
    see also   HYDROCARBONS, ALIPHATIC

Consumption as primary energy source	European countries	U 10-a	
for organic synthesis: tonnage	OECD countries	D 5-a	
tonnage	OECD countries	D 5-a	
Production (from coal derivatives): tonnage	OECD countries	D 5-a	
(from oil & natural gas): tonnage	OECD countries	D 5-a	

Methane carriers   see   TANKERS

	Territorial coverage	Title codes

METHANOL
    see also   CHEMICAL PRODUCTS
                    CHEMICALS, ORGANIC
                    ETHYL ALCOHOL

Exports by destination: tonnage	Main countries	U 2-a
tonnage	European countries, Japan & USA	U 26-a
Imports: tonnage	European countries, Japan & USA	U 26-a
Production: tonnage	European countries, Japan & USA	U 26-a

Methyl alcohol   see   CHEMICAL PRODUCTS
                                   CHEMICALS, ORGANIC

MICA

Consumption: mica & natural mica sheet: tonnage	USA	N 1-a
sheets & block splittings for electronic use: tonnage	USA	U 11-a
for other uses: tonnage	USA	U 11-a
Imports & exports by source & destination: tonnage	Main countries	B 15-a
Production: crude sheet & waste in lbs & kg	All countries	B 15-a
crude mica crystals: tonnage	All countries	U 22-a
tonnage	Malagasy Rep	E 41-a
Wholesale prices: ground mica in $ per ton	USA	N 1-a
scrap & flake mica in $ per ton	USA	N 1-a
World exports: tonnage	Brazil, India & Madagascar	U 11-a
World production: tonnage	Worldwide	N 4-a
	Main countries	N 1-a

MICA PRODUCTS

Exports: condenser film: tonnage & value in $	India	U 11-a
tonnage & value in $m	India	U 11-a

MICA SHEET
    see also   MICA PRODUCTS

Consumption: tonnage	USA	N 1-a
Government strategic stockpile: blocks, splittings & film: tonnage	USA	N 1-a
Stocks held at consumers' premises: tonnage	USA	N 1-a
Wholesale prices: mica block & film in $ per ton	USA	N 1-a
mica splittings in $ per ton	USA	N 1-a

Microlite   see   TANTALUM & NIOBIUM

Microscopes   see   OPTICAL INSTRUMENTS

MIDWIVES
    see also   HOSPITAL PERSONNEL

No employed	AASM countries	E 41-a
	Asian, Far East & Australasian countries	U 45-a

Migrant workers   see   FOREIGN MIGRANT WORKERS

MIGRATION
    see also   EMIGRATION
                    IMMIGRATION
                    POPULATION MOVEMENT

Movement of EEC area population internationally	EEC countries	E 37-a
within EEC area	EEC countries	E 37-a
Net migration by areas	EEC countries	E 38-a
from S Italy: historical table	Italy	E 37-a
total (incl net rates per 1000 population)	OECD countries	D 23-a
No of emigrants: historical table from 1815-1969	Main European countries	Z 1-a
immigrants: historical table from 1815-1969	Main European countries	Z 1-a

MIGRATION, INTER-REGIONAL

Changes in domicile within EEC area	EEC countries	E 2-a
No of persons changing domicile	EEC countries	E 38-a

MILITARY EQUIPMENT

Consumption cost: arms & military construction work	EEC countries	E 32-a

Military equipment plants   see   ORDNANCE FACTORIES

Military expenditure   see   ARMED FORCES
                                       DEFENCE EXPENDITURE

MILK
    see also   CONDENSED & EVAPORATED MILK
                    STATE PROCUREMENT (COMMUNIST COUNTRIES)

% change in farm prices (over previous yr)	EEC countries	E 34-m
	W European countries	U 30-a
% change in retail sales	E European countries & USSR	U 16-a
% fat content (average)	EEC countries	B 3-a
% of consumption from production of milk by dairy co-operatives	EEC countries	B 3-a
% of deliveries by dairy co-operatives to dairies	EEC countries	B 3-a
% of EEC total production	EEC countries	R 5-a

	Territorial coverage	Title codes
MILK, continued		
% of milk production sold by dairies as liquid fresh milk	EEC countries	B 3-a
used by dairies for production of butter	EEC countries	B 3-a
cheese	EEC countries	B 3-a
condensed milk	EEC countries	B 3-a
fresh cream	EEC countries	B 3-a
milk powder	EEC countries	B 3-a
% of production delivered to dairies	EEC countries	B 3-a
% of production: liquid milk sold ex farm gate	EEC countries	B 3-a
retained for own consumption on farms	EEC countries	B 3-a
used on farm for butter production	EEC countries	B 3-a
cheese production	EEC countries	B 3-a
to feed livestock	EEC countries	B 3-a
% share of world imports & exports	Main countries	B 1-a
% usage by kind of milk product	EEC countries	E 44-a
for producing dairy products	Main countries	A 1
for sale, farm consumption or for industrial processing	ECE countries	U 34-a
As source of fat protein & calorie intake per capita in grammes	OAS member countries	N 17-a
Consumption (as animal feed) in million gallons	Main countries	B 12-m B 4-a
tonnage	Main countries	A 1-a
Consumption as fresh milk & cream in million gallons	Main countries	B 4-a
by dairies for production of milk products	EEC countries	B 3-a
for human use projected to 1978: tonnage	OECD countries	D 15-a
industrial processing projected to 1978: tonnage	OECD countries	D 15-a
industrial processing: tonnage	Main countries	B 12-m
production of butter, cheese & other milk products: tonnage	EEC countries	E 44-a
butter projected to 1978: tonnage	OECD countries	D 15-a
tonnage	Main countries	B 12-m
cheese projected to 1978: tonnage	OECD countries	D 15-a
tonnage	Main countries	B 12-m
chocolate crumb in gallons	Main countries	B 12-m
tonnage	UK	B 12-m
condensed milk in gallons	Main countries	B 12-m
tonnage	Main countries	B 12-m
cream: tonnage	Main countries	B 12-m
dairy products (all kinds): tonnage	Main countries	B 4-a
fresh cream in gallons	Main countries	B 12-m
milk powder: tonnage	Main countries	B 12-m
products (incl skim): tonnage	EEC countries	E 44-a
projected to 1978: tonnage	OECD countries	D 15-a
of sterilised cream in gallons & tonnage	UK	B 12-m
in gallons	Main countries	B 12-m
on farms as % of total milk consumption	EEC countries	B 3-a
(incl milk fed to livestock): tonnage	EEC countries	B 3-a
tonnage	Czechoslovakia, Hungary & Poland	U 34-a
	EEC countries	B 3-a
per capita in gallons per yr	Main countries	B 4-a
in kg per yr	EEC countries	B 1-a B 3-a
	Main countries	E 3-a
	W European countries	P 5-a
	Canada, European countries, Japan & USA	E 44-a
in lbs per yr	UK	B 12-a
in litres per yr	E European countries & USSR	U 16-a
	EEC countries	E 44-a
(incl cream) in gallons per yr	USA	B 4-a
tonnage	OAS member countries	N 17-a
Deliveries for market sale & for processing: tonnage	Czechoslovakia, Hungary & Poland	U 34-a
to dairies as % of total production	EEC countries	E 44-a
to dairies & factories: tonnage	EEC countries	E 26-m
to dairies: tonnage	EEC countries	B 3-a
	European countries	U 35-q
Expenditure: intervention activity under EEC budget in £m		B 3-a
price guarantees under EEC budget in £m		B 3-a
Export prices: fresh milk in local currency	Netherlands	A 9-a
Export prices - index nos (weighted average main sources)		U 29-q
Exports by value in $m	W European countries	U 33-a
Farm prices in local currency per 100 kg	EEC countries	E 34-m
Government expenditure: price guarantees in £m	UK	P 5-a
Gross output (incl milk products) by value in $	ECE countries	U 34-a
Imports (incl cream) by value in $m	European countries	U 33-a
Inter-EEC exports by destination: tonnage	EEC countries	B 3-a
Intervention prices per 100 kg	EEC countries	B 3-a E 44-a
No of milking animals, production tonnage & milk yield per cow	All countries	A 9-a
Producer prices (all types of sale) in local currency	W European countries	U 30-a
as ratio of oilcake costs	W European countries	U 30-a
(delivered dairies) in local currency	W European countries	U 30-a
fresh cow's milk in local currency	EEC countries	B 3-a
	All countries	A 9-a
	E European countries (excl USSR)	U 30-a
	EEC countries	E 44-a
fresh goat milk in pesetas per kg	Spain	D 1-a
in local currency per ton or per 100 litres	OECD countries	D 1-a
in pence per gallon equiv	EEC countries	B 1-a
in $ & in local currency per kg	Main countries	A 5-a
(incl dairy products) - index nos	EEC countries	E 44-a
per 100 kg of fat content in local currency	European countries	E 35-a
per 100 lbs of fat content in $	W European countries	E 35-a

	Territorial coverage	Title codes	
MILK, continued			
Production: % change in output projected to 1978	OECD countries	D 15-a	
Production & consumption projected to 1985: tonnage	Main countries	A 1	
by value in local currency	EEC countries	E 44-a	
Production costs on collective farms in $ per ton	USSR	U 34-a	
in million gallons	Main countries	B 4-a	
Production: (all kinds): tonnage	Main countries	A 5-a	
condensed milk & milk powder: tonnage	EEC countries	E 26-m	
cows', goats' & buffalo milk: tonnage	OECD countries	D 1-a	
	All countries	U 43-a	
cows' milk: historical table from 1903: tonnage	Main European countries	Z 1-a	
(sterilised): tonnage	OAS member countries	N 13-a	
(unsterilised): tonnage	OAS member countries	N 13-a	
tonnage	African countries	U 44-a	
	Czechoslovakia, Hungary & Poland	U 34-a	
	E European countries & USSR (incl Ukraine)	U 16-a	
	EEC countries	B 1-a	B 3-a
		E 44-a	
	Canada, European countries, Japan, USA & USSR	E 44-a	
	Latin American countries	J 5-a	U 40-a
	Main countries	B 3-a	E 3-a
		R 5-a	
	OECD countries	D 1-a	
fresh & skim milk: tonnage & consumption in kg per capita	OECD countries	D 14-a	
goats' milk: tonnage	African countries	U 44-a	
	EEC countries	B 3-a	
goats' & sheep milk: tonnage	OECD countries	D 1-a	
imports, exports & consumption: tonnage	EEC countries	B 1-a	E 44-a
sheep milk: tonnage	African countries	U 44-a	
	EEC countries	B 3-a	
value as % of gross output (incl crops)	E European countries	U 34-a	
Production - index nos	Main countries	B 4-a	
Retail prices (comparative): whole milk in cents per litre	EEC countries	Z 3-a	
(in bottles) in local currency per litre	EEC countries	B 3-a	
in pence per pint equiv	EEC countries	B 3-a	
in local currency	Main countries	B 4-a	
	OAS member countries	N 17-a	
(maximum permitted): pasteurised milk in pence per gallon	UK	B 4-a	
Retail sales as % of total sales	EEC countries	B 3-a	
ex dairies as % of total sales	EEC countries	B 3-a	
Self-sufficiency ratios: fresh & skim milk	EEC countries	E 44-a	
milk & milk products	EEC countries	B 1-a	B 3-a
State procurement: tonnage	E European countries & USSR (incl Ukraine)	U 16-a	
	European countries	U 35-q	
Supply (net) per capita in kg per day	All countries	U 43-a	
(daily average) - index nos	EEC countries	B 3-a	
Surplus of production over requirements projected to 1978: tonnage	OECD countries	D 15-a	
Target prices (3.7% fat content) in £ per 100 kg	EEC countries	B 3-a	
in pence per gallon	EEC countries	B 1-a	
milk delivered factory in £ per 100 kg	EEC area	B 4-a	
Wholesale prices in local currency	OAS member countries	N 17-a	
Yield per milking cow in gallons per yr	Main countries	B 4-a	
	EEC countries	B 3-a	E 44-a
in kg per yr	European countries	U 35-a	
	Latin American countries	J 5-a	
- index nos	Main countries	B 4-a	
Milk, fermented (yoghurt) see MILK PRODUCTS			
MILK FAT, ANHYDROUS			
Bilateral food aid shipments ex EEC area: tonnage		B 3-a	
Exports: butter-oil by destination: tonnage	Main countries	B 12-m	
tonnage	Main countries	B 4-a	
Food aid ex EEC area: tonnage	Recipient world regions	B 3-a	
expenditure on butter-oil shipments	EEC countries	B 3-a	
Import quotas: butter-oil in lbs	USA	B 4-a	
Imports by source: butter-oil: tonnage	UK	B 4-a	
	Main countries	B 12-m	
Multilateral aid ex EEC area shipped to International Red Cross: tonnage		B 3-a	
to UNRWA: tonnage		B 3-a	
under World Food Program: tonnage		B 3-a	
MILK MARKETING BOARD (UK)			
Realisation price: fresh milk in pence per gallon	UK	B 4-a	
milk (for processing) in pence per gallon	UK	B 4-a	
MILK POWDER			
see also WHEY POWDER			
% of production by dairy co-operatives	EEC countries	B 3-a	
of whole milk powder exported	Main countries	B 4-a	
% of skim milk production used in making milk powder	EEC countries	B 3-a	
Commonwealth % share in UK imports of whole skim powder	UK	B 4-a	
Consignments (as emergency food aid) by value in $	Recipient countries	M 1-a	

MILK POWDER, continued

Entry	Territorial coverage	Title codes	
Consumption: milk (fresh) in production of milk powder in gallons	Main countries	B 4-a	
per capita: milk powder in kg per yr	EEC countries	E 44-a	
skim milk powder in kg per yr	EEC countries	B 1-a	B 3-a
whole milk powder in kg per yr	EEC countries	B 3-a	
projected to 1978: tonnage	OECD countries	D 15-a	
tonnage	EEC countries	B 3-a	
	OAS member countries	N 17-a	
Expenditure on storage of surplus milk powder (under EEC budget) in £m		B 3-a	
Export availability & import needs projected to 1978	OECD countries	D 15-a	
Export prices in $ per ton	Australia, Eire, Netherlands & UK	A 9-a	
Export subsidies by zone per 100 kg	EEC area	B 4-a	
Exports by destination: whole milk powder: tonnage	EEC countries	B 3-a	
	Main countries	B 4-a	
skim milk powder: tonnage	Main countries	B 4-a	
tonnage	Main countries	B 12-m	
	EEC countries	B 3-a	
kind: tonnage	Main countries	B 4-a	
value in $m	W European countries	U 33-a	
tonnage & EEC area shipments as % share of world exports		B 3-a	
whole & skim powder: tonnage	EEC countries	B 3-a	
Food aid: expenditure: skim powder by EEC area in £m	Main countries (as total)	B 4-a	
expenditure under EEC budget in £m	EEC countries	B 3-a	
	Recipient world regions	B 3-a	
Import quotas: dried skim milk in lbs	USA	B 4-a	
Imports by source: skim powder: tonnage	EEC countries	B 3-a	
tonnage	Main countries	B 12-m	
whole & skim milk powder: tonnage	UK	B 4-a	
	EEC countries	B 3-a	
	Netherlands & UK	B 12-m	
whole milk powder: tonnage	EEC countries	B 3-a	
dried milk & cream by value in $	W European countries	U 33-a	
tonnage & EEC area % share of world imports		B 3-a	
tonnage	Main countries	B 4-a	
Inter-EEC imports & exports: tonnage	EEC countries	B 12-a	
Intervention & threshold prices in £ per cwt	EEC countries	B 1-a	
Intervention prices: skim powder in £ per ton	EEC countries	B 3-a	
Multilateral aid ex EEC area shipped to International Red Cross: tonnage		B 3-a	
to UNICEF: tonnage		B 3-a	
UNRWA: tonnage		B 3-a	
under World Food Program: tonnage		B 3-a	
Net surplus of production over needs projected to 1978: tonnage	OECD countries	D 15-a	
Net trade: tonnage	EEC countries	B 4-a	
Output per plant (average) per yr: tonnage	EEC countries	B 3-a	
Production & consumption per capita in kg per yr	OECD countries	D 14-a	
by kind: tonnage	Main countries	B 4-a	
Production, imports, exports, stocks & consumption: tonnage	EEC countries	E 44-a	
(incl skim powder & dry whey): tonnage	All countries	A 9-a	
(incl skim powder): tonnage	European countries	U 35-a	
projected to 1978: tonnage	OECD countries	D 15-a	
skim milk powder: tonnage	EEC countries	B 1-a	
	Main countries	B 3-a	B 4-a
	Main countries	A 5-a	
	EEC countries	E 28-q	B 3-a
		E 27-a	
whole milk powder: tonnage	Main countries	B 3-a	B 4-a
Purchase price paid by commodity credit corporation in $ per ton	USA	B 4-a	
Retail prices in local currency	OAS member countries	N 17-a	
Self-sufficiency ratios: skimmed milk powder	EEC countries	B 1-a	
milk powder	EEC countries	E 44-a	
Shipments ex EEC area under bilateral food aid: tonnage	EEC countries	B 3-a	
Stocks: dried milk & milk powder: tonnage	EEC countries	E 44-a	
skim milk powder: tonnage	Main countries	B 12-m	
	EEC countries	U 35-a	
Subsidy for production of rennet & casein in £ per ton	EEC countries	B 3-a	
Supply, production, consumption & trade: tonnage	EEC countries	B 1-a	
Wholesale prices by quality in $ per ton	Canada & USA	A 9-a	
in local currency	OAS member countries	N 17-a	
skim milk powder in £ per ton	UK	B 4-a	

MILK POWDER PLANTS

Entry	Territorial coverage	Title codes
No by size based on production over 2000 tons per yr	EEC countries	B 3-a
up to 1000 tons per yr	EEC countries	B 3-a
up to 2000 tons per yr	EEC countries	B 3-a
of milk powder processing factories in operation	EEC countries	B 3-a

Milk processing   see   CHEESE FACTORIES
CREAMERIES
DAIRIES
MILK POWDER PLANTS

MILK PRODUCTS

    see also   BUTTER
                   CHEESE
                   CONDENSED & EVAPORATED MILK
                   ICE CREAM
                   MILK POWDER

	Territorial coverage	Title codes
% of skim milk consumed in liquid form	EEC countries	B 3-a
used as animal feed	EEC countries	B 3-a
for manufacturing casein	EEC countries	B 3-a
cheese	EEC countries	B 3-a
condensed milk	EEC countries	B 3-a
milk powder	EEC countries	B 3-a
% Commonwealth share of UK imports: buttermilk & whey	UK	B 4-a
Consumption: dried skim milk projected to 1978: tonnage	OECD countries	D 15-a
(for production of animal feed): tonnage	EEC countries	P 5-a
per capita: cheese in lbs	UK	B 12-a
condensed milk in lbs	UK	B 12-a
cream in kg of milk equiv	EEC countries	B 3-a
in kg	Main countries	B 4-a
in lbs	UK	B 12-a
dried skim milk in lbs	UK	B 12-a
in kg	UK	B 12-a
whole milk powder in lbs	EEC countries	B 3-a
skim liquid milk: tonnage	UK	B 12-a
Dairy sales as % of total sales in whole milk equiv	EEC countries	B 3-a
Exports by destination: skimmed milk	EEC countries	B 3-a
whey powder	Main countries	B 12-m
Import quotas: butter, cream, skim milk & ice cream	Main countries	B 12-m
Imports by source: cream (fresh & preserved) in lbs	USA	B 4-a
fresh & canned cream & yoghurt in lbs	UK	B 12-m
Production (incl skim milk): tonnage	UK	B 12-m
skim milk powder projected to 1978: tonnage	EEC countries	E 44-a
yoghurt: tonnage	OECD countries	D 15-a
Retail prices: milk products by kind in local currency	EEC countries	B 3-a
Sales: cream by dairies in milk equiv tonnage	OAS member countries	N 17-a
skim buttermilk by dairies: tonnage	EEC countries	B 3-a
Supply, home production & imports: chocolate crumb: tonnage	EEC countries	B 3-a
Threshold prices by kind of milk product per 100 kg	UK	B 12-a
	EEC area	B 4-a

Milking cows   see   LIVESTOCK

MILKING MACHINES

    see also   DAIRY EQUIPMENT

	Territorial coverage	Title codes	
No in use & no in use per 100 dairy cows	EEC countries	E 3-a	E 44-a
No in use (incl world total)	Main countries	R 5-a	
No in use	All countries	A 9-a	
	EEC countries	B 1-a	
Production by volume: milking equipment	All countries	U 22-a	
	European countries & UK & USA	U 38-a	

MILLET

    see also   SORGHUM

	Territorial coverage	Title codes
Area harvested, production tonnage & yield per ha	All countries	A 9-a
under crop (incl buckwheat & canary grass) in ha	EEC countries	E 12-a
Crop yield (incl buckwheat & canary grass) in kg per ha	EEC countries	E 12-a
EEC levy per ton: imported millet shipped ex non-EEC sources	EEC countries	B 7-m
Producer prices received in $ per ton	Argentina, S Korea & Uganda	A 9-a
Production (incl buckwheat & canary grass): tonnage	EEC countries	E 12-a
(incl sorghum): tonnage	Asian & Far East countries	U 32-a
	European countries	U 35-a
Production, industrial usage, for fodder & seed: tonnage	OECD countries	D 14-a
tonnage	Argentina & Haiti	U 40-a
Retail prices in local currency	OAS member countries	N 17-a
Wholesale prices in local currency	India & Pakistan	A 9-a
	OAS member countries	N 17-a

MILLINERY

Sales (wholesale) by manufacturers: hats & caps by value in £m	UK	B 22-a

MILLING MACHINES

    see also   MACHINE TOOLS

	Territorial coverage	Title codes
Deliveries by industrial sector by value in $m	USA	J 2-a
(domestic) by value in $m	EEC countries	B 31-a
Exports as % of production (value basis)	EEC countries	B 31-a
by destination by value in £m	UK	B 31-a
by volume by value in $m	USA	J 2-a
Imports as % of consumption (value basis)	EEC countries	B 31-a
by source by value in £m	UK	B 31-a
by volume & by value in $m	USA	J 2-a
Inter-EEC trade by value in $m (incl % growth rates)		B 20-a
Production: automatic numerically-controlled type by volume	EEC countries	B 20-a
by value in $m	EEC countries	B 31-a
by volume: metal milling machines	EEC countries	B 31-a
Production, imports, exports & domestic sales by value in $m	EEC countries	B 20-a
Sales by type of milling machine by volume & value in $m	USA	J 2-a

	Territorial coverage	Title codes

MILLING OFFALS
    Consumption in production of animal feed: tonnage — EEC countries — P 5-a

MINERAL FERTILISERS
    see also   BASIC SLAG
                FERTILISERS, NITROGENOUS
                FERTILISERS, PHOSPHATE
                FERTILISERS, POTASH
                PHOSPHATE ROCK
                POTASH SALTS
                SULPHUR
                SUPERPHOSPHATES
    Production by kind: tonnage — All countries — N 5-a

MINERAL FUELS
    see also   COAL
                COKE
                LIGNITE
                FUELS, PATENT
                PEAT

Area covered by permits to drill by region in ha	Italy	H 4-a
Exports by value in $m	Australasian countries & Singapore	U 32-m
(incl lubricants) by value in $m & as % of total exports	ECE countries	U 15-a
Exports - index nos (quantum & value bases)	OECD countries	D 16-q
Imports by value in $m	Asian, Far East & Australasian countries	U 32-m
(incl lubricants) by value in $m & as % of total imports	ECE countries	U 15-a
Imports - index nos (quantum & value bases)	OECD countries	D 16-q
No of permits granted to search for energy	Italy	H 4-a

MINERAL FUELS BY KIND

% share of world production	All countries	N 4-a
Exports by destination: tonnage & value in $	All countries	U 12-a
tonnage	All countries	N 5-a
Imports by source: tonnage & value in $	All countries	U 12-a
tonnage	Main countries	N 5-a
Production: tonnage	All countries	N 5-a

MINERAL NUTRIENTS

% needs by kind of nutrient per lb of dry diet for chickens		P 5
for turkeys		P 5
% needs of bulls (mature) per lb of dry diet		P 5
chickens (for breeding) per lb of dry diet		P 5
(for growing) per lb of dry diet		P 5
(for laying) per lb of dry diet		P 5
(for starting) per lb of dry diet		P 5
cows (dry) per lb of dry diet		P 5
(lactating) per lb of dry diet		P 5
dairy cattle per lb of dry diet		P 5
heifers per lb of dry diet		P 5
turkeys (for breeding) per lb of dry diet		P 5
(for fattening) per lb of dry diet		P 5
(for growing) per lb of dry diet		P 5
(for starting) per lb of dry diet		P 5

Mineral oil industry   see   PETROLEUM INDUSTRY

Mineral oils   see   PETROLEUM PRODUCTS

Mineral pigments   see   PIGMENTS, MINERAL

MINERAL PROCESSING MACHINERY

Exports by destination by value in $m	Main countries	U 9-a
by value in $m	All countries	U 38-a
Imports by value in $m	All countries	U 38-a
World exports by value in $m		U 38-a

MINERAL PRODUCTS
    Exports - index nos (quantum & unit value bases) — Far East countries — U 32-q

Mineral reserves   see   WORLD MINERAL RESERVES

Mineral royalties   see   ROYALTIES, MINERAL

Mineral waters   see   SOFT DRINKS

MINERALS

% change in export earnings (incl metals)	Bolivia	U 11-a
Export prices - index nos	Worldwide	U 54-q
Exports to non-EEC area by value in $m	EEC countries	E 29-a
(incl ores & scrap) by value in $m	World regions	U 23-a
Imports shipped ex non-EEC area into EEC area by value in $m		E 29-a
Inter-EEC trade by value in $m & as % of total trade	EEC countries	E 29-a
Symbols, atomic numbers, & atomic weights of all elements		J 6-a
World market prices - index nos		U 23-a

	Territorial coverage	Title codes
MINERALS BY KIND		
% share of world production (in detail)	All countries	N 4-a
Consumption by end-use: tonnage	USA	J 3-a
tonnage	Main countries	N 5-a
Exports: tonnage	All countries	N 5-a
Import duties: rates in % ad val	USA	J 3-a
Imports: tonnage	All countries	N 5-a
Production: tonnage & value in local currency	W Indies & Caribbean countries	T 6-a
tonnage	African countries	U 44-a
	All countries	N 5-a
	Latin American countries	U 18-a
	OAS member countries	N 14-a
	USA	J 3-a
Production – index nos (quantum basis)	Worldwide	N 5-a
Reserves: tonnage (estim)	Main countries	N 5-a
Stocks held at end-period: tonnage	USA	J 3
Wholesale prices in cents per lb or in $ per ton	USA	J 3-a
World market prices – index nos		G 1-a
World production: tonnage	Main countries	J 3-a
MINIMUM LENDING RATE		
see also BANK RATE		
Changes over last 8 years by Bank of England	UK	P 1
MINING & QUARRYING		
see also COLLIERIES		
IRON ORE MINING		
ORE MINING INDUSTRY		
As % of world industrial activity (5 yr periods)		U 38
% change in gross output of mines	Latin American countries	U 18-a
% change in implicit price deflator	Developing countries	D 25-a
% contribution to national income	Developing countries	D 25-a
% growth rates in gross product	Developing countries	D 25-a
% of economically-active population employed in mining industry	EEC countries	E 33-a
% share of industrial production contributed by mining	Main countries	U 38-a
Capital formation by areas	EEC countries	E 38-a
in local currency	OAS member countries	N 16-a
in $m	EEC countries	E 32-a
Consumption: electricity by area in kWh	EEC countries	E 38-a
from own production in kWh	All countries	C 23-a
public supply in kWh	All countries	C 23-a
in kWh	All countries	C 23-a
	European countries & USA	U 1-a
manufactured gas by volume in m³	OECD countries	D 8-a
Contribution to gross domestic product (at factor cost) in local currency	European countries & USA	U 3-a
	African countries	U 44-a
	Latin American countries	U 18-a
in $m	S American countries	U 41-a
Corporate investment: US corporations in mining activities	Main countries	R 5-a
Costs: salaried staff per mth in local currency	EEC countries	E 11-a
Direct labour costs per hr in local currency	EEC countries	E 11-a
Earnings (average) in cash per employee in local currency	Singapore	U 32-m
	All countries	L 4-a
(gross) per hr by type of mine in local currency	EEC countries	E 3-a
per hr by areas in local currency	EEC countries	E 38-a
in local currency	Main countries	R 3-a
Employment – index nos	OAS member countries	N 18-a
Fatality rates: mining accidents	All countries	L 4-a
Frequency of accidents at mines	EEC countries	E 2-a
Gross product of mining as component of gross domestic product	Developing countries	D 25-a
(at current prices) in local currency	OAS member countries	N 16-a
IBRD loans approved for mining enterprises in $	OAS member countries	N 16-a
IDA loans for improving output in mines & quarries in $	OAS member countries	N 16-a
Incidence of strikes (or lock-outs)	Main countries	R 3-a
Income contribution to gross domestic product & as % total product	EEC countries	E 32-a
Income distribution from mining (at factor cost) in $	S American countries	U 41-a
Indirect taxes levied on mining industry in $	S American countries	U 41-a
Labour costs per hr (all employees) in local currency	EEC countries	E 11-a
by areas in local currency	EEC countries	E 38-a
manual workers in local currency	EEC countries	E 3-a
wage earners in local currency	EEC countries	E 11-a
Labour force employed (average) or end-period	EEC countries	E 33-a
by areas	EEC countries	E 38-a
sex: historical table from 1750-1969	Main European countries	Z 1-a
by region	EEC countries	E 18-a
(census data)	African countries	U 44-a
& status by areas	EEC countries	E 38-a
sex	EEC countries	E 18-a
status	Main countries	C 28-irr
(census data)	OAS member countries	N 18
no of labourers	AASM countries	E 41-a
managerial staff	AASM countries	E 41-a
salaried staff	AASM countries	E 41-a
	EEC countries	E 11-a
wage earners	AASM countries	E 41-a
	EEC countries	E 11-a

	Territorial coverage	Title codes
MINING & QUARRYING, continued		
Labour force employed: tin mining	Malaysia	U 32-q
Labour force employed (total)	All countries	L 4-a
	Hong Kong, Japan, S Korea & Phillipines	U 32-q
	Latin American countries	U 18-a
	OECD countries	D 23-a
Loan advances (by commercial banks) in local currency	OAS member countries	N 16-a
No of employees involved in strikes in mining industry	Main countries	R 3-a
of hrs worked per wk	All countries	L 4-a
	Main countries	R 3-m
	OAS member countries	N 18-a
per wk by region	EEC countries	E 25-a
by sex	EEC countries	E 18-a
per yr: salaried staff	EEC countries	E 11-a
wage earners	EEC countries	E 11-a
of miners & quarrymen unemployed	All countries	L 4-a
of mines & quarries in operation	African countries	U 44-a
of working days lost per employee	UK	B 29-a
lost through strikes	Main countries	R 3-a
Production by kind – index nos	Latin American countries	U 40-a
by value, employment & wages paid	Main countries	U 43-a
ores (all kinds) – index nos	Latin American countries	U 18-a
coal minerals & metals: tonnage	Latin American countries	U 40-a
metallic ores by kind: tonnage	Asian & Australasian countries	U 45-a
	S American countries	U 40-a
	African countries	U 44-a
	Asian & Far East countries	U 32-q
Production – index nos (quantum basis)	ECE countries	U 42-m
	EEC countries	E 26-m E 28-q
		E 27-a
	Asian & Australasian countries & Iran	U 32-q
	Latin American countries	J 5-a
	Main countries	N 5-a R 5-a
	OAS member countries	N 14-a
	OECD countries	D 19-m D 20-m
US government: direct investment in mining in $m	OAS member countries	N 16-a
Wage rates (daily, hourly & monthly) in local currency	OAS member countries	N 17-a
per hr by grade of employee	Main countries	R 4-q
by sex in local currency	Main countries	R 3-m C 7-a
general labourers in local currency	OAS member countries	N 17-a
in local currency	EEC countries	E 25-a2
stone, clay & sand quarry workers in local currency	OAS member countries	N 17-a
per hr – index nos	EEC countries	E 26-a2
	Main countries	R 3-a
MINING MACHINERY		
Exports by destination by value	Main countries	U 9-a
Production: tonnage	EEC countries	E 28-q E 27-a
Minting of coins see COINAGE		
Mixed feed see FEEDING STUFFS, MIXED		
Mobile cranes see SERVICE VEHICLES		
Mobile homes see TRAILERS		
Mobility, coefficients of see POPULATION MOVEMENT		
MOHAIR		
see also GOATS, ANGORA		
Exports by destination in kg	Main countries	K 6-a
in million lbs	S Africa, Turkey & USA	B 10-a
Imports by source in million lbs	UK	B 10-a
Production (greasy basis) in kg	Lesotho, S Africa, Turkey & USA	K 6-a
in million lbs	Lesotho, S Africa, Turkey & USA	B 10-a
Wholesale prices by kind of mohair in pence per kg on London market	UK	K 6-m
(summer & winter) in cents per lb (average)	S Africa	B 10-a
Texas mohair by quality in pence per lb	UK	B 10-m
Molasses see SYRUP		
MOLLUSC PRODUCTS		
see also CRUSTACEANS & MOLLUSCS		
Exports: tinned products by kind: tonnage	All countries	A 21-a
Imports & exports: tonnage & value in $m	All countries	A 21-a
Production: oysters, mussels (et al): tonnage	All countries	A 21-a
tinned products by kind: tonnage	Main countries	A 21-a
Molybdenite see MOLYBDENUM ORE		
MOLYBDENUM		
see also FERRO-MOLYBDENUM		
Consumption in ferro-alloy production: tonnage	UK	T 4-a
metallic molybdenum in lbs	USA	N 1-a
Imports & exports by source & destination: tonnage	Main countries	B 15-a

	Territorial coverage	Title codes	
MOLYBDENUM, continued			
Production (based on metal content of ore): tonnage	All countries	B 15-a	U 22-a
		U 43-a	
tonnage	Chile, Peru & Mexico	U 40-a	
Wholesale prices in $ per lb	USA	N 1-a	
World production in lbs	Main countries	N 1-a	
(based on metal content of ore): tonnage		C 30-a	N 4-a
World reserves: tonnage (estim)	Main countries	N 1-a	
MOLYBDENUM COMPOUNDS			
Consumption: ammonium molybdate in lbs	USA	J 6-a	
by kind by end-use in lbs	USA	J 6-a	
ferro-molybdenum in lbs	USA	J 6-a	
molybdenum powder in lbs	USA	J 6-a	
molybdic oxides in lbs	USA	J 6-a	
sodium molybdate in lbs	USA	J 6-a	
MOLYBDENUM CONCENTRATES			
Consumption: tonnage	USA	T 4-a	
Production, trade, consumption & stocks: tonnage	USA	J 6-a	
Stocks held at mines & at users' plants: tonnage	USA	N 1-a	
World market price in £ per lb		T 4-m	
MOLYBDENUM ORE			
Exports by destination: tonnage	USA	T 4-a	
Imports by source: tonnage	Main countries	T 4-a	
Production (based on metal content of ore): tonnage	All countries	C 12-a	
Wholesale prices: climax lump in $ per lb	USA	C 12-m	
World production (based on metal content of ore): tonnage	Worldwide	C 12-a	
	Main countries	T 4-a	
MOLYBDENUM POWDER			
Consumption by industrial end-use in lbs	USA	J 6-a	

Monazite   see   RARE EARTH MINERALS

Monetary reserves   see   FOREIGN EXCHANGE
GOLD HOLDINGS
RESERVES

MONEY MARKET RATES

see also   BANK RATE
DISCOUNT RATES
INTEREST RATES
MINIMUM LENDING RATE

	Territorial coverage	Title codes	
% interest rates by kind per annum	Main countries	M 7-a	
on call money & treasury bills per annum	EEC countries	E 26-m	
	Main countries	U 27-m	U 43-a
call money per annum	OECD countries	D 26-q	
discounted bills per annum	Main countries	E 3-a	
Eurodollars per annum	All countries	F 5-m	F 6-q
treasury bills per annum	All countries	F 5-m	F 6-q
	Main countries	E 3-a	M 7-a
	OECD countries	D 26-q	
% official discount rates per annum	Main countries	M 7-a	
% yields on government securities per annum	Main countries	M 7-a	

MONEY SUPPLY

	Territorial coverage	Title codes	
% annual rate of change (compounded)	Main countries	N 7-a	
% change (incl quasi-money in circulation)	ECAFE countries	U 17-a	
	EEC countries	E 13-m	
% growth rate: means of payment (total)	All countries	M 6-a	
money (incl quasi money) in circulation	EEC countries	E 13-a	
Balances in circulation (at end-yr)	OAS member countries	N 16-a	
Banknotes in circulation by value: historical table in local currency	Main European countries	Z 1-a	
Coins in circulation in local currency	OAS member countries	N 16-a	
Countries listed by % rate of change in money supply		U 54-a	
Currency (& all other means of payment) in circulation	EEC countries	E 3-a	
	African countries	U 44-a	
	All countries	F 5-m	F 6-q
demand deposits in $	Asian, Far East & Australasian countries	U 45-a	
held by banking system in local currency	OAS member countries	N 16-a	
in circulation & deposits made in local currency	Main countries	E 3-a	
in local currency	OAS member countries	N 16-a	
	African countries	U 44-a	
	ECE countries	U 42-m	
	EEC countries	E 26-m	
	OECD countries	D 26-q	
in $m	EEC area	E 13-a	
Demand deposits (incl currency in circulation) in $	Latin American countries	J 5-a	
in local currency	African countries	U 44-a	
No of notes & coins in circulation in local currency (end-yr)	Main countries	N 7-a	R 5-a
	OAS member countries	N 16-a	
Private sector: currency & deposits held in $m	Main countries	U 27-m	U 43-a
Reserves & banking liabilities in $m	Main countries	U 27-m	U 43-a

	Territorial coverage	Title codes
Monofil see SYNTHETIC MONOFIL		
MONOPOLY PROFITS, GOVERNMENT		
Receipts in local currency	Panama	J 5-a
MONOPOLY TAXES		
Revenue: historical table from 1845 in local currency	Main European countries	Z 1-a
Mopeds see CYCLES & MOPEDS		
MORPHINE		
Consumption in manufacture of codeine in kg	All countries	U 46-a
drugs (for export) in kg	All countries	U 46-a
ethylmorphine & other drugs in kg	All countries	U 46-a
pholcodine in kg	All countries	U 46-a
(total) & per million population in kg	All countries	U 46-a
opium in production of morphine in kg	All countries	U 46-a
poppy straw in production of morphine in kg	Netherlands & Poland	U 46-a
Exports by destination in kg	Main countries	U 46-a
Illicit traffic: seizures in kg	All countries	U 46-a
Production from opium in kg	All countries	U 46-a
poppy straw & straw concentrates in kg	All countries	U 46-a
World requirements in kg (estim)		U 19-a
Mortality see DEATHS		
Mortality rates see DEATH RATES		
Mortgage taxes see TAXATION		
MORTGAGES		
see also BUILDING SOCIETIES		
% interest rates charged by building societies for house purchase	OECD countries	D 12-a
by local authorities for house purchase	OECD countries	D 12-a
MOTELS		
No of beds available for use of visitors & tourists	OECD countries	D 47-a
Mother ships see SUPPLY VESSELS		
Motor cars see PASSENGER CARS		
Motor cars, second-hand see PASSENGER CARS, SECOND-HAND		
Motor coaches see BUSES & COACHES		
MOTOR CULTIVATORS		
see also GARDEN TRACTORS		
Production by volume	EEC countries	E 28-q E 27-a
MOTOR CYCLE INDUSTRY		
Investment in buildings in local currency	EEC countries	E 40-a
machinery in local currency	EEC countries	E 40-a
MOTOR CYCLES & SCOOTERS		
% changes in retail sales	E European countries	U 16-a
Exports by value in $m	OECD countries	D 9-a
Exports: motor cycles by value in $m	All countries	U 38-a
Imports by value in $m	All countries	U 38-a
No in use (incl no exceeding 125 cc capacity)	European countries	U 8-a
No in use	EEC countries	E 43-a
	European countries & USA	U 47-a
	Great Britain	V 1-a
	Main countries	E 3-a S 24-a
		V 4-a
	W Indies & Caribbean countries	T 6-a
of km run (estim)	European countries & USA	U 47-a
new registrations	European countries & USA	U 47-a
	Main countries	S 24-a
Production: machines over 50 cc capacity	EEC countries	E 28-q E 27-a
by volume	All countries	U 22-a
Sales demand per 1000 population (estim)	E European countries	U 16-a
World exports: motor cycles by value in $m		U 38-a
Motor fuel see MOTOR SPIRIT		
MOTOR FUEL TAXATION		
% content of taxes in minimum prices of diesel oil	Main countries	S 24-a
motor spirit	Main countries	S 24-a
Government revenue accruing from petrol taxation in £m	UK	V 1-a
Motor lorries see COMMERCIAL VEHICLES		

	Territorial coverage	Title codes	
Motor ships see MERCHANT SHIPPING FLEETS SHIPS & BOATS TANKERS, OIL			

MOTOR SPIRIT

	Territorial coverage	Title codes	
% consumption of world supply	Latin American countries	U 18-a	
% growth in demand	World regions & Japan	G 1-a	
% of consumption used by road vehicles	Main countries	S 24-a	
% of EEC area production (incl aviation fuel)	EEC countries	R 5-a	
% tax element in minimum retail prices	Main countries	S 24-a	
	W European countries	C 14-a	
Consumption by motor vehicles & lorries: tonnage	EEC countries	E 14-a	
	European countries	U 8-a	
	OECD countries	D 31-a	
	AASM countries	E 41-a	
by volume in m³	World regions	C 3-a	
in barrels per day	OAS member countries	N 17-a	
in litres	All countries	U 55-a	
per capita in litres	Italy	H 4-a	
petrol ex own refineries: tonnage	Main countries	C 14-a	S 24-a
tonnage	EEC countries	E 44-a	
Cost of engine fuel for farm machinery - index nos	EEC countries	E 16-m	E 15-a
Deliveries for domestic consumption: tonnage	OECD countries	D 31-a	
for domestic consumption & exports: tonnage	Main countries	C 21-a	
Demand domestic (all types of gasolines) in gallons	Netherlands Antilles	R 2-m	
Export prices: 80 octane in cents per gallon fob, Aruba	Iran	R 2-m	
90 octane in cents per gallon fob	Netherlands	R 2-m	
92 octane in $ per ton fob	Netherlands Antilles	R 2-m	
98 octane in cents per gallon fob, Aruba	Worldwide	H 4-a	
in cents per gallon fob (at main ports)	All countries	B 15-a	
Imports & exports by source & destination: tonnage	OECD countries	D 31-a	
by source: tonnage	Main countries	S 24-a	
Minimum prices in cents per litre	Worldwide	C 3-a	
Prices posted at specific ports in cents per gallon fob	Main countries	H 4-a	
Producer prices by grade (ex refineries) in $ per ton	Italy	H 4-a	
(controlled) by grade in lire per litre	OPEC member countries	C 3-a	
Production in barrels per day	All countries	N 5-a	
	All countries	R 5-a	
(incl aviation fuel): tonnage	Main countries	U 27-q	
tonnage (see no 1, 4, 7, 10)	All countries	U 55-a	
Production, trade & consumption: tonnage	AASM countries	E 41-a	
tonnage	African countries	U 39-a	U 44-a
	All countries	U 22-a	U 43-a
	EEC countries	E 26-m	E 28-q
		E 14-a	E 27-a
	Latin American countries	J 5-a	
	Main countries	B 15-a	E 3-a
		R 5-a	
volume in m³	OECD countries	D 44-a	
	OAS member countries	N 14-a	
	S American countries, Cuba & Mexico	U 40-a	
Receipts from taxes on hydrocarbon oils in local currency	EEC countries	E 42-a	
Refinery output, imports, consumption & supply: tonnage	Main countries	S 24-a	
	OECD countries	D 31-a	
Retail prices (incl tax element in price) by grade	EEC countries	E 15-a	
at garages by octane ratings per 100 litres	EEC countries	E 34-m	
per gallon	Main countries	C 3-a	
(comparative) per litre	EEC countries	Z 3-a	
for agricultural machinery use per 100 litres	EEC countries	E 34-m	
in local currency	OAS member countries	N 17-a	
low & high grade motor spirit in cents per gallon	Main countries	U 18-a	
per litre (at end-yr)	W European countries	C 14-a	
Wholesale prices in local currency	OAS member countries	N 17-a	

Motor spirit additives see ANTI-KNOCK ADDITIVES

MOTOR VEHICLE DUTIES

	Territorial coverage	Title codes
Rates charges & basis of assessment	EEC countries	E 31-a
Receipts from road fund taxes: passenger cars	EEC countries	E 41-a

MOTOR VEHICLES

see also AMBULANCES
BUSES & COACHES
COMMERCIAL VEHICLES
HEARSES
MOTOR CYCLES & SCOOTERS
PASSENGER CARS
PUBLIC SERVICE VEHICLES
TAXI CABS

	Territorial coverage	Title codes
% growth rate in demand & projected to 1977	UK	B 28
% increase in demand projected to 1977	UK	B 28
in imports & exports projected to 1977	UK	B 28
% of exports by value: cars (assembled)	UK	B 28-a
(unassembled)	UK	B 28-a
commercial vehicles	UK	B 28-a
replacement parts & accessories	UK	B 28-a

	Territorial coverage	Title codes	
MOTOR VEHICLES, continued			
% of imports by value: cars (assembled)	UK	B 28-a	
(unassembled)	UK	B 28-a	
commercial vehicles	UK	B 28-a	
replacement parts & accessories	UK	B 28-a	
Assembly by make of vehicle by volume	All countries	V 4-a	
(mainly from imported parts) by volume	All countries	U 27-m	U 43-a
passenger cars by volume	All countries	V 4-a	
trucks & buses by volume	All countries	V 4-a	
Consumption cost to private sector in local currency	EEC countries	E 32-a	
(or sales) by volume	Latin American region	U 38-a	
tonnage	Central African countries	U 38-a	
Domestic demand projected to 1977 (at 1972 prices)	UK	B 28	
Driving licence fees in local currency	Main countries	S 24-a	
Excise duties: rates levied	Main countries	S 24-a	
Exports by destination by value in $m	Main countries	U 9-a	
value in $m (incl % growth rates)	Main countries	U 38-a	
in $m	All countries	U 38-a	
in £m projected to 1977	UK	B 28	
volume: cars, trucks & buses	All countries	V 4-a	
	OECD countries	D 9-a	
historical table	Main countries	V 4-a	
motor vehicles by value in £m	UK	V 1-m	
replacement parts (incl tyres) by value in £m	UK	V 1-a	
Import duties: rates & basis of assessment	Main countries	S 24-a	
Imports by value in $m	All countries	U 38-a	
in £m projected to 1977	UK	B 28	
by volume	Latin American region	U 38-a	
(net): no & value in £m: historical table	UK	V 1-a	
Mileage covered by kind of motor vehicle (estim)	UK	V 1-a	
No in use by year of first registration & engine capacity in cc	UK	V 1-q	
(all kinds)	Main countries	V 1-a	V 3-a
buses & coaches	European countries & USA	U 47-a	
by kind	AASM countries	E 41-a	
goods vehicles	European countries & USA	U 47-a	
	Main countries	V 4-a	
hearses	Main countries	V 4-a	
mopeds	European countries & USA	U 47-a	
motor cycles	European countries & USA	U 47-a	
	Main countries	V 4-a	
per 1000 population	Latin American countries	U 40-a	
private cars & commercial vehicles	All countries	U 43-a	
private cars	European countries & USA	U 47-a	
	Main countries	V 4-a	
public service vehicles	Main countries	V 4-a	
of motor vehicles locally-assembled by kind of engine fuel used	Main countries	V 2-a	
passenger cars locally-assembled by kind	Main countries	V 2-a	
by make	Main countries	V 2-a	
by model	Main countries	V 2-a	
jeeps locally-assembled	Main countries	V 2-a	
light vans locally-assembled	Main countries	V 2-a	
lorries locally-assembled	Main countries	V 2-a	
pick-ups locally-assembled	Main countries	V 2-a	
new registrations of motor vehicles	African countries	U 44-a	
persons per vehicle in use	All countries	V 4-a	
	Main countries	V 1-a	
registrations & no in use	All countries	V 4-a	
(incl world total)	World regions	V 3-a	
by class of vehicle	Latin American countries	J 5-a	
cars, commercial vehicles & buses	Latin American countries	U 38-a	
historical table from 1928	Main countries	V 4-a	
(all vehicles) (see no 3, 6, 9, 12)	Main countries	U 27-q	
Production & assembly by make by volume	Main countries	V 4-a	
historical table by volume	Main countries	V 4-a	
Production, imports & consumption by volume	Latin American countries	U 38-a	
Production: passenger cars & trucks by volume	All countries	U 27-m	U 43-a
passenger cars by volume	All countries	V 3-a	
trucks & buses by volume	All countries	V 3-a	
Purchase taxes levied in local currency	Main countries	S 24-a	
Registration fees levied in local currency	Main countries	S 24-a	
Revenue from taxation in $	OECD countries	D 42-a	
Road fund taxes levied in local currency	Main countries	S 24-a	
Sales taxes levied on vehicle fuels	Main countries	S 24-a	
Taxes (excise) levied on replacement parts for vehicles	Main countries	S 24-a	
road licence fees levied	Main countries	S 24-a	
levied on commercial vehicles	Main countries	S 24-a	
diesel fuel for motor vehicles	Main countries	S 24-a	
heavy lorries & trailers	Main countries	S 24-a	
motor vehicle accessories	Main countries	S 24-a	
motor spirit & lubricating oils	Main countries	S 24-a	
re-sale of vehicles & transfer of ownership	Main countries	S 24-a	
tyres (for vehicles)	Main countries	S 24-a	
vehicle inspection	Main countries	S 24-a	
vehicle insurance	Main countries	S 24-a	
Taxes (local) on passenger car ownership	Main countries	S 24-a	
(luxury) on passenger car ownership	Main countries	S 24-a	
Turnover taxes levied on passenger cars	Main countries	S 24-a	

	Territorial coverage	Title codes
MOTOR VEHICLES, continued		
Value added tax (VAT) levied on motor vehicles	Main countries	S 24-a
Value added in manufacture of motor vehicles in $m	OECD countries	D 9-a
Weight, size & axle load regulations in force	Latin American countries	U 40-a
World production: vehicles assembled from imported parts by volume	Worldwide	C 4-a
historical table by volume	Worldwide	V 4-a
MOTOR VEHICLES, TAX-EXEMPT		
No in use	Great Britain	V 1-a
of registrations: new buses & coaches	UK	V 1-a
new cars	UK	V 1-a
new motor cycles	UK	V 1-a
Registrations: new vehicles	N Ireland	V 1-q
MOTOR VEHICLES BY KIND		
Exports: buses & coaches by value in £m	UK	B 28-a
by destination by CST classes: tonnage & value in $m	EEC countries	E 48-a
SITC classes by value in $m	Main countries	D 2-q
tonnage & value in $m	OECD countries	D 3-a2
tonnage & value in $m	All countries	U 12-a
cars (incl taxis) by value in £m	UK	B 28-a
goods vehicles by value in £m	UK	B 28-a
replacement parts for vehicles by value in £m	UK	B 28-a
Imports: buses & coaches by value in £m	UK	B 28-a
by source by CST classes: tonnage & value in $m	EEC countries	E 21-a
SITC classes by value in $m	Main countries	D 2-q
tonnage & value in $m	OECD countries	D 3-a2
by source: tonnage & value in $m	All countries	U 12-a
cars (incl taxis) by value in £m	UK	B 28-a
goods vehicles by value in £m	UK	B 28-a
replacement parts for vehicles by value in £m	UK	B 28-a
Maximum authorised size & wt of motor vehicles in kg	EEC countries	E 43-a
No in use & projected vehicle park by 1980	E African countries	U 38-a
by areas	EEC countries	E 38-a
cars, buses & motor cycles	EEC countries	E 43-a
	European countries	U 8-a
cars & buses	Latin American countries	U 40-a
at end-yr (all vehicles)	Main countries	V 1-a
	European countries & USA	U 47-a
of motor vehicles licenced	Great Britain	V 1-q
motor vehicle licences (tax-exempt)	Great Britain	V 1-q
new registrations (incl world total)	All countries	N 8-a
new registrations	European countries & USA	U 47-a
	Main countries	S 24-a
Production & assembly by volume	Main countries	E 3-a
Production by overseas subsidiaries by volume	Main countries	V 2-a
volume: historical tables	UK	V 1-a
by specific companies	All countries	V 4-a
volume	All countries	N 8-a
	EEC countries	E 28-q E 27-a
Trade between Canada & USA in motor vehicles by value in $m		G 1-a
MOTOR VEHICLES BY MAKE		
Assembly by overseas subsidiaries by volume	Main countries	V 2-a
Production by volume: passenger cars	All countries	V 3-a
trucks & buses	All countries	V 3-a
MOTOR VEHICLES BY MODEL		
Assembly volume by names or model nos by overseas subsidiaries (in detail)	Main countries	V 2-a
MOTOR VEHICLES INDUSTRY		
see also COMMERCIAL VEHICLES INDUSTRY		
% production increase projected to 1977	UK	B 26
% usage of machine tool park by vehicles manufacturing companies	EEC countries	B 20-a
Assets of motor vehicle corporations as % of liabilities	USA	J 2-a
Capital formation in vehicles industry as % of all manufacturing industry	UK	B 28
in $m	Main countries	U 21-a
Cash flow in motor manufacturing industry in £m	UK	B 28
Consumption of electricity in kWh	EEC countries	E 15-a
iron castings: tonnage	UK	B 25-a
metals by kind: tonnage	USA	J 3-a
steel castings: tonnage	UK	B 25-a
Costs: salaried staff per mth in local currency	EEC countries	E 11-a
Depreciation: corporate assets as % of sales turnover	USA	J 2-a
Earnings (corporate) as % of sales turnover	USA	J 2-a
female workers per hr in FrS	Main countries	C 2-a
(net) & cash flow in £m	UK	B 28
per hr by sex in local currency	Main countries	R 3-a
in FrS	Main countries	C 2-a
piece rates per hr in FrS	Main countries	C 2-a
semi-skilled workers per hr in FrS	Main countries	C 2-a
skilled workers per wk in £	UK	B 28-a
per hr in FrS	Main countries	C 2-a
time rates per hr in FrS	Main countries	C 2-a
unskilled workers per hr in FrS	Main countries	C 2-a

	Territorial coverage	Title codes
MOTOR VEHICLES INDUSTRY, continued		
Employment by occupation projected to 1977	UK	B 28
by sex projected to 1977	UK	B 28
Exports by value in £m	UK	V 1-m
Frequency of accidents at work	EEC countries	E 2-a
Gross output by value in £m projected to 1977	UK	B 28
in $m	Main countries	U 21-a
IDA loans granted for automotive assembly projects in $	OAS member countries	N 16-a
Labour costs as % of total costs	EEC countries	E 8-a
by status of employees in local currency	EEC countries	E 8-a
female workers per hr in FrS	Main countries	C 2-a
in DM million	W Germany	H 3-a
per hr in FrS	Main countries	C 2-a E 11-a
(incl staff) in local currency	EEC countries	E 2-a
semi-skilled workers per hr in FrS	Main countries	C 2-a
skilled workers per hr in FrS	Main countries	C 2-a
social levies as % of total labour costs	EEC countries	B 28-a
unskilled workers per hr in FrS	Main countries	C 2-a
wage earners per hr in local currency	EEC countries	E 11-a
wages as % of total costs	EEC countries	B 28-a
Labour force employed as % of labour force in engineering industries	UK	B 28-a
by age groups & sex	UK	B 28-a
by sex (semi-skilled)	UK	B 28-a
(skilled)	UK	B 28-a
(unskilled)	UK	B 28-a
occupation	Main countries	C 2-a
no of operatives employed	EEC countries	E 2-a
	Main countries	U 21-a
production workers employed	Main countries	C 2-a
salaried staff employed	EEC countries	E 11-a
	Main countries	C 2-a
wage earners & salaried staff employed	EEC countries	E 8-a E 11-a
workers (skilled) employed by occupation	UK	B 28-a
Loss of production by cause	UK	B 28-a
No of employees involved in strikes	UK	B 28-a
fitters employed as % of total labour force	UK	B 28-a
hrs worked per wk	Main countries	R 3-m
per wk by region	EEC countries	E 25-a
per yr: salaried staff	EEC countries	E 11-a
wage earners	EEC countries	E 11-a
per yr	EEC countries	E 8-a
inspectors employed as % of total labour force	UK	B 28-a
labour disputes causing strikes	UK	B 28-a
manual workers employed in assembly & sub-assembly shops	UK	B 28-a
in machine shops	UK	B 28-a
in packing departments	UK	B 28-a
in trim & finish shops	UK	B 28-a
times inventory turned by corporations	USA	J 2-a
stoppages due to labour disputes	UK	B 28-a
tool operators employed as % of total labour force	UK	B 28-a
tool setters employed as % of total labour force	UK	B 28-a
toolmakers employed as % of total labour force	UK	B 28-a
working days lost per 1000 workers	UK	B 28-a
through strikes	UK	B 28-a
Output & employment – index nos	UK	B 28-a
Production by kind of vehicle by volume	Main countries	C 2-a
Productivity in vehicle manufacturing industry – index nos	UK	B 28-a
Profits of corporations as % of turnover	USA	J 2-a
Receipts: aluminium products: tonnage	OECD countries	D 21-a
steel for fabrication: tonnage	OECD countries	D 22-a
Turnover in vehicle manufacturing industry in DM million	W Germany	H 3-a
Value added in manufacture of vehicles in $m	OECD countries	D 9-a
Wage rates: differentials by sex	EEC countries	B 28-a
per hr in DM	W Germany	H 3-a
in local currency	Main countries	C 2-a
	EEC countries	E 25-a2
	OAS member countries	N 17-a
by grade per hr in local currency	Main countries	R 4-q
by sex per hr in local currency	Main countries	R 3-m C 7-a
Wages & salary costs in vehicles manufacturing industry in $m	Main countries	U 21-a
Motor-bicycles see MOTOR CYCLES & SCOOTERS		
MOTORCYCLES & SCOOTERS		
Exports by volume	All countries	S 24-a
No in use	All countries	S 13-a
Production by volume	All countries	S 24-a
Motorway traffic see MOTORWAYS		
ROAD TRAFFIC		
MOTORWAYS		
Length of main autoroutes by regions in km	EEC countries	E 38-a
in km	ECE countries	U 15-a
Traffic volume in ton-km (incl % rate of increase)	ECE countries	U 15-a
Mouldboard & disc ploughs see PLOUGHS		

	Territorial coverage	Title codes

MOUNTAIN HUTS & SHELTERS
    No of beds available for climbers   OECD countries   D 47-a

Movement of population   see   POPULATION MOVEMENT

Mowing machines   see   MACHINERY, AGRICULTURAL

MULES & ASSES
    Population: asses   OAS member countries   N 13-a
        historical table from 1860   Main European countries   Z 1-a
        in 1000 head   AASM countries   E 41-a
        (incl donkeys)   EEC countries   E 1-a
        mules   OAS member countries   N 13-a
        (total)   All countries   A 9-a   U 43-a
              OECD countries   D 1-a

MULLITE, SYNTHETIC
    see also   KYANITE
    Wholesale prices in $ per ton   USA   N 1-a

Multi-decker carriers   see   CARGO SHIPS

Multi-national corporations
        see   INVESTMENT, CORPORATE OVERSEAS
                 TRANSFER PAYMENTS, CORPORATE

Multi-purpose farm implements (single axle)
        see   IMPLEMENTS, MULTI-PURPOSE FARM

MULTILATERAL AID
    see also   DEVELOPMENT AID
                 INVESTMENT, PRIVATE OVERSEAS
                 INVESTMENT, PUBLIC OVERSEAS
    Aid received in $m   Recipient countries   D 7-a
    Butter-oil (as food aid) ex EEC area: tonnage   B 3-a
    Contributions to funds of institutions in $ OECD countries   D 13-a
    Disbursements to developing areas in $ Recipient countries   U 43-a
    Loans (official) granted in $m   Developing countries   M 4-a
    Milk powder (as food aid) ex EEC area: tonnage   B 3-a
    Portfolio investment in overseas bonds in $m   Main countries   M 3-a
    Public flow to multilateral agencies in $ Main countries   D 7-a
    Public grants to UN agencies in $m   Main countries   D 7-a

MULTIPLE STORES
    % market share: non-food items   EEC countries   B 29-a
                 clothing sales   UK   B 22-a
    Labour force employed: retail clothing stores   UK   B 22-a
    Retail trade turnover by type of store - index nos   EEC countries   E 26-m
    Sales: clothing by kind by value in £m   UK   B 29-a

MUNICIPAL BONDS
    Nominal & market valuations in £m   UK   F 8-q
    Value sold (on stock exchanges) in local currency   OAS member countries   N 16-a

Municipal expenditure   see   EXPENDITURE, MUNICIPAL

Municipalities   see   LOCAL AUTHORITIES

Murder   see   HOMICIDE

Muriate of potash   see   FERTILISERS

MUSEUMS
    No of national, private & public museums in use   All countries   U 62-a
        of visitors to museums (open to public)   All countries   U 62-a

Mushrooms   see   VEGETABLES, FRESH

MUSICAL INSTRUMENTS BY KIND
    Exports by destination by CST classes by value in $ EEC countries   E 48-a
                 SITC classes by value in $ Main countries   D 2-q
                             tonnage & value in $ OECD countries   D 3-a2
    Imports by source by CST classes by value in $ EEC countries   E 21-a
                 SITC classes by value in $ Main countries   D 2-q
                             tonnage & value in $ OECD countries   D 3-a2

MUSICAL INSTRUMENTS INDUSTRY
    Investment in buildings in local currency   EEC countries   E 40-a
                 land purchase in local currency   EEC countries   E 40-a
                 machinery in local currency   EEC countries   E 40-a

Mussels   see   CRUSTACEANS & MOLLUSCS

		Territorial coverage	Title codes
MUSTARD SEED			
	Export prices in local currency	Netherlands	A 9-a
	Exports: tonnage	Canada, Denmark, Ethiopia, Italy & Netherlands	B 19-a
	Imports: tonnage	Main countries	B 19-a
MUSTARD SEED OIL			
	Export prices in local currency	Sweden	A 9-a

Mutton   see   LAMB & MUTTON

N.C. Machine tools   see   MACHINE TOOLS, AUTOMATIC

NAPHTHA			
	Consumption by petrochemical industry & other users: tonnage	OECD countries	D 31-a
	Deliveries for home consumption & exports: tonnage	OECD countries	D 31-a
	Exports by destination: tonnage	USA	B 15-a
	Imports by source: tonnage	OECD countries	D 31-a
	Production: petroleum distillates: tonnage	All countries	U 22-a
	solvent naphtha: tonnage	All countries	B 15-a U 43-a
	tonnage	African countries	U 44-a
		Canada	B 15-a
		European countries, USA & USSR	U 4-a
	Refinery output, imports, consumption & supply: tonnage	OECD countries	D 31-a

NAPHTHALENE
    see also   CHEMICAL PRODUCTS
               HYDROCARBONS, AROMATIC

	Consumption (total) & for organic synthesis: tonnage	OECD countries	D 5-a
	Exports: tonnage	European countries, Japan & USA	U 26-a
	Imports: tonnage	European countries, Japan & USA	U 26-a
	Production from coal derivatives: tonnage	OECD countries	D 5-a
	from oil & natural gas: tonnage	OECD countries	D 5-a
	tonnage	European countries, Japan & USA	U 26-a

Narcotic drugs   see   DRUGS & MEDICINES
                         SYNTHETIC NARCOTICS

National accounts   see   BUDGET ACCOUNTS
                            DEFENCE EXPENDITURE
                            EXPORT DUTIES
                            GDP
                            GOVERNMENT EXPENDITURE
                            IMPORT DUTIES
                            INCOME TAX
                            NATIONAL INCOME
                            OVERSEAS INVESTMENT INCOME
                            SUBSIDIES

National bonds   see   GOVERNMENT BONDS

National disposable income   see   NATIONAL INCOME

NATIONAL HEALTH INSURANCE
    see also   SICKNESS BENEFITS
               SOCIAL SECURITY BENEFITS

	No of employed persons covered	All countries	L 2-a
	of non-active persons covered	All countries	L 2-a
	of persons covered by State Health Insurance Schemes	All countries	L 2-a

NATIONAL INCOME
    see also   GDP
               GNP

	% breakdown: composition of national income	EEC countries	E 2-a
	% change (in money terms)	E European countries & USSR	U 16-a
	% disposal: consumption or assets	Main countries	E 3-a
	wages, profits & interest payments	Main countries	E 3-a
	% growth rates: (actual)	E European countries & USSR	U 54-a
	(planned)	E European countries & USSR	U 54-a
	& national disposable income in local currency	African countries	U 44-a
	& per capita in $m	All countries	U 60-a
	of working population in $	EEC countries	E 32-a
	At current values (incl wages & salary component)	EEC countries	E 26-a
	in local currency	OAS member countries	N 16-a
	in $m	OPEC member countries	C 3-a
		Main countries	U 27-a U 43-a
	At factor cost in local currency	All countries	L 2-a
	By component (at current prices) in local currency	OAS member countries	N 16-a
		All countries	U 60-a
		Asian, Far East & Australasian countries	U 45-a
	By kind of factor income in local currency	OAS member countries	N 16-a
	in $m	Main countries	U 27-a

	Territorial coverage	Title codes
NATIONAL INCOME, continued		
Corporate savings as component in national income in local currency	OAS member countries	N 16-a
Direct taxes levied on corporations as factor in national income	OAS member countries	N 16-a
Disposable income in local currency	Developing countries	D 25-a
in purchasers' values in $m	OECD countries	D 30-a
Disposable income (net): private sector in $m	EEC countries	E 32-a
Distribution: households, corporations & government in $m	EEC countries	E 32-a
in local currency	E European countries	U 16-a
	OAS member countries	N 16-a
per wage earner by industrial sectors in $	EEC countries	E 32-a
wages & salaries at factor cost in $m	OAS member countries	N 16-a
Domestic personal savings as component in national income in local currency	OAS member countries	N 16-a
Employers' contributions to social security	OAS member countries	N 16-a
In local currency	Main countries	R 5-a
Income from agriculture at factor cost in local currency	OAS member countries	N 16-a
corporate transfer payments at factor cost in local currency	OAS member countries	N 16-a
interest & dividends at factor cost in local currency	OAS member countries	N 16-a
property at factor cost in local currency	OAS member countries	N 16-a
rents in local currency	OAS member countries	N 16-a
Net interest payments as component in national income in local currency	OAS member countries	N 16-a
Pay costs of armed forces at factor cost in local currency	OAS member countries	N 16-a
Per capita in £m	UK	C 27-a
in $m	Main countries	C 4-a
	All countries	U 43-a
in local currency & in $m	OAS member countries	N 16-a
Profits as component in national income in local currency	OAS member countries	N 16-a
Receipts from external transactions in local currency	African countries	U 44-a
Savings of corporations os component in national income in local currency	OAS member countries	N 16-a

NATIONAL INSURANCE
    see also   DEATH BENEFITS
                  FAMILY ALLOWANCES
                  INJURY & DISABLEMENT BENEFITS
                  MATERNITY BENEFITS
                  OLD AGE PENSIONS
                  PENSIONS, INFIRMITY
                  PENSIONS, INVALID
                  PENSIONS, WAR
                  PUBLIC ASSISTANCE
                  PUBLIC HEALTH
                  REDUNDANCY
                  SICKNESS BENEFITS
                  SOCIAL SECURITY BENEFITS
                  UNEMPLOYMENT BENEFITS
                  WIDOW'S & ORPHAN'S BENEFITS

Contributions of employees & firms	All countries	L 2-a
No of employees covered by social welfare schemes	OAS member countries	N 18-a

National Insurance Contributions   see   SOCIAL SECURITY LEVIES

National libraries   see   LIBRARIES, NATIONAL

NATIONAL SAVINGS
    see also   GOVERNMENT SAVINGS

% change associated with rise in gross national product	OECD countries	D 11
% changes in bank deposits held	E European countries & USSR	U 16-a
% interest rates paid to depositors per annum	OECD countries	D 12-a
As % of disposable income	Latin American countries	J 5-a
investment in private sector	All countries	M 6-a
gross domestic product	All countries	M 6-a
public investment	All countries	M 6-a
(total) & as % of disposable income	All countries	U 60-a
As component in national income in local currency	OAS member countries	N 16-a
As financing media in capital formation in $m	EEC countries	E 32-a
By public corporations as % of total investment	All countries	M 6-a
Deposits in financial institutions (incl insurance equity) in $m	OECD countries	D 12-a
(total) in local currency	EEC countries	E 26-m
	E European countries	U 16-a
Excess of private incomes over private expenditure in local currency	OAS member countries	N 16-a
Gross domestic savings as % of gross national product	ECAFE countries	U 17-a
Private savings transactions in $m	EEC countries	E 32-a
as % of total national savings	Latin American countries	J 5-a
Ratios of incremental savings to income	E European countries	U 16-a
Savings of private sector, banks & corporations in $m	OECD countries	D 12-a
Time deposits held in banks by administrative areas in $m	EEC countries	E 38-a
Volume of national savings in local currencies	All countries	F 5-m F 6-q

Nationalisation   see   PUBLIC CORPORATIONS
                              STATE-CONTROLLED ENTERPRISES

	Territorial coverage	Title codes

Nationalised industries   see   COAL MINING
                                PUBLIC CORPORATIONS
                                RAILWAYS
                                STATE-CONTROLLED ENTERPRISES

Natural abrasives   see   ABRASIVES, NATURAL

Natural black lead   see   GRAPHITE

NATURAL DISASTERS

Compensation & welfare payments in local currency	EEC countries	E 6-a
Payments as % of expenditure on social welfare	EEC countries	E 6-a

Natural fertilisers   see   FERTILISERS, NITROGENOUS
                            FERTILISERS, PHOSPHATE
                            FERTILISERS, POTASH
                            FISH MEAL
                            MANURE
                            POTASH SALTS
                            UREA

Natural fibres   see   COTTON
                       FLAX
                       HEMP
                       JUTE
                       SILK, RAW
                       WOOL, GREASY RAW

NATURAL GAS

see also   MANUFACTURED GAS
           NATURAL GAS LIQUIDS

	Territorial coverage	Title codes	
% share in consumption of energy	Latin American countries	U 18-a	
of total energy supply sources	ECE countries	U 16-a	
As % of all energy sources consumed	Main countries	H 4-a	
As source of benzene production	European countries, Japan & USA	U 26-a	
of toluene production	European countries, Japan & USA	U 26-a	
of xylene production	European countries, Japan & USA	U 26-a	
Calorific value (average)	European countries & USA	U 3-a	
compared with refined petroleum fuels		C 21	
Capacity: subterranean storage installations in m³	EEC countries	E 15-a	
Changes in stocks in coal equiv tonnage	EEC countries	E 14-a	
Consumption as % of consumption of all primary energy sources	ECE regions	U 10-a	
	European countries	U 10-a	
by volume in m³	Italy	H 4-a	
	EEC countries	E 7-a	
	Main countries	H 4-a	
	OAS member countries	N 17-a	
in cu ft	USA	N 1-a	
in coal equiv tonnage	EEC countries	E 16-q	E 14-a
		E 15-a	
	EEC area	E 7-a	
	ECE countries	U 15-a	
	Main countries	E 3-a	
	UK	E 7-a	
(household) in coal equiv tonnage	EEC area	E 7-a	
(industrial) by volume in m³	Italy	H 4-a	
& by households in coal equiv tonnage	EEC countries	E 16-q	E 15-a
in calorific value	Main countries	H 4-a	
in coal equiv tonnage	EEC countries	E 14-a	
chemical industry in coal equiv tonnage	EEC countries	E 14-a	
by volume in m³	OECD countries	D 5-a	
iron & steel industries in coal equiv tonnage	EEC countries	E 14-a	
non-ferrous metals fabricating industry in coal equiv tonnage	EEC countries	E 14-a	
non-metallic minerals industry in coal equiv tonnage	EEC countries	E 14-a	
power stations (for electricity production) by volume in m³	UK	U 10-a	
& gasworks in coal equiv tonnage	EEC countries	E 16-q	E 15-a
publically-owned electricity generation plants in coal equiv tonnage	European countries	U 1-a	
road transportation in calorific value	Main countries	H 4-a	
steel industries in calorific value	Main countries	H 4-a	
by volume in m³	ECE countries	U 6-a	U 7-a
	Main countries	H 3-a	
in electricity generation in coal equiv tonnage	EEC countries	E 16-m	E 14-a
		E 15-a	
in gasworks in coal equiv tonnage	EEC countries	E 14-a	
in open-hearth furnaces by volume in m³	ECE countries	U 6-a	U 7-a
	Main countries	H 3-a	
in thermal power stations by volume in m³	OECD countries	D 8-a	
(incl imports) in coal equiv tonnage	All countries	U 55-a	
natural gas per capita in coal equiv tonnage	All countries	U 55-a	
tonnage	UK	U 10-m	
Deliveries to EEC area & exports: tonnage	European countries, USA & USSR	U 4-a	
to other EEC area countries: tonnage	EEC countries	E 16-q	E 15-a
Exports by destination in calorific value	EEC countries	E 14-a	
	European countries & USA	U 3-a	
shipped to non-EEC area in coal equiv tonnage	EEC countries	E 14-a	

	Territorial coverage	Title codes	
NATURAL GAS, continued			
Imports & supply: tonnage	OECD countries	D 39-q	
by source in calorific value	European countries & USA	U 3-a	
tonnage	OECD countries	D 31-a	
by volume in m³	EEC countries	E 7-a	
Imports & exports in coal equiv tonnage	EEC countries	E 16-q	E 15-a
by source & destination: tonnage	Canada, Mexico & USA	B 15-a	
by volume in m³ (incl world total)	Main countries	C 3-a	
in coal equiv tonnage	EEC countries	E 14-a	
into world areas: tonnage	Main world regions	D 31-a	
(net) as % of consumption	E European countries & USSR	U 16-a	
	EEC countries	U 16-a	
Known reserves by volume in m³	Latin American countries	U 18-a	
No of drillings made & no of drillings proven unproductive	All countries	C 14-a	
Price (free frontier) in DM per 100 m³	W Germany	R 2-m	
Production by areas by volume in m³	EEC countries	E 38-a	
	EEC countries	E 15-a	
by fields & regions in coal equiv tonnage	EEC countries	E 16-q	E 15-a
in calorific value	European countries & USSR	U 4-a	
	African countries	U 39-a	
	All countries	U 22-a	U 55-a
in coal equiv tonnage	ECE countries	U 15-a	
	EEC countries	E 16-q	E 14-a
		E 15-a	
	European countries & USSR	U 4-a	
	Main countries	E 3-a	
	All countries	U 27-m	B 15-a
		N 5-a	
by volume in cu ft	All countries	C 3-a	
in m³ (incl world total)	Main European countries	Z 1-a	
historical table from 1899	All countries	C 14-a	
from 1938	African countries	U 44-a	
in m³	All countries	R 5-a	
	Barbados & Venezuela	T 6-a	
	Congo Republic, Gabon & Rwanda	E 41-a	
	E European countries & USSR	U 16-a	
	ECAFE countries	U 32-q	
	EEC countries	E 26-m	E 28-q
		E 7-a	E 27-a
	Latin American countries	J 5-a	U 18-a
	Main countries	E 3-a	
	OAS member countries	N 14-a	
	OPEC member countries	C 3-a	
	Venezuela	C 3-a	
in petroleum equiv tonnage	Latin American countries	U 18-a	
Production re-injected by volume in m³	OPEC member countries	C 3-a	
Production & reserves in calorific value	All countries	U 43-a	
exploited (incl exports) by volume in m³	Main countries	H 4-a	
Production, imports & resources by volume in m³	Italy	H 4-a	
exports & supply: tonnage	OECD countries	D 39-q	D 31-a
Production, trade & consumption: tonnage	All countries	U 55-a	
transformed into liquids: tonnage	Venezuela	C 3-a	
used by oil industry by volume in m³	Venezuela	C 3-a	
utilised & flared by volume in m³	OPEC member countries	C 3-a	
Proven & estimated reserves by volume in m³	EEC countries	E 15-a	
	Main countries	E 3-a	
	African countries	U 39-a	
Resources & changes in stocks in coal equiv tonnage	EEC countries	E 16-q	E 15-a
Sales by main oil companies by volume in cu ft	Worldwide	C 3-a	
Selling price in cents per m³ to users	Netherlands	R 2-m	
in Frs per m³ to users	France	R 2-m	
Stocks by volume in cu ft	USA	N 1-a	
Supply ex EEC area production & from imports in coal equiv tonnage	EEC countries	E 16-q	E 14-a
		E 15-a	
		C 14-a	
World consumption in coal equiv tonnage	World regions	U 55-a	
movement between regions by volume in m³	Main countries	N 1-a	
production by volume in cu ft		C 14-a	E 15-a
in coal equiv tonnage		N 4-a	
marketed by volume in cu ft	Main countries	N 1-a	
reserves by volume in cu ft (estim)		C 14-a	
(proven)			

Natural gas, known reserves   see   APPENDIX 4

NATURAL GAS LIQUIDS

% consumption: liquefied petroleum gas	Latin American countries	U 18-a	
Consumption by end-use sectors: tonnage	OECD countries	D 31-a	
liquefied petroleum gas: tonnage	OAS member countries	N 17-a	
by vehicles: tonnage	European countries	U 8-a	
per capita in kg	All countries	U 55-a	
propane: tonnage	OAS member countries	N 17-a	
tonnage	Italy	H 4-a	
	Main countries	C 14-a	
Deliveries, home consumption & exports: tonnage	OECD countries	D 31-a	
Demand (domestic) in 42 gallon barrels	USA	N 1-a	
Excise duties: rates levied on liquefied petroleum gas	EEC countries	E 31-a	
Imports by source: tonnage	OECD countries	D 31-a	
by world areas: tonnage	Main world regions	D 31-a	

	Territorial coverage	Title codes	
NATURAL GAS LIQUIDS, continued			
Production & consumption: tonnage	OECD countries	D 44-a	
butane & propane: tonnage	All countries	U 22-a	
in 42 gallon barrels	USA	N 1-a	
liquefied gas from oil by volume in m³	OAS member countries	N 14-a	
tonnage	Main countries	E 3-a	
African countries		U 39-a	U 44-a
All countries		U 43-a	
EEC countries		E 16-m	E 15-a
European countries, USA & USSR		U 4-a	
Latin American countries		J 5-a	
Production, imports & supply: tonnage	OECD countries	D 44-a	
Production, trade & consumption: tonnage	OECD countries	D 31-a	
Refinery output, imports, supply & consumption: tonnage	All countries	U 55-a	
OECD countries		D 31-a	
Value (at refineries) in $ per 42 gallon barrel	USA	N 1-a	
NATURAL GAS PIPELINES			
see also GAS PIPELINES			
Length of existing transmission lines in km	EEC countries	E 15-a	
in km & diameter of pipe	Main pipelines worldwide	C 14-a	
Location & diameter in inches	OPEC member countries	C 3-a	
& pipe length in miles	OPEC member countries	C 3-a	
Route & name of operating company	OPEC member countries	C 3-a	
NATURAL GUMS			
% contribution to export earnings	Sudan & Chad	E 45-a	
Exports: tonnage & value in $m	Sudan	E 45-a	
Production & exports: tonnage	All countries	A 23-a	
Wholesale prices: dry resin – index nos	Main European countries	A 26-a	
NATURAL NITRATES			
Consumption: Guano: tonnage	OAS member countries	N 17-a	
tonnage	USA	N 1-a	
Stocks held at producers' premises: tonnage	USA	N 1-a	
Wholesale prices: sodium nitrate in $ per ton	USA	N 1-a	
World production: tonnage	Main countries	N 1-a	
Natural phenol see COAL BY-PRODUCTS			
NATURAL PHOSPHATES			
see also BASIC SLAG			
FERTILISERS			
FISH MEAL			
PHOSPHATE OF LIME			
PHOSPHATE ROCK			
PHOSPHATES			
Consumption by chemical industry: tonnage	Main countries	U 25-a	
tonnage	OAS member countries	N 17-a	
Exports (total) & to EEC area: tonnage & value in UA	AASM countries	E 41-a	
Imports & exports: tonnage	Main countries	B 15-a	
Production (excl Guano): tonnage	All countries	U 22-a	
(incl Apatite & Guano): tonnage	Latin American countries	J 5-a	
(incl world total): tonnage	All countries	R 5-a	
tonnage	All countries	U 43-a	
OAS member countries		N 14-a	
World market prices in $ per ton	USA	E 41-a	
NATURAL RUBBER			
% contribution to export earnings	Liberia	E 45-a	
% share in consumption of rubber (all kinds)	Main countries	A 1-a	
Area under rubber trees on plantations in ha	All countries	C 18-a	
on smallholdings in ha	All countries	C 18-a	
in ha & harvest: tonnage	All countries	R 5-a	
Consumption as % of total rubber consumption	Worldwide	U 26-a	
by end-product: tonnage	Main countries	C 18-q	
by industrial sector: tonnage	Main countries	A 1-a	
for production of belting & cables: tonnage	USA	C 18-q	
commercial vehicles & farm tractor	UK	C 18-a	
tyres: tonnage	UK	C 18-a	
Main countries		B 13-a	
footwear & soles: tonnage	UK	C 18-a	
hose & tubing: tonnage	UK	C 18-a	
inner tubes for tyres: tonnage	UK	C 18-a	
latex foams: tonnage	UK	C 18-a	
motor cycle tyres: tonnage	UK	C 18-a	
sponge rubber: tonnage	UK	C 18-a	
tyre repair material: tonnage	UK	C 18-a	
forecast for 1975: tonnage	Main countries	A 1	
(industrial): tonnage	Main countries	C 18-q	
in manufacturing industry: tonnage	Main countries	B 13-a	
per capita in lbs per yr	Main countries	B 13-a	
tonnage & per capita in lbs per yr	Main countries	U 43-a	
(incl world total)	Main countries	A 5-a	B 2-a

NATURAL RUBBER, continued

	Territorial coverage	Title codes	
Consumption: tonnage	E European countries, IRSG area & China	C 18-m	
	IRSG member countries	C 18-m	
	OAS member countries	N 17-a	
	W European countries, Japan & USA	C 17-m	
	Australia, UK & USA	C 18-m	
Deliveries ex government stocks: tonnage	USA	U 11-a	
Disposals ex US government stockpile: tonnage	USA	R 2-m	
Export prices in cents per lb ex dock, New York	Main countries	A 9-a	
in local currency fob	Singapore	U 17-m	
in $ per 100 lbs fob	Indonesia, Singapore & Sri Lanka	U 32-m	
per ton fob	Thailand	U 32-m	
unit value in Bahts per kg fob		U 29-q	U 54-q
Export prices - index nos (weighted average main sources)	Main countries	B 13-a	
Exports as % of value of total exports	Malaysia & Singapore	C 17-m	
by main destinations: tonnage	Main countries	B 13-a	
by value in local currency per ton	Burma, Indonesia, Malaysia & Thailand	U 32-m	
in $ per ton	W European countries	U 33-a	
in $	EEC countries	E 24-a	
shipped to EEC & non-EEC areas by value in $m	Liberia	E 45-a	
tonnage & value in $m	Main countries	B 2-a	
	Asian & Far East areas	U 32-q	
tonnage	ECAFE countries	U 32-m	
	Main countries	C 18-m	B 13-a
(total) & shipped to EEC area: tonnage & value in UA	AASM countries	E 41-a	
Import prices at port in £ per ton cif	UK	U 32-m	A 9-a
by grade in local currency per ton cif	Singapore, UK & USA	C 18-m	
in £ per ton cif	European & UK ports	C 17-m	
in pence per kg cif	UK	R 2-m	
Imports by source: tonnage	Main countries	B 13-a	
by value in $m	W European countries	U 33-a	
ex EEC & non-EEC areas by value in $m	EEC countries	E 24-a	
(net) into consuming areas: tonnage	Main countries	C 18-m	
programmed: tonnage	Centrally-planned economies	U 11-a	
tonnage	Canada, European countries, USA & USSR	A 11-a	
Prices (3 months forward) in £ per ton	Singapore, UK & USA	C 18-m	
(spot) on London, New York & Singapore markets in £ per ton		C 18-m	
Producer prices in M$ per kg fob	Singapore	R 2-m	
Production (incl forward projections): tonnage	Main countries	A 1	
on plantations: tonnage	Main countries	C 18-m	
on smallholdings: tonnage	Malaysia & Indonesia	C 18-m	
Production, consumption & stocks: tonnage	IRSG member countries	C 18-m	
Production & exports of Commonwealth countries as % of world totals		B 13-a	
(incl world total): tonnage	Main countries	A 5-a	B 2-a
(incl latex): tonnage	All countries	U 43-a	
	AASM countries	E 41-a	
tonnage	All countries	A 9-a	
	Asian & Far East countries	U 32-q	
	Indonesia, Malaysia & Sri Lanka	C 17-m	
	Ivory Coast, Cameroun & Zaire	E 41-a	
	Main countries	C 18-m	U 27-m
		B 13-a	
Re-exports (incl latex) by destination: tonnage	UK & USA	C 18-m	
Stockpile releases: tonnage	All countries	U 11-a	
Stocks afloat: tonnage (estim)	IRSG member countries	C 18-m	
in transit: tonnage	Worldwide	B 2-a	
(commercial) held by consumers: tonnage	IRSG member countries	C 18-m	
(end-year): tonnage	Main countries	B 13-a	
held at ports: tonnage	Malaysia	C 18-m	
by dealers: tonnage	Malaysia, Sri Lanka & S Vietnam	C 18-a	
in consuming countries: tonnage	IRSG member countries	C 18-m	
	All countries	B 2-a	
in producing countries: tonnage	IRSG member countries	C 18-m	B 2-a
on estates: tonnage	Malaysia, Indonesia & Vietnam	C 18-m	
tonnage	Main consuming & producing countries incl tonnage afloat	C 17-m	
Wholesale prices in cents per kg	Singapore & USA	A 5-a	
	USA	B 2-a	
(forward) on London terminal market in £ per ton	UK	C 17-m	
pool price in cents per lb	Papua New Guinea	U 32-m	
(spot) ex Malaysia on London terminal market in £ per ton	UK	B 2-a	
	Sri Lanka, Thailand, UK & USA	U 27-m	A 9-a
in local currency per ton	Main Commodity Markets	B 13-m	
		C 18-m	
World capacity for reclaiming rubber: tonnage (estim)	Worldwide excl centrally-planned economies	B 13-a	
World consumption: tonnage		C 18-m	U 11-a
		U 26-a	
World exports by value in $m	World regions	A 5-a	
unit value in $ per ton	Worldwide	A 11-a	
World consumption projected to 1980: tonnage		U 26-a	
World market prices - index nos		G 1-a	
World market prices: natural rubber ex Malaysia in pence per lb	UK	E 41-a	
World production, stockpile & deliveries: tonnage		B 13-a	
World production: tonnage		C 17-m	U 11-a
		U 26-a	
		G 1-a	
World stocks (end-yr): tonnage			
World supply position: tonnage		B 13-a	U 11-a

	Territorial coverage	Title codes

NATURAL SCIENCES
- % of students enrolled studying natural sciences — ECAFE countries — U 17
- No of full & part-time research staff employed — All countries — U 62-a
- new book titles published on natural sciences — All countries — U 62-a
- book translations published on natural sciences — OAS member countries — N 19-a
- students abroad by origin studying natural sciences — All countries — U 64-a
- enrolled on university courses in natural sciences — OAS member countries — N 19-a
- university degrees gained in natural sciences — All countries — U 62-a

Natural silk   see   SILK, RAW

Natural stone   see   BUILDING MATERIALS

NATURAL WAX
- Production & exports: tonnage — All countries — A 23-a

Navigational aid equipment   see   ELECTRONIC EQUIPMENT

Neoprene   see   SYNTHETIC RUBBER

NEPHELINE SYENITE
- Production: tonnage — Canada & Norway — B 15-a

NET MATERIAL PRODUCT
   see also   CAPITAL ACCUMULATION
                CAPITAL FORMATION
                CAPITAL OUTPUT RATIOS
- As ratio to capital formation — E European countries — U 16-a
- By components: % change distributed — E European countries — U 16-a
- produced — E European countries — U 16-a
- % growth rates — E European countries & USSR — U 60-a
- By kind of activity (in %) — Cuba, E European countries & Yugoslavia — U 43-a
- By use: consumption in $m — Cuba, E European countries & Yugoslavia — U 43-a
- In agriculture & forestry in $m — E European countries — U 34-a
- In local currency — E European countries & USSR — U 16-a
- Per capita: % growth rates — All countries — U 60-a
- % change in consumption (personal & social) — E European countries — U 16-a
- % change (planned & actual) — E European countries & USSR — U 16-a
- % distribution by use — All countries — U 60-a
- % growth rates — All countries — U 60-a
- Historical tables from 1850 in local currency — E European countries, Cuba & Yugoslavia — U 43-a
- — Main European countries — Z 1-a

NEW ORDERS
   see also   DELIVERIES
- Bulk & combined carriers: tonnage — Worldwide — S 22-2a
- by size classes — Country of build — S 22-2a
- by year of delivery — Worldwide — S 22-2a
- volume — Country of registration — S 22-2a
- Iron & steel industry by product (incl index nos) — EEC countries — E 30-m
- Machine tools (metal-cutting type) for export by value in $m — USA — J 2-a
- for home market by value in $m — USA — J 2-a
- (metal-forming type) for export by value in $m — USA — J 2-a
- for home market by value in $m — USA — J 2-a
- Nuclear power stations: construction by capacity in mWe — All countries — H 4-a
- by reactor types by capacity in mWe — All countries — H 4-a
- Tankers by size classes: volume — Worldwide — S 22-2a
- by year of delivery: volume — Worldwide — S 22-2a
- tonnage — Worldwide — S 22-2a
- — Country of build — S 22-2a
- — Country of registration — S 22-2a
- World order-books: no & tonnage: bulk carriers — S 15-a
- tankers — S 15-a

New plant installation   see   PLANT CAPACITY

NEWS & PUBLIC AFFAIRS
- No of hrs of radio broadcast time — All countries — U 62-a
- of television broadcast time — All countries — U 62-a

NEWSPAPERS
- Circulation & circulation per 1000 population — All countries — U 43-a
- daily newspapers published per 1000 population — Developing world regions — U 23-a
- non-daily papers in 1956 — World regions — U 63
- No of general news interest newspapers published in 1956 — Worldwide — U 63
- published & circulation — Asian, Far East & Australasian countries — U 45-a
- daily & non-daily newspapers — All countries — U 43-a
- Prices at newsagents in local currency — OAS member countries — N 17-a

	Territorial coverage	Title codes

NEWSPAPERS, DAILY

Circulation (estim)
	All countries	U 62-a
evening papers in 1956	All countries	U 63
in 1956	World regions	U 63
morning papers in 1956	All countries	U 63
per 1000 population (average)	OAS member countries	N 19-a
No & circulation per 1000 population	Latin American countries	J 5-a
	World regions	
	All countries	U 63
of general news interest newspapers published	All countries	U 62-a
of pages per paper (average)	All countries	U 63
of daily newspapers published & circulation (average)	OAS member countries	N 19-a
circa 1956	All countries	U 63
by language	All countries	U 63

Newspapers, non-daily   see   PERIODICALS

NEWSPRINT

Consumption: change per $1000 increase in gross national product	Main countries	D 32-a
Consumption - index nos	E European countries (excl USSR)	A 24-a
per $1000 of gross national product in kg	Main countries	D 32-a
per capita in kg	World economic areas	D 32-a
	All countries	U 62-a
tonnage & in kg	Main countries	U 43-a
	USA	J 7-a
in lbs	Latin American countries	J 5-a
	Main countries	D 40-a
	OAS member countries	N 17-a
	OECD countries	D 40-a
tonnage	USA	J 4-m
Domestic shipments received: tonnage	USA	J 4-a
Export prices in $ per ton	Finland	A 9-a
Exports by destination: tonnage	All countries	D 40-a
historical table from 1902: tonnage	Finland	Z 1-a
	Canada	J 4-a
tonnage & value in $m	All countries	A 23-a
(incl world total)	All countries	A 5-a
tonnage	Canada, European countries & USSR	A 13-q
	Main countries	J 7-a
	OECD countries	D 41-q
Import prices in $ per ton	UK	A 9-a
Imports & exports: tonnage & value in $m	All countries	A 23-a
ex Canada & European area: tonnage	EEC area & USA	J 4-a
tonnage	All countries	
	Canada, Egypt, European countries, Israel, USA & USSR	A 13-q
	Canada, European & Far East countries, USA & USSR	A 11-a
	OECD countries	D 41-q
Loss of consumption of newsprint due to newspaper strikes: tonnage	USA	J 4-a
Marginal propensity to consume newsprint per $1000 of gross national product in kg	Main countries	D 32-a
New plant construction (actual) & new capacity installed: tonnage	All countries	J 4-a
planned & capacity thereof: tonnage	All countries	J 4-a
Production (actual) as % of existing capacity	All countries	J 4-a
(incl reserve capacity): tonnage	Canada	A 5-a
tonnage (incl world total)	All countries	U 27-m A 23-a
	All countries	J 7-a U 22-a
		U 43-a
	EEC countries	E 28-q E 27-a
	Finland, Norway & Sweden	J 4-a
	Latin American countries	U 40-a
	Main countries	E 3-a
	OECD countries	D 41-q D 40-a
Production capacity: tonnage	All countries	J 4-a
Wholesale prices in local currency per ton	Canada, Finland, France & UK	A 13-m
in $ per ton	USA	U 27-m
	Canada	A 9-a
World capacity for newsprint production: historical table: tonnage		J 4-a
World demand as % of world production capacity: tonnage		J 4-a
historical table: tonnage & annual % change		J 4-a
tonnage	World regions	J 4-a
World production capacity: tonnage	World regions	J 4-a

NICKEL

see also   FERRO-NICKEL

Consumption as ferro-nickel: tonnage	USA	T 4-a
as matte nickel: tonnage	USA	T 4-a
as nickel oxide: tonnage	USA	T 4-a
as nickel salts: tonnage	USA	T 4-a
by end-use: tonnage	Italy	C 12-a
in production of cast iron: tonnage	USA	J 6-a T 4-a
of copper-nickel alloys: tonnage	USA	T 4-a
of electric resistance steel: tonnage	USA	J 6-a
of electro-plating anodes: tonnage	USA	J 6-a T 4-a

	Territorial coverage	Title codes	
NICKEL, continued			
Consumption in production of ferro-alloys: tonnage	UK	T 4-a	
high-temperature alloys: tonnage	USA	T 4-a	
high-temperature steel: tonnage	USA	J 6-a	
nickel alloys by kind: tonnage	USA	J 6-a	
stainless steels: tonnage	USA	J 6-a	T 4-a
metallic nickel: tonnage	USA	J 6-a	
nickel matte: tonnage	USA	J 6-a	
nickel oxide: tonnage	USA	J 6-a	
nickel salts: tonnage	USA	J 6-a	
refined metallic nickel: tonnage	All countries	C 30-q	
	OECD countries	D 21-q	
tonnage	OAS member countries	N 17-a	
Contract prices: refined metallic nickel in £ per ton	UK	R 2-m	
Export prices ex warehouse in cents per lb fob	Canada	T 4-m	
Export prices - index nos (weighted average main sources)		U 29-q	
Exports by destination: tonnage	Canada, Norway & UK	T 4-a	
refined metallic nickel by destination: tonnage	OECD countries	D 21-q	
tonnage	New Caledonia	T 4-a	
Import prices: refined metallic nickel in $ per lb cif	UK	R 2-m	
Imports & exports by source & destination: tonnage	Main countries	B 15-a	
Imports by source: tonnage	W Germany, Italy, Sweden & UK	T 4-a	
refined metallic nickel: tonnage	OECD countries	D 21-q	
unwrought metal & nickel scrap: tonnage	Italy	C 12-a	
Producer prices: electrolytic nickel & cathodes in $ per ton	USA	H 2-a	
refined metallic nickel in local currency	W Germany & UK	H 2-a	
Production based on metal content of ore: tonnage	All countries	B 15-a	U 22-a
		U 43-a	
primary metal smelted from local ores: tonnage	Brazil & Cuba	U 40-a	
refined metallic nickel: tonnage	USA	T 4-a	
	All countries	C 30-m	C 12-a
	OECD countries	D 21-q	
tonnage	Main countries	J 6-a	N 1-a
	OAS member countries	N 14-a	
Wholesale prices in £ per ton on London Metal Exchange	UK	C 12-m	
in $ per ton	Norway, UK & USA	U 27-m	
refined metallic nickel in local currency per kg	Main countries	T 4-m	
World consumption: refined metallic nickel: tonnage	Main countries	T 4-a	
	All countries	C 12-a	
tonnage		C 30-a	
World production (incl nickel ore smelted): tonnage		C 30-a	
at mines & smeltered: tonnage		C 30-a	
mines: tonnage	Main countries	N 1-a	
smelters: tonnage	All countries	T 4-a	
refined nickel: tonnage	All countries	C 12-a	
tonnage		N 4-a	
World reserves: tonnage (estim)	Main countries	N 1-a	
NICKEL ALLOYS			
Usage of nickel in production of nickel alloys: tonnage	USA	J 6-a	
Nickel cathodes see CATHODES, NICKEL			
NICKEL ORE			
% share of world reserves (estim)	Latin American countries	U 18-a	
Export prices - index nos (weighted average)		U 29-q	
Exports by destination: tonnage	Canada & New Caledonia	T 4-a	
Production at mines: tonnage	Main countries	C 30-m	
World production at mines: tonnage	All countries	T 4-a	
based on metal content: tonnage		C 12-a	
NICKEL POWDER			
Exports: tonnage	USA	T 4-a	
NICKEL PRODUCTS, SEMI-FINISHED			
see also PLATES SHEETS STRIP, NICKEL			
RODS BARS SECTIONS, NICKEL			
TUBES & PIPES, NICKEL			
Export prices: cold-rolled sheet in $ per ton	USA	T 4-m	
Exports by destination: tonnage	Main countries	T 4-a	
Wholesale prices: sheet & strip in Fr per ton	France	T 4-m	
NICKEL SCRAP			
Consumption by kind of scrap at smelters & refineries: tonnage	USA	T 4-a	
of monel metal at smelters: tonnage	USA	T 4-a	
of nickel residues at smelters: tonnage	USA	T 4-a	
of nickel-silver scrap at smelters: tonnage	USA	T 4-a	
Exports by destination: tonnage	Canada, UK & USA	T 4-a	
Imports by source: tonnage	W Germany & UK	T 4-a	
Production by method of recovery: tonnage	USA	T 4-a	
Recovery (as nickel alloys) by kind: tonnage	USA	T 4-a	
(as unalloyed metallic nickel): tonnage	USA	T 4-a	
Wholesale prices: anode scrap nickel in £ per ton	UK	R 2-m	
ex merchants' yards in £ per ton	UK	T 4-w	

	Territorial coverage	Title codes

NICKEL-SILVER SCRAP
    Wholesale prices in £ per ton — UK — T 4-w

Nickel-silver sheets   see   SHEETS, NICKEL-ALLOY

Nickel-silver strip   see   STRIP, NICKEL-ALLOY

Nickel-silver wire   see   WIRE, NICKEL-ALLOY

Nicotine   see   INSECTICIDES

NIGER SEED
    Exports: tonnage — Ethiopia — B 19-a
    Imports: tonnage — Italy & Japan — B 19-a

Nightwear   see   CLOTHING

Niobium   see   TANTALUM & NIOBIUM

Niobium ore   see   COLUMBIUM ORE

NITRATE
    see also   NATURAL NITRATES
                 NATURAL PHOSPHATES
                 PHOSPHATIC GUANO
    Production: aquatic bird guano: tonnage — All countries — U 22-a
                                              — Argentine, Peru & S Africa, Rep of — A 22-a
                                              — Chile — U 40-a

Nitrated acids   see   ACIDS, ORGANIC

NITRIC ACID
    Consumption: tonnage — OAS member countries — N 17-a
    Production: pure nitric acid: tonnage — All countries — U 22-a   U 43-a
                            tonnage — African countries — U 44-a
                                   — Main countries — R 5-a
                                   — OAS member countries — N 14-a

Nitrogen compounds   see   AMMONIA, SYNTHETIC
                                           FERTILISERS, NITROGENOUS

NITROGEN, ELEMENTAL
    Consumption: tonnage — USA — N 1-a
    Stocks held at producers' plants: tonnage — USA — N 1-a
    Wholesale prices (as bulk liquid) in $ — USA — N 1-a
                     (as pipeline gas) in $ — USA — N 1-a
    World production: tonnage — Main countries — N 1-a

NITROGEN, FIXED
    see also   AMMONIA
    Consumption: tonnage — USA — N 1-a
    Stocks held at producers' plants: tonnage — USA — N 1-a
    Wholesale prices: ammonia in $ per ton — USA — N 1-a
    World production: tonnage — Main countries — N 1-a

Nitrogenous fertilisers   see   FERTILISERS, NITROGENOUS

Nitrosated acid derivatives   see   ACIDS, ORGANIC

Noise research   see   RESEARCH & DEVELOPMENT

Nominal valuations   see   GOVERNMENT BONDS
                                     INDUSTRIAL SHARES
                                     MUNICIPAL BONDS
                                     PRIVATE BONDS
                                     SHARES, COMMON
                                     SHARES, PREFERENCE

Non-carbon compounds   see   CHEMICALS, INORGANIC

Non-cellulosic fabrics   see   WOVEN NON-CELLULOSIC FABRICS
                                       WOVEN NON-CELLULOSIC SPUN
                                                             YARN FABRICS

NON-CELLULOSIC FIBRES
    % utilisation of plant capacity — European countries, Japan & USA — D 27-a
    Acrylic fibres as % of total non-cellulosic fibre production — European countries, Japan & USA — D 27-a
    Consumption: acrylic fibres by sector of textile industry: tonnage — OECD countries — D 46-a
                                           in spinning mills: tonnage — OECD countries — D 46-a
                     by end-use: tonnage — Japan & USA — A 1-a
                     by sector of clothing manufacturing industry: tonnage — EEC countries — K 4-a
                     in spinning mills: tonnage — All countries — A 6-a
                                        — W European countries — K 2-q
                     in production of carpets: tonnage — EEC countries — K 4-a
                                 of pneumatic tyres: tonnage — EEC countries — K 4-a

	Territorial coverage	Title codes
NON-CELLULOSIC FIBRES, continued		
Consumption: polyamide fibres by textile industry: tonnage	OECD countries	D 46-a
in spinning mills: tonnage	OECD countries	D 46-a
polyester fibres by textile industry: tonnage	OECD countries	D 46-a
in spinning mills: tonnage	OECD countries	D 46-a
synthetic fibres in spinning mills: tonnage	World regions	K 5-a
tonnage	European countries, Canada, Japan & USA	D 27-a
	OAS member countries	N 17-a
Export prices: nylon fibre in cents per lb fob	USA	R 2-m
Exports as % of production	European countries, Canada, Japan & USA	D 27-a
tonnage	All countries	A 6-a
	OECD countries	D 46-a
Imports as % of production	European countries, Canada, Japan & USA	D 27-a
tonnage	All countries	A 6-a
	OECD countries	D 46-a
Plant capacity: tonnage	European countries, Canada, Japan & USA	D 27-a
Polyamide fibres as % of total fibre production	European countries, Japan & USA	D 27-a
Polyester fibres as % of total fibre production	European countries, Japan & USA	D 27-a
Production: acrylic fibres: tonnage	OECD countries	D 46-a
continuous fibres: tonnage	All countries	U 22-a
filament yarn: tonnage	All countries	B 10-a
	Main countries	E 3-a
	Canada, European countries, Japan & USA	D 27-a
polyamide fibres: tonnage	OECD countries	D 46-a
polyester fibres: tonnage	OECD countries	D 46-a
staple & fibres: tonnage	All countries	B 10-a U 22-a
staple: tonnage	Canada, European countries, Japan & USA	D 27-a
synthetic fibres: tonnage	EEC countries	E 26-m
synthetic filament: tonnage	All countries	U 27-m U 43-a
	European countries, Japan & USA	U 26-a
tonnage	All countries	A 6-a
	EEC countries	E 28-q E 27-a
	OAS member countries	N 14-a
	OECD countries	D 46-a
	S American countries	U 40-a
Wholesale prices: "Courtelle" staple in £ per ton	UK	B 10-m
nylon fibre in pence per kg	UK	R 2-m
nylon staple in £ per ton	UK	B 10-m
nylon yarn in £ per ton	UK	B 10-m
terylene staple in £ per ton	UK	B 10-m
World consumption per capita in kg		A 6-a
synthetic fibres: tonnage		B 29
tonnage		A 6-a
World exports in lbs	Main countries	B 10-a
World imports in lbs	Main countries	B 10-a
World production: all non-cellulosic yarns & staple in lbs		B 10-a
acrylic yarns & staple in lbs		B 10-a
polyamide yarns & staple in lbs		B 10-a
polyester yarns & staple in lbs		B 10-a

Non-commercial transactions rate   see   EXCHANGE RATES

Non-ferrous metal ores   see   METAL ORES

NON-FERROUS METALS

    see also   ALUMINIUM
                ANTIMONY
                ARSENIC
                BAUXITE
                BERYLLIUM
                BISMUTH
                CADMIUM
                CHROMIUM
                COBALT
                COLUMBIUM ORE
                COPPER
                GERMANIUM
                GOLD
                INDIUM
                LEAD
                LITHIUM MINERALS
                MAGNESIUM
                MANGANESE
                MERCURY
                MOLYBDENUM
                NICKEL
                PLATINUM
                PLATINUM-GROUP METALS
                PLATINUM, REFINED
                PYRITES
                RARE EARTH MINERALS
                SELENIUM
                SILVER
                TANTALUM & NIOBIUM
                TELLURIUM
                THORIUM
                TIN
                TITANIUM MINERALS

	Territorial coverage	Title codes	
NON-FERROUS METALS, continued			
see also TUNGSTEN			
URANIUM			
VANADIUM			
ZINC			
ZIRCONIUM			
% share of EEC area imports	Developing countries	U 52-a	
Export prices - index nos (weighted average)		U 29-q	U 54-q
Exports by value in $m	Main countries	U 23-a	
	Asian & Far East countries	U 32-a	
	Developing countries	U 52-a	
shipped to Communist area by value in $m	EEC countries	E 24-a	
to EEC & non-EEC areas by value in $m	Developing countries	U 52-a	
Imports by value in $m	EEC countries	E 24-a	
ex EEC & non-EEC areas by value in $m	Developing countries	U 52-a	
shipped to EEC area by value in $m	EEC countries	E 28-q	E 27-a
Production: semi-manufactured non-ferrous metal products: tonnage	OECD countries	D 19-m	D 20-m
Production - index nos			
NON-FERROUS METALS BY KIND			
Consumption: tonnage	World regions	C 12-a	
Export prices in local currency per ton fob	Main countries	T 4	
Export prices - index nos		G 1-a	
Exports by destination by CST classes: tonnage & value in $m	EEC countries	E 48-a	
SITC classes by value in $m	Main countries	D 2-q	
tonnage & value in $m	OECD countries	D 3-a2	
tonnage & value in $m	All countries	U 12-a	
NIMEXE classes by value in $m	All countries	E 20-a	
SITC classes: tonnage & value in $m	All countries	U 50-a	U 59-a
Government strategic stockpile: tonnage	USA	T 4-a	
Import duties in % ad val	EEC countries & USA	T 4	
Import prices in local currency per ton cif	Main countries	T 4	
Imports by NIMEXE classes: tonnage & value in $m	All countries	E 20-a	
SITC classes: tonnage & value in $m	All countries	U 50-a	U 59-a
source by CST classes: tonnage & value in $m	EEC countries	E 21-a	
SITC classes by value in $m	Main countries	D 2-q	
tonnage & value in $m	OECD countries	D 3-a2	
tonnage & value in $m	All countries	U 12-a	
Production & consumption: tonnage	All countries	H 2-a	
tonnage	All countries	N 5-a	
	World regions	C 12-a	
Production - index nos	S American countries	U 40-a	
Wholesale prices in local currency per ton	Main countries	N 5-q	T 4-a
NON-FERROUS METALS INDUSTRY			
Capital formation in $m	Main countries	U 21-a	
Consumption: coal & agglomerate: tonnage	EEC countries	E 14-a	
coke oven gas by volume in m³	EEC countries	E 14-a	
coke: tonnage	EEC countries	E 14-a	
diesel oil: tonnage	EEC countries	E 14-a	
electric power in kWh	European countries	U 1-a	
	All countries	C 23-a	
	OECD countries	D 8-a	
	EEC countries	E 14-a	
fuel oil: tonnage	EEC countries	E 14-a	
lignite: tonnage	EEC countries	E 14-a	
natural gas by volume in m³	EEC countries	E 14-a	
Costs for salaried staff per month	EEC countries	E 11-a	
Gas consumed in production in m³	European countries & USA	U 3-a	
Gross output by value in $m	Main countries	U 21-a	
Investment in buildings in local currency	EEC countries	E 40-a	
in land purchase in local currency	EEC countries	E 40-a	
in machinery in local currency	EEC countries	E 40-a	
Labour costs as % of total costs	EEC countries	E 8-a	
by status of employee in local currency	EEC countries	E 8-a	
in DMm	W Germany	H 3-a	
per hr in local currency	EEC countries	E 2-a	
per hr: all employees	EEC countries	E 11-a	
wage earners	EEC countries	E 11-a	
Labour force: no employed by status	EEC countries	E 8-a	
no employed	Main countries	U 21-a	
salaried staff	EEC countries	E 11-a	
wage earners	EEC countries	E 11-a	
No of hrs worked by labour force per wk	EEC countries	E 8-a	
	Main countries	R 3-m	
per wk by region	EEC countries	E 25-a	
salaried staff	EEC countries	E 11-a	
wage earners	EEC countries	E 11-a	
Turnover of non-ferrous metals industry in DMm	W Germany	H 3-a	
Wage rates per hr in local currency (average)	EEC countries	E 25-a2	
by sex in local currency	Main countries	R 3-m	
in DM	W Germany	H 3-a	
Wages & salary costs in $m	Main countries	U 21-a	

	Territorial coverage	Title codes
NON-METALLIC MINERAL INDUSTRY		
% contribution to gross national product	Main countries	U 38-a
% share of industrial production (value basis)	Main countries	U 38-a
Consumption coal: tonnage	EEC countries	E 14-a
coke oven gas by volume in m³	EEC countries	E 14-a
coke: tonnage	EEC countries	E 14-a
diesel oil: tonnage	EEC countries	E 14-a
electricity in kWh	EEC countries	E 14-a
fuel oil: tonnage	EEC countries	E 14-a
lignite: tonnage	EEC countries	E 14-a
natural gas by volume in m³	EEC countries	E 14-a
Earnings in local currency (average)	All countries	L 4-a
Employment level (total)	EEC countries	E 2-a
	OECD countries	D 23-a
Fixed capital investment in $m	EEC countries	E 38-a
Gas: consumption by volume in m³	European countries & USA	U 3-a
Investment in buildings in local currency	EEC countries	E 40-a
in land purchase in local currency	EEC countries	E 40-a
in machinery in local currency	EEC countries	E 40-a
Labour costs by status of employees	EEC countries	E 8-a
per hr	EEC countries	E 2-a
Labour force employed by status of employees	EEC countries	E 8-a
no of salaried staff employed	EEC countries	E 11-a
of wage earners employed	EEC countries	E 11-a
Labour force employed - index nos	All countries	L 4-a
No of hrs worked per wk by region	EEC countries	E 25-a
per wk	All countries	L 4-a
	OAS member countries	N 18-a
per yr	EEC countries	E 8-a
of establishments in operation	African countries	U 44-a
Production as % of world production (value basis)		U 38
Structure of labour costs as % total costs	EEC countries	E 8-a
Wage rates: brick furnace workers in local currency per hr	OAS member countries	N 17-a
cement workers in local currency per hr	OAS member countries	N 17-a
ceramists in local currency per hr	OAS member countries	N 17-a
glass-making workers in local currency per hr	OAS member countries	N 17-a
mosaic workers in local currency per hr	OAS member countries	N 17-a
moulders in local currency per hr	OAS member countries	N 17-a
non-metallic mineral industry in local currency per hr	EEC countries	E 25-a2
plastics workers in local currency per hr	OAS member countries	N 17-a
pottery workers in local currency per hr	OAS member countries	N 17-a
NON-METALLIC MINERAL PRODUCTS		
Consumption by value in $m	World regions	U 23-a
Exports as % of consumption (value basis)	World regions	U 23-a
shipped to EEC & non-EEC areas by value in $m	EEC countries	E 24-a
Imports as % of consumption (value basis)	World regions	U 23-a
shipped ex EEC & non-EEC areas by value in $m	EEC countries	E 24-a
Production by kind: tonnage	All countries	N 5-a
- index nos	S American countries	U 40-a
NON-METALLIC MINERALS BY KIND		
% share of world production (value basis)	All countries	N 4-a
Exports by regions of source by value in $m	EEC countries	E 38-a
tonnage	All countries	N 5-a
Imports: tonnage	Main countries	N 5-a
Production: tonnage	All countries	N 5-a
	OAS member countries	N 14-a
World production: tonnage		N 4-a

Non-scheduled airline operators   see   AIRLINE COMPANIES, NON-SCHEDULED

North sea oil   see   OIL EXPLORATION, NORTH SEA

Notch bars   see   INGOTS, ALUMINIUM

Notes in circulation   see   MONEY SUPPLY

NOVELS, PAPERBACK

Retail prices (comparative) in $	EEC countries	Z 3-a

NUCLEAR ENERGY

% production: electric power by reactor type	All countries	H 4-a	
% share of total energy supply sources	ECE countries	U 16-a	
Capacity: power stations in operation in MWe	All countries	H 4-a	
Consumption: primary energy source in kWh	European countries	U 10-a	
Generation: electricity by reactor types in K	Worldwide	H 4-a	
	All countries	H 4-a	
in kWh	All countries	H 4-a	
	EEC countries	E 16-m	E 15-a
	European countries, USA & USSR	U 4-a	

NUCLEAR EQUIPMENT MANUFACTURING COMPANIES

Orders completed in MW	EEC countries	B 30-a
in hand in MW	EEC countries	B 30-a

	Territorial coverage	Title codes
NUCLEAR FUEL INDUSTRY		
Labour costs as % of total costs	EEC countries	E 8-a
by status of employee in local currency	EEC countries	E 8-a
per hr: all employees	EEC countries	E 11-a
wage earners	EEC countries	E 11-a
salaried staff per month	EEC countries	E 11-a
Labour force employed (total)	EEC countries	E 8-a
no of salaried staff employed	EEC countries	E 11-a
of wage earners employed	EEC countries	E 11-a
No of hrs worked by labour force per yr	EEC countries	E 8-a
salaried staff per yr	EEC countries	E 11-a
wage earners per yr	EEC countries	E 11-a
NUCLEAR FUELS		
Consumption (domestic) in kg	Italy	H 4-a
Imports: enriched uranium & plutonium	EEC countries	E 15-a

Nuclear generators   see   GENERATORS, NUCLEAR

Nuclear power   see   POWER STATIONS, NUCLEAR

NUCLEAR REACTOR CONTROL DEVICES
    see also   CONTROL INSTRUMENTATION, NUCLEONIC

	Territorial coverage	Title codes
Deliveries by value in £m	UK	C 24-a
NUCLEAR REACTORS		
see also POWER STATIONS, NUCLEAR		
POWER GENERATING EQUIPMENT		
Capacity projected in MW	EEC area	E 7-a
Deliveries by size in MWe	European countries, Japan & USA	D 45-a
Exports as % of production	European countries, Japan & USA	D 45-a
by destination by value in $m	Main countries	U 9-a
by value in $m	All countries	U 38-a
Generating capacity: gas-cooled type in GW	Worldwide	D 48
heavy-water type in GW	Worldwide	D 48
high temperature type in GW	Worldwide	D 48
light-water type in GW	Worldwide	D 48
Magnox type in GW	Worldwide	D 48
Imports by value in $m	All countries	U 38-a
New orders (incl orders in hand) in MWe	European countries, Japan & USA	D 45-a
Production by size in MWe	European countries, Japan & USA	D 45-a
World export trade by value in $m		U 38-a
NUCLEAR REACTORS BY TYPE		
% of total electric power generation	All countries	H 4-a
Generating capacity in GW	Worldwide	D 48
Production: electric power in kWh	All countries	H 4-a
Uranium: consumption (first fuel charge)		D 48
running charges per ton		D 48

Nuclear research   see   RESEARCH & DEVELOPMENT, NUCLEAR

Number of times turned   see   INVENTORIES

Nursery schools   see   KINDERGARTENS

NURSES
    see also   HOSPITAL PERSONNEL

	Territorial coverage	Title codes
No employed by kind & ratio per 10,000 population	Latin American countries	J 5-a
of nursing personnel employed	Asian, Far East countries & Australasia	U 45-a
	AASM countries	E 41-a
NURSES, INDUSTRIAL		
No of hrs worked per wk	Main countries	L 1-a
Salaries per mth in local currency	All countries	L 1-a

Nutmegs & mace   see   SPICES & ESSENCES

NUTRIENT CONTENT

	Territorial coverage	Title codes
% content: basic slag	W European countries	U 30-a
mixed fertilisers	W European countries	U 30-a
nitrogenous & phosphate fertilisers	W European countries	U 30-a
potassic fertilisers & superphosphates	W European countries	U 30-a
urea	W European countries	U 30-a

Nutrient requirements   see   MINERAL NUTRIENTS
                                          PROTEIN
                                          VITAMINS

		Territorial coverage	Title codes

NUTRITION

see also PROTEIN

% needs: calorie consumption per capita	World regions	C 27-a
% of human calorie intake obtained from cereals by kind	World regions	C 27-a
Calorie consumption per capita per yr	World regions	C 27-a
intake per capita (as % known standards)	Main countries	M 4-a
per day from cereals	Main countries	A 19-a
from foodstuffs	OAS member countries	N 17-a
from rice	Main countries	A 19-a
of animal origin	OAS member countries	N 17-a
of vegetable origin	OAS member countries	N 17-a
per day	Developing countries	U 23-a
	ECE countries	U 15-a
Consumption per capita: animal fats in grammes per day	OAS member countries	N 17-a
other fats in grammes per day	OAS member countries	N 17-a
protein in grammes per day	OAS member countries	N 17-a
Feed characteristics: cereals by kind & % protein content		A 12-a
in calories per kg		A 12-a
Net supply by foodstuff: calories per capita per day	OAS member countries	N 17-a
fats per capita per day	OAS member countries	N 17-a
protein per capita per day	OAS member countries	N 17-a

NUTS BY KIND

see also   ALMONDS
             BABASSO KERNELS
             BRAZIL NUTS
             CASHEW KERNELS
             CHESTNUTS
             HAZELNUTS
             ILLIPE NUTS
             SHEA NUTS
             TUNG NUTS
             WALNUTS

Export prices in $ per ton	Main countries	A 9-a
Exports by value in local currency	Iran	U 32-m
edible nuts by value in $m	W European countries	U 33-a
(in shell): tonnage	Main countries	P 4-m
Import prices: almonds in $ per ton cif	W Germany	A 9-a
by grade in £ per ton c & f	UK	P 4-m
Imports: edible nuts by value in $m	W European countries	U 33-a
(in shell): tonnage	Main countries	P 4-m
Producer prices in $ per ton	All countries	A 9-a
Production, stocks & consumption: tree nuts	OECD countries	D 14-a
Production: almonds: tonnage	Turkey	D 37-a
crop: tonnage	Main countries	P 4-a
edible nuts (all kinds): tonnage	OECD countries	D 1-a
hazelnuts: tonnage	Turkey	D 37-a
pistachio nuts: tonnage	Turkey	D 37-a
processed, salted & roasted nuts: tonnage	OECD countries	D 37-a
walnuts: tonnage	Turkey	D 37-a
tonnage (all kinds)	All countries	A 9-a
Wholesale prices in local currency per ton	Spain, Turkey & USA	A 9-a
nuts, kernels & vegetable seeds in $ per ton	OAS member countries	N 17-a

Nuts screws bolts   see   HARDWARE

Nylon   see   NON-CELLULOSIC FIBRES

Nylon fabrics   see   WOVEN NON-CELLULOSIC FABRICS

OATS

% changes: producer prices (over previous yr)	EEC countries	E 34-m
	W European countries	U 30-a
Area harvested, production & yield per ha	All countries	A 9-a
under crop in acres	Main countries	B 8-a
in ha (incl harvest tonnage)	Main countries	R 5-a
historical tables from 1815	Main European countries	Z 1-a
in ha	All countries	C 16-a
	EEC countries	B 1-a E 12-a
		E 44-a
	OAS member countries	N 13-a
	OECD countries	D 1-a
Carry-over stocks (end-season): tonnage	Main countries	C 16-a
Consignments (as emergency food aid) by value in $m	Recipient countries	M 1-a
Consumption & consumption per capita per day	OECD countries	D 14-a
(domestic) as animal feed: tonnage	EEC countries	E 44-a
	Main countries	B 8-a
for human food: tonnage	UK	B 8-a
for seed: tonnage	UK	B 8-a
tonnage	EEC countries	E 44-a
	Main countries	B 8-a

	Territorial coverage	Title codes	
OATS, continued			
Consumption (incl barley) for human food: projected to 1978: tonnage	UK	P 5-a	
per capita in kg	EEC countries	B 1-a	E 44-a
tonnage	OAS member countries	N 17-a	
Crop yield in 100 kg per ha	EEC countries	E 12-a	
in cwt per acre	Main countries	B 8-a	
in kg per ha	EEC countries	B 1-a	
	Main countries	R 5-a	
	OAS member countries	N 13-a	
	OECD countries	D 1-a	
in quintals per ha	E European countries & USSR (incl Ukraine)	U 16-a	
Deliveries by farmers: tonnage	Main countries	B 7-a	
EEC levy per ton charged on imported oats shipped ex non-EEC area		B 7-m	
Ex-farm prices: domestic grain (for milling) in £ per ton	UK	B 7-m	
Export prices by grade (as fodder) in local currency per ton fob	Canada & USA	R 2-m	
by quality in £ per ton fob	Main countries	B 8-a	
in $ per ton fob: feed oats	Canada (E Coast ports)	C 16-m	
in $ per ton	Argentina, Australia, Canada, Netherlands & Sweden	A 9-a	
	Canada	U 35-a	
Export subsidies in £ per ton	EEC countries	B 8-a	
Exports by destination: tonnage	China, E European countries & USSR	A 17-a	
	Main countries	B 8-a	
(incl world total): tonnage	Main countries	C 16-a	
tonnage	All countries	A 17-a	
	European countries	U 35-a	
Government expenditure: price guarantees in £m	UK	P 5-a	
Import prices ex Argentine in $ per ton	European countries	U 35-a	
ex Australia & Canada (for feed) in £ per ton	UK	B 8-a	
Imports by port of entry: tonnage	UK	B 7-m	P 5-a2
by source: tonnage	EEC area	B 8-a	
	Main countries	B 8-a	
(for production of animal feeding stuffs): tonnage	UK	P 5-a	
shipped into E European countries & USSR: tonnage	Non-Communist countries	A 17-a	
tonnage	All countries	A 17-a	
	European countries	U 35-a	
	W European countries	B 8-a	
Intervention prices (fixed by Commission) for EEC area in local currency		E 44-a	
Prices received by farmers as animal feed (prime quality) in $ per ton	W European countries	U 30-a	
Producer prices in £ per cwt	EEC countries	B 1-a	
in local currency per kg	EEC countries	E 34-m	E 44-a
per 100 kg	European countries	E 35-a	
per ton	OECD countries	D 1-a	
in $ per bushel	USA	E 35-a	
Production, stocks & usage (for fodder & seed): tonnage	OECD countries	D 14-a	
Production by administrative areas: tonnage	EEC countries	E 38-a	
historical tables: tonnage	Main European countries	Z 1-a	
tonnage & value of output in £m	EEC countries	B 1-a	
tonnage	African countries	U 44-a	
	All countries	U 43-a	
	Canada, European countries, Japan, USA & USSR	E 44-a	
	European countries	U 35-a	
	E European countries & USSR (incl Ukraine)	U 16-a	
	EEC countries	E 12-m	E 44-a
	Main countries	B 7-a	B 8-a
		E 3-a	P 5-a
	OAS member countries	N 13-a	
	OECD countries	D 1-a	
	S American countries	U 40-a	
Proportion of harvest exported	Argentine, Australia & USA	B 8-a	
Retail prices: oats by kind in local currency per ton	OAS member countries	N 17-a	
Sales ex farm: tonnage	England & Scotland	B 7-m	
	EEC countries	E 12-m	
Self-sufficiency ratios	EEC countries	B 1-a	
Stocks (end-season): tonnage	Argentine, Canada & USA	B 8-a	
	Main countries	B 7-a	B 8-a
held at wholesalers' premises: tonnage	EEC countries	E 12-m	
held on farms (end-mth): tonnage	EEC countries	E 12-m	
	Main countries	B 7-a	
Supply & disposal by purpose: tonnage	Main countries	B 8-a	
(output plus net imports): tonnage	EEC countries, USA & USSR	B 8-a	
Supply, production, consumption & trade: tonnage	EEC countries	B 1-a	
Threshold prices in £ per cwt	EEC countries	B 1-a	
Wholesale prices: % change (over previous yr)	EEC countries	E 34-m	
by grade in local currency per ton	OAS member countries	N 17-a	
in local currency per kg	EEC countries	E 34-m	
	Main countries	A 9-a	
World production: tonnage		C 16-a	

Obeche   see   HARDWOOD LOGS
                      HARDWOOD, SAWN

Occupational diseases   see   DISEASES, INDUSTRIAL

	Territorial coverage	Title codes
OCEAN FREIGHT RATES		
% increases by name of conference	Worldwide	U 37-a
Bulk cargo - index nos	W Germany	S 16-m
By type & charter - index nos (see No 3, 6, 9 & 12)		U 27-q
Cereals shipped Gulf ports in £ per ton	UK	U 33-m
main routes (single voyage)		S 16-a
Coal: main routes (single voyage)		S 16-a
trade ex USA: single voyage in $ per ton		N 2-a
Comparison by product (main routes) in £ or $ per ton		S 16-a
Dry cargo (time charter basis) - index nos		D 28-m U 37-m
		A 9-a
(voyage charter basis) - index nos		U 37-m D 28-q
		D 28-a
General cargo: freight rate index as % of worldscale		C 3-m
General cargo freight - index nos	Worldwide	S 16-a
	W Germany	S 16-m
Grain & sugar shipped to European area ex selected ports in £ per ton		A 9-a
Index nos (weighted freight basis)		D 28-a
Iron ore shipped by source to Japan in $ per ton		U 56-a
to UK in $ per ton		U 56-a
to W Germany in $ per ton		U 56-a
Liner rates - index nos	Worldwide	U 37-m
Metallic ores: main routes (single voyage)		S 16-a
Minerals: trip & time charter - index nos		N 5-q
Oil tankers by size: worldscale basis (average)		H 4-m
Oil tankers - index nos	W Germany	S 16-m
Rate (spot) by route as % of worldscale		C 3-w
Ratio to value of selected commodity prices (cif basis)		U 37-a
Sugar: main routes (single voyage)		S 16-a
Super-tankers (up to 160,000 tons) - index nos		S 16-m
Tanker freight rate: assessment as % worldscale		C 3-m
assessments (AFRA) intascale		S 17-a
worldscale		S 17-q
Tanker freight rate - index nos	Worldwide	S 16-m
	Main countries	R 5-a
Tankers: all-purpose rates - index nos		S 16-m
by size & routes (worldscale)		S 17-m
"clean trade" by routes (worldscale)		S 17-m
"dirty trade" by routes (worldscale)		S 17-m
medium-sized tanker rates		S 16-m
single voyage "dirty load" - index nos		S 16-m
Tankers - index nos (worldscale)		U 37-m S 15-a
index nos	W Germany	S 16-m
voyage charter basis - index nos		D 28-q D 28-a
voyage charter rates (worldscale) major routes		D 28-a
Time charter: 1-2 mths - index nos		S 16-w
2-3 mths - index nos		S 16-w
6-12 mths duration in £ per ton		S 16-a
in excess of 1 yr duration in £ per ton		S 16-a
less than 1 mth - index nos		S 16-w
over 6 mths - index nos		S 16-w
short-term employment rates in £ per ton		S 16-a
Time charter - index nos	Worldwide	S 16-m
Tramp shipping - index nos	All countries	F 5-m F 6-q
	Main countries	R 5-a
	W Germany	S 16-m
	World regions	S 16-m
Trip charter - index nos	Worldwide	S 16-m
Wheat by route in £ per ton	Main importing countries	C 16-m
ex main suppliers shipped to European ports in £ per ton		C 16-m
shipped to Antwerp & Rotterdam in $ per ton	Canada & USA	B 7-m
European ports by source in $ per ton		C 16-m
ex Argentina, Australia & USA in $ per ton		U 35-a
UK ex Argentina, Canada & USA in £ per ton		B 7-m
Worldwide index (compiled by "Norwegian Shipping News")		S 16-m
Ocean freight rates see SEABORNE FREIGHT		
Ocean liners see PASSENGER VESSELS		
WORLD FLEETS		
OCEAN PASSENGER TRAFFIC		
Accommodation available on cargo ships by flag		S 16-a
Arrivals & departures at main ports	EEC countries	E 38-a E 43-a
by flags	EEC countries	E 43-a
No of passengers carried by sea by Atlantic routes		S 21-a
in passage through each port	Mozambique	S 16-a
Oceanographic research see RESEARCH & DEVELOPMENT		
OCTYL-ALCOHOL		
Production: tonnage	European countries	U 26-a

	Territorial coverage	Title codes	
OFFAL, EDIBLE			
see also MILLING OFFALS			
Consumption as % of total meat consumed (wt basis)	EEC countries	E 1-a	
per capita in lbs per yr	UK	B 12-a	
	Main countries	B 11-a	
Exports by destination: tonnage	Main countries	B 12-m	B 11-a
fresh, frozen & chilled offal: tonnage	Main countries	B 11-a	
Imports by kind by source: tonnage	UK	B 11-a	
tonnage	Main countries	B 11-a	
Imports - index nos (wt basis)	European area	U 36-a	
Production (estim): tonnage	Main countries	B 11-a	
(for export): tonnage	Main countries	B 12-a	
tonnage & consumption per capita in kg	OECD countries	D 14-a	
tonnage	All countries	A 9-a	
	OECD countries	D 1-a	
Retail prices in local currency per ton	OAS member countries	N 17-a	
Stocks: imported frozen offal: tonnage	UK	B 12-w	
Supply available for consumption: tonnage	Main countries	B 11-a	
offal of animal origin by kind: tonnage	EEC countries	E 1-a	
Office building see BUILDING CONSTRUCTION, NON-RESIDENTIAL			
OFFICE MACHINERY			
see also ACCOUNTING MACHINES			
CALCULATORS, DESK-TYPE			
ELECTRONIC CALCULATORS, DESK-TYPE			
TYPEWRITERS			
TYPEWRITERS, PORTABLE			
% share of world exports held (value basis)	UK	B 27-a	
	All countries	U 38-a	
shipped to developed countries	Developing countries	U 38-a	
Consumption: tonnage	Central African countries	U 38	
Exports by destination: value in $m	Main countries	U 9-a	
kind by destination: tonnage & value in $m	All countries	U 12-a	
value in $m	Main countries	U 38-a	
calculators & computers: volume	OECD countries	D 9-a	
Imports by kind by source: tonnage & value in $m	All countries	U 12-a	
value in $m	All countries	U 38-a	
Production by kind: volume	All countries	U 38-a	
volume	EEC countries	E 28-q	E 27-a
OFFICE MACHINERY INDUSTRY			
Capital formation in $m	Main countries	U 21-a	
Consumption: aluminium in production of office machinery: tonnage	EEC countries, Japan & USA	C 12-a	
Gross value of output in $m	Main countries	U 21-a	
Investment in buildings in local currency	EEC countries	E 40-a	
land purchase in local currency	EEC countries	E 40-a	
machinery in local currency	EEC countries	E 40-a	
Labour costs as % of total costs in the industry	EEC countries	E 8-a	
by status of employees	EEC countries	E 8-a	
wages & salaries in $m	Main countries	U 21-a	
Labour force employed: wage earners & salaried staff	EEC countries	E 8-a	
No of hrs worked by labour force per yr	EEC countries	E 8-a	
per wk	Main countries	R 3-m	
of operatives employed	Main countries	U 21-a	
Wage rates by sex in local currency per hr	Main countries	R 3-m	

Official buying rates   see   EXCHANGE RATES

Official capital flows   see   INVESTMENT, PUBLIC OVERSEAS

Official certificate buying & selling rates   see   EXCHANGE RATES

Official development assistance (ODA)   see   DEVELOPMENT AID

Official organisations   see   PUBLIC CORPORATIONS

Official selling rates   see   EXCHANGE RATES

Oil by kind   see   CRUDE PETROLEUM
                        DIESEL OIL
                        FATS & OILS
                        FISH OILS & FATS
                        FUEL OIL
                        LUBRICATING OIL
                        PETROLEUM
                        TUNG OIL
                        VEGETABLE OILS

	Territorial coverage	Title codes
OIL COMPANIES		
see also PETROLEUM INDUSTRY		
% equity held: oil-producing companies	OPEC member countries	C 3-a
% of world production: crude oil by specific oil companies		H 4-a
petroleum products by specific oil companies		H 4-a
Costs, deductions & taxation: specific oil companies in $m		C 3-a
Depreciation charges: specific oil companies in $m		C 3-a

	Territorial coverage	Title codes

OIL COMPANIES, continued
   Expenditure: major oil companies: exploration costs in $m   C 3-a
                                           marketing costs in $m   C 3-a
                                           transportation costs in $m   C 3-a
   Gross receipts: specific oil companies in $m   C 3-a
   Interest charges paid: specific oil companies in $m   C 3-a
   Net assets per share: specific oil companies in $ C 3-a
   Net income (after tax): specific oil companies in $m   C 3-a
                                  as % of gross revenue   C 3-a
                                  per share in $ C 3-a
   No of ordinary shares issued by specific oil companies   C 3-a
   Operating costs: specific oil companies as % of gross revenue   C 3-a
                                  in $m   C 3-a
   Ordinary share dividends: specific oil companies in $ per share   C 3-a
   Production: crude petroleum by specific oil companies by value in $m   C 3-a
                                  tonnage   H 4-a
              petroleum products by specific oil companies: tonnage   H 4-a
              refined chemicals by specific oil companies by value in $m   C 3-a
   Refining capacity available in barrels per day   OPEC member countries   C 3-a
   Sales: refined petroleum products by specific oil companies: tonnage   H 4-a
   Taxation paid: specific oil companies as % of gross revenue   C 3-a

Oil derivatives   see   BITUMEN
                               CHEMICALS
                               NAPHTHA
                               PARAFFIN WAX

Oil distillates   see   PETROLEUM PRODUCTS

OIL EXPLORATION
   Expenditure by each major oil company in $m   Worldwide   C 3-a
   No of drilling rigs in position by sea areas (end-yr)   Worldwide   S 16-a
           of offshore drilling units being produced by firm   Worldwide   S 16-a
           of wells drilled by sea area (end-yr)   Worldwide   S 16-a

OIL EXPLORATION, NORTH SEA
   No of wells drilled   Denmark, Norway & UK   S 16-a
           of wells drilled: Celtic Sea areas   Eire & UK   S 16-a
                          Irish Sea area   Eire   S 16-a
                          West Shetlands sea area   S 16-a

OIL PALMS
   Area under oil palm trees in acres   Indonesia & Malaysia   B 19-a

Oil pipelines   see   CRUDE OIL PIPELINES
                             REFINED OIL PIPELINES

Oil refineries   see   PETROLEUM REFINERIES

Oil royalties   see   ROYALTIES, OIL

OIL SHALE
   Production: tonnage   All countries   N 5-a
                        Austria, France, W Germany & Sweden   B 15-a

Oil tanker freight rates   see   OCEAN FREIGHT RATES

Oil tankers   see   TANKERS, OIL

Oil transportation   see   CRUDE OIL PIPELINES
                                       REFINED OIL PIPELINES
                                       TANKERS, OIL

OIL WELLS
   Average depth in ft   OPEC member countries   C 3-a
   No of wells being drilled   OPEC member countries   C 3-a
           of drillings completed proving dry   OPEC member countries   C 3-a
                             yielding crude oil   OPEC member countries   C 3-a
                             natural gas   OPEC member countries   C 3-a
           of exploratory wells completed   Latin American countries   U 18-a
           of producing wells flowing (incl artificial lift)   OPEC member countries   C 3-a

OILCAKE & MEAL
        see also   COPRA CAKE
                     COTTONSEED MEAL
                     FEEDING STUFFS
                     GROUNDNUT CAKE
                     LINSEED CAKE
                     PALM KERNEL CAKE
                     RAPESEED CAKE
                     SOYBEAN MEAL
   % contribution to export earnings   Sudan, Senegal, Gambia & Dahomey   E 45-a
   % price changes (as animal feed)   W European countries   U 30-a
   Consumption: glutenfeed in production of animal feed: tonnage   EEC countries   P 5-a
   Export prices - index nos (weighted average)   U 29-q

	Territorial coverage	Title codes	
OILCAKE & MEAL, continued			
Exports by value in $m	India & Indonesia	U 32-m	
tonnage & value in $m	W European countries	U 33-a	
(total) & shipped to EEC area: tonnage & value in UA	African, Caribbean countries & Pacific Is	E 45-a	
Import prices by kind in £ per ton cif	AASM countries	E 41-a	
Imports (all kinds) by source: tonnage	European & UK ports	P 1-m	
maize meal & flour: tonnage	UK	P 5-a	
sunflower seed cake (as animal feed): tonnage	UK	P 5-a	
tonnage & value in $m	UK	P 5-a	
Prices as ratio of prices received by farmers for milk	W European countries	U 33-a	
paid by farmers (as animal feed) in $ per ton	W European countries	U 30-a	
coconut cake in $ per ton	USA	U 30-a	
cottonseed cake in $ per ton	W European countries	U 30-a	
flax cake in $ per ton	W European countries	U 30-a	
groundnut cake in $ per ton	Italy	U 30-a	
linseed cake in $ per ton	W European countries	U 30-a	
maize cake in $ per ton	W European countries	U 30-a	
soybean cake in $ per ton	Italy	U 30-a	
sunflower seed cake in $ per ton	W European countries	U 30-a	
by state farms (as animal feed) in $ per ton	Turkey	U 30-a	
Production: copra cake: tonnage	E European countries	U 30-a	
flax cake: tonnage	France	N 10-a	
rapeseed cake: tonnage	France	N 10-a	
soybean meal: tonnage	France	N 10-a	
sunflower seed cake: tonnage	France	N 10-a	
tonnage	W Germany	N 10-a	
Supply, production, consumption & trade: tonnage	AASM countries	E 41-a	
Wholesale price (spot Colombo): Poonac in Rs per ton	EEC countries	E 28-q	E 27-a
World exports by value in $m	EEC countries	B 1-a	
World market prices oilcakes (all kinds) - index nos	Sri Lanka	A 4-m	
(fish-based) - index nos	World regions	A 5-a	
(vegetable-based) - index nos		A 5-a	
World production: oilcake (from copra): tonnage		A 5-a	
(from cottonseed): tonnage		A 5-a	
(from fish meal): tonnage		A 5-a	
(from groundnuts): tonnage		A 5-a	
(from linseed): tonnage		A 5-a	
(from palm kernels): tonnage		A 5-a	
(from rapeseed): tonnage		A 5-a	
(from sesame seed): tonnage		A 5-a	
(from soybeans): tonnage		A 5-a	
(from sunflower seed): tonnage		A 5-a	
vegetable-based oilcakes: tonnage		A 5-a	
OILS & FATS			
see also ANIMAL FATS & OILS			
ESSENTIAL OILS			
FATS & OILS			
FATTY OILS			
FISH OILS & FATS			
VEGETABLE OILS			
WHALE OIL			
Consumption in production of animal feed: tonnage	EEC countries	P 5-a	
OILS FOR PERFUMES			
see also ESSENTIAL OILS			
Exports (total) & shipped to EEC area by value in UA	Madagascar	E 41-a	
tonnage	Madagascar	E 41-a	
World market prices: perfumery oils ex Madagascar in Fr per kg		E 41-a	

Oils, hard   see   COPRA OIL
PALM KERNEL OIL
PALM OIL

Oils, soft   see   COTTONSEED OIL
GROUNDNUT OIL
OLIVE OIL
RAPESEED OIL
SAFFLOWER OIL
SESAME SEED OIL
SOYBEAN OIL
SUNFLOWER SEED OIL

Oils, technical   see   CASTOR OIL
LINSEED OIL
OITICICA OIL
TUNG OIL

Oilseed cake   see   OILCAKE & MEAL

Oilseed expellers   see   OILCAKE & MEAL

	Territorial coverage	Title codes

OILSEEDS

see also CASTOR SEED
COPRA
COTTONSEED
GROUNDNUTS
LINSEED
PALM KERNELS
PALM OIL
RAPESEED
SESAME SEED
SOYBEANS
SUNFLOWER SEED

	Territorial coverage	Title codes	
Area under crop (for vegetable oil production) in ha	EEC countries	E 44-a	
in ha	EEC countries	B 1-a	
Crop yield in quintals per ha	E European countries & USSR	U 16-a	
Crushings: copra: tonnage	Netherlands & W Germany	N 10-a	
flax seed: tonnage	Canada & Netherlands	N 10-a	
for vegetable oil production: tonnage	UK	B 19-a	
palm kernels: tonnage	Netherlands & W Germany	N 10-a	
rapeseed: tonnage	Canada, Netherlands & W Germany	N 10-a	
soybeans: tonnage	Canada, Netherlands & W Germany	N 10-a	
sunflower seed: tonnage	Netherlands & W Germany	N 10-a	
Distribution for feeding stuffs: tonnage	Czechoslovakia, Hungary & Poland	U 34-a	
for market sales: tonnage	Czechoslovakia, Hungary & Poland	U 34-a	
for own farm use: tonnage	Czechoslovakia, Hungary & Poland	U 34-a	
Export prices - index nos (weighted average main sources)	Worldwide	U 54-q	
Exports by value in $m	W European countries	U 33-a	
(incl oil nuts & kernels): tonnage	Asian & Far East countries	U 32-q	
shipped to EEC & non-EEC areas by value in $m	EEC countries	E 24-a	
tonnage & value in $m	African & Caribbean countries & Pacific Is	E 45-a	
Import duties: rates levied in local currency	Canada, EEC area, Japan, main European countries & USA	B 19-a	
Imports by kind & by source: tonnage	Main countries	B 18-a	
by value in $m	W European countries	U 33-a	
tonnage & value in $m	W European countries	U 33-a	
ex EEC & non-EEC areas by value in $m	EEC countries	E 24-a	
(incl oil nuts & kernels) by value in $m	Japan	U 32-m	
in oil equiv tonnage	Main countries	B 19-a	
Prices as % of world market prices	EEC countries	E 44-a	
Production & exports (incl oil nuts): tonnage	All countries	A 23-a	
by administrative areas: tonnage	EEC countries	E 38-a	
main oilseed crop (estim): tonnage	China	B 18-a	
tonnage	E European countries & USSR	U 16-a	
	EEC countries	B 1-a	E 44-a
	OECD countries	D 1-a	
Supply, production, consumption & trade: tonnage	EEC countries	B 1-a	
Wholesale prices in $ per ton	European countries	U 27-m	
World market prices (incl fats & oils) - index nos		G 1-a	U 30-a
vegetable oils & fats - index nos		U 23-a	
World market prices - index nos		A 4-m	

OILSEEDS BY KIND

	Territorial coverage	Title codes	
% contribution to export earnings	African & Caribbean countries & Pacific Is	E 45-a	
Area under crop in acres	USA	B 18-a	
in ha	EEC countries	E 12-a	
vegetable oilseeds in acres	Main countries	B 18-a	
Consumption (for oil extraction): tonnage	Main countries	B 18-a	
Crop (incl estim world total): tonnage	All countries	P 1-a	
Crop yield in 100 kg per ha	EEC countries	E 12-a	
Exports by destination by CST classes: tonnage & value in $m	EEC countries	E 48-a	
SITC classes by value in $m	Main countries	D 2-q	
tonnage & value in $m	OECD countries	D 3-a2	
tonnage	Commonwealth countries	B 19-a	
	French Zone of W Africa	B 18-a	
by NIMEXE classes: tonnage & value in $m	All countries	E 20-a	
SITC classes: tonnage & value in $m	All countries	U 50-a	U 59-a
(in detail): tonnage	World regions	A 11-a	
tonnage	Main countries	B 18-m	
Harvest: estimates for ensuing crop yr	Main world regions	P 1-a	
Import prices in £ per ton cif	W European countries	B 18-m	
Imports by NIMEXE classes: tonnage & value in $m	All countries	E 20-a	
SITC classes: tonnage & value in $m	All countries	U 50-a	U 59-a
by source by CST classes: tonnage & value in $m	EEC countries	E 21-a	
SITC classes by value in $m	Main countries	D 2-q	
tonnage & value in $m	OECD countries	D 3-a2	
tonnage	Canada, European countries, USA & USSR	A 11-a	
Production: tonnage (in detail)	World regions	A 11-a	
tonnage	EEC countries	E 12-a	
	Main countries	B 18-a	
Wholesale prices in £ per ton	UK	P 1-a	
(for margerine production) in £ per ton	UK	B 12-m	
in local currency per ton	OAS member countries	N 17-a	
World exports: unit value in $ per ton		A 11-a	

OITICICA OIL

	Territorial coverage	Title codes
Exports: tonnage	Brazil	B 19-a
Imports: tonnage	Main countries	B 19-a
World production: tonnage		N 10-a

396

age pensioners   see   POPULATION, ECONOMICALLY-INACTIVE

Territorial coverage | Title codes

OLD AGE PENSIONS

	Territorial coverage	Title codes
Cost to National Exchequer in local currency	All countries	L 2-a
Incl death benefits as % of gross national product	EEC countries	E 6-a
No of retirement pensions paid out	OECD countries	D 11-a
Payments made as % of total expenditure on Social Welfare	OAS member countries	N 18-a
from Social Security funds in local currency	EEC countries	E 6-a
Per capita: aged 60 yrs & over in FrB	EEC countries	E 3-a
for population over 60 yrs of age - index nos	EEC countries	E 6-a
	EEC countries	E 6-a

Oleum   see   SULPHURIC ACID

OLIVE OIL

	Territorial coverage	Title codes	
% change: wholesale prices (over previous yr)	W Germany	E 34-m	
Consumption: tonnage	Main countries	U 11-a	
Export prices: edible oil in £ per ton fob	Spain	B 19-a	
Export prices - index nos (weighted average main sources)		U 29-q	
Exports by destination: tonnage	Spain, Tunisia & Turkey	B 19-a	
tonnage	All countries	U 11-a	
Import prices: olive oil (ex Spain) in barrels in £ per ton cif	Main countries	B 19-a	
in $ per ton cif	UK	R 2-m	
in $ per ton cif	USA	R 2-m	
Imports: tonnage	European countries & USA	A 9-a	
Intervention prices (fixed by Commission) in local currency	Main countries	B 19-a	
in UA per ton	EEC area	E 44-a	
Prices as % of world market prices	EEC area	B 19-a	
Producer prices in local currency per 100 litres	EEC area	E 44-a	
Production & consumption per capita in kg	Portugal & Spain	D 1-a	
by administrative areas: tonnage	Greece & Yugoslavia	D 14-a	
(crude & refined): tonnage	EEC countries	E 38-a	
for ensuing yr (estim): tonnage	All countries	U 22-a	
(incl world total): tonnage	World regions	P 1-a	
	All countries	B 18-a	U 11-a
tonnage	African countries	U 44-a	
	All countries	N 10-a	P 1-a
Retail prices in local currency per ton	Main producing countries	B 19-a	
Stocks held: tonnage	OECD countries	D 1-a	
Target prices in UA per ton	OAS member countries	N 17-a	
paid to producers in £ per ton	Producing countries	U 11-a	
in UA per ton	EEC countries	B 19-a	
Threshold prices in UA per ton	EEC countries	B 1-a	
Value of production in local currency	EEC countries	B 19-a	
Wholesale prices in DM per 100 litres	EEC countries	B 19-a	
(in drums) in cents per lb on New York market	EEC countries	E 44-a	
(extra fine grade) in lire per kg	W Germany	E 34-m	
World & Commonwealth production: tonnage	USA	B 19-a	
World market price - index nos	Italy	R 2-m	
World production (estim): tonnage		B 19-a	
forecast by 1975: tonnage		A 4-m	
tonnage	All countries	P 1-a	
		A 1	
		A 4-a	A 5-a
		N 10-a	

OLIVE TREES

	Territorial coverage	Title codes	
Area under olive trees in ha: historical tables	Main European countries	Z 1-a	
in ha	EEC countries	B 1-a	E 3-a
		E 44-a	

OLIVES

	Territorial coverage	Title codes
Export prices: table olives in local currency	Greece	A 9-a
Production & consumption: table olives: tonnage	Greece & Spain	D 14-a
tonnage harvested: historical tables	Main European countries	Z 1-a

ONIONS

	Territorial coverage	Title codes
Area harvested in ha, production tonnage & yield (incl shallots) per ha	All countries	A 9-a
Imports: tonnage	USSR	U 20-a
Producer prices in local currency per ton	All countries	A 9-a
Production: dried onions: tonnage	African countries	U 44-a
tonnage	Latin American countries	U 40-a
	Main E European countries	U 20-a
Wholesale prices in local currency per ton	Egypt & UK	A 9-a

Oolong   see   TEA

Open-hearth plants   see   STEELWORKS

Open-hearth steel   see   CRUDE STEEL

OPERATING COSTS, AIRLINE

	Title codes
Aircraft of IATA membership	S 21-a
Costs (by item) in cents per ton-km flown	S 6-a
Depreciation: equipment in $m by airline company	S 11-a
in $m	S 21-a
Flight operations in $m by airline company	S 11-a

	Territorial coverage	Title codes

OPERATING COSTS, AIRLINE   continued
    Flight operations in $m — S 21-a
    Ground & station maintenance in $m — S 21-a
    Maintenance & aircraft overhaul in $m — S 21-a
        by airline company in $m — S 11-a
    Operating costs (total) by airline company in $m — S 11-a
    Passenger services in $m — S 21-a
    Sales promotion in $m — S 21-a
    Ticketing costs in $m — S 21-a

Operating expenses, agricultural   see   FARM COSTS

Operating profit ratios   see   FINANCIAL RATIOS, CORPORATE

Ophthalmic instruments   see   OPTICAL INSTRUMENTS

OPIUM

	Territorial coverage	Title codes
Area under poppy crop in ha	Main countries	U 46-a
Consumption (for manufacture of morphine) in kg	Main countries	U 46-a
(for non-medical purposes) in kg	Main countries	U 46-a
Exports by destination in kg	Main countries	U 46-a
shipped to morphine-producing countries in kg	All countries	U 46-a
Harvest & yield per ha in kg	Main countries	U 46-a
Illicit traffic seizures in kg	All countries	U 46-a
Maximum stocks permitted by International Narcotic Control Board in kg	All countries	U 46-a
Production in kg	All countries	U 46-a
World requirements in kg (estim)		U 19-a

OPIUM ALKALOIDS

	Territorial coverage	Title codes
Exports by destination: cocaine, caffeine & quinine by value in $m	Main countries	U 2-a
Production: codeine in kg	All countries	U 46-a
dihydrocodeine in kg	All countries	U 46-a
dionine in kg	All countries	U 46-a
oxycodone in kg	All countries	U 46-a
pholcodine in kg	All countries	U 46-a
thebaine in kg	All countries	U 46-a

OPTICAL INSTRUMENTS

	Territorial coverage	Title codes
Deliveries by kind by value in £	UK	C 24-a
microscopes by value in £	UK	C 24-a
opthalmic instruments by value in £	UK	C 24-a
surveying instruments by value in £	UK	C 24-a
telescopes & binoculars by value in £	UK	C 24-a
Demand (domestic) by value in £	UK	C 24-a

OPTICAL INSTRUMENTS INDUSTRY

	Territorial coverage	Title codes
Investment in buildings in local currency	EEC countries	E 40-a
in land purchase in local currency	EEC countries	E 40-a
in machinery in local currency	EEC countries	E 40-a
No of hrs worked per wk	Main countries	R 3-m
Wage rates by sex per hr	Main countries	R 3-m

Orange juice   see   FRUIT JUICES, CITRUS

Oranges & tangerines   see   CITRUS FRUITS

ORCHARDS
    see also   FRUIT TREES
              LAND UTILISATION

	Territorial coverage	Title codes
Area under fruit in ha	EEC countries	B 1-a

Orders   see   NEW ORDERS

Ordinary shares   see   SHARES, COMMON

Ordnance & small arms   see   MILITARY EQUIPMENT

ORDNANCE FACTORIES

	Territorial coverage	Title codes
No of numerically-controlled type machine tools in use	USA	J 2-a

Ore carriers (shipping)   see   BULK CARRIERS

ORE MINING INDUSTRY
    see also   IRON ORE MINING
              MINING & QUARRYING

	Territorial coverage	Title codes
Costs: salaried staff per mth	EEC countries	E 11-a
Gross output by value in $m	Main countries	U 21-a
Investment in buildings in local currency	EEC countries	E 40-a
land purchase in local currency	EEC countries	E 40-a
machinery in local currency	EEC countries	E 40-a
Labour costs by status of employees in local currency	EEC countries	E 8-a
per hr all employees	EEC countries	E 11-a
wage earners	EEC countries	E 11-a

	Territorial coverage	Title codes

ORE MINING INDUSTRY, continued

	Territorial coverage	Title codes
Labour force: no of salaried staff employed	EEC countries	E 11-a
of wage earners employed	EEC countries	E 11-a
of wage earners & salaried staff employed	EEC countries	E 8-a
No of hrs worked by region per wk	EEC countries	E 25-a
per yr: salaried staff	EEC countries	E 11-a
wage earners	EEC countries	E 11-a
per yr	EEC countries	E 8-a
Structure of labour costs as % of total costs	EEC countries	E 8-a
Wage rates in local currency per hr	EEC countries	E 25-a2
	Main countries	R 3-m

Ores   see   METAL ORES

Organic chemicals   see   CHEMICALS, ORGANIC

ORGANS

Production: keyboard wind instruments by volume	All countries	U 22-a

Orlon   see   MAN-MADE FIBRES
                NON-CELLULOSIC FIBRES

Osmiridium   see   PLATINUM-GROUP METALS

Osmium   see   PLATINUM, REFINED

OUTERWEAR, TAILORED

% import penetration: male & female garments (value basis)	UK	B 22-a
Sales by manufacturers for male & female use by value in £m	UK	B 22-a

OUTERWEAR, WEATHERPROOF

% import penetration to sales (value basis)	UK	B 22-a
Net output by value in £m	UK	B 22-a
per capita in £	UK	B 22-a
Sales by manufacturers in £m	UK	B 22-a

OUTPUT PER CAPITA

% growth rate: agriculture to 1980 (estim)	Main countries	D 17-a
industry to 1980 (estim)	Main countries	D 17-a
services to 1980 (estim)	Main countries	D 17-a

OVENS, DOMESTIC

Production by volume (all types)	All countries	U 22-a
electric cookers	OAS member countries	N 14-a
stoves, ranges & cookers	All countries	U 38-a

Overalls   see   CLOTHING

OVERCOATS & RAINCOATS

Production by volume	All countries	U 22-a
	EEC countries	K 4-a

Overcrowding   see   DWELLINGS

Overdraft rates   see   COMMERCIAL BANKS
                          INTEREST RATES

Overseas aid   see   DEVELOPMENT AID

Overseas banks   see   FOREIGN BANKS

Overseas debts   see   BALANCE OF PAYMENTS
                         FOREIGN DEBT

Overseas earnings   see   REMITTANCES

OVERSEAS INVESTMENT INCOME

As component of balance of payments in local currency	African countries	U 44-a	
in $m	All countries	F 1-a	
	Latin American countries	U 18-a	
	OAS member countries	N 16-a	
	S American countries	U 41-a	
gross domestic product	All developing countries	D 25-a	
national product	OAS member countries	N 16-a	
In local currency	All countries	M 6-a	U 60-a
(Net) in $m	EEC countries	E 4-a	E 32-a
% contribution to invisible income	Main countries	M 9-a	
Contribution to gross domestic product in $m	S American countries	U 41-a	
Credits on government transactions in $m	EEC countries	E 26-q	

Overseas investment transfers   see   TRANSFER PAYMENTS

Overseas property income   see   PROPERTY INCOME, OVERSEAS

Overseas trade in transit   see   RE-EXPORT TRADE
                                    TRANSIT TRADE

	Territorial coverage	Title codes

Overtime   see   HOURS OF WORK

Ox hides   see   HIDES

Oxen   see   CATTLE

Oxycodone   see   OPIUM ALKALOIDS

OXYGEN
    Consumption: tonnage — USA — N 1-a
    Wholesale prices (as liquid in cylinders) in $ per ton — USA — N 1-a
        (as pipeline gas) in $ per ton — USA — N 1-a
    World production: marketable oxygen gas: tonnage — Main countries — N 1-a

Oxygen-blown steel   see   CRUDE STEEL

Oysters & mussels   see   CRUSTACEANS & MOLLUSCS

P.A.Y.E. (Pay-as-you-earn) — OECD countries — D 42-a
    Deductions from wage & salary payments in $m

Packaged soup   see   CONVENIENCE FOODS

PACKAGING INDUSTRY
    Consumption: aluminium: tonnage — EEC countries, Japan & USA — C 12-a
     — Main countries — T 4-a
    Receipts: aluminium products: tonnage — OECD countries — D 21-a

PACKAGING MACHINERY
    % share of world exports held (value basis) — UK — B 27-a
    Exports by destination & value in $m — Main countries — U 9-a
        by value in $m — All countries — U 38-a
     — OECD countries — D 9-a
    Imports by value in $m — All countries — U 38-a

Packaging paper   see   WRAPPING PAPER

Packed meals   see   FROZEN MEALS, PREPARED

PACKING CONTAINERS
    Production: paper bags & cartons: tonnage — All countries — U 22-a
    Usage of plastic materials in production of containers as % of total usage of plastics — European countries — U 26-a

PADDY RICE
    Area harvested in acres — All countries — B 14-a
        in ha — All countries — A 19-a
    Area harvested, production tonnage & yield per ha — All countries — A 9-a
        upland rice crop in ha — All countries — A 19-a
        irrigated for paddy production in ha — All countries — A 19-a
        under crop & area harvested in ha — Burma — A 10-a
            by method of planting in ha — All countries — A 19-a
            in ha — All countries — A 19-a
     — OAS member countries — N 13-a
        used for double cropping of paddy in ha — All countries — A 19-a
    Consumption: locally-harvested paddy: tonnage — Burma — A 10-a
        tonnage — OAS member countries — N 17-a
    Crop yield in kg per ha — Burma — A 10-a
     — OAS member countries — N 13-a
     — OECD countries — D 1-a
    Export subsidies levied in £ per ton — EEC countries — B 8-a
    Exports: tonnage — Burma — A 10-a
    Producer prices received by farmers in $ per ton — All countries — A 9-a
    Production: tonnage & yield per 100 ha — Latin American countries — J 5-a
        tonnage — African countries — U 44-a
     — All countries — B 14-a
     — Asian & Far East countries — U 32-a
     — Burma — A 10-a
     — Main countries — A 10-a
     — Main producing countries — B 8-a
     — OECD countries — D 1-a
     — OAS member countries — N 13-a
    Wholesale prices in local currency per ton — OAS member countries — N 17-a
     — Thailand & S Vietnam — A 9-a
    World market prices: paddy rice by grade - index nos — — A 10-a
    World market prices: paddy rice by grade (private trade) in $ per ton — — A 10-a
        (under government contract) in $ per ton — — A 10-a
    World production: historical table from 1909 to 1962: tonnage — All countries — A 19-a
        tonnage — World regions — C 16-a   U 11-a
    World stocks (end-yr): tonnage — — G 1-a

	Territorial coverage	Title codes

Paid annual holidays   see   HOLIDAYS, INDUSTRIAL

PAINT MANUFACTURING INDUSTRY

No of hrs worked per wk	Main countries	R 3-m
Wage rates by sex in local currency per hr	Main countries	R 3-m
per wk: chemical workers employed in paint manufacturing industry in £	UK	R 4-a

Paint solvents   see   WHITE SPIRIT

Painting & sculpture   see   FINE ARTS

PAINTS & VARNISHES

see also   ARTISTS' COLOURS
           MASTICS
           PIGMENTS
           PRINTING INK

Consumption: linseed oil in production of paints: tonnage	USA	B 19-a	
mercury in production of special paints	USA	T 4-a	
paints: tonnage	OAS member countries	N 17-a	
per capita in kg	OECD countries	D 5-a	
soybean oil in production of paints: tonnage	USA	B 19-a	
Exports by destination by CST classes: tonnage & value in $	EEC countries	E 48-a	
SITC classes by value in $	Main countries	D 2-q	
tonnage & value in $	OECD countries	D 3-a2	
by NIMEXE classes by value in $	All countries	E 20-a	
SITC classes by value in $	All countries	U 50-a	U 59-a
metal oxides for production of paints by value in $	Main countries	U 2-a	
tonnage & value in $	OECD countries	D 5-a	
Imports by NIMEXE classes by value in $	All countries	E 20-a	
SITC classes by value in $	All countries	U 50-a	U 59-a
by source by CST classes: tonnage & value in $	EEC countries	E 21-a	
SITC classes by value in $	Main countries	D 2-q	
tonnage & value in $	OECD countries	D 3-a2	
tonnage & value in $	OECD countries	D 5-a	
Production by kind: tonnage	EEC countries	E 28-q	E 27-a
cellulosic paints: tonnage	All countries	U 22-a	
in litres	OECD countries	D 5-a	
lithopone: tonnage	OAS member countries	N 14-a	
paints (all kinds): tonnage	All countries	U 22-a	
paste colours: tonnage	OECD countries	D 5-a	
	OECD countries	D 5-a	
tonnage	OECD countries	D 5-a	
water paints & distempers: tonnage	AASM countries	E 41-a	
unit value in $ per ton	All countries	U 22-a	
Value of output (gross & net) in £m	OECD countries	D 5-a	
	UK	B 21-a	

Palladium   see   PLATINUM, REFINED

PALM KERNEL CAKE

Export prices in $ per ton	Netherlands	A 9-a
Exports: tonnage & value in $m	Main countries	B 2-a
Production: tonnage	W Germany	N 10-a

PALM KERNEL OIL

Export prices - index nos (weighted average main sources)		U 29-q	
Export prices in $ per ton cif	Netherlands & UK	A 9-a	
Exports by destination: tonnage	Main countries	B 18-a	
tonnage & value in $m	Main countries	B 2-a	
	Benin	E 45-a	
tonnage	Main countries	B 18-q	B 19-a
		P 1-a	
(total) & shipped to EEC area: tonnage & by value in UA	Benin & Zaire	E 41-a	
Import prices: crude kernel oil in £ per ton cif	UK	P 1-a	
(ex W Africa) in £ per ton cif at European ports		B 19-m	A 9-a
		B 2-a	
Imports: tonnage	Main countries	B 19-a	
Production: tonnage	Indonesia & Malaysia	B 19-a	
	Main countries	B 19-a	P 1-a
	W Germany	N 10-a	
Usage in production of cooking fats: tonnage	Japan & UK	A 4-a	
	UK	B 19-a	
of detergents: tonnage	Japan	B 19-a	
of margarine: tonnage	Main countries	B 19-a	
	Portugal, Japan & UK	A 4-a	
of soap & detergents: tonnage	Main countries	A 4-a	
World & Commonwealth production: tonnage		B 19-a	
World market prices (based Marseille Docks) in Fr per kg		E 41-a	
World production: projected to 1977: tonnage		A 1	
tonnage		A 4-a	A 5-a
		N 10-a	

		Territorial coverage	Title codes	

PALM KERNELS
    % contribution to earnings — Nigeria, Sierra Leone & Togo — E 45-a
    Crop (incl world total): tonnage — All countries — P 1-a
    Deliveries to mills (incl oil yields): tonnage — Benin — B 18-m
    Export prices – index nos (weighted average main sources) — — U 29-q
    Export prices in $ per ton — Cameroon & Ghana — A 9-a
    Exports by destination: tonnage — Main countries — B 18-a
        — Nigeria & Sierra Leone — B 19-a
        tonnage & value in $m — Main countries — B 2-a
        — Sierra Leone — E 45-a
        — Indonesia & W Malaysia — U 32-m
        — Main countries — B 18-q   B 19-a
        (total) & shipped to EEC area: tonnage & value in UA — AASM countries — E 41-a
    Harvest estimates (for ensuing crop yr): tonnage — World regions — P 1-a
    Import prices ex Nigeria in £ per ton cif — UK — P 1-m   R 2-m
        — — B 19-q
        in £ per ton cif at European ports — — B 19-m
        in $ per ton at European ports — — A 9-a
    Imports by source: tonnage — EEC countries — B 19-a
        (for production of animal feed): tonnage — UK — P 5-a
        tonnage (incl oil conversion equiv) — UK — P 1-a
        tonnage — Main countries — B 19-a
    Production (incl world total): tonnage — All countries — A 9-a   B 18-a
        — Main countries — B 2-a
        tonnage — Main countries — B 19-a
        — AASM countries — E 41-a
        — Indonesia & Malaysia — B 19-a
    Stocks (end-yr): tonnage — Indonesia & Malaysia — B 19-a
    Wholesale prices ex Nigeria in £ per ton cif — UK — B 2-a   P 1-a
        in $ per ton — European countries — U 27-m
    World market prices ex West Africa in Fr per kg — — E 41-a

PALM OIL
    % contribution to export earnings — Benin & Zaire — E 45-a
    Consumption in production of cooking fats: tonnage — UK & USA — B 19-a
        — Japan, UK & USA — A 4-a
        margarine: tonnage — Main countries — B 19-a
        — Portugal, Japan & UK — A 4-a
        soap & detergents: tonnage — Netherlands & Portugal — A 4-a
        soap: tonnage — UK — B 19-a
    Export prices in $ per picul fob — Singapore — U 32-m
        in $ per ton — Cameroon, Malaysia & Netherlands — A 9-a
    Export prices – index nos (weighted average main sources) — — U 29-q
    Exports by destination: tonnage — Ivory Coast, Malaysia & Nigeria — B 19-a
        — Main countries — B 18-a
        — Nigeria & Singapore — B 19-a
        by value in local currency — Singapore — U 32-m
        tonnage & value in $m — Main countries — B 2-a
        — Benin & Zaire — E 45-a
        tonnage — Indonesia & W Malaysia — U 32-m
        — Main countries — B 19-a
        (total) & shipped to EEC area: tonnage & value in UA — AASM countries — E 41-a
        unit value in $ per 100 lbs — Indonesia — U 32-m
    Import prices ex Malaysia in £ per ton cif — European countries — B 19-m
        (in bulk) in £ per ton cif — UK — P 1-a
        in $ per ton cif — European countries — A 9-a
    Imports by source: tonnage — EEC countries — B 19-a
        tonnage — Main countries — B 19-a   P 1-a
    Production (incl world total): tonnage — All countries — B 18-a
        for ensuing yr (estim): tonnage — World regions — P 1-a
        (incl kernels): tonnage — All countries — U 43-a
        tonnage — AASM countries — E 41-a
        — Main countries — B 19-a   P 1-a
    Stocks (end-yr): tonnage — Malaysia — U 32-q
    Wholesale prices (ex Malaysia) in £ per ton (on London market) — Indonesia & Malaysia — B 19-a
        in $ per ton — UK — B 2-a
        — Singapore & USA — A 9-a
        (refined) in tanks in cents per lb (on New York market) — European countries — U 27-m
        — USA — R 2-m
    World & Commonwealth production: tonnage — — B 19-a
    World market prices (based ex Malaysia) in £ per ton (on London market) — — E 41-a
    World production: forward estimates: tonnage — — A 1-a
        tonnage — — A 4-a

Palm oil estates   see   PLANTATIONS, PALM OIL

Palm oils   see   BABASSO OIL
                COCONUT OIL
                PALM KERNEL OIL
                PALM OIL

PAMPHLETS
    No of first editions published by subject groups — All countries — U 62-a
        published by subject groups (in detail) — All countries — U 62-a

	Territorial coverage	Title codes	
PANAMA CANAL			
Cargo traffic (eastwards): crude oil & petroleum products: tonnage		D 28-a	
fish meal: tonnage		D 28-a	
iron & steel products, iron ore & other metallic ores: tonnage		D 28-a	
lumber & wood products: tonnage		D 28-a	
refrigerated food: tonnage		D 28-a	
sugar: tonnage		D 28-a	
total (all goods): tonnage		D 28-a	
using canal by commodity groups (in both directions): tonnage		D 28-a	
main products carried: tonnage		S 16-m	
shipping routes: tonnage	Worldwide	S 16-m	
(westwards): alumina & bauxite: tonnage		D 28-a	
cereals: tonnage		D 28-a	
chemicals: tonnage		D 28-a	
coal & coke: tonnage		D 28-a	
crude oil & petroleum products: tonnage		D 28-a	
iron & steel products & metallic scrap: tonnage		D 28-a	
machinery: tonnage		D 28-a	
phosphates: tonnage		D 28-a	
sugar: tonnage		D 28-a	
total (all goods): tonnage		D 28-a	
Exports ex all sources passing through canal zone by value in $m		U 18-a	
Income from services provided to shipping in canal zone in balboas million	Panama	U 18-a	
transport services (incl ships' supplies & other sales) in $m	Panama	U 18-a	
Movement through canal zone: mineral cargoes by kind: tonnage		N 5-a	
Ocean traffic (commercial) of Panama Canal by type of vessel: tonnage		N 5-a	
Wages & salaries paid: canal zone services in $m		U 18-a	
PAPER & BOARD INDUSTRY			
% contribution to gross national product	European countries, Japan & USA	U 38-a	
% share of capital investment in industry	E European countries	U 16-a	
of industrial production (value basis)	Main countries	U 38-a	
Capital formation in $m	Main countries	U 21-a	
Consumption: electricity by areas in kWh	EEC countries	E 38-a	
in kWh	All countries	C 23-a	
pulp by kind: tonnage	OECD countries	D 40-a	
Costs: salaried staff in $ per mth	EEC countries	E 11-a	
Earnings by administrative areas in $ per hr	EEC countries	E 38-a	
in $ per hr	All countries	L 4-a	
Employment - index nos	All countries	L 4-a	
Fixed capital investment by administrative areas in $m	EEC countries	E 38-a	
Gross output by value in $m	Main countries	U 21-a	
IDA loans approved for paper industry in $m	OAS member countries	N 16-a	
Investment in buildings in local currency	EEC countries	E 40-a	
in land purchase in local currency	EEC countries	E 40-a	
in machinery in local currency	EEC countries	E 40-a	
Labour costs as % of total costs	EEC countries	E 8-a	
by status of employees in local currency	EEC countries	E 8-a	
per hr (incl staff) in local currency	EEC countries	E 2-a	E 11-a
by administrative areas in $	EEC countries	E 38-a	
wage earners in local currency	EEC countries	E 11-a	
Labour force employed (incl printing industry)	EEC countries	E 38-a	
Labour force: no of salaried staff employed	EEC countries	E 11-a	
of wage earners employed	EEC countries	E 11-a	
of wage earners & salaried staff employed	EEC countries	E 8-a	
No of hrs worked per mth: salaried staff	EEC countries	E 11-a	
per wk (average) by region	EEC countries	E 25-a	
wage earners	EEC countries	E 11-a	
per wk	All countries	L 4-a	
	Main countries	R 3-m	
per yr	EEC countries	E 8-a	
No of operatives employed (incl printing industry)	OECD countries	D 23-a	
of operatives employed	EEC countries	E 2-a	
	Main countries	U 21-a	
Production of paper & board industry as % of general world activity		U 38	
Production - index nos	Asian & Far East countries	U 32-q	
	Australia	U 32-q	
	EEC countries	E 28-q	E 27-a
	Latin American countries	J 5-a	
	OAS member countries	N 14-a	
Wage rates: cardboard makers per hr in local currency	OAS member countries	N 17-a	
cellulose workers per hr in local currency	OAS member countries	N 17-a	
paper-making sector per hr in local currency	OAS member countries	N 17-a	
per hr by sex in local currency	Main countries	R 3-m	C 7-a
in local currency	EEC countries	E 25-a2	
skilled workers by sex in local currency	Main countries	R 4-q	
unskilled workers by sex in local currency	Main countries	R 4-q	
Wages & salary costs in paper & board industry in $	Main countries	U 21-a	

	Territorial coverage	Title codes	
PAPER & PAPERBOARD			
see also CIGARETTE PAPER			
NEWSPRINT			
PHOTOGRAPHIC PAPER			
PRINTING PAPER			
SANITARY PAPER			
WASTE PAPER			
WRAPPING PAPER			
% changes in production	OECD countries	D 40-a	
% consumption increase per 1% in change in gross national product	Main countries	D 32-a	
% of total EEC area production	EEC countries	R 5-a	
% production increase per 1% change in gross domestic product	OECD countries	D 40-a	
Consumption coefficient based on gross national product	Main countries	D 32-a	
Consumption: construction board: tonnage	OECD countries	D 40-a	
cultural paper: tonnage	Main countries	D 32-a	
folding box-board: tonnage	OECD countries	D 40-a	
foodboard: tonnage	OECD countries	D 40-a	
industrial paper: tonnage	Main countries	D 32-a	
kraft paper & board: tonnage	Main countries	D 32-a	
liner board: tonnage	OECD countries	D 40-a	
mercury in production of pulp for paper-making	USA	T 4-a	
per $1000 of gross national product in kg	Main countries	D 32-a	
per capita: cultural paper in kg	Main countries	D 32-a	
in kg	W European area	D 32-a	
in lbs	USA	J 7-a	
industrial paper in kg	Main countries	D 32-a	
printing & writing paper: tonnage	Main countries	D 32-a	
straw board: tonnage	OECD countries	D 40-a	
tonnage	Canada, European countries, Japan & USA	D 40-a	
	Canada, W European countries & USA	D 32-a	
	OAS member countries	N 17-a	
Exports by destination by CST classes: tonnage & value in $	EEC countries	E 48-a	
SITC classes by value in $	Main countries	D 2-q	
tonnage & value in $	OECD countries	D 3-a2	
by destination: construction board: tonnage	All countries	D 40-a	
folding box-board: tonnage	All countries	D 40-a	
foodboard: tonnage	All countries	D 40-a	
liner board: tonnage	All countries	D 40-a	
strawboard: tonnage	OECD countries	D 40-a	
by destination regions by value in $	EEC countries	E 38-a	
by NIMEXE classes by value in $	All countries	E 20-a	
SITC classes by value in $	All countries	U 50-a	U 59-a
printing & writing paper: tonnage	OECD countries	D 41-q	
shipped to EEC & non-EEC areas by value in $	EEC countries	E 24-a	
tonnage & value in $	All countries	E 23-a	
historical table from 1860	Sweden	Z 1-a	
(incl world total)	All countries	A 5-a	
tonnage	Main countries	J 7-a	
Imports by kind: tonnage & value in $	All countries	A 23-a	
by NIMEXE classes by value in $	All countries	E 20-a	
SITC classes by value in $	All countries	U 50-a	U 59-a
by source by CST classes: tonnage & value in $	EEC countries	E 21-a	
SITC classes by value in $	Main countries	D 2-q	
tonnage & value in $	OECD countries	D 3-a2	
by value in local currency	Iran	U 32-m	
printing & writing paper: tonnage	OECD countries	D 41-q	
shipped ex EEC & non-EEC areas by value in $	EEC countries	E 24-a	
Marginal propensity to consume in kg	Main countries	D 32-a	
Production by administrative areas: tonnage	EEC countries	E 38-a	
by kind: tonnage	EEC countries	E 28-q	E 27-a
cardboard: tonnage	OAS member countries	N 14-a	
construction board: tonnage	OECD countries	D 41-q	D 40-a
fine paper: tonnage	Main countries	J 7-a	
folding box-board: tonnage	OECD countries	D 40-a	
for periodicals: tonnage	OAS member countries	N 14-a	
for printing: tonnage	OAS member countries	N 14-a	
kraft paper: tonnage	All countries	U 22-a	
paper (all kinds): tonnage	Asian & Far East countries	U 32-q	
paperboard: tonnage	Main countries	J 7-a	
printing & writing paper: tonnage	OECD countries	D 41-q	
trade goods made of paper: tonnage	All countries	A 23-a	
wrapping & tissue paper: tonnage	All countries	A 23-a	
wrapping paper: tonnage	Main countries	J 7-a	
writing paper: tonnage	Main countries	R 5-a	
tonnage	African countries	U 44-a	
	All countries	U 43-a	
	Australia, European countries, Japan & USA	D 40-a	
	E European countries & USSR	U 16-a	
	ECAFE countries	U 32-q	
	ECE countries	U 15-a	
	EEC countries	E 26-m	
	Latin American countries	U 40-a	
	Main countries	A 5-a	E 3-a
		R 5-a	
Production - index nos (quantum basis)	OECD countries	R 5-a	
	S American countries	U 40-a	
World demand: forecast to 1985: tonnage	EEC countries	E 26-m	
		A 1	

	Territorial coverage	Title codes
PAPER & PAPERBOARD BY KIND		
Consumption - index nos	European area	A 24-a
Consumption per capita in kg	Main countries	D 32-a
kraft paper in kg	Main countries	D 32-a
printing paper in kg	Main countries	D 32-a
tonnage	W European countries, Canada & USA	D 32-a
Exports: tonnage	Canada, European countries & USA	A 13-q
Imports: tonnage	Canada, European countries & USA	A 13-q
Production: tonnage	All countries	A 23-a
	OECD countries	D 40-a
PAPER & PAPERBOARD, CULTURAL		
Consumption per $1000 of gross national product	Main countries	D 32-a
Consumption - index nos	World regions	D 32-a
Marginal propensity to consume in kg	Main countries	D 32-a
PAPER & PAPERBOARD, INDUSTRIAL		
Consumption per $1000 of gross national product	Main countries	D 32-a
Consumption - index nos	World regions	D 32-a
Marginal propensity to consume	Main countries	D 32-a
PAPER & PULP MACHINES		
% share of world export trade held	UK	B 27-a
Exports by destination by value in $m	Main countries	U 9-a
by value in $m	Main countries	U 38-a
Imports by value in $m	All countries	U 38-a
World exports by value in $m		U 38-a

Paper bags & cartons   see   PACKING CONTAINERS

Paper waste   see   WASTE PAPER

PAPER, GREASE-PROOF

Consumption: tonnage	Canada, European countries, Japan & USA	D 40-a
Exports by destination: vegetable parchment: tonnage	All countries	D 40-a

Paper, household   see   SANITARY PAPER

Paperback novels   see   NOVELS, PAPERBACK

PAR VALUES

Currency units in terms of gold	All countries	F 7
of US dollars	All countries	F 7
per troy oz of fine gold	All countries	F 7
per US dollars	All countries	F 7
Exchange rates: parity movements (incl averages)	All countries	M 8-a
Gold parities as basis of comparison of exchange rates		R 1-m
of international levels of cost of living		R 1-m
In grammes of fine gold per currency unit	All countries	F 7
US cents per foreign currency unit		E 26-a
Parities: EEC currencies against US dollar & yen - index nos	All countries	F 7

Paraffin   see   KEROSENE

PARAFFIN WAX

Deliveries, home consumption & exports: tonnage	OECD countries	D 31-a	
Imports & exports by source & destination: tonnage	All countries	B 15-a	
by source: tonnage	OECD countries	D 31-a	
Production: tonnage	All countries	U 22-a	U 43-a
	Main countries	B 15-a	
Refinery output, imports & supply: tonnage	OECD countries	D 31-a	

Parathion   see   INSECTICIDES

Parchment, vegetable   see   PAPER, GREASE-PROOF

Parities   see   PAR VALUES
                   PURCHASING POWER PARITIES

Parmesan   see   CHEESE BY VARIETY

Part-time employment   see   EMPLOYMENT, PART-TIME

PARTICLE & CHIPBOARD

        see also   FIBREBOARD
                       PLYWOOD & BLOCKBOARD
                       WOOD-BASED PANELS

Consumption - index nos	European countries excl USSR	A 24-a
Consumption per capita by volume in m³	All countries	A 25-a
raw materials in production of particle board: tonnage	All countries	A 26-a
tonnage	Main countries	A 26-a
Exports by destination by volume in m³	European countries	A 13-q
by volume in m³	All countries	A 5-a
	Main countries	A 25-a2

405

	Territorial coverage	Title codes	
PARTICLE & CHIPBOARD, continued			
Exports: tonnage	Main countries	A 26-a	
Imports by source by volume in m³	European countries	A 13-q	
particle board: tonnage	UK	A 25-a2	
by value (average) - index nos	W Germany	A 25-m	
by volume in m³	Main countries	A 25-a2	
tonnage	Main countries	A 26-a	
unit value in £ per ton	UK	A 25-m	
No of factories by production method in operation	All countries	A 26-a	
in operation	Main countries	A 25-a	
Production & requirement forecast: tonnage	European countries	A 24-a	
by extrusion process: tonnage	All countries	A 26-a	
Production capacity: tonnage	All countries	A 26-a	
Production, consumption & trade by volume in m³	Main countries	A 25-a2	
flat-pressed board: tonnage	All countries	A 26-a	
non-wood based board by volume in m³	European countries	A 25-a2	
by volume in m³ (incl world total)	All countries	A 5-a	
by volume in m³	ECE countries	U 15-a	
	Canada, European countries, USA & USSR	A 13-q	
tonnage	Main countries	A 26-a	
	Sweden	U 5-a	
wood-based board by volume in m³	European countries	A 25-a2	
Parts see REPLACEMENT PARTS			
PASSENGER CARS			
see also MOTOR VEHICLES			
% changes: retail sales of motor cars	E European countries	U 16-a	
% exports by destination areas (value basis)	UK	B 28-a	
% household by social classes: no of cars owned	W European countries	Z 3	
% households owning a motor car	Main countries	V 4-a	
a new motor car	W European countries	Z 3	
more than one motor car	Main countries	V 4-a	
motor cars by engine size in c.c.	W European countries	Z 3	
motor car (foreign make) by source	W European countries	Z 3	
using motor car by no of km used per yr	W European countries	Z 3	
% increase projected to 1977: demand	UK	B 28	
exports & imports	UK	B 28	
% of total EEC area production (volume basis)	EEC countries	R 5-a	
% of world exports in motor cars held	Main countries	B 28	
shipped to developed countries		U 38-a	
to developing countries		U 38-a	
% of world production of motor cars	Main countries	B 28	
% owners having a garage available	W European countries	Z 3	
of cars with fitted radios	W European countries	Z 3	
% share of each manufacturing company	All countries	V 4-a	
% share held of main car markets (incl taxis) by value in £m	UK	V 1-a	
Assembly (by overseas subsidiaries): volume by make	Main countries	V 2-a	
by model	Main countries	V 2-a	
volume by engine hp	All countries	V 1-a	
mainly from imported parts	All countries	U 22-a	U 43-a
		V 1-a	
volume	ECE countries	U 15-a	
Consumption (or sales volume)	Latin American region	U 38-a	
Demand projected to 1980	E African countries	U 38-a	
Distance covered in km per yr (estim) by passenger cars	Main countries	S 24-a	
Exports: assembled motor vehicles	All countries	V 4-a	
by destination by CST classes: tonnage & value in $m	EEC countries	E 48-a	
SITC classes by value in $m	Main countries	D 2-q	
tonnage & value in $m	OECD countries	D 3-a2	
by volume	All countries	V 1-a	V 3-a
	UK	V 1-a	
	USSR	V 1-a	
no, value & engine capacity in c.c.	W Germany	V 1-a	
no & value in $m: assembled cars	USA	V 1-a	
unassembled cars	USA	V 1-a	
used models	USA	V 1-a	
by engine capacity up to 500 c.c.	UK	V 1-a	
500-1000 c.c.	UK	V 1-a	
1000-1600 c.c.	UK	V 1-a	
1600-2200 c.c.	UK	V 1-a	
2200-2800 c.c.	UK	V 1-a	
2800-3500 c.c.	UK	V 1-a	
3500 c.c. & over	UK	V 1-a	
estate cars	UK	V 1-a	
in £m	UK	V 1-a	
	Canada, European countries & Japan	V 1-a	
tonnage & value in $m	All countries	U 12-a	
by engine size: no & value in £m: assembled & unassembled	UK	V 1-a	
by NIMEXE classes by value in $m	All countries	E 20-a	
SITC classes by value in $m	All countries	U 50-a	U 59-a
by value in $m	All countries	U 38-a	
by volume: historical table	All countries	V 1-a	
unassembled motor cars	All countries	V 4-a	
by volume	OECD countries	D 9-a	
	All countries	S 24-a	
chassis & engines: volume	All countries	V 4-a	
(incl taxis) by value in £m	UK	B 28-a	
historical table in £m	UK	V 1-a	

	Territorial coverage	Title codes	
PASSENGER CARS, continued			
Exports: new motor cars (assembled & unassembled) by value in £	UK	B 28	
shipped to USA (assembled): volume	Main countries	V 4-a	
(unassembled): volume	Main countries	V 4-a	
Exports – index nos (value basis)	UK	V 1-m	
Imports: assembled motor cars (incl taxis): volume	Main countries	V 4-a	
by NIMEXE classes by value in $m	All countries	E 20-a	
SITC classes by value in $m	All countries	U 50-a	U 59-a
by source: assembled motor cars by engine capacity in c.c.	UK	V 1-a	
no & value in £m	UK	V 1-a	
no & value by engine hp	UK	V 1-a	
station wagons: no & value in £	UK	V 1-a	
unassembled motor cars (incl chassis) by value in £m	UK	V 1-a	
tonnage & value in $m	All countries	U 12-a	
by value in local currency	Iran	U 32-m	
in $m	All countries	U 38-a	
by volume	Latin American countries	U 38-a	
	Main countries	S 24-a	
unassembled motor cars (incl taxis): volume	Main countries	V 4-a	
Long-range market absorption trends	Main countries	V 4-a	
sales forecasts	Main countries	V 4-a	
New registrations (during yr)	European countries & USA	U 47-a	
No in use & % rate of increase	ECE countries	U 15-a	
& per 1000 population	Main countries	E 3-a	
	OECD countries	R 5-a	
& projected by 1980	E African countries	U 38-a	
(at end-yr)	European countries & USA	U 47-a	
	Main countries	S 24-a	
by administrative areas	EEC countries	E 38-a	
by kind	AASM countries	E 41-a	
historical tables from 1906	Main European countries	Z 1-a	
(incl taxis)	European countries	U 8-a	
per 1000 population	Developing countries	U 23-a	
	Main countries	R 5-a	S 24-a
per capita by administrative areas	EEC countries	E 38-a	
(incl world total)	World regions	N 8-a	
(total)	African countries	U 44-a	
	All countries	V 3-a	V 4-a
	Asian, Far East & Australasian countries	U 45-a	
	EEC countries	E 43-a	
	Main countries	R 5-a	U 43-a
		V 1-a	
	UK	V 1-a	
	W Indies, & Caribbean countries	T 6-a	
	Worldwide	S 13-a	
No of current licences by engine capacity in c.c.	Great Britain	V 1-q	
by licencing authority	UK	V 1-q	
foreign-owned motor cars crossing frontiers	European countries	U 8-a	
km run (estim)	European countries & USA	U 47-a	
locally-assembled motor cars by make	Main countries	V 2-a	
locally-assembled motor cars	Main countries	V 2-a	
new registrations of motor cars	Main countries	S 24-a	
private cars in use & % rate of increase	ECE countries	U 15-a	
No registered for use on public roads	OAS member countries	N 15-a	
Ownership in units per 1000 population	Main countries	V 4-a	
Population per car in use	Main countries	V 1-a	
per licenced car by areas	UK	V 1-q	
per registered car	All countries	N 8-a	V 3-a
		V 4-a	
Production by overseas subsidiaries: volume	Main countries	V 2-a	
by type & engine hp: volume	All countries	V 1-a	
(or assembly): volume	African countries	U 44-a	
	All countries	C 4-a	
	Main countries	E 3-a	
	OAS member countries	N 14-a	
volume & % of production exported	Main countries	V 1-a	
by engine capacity in c.c.	Main countries	V 4-a	
	UK	V 1-m	
by make	All countries	V 1-a	V 3-a
by manufacturing firms	All countries	V 4-a	
	Main countries	V 4-a	
for home sale & for export	All countries	U 49-a	
historical table from 1900	European countries	Z 1-a	
historical table	UK	V 1-a	
volume	All countries	U 27-m	N 8-a
		S 24-a	U 22-a
		U 38-a	
	E European countries & USSR	U 16-a	
	ECE countries	U 15-a	
	EEC countries	E 26-m	
	Latin American region	U 38-a	
	Main countries	C 2-a	
	OECD countries	D 26-m	R 5-a
Projection: % households not owning a motor car by 1977	UK	B 28	
owning a motor car by 1977	UK	B 28	
2 motor cars by 1977	UK	B 28	
demand by 1977	W European area	B 28	
no in use by 1977	UK	B 28	
	W European area	B 28	

407

	Territorial coverage	Title codes
PASSENGER CARS, continued		
Projection: no in use per 100 population by 1977	UK	B 28
Registrations (incl world total)	All countries	N 8-a
new motor cars by administrative areas	World regions	V 3-a
by engine capacity in cc	UK	V 1-a
	UK	V 1-q
by make & model: home production	N Ireland	V 1-q
imported	UK	V 1-a
	UK	V 4-a
by volume	Main countries	B 28-a
diesel-driven motor cars	Main countries	V 4-a
petrol-driven motor cars	Main countries	V 4-a
station wagons	Main countries	V 4-a
vehicles (all types)	ECE countries	U 42-m
	EEC countries	E 26-m
	Eire	V 1-a
	Latin American countries	J 5-a
	UK	V 1-a
(total)	Latin American region	U 38-a
Registrations (see no 3, 6, 9, 12)	Main countries	U 27-q
Retail sales: volume by model	All countries	V 4-a
volume: home & export by make	UK	V 1-a
Tax receipts by government from car owners	Main countries	S 24-a
Taxes (luxury) levied on private vehicles in FrB	Belgium	S 24-a
Traffic: volume in million car-km	Main countries	S 24-a
World assembly from imported parts: volume		V 4-a
World exports: motor cars by value in $m		U 38-a
World production: volume		V 1-a V 4-a
PASSENGER CARS, SECOND-HAND		
% households owning a used car by age of vehicle	W European countries	Z 3
Exports by destination: no & value in £	UK	V 1-a
	W European countries	V 1-a
Imports by source: no & value in £	UK	V 1-a

Passenger co-efficients   see AIR TRANSPORT

PASSENGER FERRIES		
Deliveries: new vessels	Netherlands	S 16-a

Passenger load factors   see AIR PASSENGER TRAFFIC

Passenger planes   see AIRCRAFT

Passenger traffic   see AIR PASSENGER TRAFFIC
                          OCEAN PASSENGER TRAFFIC
                          RAIL PASSENGER TRAFFIC
                          ROAD TRANSPORT

PASSENGER VESSELS		
No & gross tonnage: vessels by flag	Main countries	S 16-a
liners in service by flag		S 2-a
vessels laid up by flag		S 16-a

Passion fruit, guava, lychees & paw paw   see TROPICAL FRUITS

Pasture   see LAND UTILISATION

PATENT FEES		
Receipts from abroad as component of invisible income in $m		F 1-a

Patent solid fuels   see FUELS, PATENT

Pawpaw (papaya)   see TROPICAL FRUITS, CANNED

Payload capacity   see AIR PASSENGER TRAFFIC
                       AIR TRANSPORT
                       AIRCRAFT CO-EFFICIENTS

Payments balances   see BALANCE OF PAYMENTS

Payroll taxes   see REVENUE
                TAXATION

Peaches   see FRUIT, FRESH

Peanuts   see GROUNDNUTS

Pearls   see AQUATIC ANIMAL PRODUCTS

Pears   see AVOCADOS
            FRUIT, FRESH

	Territorial coverage	Title codes

PEAS & BEANS
    see also CHICK PEAS
                DRY PEAS

Area harvested, production & yield per ha	All countries	A 9-a
under crop: pulses (all kinds) in ha	EEC countries	E 3-a
(for fodder) in ha	EEC countries	E 12-a
kidney beans in ha	EEC countries	E 12-a
Crop yield (for fodder) in 100 kg per ha	EEC countries	E 12-a
kidney beans in 100 kg per ha	EEC countries	E 12-a
Income elasticity of demand for pulses	USA	C 27-a
Production, stocks & consumption: tonnage	OECD countries	D 14-a
Production: dried pulses: tonnage	Latin American countries	U 40-a
green beans: tonnage	Main E European countries	U 20-a
kidney beans: tonnage	EEC countries	E 12-a
peas: tonnage	Main E European countries	U 20-a
tonnage (all pulses)	AASM countries	E 41-a
	EEC countries	B 1-a E 12-a
	OECD countries	D 1-a
Supply, production, consumption & trade: dried pulses	EEC countries	B 1-a

PEAT

% of production comprising moss peat	USA	N 1-a
peat humus	USA	N 1-a
reed-sedge peat	USA	N 1-a
Consumption (as primary energy source) in coal equiv tonnage	European countries	U 10-a
by public electricity supply plants: tonnage	European countries	U 1-a
in thermal electricity supply plants	OECD countries	D 8-a
tonnage	European countries, USA & USSR	U 4-a
	USA	N 1-a
Production: tonnage	All countries	N 5-a U 22-a
	Eire	E 16-m E 15-a
	European countries, USA & USSR	U 4-a
Sales (commercial) for farming & horticultural purposes: tonnage	USA	N 1-a
Wholesale prices in $ per ton	USA	N 1-a
World production: tonnage		N 1-a N 4-a

PEAT BRIQUETTES
    see also HARD COAL BRIQUETTES

Consumption: tonnage	Eire	E 16-q E 15-a
	European countries, USA & USSR	U 4-a
Production: tonnage	Eire	E 16-q E 15-a

PECTIN

Production: tonnage	W Germany	D 37-a

Pellets (sinter) see IRON ORE

PENAL INSTITUTIONS

No of prisoners held in jails & per 100,000 population	OAS member countries	N 20-a

Penecillin see ANTIBIOTICS

PENSION FUNDS
    see also RETIREMENT

Equity on insurance reserves held by banks in $m	OECD countries	D 12-a
Funds invested in $m	All countries	F 6-q F 5-m

PENSION SCHEMES, STATUTORY

No of economically-active persons covered by national pension schemes	All countries	L 2-a

Pensioners see POPULATION, ECONOMICALLY-INACTIVE

PENSIONS

Cost of pensions as % of social services expenditure	All countries	L 2-a
of war pensions to national funds in $m	All countries	L 2-a
Payments for infirmity from Social Security funds in local currency	EEC countries	E 3-a
to invalids as % of expenditure on social welfare	EEC countries	E 6-a
from Social Security funds in local currency	EEC countries	E 3-a E 6-a

Pensions, retirement see OLD AGE PENSIONS

PEPPER

Consumption: tonnage	Main countries	B 2-a
Export prices in local currency per cwt	Indonesia & Malaysia	U 32-m
Exports & re-exports (ex Singapore) in cwt	Main countries	A 9-a
by destination in cwt	Main countries	B 18-q
by value in local currency	Main countries	B 13-a
tonnage & value in $m	Sarawak & Singapore	U 32-m
(total) & shipments to EEC area: tonnage & value in UA	Main countries	B 2-a U 11-a
unit value in cents per kg	AASM countries	E 41-a
	India, Indonesia & Sarawak	U 11-a

	Territorial coverage	Title codes	
PEPPER, continued			
Import prices by kind (at London Docks) in £ per ton cif	UK	B 13-m	B 18-m
(at New York) in cents per lb cif	USA	B 13-m	B 18-m
(ex Malabar & Sarawak) in £ per ton cif	UK	B 2-a	
in $ per ton cif	France & UK	A 9-a	
Imports by source in cwt	Main countries incl USSR	B 18-q	B 13-a
tonnage	Main countries	A 5-a	
Producer prices in $ per ton	Khmer Republic	A 9-a	
Production & exports of Commonwealth countries as % of world total		B 13-a	
Production in 1000 cwt (incl world total)	All countries	B 13-a	
tonnage	AASM countries	E 41-a	
	Cameroon, Central African Republic & Madagascar	E 41-a	
	Main countries	B 2-a	
Re-exports in 1000 cwt	Hong Kong & Singapore	B 13-a	
Retail prices: black pepper in local currency	OAS member countries	N 17-a	
Stocks (end-yr): black & white pepper held on London market: tonnage	UK	B 2-a	
(held on London market) in cwt	UK	B 13-m	
Supply, production, consumption & trade: tonnage	EEC countries	B 1-a	
Wholesale prices by kind in local currency per ton	Singapore, UK & USA	A 5-a	
(Malabar & Lampong grades) in $ per ton	India & Singapore	U 32-m	
World consumption: tonnage	Main countries	B 2-a	
World export trade: tonnage & value in $m		B 2-a	
World market prices: Malabar black pepper in £ per cwt cif	UK	E 41-a	
World production: tonnage	All countries	A 5-a	U 11-a
Peppers, green see VEGETABLES, FRESH			
PERAMBULATORS & PUSH-CHAIRS			
Production: volume	All countries	U 22-a	
PERFUMERY			
see also ESSENTIAL OILS			
TOILET PREPARATIONS			
Exports by destination (incl cosmetics & dentifrice) by value in $m	Main countries	U 2-a	
Production by value (based on selling prices) in $m	OECD countries	D 5-a	
Perfumery oils see OILS FOR PERFUMES			
PERIODICALS			
Circulation by frequency (circa 1957)	All countries	U 63	
(total) & per 1000 population	All countries	U 62-a	
No of periodicals by frequency of publication (circa 1956)	All countries	U 62-a	U 63
& circulation	All countries	U 63	
& subject content	All countries	U 63	
frequency (circa 1957)	All countries	U 63	
language	All countries	U 63	
subject content & circulation	All countries	U 62-a	
subject content (circa 1956)	Latin American countries	U 63	
covering education, medicine & social science subjects in 1956	Worldwide	U 63	
PERLITE			
see also VERMICULITE			
% usage in production of filter aids	USA	N 1-a	
horticultural aggregates	USA	N 1-a	
insulation board	USA	N 1-a	
Consumption: tonnage	USA	N 1-a	
Production: tonnage	All countries	B 15-a	
Wholesale prices (ex mine) paid by expanders in $ per ton	USA	N 1-a	
World production at mines: tonnage	Main countries	N 1-a	
Permanent grassland see LAND UTILISATION			
Permits, construction see BUILDING PERMITS			
Personal credit see PRIVATE BORROWING			
Personal expenditure see HOUSEHOLD BUDGETS			
PRIVATE CONSUMPTION			
PRIVATE EXPENDITURE			
PERSONAL INCOME			
% change associated with 1% increase in gross national product	OECD countries	D 11	
in credit received	E European countries	U 16-a	
farm income	E European countries & USSR	U 16-a	
money income	E European countries & USSR	U 16-a	
pensions	E European countries & USSR	U 16-a	
social benefits	E European countries	U 16-a	
wage incomes	E European countries & USSR	U 16-a	
% of national income distributed to households	EEC countries	E 32-a	
% regional share in total direct incomes	EEC countries	E 37-a	
By regions in local currency	EEC countries	E 37-a	
Earnings per capita per yr in $	Main countries	M 4-a	
From ownership of property in local currency	EEC countries	E 32-a	
From ownership of property & interest on debts in local currency	OAS member countries	N 16-a	
From private enterprise business in local currency	OAS member countries	N 16-a	

	Territorial coverage	Title codes
PERSONAL INCOME, continued		
In local currency	Latin American countries	J 5-a
Of employees as % of national income	All countries	L 4-a
Net income of population in urban & rural areas in local currency	OAS member countries	N 16-a
Per capita in local currency	EEC countries	E 37-a
Private transfers of income in local currency	AASM countries	E 41-a
Wage & salaries (net) in local currency	AASM countries	E 41-a
	OAS member countries	N 16-a
Wages, salaries & allowances in $m	EEC countries	E 32-a
PESTICIDES		
Consumption by kind on farms & purpose: tonnage	OAS member countries	N 13-a
	All countries	A 9-a
on farms: tonnage	Asian, Far East & Australasian countries	U 45-a
Costs of pesticides as % of farm operating expenses	Hungary & Poland	U 34-a
	ECE countries	U 34-a
of value of gross farm output	ECE countries	U 34-a
	Hungary & Poland	U 34-a
as item in farm operating expenses in $m	Hungary & Poland	U 34-a
Farm expenditure on pesticides as % of total operating costs	ECE countries	U 34-a
in $ (incl index nos)	ECE countries	U 34-a
Imports & exports by value in $m	All countries	A 14-a
PET FOODS		
% of households owning dogs or cats buying biscuit meal, fish, meat or tinned pet foods	W European countries	Z 3
Petalite see LITHIUM MINERALS		
PETHIDINE		
see also SYNTHETIC NARCOTICS		
Consumption in kg & per million population	All countries	U 46-a
Exports by destination in kg	Main countries	U 46-a
Production by grade in kg	Main countries	U 46-a
Quantities converted into intermediates in kg	Main countries	U 46-a
World requirements (estim) in kg		U 19-a
Petro-chemicals see BENZENE		
BUTADIENE		
ETHYLENE		
PROPYLENE		
XYLENE		
PETROCHEMICAL INDUSTRY		
Consumption: gas fuel, oils & naphtha: tonnage	OECD countries	D 31-a
petroleum products: tonnage	Italy	H 4-a
	EEC countries	E 16-q E 15-a
IDA loans for improving facilities in petrochemical industry in $m	OAS member countries	N 16-a
Petrol see MOTOR SPIRIT		
PETROLEUM		
see also CRUDE PETROLEUM		
CRUDE OIL PIPELINES		
DISTILLATION CAPACITY		
% change: petroleum output & consumption	E European countries & USSR	U 16-a
Consumption: tonnage	UK	U 10-m
Export prices - index nos (weighted average main sources)		U 54-q
Exports: crude oil & petroleum products: tonnage	E European countries & USSR	U 16-a
Imports: crude oil & petroleum products: tonnage	E European countries & USSR	U 16-a
(net) as % of consumption	E European countries & USSR	U 16-a
Inter-regional movements: crude oil & petroleum products	World regions	C 21-a
Production (incl natural gas liquids): tonnage	All countries	C 13-a
tonnage & in barrels per day	All countries	C 13-a
tonnage	E European countries & USSR	U 16-a
	European area of OECD	D 31-a
Trade balance of oil & petroleum products in $bn	Main countries	G 1-a
Wholesale prices: indigenous product in $ per barrel	USA	U 27-m
Wholesale prices in $ per barrel	Kuwait, Saudi Arabia, Venezuela & UK	U 27-m
Petroleum, known reserves see APPENDIX 4		
PETROLEUM INDUSTRY		
see also OIL COMPANIES		
PETROLEUM REFINERIES		
Corporate investment of US companies overseas in $m	Main countries	R 5-a
Costs: salaried staff per mth	EEC countries	E 11-a
specific major oil companies in $m	Worldwide	C 3-a
Depreciation costs as % of sales revenue	Venezuela	T 6-a
Direct investment of US government in $m	OAS member countries	N 16-a
Distribution: profits received by government in $m	Venezuela	T 6-a
to oil companies in $m	Venezuela	T 6-a
Electricity: consumption from public supply in kWh	All countries	C 23-a
Government income from oil production in $m	Venezuela	T 6-a
Government taxation as % of sales revenue	Venezuela	T 6-a

	Territorial coverage	Title codes	
PETROLEUM INDUSTRY, continued			
Investment by oil & natural gas industries in buildings in local currency	EEC countries	E 40-a	
land purchase in local currency	EEC countries	E 40-a	
machinery in local currency	EEC countries	E 40-a	
Labour costs per hr: all employees	EEC countries	E 11-a	
wage earners	EEC countries	E 11-a	
Labour force: no of salaried staff employed	EEC countries	E 11-a	
of wage earners employed	EEC countries	E 11-a	
No of hrs worked per wk	Main countries	R 3-m	
per wk by region	OAS member countries	N 18-a	
per yr: salaried staff	EEC countries	E 25-a	
wage earners	EEC countries	E 11-a	
of operatives employed	EEC countries	E 11-a	
Oil company income as % of sales revenue	Venezuela	E 2-a	
Operating costs as % of sales revenue	Venezuela	T 6-a	
Production: oil crude by specific companies: tonnage		T 6-a	
oil (refined) by specific companies: tonnage		H 4-a	
Wage rates (daily, hourly, monthly) in local currency	OAS member countries	H 4-a	
in local currency	OAS member countries	N 17-a	
in petroleum & natural gas industries in local currency per hr	EEC countries	N 17-a	
oil derivatives sector in local currency	OAS member countries	E 25-a2	
per hr by sex in local currency	Main countries	N 17-a	
in local currency	EEC countries	R 3-m	
		E 25-a2	
PETROLEUM PRODUCTS			
see also AVIATION FUEL			
BITUMEN			
DIESEL OIL			
FUEL OIL			
KEROSENE			
LUBRICATING OIL			
MOTOR SPIRIT			
NAPHTHA			
PARAFFIN WAX			
REFINERY GAS			
WHITE SPIRIT			
% changes in demand by kind	Main countries	C 21-a	
% growth in demand: distillates	World regions	G 1-a	
% of total consumption taken by economic sectors	Latin American countries	U 18-a	
electricity generation	Latin American countries	U 18-a	
households	Latin American countries	U 18-a	
manufacturing industry	Latin American countries	U 18-a	
transportation	Latin American countries	U 18-a	
% contribution to export earnings	Chad, Fiji, Madagascar & Senegal	E 45-a	
% of world production by specific oil companies	Worldwide	H 4-a	
% of world sales by specific oil companies	Worldwide	H 4-a	
% share in consumption of energy (all kinds)	Latin American countries	U 18-a	
of EEC area imports	Developing countries	U 52-a	
of seaborne freight: tonnage	World regions	U 37-a	
of total energy supply sources	ECE countries	U 16-a	
Availability (ex refineries) & imports: tonnage	Main countries	C 14-a	
Changes in stocks: tonnage	EEC countries	E 14-a	
Coastal shipping: oil products: tonnage	EEC countries	E 43-a	
Consumption as % of world supply	All countries	C 21-a	
bunkers: tonnage	Main countries	C 14-a	H 4-a
	EEC countries	E 16-q	E 15-a
at power stations & gasworks: tonnage	EEC countries	E 16-q	E 15-a
by chemical industry: tonnage	OECD countries	D 5-a	
	EEC countries	E 14-a	
gas, oil & iron & steel industries: tonnage	OECD countries	D 22-a	
industrial sector by areas: tonnage	EEC countries	E 38-a	
in calorific value	Main countries	H 4-a	
iron & steel industry: tonnage	EEC countries	E 14-a	
main industries: tonnage	OECD countries	D 31-a	
	EEC countries	E 16-q	E 14-a
		E 15-a	
non-ferrous metals industry: tonnage	EEC countries	E 14-a	
non-metallic minerals industry: tonnage	EEC countries	E 14-a	
petrochemical industry: tonnage	Italy	H 4-a	
road transport in calorific value	Main countries	H 4-a	
steel industry in calorific value	Main countries	H 4-a	
transportation in calorific value	Main countries	H 4-a	
value in $m	Main countries	U 23-a	
(domestic) as bunkers & exports: tonnage	OECD countries	D 39-q	D 31-a
tonnage	Main countries	C 14-a	H 4-a
in agriculture & fishing: tonnage	EEC countries	E 16-q	E 15-a
barrels per day	OPEC member countries	C 3-a	
electricity generation tonnage	EEC countries	E 16-m	E 14-a
		E 15-a	
gasworks: tonnage	EEC countries	E 16-q	E 14-a
		E 15-a	
(incl bunkers): tonnage	Main countries	T 3-a	
mineral oils: tonnage	European countries	U 10-a	
tonnage	Main countries	C 13-a	
	OECD countries	D 5-a	

412

	Territorial coverage	Title codes	
PETROLEUM PRODUCTS, continued			
Deliveries for energy purposes & other uses: tonnage	EEC countries	E 16-q	E 15-a
for home consumption & bunkers: tonnage	OECD countries	D 31-a	
to EEC area countries: tonnage	EEC countries	E 14-a	
Demand (domestic): tonnage	OECD countries	D 31-a	
Excise duties levied: mineral oils	EEC countries	E 31-a	
Export prices in $ per barrel fob	Venezuela	U 18-a	
Export prices – index nos	Latin American countries	U 18-a	
	S American countries	U 40-q	
Exports as % of consumption	Main countries	U 23-a	
by destination in barrels per day	OPEC member countries	C 3-a	
sea, inland waters, road & rail: tonnage	European countries	U 8-a	
value in $ per barrel	Indonesia	U 32-m	
in $m	African, Caribbean countries & Pacific Is	E 45-a	
	Indonesia & Singapore	U 32-m	
volume in m³	Latin American countries	U 18-a	
historical table from 1900: tonnage	Main countries	Z 1-a	
in order of importance in barrels	Main countries	C 14-a	
(incl bunkers): tonnage	World regions	D 31-a	
shipped to non-EEC area: tonnage	EEC countries	E 14-a	
	Main countries	C 14-a	
tonnage	Malaysia & Sarawak	U 32-m	
	OECD countries	D 31-a	
	World regions	T 3-a	
Imports, exports & changes in stocks: tonnage	EEC countries	E 16-q	E 15-a
Imports & exports by source & destination by rail: tonnage	EEC countries	E 43-a	
by road: tonnage	EEC countries	E 43-a	
by sea: tonnage	EEC countries	E 43-a	
Imports (all fuel oils): tonnage	ECE countries	U 15-a	
as % of consumption	Main countries	U 23-a	
by sea, inland waters, road & rail: tonnage	European countries	U 8-a	
source: tonnage	OECD countries	D 31-a	
	World regions	D 31-a	
	Developing countries	U 52-a	
	Asian, Far East & Australasian countries	U 32-m	
value in $m	Latin American countries	U 18-a	
	EEC countries	E 14-a	
volume in m³	Main European countries	Z 1-a	
ex non-EEC area: tonnage	All countries	C 3-a	
historical table from 1920: tonnage	Main countries	C 14-a	
in barrels per day (incl world total)	ECE countries	U 16-a	
in order of importance in barrels	Developing countries	U 52-a	
(net) as % of consumption	World regions	T 3-a	
shipped into EEC area by value in $m	India	S 16-a	
tonnage	EEC countries	E 2-a	
	EEC countries	E 14-a	
via Port of Karachi: tonnage	EEC countries	E 38-a	
Labour costs for processing per hr	Worldwide	H 4-a	
Production: all kinds: tonnage	OECD countries	D 44-a	
by administrative areas: tonnage	OAS member countries	N 14-a	
by specific large oil companies: tonnage	OPEC member countries	C 3-a	
by kind of fuel: tonnage	EEC countries	E 3-a	
distilled fuel oils by volume in m³	OECD countries	D 39-q	D 31-a
in barrels	EEC countries	E 16-q	E 15-a
ex refineries: tonnage	Latin American countries	U 18-a	
imports & supply: tonnage	OAS member countries	N 14-a	
in coal equiv tonnage	OPEC member countries	C 3-a	
in petroleum equiv tonnage	OAS member countries	N 14-a	
kerosene & jet fuel by volume in m³	OPEC member countries	C 3-a	
kerosene in barrels	EEC countries	E 16-q	E 15-a
lubricating oil by volume in m³	EEC countries	E 16-q	E 15-a
motor fuels in barrels	OAS member countries	N 14-a	
non-gaseous products in coal equiv tonnage	OPEC member countries	C 3-a	
refined products: tonnage	ECAFE countries	U 32-q	
residual fuel oils by volume in m³	EEC countries	E 26-m	
in barrels	Latin American countries	J 5-a	
tonnage	Italy	H 4-a	
	OECD countries	D 31-a	
Production, trade & consumption: tonnage	W European countries	S 16-a	
Refinery output, imports & supply: tonnage	EEC countries	E 14-a	
Refinery output: tonnage	EEC countries	E 43-a	
Resources (ex indigenous production & imports): tonnage	Worldwide	H 4-a	
Road transport of fuel oils by kind over frontiers: tonnage	Worldwide	C 3-a	
Sales by specific oil companies: tonnage	Worldwide	U 37-a	
in barrels per day		D 28-a	
Seaborne freight as % of total freight			
Shipments: mineral oils through Kiel Canal: tonnage	OECD countries	D 31-a	
Supply, refinery output & deliveries: tonnage	EEC countries	E 16-q	E 15-a
Trade: non-gaseous products in coal equiv tonnage	UK & USA	U 27-m	
Wholesale prices: fuel oil distillate in $ per ton		T 3-a	
World consumption (incl bunkers): tonnage		D 28-a	
World seaborne trade (estim): tonnage			
World production in barrels per day	All countries	C 3-a	
PETROLEUM PRODUCTS BY KIND			
% yields in crude oil refining	USA	C 21-a	
Consumption by transport system: tonnage	Italy	H 4-a	
in litres	OAS member countries	N 17-a	
tonnage	Main countries	C 14-a	
(total) & from own production: tonnage	Italy	H 4-a	
Demand (domestic): tonnage	All countries	C 21-a	

	Territorial coverage	Title codes	
PETROLEUM PRODUCTS BY KIND, continued			
Exports by destination by CST classes: tonnage & value in $m	EEC countries	E 48-a	
SITC classes by value in $m	Main countries	D 2-q	
tonnage & value in $m	OECD countries	D 3-a2	
tonnage	Italy	H 4-a	
tonnage & value in $m	All countries	U 12-a	
by NIMEXE classes by value in $m	All countries	E 20-a	
SITC classes by value in $m	All countries	U 50-a	U 59-a
Imports & exports: tonnage	All countries	B 15-a	
Imports by NIMEXE classes by value in $m	All countries	E 20-a	
SITC classes by value in $m	All countries	U 50-a	U 59-a
by source by CST classes: tonnage & value in $m	EEC countries	E 21-a	
SITC classes by value in $m	Main countries	D 2-q	
tonnage & value in $m	OECD countries	D 3-a2	
tonnage	Italy	H 4-a	
tonnage & value in $m	All countries	U 12-a	
Prices posted at specific ports in $ per ton fob	Worldwide	C 3-a	
Production: tonnage	AASM countries	E 41-a	
	All countries	U 43-a	
	Main countries	U 27-q	B 15-a
		E 3-a	
Rail freight (inland & abroad): tonnage	EEC countries	E 43-a	
Retail prices in local currency	OAS member countries	N 17-a	
Seaborne freight: tonnage	EEC countries	E 43-a	
PETROLEUM REFINERIES			
see also DISTILLATION CAPACITY			
FEEDSTOCKS			
As source of benzene production: tonnage	European countries, Japan & USA	U 26-a	
of toluene production: tonnage	European countries, Japan & USA	U 26-a	
of xylene production: tonnage	European countries, Japan & USA	U 26-a	
% growth rate in oil refining capacity	Latin American countries	U 18-a	
in oil refining performance	Latin American countries	U 18-a	
% yield in refining of crude oil	W European countries	C 21-a	
Capacity tonnage & % degree of utilisation of plant	EEC countries	E 15-a	
& plant locations	EEC countries	E 15-a	
as % of world total capacity	Main countries	H 4-a	
by area per yr: tonnage	EEC countries	E 38-a	
for cracking & reforming: tonnage	Main countries	E 3-a	
for distillation: tonnage	Main countries	E 3-a	
of specific oil companies in barrels million	Venezuela	T 6-a	
in barrels per day	All countries	C 3-a	N 5-a
	OPEC member countries	C 3-a	
refineries owned by ENI group: tonnage	Italy	H 4-a	
by foreign oil companies: tonnage	Italy	H 4-a	
by other Italian oil companies: tonnage	Italy	H 4-a	
tonnage & barrels per yr	All countries	C 13-a	
tonnage by region per yr	Italy	H 4-a	
per yr	All countries	C 14-a	T 3-a
		U 43-a	U 55-a
	EEC countries	B 30-a	
	African countries	U 39-a	
	Main countries	H 4-a	
	OECD countries	D 31-a	
Consumption: electricity in kWh	USA	U 1-a	
	All countries	C 23-a	
gas (all kinds) by volume in m³	OECD countries	D 44-a	
Crude petroleum: refinery output of products by volume in m³	Latin American countries	U 18-a	
through-put by refineries in barrels per day	EEC countries	E 26-m	
	OPEC countries	C 3-a	
	African countries	U 39-a	
	Main countries	C 14-a	
tonnage	World regions	C 21-a	
	European countries	D 31-a	
Intake: crude oil & feedstocks: tonnage	OECD countries	D 39-q	D 31-a
(incl refinery output): tonnage	Main countries	E 3-a	
tonnage	EEC countries	E 40-a	
Investment in buildings in local currency	EEC countries	E 40-a	
in land purchase in local currency	EEC countries	E 40-a	
in machinery in local currency	EEC countries	E 8-a	
Labour costs as % of total costs in refineries	EEC countries	E 8-a	
by status of employees in local currency	African countries	U 39-a	
Labour force employed & wages & salary costs in refineries in $m	EEC countries	E 11-a	
Labour force: no of salaried staff employed	EEC countries	E 11-a	
of wage earners employed	EEC countries	E 8-a	
of wage earners & salaried staff employed	EEC countries	E 8-a	
No of hrs worked per yr	Main countries	R 3-m	
per wk	Italy	H 4-a	
of refining plants (by size of output) in operation: tonnage	Main countries	E 3-a	
Production by kind of fuel: tonnage	OECD countries	D 31-a	
petroleum products: tonnage	Latin American countries	U 18-a	
Storage capacity (in & outside of refining plants): tonnage	EEC countries	E 15-a	
Wage rates by grade of worker in lire per hr	Italy	R 4-a	
by sex in local currency per hr	Main countries	R 3-m	
World refining & distillation capacity (end-yr): tonnage		H 4-a	T 3-a
in barrels per day		C 3-a	

Petroleum wells   see   OIL WELLS

	Territorial coverage	Title codes

PETS
    % of households (by social classes) owning cage birds, cats & dogs   W European countries   Z 3
                                                             owning no pets of any kind   W European countries   Z 3

PEWTER
    Tin: consumption in manufacture of pewter: tonnage   Italy   C 12-a

PHARMACEUTICAL INDUSTRY
    No of hrs worked per wk   Main countries   R 3-m
    Wage rates per hr by sex   Main countries   R 3-m
                per wk by sex   UK   R 4-a

PHARMACEUTICAL PRODUCTS
        see also   DRUGS & MEDICINES
    % changes in export & import trade (value basis)   Main countries   U 25-a
    Consumption: bismuth in production of pharmaceuticals: tonnage   USA   T 4-a
                      mercury in production of pharmaceuticals in flasks   USA   T 4-a
    Exports by destination by value in $m   Main countries   U 2-a
             by value in $m   European countries, Japan & USA   U 26-a
             shipped to EEC & non-EEC areas by value in $m   EEC countries   E 24-a
    Exports - index nos   European countries, Japan & USA   U 26-a
    Imports by value in $m   European countries, Japan & USA   U 26-a
             in $m & as % of imports of all chemicals   Main countries   U 25-a
             shipped ex EEC & non-EEC areas by value in $m   EEC countries   E 24-a
    Imports - index nos   European countries, Japan & USA   U 26-a
    Plant investment for production & capital expenditure in £m   UK   B 21-a
    Production (based on sales value) in $m   OECD countries   D 5-a
           by value in $m   Communist countries   U 26-a
                             European countries, Japan & USA   U 26-a
    Production - index nos   European countries, Japan & USA   U 26-a
    Value of output (gross & net) in £m   UK   B 21-a

PHARMACEUTICAL PRODUCTS BY KIND
    Exports by destination by CST classes: tonnage & value in $ EEC countries   E 48-a
                     SITC classes by value in $ Main countries   D 2-q
                               tonnage & value in $ OECD countries   D 3-a2
             NIMEXE classes by value in $ All countries   E 20-a
             SITC classes by value in $ All countries   U 50-a   U 59-a
    Imports by NIMEXE classes by value in $ All countries   E 20-a
             SITC classes by value in $ All countries   U 50-a   U 59-a
             source by CST classes by value in $ EEC countries   E 21-a
                     SITC classes by value in $ Main countries   D 2-q
                              tonnage & value in $ OECD countries   D 3-a2

PHARMACISTS
    No in practice & no per 100,000 population by administrative areas   EEC countries   E 38-a
          (or employed in hospitals)   African countries   U 44-a
                                             AASM countries   E 41-a

PHARMACY
    No of students enrolled on university courses in pharmacy   OAS member countries   N 19-a

Phenol   see   CHEMICAL PRODUCTS

Phenol, distilled   see   CHEMICALS, ORGANIC

Phenol, natural   see   COAL BY-PRODUCTS

Phenol, synthetic   see   CHEMICALS, ORGANIC

PHILOLOGY
    No of new book titles published on the science of language   All countries   U 62-a

PHILOSOPHY
    No of new book titles published on philosophical subjects   All countries   U 62-a
                                                      OAS member countries   N 19-a

Phlogopite   see   MICA SHEET

Pholcodine   see   DRUGS & MEDICINES
                        OPIUM ALKALOIDS

Phosphate fertilisers   see   FERTILISERS, PHOSPHATE
                                      NATURAL FERTILISERS
                                      PHOSPHATE OF LIME
                                      PHOSPHATE ROCK
                                      PHOSPHATIC GUANO
                                      SUPERPHOSPHATES

PHOSPHATE OF LIME
    Production: tonnage (estim)   Main countries   B 15-a

	Territorial coverage	Title codes	
PHOSPHATE ROCK			
Consumption as chemical fertilisers: tonnage	OECD countries	D 5-a	
in production of chemicals: tonnage	OECD countries	D 5-a	
of phosphorous: tonnage	OECD countries	D 5-a	
tonnage (incl % change)	All countries	C 15-a	
tonnage	All countries	T 5-a	
	USA	N 1-a	
Deliveries by grade: tonnage	World regions	U 25-a	
(domestic): tonnage	World excl Communist countries	C 15-a	
Exports by destination: tonnage	All countries	C 15-a	
Freight by cargo source: tonnage	All countries	C 15-a	
Import demand (for fertiliser production): tonnage	Main countries	D 28-a	
Imports & exports by source & destination: tonnage	Developed countries	U 11-a	
Imports: tonnage	Main countries	B 15-a	
Production by grade: tonnage	All countries	C 15-a	
ground rock (for direct use): tonnage	World excl Communist countries	C 15-a	
tonnage (incl apatite)	Main countries	A 2-a	
(incl world total)	Main countries	B 15-a	
	All countries	C 15-a	N 1-a
		U 11-a	
tonnage	AASM countries	E 41-a	
	African countries	U 44-a	
	All countries	A 2-a	T 5-a
	Senegal & Togo	E 41-a	
	World regions	U 25-a	
Stocks held at producers' plants: tonnage	USA	N 1-a	
Wholesale prices (ex plant) in $ per ton	USA	N 1-a	
World consumption: tonnage		T 5-a	
World exports: tonnage & value in $m	Main countries	U 11-a	
World production & world consumption: tonnage		U 25-a	
tonnage		N 4-a	T 5-a
World reserves: tonnage (estim)	Main countries	N 1-a	
PHOSPHATES			
see also FERTILISERS, PHOSPHATE			
PHOSPHATE OF LIME			
PHOSPHATE ROCK			
PHOSPHATIC GUANO			
SUPERPHOSPHATES			
% contribution to export earnings	Senegal & Togo	E 45-a	
Exports by kind: tonnage	Main countries	B 15-a	
(incl hypophosphates) by destination: tonnage	Main countries	U 2-a	
tonnage & value in $m	Senegal & Togo	E 45-a	
Imports by kind: tonnage	Main countries	B 15-a	
Production: commercial phosphatic fertiliser: tonnage	Latin American countries	J 5-a	
incl tribasic phosphate: tonnage	African countries	U 44-a	
tonnage	EEC countries	E 28-q	E 27-a
Shipments through Panama Canal: tonnage		D 28-a	
World production & world demand: tonnage		U 25-a	
PHOSPHATIC GUANO			
Consumption: tonnage	OAS member countries	N 17-a	
Exports: tonnage	Mauritius & Seychelles	B 15-a	
Phosphor-bronze rods see RODS & BARS, BRONZE-ALLOY			
Phosphor-bronze wire see WIRE, PHOSPHOR-BRONZE			
PHOSPHORIC ACID			
see also FERTILISERS, PHOSPHATE			
Consumption: tonnage	OAS member countries	N 17-a	
Exports by destination: tonnage	Main countries	U 2-a	
tonnage	European countries, Japan & USA	U 25-a	
Imports: tonnage	European countries, Japan & USA	U 25-a	
Production by reaction process: tonnage	OECD countries	D 5-a	
by thermal process: tonnage	OECD countries	D 5-a	
tonnage	European countries, Japan & USA	U 25-a	
PHOSPHORUS PENTOXIDE			
Exports (incl phosphoric acid) by destination: tonnage	Main countries	U 2-a	
PHOTOGRAPHIC APPARATUS			
% of households (by social classes) owning cameras by kind	W European countries	Z 3	
Exports: cameras & equipment therefor by value in $	OECD countries	D 9-a	
Production: cameras & cinematographic apparatus: volume	All countries	U 22-a	
Retail prices (comparative): cameras in $	EEC countries	Z 3-a	
PHOTOGRAPHIC FILM			
Production: sensitised roll film	All countries	U 22-a	
Retail prices (comparative): 35mm colour film	EEC countries	Z 3-a	

	Territorial coverage	Title codes	

PHOTOGRAPHIC MATERIALS
    see also   PHOTOGRAPHIC FILM
                    PHOTOGRAPHIC PAPER
    Exports by destination by value in $ Main countries   U 2-a

PHOTOGRAPHIC PAPER
    Production: sensitised paper   All countries   U 22-a

PHOTOGRAPHIC SUPPLY INDUSTRY
    Consumption of silver in production of photographic materials in oz   USA   T 4-a
    Production - index nos   OECD countries   D 5-a
    Turnover in $m   OECD countries   D 5-a

Phthalic anhydride   see   CHEMICAL PRODUCTS

Physicians   see   MEDICAL PERSONNEL

PIANOS
    Production (all types): volume   All countries   U 22-a

Pick-ups   see   MOTOR VEHICLES

Piece goods   see   COTTON PIECE GOODS
                         CLOTHING
                         RAYON PIECE GOODS

Piece-work rates   see   EARNINGS
                                WAGE RATES

PIG IRON
    see also   FERRO-ALLOYS
                    FOUNDRY IRON

	Territorial coverage	Title codes	
% of agglomerates used in furnace ore charge	All countries	U 49-a	
% of steel industry investment: blast furnaces	OECD countries	D 22-a	
% of EEC area production (incl ferro-alloys)	EEC countries	E 29-a	R 5-a
by grade	EEC countries	E 29-a	
Consumption for production of Converter steel: tonnage	ECE countries	U 7-q	U 6-a
	Main countries	H 3-a	
of Electric steel: tonnage	ECE countries	U 7-q	U 6-a
	EEC countries	E 29-a	
	Main countries	H 3-a	
of Foundry castings: tonnage	ECE countries	U 7-q	U 6-a
	EEC countries	E 30-q	E 29-a
	Main countries	H 3-a	
of L.D. steel: tonnage	ECE countries	U 7-q	U 6-a
	Main countries	H 3-a	
of Open-hearth steel: tonnage	ECE countries	U 7-q	U 6-a
	Main countries	H 3-a	
in Siemens Martin furnaces: tonnage	EEC countries	E 29-a	
in steel furnaces: tonnage	OAS member countries	N 17-a	
	EEC countries	E 30-q	E 29-a
	ECE countries	U 7-q	U 6-a
	Main countries	T 1-a	
in Thomas steel converters: tonnage	EEC countries	E 29-a	
of blast furnace alloys: tonnage	ECE countries	U 7-q	U 6-a
	Main countries	H 3-a	
of coke in blast furnaces: tonnage	EEC countries	E 16-q	E 15-a
of ferro-manganese: tonnage	ECE countries	U 7-q	U 6-a
	Main countries	H 3-a	
of sinter per ton of pig iron produced	EEC countries	E 30-q	
of spiegeleisen: tonnage	ECE countries	U 7-q	U 6-a
	Main countries	H 3-a	
per ton of Electric steel produced	EEC countries	E 29-a	
of Siemens Martin steel produced	EEC countries	E 29-a	
of Thomas steel produced	EEC countries	E 29-a	
tonnage	EEC countries	E 30-q	
	USA	N 1-a	
Deliveries by destination: tonnage	EEC area & world regions	E 29-a	
for domestic smelting: tonnage	EEC countries	E 30-m	E 29-a
for export to non-EEC area: tonnage	EEC countries	E 29-a	
(overseas) by destination: tonnage	EEC countries	E 29-a	
Siemens Martin grade for steel production: tonnage	EEC countries	E 29-a	
Thomas grade for steel production: tonnage	EEC countries	E 29-a	
to EEC area: tonnage	EEC countries	E 29-a	
Exports (incl ferro-alloys) by destination: tonnage & value in $m	All countries	U 12-a	
tonnage	OECD countries	D 22-a	
	EEC countries	E 5-q	E 29-a
shipped to non-EEC area by value in $m	EEC countries	E 29-a	
shipped to EEC area by destination: tonnage	EEC area	E 3-a	
tonnage	Australia, Belgium, Netherlands, Japan & Sweden	T 2-m	
	ECE countries, Japan & USA	U 7-m	U 6-a
	Main countries	H 3-a	
	Canada, Japan, Main European countries & USA	C 5-m	
	USSR	T 1-a	
Import demand (net): tonnage	Developed countries (as group)	U 11-a	

417

	Territorial coverage	Title codes	
PIG IRON, continued			
Imports by source: tonnage	EEC countries	E 5-q	E 29-a
	Main countries	T 1-a	
		E 29-a	
ex non-EEC area by value in $m	OECD countries	D 22-a	
(incl ferro-alloys) by source: tonnage	All countries	U 12-a	
tonnage & value in $m	Main countries	B 15-a	
Imports & exports by source & destination: tonnage	Non-EEC area	E 3-a	
shipped into EEC area by source: tonnage	ECE countries, Japan & USA	U 7-m	U 6-a
tonnage	Main countries	H 3-a	
	Canada, Japan, Main European countries & USA	C 5-m	
Input of ferrous scrap in blast furnaces: tonnage	Main countries	T 4-a	
Inter-EEC area imports: tonnage		E 3-a	
imports & exports as % of world trade		E 30-q	
by value & as % of total trade		E 29-a	
New orders for domestic smelting: tonnage	EEC countries	E 29-a	
for export outside EEC area: tonnage	EEC countries	E 29-a	
for shipment within EEC area: tonnage	EEC countries	E 29-a	
received by iron & steel industry: tonnage	EEC countries	E 30-m	
Prices fixed by ECSC: Hematite pig iron by grade in local currency per ton	EEC countries	T 4-a	
Phosphoric pig iron by grade in local currency per ton	EEC countries	T 4-a	
Prices in $ per ton	USA	N 1-a	
(less tax but incl rebates) at main centres in local currency per ton	EEC countries	E 30-a2	
Production capacity: tonnage forecast to 1976	OECD countries	D 22-a	
maximum with existing plant	EEC countries	E 30-a	
Production potential by regions: tonnage	EEC countries	E 46-a	
Production: blast furnace ferro-alloys: tonnage	ECE countries	U 7-m	U 6-a
	Main countries	H 3-a	
by grade: historical table: tonnage	EEC countries	E 29-a	
by grade: non-phosphoric: tonnage	EEC countries	E 29-a	
phosphoric: tonnage	EEC countries	E 29-a	
tonnage	France	C 5-m	
by process: tonnage	All countries	B 15-a	
	ECE countries	U 7-m	U 6-a
	Main countries	H 3-a	
by region: tonnage	France	C 5-m	
	France & W Germany	E 29-a	
charcoal pig iron: tonnage	ECE countries	U 7-m	U 6-a
	Main countries	H 3-a	
coke pig iron: tonnage	ECE countries	U 7-m	U 6-a
	Main countries	H 3-a	
electric pig iron: tonnage	ECE countries	U 7-m	U 6-a
	Main countries	H 3-a	
ferro-manganese: tonnage	ECE countries	U 7-m	U 6-a
	Main countries	H 3-a	
for foundry castings: tonnage	ECE countries	U 7-m	U 6-a
	Main countries	H 3-a	
for steel-making: tonnage	ECE countries	U 7-m	U 6-a
	Main countries	H 3-a	
historical table from 1780: tonnage	Main European countries	Z 1-a	
in electric furnaces: tonnage	EEC countries	E 29-a	
(incl ferro-alloys) & world total: tonnage	All countries	R 5-a	
	African countries	U 44-a	
	All countries	B 15-a	N 5-a
		T 1-a	
	ECE countries	U 6-a	U 7-m
	Main countries	C 5-m	H 3-a
	OAS member countries	N 14-a	
	World regions	D 22-a	
low-shaft furnace iron: tonnage	ECE countries	U 7-m	U 6-a
	Main countries	H 3-a	
(over last decade): tonnage	EEC countries	E 29-a	
pig iron & ferro-alloys (all kinds): tonnage	All countries	U 27-m	U 43-a
pig iron: special qualities: tonnage	EEC countries	E 29-a	
spiegeleisen: tonnage	ECE countries	U 7-m	U 6-a
	Main countries	H 3-a	
Production tonnage & as % of crude steel production	EEC countries	E 30-m	
tonnage as % of existing capacity	EEC countries	E 30-a	
as % of world steel production	All countries	E 29-a	
tonnage	All countries	T 2-m	T 4-a
	E European countries & USSR	U 16-a	
	EEC countries	E 26-m	
	Main countries	E 3-a	
	S American countries & Mexico	U 40-a	
Receipts from EEC area: tonnage	EEC countries	E 29-a	
Shipments (ex steelworks): tonnage	USA	N 1-a	
Stocks held at works & users' premises: tonnage	USA	N 1-a	
Supply, domestic consumption & trade: tonnage	ECE countries	U 49-a	
Wholesale prices: Hematite iron in $ per ton	EEC countries	E 29-a2	
pig iron in $ per ton	Belgium, France, W Germany, UK & USA	U 27-m	
World production: historical table since 1870: tonnage		E 29-a	
(incl ferro-alloys): tonnage		C 30-a	N 4-a
		T 1-a	
	World regions	U 11-a	U 49-a
	Main countries	N 1-a	T 4-a

418

	Territorial coverage	Title codes

PIG IRON BY KIND
    Consumption: tonnage   ECE countries   U 7-q   U 6-a
          Main countries   H 3-a
    Domestic prices (basic) in local currency per ton   Main countries   T 4-a
    Imports: Hematite pig iron: tonnage   Main countries   T 1-a
            Phosphorous pig iron: tonnage   Main countries   T 1-a
    Production: tonnage   All countries   U 22-a
          ECE countries, Japan & USA   U 7-m   U 6-a
          EEC countries   E 30-m
          Main countries   H 3-a

PIG-MEAT
    see also   BACON
                   HAM
                   PORK
    Availability for consumption: tonnage   Main countries   B 11-a
    Consumption per capita in kg per yr   OECD countries   D 1-a
                     in lbs per yr   Main countries   B 11-a
    Exports by destination: tonnage   Main countries   B 12-m
          EEC countries   E 47-m
    Imports by source: tonnage   EEC countries   B 11-a
    Inter-EEC imports & exports: tonnage   EEC countries   E 47-m   B 12-a
    Price factors in EEC area trade: compensation payments in £ per ton   C 9-m
                                   export restitution payments in £ per ton   C 9-m
                                   import levies in £ per ton   C 9-m
                                   sluice-gate price-fixing in £ per ton   C 9-m
                                   supplementary levies in £ per ton   C 9-m
    Production (incl bacon): tonnage   OECD countries   D 1-a
                     tonnage (estim)   Main countries   B 11-a
    Reference prices in £ per score (dead wt)   EEC countries   C 9-m
    Retail prices - index nos   EEC countries   C 9-m
    Sluice-gate prices by kind of pig meat in $ per 100 kg   EEC countries   B 11-a
    Wholesale prices - index nos   EEC countries   C 9-m
    World production: pork, bacon & ham: tonnage   World regions   A 5-a

Pig-meat, preserved   see   PORK, SALTED OR DRIED

PIGMENTS, MINERAL
    see also   CHEMICAL PRODUCTS
                   IRON OXIDE
                   LITHARGE
                   LITHOPONE
                   PAINTS & VARNISHES
                   RED LEAD
                   TITANIUM DIOXIDE
                   WHITE LEAD
    Consumption: cobalt in production of pigments in lbs   USA   T 4-a
                    sulphuric acid in production of pigments: tonnage   OECD countries   D 5-a
    Exports: battery oxides: tonnage   USA   J 6-a
            litharge: tonnage   USA   J 6-a
            mineral pigments & paints by destination by value in $ Main countries   U 2-a
            red & white lead: tonnage   USA   J 6-a
    Imports & exports by source & destination: zinc oxide: tonnage   All countries   B 15-a
            litharge: tonnage   USA   J 6-a
            red & white lead: tonnage   USA   J 6-a
    Production: iron oxide: tonnage   OECD countries   D 5-a
               lithopone: tonnage   OECD countries   D 5-a
               titanium dioxide: tonnage   OECD countries   D 5-a

PIGS
    see also   PORK
    % change: auction prices of live pigs (over previous yr)   EEC countries   E 34-m
    % distribution for own consumption on farm   Czechoslovakia, Hungary & Poland   U 34-a
                    for sale & processing   Czechoslovakia, Hungary & Poland   U 34-a
                    for sale, consumption & processing   EEC countries   U 34-a
    % of EEC area pig population   EEC countries   R 5-a
    % price increases: compound feed for pigs   W European countries   U 30-a
    Auction prices: bacon pigs & hogs in £ per score   Main countries   B 12-a
                 live pigs (at local markets) per kg   EEC countries   E 34-m
    Average wt (at slaughter) in kg per head   OAS member countries   N 14-a
    Deliveries to bacon factories: volume   Eire   B 12-m
    Exports by destination: live pigs for slaughter: volume   EEC countries   E 47-m
                                  volume   Main countries   B 12-m
                    live pigs: volume   European countries   U 36-a
          Main countries   B 11-a
    Feed requirements per kg of pork production projected to 1985   Main countries   P 5-a
    Government expenditure: price guarantees for pig rearing in £m   UK   P 5-a
    Gross value: output (at current prices)   ECE countries   U 34-a
    Imports by source: volume   EEC countries   B 11-a
          Main countries   B 12-m
                     live pigs: volume   E & W European countries   U 36-a
          Main countries   B 11-a
    Inter-EEC imports & exports: tonnage   EEC countries   B 12-a
                    shipments: live pigs: volume   EEC countries   E 47-m
    Population & no of pigs per 100 ha   EEC countries   E 1-a   E 44-a

	Territorial coverage	Title codes	
PIGS, continued			
Population as % of total livestock population	EEC countries	E 44-a	
boars	EEC countries	C 9-m	
by administrative areas	EEC countries	E 38-a	
by age: breeding sows, boars & fattened pigs	EEC countries	E 1-a	
piglets & breeding sows	EEC countries	E 44-a	
census data	E European countries, & USSR (incl Ukraine)	U 16-a	
gilts, sows in pig & sows (for slaughter)	Denmark	B 12-m	
historical tables from 1816	Main European countries	Z 1-a	
in 1000 head (incl world total)	Main countries	R 5-a	
in 1000 head	AASM countries	E 41-a	
	African countries	U 44-a	
in million head	All countries	A 9-a	U 43-a
	European countries incl USSR	U 36-a	
	Main countries	B 11-a	E 3-a
	OAS member countries	N 13-a	
on state farms & collectives in million head	USSR	B 12-a	
piglets by wt: suckling pigs & boars	USSR	B 12-a	
pigs & sows	Denmark	B 12-m	
pigs in 1000 head (incl world total)	OECD countries	D 1-a	
	Main countries	R 5-a	
pigs under 6 mths, boars & breeding sows	EEC countries	B 1-a	
slaughter pigs (by wt classes)	EEC countries	C 9-m	
sows & gilts in pig	EEC countries	C 9-m	
sows (incl % change)	EEC countries	C 9-a	
suckling pigs (under 44lb wt)	EEC countries	C 9-m	
Prices paid (as state purchases) for pigs for slaughter in $	Poland	U 30-a	
Producer prices (all grades)	W European countries	U 30-a	
at auction in $	European countries	U 36-q	
in local currency per ton	OECD countries	D 1-a	
in £ per score	EEC countries	B 1-a	
pigs under & over 100 kg wt	EEC countries	E 44-a	
pigs (for bacon) in local currency per kg	Eire	D 1-a	
per 100 kg (live wt) in local currency	W European countries	E 35-a	
per 100 lbs (live wt) in $	USA	E 35-a	
Production costs on collective farms per ton	USSR	U 24-a	
Production by value & % gross farm output (incl crops)	E European countries	U 34-a	
by value in £m	EEC countries	B 1-a	
Production, imports, exports & consumption: tonnage	EEC countries	E 44-a	
tonnage	Czechoslovakia, Hungary & Poland	U 34-a	
volume	Latin American countries	J 5-a	
Ratios: barley prices to pig prices (live wt)	W European countries	U 30-a	
feeding stuff prices to pig prices (live wt)	W European countries	U 30-a	
maize prices to pig prices (live wt)	W European countries	U 30-a	
Slaughterings & carcase wt in kg (average)	EEC countries	E 1-a	E 44-a
tonnage (carcase wt)	European countries	U 36-q	
	Main countries	B 12-m	
volume (actual & foreward forecast)	EEC countries	C 9-a	
volume	All countries	A 9-a	
	Main countries	B 11-a	
Sluice-gate prices: live pigs & farrowed sows in $	EEC area	B 11-a	
Unit value (for slaughter) - index nos	W European countries	U 30-a	
Wholesale prices: ex abattoirs in Fr per 100 kg	France	E 34-m	
for slaughter in local currency	OAS member countries	N 17-a	
gilts, barrows & dressed hogs in $	Canada & USA	B 11-a	
in $ per 100 lbs (live wt) at Chicago Market	USA	R 2-m	
in local currency per kg	Argentina, W Germany & USA	A 9-a	
pigs (for bacon) & fat prices per ton	European countries	B 11-a	
Wholesale prices in local currency per ton	Canada, Eire, UK & USA	B 12-m	
PIGSKINS			
Production: skins (untanned): tonnage	OAS member countries	N 14-a	
Piling see STEEL SHEET PILING			
PILING, WOODEN			
Exports: posts & poles: tonnage	Canada, European countries, USA & USSR	A 13-q	
Imports: posts & poles: tonnage	Canada, European countries, USA & USSR	A 13-q	
Pilots & co-pilots see AIRCRAFT PERSONNEL			
Pimento see SPICES & ESSENCES			
Pineapple juice see FRUIT JUICES			
PINEAPPLES, CANNED			
% share of world supply (wt basis)	All countries	A 8-a	
Consumption (domestic): tonnage	Mexico	B 6-a	
per capita in kg	Main countries	A 8-a	
Exports by destination: tonnage	Malaya	B 5-a	
	Mexico	B 6-a	
by value in $	Philippines	U 32-m	
tonnage	All countries	A 8-a	
Production: tonnage	All countries	A 8-a	
	Mexico	B 6-a	
Unit import value by source in $	Main countries	A 8-a	
Wholesale prices in $ per doz cans	European countries	A 8-a	

	Territorial coverage	Title codes

PINEAPPLES, FRESH
    see also PINEAPPLES, CANNED

Imports by source: tonnage	OECD countries	D 37-a
Production: tonnage	OAS member countries	N 13-a
	All countries	A 9-a B 5-a
	Latin American countries	U 40-a
World production: tonnage	All countries	A 8-a

Pipe tobacco   see   TOBACCO

Pipelines, gas   see   GAS PIPELINES

Pipelines, natural gas   see   NATURAL GAS PIPELINES

Pipelines, oil   see   CRUDE OIL PIPELINES
                                REFINED OIL PIPELINES

PIPES, CAST-IRON

Exports by destination: tonnage	Main countries	T 4-a
pipes (incl tubes & fittings): tonnage	Main countries	T 2-m
as % of home production	UK	B 25-a
tonnage	ECE countries, Japan & USA	U 7-m U 6-a
	Main countries	H 3-a
Imports by source: tonnage	Main countries	T 4-a
tonnage	ECE countries, Japan & USA	U 7-m U 6-a
	Main countries	H 3-a
Production requirements (projected): tonnage	UK	B 25-a
tonnage	Main countries	T 4-a

Pipes, ceramic   see   EARTHENWARE PRODUCTS

Pipes, concrete   see   BUILDING MATERIALS

Pipes, lead   see   LEAD PRODUCTS, SEMI-FINISHED

Pitch   see   COAL BY-PRODUCTS

Pitprops   see   TIMBER

Placer platinum   see   PLATINUM-GROUP METALS

Plague   see   DISEASES, CONTAGIOUS

Plaice, halibut & sole   see   FISH

Planes, commercial   see   AIRCRAFT

Planning, economic   see   DEVELOPMENT PLANS

Planning, financial   see   BUDGET ACCOUNTS

Plant & equipment   see   INVESTMENT

PLANT CAPACITY
    see also REFINERY CAPACITY
                 SMELTING CAPACITY

% utilisation in production of acrylics	European countries, Japan & USA	D 27-a
of polyamides	European countries, Japan & USA	D 27-a
of polyester	European countries, Japan & USA	D 27-a
Acetaldehyde production: tonnage	European countries	U 26-a
Acetate staple & filament production: tonnage	Canada, European countries, Japan & USA	D 27-a
Acetylene production: tonnage	OECD countries	D 5-a
Acrylic staple production: tonnage	Canada, European countries, Japan & USA	D 27-a
Aluminium ingots production by specific companies: tonnage	USA	J 6-a
Aluminium reduction plants of specific companies: tonnage	Main countries	J 6-a
Ammonia production (incl world total): tonnage	Continents	U 25-a
Benzine production: tonnage	OECD countries	D 5-a
Blister copper production: tonnage by specific companies	Worldwide	C 12-a
Butadiene production: tonnage	European countries & USSR	U 26-a
Butylene production: tonnage	OECD countries	D 5-a
Caustic soda production: tonnage	OECD countries	D 5-a
Cellulosic filament production (all kinds): tonnage	Canada, European countries, Japan & USA	D 27-a
Cellulosic staple production (all kinds): tonnage	Canada, European countries, Japan & USA	D 27-a
Cement industry: % rate of plant capacity utilisation	OECD countries	D 4-a
Cement production: increase in capacity from new grinding mills	OECD countries	D 4-a
from new kilns	OECD countries	D 4-a
tonnage	Main countries	N 1-a
	OECD countries	D 4-a
Chlorine production: tonnage	OECD countries	D 5-a
Copper refining by specific companies: tonnage	Worldwide	C 12-a
Crude steel ingots production (by process): tonnage	EEC countries	E 29-a
Cycloakenes production: tonnage	OECD countries	D 5-a
Ethyl alcohol production: tonnage	OECD countries	D 5-a
Ethylene oxide production: tonnage	European countries	U 26-a
Ethylene production: tonnage	OECD countries	D 5-a
Fertiliser production: tonnage	Canada & USA	A 2-a
Fibreboard production: volume in m³	Main countries	A 25-a

	Territorial coverage	Title codes
PLANT CAPACITY, continued		
Finished steel products production: tonnage	Main countries	U 57-a
Formaldehyde production: tonnage	European countries	U 26-a
Hydrocarbons production: tonnage	OECD countries	D 5-a
Lead refining by specific companies: tonnage	Worldwide	C 12-a
Maleic anhydride production: tonnage	European countries	U 26-a
Man-made fibres production by kind: tonnage	Canada, European countries, Japan & USA	D 27-a
Metallic zinc refining by specific companies: tonnage	Worldwide	C 12-a
Methane production: tonnage	OECD countries	D 5-a
Naphthalene production: tonnage	OECD countries	D 5-a
Newsprint plants: new production capacity presently planned	Worldwide	J 4-a
under construction	Worldwide	J 4-a
Newsprint production by area: tonnage	Canada & USA	J 4-a
tonnage	All countries	J 7-a
	Finland, Norway & Sweden	J 4-a
Non-cellulosic filament production: tonnage	Canada, European countries, Japan & USA	D 27-a
man-made fibres production: world capacity in lbs		B 10-a
staple production: tonnage	Canada, European countries, Japan & USA	D 27-a
Organic chemicals production: tonnage	OECD countries	D 5-a
Paper & paperboard production: tonnage	All countries	J 7-a
	Canada, Main European countries & USA	D 40-a
Particle board (wood-based) production: volume in m³	All countries	A 25-a
Phthalic anhydride: tonnage	European countries	U 26-a
Pig iron production: tonnage	EEC countries	E 29-a
Plywood & blockboard production: volume in m³	All countries	A 25-a
Plywood & soft & hard blockboard production: volume in m³	All countries	A 26-a
Polyamide staple & filament production: tonnage	European countries, Japan & USA	D 27-a
Polyester staple & filament production: tonnage	European countries, Japan & USA	D 27-a
Poromerics production (by brand name) by volume in sq ft	Main countries	A 18-a
Power stations (by type) for electricity generation in kW	All countries	C 23-a
Propylene production: tonnage	OECD countries	D 5-a
Rayon & acetate fibre production: tonnage	All countries	J 7-a
Rayon filament & yarn production in lbs	All countries	J 7-a
Rayon staple & filament production: tonnage	Canada, European countries, Japan & USA	D 27-a
Rotary cement kilns: no existing (wet dry) & capacity: tonnage	OECD countries	D 4-a
no newly installed & capacity: tonnage	OECD countries	D 4-a
Silver-lead: refining by specific company: tonnage	All countries	J 6-a
smelting by specific company: tonnage	All countries	J 6-a
Soda ash production: tonnage	OECD countries	D 5-a
Steel axles (for rolling stock) production: tonnage	Main countries	U 57-a
coils production: tonnage	Main countries	U 57-a
plates (heavy) production: tonnage	Main countries	U 57-a
products (cold-rolled) production: tonnage	Main countries	U 57-a
(hot-rolled) production: tonnage	Main countries	U 57-a
sections (heavy, medium & light) production: tonnage	Main countries	U 57-a
sheets (under 3mm gauge) production: tonnage	Main countries	U 57-a
tubes (seamless & welded) production: tonnage	Main countries	U 57-a
wire rods production: tonnage	Main countries	U 57-a
Synthetic rubber production: tonnage	World regions	B 13-a U 26-a
Toluene production: tonnage	OECD countries	D 5-a
Uranium production: tonnage	Australia, Canada, Portugal & USA	D 48
Utilisation in manufacturing industry - index nos	USA	J 2-a
Vertical cement kilns: no & existing capacity: tonnage	OECD countries	D 4-a
no & newly-installed capacity: tonnage	OECD countries	D 4-a
Wood pulp production by kind: tonnage	All countries	J 7-a
tonnage	Canada, Main European countries & USA	D 40-a
Xylene production: tonnage	OECD countries	D 5-a
Zinc (electrolytic) production by specific companies: tonnage	Worldwide	J 6-a
slabs production (by distillation process): tonnage	USA	J 6-a
(by electrolytic process): tonnage	USA	J 6-a
smelting by specific companies: tonnage	Main countries	J 6-a
PLANTATION CROPS BY KIND		
see also COCOA		
COFFEE		
LAND UTILISATION		
RUBBER		
SPICES & ESSENCES		
TEA		
TOBACCO		
TROPICAL PRODUCTS		
Exports: unit value in $ per ton	Worldwide	A 11-a
Imports: tonnage	Main countries	A 11-a
Plantations see LAND UTILISATION		
PLANTATIONS, COFFEE		
Loan advances from banking system in local currency	OAS member countries	N 16-a
Wages: plantation workers in local currency	OAS member countries	N 17-a
PLANTATIONS, PALM OIL		
Mature planted areas in acres	Malaysia	B 19-a
No of estates in production	Indonesia & Malaysia	B 19-a

	Territorial coverage	Title codes
PLANTATIONS, RUBBER		
Area (incl smallholdings) by size in acres	Sri Lanka	B 13-a
of estates in ha	All countries	C 18-a
of smallholdings by size in groups in acres	Sri Lanka	B 13-a
in ha	All countries	C 18-a
Earnings: estate workers in M$	Malaysia	U 32-m
No of smallholdings by size groups in acres	Sri Lanka	B 13-a
Production on estates: tonnage	Main countries	C 18-m
PLANTATIONS, SUGAR		
Wages: sugar cane cutters in local currency per hr	OAS member countries	N 17-a
PLANTATIONS, TEA		
Area: extensions under crop in ha	All countries	C 1-a
replacements under crop in ha	All countries	C 1-a
replantings with crop in ha	All countries	C 1-a
under crop (at end-yr) in ha	All countries	C 1-a
No of tea estates registered (end-March)	India	P 6-a
Wages: estate workers - index nos	Sri Lanka	U 32-m

Planters & transplanting machines   see   SEEDERS & PLANTERS

Plaster   see   BUILDING MATERIALS

	Territorial coverage	Title codes	
PLASTIC-COATED TEXTILES			
Production: volume	EEC countries	E 28-q	E 27-a
PLASTICS			
see also NATURAL GUMS			
% change in exports (value basis)	European countries, Japan & USA	U 25-a	
in imports (value basis)	European countries, Japan & USA	U 25-a	
% consumption by use: agricultural uses	Main European countries	U 26-a	
by building construction industry	Main European countries	U 26-a	
consumer durables industry	Main European countries	U 26-a	
furniture industry	Main European countries	U 26-a	
packaging industry	Main European countries	U 26-a	
toy industry	Main European countries	U 26-a	
in domestic wares production	Main European countries	U 26-a	
in electrical goods production	Main European countries	U 26-a	
% rate of production increases: condensation products	Main countries	U 26-a	
polymerisation products	Main countries	U 26-a	
Consumption per capita in kg	European countries, Japan & USA	U 26-a	
	OECD countries	D 5-a	
polymerisation products in kg	OECD countries	D 5-a	
soybean oil in production of plastics & resins	USA	B 19-a	
Exports by destination: artificial resins: tonnage & value in $m	Main countries	U 2-a	
cellulosic derivatives: tonnage	OECD countries	D 5-a	
condensation products: tonnage	OECD countries	D 5-a	
plastic materials: tonnage	OECD countries	D 5-a	
polycondensation products: tonnage	Main countries	U 2-a	
polymerisation products: tonnage	Main countries	U 2-a	
	OECD countries	D 5-a	
regenerated cellulose: tonnage & value in $m	Main countries	U 2-a	
fibres: tonnage	Main countries	U 2-a	
silicones: tonnage	Main countries	U 2-a	
cellulose & artificial resins: tonnage	Main countries	U 26-a	
condensation products: tonnage	European countries, Japan & USA	U 26-a	
polyethylene: tonnage	European countries, Japan & USA	U 26-a	
polymerisation products: tonnage	European countries, Japan & USA	U 26-a	
polypropylene: tonnage	European countries, Japan & USA	U 26-a	
polystyrene: tonnage	European countries, Japan & USA	U 26-a	
polyvinylchloride: tonnage	European countries, Japan & USA	U 26-a	
regenerated cellulose: tonnage	European countries, Japan & USA	U 26-a	
tonnage	ECE countries	U 15-a	
Imports by source: cellulosic derivatives: tonnage	OECD countries	D 5-a	
condensation products: tonnage	OECD countries	D 5-a	
plastic materials: tonnage	OECD countries	D 5-a	
polymerisation products: tonnage	OECD countries	D 5-a	
by value in $m & as % of imports of all chemical products	Main countries	U 25-a	
cellulose & artificial resins: tonnage	Main countries	U 26-a	
condensation products: tonnage	European countries, Japan & USA	U 26-a	
plastics materials by value in $m	OECD countries	D 5-a	
polyethylene: tonnage	European countries, Japan & USA	U 26-a	
polymerisation products: tonnage	European countries, Japan & USA	U 26-a	
polypropylene: tonnage	European countries, Japan & USA	U 26-a	
polystyrene: tonnage	European countries, Japan & USA	U 26-a	
polyvinylchloride: tonnage	European countries, Japan & USA	U 26-a	
regenerated cellulose: tonnage	European countries, Japan & USA	U 26-a	
tonnage	ECE countries	U 15-a	
Labour costs per hr: plastic materials manufacturing industry	EEC countries	E 2-a	
Plant investment (incl in synthetic rubber production plants) in £m	UK	B 21-a	
Polyvinylchloride: % consumption for production of bottles	Main countries	U 26-a	
cables	Main countries	U 26-a	
flooring	Main countries	U 26-a	
pipes, foil & sheets	Main countries	U 26-a	
exports: tonnage	European countries, Japan & USA	U 26-a	

	Territorial coverage	Title codes	
PLASTICS, continued			
Production capacity: polyvinylchloride: tonnage	Main countries	U 26-a	
Production: aminoplastics: tonnage	OECD countries	D 5-a	
by kind (incl alykd resins): tonnage	All countries	U 22-a	
	EEC countries	E 28-q	E 27-a
by kind by value in $m	OECD countries	D 5-a	
cellulose & artificial resin: tonnage	ECE countries	U 15-a	
cellulose derivatives: tonnage	OECD countries	D 5-a	
cellulose derivatives – index nos	OECD countries	D 5-a	
condensation products: tonnage	Main countries	U 26-a	
	OECD countries	D 5-a	
hardened casein: tonnage	OECD countries	D 5-a	
(incl alkyd resins): tonnage	All countries	U 27-m	U 43-a
	E European countries & USSR	U 16-a	
per capita in kg (estim)	European countries	U 26-a	
plastic materials: tonnage	OECD countries	D 5-a	
	EEC countries	E 26-m	
polyethylene: tonnage	All countries	U 22-a	
	European countries, Japan & USA	U 26-a	
polymerisation products: tonnage	Main countries	U 26-a	
	OECD countries	D 5-a	
polymerisation products – index nos	OECD countries	D 5-a	
polyolefines: tonnage	OECD countries	D 5-a	
polypropylene: tonnage	European countries, Japan & USA	U 26-a	
	All countries	U 22-a	
polystyrene: tonnage	All countries	U 22-a	
	European countries, Japan & USA	U 26-a	
	OECD countries	D 5-a	
polyvinyl chloride: tonnage	All countries	U 22-a	
	OECD countries	D 5-a	
	European countries, Japan & USA	U 26-a	
regenerated cellulose: tonnage	Main countries	U 26-a	
synthetic resins: tonnage	Italy	C 6-a	
tonnage	All countries	R 5-a	
	European countries, Japan & USA	U 26-a	
value of output (gross & net) in £m	UK	B 21-a	
PLASTICS INDUSTRY			
Capital formation in $m	Main countries	U 21-a	
Costs: salaried staff in local currency per mth	EEC countries	E 11-a	
Gross output: value in $m	Main countries	U 21-a	
Investment in buildings in local currency	EEC countries	E 40-a	
in land purchase in local currency	EEC countries	E 40-a	
in machinery in local currency	EEC countries	E 40-a	
Labour costs (all employees) in local currency per hr	EEC countries	E 11-a	
as % of total costs	EEC countries	E 8-a	
by status of employee in local currency	EEC countries	E 8-a	
wage earners in local currency per hr	EEC countries	E 11-a	
Labour force: no of operatives employed	Main countries	U 21-a	
salaried staff employed	EEC countries	E 11-a	
wage earners employed	EEC countries	E 11-a	
wage earners & salaried staff employed	EEC countries	E 8-a	
No of hrs worked per yr	EEC countries	E 8-a	
per wk	Main countries	R 3-m	
per wk by region	EEC countries	E 25-a	
per yr: salaried staff	EEC countries	E 11-a	
wage earners	EEC countries	E 11-a	
Wage rates by sex in local currency per hr	EEC countries	E 25-a2	
	Main countries	R 3-m	
Wages & salary costs in $m	Main countries	U 21-a	
Plate glass see GLASS & GLASS PRODUCTS			
PLATES & SHEETS, ALUMINIUM			
Consumption: tonnage	UK & USA	T 4-a	
Despatches: tonnage	OECD countries	D 21-a	
	UK	C 30-a	
Exports by destination: tonnage	Main countries	T 4-a	
Imports by source: tonnage	Main countries	T 4-a	
Production: tonnage	All countries	U 22-a	
	Main countries	T 4-a	
Sales: wrought aluminium products (incl strip): tonnage	USA	J 6-a	
Wholesale prices: aluminium sheets in Fr	France	T 4-q	
PLATES & SHEETS, COPPER			
Exports by destination: tonnage	Main countries	T 4-a	
	USA	J 6-a	
Imports by source: tonnage	USA	J 6-a	
	W Germany & USA	T 4-a	
Production: tonnage	All countries	U 22-a	
	European countries, Japan, UK & USA	T 4-a	
	Japan & UK	C 12-a	
	Main countries	C 30-m	
Usage: building industry: tonnage	USA	J 6-a	
consumer products manufacturing industry: tonnage	USA	J 6-a	
electrical engineering industry: tonnage	USA	J 6-a	
machinery & equipment manufacturing industry: tonnage	USA	J 6-a	
transport equipment manufacturing industry: tonnage	USA	J 6-a	
Wholesale prices in local currency per kg	Japan & UK	T 4-w	

	Territorial coverage	Title codes	
PLATES & SHEETS, COPPER ALLOY			
Exports by destination: tonnage	Main countries	T 4-a	
Imports by source: tonnage	Main countries	T 4-a	
Production: tonnage	Main countries	T 4-a	
PLATES & SHEETS, STEEL			
see also GALVANISED SHEETS			
PLATES, UNIVERSAL			
Basic domestic prices in $ per ton	OECD countries	D 22-a	
Consumption: tonnage	EEC countries	E 29-a	
	OECD countries	D 22-a	
Deliveries (by gauge) by dealers: tonnage	EEC countries	E 30-m	E 29-a
(home & export): tonnage	OECD countries	D 22-a	
shipped to EEC area: tonnage	EEC countries	E 29-a	
Export prices in $ per ton	OECD countries	D 22-a	
Exports by destination: tonnage	EEC countries	E 5-q	E 29-a
	ECE countries	U 48-a	
	Main countries	T 4-a	
tonnage & % share	Main countries	U 49-a	
Imports by source: tonnage	EEC countries	E 5-q	E 29-a
	Main countries	T 4-a	
by value in $	Indonesia	U 32-m	
Inter-EEC trade: tonnage & value in $m	EEC countries	E 29-a	
Prices (incl hot-rolled sheets) in $ per ton	EEC countries	E 30-a	
Production by type: tonnage	All countries	U 22-a	
cold-rolled sheets: tonnage	EEC countries	E 30-m	
heavy & light gauges: tonnage	OECD countries	D 22-a	
hot-rolled plates & sheets by kind: tonnage	EEC countries	E 30-m	
plates: tonnage	Latin American countries	U 40-a	
tonnage	EEC countries	E 28-q	E 27-a
		E 29-a	
	Main countries	T 4-a	
Receipts (by dealers) by gauge: tonnage	EEC countries	E 29-a	
from EEC area: tonnage	EEC countries	E 29-a	
PLATES & SHEETS, TINNED			
Exports by destination: tonnage	Main countries	T 4-a	
Imports by source: tonnage	Main countries	T 4-a	
Production: tonnage	Main countries	T 4-a	
PLATES & SHEETS, TITANIUM			
Sales in lbs	USA	J 6-a	
PLATES, SHEETS & STRIP, NICKEL			
Exports by destination: tonnage	UK & USA	T 4-a	
PLATES, SHEETS & STRIP, ZINC			
Exports by destination: tonnage	Main countries	T 4-a	
Production (incl wire): tonnage	UK	T 4-a	
tonnage	All countries	U 22-a	
zinc sheets: tonnage	France	T 4-a	
PLATES, HEAVY			
Export prices: hot-rolled plates in $ per 100 lbs	USA	R 2-m	
over 4.75 mm gauge (Thomas quality) in FrB per ton	Belgium	R 2-m	
Exports by destination: tonnage	Main countries	T 4-a	
heavy & medium plates: tonnage	E European countries	T 1-a	
plates over 4.75 mm gauge: tonnage	European countries, Japan & USA	C 5-m	
	ECE countries	U 7-m	U 6-a
	Main countries	H 3-a	
Imports: alloy steel plates: tonnage	Main countries	T 1-a	
by quality: tonnage	Main countries	T 1-a	
by source: tonnage	Main countries	T 4-a	
high carbon steel plates: tonnage	Main countries	T 1-a	
plates over 4.75 mm gauge: tonnage	European countries & Japan	C 5-m	
	ECE countries	U 7-m	U 6-a
	Main countries	H 3-a	
stainless steel plates: tonnage	Main countries	T 1-a	
Production potential by regions: tonnage	EEC countries	E 46-a	
Production: steel plates over 4.75 mm gauge: tonnage	W Germany	C 5-m	
	ECE countries	U 7-m	U 6-a
	Main countries	H 3-a	
	OAS member countries	N 14-a	
under 4.75 mm gauge: tonnage	OAS member countries	N 14-a	
tonnage	Main countries	T 4-a	
Wholesale prices in $ per ton	Main countries	U 49-m	U 57-a
PLATES, MEDIUM			
Exports by destination: tonnage	Main countries	T 4-a	
steel plates up to 4.75 mm gauge: tonnage	ECE countries	U 7-m	U 6-a
	Main countries	H 3-a	
tonnage	European countries	C 5-m	
Imports by source: tonnage	Main countries	T 4-a	
steel plates up to 4.75 mm gauge: tonnage	ECE countries	U 7-m	U 6-a
	Main countries	H 3-a	

		Territorial coverage	Title codes	

PLATES, MEDIUM continued
    Production: steel plates up to 4.75 mm gauge: tonnage   ECE countries   U 7-m   U 6-a
                                                             Main countries   H 3-a
            tonnage   Main countries   T 4-a
                        W Germany   C 5-m

PLATES, UNIVERSAL
    Deliveries to user industries: tonnage   ECE countries   U 7-q   U 6-a
                                              Main countries   H 3-a
    Exports by destination: tonnage   Main countries   T 4-a
                         tonnage   European countries, Japan & USA   C 5-m
    Imports by source: tonnage   Main countries   T 4-a
                     tonnage   European countries, Japan & USA   C 5-m
                                    Main countries   T 1-a
    Inter-EEC trade: tonnage & value in $m   EEC countries   E 29-a
    Production: tonnage   All countries   T 1-a
                          Main countries   T 4-a

Plating anodes   see   ANODES

PLATING SALTS
        see also   ANODES
    Consumption: cadmium in production of plating salts: tonnage   UK   T 4-a

PLATINUM
    Consumption by chemical industry in oz   USA   T 4-a
                           electrical industry in oz   USA   T 4-a
                           glass manufacturing industry in oz   USA   T 4-a
                           jewellery industry in oz   USA   T 4-a
                           petroleum refining industry in oz   USA   T 4-a
                           for dental & medical purposes in oz   USA   T 4-a
                           (incl palladium) in oz   USA   J 6-a
    Contract prices: pure refined metal in £ per oz   UK   R 2-m
                                      in $ per oz   USA   R 2-m
    Export prices in $ per oz fob   USA   T 4-w
    Imports by source in oz   Main countries   T 4-a
    Imports & exports by source & destination by kind in oz   Main countries   B 15-a
    Producer prices: refined metal in $ per oz   USA   C 12-m
    Production: crude platinum metals in kg   Colombia, S Africa & USSR   B 15-a
                                           Colombia   U 40-a
                              in oz   Main countries   B 15-a
    Recovery of platinum at refineries in oz   USA   J 6-a
    Wholesale prices by grade in lire per gramme   Italy   C 12-m
                         (free market) in £ per oz   UK   T 4-w
                         in $ per oz (ex main New York dealers)   USA   C 12-m   N 1-a
                         pure refined metal in £ per oz   UK   T 4-w   R 2-m
    World production: platinum group metals in kg   C 12-a
                                tonnage   C 30-a

PLATINUM, REFINED
    Export prices: palladium in $ per oz   USA   T 4-w
    Government strategic stockpile: iridium: tonnage   USA   N 1-a
                                               palladium: tonnage   USA   N 1-a
    Imports: iridium, osmium & ruthenium in oz   Japan   T 4-a
              palladium by source in oz   Japan   T 4-a
              rhodium by source in oz   Japan   T 4-a
    Producer prices: osmium in £ per oz   UK   T 4-m
                      palladium in £ per oz   UK   T 4-m
    Production: new platinum metals by kind: tonnage   USA   B 15-a
                palladium: tonnage   Japan & Philippines   C 12-a
    Recoveries by kind at refineries in oz   USA   T 4-a
                 iridium at refineries in oz   USA   J 6-a
                 palladium at refineries in oz   USA   J 6-a
    Sales (incl palladium) for dental purposes in oz   USA   J 6-a
                         to chemical industry in oz   USA   J 6-a
                             glass industry in oz   USA   J 6-a
                             jewellery industry in oz   USA   J 6-a
                             petroleum industry in oz   USA   J 6-a
    Wholesale prices: iridium powder in local currency per oz   UK & USA   T 4-m
                        rhodium in £ per oz   UK   T 4-m
                        ruthenium in £ per oz   UK   T 4-w

PLATINUM ORE
    Exports by destination (incl concentrates): tonnage   Canada   T 4-a
                           (incl concentrates): tonnage   Canada & USA   B 15-a
    Imports (incl concentrates): tonnage   UK & USA   B 15-a

PLATINUM PRODUCTS
    Imports: platinum bars, rods, sheet & wire in oz   Main countries   B 15-a

PLATINUM SCRAP
    Imports: scrap metal & sponge: tonnage   USA   B 15-a

	Territorial coverage	Title codes
PLATINUM-GROUP METALS		
Consumption: tonnage	USA	N 1-a
Exports by destination (in ingots) in oz	UK	T 4-a
iridium, platinum alloys & palladium in oz	UK	T 4-a
rhodium in oz	UK	T 4-a
tonnage	Main countries	T 4-a
Imports by source in oz	Main countries	T 4-a
Production at mines: tonnage	USA	N 1-a
at refineries: tonnage	USA	N 1-a
in oz	All countries	J 6-a
placer platinum in oz	All countries	C 12-a
osmiridium: tonnage	S Africa	C 12-a
Recoveries at refineries: iridium, palladium & platinum in oz	USA	J 6-a
Stocks held at dealers' premises & refineries in oz	USA	N 1-a
platinum & palladium in oz	USA	T 4-a
Wholesale prices: palladium & platinum in $ per oz	USA	N 1-a
World production by kind in kg		C 12-a
in oz		N 4-a
tonnage (at mines)	Main countries	N 1-a
World reserves in oz (estim)	Main countries	N 1-a
PLATINUM-GROUP METALS BY KIND		
Exports by destination in oz	UK	T 4-a
Imports: iridium in oz	USA	J 6-a
nuggets & grains in oz	USA	J 6-a
ores & concentrates in oz	USA	J 6-a
osmiridium & osmium in oz	USA	J 6-a
palladium & platinum in oz	USA	J 6-a
platinum scrap & sponge in oz	USA	J 6-a
rhodium in oz	USA	J 6-a
ruthenium in oz	USA	J 6-a
Sales to electrical industry in oz	USA	J 6-a
to industrial users in oz	USA	J 6-a
PLOUGHS		
Production: all kinds (incl animal-drawn): volume	All countries	U 38-a
tractor & animal-drawn ploughs: volume	All countries	U 22-a

Plumbago   see   GRAPHITE

Plums   see   FRUIT, FRESH

Plutonium   see   NUCLEAR FUELS

PLYWOOD & BLOCKBOARD
    see also   WOOD-BASED PANELS

	Territorial coverage	Title codes	
% contribution to export earnings	Gabon	E 45-a	
Consumption - index nos	European countries excl USSR	A 24-a	
by volume in m³	European countries, USA & USSR	A 26-a	
plywood per capita in m³	All countries	A 25-a	
Exports by destination by volume in m³	Canada, European countries & USA	A 13-q	
by volume in m³	Main countries	A 25-a2	A 26-a
(incl veneered panels) by value in UA	AASM countries	E 41-a	
shipped to EEC area (incl veneered panels) by value in UA	AASM countries	E 41-a	
unit value in Fmk per m³	Finland	A 25-m	
Imports by source by volume in m³	Canada, European countries & USA	A 13-q	
	Canada, UK & USA	A 25-a	
by volume in m³	Main countries & USSR	A 26-a	
	Main countries	A 25-a2	
unit value in £ per ton	UK	A 25-m	
Imports - index nos (value basis)	W Germany	A 25-m	
No of factories producing blockboard	All countries	A 26-a	
plywood	All countries	A 26-a	
in production	Main countries	A 25-a	
Production & requirement forecast by volume in m³	European countries	A 24-a	
Production, consumption & trade by volume in m³	Main countries	A 25-a	
blockboard by volume in m³	All countries	A 26-a	
	European countries	A 25-a	
by volume in m³ (incl world total)	All countries	A 5-a	
by volume in m³	Canada, European countries, USA & USSR	A 13-q	A 26-a
plywood (all kinds) by volume in m³	European countries	A 25-a	
	OAS member countries	N 14-a	
(hard) by volume in m³	All countries	A 26-a	
(soft) by volume in m³	All countries	A 26-a	
Wholesale prices - index nos	W Germany	A 25-m	

PNEUMATIC TYRE INDUSTRY

Wage rates per hr in local currency	OAS member countries	N 17-a

Pneumoconiosis   see   DISEASES, INDUSTRIAL

Pneumonia   see   DISEASES

Poliomyelitis   see   DISEASES, INFECTIOUS

Polishing preparations, domestic   see   CLEANING & POLISHING
                                              PREPARATIONS

	Territorial coverage	Title codes

Pollucite concentrates   see   CESIUM ORE

Pollution research   see   AIR POLLUTION
RESEARCH & DEVELOPMENT

Polyacids   see   ACIDS, ORGANIC

Polyacrylic & polyamide (nylon) fibres   see   MAN-MADE FIBRES
NON-CELLULOSIC FIBRES

Polyamide yarn   see   YARN, NON-CELLULOSIC

Polybutadiene   see   SYNTHETIC RUBBER

POLYESTER
    see also   MAN-MADE FIBRES

Consumption: fibre by textile industry: tonnage	OECD countries	D 46-a
in spinning mills: tonnage	OECD countries	D 46-a
yarn in production of women's stockings: tonnage	EEC countries	K 4-a
Export prices: "Dacron" fibre in cents per lb	USA	R 2-m
in cents per lb	USA	K 1-m
terylene fibre in pence per kg	UK	R 2-m
Exports (incl condensation products): tonnage	Main countries	U 2-a
Plant capacity: production of polyester: tonnage	Canada, European countries, Japan & USA	D 27-a
Production as % of all synthetic fibres	Canada, European countries, Japan & USA	D 27-a
polyester fibre in lbs	Main countries	B 10-a
& yarn: tonnage	European countries, Japan & USA	K 4-a
polyester fibres: tonnage	OECD countries	D 46-a
Wholesale prices in cents per lb	USA	A 9-a

Polyester yarn   see   YARN, NON-CELLULOSIC

Polyethylene   see   PLASTICS

Polyisoprene   see   SYNTHETIC RUBBER

Polymerisation products & polyolefines   see   PLASTICS

Polypropylene & polystyrene   see   PLASTICS

Polyvinyl compounds   see   MAN-MADE FIBRES
NON-CELLULOSIC FIBRES

Polyvinylchloride (PVC)   see   PLASTICS

Poonac (coconut cake)   see   OILCAKE & MEAL

POP CORN

Area harvested in ha, production tonnage & yield per ha	All countries	A 9-a

POPPY SEED
    see also   OPIUM

Exports: tonnage	Netherlands, Poland & Turkey	B 19-a
Imports: tonnage	Austria, Denmark, W Germany & Netherlands	B 19-a
Production & domestic consumption: tonnage	Austria	D 14-a

POPPY STRAW

Exports by destination in kg	All countries	U 46-a
concentrates by destination in kg	All countries	U 46-a

POPULATION
    see also   GROSS REPRODUCTION RATES
HOUSEHOLDS
VITAL STATISTICS
WORLD POPULATION (Appendix 4)

% adults by age groups	W European countries	Z 3	
% change since 1960 (at 5 yr intervals)	E European countries	N 6	
by regions	Latin American countries	J 5-a	
(by 5 yr age groups) projected to 1990	E European countries	N 6	
% employed & unemployed by administrative areas	EEC countries	E 38-a	
in manufacturing industry	Developing countries	U 52-a	
% growth rates by administrative areas	EEC countries	E 18-a	
density of population	World regions	U 43-a	
historical table from 1900	Canada, Latin American countries & USA	J 5-a	
in 5 yr periods	Main countries	R 5	
population of working age (over decades)	ECAFE countries	U 17	
projected to 1985	All countries	A 1	U 13-a
to yr 2000	World regions	L 3	
rural & urban areas	European countries & USA	U 5-a	
rural, urban & big city populations	All countries	U 13-a	
school-age populations projected to 1980	OECD countries	D 11	
standard deviation from average natural increase	EEC countries	E 37-a	
% living in industrialised areas	EEC countries	E 37-a	
semi-industrialised areas	EEC countries	E 37-a	
urban & rural areas	African countries	U 44-a	

POPULATION, continued

	Territorial coverage	Title codes	
% of population by regional socio-economic categories	EEC countries	E 37-a	
earning a living by age groups	EEC countries	E 18-a	
of EEC area	EEC countries	E 18-a	
presently unemployed by administrative areas	EEC countries	E 18-a	
Age of population (worldwide) projected to yr 2000		L 3	
Agricultural population as % of total population	World regions	C 27-a	
And density per sq km	All countries	A 9-a	
	OPEC member countries	C 3-a	
	Main countries	R 5-a	
By administrative areas	EEC countries	E 38-a	
By age groups	OECD countries	D 23-a	
By age groups: % rates of increase projected to 1985	All countries	U 62-a	
by marital status	All countries	U 14	
from 14-65 yrs of age	EEC countries	E 18-a	
14-65 yrs of age as % of population over 14 yrs of age	EEC countries	E 2-a	
no of females & no of children	All countries	U 14	
married persons	OAS member countries	N 12-a	
persons over 60 yrs of age as % of population over 14 yrs of age	EEC countries	E 2-a	
over 65 yrs of age	EEC countries	E 18-a	
under 14 yrs of age	EEC countries	E 18-a	
of school age (estim)	ECAFE countries	U 17-a	
By age groups & sex as % of employed population	All countries	L 4-a	
of world population	Developed world regions	M 4-a	
(at census dates)	Latin American countries	J 5-a	
	EEC countries	E 33-a	
	OAS member countries	N 12-a	
	African countries	U 44-a	
	Main countries	R 5	
	OECD countries	D 23	
(at last sample survey)			
by administrative areas	EEC countries	E 18-a	E 33-a
country of birth	All countries	U 14	
of citizenship	All countries	U 14	
marital status over 15 yrs of age	OAS member countries	N 12-a	
	EEC countries	E 18-a	
religion (in detail)	All countries	U 14	
size of locality where domiciled	All countries	U 14	
child population projected to 1990	E European countries	N 6	
historical table (census data)	E European countries	Z 1	
in 5 yr age groups	EEC countries	E 33-a	
in single yrs	All countries	U 14	
	EEC countries	E 2-a	
population (estim): total	AASM countries	E 41-a	
projected to 1990	E European countries	N 6	
to yr 2000	World regions	L 3	
By educational level: persons over 15 yrs of age	All countries	U 14	
ethnic groups & tribes by sex	All countries	U 14	
language (or mother tongue) by sex	All countries	U 14	
marital status: % adults single, married or divorced	W European countries	Z 3	
professional status: wage earners & salaried staff	OECD countries	D 23-a	
regions & administrative areas	EEC countries	E 37-a	
regions: historical table	Main European countries	Z 1	
By sex (at census dates)	Latin American countries	U 40	
(end-yr) estim	EEC countries	E 33-a	
from 14-25 yrs of age as % of population over 14 yrs of age	EEC countries	E 33-a	
historical table from 1750	Main European countries	Z 1	
(incl % growth rates)	All countries	U 43	
(incl % of males & females) at census dates	OAS member countries	N 12-a	
no of economically-active persons as % of total population	EEC countries	E 33-a	
economically-inactive persons over 14 yrs of age as % of total population	EEC countries	E 33-a	
females over 14 yrs of age as % of population of same age span	EEC countries	E 2-a	
illiterates	All countries	U 14	
persons engaged in more than one occupation	EEC countries	E 18-a	
wholly in one occupation	EEC countries	E 18-a	
over 15 yrs of age	All countries	U 62	
over 60 yrs of age as % of population over 14 yrs of age	EEC countries	E 33-a	
resident in federal territories & big cities	Caribbean countries & W Indies	T 6-a	
in urban & rural areas	OAS member countries	N 12-a	
seeking first job	EEC countries	E 18-a	
under 14 yrs of age as % of total population	EEC countries	E 33-a	
unemployed & seeking employment	EEC countries	E 3-a	E 33-a
urban & rural population	Latin American countries	J 5-a	
urban population as % of total population	ECE countries	U 15-a	
By status & occupational groups	All countries	L 4-a	
By status: salaried staff, wage earners & other categories	All countries	L 4-a	
Components of population change: no of births, deaths & migration	EEC countries	E 38-a	
	OECD countries	D 23-a	
Density: agricultural land areas per sq km & per sq mile	EEC countries	B 1-a	E 44-a
by civil divisions per sq km	Latin American countries	J 5-a	
per sq km & per sq mile of total land area	EEC countries	B 1-a	
by administrative areas	OAS member countries	N 11-a	
	EEC countries	E 37-a	E 38-a
	AASM countries	E 41-a	
per sq km	All countries	M 6-a	U 62-a

	Territorial coverage	Title codes
POPULATION, continued		
Density: per sq km	EEC countries	E 13-a E 37-a
		E 44-a
	Main countries & world regions	M 4-a
	OAS member countries	N 12-a
	World regions	R 5-a U 23-a
rural population per ha	Latin American countries	J 5-a
Expected population growth assumed as basis for economic planning	Small African countries	U 39
Farm labour force as % of total population	Main countries	A 11-a
From 15-64 yrs of age (normal span of working life)	All countries	L 2-a
Growth in population related to indigenous output of staple foodstuffs	World regions	C 27-a
Inter-regional migration (net) by administrative areas	EEC countries	E 37-a
Labour force employed compared with productive output in 1970	All countries	L 3
employed & unemployed	EEC countries	E 2-a
employed by age, sex & region projected to yr 2000	World regions	L 3
historical table 1750-2150 (estim)	World regions	L 3
(male): projected increase by yr 2000	World regions	L 3
Married women as % of female population over 14 yrs of age	EEC countries	E 2-a
Migration (to overseas countries) by administrative areas	EEC countries	E 37-a
No of females employed by marital status	All countries	C 28-a
of males as % of no of females (at census dates)	OAS member countries	N 12
per 100 females projected to 1990	E European countries	N 6
of persons in employment by administrative areas	EEC countries	E 18-a
living in cities of over 100,000 inhabitants	All countries	U 14
in largest conurbations	Latin American countries	J 5-a
	OAS member countries	N 12-a
in largest conurbations: historical table	Main European countries	Z 1
within administrative areas	EEC countries	E 37-a
occasionally employed (or working part-time) by administrative areas	EEC countries	E 18-a
over 15 yrs of age: no of literates & illiterates (census data)	OAS member countries	N 19-a
60 yrs of age seeking employment by administrative areas	EEC countries	E 18-a
seeking first job by administrative areas	EEC countries	E 18-a
up to 14 yrs of age as % of total population	All countries	M 6-a
of pupils or students over 14 yrs of age by administrative areas	EEC countries	E 18-a
of self-employed persons by sex & branch of activity	All countries	L 4-a
Projected to 1980	Main ECAFE countries	U 17
to 1985 (by 5 yr age groups)	All countries	A 1 U 13-a
		U 62
to 1990 (by 5 yr age groups)	E European countries	N 6
to yr 2000 (at 5 yr intervals)	World regions	U 43
Served by piped water supply systems in rural & urban areas	OAS member countries	N 12
sewerage systems in rural & urban areas	OAS member countries	N 18-a
(Total): at end-Dec by regions (at 5 yr intervals)	OAS member countries	N 18-a
at latest census dates	EEC countries	E 2
	All countries	U 28
	ECAFE countries	U 32
	OAS member countries	N 12
at mid-yr (at 5 yr intervals) estim	All countries	U 62
by regions (incl density)	Latin American countries	U 40-a
(incl % changes) estim	All countries	U 13-a
	AASM countries	E 41-a
	ECE countries	N 15-a
	Main countries	M 5-a
	OAS member countries	N 12-a
	EEC countries	E 26-a
	All countries	U 14-a U 27-a
	European countries & USA	U 5-a
	African countries	U 44-a
	All countries	A 9-a
by sex: historical tables	ECAFE countries	U 32-a
	EEC countries	E 26-a E 13-a
	Latin American countries	J 5-a
(Total) - index nos	OECD countries	D 23-a
Urban & rural populations (at census dates) incl % growth rates	Latin American countries	U 40
projected to 1980	Main countries	W 2
at mid-yr (estim)	European countries & USA	U 5-a
projected to 1985	All countries	U 43
to yr 2000	Developed & developing world regions	M 4-a
Urban population as % of total population	World regions	L 3
by sex as % of total population	All countries	M 6-a
projected to 1985	ECE countries	U 15-a
Rural statistics: no of births, deaths & marriages	World regions	A 1
World political blocs: historical table from 1913	ECE countries	E 33-a
World population: % changes	Worldwide	C 4-a
current official estimates	Main countries	C 4-a
(estim)	Continents	U 28
		R 5-a
(latest aggregated census data)	All countries	U 28

POPULATION, ECONOMICALLY-ACTIVE
    see also   CRAFTSMEN & PROCESS WORKERS
                  EMPLOYMENT
                  FARM WORKERS
                  LABOUR FORCE
                  SALARIED STAFF
                  SERVICE EMPLOYEES

	Territorial coverage	Title codes	
POPULATION, ECONOMICALLY-ACTIVE continued			
% of female population in employment	EEC countries	E 33-a	
population over 60 yrs of age in employment	EEC countries	E 2-a	
% increase in employed population	ECE countries	U 15-a	
As % of total population	EEC countries	E 2-a	E 44-a
By industrial sector & sex of employee (at census dates)	OAS member countries	N 18	
& by regions	EEC countries	E 3-a	
(at census dates)	African countries	U 44-a	
historical table from 1750-1969	OAS member countries	N 18	
By sex (at census dates)	Main European countries	Z 1-a	
Historical table from 1950-1965	OAS member countries	N 18	
Labour force by occupational groups by sex of employees	OAS member countries	N 12-a	
by sex as % of total population	OAS member countries	N 18	
No of persons engaged in agricultural employment	EEC countries	E 2-a	E 33-a
	African countries	U 44-a	
	All countries	A 9-a	
	EEC countries	E 18-a	
building construction industry	African countries	U 44-a	
commercial occupations	African countries	U 44-a	
employment by age groups & sex (at census dates)	All countries	C 28	
by age groups & sex	All countries	L 4-a	
by kind of activity or occupation	All countries	L 4-a	
	EEC countries	E 2-a	
by sex as % of total population	All countries	C 28-a	
	Main countries	R 5-a	
by sex	EEC countries	E 33-a	
	Latin American countries	J 5-a	
	Main OECD countries	D 24-q	
mining & quarrying	African countries	U 44-a	
public utility undertakings	African countries	U 44-a	
service industries	African countries	U 44-a	
	EEC countries	E 18-a	
transportation	African countries	U 44-a	
No of employers of labour: industrial sector by sex	OAS member countries	N 18	
females in employment as % of female population	EEC countries	E 2-a	
normally-active females presently unemployed	EEC countries	E 2-a	
persons assisting in family businesses	EEC countries	E 18-a	
self-employed persons by kind of activity by sex	OAS member countries	N 18	
	EEC countries	E 18-a	
unpaid family workers by sex	OAS member countries	N 18	
wages & salary earners	EEC countries	E 18-a	
POPULATION, ECONOMICALLY-INACTIVE			
% of population from 14-24 yrs of age unemployed	EEC countries	E 2-a	
seeking work by administrative areas	EEC countries	E 18-a	
over 14 yrs of age unemployed	EEC countries	E 2-a	
60 yrs of age unemployed	EEC countries	E 2-a	
unemployed by age groups	EEC countries	E 18-a	
unemployed	EEC countries	E 33-a	
By administrative areas	EEC countries	E 38-a	
Historical table from 1950-1965	OAS member countries	N 12-a	
No of housewives not seeking gainful employment	EEC countries	E 18-a	
persons by age groups by administrative areas	EEC countries	E 38-a	
in part-time employment	EEC countries	E 18-a	
newly on labour market & seeking first job	EEC countries	E 18-a	
unemployed	EEC countries	E 18-a	
pupils & students not gainfully employed	EEC countries	E 18-a	
retired pensioners as % of population over 60 yrs of age	EEC countries	E 2-a	
not seeking gainful employment	EEC countries	E 18-a	
POPULATION MOVEMENT			
see also MIGRATION			
% share of movement of population by regions	EEC countries	E 37-a	
Coefficients of mobility	EEC countries	E 37-a	
Emigration & immigration (regional): % population movement	EEC countries	E 37-a	
Migration & natural population increase: agricultural regions	EEC countries	E 37-a	
POPULATION PLANNING			
World Bank loans & credits for population control projects in $m	Recipient countries	M 3-a	
Porcelain see EARTHENWARE PRODUCTS			
Porcelain products industry see CERAMICS INDUSTRY			
PORK			
see also PIG-MEAT			
PRESSED PORK			
% share of world imports & world exports	Main countries	B 1-a	
Basic prices: slaughtered pigs in £ per score	EEC countries	B 1-a	
Consumption per capita in kg per yr	OECD countries	D 1-a	
	European countries	U 36-a	
	EEC countries	B 1-a	E 44-a

	Territorial coverage	Title codes	
PORK, continued			
Consumption per capita in lbs per yr	UK	B 11-a	B 12-a
tonnage & per capita in kg	EEC countries	E 1-a	
tonnage	OAS member countries	N 17-a	
Export prices - index nos (weighted average main sources)		U 29-q	
Export prices in $ per ton	Australia, Netherlands, New Zealand & Poland	A 9-a	
Exports by destination: tonnage	Main countries	B 11-a	
by value in $m	W European countries	U 33-a	
tonnage	European countries	U 36-a	
Imports & exports: tonnage	EEC countries	E 1-a	
Imports by source: tonnage	France, Italy & W Germany	B 11-a	
by value in $m	European countries	U 33-a	
pork carcases: tonnage	Main countries	B 11-a	
tonnage	European countries	U 36-a	
Intervention prices fixed by EEC Commission in local currency	EEC countries	E 44-a	
Prices as % of world market level	EEC countries	E 44-a	
Production, imports, exports & net domestic supply: tonnage	EEC countries	E 1-a	
Production & stocks: pig meat & consumption per capita in kg	OECD countries	D 14-a	
by administrative areas: tonnage	EEC countries	E 38-a	
by value in local currency	EEC countries	E 44-a	
for export: tonnage	Main countries	B 12-a	
tonnage	African countries	U 44-a	
	All countries	A 9-a	U 22-a
	European countries & USSR	U 36-a	
	EEC countries	B 1-a	
	Canada, European countries, Japan, USA & USSR	E 44-a	
	Latin American countries	U 40-a	
	OAS member countries	N 14-a	
	OAS member countries	N 17-a	
Retail prices (by cut) in local currency	EEC countries	Z 3-a	
(comparative): loin chops in $ per kg	EEC countries	B 1-a	E 3-a
Self-sufficiency ratios		E 44-a	
Sluice-gate prices in £ per cwt	EEC countries	B 1-a	
Stocks (at 1st July) & % change (on previous yr)	France & W Germany	E 1-a	
imported pork held in cold storage: tonnage	UK	B 12-w	
Supply, production, consumption, imports & exports: tonnage	EEC countries	B 1-a	
Wholesale prices (at central markets) in pence per lb	UK	B 12-w	B 11-m
(by quality) in local currency	OAS member countries	N 17-a	
	Denmark, Netherlands, UK & USA	R 2-m	
World exports by value in $m	Australia, Eire & France	A 9-a	
World market prices: slaughtered pigs per 100 kg	World regions	A 5-a	
		E 34-m	
PORK, SALTED OR DRIED			
Exports by destination: tonnage	EEC countries	E 47-m	
Imports & exports: tonnage	EEC countries	E 1-a	
Inter-EEC area shipments: tonnage	EEC countries	E 47-m	

Poromerics   see   LEATHER SUBSTITUTE

Portable typewriting machines   see   TYPEWRITERS, PORTABLE

Portfolio investment   see   GOVERNMENT BONDS
INVESTMENT, PRIVATE OVERSEAS
MUNICIPAL BONDS

Portland cement   see   CEMENT

Ports   see   SEA PORTS

Post Office savings   see   INVESTMENT, PERSONAL

Postal mail   see   LETTER MAIL
MAIL FREIGHT

Poster & billboard advertising   see   ADVERTISING BY MEDIA

POTASH			
see also FERTILISERS, POTASH			
Consumption: tonnage	USA	N 1-a	
Production based on content of potash salts: tonnage	All countries	U 43-a	
	Main countries	E 3-a	
crude potash salts: tonnage	All countries	U 22-a	
historical tables from 1895: tonnage	E Germany & France	Z 1-a	
incl potash salts: tonnage	Main countries	B 15-a	
technical grade potash: tonnage	Main countries	A 2-a	
Re-exports (in form of complex fertilisers): tonnage	Main countries	A 2-a	
Stocks held at producers' plants (end-yr): tonnage	USA	N 1-a	
Wholesale prices based on content of muriate in cents per ton	USA	N 1-a	
World production: marketable potash: tonnage		N 1-a	N 4-a
World reserves: tonnage (estim)	Main countries	N 1-a	
POTASH SALTS			
Imports & exports by kind: tonnage	Main countries	B 15-a	
Production: historical table from 1861: tonnage	W Germany	Z 1-a	
tonnage	OECD countries	D 5-a	

	Territorial coverage	Title codes
Potassic fertilisers see FERTILISERS, POTASH		
Potassic slag see FERTILISERS, MIXED		
Potassium chloride & potassium muriate see FERTILISERS, POTASH		
Potassium nitrate see FERTILISERS, NITROGENOUS		
Potassium sulphate see FERTILISERS, POTASH		

POTATO FLOUR

Consumption tonnage & consumption per capita in kg	Italy	D 14-a

POTATO PRODUCTS, FROZEN

Production & consumption: tonnage	OECD countries	D 14-a

POTATOES

see also   ROOT CROPS
SEED POTATOES
STATE PROCUREMENT
SWEET POTATOES

	Territorial coverage	Title codes	
As source of fat & protein (incl calorie intake per capita)	OAS member countries	N 17-a	
% change: producer prices (over previous yr)	EEC countries	E 34-m	
retail sales	W European countries	U 30-a	
% of EEC area production	E European countries & USSR	U 16-a	
% of sales for direct or farm consumption or processing	EEC countries	R 5-a	
A.I.D. sales (under food aid programs) in $m	ECE countries	U 34-a	
Area harvested, production tonnage & yield per ha	Recipient countries	M 1-a	
	All countries	A 9-a	
	Latin American countries	J 5-a	
under crop (early & late varieties) in ha	Italy	E 12-a	
historical tables from 1815 in ha	Main countries	Z 1-a	
in ha & harvest: tonnage	Main countries	R 5-a	
in ha	EEC countries	B 1-a	E 44-a
	OAS member countries	N 13-a	
	OECD countries	D 1-a	
Availability per capita in kg per day	All countries	U 43-a	
Consumption & consumption per capita in kg per day	OECD countries	D 14-a	
(as animal feed): tonnage	EEC countries	E 44-a	
	OECD countries	D 1-a	
(as seed potatoes): tonnage	OECD countries	D 1-a	
per capita in kg per yr	Main countries	E 3-a	
	OECD countries	D 1-a	
	E European countries & USSR	U 16-a	
	EEC countries	B 1-a	E 44-a
	W European countries	P 5-a	
	Canada, European countries, USA & USSR	E 44-a	
tonnage	EEC countries	E 44-a	
Crop yield (early & late varieties) in 100 kg per ha	EEC countries	E 3-a	E 12-a
in kg per ha	Main countries	R 5-a	
	OAS member countries	N 13-a	
	OECD countries	D 1-a	
in quintals per ha	E European countries & USSR	U 16-a	
Distribution for manufacture of processed foods: tonnage	Czechoslovakia, Hungary & Poland	U 34-a	
for market sales: tonnage	Czechoslovakia, Hungary & Poland	U 34-a	
for own farm use: tonnage	Czechoslovakia, Hungary & Poland	U 34-a	
Export prices in $ per ton	Australia, Canada, Japan & Netherlands	A 9-a	
Exports by value in $m	W European countries	U 33-a	
Gross output as % of all crops (incl cereals) on value basis	ECE countries	U 34-a	
Imports by value in $m	W European countries	U 33-a	
tonnage	Canada, European & Near East countries, USA & USSR	A 11-a	
Prices paid (as state purchases) in $ per ton	Poland	U 30-a	
Prices - index nos	W European countries	U 30-a	
Producer prices in £ per cwt	EEC countries	B 1-a	
in local currency per kg	W European countries	E 35-a	
	EEC countries	E 34-m	E 44-a
	All countries	A 9-a	
in $ per cwt	USA	E 35-a	
(prime quality) in $ per ton	E European countries	U 30-a	
	E European countries & USSR	U 30-a	
Producer prices - index nos	EEC countries	E 44-a	
	E European countries excl USSR	U 30-a	
Production as % of gross farm output (value basis)	E European countries	U 34-a	
by value in local currency	EEC countries	E 44-a	
Production costs (on collective farms) per ton	USSR	U 34-a	
Production (for human consumption) - index nos	W European countries	U 30-a	
Production, imports, exports, stocks & consumption: tonnage	EEC countries	E 44-a	
Production & usage by industry & as fodder & seed: tonnage	OECD countries	D 14-a	
by administrative areas: tonnage	EEC countries	E 38-a	
(early & late varieties): tonnage	EEC countries	E 12-a	
(excl usage for seed & as animal feed): tonnage	OECD countries	D 1-a	
historical tables: tonnage	Main European countries	Z 1-a	
(incl sweet potatoes): tonnage	Latin American countries	U 40-a	
	African countries	U 44-a	
tonnage	All countries	U 43-a	
	Asian & Far East countries	U 32-a	

		Territorial coverage	Title codes	

POTATOES, continued
    Production: tonnage

	Czechoslovakia, Hungary & Poland	U 34-a	
	E European countries & USSR	U 16-a	
	EEC countries	E 44-a	
	Main countries	E 3-a	R 5-a
	OAS member countries	N 13-a	
	OECD countries	D 1-a	
value of output in £m	EEC countries	B 1-a	
Retail prices (comparative) in cents per kg	EEC countries	Z 3-a	
in local currency per kg	OAS member countries	N 17-a	
Retail prices - index nos	EEC countries	E 44-a	
Self-sufficiency ratios	EEC countries	B 1-a	E 3-a
State procurement: tonnage	E European countries & USSR incl Ukraine	U 16-a	
Stocks held at wholesalers' premises: tonnage	UK	E 12-m	
held on farms (end-month): tonnage	W Germany, Netherlands & UK	E 12-m	
Supply ex own production as % of requirements	EEC countries	E 44-a	
Supply, production, consumption & trade: tonnage	EEC countries	B 1-a	
Wholesale prices in $ per ton	Main countries	A 9-a	
World exports: unit value in $ per ton		A 11-a	
Yield in kg per ha	EEC countries	B 1-a	E 44-a

Pottery   see   EARTHENWARE PRODUCTS

Pottery industry   see   CERAMICS INDUSTRY

POULTRY

% changes: prices received by farmers	W European countries	U 30-a	
% price increases: feed for hens & broilers	W European countries	U 30-a	
% share of world import & export trade	Main countries	B 1-a	
% usage for market sales or farm consumption	ECE countries	U 34-a	
Availability (domestic): tonnage (dead wt)	EEC countries	E 1-a	
Consumption per capita (incl game) in lbs per yr	UK	B 12-a	
tonnage & consumption per capita in kg	EEC countries	E 1-a	E 44-a
Distribution for market sales: tonnage	Czechoslovakia, Hungary & Poland	U 34-a	
for own farm consumption: tonnage	Czechoslovakia, Hungary & Poland	U 34-a	
Export prices: chickens, day-old chicks & ducks in Fl per kg	Netherlands	A 9-a	
Export prices - index nos (weighted average main sources)		U 29-q	
Exports by value in $m	W European countries	U 33-a	
Feed requirements per kg of eggs produced: projection to 1985	Main countries	P 5-a	
of poultry meat produced: projection to 1985	Main countries	P 5-a	
Gross output (incl eggs) by value in $m	ECE countries	U 34-a	
Import prices: broilers (ex Holland & Belgium) in $ per kg	W Germany	U 30-q	
Imports by value in $m	European countries	U 33-a	
Imports & exports: prepared poultry products: tonnage	EEC countries	E 1-a	
Inter-EEC area shipments: live chickens: volume	EEC countries	E 47-m	
Nutrient requirements: chickens per lb of diet in milligrammes		P 5	
turkeys per lb of diet in milligrammes		P 5	
Population: chickens (& other poultry) by areas	EEC countries	E 38-a	
chickens, ducks, geese & turkeys	OECD countries	D 1-a	
chickens, ducks & turkeys	All countries	A 9-a	
chickens (incl no per 100 ha)	EEC countries	E 1-a	
chickens	European countries & USSR	U 36-a	
	OAS member countries	N 13-a	
ducks, geese, turkeys & guinea fowls	EEC countries	E 1-a	
ducks & geese	OAS member countries	N 13-a	
historical tables from 1816	Main European countries	Z 1-a	
(incl world total) in 1000 head	Main countries	R 5-a	
in million head (census data)	Main countries	B 11-a	B 12-a
laying hens & pullets by age	EEC countries	E 1-a	
laying hens, ducks & turkeys	EEC countries	B 1-a	
laying hens	Main countries	B 4-a	
	EEC countries	E 44-a	
turkeys	OAS member countries	N 13-a	
Producer prices: chickens & turkeys in $ per ton	All countries	A 9-a	
in local currency per ton	OECD countries	D 1-a	
per kg	Belgium & W Germany	E 34-m	
fowls (for boiling) in local currency per ton	Austria & Belgium	D 1-a	
(for roasting) in local currency per ton	Austria	D 1-a	
(incl broilers) in $ per ton	European countries	U 36-q	
pullets in local currency per ton	EEC countries	E 44-a	
in $ per ton	W European countries	U 30-a	
turkeys in local currency per ton	OECD countries	D 1-a	
Producer prices - index nos	EEC countries	E 44-a	
Production by value in local currency	EEC countries	E 44-a	
in £m	EEC countries	B 1-a	
dressed fresh poultry: tonnage	All countries	U 22-a	
game (incl consumption per capita in kg)	OECD countries	D 14-a	
Production, imports, exports, stocks & consumption: tonnage	EEC countries	E 44-a	
tonnage	African countries	U 44-a	
	Latin American countries	U 40-a	
value as % of gross farm output (incl crops)	E European countries	U 34-a	
Ratio: broiler feed prices to poultry prices	W European countries	U 30-a	
Retail prices: chickens, ducks, geese & turkeys in local currency per kg	OAS member countries	N 17-a	
Self-sufficiency ratios	EEC countries	E 3-a	E 44-a
Slaughterings: volume	European countries	U 36-q	
Wholesale prices (by grade) in local currency per kg	Main countries	R 2-m	
chickens in local currency per kg	France, W Germany & UK	A 9-a	
World exports by value in $m	World regions	A 5-a	
World production (incl game): tonnage	World regions	A 5-a	

	Territorial coverage	Title codes	
POULTRY BY KIND			
Imports by source: tonnage	UK	B 11-a	
Population: fowls, turkeys, ducks & geese (at end June)	UK	B 12-a	
	OAS member countries	N 13-a	
Wholesale prices in local currency per kg	OAS member countries	N 17-a	
POULTRY MEAT			
Consumption per capita in kg per yr	OECD countries	D 1-a	
	European countries	U 36-a	
	EEC countries	B 1-a	
in lbs per yr	UK	B 12-a	
	Main countries	B 11-a	B 12-a
tonnage	OAS member countries	N 17-a	
Exports by destination: tonnage	Denmark, Netherlands & USA	B 11-a	
	Main countries	B 12-m	
chickens by destination: tonnage	EEC countries	E 47-m	
tonnage	European countries & USSR	U 36-a	
	Main countries	B 11-a	
Government expenditure: price guarantees in £m	UK	P 5-a	
Imports by source: tonnage	Main countries	B 12-m	
	W Germany	B 11-a	
chickens by source: tonnage	EEC countries	E 47-m	
	UK	B 11-a	
ducks, geese & turkeys by source: tonnage	UK	B 11-a	
tonnage	European countries & USSR	U 36-a	
	Main countries	B 11-a	
Inter-EEC area shipments: chickens: tonnage	EEC countries	E 47-m	
Producer prices in $ per ton	E European countries	U 30-a	
Production by kind of poultry: tonnage	UK	B 12-a	
in dressed carcase wt: tonnage	EEC countries	B 1-a	
	OECD countries	D 1-a	
(incl game birds): tonnage	UK	B 12-a	
Production, stocks & consumption per capita in kg	OECD countries	D 14-a	
tonnage (estim)	All countries	A 9-a	
	Main countries	B 11-a	
	European countries & USSR	U 36-a	
	E European countries & USSR	U 16-a	
Retail prices: chickens in local currency per kg	OAS member countries	N 17-a	
Self-sufficiency ratios	EEC countries	B 1-a	
Sluice-gate prices by kind of poultry meat in $ per kg	EEC countries	B 11-a	
in pence per lb	EEC countries	B 1-a	
Supply available for consumption: tonnage	Main countries	B 11-a	
Supply, production, consumption & trade: tonnage	EEC countries	B 1-a	
Wholesale prices by kind of poultry meat in local currency per kg	OAS member countries	N 17-a	
in local currency per 100 kg	France & Netherlands	E 34-m	
POWER EQUIPMENT INDUSTRY			
Labour force employed	Worldwide	T 7-a	
Net profits by firm in $m	Worldwide	T 7-a	
Sales turnover by firm in $m	Worldwide	T 7-a	
POWER GENERATING EQUIPMENT			
see also ALTERNATORS			
BOILERHOUSE PLANT			
BOILERS			
ELECTRIC POWER EQUIPMENT			
GAS TURBINES			
GENERATORS			
GENERATORS, HYDRAULIC			
GENERATORS, HYDROELECTRIC			
GENERATORS, NUCLEAR			
GENERATORS, PUMPED STORAGE			
HYDRAULIC TURBINES			
STEAM TURBINES			
TRANSFORMERS			
WATER WHEELS			
% of world exports shipped to developed countries		U 38-a	
to developing countries		U 38-a	
Consumption: tonnage	Central African countries	U 38	
Exports: boilers by value in $	OECD countries	D 9-a	
by destination by Brown Boveri: volume	Switzerland	T 7-a	
by kind by CST classes: tonnage & value in $m	EEC countries	E 48-a	
SITC classes by value in $m	Main countries	D 2-q	
tonnage & value in $m	OECD countries	D 3-a2	
by kind by NIMEXE classes by value in $m	All countries	E 20-a	
SITC classes by value in $m	All countries	U 50-a	U 59-a
by value in $m	All countries	U 38-a	
Generators (hydroelectric) in use in MW	Canada & USA	T 7-a	
(normal type) in use in MW	Canada & USA	T 7-a	
(nuclear) in use in MW	Canada & USA	T 7-a	
(pumped storage type) in use in MW	Canada & USA	T 7-a	
Imports by kind by NIMEXE classes by value in $m	All countries	E 20-a	
SITC classes by value in $m	All countries	U 50-a	U 59-a
by source by CST classes: tonnage & value in $m	EEC countries	E 21-a	
SITC classes by value in $m	Main countries	D 2-q	
tonnage & value in $m	OECD countries	D 3-a2	
by value in $m	All countries	U 38-a	

	Territorial coverage	Title codes	
POWER GENERATING EQUIPMENT, continued			
Investment by steelworks in power equipment by value in UA	EEC countries	E 46-a	
New installations by specific companies in MW	USA	T 7-a	
by type of plant in MW	USA	T 7-a	
World exports: power transformers by value in $m	Japan	U 38-a	
POWER STATIONS			
see also ELECTRIC ENERGY			
ELECTRIC SUPPLY INDUSTRY			
% of consumption of petroleum products	Latin American countries	U 18-a	
% share of total capital investment	E European countries	U 16-a	
A.I.D. grants to promote increased power supplies in $m	Recipient countries	M 1-a	
Consumption: bituminous coal & lignite: tonnage	USA	N 1-a	
coal: tonnage	UK	U 10-a	
fuels by kind in oil equiv tonnage	Latin American countries	U 18-a	
fuels (all kinds): tonnage		E 16-q	E 15-a
gas (in thermo-electric plants) in m³	OECD countries	D 44-a	
natural gas in m³	UK	U 10-a	
oil: tonnage	UK	U 10-a	
Electricity: generation (total) in kWh	All countries	C 23-a	
Foreign loans granted by A.I.D. in $m	Latin American countries	U 18-a	
by EXIMBANK in $m	Latin American countries	U 18-a	
by IBRD in $m	Latin American countries	U 18-a	
by IDB in $m	Latin American countries	U 18-a	
Generating capacity by kind of fuel in kW	Latin American countries	U 18-a	
installed in kW	W Indies & Caribbean countries	T 6-a	
	OECD countries	D 8-a	
	African countries	U 44-a	
	Latin American countries	U 18-a	
	All countries	T 7-a	
	OAS member countries	N 14-a	
using coal in GW	Latin American countries	U 18-a	
diesel oil in kW	Latin American countries	U 18-a	
fuel oil in kW	Latin American countries	U 18-a	
natural gas in kW	Latin American countries	U 18-a	
vegetable fuels in kW	Latin American countries	U 18-a	
IBRD loans approved for improvements in electricity generation	OAS member countries	N 16-a	
IDA loans approved in $m	OAS member countries	N 16-a	
Increase in generating capacity achieved during 1961-70 in MW	Latin American countries	U 18-a	
Installed generating capacity per capita in watts	Latin American countries	U 18-a	
private generating plants in kW	OAS member countries	N 14-a	
public generating plants in kW	OAS member countries	N 14-a	
Investment in buildings in local currency	EEC countries	E 40-a	
in generating capacity in $m	Latin American countries	U 18-a	
in land purchase in local currency	EEC countries	E 40-a	
in machinery in local currency	EEC countries	E 40-a	
Investment needs (by type of plant) projected to ensuing yr in $m	OECD countries	D 8-a	
Planned generating capacity by type projected to 1980 in kW	Latin American countries	U 18-a	
Power generation by type of public supply plants in kWh	EEC countries	E 38-a	
Stocks: anthracite held at power stations: tonnage	USA	N 1-a	
World bank loans & credits: electricity generation projects in $m	Worldwide	M 3-a	
World generating capacity presently installed in kW		T 7-a	
POWER STATIONS, ELECTRIC			
Capacity: generating sets by type in kW	EEC countries	E 15-a	
No in use: gas turbines & power in kW	EEC countries	E 15-a	
by kind of fuel used	EEC countries	E 15-a	
by size & age of generators in kW	EEC countries	E 15-a	
POWER STATIONS, HYDROELECTRIC			
see also HYDROELECTRICITY			
% of electric power generated hydroelectrically	Main countries	H 4-a	
Capacity by kind of fuel used in kW	European countries & USA	U 1-a	
of plants in operation in kW	All countries	U 55-a	
Capacity utilisation in kW	All countries	U 55-a	
Electricity: generating capacity in kW	All countries	C 23-a	
	African countries	U 44-a	
	EEC countries	B 30-a	E 15-a
	OAS member countries	N 14-a	
	OECD countries	D 8-a	D 45-a
	Latin American countries	U 18-a	
	Main countries	E 3-a	
	EEC countries	E 38-a	
generation (actual) by area in kWh			
in kWh	All countries	C 23-a	U 55-a
	EEC countries	E 3-a	
	OAS member countries	N 14-a	
	European countries	U 1-a	
	Main countries	E 3-a	
	OECD countries	D 8-a	
Investment in hydroelectric power supply projects in $m	EEC countries	E 15-a	
Name, location & size of power stations in MW	OECD countries	D 45-a	
New generating equipment installed in MW	OECD countries	D 45-a	
No of stations in operation	OECD countries	D 45-a	
planned for ensuing 5 years	OECD countries	D 45-a	
Planned power capacity by 1980 in MW	Latin American countries	U 18-a	

	Territorial coverage	Title codes
POWER STATIONS, HYDROELECTRIC continued		
Planned power capacity proposed in MW	OECD countries	D 45-a
Storage reservoirs: capacity in kW	EEC countries	E 15-a
	European countries & USA	U 1-a
POWER STATIONS, NUCLEAR		
% of nuclear capacity by reactor type in MWe	Communist countries	H 4-a
% of electric power generated by nuclear fuels	Main countries	H 4-a
% of total orders placed for construction	All countries	H 4-a
As % of total installed capacity	All countries	H 4-a
Capacity by reactor type in MWe	Worldwide	H 4-a
existing plant in operation in MWe	EEC countries	E 7-a
	All countries	H 4-a
no of nuclear reactors projected in MWe	EEC countries	E 7-a
under construction in MWe	EEC countries	E 7-a
Capacity utilisation in MWe	All countries	U 55-a
Electricity: nuclear generating capacity in kW (incl location)	EEC countries	E 15-a
in kW	All countries	C 23-a U 55-a
	EEC countries	B 30-a
	Main countries	E 3-a
	OECD countries	D 8-a
	European countries & USA	U 1-a
Electricity generation by nuclear power in kWh (incl time utilisation)	EEC countries	E 15-a
by areas in kWh	EEC countries	E 38-a
in kWh	All countries	C 23-a H 4-a
		R 5-a U 55-a
	EEC countries	E 3-a
	European countries & USA	U 1-a
	Main countries	E 3-a
Heat output (from core) in MWth	OECD countries	D 8-a
Investment in nuclear power plants in $m	OECD countries	D 45-a
Name, location & size of nuclear power stations in MW	EEC countries	E 15-a
Electricity generation in kWh (incl time utilisation)	OECD countries	D 45-a
Orders placed for nuclear projects by size in MWe	EEC countries	E 15-a
Planned generating capacity by type by 1980	All countries	H 4-a
Power generating capacity installed by type in kW	Worldwide	D 48
by type planned by 1980	Worldwide	D 48
Power output of generators in MWe	Worldwide	D 48
Steam pressure in kg per sq cm	OECD countries	D 45-a
Usage: enriched combustible fuel	OECD countries	D 45-a
natrium coolants: tonnage	OECD countries	D 45-a
plutonium fuel	OECD countries	D 45-a
thorium carbide fuel	OECD countries	D 45-a
uranium & uranium dioxyide	OECD countries	D 45-a
water coolants: tonnage	OECD countries	D 45-a
POWER STATIONS, THERMAL		
% of electric power generated in conventional power stations	Main countries	H 4-a
Capacity utilisation in MW	All countries	U 55-a
Electricity: generation (from liquid fuels) in kWh	All countries	C 23-a
generating capacity in kW (incl location)	EEC countries	E 15-a
in kW	All countries	C 23-a U 55-a
	African countries	U 44-a
	Latin American countries	U 18-a
	EEC countries	B 30-a
	Main countries	E 3-a
	OECD countries	D 8-a D 45-a
proposed in MW	OECD countries	D 45-a
generation by areas in kWh	EEC countries	E 38-a
(by type of fuel used) in kWh	OECD countries	D 8-a
(from coal) in kWh	All countries	C 23-a
(from lignite) in kWh	All countries	C 23-a
in kWh	All countries	C 23-a U 55-a
	EEC countries	E 3-a
	European countries & USA	U 1-a
	Main countries	E 3-a
Fuels: consumption by kind at power stations: tonnage	OECD countries	D 8-a
Investment in conventional thermal power plants in $m	EEC countries	E 15-a
Maximum thermal generating capacity in kW	European countries & USA	U 1-a
Name, location & size of thermal power plants in MW	OECD countries	D 45-a
New generating equipment installed in MW	OECD countries	D 45-a
No of power stations in service using coal, lignite, liquid fuels & natural gas	OECD countries	D 45-a
privately-owned thermal power-generating plants in use	OECD countries	D 45-a
public utility companies generating electricity	OECD countries	D 45-a
thermal power stations in operation	OECD countries	D 45-a
conventional thermal power stations planned for ensuing 5 yrs	OECD countries	D 45-a
Planned generating capacity projected by 1980 in MW	Latin American countries	U 18-a
POWER TOOLS		
see also HAND TOOLS		
MACHINE TOOLS		
Exports by destination & value in $m	Main countries	U 9-a
value in $m	All countries	U 38-a
Imports by value in $m	All countries	U 38-a
World export trade: electro-mechanical hand tools by value in $m		U 38-a
by value in $m		U 38-a

	Territorial coverage	Title codes

Power transformers   see   TRANSFORMERS

POWER TRANSMISSION LINES

Length of power lines in service in km	OECD countries	D 45-a
planned for construction (in ensuing 5 yrs) in km	OECD countries	D 45-a
No of circuits in use	OECD countries	D 45-a
Tension voltage in kV	OECD countries	D 45-a

Powered industrial tractors   see   TRACTORS, INDUSTRIAL

Pozzolan and lapilli   see   ABRASIVES, NATURAL

Prawns & shrimps   see   CRUSTACEANS & MOLLUSCS

Pre-fabricated houses   see   HOUSING, PRE-FABRICATED

Precious & semi-precious stones   see   GEM STONES
                                                          DIAMONDS

Precious metals   see   GOLD
                              PLATINUM
                              PLATINUM-GROUP METALS
                              PLATINUM, REFINED

Precipitation   see   RAINFALL

Precision balances   see   MEASURING APPARATUS

Precision drawing instruments   see   SCIENTIFIC INSTRUMENTS

Precision instruments industry   see   SCIENTIFIC INSTRUMENTS
                                                                              INDUSTRY

Preference shares & preferred capital shares   see   SHARES, PREFERENCE

Premium rates of exchange   see   EXCHANGE RATES

Premiums   see   DOLLAR PREMIUMS

Prepared meals   see   FROZEN MEALS, PREPARED

Preserved fruits   see   CANNED & BOTTLED FRUIT

Press brakes   see   MACHINE TOOLS

PRESSED PORK

Exports by destination: tonnage	EEC countries	E 47-m
Imports by source: tonnage	EEC countries	E 47-m
Inter-EEC area shipments: tonnage	EEC countries	E 47-m

PRESSES

Consumption: mechanical & hydraulic presses by supply area by value in $	EEC countries	B 31-a
Deliveries by industrial sector by value in $m	USA	J 2-a
Inter-EEC trade: all types of presses by value in $m (incl % growth rates)		B 20-a

PRESSES, HYDRAULIC

    see also   MACHINE TOOLS

Deliveries (domestic) by value in $m	EEC countries	B 31-a
Exports as % of production (value basis)	EEC countries	B 31-a
Imports as % of consumption (value basis)	EEC countries	B 31-a
Production by value in $m	EEC countries	B 31-a
Production, imports, exports & sales by value in $m	EEC countries	B 20-a
Sales by type: volume & value in $m	USA	J 2-a

PRESSES, MECHANICAL

    see also   MACHINE TOOLS

Deliveries (domestic) by value in $m	EEC countries	B 31-a
Exports as % of production (value basis)	EEC countries	B 31-a
Imports as % of consumption (value basis)	EEC countries	B 31-a
Production by value in $m	EEC countries	B 31-a
Production, imports, exports & sales by value in $m	EEC countries	B 20-a
Sales by type of press: volume & value in $m	USA	J 2-a

PRESSINGS & STAMPINGS

    see also   FORGINGS & PRESSINGS

Production: steel pressings & stampings: tonnage	EEC countries	E 29-a

Price controls (EEC)   see   ECSC
                                   INTERVENTION PRICES
                                     TARGET PRICES

Price deflator, implicit   see   GDP

	Territorial coverage	Title codes

PRICE SUPPORTS
    see also   COMMODITY CREDIT CORPORATION

Barley in equiv $ per ton	All countries	B 8-a
Cattle, lambs & pigs in $ per 100 lbs	Canada	B 11-a
Cost of price guarantees: barley & oats in £m	UK	P 5-a
eggs & milk in £m	UK	P 5-a
pigs, sheep, poultry meat & cattle in £m	UK	P 5-a
Dairy products: price supports financed by Commodity Credit Corporation in $m	USA	B 4-a
Direct purchases: rice under Commodity Credit Corporation supports: tonnage	USA	B 14-a
Expenditure by EEC Commission: cereals & rice in £m		B 3-a
fruit & vegetables in £m		B 3-a
meat & poultry meat in £m		B 3-a
milk & milk products in £m		B 3-a
oils & fats in £m		B 3-a
sugar in £m		B 3-a
Expenditure: EDF disbursements for price supports overseas	AASM countries	E 41-a
Farm subsidies (under feed grain program) in $m	USA	B 8-a
Guaranteed prices: (under price reviews): cattle	UK	B 12-a
cereals (barley, oats, rye & wheat) per ton	UK	B 8-a
eggs	UK	B 12-a
fatstock by kind	UK	B 11-a
milk (by marketing areas) per gallon	UK	B 4-a B 12-a
pigs & sheep	UK	B 12-a
Loans by US government for rice transactions in $ per ton	USA	B 14-a
for warehouse-stored wheat in $ per ton	USA	B 7-a
Maize in $ per ton	All countries	B 8-a
Milk (for processing) in cents per lb of butterfat content	USA	B 4-a
Oats in $ per ton	All countries	B 8-a
Rice (by quality) in local currency per ton	All countries	A 10-a
in $ per ton	All countries	B 8-a
Rye in $ per ton	All countries	B 8-a
Soybeans in $ per bushel	USA	N 10-a
Wheat in $ per ton	All countries	B 8-a
in local currency per 100 kg	All countries	C 29-a
per specified wt	All countries	C 16-a
parity-prices & farm subsidies in $m	USA	B 8-a
under price support (end-Oct): tonnage	USA	B 7-a

PRICES
    see also   EXPORT PRICES
                  FARM PRICES
                  IMPORT PRICES
                  INFLATION
                  INTERVENTION PRICES (EEC)
                  PRODUCER PRICES
                  RETAIL PRICES
                  WHOLESALE PRICES
                  Appendix 4: WORLD MARKET PRICES

% changes in general price levels	Developed countries	U 54-a
Agricultural produce – index nos	Main countries	A 9-a
Industrial prices – index nos	All countries	F 5-m F 6-q
Main products used by manufacturing industry – index nos	Asian, Far East & Australasian countries	U 45-a
Prices received by farmers – index nos	All countries	A 9-a

Prices paid by farmers   see   FARM COSTS

Prices received by farmers   see   FARM PRICES
                                          PRODUCER PRICES

Prices, fixed   see   PRICE SUPPORTS

Prices, guaranteed   see   INTERVENTION PRICES
                              PRICE SUPPORTS
                              TARGET PRICES

Primary batteries   see   BATTERIES & ACCUMULATORS

Primary chemicals   see   CHEMICALS, ORGANIC

PRIMARY COMMODITIES

Consumption by value in $m	Main countries	U 23-a
Demand by kind projected to 1985	Main countries	A 1
Export prices by kind in $ per ton	All countries	A 9-a
main export goods in $ per ton	ECAFE countries	U 17-m
Export prices – index nos (see No. 3, 6, 9, 12)	Worldwide	U 27-q
index nos (weighted average main sources)		U 29-q
Exports as % of consumption	EEC countries, Japan & USA	U 23-a
by kind by destination: tonnage & value in $m	All countries	U 12-a
by value in $m	World regions	U 23-a
main foodstuffs by value in $m	Developing countries	U 11-a
main ores & metals by value in $m	Developing countries	U 11-a
main raw materials by value in $m	Developing countries	U 11-a
– index nos (unit value & quantum bases)	Far East countries	U 32-q

	Territorial coverage	Title codes

PRIMARY COMMODITIES, continued

Imports as % of consumption	EEC countries, Japan & USA	U 23-a
by kind by source: tonnage & value in $m	All countries	U 12-a
Imports - index nos	World regions	A 14-a
Trade: farm products (in detail) by value in $m	All countries	A 14-a
World exports of primary commodities as % of total exports (value basis)	Developed countries	M 4-a
	Developing countries	M 4-a
by value in $m	Developed countries	M 4-a
	Developing countries	M 4-a
World market prices : primary commodities by kind - index nos		G 1-a
index nos (weighted)		U 23-a
World production (in broad categories of primary commodities) - index nos		U 43-a
World production - index nos (quantum basis)		U 23-a
World trade (based on SITC classes) by value in $m	World regions	U 23-a

Primary energy see COAL
          CRUDE PETROLEUM
          ELECTRICITY
          ENERGY
          NATURAL GAS

Primary schools see SCHOOLS, PRIMARY

Prime rate (unsecured credit) see INTEREST RATES

Print advertising see ADVERTISING BY MEDIA

PRINTING & PUBLISHING
    see also BOOK TRANSLATIONS
          BOOKS
          BOOKS FOR CHILDREN
          PAMPHLETS

Book production by subject: volume	All countries	U 62-a	
Capital formation in printing & publishing industries in $m	Main countries	U 21-a	
Costs for salaried staff per mth	EEC countries	E 11-a	
Earnings (average) in local currency	All countries	L 4-a	
Electricity consumption in kWh	All countries	C 23-a	
Employment - index nos	All countries	L 4-a	
Frequency of accidents at work in printing industry	EEC countries	E 2-a	
Gross value of output in $m	Main countries	U 21-a	
Gross output - index nos (quantum basis)	S American countries	U 40-a	
IDA loans approved in $m	OAS member countries	N 16-a	
Investment in buildings in local currency	EEC countries	E 40-a	
in land purchase in local currency	EEC countries	E 40-a	
in machinery in local currency	EEC countries	E 40-a	
Labour costs as % of total costs	EEC countries	E 8-a	
by status of employees in local currency	EEC countries	E 8-a	
per hr: all employees	EEC countries	E 2-a	E 11-a
wage earners	EEC countries	E 11-a	
Labour force: no of salaried staff employed	EEC countries	E 11-a	
wage earners employed	EEC countries	E 11-a	
& salaried staff employed	EEC countries	E 8-a	
No of books produced for children	All countries	U 62-a	
of printing & publishing establishments (incl paper industry)	African countries	U 44-a	
of hrs worked by labour force per yr	EEC countries	E 8-a	
by region per wk	EEC countries	E 25-a	
per wk	All countries	L 4-a	
	Main countries	R 3-m	
	OAS member countries	N 18-a	
per yr: salaried staff	EEC countries	E 11-a	
wage earners	EEC countries	E 11-a	
of printing operatives employed	EEC countries	E 2-a	
	Main countries	U 21-a	
of pamphlets produced by subject groups	All countries	U 62-a	
Wage rates in local currency per hr (average)	EEC countries	E 25-a2	
bookbinders in local currency per hr	OAS member countries	N 17-a	
compositors & typesetters in local currency per hr	OAS member countries	N 17-a	
linotypists in local currency per hr	OAS member countries	N 17-a	
newspaper printers in local currency per hr	OAS member countries	N 17-a	
per day by grade of employee	Portugal	R 4-q	
per hr by sex	Main countries	R 3-m	
photo-engravers in local currency	OAS member countries	N 17-a	
skilled workers by sex in local currency	Main countries	R 4-q	
unskilled workers by sex in local currency	Main countries	R 4-q	
Wages & salary costs in $	Main countries	U 21-a	
Wages by sex in $ per hr	Main countries	C 7-a	

PRINTING INK

Exports: tonnage & value in $	OECD countries	D 5-a	
Imports: tonnage & value in $	OECD countries	D 5-a	
Production: tonnage	All countries	U 22-a	
	EEC countries	E 28-q	E 27-a
	OECD countries	D 5-a	
unit value in $ per ton	OECD countries	D 5-a	

	Territorial coverage	Title codes	

PRINTING MACHINERY

% share held of world exports (value basis)	UK	B 27-a	
Exports by destination by value in $m	Main countries	U 9-a	
by value in $m	Main countries	U 38-a	
Imports by value in $m	All countries	U 38-a	
Production: tonnage	EEC countries	E 28-q	E 27-a
World export trade by value in $m		U 38-a	

PRINTING MACHINERY INDUSTRY

No of hrs worked per wk	Main countries	R 3-m	
Wage rates by sex in local currency per hr	Main countries	R 3-m	

PRINTING PAPER

Consumption: % change per $1000 increase in gross national product	Main countries	D 32-a	
(incl writing paper) per $1000 of gross national product	Main countries	D 32-a	
tonnage	OECD countries	D 40-a	
	All countries	U 62-a	
Consumption - index nos	European countries excl USSR	A 24-a	
Exports by destination (incl writing paper) by value in $m	All countries	D 40-a	
(incl writing paper): tonnage	OECD countries	D 41-q	
tonnage & value in $m	All countries	A 23-a	
Imports by kind: tonnage & by value in $m	All countries	A 23-a	
(incl writing paper): tonnage	OECD countries	D 41-q	
Production: base stock for coating: tonnage	OECD countries	D 40-a	
(incl writing paper): tonnage	All countries	A 23-a	U 22-a
	Main countries	J 7-a	
	OECD countries	D 41-q	D 40-a
uncoated paper: tonnage	OECD countries	D 40-a	

Prisons   see   PENAL INSTITUTIONS

Private airline operators   see   AIRLINE COMPANIES, NON-SCHEDULED

PRIVATE BONDS

Issues: gross valuation in local currency	EEC countries	E 26-m	
Nominal & market valuations in £m	UK	F 8-q	
Transactions in US securities in $m	OAS member countries	N 16-a	

PRIVATE BORROWING

    see also   BANK ADVANCES

% change in personal credit taken up	E European countries & USSR	U 16-a	
Advances (from acceptance houses) in $m	All countries	F 5-m	F 6-q
Company indebtedness, credits & assets in $m	OECD countries	D 12-a	
Loan advances by banking system in local currency	OAS member countries	N 16-a	
to individuals & firms by administrative areas in $	EEC countries	E 38-a	
Long-term private overseas loans granted in $m	All countries	M 6-a	

Private capital flows   see   INVESTMENT, PRIVATE OVERSEAS

Private cars   see   PASSENGER CARS

PRIVATE CONSUMPTION

    see also   HOUSEHOLD BUDGETS
               PUBLIC CONSUMPTION

% by kind of expenditure: food & rent	OECD countries	D 11	
% change as demand component of gross domestic product	Main countries	U 54-a	
of gross national product	USA	G1-a2	
in implicit price deflator	Developing countries	D 25-a	
in personal expenditure on consumption	All countries	U 60-a	
	E European countries	U 16-a	
	EEC countries	E 13-a	
	Canada, W European countries & USA	U 16-a	
	Developing countries	D 25-a	
	Japan	G 1-a	
	Latin American countries	U 18-a	
	OECD countries	D 11-a	
	All countries	M 6-a	
per capita	OECD countries	D 11	
per capita projected to 1980	OECD countries	A 1	
to 1985	Main countries	D 11	
projected to 1980	OECD countries		
% of gross national product spent on private consumption	ECE countries	U 15-a	
% of personal expenditure by kind of outlay: clerical workers	EEC countries	Z 3-a	
manual workers	EEC countries	Z 3-a	
on clothing & footwear	EEC countries	Z 3-a	
education	EEC countries	Z 3-a	
entertainment	EEC countries	Z 3-a	
food, drink & tobacco	EEC countries	Z 3-a	
house furnishings & domestic appliances	EEC countries	Z 3-a	
medicines & toiletries	EEC countries	Z 3-a	
rent, fuel & electric lighting costs	EEC countries	Z 3-a	
social security contributions	EEC countries	Z 3-a	
taxation (all kinds)	EEC countries	Z 3-a	
transportation	EEC countries	Z 3-a	
As % of gross domestic product	All countries	M 6-a	U 23-a
		U 43-a	
	Developing countries	D 25-a	

	Territorial coverage	Title codes	
PRIVATE CONSUMPTION, continued			
As % of gross domestic product	EEC countries	E 13-a	E 44-a
gross domestic product projected to 1980	Main countries	E 3-a	
national income	OECD countries	D 11	
net material product	Developing countries	D 25-a	
total national resources	All countries	U 60-a	
As component of gross, domestic product in local currency	All countries	M 6-a	
of national accounts in local currency	African countries	U 44-a	
in $m	Main countries	R 5-a	
By kind of expenditure & of products in local currency	All countries	F 5-m	F 6-q
	OAS member countries	N 16-a	
	AASM countries	U 41-a	
Contribution of personal expenditure to gross domestic & gross national products in $m	Latin American countries	U 41-a	
Expenditure & expenditure per capita by administrative areas	EEC countries	E 38-a	
at current values in $m (incl % change)	EEC countries	E 26-a	
by component in $m	EEC countries	E 32-a	
	OECD countries	D 30-a	
Expenditure: growth as % change in gross domestic product projected to 1980	OECD countries	D 11	
in local currency & as % of gross domestic product	EEC countries	E 2-a	
local currency	ECE countries	U 15-a	
	Latin American countries	U 18-a	
$m (at current values)	Asian, Far East & Australasian countries	U 45-a	
(at 1960 prices)	Latin American countries	U 18-a	
Expenditure - index nos (value basis)	EEC countries	E 32-a	
	World economic areas	U 60-a	
(quantum basis)	EEC countries	E 26-a	
(incl civil expenditure) as % of gross domestic product	OECD countries	D 11-a	
on alcoholic drinks in local currency	OAS member countries	N 16-a	
chocolate & sugar confectionery in £	UK	P 2-a	
clothing as % of total personal expenditure	EEC countries	B 22-a	
	OECD countries	D 46-a	
clothing, footwear & personal items in local currency	EEC countries	E 2-a	
	OAS member countries	N 16-a	
clothing & knitwear in £m	UK	B 22-a	
clothing projected to 1977 in £m	UK	B 29	
clothing - index nos	OECD countries	D 46-a	K 4-a
consumer goods in local currency	OAS member countries	N 16-a	
domestic equipment in local currency	EEC countries	E 2-a	
durable goods in local currency	OAS member countries	N 16-a	
education in local currency	EEC countries	E 2-a	
education by kind of school in $m	All countries	U 62-a	
electrical goods in local currency	AASM countries	E 41-a	
food & beverages in local currency	EEC countries	E 2-a	
	AASM countries	E 41-a	
fuel, heating & lighting in local currency	OAS member countries	N 16-a	
	EEC countries	E 2-a	
	AASM countries	E 41-a	
furniture, household equipment & fitting in local currency	OAS member countries	N 16-a	
footwear: costs as % of total personal expenditure	Main countries	E 18-a	
household goods & furnishings as % total expenditure	UK	B 29	
in local currency	AASM countries	E 41-a	
	OAS member countries	N 16-a	
house building & construction work in local currency	All countries	U 13-a	
personal health & care requisites in local currency	OAS member countries	N 16-a	
petroleum products in $m	EEC countries	E 16-q	E 15-a
raw materials & DIY products in local currency	AASM countries	E 41-a	
recreation & entertainment in local currency	EEC countries	E 2-a	
	OAS member countries	N 16-a	
rents in local currency	AASM countries	E 41-a	
rents & fuel as % of all household expenditure	All countries	U 13-a	
in $m	All countries	U 13-a	
rents, water charges & local taxation in local currency	EEC countries	E 2-a	
	OAS member countries	N 16-a	
services received in local currency	AASM countries	E 41-a	
	OAS member countries	N 16-a	
textiles (incl clothing) in local currency	AASM countries	E 41-a	
tobacco & tobacco products in £m	UK	B 13-a	B 17-a
in local currency	EEC countries	E 2-a	
	OAS member countries	N 16-a	
transportation & fares in local currency	EEC countries	E 2-a	
	AASM countries	E 41-a	
(personal) as % of total consumption expenditure	All countries	U 60-a	
per capita in local currency (incl % change)	ECE countries	U 15-a	
	EEC countries	E 2-a	E 26-a
		E 32-a	
in $m	OECD countries	D 30-a	
projected to 1985 in $	Main countries	A 1	
per capita - index nos	EEC countries	E 26-a	E 44-a
(total) in local currency	OAS member countries	N 16-a	
	Developing countries	D 25-a	
in $m	OECD countries	D 30-a	
	USA	G 1-a2	

Private education   see   EDUCATION, PRIVATE

	Territorial coverage	Title codes

PRIVATE EXPENDITURE
    see also PRIVATE CONSUMPTION

Direct taxation: expenditure in local currency	OAS member countries	N 16-a
Indirect taxation & levies in local currency	OAS member countries	N 16-a
Of nationals resident abroad in local currency	OAS member countries	N 16-a
in $m	EEC countries	E 32-a
Overseas remittances (private) in local currency	OAS member countries	N 16-a
Private funds available for research in $m	All countries	U 62-a

Private income   see PERSONAL INCOME

Private investment   see INVESTMENT, PRIVATE

Private loans   see PRIVATE BORROWING

Private overseas investment   see INVESTMENT, PRIVATE OVERSEAS

Private overseas loans   see DEVELOPMENT AID, PRIVATE FLOW
                                    FOREIGN LOANS

Private schools   see SCHOOLS, PRIVATE

Process control systems   see CONTROL INSTRUMENTATION
                                    ELECTRONIC EQUIPMENT

Process measuring equipment   see ELECTRONIC EQUIPMENT

Process scrap   see FERROUS SCRAP
                SCRAP DEALERS

Process workers   see CRAFTSMEN & PROCESS WORKERS

Procurement   see STATE PROCUREMENT (COMMUNIST COUNTRIES)

Procurement prices   see PRICE SUPPORTS

Produce agreements, international   see INTERNATIONAL COFFEE AGREEMENT
                                                   INTERNATIONAL SUGAR AGREEMENT
                                                   INTERNATIONAL TIN AGREEMENT
                                                   INTERNATIONAL WHEAT AGREEMENT

PRODUCER GOODS
    see also CAPITAL GOODS
                CONSUMER GOODS

% change in output: producer goods	E European countries & USSR	U 16-a	
Exports by destination by kind by CST classes: tonnage & value in $m	EEC countries	E 48-a	
SITC classes by value in $m	Main countries	D 2-q	
tonnage & value in $m	OECD countries	D 3-a2	
tonnage & value in $m	All countries	U 12-a	
kind by NIMEXE classes by value in $m	All countries	E 20-a	
SITC classes by value in $m	All countries	U 50-a	U 59-a
Imports by kind by NIMEXE classes by value in $m	All countries	E 20-a	
SITC classes by value in $m	All countries	U 50-a	U 59-a
source by kind by CST classes: tonnage & value in $m	EEC countries	E 21-a	
SITC classes by value in $m	Main countries	D 2-q	
tonnage & value in $m	OECD countries	D 3-a2	
tonnage & value in $m	All countries	U 12-a	
Wholesale prices - index nos	Japan & S Korea	U 32-m	
	OAS member countries	N 17-a	

PRODUCER PRICES
    see also FARM PRICES
                WHOLESALE PRICES

% change: butter (over previous yr)	W Germany	E 34-m
cheese (Gouda) over last 12 mths	EEC countries	E 34-m
hen eggs (over previous yr)	EEC countries	E 34-m
Apples (by variety) in cents per kg	EEC countries	U 20-a
in local currency per ton	OECD countries	D 1-a
Arable crops & livestock - index nos	EEC countries	E 44-a
Bacon pigs in local currency per kg	OECD countries	D 1-a
Barley in £ per cwt	EEC countries	B 1-a
% change (over previous yr)	EEC countries	E 34-m
(as animal feed) in local currency per 100 kg	European countries	E 35-a
in $ per ton	E European countries	U 30-a
(for brewing) in $ per ton	E European countries	U 30-a
in $ per ton	OECD countries	D 1-a
£ equiv per 100 kg	EEC countries	B 3-a
local currency per kg	EEC countries	E 34-m
local currency per 100 kg	W European countries	E 35-a
	Main countries	B 8-a
	EEC countries	B 3-a
$ per bushel	USA	E 35-a
Barley - index nos	EEC countries	B 3-a
Beef cattle (live wt) in local currency per 100 kg	W European countries	E 35-a
in $ per 100 lbs	USA	E 35-a
Beef in local currency per kg	Denmark	D 1-a
Bullocks in local currency per kg	Eire	D 1-a

PRODUCER PRICES, continued

	Territorial coverage	Title codes
Butter in £ per cwt	EEC countries	B 1-a
(ex dairies) in DM per 100 kg	W Germany	E 34-m
in FrB per kg	Belgium	D 1-a
(ex farm) in FrB per kg	Belgium	D 1-a
Cadmium in $ per lb (on New York Metal Market)	USA	C 12-m
Calves in local currency per ton	OECD countries	D 1-a
Cattle (for slaughter) in $ per ton (live wt)	E European countries	U 30-a
in local currency per ton (live wt)	OECD countries	D 1-a
in £ per cwt (live wt)	EEC countries	B 1-a
Cauliflowers in cents per kg	France, Italy & Netherlands	U 20-a
Cement (type 425) in sacks in lire per ton	Italy	R 2-m
Cereals by kind in $ per 100 kg	USA	U 30-a
	E European countries	U 30-a
Cheese in £ per cwt	EEC countries	B 1-a
(Gouda) in local currency per 100 kg	Belgium, Italy & Netherlands	E 34-m
in local currency per kg	Denmark, Sweden & Switzerland	D 1-a
Chick peas in Esc per 100 kg	Portugal	D 1-a
Chickens in local currency per ton	OECD countries	D 1-a
Chicory in cents per kg	Belgium & Netherlands	U 20-a
Cobalt in $ per lb (on New York Metal Market)	USA	C 12-m
Cocoa in £ per ton	Ghana & Nigeria	P 2-a
in Fr CFA per kg	Cameroon & Ivory Coast	P 2-a
Cocoa beans in £ per ton	Ghana & Nigeria	P 3-a
in $ per ton	Ghana & Nigeria	B 2-a
Copper (refined) for export in cents per lb	USA	C 12-m
Copra in F$ per ton	Fiji	A 4-m
Cotton (raw) in local currency per ton	OECD countries	D 1-a
Cows (for slaughter) in local currency per kg	OECD countries	D 1-a
Cucumber in cents per kg	France & Netherlands	U 20-a
Eggs in local currency per kg	Denmark & Netherlands	R 2-m
per 1000	OECD countries	D 1-a
per 100	EEC countries	E 34-m
per 100 kg	W European countries	E 35-a
in pence per doz	EEC countries	B 1-a
in $ per doz	USA	E 35-a
in local currency per 100	E European countries	U 30-a
Farm prices received: animal products – index nos	OECD countries	D 1-a
crops – index nos	OECD countries	D 1-a
Farm products by kind (free market prices) in local currency	Poland	U 30-a
Food products by kind – index nos	EEC countries	E 44-a
Fowls (for boiling) in local currency per kg	Austria & Belgium	D 1-a
(for roasting) in local currency per kg	Austria	D 1-a
Goat milk in pesetas per 100 litres	Spain	D 1-a
Groundnut oil in FrB per 100 litres	Belgium	E 34-m
Groundnuts in local currency per ton	OECD countries	D 1-a
Hay in local currency per ton	OECD countries	D 1-a
Heifers (for rearing) in local currency per head or kg	OECD countries	D 1-a
Hops in £ per 100 kg	UK	D 1-a
Horses (for slaughter) in local currency per 100 kg	OECD countries	D 1-a
Industrial products – index nos	W Germany	H 3-a
Iron & steel products – index nos	W Germany	H 3-a
Lambs in local currency per ton	OECD countries	D 1-a
Lemons (normal quality) at Catania in lire per kg	Italy	A 5-a U 20-a
Lettuce in Fl per kg	Netherlands	U 20-a
Live chickens: % change (over 12 mths)	Belgium	E 34-m
in local currency per kg	Belgium, Italy & W Germany	E 34-m
Magnesium ingots in cents per lb	USA	C 12-m
Maize: % change (over previous yr)	France & Italy	E 34-m
in local currency per kg	France & Italy	E 34-m
in local currency per 100 kg	Austria, France & Italy	E 35-a
in $ per bushel	USA	E 35-a
in $ per ton	OECD countries	D 1-a
in £ per ton	Main countries	B 8-a
Margarine: % change (over previous yr)	Belgium	E 34-m
in local currency per 100 kg	Belgium & W Germany	E 34-m
Milk (fresh for cheese production) in FrS per ton	Switzerland	D 1-a
(fresh) in local currency per 100 kg	EEC countries	B 3-a
per ton	OECD countries	D 1-a
Milk (fresh) – index nos	EEC countries	B 3-m
in local currency per ton	E European countries	U 30-a
	W European countries, Hungary & Poland	U 35-q
in pence per gallon	EEC countries	B 1-a
in local currency per 100 kg of fat content	W European countries	E 35-a
in $ per 100 lbs of fat content	W European countries	E 35-a
Motor spirit (by grade) ex Genoa & Rotterdam refineries in local currency	Italy & Netherlands	H 4-a
in lire per litre	Italy	H 4-a
Natural rubber in M$ per kg	Singapore	R 2-m
Non-ferrous metals by kind in local currency per ton	W Germany, UK & USA	H 2-a
Oats: % change (over previous yr)	EEC countries	E 34-m
in local currency per kg	EEC countries	E 34-m
per 100 kg	European countries	E 35-a
in £ per cwt	EEC countries	B 1-a
in $ per ton	OECD countries	D 1-a
in £ per ton	Main countries	B 8-a
in $ per bushel	USA	E 35-a
Olive oil in local currency per 100 litres	Portugal & Spain	D 1-a
Oranges in lire per kg	Italy	U 20-a

	Territorial coverage	Title codes
PRODUCER PRICES, continued		
Peaches in local currency per kg	France & Italy	U 20-a
Pears in local currency per kg	EEC countries	U 20-a
Peas & beans in local currency per kg	Netherlands & Portugal	D 1-a
Piglets in local currency per head or per kg	OECD countries	D 1-a
Pigs in £ per score (dead wt)	EEC countries	B 1-a
(for slaughter) in local currency per ton (live wt)	E European countries	U 30-a
in local currency per ton (live wt)	OECD countries	D 1-a
per 100 kg (live wt)	W European countries	E 35-a
in $ per 100 lbs (live wt)	USA	E 35-a
Platinum (refined) in $ per oz	USA	C 12-m
Platinum (refined), osmium & palladium in £ per oz	UK	T 4-m
Potatoes in £ per cwt	EEC countries	B 1-a
% change over previous yr	EEC countries	E 34-m
in local currency per ton	E European countries	U 30-a
per kg	EEC countries	E 34-m
per 100 kg	W European countries	E 35-a
in $ per cwt	USA	E 35-a
Poultry meat in local currency per ton	E European countries	U 30-a
Primary farm products by kind in $ per ton	All countries	A 9-a
Rice: % change (over previous yr)	France & Italy	E 34-m
(bought under government procurement contracts) in $ per ton	Burma	A 10-a
in local currency per kg	France & Italy	E 34-m
per ton: historical table 1900-1964	Main countries	A 19-a
in $ per ton	OECD countries	D 1-a
Root crops by kind in local currency per ton	E European countries	U 30-a
Rye in £ per cwt	EEC countries	B 1-a
in local currency per 100 kg	W European countries	E 35-a
	Main countries	B 8-a
in $ per bushel	USA	E 35-a
Sorghum in $ per ton	OECD countries	D 1-a
Soybeans in local currency per ton	OECD countries	D 1-a
Steers (for slaughter) in local currency per kg	OECD countries	D 1-a
Sugar: % change (over previous yr)	EEC countries	E 34-m
Sugar beet in local currency per ton	OECD countries	D 1-a
	E European countries	U 30-a
per 100 kg	W European countries	E 35-a
	EEC countries	E 34-m
in $ per ton	USA	E 35-a
Table grapes in local currency per kg	France & Italy	U 20-a
Tangerines in lire per kg	Italy	U 20-a
Tobacco in local currency per ton	OECD countries	D 1-a
Tomato paste (ex factory) in $ per ton	Italy	A 7-a
Tomatoes in local currency per kg	France, Italy & Netherlands	U 20-a
(for processing) in lire per kg	Italy	U 20-a
in pesetas per 100 kg	Spain	D 1-a
Turkeys in local currency per ton	OECD countries	D 1-a
Whale oil (charged by whaling companies) in £ per ton		B 19-a
Wheat (durum) in local currency per ton	France & Italy	B 7-m
% change (over previous yr)	France & Italy	E 34-m
in local currency per kg	France & Italy	E 34-m
per ton	Main countries	B 8-a
in $ per ton	OECD countries	D 1-a
in $ per bushel	OECD countries	D 1-a
in local currency per ton	USA	E 35-a
(soft): % change (over previous yr)	EEC countries	B 7-m
in local currency per kg	EEC countries	E 34-m
	EEC countries	E 34-m
per 100 kg	OECD countries	D 1-a
in £ per cwt	W European countries	E 35-a
Wheat flour: % change (over previous yr)	EEC countries	B 1-a
in local currency per kg	EEC countries	E 34-m
Wine in local currency per 100 litres	EEC countries	E 34-m
(red) in Esc per 100 litres	OECD countries	D 1-a
(white) in Esc per 100 litres	Portugal	D 1-a
Wool (raw) in local currency per kg	Portugal	D 1-a
Zinc metal in local currency per kg	OECD countries	D 1-a
(outside N America) in £ per ton (excl duties)	Main countries	T 4-m
slabs in £ per ton	UK	U 24-m
		C 12-m

Producer returns   see   DEFICIENCY PAYMENTS
                            PRICE SUPPORTS

PRODUCTION
    see also   LABOUR PRODUCTIVITY
                 OUTPUT PER CAPITA
                 Appendix 4: WORLD PRODUCTION

	Territorial coverage	Title codes	
% change in output: foundries (iron & steel)	Main countries	C 2-a	
iron & steel industry	Main countries	C 2-a	
per person employed	Main countries	U 16-a	
shipbuilding industry	Main countries	C 2-a	
% growth rates (planned) for industrial output	E European countries	U 16-a	
for output per capita	E European countries	U 16-a	
(at constant prices)	All countries	U 54-a	
Basic metals - index nos	OECD countries	D 19-m	D 20-m
Chemical industries - index nos	Main countries	R 5-a	
Electricity, gas & water - index nos	OECD countries	D 19-m	D 20-m

445

	Territorial coverage	Title codes	
PRODUCTION, continued			
Energy requirements (of public utility undertakings) - index nos	Main countries	R 5-a	
Food, drink & tobacco industries - index nos	Main countries	R 5-a	
	OECD countries	D 19-m	D 20-m
Index nos (based on current prices)	OECD countries	R 5-a	
output by industrial sector	Main countries	R 5-a	
Investment goods industries - index nos	Main countries	R 5-a	
Iron & steel products - index nos	OECD countries	D 19-m	D 20-m
Machine tools manufacturing industry - index nos	Main countries	R 5-a	
Machinery (non-electrical) - index nos	OECD countries	D 19-m	D 20-m
Man-made fibres by kind - index nos	Main countries	B 10-a	
Manufacturing industry - index nos	OECD countries	D 19-m	D 20-m
Metal products manufacturing industries - index nos	Main countries	R 5-a	
- index nos	OECD countries	D 19-m	D 20-m
Mining & quarrying - index nos	Main countries	R 5-a	
	OECD countries	D 19-m	D 20-m
Non-ferrous metals - index nos	OECD countries	D 19-m	D 20-m
Oil, coal derivatives & rubber - index nos	OECD countries	D 19-m	D 20-m
Synthetic rubber - index nos	OECD countries	D 19-m	D 20-m
Textile industries - index nos	Main countries	R 5-a	
Textiles, clothing & leather - index nos	OECD countries	D 19-m	D 20-m
Transport equipment - index nos	OECD countries	D 19-m	D 20-m

Production, agricultural   see   AGRICULTURAL PRODUCTION

Production, industrial   see   INDUSTRIAL PRODUCTION

Production (indices)   see   INDEX NOS (Appendix No 3)
                                   PRODUCTION

Production (output statistics)   see   UNDER NAME OF PRODUCT

Production capacity   see   PLANT CAPACITY

Production costs, agricultural   see   FARM COSTS

Production costs, industrial   see   LABOUR COSTS
                                           MATERIAL COSTS
                                           WAGES

Production goods   see   CAPITAL GOODS
                           CONSTRUCTION EQUIPMENT
                           ENGINEERING INDUSTRY
                           MACHINE TOOLS
                           MACHINERY
                           PRODUCER GOODS

Production per capita   see   LABOUR PRODUCTIVITY

Production trains, automated   see   TRANSFER MACHINES

PRODUCTION WORKERS			
see also CRAFTSMEN & PROCESS WORKERS			
No employed: engineering industry (electrical)	Main countries	C 2-a	
(mechanical)	Main countries	C 2-a	
foundries (iron & steel)	Main countries	C 2-a	
iron & steel industry	Main countries	C 2-a	
motor vehicles manufacturing industry	Main countries	C 2-a	
shipbuilding & repair industry	Main countries	C 2-a	

PRODUCTIVITY		
see also FARM PRODUCTIVITY		
INDUSTRIAL PRODUCTIVITY		
LABOUR PRODUCTIVITY		
% changes recorded in output in general to 1968	Main countries	D 17
Planned % growth rates in productivity	Portugal, Spain, Turkey & Greece	D 17

Products, manufactured   see   MANUFACTURED GOODS

Products, primary   see   PRIMARY COMMODITIES
                           RAW MATERIALS

Products, semi-manufactured   see   SEMI-MANUFACTURED PRODUCTS

Professional & technical staff   see   SALARIED STAFF, PROFESSIONAL

Profit & loss accounts   see   ASSETS & LIABILITIES
                              BALANCE SHEETS

Profit margins   see   DISTRIBUTION COSTS
                    SALES MARGINS

Profit ratios   see   FINANCIAL RATIOS, CORPORATE

	Territorial coverage	Title codes

PROFITS

see also BALANCE SHEETS
BANK PROFITS
MONOPOLY PROFITS

	Territorial coverage	Title codes
As component of national income in local currency	OAS member countries	N 16-a
Electric power equipment industry by firm in $m	Worldwide	T 7-a
Hotels (international) per room by location in $	World regions	Z 5-a
(tourist) per room in $	World regions	Z 5-a
Industrial companies: key balance sheet data	Largest European companies	F 9-a
Net trading profit: largest 100 American industrial companies in $m		H 1
30 American commercial undertakings in $m		H 1
30 American public utility companies in $m		H 1
30 American transport corporations in $m		H 1
American-owned airline companies in $m		H 1

PROFITS, CORPORATE

	Territorial coverage	Title codes
As % of turnover: chemical industry	USA	J 2-a
engineering industry	USA	J 2-a
machine tools manufacturing industry	USA	J 2-a
manufacturing industry (in general)	USA	J 2-a
motor vehicles manufacturing industry	USA	J 2-a

PROFITS TAX

see also CORPORATION TAX

	Territorial coverage	Title codes
Government revenue: historical tables from 1923 in local currency	Main European countries	Z 1-a
Receipts from corporation & profit taxes levied on firms	EEC countries	E 42-a

PROJECTIONS

	Territorial coverage	Title codes
% growth rates: output per capita in farming projected to 1980	Main countries	D 17-a
in manufacturing industry projected to 1980	Main countries	D 17-a
in service industries to 1980	Main countries	D 17-a
employment as component of gross domestic product	Main countries	D 17-a
farm output as component of gross domestic product	Main countries	D 17-a
productivity as component of gross domestic product	Main countries	D 17-a
sector shift factor as component of gross domestic product	Main countries	D 17-a
specific factors mainly conditioning output	Main countries	D 17-a
whisky consumption	Main countries	Z 6-a
% of labour force engaged in farming projected to 1980	Main countries	D 17-a
in manufacturing industry projected to 1980	Main countries	D 17-a
in service industries projected to 1980	Main countries	D 17-a
% of households not owning a car projected to 1977	UK	B 28
owning one car projected to 1977	UK	B 28
owning two or more cars projected to 1977	UK	B 28
Consumption: cereals (for animal feed) projected to 1978: tonnage	UK	P 5-a
oats & barley (for human food) projected to 1978	UK	P 5-a
wheat (soft) for human food projected to 1978: tonnage	UK	P 5-a
Employment: clerical staff: motor vehicles industry projected to 1977	UK	B 28
managerial staff: motor vehicles industry projected to 1977	UK	B 28
regional motor vehicles industry projected to 1977	UK	B 28
semi-skilled workers: motor vehicles industry projected to 1977	UK	B 28
skilled workers: motor vehicles industry projected to 1977	UK	B 28
technical staff: motor vehicles industry projected to 1977	UK	B 28
unskilled workers: motor vehicles industry projected to 1977	UK	B 28
Exports: motor vehicles: projected sales by value by 1977 in £m	UK	B 28
Feed requirements per kg of beef & veal production projected to 1985	Main countries	P 5-a
cow milk production projected to 1985	Main countries	P 5-a
eggs production projected to 1985	Main countries	P 5-a
pork production projected to 1985	Main countries	P 5-a
poultry production projected to 1985	Main countries	P 5-a
Gross domestic product per capita (at 1968 prices) projected to 1980 in $	Main countries	D 17-a
Gross output: motor vehicles industry projected to 1977 by value in £m	UK	B 28
Imports: motor vehicles: projected to 1977 by value in £m	UK	B 28
New registrations: commercial vehicles: projected to 1977	W European area	B 28
No of new passenger car & commercial vehicles registrations projected to 1977	W European countries	B 28
passenger car scrappages projected to 1977 by value in $m	UK	B 28
passenger cars in use projected to 1977	UK	B 28
passenger cars in use per 100 population projected to 1977	UK	B 28

PROJECTIONS, INDUSTRIAL

	Territorial coverage	Title codes
% changes: consumer expenditure: clothing	UK	B 22-a
% changes projected to 1977: cash flow: motor vehicle manufacturing industry	UK	B 28
consumption: machine tools	UK	B 26
deliveries: machine tools	UK	B 26
demand: arms & ordnance	UK	B 27
agricultural machinery	UK	B 27
batteries, lamps & insulated wire	UK	B 23
domestic equipment by kind (in detail)	UK	B 23

	Territorial coverage	Title codes
PROJECTIONS, INDUSTRIAL continued		
% changes projected to 1977: demand: earth-moving equipment	UK	B 27
internal combustion engines	UK	B 27
machinery by kind (in detail)	UK	B 27
employment: mechanical engineering industries	UK	B 27
exports: agricultural machinery	UK	B 27
arms & ordnance	UK	B 27
earth-moving equipment	UK	B 27
internal combustion engines	UK	B 27
machine tools	UK	B 26
machinery by kind (in detail)	UK	B 27
motor vehicles	UK	B 28
plant & steelwork	UK	B 27
imports: machine tools	UK	B 26
motor vehicles	UK	B 28
production: chemical products	UK	B 21
engineering products	UK	B 26
mechanical engineering products	UK	B 27
motor vehicles	UK	B 26
% changes projected to 1980: capital formation: engineering industry	N African countries	U 38
metal fabricating industry	N African countries	U 38
transport equipment manufacturing industry	N African countries	U 38
gross domestic product (at factor cost)	Main countries	D 17-a
labour force employed in industrial occupations	Main countries	D 17-a
output (value basis): machine tools	UK	B 26
output per capita	Main countries	D 17-a
Consumption projected to 1977: iron & steel castings: tonnage	UK	B 25-a
to 1980: fibres by kind	Main countries	B 29
Demand (domestic): blankets in lbs	UK	B 29
canvas goods & sacks in lbs	UK	B 29
carpets & linoleum in lbs	UK	B 29
clothing by value in £m	UK	B 22
in lbs	UK	B 29
commercial vehicles by value in $m	E African countries	U 38
furnishing textiles in lbs	UK	B 29
hand-knitting wools & yarns & sewing thread in lbs	UK	B 29
insulated wire: tonnage	E African countries	U 38
knitted garments in lbs	UK	B 29
passenger cars by value in $m	E African countries	U 38
	W European countries	B 28
in £m	UK	B 28
radio receivers by value in $m	E African countries	U 38
road trailers by value in $m	E African countries	U 38
textiles by kind in lbs	UK	B 29
(industrial) projected to 1977: iron & steel castings: tonnage	UK	B 25-a
tyre cord in lbs	UK	B 29
Employment projected to 1977: motor vehicle manufacturing industry	UK	B 28
Expenditure (domestic) projected to 1977: clothing by value in £m	UK	B 22
commercial vehicles by wt classes	UK	B 28
Generating capacity projected to 1980: nuclear power in kW	Main countries	D 48
Production projected to 1977: textile products by value in £m	UK	B 29
to 1980: machinery by value in $m	E African countries	U 38
metal products by value in $m	E African countries	U 38
transport equipment by value in $m	E African countries	U 38
Productivity projected to 1977: motor vehicles manufacturing industry	UK	B 28
Sales projected to 1977: retailers' purchases from wholesalers: clothing by value in £m	UK	B 22
World consumption projected to 1980: natural & synthetic rubber: tonnage		U 26-a
World demand projected to 1980: elastomers: tonnage		U 26-a

Propane   see   NATURAL GAS LIQUIDS

PROPERTY DAMAGE

Claims paid by insurance companies in local currency	OAS member countries	N 16-a

PROPERTY INCOME

As % of gross national product & of taxation receipts	Main countries	E 3-a
As component of national income (at factor cost) in $m	OAS member countries	N 16-a
	All countries	U 60-a
	Main countries	U 27-a
in local currency	African countries	U 44-a
External transactions & overseas income in local currency	African countries	U 44-a
Government revenue from property ownership in $m	Latin American countries	J 5-a
Interest, dividends & rents received in $m	OECD countries	D 30-a
Personal income received from property ownership in local currency	EEC countries	E 32-a

Property shares   see   SHARES, PROPERTY

Property taxes   see   REVENUE
                         TAXATION

	Territorial coverage	Title codes

PROPYLENE
    see also CHEMICAL PRODUCTS
                 HYDROCARBONS, ALIPHATIC

Consumption (for organic synthesis): tonnage	OECD countries	D 5-a
tonnage	OECD countries	D 5-a
Production from oil & natural gas: tonnage	OECD countries	D 5-a
tonnage	European countries, Japan & USA	U 26-a
Refining capacity available in tons per yr	EEC countries	B 30-a

PROTEIN
    see also HARDENED PROTEINS (PLASTICS)
                 NUTRITION

% needs of dairy cattle per lb of dry diet		P 5
Consumption: animal protein per capita in grammes per day	OECD countries	D 1-a
per capita in grammes per day	ECE countries	U 15-a
per capita in grammes per day	OAS member countries	N 17-a
	OECD countries	D 1-a
vegetable protein per capita in grammes per day	OECD countries	D 1-a
Content in mixed animal feeding stuffs	European countries	U 30-a
Feed characteristics: cereals by kind & % content (incl lysine)		A 12-a
cereals: energy-protein ratios		A 12-a
Net supply: animal protein per capita in grammes per day	Main countries	M 4-a
per capita by kind of foodstuff in grammes	OAS member countries	N 17-a
in grammes per day	Main countries	M 4-a

Proton accelerators see ACCELERATORS, ELECTRON & PROTON

PROVIDENT FUNDS, STATUTORY

No of persons & of economically-active population covered	All countries	L 2-a

Provincial (or state) expenditure see EXPENDITURE, PROVINCIAL

Provolone see CHEESE BY VARIETY

PRUNES
    see also FRUIT, DRIED

Producer prices in $ per ton	USA	A 9-a
Production: tonnage	All countries	B 5-a
	Main countries	A 5-a

Public administration see ADMINISTRATION, PUBLIC SECTOR

PUBLIC ASSISTANCE

Cash benefits paid out in $m	All countries	L 2-a
Costs defrayed by central government in $m	All countries	L 2-a
by local authorities in $m	All countries	L 2-a
of medical benefits in $m	All countries	L 2-a

Public broadcasting equipment see ELECTRONIC EQUIPMENT

Public catering see RESTAURANT MEALS

PUBLIC CONSUMPTION
    see also NET MATERIAL PRODUCT
                 PRIVATE CONSUMPTION

% change: public consumption expenditure	W European countries, Canada & USA	U 16-a	
public expenditure as component of gross domestic product	Main countries	U 54-a	
% growth rates: public consumption expenditure	All countries	U 60-a	
	Developing countries	D 25-a	
	Latin American region	U 18-a	
	ECE countries	U 15-a	
% of gross national product spent by government (or its agencies)	S American countries	U 41-a	
Public expenditure as factor in gross domestic & gross national product in $m		U 44-a	
in gross domestic product in local currency	African countries	F 5-m	F 6-q
in national accounts in $m	All countries	M 6-a	U 43-a
as % of gross domestic product	All countries	E 3-a	
	Main countries	M 6-a	
of gross national product	All countries	D 11	
	OECD countries	D 25-a	
	Developing countries	D 11	
of gross national product projected to 1980	OECD countries	E 26-a	
at current values (incl % change) in $m	EEC countries	N 16-a	
in local currency	OAS member countries	E 41-a	
	AASM countries	D 25-a	
	Developing countries	U 18-a	
	Latin American countries	U 60-a	
in $m	All countries	E 32-a	
	EEC countries	D 30-a	
	OECD countries	U 45-a	
	Asian, Far East & Australasian countries	U 27-a	
	Main countries	D 30-a	
by kind of outlay in $m	OECD countries		

449

	Territorial coverage	Title codes

PUBLIC CONSUMPTION, continued
    Public expenditure in $m (at 1960 prices) — Latin American countries — U 45-a
        (incl defence expenditure) as % of gross national product — OECD countries — D 11
        on building construction & housing in $m — All countries — U 13-a
           fixed capital goods & machinery purchases — OECD countries — D 30-a
           subsidies in UA — AASM countries — E 41-a
           wages & salaries of the labour force in UA — AASM countries — E 41-a
    Public expenditure - index nos — EEC countries — E 32-a
           — World economic areas — U 60-a
    Rate of growth in public consumption as % of projected change in gross national product by 1980 — OECD countries — D 11

PUBLIC CORPORATIONS
    see also   STATE-CONTROLLED ENTERPRISES
    Assets, investments & loans granted in $m — OECD countries — D 12-a
    Loans & advances granted by banking system in local currency — OAS member countries — N 16-a
    Savings of corporations as % of total savings — All countries — U 60-a

PUBLIC DEBT
    see also   DOMESTIC DEBT
                FOREIGN DEBT
    Amounts outstanding in budget accounts in $m — Main countries — U 43-a
        owed by type of creditor in $m — Latin American countries — J 5-a
    Central government debt in $m — EEC countries — E 26-m
        foreign & domestic debt in $m — Main countries — E 3-a
    External debt as % of gross national product — All countries — M 6-a
    Government expenditure: debt servicing in local currency — African countries — U 44-a
                loan repayments in local currency — African countries — U 44-a
                repayment of domestic loans in local currency — African countries — U 44-a
                of foreign loans in local currency — African countries — U 44-a
    Gross bonded debt in local currency — W Indies & Caribbean countries — T 6-a
    In local currency — OECD countries — R 5-a
    Servicing payments & amortization costs in $m — All countries — M 6-a
        as % of total government expenditure — All countries — M 6-a
           of gross domestic product — Main countries — E 3-a
           — OECD countries — D 11-a
        on loans as % of value of exports — Latin American countries — J 5-a

Public electricity supply   see   PUBLIC UTILITIES

PUBLIC EMPLOYEES
    No of civil servants employed by ministry — OAS member countries — N 20-a
    Salary (average) per civil servant in local currency — OAS member countries — N 20-a
    Salary bill: civil service by ministry in local currency — OAS member countries — N 20-a

Public enterprise   see   STATE-CONTROLLED ENTERPRISES

Public expenditure   see   GOVERNMENT EXPENDITURE

PUBLIC FINANCE
    Deficit & surplus on government financing in $m — All countries — F 5-m   F 6-q
    Receipts & expenditure: government in local currency — Main countries — R 5-a
                local authorities in local currency — Main countries — R 5-a

PUBLIC HEALTH
    see also   HEALTH
                SANITATION
    % allocation of gross national product to health services — OECD countries — D 11
    Contributions of employers & employees in $ — All countries — L 2-a
    Cost of health service as % of total social expenditure — All countries — L 2-a
    Development aid authorisations in $m — Recipient countries — M 1-a
    Difference between receipts & costs in $m — All countries — L 2-a
    Expenditure by main kinds of costs in $m — All countries — L 2-a
        administration in $m — All countries — L 2-a
        cash benefits in $m — All countries — L 2-a
        medical & hospital care in $m — All countries — L 2-a
    Government expenditure (incl welfare) in local currency — OAS member countries — N 16-a   N 18-a
        in local currency — W Indies & Caribbean countries — T 6-a
        on medical research & per capita in local currency — Latin American countries — J 5-a
    Local authority cost & participation in $m — EEC countries — E 36-a
    No of medical personnel by kind in practice — All countries — L 2-a
    Public & private expenditure on health as % of gross national product — African countries — U 44-a
    Public expenditure on health services in local currency — OECD countries — D 11
        per capita in local currency — Main countries — W 2-a
    Receipts: health service in $m — Main countries — W 2-a
    Revenue contributions (from state funds) in $m — All countries — L 2-a
    — All countries — L 2-a

Public investment   see   CENTRALISED STATE INVESTMENT
                          GOVERNMENT EXPENDITURE

Public libraries   see   LIBRARIES, PUBLIC

	Territorial coverage	Title codes
PUBLIC LIGHTING		
Consumption: electricity in kWh	All countries	C 23-a
from public supply in kWh	All countries	C 23-a
on road lighting in kWh	European countries	U 1-a
PUBLIC LOANS		
see also PRIVATE BONDS		
As component in balance of payments in $m	Latin American countries	U 18-a
% interest rates paid on municipal loans per annum	OECD countries	D 12-a
Government advances in $m	Asian, Far East & Australasian countries	U 45-a
Government expenditure loan repayments in local currency	African countries	U 44-a
Issues of bonds (gross value) in local currency	EEC countries	E 26-m
Public ownership see STATE-CONTROLLED ENTERPRISES		
Public Sector Borrowing Requirement see GOVERNMENT BORROWING		
GOVERNMENT EXPENDITURE		
PUBLIC DEBT		
PUBLIC FINANCE		
PUBLIC SERVICE VEHICLES		
No in use	Main countries	V 4-a
No of registrations: ambulances	Main countries	V 4-a
Public transport services see BUSES & COACHES		
RAILWAYS		
TRANSPORT SERVICES		
PUBLIC TRANSPORT		
Fares - index nos	EEC countries	E 26-m
PUBLIC UTILITIES		
see also ELECTRICITY SUPPLY INDUSTRY		
GAS SUPPLY INDUSTRY		
WATER SUPPLY INDUSTRY		
% change in implicit price deflator	Developing countries	D 25-a
% contribution of public utility companies to national income	Developing countries	D 25-a
% growth rates: gross output of public utilities	Developing countries	D 25-a
in output of gas & electricity	Main countries	U 38
% of persons working in gas, water & electricity supply industries	EEC countries	E 33-a
% rate of change in gross product output of public utilities	Latin American countries	U 18-a
% share of gas & electricity production of industrial activity (in general)	Main countries	U 38-a
Capacity: power generating plants in kW	All countries	U 55-a
Capital formation in public utilities in local currency	OAS member countries	N 16-a
in $m	Main countries	U 21-a
Consumption: fuels for electric power generation: tonnage	OECD countries	D 8-a
of electric power by public utilities in kWh	All countries	C 23-a
by gasworks in kWh	European countries	U 1-a
Contribution of power & gas production to gross domestic product	S American countries	U 41-a
to gross domestic product (at factor cost) in local currency	African countries	U 44-a
	Latin American countries	U 18-a
	EEC countries	E 11-a
Costs: salaried staff per mth in local currency		
Details of 30 largest public utility companies	USA	H 1
Direct investment by US Government in $m	OAS member countries	N 16-a
Employment by sex & status by administrative areas	EEC countries	E 38-a
electricity, gas & water supply industries	EEC countries	E 2-a E 33-a
	Australasian & Far East countries	U 32-q
wages: electricity & gas supply industries in $ per hr	All countries	U 43-a
Employment - index nos	OAS member countries	N 18-a
Energy requirements - index nos	Main countries	R 5-a
Foreign loans granted to electricity supply industry in $m	Latin American countries	U 18-a
Frequency: industrial accidents in public utility plants	EEC countries	E 2-a
Generation: electricity by public supply undertakings in kWh	European countries & USA	U 4-a
by type of plant	European countries	U 1-a
in kWh (planned)	OECD countries	D 8-a
in kWh	OECD countries	D 8-a
	All countries	U 55-a
Gross capital formation: gas & power plants in local currency	EEC countries	E 32-a
Gross output by value in $m	Main countries	U 21-a
Gross product as component in gross domestic product in $m	Developing countries	D 25-a
(at current prices) in local currency	OAS member countries	N 16-a
IDA loans approved for water supply projects in $m	OAS member countries	N 16-a
Income contribution to gross domestic product & as % of total	EEC countries	E 32-a
at factor cost in $m	S American countries	U 41-a
Indirect taxes levied on power, gas & water consumers	S American countries	U 41-a
Investment in buildings in local currency	EEC countries	E 40-a
in land purchase in local currency	EEC countries	E 40-a
in machinery purchase in local currency	EEC countries	E 40-a
in power supply equipment (planned) in $m	OECD countries	D 8-a
Labour costs: all employees in local currency per hr	EEC countries	E 11-a
as % of total costs in public utility enterprises	EEC countries	E 8-a
by status of employees in local currency	EEC countries	E 8-a
gas, water & power supply companies by sex	EEC countries	E 18-a
manual workers in local currency per hr	EEC countries	E 3-a

	Territorial coverage	Title codes

PUBLIC UTILITIES, continued

Labour costs: salaried staff in local currency per mth	EEC countries	E 3-a
wage earners in local currency per hr	EEC countries	E 11-a
Labour force employed by occupation in water supply companies	All countries	W 2-a
by sex (at census dates)	African countries	U 44
	OAS member countries	N 18
by status	Main countries	C 28
electricity, gas & water supply industries	All countries	L 4-a
	OECD countries	D 23-a
Labour force: no of salaried staff employed	EEC countries	E 8-a
of wage earners employed	EEC countries	E 11-a
(total)	EEC countries	E 11-a
Loan advances granted by commercial banking system in local currency	Main countries	U 21-a
	OAS member countries	N 16-a
Names of largest American public utilities incl % change in turnover	USA	H 1
labour force employed	USA	H 1
turnover & net profits in $m	USA	H 1
No of public utility enterprises in operation	African countries	U 44-a
of hrs worked per wk by sex	EEC countries	E 18-a
per wk: electricity generation	Main countries	R 3-m
gas supply industry	Main countries	R 3-m
water supply industry	Main countries	R 3-m
per wk	Main countries	R 3-m
per yr: salaried staff	EEC countries	E 11-a
wage earners	EEC countries	E 11-a
per yr	EEC countries	E 8-a
of power & gas industry workers presently unemployed	All countries	L 4-a
of wage & salary earners employed by sex by region	EEC countries	E 18-a
Power generating capacity by type of plant in kW	European countries & USA	U 1-a
Production: electricity & gas - index nos	African countries	U 44-a
	Far East countries	U 32-q
	Main countries	U 38-a
	OECD countries	D 19-m D 20-m
	Australasian countries	U 32-q
in public utility plants as % of general world activity		U 38
Stocks: anthracite held at electricity generating plants: tonnage	USA	N 1-a
Wage rates by sex in local currency per hr	Main countries	R 3-m
electricity generating plants in £ per wk	UK	R 4-a
gas equipment installation engineers in £ per wk	UK	R 4-a
Wages & salary costs incurred by public utility companies in $m	Main countries	U 21-a
Water supply companies: no of artisans employed	All countries	W 2-a
chemists & biologists employed	All countries	W 2-a
clerical staff employed	All countries	W 2-a
drillers & engineers employed	All countries	W 2-a
salaried staff & supervisors employed	All countries	W 2-a

Public utility profits   see   PROFITS

PUBLIC WORKS

see also   BUILDING CONSTRUCTION

Electricity: consumption from public supply companies in kWh	All countries	C 23-a

Publishing   see   PRINTING & PUBLISHING

Pullets   see   POULTRY

Pulp   see   PULP, FIBROUS NON-WOOD
             WOOD PULP

Pulp & purée, tomato   see   TOMATO PRODUCTS

PULP, FIBROUS NON-WOOD

Consumption: tonnage	OECD countries	D 40-a
Exports by destination: tonnage	All countries	D 40-a

Pulp, soda sulphate & sulphite   see   WOOD PULP, CHEMICAL

Pulping machines   see   PAPER & PULP MACHINES

PULPWOOD

% contribution to export earnings	Bahamas	E 45-a
Exports by destination by volume in m³	European countries	A 13-q
tonnage	Canada, European countries & USSR	A 13-q
Imports by source by volume in m³	European countries	A 13-q
tonnage	European countries	A 13-q
by volume in m³	Main countries	A 5-a
Production (all kinds) by volume in m³	Main countries	A 5-a
broadleaved timber by volume in m³	Canada, European countries & USA	A 13-a
coniferous timber by volume in m³	Canada, European countries & USA	A 13-a
Wholesale prices in local currency per ton	Main countries	A 13-m

	Territorial coverage	Title codes

PULSES
    see also PEAS & BEANS

As source of fat, protein & calorie intake per capita	OAS member countries	N 17-a
Producer prices: peas & beans in local currency per kg	Netherlands & Portugal	D 1-a
Production: beans, peas, lentils (et al)	All countries	A 9-a
by administrative areas: tonnage	EEC countries	E 38-a

PUMICE

% consumption: volcanic cinder (as concrete aggregates)	USA	N 1-a
(as railroad ballast)	USA	N 1-a
(on road construction)	USA	N 1-a
Consumption: pumice & volcanic cinder: tonnage	USA	N 1-a
Stocks held at mines or users' premises: tonnage	USA	N 1-a
Wholesale prices (at mines or mills) in $ per ton	USA	N 1-a
World production: tonnage	Main countries	N 1-a

Pumice stone   see ABRASIVES, NATURAL

Pumped storage generators   see GENERATORS, PUMPED STORAGE

PUMPS

% share held of world exports (value basis)	UK	B 27-a	
Exports by destination by value in $m	Main countries	U 9-a	
(incl centrifuges) by value in $m	All countries	U 38-a	
Imports (incl centrifuges) by value in $m	All countries	U 38-a	
Production: industrial pumps for liquids: volume	All countries	U 22-a	U 38-a
	EEC countries	E 28-q	E 27-a
World exports (incl centrifuges) by value in $m		U 38-a	

PUNCH & SHEARING MACHINES
    see also MACHINE TOOLS

Deliveries by industrial sector by value in $m	USA	J 2-a

Pupil-teacher ratios   see EDUCATION

PUPILS
    see also STUDENTS

No attending primary schools: historical table from 1830	Main European countries	Z 1-a
secondary schools: historical table from 1830	Main European countries	Z 1-a
enrolled by grade in schools as % of total enrolment	World regions	U 62
in kindergarten & as % of private education	All countries	U 62-a
of girl pupils enrolled by grade	World regions	U 62

PUPILS BY SEX

No enrolled & courses taken: secondary schools	OAS member countries	N 19-a
in kindergarten	All countries	U 62-a
in primary schools (all kinds)	All countries	U 62-a
(private)	OAS member countries	N 19-a
(public)	OAS member countries	N 19-a
in secondary schools (public)	OAS member countries	N 19-a
in special schools	All countries	U 62-a
on vocational courses	OAS member countries	N 19-a

Purchase prices (government agencies)   see COMMODITY CREDIT CORPORATION

PURCHASE TAX
    see also VALUE ADDED TAX

Government receipts from purchase taxes on motor vehicles	Main countries	S 24-a
on articles sold in general	UK	E 42-a

Purchasing power of export income   see TERMS OF TRADE

PURCHASING POWER PARITIES
    see also INFLATION

% relationship of parities to exchange rates	Main countries	C 2-a

Push-chairs   see PERAMBULATORS & PUSH-CHAIRS

PVC (Polyvinylchloride)   see PLASTICS

Pyrethrum   see INSECTICIDES

Pyridine   see CHEMICALS, ORGANIC

PYRITES
    see also IRON PYRITES
             SULPHUR

% consumption in production of sulphuric acid	Main countries	U 25-a	
Consumption by chemical industry: tonnage	European countries, Japan & USA	U 25-a	
in blast furnaces: tonnage	EEC countries	E 29-a	
in sinter plants: tonnage	EEC countries	E 29-a	
in sinter plants & furnaces: tonnage	EEC countries	E 30-q	
of pyrites residues in production of agglomerates: tonnage	ECE countries	U 7-q	U 6-a
in production of sinter: tonnage	UK	T 2-q	

	Territorial coverage	Title codes	
PYRITES, continued			
Consumption of sulphurous materials by kind: tonnage	OECD countries	D 5-a	
	Main countries	H 3-a	
Exports by destination: tonnage	OECD countries	D 5-a	
pyrites residues: tonnage	ECE countries	U 7-m	U 6-a
	Main countries	H 3-a	
Imports & exports: ferrous & cupreous pyrites: tonnage	All countries	B 15-a	
Imports by source: tonnage	OECD countries	D 5-a	
pyrites residues: tonnage	ECE countries	U 7-m	U 6-a
	Main countries	H 3-a	
Production (incl other sulphides): tonnage	European countries, Japan & USA	U 25-a	
& sulphur content: tonnage	Main countries	B 15-a	
tonnage	All countries	T 5-a	
	OECD countries	D 5-a	
World production (incl cupreous pyrites): tonnage		N 4-a	
	Main countries	T 4-a	

Pyrochloric concentrates   see   COLUMBITE CONCENTRATES

Pyrophoric alloys & ferro-cerium   see   RARE EARTH MINERALS

Pyrophyllite   see   TALC

PYROTECHNIC PRODUCTS
    see also EXPLOSIVES

Exports (incl explosives) by destination by value in $	Main countries	U 2-a

QUALITY STANDARDS, METAL

Permissible % impurities in metals by kind	Italy	C 12

QUARTZ CRYSTAL

Consumption: imported natural quartz: tonnage	USA	N 1-a
Government strategic stockpile (incl sales) in lbs	USA	N 1-a
Stocks held at users' premises in lbs	USA	N 1-a
Wholesale prices: electronic grade of quartz crystal in $ per lb	USA	N 1-a
World production (at mines) in lbs	USA	N 1-a

Quasi-money   see   MONEY SUPPLY

QUEBRACHO

Export prices - index nos	S American countries	U 40-q

Quicksilver   see   MERCURY

Quinine   see   OPIUM ALKALOIDS

Quotas   see   EXPORT QUOTAS
              IMPORT QUOTAS
              SUPPLY QUOTAS

RABBIT MEAT

Production & consumption per capita in kg	OECD countries	D 14-a
(incl game): tonnage	OECD countries	D 1-a
Retail prices in local currency	OAS member countries	N 17-a

RABIES

No of reported cases of infection	OAS member countries	N 18-a

Radar equipment   see   ELECTRONIC EQUIPMENT

RADIATION DETECTION EQUIPMENT

Deliveries by value in £m	UK	C 24-a

Radio advertising   see   ADVERTISING BY MEDIA

RADIO COMMUNICATIONS

No of amateur radio stations licenced	All countries	S 18-a
coastal stations in operation for public use	All countries	S 18-a
with radiotelegraph & radio-telephone	All countries	S 18-a
medical advices transmitted by radio	All countries	S 18-a
radiotelegrams received & transmitted	All countries	S 18-a
radiotelephone calls made	All countries	S 18-a
ship & shore stations by kind in operation	All countries	S 18-a
with radiotelephone installation	All countries	S 18-a

	Territorial coverage	Title codes

Radio communications equipment   see   ELECTRONIC EQUIPMENT

RADIO PROGRAMMES
Broadcast time by type of programme in hrs	All countries	U 62-a

RADIO RECEIVERS
see also   TELEVISION RECEIVERS

% changes in volume of retail sales	E European countries & USSR	U 16-a	
% of households owning radio receivers by social classes	W European countries	Z 3	
Demand projected to 1980: volume	African countries	U 38	
Exports by destination by CST classes: tonnage & value in $	EEC countries	E 48-a	
SITC classes by value in $	Main countries	D 2-q	
tonnage & value in $	OECD countries	D 3-a2	
by value in $m	Main countries	U 9-a	
NIMEXE classes by value in $	All countries	E 20-a	
SITC classes by value in $	All countries	U 50-a	U 59-a
value in $m	Main countries	U 38-a	
volume	OECD countries	D 9-a	
Imports by NIMEXE classes by value in $	All countries	E 20-a	
SITC classes by value in $	All countries	U 50-a	U 59-a
source by CST classes: tonnage & value in $	EEC countries	E 21-a	
SITC classes by value in $	Main countries	D 2-q	
tonnage & value in $	OECD countries	D 3-a2	
value in $m	All countries	U 38-a	
No in use & no in use per 1000 population	OAS member countries	N 19-a	
per 1000 population	All countries	U 43-a	
	ECE countries	U 15-a	
	Latin American countries	J 5-a	
	OECD countries	R 5-a	
No in use	African countries	U 44-a	
	All countries	U 62-a	
No of radio receiver licences issued (at end-yr)	Main countries	R 5-a	
	Asian, Far East & Australasian countries	U 45-a	
historical table from 1924	Main European countries	Z 1-a	
Production: transistor radios: volume	Zaire	E 41-a	
(incl transistor radios): volume	Main countries	R 5-a	
volume (all types)	African countries	U 44-a	
	All countries	U 22-a	U 43-a
	E European countries & USSR	U 16-a	
	EEC countries	E 28-q	E 27-a
	Canada, European countries, Japan & USA	U 38-a	
	OAS member countries	N 14-a	
Sales demand for radio receivers per 1000 population	E European countries & USSR	U 16-a	
World exports by value in $m		U 38-a	

RADIO STATIONS
see also   TELEVISION TRANSMITTERS

No of transmitters in operation & transmission power in kW	All countries	U 62-a
in operation	Latin American countries	J 5-a
	World regions	U 62-a
operated by public corporations	OAS member countries	N 19-a
Transmission power (long & short-wave stations) in kW	All countries	U 62-a

RADIO STATIONS, PRIVATE
No of transmitters in operation by kind	All countries	U 62-a
Transmission power in kW	All countries	U 62-a

RADIO STATIONS, PUBLIC
No of transmitters in operation by kind	All countries	U 62-a
Transmission power in kW	All countries	U 62-a

Radio telegraph & radio telephone services   see   RADIO COMMUNICATIONS

RADIOACTIVE MATERIALS
Exports by destination by value in $m	Main countries	U 2-a

RADIUM
% of imports by source: isotopes & radium compounds	USA	N 1-a
% usage in cancer therapy	USA	N 1-a
in production of luminous materials	USA	N 1-a
Wholesale prices (by wt groups) in $ per milligramme	USA	N 1-a

Rags   see   FIBROUS WASTE

RAIL FREIGHT
see also   CONTAINER TRAFFIC
RAIL PASSENGER TRAFFIC

Anthracite: domestic transport: tonnage	USA	N 1-a
Carried in ton-km: historical table from 1870	Main European countries	Z 1-a
in ton-km	Asian & Far East countries	U 32-q
	Main countries	U 43-a
Consignment distances in ton-km	EEC countries	E 43-a
	European countries	U 8-a

	Territorial coverage	Title codes	
RAIL FREIGHT, continued			
Exports by rail: building materials & timber: tonnage	European countries	U 8-a	
cereals & farm products by kind: tonnage	European countries	U 8-a	
chemical products & fertilisers: tonnage	European countries	U 8-a	
machinery: tonnage	European countries	U 8-a	
metal ores: tonnage	European countries	U 8-a	
petroleum products & solid fuels: tonnage	European countries	U 8-a	
Freight carriage (wet) in ton-km	OAS member countries	N 15-a	
Goods entered (incl transit) as % of total freight carried	European countries	U 8-a	
Goods transport in ton-km	Main countries	S 24-a	
tonnage	Main countries	S 24-a	
Hinterland traffic by route (via Hamburg): tonnage	W Germany	S 16-a	
Imports & exports: all goods (incl transit): tonnage	European countries	U 8-a	
Imports: building materials & timber: tonnage	European countries	U 8-a	
cereals & farm products by kind: tonnage	European countries	U 8-a	
chemical products & fertilisers: tonnage	European countries	U 8-a	
machinery: tonnage	European countries	U 8-a	
metal ores: tonnage	European countries	U 8-a	
petroleum products & solid fuels: tonnage	European countries	U 8-a	
Index nos (volume basis) see no 1	Continents	U 27-a	
Inter-regional rail freight flow within EEC area: tonnage	EEC countries	E 38-a	
Mode of loading: (containers or pallets): tonnage	EEC countries	E 43-a	
(wagon-loaded or parcelled): tonnage	EEC countries	E 43-a	
Goods loaded & carried in transit: tonnage	European countries	U 8-a	
loaded & unloaded from wagons: tonnage	EEC countries	E 43-a	
Inland & international freight by rail by classes of goods: tonnage	EEC countries	E 43-a	
International goods traffic by rail: tonnage	EEC countries	E 43-a	
No of freight-km covered	Main countries	R 5-a	
	European countries	U 8-a	
Tonnage & length of haul per ton of load (average)	European countries	U 8-a	
Tonnage carried: historical tables from 1855	Main European countries	Z 1-a	
Transit goods: rail traffic: tonnage	EEC countries	E 43-a	
Volume of rail freight carried in ton-km	African countries	U 44-a	
	AASM countries	E 41-a	
	Asian, Far East & Australasian countries	U 32-m	U 45-a
	ECE countries	U 42-m	U 15-a
	EEC countries	E 3-a	
	Latin American countries	J 5-a	
	Main countries	E 3-a	
	S American countries, Costa Rica & Mexico	U 40-a	
Wagon loads & wagon capacity: tonnage	European countries	U 8-a	
World rail traffic: volume - index nos	Continents	U 43-a	
RAIL PASSENGER TRAFFIC			
In passenger-km	Asian & Far East countries	U 32-q	
No of passengers carried by class of carriage	EEC countries	E 43-a	
by length of journey	European countries	U 8-a	
(total)	Latin American countries	J 5-a	
	Asian, Far East & Australasian countries	U 45-a	
	S American countries, Costa Rica & Mexico	U 40-a	
historical table from 1834	Main European countries	Z 1-a	
passenger-km: historical table from 1841	Main European countries	Z 1-a	
passenger-km run	AASM countries	E 41-a	
	African countries	U 44-a	
	ECAFE countries	U 32-q	
	Main countries	E 3-a	R 5-a
		S 24-a	U 43-a
	OAS member countries	N 15-a	
Rail passenger vehicles see ROLLING STOCK			
RAIL TRAFFIC			
see also RAIL FREIGHT			
RAIL PASSENGER TRAFFIC			
Freight: tonnage & no of passengers carried	EEC countries	E 26-m	
	Main countries	U 43-a	
Rail transport see CONTAINER TRAFFIC			
RAIL FREIGHT			
RAIL PASSENGER TRAFFIC			
RAILS & TRACK-LAYING MATERIAL			
see also SLEEPERS, STEEL			
Consumption: tonnage	EEC countries	E 29-a	
Deliveries to EEC area: tonnage	EEC countries	E 29-a	
to user industries: tonnage	ECE countries	U 7-q	U 6-a
	Main countries	H 3-a	
tonnage	OECD countries	D 22-a	
Exports by destination: tonnage	EEC countries	E 5-q	E 29-a
	ECE countries	U 48-a	
	Main countries	T 4-a	
tonnage	ECE countries	U 7-m	U 6-a
	European countries, Japan & USA	C 5-m	
	Main countries	H 3-a	
Imports by source: tonnage	EEC countries	E 5-q	E 29-a
	Main countries	T 4-a	

	Territorial coverage	Title codes	
RAILS & TRACK-LAYING MATERIALS, continued			
Imports: fishplates: tonnage	Main countries	T 1-a	
heavy rails: tonnage	Main countries	T 1-a	
light rails: tonnage	Main countries	T 1-a	
points, etc: tonnage	All countries	T 1-a	
tonnage	Developing world regions	U 57-a	
	ECE countries	U 7-m	U 6-a
	European countries, Japan & USA	C 5-m	
	Main countries	H 3-a	
Inter-EEC trade: tonnage	EEC countries	E 29-a	
Production: tonnage	All countries	T 1-a	U 22-a
	ECE countries	U 7-m	U 6-a
	EEC countries	E 30-m	E 28-a
		E 27-a	E 29-a
	European countries & Japan	C 5-m	
	Main countries	H 3-a	T 4-a
	OECD countries	D 22-a	
Receipts ex EEC area: tonnage	EEC countries	E 29-a	
RAILS, STEEL			
see also HEAVY SECTIONS, STEEL			
Exports by destination: tonnage & value in $m	EEC countries	E 5-q	
Imports by source: tonnage	EEC countries	E 5-q	

Rails, steel (second-hand)   see   FERROUS SCRAP

Railway accidents   see   ACCIDENTS, RAILWAY

Railway coaches   see   ROLLING STOCK

Railway engines   see   LOCOMOTIVES

Railway equipment   see   LOCOMOTIVES
                                    ROLLING STOCK

Railway scrap   see   FERROUS SCRAP
                             SCRAP DEALERS

	Territorial coverage	Title codes
RAILWAY SLEEPERS, WOOD		
Production, imports & exports: tonnage	All countries	A 23-a
tonnage	All countries	U 22-a
RAILWAY TRAINS		
Distances covered: passenger & goods trains in km	EEC countries	E 43-a
No & hp: electric & diesel-driven trains in service	EEC countries	E 43-a
	European countries	U 8-a
No of carriages (by class) on electric & diesel trains	EEC countries	E 43-a
of passenger seats (by class) on electric & diesel trains	EEC countries	E 43-a

Railway locomotive wheels & axles   see   WHEELS TYRES AXLES, STEEL

	Territorial coverage	Title codes	
RAILWAYS			
see also TRANSPORT SERVICES			
Consumption: coal & agglomerates: tonnage	EEC countries	E 14-a	
coal & coke-oven coke: tonnage	Main countries	N 2-a	
coke: tonnage	EEC countries	E 14-a	
diesel oil: tonnage	EEC countries	E 14-a	
	OECD countries	D 44-a	
electric power in coal equiv tonnage	EEC countries	E 14-a	
fuel oil: tonnage	EEC countries	E 14-a	
iron castings: tonnage	UK	B 25-a	
lignite & briquettes: tonnage	EEC countries	E 14-a	
patent fuels: tonnage	Main countries	N 2-a	
petroleum products by kind: tonnage	OECD countries	D 31-a	
tonnage	EEC countries	E 16-q	E 14-a
		E 15-a	
Distance covered by trains by type of traction in km	EEC countries	E 43-a	
Fatality rates: accidents on railways	All countries	L 4-a	
Freight traffic (inter-regional) by rail within EEC area: tonnage	EEC countries	E 38-a	
IBRD loans approved for railway construction projects in $m	OAS member countries	N 16-a	
Length of track (for passenger or goods or both) in km	EEC countries	E 43-a	
historical table from 1825 in km	Main European countries	Z 1-a	
in km & no of km per 1000 population	Latin American countries	J 5-a	
km per 1000 population	OAS member countries	N 15-a	
km per 1000 sq km of land area	OAS member countries	N 15-a	
use by type of railway in km	EEC countries	E 43-a	
in km	AASM countries	E 41-a	
	African countries	U 44-a	
	Main countries	E 3-a	
	Asian, Far East & Australasian countries	U 45-a	
laid down in km	OAS member countries	N 15-a	
not used for passenger transport in km	European countries	U 8-a	
single & double track (electrified)	European countries	U 8-a	
single & normal track in km	EEC countries	E 43-a	
No of containers used for freight transport	European countries	U 8-a	
freight wagons (all types) in use	AASM countries	E 41-a	

	Territorial coverage	Title codes

RAILWAYS, continued
   No of locomotives in use — AASM countries — E 41-a
      of passengers carried & passenger-km run by type of line — EEC countries — E 43-a
   Traffic volume in ton-km (incl rate of increase) — ECE countries — U 15-a
   Wage rates: railway employees in local currency per wk — OAS member countries — N 17-a

RAILWAYS, UNDERGROUND
   Length in use in km & location of underground network — OAS member countries — N 15-a
      under construction in km — OAS member countries — N 15-a
   No of passengers carried by location of underground network — OAS member countries — N 15-a
      of stations in use & location — OAS member countries — N 15-a

Raincoats   see   OUTERWEAR, WEATHERPROOF
                  OVERCOATS & RAINCOATS

RAINFALL
     see also   TEMPERATURE
   In coconut-growing areas in inches — Worldwide — A 4-m
   In major European cities: historical table from 1800-1969 in mm (average) — — Z 1-a
   % cloud cover (maximum & minimum) — All countries — R 5
   Mean precipitation by region in mm — OAS member countries — N 11-a
      (highest & lowest) in cm — All countries — R 5
   Total recorded precipitation by region in mm — OAS member countries — N 11-a

RAISINS & CURRANTS
     see also   FRUIT, DRIED
   Export prices in $ per ton — Australia & Greece — A 9-a
   Exports by destination: currants: tonnage — Greece — B 6-a
      historical table from 1858: tonnage — Greece — Z 1-a
      raisins: tonnage & value in $ — Main countries — U 11-a
      tonnage — Main countries — B 5-a
             — Turkey — D 37-a
   Import prices in £ per ton cif — UK — A 9-a
   Imports by kind: tonnage — Main countries — B 5-a
      by source: currants: tonnage — OECD countries — D 37-a
      tonnage — All countries — B 5-a
   Producer prices: raisins in $ per ton — USA — A 9-a
   Production: tonnage — All countries — A 9-a
               — Main countries — A 5-a   B 5-a
               — Turkey — D 37-a
   Supply, production, consumption & trade: tonnage — EEC countries — B 1-a
   Unit value: exports of raisins in $ per ton — Main countries — U 11-a
   Wholesale prices: raisins in local currency — Australia, Turkey & USA — A 9-a

Ramie yarn   see   FLAX YARN

Ramin   see   HARDWOOD, SAWN

Rams   see   SHEEP

RAPESEED
   Area harvested in ha, production tonnage & yield per ha — All countries — A 9-a
      under crop (for seed) in acres — Main countries — B 18-a
         in acres & ha — Austria, Australia & France — N 10-a
         in acres — Main countries — B 19-a
         rape & colza in ha — EEC countries — E 12-a
   Consumption (domestic): tonnage — Main countries — B 18-a
   Crop yield: rape & colza in 100 kg per ha — EEC countries — E 12-a
   Export prices in $ per ton cif — Canada, Netherlands & Sweden — A 9-a
   Exports by destination: tonnage — Canada — B 19-a
      tonnage — Main countries — B 18-q   B 19-a
   Harvest (for ensuing crop yr): tonnage (estim) — World regions — P 1-a
   Import prices (ex Canada) in £ per ton cif — UK — B 19-q
         — W European ports — A 9-a   B 19-a
   Imports by source: tonnage — EEC countries — B 19-a
      in vegetable oil equiv tonnage — EEC countries — P 5-a
      tonnage — UK — P 1-a
         — Main countries — B 19-a
   Intervention prices (fixed by EEC Commission) — EEC countries — E 44-a
      in UA per ton — EEC countries — B 19-a
   Market & target prices in UA per ton — EEC countries — B 19-a
   Producer prices in local currency per ton — France & Sweden — A 9-a
   Production (incl world total): tonnage (estim) — Main countries — P 1-a
      rape & colza: tonnage — EEC countries — E 12-a
      turnip rape: tonnage & yield per ha — Finland — N 10-a
      tonnage — Main countries — B 19-a
   Target prices: rapeseed & colza in £ per cwt — EEC countries — B 1-a
   Wholesale prices in cents per bushel — Canada — N 10-m
      in $ per ton — India — A 9-a
   World crop: tonnage (estim) — All countries — B 18-a   P 1-a

RAPESEED CAKE
   Export: prices in Fl per ton — Netherlands — A 9-a
   Production: tonnage — W Germany — N 10-a
   Wholesale prices in cents per lb — Canada — N 10-m

	Territorial coverage	Title codes
RAPESEED OIL		
Consumption in production of cooking fats: tonnage	UK	B 19-a
margarine & cooking fats: tonnage	UK	A 4-a
margarine: tonnage	Main countries	B 19-a
Export prices in S Kr per ton fob	Sweden	A 9-a
Exports by destination: tonnage	Canada, Denmark, France & Sweden	B 19-a
tonnage	Main countries	B 19-a
	Primary producing countries	B 18-q
		B 19-a
Import prices in £ per ton cif at W European ports		
Imports: tonnage	Main countries	B 19-a
Production for ensuing yr (estim): tonnage	Main world regions	P 1-a
tonnage	Main countries	B 19-a P 1-a
Wholesale prices in cents per lb	W Germany	N 10-a
World & Commonwealth production: tonnage	Canada	N 10-m
World production for ensuing yr (estim): tonnage		B 19-a
		A 1-a
tonnage		A 4-a A 5-a
		N 10-a
RARE EARTH MINERALS		
% consumption: thorium in production of gas mantles	USA	N 1-a
of refractories	USA	N 1-a
of special alloys	USA	N 1-a
Consumption (industrial): tonnage	USA	N 1-a
thorium: tonnage	USA	N 1-a
Export prices: thorium in $ per ton	European countries	T 4-m
Exports: bastnaesite: tonnage	USA	N 1-a
ferro-cerium & pyrophoric alloys: tonnage	USA	N 1-a
Government strategic stockpile & sales: tonnage	USA	N 1-a
thorium nitrate: tonnage	USA	N 1-a
Imports & exports by kind: tonnage	All countries	B 15-a
Imports: monazite metal, alloys & compounds: tonnage	USA	N 1-a
Production by kind: tonnage	All countries	B 15-a
Stocks: rare earth oxides: tonnage	USA	N 1-a
thorium held at premises of industrial users: tonnage	USA	N 1-a
Wholesale prices: bastnaesite concentrate in $ per ton	USA	N 1-a
cerium metal in $ per ton	USA	N 1-a
lutetium in $ per ton	USA	N 1-a
monazite concentrates in $ per ton	USA	N 1-a
thorium nitrate & oxide in $ per ton	USA	N 1-a
pellets in $ per ton	USA	N 1-a
yttrium in $ per ton	USA	N 1-a
World production: thorium: tonnage	Main countries	N 1-a
tonnage	Main countries	N 1-a
World reserves: thorium: tonnage (estim)	USA	N 1-a
RATES & WATER CHARGES		
see also RENTS		
Cost: rates & water charges to consumers - index nos	EEC countries	E 26-m
to private sector in local currency	AASM countries	E 41-a
	OAS member countries	N 17-a
(incl rents) in local currency	EEC countries	E 32-a
Rates of exchange see EXCHANGE RATES		
Rates of interest see INTEREST RATES		
Raw cattle hides & skins see HIDES		
Raw cork see CORK, RAW		
RAW MATERIALS		
see also BUILDING MATERIALS		
% change in exports by destination (on previous yr)	EEC countries	E 23-a
in imports by source (on previous yr)	EEC countries	E 23-a
Consumption by industrial sector by value in $m	OAS member countries	N 14-a
cellulosic fibres for production of yarn: tonnage	All countries	K 5-a
chemical industry for production of alcohol: tonnage	OECD countries	D 5-a
in cotton looms: tonnage	W European countries	K 2-q
spindles: tonnage	W European countries	K 2-a
non-cellulosic fibres for production of yarn: tonnage	All countries	K 5-a
raw cotton for production of yarn: tonnage	All countries	K 5-a
timber: blockboard manufacturing industry: tonnage	All countries	A 26-a
Costs for sulphuric acid production in $ per ton	Main countries	U 25-a
Disposals ex US strategic stockpile: abaca, hemp & sisal: tonnage		U 11-a
aluminium, copper, lead, tin & zinc: tonnage		U 11-a
natural rubber: tonnage		U 11-a
Expenditure by industrial sectors on raw materials in $m	OAS member countries	N 14-a
Export prices: non-food farm products - index nos	Worldwide	U 29-q
Exports by destination by value in UA	EEC countries	E 23-a
by sea, inland waters, road, rail & air: tonnage	European countries	U 8-a
by value in $m	Australia, India, Japan & S Korea	U 32-m
	Main countries	E 24-a
	Main countries & world regions	U 23-a
Exports - index nos (quantum & value bases)	OECD countries	D 16-q
(value basis)	World regions	A 11-a

459

	Territorial coverage	Title codes	
RAW MATERIALS, continued			
Exports shipped to non-EEC area by value in UA	EEC countries	E 24-a	
Household expenditure on materials for own use in local currency	AASM countries	E 41-a	
Imports (as industrial supplies): tonnage	AASM countries	E 41-a	
ex EEC area by value in UA	AASM countries	E 41-a	
by sea, inland waters, road, rail & air: tonnage	European countries	U 8-a	
source by value in UA	EEC countries	E 23-a	
value in local currency	Asian, Far East & Australasian countries	U 32-m	
in $m	African, Caribbean countries & Pacific Is	E 45-a	
	Main countries	E 24-a	
for production of capital goods by value in $m	Asian countries	U 32-q	
consumable goods by value in $	Asian countries	U 32-q	
shipped ex EEC area by value in UA	African, Caribbean countries & Pacific Is	E 45-a	
ex non-EEC area by value in UA	EEC countries	E 24-a	
Imports - index nos (quantum & value bases)	OECD countries	D 16-q	
(value basis)	World regions	A 11-a	
Inter-EEC area exports by value in UA	EEC countries	E 22-m	E 24-a
imports by value in UA	EEC countries	E 22-m	E 24-a
Production for fabrication by textile industry: tonnage	OECD countries	D 46-a	
Value of stock of raw materials in hand in $m	OAS member countries	N 14-a	
Wholesale prices - index nos	OAS member countries	N 17-a	
	OECD countries	D 26-m	
	Pakistan & S Vietnam	U 32-m	
	W Germany	H 3-a	
World market prices: raw materials - index nos		U 30-a	
textile materials - index nos		U 23-a	
World production - index nos (quantum basis)		U 23-a	
index nos (see No 2, 5, 8, 11)		U 27-q	

RAW MATERIALS, AGRICULTURAL

    see also   COTTON
                    HIDES
                    NATURAL RUBBER
                    TIMBER
                    WOOD PULP
                    WOOL

Exports by kind by value in $m	World regions	A 5-a	
Wholesale prices - index nos	W Germany	H 3-a	
World market prices by kind - index nos		G 1-a	

RAW MATERIALS BY KIND

% change in foreign trade	Developing world regions	A 1	
% content used in production of sulphuric acid	Main countries	U 25-a	
Consumption by animal feed producers: tonnage	EEC countries	P 5-a	
chipboard & fibreboard manufacturing industry: tonnage	All countries	A 26-a	
textile manufacturing industry: tonnage	OECD countries	D 46-a	
veneer industry: tonnage	All countries	A 26-a	
Demand forecast: textile manufacturing industry projected to 1977	UK	B 29	
Disposals ex US strategic stockpile: tonnage		U 11-a	
Export prices - index nos	Latin American countries	U 18-a	
Exports by destination by CST classes: tonnage & value in $m	EEC countries	E 48-a	
SITC classes by value in $m	Main countries	D 2-q	
tonnage & value in $m	OECD countries	D 3-a2	
tonnage & value in $m	All countries	U 12-a	
NIMEXE classes: tonnage & value in $m	All countries	E 20-a	
SITC classes: tonnage & value in $m	All countries	U 50-a	U 59-a
shipped to EEC & non-EEC areas by value in $m	EEC countries	E 24-a	
Imports by NIMEXE classes: tonnage & value in $m	All countries	E 20-a	
SITC classes: tonnage & value in $m	All countries	U 50-a	U 59-a
source by CST classes: tonnage & value in $m	EEC countries	E 21-a	
SITC classes by value in $m	Main countries	D 2-q	
tonnage & value in $m	OECD countries	D 3-a2	
tonnage & value in $m	All countries	U 12-a	
shipped ex EEC & non-EEC areas by value in $m	EEC countries	E 24-a	
Production - index nos (see No 2, 5, 8, 10)	Worldwide	U 27-q	
Supply & demand for raw materials: textile industry in lbs	UK	B 29-a	
Wholesale prices in local currency per ton	OAS member countries	N 17-a	

Raw steel   see   CRUDE STEEL
                        INGOTS, STEEL

Rayon cloth   see   WOVEN RAYON

Rayon fibres   see   CELLULOSIC FIBRES

RAYON PIECE GOODS

    see also   CLOTHING
                    STOCKINGS & TIGHTS

Exports: tonnage	Main countries	K 1-q	
Imports: tonnage	Main countries	K 1-q	
Production: tonnage	Main countries	K 1-q	
volume by kind	EEC countries	K 4-a	

Rayon staple   see   CELLULOSIC FIBRES
                         MAN-MADE FIBRES

	Territorial coverage	Title codes

RAYON YARN
    see also WOVEN RAYON

Exports (incl acetate yarns) in lbs	Main countries	B 10-a
Production (by process) as % of total production	All countries	B 10-a
(incl acetate fibres): tonnage	All countries	U 27-m U 43-a
(incl acetate yarn): tonnage	Main countries	K 1-q
tonnage	African countries	U 44-a
	EEC countries	E 26-m E 28-q
		E 27-a
Production capacity in lbs	All countries	J 7-a
Wholesale prices: filament & staple fibre in local currency per lb	UK & USA	B 10-m
in local currency	Japan, UK & USA	U 27-m
viscose (120 denier) in yen per kg	Japan	U 32-m
World consumption in lbs (incl fibre usage)		B 10-a
World production (incl acetate) by process as % of total production	Worldwide	B 10-a
in lbs (incl Commonwealth countries as % world total)		B 10-a

RAZOR BLADES

Production for safety razors: volume	All countries	U 22-a
Retail prices (comparative) per 10 blades in $	EEC countries	Z 3-a
in local currency	OAS member countries	N 17-a

RAZORS, ELECTRIC

Production: volume	EEC countries	E 28-q E 27-a

RE-DISCOUNT RATES
    see also DISCOUNT RATES

Of Central Banks (at end-yr) in % per annum	OAS member countries	N 16-a

RE-EXPORT TRADE
    see also TRANSIT TRADE

Butter & cheese by destination: tonnage	UK	B 12-a
Cinnamon, cassia, cloves, nutmegs & mace in cwt	Hong Kong & Singapore	B 13-a
Cocoa beans: tonnage	Main countries	A 3-a
Copper (electrolytic): tonnage	UK	J 6-a
Fertilisers (manufactured from imported potash): tonnage	Main countries	A 2-a
Ginger (dried) in cwt	Singapore	B 13-a
Natural rubber & latex by destination: tonnage	UK & USA	C 18-m
Pepper in 1000 cwt	Hong Kong & Singapore	B 13-a
tonnage	Singapore	A 5-a
Rice by destination: tonnage	Main countries	B 14-q
Tea by destination in lbs	UK	B 13-a
tonnage	Netherlands, UK & USSR	C 1-a
Tea by source of leaf: tonnage	UK	P 6-a
Wheat (consigned ex South-East Asian ports): tonnage	Singapore	B 7-q

Re-rolling mills, steel   see STEEL RE-ROLLING PLANTS

Re-valuation   see EXCHANGE RATES

Reactors   see NUCLEAR REACTORS

Ready-made clothing   see CLOTHING, READY-MADE

Ready-made clothing industry   see CLOTHING INDUSTRY

REAL ESTATE COMPANIES

Loan advances from banking system in local currency	OAS member countries	N 16-a

Real estate taxes   see TAXATION

REAL INCOME

% changes in real wages (plus family allowances)	Latin American countries	U 18-a
	E European countries	U 16-a
% changes per capita (actual & planned)	E European countries & USSR	U 16-a U 54-a

Real product growth rates   see GNP

Realisation prices   see MILK MARKETING BOARD

Reaper-threshers   see COMBINED HARVESTER-THRESHERS

RECLAIMED RUBBER

Consumption: tonnage	Main countries	C 18-m
	OAS member countries	N 17-a
Exports by destination: tonnage	UK & USA	C 18-m
Imports: tonnage	Canada, W Germany, UK & USA	C 18-m
Production (from vulcanised scrap): tonnage	All countries	U 22-a
tonnage	Main countries	C 18-m
Stocks: tonnage	Main countries	C 18-m

Record players   see SOUND REPRODUCERS

	Territorial coverage	Title codes

Records   see   GRAMOPHONE RECORDS

Recovered slurry   see   COAL

RECREATION
   Private expenditure: leisure pursuits in local currency — AASM countries — E 41-a

RECREATIONAL CENTRES
   No of beds available in youth holiday centres — OECD countries — D 47-a

RED LEAD
    see also   LEAD OXIDES
              WHITE LEAD
   Exports: tonnage — USA — J 6-a
   Imports: tonnage — USA — J 6-a

REDUNDANCY
   Administrative costs: redundancy funds disbursed in $m — All countries — L 2-a
   Expenditure & receipts (total): public funds disbursed on redundancy payments in $m — All countries — L 2-a

Reference prices (EEC)   see   WHOLESALE PRICES

REFINED OIL PIPELINES
   Flow (domestic): volume in ton-km — European countries — U 8-a
   Import & export flow by volume in ton-km — European countries — U 8-a
   Length (by usage for imports & exports) in km — European countries — U 8-a
      by usage (internal) in km — European countries — U 8-a
          transit purposes in km — European countries — U 8-a
      in km, diameter in cm, capacity & location of pipelines — EEC countries — E 43-a
      in km & diameter in cm of main pipelines — Worldwide — C 14-a
      in km — Canada, European countries, USA & USSR — C 14-a
   Location & diameter of pipelines in inches — OPEC member countries — C 3-a
   No of pumping stations in use on pipelines — EEC countries — E 43-a
   Route, ownership & length of pipelines in miles — OPEC member countries — C 3-a
   Throughput in each pipeline: tonnage — EEC countries — E 43-a
   Transit flow: volume in ton-km — European countries — U 8-a

Refined petroleum products   see   AVIATION FUEL
                              BITUMEN
                              DIESEL OIL
                              FUEL OIL
                              KEROSENE
                              LUBRICATING OIL
                              MOTOR SPIRIT
                              NAPHTHA
                              PARAFFIN WAX
                              REFINERY GAS
                              WHITE SPIRIT

Refineries   see   PETROLEUM REFINERIES

REFINERY CAPACITY (NON-FERROUS METALS)
    see also   PETROLEUM REFINERIES
   Copper refining capacity by company: tonnage — All countries — J 6-a

Refinery distillates   see   FUEL OIL

REFINERY GAS
   Production: tonnage — Main countries — E 3-a

Refinery residuals   see   FUEL OIL

Refining industry, oil   see   PETROLEUM REFINERIES

Refining materials   see   LEAD RESIDUES

REFRACTORY BRICKS
   Consumption: bauxite in production of refractories: tonnage — USA — T 4-a

Refrigerated ships & refrigerated hold capacity   see   CARGO SHIPS

REFRIGERATING EQUIPMENT
   Exports by destination by value in $m — Main countries — U 9-a
      by value in $m — All countries — U 38-a
         industrial equipment: tonnage — OECD countries — D 9-a
   Imports by value in $m — All countries — U 38-a
   Production: industrial equipment: tonnage — EEC countries — E 28-q   E 27-a
              volume — All countries — U 22-a   U 38-a
   World exports by value in $m — All countries — U 38-a

	Territorial coverage	Title codes

REFRIGERATORS, DOMESTIC
    % changes: retail sales   E European countries   U 16-a

REFRIGERATORS, DOMESTIC		
% changes: retail sales	E European countries	U 16-a
Exports: volume	OECD countries	D 9-a
Production: volume	All countries	U 22-a U 38-a
	E European countries & USSR	U 16-a
	EEC countries	E 28-q E 27-a
Retail prices (comparative) in $	OAS member countries	N 14-a
Sales demand per 1000 population	EEC countries	Z 3-a
	E European countries & USSR	U 16-a

Refugee relief   see   FOOD AID

Regenerated cellulose   see   PLASTICS

Regional emigration & immigration   see   POPULATION MOVEMENT

Registration fees   see   MOTOR VEHICLES

Registrations   see   AIRCRAFT
                            BUSES & COACHES
                            COMMERCIAL VEHICLES
                            HOTELS, INTERNATIONAL
                            PASSENGER CARS

REGULUS METAL		
Consumption: historical table: tonnage	Italy	C 12-a
Export prices (in bulk) per lb at Laredo fob	USA	T 4-m
Import prices in £ per ton cif	UK	T 4-m
Imports: black coarse regulus metal: tonnage	USA	J 6-a
Production: historical table: tonnage	Italy	C 12-a
Wholesale prices (home-produced regulus metal) in £ per ton	UK	T 4-m

REINFORCING RODS, STEEL		
Deliveries shipped to EEC area: tonnage	EEC countries	E 29-a
Export prices in $ per ton fob	OECD countries	D 22-a
Exports by destination: tonnage	EEC countries	E 5-q E 29-a
	Main countries	T 4-a
Imports by source: tonnage	EEC countries	E 5-q E 29-a
	Main countries	T 4-a
tonnage	Main countries	T 1-a
Production: tonnage	EEC countries	E 29-a
	Main countries	T 4-a
	OAS member countries	N 14-a
Receipts shipped ex EEC area: tonnage	EEC countries	E 29-a
Wholesale prices in local currency per ton	Latin American countries	U 57-a
Wholesale prices - index nos	OAS member countries	N 14-a

Relays & connectors   see   ELECTRONIC COMPONENTS

Relief agencies   see   A.I.D.
                             DEVELOPMENT AID

RELIGIONS		
% of adults by religion: atheists	W European countries	Z 3
Calvinists, Lutherans, & Dutch Reform Church	W European countries	Z 3
Church of England, Protestants & Jews	W European countries	Z 3
non-Christians	W European countries	Z 3
Roman Catholics & Orthodox Catholics	W European countries	Z 3
No of new book titles published on religious subjects	All countries	U 62-a
	OAS member countries	N 19-a
Population by religious denominations & sex	All countries	U 14-a

REMITTANCES
       see also   OVERSEAS INVESTMENT INCOME

From overseas as component in gross national product in local currency	Main countries	R 5-a
	Developing countries	D 25-a
Workers' earnings remitted from abroad in $m	All countries	F 1-a

Remoulds   see   TYRES, RETREADED

Rennet   see   CASEIN

Rented accommodation   see   DWELLINGS
                                    HOUSING

RENTS
       see also   HOUSEHOLD BUDGETS
                       RATES & WATER CHARGES

(Incl fuel) as % of private consumption expenditure	All countries	U 13-a
% changes: expenditure on rents: historical table 1955-1969	OECD countries	D 11-a
Costs: (incl rates & water charges) to private sector in local currency	EEC countries	E 32-a
for living quarters (incl cost of fuel) in $	All countries	U 13-a
rents & rates as % of total household outlay	EEC countries	E 2-a
rents, fuel & lighting in household budgets - index nos	African countries	U 44-a
rents in household budgets in local currency	OAS member countries	N 17-a
Household expenditure (incl water charges) in local currency	OAS member countries	N 16-a

	Territorial coverage	Title codes
RENTS, continued		
Imputed rents (paid on government buildings) in local currency	EEC countries	E 32-a
Income (from rents) as component of national income in local currency	OAS member countries	N 16-a
Private expenditure: rents of dwellings in local currency	AASM countries	E 41-a
Receipts from taxes levied on rents from land in local currency	EEC countries	E 42-a
Rents for living accommodation - index nos	European countries & USA	U 5-a
	All countries	L 4-a
	Canada, EEC countries, Japan & USA	D 6-m
	EEC countries	E 26-m
Repair & maintenance see MAINTENANCE & REPAIRS		
REPLACEMENT PARTS		
% share of trade in main markets: tractor replacement parts	UK	V 1-a
Consumption: machine replacement parts: tonnage	Central African countries	U 38
Deliveries (for machine tool repairs) by industry by value in $m	USA	J 2-a
Exports by destination by value: for tractors by value in £m	UK	V 1-a
for trailers by value in £m	UK	V 1-a
by value in £m	UK	V 1-a
Exports: accumulators by value in £	UK	V 1-a
air & oil filters, air pumps, fans, fan belts & blowers by value in £	UK	V 1-a
automotive axles, bodies & cabs by value in £	UK	V 1-a
brake & clutch linings by value in £	UK	V 1-a
bulbs & car fittings (electric) by value in £	UK	V 1-a
chassis (less engines) by value in £	UK	V 1-a
commercial vehicle tyres by value in £	UK	V 1-a
disc brake assemblies by value in £	UK	V 1-a
engines for tractors & combined harvester-threshers by value in £	UK	V 1-a
for engines by value in £	UK	V 1-a
for road tractors by value in £	UK	V 1-a
for trucks & dumpers by value in £	UK	V 1-a
for glass windscreens by value in £	UK	V 1-a
ignition magnetos by value in £	UK	V 1-a
(incl accessories) by value in £m	UK	B 28-a
passenger car tyres & inner tubes by value in £	UK	V 1-a
shock absorbers & sparking plugs by value in £	UK	V 1-a
vehicle spare parts by value in £	UK	V 1-a
telecommunication equipment by value in £	UK	V 1-a
tractor & truck tyres & inner tubes by value in £	UK	V 1-a
transmission chains by value in £	UK	V 1-a
vehicle spare parts & accessories by value in £m	UK	B 28-a
wheels & axles (for passenger cars) by value in £	UK	V 1-a
Imports by source for tractors by value in £	UK	V 1-a
for trailers by value in £	UK	V 1-a
for works' trucks by value in £	UK	V 1-a
safety glass for passenger cars by value in £	UK	V 1-a
vehicle spares (all kinds) by value in £	UK	V 1-a
Imports: accumulators by value in £	UK	V 1-a
air pumps, fans, fan belts & blowers by value in £	UK	V 1-a
automotive axles by value in £	UK	V 1-a
bodies & cabs by value in £	UK	V 1-a
brake & clutch linings by value in £	UK	V 1-a
bulbs & car fittings (electric) by value in £	UK	V 1-a
by value in $m	All countries	U 38-a
chassis (less engines) by value in £	UK	V 1-a
commercial vehicle tyres & inner tubes by value in £	UK	V 1-a
disc brake assemblies by value in £	UK	V 1-a
engines & engine spare parts for tractors & combined harvester-threshers by value in £	UK	V 1-a
glass windscreens as replacement parts by value in £	UK	V 1-a
ignition magnetos by value in £	UK	V 1-a
(incl accessories) by value in £m	UK	B 28-a
machine components by value in UA	AASM countries	E 41-a
shipped ex EEC area by value in UA	AASM countries	E 41-a
passenger car tyres & inner tubes by value in £	UK	V 1-a
shock absorbers & sparking plugs by value in £	UK	V 1-a
telecommunication equipment by value in £	UK	V 1-a
tractor tyres & inner tubes by value in £	UK	V 1-a
transmission chains by value in £	UK	V 1-a
wheels & axles (for passenger cars) by value in £	UK	V 1-a
World exports: spare parts incl accessories by value in $m		U 38-a
Reproduction rates see GROSS REPRODUCTION RATES		
RESEARCH & DEVELOPMENT		
% expenditure by sector: chemical industry in £m	UK	U 25-a
Capital expenditure in $m	All countries	U 62-a
Credits granted for atmospheric research in $m	EEC countries	E 39-a
for environmental planning in $m	EEC countries	E 39-a
for space exploration in $m	EEC countries	E 39-a
Expenditure on bilateral projects (by objective) in $m	EEC countries	E 39-a
on multilateral projects (by objective) in $m	EEC countries	E 39-a
as % of government disbursements (total)	All countries	U 43-a
of gross national product	All countries	U 62-a
of total budget expenditure	All countries	U 62-a
on agricultural technology in $	EEC countries	E 39-a
on applied research & development in $m	All countries	U 62-a

	Territorial coverage	Title codes
RESEARCH & DEVELOPMENT, continued		
Expenditure on civil projects per capita in $	EEC countries	E 39-a
environmental problems in $m	EEC countries	E 36-a
fundamental research & development in $m	All countries	U 62-a
health protection in $	EEC countries	E 36-a
industrial productivity in $	EEC countries	E 39-a
medical pollution & noise research in $	EEC countries	E 36-a
meteorological research in $	EEC countries	E 36-a
nuclear research in $m	EEC countries	E 39-a
oceanographic research in $	EEC countries	E 36-a
space satellites in $	EEC countries	E 36-a
per capita in $	All countries	U 62-a
per scientist engaged in $	All countries	U 62-a
Foreign-donated funds available for research work in $m	All countries	U 62-a
Funds available for exploitation of resources in $	EEC countries	E 39-a
of the earth in $	EEC countries	E 39-a
for promotion of automation techniques in $	EEC countries	E 39-a
of computer science in $	EEC countries	E 39-a
of knowledge in general in $	EEC countries	E 39-a
for social science research in $	EEC countries	E 39-a
Government appropriations (by objectives) in $	EEC countries	E 36-a
assistance to research in agriculture in $	EEC countries	U 34-a
credits & appropriated in $	EEC countries	E 36-a
expenditure & per capita in $	EEC countries	E 36-a
for social research purposes in $	EEC countries	E 36-a
on research in higher education in $	EEC countries	E 36-a
on road research in $	Main countries	S 24-a
to improve produce marketing in $	EEC countries	U 34-a
Labour costs & other costs of research in $m	All countries	U 62-a
No of persons engaged on agricultural research	All countries	U 62-a
educational research	All countries	U 62-a
engineering research	All countries	U 62-a
integrated & non-integrated research & development	All countries	U 62-a
medical science research	All countries	U 62-a
natural science research	All countries	U 62-a
social science research	All countries	U 62-a
of scientists engaged on research	All countries	U 62-a
of research technicians & other personnel employed (all projects)	All countries	U 43-a U 62-a
Private research funds available in $m	All countries	U 62-a
Public & private financing: research & development in $m	EEC countries	E 36-a
	All countries	U 62-a
Public expenditure: all research projects in $m	EEC countries	E 39-a
analysed in detail in $m	EEC countries	E 39-a
bilateral projects as % of total expenditure	EEC countries	E 39-a
in $m	EEC countries	E 39-a
by objectives in $m	EEC countries	E 39-a
by project as % of gross national product	EEC countries	E 39-a
as % of total expenditure	EEC countries	E 39-a
per capita in $	EEC countries	E 39-a
on civil projects in $m	EEC countries	E 39-a
grants & credits made to firms for research in $	EEC countries	E 39-a
multilateral projects as % of total expenditure	EEC countries	E 39-a
in $m	EEC countries	E 39-a
RESEARCH & DEVELOPMENT, NUCLEAR		
Expenditure for civil purposes in $	EEC countries	E 36-a
per capita in $	EEC countries	E 36-a
International contribution to nuclear research in $m	EEC countries	E 36-a
Public expenditure in $m	EEC countries	E 39-a
RESEARCH EQUIPMENT BY KIND		
see also ACCELERATORS, ELECTRON & PROTON		
APPLIANCES, ELECTRO-MAGNETIC		
ELECTRO-MEDICAL APPARATUS		
ELECTRONIC EQUIPMENT		
MEASURING APPARATUS		
TELECOMMUNICATIONS EQUIPMENT		
Exports by value in $m (incl % growth rates)	Main countries	U 38-a
RESEARCH SHIPS		
see also FISHERIES RESEARCH SHIPS		
No & tonnage of research vessels afloat by flag	Worldwide	S 2-a
RESERVES		
see also DRAWING RIGHTS		
FOREIGN EXCHANGE		
GOLD HOLDINGS		
& in Appendix 4:-		
WORLD MINERAL RESERVES		
WORLD NATURAL GAS RESERVES		
WORLD PETROLEUM RESERVES		
Changes as % of value of imports	Main countries	U 54-a
in allocation: special drawing rights on IMF in $m	OECD countries	D 10-a
in gold & foreign convertible exchange holdings in $m	OECD countries	D 10-a
	Main countries	U 54-a
	Developed countries	U 54-a

	Territorial coverage	Title codes	
RESERVES, continued			
Changes in monetary reserve position in $m	Main countries	U 16-a	
	OECD countries	D 10-a	
Drawing rights: reserve position in IMF in $m	Main countries	U 27-m	U 43-a
	OECD countries	D 10-a	
Foreign assets, gold & convertible foreign currencies held in $m	EEC countries	E 26-m	
Gold & convertible foreign exchange holdings as % of value of imports	All countries	M 6-a	
(incl IMF reserves) in $m	All countries	M 6-a	
	EEC countries	E 3-a	E 4-a
in $m	Main countries	C 4-a	E 3-a
		U 27-a	U 43-a
	OECD countries	D 26-a	
IMF reserve position & special drawing rights in fund in $m	All countries	F 5-m	F 6-q
Monetary reserves (on current account) in $m	All countries	F 5-m	F 6-q
	Main countries	U 16-a	
Sterling reserves of the Bank of England in £m	UK	F 5-m	F 6-q
World total monetary reserves: national & international in $m		D 10-a	

Reservoirs   see   POWER STATIONS, HYDROELECTRIC

Residual fuel oil   see   FUEL OIL

Resins   see   PLASTICS

Resins, vegetable   see   NATURAL GUMS

Resistors   see   ELECTRONIC COMPONENTS

RESOURCES

see also   in Appendix 4:-
WORLD MINERAL RESERVES
WORLD PETROLEUM RESERVES

	Territorial coverage	Title codes	
% change in gross domestic product plus imports	Canada, W European countries & USA	U 16-a	
Coal & agglomerates (plus imports): tonnage	EEC countries	E 14-a	
Coke & cove oven gas (plus imports) in coal equivalent tonnage	EEC countries	E 14-a	
Consumption of resources by value in $m	E European countries & USSR	U 16-a	
Crude petroleum (plus imports): tonnage	EEC countries	E 14-a	
Electricity (plus imports) in coal equiv tonnage	EEC countries	E 7-a	E 14-a
Ex indigenous production: blast furnace gas in coal equiv tonnage	EEC countries	E 14-a	
Fuels (liquid) in coal equivalent tonnage	EEC countries	E 7-a	
(solid) tonnage	EEC countries	E 7-a	E 14-a
Lignite & briquettes: tonnage	EEC countries	E 14-a	
Natural gas in coal equivalent tonnage	EEC countries	E 7-a	
Petroleum products (plus imports): tonnage	EEC countries	E 14-a	
Public expenditure: exploitation of resources in $m	EEC countries	E 39-a	
Supply & use of resources: fixed capital value in $m	E European countries & USSR	U 16-a	
imports (net) by value in $m	E European countries & USSR	U 16-a	
national income distribution in $m	E European countries	U 16-a	
net material product in $m	E European countries	U 16-a	
stocks: goods by value in $m	E European countries	U 16-a	
World reserves: crude petroleum: tonnage	Main countries	E 14-a	

Resources, supply of   see   CAPITAL ACCUMULATION
CAPITAL FORMATION
GNP
INVENTORIES
NATIONAL INCOME
NET MATERIAL PRODUCT
OVERSEAS INVESTMENT INCOME
PERSONAL INCOME

Resources, use of   see   BANK INVESTMENTS
CONSUMPTION, DOMESTIC
CONSUMPTION, INDUSTRIAL
GOVERNMENT EXPENDITURE
INVESTMENT
INVESTMENT, PRIVATE OVERSEAS
INVESTMENT, PUBLIC OVERSEAS
PRIVATE CONSUMPTION
PUBLIC CONSUMPTION

RESTAURANT MEALS

	Territorial coverage	Title codes	
% increases in charges for food & services provided at restaurants	OECD countries	D 47-a	
Costs of meals in restaurants to consumers - index nos	European countries & USSR	U 16-a	
	EEC countries	E 26-m	

Retail credit sales   see   INSTALMENT CREDIT

Retail food trade   see   SELF-SERVICE STORES

RETAIL PRICES

see also   WHOLESALE PRICES

	Territorial coverage	Title codes	
% change in consumer prices (all items)	All countries	A 11-a	
	Canada, EEC countries, Japan & USA	D 6-m	U 16-q
	EEC countries	E 13-a	

466

	Territorial coverage	Title codes
RETAIL PRICES, continued		
% change in consumer prices (all items)	Greece, Portugal, Spain & Turkey	U 16-a
	Latin American countries	U 18-a
	Main ECAFE countries	U 17-a
(compounded)	Main countries	N 7-a
in food prices	All countries	A 11-a
	Greece, Portugal, Spain & Turkey	U 16-a
	Canada, W European countries, Japan & USA	U 16-q
in fuels & electricity charges	European countries & USA	U 16-q
Index nos: all services	Canada, EEC countries, Japan & USA	D 6-m
	E European countries & USSR	U 16-a
	Mexico	U 18-a
(based on 1958 values)	Main countries	N 7-a
clothing	AASM countries	E 41-a
	African countries	U 44-a
clothing & footwear	UK	B 22-a
food & all other costs	All countries	U 43-a
	Australasian & Far East countries	U 32-m
	Latin American countries	J 5-a
	Main countries	A 9-a
food & housing	Asian, Far East & Australasian countries	U 45-a
food, clothes, fuel, rent & rates	EEC countries	E 2-a
food, fuel & lighting	AASM countries	E 41-a
	All countries	L 4-a
food, goods & services	OECD countries	D 26-q
food: dairy, flour products & potatoes	EEC countries	E 44-a
food items only	All countries	
	African countries	U 44-a
	Asian, Far East & Australasian countries	U 32-m
	E European countries & USSR	U 16-a
	Canada, EEC countries, Japan & USA	D 6-m
	EEC countries	B 1-m
	Main countries	U 27-m
footwear	OECD countries	D 18-a
goods & services (less food)	EEC countries & USA	D 6-m
(less food & rent)	EEC countries	E 26-m
goods & services	Canada, EEC countries, Japan & USA	D 6-m
goods (less food)	Canada, EEC countries, Japan & USA	D 6-m
historical table from 1820 (on changed bases)	Main European countries	Z 1-a
from 1937	Main countries	C 4-a
non-durable goods	Mexico	U 18-a
non-food items	E European countries & USSR	U 16-a
rent	African countries	U 44-a
	Canada, EEC countries, Japan & USA	D 6-m
(Comparative within EEC area): consumables by kind: fruit, vegetables, meats, dairy products, eggs, fish, flour, coffee, tea, salt, sugar	EEC countries	Z 3-a
RETAIL PRICES BY PRODUCT		
Alcoholic drinks by kind in local currency	OAS member countries	N 17-a
in $ per 0.75 litre	EEC countries	Z 3-a
Animal fats & oils by kind in local currency	OAS member countries	N 17-a
Bacon (sliced & salted) in local currency	OAS member countries	N 17-a
Bananas: price build-up from grower to retail sales level	Main countries	A 15-a
Beef (by cuts) in local currency per kg	OAS member countries	N 17-a
Beer & beverages by kind in local currency	OAS member countries	N 17-a
Blankets in local currency	OAS member countries	N 17-a
Bread by kind in local currency	OAS member countries	N 17-a
Bunker fuels in cents per gallon	Main countries	C 3-a
Butter by kind in local currency	OAS member countries	N 17-a
in local currency per lb	Main countries	B 4-a
Camera film (35mm & colour)	EEC countries	Z 3-a
Canned fish by kind in local currency	OAS member countries	N 17-a
Canned fruit by kind in local currency	OAS member countries	N 17-a
Canned meat by kind in local currency	OAS member countries	N 17-a
Canned vegetables by kind in local currency	OAS member countries	N 17-a
Cereal preparations by kind in local currency	OAS member countries	N 17-a
Cheese (by variety) in local currency	OAS member countries	N 17-a
Chickens in local currency	OAS member countries	N 17-a
Chocolate bars in local currency per kg	Main countries	A 3-q
Cigarettes in local currency	OAS member countries	N 17-a
Citrus fruits by kind in local currency	OAS member countries	N 17-a
Clothing by kind (incl shoes)	EEC countries	Z 3-a
Coal in local currency	OAS member countries	N 17-a
Cocoa powder in local currency per kg	Main countries	A 3-q
Coconut oil in local currency	OAS member countries	N 17-a
Coffee (bag-packed) in cents per lb	Canada & USA	J 1-m
by kind in local currency	OAS member countries	N 17-a
(regular & instant) in cents per lb	USA	J 1-m
(vacuum-packed) in cents per lb	Canada & USA	J 1-m
Condensed & evaporated milk in local currency	OAS member countries	N 17-a
Consumer goods by kind in $	EEC countries	Z 3-a
in local currency	Main countries	R 5-a
Corn flour in local currency	OAS member countries	N 17-a
Cosmetics & toilet preparations in $	EEC countries	Z 3-a
Cottonseed oil in local currency	OAS member countries	N 17-a
Detergents in local currency	OAS member countries	N 17-a
Diesel oil (for agricultural use) per 100 litres	EEC countries	E 34-m
(for motor vehicle use) per 100 litres	W Germany	E 34-m
Domestic equipment by kind in $	EEC countries	Z 3-a

RETAIL PRICES BY PRODUCT, continued

	Territorial coverage	Title codes	
Duty & tax element in retail prices: bunker fuels	Main countries	C 3-a	
kerosene	Main countries	C 3-a	
lubricating oil	Main countries	C 3-a	
petrol (gasoline)	Main countries	C 3-a	
Edible offal in local currency	OAS member countries	N 17-a	
Eggs in local currency	OAS member countries	N 17-a	
Fabrics by kind in local currency	OAS member countries	N 17-a	
Fish & fish products by kind in local currency	OAS member countries	N 17-a	
(dried or smoked) in local currency	OAS member countries	N 17-a	
Food prices as factor in rise of cost of living	Main countries	U 16-q	
by kind in local currency	OAS member countries	N 17-a	
Fruit juices by kind in local currency	OAS member countries	N 17-a	
Fruits (fresh) by kind in local currency	OAS member countries	N 17-a	
Fuel prices as factor in rise of cost of living	Main countries	U 16-q	
Fuel oil (bunker C) in cents per gallon	Main countries	U 18-a	
(for agricultural use) in local currency per 100 litres	EEC countries	E 34-m	
(in major cities) by grade in local currency per 100 litres	EEC countries	E 17-q	
Groundnut oil in local currency	OAS member countries	N 17-a	
Ham by kind in local currency	OAS member countries	N 17-a	
Honey in local currency	OAS member countries	N 17-a	
Household cleaning preparations in $	EEC countries	Z 3-a	
Household textiles by kind in local currency	OAS member countries	N 17-a	
Kerosene (household) in cents per gallon	Main countries	C 3-a	U 18-a
in local currency	OAS member countries	N 17-a	
Lamb & mutton (by cuts) in local currency	OAS member countries	N 17-a	
Lamp oil in local currency	OAS member countries	N 17-a	
Lard by kind in local currency	OAS member countries	N 17-a	
Lubricating oil in cents per gallon	Main countries	C 3-a	
in local currency	OAS member countries	N 17-a	
Macaroni & semolina in local currency	OAS member countries	N 17-a	
Maize by kind in local currency	OAS member countries	N 17-a	
Manufactured gas (for domestic use) in local currency	EEC countries	E 15-a	
Manufactured tobacco in local currency	OAS member countries	N 17-a	
Margarine in local currency	OAS member countries	N 17-a	
in pence per lb (equiv)	Main countries	B 12-q	
Matches in local currency	OAS member countries	N 17-a	
Meat (dried or salted) in local currency	OAS member countries	N 17-a	
Meat preparations by kind in local currency	OAS member countries	N 17-a	
Milk (in bottles) in pence per pint (equiv)	EEC countries	B 3-a	
in local currency per litre	EEC countries	B 3-a	
in local currency	Main countries	B 4-a	
	OAS member countries	N 17-a	
(pasteurised): maximum permitted price per gallon	UK	B 4-a	
powder in local currency	OAS member countries	N 17-a	
products by kind in local currency	OAS member countries	N 17-a	
Millet in local currency	OAS member countries	N 17-a	
Mineral waters & soft drinks by kind in local currency	OAS member countries	N 17-a	
Motor spirit 3-star octane in cents per litre	EEC countries	Z 3-a	
by grade (incl tax element) in local currency per litre	EEC countries	E 15-a	
in local currency per gallon	Main countries	C 3-a	
by octane rating in local currency per 100 litres	EEC countries	E 34-m	
(for agricultural use) in local currency per 100 litres	EEC countries	E 34-m	
(high grade) in cents per gallon	Main countries	U 18-a	
in local currency	OAS member countries	N 17-a	
(low grade) in cents per gallon	Main countries	U 18-a	
Newspapers in local currency	OAS member countries	N 17-a	
Novels (paper-back) in cents each	EEC countries	Z 3-a	
Oats by kind in local currency	OAS member countries	N 17-a	
Olive oil in local currency	OAS member countries	N 17-a	
Orange juice (concentrated) in cents per can	W Germany & USA	A 5-a	
Pepper in local currency	OAS member countries	N 17-a	
Petroleum products by kind in local currency	OAS member countries	N 17-a	
Pig-meat (by cuts) in local currency	OAS member countries	N 17-a	
Poultry: chickens, ducks, geese & turkeys in local currency	OAS member countries	N 17-a	
Rabbit meat in local currency	OAS member countries	N 17-a	
Razor blades in local currency	OAS member countries	N 17-a	
in $	EEC countries	Z 3-a	
Records (for sound reproduction equipment) in $	EEC countries	Z 3-a	
Rice by kind in local currency	OAS member countries	N 17-a	
(milled) historical table 1920-1964 in local currency	Main countries	A 19-a	
Salmon in local currency	OAS member countries	N 17-a	
Salt by kind in local currency	OAS member countries	N 17-a	
Sardines & anchovies in local currency	OAS member countries	N 17-a	
Selected main consumer goods (at end-October)	Main countries	L 1-a	
Soap by kind in local currency	OAS member countries	N 17-a	
Spices & essences by kind in local currency	OAS member countries	N 17-a	
Stockings (nylon) in cents per pair	EEC countries	Z 3-a	
Sugar (by degree of refining) in local currency	OAS member countries	N 17-a	
historical table 1938-1959 in local currency per kg	Main countries	A 20-a	
(white refined) in cents per lb	Main countries	C 25-a	
Tea by kind (incl Yerba Maté) in local currency	OAS member countries	N 17-a	
Toilet preparations by kind in local currency	OAS member countries	N 17-a	
Toothpaste in local currency	OAS member countries	N 17-a	
Tractor engine fuel (low octane) in local currency per 100 litres	EEC countries	E 34-m	
Tuna fish in local currency	OAS member countries	N 17-a	
Vegetable oils by kind in local currency	OAS member countries	N 17-a	
Vegetables by kind in local currency	OAS member countries	N 17-a	
Vinegar in local currency	OAS member countries	N 17-a	

	Territorial coverage	Title codes
RETAIL PRICES BY PRODUCT, continued		
Wheat flour by kind in local currency	OAS member countries	N 17-a
Wine by kind in local currency	OAS member countries	N 17-a
(French) in $ per 0.75 litre	EEC countries	Z 3-a
Woven cotton fabrics by kind in local currency	OAS member countries	N 17-a

Retail profit margins   see   SALES MARGINS, RETAIL

RETAIL TRADE
    see also   CO-OPERATIVE SOCIETIES
                DISTRIBUTION OUTLETS
                DURABLE GOODS
                INDEPENDENT STORES
                MAIL ORDER HOUSES
                MULTIPLE STORES

	Territorial coverage	Title codes	
% change by product as ratio to changes in wage levels	E European countries	U 16-a	
in sales (total)	E European countries & USSR	U 16-a	
animal fats	E European countries & USSR	U 16-a	
beer, hard liquor & wine	E European countries & USSR	U 16-a	
bicycles, motor cycles & scooters	E European countries & USSR	U 16-a	
butter, cheese, eggs & milk	E European countries & USSR	U 16-a	
cereal products	E European countries & USSR	U 16-a	
cotton & woollen fabrics & ready-made clothing	E European countries	U 16-a	
fish & fish products	E European countries	U 16-a	
food products	E European countries & USSR	U 16-a	
footwear	E European countries & USSR	U 16-a	
fresh fruit & vegetables	E European countries	U 16-a	
furniture	E European countries & USSR	U 16-a	
meat & meat products	E European countries	U 16-a	
passenger cars	E European countries & USSR	U 16-a	
radio & television sets	E European countries & USSR	U 16-a	
refrigerators, sewing machines, vacuum cleaners & washing machines	E European countries	U 16-a	
tea, coffee & sugar	E European countries & USSR	U 16-a	
vegetable fats & oils	E European countries	U 16-a	
watches	E European countries & USSR	U 16-a	
Breakdown of retailing costs by kind of sales outlet in local currency	EEC countries	E 9-a	
wages & social charges in local currency	EEC countries	E 9-a	
Costs of family insurance (as social levy) in local currency	EEC countries	E 9-a	
of insurance against accidents at work in local currency	EEC countries	E 9-a	
against illness of workpeople in local currency	EEC countries	E 9-a	
against unemployment in local currency	EEC countries	E 9-a	
of other legally-imposed social charges in local currency	EEC countries	E 9-a	
of social levies for labour force in local currency	EEC countries	E 9-a	
Employment, wages, sales & stocks held by retail traders	Main countries	U 43-a	
Gross product in local currency	OAS member countries	N 16-a	
Income contribution to gross domestic product & as % of total	EEC countries	E 32-a	
Labour costs by type of distributive outlet	EEC countries	E 3-a	
chemist shops per mth in local currency	EEC countries	E 9-a	
in sales of clothing per mth in local currency	EEC countries	E 9-a	
cosmetics per mth in local currency	EEC countries	E 9-a	
domestic equipment per mth in local currency	EEC countries	E 9-a	
foodstuffs per mth in local currency	EEC countries	E 9-a	
household furnishings in local currency	EEC countries	E 9-a	
leather goods per mth in local currency	EEC countries	E 9-a	
newsagents & booksellers per mth in local currency	EEC countries	E 9-a	
sales outlets (in general) per mth in local currency	EEC countries	E 9-a	
No of hypermarkets in operation	W European countries	Z 2-a	
of retail trading enterprises by administrative areas	EEC countries	E 38-a	
of hrs worked per wk by kind of retail outlet	EEC countries	E 9-a	
by sales assistants	Main countries	R 3-m	L 1-a
by sex	EEC countries	E 18-a	
per yr by kind of retail outlet shop	EEC countries	E 9-a	
of self-service food stores in operation	W European countries	Z 2-a	
of self-service stores (independently-owned) in operation	W European countries	Z 2-a	
owned by consumer co-operatives in operation	W European countries	Z 2-a	
by departmental stores in operation	W European countries	Z 2-a	
by multiple stores in operation	W European countries	Z 2-a	
of supermarkets in operation	W European countries	Z 2-a	
of wage & salary earners by sex employed in retail trade by region	EEC countries	E 18-a	
Salaries: sales assistants per mth	Main countries	L 1-a	
Salary costs by type of retail business per mth	EEC countries	E 2-a	
Sales by dairies: cream in milk equiv tonnage	EEC countries	B 3-a	
liquid milk: tonnage	EEC countries	B 3-a	
skim buttermilk: tonnage	EEC countries	B 3-a	
by kind - index nos (value basis)	Main countries	U 27-m	
Sales: commercial vehicles: volume	Main countries	V 4-a	
consumer goods by kind: volume	E European countries & USSR	U 16-a	
consumer goods - index nos	EEC countries	E 13-m	
demand per 1000 population: durable goods	E European countries	U 16-a	
food, clothing & all goods - index nos	Main countries	U 43-a	
food - index nos	EEC countries	E 26-m	
household furniture & domestic equipment - index nos	EEC countries	E 26-m	
passenger cars (by model): volume	Main countries	V 4-a	
textiles, clothing & shoes - index nos	EEC countries	E 26-m	
turnover in $m	Asian, Far East & Australasian countries	U 45-a	
turnover: food in local currency	W European countries	Z 2-a	
wool yarn: tonnage & value in £	Main countries	K 3-a	

	Territorial coverage	Title codes	

RETAIL TRADE, continued

Sales - index nos (quantum & value bases)	OECD countries	D 26-m	
(value basis)	ECE countries	U 42-m	
Stocks: anthracite held by retailers: tonnage	USA	N 1-a	
consumer goods - index nos	OECD countries	D 26-m	
Turnover (actual & planned) in $m	E European countries & USSR	U 54-a	
departmental stores - index nos	EEC countries	E 26-m	
multiple stores - index nos	EEC countries	E 26-m	
Wage rates by sex in retail trade in local currency per hr	Main countries	R 3-m	

Retail trade margins   see   DISTRIBUTION COSTS

Retirement   see   POPULATION, ECONOMICALLY-INACTIVE

Retirement pensions   see   OLD AGE PENSIONS
 PENSIONS, WAR

Retreads   see   TYRES, RETREADED

REVENUE

see also   CAPITAL GAINS
 P.A.Y.E.
 TAXATION

Accruing to local authorities: passenger car taxes in local currency	Main countries	S 24-a	
to receiving agencies of Central or local authorities in local currency	EEC countries	E 42-a	
	Main countries	R 5-a	
Receipts from issue of bonds in $m	W Indies & Caribbean countries	T 6-a	

REVENUE (AIRLINES)

Earnings of airline companies in cents per ton/km: air mail freight	Worldwide	S 6-a	
in $m: air mail freight	IATA members	S 21-a	
in cents per ton/km: cargo freight traffic	Worldwide	S 6-a	
in $m: cargo freight traffic	IATA members	S 21-a	
in cents per ton/km: excess baggage	Worldwide	S 6-a	
passenger fares	Worldwide	S 6-a	
in $m: passenger fares	IATA members	S 21-a	
on scheduled & unscheduled services in $m	Worldwide	S 21-a	
of specific airline companies in $m	Worldwide	S 11-a	

Revolution counters   see   SCIENTIFIC INSTRUMENTS

RHENIUM

% consumption in production of bimetallic catalysts	USA	N 1-a	
of electronic devices	USA	N 1-a	
of vacuum tube filaments	USA	N 1-a	
Consumption: metallic rhenium: tonnage (estim)	USA	N 1-a	
Production (from roasting of molybdenite): tonnage	USA	N 1-a	

Rhine   see   INLAND WATERWAYS

Rhodium   see   PLATINUM, REFINED

RICE

see also   PADDY RICE

% change: producer prices (over previous yr)	France & Italy	E 3-m	
% contribution to export earnings	Guyana & Madagascar	E 45-a	
% milling rate: paddy to milled rice	All countries	B 14-a	
% of human calorie intake derived from rice	World regions	C 27-a	
A.I.D. sales (under food aid programs) in $m	Recipient countries	M 1-a	
Area under rice crop in acres	Main countries	B 8-a	
in ha (incl harvested tonnage)	Main countries	R 5-a	
	EEC countries	E 44-a	
in ha	France & Italy	E 12-a	
	OECD countries	D 1-a	
Availability (output plus net imports): tonnage	Main countries	B 8-a	
Consumption as animal feed: tonnage	EEC countries	E 44-a	
	Main countries	A 19-a	B 8-a
		B 14-a	
as human food: tonnage	Main countries	A 19-a	B 14-a
	UK	B 8-a	
as seed: tonnage	Main countries	A 19-a	B 14-a
for industrial food processing: tonnage	Main countries	A 19-a	B 8-a
		B 14-a	
	UK	B 8-a	
per capita by income levels per mth	India	C 27-a	
(husked rice) in kg per yr	Main countries	E 3-a	
in kg per yr	Main countries	A 19-a	
	EEC countries	E 44-a	
	Canada, European countries, Japan, USA & USSR	E 44-a	
tonnage (incl world total)	Main countries	B 2-a	
tonnage	EEC countries	E 44-a	
	Main countries	A 19-a	B 8-a
	OAS member countries	N 17-a	
Contract price (shipped to Sri Lanka) in £ per ton	Burma	U 32-m	

RICE, continued | Territorial coverage | Title codes

Crop yield in 100 kg per ha	France & Italy	E 12-a
in cwt per acre	Main countries	B 8-a
in kg per ha	Main countries	R 5-a
	EEC countries	B 1-a
Demand per capita projected to 1985 in kg	Main countries	A 1
Export levies imposed by EEC on imports of rice from non-EEC countries		B 14-m
Export prices: broken rice: historical table from 1921-1964 in £ per ton	Thailand	A 19-a
by grade (ex warehouse) in cents per lb cif	USA	R 2-m
by quality (ex Thailand) in £ per ton cif		B 14-m
(ex Thailand & USA) in £ per ton cif		B 8-m
government to government sales in £ per ton fob	Burma	B 8-a
husked rice: historical table 1951-1964 in £ per ton cif	Thailand	A 19-a
in BWI $ per ton cif	Guyana	A 19-a
in $ per 100 lbs cif	Burma & Thailand	U 17-m
parboiled rice: historical table 1955-1964 in £ per ton cif	Thailand	A 19-a
white rice: historical table 1921-1964 in £ per ton	Thailand	A 19-a
whole rice: historical table 1921-1964 in £ per ton	Thailand	A 19-a
Export prices - index nos (weighted average main sources)	Worldwide	U 29-q U 54-q
Export subsidies by grade in £ per ton	EEC countries	A 9-a
Exports by destination by quality:	EEC countries	B 8-a
(incl rice products): tonnage	Main countries	B 14-q
tonnage	Burma	A 10-q
	All countries	B 14-q
	Main countries	B 8-a
	Republic of China	B 14-q
by value as % of total value of export trade in $m	Main countries	B 8-a
(incl rice products) by value in $m	Developing countries	U 11-a
through Port of Karachi: tonnage	Burma & Thailand	U 32-m
tonnage & value in $m	India	S 16-a
	Main countries	B 2-a
(incl world total)	Guyana & Madagascar	E 45-a
tonnage	All countries	A 10-a
	All countries	B 14-q
	Burma, Pakistan & Thailand	U 32-m
(total) & shipped to EEC area: tonnage & value in UA	Madagascar	E 41-a
Import prices (at continental & UK ports) in £ per ton c & f		B 14-m
by grade in local currency per kg	European countries	R 2-m
(shipped)ex Thailand & USA) in £ per ton cif	UK	B 2-a
in £ per ton cif	UK	A 9-a
Imports by source: tonnage	EEC countries	B 8-a
by value in $	Indonesia	U 32-m
historical table 1930-1962 in milled equiv tonnage	All countries	A 19-a
(retained): tonnage	All countries & world regions	A 10-a
tonnage	India, Pakistan & W European countries	B 8-a
No of calories derived from consumption of rice per capita per day	Main countries	A 19-a
Price supports (by quality of rice) in local currency per ton	All countries	A 10-a
Prices (spot): Basmati rice (at Hapur) in Rs per 100 kg	India	B 14-m
Procurement by grade by government agency: tonnage	Burma	A 10-a
Producer prices in local currency per kg	France & Italy	E 34-m
	OECD countries	D 1-a
per ton	France & Italy	E 44-a
Production by administrative areas: tonnage	EEC countries	E 38-a
by value in local currency	EEC countries	E 44-a
husked rice: tonnage	Main countries	E 3-a
tonnage (incl value of output)	EEC countries	B 1-a
Production, imports, exports, stocks & consumption: tonnage	EEC countries	E 44-a
Production (incl consumption forecast for ensuing yr): tonnage	Main countries	A 1-a
(incl world total): tonnage	Main countries	B 2-a
paddy rice: tonnage	Asian & Far East countries	U 32-a
	Main countries	B 8-a
rough & paddy rice: tonnage	All countries	U 43-a
tonnage	AASM countries	E 41-a
	EEC countries	E 12-a E 44-a
Proportion of harvest exported	Argentine, Burma, Cambodia & USA	B 8-a
Retail prices: milled rice: historical table 1920-1964 in local currency	Main countries	A 19-a
Self-sufficiency ratios	EEC countries	B 1-a E 3-a
		E 44-a
Stocks (end-yr carryover) in milled equiv tonnage	Main countries	A 10-a
tonnage	India, Japan, Taiwan & USA	B 2-a
	Main Far East countries & USA	A 11-a
held at wholesalers' premises: tonnage	EEC countries	E 12-m
under Commodity Credit Corporation price supports: tonnage	USA	B 14-a
Subsidies paid on rice exports by quality shipped ex EEC area in £m		B 14-m
Supply & disposal of rice by purpose: tonnage	Main countries	B 8-m
Supply, production, consumption, imports & exports: tonnage	EEC countries	B 1-a
Target, intervention & threshold prices in £ per cwt	EEC countries	B 1-a
Transactions: Commodity Credit Corporation: tonnage	USA	B 14-a
Wholesale prices (at Bangkok) in bahts per ton	Thailand	U 32-m
by grade in local currency per kg	OAS member countries	N 17-a
in $ per ton	China, W Germany, Thailand & UK	U 27-m
milled rice: historical table 1920-1964 in local currency per ton	Main countries	A 19-a
Wholesale prices - index nos	S Vietnam	U 32-m
World exports by value in $m	World regions	A 5-a
historical table 1930-1962 in milled equiv tonnage	All countries	A 19-a

471

	Territorial coverage	Title codes
RICE, continued		
World exports: husked rice (ex Madagascar) in Fr per kg	France	E 41-a
tonnage & value in $m	World regions	U 11-a
Yield in milled form (as rice flour) in cwt per acre	All countries	B 14-a
RICE, HUSKED		
Consumption: tonnage & consumption per capita in kg per yr	OECD countries	D 14-a
per capita in kg per yr	OECD countries	D 1-a
Intervention price fixed by EEC Commission in local currency per ton	EEC countries	E 44-a
Prices in EEC area as % of world market prices		E 44-a
Producer prices in $ per ton	Japan	A 9-a
Production, stocks, industrial usage & consumption for animal feed: tonnage	OECD countries	D 14-a
Wholesale prices in $ per ton	Main countries	A 9-a
RICE BY KIND		
Export prices (bilateral contracts) - index nos	Worldwide	A 19-m
in £ per ton fob	China, Burma & Thailand	A 19-a
in $ per ton fob	Taiwan	A 19-a
(private trade) - index nos	Worldwide	A 19-m
Exports by destination: broken, glazed, husked, milled & parboiled rice: tonnage	All countries	A 19-a
paddy rice: tonnage	All countries	A 19-a
Imports by source: broken, glutinous, husked, milled, parboiled & polished rice: tonnage	All countries	A 19-a
paddy rice: tonnage	All countries	A 19-a
Retail prices in local currency	OAS member countries	N 17-a

River transport   see   INLAND WATERWAYS

Rivers & lakes   see   INLAND WATERWAYS

Road accidents   see   ACCIDENTS, ROAD

	Territorial coverage	Title codes
ROAD CONSTRUCTION VEHICLES		
No of registrations: new vehicles used for road-construction & maintenance	UK	V 1-a

Road fund taxes   see   MOTOR VEHICLES

Road haulage   see   ROAD TRANSPORT

Road haulage taxes   see   TAXATION

	Territorial coverage	Title codes
ROAD MAINTENANCE		
Expenditure by Central government in $m	Main countries	S 24-a
local authorities in $m	Main countries	S 24-a
regional or state governments in $m	Main countries	S 24-a

Road passenger traffic   see   ROAD TRANSPORT

Road rollers   see   SERVICE VEHICLES

	Territorial coverage	Title codes	
ROAD TRACTORS			
Exports by destination: volume & value in £m	UK	V 1-a	
No in use (end-yr)	W European countries	V 1-a	
	Main countries	S 24-a	
	EEC countries	E 43-a	
	European countries	U 8-a	
	Great Britain	V 1-a	
licenced (incl showmen's trucks)	Great Britain	V 1-q	
Production (for trailer combinations): volume	All countries	U 22-a	U 38-a
historical tables: volume	UK	V 1-a	
volume	EEC countries	E 28-q	E 27-a
Registrations: new road tractors by unladen wt	N Ireland	V 1-q	
new general-purpose haulage tractors: volume	UK	V 1-m	

	Territorial coverage	Title codes
ROAD TRAFFIC		
see also MOTORWAY TRAFFIC		
% increase in volume (based on vehicle-km)	Main countries	S 24-a
Distances run: cars & taxis in km (estim)	European countries	U 8-a
coaches & buses in km (estim)	European countries	U 8-a
goods vehicles in km (estim)	European countries	U 8-a
motor cycles in km (estim)	European countries	U 8-a
No of coach passengers crossing frontiers	European countries	U 8-a
Volume of road traffic in vehicle-km: 2-wheelers	Main countries	S 24-a
buses, goods vehicles & passenger cars	Main countries	S 24-a
in ton/km	ECE countries	U 15-a
ROAD TRAFFIC, INTERNATIONAL		
No of incoming bus passengers crossing frontiers	European countries	U 8-a
buses & coaches crossing frontiers	European countries	U 8-a
foreign-owned buses crossing frontiers	European countries	U 8-a
foreigners' cars crossing frontiers	European countries	U 8-a
goods vehicles crossing frontiers	European countries	U 8-a

	Territorial coverage	Title codes

Road traffic accidents   see   ACCIDENTS, ROAD

Road trailers   see   TRAILERS

ROAD TRANSPORT
    see also   TRANSPORT & COMMUNICATIONS

% consumption by kind of fuel used by engine	Main countries	H 4-a
Anthracite: domestic transport: tonnage	USA	N 1-a
Consumption: diesel oil: tonnage	EEC countries	E 14-a
electric power in calorific value	Main countries	H 4-a
motor spirit (incl by passenger cars): tonnage	EEC countries	E 14-a
natural gas in calorific value	Main countries	H 4-a
petroleum products by kind: tonnage	OECD countries	D 31-a
	EEC countries	E 16-q E 15-
in calorific value	Main countries	H 4-a
Domestic haulage: goods between regions: tonnage	EEC countries	E 43-a
by distances run in km	W Germany	E 43-a
Domestic & long-distance haulage: goods: tonnage	W Germany	E 43-a
Exports by road: agricultural products by kind: tonnage	European countries	U 8-a
all products (incl transit): tonnage	European countries	U 8-a
building materials & timber: tonnage	European countries	U 8-a
cereals: tonnage	European countries	U 8-a
chemical products: tonnage	European countries	U 8-a
fertilisers: tonnage	European countries	U 8-a
machinery: tonnage	European countries	U 8-a
metal ores: tonnage	European countries	U 8-a
petroleum products: tonnage	European countries	U 8-a
solid fuels: tonnage	European countries	U 8-a
Freight arrivals by road by source of freight: tonnage	EEC countries	E 43-a
despatches by road: tonnage	EEC countries	E 43-a
entering & leaving (incl in transit): tonnage	European countries	U 8-a
haulage by distance classifications in km	EEC countries	E 43-a
by load size: tonnage & distance in km	EEC countries	E 43-a
by product groups in ton-km	EEC countries	E 43-a
in ton-km	Main countries	S 24-a
in tons million	Main countries	S 24-a
(inland) by kind of freight: tonnage	EEC countries	E 43-a
over frontiers by kind of freight: tonnage	EEC countries	E 43-a
Imports: agricultural products by kind by road: tonnage	European countries	U 8-a
all goods (incl transit) by road: tonnage	European countries	U 8-a
building materials & timber by road: tonnage	European countries	U 8-a
cereals by road: tonnage	European countries	U 8-a
chemical products by road: tonnage	European countries	U 8-a
fertilisers by road: tonnage	European countries	U 8-a
machinery by road: tonnage	European countries	U 8-a
metal ores by road: tonnage	European countries	U 8-a
petroleum products by road: tonnage	European countries	U 8-a
solid fuels by road: tonnage	European countries	U 8-a
International freight by road: tonnage	EEC countries	E 43-a
Load capacity: goods vehicles in use: tonnage	European countries	U 8-a
No of firms by no of commercial vehicles owned & in use	EEC countries	E 43-a
licences & type of road licence held	EEC countries	E 43-a
trucks by type of haulage	EEC countries	E 43-a
of passengers travelling on regular & occasional routes by road	EEC countries	E 43-a
on overland road transport services	EEC countries	E 43-a
using international coach routes	EEC countries	E 43-a
Passenger traffic: volume using private transport	Main countries	S 24-a
using public transport	Main countries	S 24-a

Road vehicle licences, commercial   see   ROAD TRANSPORT

ROADS
    see also   MOTORWAYS

% macadamised, paved, concreted or surfaced with blocks	EEC countries	E 43-a
% of road surfaces paved	Main countries	S 24-a
Density of network in km per sq km	Main countries	S 24-a
Expenditure by type of highway & on new construction of roads in $m	European countries	U 8-a
on administration & research in $m	Main countries	S 24-a
improvements, road construction & maintenance in $m	All countries	S 13-a
highways in $m	Main countries	S 24-a
new road construction in $m	Main countries	S 24-a
Government expenditure on administration & research in $m	Main countries	S 24-a
highway maintenance in $m	Main countries	S 24-a
new road construction in $m	Main countries	S 24-a
servicing of highway loans in $m	Main countries	S 24-a
IBRD loans approved: highway construction in $m	OAS member countries	N 16-a
IDA loans approved: highway construction in $m	OAS member countries	N 16-a
Improvements to roads in miles per 1000 sq miles of territory	Developing world regions	U 23-a
Length: all highways in use in km & miles	All countries	S 13-a
by kind of surface in km & miles	All countries	S 13-a
in km	African countries	U 44-a
dirt roads in use in km	OAS member countries	N 15-a
earth roads (graded & drained) in use in km & miles	All countries	S 13-a
gravel or stone-surfaced roads in use in km	OAS member countries	N 15-a
main roads in use in km	Main countries	S 24-a
in use in km (incl length asphalted)	AASM countries	E 41-a
motorways in use in km	Main countries	S 24-a

	Territorial coverage	Title codes	
ROADS, continued			
Length: network by class of motorways: arterial & local roads in km	EEC countries	E 38-a	E 43-a
	European countries	U 8-a	
by type of surface in km	Latin American countries	J 5-a	U 40-a
	Asian, Far East & Australasian countries	U 45-a	
	Main countries	S 24-a	
	All countries	S 13-a	
paved roads in use in km & miles	OAS member countries	N 15-a	
in km	OAS member countries	N 15-a	
roads & tracks (unimproved) in use in km	African countries	U 44-a	
roads (improved) in use in km	OAS member countries	N 15-a	
in use by kind of surface in km	African countries	U 44-a	
(paved) in use in km	African countries	U 44-a	
(unimproved & tracks) in use in km	OAS member countries	N 15-a	
(with levelled & drained surfaces) in km	Main countries	S 24-a	
secondary regional roads in use in km	AASM countries	E 41-a	
	All countries	S 13-a	
stabilised-surface roads in use in km & miles	Main countries	S 24-a	
(total) in use in km	All countries	S 13-a	
unimproved roads in use in km & miles	Main countries	S 24-a	
Local authority expenditure: administration & road research in $m	Main countries	S 24-a	
maintenance in $m	Main countries	S 24-a	
new road construction in $m	Main countries	S 24-a	
Regional expenditure: administration & road research in $m	Main countries	S 24-a	
highway maintenance in $m	Main countries	S 24-a	
new road construction in $m	Main countries	S 24-a	

Roasted barley   see   MALT

ROASTED COFFEE INDUSTRY

Capital expenditure in $m	USA	J 1-a
Labour force employed & total wage bill in $	USA	J 1-a
No of man-hrs of labour expended	USA	J 1-a
of production workers employed	USA	J 1-a
Wage cost per production worker in $	USA	J 1-a
per man-hr in $	USA	J 1-a

ROBBERY & THEFT

Claims paid (by insurance companies) in local currency	OAS member countries	N 16-a

Robustas   see   COFFEE BY GRADE

Rock crystal   see   GEM STONES

Rock phosphate   see   PHOSPHATE ROCK

Rock salt   see   SALT

ROD & WIRE EXTRUSION BARS, TITANIUM

Sales in lbs	USA	J 6-a

RODS & BARS, BRONZE-ALLOY

Wholesale prices: phosphor-bronze bars in yen per ton	Japan	T 4-w

RODS BARS SECTIONS, COPPER-ALLOY

Exports by destination: tonnage	Main countries	T 4-a
Imports by source: tonnage	Main countries	T 4-a
Production: tonnage	Main countries	T 4-a

RODS BARS SECTIONS, COPPER

	Territorial coverage	Title codes	
Exports by destination: copper rods: tonnage	USA	J 6-a	
tonnage	Main countries	T 4-a	
Imports by source: tonnage	W Germany	T 4-a	
Production: tonnage	Japan & UK	C 12-a	
	Main countries	C 30-m	T 4-a
Usage: building industry: tonnage	USA	J 6-a	
consumer goods manufacturing industry: tonnage	USA	J 6-a	
electrical engineering industry: tonnage	USA	J 6-a	
machinery equipment manufacturing industry: tonnage	USA	J 6-a	
transport equipment industry: tonnage	USA	J 6-a	

RODS BARS SECTIONS, NICKEL

Exports by destination: tonnage	UK & USA	T 4-a

Roes   see   FISH ROES

Roll butts   see   LEATHER

Roll-on roll-off vessels   see   CARGO SHIPS

Rolled steel products   see   STEEL PRODUCTS

Rolling mills   see   STEEL RE-ROLLING PLANTS

	Territorial coverage	Title codes

ROLLING STOCK
    see also   CONTAINERS, RAIL
                  RAILWAY TRAINS

% share of world exports (incl locomotives) held (value basis)	UK	B 27-a
shipped to developed countries		U 38-a
to developing countries		U 38-a
Capacity: freight wagons in use: tonnage	European countries	U 8-a
Consumption: rail vehicles: tonnage	Central African countries	U 38-a
Distance covered by passenger & goods trains in km	EEC countries	E 43-a
Exports by destination by value in $m	Main countries	U 9-a
rail freight wagons by value in $m	All countries	U 38-a
rail passenger coaches & freight wagons by value in $m	OECD countries	D 9-a
	All countries	U 38-a
by value in $m	All countries	U 38-a
Freight wagons: turn-round time in days	European countries	U 8-a
Goods loaded on rail freight wagons: tonnage	EEC countries	E 43-a
Imports: rolling stock by value in $m	All countries	U 38-a
Locomotives by kind in use	Developing countries	U 57-a
No of freight wagons in use by kind	African countries	U 44-a
on European railways	EEC countries	E 43-a
(open covered & flat)	European countries	U 8-a
	EEC countries	E 43-a
in use	Main countries	R 5-a
loaded (at home & abroad)	EEC countries	E 43-a
insulated refrigerated wagons in use & capacity: tonnage	European countries	U 8-a
locomotives by kind in use	African countries	U 44-a
locomotives, carriages & freight wagons in use	OAS member countries	N 15-a
rail passenger carriages in use	Main countries	R 5-a
& freight wagons in use	S American countries	U 40-a
	Asian, Far East & Australasian countries	U 45-a
in use & no of seats available	European countries	U 8-a
privately-owned freight wagons in use & capacity	European countries	U 8-a
	EEC countries	E 43-a
passenger carriages in use	EEC countries	E 43-a
rail passenger carriages by kind in use	African countries	U 44-a
special freight wagons by kind & capacity in use	European countries	U 8-a
temperature-controlled tank wagons in use	EEC countries	E 43-a
wagons loaded & no crossing European frontiers	European countries	U 8-a
Production: freight wagons & vans: volume	All countries	U 22-a U 38-a
	E European countries & USSR	U 16-a
motor passenger carriages: volume	All countries	U 22-a U 38-a
rail passenger carriages & goods wagons: volume	EEC countries	E 28-q E 27-a
(all types): volume	All countries	U 22-a U 38-a
World exports: rail freight wagons by value in $m		U 38-a
rail passenger carriages by value in $m		U 38-a

Roofing tiles   see   BUILDING MATERIALS

Rooming houses   see   DWELLINGS
                           HOUSING

Rooms   see   DWELLINGS

ROOT CROPS
    see also   CARROTS
                    CASSAVA
                    POTATOES
                    SUGAR BEET
                    SWEDES & TURNIPS

Area under potatoes, sugar beet & tubers in ha	EEC countries	E 3-a
root crops by kind in ha	OAS member countries	N 13-a
(for animal feed) in ha	EEC countries	E 44-a
in ha	EEC countries	E 44-a
Crop yields by kind in kg per ha	OAS member countries	N 13-a
(for animal feed) in kg per ha	EEC countries	E 44-a
Production by kind: tonnage	OAS member countries	N 13-a
(for animal feed): tonnage	EEC countries	E 44-a
root crops by value in local currency	EEC countries	E 44-a
tonnage	Asian, Far East & Australasian countries	U 45-a
Retail prices: root crops by kind in local currency per ton	OAS member countries	N 17-a

ROPES CORDAGE & TWINE
    see also   COIR MANUFACTURES

Production: tonnage	All countries	U 22-a

Rotenone   see   INSECTICIDES

Rotor steel   see   CRUDE STEEL

Round wood   see   TIMBER

Routes, airline   see   AIR ROUTE NETWORKS

ROYALTIES

Government revenue in $m	Venezuela	J 5-a
Mineral royalties in local currency	African countries	U 44-a
Oil royalties in local currency	African countries	U 44-a

	Territorial coverage	Title codes

ROYALTIES, continued
    Income as component of payments balances in $m   Main countries   F 1-a
    Receipts: royalty payments in local currency   EEC countries   E 42-a

Rubber   see   CLOTH, RUBBERISED
                 ELASTOMERS
                 HOSE & TUBING, RUBBER
                 LATEX
                 LATEX CREPE
                 LATEX FOAM
                 NATURAL RUBBER
                 RECLAIMED RUBBER
                 SPONGE RUBBER
                 SYNTHETIC RUBBER

Rubber footwear   see   FOOTWEAR, RUBBER

RUBBER GOODS MANUFACTURING INDUSTRY
    see also   RUBBER PROCESSING INDUSTRY
    Electricity consumption in kWh   All countries   C 23-a

RUBBER MANUFACTURES
    see also   CONVEYOR BELTS
                 FOOTWEAR, RUBBER
                 GUMS, GLUES & SOLUTIONS
                 INNER TUBES, RUBBER
                 SURGICAL PRODUCTS
    Consumption by kind: tonnage   Main countries   B 13-a
                    rubber for manufacture of technical products: tonnage   France   C 18-a
    Exports shipped to EEC & non-EEC areas by value in $m   EEC countries   E 24-a
    Imports ex EEC & non-EEC areas by value in $m   EEC countries   E 24-a
    Production by kind: tonnage   EEC countries   E 28-q   E 27-a

Rubber plantations   see   PLANTATIONS, RUBBER

RUBBER PROCESSING INDUSTRY
    Consumption: electricity in kWh   EEC countries   E 15-a
                    non-vulcanised rubber: tonnage   France   C 18-a
    Costs: salaried staff in local currency per mth   EEC countries   E 11-a
    Earnings in $m   All countries   L 4-a
    Employment - index nos   All countries   L 4-a
    Investment in buildings in local currency   EEC countries   E 40-a
               in land purchase in local currency   EEC countries   E 40-a
               in machinery in local currency   EEC countries   E 40-a
    Labour costs: all employees in local currency per hr   EEC countries   E 11-a
                 as % of total costs of rubber production   EEC countries   E 8-a
                 by status of employees in local currency   EEC countries   E 8-a
                 (incl asbestos workers) in local currency per hr   EEC countries   E 1-a
                 wage earners in local currency per hr   EEC countries   E 11-a
    Labour force: no of salaried staff employed   EEC countries   E 11-a
               of wage earners employed   EEC countries   E 2-a   E 11-a
               & salary earners employed   EEC countries   E 8-a
    No of hrs worked per wk by region   EEC countries   E 25-a
        of hrs worked per wk   EEC countries   E 11-a
                             All countries   L 4-a
                             Main countries   R 3-m
                 per yr   OAS member countries   N 18-a
                 salaried staff per mth   EEC countries   E 8-a
    Production - index nos (quantum basis)   EEC countries   E 11-a
    Wage rates by grade of employee in lire per hr   S American countries   U 40-a
               by sex in local currency per hr   Italy   R 4-a
               in local currency per hr   Main countries   R 3-m   C 7-a
                             EEC countries   E 25-a2

Rubber solutions   see   GUMS, GLUES & SOLUTIONS

Rubber sports goods   see   SPORTS GOODS, RUBBER

Rubber underlay (for floor coverings)   see   SPONGE RUBBER

Rubber, arabic   see   GUM ARABIC

Rubberised cloth   see   CLOTH, RUBBERISED

Rubies   see   GEM STONES

Rugs   see   CARPETS

Rural housing   see   DWELLINGS

Ruthenium   see   PLATINUM, REFINED

Rutile concentrates   see   TITANIUM MINERALS

RYE

	Territorial coverage	Title codes	
% changes in prices received by farmers	W European countries	U 30-a	
Area under rye crop in ha	EEC countries	E 44-a	
Area harvested, production: tonnage & yield per ha	All countries	A 9-a	
under crop: historical table from 1815 in ha	Main European countries	Z 1-a	
in acres	Main countries	B 8-a	
in ha (incl harvested tonnage)	Main countries	R 5-a	
in ha	All countries	C 16-a	
	EEC countries	B 1-a	E 44-a
	OAS member countries	N 13-a	
	OECD countries	D 1-a	
under winter & spring rye crop in ha	EEC countries	E 12-a	
Availability (output plus net imports): tonnage	EEC countries, USA & USSR	B 8-a	
Consumption (as animal feed): tonnage	EEC countries	E 44-a	
	Main countries	B 8-a	
as human food: tonnage	UK	B 8-a	
per capita in kg per yr	EEC countries	B 1-a	E 44-a
tonnage & consumption per capita per day	OECD countries	D 14-a	
tonnage	EEC countries	E 44-a	
	Main countries	B 8-a	
	OAS member countries	N 17-a	
Crop yield in cwt per acre	Main countries	B 8-a	
in kg per ha	EEC countries	B 1-a	
	Main countries	R 5-a	
	OAS member countries	N 13-a	
	OECD countries	D 1-a	
in quintals per ha	E European countries & USSR	U 16-a	
(winter & spring rye) in 100 kg per ha	EEC countries	E 12-a	
Deliveries: rye by farmers: tonnage	Main countries	B 7-a	
EEC area levy on rye imported ex non-EEC area in £ per ton		B 7-m	
Export prices in $ per ton fob	Canada	U 35-a	
	Canada (E Coast ports)	C 16-m	
	Argentine	A 9-a	
(main N American grades) in cents per bushel fob	Canada & USA	B 8-a	
(normal grade) in cents per 56 lbs cif	Canada	R 2-m	
Export subsidies in £ per ton	EEC countries	B 8-a	
Exports by destination: tonnage	China, E European countries & USSR	A 17-a	
	Main countries	B 8-a	
(incl world total): tonnage	Main countries	C 16-a	
tonnage	All countries	A 17-a	
	European countries	U 35-a	
Import prices: rye shipped ex USA at European ports in $ per ton		U 35-a	
Imports by source: tonnage	EEC countries	B 8-a	
for production of animal feed: tonnage	UK	P 5-a	
into China, E European countries & USSR: tonnage	Non-Communist countries	A 17-a	
tonnage	All countries	A 17-a	
	European countries	U 35-a	
	W European region	B 8-a	
Intervention prices fixed by EEC Commission per ton	EEC countries	B 8-a	E 44-a
Producer prices & basic fixed prices in $ per ton	W European countries	U 30-a	
in local currency per ton	All countries	A 9-a	
per 100 kg	W European countries	E 35-a	
in £ per cwt	EEC countries	B 1-a	
in $ per bushel	USA	E 35-a	
Production, stocks & usage of rye for fodder & seed: tonnage	OECD countries	D 14-a	
Production by administrative areas: tonnage	EEC countries	E 38-a	
historical tables: tonnage	Main European countries	Z 1-a	
tonnage	Argentina, Brazil, Chile & Ecuador	U 40-a	
	European countries	U 35-a	
	E European countries & USSR incl Ukraine	U 16-a	
	EEC countries	B 1-a	E 44-a
	France, W Germany & Netherlands	E 12-m	
	Main countries	B 7-a	B 8-a
		E 3-a	P 5-a
	OAS member countries	N 13-a	
	OECD countries	D 1-a	
(winter & spring) rye: tonnage	EEC countries	E 12-a	
Proportion of harvest exported	Thailand & USA	B 8-a	
Sales ex farm: tonnage	France, W Germany & Netherlands	E 12-m	
Self-sufficiency ratios	EEC countries	B 1-a	
Stocks held at wholesalers' premises: tonnage	EEC countries	E 12-m	
(end-month) held on farms: tonnage	EEC countries	E 12-m	
(end-season carry-over) held on farms: tonnage	Main countries	B 7-a	
tonnage	Argentine, Canada, W Germany & USA	B 8-a	
	Main countries	B 7-a	C 16-a
Supply & disposal by purpose: tonnage	Main countries	B 8-a	
Supply, production, consumption & trade: tonnage	EEC countries	B 1-a	
Wholesale prices in $ per ton	Austria, Canada, Turkey & USA	A 9-a	
World production: tonnage		C 16-a	

RYE FLOUR

EEC levy: imported rye flour shipped ex non-EEC area in £ per ton		B 7-m	
Export subsidies in £ per ton	EEC countries	B 8-a	

	Territorial coverage	Title codes

Sack kraft   see   WRAPPING PAPER

Sacking   see   JUTE MANUFACTURES

Sacking fibres   see   HEMP
                        JUTE

Sacks   see   JUTE MANUFACTURES

SAFFLOWER OIL

Consumption in production of margarine: tonnage	USA	B 19-a
Exports: tonnage	USA	B 19-a
Imports: tonnage	Australia	B 19-a
World production: tonnage		N 10-a

SAFFLOWER SEED

Area under crop in acres	Australia	N 10-a
Exports: tonnage	Mexico & USA	B 19-a
Imports: tonnage	Japan	B 19-a
Production: tonnage	Australia	N 10-a

SAGO & TAPIOCA

Export prices: tapioca in $ per ton	Indonesia	A 9-a
Exports: tapioca products by value in $ per ton	Thailand	U 32-m
Import prices in $ per ton cif	France & UK	A 9-a
Production: tapioca: tonnage	Madagascar & Togo	E 41-a
Wholesale prices in $ per ton	Malaysia & Singapore	A 9-a

Sailing ships   see   SHIPS & BOATS

ST LAWRENCE SEAWAY

Freight by product shipped via seaway: tonnage		S 16-m
No of vessels using seaway: inland traffic		S 16-m
ocean traffic		S 16-m

St Paulin   see   CHEESE BY VARIETY

SALARIED STAFF

      see also   SALES PERSONNEL
                    WAGE EARNERS

As % of total economically-active population	EEC countries	E 2-a	E 33-a
of total labour force employed in agriculture	EEC countries	E 2-a	
in industry	EEC countries	E 2-a	
in service industries	EEC countries	E 2-a	
% breakdown: all occupations by age groups	EEC countries	E 18-a	
industrial occupations by age groups	EEC countries	E 18-a	
service industry occupations by age groups	EEC countries	E 18-a	
% growth in administrative & managerial employment	ECAFE countries	U 17	
in no of clerical workers employed	ECAFE countries	U 17	
in professional & technical employment	ECAFE countries	U 17	
% of salaries: persons engaged in administration	EEC countries	E 33-a	
Direct costs for staff employed in industry in local currency per hr	EEC countries	E 11-a	
in mining in local currency per hr	EEC countries	E 11-a	
Earnings (all industries) by sex – index nos	EEC countries	E 25-a	
briquetting industry by sex – index nos	EEC countries	E 25-a	
building industry by administrative area in local currency per mth	EEC countries	E 38-a	
by sex – index nos	EEC countries	E 25-a	
chemical industry by administrative areas in local currency per mth	EEC countries	E 38-a	
by sex – index nos	EEC countries	E 25-a	
clothing & footwear industry – index nos	EEC countries	E 25-a	
coke ovens by sex – index nos	EEC countries	E 25-a	
electrical engineering industry – index nos	EEC countries	E 25-a	
energy production industry by administrative areas in local currency per mth	EEC countries	E 38-a	
food, drink & tobacco industries in local currency per mth	EEC countries	E 38-a	
food, drink & tobacco industries – index nos	EEC countries	E 25-a	
furniture industry by sex – index nos	EEC countries	E 25-a	
instruments manufacturing industry by sex – index nos	EEC countries	E 25-a	
leather goods manufacturing industry by sex – index nos	EEC countries	E 25-a	
man-made fibres industry by sex – index nos	EEC countries	E 25-a	
manufacturing industry by sex – index nos	EEC countries	E 25-a	
mechanical engineering industry – index nos	EEC countries	E 25-a	
metals industry by administrative areas in local currency per mth	EEC countries	E 38-a	
by sex – index nos	EEC countries	E 25-a	
mining & quarrying by administrative areas in local currency per mth	EEC countries	E 38-a	
by sex – index nos	EEC countries	E 25-a	
motor vehicles manufacturing industry – index nos	EEC countries	E 25-a	
non-metallic mineral industry – index nos	EEC countries	E 25-a	
office machinery manufacturing industry – index nos	EEC countries	E 25-a	
oil & gas industry by sex – index nos	EEC countries	E 25-a	
oil refineries by sex – index nos	EEC countries	E 25-a	
ore mining industry by sex – index nos	EEC countries	E 25-a	
paper & board manufacturing industry by administrative areas in local currency per mth	EEC countries	E 38-a	
paper & board manufacturing industry by sex – index nos	EEC countries	E 25-a	
rubber & plastics industry – index nos	EEC countries	E 25-a	

SALARIED STAFF, continued   Territorial coverage   Title codes

  Earnings: textile industry by administrative areas in local currency
                                          per mth   EEC countries   E 38-a
               by sex - index nos   EEC countries   E 25-a
      transport equipment manufacturing industry - index nos   EEC countries   E 25-a
          wood-working industry by sex - index nos   EEC countries   E 25-a
  Employment of salaried personnel in private sector   AASM countries   E 41-a
                                in public sector   AASM countries   E 41-a
  Gross income by industrial sector by sex in local currency   Main countries   R 5-a
  Labour costs by industrial sector by kind in local currency per mth   EEC countries   E 3-a
              construction industry in local currency per mth   EEC countries   E 3-a
              mining industry by kind in local currency per mth   EEC countries   E 3-a
              public utility companies in local currency per mth   EEC countries   E 3-a
  No of salaried personnel employed by sex: executive staff   All countries   L 4-a
                              in abattoirs & meat preparation
                                          industries   EEC countries   E 8-a
                            aerospace equipment industry   EEC countries   E 8-a
                            agriculture & forestry   AASM countries   E 41-a
                                    by sex & age groups   EEC countries   E 33-a
                            baking & confectionery industry   EEC countries   E 8-a
                            briquetting plants   EEC countries   E 8-a
                            building industry by sex by
                                    administrative area   EEC countries   E 38-a
                            building industry (total)   EEC countries   E 8-a
                            building materials manufacturing
                                  industry   EEC countries   E 8-a
                            carpet & rug manufacturing
                                  industry   OECD countries   D 46-a
                            cement industry   EEC countries   E 8-a
                            ceramics industry   EEC countries   E 8-a
                            chemical industry   OECD countries   D 5-a
                                                                     EEC countries   E 8-a
                            clothing manufacturing industry   EEC countries   E 8-a
                                                                     OECD countries   D 46-a
                            coke oven plants   EEC countries   E 8-a
                            collieries   EEC countries   E 8-a
                            cotton textile manufacturing
                                  industry   EEC countries   E 8-a
                            credit finance companies by sex
                                by administrative area   EEC countries   E 38-a
                            dairying industry   EEC countries   E 8-a
                            drinks manufacturing industry
                                 (incl alcoholic)   EEC countries   E 8-a
                            energy production industries   EEC countries   E 8-a
                            engineering industry (electrical)   Main countries   C 2-a
                                                                     EEC countries   E 8-a
                                    (mechanical)   Main countries   C 2-a
                                                                     EEC countries   C 2-a
                            farm machinery & tractor
                                   manufacturing industry   EEC countries   E 8-a
                            food processing industry (excl
                                 sugar refining)   EEC countries   E 8-a
                            glass & glassware manufacturing
                                  industry   EEC countries   E 8-a
                            industrial occupations   EEC countries   E 8-a   E 33-a
                                                                     Main countries   R 5-a
                            industrial occupations by age
                                   & sex   EEC countries   E 33-a
                                  by sex by
                                  administrative area   EEC countries   E 38-a
                                  by sector
                                  & by sex   All countries   L 4-a
                            iron & steel foundries   Main countries   C 2-a
                                                           EEC countries   E 8-a
                            iron & steel industry   EEC countries   E 8-a
                                                           Main countries   C 2-a
                                                            W Germany   H 3-a
                            iron ore mining   EEC countries   E 29-a
                            iron-working industry   EEC countries   E 8-a
                            knitting mills   OECD countries   D 46-a
                                                                  EEC countries   E 8-a
                            leather goods manufacturing
                                  industries   EEC countries   E 8-a
                            leather & tanning industries   EEC countries   E 8-a
                            machine tools manufacturing
                                  industry   EEC countries   E 8-a
                            man-made fibre industry   OECD countries   D 5-a
                                                                  EEC countries   E 8-a
                            manufacturing industry   EEC countries   E 8-a
                            manufacturing industry by sex &
                              by administrative areas   EEC countries   E 38-a
                            metal-working industries   EEC countries   E 8-a
                            mining & quarrying   AASM countries   E 41-a
                            mining & quarrying by sex & by
                              administrative areas   EEC countries   E 38-a
                            motor vehicle manufacturing
                                industry   EEC countries   E 8-a
                                                               Main countries   C 2-a
                            non-ferrous metals industry   EEC countries   E 8-a

479

	Territorial coverage	Title codes
SALARIED STAFF, continued		
No of salaried personnel employed in non-metallic minerals industry	EEC countries	E 8-a
nuclear fuel industry	EEC countries	E 8-a
office machinery manufacturing industry	EEC countries	E 8-a
ore mining industry	EEC countries	E 8-a
paper & board manufacturing industry	EEC countries	E 8-a
petroleum & natural gas industries	EEC countries	E 8-a
plastics manufacturing & processing industry	EEC countries	E 8-a
printing & publishing	EEC countries	E 8-a
professions by sex	All countries	L 4-a
public utilities by sex & by administrative areas	EEC countries	E 8-a E 38-a
rubber-processing industry	EEC countries	E 8-a
scientific instruments manufacturing industry	EEC countries	E 8-a
service industries	EEC countries	E 33-a
by age & sex	EEC countries	E 33-a
by sex & by administrative areas	EEC countries	E 38-a
(incl commerce)	AASM countries	E 41-a
shipbuilding & repairing industries	Main countries	C 2-a
	EEC countries	E 8-a
spinning, weaving & textile finishing industries	OECD countries	D 46-a
steel industry: administrative employees	EEC countries	E 29-a
steel industry & coal & ore mining	EEC countries	E 3-a
tanneries	EEC countries	E 8-a
textile industries (all sectors)	EEC countries	E 8-a
	OECD countries	D 46-a
timber & sawmill industry	EEC countries	E 8-a
tobacco processing industry	EEC countries	E 8-a
transport equipment manufacturing industry	EEC countries	E 8-a
transport services industries	AASM countries	E 41-a
transportation by sex & by administrative areas	EEC countries	E 38-a
water supply undertakings: professional staff: chemists, engineers, finance & other managers	All countries	W 2-a
water supply undertakings (total)	EEC countries	E 8-a
wholesale & retail trade by sex	EEC countries	E 38-a
wood-working & furniture manufacturing industries	EEC countries	E 8-a
woollen textile manufacturing industry	EEC countries	E 8-a
professional & technical staff (total)	OECD countries	D 23-a
No of executive staff presently unemployed	All countries	L 4-a
of hrs worked by salaried staff in industry per yr	EEC countries	E 2-a
of professional staff presently unemployed	All countries	L 4-a
Salary costs: professional staff by industrial sectors per mth	EEC countries	E 2-a

Salaries   see   WAGES

SALES

      see also   CASH FLOW
                     CONSUMER GOODS
                     RETAIL TRADE
                     WHOLESALE TRADE

	Territorial coverage	Title codes
Chemicals & man-made fibres industry in $m	OECD countries	D 5-a
Clothing by kind by co-operatives in £m	UK	B 29-a
by independent stores in £m	UK	B 29-a
by multiple stores in £m	UK	B 29-a
Copper cathodes: sales (on London Metal Exchange) in £	UK	C 12-m
Copper wire bars (on London Metal Exchange) in £ per ton	UK	C 12-m
Electric power equipment industry by firm in $m	Worldwide	T 7-a
Electronic equipment & components by kind in £	UK	B 24-a
Forecast of demand by 1977: agricultural machinery in £m	UK	B 27
arms & ordnance in £m	UK	B 27
batteries in £m	UK	B 23
domestic electrical equipment in £m	UK	B 23
earthmoving equipment in £m	UK	B 27
electric lamps in £m	UK	B 23
electrical machines in £m	UK	B 23
internal combustion engines in £m	UK	B 27
insulated wire in £m	UK	B 23
mechanical handling equipment in £m	UK	B 27
office machinery in £m	UK	B 27
plant & steelwork in £m	UK	B 27
pumps in £m	UK	B 27
railway equipment in £m	UK	B 27

	Territorial coverage	Title codes
SALES, continued		
Forecast of demand by 1977: textile machinery in £m	UK	B 27
wheeled tractors in £m	UK	B 27
Industrial sales: % change by kind of outlet (quantum basis)	E European countries	U 16-a
Largest ten British industrial companies in £m		H 1
French industrial companies in Fr million		H 1
Italian industrial companies in Lit		H 1
twenty German industrial companies in DM million		H 1
Swiss commercial undertakings in FrS million		H 1
industrial companies in FrS million		H 1
twenty-five Japanese industrial companies in million yen		H 1
Lead (on London Metal Exchange) in £m	UK	C 12-m
Non-ferrous metals in DM million	W Germany	H 3-a
Steel foundries in DM million	W Germany	H 3-a
Tin (on London Metal Exchange) in £m	UK	C 12-m
Turnover: chemical industry in DM million	W Germany	H 3-a
coal mining industry in DM million	W Germany	H 3-a
electrical engineering industry in DM million	W Germany	H 3-a
iron & steel industry: specific companies in DM million	W Germany	H 3-a
iron ore mining industry in DM million	W Germany	H 3-a
machine tools manufacturing industry in DM million	W Germany	H 3-a
metal fabricating industries in DM million	W Germany	H 3-a
mechanical engineering industries in DM million	W Germany	H 3-a
motor vehicles manufacturing industry in DM million	W Germany	H 3-a
steel industry by sector in DM million	W Germany	H 3-a
World's 100 largest industrial companies in FrS	Worldwide	H 1
Zinc (on London Metal Exchange) in £m	UK	C 12-m
Sales demand see CONSUMER GOODS		
CONSUMPTION PER CAPITA		
DURABLE GOODS		
RETAIL TRADE		
SALES DISCOUNTS		
Usual % discount: furniture industry to customers (for cash)	W European countries	C 8-a
to retailers (for early payments)	W European countries	C 8-a
SALES MARGINS		
see also DISTRIBUTION COSTS		
Furniture: direct sales as % of factory prices	W European countries	C 8-a
retail sales margins as % of wholesale price	W European countries	C 8-a
wholesale sales margins as % of factory selling price	W European countries	C 8-a
Sales on credit terms see INSTALMENT CREDIT		
SALES PERSONNEL		
% of employed persons: commercial salesmen	EEC countries	E 33-a
No employed by sex	All countries	L 4-a
No of salesmen presently unemployed	All countries	L 4-a
SALES PROMOTION		
see also ADVERTISING		
EXPORT PROMOTION		
Expenditure on advertising (by media) in $m	Main countries	Z 4-a
per capita in $	Main countries	Z 4-a
SALES TAXES		
see also TURNOVER TAXES		
Government revenue in local currency	OAS member countries	N 16-a
in $m	Argentine & Dominican Republic	J 5-a
Levied on farm products (at point of sale)	ECE countries	U 34-a
on vehicle fuels	Main countries	S 24-a
on wool (carded or combed) in % ad val	Canada, Malaysia & Switzerland	K 3-a
Turnover taxes: passenger cars	Main countries	S 24-a
Sales, domestic see DELIVERIES, DOMESTIC		
RETAIL TRADE		
SALMON		
Catch (nominal) by species: tonnage	All countries	A 22-a
Exports: tinned salmon by kind: tonnage & value in $m	All countries	A 21-a
Landings: tonnage & value in $ (incl trout)	OAS member countries	N 13-a
tonnage & value in $: sea salmon	OECD countries	D 43-a
Production: tinned Pacific salmons: tonnage	All countries	A 21-a
Retail prices in local currency per kg	OAS member countries	N 17-a
Salt cake see SODIUM SULPHATE		
Salt taxes see MONOPOLY TAXES		
SALT		
Consumption by chemical industry: brine, rock & sea salt: tonnage	OECD countries	D 5-a
tonnage	European countries, Japan & USA	U 25-a
common salt & sea salt: tonnage	OAS member countries	N 17-a
tonnage	USA	N 1-a

	Territorial coverage	Title codes
SALT, continued		
Excise duties: % rates charged	EEC countries	E 31-a
Imports & exports by source & destination: tonnage	All countries	B 15-a
Production: brine: tonnage	OECD countries	D 5-a
rock & sea salt: tonnage	All countries	B 15-a
	OECD countries	D 5-a
salt (all kinds): tonnage	European countries, Japan & USA	U 25-a
sodium chloride: tonnage	OECD countries	D 5-a
(unrefined): tonnage	All countries	U 22-a
tonnage	AASM countries	E 41-a
	African countries	U 44-a
	Asian & Far East countries	U 32-q
	ECAFE countries	U 32-q
	Latin American countries	J 5-a
	Main countries	U 43-a
	OAS member countries	N 14-a
	OAS member countries	N 17-a
Retail prices by kind in local currency per ton	EEC countries	Z 3-a
(comparative): cooking salt in cents per kg	USA	N 1-a
Wholesale prices excl brine (at mines) in $ per ton	OAS member countries	N 17-a
by kind in local currency per kg	USA	N 1-a
packed 100 lb bags in $ per ton		N 4-a
World production: tonnage	Main countries	N 1-a

SALTED FISH
Production by kind: tonnage	Main countries	U 43-a
dried, smoked & salted fish: tonnage	All countries	U 22-a
tonnage	Main countries	A 21-a
Wholesale prices in lire per kg	Italy	A 9-a

Salted pig-meat   see   PORK, SALTED OR DRIED

Saltpetre   see   FERTILISERS

Samso   see   CHEESE BY VARIETY

Sanatoria   see   CONVALESCENT HOMES

SAND & GRAVEL
Consumption: tonnage	USA	N 1-a
Production: sand, silica & quartz: tonnage	All countries	U 22-a
tonnage	Cyprus	U 5-a
Wholesale prices (for building industry) - index nos	OAS member countries	N 14-a
in $ per ton	USA	N 1-a
Wholesale prices - index nos	European countries & Cyprus	U 5-a
World production: tonnage	USA & Others (as total)	N 1-a

SAND CASTINGS
Consumption: zinc in production of sand castings: tonnage	USA	J 6-a
Sales: aluminium sand castings: tonnage	USA	J 6-a
magnesium sand castings: tonnage	USA	J 6-a

SANITARY PAPER
Consumption (incl household paper): tonnage	OECD countries	D 40-a	
Exports by destination: tonnage	All countries	D 40-a	
(incl household paper): tonnage	OECD countries	D 41-q	
Imports (incl household paper): tonnage	OECD countries	D 41-q	
Production (incl household paper): tonnage	OECD countries	D 41-q	D 40-a
thin household paper: tonnage	OECD countries	D 40-a	

Sanitary products   see   HYGIENE REQUISITES

Sanitary ware, ceramic   see   EARTHENWARE PRODUCTS

SANITATION

    see also   PUBLIC HEALTH

A.I.D. grants to improve health standards in $m	Recipient countries	M 1-a
Costs of installing public sewage disposal systems projected to 1980	All countries	W 2
Foreign loans: sewage disposal projects in $m	All countries	W 2-a
IBRD loans: sewage disposal projects in $m	OAS member countries	N 16-a
IDB loans: sewage disposal projects in $m	OAS member countries	N 16-a
Investment: rural sewage disposal systems in $m	All countries	W 2-a
urban sewage disposal systems in $m	All countries	W 2-a
No of dwellings with mains disposal of sewage	OAS member countries	N 18-a
with toilets (flush): rural areas	OAS member countries	N 18-a
urban areas	OAS member countries	N 18-a
other than flush toilets	OAS member countries	N 18-a
without mains disposal of sewage	OAS member countries	N 18-a
of households using septic tank system of sewage disposal	All countries	W 2-a
Population (rural) served by sewage disposal systems	All countries	W 2-a
with inadequate sewage disposal systems	All countries	W 2-a
served by conventional sewage systems	All countries	W 2-a
by oxidation pond systems	All countries	W 2-a
by sewage disposal systems: rural areas	OAS member countries	N 18-a
urban areas	OAS member countries	N 18-a
Population (urban) planned to have sewage disposal systems installed by 1980	All countries	W 2

	Territorial coverage	Title codes
SANITATION, continued		
Sewage disposal targets planned to yr 1980	Worldwide	W 2-a
Urban & rural housing with sewage disposal systems installed	Latin American countries	J 5-a
Urban sewage disposal systems in operation by type of sewage treatment	All countries	W 2-a
World bank loans & credits: sewage disposal projects in $m	Worldwide	M 3-a

Sapelli   see   HARDWOOD LOGS

Sapphires   see   GEM STONES

	Territorial coverage	Title codes
SARDINES & ANCHOVIES		
Catch: tonnage & value in $	OAS member countries	N 13-a
Consumption: sardines: tonnage	OAS member countries	N 17-a
Exports: historical table from 1873: tonnage	Portugal	Z 1-a
tinned sardines: tonnage & value in $m	All countries	A 21-a
Production: tinned sardines: tonnage	Main countries	A 21-a
Retail prices in local currency	OAS member countries	N 17-a

Satellite launching research   see   RESEARCH & DEVELOPMENT

Sauerkraut   see   VEGETABLES, PROCESSED

	Territorial coverage	Title codes
SAUSAGES		
Consumption per capita in kg	W Germany	U 36-a
Consumption, production & trade: tonnage	W Germany	U 36-a
Exports by destination: tonnage	EEC countries	E 47-m
tonnage	European countries	U 36-a
Imports by kind: meat used in sausage manufacture: pork, liver & offal: tonnage	W Germany	U 36-a
by source: tonnage	EEC countries	E 47-m
tonnage	Main European countries	U 36-a
Inter-EEC area shipments: tonnage	EEC countries	E 47-m
Production: tonnage	All countries	U 22-a
	UK	B 12-a
Wholesale prices in local currency	OAS member countries	N 17-a

Savings   see   CORPORATE SAVINGS
               GOVERNMENT SAVINGS
               INVESTMENT, PERSONAL
               NATIONAL SAVINGS

Savings accounts, tax free   see   INVESTMENT, PERSONAL

	Territorial coverage	Title codes
SAVINGS BANKS		
see also CREDIT UNIONS		
Deposits: historical table from 1817 in local currency	Main European countries	Z 1-a
in local currency	Main countries	R 5-a

Savings bonds   see   GOVERNMENT BONDS
                      INVESTMENT, PERSONAL

Savings deposit rates   see   INTEREST RATES

	Territorial coverage	Title codes
SAW & FILE MACHINES		
see also MACHINE TOOLS		
Sales by type by volume & value in $m	USA	J 2-a

Sawing & metal-cutting machines   see   MACHINE TOOLS

Sawmills   see   TIMBER & SAWMILL INDUSTRY

Sawn wood   see   HARDWOOD, SAWN
                  SOFTWOOD, SAWN
                  TIMBER

Scallops   see   CRUSTACEANS & MOLLUSCS

	Territorial coverage	Title codes
SCANDIUM		
Consumption in production of high-intensity electric lamps in kg	USA	N 1-a
Imports (in concentrate & compound form): tonnage	USA	N 1-a
Production for use in research laboratories: tonnage	USA	N 1-a
Wholesale prices: distilled scandium in $ per gramme	USA	N 1-a
scandium ingots in $ per gramme	USA	N 1-a

Scarifiers   see   CULTIVATING MACHINES

Scarlet fever   see   DISEASES, INFECTIOUS

Scent oils   see   OILS FOR PERFUMES

Scents   see   PERFUMERY

Scheelite   see   TUNGSTEN ORE

	Territorial coverage	Title codes
SCHOOL ATTENDANCE		
see also EDUCATION		
Enrolment ratio by kind of school	All countries	M 6-a
No of pupils attending by age & sex	All countries	U 14

School buildings   see   BUILDING CONSTRUCTION, NON-RESIDENTIAL

School teachers   see   TEACHERS

School textbooks   see   BOOKS

SCHOOLS

see also   COLLEGES, TECHNICAL
             EDUCATIONAL INSTITUTIONS

	Territorial coverage	Title codes
% of pupils attending school by age groups	EEC countries	E 2-a
No of medical schools in use & no of graduates enrolled	Latin American countries	J 5-a
pupils by kind: kindergarten, school or colleges	EEC countries	E 2-a
school leavers qualifying for university entrance	EEC countries	E 2-a

SCHOOLS BY KIND

No of primary, secondary, private & public schools	Latin American countries	J 5-a
pupils at school by sex	Main countries	R 5-a
schools in use & no of pupils & teachers	W Indies	T 6-a
schools in use	Asian, Far East & Australasian countries	U 45-a

Schools, infant   see   KINDERGARTEN

SCHOOLS, PRIMARY

Expenditure per pupil - index nos	All countries	U 62-a
No of classrooms in primary schools	AASM countries	E 41-a
primary educational establishments in use	All countries	U 62-a
public & private primary schools: rural areas	Main W Indies & Caribbean countries	T 6-a
public & private primary schools: rural areas	OAS member countries	N 19-a
urban areas	OAS member countries	N 19-a
pupils 5-14 yrs of age by sex enrolled in primary schools	OAS member countries	N 19-a
by sex enrolled in primary schools	AASM countries	E 41-a
enrolled by age groups & sex in primary schools	OAS member countries	N 19-a
by grades & by sex in primary schools	OAS member countries	N 19-a
by sex: private schools	OAS member countries	N 19-a
public schools	OAS member countries	N 19-a
enrolled in primary schools	African countries	U 44-a
historical tables from 1830	EEC countries	E 2-a
	Main European countries	Z 1-a
pupils & teachers (incl pupil-teacher ratio) in primary schools	EEC countries	E 2-a
qualified teachers employed	OAS member countries	N 19-a
schools by kind: urban & rural areas	All countries	U 62-a
teachers employed by sex: urban & rural areas	OAS member countries	N 19-a
teachers employed	African countries	U 44-a
	AASM countries	E 41-a
historical table from 1842	Main European countries	Z 1-a
unqualified teachers employed	OAS member countries	N 19-a
Public expenditure per pupil in $	All countries	U 62-a
primary education costs in $m	All countries	U 62-a
Pupil-teacher ratios: primary schools	AASM countries	E 41-a
	Latin American countries	J 5-a
private schools	OAS member countries	N 19-a
public schools	OAS member countries	N 19-a

SCHOOLS, PRIVATE

Enrolment as % of total enrolment in educational establishments	ECAFE countries	U 17-a

SCHOOLS, SECONDARY

Expenditure per pupil - index nos	All countries	U 62-a
No by kind: general & vocational in use	OAS member countries	N 19-a
in use by kind of specialist instruction	OAS member countries	N 19-a
of classrooms in secondary schools	AASM countries	E 41-a
public & private secondary schools: rural & urban areas	OAS member countries	N 19-a
pupils by sex enrolled in secondary schools	AASM countries	E 41-a
enrolled by age groups & sex in secondary schools	OAS member countries	N 19-a
by grades & by sex in secondary schools	OAS member countries	N 19-a
in secondary schools	African countries	U 44-a
	EEC countries	E 2-a
historical table from 1830	Main European countries	Z 1-a
schools in use by kind: urban & rural areas	Latin American countries	J 5-a
students enrolled by type of courses offered	Latin American countries	J 5-a
by age groups & sex	Latin American countries	J 5-a
teachers employed by sex: private secondary schools	OAS member countries	N 19-a
public secondary schools	OAS member countries	N 19-a
historical table from 1841	Main European countries	Z 1-a
in secondary education	African countries	U 44-a
	AASM countries	E 41-a
vocational courses offered by kind	Latin American countries	J 5-a
secondary schools specialising in agricultural subjects	OAS member countries	N 19-a
in commercial subjects	OAS member countries	N 19-a
in industrial subjects	OAS member countries	N 19-a

	Territorial coverage	Title codes
SCHOOLS, SECONDARY continued		
Public expenditure in secondary education per pupil in $	All countries	U 62-a
in $m	All countries	U 62-a
SCHOOLS, SPECIALIST		
No of blind pupils enrolled by sex	OAS member countries	N 19-a
continuation schools available for adults	OAS member countries	N 19-a
elementary evening institutes in use	OAS member countries	N 19-a
full & part-time teachers employed in special schools	All countries	U 62-a
handicapped pupils enrolled by sex in special schools	OAS member countries	N 19-a
institutions in use for handicapped pupils	OAS member countries	N 19-a
mentally-retarded pupils enrolled in special schools by sex	OAS member countries	N 19-a
pupils enrolled in special schools	EEC countries	E 2-a
schools catering for adult illiteracy	OAS member countries	N 19-a
special schools providing vocation courses for adults	OAS member countries	N 19-a
students attending literacy courses	All countries	U 62-a
teachers employed in special schools & % female	All countries	U 62-a
specialising in literacy courses	All countries	U 62-a
training centres available for adults	OAS member countries	N 19-a
Pupil-teacher ratios in special schools	All countries	U 62-a
Success rates against illiteracy	All countries	U 62-a

Schwarzbunt   see   CATTLE BY BREED

Sciences   see   APPLIED SCIENCES
                      MEDICAL SCIENCE
                      NATURAL SCIENCES
                      SCIENTISTS
                      SOCIAL SCIENCES
                      TECHNICIANS

SCIENTIFIC INSTRUMENTS

    see also   CONTROL INSTRUMENTATION, ELECTRONIC
                           CONTROL INSTRUMENTATION, NUCLEONIC
                           ELECTRONIC EQUIPMENT
                           OPTICAL INSTRUMENTS

	Territorial coverage	Title codes
Deliveries: aeronautical instruments by value in £m	UK	C 24-a
(all kinds) by value in £m	UK	C 24-a
analytical laboratory equipment by value in £m	UK	C 24-a
control equipment by value in £m	UK	C 24-a
meteoroligical equipment by value in £m	UK	C 24-a
nautical gunnery instrumentation by value in £m	UK	C 24-a
non-electronic test equipment by value in £m	UK	C 24-a
precision drawing equipment by value in £m	UK	C 24-a
surveying equipment by value in £m	UK	C 24-a
Demand (domestic) for scientific instruments by value in £m	UK	C 24-a
Exports by destination: equipment by kind by value in £m	UK	C 24-a
optical & medical instruments by value in $m	OECD countries	D 9-a
Imports by source: equipment by kind by value in £m	UK	C 24-a
Value added in manufacture in $m	OECD countries	D 9-a

SCIENTIFIC INSTRUMENTS MANUFACTURING INDUSTRY

	Territorial coverage	Title codes
% usage of machine tool park	EEC countries	B 20-a
Earnings: female workers per hr in FrS	Main countries	C 2-a
per hr in FrS	Main countries	C 2-a
piece rate per hr in FrS	Main countries	C 2-a
semi-skilled workers per hr in FrS	Main countries	C 2-a
skilled workers per hr in FrS	Main countries	C 2-a
time rate per hr in FrS	Main countries	C 2-a
unskilled workers per hr in FrS	Main countries	C 2-a
Labour costs as % total costs	EEC countries	E 8-a
by status of employees in local currency	EEC countries	E 8-a
female workers in FrS	Main countries	C 2-a
per hr in FrS	Main countries	C 2-a
semi-skilled workers in FrS	Main countries	C 2-a
skilled workers in FrS	Main countries	C 2-a
unskilled workers in FrS	Main countries	C 2-a
Labour force employed by status of employees	EEC countries	E 8-a
No of hrs worked per wk	OAS member countries	N 18-a
per yr	EEC countries	E 8-a
of machine tools in use	USA	J 2-a
Wage rates per hr in local currency	OAS member countries	N 17-a
in FrS	Main countries	C 2-a

SCIENTISTS

    see also   TECHNICIANS

	Territorial coverage	Title codes
% (incl engineers) engaged in research	All countries	U 62-a
No of females (incl technicians) available	All countries	U 62-a
of full & part-time scientists by field of research	All countries	U 62-a
(incl engineers) engaged in scientific research	All countries	U 62-a
per 10,000 of population	All countries	U 62-a

Scooters   see   MOTOR CYCLES & SCOOTERS

SCOURING POWDER

	Territorial coverage	Title codes
Production: unit value in $ per ton	OECD countries	D 5-a

	Territorial coverage	Title codes	
SCRAP (METALLIC)			
see also ALUMINIUM SCRAP			
ANTIMONY SCRAP			
COPPER SCRAP			
FERROUS SCRAP			
GUNMETAL SCRAP			
LEAD SCRAP			
LEAD ALLOY SCRAP			
NICKEL SCRAP			
NICKEL-SILVER SCRAP			
SHIPPING SCRAP			
TIN WASTE & SCRAP			
ZINC SCRAP			
Shipments through Panama Canal westwards: tonnage		D 28-a	
Wholesale prices: aluminium clippings in cents per lb	USA	J 6-m	
by kind in cents per lb	USA	J 6-m	
copper (heavy) in cents per lb	USA	J 6-m	
crankcases (aluminium) in cents per lb	USA	J 6-m	
lead in cents per lb	USA	J 6-m	
tin piping in cents per lb	USA	J 6-m	
zinc chips & old zinc in cents per lb	USA	J 6-m	
SCRAP DEALERS			
Deliveries: ferrous scrap (for export): tonnage	EEC countries	E 29-a	
to EEC area consumers: tonnage	EEC countries	E 29-a	
to home consumers: tonnage	EEC countries	E 29-a	
imported ferrous scrap: tonnage	ECE countries	U 6-a	U 7-a
	Main countries	H 3-a	
process scrap: tonnage	ECE countries	U 6-a	U 7-a
	Main countries	H 3-a	
railway scrap: tonnage	ECE countries	U 6-a	U 7-a
	Main countries	H 3-a	
ship-breaking scrap: tonnage	ECE countries	U 6-a	U 7-a
	Main countries	H 3-a	
	EEC countries	E 29-a	
Sales: ferrous scrap to foundries & steelworks: tonnage	ECE countries	U 6-a	U 7-a
	Main countries	H 3-a	
to other buyers: tonnage	ECE countries	U 6-a	U 7-a
	Main countries	H 3-a	
SCRAP, STEEL			
Consumption in blast furnaces: tonnage	OECD countries	D 22-a	
in steel furnaces: tonnage	OECD countries	D 22-a	
Exports by world regions of destination: tonnage	OECD countries	D 22-a	
Imports ex world regions of supply: tonnage	OECD countries	D 22-a	
Recovery: unit value in $ per ton	OECD countries	D 5-a	
Supply of ferrous scrap originating in steelworks: tonnage	OECD countries	D 22-a	
Tankers & cargo ships broken up for scrap: tonnage	EEC countries	E 43-a	
SCRAPERS			
see also GRADERS & LEVELLERS			
Production: scrapers (for earth moving): volume	All countries	U 22-a	
	European countries & USA	U 38-a	
SCREWS NUTS & BOLTS			
Production: tonnage	EEC countries	E 28-q	E 27-a
SEA PORTS			
Freight loaded & unloaded at ports: tonnage	European countries	U 8-a	
IBRD loans (for port development) in $m	OAS member countries	N 16-a	
Maximum berthing facilities located at ore-loading ports: tonnage	Worldwide	U 56-a	
Maximum loading rate facilities for ore-loading in tons per hr	Worldwide	U 56-a	
World ports: no of ships & tonnage entering & leaving	Worldwide	S 16-a	
Sea salt see SALT			
SEABORNE FREIGHT			
% share of OECD area in inter-regional trade		D 28-a	
% of seaborne freight tonnage taken up by shipments of petroleum products	Worldwide	U 37-a	
of crude petroleum	Worldwide	U 37-a	
of dry cargo	Worldwide	U 37-a	
tonnage	Worldwide	U 37-a	
Bulk carrier cargo: bauxite in ton-miles	Worldwide	D 28-a	
coal in ton-miles	Worldwide	D 28-a	
grain in ton-miles	Worldwide	D 28-a	
iron ore in ton-miles	Worldwide	D 28-a	
phosphates in ton-miles	Worldwide	D 28-a	
By broad classes of cargoes: tonnage	EEC countries	E 43-a	
By kind (shipped in bulk): tonnage	Worldwide	D 28-a	
Cargo handled at each port: tonnage	Mozambique	S 16-a	
imported & exported via Port of Karachi: tonnage	India	S 16-a	
loaded & unloaded at ports: tonnage	OAS member countries	N 15-a	
Coastal & overseas shipments by cargo classes: tonnage	EEC countries	E 43-a	

	Territorial coverage	Title codes

SEABORNE FREIGHT, continued

Dry cargo shipped: historical table: tonnage	Worldwide	D 28-a	U 37-a
Exports by sea: agricultural products by kind: tonnage	European countries	U 8-a	
building materials & timber: tonnage	European countries	U 8-a	
cereals: tonnage	European countries	U 8-a	
chemical products & fertilisers: tonnage	European countries	U 8-a	
machinery: tonnage	European countries	U 8-a	
metal ores: tonnage	European countries	U 8-a	
petroleum products: tonnage	European countries	U 8-a	
solid fuels: tonnage	European countries	U 8-a	
Freight traffic by kind of carrying vessel: tonnage	EEC countries	E 43-a	
Goods loaded & unloaded: tonnage	AASM countries	E 41-a	
	Latin American countries	J 5-a	
by port (see No. 2 1974)	Worldwide	U 27-a	
Imports & exports: transit freight through Port of Antwerp: tonnage	Belgium	S 16-a	
Imports by sea: agricultural products by kind: tonnage	European countries	U 8-a	
building materials & timber: tonnage	European countries	U 8-a	
cereals: tonnage	European countries	U 8-a	
chemical products & fertilisers: tonnage	European countries	U 8-a	
machinery: tonnage	European countries	U 8-a	
metal ores: tonnage	European countries	U 8-a	
petroleum products: tonnage	European countries	U 8-a	
solid fuels: tonnage	European countries	U 8-a	
Incoming & outgoing seaborne freight: agricultural products: tonnage	EEC countries	E 43-a	
building materials: tonnage	EEC countries	E 43-a	
by flags of vessels: tonnage	EEC countries	E 43-a	
by main ports: tonnage	EEC countries	E 43-a	
chemical products: tonnage	EEC countries	E 43-a	
fertilisers: tonnage	EEC countries	E 43-a	
machinery: tonnage	EEC countries	E 43-a	
metal ores: tonnage	EEC countries	E 43-a	
petroleum products: tonnage	EEC countries	E 43-a	
solid fuels: tonnage	EEC countries	E 43-a	
steel products: tonnage	EEC countries	E 43-a	
Iron ore by destination in ton-km	All countries	U 56-a	
Landed at & shipped from regional ports: tonnage	EEC countries	E 38-a	
Loaded & unloaded at specific large ports: tonnage	Worldwide	U 43-a	
tonnage	All countries	U 43-m	
	Main countries	U 27-m	
Loadings & unloadings: tonnage	Main countries	R 5-a	
coastal & international freight: tonnage	Main countries	U 27-a	
No of freight carriers in use by size of firms owning them	EEC countries	E 43-a	
of vessels clearing ports (incl tonnage)	OAS member countries	N 15-a	
entering ports (incl tonnage)	OAS member countries	N 15-a	
Oil shipped by tankers: historical table: tonnage	Worldwide	D 28-a	
Tanker cargo: historical table: tonnage	Worldwide	U 37-a	
Tanker dry cargo: tonnage (see No. 1)	Main countries	U 27-a	
Traffic (by product groups) through Port of Ghent: tonnage	Belgium	S 16-a	
tonnage	W Germany	S 16-m	
cleared through specific ports: tonnage	W Germany	S 16-m	
Transport performance in laden ton-miles	Worldwide	D 28-a	
World freight: shipments in ton-miles		S 15-a	
tonnage (estim)		S 15-a	
World inter-regional dry & bulk cargo shipping movements: tonnage	World regions	D 28-a	
World maritime cargo: tonnage (estim)		D 28-a	

Seaborne freight rates   see   OCEAN FREIGHT RATES

SEABORNE SHIPPING
    see also   CONTAINER TRAFFIC

% freight carried on UK-registered vessels		S 16-a	
Bulk cargo carried in British vessels in ton-miles	UK	S 16-a	
Cargo (all kinds) in ton-miles	UK	S 16-a	
Consumption: petroleum products by shipping	EEC countries	E 16-q	E 15-a
Crude petroleum shipped by destination areas: tonnage	Main countries	H 4-a	
Dry cargo carried in British vessels in ton-miles	UK	S 16-a	
Freight by type: loaded & unloaded: tonnage	All countries	U 43-a	
	African countries	U 44-a	
carried in British vessels in ton-miles: bulk carriers, cargo ships & tankers	UK	S 16-a	
loaded & unloaded: tonnage	ECAFE countries	U 32-m	
Imports unloaded at main ports: tonnage & value in $m	W Indies	T 6-a	
Loadings & unloadings: tonnage	Asian, Far East & Australasian ports	U 45-a	
No of cargo ships afloat (by tonnage classes)	Worldwide	E 43-a	
of ships (incl tonnage) arriving & leaving Port of Singapore		S 16-m	
clearing main ports	Mozambique	S 16-a	
entered & cleared at ports	Worldwide	U 43-a	
& tonnage	Latin American countries	J 5-a	
Overseas seaborne freight: tonnage	Asian & Far East countries	U 32-q	
Petroleum & dry cargo loaded: tonnage	Main countries	U 43-a	
Tanker cargo carried in British vessels in ton-miles	UK	S 16-a	
World cargo shipped ex EEC area by size of vessels: tonnage		E 43-a	

SEALS
    see also   FISHERIES

Catches by species by fishing areas: tonnage	All countries	A 22-a

	Territorial coverage	Title codes
SEASONAL WORKERS		
Earnings: farming occupations in $	All countries	L 4-a
Seaweed see AQUATIC PLANTS		
Second-hand cars see PASSENGER CARS, SECOND-HAND		
Second-hand commercial vehicles see COMMERCIAL VEHICLES, SECOND-HAND		
Secondary schools see SCHOOLS, SECONDARY		
Section mills see STEEL RE-ROLLING PLANTS		
Section-forming machines see MACHINE TOOLS		
Securities see GOVERNMENT BONDS / INDUSTRIAL SHARES		
Securities, fixed interest see GOVERNMENT BONDS		
SEED POTATOES		
Consumption: tonnage	OECD countries	D 1-a
SEEDERS & PLANTERS		
Production (all types): volume	All countries	U 22-a
	European countries & USA	U 38-a
SEEDS		
see also CASTOR SEED		
COTTON SEED		
HEMP SEED		
KAPOK SEED		
LINSEED		
MUSTARD SEED		
NIGER SEED		
POPPY SEED		
RAPESEED		
SAFFLOWER SEED		
SESAME SEED		
SUNFLOWER SEED		
Consumption: barley (as seed): tonnage	Main countries	B 8-a
cereals (all kinds) as seed: tonnage	OECD countries	D 1-a
oats (as seed): tonnage	Main countries	B 8-a
rice (as seed): tonnage	Main countries	B 8-a
rye (as seed): tonnage	Main countries	B 8-a
seed potatoes: tonnage	OECD countries	D 1-a
wheat & rye (as seed): tonnage	OECD countries	D 1-a
wheat (as seed): tonnage	EEC countries	E 44-a
	Main countries	B 7-a
	UK	B 8-a
tonnage	EEC countries	E 44-a
Cost of seeds (as factor in farm expenditure) - index nos	ECE countries	U 34-a
Expenditure: seeds as % of gross value of farm output	ECE countries	U 34-a
Production by value in $m	EEC countries	E 44-a
for cultivation of wheat & other cereal crops: tonnage	EEC countries	E 3-a
SELECTIVE EMPLOYMENT TAX		
Receipts by Treasury in £m	UK	E 42-a
SELENIUM		
% consumption in production of ceramics & glass	USA	N 1-a
of chemical products	USA	N 1-a
of electronic components	USA	N 1-a
tonnage	USA	N 1-a
Government strategic stockpile & sales: tonnage	USA	N 1-a
Imports by source in lbs	UK & USA	T 4-a
in kg	Main countries	T 4-a
Imports & exports by source & destination in lbs	All countries	B 15-a
Production (incl compounds) in lbs & kg	All countries	B 15-a
	USA	J 6-a
Stocks held at producers' plants (end-yr): tonnage	USA	N 1-a
Wholesale prices by grade in $ per lb	USA	T 4-m
(ex Canada) in $ per lb	UK	T 4-w
(ex store Tokyo Market) in yen per kg	Japan	T 4-m
metallic selenium in $ per lb	USA	N 1-a
World exports in kg	All countries	T 4-a
World production: selenium metal in kg	All countries	T 4-a
tonnage	Non-Communist countries only	C 30-a N 4-a
	Main countries	N 1-a
World reserves: tonnage (estim)	Main countries	N 1-a
SELF-EMPLOYED PERSONS		
% breakdown (all occupations) by age groups	EEC countries	E 18-a
% engaged in farming occupations	EEC countries	E 18-a
in industrial occupations	EEC countries	E 18-a

	Territorial coverage	Title codes	
SELF-EMPLOYED PERSONS, continued			
% engaged in service industries	EEC countries	E 18-a	
As % of total employed persons by region	EEC countries	E 33-a	
No of persons by age & sex engaged in farming occupations	EEC countries	E 18-a	E 33-a
in industrial occupations	EEC countries	E 18-a	E 33-a
in service industries	EEC countries	E 18-a	E 33-a
by occupational groups	Main countries	R 5-a	
of hrs worked by sex in farming	EEC countries	E 33-a	
of self-employed persons	EEC countries	E 18-a	
SELF-SERVICE STORES			
% growth rate in self-service retailing	W European countries	Z 2-a	
Increase in number of store by kind of ownership	W European countries	Z 2-a	
No of food stores as % of all food retailing outlets	W European countries	Z 2-a	
in operation by kind of ownership	W European countries	Z 2-a	
per sq km area	W European countries	Z 2-a	
of hypermarkets in operation	W European countries	Z 2-a	
of inhabitants per self-service food store	W European countries	Z 2-a	
per self-service store	W European countries	Z 2-a	
of self-service stores by size of floor area in m²	W European countries	Z 2-a	
in operation	W European countries	Z 2-a	
per sq km	W European countries	Z 2-a	
of supermarkets as % of all self-service stores	W European countries	Z 2-a	
in operation	W European countries	Z 2-a	
independently-owned	W European countries	Z 2-a	
owned by consumer co-operatives	W European countries	Z 2-a	
by departmental stores	W European countries	Z 2-a	
by multiple stores	W European countries	Z 2-a	
owned by consumer co-operatives	W European countries	Z 2-a	
departmental stores	W European countries	Z 2-a	
independent retailers	W European countries	Z 2-a	
multiple store companies	W European countries	Z 2-a	
Turnover as % of sales of all food retailers	W European countries	Z 2-a	
in local currency	W European countries	Z 2-a	
SELF-SUFFICIENCY			
In supply of beef, lamb, mutton, pork & veal	EEC countries	E 44-a	
butter, cheese, fresh milk & milk powder (skim & whole)	EEC countries	B 1-a	B 3-a
		E 44-a	
butter & cheese	EEC countries	B 1-a	B 3-a
casein	Denmark, France, W Germany & UK	B 3-a	
citrus fruit & fresh fruit (all kinds)	EEC countries	B 1-a	E 3-a
		E 44-a	
condensed milk	EEC countries	B 3-a	
cotton	Developed countries	U 11-a	
dairy products	EEC countries	E 3-a	
eggs	EEC countries	B 1-a	E 44-a
fats & oils, fish & fish oils, margarine & vegetable oils	EEC countries	E 3-a	E 44-a
fats & vegetable oils	Developed countries	U 11-a	
fish (from own catch)	EEC countries	E 3-a	E 44-a
grains by kind	EEC countries	B 1-a	E 3-a
		E 44-a	
lamb & mutton, beef & veal	EEC countries	B 1-a	
maize & barley	EEC countries	B 1-a	
milk & milk products	EEC countries	B 1-a	B 3-a
oats	EEC countries	B 3-a	
pork	EEC countries	B 1-a	
potatoes	EEC countries	B 1-a	E 3-a
		E 44-a	
poultry & poultry meat	EEC countries	B 1-a	E 44-a
products (agricultural) in general	EEC countries	B 1-a	
rice	EEC countries	B 1-a	E 44-a
rye	EEC countries	E 44-a	
sugar (raw)	EEC countries	E 44-a	
(refined)	EEC countries	E 3-a	E 44-a
	Developed countries	U 11-a	
tobacco	Developed countries	U 11-a	
vegetable oils	EEC countries	B 1-a	E 44-a
vegetables	EEC countries	B 1-a	E 3-a
		E 44-a	
whey powder	EEC countries	B 3-a	
wine	EEC countries	B 1-a	E 3-a
		E 44-a	
Imports as % of consumption: basic metals	Main countries	U 23-a	
chemicals	Main countries	U 23-a	
coal, oil & gas	Main countries	U 23-a	
farm products	Main countries	U 23-a	
food & tobacco	Main countries	U 23-a	
machinery	Main countries	U 23-a	
mineral ores	Main countries	U 23-a	
oil & coal products	Main countries	U 23-a	
rubber	Main countries	U 23-a	
timber products	Main countries	U 23-a	
transport equipment	Main countries	U 23-a	

Selling rates for exchange certificates   see   EXCHANGE RATES

Semi-conductors   see   ELECTRONIC COMPONENTS

	Territorial coverage	Title codes	
SEMI-MANUFACTURED PRODUCTS (INDICES)			
see also STEEL, SEMI-FINISHED			
Exports - index nos (quantum & value bases)	OECD countries	D 16-q	
Imports - index nos (quantum & value bases)	OECD countries	D 16-q	
Wholesale prices - index nos	OAS member countries	N 17-a	
	S Vietnam	U 32-m	
Semi-trailers see TRAILERS			
Semis see STEEL, SEMI-FINISHED			
SEMOLINA			
Production: tonnage	EEC countries	E 28-a	E 27-a
Retail prices in local currency	OAS member countries	N 17-a	
SERVICE INDUSTRIES			
see also LOCAL GOVERNMENT SERVICES			
% change as component of gross domestic product	S European countries	U 16-a	
in charges of hotels	OECD countries	D 47-a	
of restaurants	OECD countries	D 47-a	
% contribution to gross domestic product	AASM countries	E 41-a	
to national income	Developing countries	D 25-a	
% growth rates: output per capita projected to 1980	Main countries	D 17-a	
labour force employed	ECAFE countries	U 17-a	
% of employed persons in service industries by region	EEC countries	E 33-a	
% of married women employed in service industries	EEC countries	E 2-a	
% of population 14-24 yrs employed in service industries	EEC countries	E 2-a	
over 60 yrs employed in service industries	EEC countries	E 2-a	
Capital formation in local currency	OAS member countries	N 16-a	
Contribution to gross domestic product in local currency	African countries	U 44-a	
to gross domestic product & as % of total product	EEC countries	E 32-a	
Employment in service industries as % of total labour force by region	EEC countries	E 2-a	
(average or at yr-end)	EEC countries	E 33-a	
by sex & status by administrative areas	EEC countries	E 38-a	
Family helpers as % of labour force employed	EEC countries	E 18-a	
Government revenue: taxes on services in local currency	EEC countries	E 42-a	
Gross product of service industries as component of gross domestic product	Developing countries	D 25-a	
Labour force employed as % of total employed population	EEC countries	E 33-a	
by sex (at census dates)	African countries	U 44-a	
	OAS member countries	N 18	
by sex: catering industry	EEC countries	E 18-a	
credit & insurance	EEC countries	E 18-a	
local government services	EEC countries	E 18-a	
retail trade	EEC countries	E 18-a	
transportation	EEC countries	E 18-a	
by status	Main countries	C 28(irr)	
(incl % rate of change)	ECE countries	U 15-a	
	EEC countries	E 26-a	
no of managerial staff in service industries	AASM countries	E 41-a	
salaried staff in service industries	AASM countries	E 41-a	
unskilled workers in service industries	AASM countries	E 41-a	
wage earners in service industries	AASM countries	E 41-a	
(total) in service industries	All countries	L 4-a	
	EEC countries	E 18-a	
Loan advances (from commercial banks) in local currency	OAS member countries	N 16-a	
No of hrs worked per wk by sex	EEC countries	E 2-a	E 33-a
service industry employees in 14-24 yrs age group	EEC countries	E 3-a	
over 60 yrs of age	EEC countries	E 3-a	
salaried staff employed as % of total employed in service industries	EEC countries	E 2-a	
self-employed persons as % of total labour force	EEC countries	E 18-a	
wage & salary earners as % of total labour force	EEC countries	E 18-a	
workers normally working in service industry presently unemployed	All countries	L 4-a	
working days lost per employee in service industries	UK	B 29-a	
Retail cost of services - index nos	EEC countries	D 6-m	
Retail prices charged in service industries - index nos	E European countries & USSR	U 16-a	
Wage rates in service industries: bricklayers & masons in FrS per hr	Switzerland	R 4-a	
carpenters & joiners in FrS per hr	Canada & Switzerland	R 4-a	
electrical fitters in FrS per hr	Canada & Switzerland	R 4-a	
gas installation engineers in FrS per hr	Switzerland & UK	R 4-q	
painters & decorators in FrS per hr	Switzerland	R 4-a	
Service personnel see ARMED FORCES			
SERVICE VEHICLES			
No of ambulances, fire engines (et al) in use	EEC countries	E 43-a	
Registrations (new): ambulances	Main countries	V 4-a	
	UK	V 1-a	
fire appliances	UK	V 1-a	
mobile cranes	N Ireland	V 1-q	
	UK	V 1-a	
road construction equipment, road rollers & snow ploughs	UK	V 1-a	

	Territorial coverage	Title codes
SERVICES, DOMESTIC		
see also SERVICE INDUSTRIES		
Contribution to gross domestic product in local currency	African countries	U 44-a
Servicing of debts see DEBT SERVICING		
SESAME SEED		
Area harvested, production: tonnage & yield per ha	All countries	A 9-a
under crop in acres	Main countries	B 19-a
in ha	OAS member countries	N 13-a
Crop: tonnage (incl domestic consumption)	Greece	D 14-a
(incl world total)	All countries	B 18-a P 1-a
tonnage	Latin American countries	U 40-a
Crop yield in kg per ha	OAS member countries	N 13-a
Export prices in $ per ton cif	Sudan	A 9-a
Exports by destination: tonnage	Nigeria & Sudan	B 19-a
tonnage	Main countries	B 19-a
Harvest (for ensuing crop-yr): tonnage (estim)	World regions	P 1-a
Import prices (ex Sudan) in £ per ton cif at European ports		B 19-q
Imports: tonnage	Main countries	B 19-a
Producer prices in $ per ton	Cyprus & Khmer Rep	A 9-a
Production: tonnage	African countries	U 44-a
	Main countries	B 19-a
	OAS member countries	N 13-a
SESAME SEED OIL		
Consumption: tonnage	OAS member countries	N 17-a
Exports: tonnage	Main countries	B 19-a
Imports: tonnage	Main countries	B 19-a
Production: tonnage	Denmark, Italy & Japan	P 1-a
	India, Mexico & Venezuela	B 19-a
Wholesale prices (in drums) in cents per lb	USA	B 19-q
World & Commonwealth production: tonnage		B 19-a
World production: tonnage		A 4-a A 5-a
		N 10-a
Sewage systems see SANITATION		
Sewing see HOME SEWING		
SEWING MACHINES		
% change in retail sales	E European countries & USSR	U 16-a
Exports by destination by value in $m	Main countries	U 9-a
by value in $m	OECD countries	D 9-a
	All countries	U 38-a
Imports by value in $m	All countries	U 38-a
Production (domestic type): volume	Main countries	R 5-a
for home & industrial use: volume	All countries	U 22-a
volume	All countries	U 38-a
	OAS member countries	N 14-a
	EEC countries	E 28-q E 27-a
Sales demand: sewing machines per 1000 population	E European countries & USSR	U 16-a
World exports by value in $m		U 38-a
SEWING THREAD		
Demand (domestic) projected to 1977 in lbs (estim)	UK	B 29
Exports: cotton twist & thread by value in $	Pakistan	U 32-m
Production: tonnage	EEC countries	E 28-q E 27-a
Shale oil see CRUDE PETROLEUM		
Shallots see ONIONS		
Shampoos & hair dressings see TOILET PREPARATIONS		
Shaping machines see MACHINE TOOLS		
SHARE CAPITAL		
Industrial company share capital: nominal values	Main European companies	F 9-a
SHARES & SECURITIES		
see also INDUSTRIAL SHARES		
STOCK EXCHANGE		
INVESTMENT, PERSONAL		
Nominal & market valuations by sector in £m	UK	F 8-q
Stock Exchange values: British funds in £m	UK	F 8-q
Commonwealth bonds in £m	UK	F 8-q
fixed interest stocks by kind in £m	UK	F 8-q
municipal bonds in £m	UK	F 8-q
preference shares in £m	UK	F 8-q
SHARES, COMMON		
Government revenue: taxes on transfers of shares in local currency	EEC countries	E 42-a
No of new issues by value (incl % yields)	EEC countries	E 26-m
	All countries	F 5-m F 6-q

	Territorial coverage	Title codes

SHARES, COMMON   continued
    Nominal & market valuations in £m   Eire & UK   F 8-q
    Stock Exchange quotations (incl % yields)   Main European companies   F 9-a
    Stock Exchange quotations - index nos   EEC countries   E 3-a
    Value of shares sold on Stock Exchanges in local currency   OAS member countries   N 16-a

SHARES, PREFERENCE
    Nominal & market valuations in £m   Eire & UK   F 8-q
    Value of shares sold on Stock Exchanges in local currency   OAS member countries   N 16-a

Shark (edible)   see   FISH

Shaving soap   see   SOAP, SHAVING

SHEA NUT OIL
    Exports: tonnage   Mali & Upper Volta   B 19-a
    Imports: tonnage   Sweden   B 19-a

SHEA NUTS
    Exports: tonnage   E African countries   B 19-a
    Imports: tonnage   Denmark, Japan, Sweden & UK   B 19-a

Shearing machines   see   MACHINE TOOLS
                         PUNCH & SHEARING MACHINES

SHEEP
    % contribution to export earnings   Upper Volta, Ethiopia & Somalia   E 45-a
    Distribution for market sales: volume   Czechoslovakia, Hungary & Poland   U 34-a
                       for own farm consumption: volume   Czechoslovakia, Hungary & Poland   U 34-a
    Exports by destination: live sheep & lambs: volume   Main countries   B 12-m
                   live sheep: volume   Main countries   B 11-a
                           tonnage & value in $m   African, Caribbean countries & Pacific Is   E 45-a
    Government expenditure: price guarantees in £m   UK   P 5-a
    Gross output (incl wool) by value in $m   ECE countries   U 34-a
    Imports by source: volume   Main countries   B 12-m
                live sheep by value in $m   European countries   U 36-a
                               in £m   Main countries   B 11-a
    Inter-EEC area imports & exports: tonnage   EEC countries   B 12-a
    Population by age: over & under 1 yr of age by sex   EEC countries   E 1-a
                   ewes for breeding, rams & other kinds of sheep   Eire   B 12-a
                   historical tables from 1816   Main European countries   Z 1-a
                   in 1000 head   AASM countries   E 41-a
                   in million head   All countries   A 9-a   K 6-a
                                          U 43-a
                                    Main countries   B 11-a
                                    African countries   U 44-a
                                    OECD countries   D 1-a
                   incl goats   Main countries   E 3-a
                   incl goats & no per 100 ha   EEC countries   E 1-a
                   incl goats (census data)   E European countries   U 16-a
                   incl goats on all holdings in million head   USSR   B 12-a
                                          European countries & USSR   U 36-a
                             on state farms in million head   USSR   B 12-a
                   (incl world total) in 1000 head   Main countries   R 5-a
                   under 1 yr of age: rams & breeding ewes   EEC countries   B 1-a
    Producer prices (at auction) in $ per ton   European countries & Turkey   U 36-a
                   lambs in local currency per ton   OECD countries   D 1-a
                   sheep & lambs in $ per ton   All countries   A 9-a
    Production costs on collective farms per ton   USSR   U 34-a
    Production (incl goats) by value in £m   EEC countries   B 1-a
    Production, imports & exports (incl goats): volume   EEC countries   E 44-a
                   volume   Latin American countries   J 5-a
    Slaughterings: lambs, ewes & rams: volume (incl % change)   Main countries   C 9-q
                 sheep & goats: volume   EEC countries   E 1-a
                 sheep & lambs: tonnage (dead wt)   Main countries   B 12-m
                       volume   All countries   A 9-a
                                    European countries   U 36-a
    Wholesale prices: sheep & lambs (live wt) in $ per ton   Main countries   A 9-a
    World population: woolled sheep (end-season) in million head   Main countries   B 10-a
    Weight (average at slaughter) incl goats in kg per head   OAS member countries   N 14-a

SHEEPSKINS
         see also   LEATHER, SHEEP & GOATSKIN
    % contribution to export earnings   Somalia   E 45-a
    % consumption (incl lambskins) for production of footwear & gloves   USA   A 18-a
                               tonnage (dry wt)   OECD countries   D 18-a
    Exports by destination: tonnage   OECD countries   D 18-a
                         (incl lambskins): tonnage   Main countries   B 9-m
                         sheep & lamb skins: tonnage   Main countries   B 2-a
                         tonnage & value in $m (incl world total)   World regions   A 5-a
                         tonnage   European OECD countries   D 18-a
                                    Main countries   A 18-a
    Imports by source: tonnage & value in $m   OECD countries   D 18-a
                   ex non-OECD area: tonnage (dry wt)   OECD countries   D 18-a
                   (incl lambskins): tonnage   Main countries   B 9-m   A 18-a
    Intra-European trade: tonnage   European economic areas   D 18-a

	Territorial coverage	Title codes	
SHEEPSKINS, continued			
Production: hides (untanned): tonnage	OAS member countries	N 14-a	
(incl goatskins) forecast to 1985: tonnage		A 18-a	
(incl goatskins): tonnage	Main countries	B 2-a	
(incl lambskins) for production of fancy goods, gloves, & shoes	France	B 9-a	
of parchment	France	B 9-a	
leather from sheep & lambs: tonnage	Main countries	B 9-a	
per 1000 sheep slaughtered	European countries	A 18-a	
tonnage (dry wt)	OECD countries	D 18-a	
volume & as % of sheep population	All countries	A 18-a	
volume	Main producing world regions	A 5-a	
Utilisation of sheepskins for production of leather: tonnage	Main countries	B 9-a	
(incl goatskins): tonnage	Main countries	A 18-a	
Wholesale prices (ex Australia) in pence per kg	UK	B 2-a	
in Rs per 100 pieces	Pakistan	U 32-m	
lambskins - index nos	OECD countries	D 18-a	
shearlings - index nos	OECD countries	D 18-a	
World production: volume	Main countries	A 18-a	
Weight per skin (dewoolled average) in kg	W European countries	A 18-a	
Sheet glass see GLASS & GLASS PRODUCTS			
Sheets & pillowcases see HOUSEHOLD TEXTILES			
Sheets & plates, magnesium see MAGNESIUM PRODUCTS, SEMI-FINISHED			
Sheets & strip, nickel see NICKEL PRODUCTS, SEMI-FINISHED			
Sheets, brass see BRASS PRODUCTS, SEMI-FINISHED			
SHEETS, GALVANISED			
see also PLATES & SHEETS			
Deliveries shipped to EEC area: tonnage	EEC countries	E 29-a	
Export prices: 17-20 gauge sheets in $ per ton	Belgium	R 2-m	
Exports by destination: tonnage	EEC countries	E 5-q	E 29-a
	Main countries	T 4-a	
galvanised corrugated sheets: tonnage	Main countries	T 4-a	
tonnage	European countries, Japan & USA	C 5-m	
Imports by kind: tonnage	Main countries	T 1-a	
by source: tonnage	EEC countries	E 5-q	E 29-a
	Main countries	T 4-a	
corrugated sheets: tonnage	Main countries	T 4-a	
tonnage	Main countries	T 1-a	
electro-zinc sheets: tonnage	Main countries	T 1-a	
tonnage	European countries, Japan & USA	C 5-m	
Production: galvanised corrugated sheets: tonnage	Main countries	T 4-a	
tonnage (incl world total)	All countries	T 1-a	
tonnage	ECE countries	U 7-m	U 6-a
	All countries	U 22-a	
	EEC countries	E 30-m	E 29-a
	Main countries	H 3-a	T 4-a
	OECD countries	D 22-a	
Receipts from EEC area: tonnage	EEC countries	E 29-a	
Wholesale prices (for building industry) - index nos	Iceland	U 5-a	
Sheets, lead see LEAD PRODUCTS, SEMI-FINISHED			
SHEETS, NICKEL-ALLOY			
Wholesale prices in local currency per kg	Japan & UK	T 4-w	
Sheets, titanium see TITANIUM PRODUCTS, SEMI-FINISHED			
SHELLAC			
Exports: tonnage & value in $m	India & Thailand	U 11-a	
unit value in cents per kg	India & Thailand	U 11-a	
World production by kind: sticklac, seedlac & shellac: tonnage		U 11-a	
Shellfish see CRUSTACEANS & MOLLUSCS			
Ship machinery see MACHINERY, MARINE			
Ship-breaking scrap see FERROUS SCRAP / SCRAP DEALERS			
SHIPBUILDING			
% change in output & labour force employed	Main countries	C 2-a	
% usage of machine tool park in shipbuilding & repairing industry	EEC countries	B 20-a	
Capital formation in $m	Main countries	U 21-a	
Completions of vessels constructed	Country of construction	U 37-a	
Consumption of electrical power in kWh	EEC countries	E 15-a	
iron & steel castings: tonnage	UK	B 25-a	
Costs: salaried staff per mth	EEC countries	E 11-a	
Deliveries: no & tonnage by shipyard	W Germany	S 16-a	
of barges by kind	Netherlands	S 16-a	
cargo ships	Netherlands	S 16-a	

	Territorial coverage	Title codes
SHIPBUILDING, continued		
Deliveries: no of container ships	Netherlands	S 16-a
dredgers by kind	Netherlands	S 16-a
fish factory ships	Netherlands	S 16-a
fishing research ships	Netherlands	S 16-a
fishing vessels (conventional) & trawlers	Netherlands	S 16-a
floating cranes	Netherlands	S 16-a
passenger ships & ferries	Netherlands	S 16-a
supply vessels	Netherlands	S 16-a
tugs (coastal) & pushers	Netherlands	S 16-a
(sea-going)	Netherlands	S 16-a
Earnings in shipbuilding in FrS per hr	Main countries	C 2-a
piece rates: female workers in FrS per hr	Main countries	C 2-a
in FrS per hr	Main countries	C 2-a
semi-skilled workers in FrS per hr	Main countries	C 2-a
skilled workers in FrS per hr	Main countries	C 2-a
unskilled workers in FrS per hr	Main countries	C 2-a
time rates: female workers in FrS per hr	Main countries	C 2-a
in FrS per hr	Main countries	C 2-a
semi-skilled workers in FrS per hr	Main countries	C 2-a
skilled workers in FrS per hr	Main countries	C 2-a
unskilled workers in FrS per hr	Main countries	C 2-a
Electricity: consumption from own generation in kWh	All countries	C 23-a
from public supply in kWh	All countries	C 23-a
Employment: labour force by occupational groups	Main countries	C 2-a
Frequency of accidents at shipyards	EEC countries	E 2-a
Gross output (incl repairs) by value in $m	Main countries	U 21-a
Investment in buildings in local currency	EEC countries	E 40-a
in machinery in local currency	EEC countries	E 40-a
Labour costs as % of total costs	EEC countries	E 8-a
by status of employees in local currency	EEC countries	E 8-a
female workers in FrS per hr	Main countries	C 2-a
(incl staff salaries) in FrS per hr	EEC countries	E 2-a
in local currency per hr	EEC countries	E 11-a
in FrS per hr	Main countries	C 2-a
semi-skilled workers in FrS per hr	Main countries	C 2-a
skilled workers in FrS per hr	Main countries	C 2-a
unskilled workers in FrS per hr	Main countries	C 2-a
wage earners in local currency per hr	EEC countries	E 11-a
Labour force employed (total)	Main countries	U 21-a
Labour force: no of production workers employed	Main countries	C 2-a
of salaried staff employed	EEC countries	E 11-a
	Main countries	C 2-a
of wage earners & salaried staff employed	EEC countries	E 8-a
of wage earners employed	EEC countries	E 11-a
Launchings: ships (all types): tonnage	Main countries	C 2-a
New construction: requirements projected to 1980: tonnage	Worldwide	D 28-a
New orders as % of output - index nos	W Germany	S 16-m
No & tonnage of ships built: overseas orders, completed & delivered	W Germany	S 16-m
by type launched at each yard	UK	S 16-a
launched	EEC countries	E 28-q E 27-a
started	Main countries	U 49-a
under construction by type & by firm	UK	S 16-a
under construction	W Germany & UK	S 16-m
of hrs worked in shipbuilding & repairing industry per wk by region	EEC countries	E 25-a
	Main countries	R 3-m
per yr: all employees	EEC countries	E 8-a
per yr: salaried staff	EEC countries	E 11-a
per yr: wage earners	EEC countries	E 11-a
of vessels under construction by type (see No 3, 6, 9, 12)	Worldwide	U 27-q
(end-yr): tonnage	Main countries	R 5-a
Output: tonnage	UK	S 16-a
Prices: vessels by type & tonnage in £m	UK	S 16-a2
Receipts: steel supplies by shipbuilding industry: tonnage	OECD countries	D 22-a
Value added in ship construction in $m	OECD countries	D 9-a
Wage rates & earnings per hr in local currency	Main countries	C 2-a
in local currency per hr	Main countries	R 3-m
	EEC countries	E 25-a2
Wages & salary costs in $m	Main countries	U 21-a
by sex in FrS per hr	Main countries	C 7-a
Shipments see SEABORNE SHIPPING		
Shipping see COASTAL SHIPPING		
SEABORNE SHIPPING		
TRAMP SHIPPING		
SHIPPING FLEETS		
see also MERCHANT SHIPPING FLEETS		
(Appendix 4) WORLD MARITIME FLEETS		
Building permits issued: cargo ships & oil tankers	Japan	S 16-a
ships for export	Japan	S 16-a
No & tonnage afloat by type of vessel & by flag	Worldwide	S 2-a
car, bulk cargo & chemical carriers	Japan	S 16-a
combined cargo & oil tankers	Japan	S 16-a
container ships	W Germany & Japan	S 16-a

	Territorial coverage	Title codes
SHIPPING FLEETS, continued		
No & tonnage afloat: deep-sea fishing trawlers	W Germany	S 16-a
dry cargo ships	Main countries	S 16-a
general cargo ships	Japan	S 16-a
	Main countries	S 16-a
liquefied gas carriers	Japan	S 16-a
lumber carriers	Japan	S 16-a
multi-purpose vessels	W Germany	S 16-a
oil tankers	Japan	S 16-a
ore & bulk cargo carriers	Japan	S 16-a
owned by each shipping company	Finland	S 16-a
passenger vessels	Main countries	S 16-a
	Japan	S 16-a
refrigerated ships	Main countries	S 16-a
roll-on roll-off ships	W Germany	S 16-a
ships by type laid up	Worldwide	S 17-a
special cargo ships	Japan	S 16-a
World bulk carrier fleet in dwt million		U 37-a
SHIPPING INDUSTRY		
Costs for goods, supplies & services	Norway	S 16-a
inland navigation fees	Norway	S 16-a
new tonnage bought	Norway	S 16-a
rents, dividends & taxes	Norway	S 16-a
ship repairs	Norway	S 16-a
wages (incl foreign exchange costs)	Norway	S 16-a
Shipping loss see ACCIDENTS, MARITIME		
SHIPPING SCRAP		
Break-up prices in $ per ton	World regions	S 16-a
Broken-up: all vessels: tonnage	World regions	S 16-m
dry cargo ships by flag: tonnage	World regions	S 16-a
tankers: tonnage	World regions	S 16-m
No & tonnage: ships broken up for scrap by flag	Worldwide	S 2-a
SHIPS & BOATS		
see also BARGES		
BULK CARRIERS		
CARGO SHIPS		
CONTAINER SHIPS		
FISH FACTORY SHIPS		
FISHERIES RESEARCH SHIPS		
MERCHANT SHIPPING FLEETS		
PASSENGER FERRIES		
PASSENGER VESSELS		
RESEARCH SHIPS		
SHIPPING FLEETS		
TANKERS		
TRAMP SHIPPING		
TRAWLERS		
WORLD FLEETS		
YACHTS & SPORTING CRAFT		
% of world exports sold to developed countries		U 38-a
to developing countries		U 38-a
Consumption: tonnage	Central African countries	U 38
Exports by destination by value in $m	Main countries	U 9-a
by value in $m	All countries	U 38-a
Exports: passenger, cargo ships	OECD countries	D 9-a
Imports by value in $m	All countries	U 38-a
No of arrivals & departures by flag: tonnage	EEC countries	E 43-a
cargo boats in use on inland waterways	Main countries	R 5-a
merchant ships registered & tonnage: historical table from 1788	Main European countries	Z 1-a
sailing ships registered & tonnage: historical table from 1788	Main European countries	Z 1-a
steam cargo ships registered & tonnage: historical table from 1814	Main European countries	Z 1-a
& tonnage of ships afloat	Countries of registration & build	S 3-q S 1-a
completed	Country of build	S 1-a
launched	Country of build	S 1-a S 2-a
new construction	Country of build	S 2-a
on order & being built	All countries	S 3-q
but not yet started	Country of build	S 3-q
world fleets: motorships & steamships by flag	All countries	S 2-a
World exports by value in $m		U 38-a
SHIPS & BOATS BY KIND		
% of households owning a boat	W European countries	Z 3
Exports by destination by CST classes: tonnage & value in $m	EEC countries	E 48-a
SITC classes by value in $	Main countries	D 2-q
tonnage & value in $m	OECD countries	D 3-a2
NIMEXE classes by value in $m	All countries	E 20-a
SITC classes by value in $m	All countries	U 50-a U 59-a
Imports by NIMEXE classes by value in $m	All countries	E 20-a
SITC classes by value in $m	All countries	U 50-a U 59-a
source by CST classes: tonnage & value in $m	EEC countries	E 21-a
SITC classes by value in $m	Main countries	D 2-q

	Territorial coverage	Title codes
SHIPS & BOATS BY KIND, continued		
Imports by source by SITC classes: tonnage & value in $m	OECD countries	D 3-a2
No & tonnage of ships afloat by flag		S 2-a
SHIPS & BOATS, SECOND-HAND		
Export sales: no & tonnage	Norway	S 15-a

Ships, refrigerated   see   CARGO SHIPS

Shirts   see   CLOTHING

Shock absorbers   see   REPLACEMENT PARTS

Shoe manufacturing industry   see   FOOTWEAR INDUSTRY

Shop owners   see   RETAILERS, INDEPENDENT

Shop-floor workers   see   PRODUCTION WORKERS

Shops, retail   see   CO-OPERATIVE SOCIETIES, RETAIL
INDEPENDENT STORES
MULTIPLE STORES

	Territorial coverage	Title codes
SHORT TIME WORKING		
see also ABSENTEEISM		
No of collieries affected by strikes	EEC countries	E 15-a
of days lost per worker per yr (all activities)	Main countries	R 3-a

Shortening   see   COOKING FATS

Shorthorns   see   CATTLE BY BREED

	Territorial coverage	Title codes
SICKNESS BENEFITS		
see also INJURY & DISABLEMENT BENEFITS		
Expenditure in local currency	EEC countries	E 6-a
on health service in $m	All countries	L 2-a
(Incl mental welfare benefits) as % of gross domestic product	OECD countries	D 11
No of benefits paid out (incl maternity benefits)	OAS member countries	N 18-a
of days covered by benefits paid out	OAS member countries	N 18-a
of disability benefits paid out	OAS member countries	N 18-a
Paid out per capita in FrB	EEC countries	E 6-a
per capita - index nos	EEC countries	E 6-a
Payments made as % of total expenditure on social welfare	EEC countries	E 6-a
from social security funds in local currency	EEC countries	E 3-a
Population & no of workers covered by government sickness benefit schemes	All countries	L 2-a

Siemens-Martin steel   see   CRUDE STEEL

Silica & quartz   see   SAND

Silico-manganese   see   FERRO-ALLOYS

	Territorial coverage	Title codes	
SILICON			
see also FERRO-SILICON			
Consumption: tonnage	Main countries	N 1-a	
Export prices in cents per lb fob	USA	T 4-m	
Exports by destination: tonnage	Italy, Norway & Sweden	T 4-a	
Imports by source: high-purity metallic silicon: tonnage	UK	T 4-a	
Production: metallic silicon: tonnage	Italy	T 4-a	
Stocks held at producers' & consumers' plants: tonnage	USA	N 1-a	
Wholesale prices: metallic silicon in £ per ton	UK	C 12-m	T 4-m
in cents per lb	USA	N 1-a	
in lire per kg	Italy	C 12-m	
World production: tonnage	Main countries	N 1-a	

Silicones   see   PLASTICS

Silk fabrics   see   WOVEN SILK FABRICS

	Territorial coverage	Title codes
SILK INDUSTRY		
Investment in buildings in local currency	EEC countries	E 40-a
in land purchase in local currency	EEC countries	E 40-a
in machinery in local currency	EEC countries	E 40-a
No of hrs worked per wk	Main countries	R 3-m
Wage rates by sex in local currency per hr	Main countries	R 3-m
in £ per hr	UK	R 4-a
SILK WASTE		
Consumption by textile industry: tonnage	OECD countries	D 46-a
in spinning mills: tonnage	OECD countries	D 46-a

	Territorial coverage	Title codes
SILK YARN		
Consumption in knitting mills: tonnage	OECD countries	D 46-a
in weaving industry: tonnage	OECD countries	D 46-a
Production: spun silk: tonnage	OECD countries	D 46-a
SILK, RAW		
Consumption in million lbs	Main countries	B 10-a
tonnage	OAS member countries	N 17-a
Export prices (20-22 denier) in yen per kg fob (shipped Yokohama)	Japan	R 2-m
in local currency per kg	Italy & Japan	A 9-a
Exports by destination in lbs	China & Japan	B 10-a
(incl waste) in lbs	Main countries	B 10-a
Import prices (20-22 denier) in $ per lb	USA	R 2-m
Imports (incl waste & cocoons) in lbs	Main countries	B 10-a
Production in lbs million (incl world total)	All countries	B 10-a
raw silk & waste: tonnage	All countries	A 9-a
Stocks held by user industries in lbs	France, Italy, Japan, UK & USA	B 10-a
Wholesale prices (ex China & Japan) in £ per lb	UK	B 10-a
in $ per lb	Japan & USA	A 9-a
silk raw (ex Japan) - index nos	UK	B 10-m
World consumption in million lbs (& as % of total consumption of apparel fibres)		B 10-a
tonnage & consumption per capita in kg		A 6-a
World production in lbs million		B 10-a
tonnage		K 4-a
World stocks: tonnage (estim)	Worldwide excl Sino-Soviet areas	B 10-a
SILLIMANITE		
see also KYANITE		
Imports & exports by source & destination: tonnage	All countries	B 15-a
Production: tonnage	Australia, India & S Africa	B 15-a
SILVER		
see also BULLION		
Consumption for art work & jewellery manufacture in oz	All countries	J 6-a T 4-a
	USA	T 4-a
for minting of coinage in oz	USA	N 1-a T 4-a
for production of batteries in oz	All countries	J 6-a
bearings in oz	USA	T 4-a
brazing alloys & solder in oz	USA	T 4-a
catalysts in oz	USA	T 4-a
dental supplies in oz	USA	T 4-a
electrical contacts & conductors in oz	USA	T 4-a
electroplated & sterling silver ware in oz	USA	T 4-a
glass mirrors in oz	USA	T 4-a
photographic materials in oz	USA	T 4-a
(industrial) by end-uses in oz	USA	T 4-a
in oz	USA	N 1-a
refined sterling silver in oz	OAS member countries	N 17-a
Exports by destination: mint bullion silver in oz	OAS member countries	N 17-a
metallic silver (excl coinage) in oz	Main countries	T 4-a
refined metallic silver in oz	USA	N 1-a
silver (beaten, drawn & rolled) in oz	USA	J 6-a
Government strategic stockpile in oz	All countries	B 15-a
Imports by source (as base bullion) in oz	USA	N 1-a
(as refined bullion) in oz	USA	J 6-a
silver (beaten, drawn & rolled) in oz	USA	J 6-a
Prices (3 & 7 months forward) on London Metal Market in pence per oz	All countries	B 15-a
(for cash) on London Metal Market in pence per oz	UK	T 4-m
Producer prices in local currency per oz	UK	T 4-m
Production (based on metal content of ore) in oz	W Germany, UK & USA	H 2-a
tonnage	All countries	B 15-a
	All countries	C 12-a R 5-a
		U 22-a U 43-a
	Latin American countries	J 5-a U 40-a
	Argentine, Bolivia, Mexico & Peru	U 18-a
by large mining companies in oz	Main countries	J 6-a
by large refineries in oz	USA	J 6-a
in refineries by regions in oz	USA	J 6-a
in kg	OAS member countries	N 14-a
	Zaire	E 41-a
Recovery: metallic silver from ores by kind in oz	USA	J 6-a
Refinery production: primary metallic silver in oz	USA	N 1-a
secondary metallic silver (from scrap) in oz	USA	N 1-a
Stocks held by industrial users in oz	USA	N 1-a
by US Treasury (as bullion) in oz	USA	J 6-a
(as other coinage) in oz	USA	J 6-a
(as silver dollars) in oz	USA	J 6-a
in oz	USA	N 1-a
in government strategic stockpile in oz	USA	N 1-a
Wholesale prices in local currency per oz	Canada, UK & USA	J 6-m
(London dealers' quotation) in pence per oz	UK	T 4-m
metallic silver: historical table from 1875 in £ per ton	UK	T 4-a

	Territorial coverage	Title codes	
SILVER, continued			
Wholesale prices: metallic silver in cents per oz	USA	C 12-m	N 1-a
refined metallic silver in lire per kg	Italy	C 12-m	
in pence per oz	UK	C 12-m	
silver bars in $ per oz	UK & USA	R 2-m	
World consumption by industry & the arts in oz		T 4-a	
(for coinage) in oz	Main countries	T 4-a	
in oz	Main countries	J 6-a	
World production (based on metal content of ore): tonnage		C 12-m	C 30-a
	All countries	J 6-a	
in oz	Worldwide	N 4-a	
SILVER ORE			
Exports by destination (incl concentrates) in oz	Canada	T 4-a	
(incl bullion) in oz & value in $	USA	J 6-a	
(incl concentrates) in oz	All countries	B 15-a	
Imports by source (incl concentrates) in oz	USA	T 4-a	
(incl bullion) in oz & value in $	USA	J 6-a	
World production (at mines): tonnage	All countries	T 4-a	
Simmental see CATTLE BY BREED			
SINTER			
see also SPONGE IRON			
Consumption in blast furnaces: tonnage	UK	T 2-m	
	EEC countries	E 29-a	
in steel furnaces: tonnage	EEC countries	E 30-q	
per ton of pig iron produced in kg	EEC countries	E 30-q	E 29-a
iron ore in production of sinter: tonnage	UK	T 2-q	
limestone in production of sinter: tonnage	UK	T 2-q	
pyrites residue in production of sinter: tonnage	UK	T 2-q	
scrap & black oxide in production of sinter: tonnage	UK	T 2-q	
slag scale & flue dust in production of sinter: tonnage	UK	T 2-q	
Production in iron & steelworks: tonnage	OECD countries	D 22-a	
(incl agglomerates) in steel industry: tonnage	EEC countries	E 30-q	
sinter agglomerates: tonnage	EEC countries	E 29-a	
sintered iron ore: tonnage	ECE countries	U 7-m	U 6-a
	Main countries	H 3-a	
tonnage	UK	T 2-q	
Production potential: sinter (incl sponge iron): tonnage	EEC countries	E 46-a	
Sinter pellets see IRON ORE			
Sipo see HARDWOOD LOGS			
HARDWOOD, SAWN			
Sisal see HEMP			
Skate & turbot see FISH			
Skilled workers see CRAFTSMEN & PROCESS WORKERS			
Skim milk see MILK PRODUCTS			
MILK POWDER			
Skins see HIDES			
Skirts & slacks see CLOTHING			
Slabbing mills see STEEL RE-ROLLING MILLS			
SLABS & BLOCKS, ALUMINIUM			
Imports by source: tonnage	UK	C 30-a	
Slag see FURNACE SLAG			
ZINC FUMING			
SLATE			
Production: tonnage	All countries	U 22-a	
Slaughterhouses see ABATTOIRS			
Slaughtering premiums (livestock) see EEC BUDGET			
SLEEPERS, STEEL			
see also RAILS & TRACK-LAYING MATERIAL			
SLEEPERS, WOODEN			
Deliveries shipped to EEC area: tonnage	EEC countries	E 29-a	
Exports by destination: tonnage & value in $	EEC countries	E 5-q	
tonnage	EEC countries	E 29-a	
	Main countries	T 4-a	
Imports by source: tonnage	EEC countries	E 5-q	E 29-a
	Main countries	T 4-a	
tonnage	Main countries	T 1-a	
Inter-EEC area trade: tonnage & value in $	EEC countries	E 29-a	
Production: tonnage	Main countries	T 4-a	
Receipts ex EEC area: tonnage & value in $	EEC countries	E 29-a	

	Territorial coverage	Title codes

SLEEPERS, WOODEN
    Exports by destination by volume in m³ — European countries — A 13-q
    Imports by source by volume in m³ — European countries — A 13-q
    Production by volume in m³ — Canada, European countries, USA & USSR — A 13-q

Slippers & house shoes   see   FOOTWEAR

Sluice-gate prices   see   EGGS, HEN
                               PORK
                               POULTRY MEAT
                               PIGS
                               PIG-MEAT

Slurry, recovered   see   COAL

Smallholdings   see   AGRICULTURAL HOLDINGS

Smallpox   see   DISEASES, CONTAGIOUS

SMELTING CAPACITY (NON-FERROUS METALS)
    see also   REFINERY CAPACITY
    Copper by company in tons per yr — All countries — J 6-a

Snoek flathead & marwong   see   FISH

Snow ploughs   see   SERVICE VEHICLES

Snuff   see   TOBACCO

SOAP
    see also   HYGIENE REQUISITES
    Consumption of coconut oil in production of soap: tonnage — USA — B 19-a
                 of vegetable oils by kind in production of soap: tonnage — Main countries — A 4-a
    Exports (incl medicated soaps): tonnage & value in $ — OECD countries — D 5-a
    Plant investment: capital expenditure on manufacture of soaps & detergents in £m — UK — B 21-a
    Production (all kinds): tonnage — All countries — U 22-a
                                  AASM countries — E 41-a
                                  Main countries — A 4-a   B 19-a
            household soap: tonnage — European countries & Japan — D 5-a
            industrial soap: tonnage — European countries & Japan — D 5-a
            products derived from soap: tonnage — European countries & Japan — D 5-a
            soap powder & soft soap: tonnage — European countries & Japan — D 5-a
            toilet & shaving soap: tonnage — European countries & Japan — D 5-a
    Value of output (gross & net) in £m — UK — B 21-a

SOAP, HOUSEHOLD
    Production: detergents: tonnage — OAS member countries — N 14-a
                toilet soap: tonnage — OAS member countries — N 14-a
                washing soap: tonnage — OAS member countries — N 14-a
                tonnage — OAS member countries — N 14-a
                 — OECD countries — D 5-a

SOAP, INDUSTRIAL
    Production: (all grades): tonnage — OECD countries — D 5-a

SOAP, SHAVING
    Exports: cream & sticks: tonnage & value in $ — OECD countries — D 5-a
    Production: cream & sticks: tonnage — OECD countries — D 5-a

SOAP, TOILET
    Production (incl perfumed soap): tonnage — OECD countries — D 5-a
               tonnage — OAS member countries — N 14-a
    Retail prices (comparative): toilet soap of similar quality in $ — EEC countries — Z 3-a

SOAP BY KIND
    Exports by destination by value in $ — Main countries — U 2-a
    Production: soap with potash base: tonnage — OECD countries — D 5-a
                tonnage — EEC countries — E 28-q   E 27-a
                 — European countries & Japan — D 5-a
    Retail & wholesale prices in local currency — OAS member countries — N 17-a

SOAP POWDER
    Production: tonnage — OECD countries — D 5-a

Soapstone   see   TALC

SOCIAL ASSISTANCE GRANTS
    As component of government expenditure in $m — OECD countries — D 30-a
    Government assistance granted to farming community in $m — ECE countries — U 34-a

	Territorial coverage	Title codes
SOCIAL CHARGES		
see also LABOUR COSTS		
WAGES		
As labour cost: transport service drivers in local currency	EEC countries	E 10-a
Costs to employer by industry as % of wages cost	Main countries	C 2-a
Employers' costs: industrial staff in local currency per mth	Main countries	R 3-a
industrial workers in local currency per wk	Main countries	R 3-a
Expenditure by industrial sector in $m	OAS member countries	N 14-a
Jute products industry as % of wages paid	W European countries	C 22-a
Social expenditure accounts see SOCIAL FUNDS		
SOCIAL FUNDS		
% of contributions made by employers & employees	EEC countries	B 29
% of receipts by sector of origin	EEC countries	E 6-a
from business enterprises	EEC countries	E 6-a
central & local government	EEC countries	E 6-a
employees' & employers' contributions	EEC countries	E 6-a
government contributions	EEC countries	E 6-a
households	EEC countries	E 6-a
income on capital funds	EEC countries	E 6-a
social institutions	EEC countries	E 6-a
Budgeted expenditure by EEC Commission in £m	EEC countries	B 1-a
Deficits: expenditure over receipts in local currency	EEC countries	E 6-a
Expenditure (social) as % of gross domestic product	EEC countries	E 6-a
administrative cost of paying out social benefits	EEC countries	E 3-a E 6-a
	OAS member countries	N 18-a
by function as % of gross national product	OECD countries	D 11
by social security departments in local currency	OAS member countries	N 18-a
on benefits paid out in local currency	OAS member countries	N 18-a
on social welfare per capita in local currency	EEC countries	E 6-a
(total) - index nos	EEC countries	E 6-a
Proportion of income of social funds accruing from investment	All countries	L 2-a
Receipts (by kind of financing) as % of total receipts paid into social funds	EEC countries	E 6-a
by source: contributions & other income in local currency	EEC countries	E 3-a
	All countries	L 2-a
from employees' contributions in local currency	EEC countries	E 6-a
employers' contributions in local currency	EEC countries	E 6-a
taxation to cover social welfare requirements in local currency	EEC countries	E 42-a
& contributions of employees & employers in local currency	EEC countries	E 42-a
government in local currency	EEC countries	E 6-a
in $m	All countries	L 2-a
local authorities in $m	All countries	L 2-a
income on capital in local currency	EEC countries	E 6-a
Social insurance see NATIONAL INSURANCE		
SOCIAL SCIENCE RESEARCH		
see also RESEARCH & DEVELOPMENT		
Public expenditure on research in social sciences in $m	EEC countries	E 39-a
SOCIAL SCIENCES		
% of all students enrolled studying social sciences	ECAFE countries	U 17
No of book titles published on social science subjects	OAS member countries	N 19-a
book translations published on social science subjects	OAS member countries	N 19-a
full & part-time research staff engaged in social problems	All countries	U 62-a
new book titles published on sociology	All countries	U 62-a
students by origin studying sociology abroad	All countries	U 64-a
enrolled on university courses in social sciences	OAS member countries	N 19-a
taking courses in social sciences at universities	All countries	U 62-a
university degrees granted in social sciences	All countries	U 62-a
SOCIAL SECURITY BENEFITS		
see also DEATH BENEFITS		
FAMILY ALLOWANCES		
INJURY & DISABLEMENT BENEFITS		
MATERNITY BENEFITS		
OLD AGE PENSIONS		
PENSIONS, INFIRMITY		
PENSIONS, INVALID		
PENSIONS, WAR		
PUBLIC ASSISTANCE		
REDUNDANCY		
SICKNESS BENEFITS		
UNEMPLOYMENT BENEFITS		
WIDOW'S & ORPHAN'S BENEFITS		
% change in level of benefits (incl pensions)	E European countries	U 16-a
% of social security expenditure paid out as family allowances	EEC countries	E 6-a
invalid & sickness benefits	EEC countries	E 6-a
maternity benefits	EEC countries	E 6-a
old age pensions	EEC countries	E 6-a
result of natural disasters	EEC countries	E 6-a

	Territorial coverage	Title codes
SOCIAL SECURITY BENEFITS, continued		
% of social security expenditure paid out as unemployment benefits	EEC countries	E 6-a
for injury sustained at place of work	EEC countries	E 6-a
Administrative costs in $m	All countries	L 2-a
And levies as % of national income	EEC countries	E 2-a
As % of private consumption expenditure	OECD countries	D 11
of private incomes of households	EEC countries	E 2-a
of total government expenditure	All countries	L 2-a
As component of public expenditure in $m	OECD countries	D 30-a
By kind & purpose of payment in local currency	EEC countries	E 2-a
as % of total benefits paid	EEC countries	E 6-a
of assistance granted in $	All countries	L 2-a
Cash payments (once only) as % of total disbursements	EEC countries	E 6-a
(regular) as % of total disbursements	EEC countries	E 6-a
Cost of social welfare by kind of benefit in $m	All countries	L 2-a
Expenditure in local currency	EEC countries	E 6-a
in $m	All countries	L 2-a
Goods & services costs as % of total social welfare costs	EEC countries	E 6-a
Income of households from benefits in $	OECD countries	D 30-a
No of benefits paid out	OAS member countries	N 18-a
(Non-monetary) as % of total consumption expenditure	EEC countries	E 6-a
Payments arising from natural disasters in local currency	EEC countries	E 6-a
by bases for claims in local currency	EEC countries	E 2-a
by kind of contingency in local currency	EEC countries	E 3-a
by purpose in local currency	EEC countries	E 6-a
family allowances in local currency	EEC countries	E 6-a
for disablement in local currency	EEC countries	E 6-a
for injuries sustained at place of work in local currency	EEC countries	E 3-a E 6-a
invalid benefits in local currency	EEC countries	E 6-a
maternity benefits in local currency	EEC countries	E 6-a
sickness benefits in local currency	EEC countries	E 6-a
under general schemes in local currency	EEC countries	E 6-a
special schemes in local currency	EEC countries	E 6-a
statutory schemes in local currency	EEC countries	E 6-a
supplementary schemes in local currency	EEC countries	E 6-a
voluntary schemes in local currency	EEC countries	E 6-a
unemployment benefits in local currency	EEC countries	E 6-a
Per capita paid out to persons 15-64 yrs of age in $	All countries	L 2-a
	Main countries	E 3-a
in local currency	All countries	L 2-a
	Main countries	E 3-a
	EEC countries	E 2-a
Public expenditure: social funds in local currency	EEC countries	E 32-a
Reimbursements as % of total social benefits in local currency	EEC countries	E 6-a
Transfer of social benefits to households as % of gross domestic product	OECD countries	D 11
SOCIAL SECURITY LEVIES		
Administration costs of social welfare as % of receipts of levies	All countries	L 2-a
As % of farm wages costs for hired labour	ECE countries	U 34-a
gross domestic product & of government revenue	OECD countries	D 42-a
gross domestic product to 1969	OECD countries	D 11
public expenditure on consumption	EEC countries	E 2-a
total gross income of government	Main countries	E 3-a
total tax revenue of government	OECD countries	D 11
	All countries	M 6-a
As contribution to gross income of government in local currency	S American countries	U 41-a
Payments of social levies by industry as % of industrial costs	EEC countries	E 2-a
by employees & employers in local currency	OAS member countries	N 18-a
from state funds in local currency	OAS member countries	N 18-a
Proportion of social levies accruing from special taxes	All countries	L 2-a
paid by employees & employers	All countries	L 2-a
Receipts of social levies by origin of payments in $m	All countries	L 2-a
from employees & employers in local currency	EEC countries	E 3-a
SOCIAL SERVICES		
see also LOCAL GOVERNMENT SERVICES		
MENTAL WELFARE		
% of government expenditure on welfare	Main countries	R 5-a
A.I.D. grants to improve social welfare in $m	All countries	M 1-a
Benefits per capita - index nos	All countries	L 2-a
Development aid authorisations in $m	Recipient countries	M 1-a
Distribution of cost of social services by purpose	All countries	L 2-a
Expenditure & benefits paid out in $m	All countries	L 2-a
as % of gross domestic product	EEC countries	E 6-a
	All countries	L 2-a
	Main countries	E 3-a
of net national disposable income	EEC countries	E 6-a
in local currency	EEC countries	E 6-a
of government agencies in $m	Asian, Far East & Australasian countries	U 45-a
on benefits as % of gross domestic product	All countries	L 2-a
per capita in local currency	EEC countries	E 6-a
in $m	All countries	L 2-a
15-64 yrs of age	All countries	L 2-a
per capita - index nos	All countries	L 2-a
Family benefits costs: as % of total social welfare expenditure	All countries	L 2-a

	Territorial coverage	Title codes

SOCIAL SERVICES, continued
    Government expenditure in local currency — OAS member countries — N 16-a
        in $m — Latin American countries — J 5-a
    Industrial accidents: benefits as % of total social expenditure — All countries — L 2-a
    Labour force employed by social service departments by sex (at census dates) — OAS member countries — N 18
        in community & personal service occupations — OECD countries — D 23-a
    Medical care: costs as % of total social welfare expenditure — All countries — L 2-a
    Pensions: costs as % of total social expenditure — All countries — L 2-a
    Public health: costs as % of total social welfare expenditure — All countries — L 2-a
    Receipts as % of gross domestic product — All countries — L 2-a
        per capita (for population 15-64 yrs of age) — All countries — L 2-a
        per capita - index nos — All countries — L 2-a
    Unemployment benefits: costs as % of total expenditure — All countries — L 2-a

Social welfare contributions   see   SOCIAL FUNDS

Sociology   see   SOCIAL SCIENCES

SOCKS
    see also   STOCKINGS & TIGHTS
    Consumption: wool for production of socks in kg — Main countries — K 6-a
    Production: socks: volume — All countries — U 22-a

SODA ASH
    Consumption: natural & manufactured soda ash: tonnage — USA — N 1-a
        tonnage — OAS member countries — N 17-a
    Exports by destination: sodium carbonate: tonnage — Main countries — U 2-a
        tonnage — European countries, Japan & USA — U 25-a
        — OECD countries — D 5-a
    Imports: tonnage — European countries, Japan & USA — U 25-a
        — OECD countries — D 5-a
    Production capacity: tonnage — OECD countries — D 5-a
    Production: soda ash (mainly from brine): tonnage — USA — N 1-a
        sodium bicarbonate: tonnage — All countries — U 22-a   U 43-a
        tonnage — European countries, Japan & USA — U 25-a
        — Kenya & USA — B 15-a
        — Main countries — R 5-a
        — OECD countries — D 5-a
        — OAS member countries — N 14-a
    Production - index nos — OECD countries — D 5-a
    Wholesale prices: manufactured soda ash in $ per ton — USA — N 1-a
        natural soda ash (at mine) in $ per ton — USA — N 1-a
    World production: tonnage — Chad, Kenya & USA — N 1-a

Soda wood pulp   see   WOOD PULP, BLEACHED SULPHATE
        WOOD PULP, UNBLEACHED SULPHATE

Sodium bicarbonate & sodium carbonate   see   SODA ASH

Sodium chloride   see   SALT

Sodium compounds   see   CAUSTIC SODA
        FERTILISERS
        SALT
        SODA ASH

Sodium hydroxide   see   CAUSTIC SODA

Sodium molybdate   see   MOLYBDENUM COMPOUNDS

Sodium nitrate   see   FERTILISERS
        NATURAL NITRATES

SODIUM SULPHATE
    % consumption in production of kraft paper & pulp — USA — N 1-a
        of detergents — USA — N 1-a
    Consumption: natural & manufactured sulphate: tonnage — USA — N 1-a
    Production: tonnage — All countries — B 15-a
    Wholesale prices: manufactured cake in $ per ton — USA — N 1-a
        natural mined sulphate in $ per ton — USA — N 1-a
    World production: tonnage — Main countries — N 1-a

SOFT DRINKS
    see also   BEVERAGES
        MINERAL WATERS
    % of households consuming beer, stout or lager — W European countries — Z 3
        cola drinks, soda or tonic waters — W European countries — Z 3
        fruit drinks (aerated) — W European countries — Z 3
        fruit juices, squashes or syrups — W European countries — Z 3
    Production: volume — All countries — U 22-a
    Retail prices by kind in local currency — OAS member countries — N 17-a
        (comparative): coca cola per 0.75 litres — EEC countries — Z 3-a
        mineral waters in local currency — OAS member countries — N 17-a

Soft furnishings   see   HOUSEHOLD TEXTILES

	Territorial coverage	Title codes

Soft oils   see   COTTONSEED OIL
                    GROUNDNUT OIL
                    RAPESEED OIL
                    SAFFLOWER OIL
                    SOYBEAN OIL
                    SUNFLOWER SEED OIL

Soft wheat   see   WHEAT, SOFT

SOFTWOOD, SAWN

see also   TIMBER, CONIFEROUS

Consumption by volume in m³	Canada, European countries & USA	A 24-a
	OAS member countries	N 17-a
per capita by volume in m³	Main countries	A 24-a
Consumption - index nos	European countries (excl USSR)	A 24-a
Contracts placed by British & Dutch importers by source		A 24-a
Domestic requirements: forecast	Canada, European countries & USA	A 24-a
Export prices in $ per m³ fob	Finland	A 24-a
Exports by destination by volume in m³	Canada, European countries & USA	A 13-q
	Finland & Sweden	A 24-a
by volume in m³	Main countries	A 5-a A 24-a
Fellings by volume in m³	Main countries	R 5-a
Freight by cargo source: tonnage	Main importing countries	D 28-a
Import prices in $ per m³	UK	A 9-a
red deal battens in £ per m³ cif	UK	R 2-m
white deal battens in £ per m³ cif	UK	R 2-m
Imports by source by volume in m³	European countries	A 13-q
	W European countries	A 24-a
Prices by kind of timber: forward sales in $ per m³	Scandinavian countries & USSR	A 24-a
Production & forecast requirements: volume in m³	European area	A 24-a
Production: coniferous logs by volume in m³	All countries	A 5-a
	World regions	J 7-a
for industrial use or as fuel by volume in m³	Canada, European countries, USA & USSR	A 13-q
in m³	Main countries	A 24-a
	OECD countries	R 5-a
in standards: historical table from 1910: tonnage	Main European countries	Z 1-a
Stocks (end-period) by volume in m³	Canada, European countries & USA	A 24-a
Wholesale prices: beech planks in lire per m³	Italy	R 2-m
in $ per m³	Canada, European countries & USA	A 13-m
roundwood - index nos	European countries	A 26-a

SOFTWOOD LOGS

Exports by destination by volume in m³	European countries, USA & USSR	A 13-q
Imports by source by volume in m³	Canada, European countries & USA	A 13-q
Wholesale prices in local currency	European countries	A 13-m

SOLDER

see also   BRAZING METALS
            WHITE METAL

Consumption: lead in production of solder: tonnage	European countries	C 12-a
	USA	J 6-a
silver in production of solder (incl brazing metals) in oz	USA	T 4-a
tin in production of solder: tonnage	USA	J 6-a
	European countries & USA	C 12-a
	All countries	C 20-m
tin scrap in production of solder: tonnage	USA	T 4-a
Exports by destination: tonnage	Main countries	C 20-m
Imports by source: tonnage	Main countries	C 20-m
Production: tonnage	European countries & USA	C 12-a
	Italy	H 2-a

SOLES FOR FOOTWEAR, LEATHER

see also   FOOTWEAR UPPERS, LEATHER

Consumption: tonnage	OECD countries	D 18-a
Exports by destination by value in $	OECD countries	D 18-a
tonnage	OECD countries	D 18-a
into non-EEC area ex OECD area: tonnage		D 18-a
Imports by source: tonnage & value in $	OECD countries	D 18-a
Production: tonnage	Main countries	A 18-a
	OECD countries	D 18-a

SOLES FOR FOOTWEAR, RUBBER

Consumption of rubber in production of soles	France & UK	C 18-a

Soluble coffee   see   INSTANT COFFEE

Solutions, rubber   see   GUMS GLUES SOLUTIONS

SORGHUM

see also   MILLET

Area harvested, production: tonnage & yield per ha	All countries	A 9-a
under crop in ha	EEC countries	E 12-a
Consignments (as emergency food aid) in $	Recipient countries	M 1-a
Consumption (as animal feed): tonnage	Main countries	A 12-a
tonnage	OAS member countries	N 17-a

503

	Territorial coverage	Title codes	
SORGHUM, continued			
Crop yield in 100 kg per ha	EEC countries	E 12-a	
EEC levy: sorghum imported from non-EEC area in £ per ton	EEC countries	B 7-m	
Export prices in $ per ton fob	USA	C 16-m	A 9-a
		U 35-a	
Exports (incl millet) by destination: tonnage	China, E European countries & USSR	A 17-a	
tonnage	Main countries	A 17-a	
	All countries	A 17-a	
	European countries	U 35-a	
tonnage (incl world total)	Main countries	C 16-a	
Import prices at European ports: sorghum shipped ex USA in $ per ton cif	European countries	U 35-a	
in $ per ton	UK	A 9-a	
shipped ex Argentine & USA in $ per ton cif	UK	B 7-m	
Imports (incl millet) by port of entry: tonnage	UK	B 7-m	P 5-a2
into E European countries & USSR: tonnage	Non-Communist countries	A 17-a	
tonnage	All countries	A 17-a	
	European countries	U 35-a	
Income elasticity of demand for Jowar in rural & urban areas	India	C 27-a	
Producer prices in local currency per ton	OECD countries	D 1-a	
	All countries	A 9-a	
Production, stocks, industrial usage & consumption as fodder & seed: tonnage	OECD countries	D 14-a	
Production (incl millet & fonium): tonnage	AASM countries	E 41-a	
tonnage	African countries	U 44-a	
	Argentine & USA	P 5-a	
	EEC countries	E 12-a	
	Latin American countries	U 40-a	
Stocks (at end-season): tonnage	Argentine & USA	B 7-a	
	Main countries	C 16-a	
held at wholesalers' premises: tonnage	EEC countries	E 12-m	
Wholesale prices in $ per ton	Ethiopia, India, Pakistan & USA	A 9-a	
World production (incl millet): tonnage		C 16-a	
SOUND REPRODUCERS			
% households owning sound reproducing equipment by social classes	W European countries	Z 3	
record players & tape recorders by kind	W European countries	Z 3	
Production: record players: volume	All countries	U 22-a	
sound recorders: volume	All countries	U 22-a	

Soup   see   CANNED SOUP

Sows, breeding   see   PIGS

Soya beans   see   SOYBEANS

Soya oilseed cake   see   SOYBEAN MEAL

	Territorial coverage	Title codes	
SOYBEAN MEAL			
Export prices: meal & cake in $ per ton	Brazil, Netherlands & USA	A 9-a	
Exports: tonnage & value in $m	Main countries	U 33-a	
Imports (as animal feed): tonnage	UK	P 5-a	
tonnage & value in $m	Main countries	U 33-a	
Prices paid by farmers (as animal feed) in $ per ton	W European countries	U 30-a	
in £ per ton (equiv)	EEC countries	B 3-a	
in local currency per 100 kg	EEC countries	B 3-a	
Production: tonnage	W Germany	N 10-a	
Wholesale prices in cents per lb	Canada	N 10-m	
World market prices (as animal feed) per 100 kg		E 34-m	
SOYBEAN OIL			
Consumption for production of cooking fats: tonnage	UK & USA	A 4-a	B 19-a
	USA	B 19-a	
margarine: tonnage	Main countries	B 19-a	
	USA	B 19-a	
paint & varnishes: tonnage	Japan, UK & USA	A 4-a	
	USA	B 19-a	
plastics & resin: tonnage	USA	B 19-a	
Donations through voluntary relief agencies: tonnage	USA	B 19-a	
Export prices in $ per ton fob	Netherlands & USA	A 9-a	
raw soybean oil in cents per lb fob	USA	B 19-m	R 2-m
Export prices - index nos (weighted average main sources)		U 29-q	
Exports by destination (donated for relief): tonnage	USA	B 18-q	
tonnage	USA	B 19-a	
(on barter basis) as food aid: tonnage	USA	B 19-a	
tonnage & value in $m	Main countries	U 33-a	
tonnage	Main countries	B 18-q	B 19-a
(under A.I.D. relief programs): tonnage	USA	B 19-a	
(under US Government relief programs): tonnage	USA	B 19-a	
Import prices (ex tank Rotterdam) in £ per ton cif	UK	B 19-m	
in $ per ton cif	European countries	A 9-a	
(under contract) in $ per ton cif	UK	R 2-m	
Imports: tonnage & value in $m	W European countries	U 33-a	
tonnage	Main countries	P 1-a	
Production (for ensuing yr): tonnage (estim)	Main world regions	P 1-a	
refined soybean oil: tonnage	All countries	U 22-a	
tonnage	Main countries	B 19-a	P 1-a
	W Germany	N 10-a	

	Territorial coverage	Title codes	
SOYBEAN OIL, continued			
Sales against long-term dollar credit: tonnage	USA	B 19-a	
under government to government donations as relief: tonnage	USA	B 19-a	
Wholesale prices: crude soybean oil ex mill in £ per ton	UK	P 1-m	P 1-a
in cents per lb	Canada	N 10-m	
	European countries	U 27-m	
	USA	A 9-a	
		B 19-a	
World & Commonwealth production: tonnage		E 34-m	
World market prices per 100 kg cif at North Sea ports	European countries	A 1	
World production projected to 1975: tonnage		A 4-a	A 5-a
tonnage		N 10-a	
SOYBEANS			
Area harvested, production: tonnage & yield per ha	All countries	A 9-a	
under crop in acres	Main countries	B 18-a	B 19-a
	USA	N 10-a	
in ha (incl harvested tonnage)	All countries	R 5-a	
in ha	OAS member countries	N 13-a	
Consumption & consumption per capita per day	OECD countries	D 14-a	
for animal feed (incl wastage): tonnage	USA	B 19-a	
for oil crushing: tonnage	USA	B 19-a	
for seed: tonnage	USA	B 19-a	
Crop yield in bushels per acre	USA	N 10-a	
in kg per ha	OAS member countries	N 13-a	
Export prices in cents per bushel fob	USA	B 19-m	
in $ per ton	Brazil, Canada & USA	A 9-a	
Export prices - index nos (weighted average main sources)		U 29-q	
Exports by destination: tonnage	Main countries	B 18-a	
	USA	B 19-a	
by value in $m	W European countries	U 33-a	
tonnage & value in $m	Main countries	U 33-a	
tonnage	Main countries	B 18-q	B 19-a
Harvest estimates (for ensuing crop yr): tonnage	Main world regions	P 1-a	
Import prices: American Yellow grade in £ per ton cif	UK	B 19-m	P 1-a
ex USA in £ per ton cif	UK	P 1-m	B 19-q
in $ per ton cif	UK	A 9-a	
Imports by source: tonnage	EEC countries	B 19-a	
	Main European countries & Japan	B 19-a	
	W European countries	U 33-a	
by value in $m	UK	P 5-a	
(for production of animal feed): tonnage	EEC countries	P 5-a	
in vegetable oil equiv tonnage	EEC countries	P 5-a	
(incl soybean oil): tonnage	UK	P 1-a	
tonnage & in vegetable oil equiv & value in $m	W European countries	U 33-a	
tonnage	Main countries	B 19-a	
Price supports in $ per bushel	USA	N 10-a	
Prices paid by collective farms (as animal feed) in $ per ton	E European countries	U 30-a	
by farmers (as animal feed) in $ per ton	USA	U 30-a	
Producer prices in local currency per ton	OECD countries	D 1-a	
in $ per ton	USA	A 9-a	
Production, stocks, industrial usage, & consumption as fodder & seed: tonnage	OECD countries	D 14-a	
Production, supply, stocks & industrial usage: tonnage	France & USA	N 10-a	
tonnage (incl world total)	All countries	B 18-a	U 43-a
tonnage	Main countries	B 19-a	
	OAS member countries	N 13-a	
	Argentine, Brazil, Colombia, Paraguay & Mexico	U 40-a	
Stocks (initial & end-yr): tonnage	USA	B 19-a	
Wholesale prices in cents per bushel	Canada	N 10-m	
in cents per 60 lbs (on Chicago Market)	USA	R 2-m	
in $ per ton	European countries	U 27-m	
World crop: tonnage (estim)	USA	A 9-a	
World market prices based ex USA in $ per 100 kg	All countries	P 1-a	
		E 34-m	

Space exploration   see   RESEARCH & DEVELOPMENT

Space heaters, electric   see   HEATING APPLIANCES, ELECTRIC

Spaghetti   see   MACARONI & SPAGHETTI

Spare parts & sparking plugs   see   REPLACEMENT PARTS

Special schools   see   SCHOOLS, SPECIALIST

Special steels   see   ALLOY STEEL
CRUDE STEEL
TOOL STEEL

Specification requirements   see   BRITISH STANDARDS

Spectacle lenses   see   LENSES & FRAMES

Spelt   see   WHEAT

Sperm oil   see   WHALE OIL

Spice seeds   see   SPICES & ESSENCES

SPICES & ESSENCES
    see also   CURRY POWDER
                 GINGER
                 PEPPER
                 VANILLA & CLOVES

	Territorial coverage	Title codes
% contribution to export earnings	Madagascar & Tanzania	E 45-a
Area under cinnamon crop in acres	Sri Lanka	B 13-a
Exports by destination: capsicums in cwt	Main countries	B 13-a
cardamoms in cwt	India & Sri Lanka	B 13-a
cumin seed in cwt	India & Iran	B 13-a
mace in cwt	Grenada	B 13-a
nutmegs in cwt	Grenada	B 13-a
pimento in cwt	Jamaica	B 13-a
turmeric in cwt	India	B 13-a
by kind as % of total exports (value basis)	Main countries	B 13-a
by value in £m	Main countries	B 13-a
in $m	India	U 32-m
tonnage	ECAFE countries	U 32-m
capsicums & chillies in cwt	Main countries	B 18-q
cardamoms in cwt	India & Thailand	B 18-q
cassia in cwt	China, Madagascar & S Vietnam	B 13-a
cinnamon bark quills in cwt	Seychelles	B 13-a
cinnamon & cassia in cwt	Main countries	B 18-q
coriander seed in cwt	India & Morocco	B 13-a
	India, Morocco & Pakistan	B 18-q
cumin seed in cwt	India & Cyprus	B 18-q
fenugreek seed in cwt	India	B 13-a
nutmegs & mace in cwt	Indonesia & W Indies	B 18-q
pimento in cwt	Jamaica, Guatemale & Mexico	B 13-a
	Jamaica & British Honduras	B 18-q
tonnage & value in $m	African, Caribbean countries & Pacific Is	E 45-a
tonnage	Asian & Far East countries	U 32-q
turmeric in cwt	India	B 18-q
vanilla in cwt	All countries	B 18-q
Import prices: cardamoms in pence per lb cif	UK	B 18-m
cinnamon & cassia in pence per lb cif	UK	B 18-m
nutmeg & mace by kind in pence per lb cif	UK	B 18-m
pimento in £ per ton cif	UK	B 18-m
turmeric in £ per ton cif	UK	B 18-m
Imports by source: capsicums in cwt	All countries	B 13-a
	EEC countries & USA	B 18-m
cardamoms in cwt	Main countries	B 13-a
chillies in cwt	EEC countries & USA	B 18-m
nutmegs & mace in cwt	EEC countries	B 13-a
pimento in cwt	Main countries	B 18-q
cardamoms in cwt	Finland & Sweden	B 18-q
	Main countries	B 18-q
cinnamon & cassia in cwt	Main countries	B 13-a
coriander seed in cwt	Main countries	B 18-q
	Sri Lanka & USA	B 13-a
cumin seed in cwt	India, Sri Lanka & USA	B 13-a
turmeric in cwt	Main countries	B 18-q
	Sri Lanka, Iran & USA	B 13-a
Production: cinnamon in cwt	Sri Lanka	B 13-a
cracked nutmegs & cured mace in cwt	Grenada	B 13-a
pimento in cwt	Jamaica	B 13-a
Re-exports by destination: nutmegs & mace in cwt	Singapore	B 13-a
cinnamon & cassia in cwt	Singapore	B 13-a
Retail prices by kind in local currency	OAS member countries	N 17-a
Wholesale prices: cardamoms in £ per ton	UK	B 13-m
cassia by kind in £ per ton	UK	B 13-m
chillies in £ per ton	UK	B 13-m
cinnamon in £ per ton	UK	B 13-m
cloves by kind in £ per ton	UK	B 13-m
ginger by kind in £ per ton	UK	B 13-m
mace (ex W Indies) in £ per ton	UK	B 13-m
nutmegs by kind in £ per ton	UK	B 13-m
pimento in £ per ton	UK	B 13-m
turmeric in £ per ton	UK	B 13-m

Spiegeleisen   see   FERRO-MANGANESE

Spinach   see   VEGETABLES, GREEN

Spindles & twisting machines   see   TEXTILE MACHINERY

SPINNING & WEAVING INDUSTRY
    see also   TEXTILE INDUSTRY

	Territorial coverage	Title codes
Gross output by value in $m	OECD countries	D 46-a
Investment in $m	OECD countries	D 46-a
Labour force employed (incl finishers)	OECD countries	D 46-a
Production by kind of yarn: tonnage	OECD countries	D 46-a
Production - index nos	OECD countries	D 46-a
Wage rates by sex in local currency per hr	Main countries	R 3-m
in local currency per hr	OAS member countries	N 17-a

	Territorial coverage	Title codes
Spirits, distilled see ALCOHOLIC DRINKS		
SPONGE IRON		
see also SINTER		
Imports (incl powders): tonnage	Main countries	T 1-a
Production: tonnage	Main countries	H 3-a
	Spain & Sweden	U 6-a U 7-a
Sponge metal see TITANIUM MINERALS		
SPONGE RUBBER		
Consumption: rubber in production of sponge: tonnage	France & UK	C 18-a
Sponges see AQUATIC ANIMAL PRODUCTS		
SPORTS		
see also RECREATIONAL CENTRES		
Attendances at boxing matches (incl no of matches held)	OAS member countries	N 19-a
football matches (incl no of public games played)	OAS member countries	N 19-a
horse-races (incl no of meetings held)	OAS member countries	N 19-a
SPORTS GOODS		
Consumption: rubber in production of sports goods: tonnage	France	C 18-a
Sports goods industry see TOYS & SPORTS GOODS INDUSTRY		
Sprats see FISH		
Spun yarn see MAN-MADE FIBRE YARN		
Spun yarn fabrics		
see WOVEN NON-CELLULOSIC SPUN YARN FABRICS		
WOVEN CELLULOSIC SPUN YARN FABRICS		
Squid, cuttlefish & octopus (edible) see CRUSTACEANS & MOLLUSCS		
Stabilisation prices see INTERVENTION PRICES		
PRICE SUPPORTS		
Staff, administrative see SALARIED STAFF		
Staff, managerial see SALARIED STAFF, EXECUTIVE		
Staff, technical see SCIENTISTS		
TECHNICIANS		
STAINLESS STEEL		
see also ALLOY STEEL		
INGOTS, STAINLESS STEEL		
Consumption: cobalt in production of stainless steel: tonnage	USA	T 4-a
nickel in production of stainless steel: tonnage	USA	J 6-a
Exports by destination: tonnage	Main countries	T 4-a
Imports: bars & rods: tonnage	Main countries	T 1-a
blooms, billets & slabs: tonnage	Main countries	T 1-a
by source: tonnage	Main countries	T 4-a
cold-rolled stainless steel bars: tonnage	Main countries	T 1-a
cold-rolled stainless steel strip: tonnage	Main countries	T 1-a
heavy plates over 3mm gauge: tonnage	Main countries	T 1-a
hot-rolled stainless steel coil: tonnage	Main countries	T 1-a
hot-rolled stainless steel strip: tonnage	Main countries	T 1-a
steel ingots (stainless): tonnage	All countries	T 1-a
steel stainless sheets: tonnage	Main countries	T 1-a
steel stainless wire: tonnage	Main countries	T 1-a
Production: stainless steel castings as % of all steel castings produced	UK	B 25-a
tonnage & value in £m	UK	B 25-a
tonnage	Main countries	T 4-a
STAMP DUTIES		
see also TAXATION		
As component in revenue receipts in $m	OECD countries	D 42-a
Government revenue: registration fees in local currency	EEC countries	E 42-a
	Asian, Far East & Australasian countries	U 45-a
in $m	Jamaica	J 5-a
Rates charged (incl basis of assessment)	EEC countries	E 31-a
STAND-BY CREDITS		
Position in International Monetary Fund in $	All countries	F 5-m F 6-q

	Territorial coverage	Title codes

Standard of living   see   GDP PER CAPITA
    HOUSEHOLD BUDGETS
    PRIVATE CONSUMPTION

Staple   see   CELLULOSIC FIBRES
    MAN-MADE FIBRES
    NON-CELLULOSIC FIBRES
    SYNTHETIC FIBRES

STARCH

	Territorial coverage	Title codes
Exports (incl gluten & albuminoidal substances) by value in $	Main countries	U 2-a
Wholesale prices in local currency per ton	OAS member countries	N 17-a

State co-operatives   see   COLLECTIVE FARMS
    HOUSING, STATE-FINANCED

State farms   see   COLLECTIVE FARMS

State investment   see   CENTRALISED STATE INVESTMENT

STATE LOTTERIES

	Territorial coverage	Title codes
Government revenue from lotteries in $m	Dominican Republic	J 5-a
Taxes on betting & gambling: rates charged	EEC countries	E 31-a

State planning   see   ECONOMIC PLANNING

STATE PROCUREMENT

    see also   ECONOMIC PLANNING

	Territorial coverage	Title codes
Bread grains & cereals: tonnage	E European countries & USSR	U 16-a
Government purchases: rice by grade: tonnage	Burma	A 10-a
Hen eggs: volume	E European countries	U 16-a
Meat: tonnage (live wt)	E European countries	U 16-a
Milk: tonnage	E European countries & USSR	U 16-a
Potatoes: tonnage	E European countries & USSR	U 16-a
Producer prices paid by government for rice	Burma	A 10-a
Sugar beet: tonnage	E European countries	U 16-a
Sunflower seed: tonnage	E European countries	U 16-a

STATE-CONTROLLED ENTERPRISES

	Territorial coverage	Title codes
% of state supervision held in control of enterprises	Chile	U 18-a
% production of crude oil by state agencies	Latin American countries	U 18-a
% refining of crude oil by state agencies	Latin American countries	U 18-a
% share of state agencies in value of gross output	Chile	U 18-a

Station wagons   see   PASSENGER CARS

Statistical machines   see   CALCULATING MACHINES

Status, industrial   see   SALARIED STAFF
    WAGE EARNERS

Steam condensers   see   BOILERHOUSE PLANT

Steam generating boilers   see   BOILERS, STEAM

Steam locomotives   see   LOCOMOTIVES, STEAM

STEAM TURBINE GENERATORS

	Territorial coverage	Title codes
Power of generators produced in kW	All countries	U 38-a
Production: volume	All countries	U 38-a

STEAM TURBINES

    see also   GENERATORS, THERMAL
    POWER GENERATING EQUIPMENT

	Territorial coverage	Title codes	
% market share: domestic sales by firm	W Germany	T 7-a	
Deliveries by size in MW	European countries, Japan & USA	D 45-a	
Exports by destination by size in MW	W Germany	T 7-a	
generators by Brown Boveri in MW	Switzerland	T 7-a	
in MW	W European countries & Japan	T 7-a	
installed by Brown Boveri in MW	Switzerland	T 7-a	
by make in MW	W Germany	T 7-a	
New orders & orders in hand in MW	European countries, Japan & USA	D 45-a	
No of steam turbines installed by size in MW	USA	T 7-a	
planned for installation by size in MW	Japan	T 7-a	
Plant installed by make: volume & in MW	Japan	T 7-a	
Production in MW	W European countries & Japan	T 7-a	
tonnage (or capacity) in MW	EEC countries	E 28-q	E 27-a
volume & by power class in MW	All countries	U 22-a	U 38-a

Steamships   see   MERCHANT SHIPPING FLEETS
    SHIPS & BOATS
    TANKERS, OIL

Steatite   see   TALC

Steel, corrosion-resistant & high-speed   see   ALLOY STEEL

	Territorial coverage	Title codes

Steel, manganese & silicon   see   ALLOY STEEL

STEEL, SEMI-FINISHED
see also   RE-ROLLING PLANTS

Deliveries by dealers: tonnage	EEC countries	E 29-a
Exports: blooms & billets: tonnage	E European countries	T 1-a
by destination: tonnage	OECD countries	D 22-a
	EEC countries	E 5-q
by kind: tonnage	Main countries	T 2-m
by regions of destination: tonnage	Main countries	U 57-a
Imports: alloy billets: tonnage	All countries	T 1-a
alloy wire rods: tonnage	Main countries	T 1-a
by source: tonnage	EEC countries	E 5-q
	OECD countries	D 22-a
high carbon billets: tonnage	Main countries	T 1-a
high carbon wire rods: tonnage	Main countries	T 1-a
stainless steel semis: tonnage	Main countries	T 1-a
steel slabs: tonnage	Main countries	T 1-a
Inter-EEC area trade: tonnage & value in $m	EEC countries	E 29-a
Prices: re-rolling slabs & forging steel in local currency per ton	EEC countries	E 30-a
Production of semis as % of crude steel production	EEC countries	E 29-a
by kind (in detail): tonnage	Main countries	T 4-a
for sale: tonnage	ECE area	U 7-m U 6-a
	EEC countries	E 29-a
	Main countries	H 3-a
	OECD countries	D 22-a
Receipts of semis at re-rolling plants: tonnage	EEC countries	E 29-a
by dealers: tonnage	EEC countries	E 29-a
Stocks: tonnage (incl % change)	EEC countries	E 29-a

STEEL, SEMI-FINISHED ALLOY

Exports by destination: tonnage	Main countries	T 4-a
Imports by source: tonnage	Main countries	T 4-a
Production: tonnage	Main countries	T 4-a

Steel alloys   see   ALLOY STEEL

STEEL CASTINGS
see also   CRUDE STEEL
           PIG IRON
           STEEL FOUNDRIES

Consumption: chemical industry: tonnage	UK	B 25-a
electrical engineering industry: tonnage	UK	B 25-a
iron & steel industry: tonnage	UK	B 25-a
iron foundries: tonnage	UK	B 25-a
machine tools manufacturing industry: tonnage	UK	B 25-a
mechanical engineering industry: tonnage	UK	B 25-a
motor vehicle manufacturing industry: tonnage	UK	B 25-a
shipbuilding & repair industry: tonnage	UK	B 25-a
for production of railway equipment: tonnage	UK	B 25-a
(industrial): tonnage	UK	B 25-a
Deliveries for production of construction plant: tonnage	UK	B 25-a
farm machinery & wheeled tractors: tonnage	UK	B 25-a
industrial engines: tonnage	UK	B 25-a
industrial steelwork: tonnage	UK	B 25-a
mechanical handling equipment: tonnage	UK	B 25-a
office machinery: tonnage	UK	B 25-a
ordnance & small arms: tonnage	UK	B 25-a
pumps, valves & compressors: tonnage	UK	B 25-a
railway rolling stock: tonnage	UK	B 25-a
textile machinery: tonnage	UK	B 25-a
to user industries: tonnage	ECE countries	U 7-q U 6-a
	Main countries	H 3-a
Demand & required production projected to 1977: tonnage	UK	B 25-a
Exports by destination: tonnage	EEC countries	E 5-q
	Main countries	T 4-a
tonnage & as % of home production	UK	B 25-a
tonnage	ECE countries, Japan & USA	U 7-m U 6-a
	Main countries	H 3-a
Imports & exports by source & destination: tonnage	All countries	B 15-a
by source: tonnage	EEC countries	E 5-q
	Main countries	T 4-a
tonnage	ECE countries, Japan & USA	U 7-m U 6-a
	Main countries	H 3-a T 1-a
Prices (on production value basis) in £ per ton	UK	B 25-a
Production: alloy steel: tonnage & value in £m	UK	B 25-a
Bessemer quality: tonnage	All countries	B 15-a
by process: tonnage	All countries	B 15-a
by quality: tonnage & value in £m	UK	B 25-a
carbon steel quality: tonnage & value in £m	UK	B 25-a
Electric steel quality: tonnage	All countries	B 15-a
Open Hearth steel quality: tonnage	All countries	B 15-a
rough castings: tonnage	All countries	U 22-a
	EEC countries	E 30-a
stainless steel: tonnage & value in £m	UK	B 25-a
tonnage & value in £m	France, W Germany & UK	B 25-a

	Territorial coverage	Title codes	
STEEL CASTINGS, continued			
Production: tonnage	EEC countries	E 29-a	
Shipments ex steelworks: tonnage	Main countries	T 4-a	
Value in local currency per ton	USA	N 1-a	
World production: tonnage	France, W Germany & UK	B 25-a	
	Main countries	B 25-a	
STEEL COILS			
see also COLD-ROLLED STRIP			
HOT-ROLLED STRIP			
Consumption: tonnage	EEC countries	E 29-a	
Deliveries ex EEC area: tonnage	EEC countries	E 29-a	
shipped to EEC area: tonnage	EEC countries	E 29-a	
Exports by destination: tonnage	ECE countries	U 48-a	
	EEC countries	E 5-q	E 29-a
	Main countries	T 4-a	
Imports by quality: tonnage	Main countries	T 1-a	
by source: tonnage	EEC countries	E 5-q	E 29-a
	Main countries	T 4-a	
Electric steel coils: tonnage	Main countries	T 1-a	
hot-rolled carbon steel coils: tonnage	Main countries	T 1-a	
stainless steel coils: tonnage	Main countries	T 1-a	
Inter-EEC trade: tonnage & value in $m	EEC countries	E 29-a	
Production capacity: tonnage	Main countries	U 57-a	
potential by regions: tonnage	EEC countries	E 46-a	
for further processing: tonnage	EEC countries	E 30-m	
tonnage	EEC countries	E 29-a	
	Main countries	T 4-a	
	W Germany	C 5-m	
Supply available for further processing: tonnage	EEC countries	E 30-m	
Steel converters, oxygen-blown see CRUDE STEEL			
STEEL FABRICATION INDUSTRY			
Labour costs in DM million	W Germany	H 3-a	
Wage rates in DM per hr	W Germany	H 3-a	
Steel for castings see CRUDE STEEL			
Steel forgings see FORGINGS & PRESSINGS, STEEL			
STEEL FOUNDRIES			
Consumption: carbonisation coke: tonnage	EEC countries	E 29-a	
coal, briquettes, coke, semi-coke, lignite & dust: tonnage	EEC countries	E 29-a	
electric power in kWh	EEC countries	E 30-q	E 29-a
gas in m³ & electric power in kWh	EEC countries	E 30-q	E 29-a
liquid fuels: tonnage	EEC countries	E 29-a	
pig iron, spiegeleisen & ferro-alloys: tonnage	EEC countries	E 29-a	
raw materials by kind: tonnage	EEC countries	E 30-q	
scrap (total) & from own plant: tonnage	EEC countries	E 29-a	
Costs: fuel & power in £ per ton	UK	B 25-a	
profit & depreciation in £ per ton	UK	B 25-a	
raw materials in £ per ton	UK	B 25-a	
wages & salaries in £ per ton	UK	B 25-a	
Investment as % of value of output of steel castings	France, W Germany & UK	B 25-a	
by regions in UA	EEC countries	E 46-a	
Labour force employed (at mid-yr)	France, W Germany & UK	B 25-a	
No of fatalities through lung diseases endemic to foundries	UK	B 25-a	
of steel foundries in operation & no of net closures	UK	B 25-a	
by size of labour force employed	UK	B 25-a	
of output in tonnage of castings	UK	B 25-a	
of steel foundries in operation	France, W Germany & UK	B 25-a	
Production: tonnage	France, W Germany & UK	B 25-a	
Productivity in tons per man-yr	UK	B 25-a	
Steel furnaces see FURNACES, STEEL			
Steel ingots see CRUDE STEEL			
STEEL PRODUCTS			
see also ALLOY STEEL			
BLANKS FOR TUBES, STEEL			
BRIGHT STEEL BARS			
COLD-ROLLED STRIP			
FERROUS SCRAP			
FORGINGS & PRESSINGS			
GALVANISED SHEETS			
HEAVY SECTIONS, STEEL			
HOT-ROLLED STRIP			
LIGHT SECTIONS, STEEL			
MERCHANT BARS, STEEL			
PLATES, HEAVY			
PLATES, MEDIUM			
PLATES, UNIVERSAL			
PLATES & SHEETS			

	Territorial coverage	Title codes
STEEL PRODUCTS, continued		
see also RAILS, STEEL (SECOND-HAND)		
RAILS & TRACK-LAYING MATERIAL		
RE-INFORCING RODS, STEEL		
SLEEPERS, STEEL		
STEEL CASTINGS		
STEEL COILS		
STEEL SHEET PILING		
STEEL SHEETS, COATED		
STEEL SHEETS, COLD-ROLLED		
STEEL SHEETS, HOT-ROLLED		
STEEL SHEETS, MAGNETIC		
STRUCTURAL STEEL PRODUCTS		
TINPLATE		
TOOL STEEL		
TUBES, STEEL		
WHEELS TYRES AXLES, STEEL		
WIRE, STEEL		
WIRE ROD		
% of EEC area production: rolled steel products	EEC countries	E 29-a R 5-a
Basic domestic prices: steel products by kind in $ per ton	OECD countries	D 22-a
Coastal shipping: iron & steel products: tonnage	EEC countries	E 43-a
Consumption (domestic) by product: tonnage	OECD countries	D 22-a
in crude steel equiv tonnage	World regions	U 57-a
per capita in kg	Developing countries	U 57-a
	EEC countries	E 3-a
rolled steel products: tonnage	OAS member countries	N 17-a
semis for re-rolling: tonnage	EEC countries	E 29-a
Deliveries & receipts: steel products by kind: home & export sales: tonnage	EEC countries	E 30-m
by destination: tonnage	EEC area & world regions	E 29-a
(domestic) for final processing: tonnage	OECD countries	D 22-a
	EEC countries, Japan & UK	U 49-a
finished steel products: home & export sales: tonnage	EEC countries	E 30-a
tonnage	EEC countries	E 29-a
for export: tonnage	EEC countries, Japan & UK	U 49-a
overseas by destination: tonnage	EEC countries	E 29-a
semi-manufactured steel products: tonnage	EEC countries	E 30-m
to end-users: tonnage	OECD countries	D 22-a
tonnage	OECD countries	D 22-m
Export prices fixed by ECSC: steel products by kind in local currency per ton		T 4
Exports by destination: steel products by kind (in detail): tonnage	EEC countries	E 30-q
by world regions: tonnage	Main countries	U 57-a
tonnage	OECD countries	D 22-a
by kind (in detail): tonnage	EEC countries	E 30-q
ex European sources: tonnage	World regions	U 49-a
(incl semis): tonnage	Main countries	U 49-a
ingots, semis & finished steel products: tonnage	Main countries	C 5-m
shipped to non-EEC area by value in $m	EEC countries	E 29-a
Imports as % of consumption	Developing countries	U 57-a
by source: steel products by kind (in detail): tonnage	EEC countries	E 30-q
tonnage	OECD countries	D 22-a
shipped ex non-EEC area by value in $m	EEC countries	E 29-a
handled via Port of Karachi: tonnage	India	S 16-a
ingots, semis & finished steel products: tonnage	Main countries	C 5-m
Inter-EEC area trade by value in $m (& as % of total)	EEC countries	E 29-a
Inter-European trade (incl semis): tonnage		U 49-a
New orders received: export sales: tonnage	EEC countries & Japan	U 49-a
home & export sales - index nos	Japan	D 22-m
home market sales: tonnage	EEC countries & Japan	U 49-a
shipments & unfilled orders: tonnage	USA	D 22-m
total order book: tonnage	OECD countries	D 22-m
Production: bars & rods: tonnage	All countries	T 1-a
finished rolled steel products: tonnage	Main countries	E 3-a
galvanised sheets: tonnage	All countries	T 1-a
heavy steel profiles & plates: tonnage	EEC countries	E 26-m
heavy steel sections: tonnage	All countries	T 1-a
hot-rolled steel products (all kinds): tonnage	All countries	T 1-a
hot-rolled steel strip: tonnage	All countries	T 1-a
light steel sections: tonnage	All countries	T 1-a
railway permanent way material: tonnage	All countries	T 1-a
rolled steel products by area: tonnage	EEC countries	E 38-a
by kind: tonnage	OAS member countries	N 14-a
tonnage	E European countries & USSR	U 16-a
	OECD countries	R 5-a
seamless tubes: tonnage	All countries	T 1-a
steel coils: tonnage	EEC countries	E 46-a
steel products as % of crude steel production	EEC countries	E 29-a
steel tube rounds: tonnage	All countries	T 1-a
tinplate: tonnage	All countries	T 1-a
uncoated steel sheets: tonnage	All countries	T 1-a
universal plates: tonnage	All countries	T 1-a
welded steel tubes: tonnage	All countries	T 1-a
wire rod: tonnage	All countries	T 1-a
tonnage	EEC countries	E 29-a
Production capacity: all finished steel products: tonnage	Main countries	U 57-a
cold-rolled steel products: tonnage	Main countries	U 57-a
sheets: tonnage	Main countries	U 57-a

	Territorial coverage	Title codes	
STEEL PRODUCTS, continued			
Production capacity: flat rolled steel products: tonnage	Main countries	U 57-a	
heavy steel plates: tonnage	Main countries	U 57-a	
heavy steel sections: tonnage	Main countries	U 57-a	
hoop, coils & strip: tonnage	Main countries	U 57-a	
hot-rolled steel products: tonnage	Main countries	U 57-a	
medium steel sections: tonnage	Main countries	U 57-a	
steel sheets (under 3 mm gauge): tonnage	Main countries	U 57-a	
wire rods: tonnage	Main countries	U 57-a	
Production potential by regions: tonnage	EEC countries	E 46-a	
cold-reduced sheets: tonnage	EEC countries	E 46-a	
hoop & strip: tonnage	EEC countries	E 46-a	
hot-rolled steel sheets: tonnage	EEC countries	E 46-a	
steel plates over 3 mm gauge: tonnage	EEC countries	E 46-a	
steel sections: tonnage	EEC countries	E 46-a	
wire rod: tonnage	EEC countries	E 46-a	
Receipts by dealers (ex home production): tonnage	EEC countries	E 29-a	
(ex EEC area production): tonnage	EEC countries	E 29-a	
finished steel products ex EEC area plants: tonnage	EEC countries	E 29-a	
special steel products ex EEC area plants: tonnage	EEC countries	E 29-a	
Shipments (ex steelworks): tonnage	USA	N 1-a	
Supply (for further processing) incl semis: tonnage	EEC countries	E 30-m	
Wholesale prices - index nos	EEC countries	E 29-a	
Wholesale prices in $ per ton	Belgium, France, W Germany & Japan	U 27-m	
steel sheets, bars & plates in $ per ton	UK & USA	U 27-m	
STEEL PRODUCTS BY KIND			
Base prices in $ per ton	EEC countries	U 57-a	
Basic price supports in $ per ton	EEC countries	E 29-a	
Consumption per capita: tonnage	Main countries	U 57-a	
Deliveries (domestic): tonnage	Canada & USA	T 2-m	
to E Berlin sector: tonnage & value in DM	W Germany	H 3-a	
to W Berlin sector: tonnage & value in DM	W Germany	H 3-a	
Delivery patterns in detail: tonnage	Main countries	U 57-a	
Exports by destination (in detail): tonnage	W Germany	H 3-a	
tonnage & value in $	EEC countries	E 5-q	
tonnage	Main countries	T 4-a	
	ECE countries	U 7-m	U 6-a
	Main countries	T 2-m	H 3-a
Imports by source (in detail): tonnage	W Germany	H 3-a	
tonnage	EEC countries	E 5-q	
	Main countries	T 4-a	
tonnage	ECE countries	U 7-m	U 6-a
	Main countries	H 3-a	
Inter-EEC area trade: tonnage & value in UA	EEC countries	E 29-a	
Prices (less tax): semi-finished steel products in local currency per ton	EEC countries	E 30-a2	
Production & stocks: tonnage (incl % change)	EEC countries	E 29-a	
Production as % of consumption	Developing countries	U 57-a	
(& as % of all steel products): tonnage	EEC countries	E 30-m	
(in detail): tonnage	Main countries	T 4-a	
rolled steel products: tonnage	ECE countries	U 7-m	U 6-a
	Main countries	H 3-a	
semi-finished steel products: tonnage	EEC countries	E 3-a	
	Latin American countries	U 40-a	
tonnage	All countries	N 5-a	T 1-a
	EEC countries	E 28-q	E 27-a
		E 29-a	
	Latin American countries	U 57-a	
	Main countries	T 2-m	
	OECD countries	D 22-a	
	USA	J 3-a	
Wholesale prices in $ per 100 lbs	Canada	T 4-m	
per ton	Main countries	T 4-w	
STEEL RE-ROLLING PLANTS			
As source of ferrous scrap: tonnage	ECE countries	U 6-a	U 7-a
	Main countries	H 3-a	
% share of world exports held (value basis)	UK	B 27-a	
% of steel industry investment allocated to re-rolling mills	OECD countries	D 22-a	
Investment: blooming mills in UA	EEC countries	E 46-a	
flat product mills in UA	EEC countries	E 46-a	
funds allocated to new projects in $m	EEC countries	E 29-a	
in $m	EEC countries	E 29-a	
section mills in UA	EEC countries	E 46-a	
(total) by regions in UA	EEC countries	E 46-a	
Labour force employed: hot & cold re-rolling mills	EEC countries	E 29-a	
Projected investments planned in $m	EEC countries	E 30-a2	
Steel scrap see FERROUS SCRAP			
STEEL SHEET PILING			
Exports by destination: tonnage	Main countries	T 4-a	
Imports by source: tonnage	Main countries	T 4-a	
tonnage	Main countries	T 1-a	
Inter-EEC area trade: tonnage & value in $m	EEC countries	E 29-a	
Production: tonnage	Luxembourg & W Germany	C 5-m	
	Main countries	T 4-a	

	Territorial coverage	Title codes
STEEL SHEETS, COATED		
see also GALVANISED SHEETS		
Deliveries to EEC area: tonnage	EEC countries	E 29-a
Exports by destination: tonnage	EEC countries	E 5-q E 29-a
	Main countries	T 4-a
Imports: alloy steel: tonnage	Main countries	T 1-a
by source: tonnage	EEC countries	E 5-q E 29-a
	Main countries	T 4-a
Production: tonnage	EEC countries	E 30-m E 29-a
	Main countries	T 4-a
Receipts ex EEC area: tonnage	EEC countries	E 29-a
STEEL SHEETS, COLD-ROLLED		
Basic domestic prices in $ per ton	OECD countries	D 22-a
Consumption: tonnage	OECD countries	D 22-a
Deliveries: home & export sales: tonnage	OECD countries	D 22-a
Export prices in FrB per ton fob	EEC countries	U 49-m
in $ per ton	Belgium	R 2-m
	OECD countries	D 22-a
Exports by destination: tonnage	Main countries	T 4-a
tonnage	European countries, Japan & USA	C 5-m
Imports by source: tonnage	Main countries	T 4-a
tonnage	European countries, Japan & USA	C 5-m
Production potential: tonnage	EEC countries	E 46-a
Production: tonnage	ECE countries	U 7-m U 6-a
	European countries, & Japan	C 5-m
	Main countries	H 3-a T 4-a
	OECD countries	D 22-a
Wholesale prices in $ per ton	Main countries	U 57-a
	Latin American countries	U 57-a
STEEL SHEETS, HOT-ROLLED		
Consumption: tonnage	OECD countries	D 22-a
Deliveries: home & export sales: tonnage	OECD countries	D 22-a
under 3 mm gauge to user industries: tonnage	EEC countries	U 7-q U 6-a
	Main countries	H 3-a
Export prices in $ per 100 lbs	USA	R 2-m
Exports by destination: tonnage	Main countries	T 4-a
tonnage	European countries, Japan & USA	C 5-m
	E European countries & USSR	T 1-a
Imports: alloy steel sheets: tonnage	Main countries	T 1-a
by quality: tonnage	Main countries	T 1-a
by source: tonnage	Main countries	T 4-a
carbon steel quality: tonnage	Main countries	T 1-a
Electric steel quality: tonnage	Main countries	T 1-a
stainless steel sheets: tonnage	Main countries	T 1-a
tonnage	European countries, Japan & USA	C 5-m
Production: sheets under 3 mm gauge: tonnage	ECE countries	U 7-m U 6-a
	All countries	T 1-a
	Main countries	H 3-a
	OECD countries	D 22-a
tonnage	European countries & Japan	C 5-m
	Main countries	T 4-a
Production potential: tonnage	EEC countries	E 46-a
Wholesale prices in $ per ton	Main countries	U 57-a
	Latin American countries	U 57-a
STEEL SHEETS, MAGNETIC		
Deliveries to EEC area: tonnage	EEC countries	E 29-a
Exports by destination: tonnage	Main countries	T 4-a
	EEC countries	E 5-q E 29-a
tonnage	European countries, Japan & USA	C 5-m
Imports by source: tonnage	EEC countries	E 5-q E 29-a
	Main countries	T 4-a
tonnage	European countries, Japan & USA	C 5-m
Inter-EEC area trade: tonnage & value in $m	EEC countries	E 29-a
Production: dynamo sheets: tonnage	ECE countries	U 7-m U 6-a
	EEC countries	E 30-m
	Main countries	H 3-a
tonnage	EEC countries	E 30-m E 29-a
	Main countries	T 4-a
	OECD countries	D 22-a
Receipts ex EEC area: tonnage	EEC countries	E 29-a
STEEL STOCKHOLDERS		
Deliveries: drawn wire: tonnage	EEC countries	E 29-a
merchant bars: tonnage	EEC countries	E 29-a
plates & sheets by gauge: tonnage	EEC countries	E 29-a
semi-finished steel products: tonnage	EEC countries	E 29-a
steel sections & profiles: tonnage	EEC countries	E 29-a
Receipts: drawn steel wire: tonnage	EEC countries	E 29-a
merchant bars: tonnage	EEC countries	E 29-a
plates & sheets: by gauge: tonnage	EEC countries	E 29-a
semi-finished steel products: tonnage	EEC countries	E 29-a
steel products (all kinds): tonnage	OECD countries	D 22-a
steel sections & profiles: tonnage	EEC countries	E 29-a

	Territorial coverage	Title codes	

Steel tubes   see   TUBES, STEEL

Steel tyres   see   WHEELS TYRES AXLES, STEEL

Steel wire   see   WIRE, STEEL

Steelwork   see   INDUSTRIAL PLANT & STEELWORK

STEELWORKS
    see also   STEEL RE-ROLLING PLANTS

	Territorial coverage	Title codes	
Consumption: brown coal briquettes: tonnage	ECE countries	U 6-a	U 7-a
	Main countries	H 3-a	
coke oven gas by volume in m³	ECE countries	U 6-a	U 7-a
	Main countries	H 3-a	
diesel & gas oils: tonnage	ECE countries	U 6-a	U 7-a
	Main countries	H 3-a	
electric power in kWh	ECE countries	U 6-a	U 7-a
	Main countries	H 3-a	
fuel oils: tonnage	ECE countries	U 6-a	U 7-a
	Main countries	H 3-a	
hard coal: tonnage	ECE countries	U 6-a	U 7-a
	Main countries	H 3-a	
lignite & brown coal: tonnage	ECE countries	U 6-a	U 7-a
	Main countries	H 3-a	
liquid fuels by kind: tonnage	ECE countries	U 6-a	U 7-a
	Main countries	H 3-a	
natural gas by volume in m³	ECE countries	U 6-a	U 7-a
	Main countries	H 3-a	
patent solid fuels: tonnage	ECE countries	U 6-a	U 7-a
	Main countries	H 3-a	
scrap in production of foundry iron: tonnage	Main countries	T 4-a	
of pig iron: tonnage	Main countries	T 4-a	
tar & pitch: tonnage	ECE countries	U 6-a	U 7-a
	Main countries	H 3-a	
Investment: Community funds in new steelworks projects in $m	EEC countries	E 29-a	
in basic Bessemer steel plants by region in UA	EEC countries	E 46-a	
in bottom-blown & other types of steel plants in UA	EEC countries	E 46-a	
in Electric steel furnaces by regions in UA	EEC countries	E 46-a	
in L.D. & Kaldo steel plants by regions in UA	EEC countries	E 46-a	
in Open-Hearth steel plants by regions in UA	EEC countries	E 46-a	
projected in $m	EEC countries	E 30-a2	
(total) by regions in UA	EEC countries	E 46-a	
Labour force employed: steel production	EEC countries	E 29-a	
No of associated plants in production in EEC area	EEC countries	E 29-a	
of plants in operation by size of output & % of production within EEC area	EEC countries	E 29-a	
Purchases by steelworks: ferrous scrap (from dealers): tonnage	ECE countries	U 6-a	U 7-a
	Main countries	H 3-a	

Sterling, spot value of   see   EXCHANGE RATES

Stock Exchange turnover taxes   see   TAXATION

STOCK EXCHANGE

	Territorial coverage	Title codes
Listed securities: valuation (public sector) in £m	UK	F 8-q
Market valuation: agricultural sector shares in local currency	OAS member countries	N 16-a
bank shares in local currency	OAS member countries	N 16-a
bonds & securities in local currency	OAS member countries	N 16-a
British guaranteed bonds in £m	UK	F 8-q
common stocks & shares in local currency	OAS member countries	N 16-a
Commonwealth bonds in £m	UK	F 8-q
company convertible stocks in £m	UK	F 8-q
debentures in local currency	OAS member countries	N 16-a
finance company shares in local currency	OAS member countries	N 16-a
foreign government bonds in £m	UK	F 8-q
industrial company shares in local currency	OAS member countries	N 16-a
Irish company equities in £m	UK	F 8-q
loan stocks in £m	UK	F 8-q
preference stocks in £m	UK	F 8-q
Irish government bonds in £m	UK	F 8-q
local authority bonds in £m	UK	F 8-q
mining sector shares in local currency	OAS member countries	N 16-a
municipal & mortgage bonds in local currency	OAS member countries	N 16-a
national bonds in local currency	OAS member countries	N 16-a
overseas company loan stocks in £m	UK	F 8-q
preference shares in £m	UK	F 8-q
preference stocks & shares in local currency	OAS member countries	N 16-a
public board bonds in £m	UK	F 8-q
shares by sector in £m	UK	F 8-q
stocks & debentures in local currency	OAS member countries	N 16-a
transactions (total) in local currency	OAS member countries	N 16-a
Treasury bonds in local currency	OAS member countries	N 16-a
UK company equities in £m	UK	F 8-q
loan stocks in £m	UK	F 8-q
preference shares in £m	UK	F 8-q
No of applications for share quotations on Stock Exchange by sector	UK	F 8-q
of bargains completed & value in £m	UK	F 8-q
of clearings by dealing periods	UK	F 8-q

	Territorial coverage	Title codes	
STOCK EXCHANGE, continued			
No of share deliveries by stock payment office	UK	F 8-q	
of Stock Exchange share quotation cancellations by company	UK	F 8-q	
share suspensions (temporary) by company	UK	F 8-q	
Nominal & market valuation: convertible stocks in £m	UK	F 8-q	
Share prices (average) - index nos	Main countries	R 5-a	
Turnover on Eire government bonds in £m	UK	F 8-q	
fixed-interest stocks in £m	UK	F 8-q	
foreign bonds in £m	UK	F 8-q	
ordinary shares in £m	UK	F 8-q	
UK municipal bonds in £m	UK	F 8-q	
share transactions by type in £m	UK	F 8-q	
in local currency	EEC countries	E 26-m	
tax rates charged on share transfers	EEC countries	E 31-a	
STOCKFISH			
Catch by kind: tonnage & value in $m	OECD countries	D 43-a	
cod (& similar species): tonnage & value in $	OAS member countries	N 13-a	
tonnage	World regions	A 21-a	
cod, hake, haddock (et al): tonnage	Main countries	A 21-a	
Exports by kind: tonnage & value in $m	Main countries	A 21-a	
STOCKINGS & TIGHTS			
Production: hosiery: volume	Zaire	E 41-a	
volume	All countries	U 22-a	
	EEC countries	E 28-q	E 27-a
		K 4-a	
	OECD countries	D 46-a	
Retail prices (comparative): nylon stockings	EEC countries	Z 3-a	
STOCKPILES, GOVERNMENT			
see also ABACA			
ALUMINIUM			
COTTON			
FATS & OILS			
HARD FIBRES			
HEMP			
LEAD			
NATURAL RUBBER			
NON-FERROUS METALS			
RAW MATERIALS			
SUGAR			
TIN			
ZINC			
Aluminium: tonnage (incl sales ex stock)	USA	N 1-a	
Amosite, chrysotile & crocidolite: tonnage	USA	N 1-a	
Antimony: tonnage (incl sales ex stock)	USA	N 1-a	
Asbestos by kind: tonnage	USA	N 1-a	
Beryl ore & beryllium metal: tonnage	USA	N 1-a	
Beryllium-copper alloy: tonnage	USA	N 1-a	
Bismuth: tonnage in stock	USA	N 1-a	
Cadmium: tonnage (incl sales ex stock)	USA	N 1-a	
Celestite: tonnage (incl sales ex stock)	USA	N 1-a	
Chromite (chemical grade): tonnage	USA	N 1-a	
(metallurgical grade): tonnage	USA	N 1-a	
(refractory grade): tonnage	USA	N 1-a	
Chromium metal & alloys: tonnage	USA	N 1-a	
Cobalt metal: tonnage (incl sales ex stock)	USA	N 1-a	
Columbite concentrates: tonnage	USA	N 1-a	
Columbium carbide powder: tonnage	USA	N 1-a	
Columbium metal: tonnage	USA	N 1-a	
Columbium oxide powder: tonnage	USA	N 1-a	
Ferro-columbium: tonnage	USA	N 1-a	
Ferro-manganese: tonnage	USA	N 1-a	
Ferro-molybdenum in lbs	USA	N 1-a	
Ferro-vanadium in lbs	USA	N 1-a	
Fluorspar (by grade): tonnage	USA	N 1-a	
Graphite (amorphous lumps): tonnage	USA	N 1-a	
(crystalline flakes): tonnage	USA	B 10-a	
Hard fibres: tonnage (incl sales ex stock)	USA	N 1-a	
Industrial diamonds: tonnage (incl sales ex stock)	USA	N 1-a	
Iodine in lbs	USA	N 1-a	
Iridium: tonnage	USA	N 1-a	
Kyanite (in lump form): tonnage	USA	U 24-m	
Lead (commercial): official commitment: tonnage	USA	N 1-a	
Manganese (electrolytic): tonnage	USA	N 1-a	
Manganese ore (chemical): tonnage	USA	N 1-a	
(metallurgical): tonnage	USA	N 1-a	
(natural): tonnage	USA	N 1-a	
Manganese oxide (synthetic): tonnage	USA	N 1-a	
Mercury in 76 lb flasks	USA	N 1-a	
Mica blocks (Muscovite): tonnage	USA	N 1-a	
(Phlogopite): tonnage	USA	N 1-a	
film & splittings: tonnage	USA	N 1-a	
Molybdenum disulphide in lbs	USA	N 1-a	
Molybdic oxide in lbs	USA	N 1-a	
Natural rubber: sales ex stock: tonnage	UK & USA	C 18-m	

	Territorial coverage	Title codes	
STOCKPILES, GOVERNMENT continued			
Non-ferrous metals (strategic): tonnage	USA	T 4-a	
Palladium: tonnage	USA	N 1-a	
Pig tin: tonnage (incl sales ex stock)	USA	N 1-a	
Quartz crystal in lbs (incl sales ex stock)	USA	N 1-a	
Rare earth oxide: tonnage (incl sales ex stock)	USA	N 1-a	
Raw materials by kind: sales ex stock: tonnage	USA	U 11-a	
Rutile concentrates: tonnage (incl sales ex stock)	USA	N 1-a	
Selenium metal: (incl sales ex stock) tonnage	USA	N 1-a	
Silico-manganese: tonnage	USA	N 1-a	
Silver in oz	USA	N 1-a	
Steatite talc lumps: tonnage (incl sales ex stock)	USA	N 1-a	
Tantalum & tantalum minerals: tonnage (incl sales ex stock)	USA	N 1-a	
Tantalum carbide powder: tonnage (incl sales ex stock)	USA	N 1-a	
Thorium nitrate: tonnage (incl sales ex stock)	USA	N 1-a	
Tin: sales to A.I.D. & other agencies: tonnage	USA	C 20-m	
tonnage (incl sales ex stock)	USA	C 20-m	
Titanium sponge metal: tonnage (incl sales ex stock)	USA	N 1-a	
Tungsten & tungsten carbide: tonnage	USA	N 1-a	
Tungsten ore & concentrates: tonnage	USA	U 53-q	N 1-a
sales ex stock: tonnage	UK & USA	U 53-q	
Vanadium pentoxide in lbs	USA	N 1-a	
Yttrium oxide: tonnage	USA	N 1-a	
Zinc (commercial): official commitment: tonnage	USA	U 24-m	
Zinc: tonnage (incl sales ex stock)	USA	N 1-a	

Stocks   see   INDUSTRIAL SHARES
                    INVENTORIES

Stocks, gilt-edged   see   GOVERNMENT BONDS
                            GOVERNMENT BONDS, COMMONWEALTH
                            GOVERNMENT BONDS, FOREIGN

Stoking furnaces & ovens   see   FURNACES, INDUSTRIAL

Stone, crushed & natural   see   BUILDING MATERIALS

Stoppages of work   see   ABSENTEEISM
                          SHORT-TERM WORKING
                          STRIKES & LOCK-OUTS

Storage generators   see   GENERATORS, PUMPED STORAGE

Storage reservoirs   see   HYDROELECTRICITY
                         POWER STATIONS, HYDROELECTRIC

STOVES & COOKERS

    see also   ELECTRIC COOKERS
                   OVENS, DOMESTIC

	Territorial coverage	Title codes
Production by kind: tonnage	EEC countries	E 28-q
volume	EEC countries	E 27-a
electric cookers: volume	OAS member countries	N 14-a

Strategic stocks & disposals   see   STOCKPILES, GOVERNMENT

Straw paper & board   see   PAPER & PAPERBOARD, STRAW

Strawberries   see   FRUIT, FRESH

Street cleaning equipment (motorised)   see   SERVICE VEHICLES

Streptomycin   see   ANTIBIOTICS

STRIKES & LOCK-OUTS

    see also   ABSENTEEISM
                   SHORT-TIME WORKING

	Territorial coverage	Title codes	
Collieries: % absence due to labour disputes	EEC countries	E 15-a	
no of working days & tonnage of coal lost	EEC countries	E 15-a	
Effect of strikes on consumption of newprint	USA	J 4-a	
Industry (in general) no of employees involved in strikes	UK	B 28-a	
of stoppages & no of working days lost	UK	B 28-a	
Labour force: no involved in strikes & no of working days lost	EEC countries	E 26-m	
Motor vehicle industry: no of working days lost & lost per 1000 workers	UK	B 28-a	
employees involved in strikes	UK	B 28-a	
stoppages of work due to strikes reported	UK	B 28-a	
No of disputes, labour force involved & no of days lost	All countries	L 4-a	
employees involved in strikes: historical table from 1888	Main European countries	Z 1-a	
employees involved in strikes	Main countries	R 3-a	
industrial disputes by sector	Main countries	R 3-a	
reported	Main European countries	Z 1-a	
labour disputes reported	Main countries	R 3-a	R 5-a
	OAS member countries	N 18-a	
man-days of work lost through strikes & lock-outs	OAS member countries	N 18-a	
workers involved in labour disputes	Main countries	R 5-a	
	OAS member countries	N 18-a	

	Territorial coverage	Title codes
STRIKES & LOCK-OUTS, continued		
No of working days lost by industrial sector & by region	EEC countries	E 33-a
in labour disputes: historical table from 1888	Main European countries	Z 1-a
in labour disputes	Main countries	R 3-a R 5-a
per man employed: building industry	UK	B 29-a
engineering industry	UK	B 29-a
mining & quarrying	UK	B 29-a
service industries	UK	B 29-a
textile industry	UK	B 29-a
transportation (public)	UK	B 29-a
STRIP IN COIL, ALUMINIUM		
Consumption: tonnage	UK	T 4-a
Despatches: tonnage	UK	C 30-a
Exports by destination: tonnage	Main countries	T 4-a
Production: tonnage	Main countries	T 4-a
STRIP IN COIL, COPPER		
Exports by destination: tonnage	W Germany & Italy	T 4-a
Imports by source: tonnage	W Germany & USA	T 4-a
Production: tonnage	Japan	T 4-a
Wholesale prices in £ per kg	UK	T 4-w
STRIP, BERYLLIUM-COPPER		
Wholesale prices in £ per lb	UK	T 4-w
STRIP, NICKEL-ALLOY		
Wholesale prices in £ per kg	France & UK	T 4-w
STRONTIUM		
Consumption: strontium minerals: tonnage	USA	N 1-a
Government stockpile: celestite tonnage (incl sales ex stock)	USA	N 1-a
Imports & exports: strontium minerals: tonnage	All countries	B 15-a
Production: celestite: tonnage	All countries	B 15-a
strontium minerals: tonnage	USA	N 1-a
Wholesale prices: imported strontium minerals in $ per ton	USA	N 1-a
World production: strontium minerals: tonnage	Main countries	N 1-a N 4-a
STRUCTURAL STEEL PRODUCTS		
see also HEAVY SECTIONS		
Exports by destination: tonnage	Main countries	T 4-a
	EEC countries	E 5-q
(incl replacement parts): tonnage	OECD countries	D 9-a
Imports by source: tonnage	EEC countries	E 5-q
	Main countries	T 4-a
Production: tonnage	EEC countries	E 30-m E 29-a
	Main countries	T 4-a
Value added in manufacture in $m	OECD countries	D 9-a
Student graduation see UNIVERSITY DEGREES		
STUDENTS		
see also PUPILS		
Enrolment abroad by country of origin	All countries	U 64-a
by country of study	All countries	U 64-a
grade of educational institution	African countries	U 44-a
type of school & sex of student	Latin American countries	J 5-a
type of school	Asian, Far East & Australasian countries	U 45-a
in adult education institutes by kind	OAS member countries	N 19-a
higher education institutions & universities	Latin American countries	J 5-a
by grade level	Latin American countries	J 5-a
by type of course	Latin American countries	J 5-a
universities: historical table from 1817	Main European countries	Z 1-a
on teacher training courses by age groups	All countries	U 62-a
university courses by field of study & by sex	OAS member countries	N 19-a
by grade & sex	OAS member countries	N 19-a
vocational training courses	All countries	U 62-a
No of full-time students & as % of total population	EEC countries	E 3-a
of school children & students as % of population in 14-24 yrs age group	EEC countries	E 2-a
of students over 14 yrs of age (incl school pupils) by administrative areas	EEC countries	E 18-a
of university degrees granted by faculties	Latin American countries	J 5-a
STUDENTS BY SEX		
Enrolment: abroad by field of study	All countries	U 64-a
by field of study	All countries	U 64-a
of foreign & national students	All countries	U 64-a
in higher education institutions	OAS member countries	N 19-a
universities	OAS member countries	N 19-a
on adult education courses	Latin American countries	J 5-a
vocational courses	All countries	U 62-a

	Territorial coverage	Title codes
STUDENTS, FOREIGN		
Enrolment by country of study	All countries	U 64-a
by field of study & by nationality of students	All countries	U 62-a
by sex as % of total no of students	All countries	U 62-a
by sex by field of study	All countries	U 64-a
STUDENTS, UNIVERSITY		
% of university entrants by socio-economic origin	Main ECAFE countries	U 17
% of students formerly employed as clerical workers	ECAFE countries	U 17
farm workers or farmers	ECAFE countries	U 17
government officials	ECAFE countries	U 17
policemen or soldiers	ECAFE countries	U 17
professional employees	ECAFE countries	U 17
self-employed persons	ECAFE countries	U 17
No of university entrants studying: agriculture	All countries	U 62-a
education	All countries	U 62-a
engineering	All countries	U 62-a
fine arts & humanities	All countries	U 62-a
jurisprudence	All countries	U 62-a
medical science	All countries	U 62-a
natural sciences & technology	All countries	U 62-a
social sciences	All countries	U 62-a

Study courses   see   AGRICULTURE
                          AGRONOMY
                          BUILDING SCIENCES
                          BUSINESS STUDIES
                          CHEMISTRY
                          DENTISTRY
                          ECONOMICS
                          EDUCATION
                          ENGINEERING
                          FINE ARTS
                          HUMANITIES
                          LAW
                          MEDICAL SCIENCE
                          NATURAL SCIENCES
                          PHARMACY
                          SOCIAL SCIENCES
                          VETERINARY MEDICINE

	Territorial coverage	Title codes
STURGEON		
Catch by species: tonnage	World fishing areas	A 22-a

Styrene   see   CHEMICALS, ORGANIC

SUBSIDIES

        see also   EXPORT SUBSIDIES
                          GOVERNMENT ASSISTANCE
                          INTERVENTION PRICES

	Territorial coverage	Title codes
As % of government expenditure	All countries	M 6-a
of gross domestic product (annual averages)	OECD countries	D 11-a
As component in gross domestic product in local currency	Developing countries	D 25-a
	EEC countries	E 32-a
Country listing by % range of subsidy payments made on fertilisers		A 2-a
Government assistance for development of tourism in $m	OECD countries	D 47-a
Government expenditure on subsidies as component in budget		
accounts in $m	Main countries	U 43-a
in local currency	OAS member countries	N 16-a
	AASM countries	E 41-a
paid to official corporations		
in local currency	Caribbean countries	T 6-a
Subsidy payments made by provincial authorities in local currency	OAS member countries	N 16-a
Tax concessions granted to aid tourism	OECD countries	D 47-a

SUBSIDIES, AGRICULTURAL

        see also   DEFICIENCY PAYMENTS

	Territorial coverage	Title codes
Acreage subsidy in £ per ton: cottonseed	EEC countries	B 1-a
As component in gross domestic product	EEC countries	E 32-a
Compensation paid (against losses in farming)	ECE countries	U 34-a
Flax subsidy in £ per ton	EEC countries	B 1-a
Government expenditure: subsidy payments in local currency	Czechoslovakia & Poland	U 34-a
	ECE countries	U 34-a
in $m	OAS member countries	N 16-a
Hemp subsidy in £ per ton	EEC countries	E 44-a
No of applications to plant fruit trees (under subsidy payments)	EEC countries	B 1-a
Subsidy payments paid (net) in £m	EEC countries	U 20-a
as % of gross farm product	EEC countries	B 1-a
for storage (private): butter in £m	ECE countries	U 34-a
cheese in £m	EEC countries	B 3-a
on cheap sales to manufacturers in £m	EEC countries	B 3-a
on fertilisers in $	EEC countries	B 3-a
on inputs as % of gross farm output	E European countries	U 30-a
on output as % of gross farm output	ECE countries	U 34-a
on non-profit making sales to institutions in £m	ECE countries	U 34-a
	EEC countries	B 3-a

	Territorial coverage	Title codes

SUBSIDIES, AGRICULTURAL   continued
    Subsidy payments paid on package sales: butter to consumers in £m   EEC countries   B 3-a
        skim milk (for rennet & casein production) in UA per ton   EEC countries   B 3-a
        milk (liquid) as animal feed in pence per gallon   EEC countries   B 3-a
        milk powder (as animal feed) in £ per ton   EEC countries   B 3-a
        specific farm input items in $m   EEC countries   U 34-a
        under calf subsidy scheme in £m   UK   B 11-a
        fatstock guarantees in £m   UK   B 11-a
        hill cattle & sheep scheme in £m   UK   B 11-a

Succession taxes (on inheritance)   see   TAXATION

Sucrose recovery rate   see   SUGAR CANE

SUEZ CANAL
    Dues collected for passage of shipping in $m   Egypt   F 5-m   F 6-q
    Freight tariff surcharges to main ports after closure in $ U 37-a
    Freight traffic: crude oil & petroleum products to yr 1966: tonnage   U 37-a
        volume: South & North-bound traffic up to closure in 1966   U 37-a
    Maritime distances between world ports before & after closure of canal   U 37-a
    No of oil tankers using canal: North-South direction   C 14-a
        South-North direction   C 14-a
    vessels using canal: North-South direction   C 14-a
        South-North direction   C 14-a

SUGAR, BEET
    Production as % of world production of sugar (all kinds)   All countries   C 25-a
        (incl world total): tonnage   All countries   B 13-a
        tonnage   All countries   A 20-a   C 25-a
    Wholesale prices in $ per ton   Main European countries   A 9-a
    World production: historical table 1880-1960: tonnage   All countries   A 20-a
        tonnage   All countries   C 25-a

SUGAR, CANE
    Import prices in $ per ton cif   UK & USA   A 9-a
    Production as % of world production of sugar (all kinds)   C 25-a
    Production, consumption & stocks: tonnage   India   B 13-a
        (incl world total): tonnage   All countries   B 13-a
        tonnage   All countries   A 20-a   C 25-a
    Wholesale prices in $ per ton   Main countries   A 9-a
    World production: historical table 1880-1960: tonnage   All countries   A 20-a
        tonnage   All countries   C 25-a

SUGAR, NON-CENTRIFUGAL
    Consumption per capita in kg   Main countries   A 20-a
        tonnage   Main countries   A 20-a
    Imports: historical table from 1890: tonnage   Main countries   A 20-a
    Production: historical table from 1880: tonnage   All countries   A 20-a
        tonnage   All countries   B 13-a
    World exports: tonnage   Main countries   A 20-a

SUGAR, RAW CENTRIFUGAL
    Commonwealth negotiated price in cents per lb   A 5-a
    Consumption per capita in kg   Main countries   A 20-a   C 25-a
        tonnage   All countries   C 19-a   C 25-a
            Hawaii & Puerto Rico   C 25-a
            Main countries   A 20-a   C 13-a
    Export prices: historical table from 1900 in cents per lb cif   USA   A 20-a
        in $ per ton cif   Main countries   A 9-a
        (less duty) in $ per ton cif   USA   A 5-a
        shipped to UK in cents per lb cif   USA   C 25-a
    Exports by destination: tonnage   All countries   C 25-a
        by value in $m   Philippines   U 32-m
        tonnage   All countries   C 19-a
        (total) & shipped to EEC area: tonnage & value in UA   AASM countries   E 41-a
    Import levies in local currency per 100 kg   EEC countries   B 13-m
        prices: historical table from 1900 in £ per cwt   UK   A 20-a
        in £ per ton cif   UK   C 25-a
    Imports by areas of source: tonnage   EEC countries   B 13-a
        by source: tonnage   Main countries   C 25-a
            I.S.O. countries   C 19-m
        historical table from 1890: tonnage   Main countries   A 20-a
        tonnage   All countries   C 19-a
    Negotiated prices under Sugar Agreement in £ per ton   UK   C 25-a
    Production: raw beet & cane sugar: tonnage   All countries   U 22-a
        tonnage   African countries   U 44-a
            All countries   A 9-a   C 19-a
            ECAFE countries   U 32-q
            Hawaii & Puerto Rico   C 25-a
            Main countries   R 5-a
            OECD countries   D 1-a
            All countries   C 19-a   C 25-a
    Stocks (end-yr): tonnage   Main countries   B 13-a

	Territorial coverage	Title codes	
SUGAR, RAW CENTRIFUGAL continued			
Wholesale prices in $ per ton at Manila	Philippines	U 32-m	
World consumption: tonnage		U 11-a	
World contract prices: raw sugar by grade in cents per lb		R 2-m	
World exports by value in $m		B 13-a	
tonnage	All countries	C 25-a	
	Main countries	A 20-a	
World market price in $ per 100 kg		E 34-m	
$ per ton Caribbean ports fob		A 5-a	
local currency	UK & USA	C 25-a	
World production from beet: tonnage		A 5-a	B 13-a
		U 11-a	
cane: tonnage		A 5-a	B 13-a
		U 11-a	
tonnage	All countries	A 20-a	C 25-a
World stocks (end-yr): tonnage		C 25-a	
SUGAR, REFINED			
see also GLUCOSE			
IMPORT QUOTAS			
INTERNATIONAL SUGAR AGREEMENT			
MAPLE SUGAR			
% change: factory selling price (over previous yr)	EEC countries	E 34-m	
retail sales	E European countries & USSR	U 16-a	
% content of sugar beet crop	W European countries	E 35-a	
% contribution to export earnings	Trinidad, Mauritius, Jamaica, Fiji & Barbados	E 45-a	
As source of fat, protein & calorie intake per capita in grammes	OAS member countries	N 17-a	
Availability per capita per day	All countries	U 43-a	
tonnage (incl home production as % of supply)	All countries	U 43-a	
Consumption: all kinds (incl world total): tonnage	Main countries	B 2-a	
	EEC countries	E 44-a	
(as animal feed): tonnage	EEC countries	E 44-a	
(incl industrial usage): tonnage	EEC countries	E 3-a	
per capita in kg per yr	Main countries	E 3-a	
	Canada, European countries, Japan & USA	E 44-a	
	OECD countries	D 1-a	
	E European countries & USSR	U 16-a	
	EEC countries	B 1-a	E 44-a
in lbs per yr	Main countries	B 13-a	
white sugar in kg per yr	W European countries	P 5-a	
tonnage & per capita in kg	Main countries	U 43-a	
tonnage	I.S.O. countries	C 19-m	
	OAS member countries	N 17-a	
	World regions	A 5-a	
Demand, consumption & exports: tonnage	All countries	C 19-a	
Excise duties: sugar & sweeteners: rates charged	EEC countries	E 31-a	
Expenditure: price guarantees on sugar under EEC budget in £m		B 3-a	
Export prices: refined grades in $ per ton fob	Main countries	B 13-a	
granulated sugar in £ per ton fob	UK	R 2-m	
in $ per 100 lbs fob	Philippines	U 17-m	
Export prices - index nos (weighted average main sources)		U 29-q	U 54-q
	S American countries	U 40-q	
Export quotas agreed by US government: tonnage	Recipient countries	C 25-a	
under Commonwealth Sugar Agreement: tonnage		C 25-a	
Exports as % of value of export trade (total)	Main countries	B 13-a	
by destination by CST classes: tonnage & value in $m	EEC countries	E 48-a	
SITC classes by value in $m	Main countries	D 2-q	
tonnage & value in $m	OECD countries	D 3-a2	
	All countries	C 25-a	
tonnage	I.S.O. countries	C 19-m	
	Main countries	A 20-a	B 13-a
by value in $m	W European countries	U 33-a	
	Developing countries	U 11-a	
in local currency	Fiji, India & Philippines	U 32-m	
historical table from 1876: tonnage	Main countries	B 13-a	
(incl honey) as % of exports of farm products (value basis)	Russia	Z 1-a	
by value in $m	W European countries	U 20-a	
	OECD countries	D 1-a	
shipped to E European area by value in $m	W European countries	U 20-a	
(incl sugar products) by NIMEXE classes: tonnage & value in $m	W European countries	U 20-a	
by SITC classes: tonnage & value in $m	All countries	E 20-a	
shipped to EEC and non-EEC areas by value in $m	All countries	U 50-a	U 59-a
(net) shipped to non-Communist area: tonnage	EEC countries	E 24-a	
tonnage & value in $m	All countries	C 19-a	
	Main countries	B 2-a	
tonnage	African, Caribbean countries & Pacific Is	E 45-a	
	Asian, & Far East countries	U 32-q	
Factory selling price in local currency per kg	Fiji, India, Philippines & Thailand	U 32-m	
Freight (by source of cargo): tonnage	EEC countries	E 34-m	
Import levies: refined sugar in local currency per 100 kg	Main countries	D 28-a	
Import prices: refined sugar ex Caribbean area in cents per lb cif	EEC countries	B 13-a	
(in bulk London market) in £ per ton cif	UK & USA	R 2-m	
Imports by source by CST classes: tonnage & value in $m	UK	B 2-a	
	EEC countries	E 21-a	
	EEC area & I.S.O. countries	C 19-m	
tonnage	All countries	C 25-a	

520

SUGAR, REFINED   continued

	Territorial coverage	Title codes	
Imports by source: tonnage	Main countries	A 20-a	B 13-a
by value in local currency	EEC countries	B 13-a	
in $m	Asian, Far East & Australasian countries	U 33-a	
historical table from 1890: tonnage	W European countries	U 33-a	
(incl honey) as % of imports of farm products (value basis)	Main countries	A 20-a	
by value in $m	W European countries	U 20-a	
	W European countries	U 20-a	
shipped ex E European area by value in $m	OECD countries	D 1-a	
(incl sugar products) by NIMEXE classes: tonnage & value	W European countries	U 20-a	
in $m	All countries	E 20-a	
SITC classes: tonnage & value in $m	All countries	U 50-a	U 59-a
source by SITC classes by value in $m	Main countries	D 2-q	
tonnage & value in $m	OECD countries	D 3-a2	
shipped ex EEC & non-EEC areas by value in $m	EEC countries	E 24-a	
(net) shipped ex non-Communist area: tonnage	All countries	C 19-a	
sugar products (by areas of source): tonnage	EEC countries	B 13-a	
tonnage	Main countries	A 11-a	B 13-a
International Agreement price ex Caribbean area in cents per lb fob		U 20-q	
Intervention prices fixed by EEC Commission in $ per ton	EEC countries	E 44-a	
Intervention, target & threshold prices in £ per ton	EEC countries	B 13-a	
Ocean freight rates for sugar (main routes single voyage) in £ or $ per ton		S 16-a	
Output, stocks, imports, exports & domestic consumption: tonnage	EEC countries	E 3-a	
Prices in EEC area as % of world market prices		E 44-a	
Prices: daily quotations: bulk refined sugar per ton	UK & USA	C 19-m	
under I.S.A. (annual average)		B 13-a	
(daily quotations)		C 19-m	
ex Caribbean area in cents per lb fob		U 33-q	
Production, imports, exports, consumption & stocks: tonnage	EEC countries	E 44-a	
Production & consumption projected to 1985: tonnage	Main world regions	A 1	
& exports ex Commonwealth as % of world exports of refined sugar		B 13-a	
beet sugar (incl world total): tonnage	Main countries	B 2-a	
by kind: beet or cane by region: tonnage	USA	B 13-a	
	EEC area & I.S.O. countries	C 19-m	
	Latin American countries	U 40-a	
by main areas: tonnage	Hawaii, Puerto Rico & USA	C 19-m	
cane sugar (incl world total): tonnage	Main countries	B 2-a	
centrifugal sugar processed from beet & cane: tonnage	All countries	U 43-a	
for human consumption: tonnage	Worldwide	B 13-a	
processed from beet or cane: tonnage	Latin American countries	J 5-a	
tonnage	All countries	U 22-a	
	OECD countries	D 1-a	
	AASM countries	E 41-a	
	African countries	U 44-a	
	Asian & Far East countries	U 32-q	
	E European countries & USSR	U 16-a	
	Main countries	E 3-a	
	OAS member countries	N 14-a	
Quota-exempt imports by source: tonnage	USA	C 19-m	
Retail prices by kind of sugar in local currency	OAS member countries	N 17-a	
(comparative): white granulated sugar in cents per kg	EEC countries	Z 3-a	
historical table from 1938-1959 in local currency per kg	Main countries	A 20-a	
white refined sugar in cents per lb	Main countries	C 25-a	
Self-sufficiency ratios	EEC countries	E 3-a	E 44-a
Shipments through Panama Canal (East & West): tonnage		D 28-a	
trip & period charter: tonnage	Worldwide	S 17-m	
Stocks (end-mth): tonnage	I.S.O. countries	C 19-m	
	EEC countries	E 44-a	
	Main countries	A 20-a	
(end-season) carry-over: tonnage	Worldwide	A 5-a	A 11-a
		B 13-a	
(end-yr): tonnage	Main countries	B 2-a	
held in producer & importing countries: tonnage		C 19-a	
Supply, production, consumption & trade: tonnage	EEC countries	B 1-a	
Supply, production, imports & stocks: tonnage	All countries	C 19-a	
Supply quotas: final adjusted quotas agreed by US authorities: tonnage	Recipient countries	B 13-a	
Target, intervention & threshold prices in £ per cwt	EEC countries	B 1-a	
Tramp shipping freight rates - index nos	Worldwide	U 37-m	
Wholesale prices ex factory in Rs per quintal	India	U 32-m	
ex warehouse: historical table from 1900 in cents per lb	Cuba	A 20-a	
historical table from 1900 in local currency per kg	Main countries	A 20-a	
in $ per ton: C.S.A. contract price for UK & USA (incl world market price)		U 27-m	
in local currency	OAS member countries	N 17-a	
sugar products by kind in local currency per ton	OAS member countries	N 17-a	
spot & average of daily quotations	UK & USA	C 25-m	
under Commonwealth Agreement in £ per ton	Main countries	C 25-a	
white sugar in cents per lb	Main countries	C 25-a	
World consumption: tonnage		B 13-a	
World exports by value in $m		M 4-a	
	World regions	A 5-a	B 13-a
tonnage	All countries	B 13-a	
	Main countries	A 20-a	
unit value in $ per ton		A 11-a	

	Territorial coverage	Title codes	
SUGAR, REFINED continued			
World market prices – index nos		G 1-a	M 4-a
in cents per lb (on New York market)	USA	E 41-a	
World production: tonnage		B 13-a	
World stocks (end-yr): tonnage		G 1-a	

SUGAR BEET

see also STATE PROCUREMENT (COMMUNIST COUNTRIES)

	Territorial coverage	Title codes	
% change: prices received by farmers	W European countries	U 30-a	
% of total EEC area production	EEC countries	R 5-a	
% sugar content of sugar beet crop	W European countries	E 35-a	
Area harvested, production : tonnage & yield per ha	All countries	A 9-a	
under crop: historical table from 1815 in ha	Main European countries	Z 1-a	
(in 5 yr averages) in ha	Main countries	A 20-a	
in ha (incl harvested tonnage)	All countries	R 5-a	
	Developing countries & E European area	U 11-a	
in ha	EEC countries	B 1-a	E 12-a
		E 44-a	
Consumption: tonnage	OECD countries	D 1-a	
	EEC countries	E 44-a	
Crop yield in kg per ha	EEC countries	B 1-a	E 12-a
	OECD countries	D 1-a	
in quintals per ha	Developed countries	D 11-a	
	E European countries & USSR	U 11-a	U 16-a
sugar & fodder beet in kg per ha	EEC countries	E 3-a	
Distribution for market sales: tonnage	Czechoslovakia, Hungary & Poland	U 34-a	
for sugar refining: tonnage	Czechoslovakia, Hungary & Poland	U 34-a	
Gross output of sugar beet crop by value as % of all crops	ECE countries	U 34-a	
Intervention prices fixed by EEC Commission in $ per ton		E 44-a	
Minimum price (in & outside basic quota) in £ per cwt	EEC countries	B 1-a	
Prices: average harvest selling prices in local currency per ton	W European countries	U 30-a	
basic: beet imported under quotas in £ per cwt	EEC countries	B 13-a	
Producer prices in local currency per ton	OECD countries	D 1-a	
per 100 kg	W European countries	E 35-a	
	All countries	A 9-a	
	E European countries	U 30-a	
	EEC countries	E 44-a	
in $ per ton	USA	E 35-a	
	W European countries	U 30-a	
(on contract) in local currency per ton	EEC countries	E 44-a	
Producer prices – index nos	USSR	U 34-a	
Production costs on collective farms in $ per ton	Main countries	R 5-a	
Production based on sugar content: tonnage	EEC countries	E 44-a	
by value in $m	All countries	A 20-a	
historical table (in 5 yr averages) from 1880	Main European countries	Z 1-a	
tonnage	EEC countries	B 1-a	
tonnage & value in £ per ton	African countries	U 44-a	
tonnage	Czechoslovakia, Hungary & Poland	U 34-a	
	Developed countries & E European countries	U 11-a	
	E European countries & USSR	U 16-a	
	EEC countries	E 12-a	E 44-a
	I.S.O. countries	C 19-m	
	Main countries	E 3-a	
	OECD countries	D 1-a	
	E European countries	U 34-a	
value as % of gross farm output	E European countries & USSR incl Ukraine	U 16-a	
State procurement: tonnage			

SUGAR CANE

	Territorial coverage	Title codes
Area harvested, production: tonnage & yield per ha	All countries	A 9-a
under crop & yield per ha	Latin American countries	J 5-a
historical tables in ha	Main European countries	Z 1-a
(incl harvested tonnage) in ha	All countries	R 5-a
(in 5 yr averages)	Main countries	A 20-a
in ha	OAS member countries	N 13-a
Crop yield in kg per ha	OAS member countries	N 13-a
in tons per acre	India	B 13-a
Crushings at central sugar factories: tonnage	India	B 13-a
Producer prices in $ per ton	All countries	A 9-a
Production: historical table (in 5 yr averages) from 1880	All countries	A 20-a
tonnage & value in $	W Indies & Caribbean countries	T 6-a
tonnage	Main European countries	Z 1-a
	AASM countries	E 41-a
	I.S.O. countries	C 19-m
	OAS member countries	N 13-a
	OECD countries	D 1-a
Sucrose recovery as % of sugar crushings	India	B 13-a

Sugar plantations see PLANTATIONS, SUGAR

SUGAR REFINING INDUSTRY

	Territorial coverage	Title codes
Investment in buildings in local currency	EEC countries	E 40-a
in land purchase in local currency	EEC countries	E 40-a
in machinery in local currency	EEC countries	E 40-a
No of hrs worked per wk	Main countries	R 3-m
Wage rates by sex in local currency per hr	Main countries	R 3-m

	Territorial coverage	Title codes	
SUICIDE			
Death rates per 100,000 population	All countries	W 2-m	
No of deaths reported by cause	OAS member countries	N 20-a	
resulting from strangulation	OAS member countries	N 20-a	
from use of firearms	OAS member countries	N 20-a	
of poison	OAS member countries	N 20-a	
through self-inflicted injury (all kinds)	Main countries	W 1-a	
	OAS member countries	N 12-a	

Suitcases   see   LUGGAGE, LEATHER

Suits   see   CLOTHING

Sulfonated acids   see   ACIDS, ORGANIC

Sulphate of potash   see   FERTILISERS

Sulphate of soda   see   CHEMICAL PRODUCTS

Sulphate of zinc   see   ZINC COMPOUNDS

Sulphite wrapping   see   WRAPPING PAPER

SULPHUR
    see also   PYRITES

	Territorial coverage	Title codes	
% consumption in production of farm fertilisers	USA	N 1-a	
paints, plastics & synthetics	USA	N 1-a	
sulphuric acid	Main countries	U 25-a	
	USA	N 1-a	
Consumption: frasch sulphur (recovered) & pyrites: tonnage	USA	N 1-a	
(incl lime sulphur) in agriculture: tonnage	All countries	A 9-a	
sulphurous materials by kind: tonnage	OECD countries	D 5-a	
tonnage	All countries	T 5-a	
	European countries, Japan & USA	U 25-a	
Exports by destination: tonnage	OAS member countries	N 17-a	
Imports & exports: crude & refined sulphur: tonnage	OECD countries	D 5-a	
Imports by source: tonnage	All countries	B 15-a	
Production based on content of pyrites concentrates: tonnage	OECD countries	D 5-a	
by kind: tonnage	All countries	B 15-a	U 43-a
	OECD countries	D 5-a	
crude & refined sulphur: tonnage	All countries	U 22-a	
crude sulphur: tonnage	All countries	B 15-a	
	All countries	U 22-a	
	EEC countries	E 28-q	E 27-a
	OAS member countries	N 14-a	
	S American countries	U 40-a	
elemental distillate (pyritic): tonnage	Latin American countries	J 5-a	
frasch sulphur: tonnage	USA	N 1-a	
historical table from 1861: tonnage	W Germany & Italy	Z 1-a	
recovered sulphur: tonnage	OAS member countries	N 14-a	
	USA	N 1-a	
sulphur residues: tonnage	Cuba & USA	N 14-a	
tonnage	African countries	U 44-a	
	Communist world regions	T 5-a	
	European countries, Japan & USA	U 25-a	
	Non-Communist world regions	T 5-a	
Stocks held at producers' plants: tonnage	USA	N 1-a	
Tramp shipping freight rates: crude sulphur - index nos	Worldwide	U 37-m	
Wholesale prices: crude sulphur in $ per ton	USA	N 1-a	
World production: crude sulphur by-products: tonnage		N 4-a	
native sulphur: tonnage		N 4-a	
tonnage	Main countries	N 1-a	
World reserves: tonnage (estim)	Main countries	N 1-a	

Sulphur anhydrite   see   BUILDING MATERIALS

SULPHUR COMPOUNDS
    see also   SULPHURIC ACID

	Territorial coverage	Title codes
Consumption in agriculture: tonnage	OECD countries	D 5-a
	All countries	A 9-a
sulphur dioxide: tonnage	OECD countries	D 5-a
Imports by source: pyrites: tonnage	OECD countries	D 5-a
sulphides of lead & copper: tonnage	OECD countries	D 5-a
Production: sulphides of lead & copper: tonnage	OECD countries	D 5-a

Sulphur dioxide   see   SULPHUR COMPOUNDS

SULPHURIC ACID

	Territorial coverage	Title codes
% of consumption used in metallurgy	Main countries	U 25-a
in production of detergents	Main countries	U 25-a
fertilisers	USA	U 25-a
fibres	Main countries	U 25-a
paints	USA	U 25-a
plastics	Main countries	U 25-a
steel (pickling)	Main countries	U 25-a

	Territorial coverage	Title codes	
SULPHURIC ACID, continued			
% usage of anhydrite gypsum in production of acid	Main countries	U 25-a	
of pyrites in production of acid	Main countries	U 25-a	
	OECD countries	D 5-a	
of spent oxides in production of acid	Main countries	U 25-a	
of sulphides & sulphur in production of acid	Main countries	U 25-a	
	OECD countries	D 5-a	
Consumption by chemical industry: tonnage	OECD countries	D 5-a	
by petro-chemical industry: tonnage	OECD countries	D 5-a	
by textile industry: tonnage	OECD countries	D 5-a	
in metallurgy: tonnage	OECD countries	D 5-a	
in production of pigments: tonnage	OECD countries	D 5-a	
tonnage	Communist world regions	T 5-a	
	Non-Communist world regions	T 5-a	
	OAS member countries	N 17-a	
	OECD countries	D 5-a	
Exports (incl oleum) by destination: tonnage	Main countries	U 2-a	
tonnage	ECE countries	U 15-a	
	European countries, Japan & USA	U 25-a	
Imports (incl oleum): tonnage	ECE countries	U 15-a	
	European countries, Japan & USA	U 25-a	
Production costs in sulphuric acid plants for coke in $ per ton	Main countries	U 25-a	
cooling water in $ per ton	Main countries	U 25-a	
depreciation of equipment in $ per ton	USA	U 25-a	
electricity consumed by value in $	Main countries	U 25-a	
labour supervision in $ per ton	USA	U 25-a	
maintenance of equipment & plant in $ per ton	USA	U 25-a	
natural gas consumed in $ per ton	Main countries	U 25-a	
overheads in $ per ton	USA	U 25-a	
raw materials used in $ per ton	Main countries	U 25-a	
sand & ash used in $ per ton	Main countries	U 25-a	
sulphur consumed in $ per ton	Main countries	U 25-a	
(total) in $ per ton of sulphuric acid produced	USA	U 25-a	
Production: historical tables from 1860: tonnage	Main European countries	Z 1-a	
(incl oleum): tonnage	ECE countries	U 15-a	
	European countries, Japan & USA	U 25-a	
pure mono-hydrate acid: tonnage	All countries	U 27-m	
tonnage	African countries	U 44-a	
	All countries	R 5-a	T 5-a
		U 22-a	U 43-a
	Communist world regions	T 5-a	
	E European countries & USSR	U 16-a	
	EEC countries	E 26-m	E 28-q
		E 27-a	
	Main countries	E 3-a	
	Non-Communist world regions	T 5-a	
	OAS member countries	N 14-a	
	OECD countries	D 5-a	
	Zaire	E 41-a	

Sulphurous raw materials   see   PYRITES
                                    SULPHUR
                                    SULPHUR COMPOUNDS

SUNFLOWER SEED

    see also   STATE PROCUREMENT (COMMUNIST COUNTRIES)

	Territorial coverage	Title codes
Area harvested, production: tonnage & yield per ha	All countries	A 9-a
under crop (for seed) in acres	Main countries	B 18-a
in acres or ha	Main countries	N 10-a
in acres	Main countries	B 19-a
in ha	EEC countries	E 12-a
	OAS member countries	N 13-a
Crop (incl world total): tonnage (estim)	All countries	P 1-a
yield in 100 kg per ha	EEC countries	E 12-a
in kg per ha	OAS member countries	N 13-a
Exports: tonnage & value in $m	Main countries	B 2-a
tonnage	Main countries	B 19-a
Harvest: estimate (for ensuing crop): tonnage	Main world regions	P 1-a
Imports by source: tonnage	EEC countries	B 19-a
in vegetable oil equiv tonnage	EEC countries	P 5-a
tonnage	Main countries	B 19-a
Intervention price fixed by EEC Commission in $ per ton	EEC countries	E 44-a
in UA per ton	EEC countries	B 19-a
Market & target prices in UA per ton	EEC countries	B 19-a
Prices paid by farmers (as animal feed) in $ per ton	E European countries	U 30-a
Producer prices received in $ per ton	Uruguay	A 9-a
Production (incl world total): tonnage	All countries	B 18-a
	Main countries	B 2-a

	Territorial coverage	Title codes	
SUNFLOWER SEED, continued			
Production: tonnage	Argentina, Chile, Peru & Uraguay	U 40-a	
	EEC countries	E 12-a	
	Main countries	B 19-a	
	OAS member countries	N 13-a	
State procurement: tonnage	E European countries & USSR	U 16-a	
Target & intervention prices in £ per cwt	EEC countries	B 1-a	
Wholesale prices (ex tank Rotterdam) in £ per ton	Netherlands	B 2-a	
SUNFLOWER SEED CAKE			
see also OILCAKE & MEAL			
Exports: tonnage & value in $m	Main countries	B 2-a	
Wholesale prices in £ per ton	UK	B 2-a	
SUNFLOWER SEED OIL			
Consumption in production of cooking fats: tonnage	UK	B 19-a	
of margarine: tonnage	Main countries	B 19-a	
Exports by destination: tonnage	UK & USA	A 4-a	
tonnage & value in $m	Argentine & USSR	B 19-a	
tonnage	Main countries	B 2-a	
Import prices (ex tank Rotterdam) in $ per ton cif	Main countries	B 19-a	
in Fl per kg cif at Rotterdam	UK	B 19-m	
under contract in £ per ton cif	Netherlands	R 2-m	
Imports: tonnage	UK	R 2-m	
Production (for ensuing yr): tonnage (estim)	Main countries	B 19-a	
tonnage	World regions	P 1-a	
	Argentine, Romania & USSR	P 1-a	
	Main countries	B 19-a	
	W Germany	N 10-a	
World & Commonwealth production: tonnage		B 19-a	
World production: tonnage (forecast)		A 1-a	
tonnage		A 4-a	A 5-a
		N 10-a	
Supermarkets see SELF-SERVICE STORES			
SUPERPHOSPHATES			
see also FERTILISERS			
% change: prices paid to farmers	EEC countries	E 34-m	
Average phosphate content of superphosphates produced	All countries	C 26-a	
Consumption by grade for production of fertiliser compounds: tonnage	All countries	C 26-a	
for direct farm use: tonnage	All countries	C 26-a	
tonnage	All countries	A 2-a	
concentrated grade: tonnage	All countries	A 2-a	C 26-a
single grade: tonnage	All countries	C 26-a	
tonnage	OAS member countries	N 17-a	
Exports by destination: concentrated grade: tonnage	All countries	C 26-a	
concentrated grade: tonnage	All countries	A 2-a	C 26-a
single grade: tonnage	All countries	A 2-a	C 26-a
Farm costs (18-20% phosphate content) in local currency per bag	EEC countries	E 34-m	
Imports: concentrated grade: tonnage	All countries	A 2-a	C 26-a
single & concentrated grades: tonnage	OECD countries	D 5-a	
	All countries	A 2-a	C 26-a
Prices paid by farmers in $ per ton	W European countries	U 30-a	
Production: % phosphate content	All countries	C 26-a	
by kind: tonnage	Main countries	B 15-a	
concentrated grade: tonnage	All countries	A 2-a	C 26-a
hyperphosphates: tonnage	African countries	U 44-a	
single & concentrated grades: tonnage	OECD countries	D 5-a	
single grade: tonnage	All countries	A 2-a	C 26-a
	African countries	U 44-a	
tonnage	All countries	U 22-a	
	Australasian countries, India & Japan	U 32-q	
	EEC countries	E 26-m	E 28-q
		E 27-a	
	Main countries	R 5-a	
Wholesale prices in $ per ton	OECD countries	D 5-a	
World exports by destination: concentrated grade: tonnage	France, W Germany, Italy & UK	A 9-a	
		C 26-a	

Supply meters   see   METERS, ELECTRICITY SUPPLY
                         METERS, GAS SUPPLY
                         METERS, WATER SUPPLY

SUPPLY QUOTAS
   Sugar: final adjusted quotas by recipients: tonnage   USA   B 13-a

Supply, indigenous (as % of requirements)   see   SELF-SUFFICIENCY

Support prices   see   DEFICIENCY PAYMENTS
                     INTERVENTION PRICES
                     PRICE SUPPORTS

Support services   see   ADVISORY SERVICES, OFFICIAL

Supporting assistance programs   see   DEVELOPMENT AID

	Territorial coverage	Title codes
Surgical & ophthalmic instruments see OPTICAL INSTRUMENTS		

SURGICAL PRODUCTS, RUBBER
Consumption: rubber in production of surgical products: tonnage	France	C 18-a
Production: tonnage	EEC countries	E 28-q E 27-a

SURTAX
see also   TAXATION

Receipts of taxes levied on surtax payers in local currency	EEC countries	E 42-a
in $m	OECD countries	D 42-a

Surveying equipment   see   OPTICAL INSTRUMENTS
　　　　　　　　　　　　　　SCIENTIFIC INSTRUMENTS

Sweaters   see   CLOTHING

SWEDES & TURNIPS
Area under crop: swedes in ha	EEC countries	E 12-a
Crop yield in 100 kg per ha	EEC countries	E 12-a
Production: tonnage	EEC countries	E 12-a

SWEET POTATOES & YAMS
Area under crop in ha	OAS member countries	N 13-a
(incl yield per ha)	All countries	A 9-a
	Latin American countries	J 5-a
Consumption: tonnage	OAS member countries	N 17-a
Crop yield in kg per ha	OAS member countries	N 13-a
Producer prices in $ per ton	Argentine, Brazil, Japan, S Korea & USA	A 9-a
Production & usage by industry & for fodder & seed: tonnage	OECD countries	D 14-a
Production (incl yams): tonnage	Asian & Far East countries	U 32-a
tonnage	OAS member countries	N 13-a

Swimwear   see   CLOTHING

SWITCHGEAR, ELECTRIC
% imports by source: circuit breakers	Main countries	T 7-a

Synthesis   see   CHEMICAL INDUSTRY
　　　　　　　　　CHEMICALS, ORGANIC

Synthetic ammonia   see   AMMONIA, SYNTHETIC

Synthetic dyestuffs   see   DYESTUFFS, SYNTHETIC

Synthetic fabrics   see   WOVEN NON-CELLULOSIC FABRICS
　　　　　　　　　　　　　WOVEN NON-CELLULOSIC SPUN YARN FABRICS

Synthetic fibres   see   MAN-MADE FIBRES
　　　　　　　　　　　　NON-CELLULOSIC FIBRES
　　　　　　　　　　　　POLYESTER

Synthetic fibres industry   see   MAN-MADE FIBRES INDUSTRY

Synthetic latices   see   SYNTHETIC RUBBER

Synthetic leather   see   LEATHER SUBSTITUTE

SYNTHETIC MONOFIL
Exports by destination: monofil incl strip: tonnage	Main countries	K 4-a
Imports by source: monofil incl strip: tonnage	Main countries	K 4-a

SYNTHETIC NARCOTICS
Consumption by name of drug per million population in kg	All countries	U 46-a
dextromoramide in kg	All countries	U 46-a
methadone in kg	All countries	U 46-a
Production by name of drug (in detail) in kg	All countries	U 46-a
dextromoramide in kg	Netherlands	U 46-a
diphenoxylate in kg	All countries	U 46-a
hydrocodone in kg	All countries	U 46-a
methadone in kg	All countries	U 46-a
opium alkaloids in kg	All countries	U 46-a
pethidine in kg	All countries	U 46-a
trimeperidine in kg	All countries	U 46-a

Synthetic resins   see   PLASTICS

SYNTHETIC RUBBER
% changes in exports (value basis)	European countries, Japan & USA	U 25-a
in imports (value basis)	European countries, Japan & USA	U 25-a
Consumption & demand by yr 1975 (estim): tonnage	Main countries	A 1
& per capita in lbs	Main countries	B 13-a U 43-a
by industrial sector: tonnage	Main countries	A 1-a
by kind of synthetic rubber by industrial sector: tonnage	USA	C 18-q
of end-product: tonnage	Main countries	C 18-a
tonnage	Canada & USA	C 18-m

		Territorial coverage	Title codes	
SYNTHETIC RUBBER, continued				
Consumption for production of belting: tonnage		UK	C 18-a	
cables: tonnage		UK	C 18-a	
hose & tubing: tonnage		UK	C 18-a	
latex foams: tonnage		UK	C 18-a	
manufactured goods: tonnage		Main countries	B 13-a	
soles for footwear: tonnage		UK	C 18-a	
sponge rubber: tonnage		UK	C 18-a	
tyre repair materials: tonnage		UK	C 18-a	
tyres: tonnage		Main countries	B 13-a	
(industrial): tonnage		Main countries	C 18-q	
neoprene: tonnage		USA	C 18-m	
synthetic latices: tonnage		Main countries	C 18-m	
tonnage (incl world total)		All countries	A 5-a	
tonnage		Main countries	C 17-m	C 18-m
			B 2-a	U 43-a
Exports by destination by kind: tonnage		OAS member countries	N 17-a	
by value in $m		USA	C 18-m	
tonnage		Main countries	U 2-a	
		Main countries	C 18-m	B 13-a
			U 2-a	
		OECD countries	D 5-a	
rubber substitutes: tonnage		European countries, Japan & USA	U 26-a	
& value in $m		Main countries	C 18-m	
Imports by source: tonnage		Main countries	B 2-a	
by value in $m (& as % of imports of all chemical products		Main countries	B 13-a	
		Main countries	U 25-a	
		OECD countries	D 5-a	
rubber substitutes: tonnage		European countries, Japan & USA	U 26-a	
Production capacity: tonnage		World regions	B 13-a	
Production by kind: tonnage		Brazil, Canada & USA	C 18-m	
Production, consumption & stocks: tonnage		IRSG member countries	C 18-m	
(incl world total): tonnage		All countries	C 4-a	
		Main countries	A 5-a	B 2-a
butyl rubber: tonnage		Canada & USA	C 18-m	
incl reclaimed rubber: tonnage		All countries	U 43-a	
latices: tonnage		Main countries	C 18-m	
polisoprene: tonnage		USA	C 18-m	
polybutadiene: tonnage		USA	C 18-m	
rubber substitutes: tonnage		European countries, Japan & USA	U 26-a	
tonnage		All countries	U 27-m	U 22-a
		EEC countries	E 28-q	E 27-a
		Main countries	C 18-m	R 5-a
		OECD countries	D 5-a	
Production - index nos		OECD countries	D 19-m	D 20-m
Stocks by kind: tonnage		USA	C 18-m	
tonnage		Canada, France, Japan, UK & USA	B 2-a	
		Main countries	C 18-m	B 13-a
Supply: tonnage		All countries	B 13-a	
Value of output (gross & net) in £m		UK	B 21-a	
Wholesale prices in $ per ton		USA	U 27-m	A 9-a
World consumption		All countries (excl centrally-planned regions)	B 13-a	
World consumption: projected to 1980: tonnage			U 26-a	
tonnage			U 26-a	
World production		All countries (excl centrally-planned regions)	B 13-a	
World production: tonnage			U 26-a	
World supply		All countries (excl centrally-planned regions)	B 13-a	

Synthetic staple   see   CELLULOSIC FIBRES
                              MAN-MADE FIBRES
                              NON-CELLULOSIC FIBRES

Synthetic tyre fabric   see   TYRE FABRIC, SYNTHETIC

Synthetic waste   see   FIBRES, SYNTHETIC WASTE

Synthetic woven fabrics   see   WOVEN NON-CELLULOSIC FABRICS

Synthetic yarn   see   MAN-MADE FIBRE YARN
                              YARN, NON-CELLULOSIC

SYRUP

% contribution to export earnings: mollasses	Mauritius	E 45-a	
Consumption: molasses in production of animal feed: tonnage	EEC countries	P 5-a	
tonnage	OAS member countries	N 17-a	
Exports: molasses: tonnage & value in $m	Madagascar	E 45-a	
Production & consumption (total) & per capita in grammes per day	OECD countries	D 14-a	
Production: molasses in gallons & by value in $	W Indies & Caribbean countries	T 6-a	

Tablecloths   see   HOUSEHOLD TEXTILES

Tailored clothing   see   OUTERWEAR, TAILORED

Tailoring, bespoke   see   CLOTHING, READY-MADE

	Territorial coverage	Title codes	
TALC			
Consumption: talc, soapstone & pyrophyllite: tonnage	USA	N 1-a	
Government strategic stockpile & sales: steatite lumps: tonnage	USA	N 1-a	
Imports & exports by kind: tonnage	All countries	B 15-a	
Production by kind (incl steatite): tonnage	All countries	B 15-a	
World production (incl soapstone & pyrophyllite): tonnage		N 1-a	N 4-a
World reserves (incl soapstone & pyrophyllite): tonnage	Main countries	N 1-a	
TALLOW			
Export prices in $ per ton fob	USA	A 9-a	
Import prices (ex Australia & USA) in £ per ton cif	UK	P 1-a	
in $ per ton cif (at Rotterdam)	Netherlands	P 1-a	
Imports (incl edible & technical tallow): tonnage	Main countries	P 1-a	
Production for ensuing yr (estim): tonnage	World regions	P 1-a	
tonnage (estim)	Argentine, Australia & USA	P 1-a	
tonnage	All countries	A 9-a	
Usage in production of detergents: tonnage	Norway, Portugal & USA	A 4-a	
	Japan	B 19-a	
of margarine & cooking fats: tonnage	Japan	A 4-a	
of soap: tonnage	Japan, Norway, Portugal & USA	A 4-a	
(incl grease) in production of soap: tonnage	UK & USA	B 19-a	
Wholesale prices: bleachable fancy tallow in cents per lb	USA	R 2-m	
(grade 2) ex works in £ per ton	UK	R 2-m	
in $ per ton	UK & USA	U 27-m	A 9-a
World market prices (incl palm & fish oils) - index nos		A 4-m	
in $ per 100 kg		E 34-m	
World production (incl greases): tonnage		A 4-a	A 5-a
		N 10-a	
projected to 1975: tonnage		A 1	
World supply (incl greases): tonnage		B 19-a	

Tanker fleet (in reserve)   see   WORLD FLEETS

Tanker freight rates   see   OCEAN FREIGHT RATES

TANKERS

     see also   BULK CARRIERS
                 CARGO SHIPS
                 WORLD FLEETS

	Territorial coverage	Title codes	
% capacity of ships by age groups	European countries	U 8-a	
% craft used on inland waterways by age & by type	European countries	U 8-a	
% distribution by size: tonnage afloat	Worldwide	C 13-a	
Age distribution: tankers afloat by 5 yr age groups	Worldwide	U 37-a	
Charterings by sea routes: clean & dirty cargo by charterers	Worldwide	S 17-m	
Company & independent-owned tankers afloat by size classes	Worldwide	S 17-m	
Conversion tonnage & sales of tankers abroad in dwt	EEC countries	E 43-a	
Craft in service by load capacity & by type in dwt	European countries	U 8-a	
Deliveries: new tankers: no & tonnage in dwt	Worldwide	S 17-m	
Draft distribution by tonnage classes in ft		S 22-a	
Exports: second-hand tankers: no & tonnage	Norway	S 15-a	
Freight rate assessments (A.F.R.A.) intascale & worldscale		S 17-q	
by size of vessel & by routes: clean & dirty trade		S 17-m	
on A.F.R.A. worldscale by dwt groups		E 16-m	E 15-a
Freight rates - index nos	Worldwide	U 37-a	
Growth of sizes: tankers in service in dwt	Worldwide	C 21-a	
Hold capacities: pressurised for transport of LPG	Worldwide	U 25-a	
refrigerated for transport of LPG	Worldwide	U 25-a	
Loading capacity by age classification in BRT	EEC countries	E 43-a	
by size classification in BRT	EEC countries	E 43-a	
New construction in progress & on order (at end-yr) in dwt	All countries	C 21-a	
launched in dwt	All countries	U 43-a	
no & tonnage (incl scheduled deliveries) in dwt	Worldwide	S 17-a2	
delivered to Norwegian companies in dwt		S 15-a	
no & tonnage delivered in dwt	Worldwide	S 15-a	
launched in dwt	All countries	U 22-a	U 38-a
tonnage completed by country of build in dwt		D 28-a	
by flag in dwt	Country of construction	S 4-a	
in dwt	World regions	U 37-a	
tonnage, hp of vessels & overseas purchases in dwt	EEC countries	E 43-a	
No & tonnage: acquisitions: new & second-hand tankers by flag in dwt	Worldwide	U 37-a	
afloat in dwt	OAS member countries	N 15-a	
broken up for scrap by flag	Worldwide	S 16-m	
built by size classes & kind of ownership in dwt	Worldwide	S 17-m	
employed in grain trade in dwt & tonnage of cargo carried	Worldwide	S 15-a	
for shipping of chemicals & solvents in dwt	Norway	S 15-a	
of gas by kind in dwt	Norway	S 15-a	
laid up for lack of cargo by flag in dwt		S 23-m	
by year of build in dwt	Worldwide	S 23-m	
laid up in dwt	Worldwide	S 17-m	S 15-a
new orders in dwt		S 17-m	S 15-a
world fleet: methane carriers in dwt	EEC countries	E 15-a	
world fleet in dwt		S 17-a	
on order by size in dwt	Norway	S 15-a	
by Norwegian companies in dwt	Country of build	S 15-a	
in dwt	Country of registration	S 22-a	
world fleet by type of propulsion: steam or motor in dwt		C 13-a	

	Territorial coverage	Title codes	
TANKERS, continued			
No of tanker charterings & tonnage by length of charter in mths	Worldwide	S 17-m	
by length of charter in mths		S 17-m	
by sea routes & kind of cargo: clean & dirty trade: tonnage	Worldwide	S 17-m	
& kind of cargo: tonnage by charterers	Worldwide	S 17-m	
release date period commitments: tonnage	Worldwide	S 17-m	
tankers afloat	Country of registration	C 13-a	
tankers afloat over 10,000 tons gross wt	Country of registration	S 22-a	
by age, size & type of propulsion in service	All countries	C 21-a	
by engine capacity in hp & yr of construction	EEC countries	E 43-a	
using inland waterways by type	European countries	U 8-a	
tonnage & engine hp	EEC countries	E 43-a	
Ocean freight rates by range of tonnages (worldscale basis)		D 28-m	
Pattern: crude oil trade by sizes of vessels	All countries	C 21-a	
Sales: tankers by name, age, speed, price, name of buyer or seller in dwt	Worldwide	S 17-m	
Seaborne freight: tankers in ton-miles	UK	S 16-a	
Selling prices by age & by tonnage: second-hand vessels in $m		S 16-a	
by tonnage sizes (ex shipyards) by value in £m		S 16-a2	
Tonnage: tankers afloat & as % of world fleets		D 28-a	U 37-a
by flag	Worldwide	D 28-a	S 4-a
by size classes in dwt	Worldwide	S 22-a	
forward estimates in dwt	Worldwide	S 15-a	
broken up for scrap by engine hp in dwt	EEC countries	E 43-a	
for scrap in dwt	Worldwide	D 28-a	S 15-a
laid up for lack of employment by flag in dwt	Worldwide	D 28-a	
on order (by year of planned future delivery) in dwt	Worldwide	S 22-a	
over 10,000 tons (by size classes) in dwt	Worldwide	S 22-a	
	Country of construction	S 22-a	
on order in dwt	Worldwide	S 15-a	S 22-a
	Country of construction	D 28-a	
Utilisation: proportion of fleets in service by sea areas	All countries	C 21-a	
World tanker fleet by flags & "convenience" registration in dwt		C 21-a	
by ownership & flags in dwt	All countries	C 21-a	
by size groups in dwt		C 21-a	
hold: capacity for transport of ammonia by volume in m³		U 25-a	
of liquefied petroleum gas by volume in m³		U 25-a	
in dwt	Countries of registration	E 15-a	
TANKERS, OIL			
% distribution by yr of construction by main flags		S 4-a	
% of fleet by size categories in dwt		T 3-a	
% of registered world fleets by flag		H 4-a	
Charter fixtures, shipping route, cargo tonnage & name of ship		S 17-m	
Charter-ownership ratio: independent oil companies	Worldwide	S 19-a	
main oil companies	Worldwide	S 19-a	
Deliveries: new tankers: no & tonnage (of unfixed order)	Worldwide	S 19-a	
to major oil companies	Worldwide	S 19-a	
to private owners	Worldwide	S 19-a	
Distances per loaded voyage in miles	Worldwide	S 16-a	
Existing crude oil carrying capacity: tonnage	Worldwide	D 28-q	
Fleet tonnages: company-owned oil tankers	Worldwide	S 4-a	
independently-owned oil tankers	Worldwide	S 4-a	
Fleets (owned by major oil companies): tonnage & date of construction	Worldwide	S 19-a	
& name of tanker	Worldwide	S 19-a	
(privately-owned) by date of construction in dwt	Worldwide	S 19-a	
date charter expires in dwt	Worldwide	S 19-a	
name of charterer in dwt	Worldwide	S 19-a	
of owner in dwt	Worldwide	S 19-a	
in dwt	Worldwide	S 19-a	
List: tankers in service: ownership in dwt	Worldwide	S 19-a	
Name, age & tonnage owned & operated by specific oil companies	Worldwide	S 20-a	
by independent oil companies	Worldwide	S 20-a	
privately-owned oil tankers	Worldwide	S 20-a	
New construction by shipyard for oil companies in dwt	Worldwide	S 20-a	
for private companies in dwt	Worldwide	S 20-a	
delivery date & ownership in dwt	Worldwide	S 19-a	
No afloat by tonnage classes & as % of total tonnage	Worldwide	H 4-a	
by tonnage classes	EEC countries	E 43-a	
	Italy	H 4-a	
over 100,000 dwt	Worldwide	S 22-a	
by age groups	All countries	S 2-a	
independently-owned in service & on order	Worldwide	S 19-a	
on charter	Worldwide	C 14-a	
owned by oil companies	Worldwide	C 14-a	
No of motorships afloat	Worldwide	T 3-a	
oil tankers under construction (at 1st Jan) in dwt	All countries	C 14-a	
ships (incl total fleet) afloat in dwt	Norway	S 15-a	
by tonnage groups analysed by breadth in ft	Worldwide	S 2-a	
draught in ft	Worldwide	S 2-a	
length in ft	Worldwide	S 2-a	
steam-engined oil tankers afloat	Worldwide	T 3-a	
No & tonnage afloat by flag in dwt	Worldwide	S 2-a	
in dwt & as % of world fleets	Italy	H 4-a	

	Territorial coverage	Title codes	
TANKERS, OIL continued			
No & tonnage completed in dwt	Country of construction	S 3-q	S 1-a
diesel oil-engined oil tankers by loading space in cu ft by flag	Worldwide	S 16-a	
fuel oil-engined oil tankers by loading space in cu ft by flag	Worldwide	S 16-a	
laid up by flag in dwt	Worldwide	S 16-a	
launched in dwt	Country of construction	S 3-q	S 1-a
motorships afloat by flag in dwt	Worldwide	S 2-a	
oil-loading capacity in cu ft by flag	Worldwide	S 16-a	
on order (but not started) in dwt	All countries	S 3-q	
owned by major oil companies in service in dwt	Worldwide	S 20-a	
under construction in dwt	Worldwide	S 20-a	
registered by flag in dwt	OPEC member countries	C 3-a	
steamships afloat by flag in dwt	OPEC member countries	S 2-a	
under construction by shipyard in dwt	All countries	S 19-a	
in dwt	All countries	S 3-q	
Tonnage afloat in dwt & as % of total by age groups	Worldwide	H 4-a	
by age & by flag	Worldwide	C 14-a	
country of registration	Worldwide	R 5-a	
flag in dwt	Countries of registration	H 4-a	
year of build & engine type	Worldwide	C 14-a	
in dwt	Worldwide	H 4-a	
owned by independent companies	Worldwide	H 4-a	
by oil companies	Worldwide	H 4-a	
Tonnage: oil tankers scrapped in dwt	Worldwide	H 4-a	
under construction in dwt	Worldwide	E 14-a	H 4-a
Voyage charter fixtures: oil tankers by destination - index nos		S 16-m	
World fleets: oil tankers in service by flag	Worldwide	C 14-a	
in service in dwt	Worldwide	E 14-a	
tonnage launched in dwt	Worldwide	E 14-a	
no: oil tankers by size classes in oil company service	Worldwide	S 19-a	
on order by oil companies	Worldwide	S 19-a	
TANKERS BY AGE			
No & tonnage laid up	Worldwide	S 17-m	
No by size in dwt & by yr of build	Worldwide	C 3-a	
Tonnage afloat by flag as % of world fleet of tankers	Worldwide	D 28-a	
diesel-driven by yr of construction	Worldwide	S 4-a	
steam-driven by yr of construction	Worldwide	S 4-a	
by year of construction	Worldwide	S 22-a	
TANKERS BY SIZE			
Completions: no & tonnage	Japan & world regions	S 17-m	
No in dwt by year of construction		C 3-a	
steam & diesel-driven in dwt (company-owned)		S 4-a	
(independently-owned)		S 4-a	
under construction & dwt (company-owned)		S 17-m	
(independently-owned)		S 17-m	
TANKS & VATS			
see also CANS, METAL			
HOLLOWARE			
Production: containers made of any material: tonnage	All countries	U 22-a	
TANNERIES			
see also HIDES			
LEATHER INDUSTRY			
Calfskins & cattle hides processed: tonnage	Main countries	B 2-a	
Consumption: hides & skins by kind: tonnage	Main countries	B 9-a	
for leather production: tonnage	Main countries	B 9-a	
hides (domestic origin): tonnage	Netherlands	B 9-a	
(imported): tonnage	Netherlands	B 9-a	
Costs: salaried staff per mth	EEC countries	E 11-a	
Investment in buildings in local currency	EEC countries	E 40-a	
land purchase in local currency	EEC countries	E 40-a	
machinery in local currency	EEC countries	E 40-a	
Labour costs as % of total costs	EEC countries	E 8-a	
by status of employees in local currency	EEC countries	E 8-a	
per hr: all employees	EEC countries	E 11-a	
wage earners	EEC countries	E 11-a	
Labour force employed (total)	EEC countries	E 8-a	
Labour force: no of salaried staff employed	EEC countries	E 11-a	
of wage earners employed	EEC countries	E 11-a	
No of large tanneries in operation	W European countries & USA	A 18-a	
hrs worked by labour force per yr	EEC countries	E 8-a	
salaried staff per yr	EEC countries	E 11-a	
wage earners per yr	EEC countries	E 11-a	
TANNING BARK			
Production & exports: tonnage	All countries	A 23-a	
Tanning extracts see DYESTUFFS, SYNTHETIC			
Tantalite see COLUMBIAN ORE			

	Territorial coverage	Title codes
TANTALUM & NIOBIUM		
see also COLUMBIUM-TANTALUM CONCENTRATES		
% consumption in production of electronic components	USA	N 1-a
of machinery	USA	N 1-a
of nuclear reactors	USA	N 1-a
Consumption (based on content of concentrate): tonnage	USA	N 1-a
Exports in kg	W Germany & USA	T 4-a
Government strategic stockpile: carbide powder: tonnage	USA	N 1-a
columbiam: tonnage	USA	N 1-a
tantalum minerals: tonnage	USA	N 1-a
Import prices (at European ports) in $ per lb cif	European countries	T 4-m
Imports & exports by kind: tonnage	All countries	B 15-a
in kg	W Germany, UK & USA	T 4-a
Production by kind: tonnage	All countries	B 15-a
colombo-tantalite: tonnage	Zaire	E 41-a
niobium concentrates: tonnage	Canada	T 4-a
World production: niobium concentrates in lbs	Main countries	N 1-a
World reserves: tonnage (estim)	Main countries	N 1-a

Tap machines   see   MACHINE TOOLS, THREAD & TAP MACHINES

Tape recorders   see   SOUND RECORDERS

Tapioca   see   SAGO & TAPIOCA

TAR
see also COAL BY-PRODUCTS

	Territorial coverage	Title codes
Consumption: fuel distillate in production of manufactured gas: tonnage	European countries & USA	U 3-a
Exports by destination: tar distilled from coal, oil & natural gas by value in $	Main countries	U 2-a
by sea, inland waterways, road & rail: tonnage	European countries	U 8-a
Imports by sea, inland waterways, road & rail: tonnage	European countries	U 8-a
Production: coal tar (by chemical industry): tonnage	OECD countries	D 5-a
tonnage	All countries	B 15-a

TARGET PRICES
see also INTERVENTION PRICES

	Territorial coverage	Title codes	
Barley in £ per cwt	EEC countries	B 1-a	
Maize in £ per cwt	EEC countries	B 1-a	
Milk (3.7% fat content) in UA per 100 kg & in pence per gallon	EEC countries	B 3-a	
in pence per gallon equiv	EEC countries	B 1-a	B 3-a
Milk - index nos	EEC countries	B 3-a	
Minimum agreed price level: import prices for barley, maize, oats, sorghum & wheat in £ per ton	UK	B 8-a	
import prices for wheat flour in £ per ton	UK	B 8-a	
Olive oil in UA per ton	EEC countries	B 19-a	
price paid to producers in £ per ton	EEC countries	B 1-a	
Rapeseed & colza in £ per cwt	EEC countries	B 1-a	
in UA per ton	EEC countries	B 19-a	
Rice in £ per cwt	EEC countries	B 1-a	
Rye in £ per cwt	EEC countries	B 1-a	
Sugar (raw & refined) incl threshold prices in £ per ton	EEC countries	B 13-a	
(refined) in £ per cwt	EEC countries	B 1-a	
Sunflower seed in £ per cwt	EEC countries	B 1-a	
in UA per ton	EEC countries	B 19-a	
Wheat (durum) in £ per cwt	EEC countries	B 1-a	
(soft) in £ per cwt	EEC countries	B 1-a	

TAROS -

	Territorial coverage	Title codes
Export prices in $ per ton fob	Western Samoa	A 9-a

TAXATION
see also   CORPORATION TAX
EXCISE TAX
EXPORT DUTIES
IMPORT DUTIES
INCOME TAX
LAND TAXES
LICENCE FEES
MONOPOLY TAXES
P.A.Y.E.
PROFITS TAX
PURCHASE TAX
SALES TAXES
SELECTIVE EMPLOYMENT TAX
SOCIAL SECURITY LEVIES
STAMP DUTIES
SURTAX
TURNOVER TAXES
VALUE ADDED TAX
WEALTH TAXES

	Territorial coverage	Title codes
% change in government income from taxation	EEC countries	E 13-a
resulting from changes in gross national product	OECD countries	D 11

TAXATION, continued

Topic	Territorial coverage	Title codes	
% contribution to government income by kind of tax	Main countries	R 5-a	
% of government income arising from Company & Corporation taxes	Main countries	R 5-a	
Customs duties paid	Main countries	R 5-a	
Income tax (personal)	Main countries	R 5-a	
Inheritance taxes levied	Main countries	R 5-a	
taxes levied on consumption	Main countries	R 5-a	
Turnover taxes levied on sale of goods	Main countries	R 5-a	
taken by central authorities to cover public expenditure	All countries	M 6-a	
Elasticity of tax revenues associated with changes in the level of gross domestic product	OECD countries	D 42-a	
Government revenue & expenditure in local currency	OAS member countries	N 16-a	
(incl deficits) in $m	All countries	F 5-m	F 6-q
	Latin American countries	U 18-a	
Government tax revenue as % of gross domestic product	All countries	M 6-a	
	ECAFE countries	U 17	
	EEC countries	E 13-a	
	Main countries	E 3-a	
	OECD countries	D 42-a	
gross national product by kind of tax to yr 1969	OECD countries	D 11	
national income	All countries	M 6-a	
total government income	Main countries	E 3-a	
total OECD area revenue	OECD countries	D 42-a	
as component of Budget accounts in $m	Main countries	U 43-a	
of national income in local currency	OAS member countries	N 16-a	
by kind of tax as % of total public revenue	All countries	M 6-a	
	Main countries	E 3-a	
	OECD countries	D 42-a	
historical table in local currency	Main European countries	Z 1-a	
in local currency	EEC countries	E 42-a	
in $m	Asian, Far East & Australasian countries	U 45-a	
	Latin American countries	J 5-a	
	Main countries	E 3-a	
	OECD countries	D 30-a	D 42-a
	W Indies & Caribbean countries	T 6-a	
from: aerodrome landing charges for aircraft in local currency	EEC countries	E 31-a	
agricultural levies in local currency	EEC countries	E 42-a	
apprenticeship tax: rates & basis of assessment	EEC countries	E 31-a	
betting & gaming taxes in local currency	EEC countries	E 42-a	
rates & basis of assessment	EEC countries	E 31-a	
bills of exchange tax: rates & basis of assessment	EEC countries	E 31-a	
business profits tax: rates & basis of assessment	EEC countries	E 31-a	
capital assets & capital gains tax in local currency	EEC countries	E 42-a	
capital yields tax: rates & basis of assessment	EEC countries	E 31-a	
consumption tax: rates & basis of assessment	EEC countries	E 31-a	
corporation tax as % of gross national product	OECD countries	D 42-a	
of total government revenue	OECD countries	D 42-a	
in local currency	EEC countries	E 42-a	
	OAS member countries	N 16-a	
rates & basis of assessment	EEC countries	E 31-a	
customs duties: historical table from 1750 in local currency	Main European countries	Z 1-a	
in local currency	OAS member countries	N 16-a	
death duties in local currency	EEC countries	E 42-a	
diesel fuel tax (for motor vehicles) in local currency	Main countries	S 24-a	
direct & indirect taxes in $m	Latin American countries	U 18-a	
	OECD countries	D 30-a	
dividend tax: rates & basis of assessment	EEC countries	E 31-a	
entertainment tax: rates & basis of assessment	EEC countries	E 31-a	
estate duty: rates & basis of assessment	EEC countries	E 31-a	
excise duties: historical table from 1750 in local currency	Main European countries	Z 1-a	
in local currency	African countries	U 44-a	
levied on beer, matches, spirits & wine in £m	UK	E 42-a	
export duties in local currency	African countries	U 44-a	
fire insurance & fire service taxes: rates & basis of assessment	EEC countries	E 31-a	
gift tax: rates & basis of assessment	EEC countries	E 31-a	
import duties & excise duties in local currency	EEC countries	E 42-a	

TAXATION, continued

	Territorial coverage	Title codes
Government tax revenue from: import duties in local currency	African countries	U 44-a
income & profits taxes in local currency	EEC countries	E 42-a
income & wealth taxes as % of gross national product	OECD countries	D 42-a
as % of total government revenue	OECD countries	D 42-a
income tax (personal) in $m	W Indies & Caribbean countries	T 6-a
inheritance taxes in local currency	OAS member countries	N 16-a
rates & basis of assessment	EEC countries	E 31-a
interest payments, dividends & rents in $m	OECD countries	D 30-a
land taxes: historical table from 1750 in local currency	Main European countries	Z 1-a
(incl buildings) in local currency	EEC countries	E 42-a
lottery tax: rates & basis of assessment	EEC countries	E 31-a
lubricating oil tax (for motor vehicles) in local currency	Main countries	S 24-a
mineral royalty payments in local currency	African countries	U 44-a
	W Indies & Caribbean countries	T 6-a
monopoly taxes: historical table from 1845 in local currency	Main European countries	Z 1-a
mortgage taxes: rates & basis of assessment	EEC countries	E 31-a
motor vehicle taxes by kind of tax in local currency	Main countries	S 24-a
driving licence fees in local currency	Main countries	S 24-a
fuel taxes in local currency	Main countries	S 24-a
in £m	UK	V 1-a
goods vehicles purchase in £m	UK	V 1-a
import duties paid in local currency	Main countries	S 24-a
insurance taxes in local currency	Main countries	S 24-a
petrol tax in £m	UK	V 1-a
private cars in £m	UK	V 1-a
purchase tax paid	Main countries	S 24-a
purchase tax paid in £m	UK	V 1-a
rates & basis of assessment	EEC countries	E 31-a
re-sale taxes in local currency	Main countries	S 24-a
registration fees in local currency	Main countries	S 24-a
Road Fund taxes in local currency	Main countries	S 24-a
	EEC countries	E 42-a
road tractors in £m	UK	V 1-a
sales taxes in local currency	Main countries	S 24-a
taxis & hackney carriages in £m	UK	V 1-a
tyre taxes in local currency	Main countries	S 24-a
vehicles (luxury) taxes in local currency	Main countries	S 24-a
vehicle licencing fees in £m	UK	V 1-a
	Main countries	S 24-a
vehicle taxes as % of total government revenue	Main countries	S 24-a
	Main countries	U 18-a
oil royalty payments in $m	OPEC member countries	C 3-a
payroll tax: rates & basis of assessment	EEC countries	E 31-a
payroll, wealth & property taxes in $m	OECD countries	D 42-a
property tax in local currency	OAS member countries	N 16-a
rates & basis of assessment	EEC countries	E 31-a
profits tax: historical table from 1750 in local currency	Main European countries	Z 1-a
in local currency	EEC countries	E 42-a
	OAS member countries	N 16-a
in $m	Latin American countries	J 5-a
purchase tax in local currency	UK	E 42-a
real estate tax: rates & basis of assessment	EEC countries	E 31-a
road haulage tax: rates & basis of assessment	EEC countries	E 31-a
road vehicle taxes as % of total government revenue	Main countries	S 24-a

	Territorial coverage	Title codes
TAXATION, continued		
Government tax revenue from: sales taxes in local currency	OAS member countries	N 16-a
selective employment tax in £m	UK	E 42-a
social security taxes as % of total government revenue	All countries	M 6-a
spirits (alcoholic) taxes on sales: rates & basis of assessment	EEC countries	E 31-a
stamp duties in local currency	EEC countries	E 42-a
rates & basis of assessment	EEC countries	E 31-a
Stock Exchange: turnover taxes on share transfers in £m	UK	E 42-a
turnover taxes rates & basis of assessment	EEC countries	E 31-a
Surtax (on private incomes) in local currency	EEC countries	E 42-a
tobacco duties in local currency	EEC countries	E 42-a
transmission tax on wealth transfers: rates & basis of assessment	EEC countries	E 31-a
transport taxes levied on commercial vehicles in local currency	Main countries	S 24-a
turnover taxes: historical table from 1950 in local currency	Main European countries	Z 1-a
in local currency	EEC countries	E 42-a
Value Added Tax (VAT) in local currency	EEC countries	E 42-a
Wealth tax (incl tax on property ownership) as % of total government revenue	OECD countries	D 42-a
rates & basis of assessment	EEC countries	E 31-a
linked to output & paid to EEC area organisations in local currency	EEC countries	E 42-a
per capita in $	OECD countries	D 42-a
(total): all taxes (incl social levies) in local currency	EEC countries	E 26-m E 32-a
by kind of tax (in detail) in local currency	OECD countries	D 42-a
historical table from 1750 in local currency	Main European countries	Z 1-a
in local currency	AASM countries	E 41-a
	African countries	U 44-a
	EEC countries	E 13-a
	OAS member countries	N 16-a
	OPEC member countries	C 3-a
	W Indies & Caribbean countries	T 6-a
in $m	OECD countries	D 11
Levied on businesses as % of gross national product	EEC countries	E 42-a
betterment levies in local currency	All countries	M 6-a
corporations as % of total government revenue		
dividends & interest payments received on investments in local currency	EEC countries	E 42-a
farm tractor purchases in £m	UK	V 1-a
general consumption as % of gross national product	OECD countries	D 42-a
goods (specific) bought in $m	OECD countries	D 42-a
goods & services as % of gross national product	OECD countries	D 42-a
households as % of gross national product	OECD countries	D 11
in local currency	AASM countries	E 41-a
hydro-carbon oils in local currency	EEC countries	E 42-a
rents (from land ownership) in local currency	EEC countries	E 42-a
royalty payments received in local currency	EEC countries	E 42-a
services, land & buildings in local currency	EEC countries	E 42-a
specific oil-producing companies in $m	Worldwide	C 3-a
trade licences in £m	UK	V 1-a
vehicles (all kinds) in $m	Main countries	S 24-a
Rates & basis of assessment: taxes levied on advertising	EEC countries	E 31-a
appreciation of value: building sites	EEC countries	E 31-a
automatic amusement machines	EEC countries	E 31-a
bills	EEC countries	E 31-a
fees paid to Company directors	EEC countries	E 31-a
householders letting furnished accommodation	EEC countries	E 31-a
improvements made on property	EEC countries	E 31-a
incomes of farming community	EEC countries	E 31-a
of land-owning community	EEC countries	E 31-a
movable wealth	EEC countries	E 31-a
non-residents income	EEC countries	E 31-a
services of insurance brokers	EEC countries	E 31-a
TAXATION, INDIRECT		
% content of minimum retail prices: diesel oil	Main countries	S 24-a
	W European countries	C 14-a
motor spirit (petrol)	Main countries	S 24-a
	W European countries	C 14-a
% contribution to government income	Main countries	R 5-a

	Territorial coverage	Title codes
TAXATION, INDIRECT continued		
As % of gross national product to year 1969	OECD countries	D 11
of total government revenue	All countries	M 6-a
	Main countries	E 3-a
	OECD countries	D 11-a
As component of gross domestic product in local currency	EEC countries	E 32-a
of gross national product in local currency	Developing countries	D 25-a
	Main countries	R 5-a
By kind levied on agricultural producers - index nos	ECE countries	U 34-a
in $m	ECE countries	U 34-a
	EEC countries	E 44-a
on forestry undertakings in $m	EEC countries	E 44-a
(Incl land taxes) in $m	Czechoslovakia & Poland	U 34-a
(Net of subsidies) as cost factor in gross domestic product in local currency	African countries	U 44-a
by industrial origin in $m	S American countries	U 41-a
in local currency	OAS member countries	N 16-a
in $m	All countries	U 60-a
	OECD countries	D 30-a
Revenue (total) in local currency	African countries	U 44-a
	EEC countries	E 13-a
in $m	OAS member countries	N 16-a
Tax element: prices charged for domestic gas supply	EEC countries	E 15-a
retail prices: oils & fuel	EEC countries	E 17-q
petrol (for motor vehicles)	EEC countries	E 15-a

Taxes on monopolies   see   MONOPOLY TAXES

TAXI CABS

No of hackney carriages licenced by seating capacity	Great Britain	V 1-q
Registrations: new diesel-driven taxis	Main countries	V 4-a
new petrol-driven taxis	Main countries	V 4-a

TEA
    see also   INSTANT TEA
                 PLANTATIONS, TEA
                 YERBA MATÉ

% changes in retail sales	E European countries & USSR	U 16-a	
% contribution to export earnings	Rwanda, Uganda, Mauritius & Malawi	E 45-a	
Area harvested, production: tonnage & yield per ha	All countries	A 9-a	
under crop by main districts in ha	All countries	P 6-a	
estates & plantations (at end-yr) in ha	All countries	C 1-a	
in acres	Main countries	B 13-a	
in ha (incl yield by district in tons per ha)	India	P 6-a	
small holdings (at end-yr) in ha	All countries	C 1-a	
Auction prices (at Calcutta, Cochin & Colombo) in pence per lb	India & Sri Lanka	B 13-m	
(at Chittagong & Mombasa) in pence per lb	India & Kenya	B 13-a	
(at Colombo & Calcutta) in cents per lb	India & Sri Lanka	U 32-m	
tea by grade in pence per kg	UK	R 2-m	
ex Ceylon, India, Malawi & Kenya in pence per kg		B 2-a	
Consumption & demand projections to 1985: tonnage	Main countries	A 1	
Consumption in lbs	Main countries	B 13-a	
(incl world total): tonnage	Main countries	B 2-a	
per capita in decagrams	E European countries & USSR	U 16-a	
in kg per yr	Main countries	C 1-a	
in lbs per yr	Main countries	B 13-a	
tonnage & per capita in kg	Main countries	U 43-a	
tonnage	Main countries	C 1-a	
	OAS member countries	N 17-a	
Crop disposal: direct shipment of tea (to destinations excl UK): tonnage	India	P 6-a	
(to UK): tonnage	India	P 6-a	
tea auctioned in local markets: tonnage	India	P 6-a	
Crop yield by district in kg per ha	India	P 6-a	
Excise duties: rates charged	EEC countries	E 31-a	
Export duty (levied Colombo) in pence per lb	Sri Lanka	B 13-m	
Export prices (at Colombo & Calcutta) in Rs per kg	India & Sri Lanka	A 5-a	
in $ per 100 lbs	Sri Lanka	U 17-m	
in $ per ton	Brazil, India, Japan, Kenya & Malawi	A 9-a	
unit value in $ per 100 lbs	Indonesia	U 32-m	
Export prices - index nos (weighted average main sources)		U 29-q	U 54-q
Export quotas: black tea proposed by FAO: tonnage	All countries	C 1-a	
(internationally-agreed) in lbs	All countries	B 13-a	
Exports by destination by CST classes: tonnage & value in $	EEC countries	E 48-a	
SITC classes by value in $	Main countries	D 2-q	
tonnage & value in $	OECD countries	D 3-a2	
by value in Rs	India	P 6-a	
in lbs	Main countries	B 13-a	
tonnage	All countries	C 11-m	C 1-a
	E African countries, Indonesia & Sri Lanka	P 6-a	
	UK	C 11-m	
unit value in Rs per kg	India	P 6-a	
by NIMEXE classes: tonnage & value in $	All countries	E 20-a	
SITC classes: tonnage & value in $	All countries	U 50-a	U 59-a
by value as % of total exports	Main countries	B 13-a	
in $	All countries	C 1-a	
	Developing countries	U 11-a	
	India, Indonesia, Japan, Sri Lanka & S Vietnam	U 32-m	

	Territorial coverage	Title codes	
TEA, continued			
Exports by value in local currency	Main countries	B 13-a	
direct to UK (for London auction) ex India: tonnage		P 6-a	
(under private contract) ex India: tonnage		P 6-a	
in lbs	Main countries	B 13-a	
tonnage & value in $m	African countries, India & Sri Lanka	U 11-a	
	African, Caribbean countries & Pacific Is	E 45-a	
in $ per ton	Main countries	B 2-a	
(incl world total): tonnage	Main countries	A 5-a	
tonnage	All countries	C 1-a	P 6-a
	Asian & Far East area	U 32-q	
	India, Indonesia, Japan, Sri Lanka & S Vietnam	U 32-m	
(total) & shipments to EEC area: tonnage & value in UA	AASM countries	E 41-a	
unit value in cents per kg	African countries, India & Sri Lanka	A 5-a	U 11-a
Imports by NIMEXE classes: tonnage & value in $	All countries	E 20-a	
SITC classes: tonnage & value in $	All countries	U 50-a	U 59-a
by source: black tea by kind: tonnage	USA	C 11-m	C 1-a
by SITC classes by value in $	Main countries	D 2-q	
tonnage & value in $	OECD countries	D 3-a2	
green tea by kind: tonnage	USA	C 1-a	
in lbs	Main countries	B 13-a	
Oolong tea by quality: tonnage	USA	C 1-a	
passed by examiners for admission: tonnage	USA	C 1-a	
retained for consumption: tonnage	UK	C 1-a	
tonnage	Main countries	C 11-m	P 6-a
	All countries	C 1-a	
	UK	C 11-m	
by value in local currency	Afghanistan	U 32-m	
green tea (ex Japan): tonnage	USA	C 11-m	
in lbs	Main countries	B 13-a	
Oolong tea: tonnage	USA	C 11-m	
tonnage	Main countries	A 11-a	
Price quotations (at London auctions) in pence per kg	UK	C 1-m	
Producer prices received in $ per ton	Japan, Kenya, Peru & Uganda	A 9-a	
Production & export availability: forecast to 1975	Main world regions	A 1	
Production & exports: Commonwealth countries as % of world totals		B 13-a	
by main districts: tonnage	All countries	P 6-m	
by regions: tonnage	Main countries	C 1-a	
green, orthodox & legg-cut grades: tonnage	India	P 6-a	
harvested (incl world total): tonnage	All countries	R 5-a	
in lbs	Main countries incl China	B 13-a	
(incl world total): tonnage	Main countries	B 2-a	
on plantations & estate factories: tonnage	Main countries	U 43-a	
tonnage	All countries	C 11-m	
	Argentina, Brazil & Peru	U 40-a	
	Asian & Far East countries	U 32-a	
	Cameroun, Mauritius, Rwanda & Zaire	E 41-a	
	India, Indonesia, Japan, Pakistan & Sri Lanka	U 32-q	
Re-exports (by countries of origin & destination: tonnage	Main countries	A 5-a	P 6-a
by destination: tonnage	UK	P 6-a	
Retail prices (comparative) in $ per kg	Netherlands, UK & USSR	C 1-a	
in local currency	EEC countries	Z 3-a	
Sales (at auctions) by source (at London Tea Market): tonnage	OAS member countries	N 17-a	
(at Antwerp, Hamburg & London markets): tonnage	UK	C 11-w	
leaf tea at Calcutta by quality in chests	India	C 1-a	
at Calcutta, Cochin, Colombo: tonnage	India & Sri Lanka	P 6-a	
at Chittagong & Mombasa: tonnage	India & Kenya	C 11-w	
tonnage	Bangladesh, India & Sri Lanka	C 1-a	
tea dust (at Calcutta, Cochin & Mombasa): tonnage	India & Kenya	C 11-w	
tonnage	Bangladesh, India & Sri Lanka	C 1-a	
at local auctions: leaf tea by quality: tonnage	India	P 6-a	
at London auctions by source of consignment: tonnage	UK	P 6-a	
green, orthodox, legg-cut & Darjeeling grades: tonnage	India	P 6-a	
leaf tea & tea dust: tonnage	India	P 6-m	
Stocks afloat (en route to UK port): tonnage		P 6-m	
entered for Customs clearance: tonnage	UK	C 11-m	
(excl primary wholesaler stocks): tonnage	UK	C 1-m	
held at private warehouses & at ports: tonnage	India	C 1-q	
at public warehouses & at ports: tonnage	India	C 1-q	
at warehouses & at ports: tonnage	Bangladesh & Sri Lanka	C 1-a	
by primary wholesalers (at end-period): tonnage	UK	C 1-q	C 11-q
(end-yr): tonnage	India, Pakistan, Sri Lanka & UK	B 2-a	
in bonded warehouses (at end-mth): tonnage	UK	C 11-m	P 6-m
in lbs	Bangladesh, India, Sri Lanka & UK	B 13-q	
Supply, production, consumption, imports & exports: tonnage	EEC countries	B 1-a	
Wholesale prices at Hamburg auction in DM per 500 grammes	W Germany	C 1-a	
(average): leaf & dust by district in Rs per kg	India	P 6-m	
by grade (at London auctions) in pence per kg	UK	P 6-a	
by kind (at Calcutta sales) in Rs per kg	India	P 6-a	
by source (at London auctions) in pence per kg	UK	C 1-a	
in pence per lb	UK	B 13-m	
(ex India, Africa & Sri Lanka) in pence per kg	UK	A 5-a	
(ex Indonesia) at Antwerp auction in pence per kg	Belgium	C 1-a	
leaf tea (by districts) in local currency per kg	Main countries	A 9-a	C 1-a
in local currency per kg	Main countries	C 11-w	C 1-a
in Rs per kg	India	P 6-a	
tea dust by districts in local currency per kg	Main countries	C 1-a	
in cents per kg	India, Sri Lanka & UK	U 27-m	

	Territorial coverage	Title codes
TEA, continued		
World consumption in lbs (excl USSR, China, Iran & Japan)	Worldwide	B 13-a
tonnage	Main countries	B 2-a
World demand per capita per yr projected to 1985	Main countries	A 1
World exports by value in $m	World regions	A 5-a
World market prices: auction price in £ per 100 kg (on London market)	UK	E 34-m
in cents per lb		B 13-a
World market prices - index nos		G 1-a
World production: tonnage	Main countries	U 11-a
World stocks (at end-yr): tonnage		G 1-a
World supply & absorption in lbs		B 13-a
(excl USSR, China, Iran & Japan)	Worldwide	B 13-a

Tea bags   see   INSTANT TEA

TEA DUST

	Territorial coverage	Title codes
Sales at auctions at Calcutta, Cochin & Chittagong: tonnage	India	C 11-w
at Calcutta by kind in chests	India	P 6-a
tonnage	Bangladesh, Ceylon & India	C 1-a
by kind in local districts: tonnage	India	P 6-a
Wholesale prices at district auctions in local currency per kg	Main countries	C 11-w
in Rs per kg	India	P 6-a
in local currency per kg	Main countries	C 1-a
by kind of tea at Calcutta sales in Rs per kg	India	P 6-a

Tea estates   see   PLANTATIONS, TEA

TEACHER TRAINING

	Territorial coverage	Title codes
Expenditure per student-teacher - index nos	All countries	U 62-a
in $	All countries	U 62-a
No of lecturers employed by sex in training colleges	All countries	U 62-a
of student-teachers by age of admission & duration of courses	All countries	U 62-a
by grade & age in yrs	All countries	U 62-a
by sex enrolled in colleges	All countries	U 62-a
enrolled & % female	All countries	U 62-a

Teacher training colleges   see   COLLEGES, VOCATIONAL

TEACHERS

	Territorial coverage	Title codes
% of unqualified teachers employed in primary schools	ECAFE countries	U 17-a
in secondary schools	ECAFE countries	U 17-a
No of academically-qualified teachers employed in secondary schools	Latin American countries	J 5-a
of teachers employed by grade & by kind of educational institution	African countries	U 44-a
as % of total employment in teaching profession	World regions	U 62
grade - index nos	World regions	U 62-a
grade	Asian, Far East & Australasian countries	U 45-a
kind of school: urban & rural	Latin American countries	J 5-a
	W Indies & Caribbean countries	T 6-a
sex by kind of school	Latin American countries	J 5-a
by teaching specialisation	Latin American countries	J 5-a
in adult education institutes	Latin American countries	J 5-a
elementary evening institutes	OAS member countries	N 19-a
higher education & universities	Latin American countries	J 5-a
kindergarten	All countries	U 62-a
primary schools	OAS member countries	N 19-a
schools for adult illiteracy	OAS member countries	N 19-a
for blind pupils	OAS member countries	N 19-a
for deaf-mutes	OAS member countries	N 19-a
for physically-handicapped pupils	OAS member countries	N 19-a
for mentally-retarded pupils	OAS member countries	N 19-a
primary schools	All countries	U 62-a
secondary schools	OAS member countries	N 19-a
special schools	All countries	U 62-a
training centres (for adults)	OAS member countries	N 19-a
in continuation schools (for adults)	OAS member countries	N 19-a
high schools & universities	AASM countries	E 41-a
primary & secondary schools	African countries	U 44-a
schools: all staff	AASM countries	E 41-a
historical table from 1842	Main European countries	Z 1-a
secondary schools: all staff	AASM countries	E 41-a
historical table from 1841	Main European countries	Z 1-a
teacher training colleges	African countries	U 44-a
	AASM countries	E 41-a
technical colleges & universities	African countries	U 44-a
vocational training centres (for adults)	OAS member countries	N 19-a
	African countries	U 44-a
	AASM countries	E 41-a
	AASM countries	E 41-a
Pupil-teacher ratios: primary schools	OAS member countries	N 19-a
private schools	OAS member countries	N 19-a
public schools	All countries	U 62-a
Salaries: teachers as % of total costs of education	All countries	U 62-a

	Territorial coverage	Title codes

Teak see HARDWOOD, SAWN

TECHNICAL ASSISTANCE

A.I.D. appropriations in $m	All countries	M 1-a
costs of commodities supplied ex US sources in $m	Recipient countries	M 1-a
on contract in $m	Recipient countries	M 1-a
contract staff service payments in $m	Recipient countries	M 1-a
direct staff service payments in $m	Recipient countries	M 1-a
indirect staff service payments in $m	Recipient countries	M 1-a
grants to assist agriculture in $m	Recipient countries	M 1-a
education in $m	Recipient countries	M 1-a
housing projects in $m	Recipient countries	M 1-a
industry & mining projects in $m	Recipient countries	M 1-a
labour supply projects in $m	Recipient countries	M 1-a
power supply improvement schemes in $m	Recipient countries	M 1-a
public administration in $m	Recipient countries	M 1-a
sanitation projects in $m	Recipient countries	M 1-a
social welfare projects in $m	Recipient countries	M 1-a
transportation improvements in $m	Recipient countries	M 1-a
technical support grants in $m	Recipient countries	M 1-a
Bilateral disbursements in $m	Main countries	D 7-a
Costs incurred by European Development Fund in UA	Developing countries	E 19-a
Disbursements by major recipients in $m	USA	D 13-a
by European Development Fund in $m		D 13-a
on appointment of administrators in $m	Main countries	D 7-a
advisors in $m	Main countries	D 7-a
experts & volunteers in $m	Main countries	D 7-a
personnel by kind in $m	OECD countries	D 13-a
students & trainees in $m	Main countries	D 7-a
teachers in $m	Main countries	D 7-a
European Development Fund: aid by project (in detail) in UA	Developing countries	E 19-a
Expenditure ex European Development Fund appropriations in UA	AASM countries	E 41-a
Granted through US aid organisations in $m		R 5-a
No of experts, advisers & teachers used	OECD countries	D 13-a
	Main countries	D 7-a
of months of activity of advisors & experts	Main countries	D 7-a
students, trainees & volunteers	Main countries	D 7-a
of students & trainees used: local & foreign	OECD countries	D 13-a
Public disbursements in $m	Main countries	D 7-a

TECHNICAL ASSISTANCE, BILATERAL

see also A.I.D.
BILATERAL AID
DEVELOPMENT AID
MULTILATERAL AID

Disbursements in $m	OECD countries	D 13-a

Technical colleges see COLLEGES, TECHNICAL

Technical oils see CASTOR OIL
LINSEED OIL
OITICICA OIL
TUNG OIL

TECHNICIANS

see also SCIENTISTS

% engaged in research projects	All countries	U 62-a
No engaged by A.I.D.: directly-employed	All countries	M 1-a
indirectly-employed	All countries	M 1-a
working on contract	All countries	M 1-a
on overseas aid programs	All countries	M 1-a
in research & development	All countries	U 62-a
per 10,000 total population	All countries	U 62-a

Technology see RESEARCH & DEVELOPMENT

TELECOMMUNICATIONS EQUIPMENT

see also ELECTRONIC EQUIPMENT
TELEPHONE EXCHANGES

% of world exports shipped to developed countries		U 38-a	
to developing countries		U 38-a	
Consumption: tonnage	Central African countries	U 38	
Domestic sales by value in £m	UK	B 24-a	
Exports by destination by kind: tonnage & value in $m	All countries	U 9-a	U 12-a
NIMEXE classes by kind by value in $m	All countries	E 20-a	
SITC classes by kind by value in $m	All countries	U 50-a	U 59-a
value in $m	All countries	U 38-a	
in $m & % growth rates	Main countries	U 38-a	
Home sales: telephone exchanges	UK	B 24-a	
Imports by NIMEXE classes by kind by value in $m	All countries	E 20-a	
SITC classes by kind by value in $m	All countries	U 50-a	U 59-a
source by kind: tonnage & value in $m	All countries	U 12-a	
value in $m	All countries	U 38-a	
Production by value in £m	UK	B 24-a	
Size of market by value in £m	European countries	B 24	
World Bank loans & credits for telecommunication projects in $m	Worldwide	M 3-a	
World exports by value in $m		U 38-a	

	Territorial coverage	Title codes
TELEGRAMS		
No despatched: historical table from 1848	Main European countries	Z 1-a
to home & overseas addresses	All countries	U 43-a
	OAS member countries	N 15-a
to home addresses	Main countries	R 5-a
(total)	All countries	S 18-a
	Asian, Far East & Australasian countries	U 45-a
No of full-rate telegrams despatched overseas	All countries	S 18-a
of letter-telegrams despatched overseas	All countries	S 18-a
of phototelegrams despatched overseas	All countries	S 18-a

TELEGRAPH SERVICE
  see also   RADIO COMMUNICATIONS
             TELEX SERVICE

No of phototelegrams sent to domestic addresses	All countries	S 18-a

Telemetry equipment   see   ELECTRONIC EQUIPMENT

TELEPHONE EXCHANGES		
Export installation by value in £m	UK	B 24-a
Home installation by value in £m projected to 1977	UK	B 24-a
IBRD loans approved for installation of telephone exchanges in $	OAS member countries	N 16-a
IDB loans approved for installation of telephone exchanges in $	OAS member countries	N 16-a
TELEPHONE SERVICE		
Wage rates: engineers per hr in local currency	OAS member countries	N 17-a
linesmen per hr in local currency	OAS member countries	N 17-a

TELEPHONES
  see also   RADIO COMMUNICATIONS

No of telephones in service & % growth rates	Main countries	S 25-a
& as % of world total	Continents	S 25-a
& no per 100 population installed	Latin American countries	J 5-a
per 1000 population installed	Main countries	E 3-a
& per capita of total population by administrative areas	EEC countries	E 38-a
& population served	OAS member countries	N 15-a
connected with Bell system	Continents	S 25-a
for business purposes	All countries	S 25-a
for private household use	All countries	S 25-a
manually-operated	All countries	S 18-a
	Continents	S 25-a
on automatic exchanges	Continents	S 25-a
	All countries	S 18-a
per 1000 population	All countries	U 43-a
	Developing countries	U 23-a
	ECE countries	U 15-a
per 100 population	All countries	S 18-a
	OAS member countries	N 15-a
with extension & p.b.x.	All countries	S 25-a
(total)	African countries	U 44-a
	Asian, Far East & Australasian countries	U 45-a
	Countries (with minimum of half million in use)	S 25-a
	Latin American countries	U 40-a
	Main countries	R 5-a
	W Indies & Caribbean countries	T 6-a
installed in world's largest cities & installed per 100 population		S 25-a
No of telephone calls made: historical table from 1864 in million	Main European countries	Z 1-a
inter-urban calls (pulse-metered)	All countries	S 25-a
(total)	All countries	S 25-a
	All countries	S 18-a
local & overseas calls	OAS member countries	N 15-a
calls (pulse-metered)	All countries	S 25-a
(total)	All countries	S 25-a
long-distance calls	OAS member countries	N 15-a
on fixed charge basis	All countries	S 18-a
overseas calls (outgoing)	All countries	S 25-a
recorded automatically	All countries	S 18-a
recorded manually	All countries	S 18-a
per capita per yr	OAS member countries	N 15-a
total (pulse-metered)	All countries	S 18-a
(recorded automatically)	All countries	S 18-a
(recorded manually)	All countries	S 18-a
Production: telephone instruments: volume	All countries	U 22-a
	Canada, European countries, Japan & USA	U 38-a

Telescopes   see   OPTICAL INSTRUMENTS

Television advertising   see   ADVERTISING BY MEDIA

TELEVISION RECEIVERS
  see also   RADIO RECEIVERS

% changes in retail sales	E European countries	U 16-a
% of households owning a set by social classes	W European countries	Z 3

	Territorial coverage	Title codes
TELEVISION RECEIVERS, continued		
Exports by destination by CST classes: tonnage & value in $m	EEC countries	E 48-a
SITC classes by value in $m	Main countries	D 2-q
tonnage & value in $m	OECD countries	D 3-a2
by value in $m	Main countries	U 9-a
NIMEXE classes by value in $m	All countries	E 20-a
SITC classes by value in $m	All countries	U 50-a U 59-a
value in $m	All countries	U 38-a
(incl estimate for 1977) in $m	UK	B 24-a
volume	OECD countries	D 9-a
Home sales by value (incl estim for 1977) in £m	UK	B 24-a
Imports by NIMEXE classes by value in $m	All countries	E 20-a
SITC classes by value in $m	All countries	U 50-a U 59-a
source by CST classes: tonnage & value in $m	EEC countries	E 21-a
SITC classes by value in $m	Main countries	D 2-q
tonnage & value in $m	OECD countries	D 3-a2
value in $m	All countries	U 38-a
(incl estimate for 1977) in £m	UK	B 24-a
volume	OECD countries	D 9-a
No of television sets in use & no of licences issued	All countries	U 62-a
per 1000 population	OAS member countries	N 19-a
	All countries	U 43-a
	ECE countries	U 15-a
	Latin American countries	J 5-a
	OECD countries	R 5-a
	Main countries	E 3-a
by areas	EEC countries	E 38-a
in use	African countries	U 44-a
	Asian, Far East & Australasian countries	U 45-a
	Main countries	R 5-a
of licences issued to users: historical table from 1947	Main European countries	Z 1-a
Production by value (incl estim for 1977) in £m	UK	B 24-a
volume	African countries	U 44-a
	All countries	U 22-a U 43-a
	E European countries & USSR	U 16-a
	European countries, Japan & USA	U 38-a
	Main countries	R 5-a
	OAS member countries	N 14-a
Sales demand per 1000 population	E European countries	U 16-a
World exports by value in $m		U 38-a
TELEVISION TRANSMITTERS		
No of private transmitters in service	All countries	U 62-a
transmitters controlled by public corporations in service	All countries	U 62-a
transmitters (all kinds) in service	OAS member countries	N 19-a
	Latin American countries	J 5-a
	World regions	U 62-a
Television tubes see ELECTRONIC TUBES		
TELEVISION		
% of adults viewing television programs by no of hrs per wk	W European countries	Z 3
by social classes	W European countries	Z 3
No of hrs of locally-produced television broadcasts	All countries	U 62-a
TELEX SERVICE		
No of chargeable minutes of telex service	All countries	S 18-a
circuits installed	Asian, Far East & Australasian countries	U 45-a
domestic telex connections by subscribers	All countries	S 18-a
overseas telex connections by subscribers	All countries	S 18-a
TELLURIUM		
% consumption in production of chemical products	USA	N 1-a
of iron & steel products	USA	N 1-a
of non-ferrous metal products	USA	N 1-a
of rubber products	USA	N 1-a
Consumption in lbs	USA	N 1-a
Production (as by-product of electro-copper refining) in lbs	USA	N 1-a
in kg	Canada, Japan, Peru & USA	T 4-a
in lbs	USA	J 6-a
tonnage	Canada, Japan, Peru & USA	B 15-a
Wholesale prices in $ per lb	Worldwide (excl Communist countries)	C 30-a
(lump & powder) in £ per lb	USA	N 1-a
(slab form) in $ per lb	UK	T 4-a
World production in lbs	USA	T 4-m
tonnage	Main countries	N 1-a
		N 4-a
TEMPERATURE		
see also RAINFALL		
Average during winter in degrees centigrade	European cities	U 10-a
(in centigrade & fahrenheit) in degrees by region	OAS member countries	N 11-a
Mean air temperature: range in degrees centigrade	All countries	R 5
Minima & maxima in degrees centigrade by region	OAS member countries	N 11-m
Tenure, agricultural see AGRICULTURAL HOLDINGS		

	Territorial coverage	Title codes	

TERMS OF TRADE

Based on unit values expressed in $

	Main countries	G 1-a	
	ECAFE countries	U 32-m	

Index nos (excl petroleum fuels)
    manufactured goods
    projections (tentative)
    (see no. 2, 5, 8, 11)
        unit value basis
Index nos

		U 23-a	
	Developing countries	U 23-a	
	World regions	U 27-a	
	World regions	U 23-a	
	African countries	U 44-a	
	All countries	M 6-a	
	Asian, Far East & Australasian countries	U 45-a	
	Developing African countries	U 39-irr	
	ECE countries	U 42-m	
	EEC countries	E 22-m	E 26-m
		E 22-a	
	Main European countries	U 16-q	
	World regions	M 4-a	U 23-a

Ternary   see   FERTILISERS, MIXED

Terylene   see   POLYESTER

Testing equipment   see   SCIENTIFIC INSTRUMENTS

Textbooks   see   BOOKS

TEXTILE FABRICS

see also   FABRICS
           WOVEN COTTON FABRICS
           WOVEN JUTE FABRICS
           WOVEN LINEN FABRICS
           WOVEN SILK FABRICS
           WOVEN WOOLLEN FABRICS
           WOVEN WORSTED FABRICS

Exports by value in $m	Hong Kong, Japan & S Korea	U 32-m	
Imports by value in $m	Afghanistan, Indonesia & S Vietnam	U 32-m	
Production: clothing & leather - index nos	OECD countries	D 19-m	D 20-m
- index nos	African countries	U 44-a	
Wholesale prices by kind in local currency per ton	OAS member countries	N 17-a	
- index nos	Thailand	U 32-m	

TEXTILE FIBRES

see also   ABACA
           CELLULOSIC FIBRES
           FLAX
           HARD FIBRES
           HEMP
           JUTE
           MAN-MADE FIBRES
           NON-CELLULOSIC FIBRES
           POLYESTER
           SILK, RAW

% of consumption for production of clothing	European countries & USA	U 26-a	
of motor vehicle tyres	European countries & USA	U 26-a	
for household purposes	European countries & USA	U 26-a	
for technical purposes	European countries & USA	U 26-a	
Export prices - index nos (weighted average main sources)		U 29-q	U 44-q
Exports by value in $m	W European countries	U 33-a	
(incl yarns) by value in $m	Asian & Far East countries	U 32-a	
Imports by value in $m	W European countries	U 33-a	
raw materials by value in yen million	Japan	U 32-m	
Production (all kinds): historical table from 1909: tonnage	Main countries	C 4-a	

TEXTILE FIBRES BY KIND

% change in trade	Developing countries	A 1-a	
Consumption in production of clothing: tonnage	EEC countries	K 4-a	
of household textile products: tonnage	EEC countries	K 4-a	
per capita in kg	Main countries	U 26-a	
tonnage	OAS member countries	N 17-a	
Exports by destination by CST classes: tonnage & value in $	EEC countries	E 48-a	
SITC classes by value in $	Main countries	D 2-q	
tonnage & value in $	OECD countries	D 3-a2	
NIMEXE classes by value in $	All countries	E 20-a	
SITC classes by value in $	All countries	U 50-a	U 59-a
shipped to EEC & non-EEC areas by value in $	EEC countries	E 24-a	
Imports by NIMEXE classes by value in $	All countries	E 20-a	
SITC classes by value in $	All countries	U 50-a	U 59-a
source by CST classes: tonnage & value in $	EEC countries	E 21-a	
SITC classes by value in $	Main countries	D 2-q	
tonnage & value in $	OECD countries	D 3-a2	
shipped ex EEC & non-EEC areas by value in $	EEC countries	E 24-a	
Wholesale prices in local currency in tons	OAS member countries	N 17-a	
World production: tonnage		K 4-a	

	Territorial coverage	Title codes

TEXTILE INDUSTRY
    see also CARPET MANUFACTURING INDUSTRY
                 CLOTHING INDUSTRY
                 KNITTING MILLS
                 SPINNING & WEAVING INDUSTRY

	Territorial coverage	Title codes	
% contribution to gross national product	Canada, European countries, Japan & USA	U 38-a	
% share of capital investment	E European countries	U 16-a	
of industrial production	European countries, Japan & USA	U 38-a	
Capacity installed: combs, looms & spindles by kind	Main countries	K 6-a	
Capital expenditure by sector in £m	UK	B 29-a	
Consumption: acetate fibres: tonnage	OECD countries	D 46-a	
acrylic fibres: tonnage	OECD countries	D 46-a	
artificial fibres by kind: tonnage	OECD countries	D 46-a	
cotton fibres (at mills) in lbs	UK	B 29-a	
cotton waste: tonnage	OECD countries	D 46-a	
electricity by area in kWh	EEC countries	E 38-a	
in kWh	OECD countries	D 8-a	
fibres (for carpets): tonnage	Main countries	K 4-a	
(for knitting): tonnage	Main countries	K 4-a	
(for weaving): tonnage	Main countries	K 4-a	
flax tow: tonnage	OECD countries	D 46-a	
hemp, tow & sisal: tonnage	OECD countries	D 46-a	
jute: tonnage	OECD countries	D 46-a	
man-made fibre waste & tops: tonnage	OECD countries	D 46-a	
man-made fibres (at mills) in lbs	UK	B 29-a	
manila hemp: tonnage	OECD countries	D 46-a	
manufactured gas by volume in cu ft	European countries & USA	U 3-a	
polyamide fibres: tonnage	OECD countries	D 46-a	
polyester: fibres: tonnage	OECD countries	D 46-a	
raw cotton: tonnage	OECD countries	D 46-a	
scutched flax: tonnage	OECD countries	D 46-a	
silk waste: tonnage	OECD countries	D 46-a	
sulphuric acid: tonnage	OECD countries	D 5-a	
synthetic fibres by kind: tonnage	OECD countries	D 46-a	
virgin wool: tonnage	OECD countries	D 46-a	
viscose fibres: tonnage	OECD countries	D 46-a	
wool & animal hair (at mills): tonnage	UK	B 29-a	
wool (at carding stage): tonnage	European countries	B 10-a	
wool tops: tonnage	OECD countries	D 46-a	
Costs: salaried staff per mth	EEC countries	E 11-a	
Earnings by administrative areas in $ per hr	EEC countries	E 38-a	
by sex in local currency per hr	Main countries	R 3-a	
in pence per hr (equiv)	EEC countries	B 29	
in local currency per hr	All countries	L 4-a	
Electricity consumption (incl leather industry) in kWh	All countries	C 23-a	
Employment by occupational sectors by regions	UK	B 29-a	
Exports (incl leather) by region of origin: tonnage	EEC countries	E 38-a	
Female earnings as % of male earnings in textile industry	EEC countries	B 29	
Fixed capital investment by administrative areas in $	EEC countries	E 38-a	
Frequency of accidents at work in textile industry	EEC countries	E 2-a	
Gross value of output in textile industry in local currency	OECD countries	D 46-a	
IDA loans for improving facilities in $	OAS member countries	N 16-a	
Investment in $m	OECD countries	D 46-a	
Labour costs: all employees per hr	EEC countries	E 11-a	
as % of total costs	EEC countries	E 8-a	
by administrative areas in $ per hr	EEC countries	E 38-a	
by status of employees in local currency	EEC countries	E 8-a	
in pence per hr	EEC countries	B 29	
wage earners per hr	EEC countries	E 11-a	
wool & cotton processing per hr	EEC countries	E 2-a	
No of establishments in operation	African countries	U 44-a	
hrs worked by labour force per yr	EEC countries	E 8-a	
hrs worked per wk	OECD countries	D 46-a	
	All countries	L 4-a	
	EEC countries	B 29	E 25-a
	OAS member countries	N 18-a	
per yr: salaried staff	EEC countries	E 11-a	
wage earners	EEC countries	E 11-a	
operatives employed	EEC countries	E 2-a	
	Main countries	U 21-a	
	OECD countries	D 46-a	
employed by area	EEC countries	E 38-a	
(incl leather industry)	OECD countries	D 23-a	
operatives employed - index nos	All countries	L 4-a	
salaried staff employed	EEC countries	E 11-a	
wage earners & salaried staff employed	EEC countries	E 8-a	
employed	EEC countries	E 11-a	
paid annual holidays in days	EEC countries	B 29	
working days lost per employee	UK	B 29-a	
Production as % of general world activity		U 38	
Production - index nos (quantum basis)	S American countries	U 40-a	
	Asian & Far East countries	U 32-q	
	Australia, India & Japan	U 32-q	
	ECE countries	U 42-m	
	EEC countries	E 26-m	E 28-q
		E 27-a	
	Australia, European countries & USA	D 46-a	
	Latin American countries	J 5-a	
	Main countries	R 5-a	
	OAS member countries	N 14-a	

	Territorial coverage	Title codes
TEXTILE INDUSTRY, continued		
Shortage of skilled labour in textile production by sector	UK	B 29
Wage rates by sector in Esc per day	Portugal	R 4-q
by sex in local currency per hr	EEC countries	E 25-a2
	Main countries	R 3-m C 7-a
cotton fibre combers in local currency per hr	OAS member countries	N 17-a
cotton operatives in local currency per hr	OAS member countries	N 17-a
cotton spinners & weavers in local currency per hr	OAS member countries	N 17-a
skilled workers by sex in local currency per hr	Main countries	R 4-q
unskilled workers by sex in local currency per hr	Main countries	R 4-q
Wage rates - index nos	EEC countries	E 26-a2
	Main countries	R 3-a
TEXTILE INDUSTRY, COTTON		
% projected productivity increase to 1977	UK	B 29
Investment in buildings in local currency	EEC countries	E 40-a
in land purchase in local currency	EEC countries	E 40-a
in machinery purchase in local currency	EEC countries	E 40-a
Labour costs as % of total costs	EEC countries	E 8-a
by status of employees in local currency	EEC countries	E 8-a
Labour force employed projected to 1977	UK	B 29-a
Labour force: no of salaried staff employed	EEC countries	E 11-a
of wage earners employed	EEC countries	E 11-a
of wage earners & salaried staff employed	EEC countries	E 8-a
No of hrs worked by employees per wk	EEC countries	E 25-a
	Main countries	R 3-m
per yr	EEC countries	E 8-a
	W European countries	K 2-a
loom-hrs worked per yr	All countries	K 5-a
	W European countries	K 2-a
looms in use	All countries	K 5-a
	W European countries	K 2-a
installed	All countries	K 5-a
installed & in use	OECD countries	D 46-a
spindle-hrs worked per yr	All countries	K 5-a
	W European countries	K 2-a
spindles in use	All countries	K 5-a
	W European countries	K 2-a
installed	All countries	K 5-a
installed & in use	OECD countries	D 46-a
Wage rates by sex in local currency per hr	Main countries	R 3-m
in local currency per hr	EEC countries	E 25-a2
Wages: costs (in Bombay mills) in Rs per mth	India	U 32-m
TEXTILE INDUSTRY, WOOLLEN		
% productivity increase projected to 1977	UK	B 29
% raw material used (at carding stage)	Main countries	A 5-a
Capital expenditure in £m	UK	B 29-a
Exports by value in $m	Main countries	A 5-a
Investment in buildings in local currency	EEC countries	E 40-a
in land purchase in local currency	EEC countries	E 40-a
in machinery in local currency	EEC countries	E 40-a
Labour costs as % of total costs	EEC countries	E 8-a
by status of employees in local currency	EEC countries	E 8-a
Labour force employed projected to 1977	UK	B 29-a
Labour force: no of salaried staff employed	EEC countries	E 11-a
of wage earners employed	EEC countries	E 11-a
of wage earners & salaried staff employed	EEC countries	E 8-a
No of hrs worked per wk	EEC countries	E 25-a
	Main countries	R 3-m
per yr	EEC countries	E 8-a
looms installed	OECD countries	D 46-a
spindles installed & no in use	OECD countries	D 46-a
Wage rates by sex in local currency per hr	Main countries	R 3-m
in local currency per hr	EEC countries	E 25-a2
TEXTILE MACHINERY		
% share of world exports held	UK	B 27-a
% of world exports shipped to developed countries		U 38-a
to developing countries		U 38-a
Consumption: tonnage	Central African countries	U 38
Exports (incl leather-working machinery) by value in $m	Main countries	U 38-a
tonnage	OECD countries	D 9-a
Imports by value in $m	All countries	U 38-a
No of automatic spinning frames in operation: jute industry	W European countries	C 22-a
cotton spindles in use: historical table from 1834	Main European countries	Z 1-a
loom-hrs worked: cotton industry	W European countries	K 2-q
looms (automatic) in use	W European countries	K 2-a
installed	W European countries	K 2-a
(circular) in operation: jute industry	W European countries	C 22-a
in use: cotton mills	World regions	K 5-a
	OAS member countries	N 14-a
	W European countries	K 2-a
installed: cotton industry	OECD countries	D 46-a
woollen industry	OECD countries	D 46-a
(rectilinear) in use: jute industry	W European countries	C 22-a
(standard) in use	W European countries	K 2-a
installed	W European countries	K 2-a

	Territorial coverage	Title codes	
TEXTILE MACHINERY, continued			
No of looms (standard & automatic) in use	W European countries	K 2-a	
manual spinning frames in use: jute industry	W European countries	C 22-a	
spindle-hrs worked: cotton industry	W European countries	K 2-q	
spindles & looms in use: cotton industry	Main countries	E 3-a	
wool industry	Main countries	E 3-a	
in use: cotton industry	World regions	K 5-a	
	OAS member countries	N 14-a	
jute industry	W European countries	C 22-a	
installed & in use: textile industries	W European countries	K 2-a	
cotton industry	OECD countries	D 46-a	
woollen industry	OECD countries	D 46-a	
worsted industry	OECD countries	D 46-a	
Production by type: textile machines: volume	EEC countries	E 28-q	E 27-a
looms: volume	All countries	U 22-a	U 38-a
spinning machines: volume	All countries	U 22-a	U 38-a
World exports (incl leather-working machinery) by value in $m		U 38-a	
TEXTILE MACHINERY BY KIND			
Exports by destination by CST classes: tonnage & value in $	EEC countries	E 48-a	
SITC classes by value in $	Main countries	D 2-q	
tonnage & value in $	OECD countries	D 3-a2	
NIMEXE classes: volume & value in $	All countries	E 20-a	
SITC classes: volume & value in $	All countries	U 50-a	U 59-a
Imports by NIMEXE classes: volume & value in $	All countries	E 20-a	
SITC classes: volume & value in $	All countries	U 50-a	U 59-a
source by CST classes by value in $	EEC countries	E 21-a	
SITC classes by value in $	Main countries	D 2-q	
tonnage & value in $	OECD countries	D 3-a2	
TEXTILE MACHINERY MANUFACTURING INDUSTRY			
Investment in buildings in local currency	EEC countries	E 40-a	
land purchase in local currency	EEC countries	E 40-a	
machinery in local currency	EEC countries	E 40-a	
No of hrs worked per wk	Main countries	R 3-m	
Wage rates by sex in local currency per hr	Main countries	R 3-m	

Textile products   see   MANUFACTURED TEXTILE PRODUCTS

Textile waste   see   FIBROUS WASTE

	Territorial coverage	Title codes	
TEXTILE YARNS			
Consumption by value in $m	Main countries	U 23-a	
Exports as % of consumption	EEC countries, Japan & USA	U 23-a	
by destination by value in £m	UK	B 29-a	
Imports as % of consumption	EEC countries, Japan & USA	U 23-a	
by source by value in £m	UK	B 29-a	
value in $m	Indonesia	U 32-m	
Production: flax, hemp, jute & ramie yarns: tonnage	All countries	U 27-m	U 43-a
yarns (from vegetable fibres): tonnage	All countries	U 22-a	
tonnage	OECD countries	D 46-a	
TEXTILE YARNS BY KIND			
Consumption in production of clothing: tonnage	EEC countries	K 4-a	
of household textiles: tonnage	EEC countries	K 4-a	
tonnage	W European countries	K 2-q	
Deliveries to textile industry - index nos	UK	B 29-a	
Exports by destination by CST classes: tonnage & value in $m	EEC countries	E 48-a	
SITC classes by value in $m	Main countries	D 2-q	
tonnage & value in $m	OECD countries	D 3-a2	
NIMEXE classes by value in $m	All countries	E 20-a	
SITC classes by value in $m	All countries	U 50-a	U 59-a
Imports by NIMEXE classes by value in $m	All countries	E 20-a	
SITC classes by value in $m	All countries	U 50-a	U 59-a
source by CST classes: tonnage & value in $m	EEC countries	E 21-a	
SITC classes by value in $m	Main countries	D 2-q	
tonnage & value in $m	OECD countries	D 3-a2	
Imports & exports (incl trade balance) in lbs	UK	B 29-a	
Production (forecast to 1977) in lbs	UK	B 29	
tonnage	EEC countries	E 28-q	E 27-a
THALLIUM			
% usage by electrical industry	USA	N 1-a	
for agricultural purposes	USA	N 1-a	
in production of pharmaceutical products	USA	N 1-a	
World reserves: tonnage (estim)		N 1-a	

Thebacon & thebaine   see   OPIUM ALKALOIDS

Theft   see   ROBBERY & THEFT

Theology   see   RELIGION

Therapeutics & prophylactics   see   PHARMACEUTICAL PRODUCTS

Thermal alternators   see   ALTERNATORS, THERMAL

Thermal generators   see   GENERATORS, THERMAL

	Territorial coverage	Title codes

Thermal power   see   POWER STATIONS, THERMAL

Thermometers   see   MEASURING APPARATUS

Thomas converters   see   FURNACES, STEEL

Thomas slag   see   FURNACE SLAG

Thorium   see   RARE EARTH MINERALS

THREAD & TAP MACHINES
    Production, imports, exports & sales by value in $m   EEC countries   B 20-a

THRESHING MACHINES
    see also   COMBINED HARVESTER-THRESHERS
    Production: volume   All countries   U 22-a
          E European countries, France & Japan   U 38-a

Threshold prices   see   INTERVENTION PRICES

Tiles, roofing & floor   see   BUILDING MATERIALS

Tilsit   see   CHEESE BY VARIETY

TIMBER
    see also   FORESTRY
                HARDWOOD, SAWN
                HARDWOOD LOGS
                MANUFACTURED TIMBER PRODUCTS
                PULPWOOD
                SOFTWOOD, SAWN
                SOFTWOOD LOGS

	Territorial coverage	Title codes	
% contribution to export earnings	Ivory Coast & Central African Republic	E 45-a	
Consumption (as fuelwood): tonnage	Italy	H 4-a	
(as primary energy source): tonnage	Main countries	N 2-a	
pulpwood (by kind) for production of wood pulp: tonnage	Canada	J 7-a	
per ton of wood pulp produced	Canada	J 7-a	
roundwood for production of wood pulp by process: tonnage	Canada	J 7-a	
Export prices: redwood lumber in S Kr per ton	Sweden	A 9-a	
Export prices - index nos (weighted average main sources)	Worldwide	U 29-q	U 54-q
Exports by destination (incl sawnwood) by CST classes: tonnage & value in $	EEC countries	E 48-a	
SITC classes by value in $	Main countries	D 2-q	
tonnage & value in $	OECD countries	D 3-a2	
pitprops by volume in m³	European countries & USSR	A 13-q	
by sea, inland waterways, road & rail: tonnage	European countries	U 8-q	
fuelwood by volume in m³	Canada, Egypt, European countries, USA & USSR	A 13-q	
historical table from 1836 by volume in m³	Scandinavian countries	Z 1-a	
(incl cork) shipped to EEC & non-EEC areas by value in $m	EEC countries	E 24-a	
(incl sawnwood) by NIMEXE classes by value in $	All countries	E 20-a	
SITC classes by value in $	All countries	U 50-a	U 59-a
pitprops, piling posts (et al) by volume in m³	All countries	A 23-a	
rough wood: tonnage & value in $m	Liberia & Congo Rep	E 45-a	
roundwood by volume in m³	Canada, European countries, USA & USSR	A 13-q	
wood & lumber: tonnage	Asian & Far East countries	U 32-q	
Fuelwood by volume in m³	African countries	U 44-a	
Growing stock: conifers by volume in m³	World regions	A 16	
in m³ per ha	World regions	A 16	
non-conifers by volume in m³	World regions	A 16	
in m³ per ha	World regions	A 16	
Imports & exports: sawn logs by source or destination by volume in m³	All countries	A 23-a	
Imports by sea, inland waterways, road & rail: tonnage	European countries	U 8-a	
by source (incl sawnwood) by CST classes: tonnage & value in $	EEC countries	E 21-a	
SITC classes by value in $	Main countries	D 2-q	
	OECD countries	D 3-a2	
pitprops by volume in m³	European countries	A 13-q	
fuelwood by volume in m³	Canada, Egypt, European countries, USA & USSR	A 13-q	
(incl cork) shipped ex EEC & non-EEC areas by value in $m	EEC countries	E 24-a	
(incl sawnwood) by NIMEXE classes by value in $	All countries	E 20-a	
SITC classes by value in $	All countries	U 50-a	U 59-a
roundwood by volume in m³	Canada, European countries, Israel, USA & USSR	A 13-q	
wood lumber (incl cork) by value in yen million	Japan	U 32-m	
Labour costs: timber fabrication in local currency per hr	EEC countries	E 2-a	
Production (as fuel or for production of charcoal) by volume in m³	All countries	A 23-a	
as fuelwood by volume in m³	AASM countries	E 41-a	
	Main countries	A 5-a	
(incl European requirement forecast) by volume in m³:			
sawn hardwood		A 24-a	
sawn softwood		A 24-a	
pitprops by volume in m³	Canada, European countries, USA & USSR	A 13-q	
pulpwood & pitprops by volume in m³	African countries	U 44-a	
roundwood & pitprops by volume in m³	All countries	A 23-a	
roundwood (for industry) by volume in m³	Main countries	A 5-a	
sawnwood & plywood by volume in m³	OAS member countries	N 14-a	

545

	Territorial coverage	Title codes
TIMBER, continued		
Production: sawnwood by volume in m³	ECE countries	U 15-a
(for production of railway sleepers) by volume in m³	Latin American countries	J 5-a
hard & soft by volume in m³	All countries	A 23-a
wood-based panels, plywood & veneer by volume in m³	Main countries	E 3-a
	All countries	A 23-a
Production - index nos (quantum basis)	S American countries	U 40-a
Removals: commercial timber by kind by volume in m³	Main countries	R 5-a
conifers (as fuelwood) by volume in m³	World regions	A 16
(as industrial wood) by volume in m³	World regions	A 16
fuelwood, pitprops, railway sleepers, sawnwood & veneer by volume in m³	Main countries	R 5-a
industrial roundwood by volume in m³	African countries	U 44-a
	ECE countries	U 15-a
logs, industrial wood & sawnwood by volume in m³	All countries	A 23-a
non-conifers (as fuelwood) by volume in m³	World regions	A 16
(as industrial wood) by volume in m³	World regions	A 16
roundwood (all kinds) by volume in m³	All countries	U 43-a
	ECE countries	U 15-a
sawn logs, veneer logs & sleeper wood by volume in m³	African countries	U 44-a
(total): all types of timber (incl world total) by volume in m³	Main countries	R 5-a
Shipments (incl wood products) through Panama Canal eastwards: tonnage		D 28-a
through Kiel Canal westwards: tonnage		D 28-a
Tramp shipping: freight rates for timber - index nos		U 37-m
Wholesale prices: fuelwood in local currency	Austria, Finland, W Germany & Switzerland	A 13-a
lumber in local currency	Canada, Finland, Sweden & USA	U 27-m
	W Germany & USA	A 9-a
sawnwood (for building industry) - index nos	European countries	U 5-a
	OAS member countries	N 14-a
World market prices - index nos		G 1-a
World production: industrial roundwood by volume in m³		A 5-a
TIMBER, CONIFEROUS		
Consumption in production of blockboard by volume in m³	All countries	A 26-a
of plywood by volume in m³	All countries	A 26-a
Growing stock by volume in m³	World regions	A 16
	All countries	A 16-a
in m³ per ha	World regions	A 16
Increase in growing stock by volume in m³	All countries	A 16-a
Production by volume in m³	Canada, European countries, USA & USSR	A 13-q
roundwood logs by volume in m³	OAS member countries	N 13-a
sawn logs & pitprops by volume in m³	All countries	A 23-a U 22-a
Removals (as fuelwood) by volume in m³	All countries	A 16-a
(as industrial wood) by volume in m³	All countries	A 16-a
by kind: sawn wood logs by volume in m³	All countries	A 23-a
by volume in m³	All countries	A 16-a
TIMBER, DECIDUOUS		
Consumption in production of plywood by volume in m³	All countries	A 26-a
Growing stock by volume in m³	All countries	A 16-a
Increase in growing stock by volume in m³	All countries	A 16-a
Production by volume in m³	Canada, European countries, USA & USSR	A 13-q
roundwood logs by volume in m³	OAS member countries	N 13-a
Removals (as fuelwood) by volume in m³	All countries	A 16-a
(as industrial wood) by volume in m³	All countries	A 16-a
by volume in m³	All countries	A 16-a
TIMBER, TROPICAL		
Exports by value in $A	British Solomon Is	U 32-m
tonnage	ECAFE countries	U 32-m
(total) & shipped to EEC area: tonnage in value in UA	AASM countries	E 41-a
Imports: hardwood logs (ex tropics) by volume in m³	Main European countries	A 25-a
sawn hardwood by volume in m³	European countries	A 25-a2
World market prices: mahogany (ex Lagos) in £ per ton	UK	E 41-a
TIMBER BY KIND		
Consumption in production of particle board	All countries	A 26-a
Production by volume in m³	Asian, Far East & Australasian countries	U 45-a
(incl pulpwood) in m³	Main countries	A 5-a
conifer & deciduous timber by value in $	EEC countries	E 44-a
sawn wood by volume in m³	All countries	U 43-a
Removals: conifers (for all purposes) by volume in m³	World regions	A 16
non-conifers (for all purposes) by volume in m³	World regions	A 16
roundwood (incl consumption by purpose) by volume in m³	World regions	J 7-a
in m³	African countries	U 44-a
volume (incl consumption) in m³	Latin American countries	J 5-a
in m³	Main countries	R 5-a
World demand by volume projected to 1985 in m³		A 1
TIMBER PRODUCTS		
% share of EEC area imports	Developing countries	U 52-a
Imports (incl furniture) by value in $m	Developing countries	U 52-a
into EEC area shipped ex developing countries by value in $m		U 52-a

	Territorial coverage	Title codes	
TIMBER & SAWMILL INDUSTRY			
see also WOOD-WORKING INDUSTRY			
Costs: salaried staff in local currency per mth	EEC countries	E 11-a	
Investment in buildings in local currency	EEC countries	E 40-a	
in land purchase in local currency	EEC countries	E 40-a	
in machinery in local currency	EEC countries	E 40-a	
Labour costs: all employees in local currency per hr	EEC countries	E 11-a	
as % of total costs in timber industry	EEC countries	E 8-a	
by status of employees in local currency	EEC countries	E 8-a	
wage earners in local currency per hr	EEC countries	E 11-a	
Labour force: no of salaried staff employed	EEC countries	E 11-a	
of wage earners employed	EEC countries	E 11-a	
of wage earners & salaried staff employed	EEC countries	E 8-a	
No of hrs worked per wk	Main countries	R 3-m	
per yr	EEC countries	E 8-a	
salaried staff per mth	EEC countries	E 11-a	
wage earners per wk	EEC countries	E 11-a	
Production: historical table from 1848 by volume in m³	W Germany	Z 1-a	
Wage rates by sex in local currency per hr	Main countries	R 3-m	C 7-a
lumberjacks in local currency per hr	Canada	R 4-a	
sawyers in local currency per hr	OAS member countries	N 17-a	

Time charter (shipping)   see   CHARTERINGS

Time charter rates   see   OCEAN FREIGHT RATES

Time deposit rates (banking)   see   INTEREST RATES

Time rates   see   EARNINGS
                   WAGE RATES

Times turned   see   INVENTORIES

TIN

Ceiling & floor prices (under International Tin Agreement) in £ per ton		C 20	
Consumption by chemicals industry: tonnage	OECD countries	D 21-a	
by end-use: tonnage	European countries & USA	C 12-a	
by kind of manufactured product: tonnage	Main countries	T 4-a	U 43-a
of usage & manufactured product: tonnage	All countries	J 6-a	
for industrial tinning of sheets: tonnage	OECD countries	D 21-a	
in production of anodes: tonnage	USA	C 20-m	
anti-friction & babbitt metal: tonnage	France, Italy, W Germany & USA	C 12-a	
	USA	C 20-m	J 6-a
		T 4-a	
bearing metal alloys: tonnage	All countries	C 20-m	
	Main countries	T 4-a	
bronze & brass: tonnage	Main countries	T 4-a	
	France	C 20-q	
	UK & USA	C 20-m	
bronze, brass & gunmetal: tonnage	UK & USA	C 30-m	J 6-a
bronze: tonnage	European countries & USA	C 12-a	
chemical compounds & oxides: tonnage	France & USA	C 20-m	T 4-a
	European countries & USA	C 20-m	C 12-a
collapsible tubes & foil: tonnage	UK & USA	C 30-m	J 6-a
		T 4-a	
costume jewellery: tonnage	France	C 20-q	
foil capsules (for bottles): tonnage	W Germany	C 12-a	
pewter: tonnage	France	C 20-q	T 4-a
	Italy	C 12-a	
pipes & tubing: tonnage	UK & USA	C 20-m	T 4-a
pipes & wire: tonnage	UK	C 30-m	
semi-finished tin products: tonnage	OECD countries	D 21-a	
	European countries & USA	C 12-a	
solder & fusible alloys: tonnage	Main countries	T 4-a	
solder: tonnage	European countries & USA	C 12-a	
	All countries	C 20-m	J 6-a
	UK	C 30-m	
terneplate: tonnage	France	T 4-a	
	USA	J 6-a	
tin alloys by kind: tonnage	UK	C 30-m	
tonnage	OECD countries	D 21-a	
	USA	C 20-m	
tin foil & sheets: tonnage	UK	C 30-m	
tin oxides & chemicals: tonnage	UK & USA	J 6-a	
tin oxides & powder: tonnage	UK	C 30-m	
	France	T 4-a	
	All countries	C 20-q	
tin piping & foil capsules (for bottles): tonnage	UK	J 6-a	
tin powder: tonnage	France & USA	T 4-a	
	France	C 20-q	
	USA	C 20-m	C 12-a
tinplate, solder, bronze & brass: tonnage	USA	H 2-a	
tinplate: tonnage	European countries & USA	C 12-a	
	Main countries	T 4-a	
	All countries	C 20-m	J 6-a
	UK	C 30-m	

TIN, continued   Territorial coverage   Title codes

    Consumption in production of tubes & tin foil: tonnage   UK & USA   C 20-m
        tubes & piping: tonnage   USA   J 6-a   J 6-a
        type metal: tonnage   USA   C 20-m
                                                                                                T 4-a
                                                                 Main countries   C 12-a
        white metal: tonnage   UK & USA   C 20-m   C 12-a
                                                                                                                    J 6-a
                                                                                     UK   C 30-m
                                                                                     USA   T 4-a
        wrought tin sheets & tin foil: tonnage   UK   J 6-a
        wrought tin: tonnage   France & UK   T 4-a
                                                                                     UK   C 30-m
                                                                                     France   C 20-q
    in tinning of copper & steel wire: tonnage   UK   C 30-m
    in tinning processes: tonnage   Main countries   T 4-a
                                                                                     USA   C 20-m
                                                                                     UK & USA   J 6-a
    in wire-coating processes: tonnage   W Germany   C 12-a
    primary & secondary tin: tonnage   All countries   J 6-a
                                                                                     USA   N 1-a
    primary metallic tin: tonnage   Main countries   C 20-m   U 11-a
                                                                                     OAS member countries   N 17-a
    pure metallic tin by main trades & uses: tonnage   France & UK   H 2-a
    recovered metallic tin: tonnage   OAS member countries   N 17-a
    refined metallic tin: historical table: tonnage   World regions   C 12-a
        tonnage   All countries   C 30-q   C 12-a
                                                                                     EEC countries   C 12-a
                                                                                     Main countries   B 2-a
                                                                                     OECD countries   D 21-q
                                                                                     World regions   C 12-a
                                                                                     Worldwide excl Communist countries T 4-a
Disposals ex US government strategic stockpile: tonnage   USA   C 20-m   U 11-a
Export prices in $ per 100 lbs fob   Singapore   U 17-m
Export prices - index nos (weighted average main sources)   U 29-q

Exports by destination (incl scrap & alloys): tonnage   S American countries   U 40-q
    refined metallic tin: tonnage   Main countries   H 2-a
        tonnage   OECD countries   D 21-q
    concentrates: tonnage & value in $m   Main countries   T 4-a
        tonnage   Main countries   B 2-a
                                                                                     Bolivia   C 20-m
    metallic tin by destination: tonnage   Main countries   C 20-m
        by value in local currency   W Malaysia   U 32-m
        tonnage   Indonesia, W Malaysia & Thailand U 32-m
    pigs blocks (incl metallic tin bars): tonnage   USA   J 6-a
    tin concentrates by destination: tonnage   Main countries   C 20-m
        unit value in $ per 100 lbs   Indonesia   U 32-m
Government strategic stockpile: pig tin & sales: tonnage   USA   N 1-a
Import prices in £ per ton cif   European countries   C 20-m
    (on London & New York Metal Markets) in £ per ton cif   UK & USA   B 2-a
Imports & exports: unwrought semis, tin scrap & alloys: tonnage   All countries   B 15-a
Imports by source (incl scrap & alloys): tonnage   Main countries   H 2-a
    refined metal: tonnage   OECD countries   D 21-q
        tonnage   Main countries   T 4-a
    concentrates (based on metal content): tonnage   USA   J 6-a
    pigs, blocks & bars: tonnage   USA   J 6-a
    tin concentrates by source: tonnage   Main countries   C 20-m
Plant capacity: tin refining by company: tonnage   Worldwide   C 12-a
Prices (at mines): straits tin in M$ (at Penang)   W Malaysia   R 2-m
Producer prices: pure metallic tin in local currency per ton   W Germany, UK & USA   H 2-m
Production (at mines & smelter), imports, exports & consumption:
        tonnage   Main countries   H 2-a
    (at smelter): tonnage   All countries   J 6-a
    (based on metal content of concentrates): tonnage   Latin American countries   J 5-a   U 18-a
                                                                                     All countries   U 27-m   B 15-a
                                                                                                                    R 5-a   U 22-a
                                                                                                                    U 43-a
    by hydraulicing method: tonnage   Malaysia & Thailand   C 20-m
    by use of dredges: tonnage   Malaysia & Thailand   C 20-m
        of dulang washers: tonnage   Malaysia & Thailand   C 20-m
        of gravel pumps: tonnage   Malaysia & Thailand   C 20-m
    concentrates by mining method: tonnage   Malaysia & Thailand   C 20-m
        (incl world total): tonnage   Main countries   B 2-a
        tonnage   All countries   C 20-m
                                                                                     ECAFE countries   U 32-q
    from open cast mining: tonnage   Malaysia   C 20-m
    from tungsten-tin ores: tonnage   All countries   U 53-a
    from underground mining: tonnage   Malaysia   C 20-m
    primary metallic tin & concentrates: tonnage   Asian & Far East countries   U 32-q
        tonnage   All countries   C 20-m   U 27-m
                                                                                                                    R 5-a   U 43-a
                                                                                     Australia, Malaysia & Thailand U 32-q
    refined metallic tin: historical table: tonnage   World regions   C 12-a
        tonnage   All countries   C 30-q   C 12-a
                                                                                     EEC countries   C 12-a
                                                                                     Main countries   E 3-a
                                                                                     World regions   C 12-a
                                                                                     Zaire   E 41-a
    secondary metallic tin (from scrap): tonnage   USA   H 2-a
                                                                                     All countries   C 20-m

	Territorial coverage	Title codes	
TIN, continued			
Production: smelter & recovered metal: tonnage	All countries	B 15-a	
tonnage	USA	N 1-a	
	Argentine, Bolivia, Brazil & Mexico	U 18-a	
	OAS member countries	N 14-a	
	S American countries	U 40-a	
unwrought virgin tin: tonnage	All countries	U 22-a	
Recovery (from scrap tin, bronze or brass): tonnage & value in $	USA	C 20-m	
Sales ex US government strategic stockpile to A.I.D.: tonnage	USA	C 20-m	
Stocks held as buffer stocks by International Tin Council: tonnage		C 20-m	
at consumers' premises & warehouses: tonnage	UK	C 30-q	T 4-a
at dealers' & consumers' premises: tonnage	USA	N 1-a	
at London Metal Exchange warehouses: tonnage	UK	T 4-a	
at mines: tonnage	Brazil, Japan, Malaysia, Nigeria & Thailand	C 20-m	
at smelters' premises: tonnage	Main countries	C 20-m	
by importers or jobbers: tonnage	USA	T 4-a	
in internal transit: tonnage	USA	T 4-a	
of concentrates in transit: tonnage	Country of destination	C 20-m	
of ore & concentrates (based on metal content): tonnage	UK	J 6-a	
of pig tin held at consumers' premises: tonnage	USA	J 6-a	
(in processing stage) held at processing plants: tonnage	USA	T 4-a	
of primary metal in transit: tonnage	Country of destination	C 20-m	
of refined metal held at consumers' premises: tonnage	UK	J 6-a	
at London Metal Exchange warehouses: tonnage	UK	J 6-a	
tonnage	Main countries	B 2-a	
Transit trade by source & destination: tonnage	Country of transit	C 20-m	
Wholesale prices (3 mths forward) in £ per ton on London Metal Exchange	UK	C 12-m	T 4-m
in cents per lb (at Penang)	W Malaysia	N 1-a	
cents per lb	Belgium, Singapore, UK & USA	U 27-m	
DM per 100 kg	W Germany	R 2-m	
lire per kg	Italy	C 12-m	
M$ per picul	W Malaysia	C 20-m	
ex Malaya (on New York market) in cents per lb	USA	J 6-m	
ex works in $ per picul	Singapore	U 32-m	
for cash (on New York market) in cents per lb	USA	C 12-m	C 20-m
for cash or forward (on London market) in £ per ton	UK	C 20-m	J 6-m
on London & New York markets in cents per lb	UK & USA	N 1-a	
(spot) in local currency per kg	Main countries	T 4-w	
Straits tin (ex warehouse) in £ per ton	UK	R 2-m	
in cents per lb at docks	USA	R 2-m	
World consumption: refined metallic tin historical table: tonnage		C 12-a	
tonnage	Worldwide	C 30-a	U 11-a
World exports by destination: tonnage	All countries	J 6-a	
World market prices in cents per lb (on London & New York markets)	Worldwide excl Communist countries	T 4-a	
metallic tin: historical table from 1875 in £ per ton		U 18-a	
World production (at mines): tonnage		T 4-m	
(based on content of ore mined): tonnage		U 11-a	
concentrates: tonnage	Main countries	C 12-a	
ore mined & tin refined: tonnage		U 11-a	
refined metallic tin: tonnage	Main countries	C 30-a	
tonnage	Main countries excl Communist area	N 4-a	U 11-a
World stocks: primary & secondary metal in transit: tonnage		T 4-a	
tonnage		T 4-a	
TIN ALLOYS			
see also ANTI-FRICTION METALS			
BRONZE			
WHITE METAL			
Consumption: tin in production of alloys: tonnage	UK & USA	C 20-m	
Exports by destination: tin alloys by kind: tonnage	Main countries	C 20-m	
Transit trade by source & destination: tonnage	Country of transit	C 20-m	
TIN FOIL			
see also ALUMINIUM FOIL			
COPPER FOIL			
LEAD FOIL			
Consumption: tin scrap in production of tin foil: tonnage	USA	T 4-a	
Tin ingots see INGOTS, TIN			
TIN MINES			
Labour force employed in tin mining	Malaysia, Nigeria & Thailand	C 20-m	
	Malaysia	U 32-q	
Machinery: usage in tin mining in Bhp	Nigeria	C 20-m	
No of tin mines in operation (open cast & underground)	Malaysia	C 20-m	
by method of extraction	Malaysia & Thailand	C 20-m	
using hydraulicing method	Malaysia & Thailand	C 20-m	
with dredges & gravel pumps	Malaysia & Thailand	C 20-m	

	Territorial coverage	Title codes	
IN ORE			
% of contribution to export earnings	Rwanda	E 45-a	
% share of world reserves (estim)	Latin American region	U 18-a	
Export prices - index nos (weighted average main sources)		U 29-q	
Exports by destination (as concentrates): tonnage	Main countries	T 4-a	
tonnage	Main countries	H 2-a	
by value in local currency	Indonesia & Laos	U 32-m	
(incl tin concentrates): tonnage	Asian & Far East countries	U 32-q	
tonnage & value in $m	Rwanda	E 45-a	
(total) & shipped to EEC area: tonnage & value in UA	AASM countries	E 41-a	
Import prices by grade of tin ore in £ per ton cif	European countries	T 4-m	
Imports by source (as concentrates): tonnage	Main countries	T 4-a	
tonnage	Main countries	H 2-a	
Production (based on metal content of ore): tonnage	All countries	J 6-a	
	AASM countries	E 41-a	
historical table from 1750: tonnage	W Germany & UK	Z 1-a	
tonnage	All countries	C 30-q	
	OAS member countries	N 14-a	
Stocks (as concentrates) in transit: tonnage	Worldwide	T 4-a	
(incl concentrates) based on metal content of ore: tonnage	UK	C 30-q	
Wholesale prices (at Bangkok) in baht per ton	Thailand	U 32-m	
World market prices (70% metal content) per ton	European countries	E 41-a	
World production (as concentrates): tonnage	Main countries	T 4-a	
	Main countries	C 12-a	N 1-a
based on metal content of ore: tonnage	All countries	J 6-a	
tonnage	Worldwide, excl USA	N 4-a	
World reserves: tonnage (estim)	Main countries	N 1-a	
TIN OXIDE			
Consumption: tin in production of oxides & chemicals: tonnage	USA	J 6-a	
TIN POWDER			
Consumption: tin in production of tin powder: tonnage	USA	C 20-m	C 12-a
TIN PRODUCTS, SEMI-FINISHED			
Consumption: tin in production of manufactured tin products: tonnage	European countries & USA	C 12-a	
TIN WASTE & SCRAP			
Consumption in production of babbitt metal: tonnage	USA	T 4-a	
bronze & brass: tonnage	USA	T 4-a	
pipes & piping: tonnage	USA	T 4-a	
solder: tonnage	USA	T 4-a	
tubes & tin foil: tonnage	USA	T 4-a	
in tinning processes: tonnage	USA	T 4-a	
secondary tin scrap by uses: tonnage	USA	T 4-a	
tonnage	OAS member countries	N 17-a	
Exports by destination: tonnage	USA	C 20-m	
Recovery by sources of waste & scrap: tonnage	USA	T 4-a	
Wholesale prices: tin piping in cents per lb	USA	J 6-m	
World production: secondary tin: tonnage	Main countries	T 4-a	

Tinned sheets   see   TINPLATE

Tinned soup   see   CANNED SOUP
    CONVENIENCE FOODS

TINPLATE			
Consumption (incl blackplate): tonnage	OECD countries	D 22-a	
tin in production of tinplate: tonnage	European countries & USA	C 12-a	
	All countries	C 20-m	
& terneplate: tonnage	USA	J 6-a	
tonnage	All countries	C 20-m	
	OAS member countries	N 17-a	
Deliveries (home & export) incl blackplate: tonnage	OECD countries	D 22-a	
to user industries: tonnage	ECE countries	U 7-q	U 6-a
	Main countries	H 3-a	
Exports by destination: blackplate: tonnage	Main countries	T 4-a	
electrolytic tinplate: tonnage	USA	C 20-m	
hot-dipped tinplate: tonnage	USA	C 20-m	
terneplate: tonnage	Main countries	T 4-a	
tonnage	ECE countries	U 48-a	
	EEC countries	E 5-q	
	Main countries	C 20-m	H 2-a
		T 4-a	
tonnage (incl % share)	Main countries	U 49-a	
tonnage	ECE countries, Japan & USA	U 7-m	U 6-a
	European countries, Greece & USSR	T 1-a	
	Main countries	H 3-a	
Imports by source: blackplate & terneplate: tonnage	Main countries	T 4-a	
tonnage	EEC countries	E 5-q	
	Main countries	C 20-m	H 2-a
		T 4-a	
lacquered tinplate (for manufacture of boxes): tonnage	Main countries	T 1-a	
tonnage	ECE countries	U 7-m	U 6-a
	Main countries	H 3-a	T 1-a
Inter-EEC area trade: tonnage & value in $	EEC countries	E 29-a	
Production: blackplates: tonnage	Main countries	T 4-a	

	Territorial coverage	Title codes	
TINPLATE, continued			
Production: by hot-dipped process: tonnage	Main countries	C 20-m	T 4-a
	USA	J 6-a	
electrolytic tinplate: tonnage	Main countries	C 20-m	T 4-a
	USA	J 6-a	
terneplate: tonnage	Main countries	T 4-a	
	USA	J 6-a	
tonnage	All countries	C 20-m	T 1-a
		U 22-a	
	ECE countries	U 7-m	U 6-a
	EEC countries	E 28-q	E 27-a
		E 29-a	
	Main countries	H 3-a	T 4-a
	OECD countries	D 22-a	
	S American countries & Mexico	U 40-a	
	UK	H 2-a	
World consumption: tonnage	Main countries	T 4-a	
TITANIUM			
Wholesale prices: metal billets (round) in £ per ton	UK	T 4-m	
titanium metal sponge in £ per ton	UK	T 4-a	
TITANIUM CONCENTRATES			
Production: ilmenite & rutile: tonnage	USA	J 6-a	
(incl shipment ex mines): tonnage	USA	J 6-a	
TITANIUM DIOXIDE			
see also PIGMENTS, MINERAL			
Exports: tonnage	OECD countries	D 5-a	
Imports: tonnage	OECD countries	D 5-a	
Production: tonnage	OECD countries	D 5-a	
Titanium ingots see INGOTS, TITANIUM			
TITANIUM MINERAL SCRAP			
Consumption: tonnage	USA	J 6-a	
TITANIUM MINERALS			
see also FERRO-TITANIUM			
Consumption: ilmenite concentrates: tonnage	USA	N 1-a	
rutile concentrates: tonnage	USA	N 1-a	
sponge metal: tonnage	USA	J 6-a	T 4-a
titanium ingots: tonnage	USA	T 4-a	
tonnage (all kinds)	USA	N 1-a	
Export prices: ilmenite in $ per ton fob	USA	N 1-a	
Exports: ilmenite & rutile: tonnage	Main countries	T 4-a	
Government strategic stockpile: rutile concentrates: tonnage	USA	N 1-a	
sponge metal: tonnage	USA	N 1-a	
Import prices: ilmenite concentrates in $A per ton	European countries	T 4-m	
rutile concentrates in $A per ton	European countries	T 4-m	
Imports & exports by kind: tonnage	All countries	B 15-a	
sponge metal: tonnage	USA	J 6-a	
Production by kind (incl ilmenite): tonnage	All countries	B 15-a	
ilmenite: tonnage	Main countries	N 1-a	T 4-a
	USA	J 6-a	
rutile & ilmenite: tonnage	All countries	C 12-a	
rutile: tonnage	Australia & India	T 4-a	
	USA	J 6-a	
sponge metal: tonnage	Main countries	N 1-a	
	USA	J 6-a	
titanium tetra-chloride: tonnage	USA	J 6-a	
Stocks: ilmenite: tonnage	USA	N 1-a	
titanium metal (held by industry): tonnage	USA	N 1-a	
Wholesale prices: ilmenite ore in £ per ton	UK	C 12-m	
rutile concentrates in $ per ton	USA	N 1-a	
rutile ore in £ per ton	UK	C 12-m	
titanium metal in $ per ton	USA	N 1-a	
World production: ilmenite: tonnage		C 12-a	T 4-a
		C 30-a	
ilmenite & rutile: tonnage		N 1-a	N 4-a
ilmenite concentrates: tonnage		C 12-a	N 1-a
rutile concentrates: tonnage		N 4-a	T 4-a
World reserves: ilmenite: tonnage	Main countries	N 1-a	
rutile concentrates: tonnage	Main countries	N 1-a	
TITANIUM PRODUCTS, SEMI-FINISHED			
see also FORGING BILLETS, TITANIUM			
PLATES SHEETS & STRIP, TITANIUM			
ROD & WIRE EXTRUSION BARS, TITANIUM			
TUBES & PIPES, TITANIUM			
Deliveries by kind in lbs	USA	J 6-a	
Wholesale prices: titanium sheets in £ per ton	UK	T 4-a	

TOBACCO

	Territorial coverage	Title codes	
% contribution to export earnings	Malawi	E 45-a	
A.I.D. sales (under A.I.D. programs) in $	Recipient countries	M 1-a	
Area harvested, production: tonnage & yield per ha	All countries	A 9-a	
under crop & yield per ha	Latin American countries	J 5-a	
historical table in ha	Main European countries	Z 1-a	
in acres	Main countries	B 13-a	
in ha (incl harvest): tonnage	All countries	R 5-a	
in ha	EEC countries	B 1-a	E 12-a
		E 44-a	
Auction prices by grade in cents per lb	OAS member countries	N 13-a	
in pence per lb (weekly averages)	USA	B 17-a	
Consumer expenditure on tobacco products in £m	Main countries	B 17	
Consumption & demand projections: tonnage	UK	B 13-a	
Consumption: chewing tobacco in lbs	World regions	A 1	
Commonwealth-produced tobacco leaf in lbs	Main countries	B 16-a	
cost: private sector (incl cigarettes) in local currency	UK	B 13-a	
expenditure as % of total outlay	EEC countries	E 32-a	
on tobacco products in £m	EEC countries	E 2-a	
foreign leaf in lbs	UK	B 17-a	
per adult: all tobacco products in lbs per yr	UK	B 13-a	
pipe tobacco in lbs	Main countries	B 16-a	
	Main countries	B 16-a	
	UK	B 13-a	
snuff in lbs	Main countries	B 16-a	
	UK	B 13-a	
tonnage	OAS member countries	N 17-a	
tobacco leaf by kind in lbs	S Africa	B 17-a	
tonnage	W European countries & USA	B 2-a	
Crop yield by region in lbs per acre	Japan & USA	B 17-a	
in 100 kg per ha	EEC countries	E 12-a	
in kg per ha	EEC countries	E 44-a	
	OAS member countries	N 13-a	
in lbs per acre	Main countries	B 13-a	
in quintals per ha	E European countries & USSR	U 16-a	
Distribution (for industrial processing): tonnage	Hungary & Poland	U 34-a	
(for own farm consumption: tonnage	Hungary & Poland	U 34-a	
Expenditure (private) on tobacco products in local currency	OAS member countries	N 16-a	
Export prices - index nos (weighted average main sources)	Worldwide	U 29-q	
	S American countries	U 40-q	
in local currency	Brazil, Greece, India, Malawi & Zambia	A 9-a	
Exports as % of total export trade (value basis)	Main countries	B 13-a	
by destination: flue-cured tobacco & burley in lbs	Main countries	B 17-a	
unmanufactured leaf in lbs	All countries	B 17-a	
historical table from 1858: tonnage	Greece	Z 1-a	
in $m	W European countries	U 33-a	
in local currency	Main countries	B 13-a	
(incl beverages) as % of total trade in agricultural products	W European countries	U 20-a	
(incl tobacco manufactures) by value in $	OECD countries	D 1-a	
raw leaf: tonnage & value in $m	Malawi	E 45-a	
shipped to EEC & non-EEC areas by value in $m	EEC countries	E 24-a	
tobacco products by destination by CST classes: tonnage & value in $	EEC countries	E 48-a	
SITC classes by value in $	Main countries	D 2-q	
tonnage & value in $	OECD countries	D 3-a2	
by NIMEXE classes by value in $	All countries	E 20-a	
SITC classes by value in $	All countries	U 50-a	U 59-a
tonnage & value in $m	Main countries	B 2-a	
tonnage	India, Indonesia, S Korea & Philippines	U 32-m	
(total) & shipped to EEC area: tonnage & value in UA	AASM countries	E 41-a	
unit value in $ per kg	OAS member countries	N 15-a	
unmanufactured leaf in lbs	Main countries	B 13-a	
tonnage	Asian & Far East countries	U 32-q	
Import prices in cents per lb	USA	A 9-a	
Imports by source by SITC classes by value in $	Main countries	D 2-q	
tonnage & value in $	OECD countries	D 3-a2	
in lbs	All countries	B 13-a	
tobacco products by CST classes: tonnage & value in $	EEC countries	E 21-a	
unmanufactured leaf in lbs	UK	B 17-a	
by value in $m	W European countries	U 33-a	
flue-cured & other types (stripped): tonnage	UK	B 17-a	
(unstripped): tonnage	UK	B 17-a	
(incl beverages) as % of total trade in agricultural products	W European countries	U 20-a	
(incl tobacco manufactures) by value in $	OECD countries	D 1-a	
shipped ex EEC & non-EEC areas by value in $	EEC countries	E 24-a	
tobacco products by NIMEXE classes by value in $	All countries	E 20-a	
SITC classes by value in $	All countries	U 50-a	U 59-a
tonnage	European countries & USSR	A 11-a	
unmanufactured leaf in lbs	Main countries	B 13-a	
Intervention prices fixed by EEC Commission in $ per ton		E 44-a	
Producer prices in local currency per ton	OECD countries	D 1-a	
in $ per ton	All countries	A 9-a	
	EEC countries	E 44-a	
Production & exports of Commonwealth countries as % of world totals		B 13-a	
administrative areas: tonnage	EEC countries	E 38-a	
type in lbs	Main countries	B 17-a	
(incl snuff): tonnage	EEC countries	E 28-q	

	Territorial coverage	Title codes	
TOBACCO, continued			
Production by value as % of gross farm output (incl livestock)	E European countries	U 34-a	
historical tables: tonnage	Main European countries	Z 1-a	
(incl world total): tonnage	Main countries	A 5-a	B 2-a
in million lbs	Main countries	B 13-a	
manufactured tobacco: tonnage	African countries	U 44-a	
	Main countries	E 3-a	
	All countries	U 43-a	
	All countries	U 22-a	
prepared leaf: tonnage	OECD countries	D 1-a	
raw tobacco: tonnage	African countries	U 44-a	
	AASM countries	E 41-a	
tonnage	African countries	U 44-a	
	Asian, Far East & Australasian countries	U 45-a	
	Asian & Far East countries	U 32-a	
	Czechoslovakia, Hungary & Poland	U 34-a	
	E European countries, USSR incl Ukraine	U 16-a	
	EEC countries	B 1-a	E 12-a
		E 44-a	
	Latin American countries	U 40-a	
	OAS member countries	N 13-a	
Production - index nos (quantum basis)	S American countries	U 40-a	
Receipts of government from taxes: tobacco, cigarettes & cigars in local currency	EEC countries	E 42-a	
tobacco, spirits, beer & wine	OECD countries	D 42-a	
Sales: value at auctions (weekly) in pence per lb	Main countries	B 17	
of American leaf (at auctions) in cents per lb	USA	B 17-a	
of Malawi leaf (at auctions) in £ per ton	Malawi	B 17-a	
Stocks: Burley in lbs	Canada	B 17-m	
cigar leaf in lbs	Canada	B 17-m	
fired-cured unmanufactured tobacco in lbs	Canada	B 17-m	
flue-cured unmanufactured tobacco in lbs	UK	B 17-a	
pipe tobacco in lbs	UK	B 17-m	
tonnage	Canada	B 17-m	
unmanufactured tobacco in lbs	Greece, Canada, UK & USA	A 5-a	
Supply, production, consumption & trade: tonnage	Canada & UK	B 13-a	
Value: tobacco production in $m	EEC countries	B 1-a	
Wholesale prices: flue-cured tobacco (at auctions) in $	EEC countries	E 44-a	
in local currency	Main countries	A 5-a	
Withdrawals of tobacco (from bond) in lbs (dry wt)	India, Malawi, Pakistan, Philippines & USA	A 9-a	
World exports by value in $m	UK	B 17-a	
World market prices: unmanufactured leaf ex USA in cents per lb	World regions	A 5-a	
World production (all types) in lbs		E 41-a	
Burley in lbs		B 13-a	
oriental & semi-oriental tobacco leaf in lbs		B 13-a	
sun & air-cured tobacco leaf in lbs		B 13-a	
unmanufactured tobacco leaf: tonnage	World regions	B 13-a	
		U 11-a	
TOBACCO, MANUFACTURED			
see also CIGARS			
CIGARETTES			
FOOD, DRINK & TOBACCO			
Consumption: chewing tobacco: tonnage	OAS member countries	N 17-a	
pipe tobacco: tonnage	OAS member countries	N 17-a	
Excise duties: % rates charged	EEC countries	E 31-a	
Exports by destination: cigarettes in lbs	UK	B 17-a	
Imports by source: cigarettes in lbs	UK	B 17-a	
cigars in lbs	UK	B 17-a	
Production: processed tobacco: tonnage	All countries	U 22-a	
	OAS member countries	N 14-a	
Retail prices in local currency	OAS member countries	N 17-a	
Wholesale prices in local currency	OAS member countries	N 17-a	
TOBACCO BY KIND			
Area under crop in acres	Thailand, USA & Yugoslavia	B 17-a	
Auction prices by region in cents per lb (weekly average)	USA	B 17	
Exports by destination in lbs	USA	B 17-m	
unmanufactured leaf in lbs	All countries	B 17-a	
Imports (by Customs classification) in lbs	UK	B 13-a	
by value in pence per lb	UK	B 13-a	
Production by regions in lbs	Main countries	B 17-a	
(incl snuff): tonnage	EEC countries	E 27-a	
Stocks: unmanufactured tobacco in lbs	USA	B 13-a	
World production in billion lbs		B 13-a	
Yield: cigar tobacco in lbs per acre	Canada & USA	B 13-a	
fire-cured tobacco in lbs per acre	Malawi & USA	B 13-a	
flue-cured tobacco in lbs per acre	All countries	B 13-a	
TOBACCO INDUSTRY			
see also CIGARETTE-MAKING INDUSTRY			
Labour costs: all employees in local currency per hr	EEC countries	E 11-a	
as % of total costs of tobacco-processing industry	EEC countries	E 8-a	
by status of employees in local currency	EEC countries	E 8-a	
salaried staff in local currency per mth	EEC countries	E 11-a	
wage earners in local currency per hr	EEC countries	E 11-a	

	Territorial coverage	Title codes

TOBACCO INDUSTRY, continued

	Territorial coverage	Title codes
Labour force: no of salaried staff employed	EEC countries	E 11-a
of wage earners employed	EEC countries	E 11-a
(total)	EEC countries	E 8-a
No of hrs worked per wk	OAS member countries	N 18-a
per yr: all employees	EEC countries	E 8-a
salaried staff	EEC countries	E 11-a
wage earners	EEC countries	E 11-a
Wage rates in local currency per hr	OAS member countries	N 17-a

TOBACCO SEED OIL

Exports: tonnage	India	B 19-a

Tobacco taxes   see   MONOPOLY TAXES

TOILET PREPARATIONS

see also   PHARMACEUTICAL PRODUCTS
SOAP, TOILET

% females using cosmetics by kind by social classes	W European countries	Z 3
% males using cosmetics by kind by social classes	W European countries	Z 3
Consumption: mercury in production of dental preparations	USA	T 4-a
Exports by destination: cosmetics by value in $	Main countries	U 2-a
Plant investment: capital expenditure in £m	UK	B 21-a
Retail prices: razor blades in local currency	OAS member countries	N 17-a
toothpaste in local currency	OAS member countries	N 17-a
Value of output (gross & net) in £m	UK	B 21-a

Toilet rolls   see   SANITARY PAPER

Toilet soap   see   SOAP, TOILET

TOLLS

Receipts: toll charges on roads in local currency	All countries	S 24-a

TOLUENE

see also   CHEMICAL PRODUCTS
HYDROCARBONS, AROMATIC

Consumption for organic synthesis: tonnage	OECD countries	D 5-a
tonnage	OECD countries	D 5-a
Production from coal derivatives: tonnage	OECD countries	D 5-a
	European countries, Japan & USA	U 26-a
oil & natural gas: tonnage	European countries, Japan & USA	U 26-a
	OECD countries	D 5-a
tonnage	European countries, Japan & USA	U 26-a

Toluol   see   COAL BY-PRODUCTS

TOMATO JUICE

Consumption per capita in kg	Canada & USA	A 7-a
Exports: tonnage	All countries	A 7-a
Imports by source: tonnage	UK	B 6-m
tonnage	Main countries	A 7-a
Production: tonnage	All countries	A 7-a

TOMATO PASTE

Exports by destination: tonnage	All countries	A 7-a
Imports in fresh tomato equiv: tonnage	USA	D 36-a
tonnage	All countries	A 7-a
Production: tonnage	All countries	A 7-a
Wholesale prices by grade in $ per ton	Italy	A 7-a

TOMATOES

Area harvested, production: tonnage & yield per ha	All countries	A 9-a
under crop & yield per ha by regions	OECD countries	D 36-a
in ha	OAS member countries	N 13-a
(open field) in ha by region	USA	D 36-a
in ha	OECD countries	D 29-a D 36-a
(under glass) in ha	OECD countries	D 36-a
Consumption (as fresh tomatoes): tonnage	OECD countries	D 36-a
(as processed tomatoes): tonnage	OECD countries	D 36-a
(industrial) for processing: tonnage	OECD countries	D 29-a
per capita (as fresh tomatoes) in kg	Main countries	A 7-a
	OECD countries	D 36-a
	USA	D 36-a
(as juice) in kg	USA	D 36-a
(as ketchup) in kg	USA	D 36-a
(as processed tomatoes) in kg	Main countries	A 7-a
	OECD countries	D 36-a
(as pulp & pureé) in kg	USA	D 36-a
(as sauce & paste) in kg	USA	D 36-a
in kg	EEC countries	U 20-a
tonnage	OECD countries	D 29-a
Crop yield in kg per ha	OAS member countries	N 13-a
in tons per ha (in open fields)	OECD countries	D 29-a
Export prices in $ per ton fob	Brazil	A 9-a

	Territorial coverage	Title codes
TOMATOES, continued		
Exports by value in $m	W European countries	U 33-a
tomatoes (fresh & processed): tonnage	OECD countries	D 36-a
unit value in $ per ton	Main W European countries	U 20-a
Imports by source: tomatoes (fresh): tonnage	OECD countries	D 37-a
(processed): tonnage	OECD countries	D 37-a
by value in $m	W European countries	U 33-a
(net): tonnage	OECD countries	D 29-a
tomatoes (fresh & processed): tonnage	OECD countries	D 36-a
tonnage	USSR	U 20-a
unit value in $ per ton	W European countries	U 20-a
Intervention prices in local currency per kg	EEC countries	U 20-m
Market gardens: cultivated area of tomatoes in ha	OECD countries	D 36-a
production: tonnage	OECD countries	D 36-a
yield per ha	OECD countries	D 36-a
Producer prices for consumption & processing in lire per ton	Italy	U 20-a
in pesetas per 100 kg	Spain	D 1-a
in $ per ton	All countries	A 9-a
Production & crop harvested: tonnage	USA	D 36-a
by administrative areas: tonnage	EEC countries	E 38-a
by regions: tonnage	OECD countries	D 36-a
commercially-grown (in open fields): tonnage	OECD countries	D 37-a
(under glass): tonnage	OECD countries	D 37-a
for processing: tonnage	OECD countries	D 36-a
open field & under glass: tonnage	OECD countries	D 36-a
tonnage	African countries	U 44-a
	European countries	U 20-a
	Latin American countries	U 40-a
	OAS member countries	N 13-a
	OECD countries	D 29-a
Sales: tomatoes grown in open fields: tonnage	Netherlands	U 20-a
under glass: tonnage	Netherlands	U 20-a
Stock changes: tomatoes in processed form: tonnage	Australia	D 29-a
Supply, production, consumption & trade: tonnage	EEC countries	B 1-a
Volume: tomatoes processed: tonnage	All countries	A 7-a
Wholesale prices in local currency per kg	EEC countries	U 20-m A 9-a
Yield: open field cultivation in tons per ha	OECD countries	D 36-a
under glass in tons per ha	OECD countries	D 36-a
TOMATOES, CANNED		
Exports: tonnage	All countries	A 7-a
Imports: tonnage	Canada, UK & USA	A 7-a
Production: tonnage	All countries	A 7-a
TOOL STEEL		
Exports by destination: tonnage	Main countries	T 4-a
Imports by source: tonnage	Main countries	T 4-a
Production: tonnage	Main countries	T 4-a
Tools see HAND TOOLS		
MACHINE TOOLS		
Toothpaste see TOILET PREPARATIONS		
Tops see MAN-MADE FIBRE TOPS		
WOOL TOPS		
TOURISM		
% arrivals by mode of transport: air, sea, road or rail	OECD countries	D 47-a
% of tourist-nights spent by foreign tourists	OECD countries	D 47-a
Development funds approved for tourism in the Mezzogiorno in Lit	Italy	D 38-a
Earnings from tourist expenditure in local currency	Latin American countries	U 18-a
Expenditure of foreign tourists in $m	USA	D 47-a
incoming travellers in DEG units	OAS member countries	N 15-a
outgoing travellers in DEG units	OAS member countries	N 15-a
tourists in $m	Main countries	S 14-a
	OECD countries	D 47-a
US nationals travelling abroad in $m	USA	D 47-a
in European countries in $m	USA	D 47-a
on accommodation in $m	Main countries	S 14-a
entertainment in $m	Main countries	S 14-a
meals in $m	Main countries	S 14-a
transportation in $m	Main countries	S 14-a
of visitors by nationality in $m	USA	D 47-a
on foreign travel: US nationals	Countries of visit	D 47-a
per overseas visitor (average) in $	Main countries	S 14-a
Government inducements for tourist development in $m	OECD countries	D 47-a
subsidies to aid tourist development in $m	OECD countries	D 47-a
tax concessions offered to aid development of tourism	OECD countries	D 47-a
IBRD loans approved for tourism development in $m	OAS member countries	N 16-a
IDA loans approved for tourism development in $m	OAS member countries	N 16-a
Income derived from tourist expenditure in $m	W Indies & Caribbean countries	T 6-a
	OAS member countries	N 16-a
International tourist expenditure as % of value of imports	OECD countries	D 47-a
receipts as % of value of exports	OECD countries	D 47-a
Length of stay: all visitors in days	OECD countries	D 47-a
European visitors in days	OECD countries	D 47-a
N American visitors in days	OECD countries	D 47-a
US nationals in days	OECD countries	D 47-a

	Territorial coverage	Title codes
TOURISM, continued		
No of tourist arrivals & no of nights spent in hotels	European countries	U 8-a
& receipts from tourism in $m	All countries	U 43-a
	W Indies & Caribbean countries	T 6-a
at frontiers by nationality	OECD countries	D 47-a
at registered hotel & other accommodation	OECD countries	D 47-m
based on frontier & airport records	OECD countries	D 47-a
	Main countries	S 14-m
	ECE countries	U 15-a
by country of residence	Main countries	S 14-a
mode of transport: air, sea, road & rail	Main countries	S 14-a
	OAS member countries	N 15-a
nationality	Main countries	S 14-a
	OAS member countries	N 15-a
	All countries	U 43-a
	USA	D 47-a
purpose of visit: business, health, study or vacation	Main countries	S 14-a
cruise passengers (on excursions)	Main countries	S 14-a
foreign tourists (arriving at frontiers)	OECD countries	D 47-m
	IUOTO member countries	S 14-a
	Latin American countries	J 5-a
	African countries	U 44-a
	Asian, Far East & Australasian countries	U 45-a
	OAS member countries	N 15-a
	W Indies & Caribbean countries	T 6-a
of cruise ships calling at ports	W Germany	D 47-a
foreigners employed in tourist industry	OAS member countries	N 15-a
nationals departing (as tourists)	OECD countries	D 47-a
staff employed: tourist industry by sex	OECD countries	D 47-m
tourist-nights spent at hotels	EEC countries	E 26-m
at registered accommodation	OECD countries	D 47-m
by European visitors	OECD countries	D 47-a
foreigners in private accommodation	OECD countries	D 47-a
in youth hostels	OECD countries	D 47-a
on camping sites	OECD countries	D 47-a
nationality of visitor	Main countries	S 14-a
national tourists in private accommodation	OECD countries	D 47-a
in youth hostels	OECD countries	D 47-a
on camping sites	OECD countries	D 47-a
N American visitors	OECD countries	D 47-a
tourists	African countries	U 44-a
tourists arriving by air, by overland routes, river travel or by sea	OAS member countries	N 15-a
by country of origin	OAS member countries	N 15-a
residence	OAS member countries	N 15-a
	Main countries	R 5-a
US nationals travelling abroad as tourists		D 47-a
to European countries as tourists		D 47-a
Receipts & expenditure from tourism in $m	Latin American countries	J 5-a
from international fare payments in $m	Main countries	S 14-a
on payments balances account from tourism in $m	OECD countries	D 47-a
World bank loans & credits for tourist expansion in $m		M 3-a

Tourism, income from   see   BALANCE OF PAYMENTS

TOURIST ACCOMMODATION

    see also   BOARDING HOUSES
                CAMPING SITES
                HOTELS, TOURIST
                INNS
                MOTELS
                MOUNTAIN HUTS & SHELTERS
                YOUTH HOSTELS

	Territorial coverage	Title codes
No of beds available by kind of accommodation for tourists	OECD countries	D 47-a
	African countries	U 44-a
in hotels, inns & boarding houses	OECD countries	D 47-a
holiday camps	OECD countries	D 47-a
motels	OECD countries	D 47-a
mountain huts, shelters & youth hostels	OECD countries	D 47-a
of hotel rooms available for tourists	W Indies & Caribbean countries	T 6-a
of houses & apartments available for tourists	OECD countries	D 47-a

Tourist hotels   see   HOTELS, TOURIST

Tourist rates of exchange   see   EXCHANGE RATES

Towels & towelling   see   HOUSEHOLD TEXTILES

Toxaphene   see   INSECTICIDES

TOYS

	Territorial coverage	Title codes	
Exports by destination by CST classes: tonnage & value in $	EEC countries	E 48-a	
SITC classes by value in $	Main countries	D 2-q	
tonnage & value in $	OECD countries	D 3-a2	
NIMEXE classes by value in $	All countries	E 20-a	
SITC classes by value in $	All countries	U 50-a	U 59-a

	Territorial coverage	Title codes	
TOYS, continued			
Imports by NIMEXE classes by value in $	All countries	E 20-a	
SITC classes by value in $	All countries	U 50-a	U 59-a
source by CST classes: tonnage & value in $	EEC countries	E 21-a	
SITC classes by value in $	Main countries	D 2-q	
tonnage & value in $	OECD countries	D 3-a2	
Use of plastics in toy production as % of total usage of plastics	European countries	U 26-a	

TOYS & SPORTS GOODS MANUFACTURING INDUSTRY
  Investment in buildings in local currency — EEC countries — E 40-a
          land purchase in local currency — EEC countries — E 40-a
          machinery in local currency — EEC countries — E 40-a

Track-layers   see   TRACTORS, TRACK-LAYING

TRACTOR FUEL
  Retail prices: diesel oil in local currency per 100 litres — EEC countries — E 34-m
            fuel oil in local currency per 100 litres — EEC countries — E 34-m
            motor spirit by octane in local currency per 100 litres — EEC countries — E 34-m
                low octane in local currency per 100 litres — EEC countries — E 34-m

Tractor manufacturing industry   see   FARM MACHINERY INDUSTRY

TRACTORS, AGRICULTURAL
    see also   ROAD TRACTORS

	Territorial coverage	Title codes	
% change: wages paid to tractor drivers	W European countries	U 30-a	
% of exports by destination areas	UK	B 28-a	
% share: main markets (value basis)	UK	V 1-a	
world exports (value basis)	UK	B 27-a	
Expenditure on tractors as % on all new farm equipment	ECE countries	U 34-a	
on new tractors by value in $	ECE countries	U 34-a	
Exports by destination by value in $m	Main countries	U 9-a	
tonnage & value in $m	All countries	U 12-a	
volume	USSR	V 1-a	
wheeled type by HP groups	UK	V 1-a	
NIMEXE classes by value in $m	All countries	E 20-a	
SITC classes by value in $m	All countries	U 50-a	U 59-a
value in £m	UK	B 28-a	
in $m	Main countries	U 38-a	
value - index nos	UK	V 1-m	
volume & value: historical table in £m	UK	V 1-a	
in £m	UK	V 1-a	
Imports & exports by value in $m	All countries	A 14-a	
by NIMEXE classes by value in $m	All countries	E 20-a	
SITC classes by value in $m	All countries	U 50-a	U 59-a
source: tonnage & value in $	All countries	U 12-a	
volume & value in £m	UK	V 1-a	
value in $m	All countries	U 38-a	
No in use & no in use per 100 ha	EEC countries	E 3-a	
& total HP in use per 100 ha of agricultural land	EEC countries	E 44-a	
(all types)	Great Britain	V 1-a	
by administrative areas	EEC countries	E 38-a	
(excl garden tractors)	OECD countries	D 1-a	
from 10-50 hp engine by county	UK	V 1-a	
over 80 hp engine by county	UK	V 1-a	
per 1000 ha of agricultural land	EEC countries	E 38-a	
of arable land	EEC countries	E 38-a	
(total)	EEC countries	B 1-a	
	Great Britain	V 1-q	
	UK	V 1-a	
up to 10 hp engine by county	UK	V 1-a	
wheeled & crawler types	All countries	A 9-a	U 43-a
	Asian, Far East & Australasian countries	U 45-a	
	Great Britain	V 1-a	
Park: crawlers projected to 1980	E African countries	U 38	
(incl world total park)	Main countries	R 5-a	
wheeled projected to 1980	E African countries	U 38	
Production by overseas subsidiaries: volume	Main countries	V 2-a	
by hp categories: volume	All countries	U 22-a	
historical tables: volume	UK	V 1-a	
prime movers: volume	Main countries	R 5-a	
over 10 hp engine: volume	All countries	U 38-a	
	Argentine, Brazil & Mexico	N 14-a	
	E European countries & USSR	U 16-a	
(total): volume	EEC countries	E 26-m	E 28-q
		E 27-a	
Registrations (new)	N Ireland	V 1-q	
	UK	V 1-m	
Retail prices by hp categories in $	Main countries	A 9-a	
Sales: 2-wheel drive models by engine hp categories	UK	V 1-a	
4-wheel drive models by engine hp categories	UK	V 1-a	
Wages & social charges: drivers in $	E European countries	U 30-a	
World exports by value in $m		U 38-a	

Tractors, garden   see   GARDEN TRACTORS
                      MOTOR CULTIVATORS

Tractors, general haulage   see   ROAD TRACTORS

	Territorial coverage	Title codes	
TRACTORS, TRACK-LAYING			
Exports by destination by drawbar hp	UK	V 1-a	
Park projected to 1980	E African countries	U 38	
Production by drawbar hp	UK	V 1-q	
TRADE BALANCES			
see also BALANCE OF PAYMENTS			
As component of balance of international payments on trading account in local currency	African countries	U 44-a	
By world regions in $m	Japan & USA	G 1-a	
Changes (net) in $m	Regional country groups	U 54-a	
In $m	Asian, Far East & Australasian countries	U 45-a	
	ECAFE countries	U 32-m	
	ECE countries	U 15-a	
	Main countries	G 1-a	
	OECD countries	D 16-m	D 26-m
	OPEC member countries	C 3-a	
In local currency	African countries	U 44-a	
Inter-EEC area trade (incl balances with other world Economic areas) in $m	EEC countries	E 13-a	
Inter-regional trade balances in $m	EEC countries	E 26-m	
Of E European Bloc & USSR with rest of the world in $m	Latin American countries	J 5-a	
E European countries with other E European countries in $m		U 16-a	
EEC area with rest of the world in UA		U 16-a	
EEC countries with other EEC countries in UA		E 24-a	
USA with rest of the world in $m		E 24-a	
Trend: deficits & surpluses on payment balances (trading account) in $m	Country groups	U 54-a	
	EEC countries	E 13-m	
With E European countries in $m	USA	U 16-a	
W European countries in $m	USA	U 16-a	
rest of the world in $m	USA	U 16-a	
	OAS member countries	N 15-a	
world regions & world Economic groupings of countries in $m	OECD countries	D 16-m	
world regions in $m	OAS member countries	N 15-a	
TRADE BALANCES BY COMMODITY			
Value basis: agricultural tractors with world regions of supply in £m	UK	B 28-a	
automotive accessories & parts with world regions of supply in £m	UK	B 28-a	
commercial vehicles with world regions of supply in £m	UK	B 28-a	
finished knitted goods in £m	UK	B 29-a	
iron & steel products (in detail) in DM	W Germany	H 3-a	
motor vehicles (all types) with world regions of supply in £m	UK	B 28-a	
passenger cars with world regions of supply in £m	UK	B 28-a	
petroleum & petroleum products in $m	Main countries	G 1-a	
ready-made clothing in £m	UK	B 29-a	
Volume basis: carpets in sq yds	UK	B 29-a	
cotton yarns in lbs	UK	B 29-a	
knitted fabrics in sq yds	UK	B 29-a	
man-made fibres & yarns in lbs	UK	B 29-a	
textile fibres by kind & textile yarns in lbs	UK	B 29-a	
wool yarns in lbs	UK	B 29-a	
woven cotton fabrics in sq yards	UK	B 29-a	
woollen fabrics in sq yards	UK	B 29-a	
TRADE CONVERSION FACTORS			
In local currency per $	All countries	F 5-m	F 6-q
TRADE CREDITS			
Income (net) earned on commercial credits in $	All countries	F 5-m	F 6-q
Wheat & flour: food aid granted on long-term credit in $m	USA	C 16-a	
guaranteed export credits in $m	Canada	B 8-a	
Trade margins see DISTRIBUTION COSTS			
Trade routes see WORLD TRADE ROUTES			
TRAFFIC			
see also AIR TRAFFIC			
CONTAINER TRAFFIC			
OCEAN PASSENGER TRAFFIC			
RAIL TRAFFIC			
ROAD TRAFFIC			
Volume carried on airlines in ton-km	ECE countries	U 15-a	
inland waterways in ton-km	EEC countries	U 15-a	
motorways in ton-km	ECE countries	U 15-a	
railways in ton-km	ECE countries	U 15-a	
Traffic accidents see ACCIDENTS, ROAD			

	Territorial coverage	Title codes
TRAFFIC CONTROL EQUIPMENT		
Exports by destination by value in $m	Main countries	U 9-a
by value in $m	All countries	U 38-a
Imports by value in $m	All countries	U 38-a
World exports by value in $m		U 38-a

Traffic controllers   see   AIRLINE PERSONNEL

	Territorial coverage	Title codes
TRAILERS		
% of households owning caravans by social classes	W European countries	Z 3
Caravans as % of total living quarters available	All countries	U 13-a
Demand: road trailers projected to 1980	E African countries	U 38
Exports: caravans & trailers: volume	OECD countries	D 9-a
Imports by source: caravans: volume & value in £	UK	V 1-a
No of caravans in use (at end-yr)	Main countries	S 24-a
commercial trailers in use (at end-yr)	Main countries	S 24-a
mobile homes in use (as urban housing units)	All countries	U 13-a
permanent residents living in caravans: urban & rural areas	All countries	U 13-a
road tractors in use by type & load capacity	EEC countries	E 43-a
	European countries	U 8-a
semi-trailers in use (at end-yr)	Main countries	S 24-a
trailers in use on roads	W Indies & Caribbean countries	T 6-a
	EEC countries	E 43-a
Production: caravans: historical tables: volume	UK	V 1-a
trailers for use with road tractors: volume	All countries	U 22-a
(incl semi-trailers): volume	All countries	U 38-a
Sales: caravans for touring & holiday use: volume	UK	V 1-q
(incl semi-trailers): volume	UK	V 1-q
(motorised & converted): volume	UK	V 1-q
(permanent residential types): volume	UK	V 1-q
chassis for caravans: volume	UK	V 1-q

TRAINING COLLEGES
    see also   TEACHER TRAINING
                  UNIVERSITIES

	Territorial coverage	Title codes
No of students enrolled by sex	OAS member countries	N 19-a
incl teacher training establishments	AASM countries	E 41-a
Public expenditure per student in $	All countries	U 62-a

Trains   see   RAILWAY TRAINS

Tramp charter rates   see   CARGO SHIPS
                              OCEAN FREIGHT RATES

Tramp freight rates   see   OCEAN FREIGHT RATES

TRAMP SHIPPING
    see also   CARGO SHIPS

	Territorial coverage	Title codes	
Freight rates by commodity - index nos	Worldwide	U 37-a	
voyage charter - index nos	Worldwide	D 28-m	
- index nos	All countries	F 5-m	F 6-q

TRANSACTION TAXES
    see also   TAXATION

	Territorial coverage	Title codes
Government receipts from transaction taxes in $m	Asian, Far East & Australasian countries	U 45-a

Transfer buying rates   see   EXCHANGE RATES

Transfer increase rates   see   LABOUR FORCE

TRANSFER MACHINES
    see also   MACHINE TOOLS

	Territorial coverage	Title codes
Production by value in $m	UK	B 31-a

TRANSFER PAYMENTS
    see also   BALANCE OF PAYMENTS
                  INVESTMENT
                  TRANSFER PAYMENTS, CORPORATE

	Territorial coverage	Title codes
As % of gross domestic product	OECD countries	D 11-a
As component of gross domestic product in local currency	Main countries	E 3-a
balance of payments in local currency	African countries	U 44-a
	OAS member countries	N 16-a
	All countries	F 1-a
	Latin American countries	U 18-a
exchange losses in $	Developing world regions	U 23-a
exchange receipts in $	Developing world regions	U 23-a
gross national product in local currency	Developing countries	D 25-a
Capital transfers as % of gross domestic product	Main countries	E 3-a
(net) in local currency	OAS member countries	N 16-a
(public & private) in $m	ECAFE countries	U 17-a
Corporate transfers as component of national income in local currency	OAS member countries	N 16-a
Corporate capital transfers (net) in local currency	OAS member countries	N 16-a
External transactions by kind in local currency	OAS member countries	N 16-a
Government capital transfers (net) in local currency	OAS member countries	N 16-a

	Territorial coverage	Title codes	
TRANSFER PAYMENTS, continued			
Income (net) on private transfers in $m	All countries	F 5-m	F 6-q
Lending to rest of world (net) in local currency	OAS member countries	N 16-a	
Private & official banking payments & transfer remittances in $m	Main countries	E 3-a	
	EEC countries	E 4-a	E 32-a
	Asian, Far East & Australasian countries	U 45-a	
Private capital transfers (net) in local currency	OAS member countries	N 16-a	
Purchases of goods by non-residents in local currency	African countries	U 44-a	
Transfers (net) from abroad in $m	All countries	U 60-a	

Transfer selling rates   see   EXCHANGE RATES

Transformer plates   see   STEEL SHEETS, MAGNETIC

TRANSFORMERS
     see also   ELECTRIC POWER EQUIPMENT

	Territorial coverage	Title codes	
% of imports by source (value basis)	Main countries	T 7-a	
Capacity: transformers produced in kVA	All countries	U 38-a	
Deliveries by size in MVa	European countries, Japan & USA	D 45-a	
in MVa	European countries, Japan & USA	D 45-a	
Exports as % of production	European countries, Japan & USA	D 45-a	
to world regions in MVa	Main W European countries	T 7-a	
in MVa	European countries, Japan & USA	D 45-a	T 7-a
incl switchgear by value in $m	OECD countries	D 9-a	
Imports by value in $m	All countries	U 38-a	
New orders & orders in hand in MVa	European countries, Japan & USA	D 45-a	
Production in MVa	European countries, Japan & USA	D 45-a	T 7-a
in MVa or tonnage	EEC countries	E 28-q	E 27-a
over 5 kVa	All countries	U 22-a	
over 5 kVa & by value in $m	All countries	U 38-a	

TRANSISTORS

	Territorial coverage	Title codes
Production: volume in million	European countries, Japan, UK & USA	U 38-a
volume: silicon & germanium transistors in million	All countries	U 22-a

Transit passengers   see   AIR PASSENGER TRAFFIC

TRANSIT TRADE
     see also   RE-EXPORT TRADE

	Territorial coverage	Title codes
Tin by source & destination: tonnage	Countries of transit	C 20-m
tonnage	Countries of destination	C 20-m
Tin alloys by source & destination: tonnage	Countries of transit	C 20-m

Translations   see   BOOK TRANSLATIONS

Transmission chains   see   REPLACEMENT PARTS

Transmission lines   see   POWER TRANSMISSION LINES

Transmitters   see   RADIO STATIONS

TRANSPORT & COMMUNICATIONS
     see also   AIR TRANSPORT
                   CONTAINER TRAFFIC
                   RAIL TRAFFIC
                   ROAD TRANSPORT
                   SEABORNE SHIPPING
                   TRANSPORT SERVICES
                   TRANSPORT UNDERTAKINGS

	Territorial coverage	Title codes	
% consumption by kind of energy source	Main countries	H 4-a	
petroleum products	Latin American countries	U 18-a	
to national income	Developed countries	D 25-a	
to gross national product: historical table from 1850	Main countries	Z 1-a	
to gross national product	S American countries	U 41-a	
	All countries	U 23-a	U 60-a
% growth in income as component of gross national product	All countries	U 60-a	
% growth rate: gross product of transport industries	Developed countries	D 25-a	
% of labour force employed by region	EEC countries	E 2-a	
% share of total capital investment	E European countries	U 16-a	
A.I.D. grants to promote improved transport facilities in $	Recipient countries	M 1-a	
Capital formation in $m	EEC countries	E 32-a	
Consumption: electricity by area in kWh	EEC countries	E 38-a	
in kWh	Main countries	H 4-a	
	OECD countries	D 8-a	
	European countries	U 1-a	
per capita in kWh	EEC countries	E 15-a	
natural gas by volume in m³	Main countries	H 4-a	
petroleum products: tonnage	Main countries	H 4-a	
Cost to private sector in $m	EEC countries	E 32-a	
Development aid authorisations in $m	Recipient countries	M 1-a	
Earnings (average) in $ per yr	All countries	L 4-a	
Employment (yr-end): volume	EEC countries	E 33-a	
Employment - index nos	OAS member countries	N 18-a	
Expenditure & as % of total outlay	EEC countries	E 2-a	
Frequency of accidents at work in transport industries	EEC countries	E 2-a	
Funds granted for aid projects by European Development Fund in $m		D 13-a	

	Territorial coverage	Title codes	
TRANSPORT & COMMUNICATIONS, continued			
Government expenditure on transportation research in $m	EEC countries	E 36-a	
Gross product: transportation in $m	OAS member countries	N 16-a	
Income contribution to gross domestic product in $	African countries	U 44-a	
	Developing countries	D 25-a	
	Latin American countries	U 18-a	
	EEC countries	E 32-a	
	S American countries	U 41-a	
Index nos	World economic regions	U 60-a	
Labour force employed (at census dates)	OAS member countries	N 18	
by area	EEC countries	E 2-a	E 18-a
by sex	EEC countries	E 38-a	
by status	Main countries	C 28(irr)	
(total)	All countries	L 4-a	
	Asian, Far East & Australasian countries	U 32-q	
	OECD countries	D 23-a	
unemployed	All countries	L 4-a	
No of hrs worked per wk	All countries	L 4-a	
Private expenditure on transport in local currency	OAS member countries	N 16-a	
on vehicle fares & travel in $	AASM countries	E 41-a	
Surface goods traffic by kind: tonnage	Main countries	S 24-a	
World Bank loans & credits in $m		M 3-a	
TRANSPORT EQUIPMENT			
see also BUSES & COACHES			
LOCOMOTIVES			
ROLLING STOCK			
Consumption by value in $m	Main Latin American countries	U 38-a	
Exports as % of consumption	Main countries	U 23-a	
by destination & value in $m	Main countries	U 9-a	
by value in $m (incl % growth rates)	Main countries	U 38-a	
in $m	ECE countries	U 15-a	
	Australia, Hong Kong & Japan	U 32-m	
shipped to EEC & non-EEC areas by value in $m	EEC countries	E 24-a	
Exports - index nos (quantum & value bases)	OECD countries	D 16-q	
Growth in production capacity: tonnage	African countries	U 38-a	
Imports as % of consumption	Main countries	U 23-a	
by value in $m	Main Latin American countries	U 38-a	
	All countries	U 38-a	
	Asian, Far East & Australasian countries	U 32-m	
for industrial use by value in UA	AASM countries	E 41-a	
shipped ex EEC area for industrial use by value in UA	AASM countries	E 41-a	
ex EEC & non-EEC areas by value in $m	EEC countries	E 24-a	
Imports - index nos (quantum & value bases)	OECD countries	D 16-q	
Production as % of total industrial output	Developing countries	U 38-a	
projected to 1980	N African countries	U 38	
Production - index nos (quantum basis)	S American countries	U 40-a	
	OECD countries	D 19-m	D 20-m
Purchase: transport equipment as % share of capital formation	Developing countries	U 38-a	
Receipts: steel supplies by transport equipment industry	OECD countries	D 22-a	
Sales: transport equipment by value in $m	Main countries	U 23-a	
Value added in manufacture in $m	OECD countries	D 9-a	
Wholesale prices - index nos	Thailand	U 32-m	
World exports by value in $m		U 38-a	
TRANSPORT EQUIPMENT BY KIND			
Exports by destination by CST classes by value in $m	EEC countries	E 48-a	
SITC classes by value in $m	Main countries	D 2-q	
tonnage & value in $m	OECD countries	D 3-a2	
NIMEXE classes by value in $m	All countries	E 20-a	
SITC classes by value in $m	All countries	U 50-a	U 59-a
Imports by NIMEXE classes by value in $m	All countries	E 20-a	
SITC classes by value in $m	All countries	U 50-a	U 59-a
source by CST classes by value in $m	EEC countries	E 21-a	
SITC classes by value in $m	Main countries	D 2-q	
tonnage & value in $m	OECD countries	D 3-a2	
TRANSPORT EQUIPMENT MANUFACTURING INDUSTRY			
see also MOTOR VEHICLES INDUSTRY			
Capital formation projected to 1980 in $m	N African countries	U 38	
Consumption: brass mill products: tonnage	USA	J 6-a	
copper rods, sheets, tubes & wire: tonnage	USA	J 6-a	
Earnings (average) in $ per hr	All countries	L 4-a	
Labour costs as % of total costs	EEC countries	E 8-a	
by status of employees in local currency	EEC countries	E 8-a	
Labour force employed by status of employees	EEC countries	E 8-a	
(total)	All countries	L 4-a	
No of hrs worked by area per wk	EEC countries	E 25-a	
per wk	OAS member countries	N 18-a	
	All countries	L 4-a	
per yr	EEC countries	E 8-a	
machine tools in use	USA	J 2-a	
Production - index nos	Far East countries	U 32-q	
Wage rates in local currency per hr	EEC countries	E 25-a2	
mechanics in local currency per hr	OAS member countries	N 17-a	

	Territorial coverage	Title codes

TRANSPORT SERVICES
    see also BUSES & COACHES
                RAILWAYS

% of employed population engaged in transport services	EEC countries	E 33-a
% of government expenditure paid out on transportation	Main countries	R 5-a
% of gross domestic product used on transportation facilities	OECD countries	D 11-a
% share of electricity usage as energy source for transport services	W European countries	U 16-a
oil usage as energy source for transport services	W European countries	U 16-a
Bus & underground railways: fares in local currency	OAS member countries	N 17-a
Bus fares: inter-city journeys in local currency	OAS member countries	N 17-a
local journeys in local currency	OAS member countries	N 17-a
Consumption: electricity in kWh	All countries	C 23-a
Cost to private sector in local currency	EEC countries	E 32-a
Electricity: consumption from own production in kWh	All countries	C 23-a
from public supply in kWh	All countries	C 23-a
Incidence of strikes or lock-outs by transport employees	Main countries	R 3-a
Labour costs: drivers in local currency per hr	EEC countries	E 10-a
freight transport in local currency per hr	EEC countries	E 10-a
passenger transport in local currency per hr	EEC countries	E 10-a
wage earners in transportation in local currency per hr	EEC countries	E 10-a
Labour force employed by sex: historical table 1750-1969	Main European countries	Z 1-a
(at census dates)	African countries	U 44-a
no of managerial staff employed	AASM countries	E 41-a
salaried staff employed	AASM countries	E 41-a
unskilled workers employed	AASM countries	E 41-a
wage earners employed	AASM countries	E 41-a
Loan advances (from commercial banks) in local currency	OAS member countries	N 16-a
No of employees involved in strikes	Main countries	R 3-a
of hrs worked per wk: airlines, railways & ships	Main countries	R 3-m
of working days lost per employee (all causes)	UK	B 29-a
through strikes	Main countries	R 3-a
Public expenditure on transportation in local currency	W Indies & Caribbean countries	T 6-a
Wage rates: bus conductors in shillings per hr	UK	R 4-a
bus drivers & bus inspectors in £ per wk	UK	R 4-a
in local currency per day	OAS member countries	N 17-a
	Portugal	R 4-q
by sex: airlines in local currency per hr	Main countries	R 3-m
railways in local currency per hr	Main countries	R 3-m
ships in local currency per hr	Main countries	R 3-m
lorry drivers in local currency per day	Portugal	R 4-q
per wk	Main countries	R 4-a
railway employees in local currency per wk	Australia	R 4-a
	OAS member countries	N 17-a
porters in £ per wk	UK	R 4-a
signalmen in local currency per day	OAS member countries	N 17-a
tram drivers & conductors in local currency per day	Portugal	R 4-q
train drivers in local currency per wk	OAS member countries	N 17-a
in £ per wk	UK	R 4-a
skilled & unskilled workers in local currency per hr	Main countries	R 4-q
warehousemen in £ per wk	UK	R 4-a

TRANSPORT UNDERTAKINGS

Details: 30 largest transport undertakings	USA	H 1
Name: largest Swiss companies, labour force employed & % change in turnover in Fr S		H 1
US companies, labour force employed & % change in turnover		H 1
net profits & turnover in $m		H 1

Transportation income   see   INVISIBLE TRADE

Transportation industry   see   HAULAGE INDUSTRY

Travel   see   AIR PASSENGER TRAFFIC
               BUSINESS TRAVEL
               OCEAN PASSENGER TRAFFIC
               RAIL PASSENGER TRAFFIC
               ROAD TRANSPORT
               TRANSPORT SERVICES

TRAVEL ALLOWANCES

Foreign exchange granted for travel abroad per journey in $	OECD countries	D 47-a
per person in $	OECD countries	D 47-a

Travelling bags   see   LUGGAGE, LEATHER

TRAWLERS
    see also WORLD FISHING FLEETS

No & tonnage coastal fishing fleet (unpowered)	W Germany	D 43-a	
deep-sea fishing vessels by type	OECD countries	D 43-a	
factory ships (begun & completed)	Poland	S 16-q	
by size groups in dwt	Worldwide	D 43-a	
fishing vessels afloat by flag	Worldwide	S 2-a	
(begun & completed)	Poland	S 16-q	
by size groups in dwt & by flag	Worldwide	S 2-a	
completed in dwt	Country of construction	S 3-q	
launched in dwt	Country of construction	S 3-q	S 1-a

	Territorial coverage	Title codes

TRAWLERS, continued
    No & tonnage fishing vessels on order in dwt   Country of construction   D 28-a
        long liners & purse-seiners by type   Faroes   D 43-a
        mother factory ships completed in dwt   Poland   S 16-q
        motor fishing cutters in dwt   W Germany   D 43-a
        on order (but not started) in dwt   All countries   S 3-q
        refrigerated trawlers by type in dwt   OECD countries   D 43-a
        under construction (all types) in dwt   All countries   S 3-q
    Tonnage afloat: fishing trawlers % as % of world shipping fleets   D 28-a
    World fishing fleets by size in dwt   Country of registration   D 43-a

Treasury bill rates   see   MONEY MARKET RATES

TREASURY BILLS
    see also   DISCOUNT HOUSES
                   GOVERNMENT BONDS
                   GOVERNMENT BORROWING
    Interest rates: % per annum   Main countries   M 7

Treasury bonds   see   GOVERNMENT BONDS

Treasury funds   see   BUDGET ACCOUNTS
                     CENTRAL BANKS
                     PUBLIC DEBT

Trench diggers   see   CONSTRUCTION EQUIPMENT

Trend forecasts   see   PROJECTIONS, INDUSTRIAL

Tribes   see   ETHNIC GROUPS

Trimeperidine   see   SYNTHETIC NARCOTICS

Trip charter (shipping)   see   CHARTERINGS

Tripoli powder   see   DIATOMACEOUS EARTH

TROPICAL FRUITS, CANNED
    see also   PINEAPPLES, CANNED
    Wholesale prices: guava in $ USA   A 8-a
                     lychees in $ W Germany & UK   A 8-a
                     mangoes & mango chutney in $ USA   A 8-a
                     passion fruit in $ USA   A 8-a
                     pawpaw in $ USA   A 8-a

TROPICAL FRUITS, FRESH
    see also   FRUIT JUICES
                   MANGOES
                   PINEAPPLES
    Area under passion fruit in acres   Australia & Hawaii   A 8-a
    Crop yield: passion fruit per acre   Australia & Hawaii   A 8-a
    Farm prices: passion fruit in cents per lb   Hawaii   A 8-a
    Imports: tropical fruits: tonnage & value in local currency   OECD countries   D 37-a
    Production: passion fruit: tonnage   Australia & Hawaii   A 8-a

TROPICAL PRODUCTS
    see also   COCOA
                   COFFEE
                   COMMODITIES, AGRICULTURAL
                   CROPS
                   NATURAL RUBBER
                   PEPPER
                   SPICES & ESSENCES
                   SUGAR
                   TIMBER, TROPICAL
                   TOBACCO
    % change in export earnings   Developing countries   U 11-a
    World market prices (incl sugar) - index nos   U 30-a

TROPICAL PRODUCTS BY KIND
    Production: Commonwealth countries as % of world production   B 13-a
    World exports: Commonwealth countries as % of world total   B 13-a
    World exports - index nos (quantum & value bases)   B 13-a
    World production - index nos   B 13-a

Tropical woods   see   TIMBER, TROPICAL

Trousers   see   CLOTHING

Trucks   see   COMMERCIAL VEHICLES
                 FORK LIFT TRUCKS
                 WORKS' TRUCKS

Tube blanks   see   BLANKS FOR TUBES

	Territorial coverage	Title codes	
Tube ingots & solids see INGOTS FOR TUBES			
Tube rounds & squares see BLANKS FOR TUBES			
Tuberculosis see DISEASES			
Tubers see ROOT CROPS			

TUBES, ALUMINIUM

	Territorial coverage	Title codes	
Consumption: tonnage	UK	T 4-a	
Despatches: tonnage	OECD countries	D 21-a	
	UK	C 30-a	
Exports by destination: tonnage	Main countries	T 4-a	
Imports by source: tonnage	Main countries	T 4-a	
Production: tubes & pipes: tonnage	All countries	U 22-a	
tonnage	Main countries	T 4-a	
Sales (incl tube blooms & extruded shapes): tonnage	USA	J 6-a	
Wholesale prices: 50 mm cold-drawn aluminium tubes in Fr per kg	France	T 4-q	

Tubes, brass   see   BRASS PRODUCTS, SEMI-FINISHED

TUBES, COPPER

Exports by destination: tonnage	Main countries	T 4-a	
tubes & pipes by destination: tonnage	USA	J 6-a	
Imports by source: seamless tubes: tonnage	USA	J 6-a	
tonnage	Netherlands & USA	T 4-a	
Production: tubes & pipes: tonnage	All countries	U 22-a	
tonnage	Japan & UK	C 12-a	
	Main countries	T 4-a	
Usage by building industry (for plumbing): tonnage	USA	J 6-a	
consumer products manufacturing industry: tonnage	USA	J 6-a	
electrical & electronic industries: tonnage	USA	J 6-a	
machinery & equipment manufacturing industry: tonnage	USA	J 6-a	
transport equipment manufacturing industry: tonnage	USA	J 6-a	
Wholesale prices (by diameter) in £ per kg	UK	T 4-w	
in lire per kg	Italy	C 12-m	
in local currency per kg	Main countries	T 4-w	

TUBES, COPPER ALLOY

Exports by destination: tonnage	Main countries	T 4-a	
Imports by source: tonnage	Main countries	T 4-a	
Production: tonnage	Main countries	T 4-a	
Wholesale prices 30% nickel quality copper tubes in Fr per kg	France	T 4-w	
copper-nickel condenser tubes in £ per ton	UK	T 4-w	

TUBES, LEAD
   see also   LEAD PRODUCTS, SEMI-FINISHED

Production: lead tubes & pipes: tonnage	All countries	U 22-a	

Tubes, magnesium   see   MAGNESIUM PRODUCTS, SEMI-FINISHED

TUBES, SEAMLESS STEEL

Exports by destination: tonnage	Main countries	T 4-a	
Imports by source: tonnage	Main countries	T 4-a	
Production: semis for tube-making: tonnage	All countries	U 22-a	
welded tubes: tonnage	EEC countries	E 28-q	E 27-a
tonnage	All countries	U 22-a	
	ECE countries	U 7-m	U 6-a
	Main countries	H 3-a	T 4-a

TUBES, STEEL

Consumption (incl fittings): tonnage	Developing countries	U 57-a	
Deliveries to EEC area: tonnage	EEC countries	E 29-a	
to user industries: tonnage	ECE countries	U 7-q	U 6-a
	Main countries	H 3-a	
Exports by destination: tonnage	ECE countries	U 48-a	
	EEC countries	E 5-q	E 29-a
	Main countries	T 4-a	
(incl fittings): tonnage	E European countries	T 1-a	
	ECE countries	U 7-m	U 6-a
	Main countries	H 3-a	U 49-a
Imports by kind: tonnage	Main countries	T 1-a	
quality: tonnage	Main countries	T 1-a	
source: tonnage	EEC countries	E 5-q	
	Main countries	T 4-a	
high-pressure conduits: tonnage	Main countries	T 1-a	
(incl fittings): tonnage	ECE countries	U 7-m	U 6-a
	Main countries	H 3-a	
seamless alloy steel tubes: tonnage	Main countries	T 1-a	
carbon steel tubes: tonnage	Main countries	T 1-a	
tube & pipe fittings: tonnage	Main countries	T 1-a	
welded alloy steel tubes: tonnage	Main countries	T 1-a	
carbon steel tubes: tonnage	Main countries	T 1-a	
Production (incl blanks for tubes): tonnage	EEC countries	E 30-q	
(incl fittings): tonnage	EEC countries	E 29-a	
seamless & welded steel tubes: tonnage	EEC countries	E 30-q	E 29-a

	Territorial coverage	Title codes	
TUBES, STEEL continued			
Production: seamless tubes: tonnage	All countries	T 1-a	
	OAS member countries	N 14-a	
semis (for seamless tubes): tonnage	All countries	U 22-a	
tonnage	EEC countries	E 29-a	
	Main countries	T 4-a	
Receipts ex EEC area: tonnage	EEC countries	E 29-a	
TUBES, WELDED STEEL			
Exports by destination: tonnage	Main countries	T 4-a	
Imports by source: tonnage	Main countries	T 4-a	
Production: tonnage	All countries	U 22-a	
	ECE countries	U 7-m	U 6-a
	Main countries	H 3-a	T 4-a

Tubes & fittings, cast-iron   see   PIPES, CAST-IRON

Tubes & pipes, lead   see   LEAD PRODUCTS, SEMI-FINISHED
                                                     TUBES, LEAD

	Territorial coverage	Title codes	
TUBES & PIPES, NICKEL			
Exports: tonnage	USA	T 4-a	
TUBES & PIPES, TITANIUM			
Sales in lbs	USA	J 6-a	

Tuff   see   ABRASIVES, NATURAL

	Territorial coverage	Title codes	
TUGS			
see also BARGES			
% of no in service working on inland waterways by age groups	European countries	U 8-a	
% of total capacity covered by tugs of specific age groups	European countries	U 8-a	
Deliveries: new coastal & sea-going vessels	Netherlands	S 16-a	
No & hp of engines of tugs in service on inland waterways by age groups	EEC countries	E 43-a	
& tonnage: coastal lugger fleet	W Germany	D 43-a	
in service on inland waterways (incl pusher craft)	European countries	U 8-a	
TUNA FISH			
Catch (nominal) by kind: tonnage	All countries	A 22-a	
tonnage & value in local currency	OECD countries	D 43-a	
Consumption: canned tuna fish: tonnage	OAS member countries	N 17-a	
Retail prices in local currency per ton	OAS member countries	N 17-a	
TUNA FISH, TINNED			
Exports by kind: tonnage & value in $	All countries	A 21-a	
Production: tonnage	Main countries	A 21-a	
TUNG NUTS			
Exports: tonnage & value in $m	Main countries	B 2-a	
Production: tonnage	Argentina, Brazil & Paraguay	U 40-a	
World production: tonnage		B 2-a	
TUNG OIL			
Exports by destination: tonnage	Main countries	B 18-a	
tonnage & value in $m	Main countries	B 2-a	
tonnage	Main countries	B 19-a	P 1-a
Factory consumption in manufacture of industrial products: tonnage	USA	B 19-a	
Import prices: tung oil (ex S American countries) in $ per ton cif	UK	B 19-m	
in £ per ton cif	UK	B 2-a	
in $ per ton cif	European countries	A 9-a	
Imports by source: tonnage	EEC countries	B 19-a	
tonnage	Main countries	B 19-a	
Production (incl world total): tonnage	All countries	B 18-a	
for ensuing year (estim): tonnage	World regions	P 1-a	
tonnage	Main countries incl China	B 19-a	P 1-a
Stocks (initial & end-yr): tonnage	USA	B 19-a	
Usage in production of paints & varnishes: tonnage	USA	B 19-a	
plastics & resins: tonnage	USA	B 19-a	
putty & brake-linings, etc: tonnage	USA	B 19-a	
Wholesale prices in cents per lb	USA	B 19-m	A 9-a
		B 19-a	
World (incl Commonwealth production): tonnage		A 4-a	B 2-a
World production: tonnage		N 10-a	
TUNGSTEN			
see also FERRO-TUNGSTEN			
Consumption in production of ferro-alloys: tonnage	UK	T 4-a	
metallic tungsten: tonnage	USA	N 1-a	
Exports: metallic tungsten: tonnage	France, W Germany, Sweden & USA	T 4-a	
Government strategic stockpile: metallic tungsten & tungsten carbide: tonnage	USA	N 1-a	
tungsten ore: tonnage	USA	N 1-a	
Import prices per ton of metal content in $	UK	U 11-a	

	Territorial coverage	Title codes	
TUNGSTEN, continued			
Imports & exports: ore, metal, scrap & alloys: tonnage	All countries	B 15-a	
No of mines in operation producing tungsten ores & concentrates	Main countries	U 53-a	
Production (60% concentrates) by primary producers: tonnage	USA	J 6-a	
(based on content of concentrates): tonnage	Latin American countries	J 5-a	
	All countries	B 15-a	U 22-a
		U 43-a	
tonnage	Argentina, Bolivia, Brazil, Peru & Mexico	U 40-a	
	OAS member countries	N 14-a	
Releases ex US strategic stockpile: tonnage	USA	U 11-a	
Stocks held by producers & industrial users: tonnage	USA	N 1-a	
Wholesale prices (duty-paid) in $ per ton	USA	N 1-a	
tungsten powder in £ per kg	UK	T 4-w	
World consumption: tonnage (estim)		U 11-a	
World exports (based on metal content of ore): tonnage & value in $m		U 11-a	
World production (at mines): tonnage	Main countries	N 1-a	
(based on metal content of ore): tonnage		C 12-a	C 30-a
		U 11-a	
tungsten concentrates: tonnage		N 4-a	
World reserves: scheelite: tonnage (estim)	Main countries	N 1-a	
wolframite: tonnage (estim)	Main countries	N 1-a	
TUNGSTEN ORE			
Consumers' stocks (incl concentrates): tonnage	Main countries	U 53-q	
Consumption (based on metal content of ore): tonnage	USA	T 4-a	
incl concentrates: tonnage	Main countries	U 53-q	
Exports by destination: tonnage	Main countries	U 53-q	
wolfram ore: tonnage	Australia & Portugal	T 4-a	
by value in $	Main countries	U 53-q	
tonnage	Main countries	U 53-q	
wolfram (total) & shipments to EEC area: tonnage & value in UA	AASM countries	E 41-a	
Import prices: concentrates in $ per ton	UK & USA	U 53-m	
Imports by source: tonnage	Main countries	U 53-q	
wolfram ore: tonnage	Main countries	T 4-a	
by value in $	Main countries	U 53-q	
ex Communist sources: tonnage	Main countries	U 53-q	
ex China & USSR: tonnage	Main countries	U 53-a	
Producers' stocks (incl concentrates): tonnage	Main countries	U 53-q	
Production (based on metal content of ore): tonnage	All countries	U 53-q	C 12-a
tonnage	World regions	U 53-a	
wolfram & schellite: tonnage	All countries	B 15-a	
wolframium: tonnage	Zaire	E 41-a	
Wholesale prices: tungsten ore in £ per ton	UK	C 12-m	
World exports: tungsten ore by kind: tonnage	Main countries	T 4-a	
World prices: wolfram ore in £ per ton		T 4-m	
World production: concentrates: tonnage	Main countries	T 4-a	
incl concentrates: tonnage		U 53-a	
scheelite: tonnage	Australia & Brazil	T 4-a	
wolfram: tonnage	Australia & Brazil	T 4-a	

Turbines   see   GAS TURBINES
           HYDRAULIC TURBINES
           STEAM TURBINES

TURBINES, MARINE

Production by value in yen million	Japan	S 16-a

Turbo-prop planes   see   AIRCRAFT, TURBO-PROP

Turkeys   see   POULTRY

Turmeric   see   SPICES & ESSENCES

TURNING MACHINES
    see also   MACHINE TOOLS

Inter-EEC trade: turning machines by value in $m (incl % growth rate)		B 20-a
Production, imports, exports & domestic sales by value in $m	EEC countries	B 20-a

Turnips & swedes   see   FODDER BEET

Turnover   see   CASH FLOW
           REVENUE
           SALES BY VALUE

TURNOVER TAXES
    see also   SALES TAXES

% contribution to government income	Main countries	R 5-a
% rates levied on wool (carded or combed)	Finland & Portugal	K 3-a
woollen & worsted yarn	Greece	K 3-a
woven & woollen fabrics	Greece	K 3-a
Basis of assessment & % rates of tax levied	EEC countries	E 31-a
Government revenue: historical table from 1950 in local currency	Main European countries	Z 1-a
in local currency	EEC countries	E 42-a
Incidence of turnover taxes on direct sales of farm products	ECE countries	U 34-a

	Territorial coverage	Title codes	
Turpentine substitute see WHITE SPIRIT			
Tweendeckers (shipping) see BULK CARRIERS			
Twine see ROPES, CORDAGE & TWINE			

TYPE METAL
Consumption: antimony in production of type metal: tonnage	USA	T 4-a	

TYPEWRITERS
see also   OFFICE MACHINERY

Exports by destination by value in $m	Main countries	U 9-a	
by value in $m	Main countries	U 38-a	
volume	OECD countries	D 9-a	
Imports by value in $m	All countries	U 38-a	
Production: manual & electric models: volume	All countries	U 22-a	
portable type: volume	European countries, Japan & USA	U 38-a	
standard machines: volume	All countries	U 38-a	
volume (all types)	EEC countries	E 28-q	E 27-a
	Main countries	R 5-a	
World exports by value in $m	Main countries	U 38-a	

Typhoid   see   DISEASES, INFECTIOUS

TYRE CORD & FABRIC
Imports & exports: synthetic fabric: tonnage	Main countries	K 4-a	
Production: cotton fibre for tyre cord: tonnage	USA	K 1-q	
nylon fibre for tyre cord: tonnage	USA	K 1-q	
rayon fibre for tyre cord: tonnage	USA	K 1-q	
synthetic tyre cord: tonnage	OECD countries	D 46-a	

Tyre industry   see   PNEUMATIC TYRE INDUSTRY

TYRES, PNEUMATIC
see also   INNER TUBES, RUBBER

Consumption: fibres by kind in production of pneumatic tyres: tonnage	EEC countries	K 4-a	
natural rubber in production of aircraft tyres: tonnage	France	C 18-a	
of pneumatic tyres: tonnage	Main countries	C 18-q	B 13-a
	UK	C 18-a	
rubber by kind in production of pneumatic tyres: tonnage	Canada, France & Japan	C 18-a	
	Main countries	A 1-a	
synthetic rubber by kind in production of pneumatic tyres: tonnage	UK	C 18-a	
	USA	C 18-q	
	Main countries	B 13-a	
Deliveries for farm tractors as original equipment: volume	USA	C 18-m	
as replacements: volume	USA	C 18-m	
motor cars as original equipment: volume	USA	C 18-m	
as replacements: volume	USA	C 18-m	
trucks & buses as original equipment: volume	USA	C 18-m	
as replacements: volume	USA	C 18-m	
Exports by destination: no & value for motor cars	UK	V 1-a	
for tractors	UK	V 1-a	
for trucks	UK	V 1-a	
Exports by destination by value in £m	UK	V 1-a	
Government tax receipts on sales of automotive tyres in local currency	Main countries	S 24-a	
Imports by source by value in £m	UK	V 1-a	
Production by kind incl tubes	EEC countries	E 28-q	E 27-a
pneumatic & solid tyres	All countries	U 22-a	
for commercial vehicles, earth movers & farm tractors: volume	UK	V 1-q	
for passenger cars & commercial vehicles: volume	All countries	U 27-m	
cross ply & radial ply: volume	UK	V 1-q	
historical table: volume	UK	V 1-a	
	OAS member countries	N 14-a	
	African countries	U 44-a	
pneumatic tyres & inner tubes: volume	S American countries	U 40-a	
volume	All countries	U 43-a	
tonnage	EEC countries	V 1-a	
Sales by kind as domestic replacements: volume	UK	C 18-a	
as original equipment: volume	UK	C 18-a	
on government account: volume	UK	C 18-a	
Stocks: tyres for cars, trucks, buses & farm tractors: volume	USA	C 18-m	
Trade between Canada & USA: tyres & inner tubes by value in $m		G 1-a	

TYRES, RETREADED
Consumption: natural rubber for production of retreads: tonnage	UK	C 18-a	
synthetic rubber for production of retreads: tonnage	UK	C 18-a	
Production: tyre retreads for cars: volume	UK	V 1-q	
commercial vehicles: volume	UK	V 1-q	
earth movers: volume	UK	V 1-q	
farm tractors: volume	UK	V 1-q	
historical tables: volume	UK	V 1-a	
tonnage	EEC countries	E 28-q	E 27-a

Tyres, steel   see   WHEELS TYRES AXLES, STEEL

Tyrocidine   see   ANTIBIOTICS

	Territorial coverage	Title codes

UNDP
    Net flow of aid: United Nations Development projects as % of total aid — Worldwide — M 4-a

UNESCO
    List of member states & contributions in $m — All countries — U 62-a

Under-graduates   see   STUDENTS, UNIVERSITY

Underground railways   see   RAILWAYS, UNDERGROUND

UNDERWEAR
    see also   CLOTHING
    Production by kind: volume — EEC countries — E 28-q   E 27-a
                                           K 4-a
            knitted garments: volume — OECD countries — D 46-a
        Sales by manufacturers: lingerie for females by value in £m — UK — B 22-a

UNEMPLOYMENT
    see also   REDUNDANCY
                UNFILLED VACANCIES

    % of economically-active females unemployed — EEC countries — E 33-a
                              population unemployed — EEC countries — E 33-a
                              unemployed by area — EEC countries — E 33-a   E 38-a
                              (total) — EEC countries — E 2-a   E 13-a
                                             E 33-a
                                           Developing countries — U 23-a
    % effect on gross national product of 1% change in level of unemployment — Main countries — D 17
    % of illiterate population unemployed — ECAFE countries — U 17-a
    % of labour force unemployed by educational status — ECAFE countries — U 17-a
    % of literate population unemployed — ECAFE countries — U 17-a
    % of males & females unemployed — EEC countries — E 33-a
    % of normally non-active persons presently seeking work — EEC countries — E 2-a
    % of population of diploma level unemployed — ECAFE countries — U 17-a
                    matriculation level unemployed — ECAFE countries — U 17-a
                    primary educational level unemployed — ECAFE countries — U 17-a
                    university degree level unemployed — ECAFE countries — U 17-a
                seeking work by administrative areas — EEC countries — E 18-a   E 38-a
                unemployed 14-24 yrs age group — EEC countries — E 2-a
                      by age groups — EEC countries — E 18-a
                      in 5 yr age groups & by sex — EEC countries — E 2-a
                      over 60 yrs of age — EEC countries — E 2-a
                      seeking first job — EEC countries — E 2-a   E 18-a
    % rate of unemployment: rural & urban areas — ECAFE countries — U 17-a
    % of unemployed persons seeking work through newspaper advertising — EEC countries — E 18-a
                                    official labour exchanges — EEC countries — E 18-a
                                    personal contacts — EEC countries — E 18-a
                                    private employment agencies — EEC countries — E 18-a
    % unemployed as result of dismissal from place of work — EEC countries — E 18-a
                            family exigencies — EEC countries — E 18-a
                            notice of leaving — EEC countries — E 18-a
    % of unemployed population by 5 yr age groups by sex — EEC countries — E 2-a
    Building industry: no of workers unemployed — ECE countries — U 42-m
    Building industry - index nos — European countries & USA — U 5-a
    By age: % of persons seeking work by sex — EEC countries — E 18-a
    By 5 yr age groups: % unemployed — EEC countries — E 33-a
    By duration: % without work by sex for over 1 yr — EEC countries — E 18-a
                    from 1-3 mths — EEC countries — E 18-a
                    3-6 mths — EEC countries — E 18-a
                    6-12 mths — EEC countries — E 18-a
                    less than 1 mth — EEC countries — E 18-a
            no of persons by sex unemployed: 1-3 mths — EEC countries — E 33-a
                                    3-6 mths — EEC countries — E 33-a
                                    6-12 mths — EEC countries — E 33-a
                                    less than 1 mth — EEC countries — E 33-a
                                    over 1 yr — EEC countries — E 33-a
    By industrial sectors — All countries — L 4-a
    By reason: % of employed persons dismissed by employers — EEC countries — E 33-a
                      giving notice of leaving to employers — EEC countries — E 33-a
                      leaving first job — EEC countries — E 33-a
                      leaving to assist family — EEC countries — E 33-a
        % of females dismissed by employers — EEC countries — E 33-a
                giving notice of leaving to employers — EEC countries — E 33-a
                leaving first job — EEC countries — E 33-a
                to assist family — EEC countries — E 33-a

	Territorial coverage	Title codes	
UNEMPLOYMENT, continued			
Index nos (seasonally-adjusted)	EEC countries	E 26-m	
	Main countries	E 3-m	
No & % of economically-active population presently unemployed	All countries	L 4-a	
	Latin American countries	J 5-a	
	Main countries	U 27-m	U 43-a
of economically-active persons registered as unemployed	EEC countries	E 13-m	E 18-a
unemployed and seeking first job	EEC countries	E 18-a	
unemployed by administrative area	EEC countries	E 18-a	E 38-a
as wholly unemployed	EEC countries	E 33-a	E 18-a
	OECD countries	D 26-m	
of persons unemployed as % of population	European countries, Canada & USA	U 16-a	
	EEC countries	E 2-a	
& as % of total workforce	Main European countries	Z 1-a	
by administrative area (in detail)	EEC countries	E 33-a	
age groups & sex	EEC countries	E 18-a	
occupation (in detail)	EEC countries	E 33-a	
occupational groups	EEC countries	E 2-a	
regions	EEC countries	E 2-a	
sex	All countries	L 4-a	
	EEC countries	E 2-m	E 26-m
(incl % change)	EEC countries	E 26-m	
	Main countries	C 4-a	
	OECD countries	D 26-m	
(seasonally-adjusted)	All countries	L 1-m	
(total)	ECE countries	U 42-m	
	European countries, Canada & USA	U 16-a	
	Main countries	R 5-a	
Rate of unemployment as % of industrial labour force	Main OECD countries	D 24-q	
as % of labour force employed in farming	Main OECD countries	D 24-q	
as % of total labour force by sex	Main OECD countries	D 24-q	
	Main OECD countries	D 24-q	
UNEMPLOYMENT BENEFIT			
% changes in average rates of unemployment assistance	Developed countries	U 54-a	
As % of total social expenditure	All countries	L 2-a	
Cost as % of gross domestic product	OECD countries	D 11-a	
Cost to national funds in $m	All countries	L 2-a	
Expenditure on unemployment benefit in local currency	EEC countries	E 6-a	
No of cases & no of wks compensation paid	Canada & USA	N 18-a	
of insured persons receiving benefit	All countries	L 2-a	
	Canada & USA	N 18-a	
Payments as % of expenditure on social welfare in general	EEC countries	E 6-a	
UNFILLED VACANCIES			
No of jobs arranged through national employment agencies	EEC countries	E 33-a	
on offer by sex (end-period)	EEC countries	E 2-m	
for females	EEC countries	E 33-a	
(total)	EEC countries	E 26-m	E 33-a
	ECE countries	U 42-m	
	OECD countries	D 26-m	
vacancies per unemployed female: textile industry	UK	B 29	
male: textile industry	UK	B 29	

Unit trust shares   see   INVESTMENT, PERSONAL

Unit values   see   EXPORT TRADE
                    IMPORT TRADE

United Nations Development projects   see   UNDP

United Nations Educational, Scientific & Cultural Organisation
                            see   UNESCO

Universal plates   see   PLATES, UNIVERSAL

UNIVERSITIES
      see also   TRAINING COLLEGES

	Territorial coverage	Title codes
Enrolment: students by sex	All countries	U 62-a
Expenditure per student - index nos	All countries	U 62-a
No of academic staff employed	W Indies & Caribbean countries	T 6-a
lecture rooms available (incl high schools)	AASM countries	E 41-a
institutions of university status in operation	W Indies & Caribbean countries	T 6-a
lecturers & professors employed	African countries	U 44-a
employed by sex	OAS member countries	N 19-a
students enrolled by sex & field of study (in detail)	All countries	U 62-a
by sex & grade	OAS member countries	N 19-a
by sex	AASM countries	E 41-a
by sex, nationality & faculty	OAS member countries	N 19-a
by sex studying agriculture & agronomy	OAS member countries	N 19-a
architecture, humanities & fine arts	OAS member countries	N 19-a
civil engineering	OAS member countries	N 19-a
economics, social sciences & business studies	OAS member countries	N 19-a

	Territorial coverage	Title codes

UNIVERSITIES, continued

No of students enrolled by sex studying education	OAS member countries	N 19-a
law	OAS member countries	N 19-a
medical sciences & dentistry	OAS member countries	N 19-a
natural sciences & chemistry	OAS member countries	N 19-a
veterinary medicine & pharmacy	OAS member countries	N 19-a
historical tables from 1817	Main European countries	Z 1-a
(total)	African countries	U 44-a
	W Indies & Caribbean countries	T 6-a
of teachers & lecturers employed by sex	All countries	U 62-a
employed by specialisation	Latin American countries	J 5-a
(total)	AASM countries	E 41-a
of university students enrolled & no of graduates	EEC countries	E 2-a
Public expenditure on universities education in $m	All countries	U 62-a
per student in $	All countries	U 62-a
Student-teacher ratios	AASM countries	E 41-a

UNIVERSITY DEGREES

    see also GRADUATES

No of university degrees granted by faculty	Latin American countries	J 5-a

University faculties see STUDY COURSES

University libraries see LIBRARIES, UNIVERSITY

UNSKILLED WORKERS

    see also MANUAL WORKERS

No of unskilled workers employed: iron & steel industry	W Germany	H 3-a

UPHOLSTERY

    see also HOUSEHOLD TEXTILES

% consumption: light leather hides by upholstery industry	USA	A 18-a
Consumption: wool for upholstery in kg	Main countries	K 6-a
Production: upholstery textiles by volume in m³	EEC countries	K 4-a

URANIUM

    see also NUCLEAR FUELS

% production of concentrates to world total production	All countries	H 4-a
Capacity: concentration plants (incl locations): tonnage	EEC countries	E 15-a
Consumption (for use as nuclear fuel): tonnage	USA	N 1-a
Demand: projected to 1980: tonnage	Worldwide	D 48-a
Imports & exports: uranium minerals: tonnage	All countries	B 15-a
Imports: enriched nuclear fuels (incl plutonium) in kg	EEC countries	E 15-a
Prices paid by Atomic Energy Commission in $ per lb	USA	N 1-a
Production capability (short-term): tonnage	All countries	D 48
Production capacity: tonnage	Australia, Canada & Portugal	D 48
Production & plant location: tonnage	Australia & Portugal	D 48
at mines (based on content of ore): tonnage	Main countries	N 1-a
	All countries	B 15-a
	AASM countries	E 41-a
based on uranium oxide content: tonnage	All countries	H 4-a
uranium concentrates: tonnage	All countries (excl Communist area)	D 48
	Gabon, Madagascar & Niger	E 41-a
Reserves (based on metal content) of ore: tonnage (estim)	Main countries	U 43-a
	All countries	D 48
Sales (incl deliveries) projected to 1977: tonnage	USA	D 48
Stocks held at producers' & users' plants (end-yr): tonnage	USA	N 1-a
World consumption (for power generation): tonnage	Worldwide	D 48-a
World production: tonnage	Worldwide excl Communist area	D 48

URANIUM ORE

% contribution to export earnings	Gabon	E 45-a
Exports: (total) & shipped to EEC area: tonnage & value in UA	Gabon	E 41-a
Production capacity by mine & location: tonnage	USA	D 48
Production (incl % uranium content): tonnage	EEC countries	E 15-a
per day (incl mine location): tonnage	USA	D 48
World production: tonnage	Main countries	N 1-a
	Canada, France, S Africa & USA	T 4-a

URANIUM OXIDE

World production: tonnage	Reporting countries	C 30-a N 4-c

Uranothorianite see RARE EARTH MINERALS

Urban housing see DWELLINGS

UREA

    see also FERTILISERS

Exports: tonnage	All countries	A 2-a
Imports: tonnage	All countries	A 2-a
Prices paid by farmers (as fertiliser) in local currency per ton	W European countries	U 30-a
Production: tonnage	All countries	A 2-a

	Territorial coverage	Title codes

UREA, continued
    Usage in production of nitrogenous fertilisers: tonnage — OECD countries — D 5-a
    Wholesale prices in $ per ton — USA — A 9-a

Urena & Punga   see   JUTE

Used cars   see   PASSENGER CARS, SECOND-HAND

Used commercial vehicles   see   COMMERCIAL VEHICLES, SECOND-HAND

Utility vans   see   COMMERCIAL VEHICLES

V.A.T.   see   VALUE ADDED TAX

Vacancies   see   UNFILLED VACANCIES

Vacations   see   HOLIDAYS

VACCINATION
    No of injections carried out against smallpox & yellow fever — OAS member countries — N 18-a
        of persons vaccinated by age groups — All countries — W 2-m

VACUUM CLEANERS, DOMESTIC
    % changes in retail sales — E European countries — U 16-a
    % of households owning a vacuum cleaner — W European countries — Z 3
    Production: volume — All countries — U 22-a
        — E European countries & USSR — U 16-a
        — EEC countries — E 28-q   E 27-a
        — Canada, European countries, Japan & USA — U 38-a
    Retail prices (comparative) in $ — EEC countries — Z 3-a
    Sales demand per 1000 population — E European countries & USA — U 16-a

VALUE ADDED IN PRODUCTION
    see also   GNP
                  LABOUR RATIOS
    Agriculture & livestock farming in local currency — EEC countries — E 44-a
    Building industry in $m — Main countries — U 58-a
        — Czechoslovakia, Hungary & Poland — U 25-a
    Chemical industry in $m — Main countries — U 25-a
        — Czechoslovakia, Hungary & Poland — U 25-a
        — OECD countries — D 5-a
        per employee in $ — OECD countries — D 5-a
    Engineering industry by sector in $m — OECD countries — D 9-a
    Forestry products - index nos — EEC countries — E 44-a
    Industry (in general) in $m — Main countries — U 25-a
    Machine tools industry in $m — USA — J 2-a
    Man-made fibres industry in $m — OECD countries — D 5-a
    Manufacturing industry in $m — Main countries — U 25-a
    Per employee by industrial sector in $ — UK & USA — U 52-a

Value added per capita   see   LABOUR PRODUCTIVITY

VALUE ADDED TAX
    see also   PURCHASE TAX
    % rate levied on wool (carded or combed) — Main countries — K 3-a
        on motor vehicles — Main countries — S 24-a
    Basis of assessment & % rates of tax levied — EEC countries — E 31-a
    Government revenue from VAT taxes in local currency — EEC countries — E 42-a

Valves (for electronic apparatus)   see   ELECTRONIC VALVES

Valves (mechanical) & cocks   see   ENGINEERING PRODUCTS, MECHANICAL

VANADIUM
    see also   FERRO-VANADIUM
    Consumption in production of ferro-alloys: tonnage — UK — T 4-a
    Exports: vanadium ore, concentrates & oxides: tonnage — USA — T 4-a
    Import prices: vanadium pentoxide in $ per kg cif — European countries — T 4-m
    Imports & exports: ferro-vanadium: tonnage — All countries — B 15-a
    Production (as by-product of aluminium plants): tonnage — France — T 4-a
        (based on content of ores & concentrates): tonnage — USA — J 6-a
        — All countries — B 15-a   C 12-a
        — T 4-a   U 22-a
        — U 43-a
    Stocks held by industrial consumers in lbs — USA — N 1-a
    World production (at mines) in lbs — Main countries — N 1-a
        (based on metal content of ore mined): tonnage — C 12-a
        tonnage — N 4-a   T 4-a
    World reserves in lbs (estim) — Main countries — N 1-a

Vanaspati   see   MARGARINE

	Territorial coverage	Title codes
VANILLA & CLOVES		
Export prices in $ per ton fob	Madagascar	A 9-a
Exports by destination in cwt	Main countries	B 13-a
cloves in cwt	Comoro Is, Madagascar & Tanzania	B 13-a
vanilla in cwt	Main countries	B 13-a
(total) & shipped to EEC area by value in UA	AASM countries	E 41-a
Import prices: cloves ex Zanzibar & Madagascar in £ per ton cif	UK	B 18-m
Imports by source in cwt	France, UK & USA	B 13-a
	Main countries	B 13-a
cloves in cwt	All countries	B 18-m
Production: vanilla: tonnage	Madagascar	E 41-a
Re-exports in cwt	Hong Kong & Singapore	B 13-a
World prices: vanilla (ex Tahiti) in Fr per kg	France	E 41-a

Varnishes   see   PAINTS & VARNISHES

VEAL

    see also   CALVES

Exports by destination: tonnage	Main countries	B 12-m
	Netherlands & W Germany	C 9-m
Imports & exports: dried or salted veal: tonnage	EEC countries	E 1-a
fresh or frozen veal: tonnage	EEC countries	E 1-a
Production by administrative areas: tonnage	EEC countries	E 38-a
by value in $m	EEC countries	E 44-a
for export: tonnage	Main countries	B 12-a
Production, imports, exports & net domestic supply: tonnage	EEC countries	E 1-a
stocks & consumption per capita in kg	OECD countries	D 14-a
tonnage (incl no of calves slaughtered)	EEC countries	E 1-a
tonnage	EEC countries	E 26-m
	Latin American countries	U 40-a
Self-sufficiency ratios	EEC countries	E 3-a E 44-a
Stocks: imported frozen veal in cold storage: tonnage	UK	B 12-w
Wholesale prices (by cuts): central market quotes in pence per lb	UK	B 12-w

Vegetable dyes   see   DYESTUFFS, SYNTHETIC

VEGETABLE OILS

    see also   BABASSU OIL
                    CASHEW NUTSHELL OIL
                    CASTOR OIL
                    COCONUT OIL
                    CORN OIL
                    COTTONSEED OIL
                    FATS & OILS
                    GROUNDNUT OIL
                    LINSEED OIL
                    MUSTARD SEED OIL
                    OILCAKE & MEAL
                    OITICICA OIL
                    OLIVE OIL
                    PALM KERNEL OIL
                    PALM OIL
                    RAPESEED OIL
                    SAFFLOWER OIL
                    SESAME SEED OIL
                    SHEA NUT OIL
                    SOYBEAN OIL
                    SUNFLOWER SEED OIL
                    TOBACCO SEED OIL
                    TUNG OIL

% changes in retail sales: vegetable fats & oils	E European countries	U 16-a
Consumption per capita in kg	E European countries	U 16-a
(incl fats) in kg	EEC countries	B 1-a
tonnage (incl consumption per capita in kg)	OECD countries	D 14-a
tonnage	EEC countries	E 44-a
Crushings: oilseeds (for vegetable oil extraction): tonnage	UK	B 19-a
Excise duties: % rates charged	EEC countries	E 31-a
Expenditure: price supports under EEC budget		B 3-a
Exports by sea, inland waterways, road & rail: tonnage	European countries	U 8-a
by value in $m	W European countries	U 33-a
	W Malaysia	U 32-m
(net) incl oilseeds in oil equiv tonnage	Main countries	B 19-a
shipped to EEC & non-EEC areas by value in $m	EEC countries	E 24-a
tonnage	Asian & Far East countries	U 32-q
Import duties in % ad val	Canada, Main European countries, Japan & USA	B 19-a
Imports by sea, inland waterways, road & rail: tonnage	European countries	U 8-a
by value in $m	W European countries	U 33-a
in yen	Japan	U 32-m
ex EEC & non-EEC areas by value in $m	EEC countries	E 24-a
in oil equiv tonnage	Main countries	B 19-a
tonnage	Canada, European countries, USA & USSR	A 11-a
Labour costs of production in local currency per hr	EEC countries	E 2-a
Producer prices: vegetable oils in $ per ton	EEC countries	E 44-a
Production & exports: tonnage	All countries	A 23-a
Production, imports, exports & consumption: tonnage	EEC countries	E 44-a
Production, stocks & industrial usage: tonnage	OECD countries	D 14-a
	All countries	U 22-a
Production: crude & refined vegetable oils: tonnage	EEC countries	E 28-q E 27-a
	Main countries	B 19-a

572

	Territorial coverage	Title codes	
VEGETABLE OILS, continued			
Production: tonnage	E European countries & USSR	U 16-a	
	ECAFE countries	U 32-q	
	EEC countries	B 1-a	
	Main countries	B 18-a	
Self-sufficiency ratios (incl fats)	EEC countries	B 1-a	E 3-a
		E 44-a	
Supply, production, consumption & trade: tonnage	EEC countries	B 1-a	
Wholesale prices in local currency per litre	EEC countries	E 34-m	
per ton	Spain, UK & USA	U 27-m	
World demand per capita per yr projected to 1985		A 1	
VEGETABLE OILS BY KIND			
% Commonwealth share of imports	UK	B 19-a	
Exports by destination by CST classes: tonnage & value in $	EEC countries	E 48-a	
SITC classes by value in $	Main countries	D 2-q	
tonnage & value in $	OECD countries	D 3-a2	
tonnage	USA	B 18-m	
by NIMEXE classes: tonnage & value in $	All countries	E 20-a	
SITC classes: tonnage & value in $	All countries	U 50-a	U 59-a
(for production of margarine): tonnage	All countries	B 12-a	
tonnage	Main countries	P 1-a	
Import prices in £ per ton	W European countries	B 18-m	
Imports by NIMEXE classes: tonnage & value in $	All countries	E 20-a	
SITC classes: tonnage & value in $	All countries	U 50-a	U 59-a
by source by CST classes: tonnage & value in $	EEC countries	E 21-a	
SITC classes by value in $	Main countries	D 2-q	
tonnage & value in $	OECD countries	D 3-a2	
(incl oilseeds): tonnage	EEC countries	P 5-a	
(net): tonnage	Main countries	B 19-a	
Oil conversion factors from seeds & kernels		P 1-a	
Production (for ensuing yr): tonnage (estim)	World regions	P 1-a	
tonnage	All countries	P 1-a	
Retail prices in local currency	OAS member countries	N 17-a	
Supply from domestic seed: tonnage	Main countries	B 19-a	
from imported seed: tonnage	Main countries	B 19-a	
Usage in production of cooking fat: tonnage	UK & USA	B 19-a	
of margarine: tonnage	Main countries	B 19-a	
Wholesale prices in local currency per ton	OAS member countries	N 17-a	
World exports: unit value in $ per ton		A 11-a	
World production: edible vegetable oils: tonnage		N 10-a	
World supply: tonnage		B 19-a	

Vegetable parchment   see   PAPER, GREASE-PROOF

Vegetable protein   see   PROTEIN, VEGETABLE

Vegetable textile yarns   see   TEXTILE YARNS

VEGETABLES, DRIED

see also   DRY PEAS

% contribution to export earnings	Kenya	E 45-a	
Exports: tonnage & value in $m	Ethiopia & Kenya	E 45-a	
Imports by source by kind: tonnage	UK	B 6-m	

VEGETABLES, FRESH

see also   FODDER CROPS, GREEN

% changes in retail sales	E European countries & USA	U 16-a	
% of EEC area production	EEC countries	R 5-a	
Area harvested in ha & production: tonnage	All countries	A 9-a	
under cabbages & kale (for fodder) in ha	EEC countries	E 12-a	
crops by kind in acres	USA	B 6-a	
in ha: open field	E European countries	U 20-a	
commercial crops by kind in acres	UK	B 6-a	
in ha	EEC countries	E 12-a	E 44-a
green peppers & production & yield per ha	All countries	A 9-a	
onion crop in ha	OAS member countries	N 13-a	
vegetable crops (irrigated) in ha	Romania	U 20-a	
(non-irrigated)	Romania	U 20-a	
As source of fat, protein & calorie intake per capita	OAS member countries	N 17-a	
Consumption cost: private sector (incl potatoes) in local currency	EEC countries	E 32-a	
Consumption (as animal feed): tonnage	EEC countries	E 44-a	
fresh vegetables: tonnage	OECD countries	D 37-a	
peas & beans: tonnage	OAS member countries	N 17-a	
per capita (by income levels) in lbs	USA	C 27-a	
in kg per yr	Main countries	E 3-a	
	E European countries	U 16-a	U 20-a
	EEC countries	B 1-a	E 44-a
		U 20-a	
(incl canned vegetables) in kg per yr	Canada, European countries, USA & USSR	E 44-a	
	W European countries	P 5-a	
Crop yields: cabbages (for fodder) in kg per ha	OECD countries	D 1-a	
in quintals per ha	EEC countries	E 12-a	
onions in kg per ha	E European countries	U 16-a	
	OAS member countries	N 13-a	
Exports (all kinds): tonnage	Main E European countries	U 20-a	
as % of exports of farm products (value basis)	W European countries	U 20-a	

	Territorial coverage	Title codes	
VEGETABLES, FRESH continued			
Exports by destination: tonnage	Bulgaria	U 20-a	
kind: tonnage	Main countries	B 6-a	
value in $m	W European countries	U 20-a	U 33-a
unit value in $ per ton	Main W European countries	U 20-a	
Imports (all kinds): tonnage & value in $	OECD countries	D 37-a	
tonnage	Main E European countries	U 20-a	
as % of imports of farm products (value basis)	W European countries	U 20-a	
by kind: tonnage & value in £m	UK	B 6-a	
by source: asparagus	OECD countries	D 37-a	
beans, celery, cucumbers, endives & mushrooms: tonnage	OECD countries	D 37-a	
brussel sprouts, cabbage, cauliflowers, leeks, lettuce & spinach: tonnage	OECD countries	D 37-a	
carrots, tomatoes, onions & shallots: tonnage	OECD countries	D 37-a	
by value in $m	W European countries	U 20-a	U 33-a
unit value in $ per ton	Main W European countries	U 20-a	
Income elasticity of demand for fresh vegetables	USA	C 27-a	
Producer prices by kind per 100 kg in $	EEC countries	U 20-a	
Production, imports, exports & consumption: tonnage	EEC countries	E 44-a	
Production (all kinds) in open fields: tonnage	UK	U 20-a	
as % of all food (based on value)	OECD countries	D 37-a	
as % of consumption	OECD countries	D 37-a	
by kind: tonnage	Main E European countries	U 20-a	
	Main countries	B 6-a	
by value in £m	EEC countries	B 1-a	
in $m	EEC countries	E 44-a	
in local currency	OECD countries	D 37-a	
cabbages (incl kale for feed): tonnage	EEC countries	E 12-a	
tonnage	Main E European countries	U 20-a	
carrots: tonnage	Czechoslovakia, E Germany & Poland	U 20-a	
cauliflowers: tonnage	OECD countries	D 37-a	
cucumbers: tonnage	OECD countries	D 37-a	
cucumbers & gherkins: tonnage	E European countries	U 20-a	
green beans: tonnage	Main E European countries	U 20-a	
green peppers: tonnage	Bulgaria & Hungary	U 20-a	
onions: tonnage	Main E European countries	U 20-a	
	OECD countries	D 37-a	
	OAS member countries	N 13-a	
peas: tonnage	Main E European countries	U 20-a	
tonnage (incl consumption per capita in kg)	OECD countries	D 14-a	
tonnage	African countries	U 44-a	
	E European countries, USSR incl Ukraine	U 16-a	
	EEC countries	E 12-a	
	Main E European countries	U 20-a	
	Main countries	R 5-a	
	OECD countries	D 1-a	D 37-a
under glass: lettuce, mushrooms, cucumbers & tomatoes: tonnage	UK	U 20-a	
Retail prices by kind of crop in local currency	OAS member countries	N 17-a	
(comparative): cabbage per kg	EEC countries	Z 3-a	
Sales by producers by kind of crop: tonnage	Israel	B 6-a	
by value in local currency	OECD countries	D 37-a	
cauliflowers: tonnage	Netherlands	U 20-a	
cucumbers, endives, green beans, lettuce & spinach: tonnage	Netherlands	U 20-a	
vegetables (all kinds): tonnage	OECD countries	D 37-a	
as % of sales of agricultural products (value basis)	OECD countries	D 37-a	
Self-sufficiency ratios	EEC countries	B 1-a	E 3-a
		E 44-a	
Wholesale prices: home-grown & imported by source in £ per ton	UK	B 6-a	
in local currency per ton	OAS member countries	N 17-a	
VEGETABLES, FROZEN			
see also CANNED VEGETABLES			
Consumption: tonnage	OAS member countries	N 17-a	
Imports by source: green peas & beans: tonnage	UK	B 6-m	
Production & consumption per capita in kg	OECD countries	D 14-a	
tonnage	All countries	U 22-a	
VEGETABLES, PROCESSED			
Consumption: canned vegetables (imported): tonnage	OECD countries	D 37-a	
% contribution to export earnings	Ethiopia & Malawi	E 45-a	
Exports by value in $m	W European countries	U 33-a	
Imports by value in $m	W European countries	U 33-a	
preserved vegetables by kind: tonnage	UK	B 6-m	
Production: canned beans & peas: tonnage	OECD countries	D 37-a	
canned vegetables (incl mixed): tonnage	OECD countries	D 37-a	
gherkins: tonnage	Austria & W Germany	D 37-a	
preserved cucumbers: tonnage	OECD countries	D 37-a	
sauerkraut: tonnage	Austria & W Germany	D 37-a	
tomato pulp: tonnage	OECD countries	D 37-a	
Retail prices by kind in local currency	OAS member countries	N 17-a	
Wholesale prices - index nos	EEC countries	E 26-m	

Vehicle accessories see AUTOMOTIVE ACCESSORIES

Vehicle assembly see MOTOR VEHICLES

	Territorial coverage	Title codes

VEHICLE DRIVING LICENCES
- No held (provisional & full licences) — UK — V 1-a
- Scale of fees charged — Main countries — S 24-a

Vehicle licences, commercial   see   ROAD TRANSPORT

Vehicle registrations   see   BUSES & COACHES
      COMMERCIAL VEHICLES
      MOTOR CYCLES & SCOOTERS
      PASSENGER CARS

VEHICLES
  see also   BUSES & COACHES
      COMMERCIAL VEHICLES
      MOTOR VEHICLES
      PASSENGER VEHICLES
      ROAD CONSTRUCTION VEHICLES
      ROAD TRACTORS
      SERVICE VEHICLES

- No in use by kind (at end-yr) — Main countries — S 24-a
-     — W Indies & Caribbean countries — T 6-a
-   per 1000 population — Main countries — S 24-a

Vehicles industry   see   MOTOR VEHICLES INDUSTRY

Vehicles, articulated   see   COMMERCIAL VEHICLES

VEHICLES, TWO-WHEELED
  see also   CYCLES & MOPEDS
      MOTOR CYCLES & SCOOTERS

- % adult ownership by age & social classes — W European countries — Z 3
-   bicycle or cycle (motor-assisted) — W European countries — Z 3
-   motor cycle or motor scooter — W European countries — Z 3

Vending machines   see   AUTOMATIC VENDING MACHINES

VENEER SHEETS
- Consumption by volume in m³ — All countries — A 26-a
-   raw materials in production of veneer sheets — All countries — A 26-a
- Exports by destination by volume in m³ — European countries — A 13-q
-   by volume in m³ — All countries — A 23-a
-   (incl plywood) by volume in m³ — Main countries — A 5-a
-   tonnage & value in $m — Congo Rep — E 45-a
-   (total) & shipped to EEC area: tonnage & value in UA — AASM countries — E 41-a
- Imports & exports by source or destination by volume in m³ — All countries — A 23-a
-   by volume in m³ — All countries — A 23-a
-   by source by volume in m³ — European countries — A 13-q
-   volume in m³ — Main countries — A 26-a
- No of operating plants in veneer cutting industry — All countries — A 26-a
- Production by volume in m³ — All countries — A 23-a   A 26-a
-   capacity by volume in m³ — All countries — A 26-a
-   (incl plywood) by volume in m³ — AASM countries — E 41-a

VENEREAL DISEASES
- No of reported cases: syphilis — OAS member countries — N 18-a

VERMICULITE
  see also   PERLITE

- Consumption: exfoliated vermiculite: tonnage — USA — N 1-a
- Imports & exports by source & destination: tonnage — All countries — B 15-a
- Production: tonnage — All countries — B 15-a
- Wholesale prices (ex mine) in $ per ton — USA — N 1-a
-   — Main countries — N 1-a
- World production: tonnage — World excl Communist countries — N 4-a

Vertical boring lathes   see   LATHES, VERTICAL BORING

Vessels   see   BULK CARRIERS
      CARGO SHIPS
      PASSENGER VESSELS
      SHIPS & BOATS
      SUPPLY VESSELS

VETCH
- Area under crop (for seed) in ha — Italy — E 12-a
- Crop yield (for seed) in 100 kg per ha — Italy — E 12-a
- Production: bean plants (for fodder): tonnage — All countries — A 9-a
-   (for seed) in 100 kg — Italy — E 12-a

VETERINARY MEDICINE
- No of students enrolled on university courses — OAS member countries — N 19-a

	Territorial coverage	Title codes
VINEGAR		
Production: volume	All countries	U 22-a
Retail prices in local currency	OAS member countries	N 17-a
VINEYARDS		
Area under vines: historical table in ha	Main European countries	Z 1-a
in ha	EEC countries	B 1-a E 3-a
		E 44-a
No of vineyards in use: private & collectives in ha	Yugoslavia	D 37-a

Vinyl chloride   see   CHEMICALS, ORGANIC

VITAL STATISTICS

        see also   BIRTH RATES
                       DEATH RATES
                       INFANT MORTALITY
                       LIVE BIRTHS
                       MARRIAGES

Birth, marriage & death rates by region per 1000 population	EEC countries	E 2-a
per 1000 population	All countries	U 43-a
Crude fertility rates per 1000 population	All countries	U 43
Expectation of life by sex	All countries	U 43
No of births, marriages & deaths reported by regions	EEC countries	E 2-a

VITAMINS

        see also   MINERAL NUTRIENTS

Exports (incl provitamins) by destination by value in $	Main countries	U 2-a
Needs of vitamins per lb of diet: chickens for breeding in milligrams		P 5
for growing in milligrams		P 5
for laying in milligrams		P 5
for starting in milligrams		P 5
in milligrams		P 5
turkeys for breeding in milligrams		P 5
for fattening in milligrams		P 5
for growing in milligrams		P 5
for starting in milligrams		P 5
in milligrams		P 5

Vocational education   see   EDUCATION, VOCATIONAL

Vocational institutes   see   COLLEGES, TECHNICAL
                                                     COLLEGES, VOCATIONAL

Volcanic ash   see   ABRASIVES, NATURAL

Volcanic cinder   see   PUMICE

Volkorn   see   FERTILISERS, MIXED

Voluntary restraints on deliveries   see   CHEESE

Vulcanised fibres   see   PLASTICS

WAGE EARNERS

        - see also   CLERICAL WORKERS
                            CRAFTSMEN & PROCESS WORKERS
                            FARM WORKERS
                            FOREIGN MIGRANT WORKERS
                            MANUAL WORKERS
                            POPULATION, ECONOMICALLY ACTIVE
                            SALARIED STAFF

% age distribution: all employees	EEC countries	E 2-a
employed in industrial occupations	EEC countries	E 2-a
in service industries	EEC countries	E 2-a
female employees	EEC countries	E 2-a
% breakdown: all occupations by age groups	EEC countries	E 18-a
farm workers by age groups	EEC countries	E 18-a
% of housewives having outside jobs by age groups	W European countries	Z 3
by social classes	W European countries	Z 3
% of labour force by sex & occupation	EEC countries	E 18-a
Direct industrial labour costs per hr in local currency	EEC countries	E 11-a
Direct labour costs: mining & quarrying in local currency per hr	EEC countries	E 11-a
Incomes: workers employed in forestry in local currency	France & W Germany	E 44-a
Labour costs by industrial sector in local currency per hr	EEC countries	E 2-a
Motor vehicle manufacturing industry: no employed in basic manufacturing occupations	UK	B 28-a
in engine & body assembly shops	UK	B 28-a
in packing & despatch departments	UK	B 28-a
in trim, paint & finish departments	UK	B 28-a

WAGE EARNERS, continued

	Territorial coverage	Title codes	
No of wage earners employed by sex by industrial sectors (incl salaried staff)	All countries	L 4-a	
industrial sectors	EEC countries	E 3-a	
	OAS member countries	N 14-a	
occupational groups	Main countries	R 5-a	
in abattoirs & meat preparation factories	EEC countries	E 8-a	
aerospace equipment manufacturing industry	EEC countries	E 8-a	
agriculture & forestry occupations	AASM countries	E 41-a	
baking & confectionery industry	EEC countries	E 8-a	
briquetting plants	EEC countries	E 8-a	
building construction industry	EEC countries	E 8-a	
building materials manufacturing industry	EEC countries	E 8-a	
carpet & rug manufacturing industry	OECD countries	D 46-a	
cement industry	EEC countries	E 8-a	
ceramics industry	EEC countries	E 8-a	
chemical industry	EEC countries	E 8-a	
	OECD countries	D 5-a	
clothing industry	EEC countries	E 8-a	
	OECD countries	D 46-a	
coke oven plants	EEC countries	E 8-a	
collieries & ore mines by kind	EEC countries	E 3-a	
coal-face & pit-head workers	EEC countries	E 8-a	
cotton textile manufacturing industry	EEC countries	E 8-a	
dairying industry	EEC countries	E 8-a	
drinks manufacturing industry (incl alcoholic)	EEC countries	E 8-a	
electrical engineering industry	EEC countries	E 8-a	
energy industries (all kinds)	EEC countries	E 8-a	
farm machinery & tractor manufacturing industry	EEC countries	E 8-a	
food processing industry (excl sugar refining)	EEC countries	E 8-a	
foundries (iron & steel)	EEC countries	E 8-a	
glass & glassware manufacturing industry	EEC countries	E 8-a	
industrial activity (in general)	EEC countries	E 8-a	
	Main countries	R 5-a	
iron & steel industry (by kind of product)	EEC countries	E 30-m	
(by occupation)	EEC countries	E 2-a	E 8-a
	W Germany	H 3-a	
iron ore mines	EEC countries	E 2-a	
iron-working industries	EEC countries	E 8-a	
knitting mills	OECD countries	D 46-a	
	EEC countries	E 8-a	
leather goods manufacturing industries	EEC countries	E 8-a	
leather industry & tanning	EEC countries	E 8-a	
machine tools manufacturing industry	EEC countries	E 8-a	
man-made fibres manufacturing industry	EEC countries	E 8-a	
	OECD countries	D 5-a	
manufacturing industry (all sectors)	EEC countries	E 8-a	
mechanical engineering industry	EEC countries	E 8-a	
metal-working industries	EEC countries	E 8-a	
mining & quarrying	AASM countries	E 41-a	
	EEC countries	E 8-a	
motor vehicle manufacturing industry	EEC countries	E 8-a	
non-ferrous metals industries	EEC countries	E 8-a	
non-metallic minerals industry	EEC countries	E 8-a	
nuclear fuel industry	EEC countries	E 8-a	
office machinery manufacturing industry	EEC countries	E 8-a	
ore mining industry	EEC countries	E 8-a	
paper & board manufacturing industry	EEC countries	E 8-a	
petroleum & natural gas industries	EEC countries	E 8-a	
plastics industry	EEC countries	E 8-a	
printing & publishing	EEC countries	E 8-a	
private sector	AASM countries	E 41-a	
public sector	AASM countries	E 41-a	
public utility undertakings	EEC countries	E 8-a	
rubber processing industries	EEC countries	E 8-a	
scientific instrument manufacturing industry	EEC countries	E 8-a	
service industries & commercial occupations	AASM countries	E 41-a	
shipbuilding & repairing industries	EEC countries	E 8-a	
spinning, weaving & finishing of textiles	OECD countries	D 46-a	
tanneries	EEC countries	E 8-a	
textile industries (all sectors)	EEC countries	E 8-a	
	OECD countries	D 46-a	

	Territorial coverage	Title codes
WAGE EARNERS, continued		
No of wage earners employed in timber & sawmill industry	EEC countries	E 8-a
tobacco processing industry	EEC countries	E 8-a
transport equipment manufacturing industry	EEC countries	E 8-a
water supply industry	EEC countries	E 8-a
wood-working & furniture manufacturing industries	EEC countries	E 8-a
woollen textile industry	EEC countries	E 8-a
(incl salaried staff) by occupational groups	EEC countries	E 18-a
in farming	EEC countries	E 18-a
in industry	EEC countries	E 18-a
in service industries	EEC countries	E 18-a
(total)	EEC countries	E 18-a
specialist artisans: water supply	All countries	L 2-a
companies	All countries	W 2-a
supervisors: water supply companies	All countries	W 2-a
transport service industries	AASM countries	E 41-a
No of hrs worked by wage earners by industry per yr	EEC countries	E 2-a
by sex in building industry per yr	EEC countries	E 33-a
in industry per yr	EEC countries	E 33-a
Water supply undertakings: no of clerical workers employed	All countries	W 2-a
of drillers employed	All countries	W 2-a
WAGE RATES		
As component in gross domestic product in local currency	Main countries	R 5-a
By industrial occupations by sex in local currency per hr	All countries	L 4-a
	EEC countries	E 25-a2 E 2-a2
– index nos	EEC countries	E 26-a
By industrial sectors – index nos	Asian, Far East & Australasian countries	U 45-a
in local currency per hr	EEC countries	E 25-a2
By industry by status of employees & by sex in local currency per hr	Main countries	R 3-m
	Main countries	R 4-q
historical tables from 1800	Main countries	Z 1-a
in local currency per hr	Main countries	R 5-a
By industry – index nos	Main countries	R 4-a
	Fiji	U 32-m
by main occupations – index nos	Main countries	R 4-a
By main employment sectors – index nos	Main countries	R 5-a
	All countries	L 1-a
	Asian, Far East & Australasian countries	U 45-a
By manufacturing industry in local currency per hr	All countries	L 1-m L 4-a
– index nos	OECD countries	D 26-m
By non-agricultural sectors in local currency	All countries	L 1-m L 4-a
	Latin American countries	J 5-a
By sex in local currency per hr	Main countries	C 7-a
(Incl salaries) as cost factor in gross domestic product	African countries	U 44-a
Salaries: general level in local currency per mth	OAS member countries	N 17-a
WAGE RATES, AGRICULTURAL		
see also FARM WAGES		
Cow-hands by sex in local currency per hr	Main countries	R 4-a
Earnings: farm workers in local currency	Main countries	A 9-a
	All countries	L 4-a
Farm workers in local currency per hr	Main countries	R 4-a
	OAS member countries	N 17-a
by age groups by area in local currency per hr	Eire	R 4-a
farm occupations in local currency per hr	Main countries	R 4-a
	OAS member countries	N 17-a
province in lire per hr	Italy	R 4-a
Fodder & feed supervisors in local currency per hr	Main countries	R 4-a
Historical table from 1770 in local currency per hr	Main European countries	Z 1-a
Horse-plough workers in local currency per hr	Main countries	R 4-a
Milkers & milkmaids in local currency per hr	Main countries	R 4-a
Rates per day (with free housing) in $ per hr	Canada & USA	R 4
(normal) in $ per hr	Canada & USA	R 4
Seasonal farm workers in local currency per hr	OAS member countries	N 17-a
Shepherds in local currency per hr	Main countries	R 4-a
Tractor drivers in local currency per hr	Main countries	R 4-a
WAGE RATES BY SECTOR		
Abattoirs & meat-preparation industry in local currency per hr	EEC countries	E 25-a2
Accounting assistants in local currency per hr or mth	AASM countries	E 41-a
Aircraft industry & aerospace engineering in local currency per hr	EEC countries	E 25-a2
by sex in local currency per hr	Main countries	R 3-m
Airline personnel: salaries by kind of airline company in local currency per mth	Worldwide	S 11-a
Bakers in local currency per hr	Main countries	R 4-a
Baking & confectionery industry by sex in local currency per hr	Main countries	R 3-m
in local currency per hr	OAS member countries	N 17-a
Banking & finance by sex in local currency per hr	Main countries	R 3-m
Beverage manufacturing industry by sex in local currency per hr	Main countries	C 7-a
Boot & shoe manufacturing industry by sex in local currency per hr	Main countries	C 7-a
Brewing industry by grade of worker in A Sch per hr	Austria	R 4-a
by sex in local currency per hr	Main countries	R 3-m
	OAS member countries	N 17-a

WAGE RATES BY SECTOR, continued

	Territorial coverage	Title codes
Building & civil engineering industry in local currency per hr	EEC countries	E 25-a2
Building industry: bricklayers & concreters in local currency per hr	Main countries	R 4-a
by sex in local currency per hr	Main countries	R 3-m
building site labourers in local currency per hr	OAS member countries	N 17-a
carpenters & painters in local currency per hr	Main countries	R 4-a
in local currency per hr	OAS member countries	N 17-a
electricians in local currency per hr	OAS member countries	N 17-a
painters in local currency per hr	OAS member countries	N 17-a
plumbers & electricians in local currency per hr	Main countries	R 4-a
in local currency per hr	OAS member countries	N 17-a
skilled & unskilled employees in local currency per hr	Main countries	R 4-q
Building materials & refractory clay manufacturing industry in local currency per hr	EEC countries	E 25-a2
Building materials manufacturing industry by sex in local currency per hr	Main countries	C 7-a
Bus conductors, inspectors & drivers (in London & provinces) in £ per wk	UK	R 4-a
Canned meat industry in local currency per hr	OAS member countries	N 17-a
Cement industry by sex in local currency per hr	Main countries	R 3-m
in local currency per hr	EEC countries	E 25-a2
Ceramic products industry by sex in local currency per hr	EEC countries	E 25-a2
Chemical fibre manufacturing industry by sex in local currency per hr	Main countries	R 3-m
Chemical industry by sex in local currency per hr	Main countries	R 3-m C 7-a
	EEC countries	E 25-a2
	OAS member countries	N 17-a
in DM per hr	W Germany	H 3-a
mixers & blenders in local currency per hr	Main countries	R 4-a
skilled employees by sex in local currency per hr	Main countries	R 4-q
unskilled employees & assistants by sex in local currency per hr	Main countries	R 4-q
Chemical workers: paint industry in £ per wk	UK	R 4-a
Chemists employed in pharmaceutical industry by sex in £ per wk	UK	R 4-a
Cigarette-making industry in local currency per hr	OAS member countries	N 17-a
Clerical workers in local currency per hr or mth	AASM countries	E 41-a
Clothing industry by sex in local currency per hr	EEC countries	E 25-a2
females - index nos	UK	B 22-a
in local currency per hr	OAS member countries	N 17-a
males - index nos	UK	B 22-a
skilled employees by sex in local currency per hr	Main countries	R 4-q
unskilled employees by sex in local currency per hr	Main countries	R 4-q
Clothing & shoe manufacturing industry by sex in local currency	Main countries	R 3-m
Coffee roasting industry: production workers in $ per hr	USA	J 1-a
Collieries: face workers in local currency per hr	Main countries	R 4-a
face workers, loaders & conveyor men in local currency per hr	Main countries	R 4-a
in DM per hr	W Germany	H 3-a
(in Jahria) in Rs per wk	India	U 32-m
in local currency per wk	OAS member countries	N 17-a
pit-head workers in local currency per hr	Main countries	R 4-a
& face-workers in local currency per wk	EEC countries	E 25-a2
	Main countries	R 3-m
Commercial vehicle & truck drivers in local currency per hr	Main countries	R 4-a
in £ per wk	UK	R 4-a
Commercial vehicles manufacturing industry by sex in local currency per hr	Main countries	R 3-m
Confectionery & baking industry in local currency per hr	EEC countries	E 25-a2
Construction industry by sex in local currency per hr	Main countries	C 7-a
Cotton mills (in Bombay) in Rs per mth	India	U 32-m
Cotton textile manufacturing industry by sex in local currency per hr	EEC countries	E 25-a2
	Main countries	R 3-m
Dairy products industry by sex in local currency per hr	EEC countries	E 25-a2
Differentials (males) employed in motor industry - index nos	Main countries	B 28-a
Earnings by sex in pence per hr (average)	W European countries	C 8-a
Electric power station workers in £ per wk	UK	R 4-a
Electrical engineering industry by sex in local currency per hr	Main countries	R 3-m C 7-a
in local currency per hr	EEC countries	E 25-a2
	OAS member countries	N 17-a
in FrS per hr	Main countries	C 2-a
skilled workers by sex in local currency per hr	Main countries	R 4-q
unskilled workers by sex in local currency per hr	Main countries	R 4-q
installation fitters in local currency per hr	Main countries	R 4-a
motor & generator manufacturing industry by sex in local currency per hr	Main countries	R 3-m
in DM per hr	W Germany	H 3-a
Farm machinery & tractor manufacturing industry in local currency per hr	Main countries	R 3-m
	EEC countries	E 25-a2
	Austria	R 4-a
Fish-processing industry by sex in local currency per hr	Main countries	R 3-m
Food, drink & tobacco industries by grade in local currency per hr	Main countries	R 4-q
in local currency per hr	EEC countries	E 25-a2
Food processing industry by sex in local currency per hr	OAS member countries	N 17-a
	Main countries	R 3-m C 7-a
Footwear manufacturing industry by sex in local currency per hr	EEC countries	E 25-a2
in local currency per hr	OAS member countries	N 17-a
	Austria	R 4-a

579

WAGE RATES BY SECTOR, continued

	Territorial coverage	Title codes	
Foremen & overseers in local currency per hr or mth	AASM countries	E 41-a	
Foundries (iron & steel) in local currency per hr	EEC countries	E 25-a2	
in FrS per hr	Main countries	C 2-a	
Furniture manufacturing industry by sex in local currency per hr	Main countries	R 3-m	
	EEC countries	E 25-a2	
joiners, polishers & upholsterers in local currency per hr	Main countries	R 4-a	
Gas production & gas equipment installation engineers in £ per wk	UK	R 4-a	
Glass & glassware manufacturing industry by sex in local currency per hr	EEC countries	E 25-a2	
	Main countries	R 3-m	
Glass manufacturing industry by grade of worker in A Sch per hr	Austria	R 4-a	
Grain milling industry in local currency per hr	OAS member countries	N 17-a	
In local currency per hr or mth	AASM countries	E 41-a	
Instrument engineering industry in local currency per hr	EEC countries	E 25-a2	
(incl watchmaking) in FrS per hr	Main countries	C 2-a	
Insurance industry by sex in local currency per hr	Main countries	R 3-m	
Iron & steel industry by sector in DM per hr	W Germany	H 3-a	
by sex in local currency per hr	Main countries	R 3-m	
in DM per hr	W Germany	H 3-a	
in local currency per hr	EEC countries	E 30-m	E 25-a2
		E 29-a	
	Main countries	C 2-a	C 7-a
	OECD countries	R 5-a	
Iron foundries by sex in local currency per hr	Main countries	R 3-m	
Iron ore mines in DM per hr	W Germany	H 3-a	
in local currency per hr	EEC countries	E 25-a2	
	OAS member countries	N 17-a	
surface workers in local currency per hr	EEC countries	E 29-a	
underground workers in local currency per hr	EEC countries	E 29-a	
Iron ore mining in local currency per hr	EEC countries	E 30-m	
Iron-working industry by sex in local currency per hr	Main countries	R 3-m	
Jewellery manufacturing industry by sex in local currency per hr	Main countries	R 3-m	
Jute spinning industry: female auto-spinner operators in local currency per hr	W European countries	C 22-a	
bag overedgers in local currency per hr	W European countries	C 22-a	
cop-winder operators in local currency per hr	W European countries	C 22-a	
warp-winder operators in local currency per hr	W European countries	C 22-a	
male loom weavers in local currency per hr	W European countries	C 22-a	
Knitting mills by sex in local currency per hr	EEC countries	E 25-a2	
Labourers employed in industry in local currency per hr	AASM countries	E 41-a	
Leather & shoe manufacturing industry by sex in local currency per hr	Main countries	R 3-m	
Leather goods industry by sex in local currency per hr	EEC countries	E 25-a2	
in local currency per hr	OAS member countries	N 17-a	
Leather industry by sex in local currency per hr	Main countries	C 7-a	
skilled employees in local currency per hr	Main countries	R 4-q	
unskilled employees in local currency per hr	Main countries	R 4-q	
Locomotive & rolling stock engineers in £ per wk	UK	R 4-a	
in local currency per hr	Main countries	R 3-m	
drivers in £ per wk	UK	R 4-a	
Machine tool assemblers by grade in local currency per hr	Main countries	R 4-a	
Machine tools & accessory manufacturing industry in local currency per hr	EEC countries	E 25-a2	
Machine tools manufacturing industry in DM per hr	W Germany	H 3-a	
in local currency per hr	Main countries	R 3-m	
skilled employees by sex in local currency per hr	Main countries	R 4-q	
unskilled employees & assistants by sex in local currency per hr	Main countries	R 4-q	
Man-made fibres industry by grade in lire per hr	Italy	R 4-a	
by sex in local currency per hr	EEC countries	E 25-a2	
Manufacturing industry: basic contract rates in local currency per hr	OAS member countries	N 17-a	
by sex in local currency per hr	EEC countries	R 3-m	E 25-a2
		C 7-a	
differentials - index nos	Main countries	B 28-a	
in DM per hr	W Germany	H 3-a	
in local currency per hr	OAS member countries	N 17-a	
	AASM countries	E 41-a	
skilled employees by sex in local currency per hr	Main countries	R 4-q	
unskilled employees & assistants in local currency per hr	Main countries	R 4-q	
Manufacturing industry - index nos	ECAFE countries	U 32-m	
	Main countries	C 4-a	
Mechanical engineering industry in local currency per hr	EEC countries	E 25-a2	
	OAS member countries	N 17-a	
in DM per hr	W Germany	H 3-a	
Metal industries by sex in local currency per hr	Main countries	C 2-a	
	Main countries	R 3-m	
in local currency per hr	OAS member countries	N 17-a	
	EEC countries	E 25-a2	
skilled employees by sex in local currency per hr	Main countries	R 4-q	
smelters in local currency per hr	Main countries	R 4-a	
unskilled employees & assistants by sex in local currency per hr	Main countries	R 4-q	

	Territorial coverage	Title codes	
WAGE RATES BY SECTOR, continued			
Metal products manufacturing industries in local currency per hr	EEC countries	E 25-a2	
in DM per hr	W Germany	H 3-a	
in FrS per hr	Main countries	C 2-a	
Metal-cutting machine tools industry in $ per wk	USA	J 2-a	
Metal-working industry in $ per hr	USA	J 2-a	
Mineral oil refining industry in local currency per hr	EEC countries	E 25-a2	
Mining & quarrying by grade of employee in local currency per hr	Main countries	R 3-m	
by sex in local currency per hr	Main countries	R 4-q	
	Main countries	R 3-m	C 7-a
daily, hourly & monthly rates in local currency	OAS member countries	N 17-a	
in local currency per hr	EEC countries	E 25-a2	
	OECD countries	R 5-a	
Mining & quarrying - index nos	Japan	U 32-m	
Motor vehicles manufacturing industry by grade of employee in local currency per hr	Main countries	R 4-q	
by sex in local currency per hr	Main countries	R 3-m	C 7-a
differentials by sex in local currency per hr	EEC countries	B 28-a	
in DM per hr	W Germany	H 3-a	
in local currency per hr	EEC countries	E 25-a2	
	Main countries	C 2-a	
	OAS member countries	N 17-a	
repairers & mechanics in local currency per hr	Main countries	R 4-q	
Non-ferrous metals industry by sex in local currency per hr	Main countries	R 3-m	
in DM per hr	W Germany	H 3-a	
in local currency per hr	EEC countries	E 25-a2	
Non-metallic minerals industry by sector in local currency per hr	OAS member countries	N 17-a	
Office machinery manufacturing industry by sex in local currency per hr	Main countries	R 3-m	
Optical instruments manufacturing industry by sex in local currency per hr	Main countries	R 3-m	
Ore mining industry in local currency per hr	EEC countries	E 25-a2	
Paint manufacturing industry by sex in local currency per hr	Main countries	R 3-m	
Paper & board industry by sex in local currency per hr	OAS member countries	N 17-a	
	Main countries	R 3-m	
	EEC countries	E 25-a2	
skilled employees in local currency per hr	Main countries	R 4-q	
unskilled assistants in local currency per hr	Main countries	R 4-q	
Paper & pulp industry in local currency per hr	Main countries	C 7-a	
Petroleum & natural gas industry in local currency per hr	EEC countries	E 25-a2	
industry in local currency per day & per week	OAS member countries	N 17-a	
refineries by grade of worker in lire per hr	Italy	R 4-a	
by sex in local currency per hr	Main countries	R 3-m	
Pharmaceutical industry by sex in local currency per hr	Main countries	R 3-m	
Plastics industry by sex in local currency per hr	EEC countries	E 25-a2	
	Main countries	R 3-m	
Pneumatic tyre industry in local currency per hr	OAS member countries	N 17-a	
Pottery industry by sex in local currency per hr	Main countries	R 3-m	
Printing & publishing industry: bookbinders in local currency per hr	OAS member countries	N 17-a	
	Main countries	R 4-a	
by sex in local currency per hr	Main countries	R 3-m	C 7-a
	EEC countries	E 25-a2	
compositors in local currency per hr	OAS member countries	N 17-a	
newspaper printers in local currency per hr	OAS member countries	N 17-a	
photo-engravers in local currency per hr	OAS member countries	N 17-a	
skilled employees by sex in local currency per hr	Main countries	R 4-q	
type-setters in local currency per hr	Main countries	R 4-a	
unskilled workers by sex in local currency per hr	Main countries	R 4-q	
Printing machinery manufacturing industry by sex in local currency per hr	Main countries	R 3-m	
Public utilities & dockyards - index nos	Hong Kong	U 32-m	
by sex in local currency per hr	Main countries	R 3-m	
Quarry workers in local currency per day or wk	OAS member countries	N 17-a	
Railway employees & permanent way repairers in local currency per hr	Main countries	R 4-a	
porters (London & provinces) in £ per wk	UK	R 4-a	
Ready-made clothing industry by sex in local currency per hr	Main countries	C 7-a	
Rubber processing industry by sex in local currency per hr	Main countries	R 3-m	C 7-a
	EEC countries	E 25-a2	
	Italy	R 4-a	
Salaried staff employed in industry in local currency per mth	AASM countries	E 41-a	
Scientific instruments manufacturing industry in local currency per hr	OAS member countries	N 17-a	
Semi-skilled industrial employees in local currency per hr or mth	AASM countries	E 41-a	
Shipbuilding & marine engineering industry in local currency per hr	EEC countries	E 25-a2	
	Main countries	C 2-a	C 7-a
Shipping industry by sex in local currency per hr	Main countries	R 3-m	
Silk industry: production workers by sex in £ per wk	UK	R 4-a	
	Main countries	R 3-m	
Skilled industrial workers in local currency per hr or mth	AASM countries	E 41-a	
Social workers (in public services) in local currency per hr	Main countries	R 4-a	
Soft drinks manufacturing industry by sex in local currency per hr	Main countries	R 3-m	
Spinning & weaving industry in local currency per hr	OAS member countries	N 17-a	
Steel fabrication industry in DM per hr	W Germany	H 3-a	

	Territorial coverage	Title codes
WAGE RATES BY SECTOR, continued		
Steel foundries in DM per hr	W Germany	H 3-a
Stone clay & sand quarrymen in local currency per hr or per wk	OAS member countries	N 17-a
Sugar plantations: cane cutters in local currency per hr	OAS member countries	N 17-a
Sugar processing industry by sex in local currency per hr	Main countries	R 3-m
Tailoring industry: tailors' cutters in A Sch per hr	Austria	R 4-a
Tanning industry in local currency per hr	EEC countries	E 25-a2
Telephones: service engineers in local currency per hr	OAS member countries	N 17-a
linesmen in local currency per hr	OAS member countries	N 17-a
Textile industry by sex in local currency per hr	Main countries	R 3-m C 7-a
	OAS member countries	N 17-a
skilled employees by sex in local currency per hr	Main countries	R 4-q
spinners & weavers by sex in local currency per hr	Main countries	R 3-m
unskilled employees & assistants by sex in local currency per hr	Main countries	R 4-q
Textile industry - index nos	Hong Kong	U 32-m
workers, spinners & weavers in local currency per hr	Main countries	R 4-a
Textile machinery manufacturing industry by sex in local currency per hr	Main countries	R 3-m C 7-a
Timber & sawmill industry by sex in local currency per hr	Main countries	R 3-m
Tobacco processing industry by sex in local currency per hr	Main countries	R 3-m
	OAS member countries	N 17-a
Tramway & bus drivers & conductors in local currency per hr	Main countries	R 4-a
Transport equipment manufacturing industry in local currency per hr	EEC countries	E 25-a2
	OAS member countries	N 17-a
Transport services: bus drivers in local currency per hr	OAS member countries	N 17-a
by sex in local currency per hr	Main countries	R 3-m
rail signalmen in local currency per hr	OAS member countries	N 17-a
skilled employees in local currency per hr	Main countries	R 4-q
train drivers in local currency per hr	OAS member countries	N 17-a
unskilled employees in local currency per hr	Main countries	R 4-q
Typists employed by commercial firms in local currency per hr or mth	AASM countries	E 41-a
Warehousemen in £ per wk	UK	R 4-a
Warehousemen, storesmen & stevedores in local currency per hr	OAS member countries	N 17-a
Watch-making industry by sex in local currency per hr	Main countries	R 3-m
Water supply undertakings by sex in local currency per hr	Main countries	R 3-m
Wholesale trade by sex in local currency per hr	Main countries	R 3-m
Wood-based panel industry in $ per hr	Main European countries	A 26-a
Wood-working industry by sex in local currency per hr	Main countries	R 3-m R 4-q
cabinet makers in local currency per hr	OAS member countries	N 17-a
furniture assemblers in local currency per hr	OAS member countries	N 17-a
furniture upholsterers in local currency per hr	OAS member countries	N 17-a
Woollen textile industry by sex in local currency per hr	EEC countries	E 25-a2
	Main countries	R 3-m
Workshop managers in local currency per mth	AASM countries	E 41-a

WAGES

    see also   EARNINGS
                FARM WAGES
                LABOUR COSTS
                REAL INCOME
                WAGE RATES BY SECTOR

% change: basic wages nominal & real	Latin American countries	U 18-a
nominal earnings in $	E European countries & USSR	U 16-a
rate earned per hr in cash terms	Canada, European countries & USA	U 16-q
in real terms	Canada, European countries & USA	U 16-q
real income in $	E European countries & USSR	U 16-a
wage incomes in $m	E European countries & USSR	U 16-a
% increase: wages & salary costs: chemical industry	UK	B 21-a
As % of national income	All countries	L 4-a
As component of gross income & gross national product in $m	S American countries	U 41-a
By industrial sector in $m (in detail)	Main countries	U 21-a U 52-a
Compensation of employees as component of gross national product	Developing countries	D 25-a
Costs (incl salaries) by industrial sectors in $m	OECD countries	D 9-a
labour force (incl salaried staff) in local currency	Main countries	R 5-a
skilled & unskilled workers - index nos	Philippines	U 32-m
Earnings (gross): agricultural occupations - index nos	EEC countries	E 44-a
industrial occupations - index nos	EEC countries	E 2-a
in local currency per mth	E European countries	U 16-a
(General level) in local currency per hr, per day & per wk	OAS member countries	N 17-a
(Incl salaries) as % of national income	All countries	M 6-a
as component of national accounts	EEC countries	E 32-a
	OECD countries	D 30-a
Minimum weekly wages: adult males - index nos	Australasian countries	U 32-m
Public expenditure: teachers' salaries in $m	All countries	U 62-a

Wages costs   see   LABOUR COSTS

WALLPAPER

Production: volume	EEC countries	E 28-q E 27-a

WALNUTS

Exports (shell & unshelled): tonnage	Main countries	P 4-m
Import prices (ex France & India) in £ per ton	UK	P 4-m
Imports: tonnage	Main countries	P 4-m
Production (incl world crop): tonnage	All countries	P 4-a

War pensions   see   PENSIONS, WAR

WAREHOUSING

	Territorial coverage	Title codes	
Expenditure by industrial sector in $	OAS member countries	N 14-a	
IDA loans approved for storage projects in $	OAS member countries	N 16-a	
Wage rates: stevedores in local currency per hr	OAS member countries	N 17-a	
storesmen in local currency per hr	OAS member countries	N 17-a	

WASHING MACHINES, DOMESTIC

% changes in retail sales	E European countries	U 16-a	
% of households owning a washing machine	W European countries	Z 3	
Production: volume	OAS member countries	N 14-a	
	All countries	U 22-a	U 38-a
	EEC countries	E 28-q	E 27-a
	Main countries	R 5-a	
	E European countries & USSR	U 16-a	
Sales demand per 1000 population	E European countries & USSR	U 16-a	

Washing powder   see   DETERGENTS
                              SCOURING POWDER

Washing preparations, domestic
             see   CLEANING & POLISHING MATERIALS
                   DETERGENTS
                   SCOURING POWDER

Waste   see   COTTON WASTE
              MAN-MADE FIBRE WASTE
              SILK WASTE

WASTE PAPER

Consumption & salvage rate as % of new paper produced	All countries	J 7-a
as % of consumption of fibrous materials	OECD countries	D 40-a
tonnage	Main countries	J 7-a
	OECD countries	D 40-a
Exports by destination: tonnage	All countries	D 40-a
Recovery tonnage & rate % of paper consumption	OECD countries	D 40-a
tonnage	Australia, Canada, European countries, Japan & USA	D 40-a
Stocks held at pulp & paper mills: tonnage	OECD countries	D 41-q

WATCH INDUSTRY

Investment in buildings in local currency	EEC countries	E 40-a
in land purchase in local currency	EEC countries	E 40-a
in machinery in local currency	EEC countries	E 40-a
No of hrs worked per wk	Main countries	R 3-m
Wage rates by sex in local currency per hr	Main countries	R 3-m

Watches   see   CLOCKS & WATCHES

Water facilities, piped   see   DWELLINGS

Water heaters   see   METAL PRODUCTS

WATER METERS

Production: volume	EEC countries	E 28-q	E 27-a

WATER PAINTS

Production: tonnage	OECD countries	D 5-a

WATER SUPPLY

% of houses supplied by piped connection	Main countries	W 2-a
by public standposts	Main countries	W 2-a
% increase in supply projected to 1980	ECE countries	U 15-a
to farming projected to 1980	ECE countries	U 15-a
to industry & manufacturing projected to 1980	ECE countries	U 15-a
to public supply projected to 1980	ECE countries	U 15-a
% of urban & rural population receiving water supplies	Main countries	W 2-a
Consumption per capita: water in litres	Main countries	W 2-a
water: rural areas from standpipes in litres	Main countries	W 2-a
from taps in litres	Main countries	W 2-a
urban areas from standpipes in litres	Main countries	W 2-a
from taps in litres	Main countries	W 2-a
Cost of house connection to water supplies in $m	Main countries	W 2-a
of public standposts per consumer in $	Main countries	W 2-a
of supply to urban & rural areas projected to 1980 in $m	Main countries	W 2
Investment in rural supply systems in $m	All countries	W 2-a
in urban supply systems in $m	All countries	W 2-a
No of dwellings (urban) connected to supply of piped water	Latin American countries	J 5-a
	Main countries	W 2-a
supplied by standpipes	Main countries	W 2-a
Overseas loans & grants for water supply improvements in $m	All countries	W 2-a
material supplies by value in $m	All countries	W 2-a
Population (rural) served by community water supplies	Main countries	W 2-a
to be supplied by 1980	Main countries	W 2
served by piped water systems: rural & urban areas	OAS member countries	N 18-a

	Territorial coverage	Title codes

WATER SUPPLY, continued

    Population (urban) served by community water supplies — Main countries — W 2-a
        to be supplied by 1980 — Main countries — W 2
    World Bank loans & credits for water supply projects in $m — — M 3-a

WATER SUPPLY INDUSTRY

    see also   PUBLIC UTILITIES

    Consumption: electricity for pumping in kWh — All countries — C 23-a
    Labour costs by status of employee in local currency — EEC countries — E 8-a
    Labour force employed: wage earners & salaried staff — EEC countries — E 8-a
    No of hrs worked per yr — EEC countries — E 8-a
    Structure of labour costs as % of total costs — EEC countries — E 8-a

Water supply meters   see   METERS, WATER SUPPLY

WATER WHEELS

    see also   GENERATORS, HYDROELECTRIC

    Exports by destination: wheels for generators in mW — Japan — T 7-a
        in mW — European countries, Japan & USA — T 7-a
    Production in mW — European countries, Japan & USA — T 7-a

Watertube boilers   see   BOILERS, WATERTUBE

Waterways   see   INLAND WATERWAYS

Waxes   see   NATURAL WAX
              PARAFFIN WAX

WEALTH TAXES

    Basis of assessment & % rates of tax levied — EEC countries — E 31-a
    Government revenue from taxes on wealth in local currency — Chile & El Salvador — J 5-a
        in $m — EEC countries — E 42-a

Weather   see   TEMPERATURE

Weatherproof clothing   see   OUTERWEAR, WEATHERPROOF
                                    OVERCOATS & RAINCOATS

Weaving machines   see   TEXTILE MACHINERY

Weaving (textiles)   see   SPINNING & WEAVING INDUSTRY

Weeders   see   CULTIVATING MACHINES

WEIGHING MACHINERY

    see also   MEASURING APPARATUS

    Exports by destination by value in $m — Main countries — U 9-a
        by value in $m — Main countries — U 38-a
    Imports by value in $m — All countries — U 38-a
    Production: tonnage or volume — EEC countries — E 28-q   E 27-a
    World exports: weighing machinery by value in $m — — U 38-a

Weight-load factors   see   AIRLINE COMPANIES

WEIGHTS & BALLAST

    Consumption: lead in production of weights & ballast: tonnage — USA — J 6-a

WELDING RODS

    Consumption: cobalt in production of welding rods: tonnage — USA — T 4-a

Welfare   see   SOCIAL SERVICES

Welfare state   see   NATIONAL INSURANCE

Wells, petroleum   see   OIL WELLS

Whale blubber   see   WHALE BY-PRODUCTS

WHALE BY-PRODUCTS

    see also   WHALE OIL

    Production: whale liver oil: tonnage — Worldwide — C 10-a
        meal & bone meal: tonnage — Worldwide — C 10-a
        solubles: tonnage — Worldwide — C 10-a

Whale liver oil   see   WHALE BY-PRODUCTS

Whale meat & meal   see   WHALE BY-PRODUCTS

WHALE OIL

    Consumption in production of cooking fats: tonnage — UK — B 19-a
        margarine & cooking fats: tonnage — Japan — A 4-a
        tonnage — Main countries — B 19-a
        soap & detergents: tonnage — Norway — A 4-a
        sperm oil in production of detergents: tonnage — Japan — A 4-a   B 19-a

	Territorial coverage	Title codes
WHALE OIL, continued		
Exports: whale oil by kind (incl sperm oil): tonnage	All countries	A 21-a
Import prices: whale oil in $ per ton	European countries	A 9-a
Imports: whale oil (incl other fish oils & fats): tonnage	Main countries	P 1-a
tonnage	Main European countries	B 19-a
Production by whaling areas: tonnage	Main countries	A 21-a
for ensuing yr in barrels (estim)	World regions	P 1-a
(from pelagic whaling in Antartica) in barrels		C 10-a
(in Antarctic region) in barrels		P 1-a
(in Arctic & Antarctic regions) in barrels		P 1-a
in barrels	Japan, Norway & USSR	C 10-a
sperm oil (in Arctic & Antarctic regions) in barrels	Japan	P 1-a
tonnage	Country of registration of whaling vessels	B 19-a
whale & sperm oil by flag of whaling vessels: tonnage	Whaling regions	U 43-a
Wholesale prices (ex tanks) in $ per kg	Netherlands & UK	R 2-m
World production & exports (incl fish liver oil): tonnage		A 21-a
(excl sperm oil): tonnage		A 4-a
(incl sperm oil): tonnage		A 5-a N 10-a
World supply (excl sperm oil): tonnage		B 19-a
WHALE OIL FACTORY SHIPS		
see also WHALING OPERATIONS		
Tonnage afloat by flags	Japan & USSR	S 4-a
WHALES		
No caught by kind by flag of vessels	World whaling regions	U 43-a
by sex & size in ft in Antarctic: Fin whales		C 10-a
Minke whales		C 10-a
Sei whales		C 10-a
Sperm whales		C 10-a
pregnant females in Antarctica by size in ft		C 10-a
sperm whales (incl oil produced therefrom)	Japan & USSR	C 10-a
volume	Brazil, Canada, Chile, Peru & USA	N 13-a
WHALES BY KIND		
No caught by fishing zones	All countries	A 22-a
by season in Antartica		C 10-m
by sex & length in ft		C 10-a
by zones (Antarctica South of Lat 40)		C 10-a
No of foetuses caught in Antarctic by size in ft		C 10-m
Quotas for Antarctic catch	Japan, Norway & USSR	C 10-a
WHALING OPERATIONS		
see also WHALE OIL FACTORY SHIPS		
No of floating & shore whaling stations in service	Worldwide	U 43-a
of floating factories in service in Antarctic		C 10-a
of vessels by nationality in service	Worldwide	C 10-a
WHEAT		
see also BARTER AGREEMENT		
BUCKWHEAT		
INTERNATIONAL WHEAT AGREEMENT		
% change in producer prices	W European countries	U 30-a
% of human calorie intake obtained from consumption of wheat	World regions	C 27-a
% of production exported	Main countries	B 8-a
A.I.D. sales (incl flour) under food aid programs by value in $m	All countries	M 1-a
Area under crop: historical table from 1815 in ha	Main European countries	Z 1-a
in acres	Main countries	B 7-a B 8-a
(incl harvested tonnage) in ha	Main countries	R 5-a
(incl world total) in ha	All countries	C 16-a
in ha, production: tonnage & yield per ha	All countries	A 9-a
in ha	EEC countries	E 44-a
	All countries	C 16-a
	OAS member countries	N 13-a
	OECD countries	D 1-a
	World regions excl China	U 11-a
	World regions	C 16-a
winter & spring wheat in ha	EEC countries	E 12-a
world total in acres & ha	All countries	C 29-a
Carry-over stocks (end-season): tonnage	Main countries	C 16-a
Consignments overseas (as emergency food aid) by value in $m	Recipient countries	M 1-a
Consumption & consumption per capita per day	OECD countries	D 14-a
(as animal feed): tonnage	Australia, Canada & UK	B 7-a
	EEC countries	E 3-a
	Main countries	C 27-a
	UK	B 8-a
(as human food & animal feed): tonnage	World regions	C 27-a
(as human food): tonnage	Canada & UK	B 7-a
	Main countries	C 29-a
	UK	B 8-a
(as seed): tonnage	Main countries	B 7-a
	UK	B 8-a
for flour milling purposes: tonnage	UK	B 7-a
food, industrial usage & for seed: tonnage	EEC countries	E 3-a
industrial processing: tonnage	Canada & UK	B 7-a
	UK	B 8-a

	Territorial coverage	Title codes	
WHEAT, continued			
Consumption for production of animal feed: tonnage	UK	B 7-a	
	Main countries	C 29-a	
hard & soft wheat (as animal feed): tonnage	EEC countries	E 44-a	
home-grown wheat (as animal feed): tonnage	UK	P 5-a	
(in processing plants): tonnage	UK	P 5-a	
(intake by millers): tonnage	UK	P 5-a	
(incl rye) as animal feed: tonnage	OECD countries	D 1-a	
(incl wheat flour): tonnage	Main countries	C 16-a	
(incl world total): tonnage	World regions	C 27-a	
per capita in kg	EEC countries	B 1-a	E 44-a
urban & rural areas by income levels in kg	India	C 27-a	
requirements (as animal feed): tonnage	UK	B 7-a	
(as human food): tonnage	UK	B 7-a	
tonnage	Main countries	C 27-a	C 29-a
	OAS member countries	N 17-a	
Crop yield in bushels per acre & in kg per ha	All countries	C 29-a	
in cwt per acre	Main countries	B 8-a	
(incl spelt) in kg per ha	OECD countries	D 1-a	
in kg per ha	EEC countries	E 3-a	
	Main countries	R 5-a	
	OAS member countries	N 13-a	
in quintals per ha	E European countries & USSR incl Ukraine	U 16-a	
	World regions	C 16-a	U 11-a
winter & spring wheat in 100 kg per ha	EEC countries	E 12-a	
Deliveries by farmers: tonnage	Main countries	B 7-a	
Disposal, domestic consumption & exports: tonnage	Main countries	C 29-a	
Export prices by grade (ex Argentine, Australia, Canada & USA) in			
in £ per ton fob		B 8-m	
in $ per bushel fob	Main countries	C 16-m	
durum wheat in $ per 60 lbs fob	Argentine	U 33-m	
hard red wheat in $ per 60 lbs fob Gulf Ports	USA	U 33-q	
hard winter wheat in $ per 60 lbs fob	USA	U 33-m	
in cents per 60 lbs fob	Australia	U 32-m	
in $ per ton fob	Argentine, Australia, Canada & USA	U 35-a	
Export prices - index nos (weighted average main sources)	Worldwide	U 29-q	U 54-q
	S American countries	U 40-q	
	Canada & USA	U 30-q	
	Main countries	A 9-a	
Exports by destination (incl wheat flour): tonnage	Main countries	A 17-a	C 29-a
tonnage	China & USSR	A 17-a	
	E European countries	A 17-a	
	Main countries	B 7-m	B 8-a
by value & as & of exports of agricultural products	W European countries	U 20-a	
in local currency	Australia	U 32-m	
in $m	Developing countries	U 11-a	
	W European countries	U 33-a	
(incl flour) as % of all exports (value basis)	Main countries	B 8-a	
by destination: tonnage	All countries	C 16-a	
tonnage	All countries	A 17-a	
	European countries	U 35-a	
	Main countries	B 8-a	
under government assistance programs: tonnage	Participating countries	C 16-a	
tonnage	All countries	C 29-a	
	Australia	U 32-m	
	Main countries	B 7-m	
	UK	P 5-a	
under government-assisted programs as % of total world wheat exports		C 16-a	
unit value in $ per kg	OAS member countries	N 15-a	
Freight rates (to Antwerp & Rotterdam) shipped ex N American ports			
in £ per ton		B 7-m	
(to UK) shipped ex Argentina, Australia, Canada & USA			
in £ per ton		B 7-m	
Gross output as % of all cereal crops incl rye (value basis)	ECE countries	U 34-a	
Guaranteed export credits & insurance credits granted in $m	Canada	B 8-a	
Import prices by quality in $ per ton cif	UK	A 9-a	
Canadian spring wheat (at European ports) in $ per ton	European countries	U 33-m	
in £ per ton	UK	C 29-a	
in $ per ton c & f (by grade & source)	Japan	C 16-m	C 29-m
in $ per ton cif (by grade & source)	Main countries	C 16-m	
	Netherlands	C 29-m	
Imports as % of domestic consumption	World regions	C 27-a	
by port of entry: tonnage	UK	B 7-m	P 5-a2
by source (incl flour): tonnage	EEC countries	B 8-a	
	UK	B 7-m	
tonnage	Main countries	B 8-a	
by value & as % of imports of agricultural products	W European countries	U 20-a	
in $m	W European countries	U 33-a	
in local currency	New Zealand & Pakistan	U 32-a	
(for production of animal feed): tonnage	UK	P 5-a	
(incl flour): tonnage	All countries	A 17-a	
	European countries	U 35-a	
into E European countries & China shipped ex non-Communist countries: tonnage		A 17-a	
into USSR by source: tonnage		A 17-a	
tonnage	All countries	C 29-a	
	Main countries	B 7-q	
	India, Japan, Pakistan & W European countries	B 8-a	
Industrial usage for malting purposes: tonnage	UK	C 27-a	

	Territorial coverage	Title codes

WHEAT, continued

Description	Territorial coverage	Title codes	
Industrial usage for processing: tonnage	World regions	C 27-a	
for production of starch & glucose: tonnage	UK	C 27-a	
Intervention prices (lowest derived) for wheat in £ per ton	EEC countries	B 7-m	
Ocean freight rates by route in $ per ton	Main countries	C 16-m	
to European ports ex main suppliers in $ per ton		C 16-m	U 35-a
to Japan ex main suppliers in $ per ton		C 16-m	
Price supports in local currency per 100 kg	All countries	C 29-a	
per specified wt	All countries	C 16-a	
Producer prices & basic fixed prices in local currency per ton	W European countries	U 30-a	
& intervention prices in £ per ton	EEC countries	B 7-m	
in local currency per ton	OECD countries	D 1-a	
in £ per cwt	EEC countries	B 1-a	
ton	EEC countries	B 7-m	
in $ per bushel	USA	E 35-a	
ton	All countries	A 9-a	
soft & hard wheat in $ per ton	EEC countries	E 44-a	
Production & consumption forecast for 1975: tonnage	Main countries	A 1	
& yield per 100 ha	Latin American countries	J 5-a	
by administrative areas: tonnage	EEC countries	E 38-a	
by value in $m	EEC countries	E 44-a	
historical tables: harvest tonnage	Main European countries	Z 1-a	
in bushels million	All countries	C 29-a	
(incl rye): tonnage	Czechoslovakia, Hungary & Poland	U 34-a	
(incl world total): tonnage	All countries	C 16-a	
Production, imports, consumption & supply: tonnage	UK	B 7-m	
	India	C 27-a	
Production, stocks, imports & supply: tonnage	EEC countries	B 1-a	
	Main countries	C 29-a	
Production, stocks, industrial usage & consumption: as food & seed: tonnage	EEC countries	E 3-a	E 44-a
Production, supply & import requirements: tonnage	OECD countries	D 14-a	
tonnage	UK	B 7-m	
	African countries	U 44-a	
	All countries	U 43-a	
	OECD countries	D 1-a	
	Argentine, Australia, Canada & USA	P 1-a	
	Asian & Far East countries	U 32-a	
	Continental regions	C 16-a	
	European countries	U 35-a	
	E European countries & USSR incl Ukraine	U 16-a	
	European countries, Canada, Japan, USA & USSR	E 44-a	
	Latin American countries	U 40-a	
	Main countries	B 7-a	B 8-a
		E 3-a	P 5-a
	OAS member countries	N 13-a	
	World regional areas excl China	U 11-a	
	World regions	C 16-a	
value (incl rye) as % of gross farm output	E European countries	U 34-a	
winter & spring wheat: tonnage	EEC countries	E 12-a	
Sales by growers: tonnage	England & Scotland	B 7-m	
Stocks (end-season): tonnage	Main countries	A 11-a	B 7-a
		B 8-a	
held at wholesalers' premises (end-month): tonnage	EEC countries	E 12-m	
on farms (at end-May): tonnage	UK	P 5-a	
(end-month): tonnage	EEC countries	E 12-m	
(incl unsold surpluses): tonnage (estim)	UK	B 7-a	
new crop (incl consumption & supply): tonnage	Canada	B 7-a	
(opening & closing) incl wheat flour: tonnage	Main countries	C 16-a	
Stocks, production, imports & supply: tonnage	Exporting countries	U 35-a	
Supply: (production plus net imports): tonnage	Main countries	B 8-a	
Supply & disposal by purpose: tonnage	Main countries	B 8-a	
home-produced & imported milled wheat: tonnage	UK	B 7-a	
incl wheat flour in wheat equiv tonnage	Main countries	C 16-a	
incl wheat flour: tonnage	Main countries	C 16-a	
Support prices paid to producers in $ per ton	USA	U 30-a	
Wholesale prices by quality in local currency per ton	OAS member countries	N 17-a	
in £ per ton	EEC countries	B 7-m	
in $ per ton	Australia, Canada, UK & USA	U 27-m	
	Main countries	A 9-a	
World exports by value in $m	World regions	A 5-a	
World production: tonnage (incl % change)	Main countries	C 4-a	
tonnage	World regions	U 35-a	
World stocks (end-yr): tonnage		G 1-a	

WHEAT, HARD

Description	Territorial coverage	Title codes
% change in producer prices (over previous yr)	France	E 34-m
Area under crop in ha	EEC countries	E 12-a
	Main countries	C 29-a
Common threshold price in £ per ton	EEC countries	B 7-m
Consumption: durum wheat: tonnage	Main countries	C 29-a
Crop yield in 100 kg per ha	EEC countries	E 12-a
in quintals per ha	Main countries	C 29-a
Deliveries (ex farm): tonnage	Main countries	B 7-a
Disposal, domestic consumption & exports: tonnage	Main countries	C 29-a
Ex-farm prices: domestic grain in £ per ton	UK	B 7-m
Export prices in $ per ton fob	Argentine, Canada & USA	C 29-m
red winter wheat in $ per 60 lbs fob	USA	U 20-q
Export subsidies: durum wheat in £ per ton	EEC countries	B 8-a

	Territorial coverage	Title codes	
WHEAT, HARD continued			
Exports by destination (incl flour): tonnage	All countries	C 29-a	
Import prices at Rotterdam in £ per ton cif	Netherlands	C 29-m	
shipped ex USA in $ per ton c&f	Japan	C 29-m	
Imports: durum wheat: tonnage	World trading groups	C 16-a	
Intervention price: durum wheat in £ per ton	EEC countries	B 8-a	E 44-a
	France & Italy	B 7-a	
Producer prices in lire per 100 kg	Italy	D 1-a	
in local currency per kg	France & Italy	E 34-m	
Production, supply & stocks: tonnage	Main countries	C 29-a	
Production: tonnage	EEC countries	E 12-m	
	Main countries	B 7-a	C 29-a
Sales ex farm: tonnage	EEC countries	E 12-a	
Stocks (end-season): tonnage	Main countries	C 29-a	
held at wholesalers' premises: tonnage	EEC countries	E 12-m	
on farm (end-season): tonnage	Main countries	B 7-a	
Target, intervention & threshold prices in £ per ton	EEC countries	B 1-a	
Threshold price in £ per ton	France & Italy	B 7-m	
Wholesale price in £ per ton	France & Italy	B 7-m	
WHEAT, SOFT			
% change: producer prices (over previous yr)	EEC countries	E 34-m	
Area under crop (for own consumption) in ha	EEC countries	B 1-a	
in ha	EEC countries	E 12-a	
Consumption (as human food) projected to 1978: tonnage	UK	P 5-a	
Crop yield in 100 kg per ha	EEC countries	B 1-a	E 12-a
Deliveries by farmers: tonnage	Main countries	B 7-a	
Ex-farm prices: domestic grain in £ per ton	UK	B 7-m	
Export prices by grade in local currency per ton fob	Canada & USA	R 2-m	
Export subsidies in £ per ton	EEC countries	B 8-a	
Import prices by grade in local currency per ton cif	European countries	R 2-m	
Harvest: tonnage	EEC countries	E 12-a	
Intervention price: soft wheat in £ per ton	EEC countries	B 8-a	E 44-a
Producer prices in lire per 100 kg	Italy	D 1-a	
in local currency per kg	EEC countries	E 34-m	
	W European countries	E 35-a	
Production: tonnage & value in £m	EEC countries	B 1-a	
tonnage	EEC countries	E 12-m	
	Main countries	B 7-a	
Sales ex farm: tonnage	EEC countries	E 12-a	
Stocks held at wholesalers' premises: tonnage	EEC countries	E 12-m	
on farms (end-season): tonnage	Main countries	B 7-a	
Target, intervention & threshold prices in £ per ton	EEC countries	B 1-a	
Threshold prices in local currency per ton	EEC countries	U 33-m	
Wholesale prices: % change (over previous yr)	EEC countries	E 34-m	
in local currency per kg	EEC countries	E 34-m	
WHEAT BY KIND			
Consumption (as animal feed): tonnage	EEC countries	E 44-a	
hard & soft wheat: tonnage	EEC countries	E 44-a	
Export inspections by port areas: tonnage	USA	C 29-a	
Export prices by port areas in $ per ton fob	Canada	C 29-m	
Gulf & Atlantic & Pacific ports in $ per ton fob	USA	C 29-m	
in local currency per ton fob	Main countries	C 29-m	
	EEC countries	C 29-m	
in $ per ton fob	Australia, Canada, Argentine & USA	B 7-m	
Exports by destination by grades: tonnage	Canada	B 7-m	
by grades & loading areas: tonnage	Australia & Canada	C 29-a	
Import prices in £ per ton cif	UK	B 7-m	B 8-m
Producer prices: soft & hard wheat in $ per ton	EEC countries	E 44-a	
Production, carry-over, usage & supply: tonnage	USA	C 29-a	
hard & soft wheat: tonnage	EEC countries	E 44-a	
WHEAT BRAN			
Imports: pollards & sharps for production of animal feed: tonnage	UK	P 5-a	
Producer prices in $ per ton	W Germany	A 9-a	
Wholesale prices in $ per ton	France, Italy & USA	A 9-a	
WHEAT FLOUR			
% change in producer prices (over previous yr)	EEC countries	E 34-m	
Consumption in production of farinaceous foods - index nos	EEC countries	E 44-a	
per capita in kg per yr	UK	C 27-a	
in lbs per yr	Main countries	B 8-a	
tonnage	OAS member countries	N 17-a	
EEC area levy on imported wheat flour shipped ex non-EEC area in £ per ton	EEC countries	B 7-m	
Export prices by grade in $ per ton fob	Australia, Canada, Spain & USA	C 16-m	A 9-a
Export subsidies in £ per ton	EEC countries	B 8-a	
Exports by destination: tonnage	China, E European countries & USSR	A 17-a	
	Main countries	B 7-m	A 17-a
		B 8-a	
by source areas shipped to centrally-planned economies: tonnage		C 16-a	
to developed countries: tonnage		C 16-a	
to developing countries: tonnage		C 16-a	
in wheat equiv tonnage	Main world exporting areas	C 16-a	
tonnage	Main countries	B 7-m	
Extraction rates as % of milled wheat	Main countries	C 29-a	

	Territorial coverage	Title codes	
WHEAT FLOUR, continued			
Import prices (ex Canada & Australia) in £ per ton cif	UK	R 2-m	
Imports by port of entry: tonnage	UK	B 7-m	
by source: tonnage	Main countries	B 8-a	
	USSR	A 17-a	
by value in $m	Indonesia	U 32-m	
shipped ex non-Communist countries: tonnage	N Korea & USSR	A 17-a	
tonnage	All countries	A 17-a	C 29-a
	Main countries	B 7-q	
Mill consumption: home-grown wheat: tonnage	UK	P 5-a	
Producer prices in local currency per kg	EEC countries	E 34-m	
Production: bolted flour: tonnage	All countries	U 22-a	
milled flour: tonnage	All countries	U 27-m	U 43-a
tonnage	African countries	U 44-a	
	EEC countries	E 26-m	E 28-q
		E 27-a	
	Latin American countries	J 5-a	U 40-a
	Main countries	C 29-a	
	OAS member countries	N 14-a	
Retail prices by kind of flour in local currency per kg	OAS member countries	N 17-a	
(comparative): white flour per kg	EEC countries	Z 3-a	
Supply: home-produced flour: imports & disposals: tonnage	UK	B 7-a	
Wholesale prices in local currency per kg per ton	OAS member countries	N 17-a	
in $ per ton	Canada & USA	U 27-m	
WHEELS TYRES AXLES, STEEL			
Deliveries to user industries: tonnage	ECE countries	U 7-q	U 6-a
	Main countries	H 3-a	
Exports by destination: tonnage	ECE countries	U 48-a	
	Main countries	T 4-a	
	EEC countries	E 5-q	
tonnage & % share of world exports	Main countries	U 49-a	
Imports by source: tonnage	EEC countries	E 5-q	
rolled steel locomotive wheels: tonnage	Main countries	T 4-a	
railway rolling stock wheels: tonnage	Main countries	T 1-a	
Production (for rolling stock): tonnage	All countries	U 22-a	
	Main countries	U 22-a	
	OECD countries	D 22-a	
	ECE countries	U 7-m	U 6-a
	EEC countries	E 29-a	
	Main countries	H 3-a	
WHEY POWDER			
see also MILK POWDER			
MILK PRODUCTS			
Consumption: tonnage	EEC countries	B 3-a	
Exports: tonnage	EEC countries	B 3-a	
Imports: tonnage	EEC countries	B 3-a	
Production: tonnage	EEC countries	B 3-a	
WHISKY			
see also BEVERAGES, ALCOHOLIC			
Consumption: % growth rates	Main countries	Z 6-a	
by volume in proof gallons	UK & Worldwide	Z 6-a	
Consumption - index nos	UK	Z 6-a	
Exports: blended whisky (in bulk) by volume in proof gallons	UK	Z 6-a	
bottled blends by volume in proof gallons	UK	Z 6-a	
bottled malt whisky by volume in proof gallons & value in £m	UK	Z 6-a	
by destination by volume in proof gallons	UK	Z 6-a	
by kind by volume in proof gallons	UK	Z 6-a	
by value & as % of value of total exports	UK	Z 6-a	
by volume by destination - index nos	UK	Z 6-a	
grain whisky by volume in proof gallons	UK	Z 6-a	
malt whisky (in bulk) by volume in proof gallons & value in £m	UK	Z 6-a	
Imports: blended whisky (in bottles) ex UK by volume in proof gallons	Main countries	Z 6-a	
(in bulk) ex UK by volume in proof gallons	Main countries	Z 6-a	
by kind ex UK by volume in proof gallons	Main countries	Z 6-a	
grain whisky ex UK by volume in proof gallons	Main countries	Z 6-a	
malt whisky (in bottles) ex UK by volume in proof gallons	Main countries	Z 6-a	
(in bulk) ex UK by volume in proof gallons	Main countries	Z 6-a	
World exports by volume in proof gallons & by value in $m		Z 6-a	
WHITE LEAD			
Consumption: lead (refined) in production of white lead: tonnage	UK & USA	T 4-a	
Exports: tonnage	USA	J 6-a	
Imports: tonnage	USA	J 6-a	
WHITE METAL			
see also SOLDER			
Consumption: tin in production of white metal: tonnage	USA	J 6-a	
	All countries	C 20-m	
	UK & USA	C 12-a	
Wholesale prices (43% solder) in £ per ton	UK	T 4-w	

		Territorial coverage	Title codes

WHITE SPIRIT
    see also KEROSENE

Consumption by end-users: petrochemical industry: tonnage	OECD countries	D 31-a
tonnage	Main countries	C 14-a
Deliveries for home consumption & exports: tonnage	OECD countries	D 31-a
Imports & exports by source & destination: tonnage	All countries	B 15-a
by source: tonnage	OECD countries	D 31-a
tonnage	Main countries	C 14-a
Production (as paint solvent): tonnage	All countries	U 22-a
tonnage	Main countries	B 15-a
Refinery output, imports & supply: tonnage	OECD countries	D 31-a

Whitehead Groningen   see   CATTLE BY BREED

Whiting, mullet & snapper   see   FISH

WHOLESALE PRICES
    see also RETAIL PRICES

% changes (compounded): all products	Main countries	G 1-a	N 7-a
	Greece, Portugal, Spain & Turkey	U 16-a	
Main basic manufactured products in $	Worldwide	C 4-a	
Raw materials by kind in local currency per ton	OAS member countries	N 17-a	
(inedible) in local currency per ton	OAS member countries	N 17-a	
Index nos by product groups	Main countries	R 5-a	
(based on 1958 price levels)	Main countries	N 7-a	
capital goods	Gabon	E 41-a	
consumer goods	Gabon	E 41-a	
	Japan & S Korea	U 32-m	
	OAS member countries	N 17-a	
energy	Central African Republic & Zaire	E 41-a	
export products	ECAFE countries	U 32-m	
	OAS member countries	N 17-a	
farm products & agricultural raw materials	S Korea & Thailand	U 32-m	
	W Germany	H 3-a	
	OAS member countries	N 17-a	
finished manufactured goods	ECAFE countries	U 32-m	
	Congo Republic & Gabon	E 41-a	
	India & Pakistan	U 32-m	
	OECD countries	D 26-m	
	Main countries	G 1-a	
	OAS member countries	N 17-a	
foodstuffs	Central African Republic & Zaire	E 41-a	
	ECAFE countries	U 32-m	
	OAS member countries	N 17-a	
general level: all products	All countries	M 6-a	
	African countries	U 44-a	
	ECAFE countries	U 32-m	
	ECE countries	U 42-m	
	EEC countries	E 44-a	
	Latin American countries	J 5-a	
	OECD countries	R 5-a	
all products (excl VAT)	EEC countries	E 3-a	
historical table (on changed bases) from 1750	Main European countries	Z 1-a	
from 1913	Main countries	C 4-a	
home-produced goods	ECAFE countries	U 32-m	
imported goods	ECAFE countries	U 32-m	
	African countries	U 44-a	
(incl 12 mth % changes)	Main countries	R 2-m	
inedible raw products	OAS member countries	N 17-a	
	OECD countries	D 26-m	
	Pakistan & S Vietnam	U 32-m	
industrial raw materials	W Germany	H 3-a	
metallic ores	OAS member countries	N 17-a	
producer goods	Japan & S Korea	U 32-m	
	OAS member countries	N 17-a	
selected main products	All countries	U 43-a	
	EEC countries	E 26-m	
	Main countries	U 27-m	

WHOLESALE PRICES BY PRODUCT

Agricultural products by kind in $ per ton	All countries	A 9-a	C 4-a
Agricultural products - index nos	OAS member countries	N 17-a	
Alcoholic drinks in local currency	OAS member countries	N 17-a	
Aluminium (at London, Milan & New York markets): average in local currency	Italy, UK & USA	C 12-a	
bars (30 mm diam) in Fr per kg	France	T 4-q	
in local currency per lb or ton	Canada, UK & USA	J 6-m	
ingots (ex works) in cents per lb	UK	R 2-m	
on London Metal Exchange in £ per ton	USA	R 2-m	N 1-a
on main world metal markets in local currency per kg		C 12-m	
scrap in local currency per ton	Main countries	T 4-q	
in lire per kg	Italy	C 12-m	
semi-finished products by kind in lire per kg	Italy	C 12-m	
in £ per kg	UK	T 4-q	
sheets by quality in Fr per kg	France	T 4-q	
tubes (cold-drawn): 50 mm diam in Fr per kg	France	T 4-q	

WHOLESALE PRICES BY PRODUCT, continued

Product	Territorial coverage	Title codes	
Aluminium wire (4mm gauge) in Fr per kg	France	T 4-q	
wire rod (25mm diam) in yen per kg	Japan	T 4-q	
Ammonia in $ per ton	USA	N 1-a	
Animal feeding stuffs in $ per ton	Main countries	A 9-a	
Anthracite in $ per ton	USA	N 1-a	
Anti-friction metal in lire per kg	Italy	C 12-m	
Antimony (lump sulphide ore) in $ per ton	UK	C 12-m	
metal in cents per lb	USA	N 1-a	
Argon (as gas or liquid) in $ per ton	USA	N 1-a	
Asbestos in $ per ton	USA	N 1-a	
Babbitt metal ingots in lire per kg	Italy	C 12-m	
Bacon (English, Danish, Irish & Polish) in £ per cwt	UK	B 11-m	
(home-produced & imported) in £ per ton	UK	B 12-m	
in local currency per kg	OAS member countries	N 17-a	
Bacon pigs (live) at auction in £	Main countries	B 12-w	
(dead wt) in local currency per kg	EEC countries	C 9-m	
Barley: % change over previous yr	EEC countries	E 34-m	
by quality in local currency per ton	OAS member countries	N 17-a	
in local currency per kg	EEC countries	E 34-m	
Barytes (barite) in $ per ton	USA	N 1-a	
Bastnaesite concentrates in $ per ton	USA	N 1-a	
Bauxite in $ per ton	USA	N 1-a	
(metallurgical quality) in Fr per ton	France	T 4-m	
Beef (by cuts) at central markets in pence per lb	UK	B 12-w	
(English & imported) at Smithfield Market in pence per lb	UK	B 11-m	
hindquarters ex Argentine in pence per kg	UK	U 20-q	
in local currency per kg	OAS member countries	N 17-a	
per lb	UK & USA	R 2-m	
Beef cattle (live) in cents per kg	Main countries	A 5-q	
Beryllium metal in $ per lb	USA	N 1-a	
ore (imported) in $ per 20 lbs	USA	N 1-a	
Beryllium-copper alloy ingots in £ per lb	UK	T 4-m	
rods, strip & wire in £ per lb	UK	T 4-w	
Beverages by kind in local currency	OAS member countries	N 17-a	
Bismuth (metallic) in local currency per kg	Japan & USA	T 4-m	
in $ per lb	UK	N 1-a	
Borax pentahydrate (granulated) in $ per ton	USA	N 1-a	
Brass (heavy yellow) in local currency per ton	Main countries	T 4-m	
ingots by quality in £ per ton	UK	T 4-w	
in local currency per kg	Main countries	T 4-w	
rod (free cutting) in local currency per kg	Main countries	T 4-w	
scrap by kind in local currency per ton	Main countries	T 4-w	
(heavy rod ends & swarf) in £ per ton	UK	T 4-w	
(red composition) in local currency per ton	Main countries	T 4-w	
(yellow) & turnings in local currency per ton	Main countries	T 4-w	
sheets in lire per kg	Italy	C 12-m	
in local currency per kg	Main countries	T 4-w	
tubes (36% zinc) in local currency per kg	Main countries	T 4-w	
(by diam sizes) in pence per ft	UK	T 4-w	
in lire per kg	Italy	C 12-m	
wire in lire per kg	Italy	C 12-m	
in yen per kg	Japan	T 4-w	
Bricks - index nos	Austria, Italy & Switzerland	A 13-a	
	European countries & USA	U 5-a	
	OAS member countries	N 14-a	
Bristle fibre (made of coir) in Rs per cwt	Sri Lanka	B 10-m	
Bromide (purified) in bulk in cents per lb	USA	N 1-a	
Bronze ingots by grade in lire per kg	Italy	C 12-m	
scrap by grade in lire per kg	Italy	C 12-m	
Building materials & bricks - index nos	European countries	A 13-a	
- index nos	Australasian countries	U 32-m	
	Ivory Coast & Senegal	E 41-a	
	Main countries	R 5-a	
	OAS member countries	N 17-a	
Bullocks & steers in £ per cwt	Main countries	B 12-m	
Bulls & store bullocks in local currency	EEC countries	C 9-m	
Burlap in Rs per 100 metres	India	U 32-m	
Butter by grade on London market in £ per cwt	UK	B 12-w	
kind in £ per ton	Main countries	B 12-w	
kind & grade in £ per ton	Main countries	B 12-m	
ex Australia on London market in £ per cwt	UK	U 32-m	
dairies: % change over 12 mths	EEC countries	E 34-m	
in local currency per 100 kg	EEC countries	E 34-m	
Denmark & New Zealand on London market in £ per cwt	UK	B 4-m	P 1-m
New Zealand (salted) on London market in £ per 56 lbs	UK	U 20-q	
(fresh, canned & salted) in local currency per kg	OAS member countries	N 17-a	
(home-produced) ex dairies in local currency per kg	W European countries	U 35-a	
on London market in £ per cwt	UK	B 4-m	
(standard grade) in local currency per kg	Main countries	B 4-a	
Cadmium metal (electrolytic) in Fr per kg	France	T 4-m	
(in sticks) in local currency per kg	Main countries	T 4-m	
in lire per kg	Italy	C 12-m	
(refined & secondary) in $ per lb	USA	N 1-a	
Calfskins (8 lb wt & under) in pence per kg	UK	B 2-a	
Calves in pence per lb (live wt)	EEC countries	C 9-m	
Candles in local currency per box	OAS member countries	N 17-a	
Canned apricots & peaches by grade in $	European countries	A 7-a	
Carbon black in cents per lb	USA	N 1-a	
Cardamoms in £ per ton	UK	B 13-m	

591

WHOLESALE PRICES BY PRODUCT, continued	Territorial coverage	Title codes

	Territorial coverage	Title codes
Cassia by kind in £ per ton	UK	B 13-m
Castor oil (ex tanks) in cents per lb	USA	R 2-m
Cattle & livestock in local currency	OAS member countries	N 17-a
in £ per cwt (live wt)	EEC countries	C 9-m
Cattle hides & calfskins on Chicago market in cents per kg	USA	A 5-a
Cauliflowers in local currency per kg	EEC countries	U 20-m
	OAS member countries	N 14-a
Cement (for building industry) - index nos	Austria, Canada, Italy & Switzerland	A 13-a
	European countries & USA	U 5-a
	OECD countries	D 4-a
in local currency per ton	OAS member countries	N 17-a
in $ per ton	USA	N 1-a
(Portland) in sacks in $ per ton	USA	R 2-m
Cereals & cereal preparations in local currency per kg	OAS member countries	N 17-a
Cerium metal & lutetium metals in $ per ton	USA	N 1-a
& compounds in $ per lb	USA	N 1-a
Cesium ore (pollucite) in $ per ton	USA	N 1-a
Cheese: % change (over 12 months)	France & W Germany	E 34-m
by kind in £ per ton	Main countries	B 12-m
on London market in £ per cwt	UK	B 12-m
by quality in local currency per kg	OAS member countries	N 17-a
ex dairies in cents per kg	Main European countries	U 35-q
(ex Netherlands & New Zealand) in £ per cwt	UK	B 4-m
home-produced cheddar in £ per cwt	UK	B 4-a
in local currency per kg (annual averages)	Main countries	B 4-a
per 100 kg (45% fat)	France & W Germany	E 34-m
(white) ex New Zealand in £ per 56 lbs	UK	U 20-q
Chemical products by kind in local currency per ton	OAS member countries	N 17-a
- index nos	OECD countries	D 5-a
	Japan & Philippines	U 32-m
Chickens by grade in local currency	Main countries	R 2-m
(for roasting) in FrB per kg (live wt)	Belgium	E 34-m
(live) over 12 months: % change	W Germany	E 34-m
Chillies (ex Mombasa) on London market in £ per ton	UK	B 13-m
Chromium (chemical grade) in $ per ton of ore	USA	N 1-a
in £ per lb	UK	C 12-m	T 4-m
(metallurgical grade) in $ per ton	USA	N 1-a
Cinnamon by kind in £ per ton	UK	B 13-m
Citrus fruits by kind in £ per pack	UK	B 6-m
in local currency	OAS member countries	N 17-a
cost to processors: grapefruit, lemons & oranges in $ per ton	All countries	A 7-a
Clothing by kind in local currency	OAS member countries	N 17-a
(made-up) - index nos	UK	B 22-a
Cloves by kind in £ per ton	UK	B 13-m
Coal (bituminous) & lignite at mines in $ per ton	USA	N 1-a
(ex Poland) in lire per ton	Italy	R 2-m
Cobalt metal (contract price) in £ per lb	UK	T 4-m
in $ per lb	USA	N 1-a
Cocoa beans: % change over previous yr	EEC countries	E 34-m
(ex Brazil) on New York market in cents per lb	USA	P 3-a
(ex Ghana) on London market in £ per ton	UK	P 3-a
in local currency per kg	OAS member countries	N 17-a
	EEC countries	E 34-m
on London, New York & Le Havre markets (spot) in $ per ton	France, UK & USA	A 3-m
main crop ex Ghana (spot) in $ per ton	USA	P 3-a
Cocoa butter: high & low prices: historical table since 1938 in £ per ton	UK	P 2-a
Cocoa (ex Brazil & Ghana) in cents per lb	USA	P 1-m
ex warehouse (spot) in £ per ton	UK	P 2-m
in cents per lb	USA	P 2-m
on London Terminal Market in £ per ton	UK	P 2-m
on New York Terminal Market in cents per lb	USA	P 2-m
(raw) by grade ex Ghana & Brazil (spot) in $ per ton	USA	B 13-m
ex Ghana (spot) in £ per ton	UK	B 13-m
Coconut cake (spot) in Rs per ton	Sri Lanka	A 4-m
oil (crude) Pacific Coast in cents per lb	USA	P 1-m
in cents per lb	Philippines	A 4-m
in Pesos per kg	Philippines	U 32-m
in Rs per 100 kg	India	A 4-m
on London market in £ per ton	UK	B 2-a
Coffee (Arabicus & Robustas) in cents per lb	USA	J 1-m
beans in local currency per ton	OAS member countries	N 17-a
by grade (spot) in cents per lb	USA	B 13-m	A 5-a
by source on New York market in cents per lb	USA	J 1-m
(instant) in cents per 6 oz jar	USA	J 1-m
(roasted beans) in cents per 1 lb vacuum can	USA	J 1-m
Robustas (on contract) in pence per lb	UK	J 1-m
Coir fibre (for mattresses) in Rs per cwt	Sri Lanka	B 10-m
yarn (superior anjengo) in Rs per cwt	India	B 10-m
Coke ex coke ovens (40-70 mm) in lire per ton	Italy	R 2-m
(60-90 mm) in Fr per ton	France	R 2-m
in $ per ton	USA	R 2-m
ex Ruhr area (40-90 mm) in DM per ton	W Germany	R 2-m
in local currency per ton	OAS member countries	N 17-a
Columbite concentrates (by contract) in $ per lb	USA	T 4-m
Concrete roofing tiles - index nos	UK	U 5-a

592

WHOLESALE PRICES BY PRODUCT, continued

Product	Territorial coverage	Title codes	
Condensed & evaporated milk in local currency per kg	OAS member countries	N 17-a	
	Austria, France & W Germany	U 35-a	
Confectionery made of chocolate & sugar – index nos	UK	P 2-a	
Coniferous logs in local currency per m³	European countries	A 13-m	
sawnwood in $ per m³	European countries, Canada & USA	A 13-m	
Copper alloy tubes (30% nickel) in Fr per kg	France	T 4-w	
cathodes (3 mths forward) in £ per ton	UK	C 12-m	T 4-m
(electrolytic) in FrB per ton	Belgium	T 4-w	
in cents per lb	Canada	J 6-m	
(home-refined) in cents per lb	USA	J 6-m	
on London Metal Exchange in £ per ton	UK	J 6-m	
(refined) in cents per lb	USA	N 1-a	
scrap by grade in lire per kg	Italy	C 12-m	
sheets in local currency per kg	Main countries	T 4-w	
strip (in coils) in £ per kg	UK	T 4-w	
tubes (by diam) in £ per kg	UK	T 4-w	
in local currency per kg	Main countries	T 4-w	
wire (3 mm diam) in Fr per kg	France	T 4-w	
in local currency per kg	Main countries	T 4-w	
wire bars in £ per ton (spot)	UK	B 2-a	
(electrolytic) in local currency per kg	W Germany, S Africa & UK	T 4-m	
in lire per kg	Italy	C 12-m	
Copper-nickel condenser tubes by size in pence per ft	UK	T 4-w	
Copra in £ per ton	UK	B 2-a	
(Rescada grade) in pesos per kg	Philippines	U 32-m	
Corn flour in local currency per kg	OAS member countries	N 17-a	
oil (refined) in cents per lb	USA	R 2-m	
Cotton (American) – index nos	UK	B 10-m	
cloth & shirting in local currency	India & Japan	U 32-m	
fibres by quality in local currency per kg	OAS member countries	N 17-a	
(raw) in cents per lb	Brazil, Pakistan & USA	B 2-a	
in Rs per lb	India & Pakistan	U 32-m	
middling upland grade in cents per lb	USA	R 2-m	
strict middling grade in cents per lb	UK	R 2-m	
shipped ex USA & Sudan in pence per lb	UK	B 10-m	
textiles – index nos	Nepal	U 32-m	
Cottonseed cake & meal (shipped ex Pakistan) in £ per ton	UK	B 2-a	
Cottonseed (shipped ex Nigeria) in £ per ton	UK	B 2-a	
Cottonseed oil (shipped ex Sudan) in £ per ton	UK	B 2-a	
(raw) in cents per lb	USA	R 2-m	
(refined) in £ per ton	UK	R 2-m	
(spot) on New York market in cents per lb	USA	P 1-m	
Courtelle staple in pence per lb	UK	B 10-m	
Cow & bull hides – index nos	OECD countries	D 18-a	
Cows, oxen & heifers in D Kr per kg	Denmark	R 2-m	
Crushed stone (for construction) in $ per ton	USA	N 1-a	
Diesel oil in local currency per ton	OAS member countries	N 17-a	
Dimension stone (for construction) in $ per ton	USA	N 1-a	
Domestic equipment – index nos	African countries	U 44-a	
	OAS member countries	N 17-a	
Edible oils & fats by kind in local currency per kg	OAS member countries	N 17-a	
Fat cattle & calves in local currency per kg (dead wt)	EEC countries	C 9-m	
by kind per cwt	Main countries	B 12-m	
in £ per ton & per 100 kg (live wt)	EEC countries	B 3-a	
steers (at auction) in £	Main countries	B 11-a	
dairy cattle (live wt) – index nos	EEC countries	B 3-a	
per head in £ (live wt)	EEC countries	B 3-a	
lambs in £ (live wt)	Australia, Canada, New Zealand, UK & USA	B 11-a	
sows in local currency per kg (dead wt)	EEC countries	C 9-m	
Feeding stuffs: pig-rearing meal – index nos	Netherlands	C 9-m	
Feldspar in $ per ton	USA	N 1-a	
Ferro-borom in £ per kg	UK	T 4-m	
Ferro-chromium by grade in £ per ton	UK	T 4-m	
in local currency per kg	France & Japan	T 4-m	
Ferro-colombium in £ per lb of metal content of ore	UK	T 4-m	
Ferro-manganese in local currency per ton	Main countries	T 4-w	
in $ per ton	EEC countries	E 29-a2	
Ferro-molybdenum climax lump in $ per lb	USA	C 12-m	
in £ per lb of metal content of ore	UK	T 4-w	
in £ per ton	UK	C 12-m	
in yen per kg	Japan	T 4-w	
Ferro-nickel in local currency per kg	France & Japan	T 4-m	
Ferro-silicon by grade in £ per ton	UK	T 4-m	
in cents per lb	USA	N 1-a	
in local currency per ton	France & Japan	T 4-m	
in $ per ton	USA	C 12-m	
Ferro-titanium by grade in £ per ton	USA	C 12-m	
in £ per ton	UK	T 4-m	
Ferro-tungsten in local currency per ton	Japan & UK	T 4-w	
Ferro-vanadium in £ per kg of metal content of ore	UK	C 12-m	
in cents per lb	USA	C 12-m	
in local currency per ton	Japan & UK	T 4-w	
Ferrous scrap in $ per ton	EEC countries & USA	E 29-m	
Fibre products – index nos	S Korea	U 32-m	
Fish & fish products by kind in local currency per kg	OAS member countries	N 17-a	
Flax (ex Belgium) – index nos	UK	B 10-m	
Footwear by kind in local currency	OAS member countries	N 17-a	
Foundry iron in $ per ton	EEC countries	E 29-a2	

WHOLESALE PRICES BY PRODUCT, continued | Territorial coverage | Title codes

Product	Territorial coverage	Title codes		
Fresh fruits: apples by kind (home-grown) in pence per lb	UK	B 6-m		
in pence per lb	UK	B 6-m		
in $A per bushel	Australia	D 38-a		
apples, pears & lemons in local currency per kg	EEC countries	U 20-m		
apricots (for processing) in $ per ton	All countries	A 7-a		
by kind by source in pence per lb	UK	B 6-m		
home & imported in pence per lb	UK	B 5-m		
in local currency per kg	OAS member countries	N 17-a		
in $ per kg	EEC countries	D 38-a		
oranges in cents per kg	UK & USA	A 5-a		
in local currency per kg	EEC countries	U 20-m		
peaches (for processing) in $ per ton	All countries	A 7-a		
in local currency per kg	EEC countries	U 20-m		
table grapes in local currency per kg	EEC countries	U 20-m		
tangerines in local currency per kg	EEC countries	U 20-m		
Fresh milk in local currency per litre	OAS member countries	N 17-a		
Fuelwood in local currency per ton	Austria & W Germany	A 13-m		
	Finland & Switzerland	A 13-a		
Gallium in $ per kg	USA	N 1-a		
Galvanised roofing sheets - index nos	Iceland	U 5-a		
Garnet (abrasive grade) in $ per ton	USA	N 1-a		
Germanium di-oxide in £ per kg (duty-paid)	UK	C 12-m		
in cents per gramme	USA	N 1-a		
(New York dealer prices) in $ per kg	USA	C 12-m		
Ginger by kind in £ per ton	UK	B 13-m		
Glass (for building industry) - index nos	European countries & USA	U 5-a		
Goat meat in local currency per kg	OAS member countries	N 17-a		
Goatskins in cents per kg	India	A 5-a		
in Rs per 100 pieces	India	U 32-m		
Gold bars (for industrial use) in $ per oz	UK	R 2-m		
Grapefruit (at Florida auctions) in cents per kg	USA	A 5-a		
(shipped ex Israel & S Africa) in cents per kg	UK	A 5-a		
Groundnut cake (ex factory) in Fr per kg	France	R 2-m		
oil in local currency per litre	EEC countries	E 34-m		
(raw ex tanks) in cents per lb	USA	R 2-m		
in Rs per quintal	India	U 32-m		
Groundnuts in local currency per kg	OAS member countries	N 17-a		
(shelled) in Rs per quintal	India	U 32-m		
Gunmetal ingots by quality in £ per ton	UK	T 4-w		
scrap in £ per ton	UK	T 4-w		
Gypsum (crude) in $ per ton	USA	N 1-a		
Hafnium in $ per lb	USA	N 1-a		
Hard woods: mahogany in local currency per m³	OAS member countries	N 17-a		
Hemp (ex E Africa) - index nos	UK	B 10-m		
Hen eggs (grade A4) delivered Hamburg in DM per 100	W Germany	B 4-a		
(home-produced) by size in £ per 120	UK	B 4-m		
in local currency per 100	OAS member countries	N 17-a		
shipped ex Denmark in £ per 120	UK	B 4-m		
Hessian in Rs per 100 yards	India & Pakistan	B 10-a		
Hides & skins by kind in local currency per kg	OAS member countries	N 17-a		
& thickness in £ per cwt	France, UK & USA	B 9-m		
(wet salted) in Rs per piece	Pakistan	U 32-m		
Hogs, dressed barrows & gilts in $	Canada & USA	B 11-a		
Honey in local currency per kg	OAS member countries	N 17-a		
Indium ingots in $ per oz	USA	T 4-a		
metallic bars in pence per oz	UK	T 4-m		
in $ per oz	USA	N 1-a		
Instant coffee in cents per 6 oz jar	USA	J 1-m		
in local currency per kg	OAS member countries	N 17-a		
Iridium: sponge & powder in $ per oz	UK & USA	T 4-m		
Iron & steel products - index nos	EEC countries	E 29-a		
Iron products (for building industry) - index nos	Switzerland	U 5-a		
Jute bags in Rs per 100	India	U 32-m		
(raw fibre) in Rs per 180 kg	India	U 32-m		
yarn: (seasonal average) in pence per lb	UK	B 10-a		
Kerosene in local currency per litre	OAS member countries	N 17-a		
Kerosene - index nos	Nepal	U 32-m		
Kraft wood pulp (bleached & unbleached) in $ per ton	USA	J 7-a		
Lamb by quality in pence per lb	UK	B 12-w		
(frozen carcasses) shipped ex New Zealand in pence per lb	UK	U 20-m		
(home-produced & New Zealand lamb) in pence per lb	UK	B 11-a		
in local currency per kg	OAS member countries	N 17-a		
in pence per lb	Australia, Canada & USA	B 12-m		
(incl subsidy payments) in pence per lb	UK	B 12-m		
Lambskins - index nos	OECD countries	D 18-a		
Lard in local currency per kg	OAS member countries	N 17-a		
(prime steam quality) on Chicago market in cents per lb	USA	P 1-m		
Lead (3 mths forward) on London Metal Exchange in £ per ton	UK	C 12-m	J 6-m	
		T 4-m	U 11-a	
historical table from 1875 in £ per ton	UK	T 4-a		
ingots in lire per kg	Italy	C 12-m		
on London Metal Exchange (daily & monthly averages) in £ per ton	UK	U 24		
		U 24-m		
on major overseas metal markets in local currency per ton		J 6-m		
on New York & St Louis markets in cents per lb	USA	C 12-m	U 24-m	
on New York market in cents per lb	USA	T 4-w		
oxide (dry red) in $ per ton	USA	T 4-w		
residues (for metal refining) in £ per ton	UK			

WHOLESALE PRICES BY PRODUCT, continued

Product	Territorial coverage	Title codes
Lead scrap by kind in £ per ton (delivered)	UK	T 4-w
(from batteries) in lire per kg	Italy	C 12-m
in local currency per ton	Main countries	T 4-w
(soft) in lire per kg	Italy	C 12-m
semi-finished products by kind in $ per ton	Main countries	T 4-w
sheets (3 mm thick) in yen per kg	Japan	T 4-w
sheets & pipes in £ per ton	UK	T 4-w
(full-rolled) in cents per lb	USA	T 4-w
(spot & 3 mths forward) in £ per ton	UK	U 24-m
tubes & sheets in lire per kg	Italy	C 12-m
(rolled) in lire per kg	Italy	T 4-w
(virgin soft) in local currency per ton	Main countries	T 4-w
Leather (box calf & sides) - index nos	OECD countries	D 18-q
(kid for glove-making) - index nos	OECD countries	D 18-q
roll butts - index nos	OECD countries	D 18-q
Lemons (at auction) in cents per kg	W Germany & USA	A 5-a
Light calfskins - index nos	OECD countries	D 18-a
Lime (for building industry) - index nos	OAS member countries	N 14-a
Linseed in cents per 56 lbs	European countries & USA	U 5-a
per bushel	Canada & USA	R 2-m
cake (ex store) in lire per 100 kg	Canada	N 10-m
(home-produced) in £ per ton	Italy	R 2-m
in cents per lb	UK	P 1-a
oil in cents per lb	Canada	N 10-m
(raw ex tanks) in cents per lb	Canada	N 10-m
Lithium minerals (from imported ore) in $ per ton	USA	R 2-m
Live animals (for slaughter) in local currency	USA	N 1-a
beef cattle: % change over 12 mths	OAS member countries	N 17-a
(local market price) per kg	EEC countries	E 34-m
pigs: % change over previous yr	EEC countries	E 34-m
(at local auctions) in local currency per 100 kg	EEC countries	E 34-m
Livestock products - index nos	EEC countries	E 34-m
Lubricating oil in local currency per litre	OAS member countries	N 17-a
Mace (shipped ex W Indies) on London market in £ per ton	OAS member countries	N 17-a
Machine tools (metal-cutting type) - index nos	UK	B 13-m
(metal-forming type) - index nos	USA	J 2-a
Magnesium in lire per kg	USA	J 2-a
pig ingots (electrolytic) in £ per ton	Italy	T 4-w
in lire per kg	UK	T 4-w
in cents per lb	Italy	C 12-m
powder in £ per ton	USA	T 4-w
pure metal in Fr per kg	UK	T 4-m
sandcasting alloy ingots in £ per ton	France	T 4-m
semi-finished products in local currency per ton	UK	T 4-m
Maize: % change over previous yr	Main countries	T 4-m
in local currency per kg	EEC countries	E 34-m
	OAS member countries	N 17-a
(on Chicago market) in cents per bushel	EEC countries	E 34-m
Man-made chemical fibres - index nos	USA	P 1-m
Manganese (electrolytic) in £ per ton	OECD countries	D 5-a
in lire per kg	UK	C 12-m
in £ per ton	Italy	C 12-m
(normal grade) in cents per lb	UK	T 4-m
Manufactured tobacco by kind in local currency	USA	C 12-m
Margarine: % change (over previous yr)	OAS member countries	N 17-a
in local currency per kg	France & Italy	E 34-m
per 100 kg	OAS member countries	N 17-a
Matches in local currency per pack	France & Italy	E 34-m
Meat (dried, smoked or salted) in local currency per kg	OAS member countries	N 17-a
Meat preparations by kind in local currency per kg	OAS member countries	N 17-a
Mercury in lire per flask of 76 lbs	OAS member countries	N 17-a
in local currency per flask of 76 lbs	Italy	C 12-m R 2-m
in $ per flask of 76 lbs	Japan & USA	T 4-m
	USA	C 12-m R 2-m
		N 1-a
	UK	N 1-a
Metal products - index nos	Japan & S Korea	U 32-m
Metals (basic) & minerals by kind in $ per ton	USA	J 3-m
by kind in local currency per ton	OAS member countries	N 17-a
Mica (ground) in $ per ton	USA	N 1-a
blocks & film sheets in $ per ton	USA	N 1-a
scrap & flake in $ per ton	USA	N 1-a
sheet & splittings in $ per ton	USA	N 1-a
Milk & egg products in local currency per kg	OAS member countries	N 17-a
powder in local currency per kg	OAS member countries	N 17-a
(skimmed) in £ per ton	UK	B 4-a
Millet in local currency per ton	OAS member countries	N 17-a
Mohair by kind in pence per kg	UK	K 6-m
by quality in pence per lb	S Africa & UK	B 10-m
Molybdenum metal in $ per lb	USA	N 1-a
ore (climax lump) in $ per lb	USA	C 12-m
Monazite concentrates in $ per ton	USA	N 1-a
Motor spirit in local currency per litre	OAS member countries	N 17-a
Natural rubber in cents per kg	Singapore & USA	A 5-a
	USA	B 2-a
(forward) on London Terminal Market in £ per ton	UK	C 17-m
in local currency per ton	Main commodity markets	B 13-m
(pool price) in cents per lb	Papua New Guinea	U 32-m
(spot) ex Malaysia in £ per ton	UK	B 2-a

WHOLESALE PRICES BY PRODUCT, continued

Product	Territorial coverage	Title codes	
Newsprint in $ per ton	Canada, Finland, France & UK	A 13-m	
Nickel cathodes (ex refinery) in cents per lb	USA	R 2-m	
in lire per kg	Italy	C 12-m	
in $ per lb	USA	C 12-m	
(refined) in £ per ton	UK	C 12-m	
in local currency per kg	Main countries	T 4-m	
scrap ex merchants' yards in £ per ton	UK	T 4-w	
sheets & strip (ex works) in Fr per kg	France	T 4-w	
Nickel-alloy sheets in yen per kg	Japan	T 4-w	
Nickel-silver scrap in £ per ton	UK	T 4-w	
Nitrogen (elemental) in $ per ton	USA	N 1-a	
(fixed) in $ per ton	USA	N 1-a	
Non-ferrous metals by kind in local currency per kg	Main countries	N 5-q	T 4-a
Nutmegs by kind in £ per ton	UK	B 13-m	
Nylon filament yarn in pence per lb	UK	B 10-m	
staple fibre in pence per kg	UK	R 2-m	
per lb	UK	B 10-m	
Oats: % change over previous yr	EEC countries	E 34-m	
by quality in local currency per kg	OAS member countries	N 17-a	
in local currency per kg	EEC countries	E 34-m	
Oilseeds by kind in local currency per kg	OAS member countries	N 17-a	
(used in production of margarine) in £ per ton	UK	B 12-m	
Olive oil in DM per 100 litres	W Germany	E 34-m	
(edible) in drums in cents per lb	USA	B 19-a	
(extra fine grade) in lire per kg	Italy	R 2-m	
Ox hides in pence per kg	UK	B 2-a	
Ox hides - index nos	OECD countries	D 18-a	
Oxygen (as liquid in cylinders) in $ per ton	USA	N 1-a	
(as pipeline gas) in $ per ton	USA	N 1-a	
Paddy rice in local currency per kg	OAS member countries	N 17-a	
Palladium in $ per oz	USA	N 1-a	
Palm kernels (shipped ex Nigeria) in £ per ton	UK	B 2-a	P 1-a
Palm oil (shipped ex Malaysia) in £ per ton	UK	B 2-a	
in $ per pical	Singapore	U 32-m	
(refined) in tanks in cents per lb	USA	R 2-m	
Peat in $ per ton	USA	N 1-a	
Pepper (Malabar & Lampong grades) in cents per lb	India & Singapore	U 32-m	
Perlite (ex mine for delivery to expanders) in $ per ton	USA	N 1-a	
Phosphate rock (ex plant) in $ per ton	USA	N 1-a	
Phosphor-bronze ingots in £ per ton	UK	T 4-w	
rods in local currency per kg	Japan & UK	T 4-w	
wire in local currency per kg	Japan & UK	T 4-w	
Pig iron (hematite) in $ per ton	EEC countries	E 29-a2	
Pig lead in local currency per lb or ton	Main countries	J 6-m	
Pig-meat at central markets in pence per lb	UK	B 12-w	
by quality in local currency per kg	Denmark, Netherlands, UK & USA	R 2-m	
(ex abattoirs) in Fr per 100 kg	France	E 34-m	
(home-produced) at Smithfield market in pence per lb	UK	B 11-m	
in local currency per kg	OAS member countries	N 17-a	
in £ per score (dead wt)	Main countries	C 9-m	
Pig-meat - index nos	EEC countries	C 9-m	
Pigs (for bacon) & fat pigs in £ per cwt	European countries	B 11-a	
(live for slaughter) & sucklings in local currency per kg	OAS member countries	N 17-a	
in $ per 100 lbs (at Chicago)	USA	R 2-m	
in £ per cwt	Eire, Canada, UK & USA	B 12-m	
Pimento (ex Jamaica) in £ per ton	UK	B13-m	
Pineapples (canned) in $ per doz cans	W European countries	A 8-a	
Platinum by grade in lire per gramme	Italy	C 12-m	
(ex main New York dealers) in $ per oz	USA	C 12-m	N 1-a
(free market price) in £ per oz	UK	T 4-w	
(refined metal) in £ per oz	UK	T 4-w	
Plywood - index nos	W Germany	A 25-m	
Polyester: "Courtelle" fibre in pence per kg	UK	R 2-m	
Poromerics (by brand name) in $	W Germany, UK & USA	A 18-a	
Potash in cents per ton of muriate content	USA	N 1-a	
Poultry: hens, ducks & turkeys in local currency per kg	OAS member countries	N 17-a	
Poultry meat by kind in local currency per kg	OAS member countries	N 17-a	
in local currency per 100 kg	France & Netherlands	E 34-m	
Pre-fabricated concrete building blocks - index nos	European countries	U 5-a	
Pulpwood in local currency per ton	Main countries	A 13-m	
Pumice (at mine or mills) in $ per ton	USA	N 1-a	
Radium (by wt groups) in $ per milligramme	USA	N 1-a	
Rapeseed in cents per bushel	Canada	N 10-m	
cake in cents per lb	Canada	N 10-m	
oil in cents per lb	Canada	N 10-m	
Rare earth compounds (mixed) in $ per ton	USA	N 1-a	
oxides (high-purity) in $ per ton	USA	N 1-a	
Rayon yarn, filament, staple & fibre in £	UK & USA	B 10-m	
Regulus metal (home-produced) in £ per ton	UK	T 4-m	
on Milan Metal Market in lire per kg	Italy	C 12-m	
Reinforcing steel bars in local currency per ton	Latin American countries	U 57-a	
rods (for building industry) - index nos	OAS member countries	N 14-a	
Resin (dry) delivered plant - index nos	European countries	A 26-a	
Rhodium in £ per oz	UK	T 4-w	
Rice & paddy - index nos	S Vietnam	U 32-m	
by kind in local currency per kg	OAS member countries	N 17-a	
(milled): historical table 1920-1964 in local currency per ton	Main countries	A 19-a	
(on Bangkok market) in bahts per ton	Thailand	U 32-m	
Roofing tiles - index nos	European countries	U 5-a	

WHOLESALE PRICES BY PRODUCT, continued

	Territorial coverage	Title codes	
Roundwood (coniferous) - index nos	Main European countries	A 26-a	
(deciduous) - index nos	Main European countries	A 26-a	
Ruthenium in £ per oz	UK	T 4-w	
Rutile concentrates in $ per ton	USA	N 1-a	
Sacking twills (jute) in Rs per bag	India & Pakistan	B 10-a	
Salt (excl brine) at mines in $ per ton	USA	N 1-a	
by kind in local currency per ton	OAS member countries	N 17-a	
in $ per ton (packed in 100 lb bags)	USA	N 1-a	
Sand & gravel - index nos	European countries & Cyprus	U 5-a	
(for building industry) - index nos	OAS member countries	N 14-a	
in $ per ton	USA	N 1-a	
Sausages in local currency per kg	OAS member countries	N 17-a	
Sawn hardwood: oak boards in lire per m³	Italy	R 2-m	
softwood: beech planks in lire per m³	Italy	R 2-m	
Sawnwood (for building industry) - index nos	European countries	U 5-a	
Scandium (distilled) in $ per gramme	USA	N 1-a	
ingots in $ per gramme	USA	N 1-a	
Scrap (metallic) by kind in cents per lb	USA	J 6-m	
Sea fish (incl herrings) in local currency	OECD countries	D 43-a	
Selenium by grade in $ per lb	USA	T 4-m	
(ex Canada) in $ per lb	UK	T 4-w	
ex store (on Tokyo market) in yen per kg	Japan	T 4-m	
in $ per lb	USA	N 1-a	
Semi-finished brass products by kind in local currency per ton	Main countries	T 4-w	
products - index nos	S Vietnam	U 32-m	
	OAS member countries	N 17-a	
Sesame seed oil (in drums) in cents per lb	USA	B 19-q	
Sheepskin shearlings - index nos	OECD countries	D 18-a	
Sheepskins (shipped ex Australia) in pence per kg	UK	B 2-a	
& lambskins in cents per kg	USA	A 5-a	
in Rs per 100 pieces	Pakistan	U 32-m	
Silicon in £ per ton	UK	T 4-m	
in cents per lb	USA	N 1-a	
in £ per ton	UK	C 12-m	
in lire per kg	Italy	C 12-m	
Silk (raw) shipped ex China & Japan in £ per lb	UK	B 10-m	
shipped ex Japan - index nos	UK	B 10-m	
Silver (3 & 7 mths forward) on London Metal Exchange in pence per oz	UK	T 4-m	
bars in $ per oz	UK & USA	R 2-m	
(for cash) on London Metal Exchange in pence per oz	UK	T 4-m	
historical table from 1875 in pence per oz	UK	T 4-a	
in cents per oz	USA	C 12-m	
local currency per oz	Canada, UK & USA	J 6-m	
lire per kg	Italy	C 12-m	
pence per oz	UK	C 12-m	
London dealer quotation in pence per oz	UK	T 4-m	
Soap by kind in local currency per kg	OAS member countries	N 17-a	
Soda ash (manufactured) in $ per ton	USA	N 1-a	
(natural) in $ per ton	USA	N 1-a	
Soda wood pulp in $ per ton	USA	J 7-a	
Sodium nitrate in $ per ton	USA	N 1-a	
Sodium sulphate (manufactured cake) in $ per ton	USA	N 1-a	
(natural mined sulphate) in $ per ton	USA	N 1-a	
Soybean meal in cents per lb	Canada	N 10-m	
oil (crude) ex mill in £ per ton	UK	P 1-m	P 1-a
in cents per lb	Canada	N 10-m	
Soybeans in cents per bushel of 60 lbs	USA	R 2-m	
	Canada	N 10-m	
Spiegeleisen in local currency per ton	Main countries	T 4-w	
in $ per ton	EEC countries	E 29-a2	
Starch in local currency per kg	OAS member countries	N 17-a	
Steel bars (for building industry) - index nos	European countries	U 5-a	
girders (for building industry) - index nos	European countries	U 5-a	
merchant bars in $ per ton	Main countries	U 49-m	U 57-a
plates (heavy) in $ per ton	Main countries	U 49-a	
products by kind in local currency per ton	Main countries	T 4-w	
sections (heavy) in $ per ton	Main countries	U 49-m	U 57-a
in local currency per ton	Latin American countries	U 57-a	
sheets (cold & hot-rolled) in $ per ton	Main countries	U 57-a	
in local currency per ton	Latin American countries	U 57-a	
(for home sale) - index nos	UK	T 2-m	
strip (hot & cold-rolled) in $ per ton	Main countries	U 57-a	
tubes (for home sale) - index nos	UK	T 2-m	
Stone blocks (for building) - index nos	Greece & Malta	U 5-a	
Strip (made of nickel alloys) in Fr per kg	France	T 4-w	
Strontium minerals (imported) in $ per ton	USA	N 1-a	
Sugar & sugar preparations by kind in local currency per kg	OAS member countries	N 17-a	
(ex factory) in Rs per quintal	India	U 32-m	
(ex warehouse): historical table from 1900 in cents per lb	Cuba	A 20-a	
historical table from 1900 in local currency per kg	Main countries	A 20-a	
(raw centrifugal) at Manila in Pesos per ton	Philippines	U 32-m	
(spot) & average of daily quotations in £ per ton	UK & USA	C 25-m	
Sugar Agreement: negotiated price in £ per ton	UK	C 25-a	
under International Sugar Agreement in £ per ton		B 13-a	
(white refined) in cents per lb	Main countries	C 25-a	
Sulphur (elemental) in $ per ton	USA	N 1-a	
Sunflower seed cake & meal in £ per ton	UK	B 2-a	
oil in £ per ton	Netherlands	B 2-a	

WHOLESALE PRICES BY PRODUCT, continued | Territorial coverage | Title codes

Product	Territorial coverage	Title codes	
Tallow (bleachable fancy) in cents per lb	USA	R 2-m	
(grade 2) ex works in £ per ton	UK	R 2-m	
Tantalite (columbium ore) in $ per lb	USA	N 1-a	
Tea & tea dust (at district auctions) in Rs per kg	India	P 6-a	
(at auction) in local currency per lb	India & Sri Lanka	B 13-m	
by grade (at London auctions) in pence per kg	UK	R 2-m	B 2-a
		P 6-a	
by origin (at London auctions) in pence per kg or per lb	UK	B 13-m	C 1-a
(ex India, Africa & Sri Lanka) in pence per kg	UK	A 5-a	
(ex Indonesia) at Antwerp auction in pence per kg	Belgium	C 1-a	
at Hamburg auction in DM per 500 grammes	W Germany	C 1-a	
dust (at auction) in local currency per kg	Main countries	C 11-w	
(at district auctions) in Rs per kg	India	P 6-a	
by districts in local currency per kg	Main countries	C 1-a	
leaf (at auction) in local currency per kg	Main countries	C 11-w	
(at district auctions) in Rs per kg	India	P 6-a	
by districts in local currency per kg	Main countries	C 1-a	
Tellurium in $ per lb	USA	N 1-a	
(lump & powder) in £ per lb	UK	T 4-a	
(slab form) in $ per lb	USA	T 4-m	
Terylene staple (cotton-type) in pence per lb	UK	B 10-m	
Textile fabrics by kind in local currency per kg	OAS member countries	N 17-a	
(imported) - index nos	OAS member countries	N 17-a	
fibres by kind in local currency per kg	OAS member countries	N 17-a	
Textiles (general) - index nos	Thailand	U 32-m	
Timber (for building industry) - index nos	OAS member countries	N 14-a	
Tin (3 mths forward) on London Metal Exchange in £ per ton	UK	C 12-m	J 6-m
		T 4-m	
ex works in $ per pical	Singapore	U 32-m	
in DM per 100 kg	W Germany	R 2-m	
in lire per kg	Italy	C 12-m	
ingots in lire per kg	Italy	C 12-m	
(on New York Metal Market) in cents per lb	USA	C 12-m	
price ranges ex Straits in M$ per picul	Singapore	C 20-m	
for cash or forward in cents per lb or £ per ton	UK & USA	C 20-m	
(shipped ex Straits) in £ per ton	UK	R 2-m	
in cents per lb at docks	USA	R 2-m	
on New York Market in cents per lb	USA	J 6-m	
(spot) in local currency per kg	Main countries	T 4-w	
Tin ore in baht per ton	Thailand	U 32-m	
Tinplate for home sales - index nos	UK	T 2-m	
Titanium billets & rounds in £ per ton	UK	T 4-m	
in $ per ton	USA	N 1-a	
ore: ilmenite in £ per ton	UK	C 12-m	
sheets (20 swg) in £ per lb	UK	T 4-a	
sponge in £ per ton	UK	T 4-a	
rutile in £ per ton	UK	C 12-m	
Tobacco by kind in £ per lb	Canada, Malawi & Zambia	B 13-a	
flue & fire-cured, Burley & cigar tobacco in cents per lb	USA	B 13-a	
flue-cured in cents per kg	Main countries	A 5-a	
Tomato paste by grade in $ per ton	Italy	A 7-a	
Tomatoes in local currency per kg	EEC countries	U 20-m	
Transport equipment - index nos	Thailand	U 32-m	
Tropical fruit (canned) by kind in $	USA	A 8-a	
Tung oil in cents per lb	USA	B 19-m	
Tungsten (at ports duty-paid) in $ per ton	USA	N 1-a	
ore in £ per ton	UK	C 12-m	
powder in £ per kg	UK	T 4-w	
Turmeric (Madras fingers) on London market in £ per ton	UK	B 13-m	
Vanadium pentoxide in $ per lb	USA	N 1-a	
Veal by cuts (at central markets) in pence per lb	UK	B 12-w	
Vegetable oils in local currency per litre	OAS member countries	N 17-a	
	EEC countries	E 34-m	
Vegetable seeds, nuts & kernels in local currency	OAS member countries	N 17-a	
Vegetables (fresh) by kind by source in £ per cwt	UK	B 6-m	
in local currency per kg	OAS member countrie	N 17-a	
Vermiculite (ex mine) in $ per ton	USA	N 1-a	
Wax in local currency per kg	OAS member countries	N 17-a	
Whale oil (ex tanks) in $ per kg	Netherlands & UK	R 2-m	
Wheat by quality in local currency per ton	OAS member countries	N 17-a	
in £ per ton	EEC countries	B 7-m	
(soft): % change over previous yr	EEC countries	E 34-m	
in local currency per kg	EEC countries	E 34-m	
flour for use by baking industry in £ per kg	Main countries	B 7-m	
in local currency per kg	OAS member countries	N 17-a	
White metal (43% solder) in £ per ton	UK	T 4-w	
Window glass (for building industry) - index nos	OAS member countries	N 14-a	
Wine (common red & white) at farm gate in local currency per litre	France & Spain	A 5-a	
Chianti (at Florence market) in lire per litre	Italy	A 5-a	
Wire bars (copper) on London Metal Exchange in £ per ton	UK	R 2-m	
Wire (made of nickel alloys) in Fr per kg	France	T 4-w	
Wire rods (steel) in $ per ton	Main countries	U 57-a	
in local currency per ton	Latin American countries	U 57-a	
Wood panels (for building industry) - index nos	Austria	U 5-a	
Wood pulp: % increases: mechanical pulp	European countries	D 40-a	
sulphate & sulphite pulp	European countries	D 40-a	
(bleached & unbleached sulphite) in $ per ton	USA	J 7-a	
(chemical) in $ per ton	Canada, Finland & Sweden	A 13-m	

	Territorial coverage	Title codes

WHOLESALE PRICES BY PRODUCT, continued

Wood pulp (for production of acetate yarn) in $ per ton	USA	J 7-a
(for production of viscose yarn) in $ per ton	USA	J 7-a
(mechanical) in $ per ton	Canada, Finland & Sweden	A 13-m
Wool by grade in pence per kg (clean basis)	UK	K 6-m
carded tops in FrB per kg (on Antwerp market)	Belgium	R 2-m
in pence per kg (on London market)	UK	R 2-m
(greasy raw) at auction in $	Australia & New Zealand	U 32-m
ex warehouse in cents per lb	UK	R 2-m
in local currency per kg	OAS member countries	N 17-a
Lincoln Wethers in pence per kg	UK	R 2-m
(type 78A) in cents per kg	Australia	R 2-m
(Merino crossbred) - index nos	UK	B 10-m
Wrapping paper in local currency per kg	OAS member countries	N 17-a
Xenotime, yttrium & yttrium oxide in $ per ton	USA	N 1-a
Zinc alloy ingots by grade in lire per kg	Italy	C 12-m
concentrates (at Joplin) in $ per ton	USA	J 6-m
dust in £ per ton	UK	T 4-m
(electrolytic) spot in local currency per ton	India & Japan	T 4-w
in local currency per lb or ton	Australia, Canada & UK	J 6-m
	Main countries	T 4-m
ingots by grade in lire per kg	Italy	C 12-m
in local currency per kg	France & Italy	T 4-w
(on London Metal Exchange) in £ per ton	UK	R 2-m
(normal brand) in Fr B per kg	Belgium	R 2-m
on London Metal Exchange (3 mths forward) in £ per ton	UK	T 4-m
in £ per ton	UK	J 6-m	U 24-m
on New York market in cents per lb	USA	U 24-m
on St Louis market in cents per lb	USA	J 6-m
oxide (red seal) in £ per ton	UK	T 4-m
(prime western grade) in cents per lb	USA	R 2-m
(rolled standard sizes) in Fr per kg	France	T 4-m
scrap by kind in £ per ton	UK	T 4-w
in local currency per ton	Main countries	T 4-m
(remelted) in £ per ton	UK	T 4-w
sheets (1.17mm gauge) in £ per kg	UK	T 4-m
in lire per kg	Italy	C 12-m
slabs in cents per lb	USA	C 12-m

Wholesale profit margins   see   SALES MARGINS, WHOLESALE

Wholesale trade margins   see   DISTRIBUTION COSTS

WHOLESALE TRADE

% contribution (incl retail trade) to gross domestic product	All countries	U 23-a
Employment (incl retail trading)	EEC countries	E 33-a
Employment, wages, sales & stocks in $m	Main countries	U 43-a
Food & clothing sales - index nos	Main countries	U 43-a
Gross product: wholesale trade in local currency	OAS member countries	N 16-a
Income contribution to gross domestic product & as % of total	EEC countries	E 32-a
No of enterprises in operation by administrative areas	EEC countries	E 38-a
of hrs worked per wk: clerks & typists	All countries	L 1-a
per wk	Main countries	R 3-m
Peaches, pears, apples & tomatoes: commercial sales: tonnage	OECD countries	D 29-a
Salaries: clerks & typists per mth	Main countries	L 1-a
Turnover by kind of goods - index nos (value basis)	Main countries	U 27-m
Wage rates by sex in local currency per hr	Main countries	R 3-m

Whooping cough   see   DISEASES, INFECTIOUS

WIDOW'S & ORPHAN'S BENEFITS
see also   DEATH BENEFITS

Cost to national funds in $m	All countries	L 2-a

Window glass   see   GLASS, WINDOW

WINE

% changes in retail sales	E European countries & USSR	U 16-a
% consumption for market sales or by producer	EEC countries	U 34-a
% of households consuming wines (fortified & aperitifs)	W European countries	Z 3
Consumption & per capita in litres	EEC countries	E 44-a
in litres	OAS member countries	N 17-a
per capita in kg per yr	OECD countries	D 1-a
in litres per yr	E European countries & USSR	U 16-a
	EEC countries	B 1-a	E 44-a
	European countries	E 44-a
	Main countries	E 3-a
Distribution for market sales in litres	Czechoslovakia, Hungary & Poland	U 34-a
for own farm consumption in litres	Czechoslovakia, Hungary & Poland	U 34-a
Excise duties: % rates charged on wine	EEC countries	E 31-a
Export prices - index nos (weighted average main sources)		U 29-q
Export prices in local currency per litre	Greece & Tunisia	A 9-a
Exports by value in $m	W European countries	U 33-a
by volume in hectolitres	EEC countries	E 44-a
	Main countries	A 5-a
in million gallons	All countries	B 5-a
historical tables from 1830 in hectolitres	Main European countries	Z 1-a
Import prices: common red wine ex France in DM free border	W Germany	A 5-a

	Territorial coverage	Title codes
WINE, continued		
Imports by kind: bottled, still or sparkling wines by volume in gallons	UK	B 5-a
unbottled by volume in gallons	UK	B 5-a
by value in $m	W European countries	U 33-a
by volume in hectolitres	EEC countries	E 44-a
	Main countries	A 5-a
tonnage	European countries & USSR	A 11-a
Intervention price: wine by kind fixed by EEC Commission in $ per hectolitre	EEC countries	E 44-a
Losses (in production & marketing) by volume in hectolitres	EEC countries	E 44-a
Producer prices in local currency per 100 litres	OECD countries	D 1-a
per litre	All countries	A 9-a
	France, W Germany & Italy	E 44-a
Producer prices – index nos	EEC countries	E 44-a
Production as % of gross output of all farm products (value basis)	E European countries	U 34-a
by areas in hectolitres	EEC countries	E 38-a
by value in $m	EEC countries	E 44-a
historical table from 1840 in hectolitres	Main European countries	Z 1-a
in hectolitres	All countries	U 43-a
	Czechoslovakia, Hungary & Poland	U 34-a
	Main countries	E 3-a U 22-a
	OAS member countries	N 14-a
in litres	African countries	U 44-a
in proof gallons	All countries	B 5-a
	W Indies & Caribbean countries	T 6-a
(incl produce pressed from imported grapes): tonnage	EEC countries	B 1-a
(incl world total) in litres	Main countries	A 5-a
Production, stocks, imports, exports & consumption: tonnage	EEC countries	E 3-a E 44-a
Production, stocks, industrial usage & consumption: tonnage	OECD countries	D 14-a
Production: tonnage	African countries	U 44-a
	OECD countries	D 1-a
	S American countries	U 40-a
	OAS member countries	N 17-a
Retail prices: wine by kind in local currency per litre		
(comparative): Beaujolais in local currency per 0.75 litres	EEC countries	Z 3-a
Revenue from taxes on sale of wine in $m	OECD countries	D 42-a
Self-sufficiency ratios	EEC countries	B 1-a E 3-a
		E 44-a
Supply, production, consumption, imports & exports: tonnage	EEC countries	B 1-a
Wholesale prices: Chianti at Florence market in lire per litre	Italy	A 5-a
common red & white wine at farm gate in local currency per litre	France & Spain	A 5-a
World exports by value in $m	World regions	A 5-a
World production by volume in hectolitres	Main countries	U 11-a
WIRE, ALUMINIUM		
Consumption: tonnage	UK	T 4-a
Despatches: drawn aluminium wire: tonnage	UK	C 30-a
tonnage	OECD countries	D 21-a
Exports by destination: tonnage	Main countries	T 4-a
Imports by source: tonnage	Main countries	T 4-a
Production: tonnage	All countries	U 22-a
	Main countries	T 4-a
Wholesale prices (4 mm diam) in Fr per kg	France	T 4-q
WIRE, BERYLLIUM-COPPER		
Wholesale prices in £ per lb	UK	T 4-w
Wire, brass see BRASS PRODUCTS, SEMI-FINISHED		
WIRE, COPPER		
Consumption: tin for coating copper wire: tonnage	UK	C 20-m
Exports by destination (excl insulated wire): tonnage	USA	J 6-a
tonnage	Main countries	T 4-a
Imports by source: tonnage	Netherlands	T 4-a
Production (incl wire strip): tonnage	Main countries	C 30-m T 4-a
	All countries	U 22-a
	Japan & UK	C 12-a
Wholesale prices (3 mm diam) in Fr per kg	France	T 4-w
in lire per kg	Italy	C 12-m
in local currency per kg	Main countries	T 4-w
WIRE, COPPER ALLOY		
Exports by destination: tonnage	Main countries	T 4-a
Imports by source: tonnage	USA	J 6-a
Production: tonnage	Main countries	T 4-a
Usage by building industry: tonnage	USA	J 6-a
consumer products manufacturing industry: tonnage	USA	J 6-a
electrical engineering industry: tonnage	USA	J 6-a
machinery & equipment manufacturing industry: tonnage	USA	J 6-a
transport equipment manufacturing industry: tonnage	USA	J 6-a
WIRE, GALVANISED		
Exports by destination: tonnage	Main countries	T 4-a
Imports by source: tonnage	Main countries	T 4-a
Production: tonnage	Main countries	T 4-a

	Territorial coverage	Title codes	
WIRE, NICKEL-ALLOY			
Wholesale prices in local currency per kg	France & UK	T 4-w	
WIRE, PHOSPHOR-BRONZE			
Wholesale prices in yen per kg	Japan	T 4-w	
WIRE, STEEL			
Consumption: tin for coating steel wire: tonnage	UK	C 20-m	
Deliveries by dealers: tonnage	EEC countries	E 29-a	
to EEC area: tonnage	EEC countries	E 29-a	
to user industries: tonnage	ECE countries	U 7-q	U 6-a
	Main countries	H 3-a	
Diameter by gauge in inches & wt in lbs per ft		J 3	
Exports by destination: tonnage	ECE countries	U 48-a	
	EEC countries	E 5-q	E 29-a
	Main countries	T 4-a	
drawn wire: tonnage & as % share of total exports	Main countries	U 49-a	
tonnage	E European countries & USSR	T 1-a	
wire products of steel (incl fencing & grills): tonnage	OECD countries	D 9-a	
Imports: alloy steel wire: tonnage	Main countries	T 1-a	
by quality: tonnage	Main countries	T 1-a	
by source: tonnage	EEC countries	E 5-q	E 29-a
	Main countries	T 4-a	
high carbon steel wire: tonnage	Main countries	T 1-a	
shipped ex EEC area: tonnage	EEC countries	E 29-a	
stainless steel wire: tonnage	Main countries	T 1-a	
Inter-EEC area trade: tonnage & value in $m	EEC countries	E 29-a	
Prices (net less tax) at main centres in local currency per kg	EEC countries	E 30-a	
Production by kind: tonnage	EEC countries	E 30-q	
	All countries	U 22-a	
cold-drawn steel wire: tonnage	ECE countries	U 7-m	U 6-a
	Main countries	H 3-a	T 4-a
	EEC countries	E 30-m	E 28-q
		E 27-a	E 29-a
tonnage	OAS member countries	N 14-a	
Receipts by dealers: tonnage	EEC countries	E 29-a	
WIRE & CABLE INDUSTRY			
Investment in buildings in local currency	EEC countries	E 40-a	
in land purchase in local currency	EEC countries	E 40-a	
in machinery in local currency	EEC countries	E 40-a	
WIRE BARS, BRASS			
Consumption: copper in production of brass wire-drawing bars: tonnage	USA	T 4-a	
WIRE BARS, COPPER			
Consumption: copper in production of copper wire-drawing bars: tonnage	USA	T 4-a	
Export prices: electrolytic quality in cents per lb fob	USA	R 2-m	
Exports by destination: tonnage	Belgium, Japan & UK	T 4-a	
Imports by source: tonnage	Netherlands	T 4-a	
wire-drawing bars (electrolytic): tonnage	India	T 4-a	
Prices in DM per kg	W Germany	R 2-m	
in local currency per lb	Australia	R 2-m	
wire-drawing bars (electrolytic) in cents per lb	USA	R 2-m	
Producer prices in cents per lb	USA	T 4-m	
Stocks held at user's premises: tonnage	UK	J 6-a	
Wholesale prices (on London Metal Exchange) in £ per ton	UK	R 2-m	
spot (on London Metal Exchange) in £ per ton	UK	B 2-a	
(electrolytic quality) in local currency per ton	W Germany & S Africa	T 4-m	
in Fr per kg (excl tax)	France	T 4-w	
in lire per kg	Italy	C 12-m	
in £ per ton	UK	C 12-m	
WIRE RODS, STEEL			
see also WIRE BARS, COPPER			
WIRE-DRAWING RODS, ALUMINIUM			
Consumption: tonnage	EEC countries	E 29-a	
	OECD countries	D 22-a	
Deliveries (for wire drawing): tonnage	ECE countries	U 7-q	U 6-a
	Main countries	H 3-a	
(home & export): tonnage	OECD countries	D 22-a	
to EEC area: tonnage	EEC countries	E 29-a	
Export prices: Bessemer quality in $ per 100 lbs fob	USA	R 2-m	
in $ per ton fob	OECD countries	D 22-a	
Thomas quality (5.5 mm gauge) in $ per ton fob	Belgium	R 2-m	
Exports by destination: tonnage & value in $m	EEC countries	E 5-q	
tonnage	ECE countries	U 48-a	
	Main countries	T 4-a	
	EEC countries	E 29-a	
	Main countries	U 49-a	
tonnage (incl % share)	E European countries & USSR	T 1-a	
tonnage	ECE countries, Japan & USA	U 7-m	U 6-a
	European countries, Japan & USA	C 5-m	
	Main countries	H 3-a	

WIRE RODS, STEEL continued

	Territorial coverage	Title codes	
Imports by source: tonnage	EEC countries	E 5-q	E 29-a
high carbon steel wire rods by quality: tonnage	Main countries	T 4-a	
shipped ex EEC area: tonnage	Main countries	T 1-a	
stainless steel wire rods by quality: tonnage	EEC countries	E 29-a	
tonnage	Main countries	T 1-a	
	ECE countries, Japan & USA	U 7-m	U 6-a
	European countries, Japan & USA	C 5-m	
	Main countries	H 3-a	
Production capacity: steel wire rods: tonnage	Main countries	U 57-a	
potential by regions: tonnage	EEC countries	E 46-a	
Production: tonnage (incl world total)	All countries	T 1-a	
tonnage	All countries	U 22-a	
	ECE countries	U 7-m	U 6-a
	EEC countries	E 30-m	E 28-q
		E 27-a	E 29-a
	European countries & Japan	C 5-m	
	Main countries	H 3-a	T 4-a
	OECD countries	D 22-a	
	S American countries & Mexico	U 40-a	
Wholesale prices (basic) in $ per ton	OECD countries	D 22-a	
steel wire rods in local currency per ton	Latin American countries	U 57-a	
in $ per ton	Main countries	U 57-a	

WIRE ROPE & CABLES
    see also   INSULATED WIRE & CABLES

Production: tonnage	All countries	U 22-a	

WIRE-DRAWING RODS, ALUMINIUM

Consumption: tonnage	UK	T 4-a	
Despatches: cold-rolled aluminium wire rods: tonnage	UK	C 30-a	
hot-rolled aluminium wire rods: tonnage	UK	C 30-a	
Exports by destination: tonnage	Main countries	T 4-a	
Wholesale prices (25 mm gauge) in yen per kg	Japan	T 4-q	

Wire-working machines   see   MACHINE TOOLS

Witherite   see   BARIUM MINERALS

Wolfram   see   TUNGSTEN ORES

WOLLASTONITE

Production: tonnage	Finland, India, Kenya & Mexico	B 15-a	

Women's wear   see   CLOTHING

Wood   see   PULPWOOD
                 TIMBER

Wood oil   see   TUNG OIL

Wood products   see   TIMBER PRODUCTS

WOOD PULP
    see also   PULP, FIBROUS NON-WOOD
                    PULPWOOD

% changes in production	OECD countries	D 40-a	
in stocks held at paper mills	Canada, European countries, Japan & USA	D 40-a	
at pulp mills	Canada, European countries, Japan & USA	D 40-a	
% contribution to export earnings	Swaziland	E 45-a	
Comparison: % changes in production of wood pulp to % changes in gross domestic product	OECD countries	D 40-a	
Consumption: bagasse pulp: tonnage	OECD countries	D 40-a	
bamboo pulp: tonnage	OECD countries	D 40-a	
chemical straw pulp: tonnage	OECD countries	D 40-a	
esparto grass for production of wood pulp: tonnage	OECD countries	D 40-a	
fibrous materials for production of wood pulp: tonnage	OECD countries	D 40-a	
macerated wood pulp for production of paper: tonnage	OECD countries	D 40-a	
pulp for production of paper: tonnage	OECD countries	D 40-a	
tonnage	Canada, European countries, Japan & USA	D 40-a	
	OECD countries	D 40-a	
Export prices: bleached pulp in DM per 100 kg cif	Sweden	R 2-m	
in $ per ton	Finland & Sweden	A 9-a	
unbleached pulp in DM per 100 kg cif	Sweden	R 2-m	
- index nos (weighted average main sources)		U 29-q	U 54-q
Exports by destination: tonnage	All countries	D 40-a	
historical tables from 1872: tonnage	Scandinavian countries	Z 1-a	
(incl world total): tonnage	All countries	A 5-a	
mechanical pulp: tonnage	Canada, European countries, & USA	A 13-q	
rounds, residues, split wood & chips for wood pulp production: tonnage	All countries	A 23-a	
tonnage & by value in $m	All countries	A 23-a	
Import prices: bleached pulp in lire per 100 kg cif	Swaziland	E 45-a	
	Italy	R 2-m	
unbleached pulp in lire per 100 kg cif	Italy	R 2-m	
Imports & exports by source & destination: tonnage	All countries	A 23-a	

	Territorial coverage	Title codes	
WOOD PULP, continued			
Imports: chemical pulp: tonnage	Canada, European countries & USA	A 13-q	
mechanical pulp: tonnage	Canada, European countries & USA	A 13-q	
tonnage & by value in $m	All countries	A 23-a	
tonnage	European & Far East countries & USA	A 11-a	
	Main countries	J 7-a	
Production: chemical & mechanical pulp: tonnage	All countries	A 5-a	A 23-c
		U 43-a	
chemical fibre pulp: tonnage	All countries	K 4-a	
historical table from 1887: tonnage	Main European countries	Z 1-a	
tonnage	Canada, European countries, Japan & USA	D 40-a	
	ECE countries	U 15-a	
	Latin American countries	U 40-a	
	Main countries	E 3-a	R 5-a
Shipments through Kiel Canal westwards: tonnage		D 28-a	
Stocks held at paper mills: tonnage	OECD countries	D 41-q	
at pulp mills: tonnage	OECD countries	D 41-q	
market pulp held at paper mills: tonnage	OECD countries	D 41-q	
at pulp mills: tonnage	OECD countries	D 41-q	
Wholesale prices: chemical pulp in $ per ton	Canada, Finland & Sweden	A 13-m	
in $ per ton	Canada	A 9-a	
	Finland, Canada & USA	U 27-m	
mechanical pulp in $ per ton	Canada, Finland & Sweden	A 13-m	
World exports: unit value in $ per ton		A 11-a	
World market prices - index nos		G 1-a	
WOOD PULP, DISSOLVING			
see also PULP, FIBROUS NON-WOOD			
Consumption: tonnage	OECD countries	D 40-a	
Exports by destination: tonnage	All countries	D 40-a	
tonnage	OECD countries	D 41-q	
Imports: tonnage	OECD countries	D 41-q	
Production: tonnage	OECD countries	D 41-q	
WOOD PULP, MECHANICAL			
Consumption: tonnage	OECD countries	D 40-a	
Exports by destination: tonnage	All countries	D 40-a	
Production by grade: tonnage	Main countries	J 7-a	
tonnage	OAS member countries	N 14-a	
	OECD countries	D 40-a	
Stocks held at paper mills: tonnage	OECD countries	D 41-q	
at pulp mills: tonnage	OECD countries	D 41-q	
WOOD PULP, SULPHATE & SULPHITE			
Consumption: tonnage	OECD countries	D 40-a	
Exports by destination: tonnage	All countries	D 40-a	
tonnage	OECD countries	D 41-q	
Imports: tonnage	OECD countries	D 41-q	
Production by grade: tonnage	Main countries	J 7-a	
tonnage	OECD countries	D 41-q	
	OAS member countries	N 14-a	
Stocks held at paper mills: tonnage	OECD countries	D 41-q	
at pulp mills: tonnage	OECD countries	D 41-q	
WOOD PULP BY KIND			
% increases in wholesale prices	European countries	D 40-a	
Consumption for production of paper: tonnage	All countries	J 7-a	
	OECD countries	D 40-a	
Exports by destination: tonnage	Main countries	J 7-a	
tonnage	OECD countries	D 41-q	
Imports by source: tonnage	Main countries	J 7-a	
tonnage	OECD countries	D 41-q	
Production capacity: tonnage	All countries	J 7-a	
Production by grade: tonnage	Main countries	J 7-a	
by purpose: tonnage	Main countries	J 7-a	U 22-c
tonnage	All countries	A 23-a	
	EEC countries	E 28-q	E 27-a
Stocks held at paper & pulp mills: tonnage	OECD countries	D 41-q	
Wholesale prices by grade in $ per ton	OECD countries	D 41-q	
World production: chemical & dissolving pulp: tonnage	USA	J 7-a	
		K 4-a	
Wood spirit (or wood naphtha) see METHANOL			
WOOD-BASED PANELS			
see also FIBREBOARD			
PARTICLE & CHIPBOARD			
PLYWOOD & BLOCKBOARD			
% consumption for "do-it-yourself" purposes	Main European countries	A 26-a	
in advertising industry	Main European countries	A 26-a	
in building industry	Main European countries	A 26-a	
in packaging industry	Main European countries	A 26-a	
in production of boats, caravans, furniture, road vehicles & railway carriages	Main European countries	A 26-a	
in shopfitting industry	Main European countries	A 26-a	
in transport industry	Main European countries	A 26-a	

	Territorial coverage	Title codes
WOOD-BASED PANELS, continued		
Consumption by kind – index nos	European countries	A 24-a
Exports by kind by volume in m³	Main countries	A 26-a
plywood & veneer by value in $	S Korea	U 32-m
Imports by kind by volume in m³	Main countries	A 26-a
No of operating plants	All countries	A 26-a
of plants producing wood-wool panels	All countries	A 26-a
Production by kind by volume in m³	Main countries	A 5-a
bonded wood-wool panels: tonnage	All countries	A 26-a
plywood & blockboard: tonnage	All countries	A 25-a
Production capacity: tonnage	All countries	A 26-a
Turnover of wood-based panel production industry in $m	European countries	A 26-a
Wholesale prices – index nos	Austria	U 5-a

Wood-wool board, cement bonded   see   WOOD-BASED PANELS

WOOD-WORKING INDUSTRY
     see also   FURNITURE INDUSTRY
                TIMBER & SAWMILL INDUSTRY

	Territorial coverage	Title codes	
% contribution to gross national product	European countries, Japan & USA	U 38-a	
% share of industrial production (value basis)	Main countries	U 38-a	
Capital formation in $m	Main countries	U 21-a	
Consumption: electricity in kWh	EEC countries	E 15-a	
(incl furniture industry) in kWh	All countries	C 23-a	
Costs: salaried staff per mth	EEC countries	E 11-a	
Domestic demand: furniture per capita in £	W European countries	C 8-a	
Earnings in $ per hr	All countries	L 4-a	
Employment – index nos	All countries	L 4-a	
Frequency of accidents at work	EEC countries	E 2-a	
Gross output: wood-working industry in $m	Main countries	U 21-a	
IDA loans granted to expand furniture industries in $m	OAS member countries	N 16-a	
Investment in buildings in local currency	EEC countries	E 40-a	
land purchase in local currency	EEC countries	E 40-a	
machinery in local currency	EEC countries	E 40-a	
Labour costs: all employees in local currency per hr	EEC countries	E 11-a	
furniture manufacturing industry as % of total costs	EEC countries	E 8-a	
in local currency per hr	EEC countries	E 8-a	
wage earners in local currency per hr	EEC countries	E 11-a	
Labour force employed by kind: furniture industry	EEC countries	E 8-a	
no of salaried staff employed	EEC countries	E 11-a	
of wage earners employed	EEC countries	E 11-a	
(total)	EEC countries	E 2-a	
No of establishments (incl furniture industry) in operation	Main countries	U 21-a	
of furniture factories in operation by size	African countries	U 44-a	
in operation	W European countries	C 8-a	
of hrs worked by region per wk	W European countries	C 8-a	
furniture industry per wk	EEC countries	E 25-a	
per yr	W European countries	C 8-a	
salaried staff per mth	EEC countries	E 8-a	
wage earners per wk	EEC countries	E 11-a	
per wk	EEC countries	E 11-a	
	All countries	L 4-a	
	Main countries	R 3-m	
	OAS member countries	N 18-a	
Production (incl furniture) as % of world production of goods		U 38	
Value of output: furniture industry in £m	W European countries	C 8-a	
per operative in £ per yr	W European countries	C 8-a	
Wage rates by grade in Esc per day	Portugal	R 4-q	
by sex in local currency per hr	Main countries	R 3-m	
cabinet makers & carpenters in local currency per hr	OAS member countries	N 17-a	
furniture assemblers in local currency per hr	OAS member countries	N 17-a	
furniture industry in local currency per hr	EEC countries	E 25-a2	
skilled workers by sex in local currency per hr	W European countries	C 8-a	
unskilled workers by sex in local currency per hr	Main countries	R 4-q	
upholsterers in local currency per hr	Main countries	R 4-q	
	OAS member countries	N 17-a	
Wages costs: wood-working industry in $	Main countries	U 21-a	

WOOD-WORKING MACHINERY

	Territorial coverage	Title codes	
Production as % of production of machinery	Main countries	U 38-a	
volume	All countries	U 22-a	U 38-a
	EEC countries	E 28-q	E 27-a

Wooded areas   see   FOREST LAND

Wooden posts & poles   see   PILING, WOODEN

Wool (for mending)   see   HOME SEWING

WOOL

	Territorial coverage	Title codes
% contribution to export earnings (incl mohair)	Lesotho	E 45-a
Consumption & projected demand by 1975	Main countries	A 1
at carding stage in lbs	Main countries	B 10-a
at textile mills in lbs	UK	B 29-a
tonnage	All countries	A 6-a
by end-use: production of clothing: tonnage	EEC countries	K 4-a
	W European countries, Japan & USA	A 1-a

	Territorial coverage	Title codes	
WOOL, continued			
Consumption for hand knitting in kg	Main countries	K 6-a	
home sewing & mending in kg	Main countries	K 6-a	
for production of blankets in kg	Main countries	K 6-a	
carpets (all kinds): tonnage	EEC countries & USA	K 4-a	
(handmade) in kg	Main countries	K 6-a	
(tufted) in kg	Main countries	K 6-a	
(woven) in kg	Main countries	K 6-a	
clothing by kind: tonnage	EEC countries	K 4-a	
for children in kg	Main countries	K 6-a	
for men in kg	Main countries	K 6-a	
for women in kg	Main countries	K 6-a	
felt in kg	Main countries	K 6-a	
household textiles by kind: tonnage	EEC countries	K 4-a	
jackets & coats in kg	Main countries	K 6-a	
kimonos in kg	Main countries	K 6-a	
socks in kg	Main countries	K 6-a	
suits & trousers in kg	Main countries	K 6-a	
sweaters & skirts in kg	Main countries	K 6-a	
textiles: tonnage	Main countries	U 43-a	
for upholstery purposes in kg	Main countries	K 6-a	
per capita in kg	Main countries	U 26-a	
virgin wool by purpose in kg	Main countries	K 6-a	
by textile industry: tonnage	OECD countries	D 46-a	
in kg	Main European countries, Japan & USA	K 6-m	
in spinning mills: tonnage	OECD countries	D 46-a	
Demand projections by end-use: tonnage	W European countries, Japan & USA	A 1	
Distribution for own farm use: tonnage	Czechoslovakia, Hungary & Poland	U 34-a	
for textile processing: tonnage	Czechoslovakia, Hungary & Poland	U 34-a	
Export prices by kind - index nos	S American countries	U 40-q	
in $ per kg	Asian, Far East & Australasian countries	U 45-a	
Export prices - index nos (weighted average main sources)	Worldwide	U 29-q	
Exports by destination: tonnage	Commonwealth countries	B 10-a	
scoured wool by destination in kg	Main countries	K 6-a	
virgin wool by destination in kg	Main countries	K 6-a	
Import prices (ex Australasia) by kind: clean basis in £ per ton	UK	A 5-a	
Merino crossbred (ex N Zealand & Australia) in £ per ton	UK	B 10-m	
Imports (ex British Commonwealth countries) in lbs	EEC countries	B 10-a	
Production costs (on collective farms) in $ per ton	USSR	U 34-a	
Production: (clean basis): tonnage	All countries	A 9-a	
(greasy & clean basis): tonnage	Latin American countries	J 5-a	
projection for ensuing yr: tonnage	Main countries	A 1	
pulled from imported skins: tonnage	OECD countries	D 46-a	
tonnage	E European countries & USSR incl Ukraine	U 16-a	
	S American countries	U 40-a	
	EEC countries	B 1-a	
Supply, production, consumption, imports & exports: tonnage	Main world wool-producing regions	K 6-a	
Supply, production & stocks: raw wool in kg	Australia, S Africa, UK & USA	U 27-m	
Wholesale prices by grade (clean basis) in $ per kg	UK & USA	A 9-a	
by kind in pence per kg (clean basis)	UK	K 6-m	
carded tops in FrB per kg (on Antwerp market)	Belgium	R 2-m	
in pence per kg (on London market)	UK	R 2-m	
Merino crossbred wool - index nos	UK	B 10-m	
World consumption in lbs & as % of consumption of total apparel fibres		B 10-a	
raw wool (cleaned basis) in kg	All countries	K 6-a	
tonnage & consumption per capita in kg		A 6-a	
virgin wool (clean basis) in kg	Main countries	B 10-a	
World exports by value in $m	World regions	A 5-a	
World market prices - index nos		G 1-a	U 23-a
World production (clean basis) in lbs & Commonwealth production as % of world total		B 10-a	
World stocks (end-yr): tonnage		B 10-a	G 1-a
WOOL, GREASY RAW			
Consumption by textile mills: tonnage	Main countries	K 4-a	
historical table from 1862: tonnage	France	Z 1-a	
tonnage	OAS member countries	N 17-a	
Export prices in $ per kg fob	Main countries	A 9-a	
unit value in Rs per lb	Pakistan	U 32-m	
Exports by destination in kg	Main countries	K 6-a	
by value in $m	W European countries	U 33-a	
	Developing countries	U 11-a	
	Australasian countries & Pakistan	U 32-m	
(incl mohair): tonnage & value in $m	Lesotho	E 45-a	
in lbs	Main countries	B 10-a	
tonnage & value in $m	Main countries	U 11-a	
tonnage	Asian & Far East countries	U 32-q	
	ECAFE countries	U 32-m	
	Main countries	A 5-a	
Imports by source in lbs	Main countries	B 10-a	
by value in $m	W European countries	U 33-a	
(net): historical table from 1772: tonnage	W Germany & UK	Z 1-a	
tonnage	OECD countries	D 46-a	
Net changes in commercial stocks: tonnage	Worldwide	U 11-a	
Producer prices in local currency per kg	OECD countries	D 1-a	
	Guatemala & USA	A 9-a	
Production (clean basis): tonnage	OECD countries	D 46-a	
historical table from 1816: tonnage	Main countries	Z 1-a	

	Territorial coverage	Title codes	
WOOL, GREASY RAW continued			
Production (incl world total) in kg	All countries	K 6-a	
tonnage	Main countries	A 5-a	
tonnage	All countries	A 9-a	R 5-a
		U 43-a	
	Main countries	K 4-a	
	OECD countries	D 1-a	D 46-a
Stocks (commercial): tonnage	EEC countries & Japan	A 5-a	
held: tonnage	Producing countries	A 5-a	
Wholesale prices (at auction) in $ per lb	Australasian countries	U 32-m	A 9-a
(ex warehouse) in cents per lb	USA	R 2-m	
in local currency per kg	OAS member countries	N 17-a	
Lincoln Wethers in pence per kg	UK	R 2-m	
(type 78 A) in cents per kg	Australia	R 2-m	
World consumption projected to 1980: tonnage		B 29	
World exports: tonnage	World exporting regions	U 11-a	
World production in lbs	Main countries	B 10-a	
tonnage (clean basis)		K 4-a	
tonnage	World economic regions	U 11-a	
WOOL TOPS			
Consumption: textile industry: tonnage	OECD countries	D 46-a	
spinning mills: tonnage	OECD countries	D 46-a	
Exports: crossbred Merino tops (incl hair): tonnage & value in £	Main countries	K 3-a	
tonnage	OECD countries	D 46-a	
Import duties: % rates ad val	Hungary	K 3-a	
Imports: tonnage	OECD countries	D 46-a	
Production in kg	EEC countries (excl Netherlands) & Japan	K 6-m	
(first combing) & hair: tonnage	OECD countries	D 46-a	
tonnage	Main countries	K 3-a	
	OECD countries	D 46-a	
Sales taxes: % rates ad val	Canada, Malaysia & Switzerland	K 3-a	
Value added taxes: % rates	Main countries	K 3-a	
Wholesale prices: carded wool tops in pence per kg	UK	R 2-m	
WOOL YARN			
see also HAND-KNITTING YARN			
WORSTED YARN			
% export penetration (by importing countries)	Main exporting countries	K 3-a	
% of EEC area production	EEC countries	R 5-a	
% turnover taxes levied	Finland, Greece & Portugal	K 3-a	
% value added taxes levied	Main countries	K 3-a	
Consumption in knitting mills: tonnage	OECD countries	D 46-a	
in weaving industry: tonnage	OECD countries	D 46-a	
Deliveries (incl worsted) to industry - index nos	UK	B 29-a	
Exports: fine woollen hair & yarn: tonnage & value in £m	Main countries	K 3-a	
synthetic fibre & wool yarn: tonnage & value in £m	Main countries	K 3-a	
tonnage	OECD countries	D 46-a	
woollen yarn: tonnage & value in £m	Main countries	K 3-a	
worsted yarn: tonnage & value in £m	Main countries	K 3-a	
Import duties: rates % ad val	Main countries	K 3-a	
Imports & exports (incl trade balance) in lbs	UK	B 29-a	
Imports (incl worsted yarn) as % of domestic consumption	UK	B 29-a	
tonnage	OECD countries	D 46-a	
Production by kind: tonnage	EEC countries	E 28-q	E 27-a
historical table from 1925: tonnage	Main Euorpean countries	Z 1-a	
in kg	EEC countries & Japan	K 6-m	
	Main countries	K 6-a	
(incl hair) by spinning industry: tonnage	OECD countries	D 46-a	
(incl thread): tonnage	OAS member countries	N 14-a	
(incl worsted): tonnage	OECD countries	R 5-a	
mixed & pure wool: tonnage	All countries	U 22-a	
spun worsted yarn: tonnage	All countries	U 43-a	
tonnage	African countries	U 44-a	
	EEC countries	D 46-a	
	OECD countries	D 46-a	
	Main countries	U 27-m	E 3-a
		K 3-a	R 5-a
Retail sales: tonnage & value in £	Main countries	K 3-a	
Stocks held by spinners & others in kg	Main countries	K 6-a	
Wholesale prices in cents per lb	UK & USA	U 27-m	
Woollen fabrics see WOVEN WOOLLEN FABRICS			
WORSTED YARN			
see also WOOL YARN			
Consumption: weaving industry: tonnage	OECD countries	D 46-a	
Exports: tonnage & value in £m	Main countries	K 3-a	
Import duties: rates % ad val	Main countries	K 3-a	
Production in kg	EEC countries & Japan	K 6-m	
	Main countries	K 6-a	
WOVEN CELLULOSIC FABRICS			
Exports by destination: tonnage	Main countries	K 4-a	
tonnage	All countries	A 6-a	
	Main countries	K 4-a	

	Territorial coverage	Title codes	
WOVEN CELLULOSIC FABRICS, continued			
Imports by source: tonnage	All countries	K 4-a	
tonnage	All countries	A 6-a	
	Main countries	K 4-a	
Production: rayon & acetate fabrics: tonnage	OAS member countries	N 14-a	
rayon cloth: tonnage	All countries	U 22-a	
tyre cord: tonnage	OECD countries	D 46-a	
tonnage	OECD countries	D 46-a	
	W European countries	K 2-q	
WOVEN CELLULOSIC SPUN YARN FABRICS			
Exports: tonnage	All countries	K 4-a	
Imports: tonnage	All countries	K 4-a	
WOVEN COTTON FABRICS			
% changes in retail sales	E European countries	U 16-a	
% contribution to export earnings	Fiji	E 45-a	
Consumption per capita in metres	E European countries	U 16-a	
Deliveries to textile industry - index nos	UK	B 29-a	
Exports by value in local currency per ton	Pakistan	U 32-m	
cotton cloth: tonnage	All countries	K 1-q	
tonnage	Hong Kong, India & Japan	U 32-m	
	OECD countries	D 46-a	
Imports as % of domestic consumption	UK	B 29-a	
Imports, exports & trade balance in sq yds	UK	B 29-a	
tonnage	OECD countries	D 46-a	
Production: historical table from 1913 in metres	Main European countries	Z 1-a	
1921: tonnage	Main European countries	Z 1-a	
1938 in m²	Main European countries	Z 1-a	
85% pure cotton: tonnage	OECD countries	D 46-a	
in m²	All countries	U 22-a	
	AASM countries	E 41-a	
	E European countries & USSR	U 16-a	
	ECAFE countries	U 32-q	
	Latin American countries	J 5-a	
	Main countries	R 5-a	
	OAS member countries	N 14-a	
	OECD countries	D 46-a	
mixed blends: tonnage	All countries	U 43-a	
pure mixed cotton: tonnage	African countries	U 44-a	
tonnage	All countries	K 1-q	
	Asian & Far East countries	U 32-q	
	EEC countries	E 28-q	E 27-a
	Main countries	U 27-m	E 3-a
		R 5-a	
	OECD countries	D 46-a	
	W European countries	K 2-q	
Retail prices by kind in local currency per kg	OAS member countries	N 17-a	
Wholesale prices - index nos	Nepal	U 32-m	
WOVEN JUTE FABRICS			
Exports by destination: tonnage	Main countries	C 22-a	
by value in Rs	India & Pakistan	U 32-m	
Imports by source: tonnage	W European countries	C 22-a	
jute cloth: tonnage	W European countries	C 22-a	
Production by volume in m²	All countries	U 22-a	
	EEC countries	E 28-q	E 27-a
tonnage	OECD countries	D 46-a	
WOVEN LINEN FABRICS			
Exports by destination by volume in sq yds	UK	B 10-a	
Production by volume in m²	All countries	U 22-a	
	EEC countries	E 28-q	E 27-a
tonnage	OECD countries	D 46-a	
WOVEN NON-CELLULOSIC FABRICS			
Exports by destination: tonnage	Main countries	K 4-a	
tonnage	All countries	A 6-a	
Imports by source: tonnage	Main countries	K 4-a	
tonnage	All countries	A 6-a	
Production: mixed fabrics: tonnage	OECD countries	D 46-a	
unmixed fabrics: tonnage	OECD countries	D 46-a	
tonnage	All countries	U 22-a	
	OECD countries	D 46-a	
	W European countries	K 2-q	
WOVEN NON-CELLULOSIC SPUN YARN FABRICS			
Exports: tonnage	Main countries	K 4-a	
Imports: tonnage	Main countries	K 4-a	
WOVEN RAYON FABRICS			
Exports: tonnage	All countries	K 1-q	
Production: acetate fabrics: tonnage	African countries	U 44-a	
(incl acetate fabric): tonnage	All countries	U 27-m	U 22-a
		U 43-a	

	Territorial coverage	Title codes	
WOVEN SILK FABRICS			
Production: natural silk fabrics by volume in m²	All countries	U 22-a	U 43-a
tonnage	EEC countries	E 28-q	E 27-a
	OECD countries	D 46-a	
WOVEN WOOLLEN FABRICS			
see also KNITTED FABRICS			
TEXTILE INDUSTRY, WOOLLEN			
% changes in retail sales	E European countries	U 16-a	
% export penetration by country	Main countries	K 3-a	
% turnover taxes levied	Greece	K 3-a	
Consumption per capita in metres	E European countries	U 16-a	
Deliveries to textile industry - index nos	UK	B 29-a	
Exports: cotton-wool mixture in yds & value in £	Main countries	K 3-a	
fibre-wool mixtures in yds & value in £	Main countries	K 3-a	
tonnage	OECD countries	D 46-a	
wool interlinings in yds & value in £	Main countries	K 3-a	
woollen cloth in yds & value in £	Main countries	K 3-a	
woollen & worsted cloth in yds & value in £	Main countries	K 3-a	
woollen mixtures in yds & value in £	Main countries	K 3-a	
Import duties: rates % ad val	Main countries	K 3-a	
levies by kind of woven fabric: rates % ad val	Main countries	K 3-a	
Imports as % of domestic consumption	UK	B 29-a	
Imports, exports & trade balance in sq yds	UK	B 29-a	
tonnage	OECD countries	D 46-a	
Production by kind: tonnage	EEC countries	E 28-q	E 27-a
historical table from 1925 in metres	European countries	Z 1-a	
in kg	Main countries	K 6-a	
	Main European countries & Japan	K 6-m	
in m²	Main countries	R 5-a	
	All countries	U 22-a	
	E European countries & USSR	U 16-a	
in sq yds	Main countries	K 3-a	
pure & mixed wool: tonnage	All countries	U 27-m	U 43-a
tonnage	African countries	U 44-a	
	Main countries	E 3-a	R 5-a
	OAS member countries	N 14-a	
	OECD countries	D 46-a	
Stocks held by dyers in kg	Main countries	K 6-a	
by finishers in kg	Main countries	K 6-a	
by weavers in kg	Main countries	K 6-a	
WOVEN WORSTED FABRICS			
Production in kg	Main European countries & Japan	K 6-m	
85% pure wool: tonnage	OECD countries	D 46-a	
mixed blends: tonnage	OECD countries	D 46-a	
WRAPPING PAPER			
Consumption by kind: tonnage	OECD countries	D 40-a	
change per $1000 increase in gross national product	Main countries	D 32-a	
fluting paper: tonnage	OECD countries	D 40-a	
kraft paper & board: tonnage	Main countries	D 32-a	
	OECD countries	D 40-a	
	All countries	D 40-a	
sack kraft paper: tonnage	OECD countries	D 40-a	
Exports by destination: fluting paper: tonnage	All countries	D 40-a	
kraftliners: tonnage	All countries	D 40-a	
sack kraft paper: tonnage	All countries	D 40-a	
Marginal propensity to consume: kraft paper	Main countries	D 32-a	
Production by kind: tonnage	OECD countries	D 40-a	
fluting paper: tonnage	OECD countries	D 40-a	
(incl packaging paper): tonnage	OECD countries	D 41-q	
kraftliners: tonnage	OECD countries	D 40-a	
sack kraft paper: tonnage	OECD countries	D 40-a	
sulphite wrapping paper: tonnage	OECD countries	D 40-a	
Wholesale prices in local currency per ton	OAS member countries	N 17-a	
Writing paper see PAPER & PAPERBOARD			
WROUGHT IRON, ROLLED			
Production: tonnage	Main countries	H 3-a	
	European countries	U 6-a	U 7-a
WROUGHT STEEL			
Production: historical tables: tonnage	EEC countries	E 29-a	
WROUGHT TIN PRODUCTS			
Consumption: tin in production of foil & sheets: tonnage	UK	C 20-m	
of piping & tubing: tonnage	UK	C 20-m	
of wire: tonnage	UK	C 20-m	

	Territorial coverage	Title codes
X-RAY EQUIPMENT		
Deliveries by value in £	UK	C 24-a
X-ray technicians see HOSPITAL PERSONNEL		
XYLENE		
Consumption (for organic synthesis): tonnage	OECD countries	D 5-a
tonnage	OECD countries	D 5-a
Exports: tonnage	European countries, Japan & USA	U 26-a
Imports: tonnage	European countries, Japan & USA	U 26-a
Production from coal derivatives: tonnage	European countries, Japan & USA	U 26-a
	OECD countries	D 5-a
from oil & natural gas: tonnage	European countries, Japan & USA	U 26-a
	OECD countries	D 5-a
tonnage	European countries, Japan & USA	U 26-a
Refining capacity: xylene in tons per yr	EEC countries	B 30-a
YACHTS & SPORTING CRAFT		
No & tonnage: new construction	Worldwide	S 2-a
registered craft	W Germany	S 16-a
Yams see SWEET POTATOES & YAMS		
Yarn, acrylic see MAN-MADE FIBRES		
NON-CELLULOSIC FIBRES		
YARN, CELLULOSIC		
Consumption by kind in knitting mills: tonnage	OECD countries	D 46-a
in weaving industry: tonnage	OECD countries	D 46-a
continuous yarn: tonnage	W European countries	K 2-q
discontinuous yarn: tonnage	W European countries	K 2-q
in carpet production: tonnage	EEC countries & USA	K 4-a
in pneumatic tyre production: tonnage	EEC countries & USA	K 4-a
Exports: tonnage	OECD countries	D 46-a
Imports: tonnage	OECD countries	D 46-a
Production: artificial yarn: tonnage	Main countries	U 26-a
	W European countries	K 2-q
tyre cord: tonnage	OECD countries	D 46-a
tonnage	All countries	K 4-a
Yarn, cotton waste see COTTON WASTE YARN		
YARN, NON-CELLULOSIC		
Consumption by kind in knitting mills	OECD countries	D 46-a
in weaving industry: tonnage	OECD countries	D 46-a
continuous yarn: tonnage	W European countries	K 2-q
discontinuous yarn: tonnage	W European countries	K 2-q
in carpet production: tonnage	EEC countries	K 4-a
in pneumatic tyre production: tonnage	EEC countries	K 4-a
polyamide in production of carpets: tonnage	EEC countries	K 4-a
polyamide yarn by use: tonnage	EEC countries	K 4-a
synthetic yarn: tonnage	Main countries	K 4-a
Exports by destination: tonnage	Main countries	K 4-a
synthetic spun yarn: tonnage	Main countries	K 4-a
tonnage	OECD countries	D 46-a
Imports by source: tonnage	Main countries	K 4-a
carded & combed non-cellulosic yarn & tow: tonnage	Main countries	K 4-a
synthetic spun yarn: tonnage	Main countries	K 4-a
synthetic waste: tonnage	Main countries	K 4-a
tonnage	OECD countries	D 46-a
Production: acetate yarn: tonnage	OECD countries	D 46-a
by kind: tonnage	All countries	K 4-a
polyamide yarn: tonnage	OECD countries	D 46-a
polyester yarn: tonnage	OECD countries	D 46-a
synthetic yarn: tonnage	Main countries	U 26-a
	W European countries	K 2-q
tyre cord: tonnage	OECD countries	D 46-a
YARNS		
see also COTTON YARN		
FLAX YARN		
HEMP YARN		
JUTE YARN		
LINEN YARN		
MAN-MADE FIBRE YARN		
SILK YARN		
TEXTILE YARNS		
WOOL YARN		
WORSTED YARN		
Excise duties: woven materials: % rates levied	EEC countries	E 31-a
Exports: textile yarns (all kinds): tonnage	OECD countries	D 46-a
Imports (incl fabrics & made-up articles) by value in $m	Main countries	G 1-a
textile yarns (all kinds): tonnage	OECD countries	D 46-a

	Territorial coverage	Title codes
YARNS BY KIND		
Exports: projection to 1977 in lbs	UK	B 29
Imports: projection to 1977 in lbs	UK	B 29
Production: artificial yarns: tonnage	W European countries	K 2-a
by spinning industry: tonnage	OECD countries	D 46-a
cotton yarn: tonnage	W European countries	K 2-a
synthetic yarns: tonnage	W European countries	K 2-a

Yellow fever   see   DISEASES, CONTAGIOUS

	Territorial coverage	Title codes
YERBA MATE		
Export prices in $ per ton	Brazil	A 9-a
Retail prices in local currency per ton	OAS member countries	N 17-a

Yields   see   CROP YIELDS
              GOVERNMENT BONDS
              INDUSTRIAL SHARES
              MILK-YIELD PER COW

Yoghurt   see   MILK PRODUCTS

Yolks, frozen or dried   see   EGG PRODUCTS

	Territorial coverage	Title codes
YOUTH EMPLOYMENT		
% of active population in 14-24 yrs age group employed in agriculture	EEC countries	E 2-a
in industrial occupations	EEC countries	E 2-a
in service industry occupations	EEC countries	E 2-a
in work or unemployed	EEC countries	E 2-a
YOUTH HOSTELS		
No of beds available for members of youth clubs	OECD countries	D 47-a
YTTRIUM		
see also RARE EARTH MINERALS		
Consumption: tonnage	USA	N 1-a
Government strategic stockpile: yttrium oxide: tonnage	USA	N 1-a
World production: tonnage	Main countries	N 1-a
World reserves: tonnage (estim)	Main countries	N 1-a

	Territorial coverage	Title codes	
ZINC			
% contribution to export earnings	Zambia	E 45-a	
% of EEC area production	EEC countries	R 5-a	
Consumption by chemical industry: tonnage	OECD countries	D 21-a	
main end-uses & in production of brass & bronze: tonnage	Canada & USA	H 2-a	
tonnage	Main countries	C 30-q	H 2-a
	UK & USA	T 4-a	
	USA	J 6-a	
in diecasting of alloys: tonnage	Main countries	C 30-q	
galvanising of fencing & netting: tonnage	USA	C 12-a	
semi-manufactured products: tonnage	USA	J 6-a	
steel plates: tonnage	European countries	C 12-a	
sheets: tonnage	European countries, Japan & USA	C 12-a	
strip: tonnage	European countries, Japan & USA	C 12-a	
tubes: tonnage	European countries & USA	C 12-a	
tanks & containers: tonnage	USA	C 12-a	
wire: tonnage	European countries & USA	C 12-a	
galvanising processes: tonnage	European countries & Japan	C 12-a	
	Main countries	C 30-q	T 4-a
	OECD countries	D 21-a	
	UK & USA	J 6-a	
production of alloys for die casting: tonnage	UK	J 6-a	
brass & brass products: tonnage	Main countries	C 12-a	
& other alloys: tonnage	UK	C 30-m	
bars & sections: tonnage	France & Italy	C 12-a	
castings: tonnage	Main countries	H 2-a	
	France & Italy	C 12-a	
metal: tonnage	Main countries	C 30-q	T 4-a
	UK	J 6-a	
products (finished): tonnage	USA	J 6-a	
tubing: tonnage	France, Italy & USA	C 12-a	
chemicals: tonnage	France & Italy	T 4-a	
	France, W Germany & UK	C 12-a	
copper-alloy castings: tonnage	Main countries	C 30-q	
	France & Italy	T 4-a	
semi-manufactured products: tonnage	France & Italy	T 4-a	
die-casting alloys: tonnage	European countries, Japan & USA	C 12-a	
	Main countries	T 4-a	
die-castings: tonnage	USA	J 6-a	

	Territorial coverage	Title codes	
ZINC, continued			
Consumption in production of rolled zinc: tonnage	Main countries	C 30-q	T 4-a
	UK & USA	J 6-a	
sand castings: tonnage	USA	J 6-a	
semi-finished brass products: tonnage	OECD countries	D 21-a	
products of all kinds: tonnage	Main countries	C 12-a	
	OECD countries	D 21-a	
sheets & strip: tonnage	European countries, Japan & USA	C 12-a	
wire & tubes: tonnage	Main countries	C 30-q	
tonnage	France, Italy & USA	C 12-a	
zinc alloy semi-manufactured products: tonnage	Main countries	C 30-q	
	France & Italy	C 12-a	
alloys: tonnage	USA	J 6-a	
castings: tonnage	OECD countries	D 21-a	
dust: tonnage	UK	C 12-a	J 6-a
oxide & zinc dust: tonnage	Main countries	C 30-q	
oxide: tonnage	Main countries	T 4-a	
	USA	J 6-a	
	Japan, UK & USA	C 12-a	
	France & Italy	T 4-a	
wire & tubes: tonnage	UK	C 30-m	
of zinc by grade (incl electrolytic): tonnage	UK	T 4-a	
(electrolytic): tonnage	UK	C 30-m	
remelted metal: tonnage	UK	T 4-a	
slabs by grade: tonnage	UK	C 12-a	
historical table: tonnage	World regions		
in galvanising of fencing & netting: tonnage	USA	T 4-a	
sheets & strip: tonnage	UK & USA	T 4-a	
tanks & containers: tonnage	USA	T 4-a	
tubes & fittings: tonnage	UK & USA	T 4-a	
wire: tonnage	UK & USA	T 4-a	
in galvanising processes: tonnage	UK & USA	T 4-a	
tonnage	All countries	C 30-m	
	EEC countries	C 12-a	
	USA	N 1-a	
	World regions	C 12-a	
	All countries	U 24-m	
tonnage	Argentina, Brazil, Mexico & Peru	U 18-a	
	Japan	H 2-a	
	OAS member countries	N 17-a	
	OECD countries	D 21-q	
zinc (high & low quality): tonnage	UK	T 4-a	
zinc scrap (from zinc & alloys): tonnage	UK	C 30-m	
Disposals ex US strategic stockpile: tonnage		U 11-a	
Export prices in $A per ton	Australia	T 4-m	
prime western zinc in cents per lb	Canada	R 2-m	
Export prices - index nos (weighted average main sources)	Worldwide	U 29-q	
	S American countries	U 40-q	
Exports by destination: crude zinc: tonnage	Main countries	H 2-a	
slab zinc: tonnage	France, UK & USSR	H 2-a	
	OECD countries	D 21-q	
	USA	J 6-a	
rolled zinc: tonnage	Main countries	C 30-m	C 12-a
slab zinc: tonnage	Zambia	E 45-a	
tonnage & value in $m	USA	J 6-a	
zinc blocks & slabs by destination: tonnage	Main countries	T 4-a	
	USA	J 6-a	
sheets & strip by destination: tonnage	USA	N 1-a	
Government strategic stockpile: zinc metal: tonnage	All countries	B 15-a	
Imports & exports: unwrought metal & zinc scrap: tonnage	Main countries	U 24-m	
Imports by source: bullion & refined metal: tonnage	Main countries	H 2-a	
crude zinc: tonnage	UK	C 30-m	
slab zinc by grade: tonnage	France, UK & USSR	H 2-a	
tonnage	Main countries	T 4-a	
	OECD countries	D 21-q	
	USA	J 6-a	
zinc pigs & slabs: tonnage	USA	J 6-a	
rolled zinc: tonnage	Italy & UK	C 12-a	
slab zinc by source: tonnage	Main countries	C 30-m	C 12-a
tonnage	USA	J 6-a	
Plant smelting capacity by company & by no of retorts in use	USA	J 6-a	
by output per day	USA	J 6-a	
by volume of retorts in use		C 12-a	
zinc ore: tonnage per yr	Worldwide	J 6-a	
	Main countries	U 24-m	
Producer prices in £ per ton (excl duties)	Worldwide, excl Canada & USA	T 4-m	
in local currency per kg	Main countries	R 2-m	
normal quality in £ per ton	UK	H 2-m	
primary virgin zinc in local currency per ton	W Germany, UK & USA	C 12-m	
slab zinc in £ per ton	UK	H 2-a	
Production at mines & smelters, imports & exports: tonnage	All countries	U 24-m	U 27-m
based on metal content of ore: tonnage	All countries	B 15-a	E 3-a
		R 5-a	U 22-a
		U 43-a	
	Latin American countries	J 5-a	U 18-a
		U 40-a	

611

	Territorial coverage	Title codes	
ZINC, continued			
Production by grade: slab zinc (brass grade): tonnage	USA	J 6-a	
(high grade): tonnage	USA	J 6-a	
(medium grade): tonnage	USA	J 6-a	
(prime western grade): tonnage	USA	J 6-a	
tonnage	USA	T 4-a	
distilled primary & secondary zinc: tonnage	USA	J 6-a	
electrolytic slab zinc: tonnage	USA	T 4-a	
historical table since 1897: tonnage	USA	J 6-a	
(incl concentrates): tonnage	OAS member countries	N 14-a	
metallic zinc (from imported ores): tonnage	USA	J 6-a	
(from local ores): tonnage	USA	J 6-a	
tonnage	OECD countries	R 5-a	
recoverable zinc by region: tonnage	USA	J 6-a	
secondary metallic zinc (from zinc scrap): tonnage	Main countries	H 2-a	
in slabs: tonnage	USA	J 6-a	
semi-manufactured zinc products: tonnage	EEC countries	E 28-q	E 27-a
slab & refined zinc: tonnage	All countries	C 30-m	
slab zinc (from zinc scrap): tonnage	USA	T 4-a	
tonnage	USA	J 6-a	
tonnage	All countries	C 12-a	
	Argentine, Bolivia, Brazil, Honduras, Mexico & Peru	U 18-a	
unwrought zinc: tonnage	Zaire	E 41-a	
zinc & zinc alloy castings: tonnage	All countries	U 22-a	
dust (from zinc scrap): tonnage	Main countries	H 2-a	
in concentrates by specific large companies: tonnage	USA	T 4-a	
(primary) from imported ore: tonnage	Main countries	J 6-a	
from local ore: tonnage	USA	T 4-a	
(secondary distilled): tonnage	USA	T 4-a	
slabs by specific companies: tonnage	USA	T 4-a	
historical table: tonnage	Main countries	J 6-a	
(primary): tonnage	World regions	C 12-a	
(secondary): tonnage	USA	N 1-a	
tonnage	USA	N 1-a	
	All countries	J 6-a	R 5-a
	Argentine, Mexico & Peru	U 18-a	
	EEC countries	C 12-a	
	World regions	C 12-a	
Smelting plants: no of distillation furnaces in operation	Main countries	J 6-a	
of retorts in operation	Main countries	J 6-a	
Stocks held at smelter plants: tonnage	USA	J 6-a	
	UK & USA	J 6-a	
by consumers (end-period): tonnage	Italy	C 12-a	
by producers (end-period): tonnage	European countries & USA	U 24-a	
	Italy	C 12-a	
slab zinc held at London Metal Market warehouses: tonnage	UK	J 6-a	
tonnage	UK	C 30-q	
zinc metal held at producers' & users' plants: tonnage	USA	N 1-a	
at smelters' plants: tonnage	USA	T 4-a	
at consumers' premises: tonnage	UK	T 4-a	
Wholesale prices (3 mths forward) on London market in £ per ton	UK	T 4-m	
in cents per lb at St Louis	USA	J 6-m	
on New York Metal Market	USA	C 12-m	
in cents per lb	USA	N 1-a	
	Canada, UK & USA	U 27-m	
in local currency per lb or ton	Australia, Canada & UK	J 6-m	
(normal brand) in FrB per kg	Belgium	R 2-m	
(on London Metal Exchange) in £ per ton (daily average)	UK	J 6-m	U 24-m
(on New York market) in cents per lb (daily average)	USA	U 24-m	
prime western quality zinc in cents per lb	USA	R 2-m	
(spot) in local currency per ton	Main countries	T 4-m	
virgin zinc ingots in local currency per kg	France & Italy	T 4-w	
World consumption: historical table: tonnage		C 12-a	
slab zinc: tonnage	Worldwide	C 30-a	
	All countries	C 12-a	
tonnage	All countries excl USSR	T 4-a	
World exports: tonnage	Main countries	T 4-a	
World market prices: historical table from 1875 in £ per ton		T 4-a	
in cents per lb	UK & USA	U 18-a	
World production: slab zinc: tonnage	All countries	C 12-a	
tonnage	Worldwide	C 12-a	U 11-a
	All countries excl USSR	T 4-a	
zinc ore & slab zinc: tonnage	Main countries	N 1-a	
World reserves: tonnage (estim)		C 30-a	
World smelter production: tonnage	Main countries	N 1-a	
		N 4-a	
ZINC, ELECTROLYTIC			
Consumption: tonnage	UK	T 4-a	
Imports by source: tonnage	UK	T 4-a	
Plant capacity: specific companies in tons per yr	Worldwide	J 6-a	
Production: tonnage	Main countries	B 15-a	
	USA	J 6-a	
Wholesale prices (spot) in local currency per ton	India & Japan	T 4-w	

612

	Territorial coverage	Title codes	
ZINC ALLOYS			
Consumption: magnesium in production of zinc alloys: tonnage	USA	T 4-a	
zinc in production of alloys: tonnage	USA	J 6-a	
Wholesale prices: zinc ingots by grade in lire per kg	Italy	C 12-m	
Zinc ammonium chloride see ZINC COMPOUNDS			
Zinc castings see CASTINGS, ZINC			
Zinc chloride see ZINC COMPOUNDS			
ZINC COMPOUNDS			
Production by kind (from scrap): tonnage	USA	T 4-a	
ZINC CONCENTRATES			
Exports by destination: tonnage	Australia	H 2-a	
Wholesale prices (at Joplin) in $ per ton	USA	J 6-m	
ZINC FUMING			
Oxide fume content of treated slag: tonnage	USA	J 6-a	
Recovered zinc content of treated slag: tonnage	USA	J 6-a	
Slag (hot & cold-treated): tonnage	USA	J 6-a	
Zinc ingots see INGOTS, ZINC			
ZINC ORE			
% share of world reserves (estim)	Latin American region	U 18-a	
Export prices - index nos (weighted average main sources)	Worldwide	U 29-q	
Exports by destination (incl concentrates): tonnage	All countries	T 4-a	
	OECD countries	D 21-q	
	Main countries	U 24-m	C 12-a
		H 2-a	
tonnage & by value in $m	Congo Rep	E 45-a	
Import prices: sulphide ore in $ per ton cif	European countries	T 4-w	
Imports & exports by source & destination: tonnage	All countries	B 15-a	
by source (incl concentrates): tonnage	OECD countries	D 21-q	
	Main countries	H 2-a	T 4-a
	USA	J 6-a	
(incl concentrates): tonnage	Main countries	U 24-m	C 12-a
Production based on metal content of ore: tonnage	All countries	J 6-a	T 4-a
historical table from 1837: tonnage	Main European countries	Z 1-a	
(incl concentrates): tonnage	OECD countries	D 21-q	
tonnage	African countries	U 44-a	
	All countries	C 30-m	
	EEC countries	E 28-q	E 27-a
	OAS member countries	N 14-a	
World exports (incl concentrates) by destination: tonnage	All countries	T 4-a	
World production: tonnage		C 12-a	N 4-a
		U 11-a	
Zinc oxide see CHEMICAL PRODUCTS			
PIGMENTS, MINERAL			
ZINC POWDER & DUST			
Exports: zinc dust: tonnage	USA	J 6-a	
Production: zinc dust: tonnage	USA	J 6-a	
	UK	T 4-a	
ZINC PRODUCTS, SEMI-FINISHED			
see also GALVANISED SHEETS			
PLATES SHEETS & STRIP, ZINC			
Exports by kind: tonnage	Main countries	T 4-a	
Imports & exports by kind: tonnage	All countries	B 15-a	
Production by kind: tonnage	All countries	B 15-a	
	USA	J 6-a	
tonnage	Main countries	H 2-a	
Wholesale prices: rolled zinc in Fr per ton	France	T 4-m	
zinc sheets in lire per ton	Italy	C 12-m	
in local currency per ton	UK & USA	T 4-m	
ZINC SCRAP			
Dealers' buying prices (in New York) in cents per lb	USA	T 4-m	
Exports by destination: tonnage	Main countries	T 4-a	
dross, ashes & skimmings: tonnage	USA	J 6-a	
Imports by source: tonnage	Main countries	T 4-a	
Production: die-cast zinc slabs (from scrap): tonnage	USA	T 4-a	
slab zinc (from scrap): tonnage	USA	T 4-a	
zinc compounds by kind (from scrap): tonnage	USA	T 4-a	
dust (from scrap): tonnage	USA	T 4-a	
oxide (lead-free) from scrap: tonnage	USA	T 4-a	
zinc-based chemicals (from scrap): tonnage	USA	T 4-a	
Wholesale prices: diecasting zinc in £ per ton	UK	T 4-w	
galvanizers' ashes in £ per ton	UK	T 4-w	
in local currency per ton	Main countries	T 4-m	
old zinc & re-melted zinc in £ per ton	UK	T 4-w	

	Territorial coverage	Title codes
ZINC SCRAP, continued		
Wholesale prices: zinc chips in £ per ton	UK	T 4-w
in cents per lb	USA	J 6-m
Zinc sulphate see ZINC COMPOUNDS		
Zinc-based chemicals see ZINC COMPOUNDS		
ZIRCONIUM		
see also HAFNIUM		
Production (incl concentrates): tonnage	All countries	B 15-a
ZIRCONIUM ORE		
Exports by destination: tonnage	Australia & USA	T 4-a
tonnage	Australia, W Germany, Malaysia & USA	T 4-a
Import prices: zirconium sand in local currency per ton cif	European countries	T 4-m
Imports & exports (incl concentrates): tonnage	All countries	B 15-a
by source: tonnage	Main countries	T 4-a
World production: tonnage	Main countries	T 4-a

APPENDIX 1 - EXPORTS BY PRODUCT

Product	Territorial coverage	Title codes
ABACA by value in $m	Philippines	U 32-m
ACCUMULATORS & no of cells by destination by value in £	UK	V 1-a
ACID DERIVATIVES (nitrosated) by destination by value in $	Main European countries	U 2-a
ACIDS (halogenated) by destination by value in $	Main countries	U 2-a
(nitrated) by destination by value in $	Main countries	U 2-a
(sulfonated) by destination by value in $	Main countries	U 2-a
AGRICULTURAL COMMODITIES (by product groups): tonnage	All countries	A 14-a
(by regions of origin): tonnage	EEC countries	E 38-a
AGRICULTURAL MACHINERY by value in $m	Main countries	U 38-a
AGRICULTURAL PRODUCTS		
(incl food) by value in $	OECD countries	D 1-a
as % of total exports (quantum basis)	OECD countries	D 1-a
(value basis)	W European countries	U 20-a
by areas of destination by value in $	OECD countries	D 1-a
by destination by value in $	W European countries	U 33-a
by value in $m	W European countries	U 20-a
inter-EEC exports by value in $m		U 33-a
tonnage (in detail)	World regions	A 11-a
index nos (value basis)	World regions	A 11-a
AGRICULTURAL TRACTORS by value in £m: historical table	UK	V 1-a
in $m	Main countries	U 38-a
AIR CONDITIONING MACHINERY by value in $m	Main countries	U 38-a
AIRCRAFT (incl replacement parts)		
by destination by CST classes: tonnage & value in $m	EEC countries	E 48-a
SITC classes by value in $m	Main countries	D 2-q
tonnage & value in $m	OECD countries	D 3-a2
by NIMEXE classes: no & value in $m	All countries	E 20-a
SITC classes: no & value in $m	All countries	U 50-a U 59-a
by value in $m	Main countries	U 38-a
AIRCRAFT ENGINES by value in $m	Main countries	U 38-a
ALDEHYDES by destination by value in $	Main countries	U 2-a
ALLOY STEEL by destination: tonnage & value in $	EEC area	E 5-q
tonnage	EEC countries	E 29-a
by quality by destination: tonnage	Main countries	T 4-a
ALLOY STEEL INGOTS by destination: tonnage	Main countries	T 4-a
ALMONDS: tonnage	Main countries	P 4-m
ALTERNATORS (hydraulic) in mW	European countries, Japan & USA	D 45-a
(thermal) in mW	European countries, Japan & USA	D 45-a
ALUMINA: tonnage & value in $	Guyana, Jamaica & Surinam	B 2-a
ALUMINIUM: total exports & to EEC area: tonnage & value in UA	AASM countries	E 41-a
unit value in $ per ton	Cameroons & Ghana	E 45-a
ALUMINIUM (primary) by destination: tonnage	Main countries	T 4-a
	OECD countries	D 21-q
(unwrought): tonnage	Main countries	C 12-a
ALUMINIUM BARS, RODS, PLATES, SHEETS & STRIP: tonnage	USA	J 6-a
ALUMINIUM FOIL by destination: tonnage	Main countries	T 4-a
ALUMINIUM FORGING BARS by destination: tonnage	Main countries	T 4-a
ALUMINIUM INGOTS (incl alloy ingots): tonnage	USA	J 6-a
(incl notch bars): tonnage	UK	C 30-a
ALUMINIUM OXIDE by destination: tonnage	Main countries	U 2-a
ALUMINIUM PLATES & SHEETS by destination: tonnage	Main countries	T 4-a
ALUMINIUM POWDER by destination: tonnage	Main countries	T 4-a
ALUMINIUM SCRAP by destination: tonnage	Main countries	T 4-a
tonnage	USA	J 6-a
ALUMINIUM SEMI-FINISHED PRODUCTS: tonnage	Canada	J 6-a
	OECD countries	D 21-a
	All countries	B 15-a
ALUMINIUM STRIP (in coils) by destination: tonnage	Main countries	T 4-a
ALUMINIUM TUBES by destination: tonnage	Main countries	T 4-a
ALUMINIUM WIRE by destination: tonnage	Main countries	T 4-a

APPENDIX 1 - EXPORTS BY PRODUCT

	Territorial coverage	Title codes
ALUMINIUM WIRE-DRAWING RODS by destination: tonnage	Main countries	T 4-a
AMMONIA (anhydrous & aqueous) by destination: tonnage	Main countries	U 2-a
AMMONIA: tonnage	ECE countries	U 15-a
	European countries, Japan & USA	U 25-a
ANIMAL & VEGETABLE PRODUCTS by value in $m	W European countries	U 33-a
ANIMAL FATS & OILS shipped to EEC & non-EEC areas by value in $	EEC countries	E 24-a
ANIMAL FEEDING STUFFS by value in $m	OECD countries	D 1-a
	W European countries	U 33-a
ANIMAL FEEDING STUFFS - index nos (value basis)	World regions	A 11-a
ANTHRACITE by destination: tonnage & value in $	EEC countries	E 5-q
by grade: tonnage	All countries	B 15-a
ANTIBIOTICS by kind by destination by value in $	Main countries	U 2-a
ANTIMONY (unwrought) by destination: tonnage	Italy	C 12-a
ANTIMONY METAL by destination: tonnage	Main countries	T 4-a
tonnage	All countries	B 15-a
ANTIMONY ORE by destination: tonnage	Main countries	T 4-a
ANTIMONY ORE, REGULUS METAL, SCRAP & OXIDE: tonnage	All countries	B 15-a
APPLES (fresh) by destination in bushels	Australia	D 38-a
tonnage	Main OECD countries	D 33-a
by value in $m	W European countries	U 33-a
tonnage	OECD countries	D 33-a
(processed): tonnage	OECD countries	D 33-a
unit value in $ per ton	Main European countries	U 20-a
APPLIANCES, replacement parts & machine accessories by value in $	Main countries	U 38-a
ARSENIC & DERIVATIVES: tonnage	All countries	B 15-a
ARSENIC: tonnage	All countries	B 15-a
ARTIFICIAL STAPLE FIBRES: tonnage	European countries, Japan & USA	U 26-a
ARTISTS' COLOURS: tonnage & value in $	OECD countries	D 5-a
ASBESTOS PRODUCTS by destination by CST classes: tonnage & value in $	EEC countries	E 48-a
SITC classes by value in $	Main countries	D 2-q
tonnage & value in $	OECD countries	D 3-a2
ASBESTOS PRODUCTS, fibres & crude asbestos: tonnage	All countries	B 15-a
ASPHALT & BITUMEN: tonnage	Main countries	B 15-a
ASSEMBLED CARS shipped to USA by volume	All countries	V 4-a
AUTOMATIC NUMERICALLY-CONTROLLED MACHINE TOOLS as % of total machine tool exports	EEC countries	B 20-a
by value in $m	EEC countries	B 20-a
by volume	EEC countries	B 20-a
AUTOMOTIVE ACCESSORIES: quantity & value in $	USA	V 3-a
AUTOMOTIVE CHASSIS (all types) by destination by volume	W European countries	V 1-a
AUTOMOTIVE ELECTRICAL EQUIPMENT by value in $m	Main countries	U 38-a
AUTOMOTIVE REPLACEMENT PARTS by value in £m (in detail)	UK	V 1-a
AVIATION SPIRIT (incl jet fuels) by destination: tonnage	OECD countries	D 31-a
tonnage	Main countries	B 15-a
AVIATION TURBINE FUEL: tonnage	Main countries	B 15-a
BABASSU KERNELS: tonnage	Brazil	B 19-a
BABASSU OIL: tonnage	Brazil	B 19-a
BACON & HAM as % of total exports (value basis)	Main countries	B 11-a
BACON & LARD by destination: tonnage	EEC countries	E 47-m
BANANAS as % of total exports (value basis)	Main countries	A 15-a
by destination: tonnage	Central & S American countries	B 5-a
	Main countries	B 6-a
by value in local currency	Cook Is, W Samoa & Tonga	U 32-m
tonnage	All countries	B 5-a
tonnage & value in $m	Main countries	B 2-a

APPENDIX 1 - EXPORTS BY PRODUCT

Product	Territorial coverage	Title codes	
BANANAS, continued			
total exports & to EEC area: tonnage & value in UA	AASM countries	E 41-a	
unit value in $ per ton	Jamaica & Somalia	E 45-a	
in $ per kg	OAS member countries	N 15-a	
BARIUM MINERALS, WITHERITE & BARYTES: tonnage	All countries	B 15-a	
BARLEY by destination: tonnage	China, E European countries & USSR	A 17-a	
	Main countries	A 17-a	
by value in $m	W European countries	U 33-a	
tonnage	All countries	A 17-a	
	European countries	U 35-a	
	Main countries	B 8-a	
BASIC METALS by value in $	ECAFE countries	U 32-m	
BASIC SLAG: tonnage	OECD countries	D 5-a	
BASTNAESITE (rare earth mineral): tonnage	USA	N 1-a	
BATTERIES & ACCUMULATORS by value in $m	Main countries	U 38-a	
BAUXITE by destination: tonnage	Main countries	T 4-a	
tonnage & value in $	Guyana, Jamaica & Surinam	B 2-a	
unit value in $ per ton	African, Caribbean countries & Pacific Is	E 45-a	
BEARINGS (ball & roller) by value in $m	Main countries	U 38-a	
BEEF & VEAL as % of total exports (value basis)	Main countries	B 11-a	
by destination: tonnage	Main countries	B 12-m	B 11-a
tonnage	European countries & USSR	U 36-a	
BEEF: unit value in $ per ton	Chad & Madagascar	E 45-a	
BENTONITE & BENTONITE CLAY: tonnage	All countries	B 15-a	
BENZENE: tonnage	European countries, Japan & USA	U 26-a	
BERYL: tonnage	France & USA	B 15-a	
BERYLLIUM ORE by destination: tonnage	Brazil	T 4-a	
BEVERAGES: coffee, tea & cocoa by value in $	OECD countries	D 1-a	
BEVERAGES (incl tobacco) by kind by destination: tonnage & value in $	All countries	U 12-a	
shipped to EEC & non-EEC areas by value in $	EEC countries	E 24-a	
BEVERAGES & TOBACCO as % of total agricultural trade	W European countries	U 20-a	
by value in $m	W European countries	U 33-a	
BEVERAGES (alcoholic): unit value in $ per ton	African, Caribbean countries & Pacific Is	E 45-a	
BEVERAGES BY KIND by destination by CST classes: tonnage & value in $	EEC countries	E 48-a	
SITC classes by value in $	Main countries	D 2-q	
tonnage & value in $	OECD countries	D 3-a2	
by NIMEXE classes by value in $	All countries	E 20-a	
SITC classes by value in $	All countries	U 50-a	U 59-a
BICYCLES by value in $m	Main countries	U 38-a	
BIRD'S FEATHERS by value in local currency	S Vietnam	U 32-m	
BISMUTH METAL by destination: tonnage	Main countries	T 4-a	
BISMUTH ORE & CONCENTRATES: tonnage	All countries	B 15-a	
BOILER AUXILIARIES by value in $	France, W Germany & UK	B 30-a	
BOILERHOUSE PLANT by destination by value in $	EEC countries	B 30-a	
by value in $	France, W Germany & UK	B 30-a	
feed-heaters by destination by value in $	EEC countries	B 30-a	
steam condensers by destination by value in $	EEC countries	B 30-a	
BOILERHOUSE PLANT AUXILIARIES by destination by value in $	EEC countries	B 30-a	
BORATES, BORON MINERALS & REFINED BORAX: tonnage	All countries	B 15-a	
BORING MACHINES FOR METALWORK by destination by value in £	UK	B 31-a	
no & value in $m	USA	J 2-a	
BOX-BOARD FOLDING MACHINES by destination: tonnage	All countries	D 40-a	
BRASS (rolled) by destination: tonnage	USSR	T 4-a	
BRASS SCRAP, INGOTS, BARS, PLATES, SHEETS, WIRE, PIPES, TUBES & FITTINGS: tonnage	USA	J 6-a	
BRIGHT STEEL BARS by destination: tonnage	Main countries	T 4-a	
	EEC countries	E 29-a	
tonnage & value in $	EEC countries	E 5-q	

APPENDIX 1 - EXPORTS BY PRODUCT

	Territorial coverage	Title codes	
BRISTLE FIBRE (made of coir): tonnage	Sri Lanka	B 10-a	
BROADLEAVED TIMBER LOGS by destination by volume in m³	Canada, European countries & USA	A 13-q	
BROMIDE & COMPOUNDS: tonnage	All countries	B 15-a	
BROWN COAL BRIQUETTES: tonnage	European countries	U 31-q	
BROWN COAL: tonnage	European countries	U 31-q	U 10-a
BUILDING MATERIALS BY KIND			
by destination by CST classes: tonnage & value in $	EEC countries	E 48-a	
SITC classes by value in $	Main countries	D 2-q	
tonnage & value in $	OECD countries	D 3-a2	
by NIMEXE classes: tonnage & value in $	All countries	E 20-a	
SITC classes: tonnage & value in $	All countries	U 50-a	U 59-a
BUSES & COACHES by destination by volume	USSR	V 1-a	
volume & value in £m	W European countries & Japan	V 1-a	
volume & value up to & over 14 seats in size	UK	V 1-a	
by value in £m	UK	B 28-a	
volume	Main countries	V 4-a	
volume & value by destination in $	USA	V 1-a	
BUTANOL: tonnage	European countries, Japan & USA	U 26-a	
BUTTER by destination: tonnage	Main countries	B 12-m	B 4-a
by value in $m	OECD countries	D 1-a	
	W European countries	U 33-a	
	New Zealand	U 32-m	
shipments to EEC & non-EEC areas: tonnage	EEC countries	E 44-a	
tonnage (incl world total)	All countries	B 3-a	
tonnage: historical table from 1860	Denmark	Z 1-a	
tonnage	Main countries	B 4-a	
BUTTER-OIL (anhydrous milk fat): tonnage	Main countries	B 4-a	
by destination: tonnage	Main countries	B 12-m	
CADMIUM METAL & COMPOUNDS: tonnage	All countries	B 15-a	
CADMIUM METAL by destination: tonnage	Main countries	T 4-a	
CALCIUM CARBIDE by destination: tonnage	Main countries	U 2-a	
tonnage	European countries, Japan & USA	U 25-a	
	OECD countries	D 5-a	
CALCULATING MACHINES by value in $m	Main countries	U 38-a	
CALFSKINS & KIPS: tonnage	Main countries	B 9-m	
CALFSKINS by destination: tonnage	OECD countries	D 18-a	
by value in $	OECD countries	D 18-a	
tonnage	European OECD countries	D 18-a	
	Main countries	B 2-a	
CALFSKINS (wet-salted): tonnage	Main countries	A 18-a	
CANNED & BOTTLED FRUIT BY KIND by destination: tonnage	OECD countries	B 6-a	
	All countries	B 5-a	
CANNED APRICOTS: tonnage	All countries	A 7-a	
CANNED FISH (all kinds): tonnage & value in $	OECD countries	D 43-a	
CANNED FISH PRODUCTS: tonnage & value in $m	OECD countries	D 43-a	
CANNED FRUITS BY KIND: seasonal shipments: tonnage	Australia	B 5-a	
CANNED GRAPEFRUIT PIECES: tonnage	All countries	A 7-a	
CANNED MEAT by destination: tonnage	Main countries	B 12-m	B 11-a
CANNED ORANGES: tonnage	Cyprus, Israel & Japan	A 7-a	
CANNED PEACHES by destination: tonnage	Main countries	A 7-a	
tonnage	All countries	A 7-a	
CANNED PINEAPPLES by value in $m	Philippines	U 32-m	
CANNED TOMATOES: tonnage	All countries	A 7-a	
CANNED VEGETABLES BY KIND by destination: tonnage	OECD countries	B 6-a	
CAPSICUMS & CHILLIES by destination: tonnage	India, Japan & Spain	B 13-a	
CARBON BLACK by destination: tonnage	Main countries	U 2-a	
tonnage	European countries, Japan & USA	U 25-a	

● APPENDIX 1 - EXPORTS BY PRODUCT

Product	Territorial coverage	Title codes	
CARDAMOMS by destination in cwt	India & Sri Lanka	B 13-a	
CARGO SHIPS (second-hand): no & tonnage	Norway	S 15-a	
CARPETS & RUGS by value in $	Afghanistan	U 32-m	
CARS & TAXIS (new): historical table by value in £m	UK	V 1-a	
CASEIN (incl casein derivatives): tonnage	EEC countries	B 3-a	
by destination: tonnage	Main countries	B 4-a	
by kind: tonnage	Main countries	B 12-a	
tonnage	Main countries (total)	B 4-a	
CASHEW KERNELS: shipments to Mozambique: tonnage	E African countries	P 4-m	
CASHEW NUTSHELL OIL: tonnage	Brazil, India & Mozambique	B 19-a	
CASHEW SEEDS: shipments to Mozambique, Kenya & Tanzania	E African countries	P 4-m	
CASSIA in cwt	China, Madagascar & S Vietnam	B 13-a	
CAST-IRON PIPES & FITTINGS: tonnage & as % of production	UK	B 25-a	
CAST-IRON PIPES by destination: tonnage	Main countries	T 4-a	
tonnage	ECE countries	U 7-m	U 6-a
	Main countries	H 3-a	
CAST-IRON TUBES & FITTINGS: tonnage	Main countries	T 2-m	
CASTINGS by destination: tonnage & value in $	EEC countries	E 5-q	
CASTOR OIL by destination: tonnage	Brazil & India	B 19-a	
tonnage & value in $m	Main countries	B 2-a	
tonnage	Primary producing countries	B 18-q	
CASTOR SEED by destination: tonnage	Tanzania & Thailand	B 19-a	
tonnage	Main countries	B 18-q	B 19-a
tonnage & value in $m	Main countries	B 2-a	
CATTLE by destination by volume	Main countries	B 12-m	
by kind for beef: tonnage (live wt)	EEC countries	E 1-a	
unit value in $ per ton	African, Caribbean countries & Pacific Is	E 45-a	
CATTLE HIDES by destination: tonnage & value in $	OECD countries	D 18-a	
CATTLE HIDES (incl buffalo hides): tonnage	All countries	A 18-a	
CATTLE HIDES & SKINS: tonnage	Main countries	B 9-m	B 2-a
CAUSTIC SODA by destination: tonnage	Main countries	U 2-a	
tonnage	ECE countries	U 15-a	
	European countries, Japan & USA	U 25-a	
	OECD countries	D 5-a	
CELLULOSIC DERIVATIVES by destination: tonnage	OECD countries	D 5-a	
CELLULOSIC FIBRE WASTE by destination: tonnage	Main countries	K 4-a	
CELLULOSIC FIBRES by destination: tonnage	Main countries	K 4-a	
tonnage	OECD countries	D 46-a	
CELLULOSIC FILAMENTS as % of production	Main countries	D 27-a	
CELLULOSIC SPUN YARN by destination: tonnage	Main countries	K 4-a	
tonnage	Main countries	K 4-a	
CELLULOSIC SPUN YARN FABRICS: tonnage	Main countries	K 4-a	
CELLULOSIC STAPLE (incl tow): tonnage	Main countries	K 4-a	
CELLULOSIC STAPLE as % of production of all staple	Main countries	D 27-a	
CELLULOSIC WOVEN FILAMENT FABRICS: tonnage	Main countries	K 4-a	
CELLULOSIC YARN: tonnage	Main countries	K 4-a	
	OECD countries	D 46-a	
CEMENT (incl plaster)			
by destination by CST classes: tonnage & value in $	EEC countries	E 48-a	
SITC classes by value in $	Main countries	D 2-q	
tonnage & value in $	OECD countries	D 3-a2	
by NIMEXE classes: tonnage & value in $	All countries	E 20-a	
SITC classes: tonnage & value in $	All countries	U 50-a	U 59-a
CEMENT by destination areas: tonnage	OECD countries	D 4-a	
tonnage	European countries & USA	U 5-a	
unit value in $ per ton	Bahamas	E 45-a	
	OAS member countries	N 15-a	
CEREAL PREPARATIONS by value in $m	W European countries	U 33-a	

APPENDIX 1 – EXPORTS BY PRODUCT

Product / Description	Territorial coverage	Title codes	
CEREALS (incl ceral preparations)			
shipped to EEC & non-EEC areas by value in $	EEC countries	E 24-a	
by value in $	OECD countries	D 1-a	
CEREALS: historical tables from 1750: tonnage	Main European countries	Z 1-a	
shipped to EEC & non-EEC areas: tonnage	EEC countries	E 44-a	
tonnage	Asian & Far East areas	U 32-q	
	E European countries & USSR	U 16-a	
CEREALS BY KIND by destination by CST classes: tonnage & value in $m	EEC countries	E 48-a	
SITC classes by value in $m	Main countries	D 2-q	
tonnage & value in $m	OECD countries	D 3-a2	
by NIMEXE classes: tonnage & value in $m	All countries	E 20-a	
SITC classes: tonnage & value in $m	All countries	U 50-a	U 59-a
value in $m	W European countries	U 33-a	
tonnage (in detail)	World regions	A 11-a	
tonnage	All countries	A 17-a	
CHEESE by destination: tonnage	Main countries	B 4-a	
CHEESE (incl curd) by value in NZ£	New Zealand	U 32-m	
by value in $m	W European countries	U 33-a	
shipped to EEC & non-EEC areas: tonnage	EEC countries	E 44-a	
shipped to EEC area: tonnage	EEC countries	B 3-a	
tonnage (incl world total)	All countries	B 3-a	
tonnage	Main countries (as total)	B 4-a	
CHEMICAL COMPOUNDS by kind by destination: tonnage & value in $m	All countries	U 12-a	
CHEMICAL PRODUCTS			
as % of total export trade (value basis)	World economic areas	D 5-a	
by destination by value in $m	Main countries	U 2-a	
in UA	EEC countries	E 23-a	
tonnage	OECD countries	D 5-a	
% change (value basis)	EEC countries	E 23-a	
by kind (in detail) by value in LIT	Italy	C 6-a	
shipped to EEC & non-EEC areas by value in $m	EEC countries	E 24-a	
tonnage	OECD countries	D 5-a	
by value in local currency	EEC countries	E 38-a	
shipped to non-EEC area by value in UA	EEC countries	E 22-m	
CHEMICAL PRODUCTS - index nos (quantum & value bases)	OECD countries	D 16-q	
CHEMICALS by kind by destination by CST classes: tonnage & value in $m	EEC countries	E 48-a	
SITC classes by value in $m	Main countries	D 2-q	
tonnage & value in $m	OECD countries	D 3-a2	
tonnage & value in $m	All countries	U 12-a	
by NIMEXE classes by value in $m	All countries	E 20-a	
SITC classes by value in $m	All countries	U 50-a	U 59-a
by value in LIT	EEC countries	C 6-a	
	Main countries	C 6-a	
in $m	Asian & Far East areas	U 32-a	
	ECAFE countries	U 32-m	
CHEMICALS (basic) as % of world export trade (value basis)	Communist areas	U 23-a	
	Developed countries (as group)	U 23-a	
	Developing countries (as group)	U 23-a	
CHEMICALS (organic & inorganic) by kind by destination by value in $m	Main countries	U 2-a	
CHICKENS by destination: tonnage	EEC countries	E 47-m	
CHINA CLAY: tonnage	All countries	B 15-a	
CHLORINE by destination: tonnage	Main countries	U 2-a	
tonnage	European countries, Japan & USA	U 25-a	
	OECD countries	D 5-a	
CHOCOLATE (incl chocolate products): tonnage	Main countries	A 3-m	

APPENDIX 1 - EXPORTS BY PRODUCT

Product	Territorial coverage	Title codes
CHROME ORE (incl concentrates)		
tonnage	All countries	B 15-a
total & shipments to EEC area by value in UA	AASM countries	E 41-a
CHROME ORE by destination: tonnage	Main countries	T 4-a
CHROMIUM METAL by destination: tonnage	France & UK	T 4-a
CIGARETTES by destination in lbs	UK	B 17-a
CINNAMON (incl cassia) in cwt	Main countries	B 18-q
CINNAMON BARK QUILLS & QUILLINGS in cwt	Seychelles	B 13-a
CITRUS FRUITS by kind by destination: tonnage	OECD countries	B 6-a
tonnage & value in $m	Main countries	B 2-a
tonnage (in detail)	World regions	A 11-a
	All countries	B 5-a
oranges: historical table from 1850: tonnage	Italy & Spain	Z 1-a
oranges & tangerines by value in $m	W European countries	U 33-a
CLEANING & POLISHING MATERIALS by destination by value in $	Main European countries	U 2-a
CLINKER by destination: tonnage	OECD countries	D 4-a
CLOTH manufactured of cotton & wool mixtures: yds & value in £	Main countries	K 3-a
fibre & wool mixtures: yds & value in £	Main countries	K 3-a
woollen mixtures: yds & value in £	Main countries	K 3-a
worsted yarn: yds & value in £	Main countries	K 3-a
CLOTHING (incl footwear)		
by kind by destination by CST classes: tonnage & value in $	EEC countries	E 48-a
SITC classes by value in $	Main countries	D 2-q
tonnage & value in $	OECD countries	D 3-a2
by NIMEXE classes by value in $	All countries	E 20-a
CLOTHING as % of domestic sales (value basis)	EEC countries	B 22-a
by value in local currency	Hong Kong & S Korea	U 32-m
CLOTHING (incl accessories): tonnage	OECD countries	D 46-a
CLOTHING INDUSTRY PRODUCTS by kind by value in £	UK	B 22-a
CLOTHING manufactured of cellulosic fabrics by value in $	All countries	A 6-a
of non-cellulosic fabrics by value in $	All countries	A 6-a
CLOTHING (ready-made)		
by destination by value in £m	UK	B 29-a
by value in £m	UK	B 29-a
shipped by world regions by value in $m	EEC countries	B 22-a
to EEC & non-EEC areas by value in $m	EEC countries	E 24-a
CLOVES in cwt by destination	Madagascar, Singapore & Tanzania	B 13-a
in cwt	Comoro Is, Madagascar & Tanzania	B 13-a
COAL by destination: tonnage & value in $	EEC countries	E 5-q
historical table from 1827: tonnage	Main European countries	Z 1-a
shipped to non-EEC area by value in $	EEC area	E 29-a
tonnage	Asian & Far East areas	U 32-q
	India & S Korea	U 32-m
COAL (incl agglomerates) shipped to non-EEC area: tonnage	EEC countries	E 14-a
COAL & PATENT FUELS by destination: tonnage	Main world regions	U 10-a
COAL (bituminous) by destination: tonnage	Main countries	N 2-a
COAL BRIQUETTES & LIGNITE: tonnage	Main countries	B 15-a
COAL BY-PRODUCTS by destination by value in $	Main countries	U 2-a
COAL & COKE (incl by-products): tonnage	All countries	B 15-a
COARSE GRAINS by kind: tonnage	Main countries	C 16-a
COATED STEEL SHEETS by destination: tonnage & value in $	EEC area	E 5-q
COBALT by destination: tonnage	Main countries	T 4-a
tonnage	All countries	B 15-a
unit value in $ per ton	Zambia	E 45-a
COBALT & DERIVATIVES: tonnage	All countries	B 15-a
COCA LEAF (for cocaine production) by destination in kg	All countries	U 46-a
COCAINE by destination in kg	All countries	U 46-a
COCAINE, CAFFEINE & QUININE by destination by value in $	Main countries	U 2-a

621

APPENDIX 1 - EXPORTS BY PRODUCT

Product	Description	Territorial coverage	Title codes	
COCOA	as % of total exports (value basis)	Main countries	B 13-a	
	(raw) by destination: tonnage	Cameroon, Ivory Coast & Togo	B 13-a	
		Main countries	B 18-q	
	by value in local currency	Main countries	B 13-a	
	tonnage	Main producing countries	B 13-a	
		Main exporting countries	A 3-m	A 5-a
	unit value in cents per kg	Main countries	A 5-a	
COCOA BEANS	by destination by CST classes: tonnage & value in $	EEC countries	E 48-a	
	SITC classes by value in $	Main countries	D 2-q	
	tonnage & value in $	OECD countries	D 3-a2	
	tonnage	All countries	A 3-m	
	by value in $	Main countries	A 3-a	
	in local currency	Papua New Guinea	U 32-m	
	tonnage	Main countries	A 3-m	
	tonnage (incl world total)	Main countries	B 2-a	
	tonnage: historical table from 1940	Main countries	P 2-a	
	total exports & shipments to EEC area: tonnage & value in UA	AASM countries	E 41-a	
	unit value in $ per kg	Main countries	A 3-m	
		OAS member countries	N 15-a	
	in $ per ton	African, Caribbean countries & Pacific Is	E 45-a	
COCOA BUTTER:	historical table from 1947: tonnage	UK	P 2-a	
	tonnage	Main countries	B 13-a	P 3-a
	unit value in $ per ton	African, Caribbean countries & Pacific Is	E 45-a	
COCOA PASTE & POWDER: tonnage		Main countries	B 18-a	
COCOA PASTE (incl cake): tonnage		Main countries	B 13-a	
COCOA PASTE: tonnage		Main countries	A 3-m	
COCOA POWDER: tonnage		Main countries	A 3-m	B 13-a
			P 3-a	
COCOA PRODUCTS: by value in $m		Main countries	A 3-a	
COCONUT OIL	(incl copra): tonnage	Main countries	A 4-a	
	by destination: tonnage	Sri Lanka & Singapore	B 19-a	
	by value in local currency	Fiji, Papua New Guinea & Sri Lanka	U 32-m	
	shipped to European area & USA: tonnage	Philippines	B 19-a	
	tonnage & value in $m	Main countries	B 2-a	
	tonnage	Main exporting countries	B 19-a	
		Main producing countries	B 18-q	
		W Malaysia	U 32-m	
COCONUTS	by value in $m	Philippines	U 32-m	
	unit value in $ per ton	Tanzania	E 45-a	
CODEINE	by destination in kg	All countries	U 46-a	
COFFEE	as % of total export trade (value basis)	Main countries	B 13-a	
	of world coffee exports	Main countries	J 1-a	
	by destination by CST classes: tonnage & value in $	EEC countries	E 48-a	
	SITC classes by value in $	Main countries	D 2-q	
	tonnage & value in $	OECD countries	D 3-a2	
	in bags	Main countries	B 18-q	B 13-a
			J 1-a	
	by kind (incl world total) in bags	All countries	J 1-a	
	by NIMEXE classes: tonnage & value in $	All countries	E 20-a	
	SITC classes: tonnage & value in $	All countries	U 50-a	U 59-a
	value in local currency	Main countries	B 13-a	
	in $	Indonesia	U 32-m	
	shipments under International Coffee Agreement: tonnage	Member countries of ICA	B 18-a	
	tonnage (incl world total)	Main countries	B 2-a	
	tonnage	Asian & Far East areas	U 32-q	
		India, Indonesia, Laos & Papua New Guinea	U 32-m	
	unit value in $ per kg	OAS member countries	N 15-a	
	in $ per ton	African, Caribbean countries & Pacific Is	E 45-a	

● APPENDIX 1 - EXPORTS BY PRODUCT

Product	Territorial coverage	Title codes	
COFFEE BEANS by value in $	Papua New Guinea & Singapore	U 32-m	
(roasted) by destination: tonnage	Main countries	B 13-a	
in bags	Main countries	B 13-a	
total shipments to EEC area: tonnage & value in UA	AASM countries	E 41-a	
COIR FIBRE & MANUFACTURES: tonnage	Main countries	B 10-a	
COIR MANUFACTURES: floor rugs shipped to UK & USSR: tonnage	India	B 10-a	
COIR YARN by destination: tonnage	India	B 10-a	
COKE by destination: tonnage & value in $	EEC countries	E 5-q	
tonnage	Main countries	U 10-a	
shipped to non-EEC area: tonnage	EEC countries	E 14-a	
tonnage	ECE countries, Japan & USA	U 7-m	U 6-a
	Main countries	H 3-a	
COKE-OVEN COKE: tonnage	European countries	U 31-q	
shipped to non-EEC area in coal equiv tonnage	EEC countries	E 14-a	
COLD-ROLLED STEEL SHEETS by destination: tonnage	Main countries	T 4-a	
STRIP by destination: tonnage	Main countries	T 4-a	
tonnage & value in $	EEC countries	E 5-q	
COMMERCIAL VEHICLE CHASSIS by volume	Main countries	V 4-a	
COMMERCIAL VEHICLES			
& buses by value in $m	Main European countries	U 38-a	
by destination by volume	All countries	V 1-a	
	USSR	V 1-a	
by NIMEXE classes by value in $	All countries	E 20-a	
SITC classes by value in $	All countries	U 50-a	U 59-a
by type by destination by volume	UK	V 1-a	
by value: historical table in £m	UK	V 1-a	
by value in £m	UK	B 28-a	
by volume & value by destination	UK	V 1-a	
	Canada & Japan	V 1-a	
	W European countries	V 1-a	
by volume	All countries	S 24-a	
shipped to USA by volume	Main countries	V 4-a	
tonnage, volume & value by destination in £m	UK	V 1-a	
COMMERCIAL VEHICLES (complete) by volume	Main countries	V 4-a	
	All countries	V 1-a	
(chassis only) by value in £m	UK	B 28-a	
COMPLEX PHOSPHATE FERTILISERS: tonnage	OECD countries	D 5-a	
COMPUTERS (& ancillary equipment) by value in £m	UK	B 24-a	
CONDENSATION PRODUCTS (plastics): tonnage	European countries, Japan & USA	U 26-a	
CONDENSED & EVAPORATED MILK: tonnage	EEC countries	E 44-a	
	Main countries	B 4-a	
CONDENSED MILK			
by destination: tonnage	France & UK	B 12-m	
	Main countries	B 12-m	B 4-a
tonnage	EEC countries	B 3-a	
	Main countries	B 4-a	
(unsweetened) by destination: tonnage	EEC countries	B 3-a	
CONDENSERS by value in $m	Main countries	U 38-a	
CONIFEROUS TIMBER LOGS by destination	European countries, USA & USSR	A 13-q	
CONSTRUCTION & MINING EQUIPMENT by value in $m	Main countries	U 38-a	
CONSTRUCTION BOARD: tonnage	OECD countries	D 41-q	
CONSTRUCTION MATERIALS - index nos (volume & value basis)	OECD countries	D 16-q	
CONSUMER GOODS as % of total exports (value basis)	E European countries	U 16-a	
COPPER by value in $m	Main countries	B 2-a	
unit value in $ per ton	Uganda, Zaire & Zambia	E 45-a	
(unwrought) incl semi-manufactures: tonnage	All countries	B 15-a	

APPENDIX 1 – EXPORTS BY PRODUCT

	Territorial coverage	Title codes	
COPPER ALLOY PRODUCTS by destination: bars & sections: tonnage	Main countries	T 4-a	
pipes & tubing: tonnage	Main countries	T 4-a	
plates & sheets: tonnage	Main countries	T 4-a	
wire & cables: tonnage	Main countries	T 4-a	
COPPER ALLOYS by destination: tonnage	Main countries	T 4-a	
COPPER BARS by destination: tonnage	USA	J 6-a	
COPPER BLISTER by destination: tonnage	Main countries	T 4-a	
(refined) by destination: tonnage	OECD countries	D 21-q	
tonnage	All countries	C 30-m	
	Main countries	C 12-a	
total & shipments to EEC area: tonnage & value in UA	AASM countries	E 41-a	
COPPER CONCENTRATES by value in $m	Philippines	U 32-m	
tonnage	Asian & Far East areas	U 32-q	
	Philippines	U 32-m	
COPPER (electrolytic) incl fire-refined copper: tonnage	UK	J 6-a	
tonnage	All countries	B 15-a	
COPPER FOIL by destination: tonnage	Japan	T 4-a	
COPPER ORE (based on metal content): tonnage	USA	J 6-a	
(incl concentrates) by destination: tonnage	OECD countries	D 21-q	
	Main European countries	T 4-a	
	All countries	C 30-m	B 15-a
unit value (incl residues) in $ per ton	Zambia	E 45-a	
COPPER PLATES & SHEETS by destination: tonnage	Main countries	T 4-a	
	USA	J 6-a	
COPPER POWDER by destination: tonnage	Japan	T 4-a	
COPPER PRODUCTS (semi-finished) by kind: tonnage	Main countries	T 4-a	
	UK	J 6-a	
COPPER (refined & alloyed): tonnage	All countries	B 15-a	
COPPER (refined) by destination: tonnage	USA	J 6-a	
	Main countries	T 4-a	
in ingot or bar form: tonnage	USA	J 6-a	
tonnage	All countries	C 30-m	
COPPER RODS, BARS & SECTIONS by destination: tonnage	Main countries	T 4-a	
COPPER SCRAP by destination: tonnage	Main countries	T 4-a	
	USA	J 6-a	
tonnage	All countries	B 15-a	
COPPER STRIP (in coil) by destination: tonnage	W Germany & Italy	T 4-a	
COPPER SULPHATE: tonnage	All countries	B 15-a	
COPPER TUBES & PIPES by destination: tonnage	USA	J 6-a	
	Main countries	T 4-a	
COPPER WIRE by destination: tonnage	Main countries	T 4-a	
(excl insulated) by destination: tonnage	USA	J 6-a	
COPPER WIRE BARS by destination: tonnage	Belgium, Japan & UK	T 4-a	
COPRA by destination: tonnage	Papua New Guinea	B 19-a	
by value in $ per ton	Malaysia, Papua New Guinea, Tonga & W Samoa	U 32-m	
shipped to European area & USA: tonnage	Philippines	B 19-a	
tonnage & value in $m	Main countries	B 2-a	
tonnage	Cook Is, Fiji, Indonesia & Solomon Is	U 32-m	
	Main countries	E 18-q	B 19-a
total shipments to EEC area: tonnage & value in UA	AASM countries	E 41-a	
unit value in $ per ton	Tonga & W Samoa	E 45-a	
COPRA CAKE & MEAL: tonnage & value in $m	Main countries	B 2-a	
tonnage	Main countries	A 4-a	
CORDAGE & ROPES MADE OF COIR FIBRE: tonnage	India	B 10-a	
CORK: historical table from 1873: tonnage	Portugal	Z 1-a	
CORN OIL: tonnage	Belgium, France & Netherlands	B 19-a	
CORROSION-RESISTANT ALLOY STEEL by destination: tonnage	EEC countries	E 29-a	
COSMETICS (incl dentifrice) by destination by value in $	Main countries	U 2-a	

APPENDIX 1 - EXPORTS BY PRODUCT

		Territorial coverage	Title codes	
COTTON (raw)	by destination in bales	USA	P 1-a	
	tonnage	Main countries	K 1-m	
		Commonwealth countries	B 10-a	
	by value in $m	W European countries	U 33-a	
	export earnings in $m	Main countries	A 5-a	
	in bales & tonnage	All countries	K 1-a	
	in lbs million	Main countries	B 10-a	
	tonnage & value in $m	Main countries	B 2-a	
	total & shipments to EEC area: tonnage & value in UA	AASM countries	E 41-a	
	unit value in $ per ton	African, Caribbean countries & Pacific Is	E 45-a	
COTTON SEWING THREAD by value in Rs		Pakistan	U 32-m	
COTTON YARN (incl fabrics) by value in Rs		India	U 32-m	
	tonnage	Hong Kong & Japan	U 32-m	
		OECD countries	D 46-a	
COTTONSEED	by destination: tonnage	Nicaragua, Nigeria & Sudan	B 19-a	
	tonnage & value in $m	Main countries	B 2-a	
	tonnage	Main countries	B 18-q	B 19-a
COTTONSEED CAKE & MEAL: tonnage & value in $m		Main countries	B 2-a	
COTTONSEED OIL: tonnage & value in $m		Main countries	B 2-a	
	tonnage	Main exporting countries	B 19-a	
		Main producing countries	B 18-q	
CRUDE OIL (incl fuel oils) by destination by value in £m		World regions	C 21-a	
CRUDE OILS & FATS by value in $m		Asian & Far East countries	U 32-a	
CRUDE PETROLEUM (incl petroleum products) by destination: tonnage		World regions	C 13-a	
		E European countries & USSR	U 16-a	
	by destination: tonnage	OECD countries	D 31-a	
	tonnage & value in $	All countries	U 12-a	
	in barrels	All countries	U 18-a	
	in barrels per day	OPEC countries	C 3-a	
	in m³	Latin American countries	U 18-a	
	tonnage	Asian & Far East areas	U 32-q	
		Iran	U 32-m	
		OECD countries	D 39-q	
		World regions	T 3-a	
	total & exports to EEC area: tonnage & value in UA	AASM countries	E 41-a	
	unit value in $	OAS member countries	N 15-a	
CRUDE STEEL	by destination: tonnage	Main countries	T 4-a	
		EEC countries	E 29-a	
	tonnage & value in $	EEC area	E 5-q	
CRUDE STEEL INGOTS & CASTINGS: tonnage		All countries	B 15-a	
CULTIVATING IMPLEMENTS by value in $m		Main countries	U 38-a	
CURED FISH PRODUCTS: tonnage & value in $m		OECD countries	D 43-a	
CURRANTS: historical table from 1858: tonnage		Greece	Z 1-a	
CURRENT ACCOUNT: goods, services & transfers in $m		ECE countries	U 15-a	
CURRY POWDER by destination in lbs		India & Singapore	B 13-a	
CYCLES & MOPEDS				
	by destination by CST classes: tonnage & value in $	EEC countries	E 48-a	
	SITC classes by value in $	Main countries	D 2-q	
	tonnage & value in $	OECD countries	D 3-a2	
	by NIMEXE classes by value in $	All countries	E 20-a	
	SITC classes by value in $	All countries	U 50-a	U 59-a
DAIRY EQUIPMENT by value in $m		Main countries	U 38-a	
DAIRY PRODUCTS by destination by CST classes: tonnage & value in $		EEC countries	E 48-a	
	SITC classes by value in $	Main countries	D 2-q	
	tonnage & value in $	OECD countries	D 3-a2	
	by value in local currency	Australia & New Zealand	B 4-a	

APPENDIX 1 – EXPORTS BY PRODUCT

	Territorial coverage	Title codes	
DAIRY PRODUCTS, continued			
by kind by NIMEXE classes: tonnage & value in $	All countries	E 20-a	
SITC classes: tonnage & value in $	All countries	U 50-a	U 59-a
tonnage	World regions	A 11-a	
by value in £m	Main countries	B 4-a	
tonnage	Australia & New Zealand	U 32-m	
DAIRY PRODUCTS (incl eggs) by value in $m	OECD countries	D 1-a	
shipped to EEC & non-EEC areas by value in $m	EEC countries	E 24-a	
DATES: tonnage & value in $m	Main countries	U 11-a	
DESSICATED COCONUT by value in local currency	Tonga	U 32-m	
DIAMONDS (gems & industrial stones) in carats & value	All countries	B 15-a	
total exports & to EEC area: carats & value in UA	AASM countries	E 41-a	
DIATOMACEOUS EARTH: tonnage	All countries	B 15-a	
DIESEL OIL by destination: tonnage	OECD countries	D 31-a	
tonnage	Main countries	B 15-a	
DIRECTION OF EXPORTS:			
ex developed shipped to developed countries – index nos		M 4-a	
to developing countries – index nos		M 4-a	
ex developing shipped to developed countries – index nos		M 4-a	
to developing countries – index nos		M 4-a	
DOMESTIC EQUIPMENT			
by kind by destination by CST classes by value in $m	EEC countries	E 48-a	
SITC classes by value in $m	Main countries	D 2-q	
tonnage & value in $m	OECD countries	D 3-a2	
by NIMEXE classes by volume	All countries	E 20-a	
SITC classes by volume	All countries	U 50-a	U 59-a
(electrical) by kind by destination by value in $m	All countries	U 12-a	
by value in $m	Main countries	U 38-a	
(electronic) by value in £m	UK	B 24-a	
(non-electrical) by value in $m	Main countries	U 38-a	
DRAWN WIRE by destination: tonnage & value in $	EEC countries	E 5-q	
tonnage	ECE countries	U 48-a	
	EEC countries	E 29-a	
DRIED FRUIT by kind: tonnage	All countries	B 5-a	
by destination: tonnage	OECD countries	B 6-a	
tonnage	Main countries	A 5-a	
DRILLING MACHINES: volume & value in $m	USA	J 2-a	
DRILLING MACHINES (for metal working) by destination by value in £	UK	B 31-a	
DRUGS & MEDICINES by kind by destination in kg	All countries	U 46-a	
DUMPERS & DUMP TRUCKS by destination: volume & value in £	UK	V 1-a	
DURABLE CONSUMER GOODS – index nos (quantum & value bases)	OECD countries	D 16-q	
DYEING EXTRACTS (synthetic) by destination by value in $	Main countries	U 2-a	
DYESTUFFS by destination: tonnage & value in $m	OECD countries	D 5-a	
DYESTUFFS (synthetic) by destination by value in $	Main countries	U 2-a	
DYNAMO STEEL SHEETS by destination: tonnage & value in $	EEC countries	E 5-q	
EDIBLE OFFAL by destination: tonnage	Main countries	B 12-m	
EDIBLE OFFAL (fresh, frozen & chilled): tonnage	Main countries	B 11-a	
EGG PRODUCTS by destination: tonnage	Main countries	B 12-m	
tonnage	Main countries	B 4-a	
EGGS (IN SHELL) by destination by volume	EEC countries	E 47-m	
	Belgium, Denmark, Netherlands & Poland	B 4-a	
	Main countries	B 12-m	
tonnage	EEC countries	E 47-m	
by value in $m	W European countries	U 33-a	
by volume: historical table from 1861	Denmark	Z 1-a	
in million dozen	Main countries	B 4-a	
tonnage	EEC countries	E 44-a	

APPENDIX 1 - EXPORTS BY PRODUCT

	Territorial coverage	Title codes	
ELECTRIC ENERGY by destination in kWh	European countries	U 1-a	
in kWh	All countries	C 23-a	
to EEC & non-EEC areas by value in $	EEC countries	E 24-a	
ELECTRIC FURNACES by value in $m	Main countries	U 38-a	
ELECTRIC LAMPS by value in $m	Main countries	U 38-a	
ELECTRIC POWER TRANSMISSION EQUIPMENT by value in $	Main countries	U 38-a	
ELECTRICAL APPARATUS			
by kind by destination by CST classes: tonnage & value in $m	EEC countries	E 48-a	
SITC classes by value in $m	Main countries	D 2-q	
tonnage & value in $m	OECD countries	D 3-a2	
by NIMEXE classes by value in $m	All countries	E 20-a	
SITC classes by value in $m	All countries	U 50-a	U 59-a
ELECTRICAL POWER MACHINERY by value in $m	Main countries	U 38-a	
ELECTRICITY BY LOCAL REGIONS OF ORIGIN by value in $	EEC countries	E 38-a	
ELECTRICITY in kWh	ECE countries	U 15-a	
to non-EEC area in coal equiv tonnage	EEC countries	E 14-a	
ELECTRO-MAGNETIC APPLIANCES by value in $m	Main countries	U 38-a	
ELECTRON & PROTON ACCELERATORS by value in $m	Main countries	U 38-a	
ELECTRONIC COMMUNICATIONS EQUIPMENT by value in £m	UK	B 24-a	
ELECTRONIC COMPONENTS by kind by value in £m	UK	B 24-a	
by value in £m	UK	B 24-a	
ELECTRONIC CONTROL INSTRUMENTATION by value in £m	UK	B 24-a	
ELECTRONIC EQUIPMENT by kind by value in £m	UK	B 24-a	
by value as % of total exports	UK	B 24-a	
in £m	UK	B 24-a	
ELECTRONIC VALVES & TUBES by value in $m	Main countries	U 38-a	
ENGINEERING PRODUCTS			
as % of world total exports (value basis)	All countries	U 38-a	
by value in $m	Main countries	U 38-a	
	All countries	U 38-a	
(in detail) by value in $	OECD countries	D 9-a	
inter-regional trade by value in $m	World regions	U 38-a	
ENGINES by kind by destination by CST classes by value in $m	EEC countries	E 48-a	
SITC classes by value in $m	Main countries	D 2-q	
tonnage & value in $m	OECD countries	D 3-a2	
tonnage & value in $m	All countries	U 12-a	
by NIMEXE classes: volume & value in $m	All countries	E 20-a	
SITC classes: volume & value in $m	All countries	U 50-a	U 59-a
ENGINES (industrial) by destination by value in £m	UK	V 1-a	
ENGINES (internal combustion): volume & value in £m	UK	V 1-a	
EPOXY DERIVATIVES by destination: tonnage	Main countries	U 2-a	
EPOXYESTERS by destination: tonnage	Main countries	U 2-a	
ESSENTIAL OILS by destination by value in $	Main countries	U 2-a	
ESTATE CARS & STATION WAGONS by destination: volume & value in £m	UK	V 1-a	
ESTERS (incl derivatives) by destination by value in $	Main countries	U 2-a	
ETHYL ALCOHOL by destination by value in $	Main countries	U 2-a	
tonnage	European countries, Japan & USA	U 26-a	
ETHYLENE OXIDE: tonnage	European countries	U 26-a	
ETHYLMORPHINE (dionine) by destination in kg	All countries	U 46-a	
EXPLOSIVES (incl pyrotechnic products) by destination by value in $	Main countries	U 2-a	
shipped to EEC & non-EEC areas by value in $m	EEC countries	E 24-a	
FABRICATED MATERIALS - index nos (quantum & value bases)	OECD countries	D 16-q	
FABRICATED PRODUCTS - index nos (quantum & value bases)	OECD countries	D 16-q	
FARM MACHINERY by kind by destination: tonnage & value in $	All countries	U 12-a	
FARM PRODUCTS by value in $ shipped to E Europe & USSR	EEC area	U 33-a	

APPENDIX 1 - EXPORTS BY PRODUCT

	Territorial coverage	Title codes	
FARM TRACTORS by destination areas as % of total exports	UK	B 28-a	
by destination: tonnage & value in $	All countries	U 12-a	
FATS & OILS: animal & fish oils: tonnage	EEC countries	E 44-a	
by kind by destination by CST classes by value in $	EEC countries	E 48-a	
SITC classes by value in $	Main countries	D 2-q	
tonnage & value in $	OECD countries	D 3-a2	
by NIMEXE classes: tonnage & value in $	All countries	E 20-a	
SITC classes: tonnage & value in $	All countries	U 50-a	U 59-a
FATS, OILS & OILSEEDS by value in $	OECD countries	D 1-a	
FEEDING STUFFS BY KIND			
by destination by CST classes by value in $	EEC countries	E 48-a	
SITC classes by value in $	Main countries	D 2-q	
tonnage & value in $	OECD countries	D 3-a2	
by NIMEXE classes: tonnage & value in $	All countries	E 20-a	
SITC classes: tonnage & value in $	All countries	U 50-a	U 59-a
FEEDSTOCKS (for oil refineries) by destination: tonnage	OECD countries	D 31-a	
FELDSPAR: tonnage	All countries	B 15-a	
FERRO-ALLOYS by destination: tonnage & value in $	EEC area	E 5-q	
by kind: tonnage	All countries	B 15-a	
tonnage	Belgium, Italy, Japan, Sweden & USA	T 2-m	
	E Germany & USSR	T 1-a	
FERRO-ALLOYS, FERROMANGANESE & SPIEGELEISEN: tonnage	ECE countries	U 7-m	U 6-a
	Main countries	H 3-a	
FERRO-CERIUM (incl pyrophoric alloys): tonnage	USA	N 1-a	
FERRO-CHROMIUM by destination: tonnage	France	T 4-a	
FERRO-COLUMBIUM: tonnage	UK	T 4-a	
FERRO-MANGANESE by destination: tonnage & value in $	EEC area	E 5-q	
	All countries	U 12-a	
	EEC countries	E 29-a	
tonnage	Main countries	T 4-a	
FERRO-MOLYBDENUM: tonnage	France, W Germany & UK	T 4-a	
FERRO-NICKEL by destination: tonnage	France & UK	T 4-a	
tonnage	W Germany	T 4-a	
FERRO-SILICON by destination: tonnage	Main countries	T 4-a	
FERRO-TITANIUM: tonnage	France & UK	T 4-a	
FERRO-TUNGSTEN: tonnage	France & UK	T 4-a	
FERRO-VANADIUM: tonnage	All countries	B 15-a	
	France & UK	T 4-a	
FERROUS SCRAP by destination: tonnage	Main countries	T 4-a	
tonnage & value in $	EEC area	E 5-q	
by kind (sorted & unsorted): tonnage	EEC countries	E 30-m	
shipped to non-EEC area by value in $	EEC countries	E 29-a	
tonnage	All countries	B 15-a	
	Australia, Canada, France, W Germany & USA	T 2-m	
	ECE countries, Japan & USA	U 7-m	U 6-a
	EEC countries	E 30-m	
	EEC area & world regions	E 29-a	
	Main countries	H 3-a	
FERTILISERS BY KIND			
by destination by CST classes: tonnage	EEC countries	E 48-a	
SITC classes by value in $	Main countries	D 2-q	
tonnage & value in $	OECD countries	D 3-a2	
by value in $	Main countries	U 2-a	
by NIMEXE classes: tonnage & value in $	All countries	E 20-a	
SITC classes: tonnage & value in $	All countries	U 50-a	U 59-a
(in detail): tonnage	All countries	A 2-a	

APPENDIX 1 - EXPORTS BY PRODUCT

Product	Territorial coverage	Title codes	
FERTILISERS (manufactured) shipped to EEC & non-EEC areas: tonnage	EEC countries	E 24-a	
(nitrogenous) by destination: tonnage	Main countries	U 2-a	
(phosphate) by destination: tonnage	Main countries	U 2-a	
(potash) by destination: tonnage	Main countries	U 2-a	
(synthetic) by destination by value in $	Main countries	U 2-a	
unit value in $ per ton	Trinidad	E 45-a	
FIBREBOARD: tonnage	Main countries	A 25-a2	
FIBRES BY KIND (in detail): tonnage	World regions	A 11-a	
FIBRES (discontinuous): tonnage	All countries	A 6-a	
(hard) by kind by value in $	Main countries	A 5-a	
FIBROUS NON-WOOD PULP by destination: tonnage	All countries	D 40-a	
FILAMENT FIBRES (cellulosic): tonnage	All countries	A 6-a	
(non-cellulosic): tonnage	All countries	A 6-a	
FINISHED MANUFACTURED GOODS - index nos (quantum & value bases)	OECD countries	D 16-q	
FISH by value in $m	OECD countries	D 43-a	
historical table from 1830: tonnage	Norway	Z 1-a	
tonnage	EEC countries	E 44-a	
(crustaceans & molluscs): tonnage	OECD countries	D 43-a	
(dried): unit value in $ per ton	African, Caribbean countries & Pacific Is	E 45-a	
(fresh): tonnage	Asian, Far East & Australasian countries	U 32-m	
(fresh & canned): tonnage & value in $	OECD countries	D 43-a	
(fresh & preserved): tonnage	Asian & Far East countries	U 32-q	
(incl fish preparations) by value in $	ECAFE area	U 32-m	
(processed) by value in $	British Solomon Is & Japan	U 32-m	
(salted, dried & smoked): tonnage	OECD countries	D 43-a	
FISH & FISH PRODUCTS by kind by value in $	World regions	A 11-a	
by value in $	OECD countries	D 1-a	
shipped to EEC & non-EEC areas by value in $	EEC countries	E 24-a	
tonnage & value in $	All countries	A 5-a	
	OECD countries	D 43-a	
FISH & MEAT MEAL by value in $m	W European countries	U 33-a	
FISH BODY OILS: tonnage	Main countries	B 19-a	
FISH MEAL: tonnage & value in $m & in local currency	OECD countries	D 43-a	
tonnage	Main countries	P 5-a	
FISH OILS & FATS by kind by destination by CST classes by value in $	EEC countries	E 48-a	
SITC classes by value in $	Main countries	D 2-q	
tonnage & value in $	OECD countries	D 3-a2	
by NIMEXE classes: tonnage & value in $	All countries	E 20-a	
SITC classes: tonnage & value in $	All countries	U 50-a	U 59-a
tonnage & value in $	OECD countries	D 43-a	
	Main countries	P 1-a	
FLAX FIBRE by destination: tonnage	Benelux countries, France & USSR	B 10-a	
tonnage	Main countries	B 10-a	
FLUORSPAR: tonnage	All countries	B 15-a	
FLUTING PAPER by destination: tonnage	All countries	D 40-a	
FOOD as % of total exports (value basis)	E European countries	U 16-a	
(by product groups) by value in $m	W European countries	U 33-a	
by value by world destination areas by value in $m	W European countries	U 20-a	
(main foodstuffs) in $bn	Developing countries	U 11-a	
- index nos	World regions	A 11-a	
FOOD (incl live animal products) by destination: tonnage & value in $	All countries	U 12-a	
FOOD & BEVERAGES as % of world total (value basis)	Communist countries	U 23-a	
	Developed countries (as group)	U 23-a	
	Developing countries (as group)	U 23-a	
FOOD, BEVERAGES & TOBACCO by value in $	Asian & Far East countries	U 32-a	
FOOD BY KIND shipped to EEC & non-EEC areas by value in $m	EEC countries	E 24-a	

● APPENDIX 1 – EXPORTS BY PRODUCT

	Territorial coverage	Title codes
FOOD, DRINK & TOBACCO		
by value in $m	Main countries	E 24-a
shipped to non-EEC area by value in UA	EEC countries	E 22-m
% change by destination	EEC countries	E 23-a
by destination by value in UA	EEC countries	E 23-a
by regions of origin by value in $	EEC countries	E 38-a
farm raw materials by value in $	ECE countries	U 15-a
– index nos (quantum & value bases)	OECD countries	D 16-q
FOOD PROCESSING MACHINERY by value in $m	Main countries	U 38-a
FOOD PRODUCTS as % of total trade in farm products (value basis)	W European countries	U 20-a
by value in $m	ECAFE countries	U 32-m
FOODBOARD by destination: tonnage	All countries	D 40-a
FOOTWEAR (MADE OF LEATHER)		
by destination by value in $	OECD countries	D 18-a
in pairs	OECD countries	D 18-a
shipped to non-OECD area in pairs	OECD countries	D 18-a
(MADE OF PLASTIC MATERIALS)		
by destination by value in $	OECD countries	D 18-a
in pairs	OECD countries	D 18-a
shipped to non-OECD area in pairs	OECD countries	D 18-a
(MADE OF RUBBER)		
by destination by value in $	OECD countries	D 18-a
in pairs	OECD countries	D 18-a
shipped to non-OECD area in pairs	OECD countries	D 18-a
(MADE OF TEXTILE MATERIALS)		
by destination by value in $	OECD countries	D 18-a
in pairs	OECD countries	D 18-a
shipped to non-OECD area in pairs	OECD countries	D 18-a
shipped to EEC & non-EEC areas by value in $m	EEC countries	E 24-a
FORESTRY PRODUCTS BY KIND: tonnage	World regions	A 11-a
FORGINGS & PRESSINGS by destination: tonnage & value in $	EEC countries	E 5-q
tonnage	EEC countries	E 29-a
FORK LIFT TRUCKS: no & value by destination	UK	V 1-a
FORMALDEHYDE: tonnage	European countries, Japan & USA	U 26-a
FOUNDRY PIG IRON by destination: tonnage	EEC countries	E 29-a
	OECD countries	D 22-a
tonnage & value in $	EEC countries	E 5-q
FOUNDRY SCRAP shipped to non-EEC area: tonnage	EEC countries	E 29-a
FRUIT & VEGETABLE JUICES: tonnage & value in $	W European countries	U 20-a
FRUIT & VEGETABLES by value in $	OECD countries	D 1-a
	W European countries	U 33-a
shipped to EEC & non-EEC area by value in $	EEC countries	E 24-a
FRUIT (dried) by value in $m	W European countries	U 33-a
tonnage & value in $	W European area	U 20-a
FRUIT (fresh) by destination: tonnage	Bulgaria	U 20-a
	OECD countries	B 6-a
by kind by destination by CST classes: tonnage	EEC countries	E 48-a
SITC classes by value in $	Main countries	D 2-q
tonnage & value in $	OECD countries	D 3-a2
by NIMEXE classes: tonnage & value in $	All countries	E 20-a
SITC classes: tonnage & value in $	All countries	U 50-a U 59-a
tonnage & value in $	W European countries	U 20-a
tonnage	All countries	B 5-a
	Main E European countries	U 20-a
	ECAFE countries	U 32-m
unit value in $ per ton	W European countries	U 20-a
by value in $	ECAFE countries	U 32-m
unit value in $ per ton	Main European countries	U 20-a
FRUIT (fresh, dried & preserved): tonnage	Asian & Far East countries	U 32-q

APPENDIX 1 - EXPORTS BY PRODUCT

Product	Territorial coverage	Title codes
FRUIT (frozen) by destination: tonnage	OECD countries	B 6-a
tonnage	All countries	B 5-a
unit value in $ per ton	Mauritania	E 45-a
FRUIT JUICES by kind by destination: tonnage	OECD countries	B 6-a
by volume	Main countries	B 5-a
(canned) by value in local currency	Cook Is	U 32-m
tonnage	Brazil, Israel, Italy & USA	A 5-a
FRUIT PREPARATIONS by kind by destination: tonnage	OECD countries	B 6-a
tonnage & value in $	W European countries	U 20-a
FRUIT (preserved) by value in $m	W European countries	U 33-a
FUEL OILS by destination: tonnage	OECD countries	D 31-a
tonnage	Main countries	B 15-a
FUELS (incl lubricants) by value in $ & as % of total exports	ECE countries	U 15-a
FUELS as % of world export trade (value basis)	Communist countries	U 23-a
	Developed countries (as group)	U 23-a
	Developing countries (as group)	U 23-a
by destination by value in UA	EEC countries	E 23-a
by kind shipped to EEC & non-EEC areas by value in $	EEC countries	E 24-a
by value in $m	Main countries	E 24-a
% change by destination (value basis)	EEC countries	E 23-a
FUELS (liquid) in coal equiv tonnage	EEC area	E 7-a
FUELS shipped to non-EEC area by value in UA	EEC countries	E 22-m
FUELWOOD by volume in m³	Canada, Egypt, European countries, USA & USSR	A 13-q
FULLER'S EARTH: tonnage	Morocco, Iran & USA	B 15-a
FURNITURE by destination by CST classes: tonnage & value in $	EEC countries	E 48-a
SITC classes by value in $	Main countries	D 2-q
tonnage & value in $	OECD countries	D 2-a2
by value in £	W European countries	C 8-a
shipped to EEC area by value in £	W European countries	C 8-a
EFTA area by value in £	W European countries	C 8-a
Third markets by value in £	W European countries	C 8-a
FURNITURE (incl timber products) by NIMEXE classes by value in $	All countries	E 20-a
SITC classes by value in $	All countries	U 50-a U 59-a
GALVANISED SHEETS by destination: tonnage & value in $	EEC countries	E 5-q
tonnage	EEC countries	E 29-a
(plain & corrugated) by destination: tonnage	Main countries	T 4-a
tonnage	Hong Kong	T 1-a
GALVANISED STEEL SCRAP shipped to non-EEC area: tonnage	EEC countries	E 29-a
GAS TURBINES by value in $m	Main countries	U 38-a
GASEOUS FUELS in coal equiv tonnage	ECE countries	U 15-a
GEAR PRODUCTION MACHINES: volume & value in $m	USA	J 2-a
GENERATORS (hydroelectric) in MW	Japan, USA & W European countries	T 7-a
GENERATORS (incl pumps) by kind by destination by CST classes by value in $	EEC countries	E 48-a
SITC classes by value in $	Main countries	D 2-q
tonnage & value in $	OECD countries	D 3-a2
GERMANIUM (unwrought & refined) by destination in kg	Italy	C 12-a
GINGER (dried) by destination: tonnage	India, Nigeria, & Sierra Leone	B 13-a
GLASS (incl glassware products) by kind by destination by CST classes by value in $	EEC countries	E 48-a
SITC classes by value in $	Main countries	D 2-q
tonnage & value in $	OECD countries	D 3-a2
by NIMEXE classes by value in $	All countries	E 20-a
SITC classes by value in $	All countries	U 50-a U 59-a
GLASS-WORKING MACHINERY by value in $m	Main countries	U 38-a

APPENDIX 1 - EXPORTS BY PRODUCT

	Territorial coverage	Title codes	
GLUES & GUMS by destination by value in $	Main countries	U 2-a	
GLYCERINE by destination by value in $	Main countries	U 2-a	
GOATSKINS & KIDSKINS (salted & pickled): tonnage (dry weight)	Main countries	B 9-m	A 18-a
GOATSKINS by destination: tonnage & value in $	OECD countries	D 18-a	
tonnage	European OECD countries	D 18-a	
unit value in $ per ton	Ethiopia	E 45-a	
GOLD (refined) by destination in troy oz	Main countries	T 4-a	
GOLD BULLION COIN (rolled) in troy oz	All countries	B 15-a	
GOLD ORE, BULLION & GOLD COINAGE by value in $	USA	J 6-a	
GOODS VEHICLES			
by volume	All countries	S 24-a	
no (3-7 tons) by destination & value in £m	UK	V 1-a	
(7-10 tons) by destination & value in £m	UK	V 1-a	
(over 10 tons) by destination & value in £m	UK	V 1-a	
(up to 3 tons) by destination & value in £m	UK	V 1-a	
GRAINS BY KIND: tonnage	All countries	A 17-a	
GRAPEFRUIT JUICE: tonnage	All countries	A 7-a	
GRAPES (ALL KINDS) by destination: tonnage	Main countries	B 5-a	
GRAPES (fresh for table) by value in $m	W European countries	U 33-a	
unit value in $ per ton	W European countries	U 20-a	
GRAPES: tonnage	All countries	B 5-a	
GRAPHITE: tonnage	All countries	B 15-a	
GREASE-PROOF PAPER & GLASSINE by destination: tonnage	All countries	D 40-a	
GRINDING MACHINES: volume & value in $m	USA	J 2-a	
GROUNDNUT OIL by destination: tonnage	Argentine, Gambia, Nigeria & Senegal	B 19-a	
shipments & to EEC area: tonnage & value in UA	AASM countries	E 41-a	
tonnage & value in $m	Main countries	B 2-a	
tonnage	Main countries	B 18-q	B 19-a
		P 1-a	
unit value in $ per ton	Mali	E 45-a	
GROUNDNUTS by destination: tonnage	Gambia, Nigeria, Senegal & Sudan	B 19-a	
shipments & to EEC area: tonnage & value in UA	AASM countries	E 41-a	
tonnage & value in $m	Main countries	B 2-a	
tonnage	Main countries	B 18-q	B 19-a
	Thailand	U 32-m	
unit value in $ per ton	African, Caribbean countries & Pacific Is	E 45-a	
GROUNDNUTS (incl groundnut oil by value in £m	Gambia & Nigeria	B 19-a	
in FrCFA	Niger & Senegal	B 19-a	
GYPSUM (crude calcined): tonnage	All countries	B 15-a	
HALOGEN SALTS & OXIDES by destination by value in $	Main countries	U 2-a	
HAM (cooked or prepared) by destination: tonnage	EEC countries	E 47-m	
HAND-MADE CARPETS by value in local currency	Iran	U 32-m	
HARD COAL: tonnage	European countries	U 31-q	
HARD COAL BRIQUETTES by destination: tonnage & value in $	EEC countries	E 5-q	
tonnage	Czechoslovakia & E Germany	U 10-a	
HARD FIBRES as % of total exports (value basis)	Main countries	B 10-a	
by destination: tonnage	Main countries	B 10-a	
abaca & henequen: tonnage	All countries	U 11-a	
sisal: tonnage	Brazil & Tanzania	U 11-a	
HARDENED PROTEIN (plastics): tonnage	Main countries	U 26-a	
HARDWOOD TIMBER LOGS by value in $	Malaysia, Papua New Guinea & Solomon Is	U 32-m	
by volume in m³	European countries & USA	A 25-a2	
HAZELNUTS (in shell & unshelled): tonnage	Main countries	P 4-m	
HEAVY STEEL PLATES			
over 4.75mm gauge by destination: tonnage	Main countries	T 4-a	
tonnage	ECE countries	U 7-m	U 6-a
	Main countries	H 3-a	

APPENDIX 1 - EXPORTS BY PRODUCT

Product	Territorial coverage	Title codes	
HEAVY STEEL SECTIONS by destination: tonnage	Main countries	T 4-a	
tonnage & value in $	EEC countries	E 5-q	
HEAVY STEEL SECTIONS (incl profiles): tonnage	ECE area	U 7-m	U 6-a
	Main countries	H 3-a	
HEMP (sisal): shipments (total) & to EEC area: tonnage & value in UA	AASM countries	E 41-a	
(henequen, sisal & abaca): tonnage	Main countries	A 5-a	
(henequen, sisal & sunn hemp): tonnage	All countries	B 10-a	
unit value in $ per ton	Tanzania	E 45-a	
HEMP (raw): tonnage	Asian & Far East areas	U 32-q	
	India, Philippines & Sabah	U 32-m	
HEMP SEED: tonnage	Turkey & Yugoslavia	B 19-a	
HETEROCYCLIC COMPOUNDS by destination by value in $m	Main countries	U 2-a	
HIDES & SKINS (raw)			
by kind by destination by CST classes by value in $m	EEC countries	E 48-a	
SITC classes by value in $m	Main countries	D 2-q	
tonnage & value in $m	OECD countries	D 3-a2	
by NIMEXE classes: tonnage & value in $m	All countries	E 20-a	
SITC classes: tonnage & value in $m	All countries	U 50-a	U 59-a
by value in $m	Main countries	B 2-a	
	Afghanistan	U 32-m	
	W European countries	U 33-a	
shipped to EEC & non-EEC areas by value in $m	EEC countries	E 24-a	
tonnage	Asian & Far East countries	U 32-q	
	India, Iran, Pakistan & Thailand	U 32-m	
unit value in local currency per ton	Burundi	E 45-a	
HIGH-SPEED ALLOY STEEL by destination: tonnage	EEC countries	E 29-a	
HORIZONTAL BORER-MILLING MACHINES by value in $m	EEC countries	B 20-a	
HORMONES by destination by value in $	Main countries	U 2-a	
HORSEHIDES by destination: tonnage & value in $	OECD countries	D 18-a	
HOT-ROLLED STEEL BARS: tonnage	E European countries & USSR	T 1-a	
HOT-ROLLED STEEL SHEETS by destination: tonnage	Main countries	T 4-a	
HOT-ROLLED STRIP by destination: tonnage	Main countries	T 4-a	
	EEC countries	E 29-a	
tonnage & value in $	EEC countries	E 5-q	
tonnage	E European countries & USSR	T 1-a	
HYDRAULIC TURBINES in MW	European countries, Japan & USA	D 45-a	
HYDROCARBONS BY KIND by destination: tonnage & value in $	Main countries	U 2-a	
HYPOPHOSPHATES by destination: tonnage	Main countries	U 2-a	
ILLIPE NUTS: tonnage	Indonesia & Sarawak	B 19-a	
ILMENITE & RUTILE MINERALS: tonnage	Main countries	T 4-a	
INDUSTRIAL & WORKS TRUCKS by destination: no & value in £	UK	V 1-a	
INDUSTRIAL FURNACES & OVENS by value in $m	Main countries	U 38-a	
INGOTS & SEMI-MANUFACTURED STEEL PRODUCTS by destination: tonnage	ECE countries	U 48-a	
INGOTS BILLETS & BLOOMS: tonnage	ECE countries	U 7-m	U 6-a
	Main countries	H 3-a	
INNER TUBES for motor cars: no & value by destination in £	UK	V 1-a	
tractors: no & value by destination in £	UK	V 1-a	
trucks: no & value by destination in £	UK	V 1-a	
INSECTICIDES by kind by destination by value in $	Main countries	U 2-a	
INSTANT COFFEE by destination in bags	Brazil	B 18-m	
	USA	J 1-a	
in lbs & bags	Main countries	B 13-a	
INSTANT TEA by destination in lbs	India, Sri Lanka & UK	B 13-a	
in kg	India, Uganda & UK	C 1-a	
INSULATED WIRE & CABLES by value in $m	Main countries	U 38-a	

APPENDIX 1 - EXPORTS BY PRODUCT

	Territorial coverage	Title codes
IODINE (crude sublimated): tonnage	All countries	B 15-a
IRIDIUM (unwrought or semi-manufactured) by destination in oz	UK	T 4-a
IRON & STEEL PRODUCTS		
by destination: tonnage	UK	T 2-m
tonnage & value in $	All countries	U 12-a
by kind by destination by CST classes: tonnage & value in $	EEC countries	E 48-a
SITC classes by value in $	Main countries	D 2-q
tonnage & value in $	OECD countries	D 3-a2
tonnage	EEC countries	E 5-q
by NIMEXE classes by value in $	All countries	E 20-a
SITC classes by value in $	All countries	U 50-a U 59-a
tonnage	Main countries	T 2-m
by value in $	Asian & Far East countries	U 32-a
shipped to EEC & non-EEC areas by value in $	EEC countries	E 24-a
IRON CASTINGS by destination: tonnage & value in $	EEC area	E 5-q
tonnage & as % of home production	UK	B 25-a
IRON ORE by destination: tonnage & value in $	EEC countries	E 5-q
tonnage	All countries	T 4-a
	EEC countries	E 29-a
by regions of destination: tonnage	All countries	U 56-a
by value in Rs	India	U 32-m
shipped to non-EEC area: tonnage	EEC countries	E 29-a
to world regions: tonnage	OECD countries	D 22-a
shipments (total) to EEC area: tonnage & value in UA	AASM countries	E 41-a
tonnage	Australia, France, W Germany, Sweden & USA	T 2-m
	Hong Kong, India, Korea & Malaysia	U 32-m
	World exporting regions	U 56-a
unit value in $ per ton	African, Caribbean countries & Pacific Is	E 45-a
IRON ORE (incl concentrates): tonnage	Asian & Far East areas	U 32-q
	ECE countries	U 7-m U 6-a
	Main countries	H 3-a
IRON ORE (incl manganiferous ores): tonnage	All countries	B 15-a
IRON OXIDE: tonnage	OECD countries	D 5-a
IRON PYRITES by destination: tonnage & value in $	EEC area	E 5-q
tonnage	EEC countries	E 29-a
shipped to non-EEC area: tonnage	EEC countries	E 29-a
JUTE by destination: tonnage	Pakistan	B 10-a
by value in $ & unit value in $ per ton	Main countries	A 5-a
JUTE & ALLIED FIBRES: tonnage & value in $m	Main countries	B 2-a
tonnage	Asian & Far East areas	U 32-q
	India, Pakistan & Thailand	U 32-m
JUTE (incl jute products)		
by kind by destination by CST classes: tonnage	EEC countries	E 48-a
SITC classes by value in $	Main countries	D 2-q
tonnage & value in $	OECD countries	D 3-a2
by NIMEXE classes by value in $	All countries	E 20-a
SITC classes by value in $	All countries	U 50-a U 59-a
JUTE & KENAF by destination in local currency	Pakistan & Thailand	B 10-a
JUTE BAGS & SACKS (new) by destination: tonnage	W European countries	C 22-a
JUTE CLOTH by destination: tonnage	W European countries	C 22-a
JUTE MANUFACTURES: bags & sacks by value in $	Pakistan	U 32-m
tonnage	Main countries	A 5-a
JUTE YARN by destination: tonnage	W European countries	C 22-a
by value in Rs	India & Pakistan	U 32-m
tonnage	W European countries	C 22-a

APPENDIX 1 - EXPORTS BY PRODUCT

	Territorial coverage	Title codes
KAPOK SEED: tonnage	Cambodia, Indonesia & Thailand	B 19-a
KEROSENE by destination: tonnage	OECD countries	D 31-a
tonnage	Main countries	B 15-a
KNITTED & CROCHETED FABRICS: tonnage	OECD countries	D 46-a
KRAFT LINING PAPER by destination: tonnage	All countries	D 40-a
LAMB & MUTTON		
by destination: tonnage	Main countries	B 12-m
by value in $m	W European countries	U 33-a
by value as % of total exports	Main countries	B 11-a
tonnage	European countries	U 36-a
LATEX & CRUDE RUBBER by destination: tonnage	Main countries	C 18-m
LATHES (automatic) by value in £m	EEC countries	B 20-a
(capstan & turret) by value in £m	EEC countries	B 20-a
(excl turret type) by volume & value in $m	USA	J 2-a
LEAD (based on content of ore): tonnage	All countries	T 4-a
(soft & antimonial): tonnage	All countries	C 30-m
unit value in $ per ton	Zambia	E 45-a
(unwrought), lead ore, scrap & concentrates: tonnage	All countries	B 15-a
LEAD BULLION (REFINED) by destination: tonnage	OECD countries	D 21-q
LEAD BULLION (REFINED), LEAD & LEAD ALLOYS: tonnage	UK	C 30-m
LEAD FOIL, POWDERS & FLAKES: tonnage	UK	C 30-m
LEAD ORE (incl concentrates) by destination: tonnage	OECD countries	D 21-q
	Italy	C 12-a
	Main countries	U 24-m
LEAD OXIDES (excl red lead): tonnage	UK	C 30-m
LEAD PIGS & BARS by destination: tonnage	USA	J 6-a
LEAD (REFINED) & LEAD BULLION by destination: tonnage	UK	C 30-m
LEAD (REFINED) INCL BULLION: tonnage	Main countries	U 24-m
LEAD (REFINED): tonnage	All countries	C 12-a
LEAD RODS & LEAD WIRE: tonnage	UK	C 30-m
LEAD SCRAP by destination: tonnage	Main countries	T 4-a
LEAD SHEET & STRIP: tonnage	UK	C 30-m
LEAD TUBES & LEAD PIPES: tonnage	UK	C 30-m
LEATHER (INCL LEATHER GOODS)		
by destination by CST classes by value in $	EEC countries	E 48-a
SITC classes by value in $	Main countries	D 2-q
tonnage & value in $	OECD countries	D 3-a2
by NIMEXE classes by value in $	All countries	E 20-a
SITC classes by value in $	All countries	U 50-a U 59-a
LEATHER by kind by destination: tonnage	Main countries	B 9-m
value in $m	Main countries	A 18-a
value in Rs	India	U 32-m
(heavy): tonnage	Main countries	A 18-a
(light cattle & calf): tonnage	Main countries	A 18-a
LEATHER FOOTWEAR in pairs	Main countries & USSR	A 18-a
LEATHER GOATSKINS shipped ex OECD area in sq ft	Main countries excl OECD area	D 18-a
LEATHER MADE FROM SHEEP & GOATSKINS		
by destination in sq ft & by value in $	OECD countries	D 18-a
tonnage	Main countries	A 18-a
LEATHER MADE FROM SHEEPSKIN shipped ex OECD area in sq ft	Main countries (excl OECD area)	D 18-a
LEATHER SOLES by destination: tonnage & value in $	OECD countries	D 18-a
shipped ex OECD area: tonnage	Main countries excl OECD area	D 18-a
LEATHER UPPERS by destination in sq ft & by value in $	OECD countries	D 18-a
shipped ex OECD area in sq ft	Main countries excl OECD area	D 18-a
LEATHER-WORKING MACHINERY by value in $m	Main countries	U 38-a
LEMON JUICE: tonnage	All countries	A 7-a
LEMONS & GRAPEFRUIT: unit value in $ per ton	W European countries	U 20-a

APPENDIX 1 - EXPORTS BY PRODUCT

	Territorial coverage	Title codes	
LIGHT STEEL SECTIONS by destination: tonnage	Main countries	T 4-a	
LIGHT STEEL SECTIONS (incl profiles): tonnage	ECE area	U 7-m	U 6-a
	Main countries	H 3-a	
LIGHTING EQUIPMENT by destination by CST classes by value in $	EEC countries	E 48-a	
LIGNITE (incl briquettes) shipped to non-EEC area: tonnage	EEC countries	E 14-a	
LIGNITE by destination: tonnage & value in $	EEC countries	E 5-q	
LINEN PIECE GOODS by destination in sq yds	UK	B 10-a	
LINER BOARD by destination: tonnage	All countries	D 40-a	
LINSEED by destination: tonnage	Canada	B 19-a	
tonnage & value in $m	World regions	B 2-a	
tonnage	Main countries	B 19-a	
	Main producing countries	B 18-q	
LINSEED CAKE & MEAL: tonnage & value in $m	World regions	B 2-a	
LINSEED OIL by destination: tonnage	Argentine, Uruguay & USA	B 19-a	
tonnage & value in $m	World regions	B 2-a	
tonnage	Main countries	B 19-a	P 1-a
	Main producing countries	B 18-q	
LIQUEFIED PETROLEUM GAS (LPG): tonnage	Canada	B 15-a	
LIQUID FUELS in coal equiv tonnage	EEC countries	E 14-a	
LITHIUM MINERALS: tonnage	All countries	B 15-a	
LITHOPONE: tonnage	All countries	B 15-a	
	OECD countries	D 5-a	
LIVE ANIMALS by value in $m	W European countries	U 33-a	
(incl meat & meat preparations) by value in $	OECD countries	D 1-a	
LIVE ANIMALS - index nos (quantum & value bases)	OECD countries	D 16-q	
LIVE CATTLE by destination by volume	Denmark, Eire, France & UK	B 11-a	
calves by volume	European countries & USSR	U 36-a	
by volume	Main countries	B 11-a	
LIVE PIGS by volume	European countries	U 36-a	
	Main countries	B 11-a	
(for slaughter) by destination by volume	EEC countries	E 47-m	
LIVE SHEEP by volume	Main countries	B 11-a	
LIVESTOCK (incl meat by kind): tonnage	World regions	A 11-a	
LIVESTOCK by kind by destination by CST classes: tonnage & value in $	EEC countries	E 48-a	
SITC classes by value in $	Main countries	D 2-q	
tonnage & value in $	OECD countries	D 3-a2	
tonnage	Main countries	B 12-m	
by NIMEXE classes: tonnage & value in $	All countries	E 20-a	
SITC classes: tonnage & value in $	All countries	U 50-a	U 59-a
shipped to EEC & non-EEC areas: volume	EEC countries	E 44-a	
LOCOMOTIVES (electric) by value in $m	Main countries	U 38-a	
(steam) by value in $m	Main countries	U 38-a	
LUBRICATING OIL (incl greases): tonnage	Main countries	B 15-a	
LUBRICATING OIL by destination: tonnage	OECD countries	D 31-a	
MACHINE TOOLS as % of production (value basis)	EEC countries	B 31-a	
by destination by value in $m	EEC countries	B 31-a	
in £m	EEC countries	B 20-a	
by kind by destination by CST classes by value in $m	EEC countries	E 48-a	
SITC classes by value in $m	Main countries	D 2-q	
tonnage & value in $m	OECD countries	D 3-a2	
by NIMEXE classes: volume & value in $m	All countries	E 20-a	
SITC classes: volume & value in $m	All countries	U 50-a	U 59-a
value in $m (in detail)	EEC countries	J 2-a	
volume & value in $m	USA	J 2-a	

● APPENDIX 1 - EXPORTS BY PRODUCT

	Territorial coverage	Title codes	
MACHINE TOOLS, continued			
by value in £m	UK	B 20-a	
in $m	EEC countries	B 31-a	
	Main countries	U 38-a	
by world regions by value in £m	EEC countries	B 20-a	
(numerically-controlled type) as % of total machine tool exports	EEC countries	B 20-a	
by destination: volume	EEC countries	B 20-a	
by volume & value in £m	EEC countries	B 20-a	
shipped to EEC area by value in £m	UK	B 31-a	
EFTA area by value in £m	UK	B 31-a	
MACHINERY as % of total exports (value basis)	E European countries	U 16-a	
world total exports (value basis)	Communist countries	U 23-a	
	Developed countries (as group)	U 23-a	
	Developing countries (as group)	U 23-a	
by type by destination: tonnage & value in $m	All countries	U 12-a	
by value in $m	Australia, Hong Kong & Japan	U 32-m	
MACHINERY & EQUIPMENT - index nos (quantum & value bases)	OECD countries	D 16-q	
MACHINERY & TRANSPORT EQUIPMENT			
% change by destination	EEC countries	E 23-a	
by destination by value in UA	EEC countries	E 23-a	
by value in $m	Main countries	E 24-a	
shipped to non-EEC area by value in $m	EEC countries	E 22-m	
MACHINERY (electrical)			
by kind by destination: tonnage & value in $m	All countries	U 12-a	
by CST classes by value in $m	EEC countries	E 48-a	
SITC classes by value in $m	Main countries	D 2-q	
tonnage & value in $m	OECD countries	D 3-a2	
by NIMEXE classes: volume & value in $m	All countries	E 20-a	
SITC classes: volume & value in $m	All countries	U 50-a	U 59-a
by value in $m	Main countries	U 38-a	
shipped to EEC & non-EEC areas by value in $m	EEC countries	E 24-a	
MACHINERY (mechanical)			
by kind by destination by CST classes by value in $	EEC countries	E 48-a	
SITC classes by value in $	Main countries	D 2-q	
tonnage & value in $	OECD countries	D 3-a2	
by NIMEXE classes by value in $	All countries	E 20-a	
by SITC classes by value in $	All countries	U 50-a	U 59-a
by value in $	Main countries	U 38-a	
shipped to EEC & non-EEC areas by value in $	EEC countries	E 24-a	
MACHINERY & TRANSPORT EQUIPMENT by value in $	Far East countries	U 32-a	
MACHINING CENTRES (machine tools): volume	UK	B 31-a	
MAGNESITE & DOLOMITE BY KIND: tonnage	All countries	B 15-a	
MAGNESIUM METAL by destination: tonnage	Main countries	T 4-a	
MAGNESIUM (unwrought) by destination: tonnage	Italy	C 12-a	
MAGNETIC STEEL DYNAMO SHEETS by destination: tonnage	EEC countries	E 5-q	E 29-a
MAIZE by destination: tonnage	China, E European countries & USSR	A 17-a	
	Main countries	A 17-a	
by value as % of total exports	Main countries	B 8-a	
in $m	W European countries	U 33-a	
in local currency	Burma & Thailand	U 32-m	
tonnage	All countries	A 17-a	
	Burma & Thailand	U 32-m	
	European countries	U 35-a	
	Main countries	B 7-m	B 8-a
		P 5-a	
MAN-MADE CELLULOSIC & NON-CELLULOSIC STAPLE in lbs	UK	B 10-a	
MAN-MADE FIBRE YARN by destination in lbs	UK	B 10-a	
	Main countries	K 4-a	

● APPENDIX 1 - EXPORTS BY PRODUCT

	Territorial coverage	Title codes	
MAN-MADE FIBRE YARN (cellulosic): tonnage	Main countries	K 4-a	
MAN-MADE FIBRES			
as % of fibre production (value basis)	Main countries	D 27-a	
<u>by destination</u> in lbs	UK	B 10-a	
by kind <u>by destination</u> by CST classes by value in $	EEC countries	E 48-a	
SITC classes by value in $	Main countries	D 2-q	
tonnage & value in $	OECD countries	D 3-a2	
by NIMEXE classes by value in $	All countries	E 20-a	
SITC classes by value in $	All countries	U 50-a	U 59-a
(for spinning) <u>by destination</u>: tonnage & value in $	Main countries	U 2-a	
MAN-MADE FILAMENT BY KIND: tonnage	Canada, European countries, Japan & USA	D 27-a	
MAN-MADE STAPLE & FILAMENT YARN by value in £	UK	B 29-a	
MAN-MADE STAPLE BY KIND: tonnage	Canada, European countries, Japan & USA	D 27-a	
MANGANESE ORE & CONCENTRATES: tonnage	Asian & Far East countries	U 32-q	
MANGANESE ORE			
<u>by destination</u>: tonnage & value in $	EEC area	E 5-q	
tonnage	Main countries	T 4-a	
	EEC countries	E 29-a	
shipped to non-EEC area: tonnage	EEC countries	E 29-a	
tonnage	ECE countries, Japan & USA	U 7-m	U 6-a
	India, Iran & Philippines	U 32-m	
	Main countries	H 3-a	
total shipments & to EEC area: tonnage & value in UA	AASM countries	E 41-a	
unit value in $ per ton	Gabon	E 45-a	
MANGANESE ORE, FERRO-MANGANESE & METALLIC MANGANESE: tonnage	All countries	B 15-a	
MANUFACTURED GOODS			
as % of total exports (value basis)	Communist countries	U 23-a	
	Developed countries (as group)	U 23-a	
	Developing countries (as group)	U 23-a	
<u>by destination</u>: tonnage & value in $m	All countries	U 12-a	
by kind <u>by destination</u> by CST classes by value in $m	EEC countries	E 48-a	
SITC classes by value in $m	Main countries	D 2-q	
tonnage & value in $m	OECD countries	D 3-a2	
by value in UA	EEC countries	E 23-a	
shipped to EEC & non-EEC areas by value in $m	EEC countries	E 24-a	
by NIMEXE classes by value in $m	All countries	E 20-a	
SITC classes by value in $m	All countries	U 50-a	U 59-a
by value: % change <u>by destination</u>	Main countries	N 3-a	
	EEC countries	E 23-a	
per capita in $	Developing countries	U 52-a	
shipped to Communist area by value in $m	Developed countries	U 52-a	
non-EEC area by value in UA	EEC countries	E 22-m	
US share by SITC classes (value basis)	USA	N 3-a	
MANUFACTURED GOODS - index nos (see no 3, 6, 9, 12)	Main world regions	U 27-q	
	OECD countries	D 26-q	
MANUFACTURED TEXTILE PRODUCTS & CLOTHING by value in $m	Main countries	G 1-a	
	OECD countries	D 46-a	
MANUFACTURED TIMBER PRODUCTS by kind by value in $m	World regions	A 11-a	
MARGARINE: tonnage	EEC countries	E 44-a	
	Main exporting countries	B 12-a	
	Main producing countries	B 4-a	
MARINE ENGINES (up to 200 bhp) <u>by destination</u> by volume	UK	V 1-a	
MARINE MACHINERY <u>by destination</u> by value in million yen	Japan	S 16-a	
MASTICS: tonnage & value in $	OECD countries	D 5-a	
MATS & MATTING (made of coir fibre) <u>by destination</u>: tonnage	India	B 10-a	
MATTRESS MATERIAL (made of coir fibre): tonnage	Sri Lanka	B 10-a	
MEASURING APPARATUS by value in $m	Main countries	U 38-a	

APPENDIX 1 – EXPORTS BY PRODUCT

Product	Territorial coverage	Title codes	
MEAT by kind by destination by CST classes: tonnage & value in $	EEC countries	E 48-a	
SITC classes by value in $	Main countries	D 2-q	
tonnage & value in $	OECD countries	D 3-a2	
tonnage	Main countries	B 12-m	
by NIMEXE classes: tonnage & value in $	All countries	E 20-a	
SITC classes: tonnage & value in $	All countries	U 50-a	U 59-a
by value in $	W European countries	U 33-a	
historical table from 1831: tonnage	Denmark & Eire	Z 1-a	
tonnage & value in $	Australia & New Zealand	U 32-m	
MEAT (fresh, frozen, dried & salted): tonnage	EEC countries	E 1-a	
(incl meat products) by value in £	Main countries	B 11-a	
MEAT PREPARATIONS by value in $	W European countries	U 33-a	
unit value in $ per ton	Kenya	E 45-a	
MECHANICAL ENGINEERING PRODUCTS by value in £m	UK	B 27-a	
	Main countries	B 27-a	
MECHANICAL HANDLING EQUIPMENT			
by NIMEXE classes by value in $	All countries	E 20-a	
SITC classes by value in $	All countries	U 50-a	U 59-a
value in $	Main countries	U 38-a	
MEDICAL APPARATUS by value in $m	Main countries	U 38-a	
MEDICAMENTS by destination by value in $	Main countries	U 2-a	
MEDICINAL INGREDIENTS by value in $m	Main countries	U 26-a	
MEDICINAL PLANTS & HERBS by value in local currency	Laos	U 32-m	
MEDICINAL PRODUCTS (incl drugs) by destination by value in $	Main countries	U 2-a	
MEDICINES & PHARMACEUTICAL PRODUCTS by value in $m	Main countries	U 26-a	
MEDIUM STEEL PLATES			
up to 4.75 mm guage by destination: tonnage	Main countries	T 4-a	
tonnage	ECE countries	U 7-m	U 6-a
	Main countries	H 3-a	
MERCURY (incl mercuric compounds) in lbs	All countries	B 15-a	
MERCURY by destination in flasks	Spain & Mexico	T 4-a	
tonnage	Italy	C 12-a	
METAL GOODS (incl tools)			
by kind by destination by CST classes: tonnage & value in $	EEC countries	E 48-a	
SITC classes by value in $	Main countries	D 2-q	
tonnage & value in $	OECD countries	D 3-a2	
by NIMEXE classes by value in $	All countries	E 20-a	
SITC classes by value in $	All countries	U 50-a	U 59-a
METAL GOODS BY REGIONS OF ORIGINS by value in $	EEC countries	E 38-a	
METAL GOODS, MACHINES & TRANSPORT EQUIPMENT by value in $	ECE countries	U 15-a	
METAL ORES, & METALS by value in $bn	Developing countries	U 11-a	
METAL ORES BY REGIONS OF ORIGIN by value in $	EEC countries	E 38-a	
METAL ORES & CRUDE MINERALS by value & as % of total exports	ECE countries	U 15-a	
METAL-CUTTING MACHINE TOOLS: deliveries by value in $m	USA	J 2-a	
METAL-FORMING MACHINE TOOLS: deliveries by value in $m	USA	J 2-a	
new orders (for export) in $m	USA	J 2-a	
METAL-WORKING MACHINE TOOLS by value in $m	Main countries	U 38-a	
METALLIC OXIDES (for paint production) by destination by value in $	Main countries	U 2-a	
METALS BY KIND by destination by CST classes: tonnage & value in $m	EEC countries	E 48-a	
SITC classes by value in $m	Main countries	D 2-q	
tonnage & value in $m	OECD countries	D 3-a2	
by NIMEXE classes: tonnage & value in $m	All countries	E 20-a	
SITC classes: tonnage & value in $m	All countries	U 50-a	U 59-a
METHADONE by destination in kg	Switzerland & UK	U 46-a	
tonnage	Main countries	U 2-a	
METHANOL: tonnage	European countries, Japan & USA	U 26-a	

APPENDIX 1 – EXPORTS BY PRODUCT

	Territorial coverage	Title codes
MICA BLOCKS: tonnage & value in $m	India	U 11-a
MICA (for condensers & film): tonnage & value in $m	India	U 11-a
MICA MANUFACTURES: tonnage & value in $m	India	U 11-a
MICA SHEET, CRUDE, WASTE & PROCESSED MICA: tonnage	All countries	B 15-a
MICA SPLITTINGS: tonnage & value in $m	India	U 11-a
MILK & CREAM by value in $m	W European countries	U 33-a
MILK POWDER (incl dried cream) by value in $m	W European countries	U 33-a
by destination: tonnage	Main countries	B 12-m
tonnage (incl world total)	All countries	B 3-a
(skim) by destination: tonnage	Main countries	B 4-a
shipped to EEC area: tonnage	EEC countries	B 3-a
tonnage	Main countries (as total)	B 4-a
(whole & skim): tonnage	EEC countries	B 3-a
(whole) by destination: tonnage	Main countries	B 4-a
shipped to EEC area: tonnage	EEC countries	B 3-a
tonnage	Main countries (as total)	B 4-a
MILLING MACHINES by destination by value in £m	UK	B 31-a
volume & value in $m	USA	J 2-a
MINERAL FUELS by kind by destination: tonnage & value in $	All countries	U 12-a
tonnage	All countries	N 5-a
by value in $m	Asian & Far East areas	U 32-a
	Australasian countries & Singapore	U 32-m
MINERAL FUELS – index nos (quantum & value bases)	OECD countries	D 16-q
MINERAL PIGMENTS (of lead content) by kind: tonnage	USA	J 6-a
MINERAL PROCESSING MACHINERY by value in $m	Main countries	U 38-a
MINERALS by kind: tonnage	All countries	N 5-a
shipped to non-EEC area: tonnage	EEC countries	E 29-a
MOHAIR by destination in kg	Main countries	K 6-a
in lbs	S Africa, Turkey & USA	B 10-a
MOLASSES: unit value in $ per ton	Malagasy Rep	E 45-a
MOLYBDENUM METAL, ORE & CONCENTRATES: tonnage	All countries	B 15-a
MOLYBDENUM ORE by destination: tonnage	USA	T 4-a
MORPHINE by destination in kg	All countries	U 46-a
MOTOR CARS by engine capacity: volume & value by destination in £m	UK	V 1-a
by volume by destination	USSR	V 1-a
historical table	All countries	V 1-a
volume & value by destination in local currency	Canada, Japan & W European countries	V 1-a
by engine capacity	W Germany	V 1-a
MOTOR CARS (second-hand): volume & value by destination	W European countries	V 1-a
MOTOR CYCLES by value in $m	Main countries	U 38-a
MOTOR CYCLES (incl mopeds) by volume	All countries	S 24-a
MOTOR SPIRIT by destination by value in $	OECD countries	D 31-a
tonnage	Main countries	B 15-a
MOTOR VEHICLES		
by kind by destination by CST classes by value in $m	EEC countries	E 48-a
SITC classes by value in $m	Main countries	D 2-q
tonnage & value in $m	OECD countries	D 3-a2
tonnage & value in $m	All countries	U 12-a
by NIMEXE classes by value in $m	All countries	E 20-a
SITC classes by value in $m	All countries	U 50-a U 59-a
by value in $m	Main countries	U 38-a
historical table by volume	Main countries	V 4-a
projection of export demand by 1977 by value in £m	UK	B 28
MOTOR VEHICLES INDUSTRY PRODUCTS by value in £m	UK	V 1-a

● APPENDIX 1 - EXPORTS BY PRODUCT

	Territorial coverage	Title codes
MUSICAL INSTRUMENTS BY KIND		
by destination by CST classes: tonnage & value in $	EEC countries	E 48-a
SITC classes by value in $	Main countries	D 2-q
tonnage & value in $	OECD countries	D 3-a2
by NIMEXE classes by value in $	All countries	E 20-a
SITC classes by value in $	All countries	U 50-a U 59-a
MUSTARD SEED: tonnage	Main countries	B 19-a
NAPHTHA by destination: tonnage	OECD countries	D 31-a
NAPHTHALENE: tonnage	European countries, Japan & USA	U 26-a
NATURAL ABRASIVES: tonnage	All countries	B 15-a
NATURAL GAS by destination in cu ft	OECD countries	D 31-a
by volume in cu ft	Canada & Mexico	B 15-a
shipped to non-EEC area in coal equiv tonnage	EEC countries	E 14-a
NATURAL GAS LIQUIDS by destination: tonnage	OECD countries	D 31-a
NATURAL GUMS: unit value in $ per ton	Sudan	E 45-a
NATURAL PHOSPHATES: total exports & to EEC area: tonnage & by value in UA	AASM countries	E 41-a
NATURAL RUBBER by destination: tonnage	Main countries	B 13-a
by value in $m	W European countries	U 33-a
	Indonesia, Malaysia & Thailand	U 32-m
shipped to China & USSR: tonnage	Malaysia	C 17-m
European countries & USA: tonnage	Malaysia	C 17-m
EEC & non-EEC areas by value in $m	EEC countries	E 24-a
shipments (total) & to EEC area: tonnage & value in UA	AASM countries	E 41-a
tonnage & value in $m	Main countries	B 2-a
tonnage	ECAFE countries	U 32-m
	Main countries	C 18-m A 5-a
unit value in $ per ton	Liberia	E 45-a
NATURAL TEXTILE FIBRES by value in £m	UK	B 29-a
NEWSPRINT, BOOK PAPER & FINE PAPER: tonnage	Main countries	J 7-a
NEWSPRINT by destination: tonnage	All countries	D 40-a
historical table from 1902: tonnage	Finland	Z 1-a
tonnage	All countries	J 4-a
	Canada, European countries, USA & USSR	A 13-q
	OECD countries	D 41-q
NICKEL BARS, ANGLES, SECTIONS & WIRE by destination: tonnage	UK & USA	T 4-a
NICKEL METAL: tonnage	New Caledonia	T 4-a
NICKEL (refined) by destination: tonnage	Canada, Norway & UK	T 4-a
	OECD countries	D 21-q
NICKEL ORE by destination: tonnage	Canada & New Caledonia	T 4-a
NICKEL PLATES, SHEETS & STRIP by destination: tonnage	UK & USA	T 4-a
NICKEL POWDER: tonnage	USA	T 4-a
NICKEL PRODUCTS by kind by destination: tonnage	Main countries	T 4-a
NICKEL SCRAP by destination: tonnage	Canada, UK & USA	T 4-a
NICKEL TUBES & PIPES by destination: tonnage	USA	T 4-a
NICKEL (unwrought) incl semis, scrap & alloys: tonnage	All countries	B 15-a
NIGER SEED: tonnage	Ethiopia	B 19-a
NITROGEN FERTILISER COMPOUNDS		
by destination by value in $	Main European countries	U 2-a
tonnage	OECD countries	D 5-a
by kind: tonnage	All countries	B 15-a
tonnage	All countries	A 2-a
NON-CELLULOSIC FIBRES: tonnage	OECD countries	D 46-a
NON-CELLULOSIC FILAMENTS as % of production	Main countries	D 27-a
NON-CELLULOSIC STAPLE as % of production	Main countries	D 27-a
NON-CELLULOSIC STAPLE & YARN by destination in lbs	UK & USA	B 10-a
	Main countries	K 4-a

• APPENDIX 1 - EXPORTS BY PRODUCT

	Territorial coverage	Title codes	
NON-CELLULOSIC YARN: tonnage	OECD countries	D 46-a	
NON-FERROUS METAL ORES: unit value in UA per ton	Niger	E 45-a	
NON-FERROUS METAL PRODUCTS BY KIND			
by destination by CST classes by value in $	EEC countries	E 48-a	
SITC classes by value in $	Main countries	D 2-q	
tonnage & value in $	OECD countries	D 3-a2	
by NIMEXE classes: tonnage & value in $	All countries	E 20-a	
SITC classes: tonnage & value in $	All countries	U 50-a	U 59-a
NON-FERROUS METALS			
as % of total exports (value basis)	Communist countries	U 23-a	
	Developed countries (as total)	U 23-a	
	Developing countries (as total)	U 23-a	
by kind by destination by CST classes by value in $	EEC countries	E 48-a	
SITC classes by value in $	Main countries	D 2-q	
tonnage & value in $	OECD countries	D 3-a2	
tonnage & value in $	All countries	U 12-a	
by NIMEXE classes: tonnage & value in $	All countries	E 20-a	
SITC classes: tonnage & value in $	All countries	U 50-a	U 59-a
by value in $	Asian & Far East areas	U 32-a	
shipped to EEC & non-EEC areas by value in $	EEC countries	E 24-a	
NON-METALLIC MINERAL PRODUCTS shipped to EEC & non-EEC areas: tonnage	EEC countries	E 24-a	
NON-METALLIC MINERALS by kind: tonnage	All countries	N 5-a	
by regions of origin: tonnage	EEC countries	E 38-a	
NUCLEAR REACTORS by value in $m	Main countries	U 38-a	
NUTMEG & MACE in cwt	Grenada, Indonesia & Trinidad	B 18-q	
by destination in cwt	Grenada	B 13-a	
NUTS (edible) by kind (in shell & unshelled): tonnage	Main countries	P 4-m	
by value in local currency	Iran	U 32-m	
in $m	W European countries	U 33-a	
OATS by destination: tonnage	European countries	U 35-a	
	China, European countries & USSR	A 17-a	
	Main countries	B 8-a	
tonnage	All countries	A 17-a	
OFFICE MACHINERY by kind by destination: tonnage & value in $	All countries	U 12-a	
by value in $m	Main countries	U 38-a	
OILCAKE & MEAL by value in local currency	India & Indonesia	U 32-m	
OILCAKE: unit value in $ per ton	African, Caribbean countries & Pacific Is	E 45-a	
OILS & FATS as % of total trade in agricultural products	W European countries	U 20-a	
by kind by destination: tonnage & value in $	All countries	U 12-a	
OILS & FATS - index nos (quantum & value bases)	OECD countries	D 16-q	
OILS (for production of perfumes): total shipments & to EEC area: tonnage & value in UA	AASM countries	E 41-a	
OILSEED CAKE by value in $m	W European countries	U 33-a	
shipments (total) & to EEC area: tonnage & value in UA	AASM countries	E 41-a	
OILSEEDS as % of total trade in agricultural products (value basis)	W European countries	U 20-a	
by kind by destination by CST classes: tonnage & value in $	EEC countries	E 48-a	
SITC classes by value in $	Main countries	D 2-q	
tonnage & value in $	OECD countries	D 3-a2	
tonnage	Commonwealth countries	B 19-a	
by NIMEXE classes: tonnage & value in $	All countries	E 20-a	
SITC classes: tonnage & value in $	All countries	U 50-a	U 59-a
tonnage	World regions	A 11-a	
by value in $	W European countries	U 33-a	
OILSEEDS, OILNUTS & KERNELS: tonnage	Asian & Far East areas	U 32-q	

APPENDIX 1 - EXPORTS BY PRODUCT

Product	Territorial coverage	Title codes	
OILSEEDS shipped to EEC & non-EEC areas by value in $	EEC countries	E 24-a	
unit value in UA per ton	African, Caribbean countries & Pacific Is	E 45-a	
OITICICA OIL: tonnage	Brazil	B 19-a	
OLIVE OIL by destination: tonnage	Spain, Tunisia & Turkey	B 19-a	
tonnage	Main countries	B 19-a	
OPIUM ALKALOIDS by kind by destination by value in $	Main countries	U 2-a	
OPIUM by destination in kg	Main countries	U 46-a	
shipped to morphine-producing countries in kg	All countries	U 46-a	
ORANGE JUICE by destination: tonnage	Main countries	A 7-a	
ORANGE JUICE (canned): tonnage	All countries	A 7-a	
ORANGES & TANGERINES: unit value in $ per ton	W European countries	U 20-a	
PACKAGING MACHINERY by value in $m	Main countries	U 38-a	
PADDY RICE: tonnage	Burma	A 10-a	
	World regions	C 16-a	
PAINTS (incl mineral pigments) by destination by value in $	Main countries	U 2-a	
PAINTS & VARNISHES			
by destination by CST classes: tonnage & value in $	EEC countries	E 48-a	
SITC classes by value in $	Main countries	D 2-q	
tonnage & value in $	OECD countries	D 3-a2	
by NIMEXE classes by value in $	All countries	E 20-a	
SITC classes by value in $	All countries	U 50-a	U 59-a
tonnage & value in $	OECD countries	D 5-a	
PALLADIUM (unwrought or semi-manufactured) by destination in oz	UK	T 4-a	
PALM KERNEL OIL			
shipments (total) & to EEC area: tonnage & value in UA	AASM countries	E 41-a	
tonnage & value in $m	Main countries	B 2-a	
tonnage	Main countries	B 19-a	P 1-a
	Producing countries	B 18-q	
unit value in $ per ton	Benin	E 45-a	
PALM KERNEL OILCAKE & MEAL: tonnage & value in $m	Main countries	B 2-a	
PALM KERNELS by destination: tonnage	Nigeria	B 19-a	
tonnage & value in $m	Main countries	B 2-a	
tonnage	Indonesia, & W Malaysia	U 32-m	
	Main countries	B 19-a	
	Producing countries	B 18-q	
unit value in $ per ton	Sierra Leone	E 45-a	
PALM NUTS (incl kernels)			
shipments (total) & to EEC area: tonnage & value in UA	AASM countries	E 41-a	
PALM OIL by destination: tonnage	Ivory Coast, Malaysia, Nigeria & Singapore	B 19-a	
by value in local currency	Singapore	U 32-m	
tonnage & value in $m	Main countries	B 2-a	
tonnage	Indonesia & W Malaysia	U 32-m	
	Main countries	B 19-a	
total shipments & to EEC area: tonnage & value in UA	AASM countries	E 41-a	
unit value in $ per ton	Zaire	E 45-a	
PAPER: historical table from 1860: tonnage	Sweden	Z 1-a	
PAPER & BOARD PRODUCTS			
by kind by destination by CST classes by value in $	EEC countries	E 48-a	
SITC classes by value in $	Main countries	D 2-q	
tonnage & value in $	OECD countries	D 3-a2	
by NIMEXE classes by value in $	All countries	E 20-a	
SITC classes by value in $	All countries	U 50-a	U 59-a
shipments to EEC & non-EEC areas by value in $	EEC countries	E 24-a	
tonnage	Canada, European countries & USA	U 38-a	
PAPER (incl printed matter) by regions of origin: tonnage	EEC countries	E 38-a	
PAPER & PULP-MAKING MACHINES by value in $m	Main countries	U 38-a	
PAPERBOARD: tonnage	Main countries	J 7-a	

APPENDIX 1 - EXPORTS BY PRODUCT

	Territorial coverage	Title codes	
PARTICLE BOARD (incl chipboard) by volume in m³	Main countries	A 25-a2	
by destination by volume in m³	European countries	A 13-q	
tonnage	Main countries	A 26-a	
PASSENGER CARS (assembled & unassembled) by value in £m	UK	B 28-a	
(incl taxis) by value in £m	UK	B 28-a	
(unassembled): volume	Main countries	V 4-a	
by destination areas as % of total exports (value basis)	UK	B 28-a	
by destination by volume	All countries	V 1-a	V 3-a
by volume & value in £m	W European countries	V 1-a	
by engine capacity in cc: volume & value in £m	UK	V 1-a	
by NIMEXE classes by value in $m	All countries	E 20-a	
SITC classes by value in $m	All countries	U 50-a	U 59-a
by value in $m	Main countries	U 38-a	
in £m	UK	B 28-a	
by volume	All countries	S 24-a	
PASSENGER CARS: chassis (only): volume	Main countries	V 4-a	
PASSENGER CARS, TRUCKS & BUSES: volume	All countries	V 4-a	
PATENT FUELS: tonnage	European countries	U 31-q	
PEACHES (canned) by destination: tonnage	Main OECD countries	D 35-a	
(fresh) by destination: tonnage	Main OECD countries	D 35-a	
PEARS (canned & dried): tonnage	Argentine	D 34-a	
(fresh) by destination: tonnage	Main OECD countries	D 34-a	
PENICILLIN & STREPTOMYCIN by destination by value in $	Main countries	U 2-a	
PEPPER & PIMENTO: shipments (total) & to EEC area: tonnage & value in UA	AASM countries	E 41-a	
PEPPER by value in local currency	Sarawak & Singapore	U 32-m	
by destination in cwt	Main countries	B 18-q	B 13-a
tonnage & value in $	Main countries	U 11-a	
unit value in local currency per kg	Main countries	A 5-a	
PERFUMERY by destination by value in $	Main countries	U 2-a	
PETHIDINE by destination in kg	All countries	U 46-a	
PETROLEUM by value in $m & as % of total exports (value basis)	OPEC member countries	C 3-a	
PETROLEUM PRODUCTS			
by kind by destination by CST classes by value in $m	EEC countries	E 48-a	
SITC classes by value in $m	Main countries	D 2-q	
tonnage & value in $m	OECD countries	D 3-a2	
tonnage	Italy	H 4-a	
	OECD countries	D 31-a	
tonnage & value in $m	All countries	U 12-a	
by NIMEXE classes by value in $m	All countries	E 20-a	
SITC classes by value in $m	All countries	U 50-a	U 59-a
tonnage	Main countries	B 15-a	
by value in $m	Indonesia & Singapore	U 32-m	
by volume in m³	Latin American countries	U 18-a	
in barrels per day	OPEC member countries	C 3-a	
shipped to non-EEC area: tonnage	EEC countries	E 14-a	
tonnage	Main countries	C 14-a	
	Malaysia & Sarawak	U 32-m	
	World regions	T 3-a	
PETROLEUM WAXES (incl petroleum jelly): tonnage	Main countries	B 15-a	
PHARMACEUTICAL PRODUCTS			
by destination by value in $m	Main countries	U 2-a	
by kind by destination by CST classes by value in $m	EEC countries	E 48-a	
SITC classes by value in $m	Main countries	D 2-q	
tonnage & value in $m	OECD countries	D 3-a2	
by NIMEXE classes by value in $m	All countries	E 20-a	
SITC classes by value in $m	All countries	U 50-a	U 59-a
by value in $m	Main countries	U 26-a	
shipped to EEC & non-EEC areas by value in $m	EEC countries	E 24-a	

APPENDIX 1 - EXPORTS BY PRODUCT

Product	Territorial coverage	Title codes
PHENOLS by destination: tonnage & value in $	Main countries	U 2-a
tonnage	European countries, Japan & USA	U 26-a
PHOSPHATE FERTILISERS by kind: tonnage	OECD countries	D 5-a
tonnage	All countries	A 2-a
PHOSPHATES: unit value in $ per ton	Senegal & Togo	E 45-a
PHOSPHORIC ACID by destination: tonnage	Main countries	U 2-a
tonnage	European countries, Japan & USA	U 25-a
PHOSPHORUS PENTOXIDE by destination: tonnage	Main countries	U 2-a
PHOTOGRAPHICAL MATERIALS by value in $	Main countries	U 2-a
PHTHALIC ANHYDRIDE: tonnage	European countries, Japan & USA	U 26-a
PIG IRON (incl ferro-alloys) by destination: tonnage	OECD countries	D 22-a
by kind: tonnage	All countries	B 15-a
PIG IRON by destination: tonnage & value in $	EEC countries	E 5-q
	All countries	U 12-a
tonnage	EEC countries	E 29-a
shipped to non-EEC area by value in $	EEC countries	E 29-a
tonnage	Australia, Belgium, Netherlands, Japan & Sweden	T 2-m
	ECE countries, Japan & USA	U 7-m U 6-a
	Main countries	H 3-a
	USSR	T 1-a
PIG-MEAT (chilled or frozen) by destination: tonnage	EEC countries	E 47-m
by destination: tonnage	Main countries	B 12-m
tonnage	European countries	U 36-a
PIGS (live) by destination: volume	Main countries	B 12-m
PIMENTO by destination in cwt	Jamaica	B 13-a
in cwt	Guatemala, Honduras, Jamaica & Mexico	B 13-a
PINEAPPLES (canned) by destination: tonnage	Malaysia	B 5-a
tonnage	All countries	A 8-a
PINEAPPLES (fresh): tonnage	All countries	B 5-a
PITPROPS by destination by volume in m²	European countries & USSR	A 13-q
PLASTICS by kind by destination: tonnage & value in $	Main countries	U 2-a
PLASTICS: condensation products by destination: tonnage	OECD countries	D 5-a
regenerated cellulose & artificial resins by value in $	Main countries	U 26-a
PLASTICS PRODUCTS by destination: tonnage	OECD countries	D 5-a
by NIMEXE classes by value in $	All countries	E 20-a
SITC classes by value in $	All countries	U 50-a U 59-a
PLATES & SHEETS (coated or tinned) by destination: tonnage	Main countries	T 4-a
PLATINUM ALLOYS by destination in oz	UK	T 4-a
PLATINUM INGOTS, BARS, SPONGE & POWDER by destination in oz	UK	T 4-a
PLATINUM ORE & CONCENTRATES: tonnage	All countries	B 15-a
PLATINUM ORE by destination (incl concentrates): tonnage	Canada	T 4-a
PLATINUM-GROUP METALS by destination in oz	Main countries	T 4-a
by destination by kind in oz	UK	T 4-a
PLYWOOD & BLOCKBOARD by destination by volume in m³	European countries & USA	A 13-q
by volume in m³	Main countries	A 25-a2 A 26-a
PLYWOOD & VENEERED PANELS by value in $	S Korea	U 32-m
total shipments & to EEC area by value in UA	AASM countries	E 41-a
POLYACIDS & DERIVATIVES by destination by value in $	Main countries	U 2-a
POLYCONDENSATION PRODUCTS by destination: tonnage	Main European countries	U 2-a
POLYESTER CONDENSATION PRODUCTS by destination: tonnage	Main European countries	U 2-a
POLYETHYLENE: tonnage	European countries, Japan & USA	U 26-a
POLYMERISATION PRODUCTS by destination: tonnage	Main countries	U 2-a
	OECD countries	D 5-a
tonnage	European countries, Japan & USA	U 26-a
POLYPROPYLENE: tonnage	European countries, Japan & USA	U 26-a
POLYSTYRENE: tonnage	European countries, Japan & USA	U 26-a
POLYVINYLCHLORIDE (PVC): tonnage	European countries, Japan & USA	U 26-a
POPPY SEED: tonnage	Netherlands, Poland & Turkey	B 19-a

APPENDIX 1 – EXPORTS BY PRODUCT

	Territorial coverage	Title codes	
POPPY STRAW & CONCENTRATES by destination in kg	All countries	U 46-a	
POPPY STRAW (for opium production) by destination in kg	All countries	U 46-a	
PORK CARCASES by destination: tonnage	Main countries	B 11-a	
PORK by value in $m	W European countries	U 33-a	
(salted or dried) by destination: tonnage	EEC countries	E 47-m	
POTASH FERTILISERS: tonnage	All countries	A 2-a	
unit value in $ per ton	Kinshasa	E 45-a	
POTASH SALTS by kind: tonnage	All countries	B 15-a	
POTATOES by value in $m	W European countries	U 33-a	
shipped to EEC & non-EEC areas: tonnage	EEC countries	E 44-a	
POULTRY MEAT by destination: tonnage	Main countries	B 12-m	
by value in $m	W European countries	U 33-a	
tonnage	European countries & USSR	U 36-a	
	Main countries	B 11-a	
POWER GENERATING EQUIPMENT by value in $m	Main countries	U 38-a	
POWER TOOLS by value in $m	Main countries	U 38-a	
POWER TRANSFORMERS by value in $m	Main countries	U 38-a	
in MVa	Japan, USA & W European countries	T 7-a	
PRECIOUS STONES by kind by destination by CST classes by value in $m	EEC countries	E 48-a	
SITC classes by value in $m	Main countries	D 2-q	
tonnage & value in $m	OECD countries	D 3-a2	
PRESSED PORK by destination: tonnage	EEC countries	E 47-m	
PRIMARY ENERGY SOURCES: coal, oil, gas, coke & fuels: tonnage	European countries & USSR	U 4-a	
	EEC countries	E 16-q	E 15-a
PRIMARY MATERIALS			
as % of total exports (value basis)	Communist countries	U 23-a	
	Developed countries (as total)	U 23-a	
	Developing countries (as total)	U 23-a	
by kind by destination: tonnage & value in $	All countries	U 12-a	
PRINTING & WRITING PAPER by destination: tonnage	All countries	D 40-a	
tonnage	OECD countries	D 41-q	
PRINTING INKS: tonnage & value in $	OECD countries	D 5-a	
PRINTING MACHINERY by value in $m	Main countries	U 38-a	
PULPWOOD by destination: tonnage	Canada, European countries & USSR	A 13-q	
PUMPS (incl centrifuges) by value in $m	Main countries	U 38-a	
PYRITES IRON (cupreous): tonnage	All countries	B 15-a	
PYRITES RESIDUES: tonnage	ECE countries	U 7-m	U 6-a
	Main countries	H 3-a	
PYROTECHNIC PRODUCTS by destination by value in $	Main countries	U 2-a	
RADIO RECEIVERS by destination by CST classes: tonnage & value in $m	EEC countries	E 48-a	
SITC classes by value in $m	OECD countries	D 3-a2	
	Main countries	D 2-q	
by NIMEXE classes by value in $m	All countries	E 20-a	
SITC classes by value in $m	All countries	U 50-a	U 59-a
by value in $m	Main countries	U 38-a	
RADIOACTIVE MATERIALS by destination by value in $	Main countries	U 2-a	
RAIL FREIGHT WAGONS by value in $m	Main countries	U 38-a	
RAIL PASSENGER COACHES by value in $m	Main countries	U 38-a	
RAIL VEHICLES (incl rolling stock) by value in $m	Main countries	U 38-a	
RAILS (SECOND-HAND) by destination: tonnage	EEC countries	E 29-a	
RAILS & SLEEPERS by destination: tonnage	ECE countries	U 48-a	
RAILS, SLEEPERS & TRACK-LAYING MATERIAL: tonnage	ECE countries	U 7-m	U 6-a
	Main countries	H 3-a	
by destination: tonnage	EEC area	E 5-q	
	EEC countries	E 29-a	
	Main countries	T 4-a	

● APPENDIX 1 - EXPORTS BY PRODUCT

Product	Territorial coverage	Title codes
RAISINS, CURRANTS & SULTANAS by destination: tonnage	OECD countries	B 6-a
RAISINS: tonnage & value in $m	Main countries	U 11-a
RAPESEED by destination: tonnage	Canada	B 19-a
tonnage	Main countries	B 19-a
	Producing countries	B 18-q
RAPESEED OIL by destination: tonnage	Canada, Denmark, France & Sweden	B 19-a
tonnage	Main countries	B 19-a
	Producing countries	B 18-q
RARE EARTH MINERALS by kind: tonnage	USA	N 1-a
RAW CATTLE HIDES: tonnage	European OECD countries	D 18-a
RAW COCOA: tonnage	All countries	P 3-a
RAW COTTON: tonnage	Afghanistan	U 32-m
RAW JUTE by value in local currency	Pakistan	U 32-m
RAW MATERIALS as % of world total exports (value basis)	Communist countries	U 23-a
	Developed countries (as total)	U 23-a
	Developing countries (as total)	U 23-a
by kind by destination: tonnage & value in $	All countries	U 12-a
shipped to EEC & non-EEC areas by value in $	EEC countries	E 24-a
unit value in $ per ton	African, Caribbean countries & Pacific Is	E 45-a
by value: % change by destination	EEC countries	E 23-a
by destination in UA	EEC countries	E 23-a
in $m	Main countries	E 24-a
	Australia, India, Japan & New Zealand	U 32-m
in $bn	Developing countries	U 11-a
- index nos (quantum & value bases)	OECD countries	D 16-q
(value basis)	World regions	A 11-a
shipped to non-EEC area by value in UA	EEC countries	E 22-m
RAW SUGAR by value in $m	Philippines	U 32-m
RAW WOOL: tonnage & value in $m	Australia, New Zealand & Pakistan	U 32-m
RAYON ACETATE STAPLE FIBRE in million lbs	All countries	B 10-a
RAYON PIECE GOODS: tonnage	Main countries	K 1-q
RAYON STAPLE (incl waste) by destination in million lbs	UK	B 10-a
RAYON YARN (incl acetate) in million lbs	Main countries	B 10-a
RECLAIMED RUBBER by destination: tonnage	UK & USA	C 18-m
RED LEAD & ORANGE LEAD: tonnage	UK	C 30-m
RED LEAD, WHITE LEAD & LITHARGE: tonnage	USA	J 6-a
REFRIGERATING EQUIPMENT by value in $m	Main countries	U 38-a
REGENERATED CELLULOSE by destination by value in $m	Main countries	U 2-a
tonnage	Main countries	U 2-a
tonnage	European countries, Japan & USA	U 26-a
REPLACEMENT PARTS for boilers by value in $	France, W Germany & UK	B 30-a
for track-layers by value in £m	UK	V 1-a
for tractors (wheeled) by value in £m	UK	V 1-a
RESINS (artificial) by destination: tonnage & value in $	Main countries	U 2-a
RHODIUM (unwrought or semi-manufactured) by destination in oz	UK	T 4-a
RICE by destination: tonnage	All countries	B 14-q B 8-a
by kind by destination: broken rice: tonnage	All countries	A 19-a
glazed rice: tonnage	All countries	A 19-a
husked rice: tonnage	All countries	A 19-a
milled rice: tonnage	All countries	A 19-a
paddy rice: tonnage	All countries	A 19-a
parboiled rice: tonnage	All countries	A 19-a
by value in $m	Burma & Thailand	U 32-m
(locally-produced): tonnage	World regions	A 10-a
shipped to EEC & non-EEC areas: tonnage	EEC countries	E 44-a
shipments (total) & to EEC area: tonnage & value in UA	AASM countries	E 41-a
tonnage & value in $m	Main countries	B 2-a

APPENDIX 1 - EXPORTS BY PRODUCT

	Territorial coverage	Title codes	
RICE, continued			
tonnage	All countries	A 10-a	
	Burma, Pakistan & Thailand	U 32-m	
unit value in $ per ton	Guyana & Malagasy Rep	E 45-a	
ROAD TRACTORS (for use with semi-trailers) by volume by destination	UK	V 1-a	
by destination by volume & value in £m	W European countries	V 1-a	
ROLLED STEEL PRODUCTS by kind by destination: tonnage	EEC countries	E 5-q	
ROLLED WHEELS (for railway rolling stock) by destination: tonnage	Main countries	T 4-a	
RUBBER MANUFACTURES shipped to EEC & non-EEC areas by value in $	EEC countries	E 24-a	
RYE by destination: tonnage	China, E European countries & USSR	A 17-a	
	Main countries	B 8-a	
tonnage	All countries	A 17-a	
	European countries	U 35-a	
SACK KRAFT WRAPPING by destination: tonnage	All countries	D 40-a	
SAFFLOWER OIL: tonnage	USA	B 19-a	
SAFFLOWER SEED: tonnage	Mexico & USA	B 19-a	
SALT by kind: tonnage	All countries	B 15-a	
SANITARY PAPER (incl household paper) by destination: tonnage	All countries	D 40-a	
tonnage	OECD countries	D 41-q	
SARDINES: historical table from 1873: tonnage	Portugal	Z 1-a	
SAUSAGES by destination: tonnage	EEC countries	E 47-m	
tonnage	European countries	U 36-a	
SAWN HARDWOOD: beech, oak & tropical woods by volume in m³	European countries	A 25-a	
SAWN HARDWOOD			
by destination by volume in m³	Canada, European countries & USA	A 13-q	
by volume in m³	Canada, European countries & USA	A 25-a	
teak by value in $	Burma	U 32-m	
unit value in $ per ton	Ghana & Ivory Coast	E 45-a	
SAWN SOFTWOOD by destination by volume in m³	Canada, European countries & USA	A 13-q	
	Finland & Sweden	A 24-a	
by volume in m³	Main countries	A 5-a	A 24-a
SAWNWOOD, SLEEPERS & WOOD-BASED PANELS: tonnage	All countries	A 23-a	
SCIENTIFIC INSTRUMENTS by kind by destination by value in £	UK	C 24-a	
SECOND-HAND CARS by destination: volume & value in £	W European countries	V 1-a	
SECOND-HAND TRUCKS by destination: volume & value in £	W European countries	V 1-a	
SEMI-FINISHED ALLOY STEEL PRODUCTS by destination: tonnage	Main countries	T 4-a	
SEMI-FINISHED COPPER PRODUCTS: tonnage	France	T 4-a	
SEMI-FINISHED STEEL PRODUCTS by destination: tonnage & value in $	EEC countries	E 5-q	
tonnage	OECD countries	D 22-a	
by kind: tonnage	Main countries	T 2-m	
SEMI-MANUFACTURED GOODS as % of total exports (value basis)	E European countries	U 16-a	
- index nos (quantum & value bases)	OECD countries	D 16-q	
SESAME SEED by destination: tonnage	Nigeria & Sudan	B 19-a	
tonnage	Main countries	B 19-a	
SESAME SEED OIL: tonnage	Main countries	B 19-a	
SEWING MACHINES by value in $m	Main countries	U 38-a	
SHAVING CREAMS (incl shampoos): tonnage & value in $	OECD countries	D 5-a	
SHEA NUT OIL: tonnage	Mali & Upper Volta	B 19-a	
SHEA NUTS: tonnage	E African countries	B 19-a	
SHEEP & LAMBS (live) by destination by volume	Main countries	B 12-m	
SHEEP & LAMBSKINS: tonnage	Main countries	B 9-m	A 18-a
		B 2-a	
SHEEP (live): tonnage	EEC countries	E 1-a	
unit value in $ per ton dead wt	African, Caribbean countries & Pacific Is	E 45-a	
SHEEPSKINS by destination: tonnage & value in $	OECD countries	D 18-a	
tonnage	European OECD countries	D 18-a	
SHELLAC (incl other lacs): tonnage	India & Thailand	U 11-a	
SHELLFISH: tonnage & value in $m	OECD countries	D 43-a	

● APPENDIX 1 - EXPORTS BY PRODUCT

Product		Territorial coverage	Title codes	
SHIPS & BOATS	by destination by CST classes: tonnage & value in $	EEC countries	E 48-a	
	SITC classes by value in $m	Main countries	D 2-q	
	tonnage & value in $m	OECD countries	D 3-a2	
	by NIMEXE classes by value in $m	All countries	E 20-a	
	SITC classes by value in $m	All countries	U 50-a	U 59-a
	by value in $m	Main countries	U 38-a	
SILICON METAL by destination: tonnage		Italy, Norway & Sweden	T 4-a	
SILICONES by destination: tonnage		Main countries	U 2-a	
SILK (incl waste) in lbs		Main countries	B 10-a	
SILVER	(beaten, drawn & rolled) in oz	All countries	B 15-a	
	(excl coinage) in million oz	USA	N 1-a	
	(mint bullion) by destination in million oz	All countries	T 4-a	
	in million oz	All countries	B 15-a	
	(refined) by destination in oz	USA	J 6-a	
SILVER ORE & bullion in oz & by value in $m		USA	J 6-a	
	(incl concentrates) by destination in oz	Canada	T 4-a	
	in oz	All countries	B 15-a	
SISAL by destination: tonnage		Kenya & Tanzania	B 10-a	
SKIM MILK POWDER by destination: tonnage		Main countries	B 12-m	
SLAB ZINC: tonnage		Main countries	C 12-a	
SLIPPERS (incl house shoes) shipped ex European area in pairs		Non-OECD countries	D 18-a	
	by destination in pairs & by value in $	OECD countries	D 18-a	
SOAP by kind by destination by value in $		Main countries	U 2-a	
	(incl medicated soap): tonnage & value in $	OECD countries	D 5-a	
SODA ASH by destination: tonnage		Main countries	U 2-a	
	tonnage	European countries, Japan & USA	U 25-a	
		OECD countries	D 5-a	
SOLDER by destination: tonnage		Main countries	C 20-m	
SOLID FUELS	(all kinds): tonnage	ECE countries	U 15-a	
	by kind by destination by CST classes by value in $	EEC countries	E 48-a	
	SITC classes by value in $	Main countries	D 2-q	
	tonnage & value in $	OECD countries	D 3-a2	
	by NIMEXE classes: tonnage & value in $	All countries	E 20-a	
	SITC classes: tonnage & value in $	All countries	U 50-a	U 59-a
	tonnage	All countries	B 15-a	
		Main countries	N 2-a	
SORGHUM & MILLET by destination: tonnage		Main countries	A 17-a	
		China, E European countries & USSR	A 17-a	
	tonnage	All countries	A 17-a	
		European countries	U 35-a	
SOUND RECORDERS by NIMEXE classes by value in $		All countries	E 20-a	
	SITC classes by value in $	All countries	U 50-a	U 59-a
SOYBEAN MEAL: tonnage & value in $		W European countries	U 33-a	
SOYBEAN OIL by destination: tonnage		USA	B 19-a	
	tonnage & value in $	W European countries	U 33-a	
	tonnage	Main countries	B 18-q	B 19-a
SOYBEANS	by destination: tonnage	USA	B 19-a	
	by value in $m	W European countries	U 33-a	
	tonnage & value in $m	W European countries	U 33-a	
	tonnage	Main countries	B 18-q	B 19-a
SPECIAL ALLOY STEELS by destination: tonnage		EEC countries	E 29-a	
SPICES	(incl essences) as % of total exports (value basis)	Main countries	B 13-a	
	by kind: tonnage	Main countries	B 18-q	
		Asian, Far East & Australasian countries	U 32-m	
	by value in $	India	U 32-m	
	tonnage	Asian & Far East areas	U 32-q	
	unit value in $ per ton	Kenya	E 45-a	
SPIEGELEISEN by destination: tonnage		EEC countries	E 29-a	

● APPENDIX 1 - EXPORTS BY PRODUCT

Product	Territorial coverage	Title codes	
SPRAYING MACHINES by value in $m	Main countries	U 38-a	
SPUN YARN (cellulosic): tonnage	All countries	A 6-a	
(non-cellulosic): tonnage	All countries	A 6-a	
STAINLESS STEEL INGOTS by destination: tonnage	Main countries	T 4-a	
STAINLESS STEEL PRODUCTS by destination: tonnage	Main countries	T 4-a	
STARCH, GLUTEN & ALBUMINOIDS by destination by value in $	Main countries	U 2-a	
STEAM BOILERS by destination by value in $m	Main European countries	B 30-a	
by type by destination by value in $m	EEC countries	B 30-a	
in tons-hr capacity	European countries, Japan & USA	D 45-a	
STEAM CONDENSERS (for boilers) by value in $	France, W Germany & UK	B 30-a	
STEAM ENGINES by value in $m	Main countries	U 38-a	
STEAM TURBINE GENERATORS by destination by size in mV	Japan	T 7-a	
STEAM TURBINES by destination by size in mW	W Germany	T 7-a	
by size in mW	W European countries & Japan	T 7-a	
manufactured by Brown Boveri in mW	Switzerland	T 7-a	
STEEL ANGLES, SHAPES & SECTIONS: tonnage	E European countries	T 1-a	
STEEL BLANKS (for tubes) by destination: tonnage & value in $	EEC countries	E 5-q	
tonnage	Main countries	T 4-a	
STEEL BLOOMS & BILLETS: tonnage	E European countries & USSR	T 1-a	
STEEL CASTINGS by destination: tonnage	Main countries	T 4-a	
tonnage & as % of domestic production	UK	B 25-a	
tonnage	ECE countries	U 7-m	U 6-a
	Main countries	H 3-a	
STEEL COILS by destination: tonnage & value in $	EEC area	E 5-q	
tonnage	EEC countries	E 29-a	
	Main countries	T 4-a	
STEEL COILS (for re-rolling): tonnage	ECE countries	U 7-m	U 6-a
	Main countries	H 3-a	
STEEL DRAWN WIRE: tonnage	ECE countries	U 7-m	U 6-a
	Main countries	H 3-a	
STEEL FORGINGS & PRESSINGS by destination: tonnage	Main countries	T 4-a	
tonnage	ECE countries	U 7-m	U 6-a
	Main countries	H 3-a	
STEEL HEAVY SECTIONS by destination: tonnage	EEC countries	E 29-a	
STEEL HOOP & STRIP: tonnage	ECE countries	U 7-m	U 6-a
	Main countries	H 3-a	
STEEL INGOTS by destination: tonnage	Main countries	T 4-a	
	EEC countries	E 29-a	
tonnage & as % share of world exports	Main countries	U 49-a	
STEEL INGOTS & CASTINGS by destination: tonnage & value in $	EEC countries	E 5-q	
STEEL MERCHANT BARS by destination: tonnage & value in $	EEC countries	E 5-q	
tonnage	EEC countries	E 29-a	
	Main countries	T 4-a	
STEEL PLATES by destination: tonnage	ECE countries	U 48-a	
tonnage	E European countries & USSR	T 1-a	
STEEL PLATES & SHEETS by destination: tonnage & value in $	EEC countries	E 5-q	
tonnage	EEC countries	E 29-a	
tonnage & as % share of world exports	Main countries	U 49-a	
STEEL PRODUCTS by destination: tonnage	European countries	U 49-a	
	OECD countries	D 22-a	
by destination regions: tonnage	Main European countries	U 57-a	
by kind by destination: tonnage & value in $	EEC countries	E 5-q	
tonnage	Main countries	T 4-a	
by kind (in detail) by destination: tonnage	W Germany	H 3-a	
shipped to EEC area: tonnage	EEC countries	E 30-m	
non-EEC area: tonnage	EEC countries	E 30-m	
(finished) by kind: tonnage	Main countries	T 2-m	
(incl semis): tonnage	Main countries	U 49-a	
shipped to non-EEC area by value in $m	EEC countries	E 29-a	

650

● APPENDIX 1 - EXPORTS BY PRODUCT

Product	Territorial coverage	Title codes	
STEEL RAILS by destination: tonnage & value in $	EEC area	E 5-q	
STEEL REINFORCING RODS by destination: tonnage & value in $	EEC countries	E 5-q	
tonnage	Main countries	T 4-a	
	EEC countries	E 29-a	
STEEL SCRAP: tonnage shipped by world regions	OECD countries	D 22-a	
STEEL SECTIONS by destination: tonnage	ECE countries	U 48-a	
tonnage & % share of world exports	Main countries	U 49-a	
STEEL SEMIS by destination regions: tonnage	Main countries	U 57-a	
STEEL SHEET PILING by destination: tonnage	Main countries	T 4-a	
STEEL SHEETS by destination: tonnage	ECE countries	U 48-a	
(coated) by destination: tonnage	EEC countries	E 29-a	
	Main countries	T 4-a	
(cold-reduced & uncoated): tonnage	E European countries	T 1-a	
(magnetic) by destination: tonnage	Main countries	T 4-a	
(under 3mm gauge): tonnage	ECE area	U 7-m	U 6-a
	Main countries	H 3-a	
STEEL SLEEPERS by destination: tonnage & value in $	EEC area	E 5-q	
tonnage	EEC countries	E 29-a	
	Main countries	T 4-a	
STEEL STRIP by destination: tonnage	ECE countries	U 48-a	
tonnage & % share of world exports	Main countries	U 49-a	
STEEL TUBES by destination: tonnage & value in $	EEC countries	E 5-q	
tonnage	ECE countries	U 48-a	
	EEC countries	E 29-a	
(welded & seamless) by destination: tonnage	Main countries	T 4-a	
STEEL TUBES & FITTINGS: tonnage & % share of world exports	Main countries	U 49-a	
tonnage	ECE countries	U 7-m	U 6-a
	Main countries	H 3-a	
STEEL WHEELS, TYRES & AXLES (for locomotives) by destination: tonnage	EEC countries	E 5-q	
tonnage	ECE countries	U 7-m	U 6-a
	Main countries	H 3-a	
STEEL WIRE by destination: tonnage	Main countries	T 4-a	
tonnage & as % share of world exports	Main countries	U 49-a	
tonnage	E European countries	T 1-a	
STRAW PAPER & STRAW BOARD by destination: tonnage	OECD countries	D 40-a	
STRONTIUM MINERALS: tonnage	All countries	B 15-a	
STRUCTURAL STEEL PRODUCTS by destination: tonnage & value in $	EEC countries	E 5-q	
tonnage	Main countries	T 4-a	
STYRENE by destination: tonnage	Main countries	U 2-a	
SUGAR by destination: tonnage	Main countries	A 20-a	B 13-a
by value & as % of world exports	Main countries	B 13-a	
by value in local currency	Main countries	B 13-a	
	Fiji & Philippines	U 32-m	
(non-centrifugal): historical table from 1890: tonnage	Main countries	A 20-a	
(raw centrifugal) by destination: tonnage	All countries	C 25-a	
historical table from 1890: tonnage	Main countries	A 20-a	
tonnage	All countries	C 19-a	
(raw & refined): unit value of world exports in $ per ton		B 13-a	
(refined) shipped to EEC & non-EEC areas: tonnage	EEC countries	E 44-a	
historical table from 1890: tonnage	Main countries	A 20-a	
from 1876: tonnage	Russia	Z 1-a	
shipments to non-Communist markets: tonnage	All countries	C 19-a	
(total) & to EEC area: tonnage & value in UA	AASM countries	E 41-a	
tonnage & value in $m	Main countries	B 2-a	
tonnage	Asian & Far East areas	U 32-q	
	Fiji, India, Philippines & Thailand	U 32-m	
unit value in $ per ton	African, Caribbean countries & Pacific Is	E 45-a	

APPENDIX 1 - EXPORTS BY PRODUCT

Product	Territorial coverage	Title codes
SUGAR (incl honey) by value in $m	OECD countries	D 1-a
	W European countries	U 33-a
SUGAR & SUGAR PRODUCTS		
by destination by CST classes by value in $	EEC countries	E 48-a
SITC classes by value in $	Main countries	D 2-q
tonnage & value in $	OECD countries	D 3-a2
by NIMEXE classes: tonnage & value in $	All countries	E 20-a
SITC classes: tonnage & value in $	All countries	U 50-a U 59-a
shipped to EEC & non-EEC areas by value in $	EEC countries	E 24-a
SULPHUR by destination: tonnage	OECD countries	D 5-a
by kind: tonnage	All countries	B 15-a
SULPHURIC ACID (incl oleum) by destination: tonnage	Main countries	U 2-a
	ECE countries	U 15-a
	European countries, Japan & USA	U 25-a
SUNFLOWER SEED: tonnage & value in $m	Main countries	B 2-a
tonnage	Main countries	B 19-a
SUNFLOWER SEED CAKE (incl meal): tonnage & by value in $m	Main countries	B 2-a
SUNFLOWER SEED OIL by destination: tonnage	Argentine & USSR	B 19-a
tonnage & value in $m	Main countries	B 2-a
tonnage	Main countries	B 19-a
SUPERPHOSPHATES (concentrated) by destination: tonnage	All countries	C 26-a
(single grade): tonnage	All countries	C 26-a
SYNTHETIC AMMONIA: tonnage	OECD countries	D 5-a
SYNTHETIC DETERGENTS by value in $m	Main countries	U 26-a
SYNTHETIC FIBRE & WOOL YARN: tonnage & value in £	Main countries	K 3-a
SYNTHETIC FIBRE WASTE by destination: tonnage	Main countries	K 4-a
SYNTHETIC FILAMENT YARN: tonnage	Main countries	K 4-a
SYNTHETIC MONOFIL STRIP by destination: tonnage	Main countries	K 4-a
SYNTHETIC NARCOTIC DRUGS by kind by destination in kg	All countries	U 46-a
SYNTHETIC RUBBER (incl substitutes): tonnage	European countries, Japan & USA	U 26-a
by destination: tonnage & value in $	Main countries	U 2-a
tonnage	Main countries	C 18-m B 13-a
	OECD countries	D 5-a
by kind: tonnage	USA	C 18-m
tonnage & value in $m	Main countries	B 2-a
SYNTHETIC SPUN YARN by destination: tonnage	Main countries	K 4-a
SYNTHETIC STAPLE (incl tow): tonnage	Main countries	K 4-a
SYNTHETIC STAPLE by destination: tonnage	Main countries	K 4-a
(carded & combed) & tow: tonnage	Main countries	K 4-a
(incl tow): tonnage	Main countries	U 26-a
SYNTHETIC STAPLE WASTE: tonnage	Main countries	K 4-a
SYNTHETIC WOVEN FILAMENT & FABRICS: tonnage	Main countries	K 4-a
SYNTHETIC WOVEN SPUN YARN FABRICS: tonnage	Main countries	K 4-a
TANNING EXTRACTS (synthetic) by destination by value in $	Main countries	U 2-a
TANTALUM in kg	W Germany & USA	T 4-a
TAPIOCA PRODUCTS by value in local currency	Thailand	U 32-m
TAR & PITCH: tonnage	Main countries	B 15-a
TAR (distilled from coal & natural gas) by destination by value in $	Main countries	U 2-a
TEA by destination by CST classes: tonnage & value in $	EEC countries	E 48-a
SITC classes by value in $	Main countries	D 2-q
tonnage & value in $	OECD countries	D 3-a2
by value in Rs	India	P 6-a
in lbs million	Main countries	B 13-a
tonnage	All countries	C 1-a
	UK	C 11-m

APPENDIX 1 – EXPORTS BY PRODUCT

	Territorial coverage	Title codes	
TEA, continued			
by NIMEXE classes: tonnage & value in $	All countries	E 20-a	
SITC classes: tonnage & value in $	All countries	U 50-a	U 59-a
by value as % of world exports	Main countries	B 13-a	
in local currency	Main countries	B 13-a	
in $	India, Indonesia, Japan & Sri Lanka	U 32-m	
shipped to UK (for sale at London auctions): tonnage	India	P 6-a	
(under private contract): tonnage	India	P 6-a	
shipments (total) & to EEC area: tonnage & value in UA	AASM countries	E 41-a	
tonnage (incl world total)	Main countries	B 2-a	P 6-a
tonnage	Asian & Far East areas	U 32-q	
	India, Indonesia, Japan, Sri Lanka & S Vietnam	U 32-m	
unit value in $ per ton	African, Caribbean countries & Pacific Is	E 45-a	
TELECOMMUNICATIONS EQUIPMENT			
by destination: tonnage & value in $	All countries	U 12-a	
by value in £m	UK	B 24-a	
in $m	Main countries	U 38-a	
TELEVISION RECEIVERS			
by destination by CST classes by value in $	EEC countries	E 48-a	
SITC classes by value in $	Main countries	D 2-q	
	OECD countries	D 3-a2	
by NIMEXE classes by value in $	All countries	E 20-a	
SITC classes by value in $	All countries	U 50-a	U 59-a
by value in £m	UK	B 24-a	
in $m	Main countries	U 38-a	
TEXTILE FABRICS by value in $	Hong Kong, Japan & S Korea	U 32-m	
TEXTILE FIBRES by kind by CST classes by destination by value in $	EEC countries	E 48-a	
NIMEXE classes by value in $	All countries	E 20-a	
SITC classes by value in $	All countries	U 50-a	U 59-a
by destination by value in $	Main countries	D 2-q	
tonnage & value in $	OECD countries	D 3-a2	
shipped to EEC & non-EEC areas: tonnage	EEC countries	E 24-a	
by value in $m	W European countries	U 33-a	
TEXTILE MACHINERY			
by kind by destination by CST classes by value in $	EEC countries	E 48-a	
SITC classes by value in $	Main countries	D 2-q	
tonnage & value in $	OECD countries	D 3-a2	
by NIMEXE classes: volume & value in $	All countries	E 20-a	
SITC classes: volume & value in $	All countries	U 50-a	U 59-a
by value in $	Main countries	U 38-a	
TEXTILE YARNS (all kinds): tonnage	OECD countries	D 46-a	
by kind by destination by CST classes by value in $m	EEC countries	E 48-a	
SITC classes by value in $m	Main countries	D 2-q	
tonnage & value in $	OECD countries	D 3-a2	
by NIMEXE classes by value in $m	All countries	E 20-a	
SITC classes by value in $m	All countries	U 50-a	U 59-a
by value in $m	Asian & Far East countries	U 32-a	
(incl fabrics) by destination by value in £m	UK	B 29-a	
(incl leather) by regions of origin by value in $m	EEC countries	E 38-a	
TIMBER by kind: logs, sawnwood & rounds by volume in m³	All countries	A 23-a	
by volume in m³: historical table from 1836	Scandinavian countries	Z 1-a	
TIMBER (incl cork) shipped to EEC & non-EEC areas by value in $m	EEC countries	E 24-a	
TIMBER (incl sawnwood)			
by kind by destination by CST classes by value in $m	EEC countries	E 48-a	
SITC classes by value in $m	Main countries	D 2-q	
tonnage & value in $m	OECD countries	D 3-a2	

APPENDIX 1 – EXPORTS BY PRODUCT

	Territorial coverage	Title codes	
TIMBER (incl sawnwood), continued			
by kind by NIMEXE classes by value in $m	All countries	E 20-a	
SITC classes by value in $m	All countries	U 50-a	U 59-a
TIN by destination: tonnage	Main countries	C 20-m	T 4-a
by value in local currency	W Malaysia	U 32-m	
(refined) by destination: tonnage	OECD countries	D 21-q	
(unwrought): tonnage	Indonesia, W Malaysia & Thailand	U 32-m	
(unwrought, semis, scrap & alloys): tonnage	All countries	B 15-a	
TIN CONCENTRATES by destination: tonnage	Main countries	C 20-m	
tonnage & value in $m	Main countries	B 2-a	
tonnage	Bolivia	C 20-m	
TIN ORE (incl concentrates): tonnage	Asian & Far East area	U 32-q	
by value in local currency	Indonesia & Laos	U 32-m	
(in concentrates) by destination: tonnage	Main countries	T 4-a	
total exports & to EEC area: tonnage & value in UA	AASM countries	E 41-a	
unit value in $ per ton	Rwanda	E 45-a	
TIN PIGS, BLOCKS & BARS: tonnage	USA	J 6-a	
TINPLATE (incl blackplate) by destination: tonnage & value in $	EEC countries	E 5-q	
TINPLATE by destination: tonnage	ECE countries	U 48-a	
	Main countries	C 20-m	
(electrolytic) by destination: tonnage	USA	C 20-m	
(hot-dipped) by destination: tonnage	USA	C 20-m	
tonnage & % share of world exports	Main countries	U 49-a	
tonnage	ECE countries, Japan & USA	U 7-m	U 6-a
	Greece, E European countries & USSR	T 1-a	
	Main countries	H 3-a	
TINPLATE, TERNEPLATE & BLACKPLATE by destination: tonnage	Main countries	T 4-a	
TITANIUM DIOXIDE: tonnage	OECD countries	D 5-a	
TITANIUM MINERALS: tonnage	All countries	B 15-a	
TOBACCO (incl tobacco manufactures) by value in $m	OECD countries	D 1-a	
TOBACCO Burley by kind by destination in lbs	Main countries	B 17-a	
by destination in lbs	Main countries	B 13-a	
by kind by destination in lbs (in detail)	USA	B 17-m	
by value as % of total world exports	All countries	B 13-a	
in local currency	Main countries	B 13-a	
historical table from 1858: tonnage	Greece	Z 1-a	
tonnage & value in $m	Main countries	B 2-a	
tonnage	India, Indonesia, S Korea & Philippines	U 32-m	
	Main countries	A 5-a	
unit value in $	OAS member countries	N 15-a	
(unmanufactured leaf) in lbs million	All countries	B 13-a	
by value in $m	W European countries	U 33-a	
tonnage	Asian & Far East countries	U 32-q	
total shipped to EEC area: tonnage	AASM countries	E 41-a	
TOBACCO LEAF (flue-cured) by destination: tonnage	Main countries	B 17-a	
TOBACCO PRODUCTS			
by kind by destination by CST classes by value in $m	EEC countries	E 48-a	
SITC classes by value in $m	Main countries	D 2-q	
tonnage & value in $m	OECD countries	D 3-a2	
by NIMEXE classes by value in $m	All countries	E 20-a	
SITC classes by value in $m	All countries	U 50-a	U 59-a
shipped to EEC & non-EEC areas by value in $m	EEC countries	E 24-a	
TOBACCO (raw): unit value in $ per ton	Malawi	E 45-a	
TOBACCO SEED OIL: tonnage	India	B 19-a	
TOILET PREPARATIONS by destination by value in $	Main countries	U 2-a	
TOMATO JUICE: tonnage	All countries	A 7-a	
	OECD countries	B 6-a	
TOMATO PASTE: by destination: tonnage	All countries	A 7-a	

● APPENDIX 1 — EXPORTS BY PRODUCT

Product	Territorial coverage	Title codes	
TOMATOES (fresh) by destination: tonnage	Main countries	D 36-a	
tonnage	OECD countries	D 36-a	
unit value in $ per ton	W European countries	U 20-a	
(processed) by destination: tonnage	Main countries	D 36-a	
tonnage	OECD countries	D 36-a	
TOOL STEEL by destination: tonnage	Main countries	T 4-a	
TOYS by destination by CST classes: tonnage & value in $	EEC countries	E 48-a	
SITC classes by value in $	Main countries	D 2-q	
tonnage & value in $	OECD countries	D 3-a2	
by NIMEXE classes by value in $	All countries	E 20-a	
SITC classes by value in $	All countries	U 50-a	U 59-a
TRACTORS (agricultural) by destination by hp classes by value in £m	UK	V 1-a	
by volume	USSR	V 1-a	
by volume & value in £m	UK	V 1-a	
by value in £m: historical table	UK	V 1-a	
(track-laying) by destination by hp classes by value in £m	UK	V 1-a	
TRAFFIC CONTROL EQUIPMENT by value in $m	Main countries	U 38-a	
TRANSFORMERS by size in mVa	European countries, Japan & USA	D 45-a	
TRANSPORT EQUIPMENT by kind by destination by CST classes by value in $m	EEC countries	E 48-a	
SITC classes by value in $m	Main countries	D 2-q	
tonnage & value in $	OECD countries	D 3-a2	
tonnage & value in $m	All countries	U 12-a	
by NIMEXE classes by value in $m	All countries	E 20-a	
SITC classes by value in $m	All countries	U 50-a	U 59-a
by value in $m	Main countries	U 38-a	
	Australia & Japan	U 32-m	
shipped to EEC & non-EEC areas by value in $m	EEC countries	E 24-a	
TRANSPORT EQUIPMENT – index nos (quantum & value bases)	OECD countries	D 16-q	
TROPICAL TIMBER by value in $	British Solomon Is	U 32-m	
shipments (total) & to EEC area: tonnage & value in UA	AASM countries	E 41-a	
tonnage	ECAFE countries	U 32-m	
TRUCKS & ROAD TRACTORS by destination: volume & value in £m	UK	V 1-a	
TRUCKS, TRACTOR PARTS & DUMPERS by value in £m	UK	V 1-a	
TUBES, PIPES & FITTINGS: tonnage	E European countries & USSR	T 1-a	
TUNG NUTS: tonnage & value in $m	Main countries	B 2-a	
TUNG OIL: tonnage & value in $m	Main countries	B 2-a	
tonnage	Main countries	B 19-a	P 1-a
TUNGSTEN ORE by destination: tonnage & value in $	Main countries	U 53-q	
tonnage	Main countries	U 53-a	
TUNGSTEN ORE, TUNGSTEN METAL, SCRAP & ALLOYS: tonnage	All countries	B 15-a	
TURMERIC by destination in cwt	India	B 13-a	
TYPEWRITERS by value in $m	Main countries	U 38-a	
TYRES (pneumatic) by destination by value in £m	UK	V 1-a	
for passenger cars by destination by value in £m	UK	V 1-a	
passenger cars: volume	USA	C 18-m	
tractors & farm implements: volume	USA	C 18-m	
tractors by destination by value in £m	UK	V 1-a	
trucks and buses: volume	USA	C 18-m	
trucks by destination by value in £m	UK	V 1-a	
UNCOATED STEEL SHEETS (cold-reduced): tonnage	E European countries	T 1-a	
UNIVERSAL STEEL PLATES by destination: tonnage	Main countries	T 4-a	
URANIUM MINERALS: tonnage	All countries	B 15-a	
URANIUM ORE: shipments (total) & to EEC area: tonnage & value in UA	AASM countries	E 41-a	

APPENDIX 1 – EXPORTS BY PRODUCT

	Territorial coverage	Title codes	
VANADIUM ORE (concentrates & oxides): tonnage	USA	T 4-a	
VANILLA ESSENCE in cwt	Main countries	B 13-a	
shipments (total) & to EEC area: tonnage & value in UA	AASM countries	E 41-a	
VEAL by destination: tonnage	Main countries	B 12-m	
VEGETABLE OILS by kind by destination by CST classes by value in $m	EEC countries	E 48-a	
SITC classes by value in $m	Main countries	D 2-q	
tonnage & value in $	OECD countries	D 3-a2	
by NIMEXE classes: tonnage & value in $m	All countries	E 20-a	
SITC classes: tonnage & value in $m	All countries	U 50-a	U 59-a
by value in $m	W Malaysia	U 32-m	
shipped to EEC & non-EEC areas by value in $m	EEC countries	E 24-a	
tonnage	Asian & Far East areas	U 32-q	
	EEC countries	E 44-a	
VEGETABLE PARCHMENT by destination: tonnage	All countries	D 40-a	
VEGETABLE PREPARATIONS by kind: tonnage	OECD countries	B 6-a	
VEGETABLES by destination: tonnage	Bulgaria	U 20-a	
by kind by destination by CST classes by value in $m	EEC countries	E 48-a	
SITC classes by value in $m	Main countries	D 2-q	
tonnage & value in $	OECD countries	D 3-a2	
by NIMEXE classes: tonnage & value in $m	All countries	E 20-a	
SITC classes: tonnage & value in $m	All countries	U 50-a	U 59-a
by value in $m	W European countries	U 20-a	
(dried): unit value in $ per ton	African, Caribbean countries & Pacific Is	E 45-a	
(fresh & frozen) by kind by destination: tonnage	OECD countries	B 6-a	
by value in $m	W European countries	U 33-a	
tonnage	Main E European countries	U 20-a	
unit value in $ per ton	Main European countries	U 20-a	
(prepared) by value in $m	W European countries	U 33-a	
VEHICLE REPLACEMENT PARTS (incl tyres) by value: historical table in £m	UK	V 1-a	
VEHICLE REPLACEMENT PARTS by destination by value in $m	UK	V 1-a	
VEHICLES (special purpose): volume & value by destination in £m	UK	V 1-a	
VENDING MACHINES by value in $m	Main countries	B 18-q	
VENEER SHEETS by destination by volume in m³	European countries	A 13-q	
(incl plywood) by volume in m³	All countries	A 5-a	
shipments (total) & to EEC area: tonnage & value in UA	AASM countries	E 41-a	
unit value in $ per ton	Congo Republic	E 45-a	
VITAMINS (incl provitamins) by destination by value in $	Main countries	U 2-a	
WALNUTS: tonnage (in shell & unshelled)	Main countries	P 4-m	
WASHING PREPARATIONS: tonnage & value in $	OECD countries	D 5-a	
WASTE PAPER by destination: tonnage	All countries	D 40-a	
WATER WHEELS (for hydroelectric generators) by size in mW	Main countries	T 7-a	
WEIGHING MACHINERY by value in $m	Main countries	U 38-a	
WHEAT (incl wheat flour)			
by destination: tonnage	Main countries	A 17-a	C 16-a
		C 29-a	
(commercial sales): tonnage	Main countries	C 16-a	
(special sales): tonnage	Main countries	C 16-a	
tonnage	European countries	U 35-a	
	Main countries	B 7-m	A 17-a
		B 8-a	
world shipments (excl inter-EEC sales): tonnage	Worldwide	C 29-a	

● APPENDIX 1 - EXPORTS BY PRODUCT

Product	Description	Territorial coverage	Title codes	
WHEAT	by destination: tonnage	China, E European countries & USSR	A 17-a	
		Main countries	B 8-a	
	by grade: tonnage by loading areas	Australia & Canada	C 29-a	
	by kind: export inspections by port areas: tonnage	USA	C 29-a	
	by value as % of total exports	Main countries	B 8-a	
	in $m	W European countries	U 33-a	
		Australia	U 32-m	
	(hard) by destination: tonnage	Main countries	C 29-m	
	shipped to USSR: tonnage	All countries	A 17-a	
	under government-assisted programs as % of wheat exports	Worldwide	C 16-a	
	tonnage	All countries	C 29-a	
		Australia	U 32-m	
		Main countries	B 7-q	
		UK	P 5-a	
	unit value in $ per kg	OAS member countries	N 15-a	
WHEAT FLOUR	by destination: tonnage	Main countries	A 17-a	B 8-a
		China, E European countries & USSR	A 17-a	
	tonnage	Communist countries	C 16-a	
		Developed countries	C 16-a	
		Developing countries	C 16-a	
		Main countries	B 7-q	
WHEELS, TYRES & AXLES (STEEL)	by destination: tonnage	ECE countries	U 48-a	
	tonnage & % share	Main countries	U 49-a	
WHEY POWDER	by destination: tonnage	Netherlands	B 12-m	
	tonnage	EEC countries	B 3-a	
WHISKY	by destination by volume in proof gallons	UK	Z 6-a	
	by destination - index nos (volume basis)	UK	Z 6-a	
	by kind by volume in proof gallons	UK	Z 6-a	
	by value in £ & as % of total exports (value basis)	UK	Z 6-a	
WHITE SPIRIT: tonnage		Singapore & W Germany	B 15-a	
WINE	by destination by volume in hectolitres	Main countries	B 5-a	
	by value in $m	W European countries	U 33-a	
	historical table from 1830 by volume in hectolitres	Main European countries	Z 1-a	
	shipped to EEC & non-EEC areas by volume in hectolitres	EEC countries	E 44-a	
WIRE (GALVANISED)	by destination: tonnage	Main countries	T 4-a	
WIRE RODS	by destination: tonnage & value in $	EEC countries	E 5-q	
	tonnage	ECE countries	U 48-a	
		ECE countries, Japan & USA	U 7-m	U 6-a
		EEC countries	E 29-a	
		E European countries & USSR	T 1-a	
		Main countries	H 3-a	T 4-a
	tonnage & as % share of world exports	Main countries	U 49-a	
WOLFRAM ORE	by destination: tonnage	Australia & Portugal	T 4-a	
WOLFRAM: shipments (total) & to EEC area: tonnage & value in UA		AASM countries	E 41-a	
WOOD (incl lumber): tonnage		Asian & Far East areas	U 32-q	
WOOD PULP	(all kinds) by destination: tonnage	All countries	D 40-a	
	by kind & grade: tonnage	Main countries	J 7-a	
		OECD countries	D 41-q	
	(chemical) by destination: tonnage	All countries	D 40-a	
	tonnage	Canada, European countries & USA	A 13-q	
	(dissolving) by destination: tonnage	All countries	D 40-a	
	tonnage	OECD countries	D 41-q	
	(for paper-making) by destination: tonnage	All countries	D 40-a	
	historical table from 1872: tonnage	Scandinavian countries	Z 1-a	
	(mechanical) by destination: tonnage	All countries	D 40-a	
	tonnage	Canada, European countries & USA	A 13-q	

● APPENDIX 1 - EXPORTS BY PRODUCT

	Territorial coverage	Title codes
WOOD PULP, continued		
(sulphate bleached) by destination: tonnage	All countries	D 40-a
(sulphite bleached) by destination: tonnage	All countries	D 40-a
(sulphate unbleached): tonnage	OECD countries	D 41-q
by destination: tonnage	All countries	D 40-a
(sulphite bleached): tonnage	OECD countries	D 41-q
(sulphite unbleached): tonnage	OECD countries	D 41-q
by destination: tonnage	All countries	D 40-a
unit value in $ per ton	Swaziland	E 45-a
WOOD-BASED PANELS by kind by volume in m³	Main countries	A 26-a
WOODEN SLEEPERS by destination by volume in m³	European countries	A 13-q
WOOL (incl mohair): unit value in $ per ton	Lesotho	E 45-a
WOOL by destination in lbs	Commonwealth countries	B 10-a
by kind by destination in kg	Main countries	K 6-a
WOOL (greasy raw)		
by value in $m	W European countries	U 33-a
	World regions	U 11-a
in million lbs	Main countries	B 10-a
tonnage	Asian & Far East countries	U 32-q
	Developing countries	U 11-a
	Main countries	A 5-a U 11-a
	World regions	U 11-a
WOOL TOPS by kind: tonnage & value in £	Main countries	K 3-a
tonnage	OECD countries	D 46-a
WOOL YARN by destination: tonnage	Main countries	K 6-a
by kind: tonnage & value in £	Main countries	K 3-a
tonnage	OECD countries	D 46-a
WOOLLEN CLOTH by quality in yards & value in £	Main countries	K 3-a
WOOLLEN HAIR & YARN: tonnage & value in £	Main countries	K 3-a
WOOLLEN INTERLININGS in yards & value in £	Main countries	K 3-a
WOOLLEN MANUFACTURES by value in $m	Main countries	A 5-a
WORSTED YARN: tonnage & value in £	Main countries	K 3-a
WOVEN COTTON FABRICS by value in Rs	Pakistan	U 32-m
tonnage	All countries	K 1-q
	Hong Kong, India & Japan	U 32-m
	OECD countries	D 46-a
WOVEN JUTE FABRICS by value in $	India & Pakistan	U 32-m
WOVEN KNITTED FABRICS (cellulosic): tonnage	All countries	A 6-a
WOVEN TEXTILE FABRICS: tonnage	OECD countries	D 46-a
WOVEN WOOLLEN FABRICS by destination in kg	Main countries	K 6-a
tonnage	OECD countries	D 46-a
WRAPPING, PACKAGING PAPER & BOARD: tonnage	OECD countries	D 41-q
WRAPPING PAPER: tonnage	Main countries	J 7-a
XYLENE: tonnage	European countries, Japan & USA	U 26-a
ZINC DUST: tonnage	USA	J 6-a
ZINC INGOTS & BARS by destination: tonnage	Zambia	T 4-a
ZINC METAL by destination: tonnage	Main countries	T 4-a
	OECD countries	D 21-q
ZINC: unit value in $ per ton	Zambia	E 45-a
ZINC ORE (incl concentrates) by destination: tonnage	OECD countries	D 21-q
	All countries	T 4-a
	Main countries	C 12-a
crude metal & scrap: tonnage	All countries	B 15-a
(incl concentrates): tonnage	Main countries	U 24-m
unit value in $ per ton	Congo Republic	E 45-a

● APPENDIX 1 - EXPORTS BY PRODUCT

	Territorial coverage	Title codes
ZINC OXIDE: tonnage	OECD countries	D 5-a
ZINC PLATES, SHEETS & STRIP by destination: tonnage	Main countries	T 4-a
ZINC PRODUCTS (rolled): tonnage	USA	J 6-a
(semi-finished) by kind: tonnage	Main countries	T 4-a
ZINC SCRAP by destination: tonnage	Main countries	T 4-a
ZINC SCRAP, DROSS, ASHES & SKIMMINGS: tonnage	USA	J 6-a
ZINC SHEETS & STRIP by destination: tonnage	USA	J 6-a
ZINC SLABS & BLOCKS by destination: tonnage	USA	J 6-a
ZIRCONIUM ORE by destination: tonnage	Australia & USA	T 4-a
tonnage	Australia, W Germany, Malaysia & USA	T 4-a

APPENDIX 2 - IMPORTS BY PRODUCT

	Territorial coverage	Title codes	
ACCUMULATORS by source: no of cells & by value in £	UK	V 1-a	
AGRICULTURAL MACHINERY by value in $m	All countries	U 38-a	
AGRICULTURAL PRODUCTS			
(incl food) by value in $	OECD countries	D 1-a	
as % of total imports (value basis)	OECD countries	D 1-a	
	W European countries	U 20-a	
by areas of source by value in $	OECD countries	D 1-a	
by groups by value in $	All countries	A 14-a	
by source by value in $m	W European countries	U 33-a	
by value in $m	W European countries	U 20-a	
	Main countries	U 23-a	
AGRICULTURAL PRODUCTS - index nos (value basis)	World regions	A 11-a	A 14-a
AGRICULTURAL TRACTORS by value in $m	All countries	U 38-a	
AIR CONDITIONING MACHINERY by value in $	All countries	U 38-a	
AIRCRAFT (incl replacement parts)			
by NIMEXE classes by value in $m	All countries	E 20-a	
SITC classes: volume & value in $m	All countries	U 50-a	U 59-a
by source by CST classes by value in $m	EEC countries	E 21-a	
SITC classes by value in $m	Main countries	D 2-q	
	OECD countries	D 3-a2	
AIRCRAFT by value in $m	All countries	U 38-a	
ALLOY STEEL (by quality) by source: tonnage	Main countries	T 4-a	
by source: tonnage & value in $	EEC countries	E 5-q	
ingots by source: tonnage	Main countries	T 4-a	
tonnage	EEC countries	E 29-a	
ALLOY STEEL (CORROSION-RESISTANT) by source: tonnage	EEC countries	E 29-a	
ALLOY STEEL PRODUCTS by kind: tonnage	Main countries	T 1-a	
ALMONDS: tonnage	Main countries	P 4-m	
ALUMINIUM BARS, RODS, PLATES & SHEETS: tonnage	USA	J 6-a	
ALUMINIUM BLOCKS, SLABS, BILLETS & BARS by source: tonnage	UK	C 30-a	
ALUMINIUM FOIL by source: tonnage	Main countries	T 4-a	
ALUMINIUM INGOTS (incl notch bars): tonnage	UK	C 30-a	
(incl alloy ingots): tonnage	USA	J 6-a	
ALUMINIUM LIGHT SECTIONS by source: tonnage	Main countries	T 4-a	
ALUMINIUM PLATES & SHEETS by source: tonnage	Main countries	T 4-a	
ALUMINIUM (primary) by source: tonnage	Main countries	T 4-a	
	OECD countries	D 21-q	
ALUMINIUM SCRAP by source: tonnage	Main countries	T 4-a	
tonnage	USA	J 6-a	
ALUMINIUM SEMI-MANUFACTURES (unwrought): tonnage	All countries	B 15-a	
ALUMINIUM TUBES by source: tonnage	Main countries	T 4-a	
ALUMINIUM (unwrought): tonnage	Main countries	C 12-a	
ALUMINIUM WIRE by source: tonnage	Main countries	T 4-a	
AMMONIA: tonnage	ECE countries	U 15-a	
	European countries, Japan & USA	U 25-a	
ANIMAL & VEGETABLE OILS & FATS by value in $m	W European countries	U 33-a	
ANIMAL & VEGETABLE PRODUCTS by value in $m	W European countries	U 33-a	
ANIMAL FATS & OILS ex EEC & non-EEC areas by value in $	EEC countries	E 24-a	
ANIMAL FEEDING STUFFS by value in $m	OECD countries	D 1-a	
	W European countries	U 33-a	
ex EEC & non-EEC areas by value in $	EEC countries	E 24-a	
ANIMAL FEEDING STUFFS - index nos (value basis)	World regions	A 11-a	
ANTHRACITE by source: tonnage & value in $m	EEC countries	E 5-q	
tonnage	Main countries	N 2-a	
ANTHRACITE (graded): tonnage	Main countries	B 15-a	
ANTIMONY METAL by source: tonnage	Main countries	T 4-a	
ANTIMONY METAL, ORE, REGULUS METAL & SCRAP: tonnage	All countries	B 15-a	
ANTIMONY METAL: tonnage	All countries	B 15-a	
ANTIMONY ORE by source: tonnage	Italy	C 12-a	
	Main countries	T 4-a	

APPENDIX 2 - IMPORTS BY PRODUCT

Product	Territorial coverage	Title codes	
ANTIMONY OXIDES by source: tonnage	Italy	C 12-a	
ANTIMONY (unwrought) by source: tonnage	Italy	C 12-a	
APPLES (for cider production) by source: tonnage	OECD countries	D 37-a	
(fresh) by source: tonnage	Main OECD countries	D 33-a	D 37-a
by value in $m	W European countries	U 33-a	
tonnage	OECD countries	D 33-a	
unit value in $ per ton	W European countries	U 20-a	
net imports: tonnage	OECD countries	D 29-a	
(processed): tonnage	OECD countries	D 33-a	
APRICOTS (fresh) by source: tonnage	OECD countries	D 37-a	
ARSENIC (incl derivatives): tonnage	All countries	B 15-a	
ARTIFICIAL STAPLE FIBRES: tonnage	European countries, Japan & USA	U 26-a	
ARTISTS' COLOURS: tonnage & value in $	OECD countries	D 5-a	
ASBESTOS PRODUCTS by source by CST classes: tonnage & value in $	EEC countries	E 21-a	
SITC classes by value in $	Main countries	D 2-q	
tonnage & value in $	OECD countries	D 3-a2	
ASPARAGUS by source: tonnage	OECD countries	D 37-a	
ASPHALT, BITUMEN & PITCH: tonnage	Main countries	B 15-a	
AUTOMOTIVE AXLES by source by value in £m	UK	V 1-a	
AUTOMOTIVE EQUIPMENT (electrical) by value in $	All countries	U 38-a	
AUTOMOTIVE REPLACEMENT PARTS by value in £ (in detail)	UK	V 1-a	
AVIATION SPIRIT (incl jet fuels) by source: tonnage	OECD countries	D 31-a	
AVIATION SPIRIT: tonnage	Main countries	B 15-a	
	OECD countries	D 39-q	
AVIATION TURBINE FUEL: tonnage	Main countries	B 15-a	
BABASSU OIL: tonnage	USA	B 19-a	
BACON & LARD by source: tonnage	EEC countries	E 47-m	
BACON by source: tonnage	UK	B 11-a	
BANANA PRODUCTS: purée & banana flour: tonnage	Main countries	A 5-a	
BANANAS by source: tonnage	EEC countries	B 5-a	
	OECD countries	D 37-a	
	UK	B 5-m	
(dried): tonnage	Main countries	A 5-a	
tonnage	Main countries	B 5-a	
	OECD countries	B 6-a	
	USSR	U 20-a	
unit value in $ per ton	W European countries	U 20-a	
BARIUM MINERALS: witherite & barytes: tonnage	All countries	B 15-a	
BARLEY by source: tonnage	European countries	U 35-a	
	Main countries	B 8-a	
by ports of entry: tonnage	UK	B 7-m	P 5-a
by value in $m	W European countries	U 33-a	
shipped into E European area & USSR: tonnage	Non-Communist countries	A 17-a	
tonnage	All countries	A 17-a	
BARLEY (unmilled) for production of animal feed: tonnage	UK	P 5-a	
BASIC METALS by value in $m	Asian, Far East & Australasian countries	U 32-m	
BASIC SLAG: tonnage	OECD countries	D 5-a	
BATTERIES & ACCUMULATORS by value in $m	All countries	U 38-a	
BAUXITE by source: tonnage	Main countries	T 4-a	
BEANS (green) by source: tonnage	OECD countries	D 37-a	
BEARINGS (ball & rolled) by value in $m	All countries	U 38-a	
BEEF & VEAL by source: tonnage	EEC countries	B 11-a	
tonnage	European countries & USSR	U 36-a	
BEEF & VEAL (fresh, salted & chilled): tonnage	Main countries	B 11-a	
BENTONITE (incl bentonite clay): tonnage	All countries	B 15-a	
BENZENE: tonnage	European countries, Japan & USA	U 26-a	
BERYL: tonnage	All countries	B 15-a	

•• APPENDIX 2 — IMPORTS BY PRODUCT

Product	Territorial coverage	Title codes	
BERYLLIUM ORE by source: tonnage	USA	T 4-a	
BEVERAGES (incl tobacco)			
as % of total trade in agricultural products	W European countries	U 20-a	
by kind by source: tonnage & value in $	All countries	U 12-a	
by value in $m	W European countries	U 33-a	
BEVERAGES BY KIND			
by NIMEXE classes by value in $	All countries	E 20-a	
SITC classes by value in $	All countries	U 50-a	U 59-a
by source by CST classes: tonnage & value in $	EEC countries	E 21-a	
SITC classes by value in $	Main countries	D 2-q	
tonnage & value in $	OECD countries	D 3-a2	
BEVERAGES: coffee, tea & cocoa by value in $	OECD countries	D 1-a	
shipped ex EEC & non-EEC areas by value in $m	EEC countries	E 24-a	
BICYCLES by value in $m	All countries	U 38-a	
BISMUTH (metallic) by source: tonnage	UK & USA	T 4-a	
BISMUTH (incl ore concentrates): tonnage	All countries	B 15-a	
BITUMEN by source: tonnage	OECD countries	D 31-a	
BOILERS (incl ancillaries) by value in local currency	Iran	U 32-m	
BORATES, BORON MINERALS & REFINED BORAX: tonnage	All countries	B 15-a	
BORING MACHINES (for metal) by source by value in £m	UK	B 31-a	
no & value in $m	USA	J 2-a	
BRASS PRODUCTS (semi-finished) by source: tonnage	USA	J 6-a	
BRASS SCRAP: tonnage	USA	J 6-a	
BRASS TUBES & TUBING (seamless) by source: tonnage	USA	J 6-a	
BRAZIL NUTS (in shell): tonnage	Main countries	P 4-m	
BRIGHT STEEL BARS by source: tonnage	EEC countries	E 5-q	E 29-a
	Main countries	T 4-a	
BROADLEAVED LOGS by source by volume in m³	European countries	A 13-q	
BROMIDE (incl compounds): tonnage	All countries	B 15-a	
BROWN COAL BRIQUETTES: tonnage	European countries	U 31-q	
BROWN COAL: tonnage	European countries	U 31-q	
BRUSSELS SPROUTS by source: tonnage	OECD countries	D 37-a	
BUILDING MATERIALS BY KIND			
by NIMEXE classes: tonnage & value in $	All countries	E 20-a	
SITC classes: tonnage & value in $	All countries	U 50-a	U 59-a
by source by CST classes: tonnage & value in $	EEC countries	E 21-a	
SITC classes by value in $	Main countries	D 2-q	
tonnage & value in $	OECD countries	D 3-a2	
BUSES & COACHES by value in £m	UK	B 28-a	
BUSES, COACHES & GOODS VEHICLES by volume	Main countries	S 24-a	
BUTANOL: tonnage	European countries, Japan & USA	U 26-a	
BUTTER by source: tonnage	Main countries	B 12-m	
	UK	B 4-a	
by value in $m	OECD countries	D 1-a	
	W European countries	U 33-a	
inter-EEC imports: tonnage	EEC countries	B 3-a	
shipped ex EEC & non-EEC areas: tonnage	EEC countries	E 44-a	
tonnage	Main countries	B 4-a	P 1-a
BUTTER-OIL by source: tonnage	Main countries	B 12-m	
CABBAGES by source: tonnage	OECD countries	D 37-a	
CADMIUM METAL (incl compounds): tonnage	All countries	B 15-a	
CADMIUM METAL by source: tonnage	Italy	C 12-a	
	Main countries	T 4-a	
CALCIUM CARBIDE: tonnage	European countries, Japan & USA	U 25-a	
	OECD countries	D 5-a	
CALCULATING MACHINES by value in $m	All countries	U 38-a	
CALFSKINS (incl kips): tonnage	Main countries	B 9-m	

APPENDIX 2 – IMPORTS BY PRODUCT

Product	Territorial coverage	Title codes	
CALFSKINS by source: tonnage & value in $m	OECD countries	D 18-a	
shipped ex non-OECD area: tonnage	OECD countries	D 18-a	
(wet-salted): tonnage	Main countries	A 18-a	
CANNED & BOTTLED FRUIT by kind: tonnage	OECD countries	B 6-a	
CANNED APRICOTS: tonnage	Main countries	A 7-a	
CANNED FISH (all kinds): tonnage & value in $	OECD countries	D 43-a	
CANNED FISH PRODUCTS: tonnage & value in $m	OECD countries	D 43-a	
CANNED FRUIT by source: tonnage	Main countries	B 5-a	
CANNED MEAT by kind: tonnage	UK	B 11-a	
by source by kind: tonnage	UK	B 12-a	
tonnage	Main countries	B 11-a	
CANNED PEACHES: tonnage	Main countries	A 7-a	
CANNED TOMATOES: tonnage	Canada, UK & USA	A 7-a	
CANNED VEGETABLES by kind: tonnage	OECD countries	B 6-a	
CAPITAL GOODS by value in local currency	African countries	U 44-a	
in UA	AASM countries	E 41-a	
shipped ex EEC area by value in UA	AASM countries	E 41-a	
CAPSICUMS & CHILLIES by source in cwt	Main countries	B 13-a	
CARAVAN TRAILERS by source: no & value in £	UK	V 1-a	
CARBON BLACK: tonnage	European countries, Japan & USA	U 25-a	
CARDAMONS by source in cwt	Main countries	B 13-a	
CARROTS by source: tonnage	OECD countries	D 37-a	
CASEIN (incl caseinates) by source: tonnage	Main countries	B 12-a	
by source: tonnage	Italy, Japan, UK & USA	B 4-a	
tonnage	EEC countries	B 3-a	
	Main countries	B 4-a	
CASHEW KERNELS: tonnage	Main countries	P 4-m	
CASHEW SEEDS: tonnage	India	P 4-m	
CAST IRON PIPES by source: tonnage	Main countries	T 4-a	
(incl fittings): tonnage	Main countries	T 1-a	
tonnage	ECE countries	U 7-m	U 6-a
	Main countries	H 3-a	T 1-a
CASTINGS by source: tonnage & value in $	EEC countries	E 5-q	
CASTOR OIL by source: tonnage	UK	B 19-a	
CASTOR SEED by source: tonnage	EEC countries	B 19-a	
tonnage	Main countries	B 19-a	
CATTLE & CALVES by source by volume	Main countries	B 12-m	
CATTLE (for beef) by kind: tonnage (live wt)	EEC countries	E 1-a	
CATTLE HIDES by source: tonnage & value in $	OECD countries	D 18-a	
(incl buffalo hides): tonnage	All countries	A 18-a	
shipped ex non-OECD area: tonnage	OECD countries	D 18-a	
CAULIFLOWERS by source: tonnage	OECD countries	D 37-a	
CAUSTIC SODA: tonnage	ECE countries	U 15-a	
	European countries, Japan & USA	U 25-a	
	OECD countries	D 5-a	
CELERY by source: tonnage	OECD countries	D 37-a	
CELLULOSIC DERIVATIVES by source: tonnage	OECD countries	D 5-a	
CELLULOSIC FIBRES & FIBRE WASTE by source: tonnage	Main countries	K 4-a	
tonnage	OECD countries	D 46-a	
CELLULOSIC FILAMENTS: imports as % of own production	Main countries	D 27-a	
CELLULOSIC SPUN YARN by source: tonnage	Main countries	K 4-a	
CELLULOSIC STAPLE & TOW: tonnage	Main countries	K 4-a	
CELLULOSIC STAPLE: imports as % of own production	Main countries	D 27-a	
CELLULOSIC WOVEN FILAMENT FABRICS: tonnage	Main countries	K 4-a	
CELLULOSIC WOVEN SPUN YARN FABRICS: tonnage	Main countries	K 4-a	
CELLULOSIC YARN: tonnage	Main countries	K 4-a	
	OECD countries	D 46-a	

APPENDIX 2 – IMPORTS BY PRODUCT

Product	Territorial coverage	Title codes	
CEMENT (ex world regions): tonnage	OECD countries	D 4-a	
tonnage	European countries	U 5-a	
CEMENT & PLASTER			
by NIMEXE classes: tonnage & value in $	All countries	E 20-a	
SITC classes: tonnage & value in $	All countries	U 50-a	U 59-a
by source by CST classes: tonnage & value in $	EEC countries	E 21-a	
SITC classes by value in $	Main countries	D 2-q	
tonnage & value in $	OECD countries	D 3-a2	
CEREAL PREPARATIONS by value in $m	W European countries	U 33-a	
CEREALS by value	Asian & Far East countries	U 32-m	
historical tables from 1750: tonnage	Main European countries	Z 1-a	
shipped ex EEC & non-EEC areas: tonnage	EEC countries	E 44-a	
tonnage	E European countries & USSR	U 16-a	
CEREALS (incl cereal preparations)			
ex EEC & non-EEC areas by value in $	EEC countries	E 24-a	
by value in $	OECD countries	D 1-a	
CEREALS BY KIND			
by NIMEXE classes: tonnage & value in $	All countries	E 20-a	
by ports of entry: tonnage	UK	B 7-m	
by SITC classes: tonnage & value in $	All countries	U 50-a	U 59-a
by source by CST classes: tonnage & value in $	EEC countries	E 21-a	
SITC classes by value in $	Main countries	D 2-q	
tonnage & value in $	OECD countries	D 3-a2	
by value in $	W European countries	U 33-a	
tonnage	Main countries	B 8-a	
CHEESE by source: tonnage	UK	B 4-a	
(processed blue-veined cheddar): tonnage	UK	B 12-m	
ex EEC & non-EEC areas: tonnage	EEC countries	E 44-a	
ex EEC area: tonnage	EEC countries	B 3-a	
(incl curd) by value in $m	W European countries	U 33-a	
tonnage	Main countries	B 4-a	
CHEMICAL COMPOUNDS by source by kind: tonnage & value in $	All countries	U 12-a	
CHEMICAL PRODUCTS			
by kind ex EEC & non-EEC areas: tonnage	EEC countries	E 24-a	
by value in Lit (in detail)	Italy	C 6-a	
tonnage	OECD countries	D 5-a	
by source by value in UA	EEC countries	E 23-a	
tonnage	OECD countries	D 5-a	
% change by source (value basis)	EEC countries	E 23-a	
% increase in imports	Canada, European countries, Japan & USA	D 5-a	
ex non-EEC area by value in UA	EEC countries	E 22-m	
CHEMICAL PRODUCTS – index nos (quantum & value bases)	OECD countries	D 16-q	
CHEMICALS by source by value in $m	Main countries	U 23-a	
by value in Lit	Main countries	C 6-a	
in $m	Developing countries	U 52-a	
	Asian, Far East & Australasian countries	U 32-m	
shipped ex developing countries by value in $m	EEC countries	U 52-a	
ex EEC area by value in UA	African, Caribbean countries & Pacific Is	E 45-a	
CHEMICALS BY KIND			
by NIMEXE classes by value in $	All countries	E 20-a	
SITC classes by value in $	All countries	U 50-a	U 59-a
by source by CST classes: tonnage & value in $	EEC countries	E 21-a	
SITC classes by value in $	Main countries	D 2-q	
tonnage & value in $	OECD countries	D 3-a2	
tonnage & value in $	All countries	U 12-a	
CHERRIES (fresh) by source: tonnage	OECD countries	D 37-a	
CHINA CLAY: tonnage	All countries	B 15-a	
CHLORINE: tonnage	European countries, Japan & USA	U 25-a	
CHOCOLATE (incl chocolate products): tonnage	OECD countries	D 5-a	
	Main countries	A 3-m	

APPENDIX 2 - IMPORTS BY PRODUCT

Product	Territorial coverage	Title codes	
CHROME ORE by source: tonnage	Main countries	T 4-a	
CHROME ORE (incl alloys by grade) by source: tonnage	Italy	C 12-a	
CHROME ORE, CHROMIUM METAL & CONCENTRATES: tonnage	All countries	B 15-a	
CHROMIUM METAL by source: tonnage	Sweden & USA	T 4-a	
CIGARETTES by source in lbs	UK	B 17-a	
CIGARS by source in lbs	UK	B 17-a	
CINNAMON & CASSIA by source in cwt	EEC countries & USA	B 18-q	
in cwt	Main countries	B 13-a	
CITRUS FRUITS BY KIND by source: tonnage	OECD countries	D 37-a	
tonnage	OECD countries	B 6-a	
	USSR	U 20-a	
CITRUS FRUITS: grapefruit, lemons & limes: tonnage	Main countries	A 5-a	
oranges & tangerines by value in $m	W European countries	U 33-a	
tonnage	Main countries	A 5-a	
CLINKER by source: tonnage	OECD countries	D 4-a	
CLOTHING by kind by value in £m	UK	B 22-a	
by source by value in $	EEC countries, Japan & USA	U 23-a	
by value as % of domestic sales	EEC countries	B 22-a	
in $m	Developing countries	U 52-a	
	ECAFE countries	U 32-m	
	Main countries	G 1-a	
(ex developing countries) by value in $m	EEC countries	U 52-a	
(ex EEC & non-EEC areas) by value in $m	EEC countries	E 24-a	
(ex world regions) by value in $m	EEC countries	B 22-a	
(incl accessories): tonnage	OECD countries	D 46-a	
made of cellulosic materials: tonnage	All countries	A 6-a	
made of non-cellulosic materials: tonnage	All countries	A 6-a	
(ready-made) by source by value in £m	UK	B 29-a	
CLOTHING & FOOTWEAR by kind by NIMEXE classes by value in $	All countries	E 20-a	
SITC classes by value in $	All countries	U 50-a	U 59-a
by source by CST classes by value in $	EEC countries	E 21-a	
by source by SITC classes by value in $	Main countries	D 2-q	
tonnage & value in $	OECD countries	D 3-a2	
CLOVES by source in cwt	All countries	B 18-m	
	Main countries	B 13-a	
COAL by source in kg & by value in $	EEC countries	E 5-q	
(ex non-EEC area) by value in $	EEC countries	E 29-a	
tonnage	EEC countries	E 14-a	
historical table from 1827: tonnage	Main European countries	Z 1-a	
COAL & FUELS by value in UA	AASM countries	E 41-a	
shipped ex EEC area by value in UA	AASM countries	E 41-a	
COAL (bituminous) by source: tonnage	Main countries	N 2-a	
COAL BRIQUETTES (incl lignite): tonnage	Main countries	B 15-a	
COARSE GRAINS as % of domestic consumption	World regions	C 27-a	
tonnage	All countries	A 17-a	
	EEC countries, Israel, Japan & Spain	A 12-a	
	World importing regions	C 16-a	
	Main countries	A 12-a	
COATED STEEL SHEETS by source: tonnage	EEC countries	E 5-q	
COBALT (incl derivatives): tonnage	All countries	B 15-a	
by source: tonnage	All countries	B 15-a	
(unwrought & refined) by source: tonnage	Italy	C 12-a	
COCOA BEANS by SITC classes by value in $	Main countries	D 2-q	
tonnage & value in $	OECD countries	D 3-a2	
by source by CST classes: tonnage & value in $	EEC countries	E 21-a	
historical table from 1940: tonnage	Main countries	P 2-a	
tonnage	Main countries	A 3-m	

•• APPENDIX 2 – IMPORTS BY PRODUCT

Product	Territorial coverage	Title codes	
COCOA BUTTER: historical table from 1947: tonnage	UK	P 2-a	
tonnage	Main countries	A 3-m	B 13-a
		P 3-a	
COCOA PASTE (incl powder): tonnage	Main countries	B 18-a	
(incl cake): tonnage	Main countries	B 13-a	
tonnage	Main countries	A 3-m	
COCOA POWDER: tonnage	Main countries	A 3-m	B 13-a
		P 3-a	
COCOA (raw): tonnage	Main countries	B 18-q	A 5-a
		B 13-a	P 3-a
COCONUT OIL & COPRA: tonnage	Main countries	A 4-a	
COCONUT OIL: tonnage	Main countries	B 19-a	P 1-a
COFFEE by NIMEXE classes: tonnage & value in $	All countries	E 20-a	
SITC classes: tonnage & value in $	All countries	U 50-a	U 59-a
by source by CST classes: tonnage & value in $	EEC countries	E 21-a	
SITC classes by value in $	Main countries	D 2-q	
tonnage & value in $	OECD countries	D 3-a2	
by value in cents per lb	USA	J 1-m	
COFFEE BEANS by source & customs districts: tonnage	USA	J 1-m	
in 60 kg bags	All countries	J 1-a	
	Canada	J 1-a	
tonnage	USA	J 1-m	
in 60 kg bags	Main countries	B 18-q	B 13-a
(incl world total) in 60 kg bags	Main countries	J 1-a	
(roasted) by source: tonnage	Main countries	J 1-a	
tonnage	Main countries	B 13-a	
COKE by source: tonnage & value in $	EEC countries	E 5-q	
shipped ex non-EEC area: tonnage	EEC countries	E 14-a	
tonnage	ECE countries, Japan & USA	U 7-m	U 6-a
	Main countries	B 15-a	H 3-a
		N 2-a	
COKE-OVEN COKE (for iron & steel industry): tonnage	OECD countries	D 22-a	
tonnage	European countries	U 31-q	
COLD-ROLLED STEEL SHEETS by source: tonnage	Main countries	T 4-a	
COLD-ROLLED STEEL STRIP by source: tonnage	Main countries	T 4-a	
	EEC countries	E 5-q	
COLUMBIUM ORE (incl concentrates) by source: tonnage	Main countries	T 4-a	
COMMERCIAL VEHICLES (incl buses) by value in $m	All countries	U 38-a	
	Latin American countries	U 38-a	
COMMERCIAL VEHICLES			
by NIMEXE classes by value in $m	All countries	E 20-a	
SITC classes by value in $m	All countries	U 50-a	U 59-a
by source: no & value in £m	UK	V 4-a	
by value in £m	UK	B 28-a	
(incl chassis): volume	Main countries	V 4-a	
shipped ex USA: volume	Main countries	V 4-a	
COMMODITIES by NIMEXE classes: tonnage & value in $	All countries	E 20-a	
SITC classes: tonnage & value in $	All countries	U 50-a	U 59-a
by source by CST classes: tonnage & value in $	EEC countries	E 21-a	
SITC classes by value in $	Main countries	D 2-q	
tonnage & value in $	OECD countries	D 3-a2	
COMMONWEALTH SHARE: UK imports of butter: tonnage	UK	B 4-a	
buttermilk & whey: tonnage	UK	B 4-a	
dairy products & milk powder: tonnage	UK	B 4-a	
COMPLEX PHOSPHATE FERTILISERS: tonnage	OECD countries	D 5-a	
COMPOUND ANIMAL FEEDING STUFFS: tonnage	UK	P 5-a	
COMPUTERS (incl ancillary equipment) by value in £m	UK	B 24-a	
CONDENSATION PRODUCTS (plastics): tonnage	European countries, Japan & USA	U 26-a	

•• APPENDIX 2 – IMPORTS BY PRODUCT

Product	Territorial coverage	Title codes	
CONDENSED MILK by source: tonnage	Main countries	B 12-m	
	Philippines, Thailand & UK	B 4-a	
tonnage	EEC countries	B 3-a	E 44-a
	Main countries	B 4-a	
CONDENSERS by value in $m	All countries	U 38-a	
CONSTRUCTION BOARD: tonnage	OECD countries	D 41-q	
CONSTRUCTION EQUIPMENT by value in $m	All countries	U 38-a	
CONSTRUCTION MATERIALS – index nos (quantum & value bases)	OECD countries	D 16-q	
CONSUMER GOODS as % of total imports (value basis)	E European countries	U 16-a	
by value in local currency	African countries	U 44-a	
COPPER by kind: tonnage	USA	J 6-a	
(electrolytic) by source: tonnage	UK & Yugoslavia	T 4-a	
tonnage	All countries	B 15-a	
	UK	J 6-a	
(fire-refined): tonnage	UK	J 6-a	
(refined & alloyed): tonnage	All countries	B 15-a	
(refined) by source: tonnage	Main countries	T 4-a	
tonnage	Main countries	C 30-m	
(unwrought) incl semi-manufactures: tonnage	All countries	B 15-a	
COPPER ALLOY: plates & sheets by source: tonnage	Main countries	T 4-a	
rods, bars & sections by source: tonnage	Main countries	T 4-a	
tubes by source: tonnage	Main countries	T 4-a	
COPPER ALLOY FOIL by source: tonnage	USA	J 6-a	
COPPER ALLOYS by source: tonnage	Main countries	T 4-a	
COPPER BLISTER by source: tonnage	Main countries	T 4-a	
	OECD countries	D 21-q	
tonnage	Main countries	C 30-m	C 12-a
	UK	J 6-a	
(unrefined) in pigs: tonnage	USA	J 6-a	
COPPER CATHODES (incl cathode ingots): tonnage	USA	J 6-a	
COPPER CONCENTRATES (based on metal content): tonnage	USA	J 6-a	
COPPER INGOTS by source: tonnage	Netherlands	T 4-a	
COPPER ORE (based on metal content): tonnage	USA	J 6-a	
(incl concentrates) by source: tonnage	OECD countries	D 21-q	
tonnage	Main countries	C 30-m	
COPPER PLATES & SHEETS by source: tonnage	W Germany & USA	T 4-a	
COPPER POWDER by source: tonnage	USA	T 4-a	
COPPER PRODUCTS (semi-finished) incl alloy by kind by source: tonnage	Main countries	T 4-a	
by source: tonnage	USA	J 6-a	
COPPER RODS, BARS & SECTIONS by source: tonnage	W Germany	T 4-a	
COPPER SCRAP by source: tonnage	Main countries	T 4-a	
tonnage	All countries	B 15-a	
	USA	J 6-a	
COPPER SHEETS (in rolls) incl rods by source: tonnage	USA	J 6-a	
COPPER STRIP (in coil) by source: tonnage	W Germany & USA	T 4-a	
COPPER SULPHATE: tonnage	All countries	B 15-a	
COPPER TUBES by source: tonnage	Netherlands & USA	T 4-a	
(seamless) by source: tonnage	USA	J 6-a	
COPPER WIRE by source: tonnage	Netherlands & USA	T 4-a	
COPPER WIRE BARS by source: tonnage	Netherlands	T 4-a	
(electrolytic) by source: tonnage	India	T 4-a	
COPRA by source: tonnage	EEC countries	B 19-a	
	France, W Germany, Netherlands & Japan	B 19-a	
(for production of animal feed): tonnage	UK	P 5-a	
in oil conversion equiv tonnage	UK	P 1-a	
tonnage	Main countries	B 19-a	
CORNED BEEF, CANNED VEAL & PORK PRODUCTS: tonnage	UK	B 11-a	

•• APPENDIX 2 – IMPORTS BY PRODUCT

Product	Territorial coverage	Title codes	
COTTON (ex British Commonwealth countries): tonnage	EEC countries	B 10-a	
COTTON (raw) <u>by source</u> in bales	Main countries	K 1-m	
in lbs million	Main countries	B 10-a	
by value in local currency	Hong Kong	U 32-m	
in $m	W European countries	U 33-a	
shipped ex USA & all other sources (as total): tonnage	OECD countries	D 46-a	
tonnage & in bales	All countries	K 1-a	
COTTON YARN: tonnage	Main countries	K 1-q	
	OECD countries	D 46-a	
COTTONSEED in vegetable oil equiv tonnage	UK	P 1-a	
	EEC countries	P 5-a	
(for production of animal feed): tonnage	UK	P 5-a	
tonnage	Main countries	B 19-a	
COTTONSEED MEAL (as animal feed): tonnage	UK	P 5-a	
COTTONSEED OIL (crude & refined); tonnage	Main countries	P 1-a	
tonnage	Main countries	B 19-a	
CRUDE PETROLEUM (incl petroleum products) <u>by source</u>: tonnage	World hemispheres	C 13-a	
	World regions	C 21-a	
tonnage	E European countries & USSR	U 16-a	
CRUDE PETROLEUM			
as % of total domestic supply	Main countries	H 4-a	
<u>by source</u>: tonnage	EEC countries	C 14-a	
	Italy	H 4-a	
	OECD countries	D 31-a	
tonnage & value in $	All countries	U 12-a	
by value in $m	Australia & India	U 32-m	
by volume in m³	Latin American countries	U 18-a	
ex non-EEC area: tonnage	EEC countries	E 14-a	
importing countries listed in order of volume of demand	All countries	C 14-a	
tonnage	ECE countries	U 15-a	
	EEC countries	E 26-m	
	Main countries	B 15-a	C 14-a
		E 3-a	
	OECD countries	D 39-q	
	World regions	T 3-a	
CRUDE STEEL INGOTS & CASTINGS <u>by source</u>: tonnage & value in $m	EEC countries	E 5-q	
tonnage	EEC countries	E 29-a	
	Main countries	T 4-a	
	All countries	B 15-a	
	UK	T 2-m	
CRUSTACEANS & MOLLUSCS: tonnage	OECD countries	D 43-a	
CUCUMBERS <u>by source</u>: tonnage	OECD countries	D 37-a	
CULTIVATING MACHINES by value in $m	All countries	U 38-a	
CURED FISH PRODUCTS: tonnage & value in $m	OECD countries	D 43-a	
CURRANTS <u>by source</u>: tonnage	OECD countries	D 37-a	
CURRY POWDER in lbs	Main countries	B 13-a	
CYCLES & MOPEDS			
by NIMEXE classes by value in $	All countries	E 20-a	
SITC classes: tonnage & value in $	All countries	U 50-a	U 59-a
<u>by source</u> by CST classes by value in $	EEC countries	E 21-a	
SITC classes by value in $	Main countries	D 2-q	
tonnage & value in $	OECD countries	D 3-a2	
DAIRY EQUIPMENT by value in $m	All countries	U 38-a	
DAIRY PRODUCTS (incl eggs) by value in $	OECD countries	D 1-a	
ex EEC & non-EEC areas by value in $	EEC countries	E 24-a	

•• APPENDIX 2 - IMPORTS BY PRODUCT

Product	Territorial coverage	Title codes	
DAIRY PRODUCTS BY KIND			
by NIMEXE classes: tonnage & value in $	All countries	E 20-a	
SITC classes: tonnage & value in $	All countries	U 50-a	U 59-a
by source by CST classes: tonnage & value in $	EEC countries	E 21-a	
SITC classes by value in $	Main countries	D 2-q	
tonnage & value in $	OECD countries	D 3-a2	
DIAMONDS (gem, rough & industrial) by value in local currency	All countries	B 15-a	
DIATOMACEOUS EARTH: tonnage	All countries	B 15-a	
DIESEL OIL by source: tonnage	OECD countries	D 31-a	
tonnage	Main countries	B 15-a	C 14-a
	OECD countries	D 39-q	
DOMESTIC EQUIPMENT BY KIND			
by NIMEXE classes by volume	All countries	E 20-a	
SITC classes by volume	All countries	U 50-a	U 59-a
by source by CST classes by value in $	EEC countries	E 21-a	
SITC classes by value in $	Main countries	D 2-q	
tonnage & value in $	OECD countries	D 3-a2	
DOMESTIC EQUIPMENT (electrical) by source: tonnage & value in $m	All countries	U 12-a	
by value in $m	All countries	U 38-a	
(electronic) by value in £m	UK	B 24-a	
(non-electrical) by value in $m	All countries	U 38-a	
DRAWN WIRE by source: tonnage	EEC countries	E 5-q	E 29-a
DRIED FRUIT by kind: tonnage	Main countries	B 5-a	
	OECD countries	B 6-a	
DRILLING MACHINES by source by value in £m	UK	B 31-a	
by volume & value in $m	USA	J 2-a	
DRINK & TOBACCO shipped ex EEC area by value in UA	African, Caribbean countries & Pacific Is	E 45-a	
into EEC area by value in $m	Developing countries	U 52-a	
DUMPERS (incl dump trucks) by source: no & value in £m	UK	V 1-a	
DURABLE CONSUMER GOODS - index nos (quantum & value bases)	OECD countries	D 16-q	
DURUM WHEAT: tonnage	World economic groups	C 16-a	
DYESTUFFS by source: tonnage & value in $m	OECD countries	D 5-a	
DYNAMO STEEL SHEETS by source: tonnage	EEC countries	E 5-q	
EGG PRODUCTS by source: tonnage	Main countries	B 12-m	
	W Germany & UK	B 4-a	
EGG PRODUCTS: YOLKS (frozen & dried): tonnage	Main countries	B 4-a	
EGGS by source by volume	EEC countries	E 47-m	
	Main countries	B 12-m	
tonnage	EEC countries	E 47-m	
	W Germany, Italy, Switzerland & UK	B 4-a	
by value in $m	W European countries	U 33-a	
tonnage	EEC countries	E 44-a	
ELECTRIC ENERGY			
by source in kWh	European countries	U 1-a	
ex EEC & non-EEC areas by value in $m	EEC countries	E 24-a	
ex non-EEC area in coal equiv tonnage	EEC countries	E 14-a	
in coal equiv tonnage	EEC area	E 7-a	
in kWh	All countries	C 23-a	
	ECE countries	U 15-a	
ELECTRIC LAMPS by value in $m	All countries	U 38-a	
ELECTRIC POWER EQUIPMENT by value in $m	All countries	U 38-a	
ELECTRICAL APPARATUS BY KIND			
by NIMEXE classes by value in $m	All countries	E 20-a	
SITC classes by value in $m	All countries	U 50-a	U 59-a
by source by CST classes by value in $m	EEC countries	E 21-a	
SITC classes by value in $m	Main countries	D 2-q	
	OECD countries	D 3-a2	
ELECTRICAL MACHINERY by value in local currency	Iran	U 32-m	

•• APPENDIX 2 - IMPORTS BY PRODUCT

Product	Territorial coverage	Title codes	
ELECTRONIC COMMUNICATIONS EQUIPMENT by value in £m	UK	B 24-a	
ELECTRONIC COMPONENTS by kind by value in £m	UK	B 24-a	
ELECTRONIC CONTROL INSTRUMENTATION by value in £m	UK	B 24-a	
ELECTRONIC EQUIPMENT by kind by value in £m	UK	B 24-a	
ELECTRONIC VALVES & TUBES by value in $m	All countries	U 38-a	
ENDIVES by source: tonnage	OECD countries	D 37-a	
ENERGY as % of domestic consumption	E European countries & USSR	U 16-a	
in coal equiv tonnage	E European countries & USSR	U 16-a	
(less bunkers) in coal equiv tonnage	EEC countries	E 26-q	
ENGINE REPLACEMENT PARTS (FOR TRACTORS) by source by value in £	UK	V 1-a	
ENGINEERING PRODUCTS			
by value in $m	All countries	U 38-a	
	Developing countries	U 52-a	
shipped ex developing countries by value in $	EEC countries	U 52-a	
unit value in £ per ton	Main countries	B 27-a	
ENGINES & MOTORS BY KIND			
by NIMEXE classes by value in $m	All countries	E 20-a	
SITC classes: no & value in $m	All countries	U 50-a	U 59-a
by source by CST classes by value in $m	EEC countries	E 21-a	
SITC classes by value in $m	Main countries	D 2-q	
tonnage & value in $m	OECD countries	D 3-a2	
tonnage & value in $m	All countries	U 12-a	
ENGINES (industrial) up to 200 hp by source by value in £m	UK	V 1-a	
ETHYL ALCOHOL: tonnage	European countries, Japan & USA	U 26-a	
ETHYLENE OXIDE: tonnage	European countries & USA	U 26-a	
EXPLOSIVES shipped ex EEC & non-EEC areas by value in $m	EEC countries	E 24-a	
FABRICATED MATERIALS - index nos (volume & value bases)	OECD countries	D 16-q	
FABRICATED PRODUCTS - index nos	OECD countries	D 16-q	
FARM MACHINERY by source by kind: tonnage & value in $	All countries	U 12-a	
FARM PRODUCTS shipped ex E European area & USSR by value in $m	EEC countries	U 33-a	
FARM TRACTORS by source: tonnage & value in $	All countries	U 12-a	
	UK	V 1-a	
FATS & OILS: ANIMAL & FISH OILS: tonnage	EEC countries	E 44-a	
FATS & OILS BY KIND			
by NIMEXE classes: tonnage & value in $	All countries	E 20-a	
SITC classes: tonnage & value in $	All countries	U 50-a	U 59-a
by source by CST classes: tonnage & value in $	EEC countries	E 21-a	
SITC classes by value in $	Main countries	D 2-q	
tonnage & value in $	OECD countries	D 3-a2	
FATS, OILS & OILSEEDS by value in $	OECD countries	D 1-a	
FEEDING STUFFS BY KIND			
by NIMEXE classes: tonnage & value in $	All countries	E 20-a	
SITC classes: tonnage & value in $	All countries	U 50-a	U 59-a
by source by CST classes by value in $	EEC countries	E 21-a	
SITC classes by value in $	Main countries	D 2-q	
tonnage & value in $	OECD countries	D 3-a2	
FEEDING STUFFS (incl MIXED COMPOUNDS FOR ANIMALS): tonnage	UK	P 5-a	
FEEDSTOCKS (for oil refineries) by source: tonnage	OECD countries	D 31-a	
FELDSPAR: tonnage	All countries	B 15-a	
FERRO-ALLOYS by source: tonnage & value in $	EEC countries	E 5-q	
FERRO-ALLOYS BY KIND: tonnage	Main countries	B 15-a	T 1-a
		T 4-a	
FERRO-ALLOYS, FERRO-MANGANESE & SPIEGELEISEN: tonnage	ECE countries	U 7-m	U 6-a
	Main countries	H 3-a	
FERRO-CHROMIUM by source: tonnage	Main countries	T 4-a	

•• APPENDIX 2 - IMPORTS BY PRODUCT

	Territorial coverage	Title codes	
FERRO-MANGANESE by source: tonnage & value in $	All countries	U 12-a	
	EEC countries	E 5-q	
tonnage	Italy	C 12-a	
	Main countries	T 4-a	
FERRO-MOLYBDENUM: tonnage	Italy	C 12-a	
	Main countries	T 4-a	
FERRO-NICKEL by source: tonnage	Belgium, Japan & USA	T 4-a	
FERRO-SILICON by source: tonnage	Main countries	T 4-a	
FERRO-SILICON & MANGANESE: tonnage	Italy	C 12-a	
FERRO-TITANIUM: tonnage	W Germany, Italy, Japan & Sweden	T 4-a	
FERRO-TUNGSTEN: tonnage	Main countries	T 4-a	
FERRO-VANADIUM by source: tonnage	All countries	B 15-a	
tonnage	Main countries	T 4-a	
FERROUS SCRAP by kind (sorted & unsorted): tonnage	EEC countries	E 30-m	
by source: tonnage & value in $m	EEC countries	E 5-q	
tonnage	EEC countries	E 30-m	E 29-a
	Main countries	T 1-a	T 4-a
shipped ex non-EEC area: tonnage & value in $	EEC countries	E 29-a	
tonnage	ECE countries, Japan & USA	U 7-m	U 6-a
	Main countries	B 15-a	H 3-a
FERTILISERS by kind by NIMEXE classes: tonnage & value in $	All countries	E 20-a	
SITC classes: tonnage & value in $	All countries	U 50-a	U 59-a
by source by CST classes: tonnage & value in $	EEC countries	E 21-a	
SITC classes by value in $	Main countries	D 2-q	
tonnage & value in $	OECD countries	D 3-a2	
tonnage	All countries	A 2-a	
by value in $	Indonesia	U 32-m	
(manufactured): shipped ex EEC & non-EEC areas by value in $	EEC countries	E 24-a	
FIBREBOARD: tonnage	Main countries	A 25-a2	
FIBRES (discontinuous): tonnage	All countries	A 6-a	
FIBRES: hard fibres, abaca, sisal & henequen: tonnage	Main countries	A 5-a	B 10-a
soft fibres (incl true hemp): tonnage	Main countries	B 10-a	
FILAMENT FIBRES (cellulosic): tonnage	All countries	A 6-a	
(non-cellulosic): tonnage	All countries	A 6-a	
FINISHED MANUFACTURED GOODS - index nos (value basis)	OECD countries	D 16-q	
FISH by source by kind: tonnage & value in $m	UK	D 43-a	
by value in $m	OECD countries	D 43-a	
(fresh & canned): tonnage & value in $m	OECD countries	D 43-a	
(salted dried or smoked): tonnage	OECD countries	D 43-a	
tonnage	EEC countries	E 44-a	
FISH & FISH PRODUCTS by value in $	OECD countries	D 1-a	
ex EEC & non-EEC areas by value in $	EEC countries	E 24-a	
tonnage & value in $	OECD countries	D 43-a	
FISH & MEAT MEAL (as animal feed) by value in $m	W European countries	U 33-a	
by source: tonnage	UK	P 5-a	
FISH BODY OILS: tonnage	Main countries	B 19-a	
FISH MEAL: tonnage & value in local currency & in $m	OECD countries	D 43-a	
tonnage	Main countries	P 5-a	
FISH OILS & FATS by kind by NIMEXE classes: tonnage & value in $	All countries	E 20-a	
SITC classes: tonnage & value in $	All countries	U 50-a	U 59-a
by source by CST classes: tonnage & value in $	EEC countries	E 21-a	
SITC classes by value in $	Main countries	D 2-q	
tonnage & value in $	OECD countries	D 3-a2	
tonnage & value in $	OECD countries	D 43-a	

•• APPENDIX 2 - IMPORTS BY PRODUCT

Product	Territorial coverage	Title codes	
FLAX & LINSEED in oil conversion equiv tonnage	UK	P 1-a	
FLAX FIBRE (incl tow) by source: tonnage	EEC area	B 10-a	
tonnage	Main countries	B 10-a	
FLUORSPAR: tonnage	All countries	B 15-a	
FOOD as % of value of total imports	E European countries	U 16-a	
by kind shipped ex EEC & non-EEC areas by value in $m	EEC countries	E 24-a	
by product groups by value in $m	W European countries	U 33-a	
by source (incl live animal products) by kind: tonnage & value in $	All countries	U 12-a	
by world source areas by value in $m	W European countries	U 20-a	
by value in $m	Australia, New Zealand, Asian & Far East countries	U 32-m	
FOOD - index nos (value basis)	World regions	A 11-a	
(quantum & value bases)	World regions	A 14-a	
FOOD & BEVERAGES by value in UA	AASM countries	E 41-a	
ex EEC area by value in UA	AASM countries	E 41-a	
FOOD & CONSUMPTION GOODS by value in $m	Asian & Far East countries	U 32-q	
FOOD & MANUFACTURED GOODS - index nos (value basis)	OECD countries	D 26-q	
FOOD, DRINK & TOBACCO			
% change in imports by source	EEC countries	E 23-a	
by source by value in UA	EEC countries	E 23-a	
in $m	World regions	U 23-a	
by value & as % of total imports	ECE countries	U 15-a	
in $m	Developing countries	U 52-a	
	ECAFE countries	U 32-m	
	Main countries	E 24-a	
in local currency	African countries	U 44-a	
(incl animal feed) - index nos	OECD countries	D 16-q	
shipped ex non-EEC area by value in UA	EEC countries	E 22-m	
FOOD, FUEL & MACHINERY GROUPS			
as % of total imports (value basis)	All countries	M 6-a	
FOOD PROCESSING MACHINERY by value in $	All countries	U 38-a	
FOOD PRODUCTS as % of total agricultural trade	W European countries	U 20-a	
shipped ex EEC area by value in UA	African, Caribbean countries & Pacific Is	E 45-a	
into EEC area by value in $m	Developing countries	U 52-a	
FOOTWEAR made of leather by source by value in $	OECD countries	D 18-a	
in pairs	OECD countries	D 18-a	
plastic materials by source in pairs	OECD countries	D 18-a	
by value in $	OECD countries	D 18-a	
rubber by source in pairs & by value in $	OECD countries	D 18-a	
textile materials by source by value in $	OECD countries	D 18-a	
in pairs	OECD countries	D 18-a	
shipped ex EEC & non-EEC areas by value in $m	EEC countries	E 24-a	
FORGINGS & PRESSINGS (of all metal) by source: tonnage	EEC countries	E 5-q	E 29-a
FORGINGS (iron & steel): tonnage	Main countries	T 1-a	
FORMALDEHYDE: tonnage	European countries, Japan & USA	U 26-a	
FOUNDRY IRON by source: tonnage & by value in $	EEC area	E 5-q	
tonnage	EEC countries	E 29-a	
	OECD countries	D 22-a	
FOUNDRY SCRAP shipped ex non-EEC area: tonnage	EEC countries	E 29-a	
FRESH VEGETABLES: tonnage	Main E European countries	U 20-a	
FROZEN FRUIT: tonnage	Main countries	B 5-a	
FRUIT (preserved) by value in $m	W European countries	U 33-a	
(temperate) by kind by source: tonnage	OECD countries	D 37-a	
tonnage & value in local currency	OECD countries	D 37-a	
(tropical): tonnage & value in local currency	OECD countries	D 37-a	
FRUIT & VEGETABLE JUICES: tonnage & value in $	W European countries	U 20-a	

•• APPENDIX 2 - IMPORTS BY PRODUCT

Product	Territorial coverage	Title codes	
FRUIT & VEGETABLES by value in $m	OECD countries	D 1-a	
ex EEC & non-EEC areas by value in $	W European countries	U 33-a	
FRUIT BERRIES (FRESH) by source: tonnage	EEC countries	E 24-a	
FRUIT (dried) by value in $m	OECD countries	D 37-a	
tonnage & value in $	W European countries	U 33-a	
FRUIT (fresh) as % of total fruit consumption	W European area	U 20-a	
tonnage	OECD countries	D 37-a	
FRUIT (fresh by kind)	Main E European countries	U 20-a	
by NIMEXE classes: tonnage & value in $	All countries	E 20-a	
SITC classes: tonnage & value in $	All countries	U 50-a	U 59-a
by source by CST classes: tonnage & value in $	EEC countries	E 21-a	
SITC classes by value in $	Main countries	D 2-q	
tonnage & value in $	OECD countries	D 3-a2	
tonnage	EEC countries	B 5-a	
tonnage	Main countries	B 5-a	
	OECD countries	B 6-a	
	USSR	U 20-a	
tonnage & value in $	W European countries	U 20-a	
unit value in $ per ton	W European countries	U 20-a	
FRUIT (frozen): tonnage	OECD countries	B 6-a	
FRUIT JUICES by kind: tonnage	OECD countries	B 6-a	
by volume	All countries	B 5-a	
FRUIT PREPARATIONS by kind: tonnage	OECD countries	B 6-a	
tonnage & value in $m	W European countries	U 20-a	
FUEL OILS by source: tonnage	OECD countries	D 31-a	
tonnage	Main countries	B 15-a	C 14-a
FUELS by kind ex EEC & non-EEC areas by value in $m	EEC countries	E 24-a	
by value: % change by source (on previous yr)	EEC countries	E 23-a	
by source in UA	EEC countries	E 23-a	
shipped ex EEC area by value in UA	African, Caribbean countries & Pacific Is	E 45-a	
ex non-EEC area by value in UA	EEC countries	E 22-m	
	Main countries	E 24-a	
(incl lubricants) by value in $m & as % of total imports	ECE countries	U 15-a	
(liquid) in coal equiv tonnage	EEC area	E 7-a	
(solid): tonnage	EEC area	E 7-a	
FUELWOOD by volume in m³	Canada, European countries, Egypt, USA & USSR	A 13-q	
FULLER'S EARTH: tonnage	All countries	B 15-a	
FURNITURE by kind: chairs & bedding (incl replacement parts) by value in $	EEC countries	C 8-a	
by source by CST classes: tonnage & value in $	EEC countries	E 21-a	
SITC classes by value in $	Main countries	D 2-q	
tonnage & value in $	OECD countries	D 3-a2	
by value in £m	W European countries	C 8-a	
shipped ex EEC area by value in £	W European countries	C 8-a	
ex EFTA area by value in £	W European countries	C 8-a	
in £m	W European countries	C 8-a	
FURNITURE (incl other timber products) by NIMEXE classes by value in $	All countries	E 20-a	
SITC classes by value in $	All countries	U 50-a	U 59-a
GALVANISED STEEL SHEETS by source: tonnage	EEC countries	E 5-q	E 29-a
(plain & corrugated) by source: tonnage	Main countries	T 4-a	
GALVANISED STEEL SCRAP shipped ex non-EEC area: tonnage	EEC countries	E 29-a	
GAS OIL: tonnage	Main countries	B 15-a	
GAS TURBINES by value in $m	All countries	U 38-a	
GASEOUS FUELS (all kinds) in coal equiv tonnage	ECE countries	U 15-a	

APPENDIX 2 - IMPORTS BY PRODUCT

Product	Territorial coverage	Title codes	
GEAR PRODUCTION MACHINES: volume & by value in $m	USA	J 2-a	
GENERATORS & PUMPS			
by source by CST classes: tonnage & value in $	EEC countries	E 21-a	
SITC classes by value in $	Main countries	D 2-q	
tonnage & value in $	OECD countries	D 3-a2	
GERMANIUM (unwrought & refined) by source: tonnage	Italy	C 12-a	
GINGER (DRIED) by source in cwt	Main countries	B 13-a	
GLASS (incl glassware by kind)			
by source by CST classes: tonnage & value in $	EEC countries	E 21-a	
NIMEXE classes by value in $	All countries	E 20-a	
SITC classes by value in $	All countries	U 50-a	U 59-a
GLASS (incl glassware)			
by source by SITC classes: tonnage & value in $	OECD countries	D 3-a2	
by value in $	Main countries	D 2-q	
GLASS-WORKING MACHINERY by value in $	All countries	U 38-a	
GOATSKINS & KIDSKINS (salted & pickled): tonnage	Main countries	B 9-m	
tonnage (dry wt)	Main countries	A 18-a	
GOATSKINS by source: tonnage & by value in $	OECD countries	D 18-a	
shipped ex non-OECD area: tonnage	OECD countries	D 18-a	
GOLD BULLION & COIN in troy oz	All countries	B 15-a	
GOLD ORE, BULLION & COIN by value in $m	USA	J 6-a	
GOLD (refined metal) by source in troy oz	Main countries	T 4-a	
GOODS & SERVICES:			
% volume changes	EEC countries	E 13-a	
(total) - index nos	EEC countries	E 26-a	
as % of gross domestic product	Developing countries	D 25-a	
as component of gross domestic product in $m	Developing countries	D 25-a	
	Main countries	R 5-a	
by value (incl % changes)	EEC countries	E 26-a	
in local currency	African countries	U 44-a	
GOODS (all kinds) unloaded at ports: tonnage	EEC countries	E 26-m	
GRAPEFRUIT by source: tonnage	OECD countries	D 37-a	
GRAPEFRUIT JUICE: tonnage	Main countries	A 7-a	
GRAPES (all kinds) tonnage	All countries	B 5-a	
GRAPES (for table) by source: tonnage	OECD countries	D 37-a	
by value in $m	W European countries	U 33-a	
unit value in $ per ton	Main W European countries	U 20-a	
GRAPHITE: tonnage	All countries	B 15-a	
GRINDING MACHINES: volume & value in $m	USA	J 2-a	
GROUNDNUT CAKE & MEAL (as animal feed): tonnage	UK	P 5-a	
GROUNDNUT OIL by source (shelled equiv tonnage)	UK	B 19-a	
tonnage	Main countries	B 19-a	P 1-a
GROUNDNUTS (incl groundnut oil): tonnage	Main countries	B 18-m	
GROUNDNUTS by source: tonnage	EEC countries	P 5-a	
(for production of animal feed): tonnage	UK	P 5-a	
in oil conversion equiv tonnage	UK	P 1-a	
in shelled equiv tonnage	Main countries	B 19-a	
in vegetable oil equiv tonnage	EEC countries	P 5-a	
(shelled) by source: tonnage	EEC countries	B 19-a	
GYPSUM (crude & calcined): tonnage	All countries	B 15-a	
HAM (cooked or prepared) by source: tonnage	EEC countries	E 47-m	
HARD COAL BRIQUETTES by source: tonnage & value in $	EEC area	E 5-q	
HARD COAL: tonnage	European countries	U 31-q	
HARDENED PROTEIN (PLASTICS): tonnage	Main countries	U 26-a	
HARDWOOD LOGS by source (ex tropics)	EEC countries	A 25-a	
by species: oak, beech & tropical woods	European countries	A 25-a	
HAY & FODDER (as animal feed): tonnage	UK	P 5-a	
HAZELNUTS: tonnage	Main countries	P 4-m	

•• APPENDIX 2 – IMPORTS BY PRODUCT

Product	Territorial coverage	Title codes	
HEAVY STEEL PLATES over 4.75 mm gauge by source: tonnage	Main countries	T 4-a	
over 4.75 mm gauge: tonnage	ECE countries	U 7-m	U 6-a
	Main countries	H 3-a	
HEAVY STEEL SECTIONS by source: tonnage	EEC countries	E 5-q	
	Main countries	T 4-a	
(incl profiles): tonnage	Main countries	H 3-a	
	ECE area	U 7-m	U 6-a
HEMP (ex British Commonwealth countries): tonnage	EEC countries	B 10-a	
HEMP SEED: tonnage	Main countries	B 19-a	
HESSIAN CLOTH by source: tonnage	USA	B 10-a	
HIDES & SKINS BY KIND			
by NIMEXE classes: tonnage & value in $	All countries	E 20-a	
SITC classes: tonnage & value in $	All countries	U 50-a	U 59-a
by source by CST classes by value in $	EEC countries	E 21-a	
SITC classes by value in $	Main countries	D 2-q	
tonnage & value in $	OECD countries	D 3-a2	
by value in $	W European countries	U 33-a	
ex EEC & non-EEC areas by value in $	EEC countries	E 24-a	
HIDES (dry & wet-cured) by source: tonnage	All countries	B 9-m	
HIGH CARBON STEEL PRODUCTS by kind: tonnage	Main countries	T 1-a	
HIGH-SPEED ALLOY STEEL by source: tonnage	EEC countries	E 29-a	
HORSEHIDES by source by value in $	OECD countries	D 18-a	
tonnage	OECD countries	D 18-a	
HOT-ROLLED STEEL SHEETS by source: tonnage	Main countries	T 4-a	
HOT-ROLLED STEEL STRIP by source: tonnage	EEC countries	E 5-q	E 29-a
	Main countries	T 4-a	
HOUSEHOLD DURABLES by value in UA	AASM countries	E 41-a	
shipped ex EEC area by value in UA	AASM countries	E 41-a	
HOUSEHOLD NON-DURABLES by value in UA	AASM countries	E 41-a	
shipped ex EEC area by value in UA	AASM countries	E 41-a	
ILLIPE NUTS: tonnage	Netherlands & UK	B 19-a	
INDUSTRIAL FURNACES (INCL STOVES) by value in $	All countries	U 38-a	
INDUSTRIAL HEATING & COOLING EQUIPMENT by value in $	All countries	U 38-a	
INDUSTRIAL RAW MATERIALS by value in UA	AASM countries	E 41-a	
ex EEC area by value in UA	AASM countries	E 41-a	
INGOTS, BILLETS & BLOOMS (STEEL): tonnage	ECE countries	U 7-m	U 6-a
	Main countries	H 3-a	
INNER TUBES for commercial vehicles tyres by source: no & value in £	UK	V 1-a	
for farm tractors tyres by source: no & value in £	UK	V 1-a	
for vehicle tyres by source: no & value in £	UK	V 1-a	
INSTANT COFFEE by source in bags	UK & USA	B 18-m	
	Main countries	B 13-a	
shipped into European area in bags	European countries	J 1-a	
INSTANT TEA by source in kg	UK	C 1-a	
in lbs	UK	B 13-a	
INSULATED WIRE & CABLES by value in $m	All countries	U 38-a	
INTER-EEC AREA IMPORTS:			
agricultural products by value in $m		U 33-a	
meat (fresh, frozen, dried & salted): tonnage	EEC countries	E 1-a	
pig iron by source: tonnage	EEC countries	E 3-a	
INTERMEDIATE GOODS as % of total imports (value basis)	E European countries	U 16-a	
INTERNAL COMBUSTION ENGINES by value in $	Indonesia	U 32-m	
IODINE (crude & sublimated): tonnage	All countries	B 15-a	
IRIDIUM in oz	USA	J 6-a	
IRIDIUM, OSMIUM & RUTHENIUM by source in oz	Japan & USA	T 4-a	
IRON & MANGANESE ORES by source: tonnage	EEC countries	E 30-m	

675

APPENDIX 2 - IMPORTS BY PRODUCT

	Territorial coverage	Title codes	
IRON & STEEL PRODUCTS			
by kind by NIMEXE classes by value in $m	All countries	E 20-a	
SITC classes by value in $m	All countries	U 50-a	U 59-a
by source by CST classes: tonnage & value in $m	EEC countries	E 21-a	
SITC classes by value in $m	Main countries	D 2-q	
tonnage & value in $m	OECD countries	D 3-a2	
	All countries	U 12-a	
by source: tonnage & value in $m	EEC countries	E 5-q	
by value in $m	Developing countries	U 52-a	
shipped ex EEC & non-EEC areas by value in $m	EEC countries	E 24-a	
into EEC area by value in $m	Developing countries	U 52-a	
IRON CASTINGS by source: tonnage & value in $	EEC countries	E 5-q	
tonnage	Main countries	T 1-a	
IRON ORE (incl concentrates): tonnage	ECE countries	U 7-m	U 6-a
	Main countries	H 3-a	
IRON ORE by source: tonnage & value in $	EEC countries	E 5-q	
tonnage	EEC countries	E 29-a	
	Main countries	T 1-a	U 49-a
unit value in cents per unit	UK	U 56-a	
shipped ex non-EEC area: tonnage	EEC countries	E 29-a	
ex world regions: tonnage	Main countries	U 56-a	
	OECD countries	D 22-a	
(incl manganiferous ore): tonnage	All countries	B 15-a	
tonnage & average % metallic iron content	Japan & W Germany	U 56-a	
by source & average % metallic iron content	UK	U 56-a	
IRON OXIDE: tonnage	OECD countries	D 5-a	
IRON PYRITES by source: tonnage & value in $	EEC countries	E 5-q	
tonnage	EEC countries	E 29-a	
IRON SHOT (incl wire pellets): tonnage	Main countries	T 1-a	
JUTE & JUTE PRODUCTS BY KIND			
by NIMEXE classes by value in $	All countries	E 20-a	
SITC classes by value in $	All countries	U 50-a	U 59-a
by source by CST classes by value in $	EEC countries	E 21-a	
SITC classes by value in $	Main countries	D 2-q	
tonnage & value in $	OECD countries	D 3-a2	
JUTE BAGS & SACKS (NEW) by source: tonnage	W European countries	C 22-a	
tonnage	W European countries	C 22-a	
JUTE CLOTH by source: tonnage	W European countries	C 22-a	
JUTE MANUFACTURES (ex British Commonwealth countries): tonnage	EEC countries	B 10-a	
JUTE PIECE GOODS (incl sacks): tonnage	UK	B 10-a	
JUTE (raw) shipped ex British Commonwealth countries: tonnage	EEC countries	B 10-a	
into W European area as % of world imports of jute		C 22-a	
JUTE YARN by source: tonnage	W European countries	C 22-a	
tonnage	Main countries	B 10-a	
	W European countries	C 22-a	
KAPOK SEED: tonnage	Japan	B 19-a	
KEROSENE by source: tonnage	OECD countries	D 31-a	
tonnage	Main countries	B 15-a	
KNITTED & CROCHETED FABRICS: tonnage	OECD countries	D 46-a	
LAMB & MUTTON by source: tonnage	Greece, France, Japan & USA	B 11-a	
tonnage	European countries	U 36-a	
	Main countries	B 11-a	

APPENDIX 2 – IMPORTS BY PRODUCT

Product	Territorial coverage	Title codes	
LAMB by value in $m	W European countries	U 33-a	
LARD (incl margarine & shortening): tonnage	Main countries	P 1-a	
LATEX: tonnage	Main countries	C 18-m	
LATHES (excl turret type) by volume & by value in $m	USA	J 2-a	
LEAD (soft) & antimonial lead: tonnage	Main countries	C 30-m	
tonnage (based on metal content of ore)	Main countries	T 4-a	
(unwrought) ore, scrap & concentrates: tonnage	All countries	B 15-a	
LEAD BULLION (incl refined): tonnage	UK	C 30-m	
LEAD BULLION by source: tonnage	USA	J 6-a	
(refined) by source: tonnage	OECD countries	D 21-q	
LEAD ORE (incl concentrates) by source: tonnage	Italy	C 12-a	
	OECD countries	D 21-q	
	UK	C 30-m	
(incl matte) by source: tonnage	USA	J 6-a	
tonnage	Main countries	U 24-m	
LEAD PIGS & BARS by source: tonnage	USA	J 6-a	
LEAD (refined & lead bullion) by source: tonnage	UK	C 30-m	
tonnage	Main countries	U 24-m	
LEAD (REFINED): tonnage	All countries	C 12-a	
LEAD SCRAP (incl lead alloy scrap): tonnage	UK	C 30-m	
by source: tonnage	Main countries	T 4-a	
LEATHER (goatskin) ex non-OECD area in sq ft	OECD countries	D 18-a	
(heavy): tonnage	Main countries	A 18-a	
(light cattle & calf): tonnage	Main countries	A 18-a	
(processed) by kind by source: tonnage	Main countries	B 9-m	
(sheep & goatskin) by source by value in $	OECD countries	D 18-a	
in sq ft	OECD countries	D 18-a	
tonnage	Main countries	A 18-a	
(sheepskin) shipped ex non-OECD area in sq ft	OECD countries	D 18-a	
LEATHER & FOOTWEAR by value in $	Developing countries	U 52-a	
shipped ex developing countries by value in $	EEC countries	U 52-a	
LEATHER & LEATHER GOODS by NIMEXE classes by value in $	All countries	E 20-a	
SITC classes by value in $	All countries	U 50-a	U 59-a
by source by CST classes: tonnage & value in $	EEC countries	E 21-a	
SITC classes by value in $	Main countries	D 2-q	
tonnage & value in $	OECD countries	D 3-a2	
LEATHER FOOTWEAR by volume in million pairs	Main countries incl USSR	A 18-a	
LEATHER SOLES (for footwear) by source: tonnage & value in $	OECD countries	D 18-a	
shipped ex non-OECD area: tonnage	OECD countries	D 18-a	
LEATHER UPPERS (for footwear) by source by value in $	OECD countries	D 18-a	
in sq ft	OECD countries	D 18-a	
shipped ex non-OECD area: tonnage	OECD countries	D 18-a	
LEEKS by source: tonnage	OECD countries	D 37-a	
LEMON JUICE: tonnage	Main countries	A 7-a	
LEMONS & GRAPEFRUIT: unit value in $ per ton	W European countries	U 20-a	
LEMONS by source: tonnage	OECD countries	D 37-a	
LETTUCE by source: tonnage	OECD countries	D 37-a	
LIGHT STEEL SECTIONS (incl profiles): tonnage	ECE area	U 7-m	U 6-a
	Main countries	H 3-a	
by source: tonnage	Main countries	T 4-a	
LIGHTING EQUIPMENT by source by CST classes by value in $	EEC countries	E 21-a	
SITC classes by value in $	Main countries	D 2-q	
tonnage & value in $	OECD countries	D 3-a2	
(for vehicles) by source by value in £m	UK	V 1-a	
LIGNITE by source: tonnage & value in $	EEC countries	E 5-q	
shipped ex non-EEC area: tonnage	EEC countries	E 14-a	

APPENDIX 2 - IMPORTS BY PRODUCT

Product	Territorial coverage	Title codes	
LINSEED by source: tonnage	EEC countries	B 19-a	
tonnage	Main countries	B 19-a	
LINSEED CAKE & MEAL (as animal feed): tonnage	UK	P 5-a	
LINSEED (FOR PRODUCTION OF ANIMAL FEED): tonnage	UK	P 5-a	
LINSEED OIL: tonnage	Main countries	B 19-a	P 1-a
LIQUEFIED PETROLEUM GAS: tonnage	Canada	B 15-a	
LITHIUM MINERALS: tonnage	All countries	B 15-a	
	Main countries	T 4-a	
LITHOPONE: tonnage	All countries	B 15-a	
	OECD countries	D 5-a	
LIVE PIGS by source: volume	EEC countries	E 47-m	
by volume	European countries	U 36-a	
	Main countries	B 11-a	
LIVE SHEEP: volume	Main countries	B 11-a	
LIVESTOCK (incl calves): volume	European countries incl USSR	U 36-a	
LIVESTOCK by kind by NIMEXE classes: tonnage & value in $	All countries	E 20-a	
SITC classes: tonnage & value in $	All countries	U 50-a	U 59-a
by source by CST classes: tonnage & value in $	EEC countries	E 21-a	
SITC classes by value in $	Main countries	D 2-q	
tonnage & value in $	OECD countries	D 3-a2	
by value in $	W European countries	U 33-a	
in local currency	Hong Kong	U 32-m	
volume	EEC countries	B 11-a	
ex EEC & non-EEC areas by volume	EEC countries	E 44-a	
LIVESTOCK - index nos (quantum & value bases)	OECD countries	D 16-q	
LIVESTOCK, MEAT & MEAT PREPARATIONS by value in $	OECD countries	U 38-a	
LOCOMOTIVES (electric) by value in $m	All countries	U 38-a	
(steam) by value in $m	All countries	U 38-a	
LUBRICATING OIL (incl greases): tonnage	Main countries	B 15-a	C 14-a
by source: tonnage	OECD countries	D 31-a	
MACHINE TOOLS as % of domestic consumption	EEC countries	B 31-a	
	Main countries	J 2-a	
by source by value in £m	EEC countries	B 20-a	
in $m	EEC countries	B 31-a	
numerically-controlled type by value in £m	UK	B 20-a	
by type by main source areas by value in $m	All countries	B 20-a	
by NIMEXE classes: tonnage & value in $m	All countries	E 20-a	
SITC classes: volume & value in $m	All countries	U 50-a	U 59-a
by source by CST classes by value in $m	EEC countries	E 21-a	
SITC classes by value in $m	Main countries	D 2-q	
: tonnage & value in $m	OECD countries	D 3-a2	
value in £m	EEC countries	B 20-a	
volume & value in $m	USA	J 2-a	
(in detail) by value in $m	EEC countries	J 2-a	
by value in $m	EEC countries	B 31-a	
	All countries	U 38-a	
shipped ex EEC area by value in £m	UK	B 31-a	
ex EFTA area by value in £m	UK	B 31-a	
MACHINE TOOLS (metal-cutting type) by value in $m	USA	J 2-a	
(metal-forming type) by value in $m	USA	J 2-a	
(numerically-controlled type) by volume	EEC countries	B 20-a	
MACHINERY as % of total imports (value basis)	E European countries	U 16-a	
by source by value in $m	Main countries	U 23-a	
by type: tonnage & value in $	All countries	U 12-a	

APPENDIX 2 – IMPORTS BY PRODUCT

	Territorial coverage	Title codes	
MACHINERY, continued			
by value shipped ex EEC area in UA in $m	African, Caribbean countries & Pacific Is	E 45-a	
	Asian, Far East & Australasian countries	U 32-m	
	Main Latin American countries	U 38-a	
(electrical) by kind by NIMEXE classes: volume & value in $m	All countries	E 20-a	
SITC classes: volume & value in $m	All countries	U 50-a	U 59-a
by source by CST classes by value in $m	EEC countries	E 21-a	
SITC classes by value in $m	Main countries	D 2-q	
tonnage & value in $m	OECD countries	D 3-a2	
tonnage & value in $m	All countries	U 12-a	
by value in $m	Main Latin American countries	U 38-a	
ex EEC & non-EEC areas by value in $m	EEC countries	E 24-a	
(mechanical) by kind by NIMEXE classes by value in $m	All countries	E 20-a	
SITC classes by value in $m	All countries	U 50-a	U 59-a
by source by CST classes by value in $m	EEC countries	E 21-a	
SITC classes by value in $m	Main countries	D 2-q	
tonnage & value in $m	OECD countries	D 3-a2	
shipped ex EEC & non-EEC areas by value in $m	EEC countries	E 24-a	
MACHINERY (incl ACCESSORIES) by value in UA	AASM countries	E 41-a	
ex EEC area by value in UA	AASM countries	E 41-a	
– index nos (quantum & value bases)	OECD countries	D 16-q	
MACHINERY (incl transport equipment)			
by source: % change	EEC countries	E 23-a	
by value in UA	EEC countries	E 23-a	
by value in $m	Main countries	E 24-a	
ex non-EEC area by value in UA	EEC countries	E 22-m	
MACHINING CENTRES (MACHINE TOOLS) by source by volume	UK	B 31-a	
MAGNESITE & DOLOMITE by kind: tonnage	All countries	B 15-a	
MAGNESIUM METAL by source: tonnage	Main countries	T 4-a	
MAGNESIUM (unwrought) by source : tonnage	Italy	C 12-a	
MAGNETIC STEEL DYNAMO SHEETS by source: tonnage	EEC countries	E 5-q	E 29-a
MAIZE by ports of entry: tonnage	UK	B 7-m	P 5-a
by source: tonnage	Main countries	B 8-a	
by value in $m	W European countries	U 33-a	
shipped ex non-Communist area: tonnage	China, E European countries & USSR	A 17-a	
tonnage	All countries	A 17-a	
	European countries	U 35-a	
	Main countries	A 12-a	P 5-a
(unmilled) for production of animal feed: tonnage	UK	P 5-a	
MAIZE MEAL & MAIZE FLOUR by source: tonnage	UK	P 5-a	
MAN-MADE FIBRE YARN by source: tonnage	All countries	K 4-a	
(cellulosic): tonnage	Main countries	K 4-a	
MAN-MADE FIBRES as % of fibre production	Main countries	D 27-a	
MAN-MADE FIBRES BY KIND			
by NIMEXE classes by value in $m	All countries	E 20-a	
SITC classes by value in $m	All countries	U 50-a	U 59-a
by source by CST classes by value in $m	EEC countries	E 21-a	
SITC classes by value in $m	Main countries	D 2-q	
tonnage & value in $m	OECD countries	D 3-a2	
MAN-MADE FILAMENT by kind: tonnage	Canada, European countries, Japan & USA	D 27-a	
MAN-MADE STAPLE & FILAMENT YARN by value in £	UK	B 29-a	
MAN-MADE STAPLE by kind: tonnage	Canada, European countries, Japan & USA	D 27-a	
MANDARINES & CLEMENTINES by source: tonnage	OECD countries	D 37-a	

•• APPENDIX 2 - IMPORTS BY PRODUCT

	Territorial coverage	Title codes	
MANGANESE COMPOUNDS by kind: tonnage	Italy	C 12-a	
MANGANESE METAL by source: tonnage	UK	T 4-a	
tonnage	Italy	C 12-a	
MANGANESE ORE (incl ferro-manganese): tonnage	All countries	B 15-a	
by source: tonnage & value in $	EEC countries	E 5-q	
tonnage	EEC countries	E 29-a	
	Italy	C 12-a	
	Main countries	T 4-a	
shipped ex non-EEC area: tonnage	EEC countries	E 29-a	
tonnage	ECE countries, Japan & USA	U 7-m	U 6-a
	Main countries	H 3-a	
MANUFACTURED FUELS: tonnage	Main countries	B 15-a	
MANUFACTURED GAS in coal equiv tonnage	EEC area	E 7-a	
MANUFACTURED GOODS			
by kind by NIMEXE classes by value in $m	All countries	E 20-a	
SITC classes by value in $m	All countries	U 50-a	U 59-a
by source by CST classes: tonnage & value in $m	EEC countries	E 21-a	
SITC classes by value in $m	Main countries	D 2-q	
tonnage & value in $m	OECD countries	D 3-a2	
tonnage & value in $m	All countries	U 12-a	
ex EEC & non-EEC areas by value in $m	EEC countries	E 24-a	
by source by value in $m	Main countries	U 23-a	
in UA	EEC countries	E 23-a	
by value: % change	EEC countries	E 23-a	
by value in $m	Developing countries	U 52-a	
ex EEC area by value in UA	African, Caribbean countries & Pacific Is	E 45-a	
non-EEC area by value in UA	EEC countries	E 22-m	
MANUFACTURED TEXTILES (incl clothing) by value in $m	Main countries	G 1-a	
by value in $m	OECD countries	D 46-a	
	Developing countries	U 52-a	
MARGARINE: tonnage	EEC countries	E 44-a	
	Main countries	B 4-a	B 12-a
MARINE ENGINES (up to 200 hp) by source by value in £	UK	V 1-a	
MASTICS: tonnage & value in $	OECD countries	D 5-a	
MEASURING APPARATUS by value in $m	All countries	U 38-a	
MEAT BY KIND by NIMEXE classes: tonnage & value in $m	All countries	E 20-a	
SITC classes: tonnage & value in $m	All countries	U 50-a	U 59-a
by source by CST classes: tonnage & value in $m	EEC countries	E 21-a	
SITC classes by value in $m	Main countries	D 2-q	
tonnage & value in $m	OECD countries	D 3-a2	
value in $m	W European countries	U 33-a	
MEAT PREPARATIONS by value in $m	W European countries	U 33-a	
MECHANICAL ENGINEERING PRODUCTS by value in £m	UK	B 27-a	
MECHANICAL HANDLING EQUIPMENT			
by NIMEXE classes by value in $m	All countries	E 20-a	
SITC classes by value in $m	All countries	U 50-a	U 59-a
value in $m	All countries	U 38-a	
MEDICAL EQUIPMENT by value in $m	All countries	U 38-a	
MEDICINAL INGREDIENTS by value in $m	Main countries	U 26-a	
MEDICINES (incl pharmaceuticals) by value in $m	Main countries	U 26-a	
MEDIUM STEEL PLATES by source up to 4.75 mm gauge: tonnage	Main countries	T 4-a	
up to 4.75 mm gauge: tonnage	ECE countries	U 7-m	U 6-a
	Main countries	H 3-a	
MELONS by source: tonnage	OECD countries	D 37-a	
MERCURY (incl mercuric compounds) in lbs	All countries	B 15-a	
MERCURY by source in flasks of 76 lbs	Main countries	T 4-a	
(metallic) by source: tonnage	Italy	C 12-a	

APPENDIX 2 - IMPORTS BY PRODUCT

Product	Territorial coverage	Title codes	
METAL GOODS (incl tools) by kind			
by NIMEXE classes by value in $	All countries	E 20-a	
SITC classes by value in $	All countries	U 50-a	U 59-a
by source by CST classes by value in $	EEC countries	E 21-a	
SITC classes by value in $	Main countries	D 2-q	
tonnage & value in $	OECD countries	D 3-a2	
METAL MANUFACTURES, MACHINES & TRANSPORT EQUIPMENT by value in $	ECE countries	U 15-a	
METAL ORES (incl scrap) by value in $	Japan	U 32-m	
METAL ORES (incl CRUDE MINERALS)	ECE countries	U 15-a	
METAL-CUTTING MACHINE TOOLS by type by value in $m	EEC countries	B 31-a	
METAL-WORKING MACHINE TOOLS by type by value in $m	EEC countries	B 31-a	
by value in $m	All countries	U 38-a	
METALS BY KIND by NIMEXE classes: tonnage & value in $	All countries	E 20-a	
by SITC classes: tonnage & value in $	All countries	U 50-a	U 59-a
by source by CST classes: tonnage & value in $	EEC countries	E 21-a	
SITC classes by value in $	Main countries	D 2-q	
tonnage & value in $	OECD countries	D 3-a2	
METALS (FERROUS & NON-FERROUS) by source by value in $	Main world regions	U 23-a	
METHANOL: tonnage	European countries, Japan & USA	U 26-a	
MICA SHEET (crude) incl waste & processed mica in lbs	All countries	B 15-a	
MILK & CREAM by source: tonnage	EEC countries	B 3-a	
by value in $m	W European countries	U 33-a	
MILK, CANNED CREAM & YOGHURT by value in £	UK	B 12-m	
MILK POWDER (incl dried cream) by value in $m	W European countries	U 33-a	
by source: tonnage	Main countries	B 12-m	
skim shipped ex EEC area: tonnage	EEC countries	B 3-a	
tonnage	Main countries	B 4-a	
(whole & skim) by source: tonnage	Netherlands & UK	B 4-a	B 12-m
tonnage	EEC countries	B 3-a	
(whole) shipped ex EEC area: tonnage	EEC countries	B 3-a	
MILLING MACHINES (for METAL WORKING) by source by value in £	UK	B 31-a	
volume & value in $m	USA	J 2-a	
MINED & QUARRIED ORE & ORE PRODUCTS by source by value in $	Main world regions	U 23-a	
MINERAL FUELS by kind by source: tonnage & value in $	All countries	U 12-a	
tonnage	Main countries	N 5-a	
by value in $m	Asian, Far East & Australasian countries	U 32-m	
MINERAL FUELS - index nos (quantum & value bases)	OECD countries	D 16-q	
MINERAL PIGMENTS OF LEAD by kind: tonnage	USA	J 6-a	
MINERAL PROCESSING MACHINERY by value in $	All countries	U 38-a	
MINERALS by kind: tonnage	Main countries	N 5-a	
shipped ex non-EEC area by value in $	EEC countries	E 29-a	
MOHAIR by source in lbs million	UK	B 10-a	
MOLYBDENUM COMPOUNDS by kind: tonnage	Italy	C 12-a	
MOLYBDENUM METAL, ORE & CONCENTRATES: tonnage	All countries	B 15-a	
MOLYBDENUM ORE by source: tonnage	Main countries	T 4-a	
MONAZITE ALLOYS (incl compounds): tonnage	USA	N 1-a	
MONAZITE METAL: tonnage	USA	N 1-a	
MOTOR CYCLES (incl mopeds) by volume	Main countries	S 24-a	
MOTOR CYCLES by value in $m	All countries	U 38-a	
MOTOR SPIRIT by source: tonnage	OECD countries	D 31-a	
tonnage	Main countries	B 15-a	
MOTOR VEHICLES BY KIND			
by NIMEXE classes by value in $m	All countries	E 20-a	
SITC classes by value in $m	All countries	U 50-a	U 59-a
by source by CST classes by value in $m	EEC countries	E 21-a	
SITC classes by value in $m	Main countries	D 2-q	
tonnage & value in $m	OECD countries	D 3-a2	
tonnage & value in $m	All countries	U 12-a	

APPENDIX 2 – IMPORTS BY PRODUCT

Product	Territorial coverage	Title codes	
MOTOR VEHICLES: projection of imports by 1977 by value in £m	UK	B 28	
MUSHROOMS by source: tonnage	OECD countries	D 37-a	
MUSICAL INSTRUMENTS BY KIND			
by NIMEXE classes by value in $	All countries	E 20-a	
SITC classes by value in $	All countries	U 50-a	U 59-a
by source by CST classes by value in $	EEC countries	E 21-a	
SITC classes by value in $	OECD countries	D 3-a2	
	Main countries	D 2-q	
MUSTARD SEED: tonnage	Main countries	B 19-a	
NAPHTHA by source: tonnage	OECD countries	D 31-a	
NAPHTHALENE: tonnage	European countries, Japan & USA	U 26-a	
NATURAL ABRASIVES: tonnage	All countries	B 15-a	
NATURAL GAS by source: tonnage	OECD countries	D 31-a	
by volume in cu ft	France, UK & USA	B 15-a	
by volume in m³	EEC countries	E 7-a	
by volume in m³ (incl world total)	All countries	C 3-a	
tonnage	OECD countries	D 39-q	
NATURAL GAS LIQUIDS by source: tonnage	OECD countries	D 31-a	
NATURAL RUBBER by source: tonnage	Main countries	B 13-a	
by value in $m	W European countries	U 33-a	
ex EEC & non-EEC areas by value in $	EEC countries	E 24-a	
programmed demand: tonnage	Communist countries	U 11-a	
tonnage	Main countries	C 18-m	
NATURAL TEXTILE FIBRES by value in £m	UK	B 29-a	
NEWSPRINT (ex Canada & European area): tonnage	USA	J 4-a	
(ex Canada & Scandinavian area): tonnage	EEC area	J 4-a	
	Latin American countries	J 4-a	
tonnage	All countries	J 4-a	
	Canada, Egypt, European countries, USA & USSR	A 13-q	
	OECD countries	D 41-q	
	World regions	A 5-a	
NICKEL by source: tonnage	W Germany, Italy, Sweden & UK	T 4-a	
	OECD countries	D 21-q	
NICKEL SCRAP by source: tonnage	W Germany & UK	T 4-a	
NICKEL semi-manufactures by kind by source: tonnage	Italy	C 12-a	
(unwrought) incl scrap by source: tonnage	Italy	C 12-a	
incl semis, scrap & alloys: tonnage	All countries	B 15-a	
NIGER SEED: tonnage	Italy & Japan	B 19-a	
NITROGEN FERTILISER COMPOUNDS by kind: tonnage	All countries	B 15-a	
NITROGENOUS FERTILISERS by source: tonnage	OECD countries	D 5-a	
tonnage	All countries	A 2-a	
NON-CELLULOSIC FIBRES: tonnage	OECD countries	D 46-a	
NON-CELLULOSIC FILAMENTS & STAPLE as % of total production	Main countries	D 27-a	
NON-CELLULOSIC YARN by source: tonnage	All countries	K 4-a	
tonnage	OECD countries	D 46-a	
NON-FERROUS METAL PRODUCTS BY KIND			
by NIMEXE classes: tonnage & value in $	All countries	E 20-a	
SITC classes: tonnage & value in $	All countries	U 50-a	U 59-a
by source by CST classes by value in $	EEC countries	E 21-a	
SITC classes by value in $	Main countries	D 2-q	
tonnage & value in $	OECD countries	D 3-a2	
NON-FERROUS METALS BY KIND			
by NIMEXE classes: tonnage & value in $	All countries	E 20-a	
SITC classes: tonnage & value in $	All countries	U 50-a	U 59-a
by source by CST classes: tonnage & value in $	EEC countries	E 21-a	
SITC classes by value in $	Main countries	D 2-q	
tonnage & value in $	OECD countries	D 3-a2	
by source: tonnage & value in $	All countries	U 12-a	

•• APPENDIX 2 - IMPORTS BY PRODUCT

Product	Territorial coverage	Title codes	
NON-FERROUS METALS shipped ex EEC & non-EEC areas by value in $m	EEC countries	E 24-a	
(unworked) by value in $	Developing countries	U 52-a	
NON-METALLIC METAL PRODUCTS shipped ex EEC & non-EEC areas: tonnage	EEC countries	E 24-a	
NON-METALLIC MINERALS by kind: tonnage	Main countries	N 5-a	
NUCLEAR REACTORS by value in $m	All countries	U 38-a	
NUTMEGS & MACE by source in cwt	EEC countries & USA	B 18-m	B 13-a
NUTS (in shell) by kind: tonnage	Main countries	P 4-m	
(edible) by value in $m	W European countries	U 33-a	
OATS by destination: tonnage	European countries	U 35-a	
by port of entry: tonnage	UK	B 7-m	P 5-a
by source: tonnage	Main countries	B 8-a	
shipped to E European area & USSR: tonnage	Non-Communist countries	A 17-a	
tonnage	All countries	A 17-a	
(unmilled) for production of animal feed: tonnage	UK	P 5-a	
OFFAL (edible) beef cattle, pigs, sheep & lambs: tonnage	UK	B 11-a	
tonnage	Main countries	B 11-a	
OFFICE MACHINERY by kind by source: tonnage & value in $m	All countries	U 12-a	
by value in $m	All countries	U 38-a	
OILCAKE & MEAL by kind (as animal feed): tonnage	UK	P 5-a	
by source: tonnage	UK	P 5-a	
OILS & FATS as % of trade in agricultural products	W European countries	U 20-a	
by kind by source: tonnage & value in $	All countries	U 12-a	
OILS & FATS - index nos (quantum & value bases)	OECD countries	D 16-q	
OILSEED CAKE & MEAL by value in $m	W European countries	U 33-a	
OILSEEDS as % of trade in agricultural products (value basis)	EEC countries	U 20-a	
by kind by NIMEXE classes: tonnage & value in $	All countries	E 20-a	
SITC classes: tonnage & value in $	All countries	U 50-a	U 59-a
by source by CST classes: tonnage & value in $	EEC countries	E 21-a	
SITC classes by value in $	Main countries	D 2-q	
tonnage & value in $	OECD countries	D 3-a2	
tonnage	Main countries	B 18-m	
tonnage & value in $	W European countries	U 33-a	
in oil equiv tonnage	Main countries	B 19-a	
shipped ex EEC & non-EEC areas by value in $	EEC countries	E 24-a	
OILSEEDS, VEGETABLE OILS, NUTS & KERNELS by value in $	Japan	U 32-m	
OITICICA OIL: tonnage	Main countries	B 19-a	
OLIVE OIL: tonnage	Main countries	B 19-a	
ONIONS (incl shallots) by source: tonnage	OECD countries	D 37-a	
tonnage	USSR	U 20-a	
ORANGE JUICE: tonnage	Main countries	A 7-a	
ORANGES & TANGERINES: unit value in $ per ton	Main European countries	U 20-a	
ORANGES by source: tonnage	OECD countries	D 37-a	
OSMIRIDIUM & OSMIUM in troy oz	USA	J 6-a	
PACKAGING MACHINERY by value in $m	All countries	U 38-a	
PADDY RICE: tonnage	World regions	C 16-a	
PAINTS (incl varnishes) by NIMEXE classes by value in $	All countries	E 20-a	
SITC classes by value in $	All countries	U 50-a	U 59-a
by source by CST classes: tonnage & value in $	EEC countries	E 21-a	
SITC classes by value in $	Main countries	D 2-q	
tonnage & value in $	OECD countries	D 3-a2	
tonnage & value in $	OECD countries	D 5-a	
PALLADIUM & RHODIUM by source in oz	Japan & USA	T 4-a	
PALLADIUM in troy oz	USA	J 6-a	

•• APPENDIX 2 – IMPORTS BY PRODUCT

	Territorial coverage	Title codes	
PALM KERNEL OIL: tonnage	Main countries	B 19-a	
PALM KERNELS by source: tonnage	EEC countries	B 19-a	
	France, W Germany & Netherlands	B 19-a	
(for production of animal feed): tonnage	UK	P 5-a	
in oil conversion equiv tonnage	UK	P 1-a	
tonnage	Main countries	B 19-a	
PALM OIL by source: tonnage	EEC countries	B 19-a	
tonnage	Main countries	B 19-a	P 1-a
PAPER & BOARD PRODUCTS			
by kind by NIMEXE classes by value in $	All countries	E 20-a	
SITC classes by value in $	All countries	U 50-a	U 59-a
by source by CST classes: tonnage & value in $	EEC countries	E 21-a	
SITC classes by value in $	Main countries	D 2-q	
tonnage & value in $	OECD countries	D 3-a2	
by value in local currency	Iran	U 32-m	
ex EEC & non-EEC areas by value in $	EEC countries	E 24-a	
tonnage	Canada, European countries & USA	A 13-q	
	World regions	A 5-a	
PAPER & PULP MACHINES by value in $m	All countries	U 38-a	
PARAFFIN WAX by source: tonnage	OECD countries	D 31-a	
PARTICLE BOARD (incl chipboard) by volume in m³	Main countries	A 25-a2	
PARTICLE BOARD by source by volume in m³	European countries	A 13-q	
	UK	A 25-a2	
tonnage	Main countries	A 26-a	
PASSENGER CARS (incl taxis) by value in £m	UK	B 28-a	
by NIMEXE classes by value in $m	All countries	E 20-a	
SITC classes by value in $m	All countries	U 50-a	U 59-a
by source: no by engine hp & value in £m	UK	V 1-a	
(second-hand): no & value in £	UK	V 1-a	
(unassembled incl chassis): no & value in £	UK	V 1-a	
by value in local currency	Iran	U 32-m	
in $m	All countries	U 38-a	
by volume	Latin American region	U 38-a	
	Main countries	V 4-a	
PATENT FUELS: tonnage	European countries	U 31-q	
	Main countries	B 15-a	
PEACHES (canned) by source: tonnage	Main OECD countries	D 35-a	
(fresh) by source: tonnage	OECD countries	D 29-a	D 35-a
		D 37-a	
PEARS (for perry production) by source: tonnage	OECD countries	D 37-a	
(fresh): tonnage	OECD countries	D 29-a	D 34-a
(processed) by source: tonnage	OECD countries	D 34-a	
PEPPER by source in cwt	Main countries incl USSR	B 18-q	B 13-a
tonnage	Main countries	A 5-a	
PETROLEUM & COAL PRODUCTS by source by value in $	Main world areas	U 23-a	
PETROLEUM COKE: tonnage	Main countries	B 15-a	
PETROLEUM PRODUCTS BY KIND			
by NIMEXE classes by value in $	All countries	E 20-a	
SITC classes by value in $	All countries	U 50-a	U 59-a
by source by CST classes: tonnage & value in $	EEC countries	E 21-a	
SITC classes by value in $	Main countries	D 2-q	
tonnage & value in $	OECD countries	D 3-a2	
tonnage	Italy	H 4-a	
	OECD countries	D 31-a	
	Main countries	B 15-a	
PETROLEUM PRODUCTS			
by source: tonnage & value in $	All countries	U 12-a	
by value in $	Developing countries	U 52-a	
	ECAFE countries	U 32-m	

684

•• APPENDIX 2 - IMPORTS BY PRODUCT

	Territorial coverage	Title codes	
PETROLEUM PRODUCTS, continued			
by volume in m³	Latin American countries	U 18-a	
	Main countries	C 14-a	
shipped ex non-EEC area: tonnage	EEC countries	E 14-a	
into EEC area: tonnage	Developing countries	U 52-a	
tonnage	ECE countries	U 15-a	
	Main countries	C 14-a	
	OECD countries	D 39-q	
	World regions	T 3-a	
PETROLEUM WAXES & JELLY: tonnage	Main countries	B 15-a	
PHARMACEUTICAL PRODUCTS			
by kind by NIMEXE classes by value in $	All countries	E 20-a	
SITC classes by value in $	All countries	U 50-a	U 59-a
by source by CST classes: tonnage & value in $	EEC countries	E 21-a	
SITC classes by value in $	Main countries	D 2-q	
tonnage & value in $	OECD countries	D 3-a2	
by value in $	Main countries	U 26-a	
shipped ex EEC & non-EEC areas by value in $	EEC countries	E 24-a	
PHENOL: tonnage	European countries, Japan & USA	U 26-a	
PHOSPHATE FERTILISERS by kind: tonnage	OECD countries	D 5-a	
tonnage	All countries	A 2-a	
PHOSPHATE ROCK: tonnage	All countries	C 15-a	
PHOSPHORIC ACID: tonnage	European countries, Japan & USA	U 25-a	
PHTHALIC ANHYDRIDE: tonnage	European countries, Japan & USA	U 26-a	
PIG IRON (incl FERRO-ALLOYS) by kind: tonnage	All countries	B 15-a	
by source: tonnage	OECD countries	D 22-a	
PIG IRON by source: tonnage & value in $	All countries	U 12-a	
	EEC countries	E 5-q	
tonnage	EEC countries	E 29-a	
	Main countries	T 1-a	
(hematite) by source: tonnage	Main countries	T 1-a	
inter-EEC area imports: tonnage	EEC countries	E 3-a	
(phosphoric) by source: tonnage	Main countries	T 1-a	
shipped ex non-EEC area by value in $	EEC countries	E 29-a	
tonnage	ECE countries, Japan & USA	U 7-m	U 6-a
	Main countries	H 3-a	
PIG-MEAT: tonnage	European countries	U 36-a	
by source: tonnage	EEC countries	E 47-m	
PIGS by source by volume	Main countries	B 12-m	
PIMENTO by source in cwt	W Germany, UK & USA	B 13-a	
PINEAPPLE JUICE: tonnage	Main countries	A 8-a	
PINEAPPLES (canned): tonnage	Main countries	A 8-a	
(fresh) by source: tonnage	OECD countries	D 37-a	
tonnage	Main countries	B 5-a	
PITPROPS by source by volume in m³	European countries	A 13-q	
PLASTIC MATERIALS (condensation products) by source: tonnage	OECD countries	D 5-a	
by value in $m	OECD countries	D 5-a	
PLASTIC PRODUCTS by NIMEXE classes by value in $	All countries	E 20-a	
SITC classes by value in $	All countries	U 50-a	U 59-a
PLASTICS: regenerated cellulose & artificial resins: tonnage	Main countries	U 26-a	
PLATES & SHEETS OF STEEL (uncoated & tinned) by source: tonnage	Main countries	T 4-a	
PLATINUM ORE (INCL CONCENTRATES): tonnage	All countries	B 15-a	
PLATINUM (refined) by source in oz	Japan & USA	T 4-a	
in oz	USA	J 6-a	
PLATINUM-GROUP METALS			
(incl refined metals by kind): in oz	USA	J 6-a	
nuggets & grains in oz	USA	J 6-a	
ores & concentrates in oz	USA	J 6-a	
scrap & sponge in oz	USA	J 6-a	

•• APPENDIX 2 – IMPORTS BY PRODUCT

Product	Territorial coverage	Title codes	
PLUMS & OTHER STONE FRUITS (fresh) by source: tonnage	OECD countries	D 37-a	
PLYWOOD & BLOCKBOARD by source by volume in m³	European countries & USA	A 13-q	
	Canada, UK & USA	A 25-a	
by volume in m³	Main countries	A 25-a2	A 26-a
POLYETHYLENE: tonnage	European countries, Japan & USA	U 26-a	
POLYMERISATION PRODUCTS by source: tonnage	OECD countries	D 5-a	
tonnage	European countries, Japan & USA	U 26-a	
POLYPROPYLENE: tonnage	European countries, Japan & USA	U 26-a	
POLYSTYRENE: tonnage	European countries, Japan & USA	U 26-a	
POLYVINYLCHLORIDE: tonnage	European countries, Japan & USA	U 26-a	
POPPY SEED: tonnage	Main countries	B 19-a	
PORK by source: tonnage	France, W Germany & Italy	B 11-a	
by value in $m	W European countries	U 33-a	
(chilled or frozen) by source: tonnage	UK	B 11-a	
tonnage	Main countries	B 11-a	
(fresh) shipped ex Eire & Netherlands: tonnage	UK	B 11-a	
(salted or dried) by source: tonnage	EEC countries	E 47-m	
POTASH FERTILISERS: tonnage	All countries	A 2-a	
POTASH SALTS by kind: tonnage	All countries	B 15-a	
POTATOES by value in $m	W European countries	U 33-a	
shipped ex EEC & non-EEC areas: tonnage	EEC countries	E 44-a	
POULTRY MEAT by source: tonnage	Main countries	B 12-m	
	W Germany	B 11-a	
by value in $m	W European countries	U 33-a	
tonnage	European countries incl USSR	U 36-a	
	Main countries	B 11-a	
	EEC countries	E 47-m	
POULTRY MEAT & CHICKENS by source: tonnage			
POULTRY MEAT, CHICKENS, DUCKS, GEESE & TURKEYS by source: tonnage	UK	B 11-a	
POWER GENERATING EQUIPMENT by value in $	All countries	U 38-a	
POWER TOOLS by value in $m	All countries	U 38-a	
PRECIOUS STONES BY KIND			
by source by CST classes: tonnage & value in $	EEC countries	E 21-a	
SITC classes by value in $	Main countries	D 2-q	
tonnage & value in $	OECD countries	D 3-a2	
PRESSED PORK by source: tonnage	EEC countries	E 47-m	
PRIMARY COMMODITIES by source by value in $	World regions	U 23-a	
PRIMARY ENERGY SOURCES as % of all energy consumed	ECE countries	U 16-a	
by value in $m	Main countries	U 23-a	
PRIMARY MATERIALS by kind by source: tonnage & value in $	All countries	U 12-a	
PRINTING & WRITING PAPER: tonnage	OECD countries	D 41-q	
PRINTING INKS: tonnage & value in $	OECD countries	D 5-a	
PRINTING MACHINERY by value in $m	All countries	U 38-a	
PRODUCER GOODS by value in local currency	African countries	U 44-a	
PULPWOOD by source: tonnage	European countries	A 13-q	
by volume in million m³	Main countries	A 5-a	
PUMPS (incl centrifuges) by value in $m	All countries	U 38-a	
PYRITES (incl other sulphides) by source: tonnage	OECD countries	D 5-a	
PYRITES CONCENTRATES ex non-EEC area: tonnage	EEC countries	E 29-a	
PYRITES (ferrous & cupreous): tonnage	Main countries	B 15-a	
PYRITES RESIDUES: tonnage	ECE countries	U 7-m	U 6-a
	Main countries	H 3-a	
RADIO RECEIVERS by NIMEXE classes by value in $m	All countries	E 20-a	
SITC classes by value in $m	All countries	U 50-a	U 59-a
by source by CST classes by value in $m	EEC countries	E 21-a	
SITC classes by value in $m	Main countries	D 2-q	
	OECD countries	D 3-a2	
by value in $m	All countries	U 38-a	

APPENDIX 2 – IMPORTS BY PRODUCT

Product	Territorial coverage	Title codes	
RAILS (incl track-laying material)			
by source: tonnage	EEC countries	E 5-q	E 29-a
	Main countries	T 4-a	
tonnage	ECE countries	U 7-m	U 6-a
	Developing countries	U 57-a	
	Main countries	H 3-a	T 1-a
RAILS (second-hand) by source : tonnage	EEC countries	E 29-a	
RAILWAY ROLLING STOCK by value in $m	All countries	U 38-a	
RAILWAY SCRAP (INCL USED RAILS): tonnage	Main countries	T 1-a	
RAISINS, CURRANTS & SULTANAS: tonnage	OECD countries	B 6-a	
RAPESEED & RAPESEED OIL in conversion equiv tonnage	UK	P 1-a	
RAPESEED by source: tonnage	EEC countries	B 19-a	
in vegetable oil equiv tonnage	EEC countries	P 5-a	
tonnage	Main countries	B 19-a	
RAPESEED OIL: tonnage	Main countries	B 19-a	
RAW MATERIALS by kind by source: tonnage & value in $	All countries	U 12-a	
shipped ex EEC & non-EEC area by value in $	EEC countries	E 24-a	
by source: % change (value basis)	EEC countries	E 23-a	
by value in UA	EEC countries	E 23-a	
in $m	Main countries	E 24-a	
shipped ex EEC area by value in UA	African, Caribbean countries & Pacific Is	E 45-a	
by value in $	Asian, Far East & Australasian countries	U 32-m	
(for production of capital goods) by value in $	Asian & Far East countries	U 32-q	
(for production of consumables) by value in $	Asian & Far East countries	U 32-q	
shipped ex non-EEC area by value in UA	EEC countries	E 22-m	
RAW MATERIALS - index nos (value basis)	World regions	A 11-a	
(quantum & value bases)	OECD countries	D 16-q	
RAYON & ACETATE FILAMENT YARN by source in lbs	UK	B 10-a	
RAYON & ACETATE STAPLE by source in lbs	All countries	B 10-a	
RAYON PIECE GOODS: tonnage	Main countries	K 1-q	
RAYON YARN (incl acetate) by source : tonnage	Main countries	B 10-a	
RECLAIMED RUBBER: tonnage	Canada, W Germany & UK	C 18-m	
REFRIGERATING EQUIPMENT by value in $m	All countries	U 38-a	
REGENERATED CELLULOSE (PLASTICS) by value in $	European countries, Japan & USA	U 26-a	
REGULUS METAL (BLACK & COARSE): tonnage	USA	J 6-a	
REPLACEMENT AUTOMOTIVE PARTS by source by value in £	UK	V 1-a	
REPLACEMENT ENGINES (FOR TRACTORS) by source by value in £	UK	V 1-a	
(PETROL & DIESEL) by source by value in £	UK	V 1-a	
REPLACEMENT MACHINE PARTS by value in $m	All countries	U 38-a	
in UA	AASM countries	E 41-a	
shipped ex EEC area by value in UA	AASM countries	E 41-a	
REPLACEMENT PARTS for farm tractors (wheeled) by source by value in £	UK	V 1-a	
for tracklayers by source by value in £	UK	V 1-a	
RHODIUM in oz	USA	J 6-a	
RICE by source (all kinds): tonnage	EEC countries	B 14-m	
	Main countries	B 8-a	
by value in $	Indonesia	U 32-m	
in milled equiv tonnage: historical table from 1930-1962	All countries	A 19-a	
shipped ex EEC & non-EEC areas: tonnage	EEC countries	E 44-a	
tonnage	All countries & world regions	B 14-q	A 10-a
RICE BY KIND by source: broken rice: tonnage	All countries	A 19-a	
glutinous rice: tonnage	All countries	A 19-a	
husked rice: tonnage	All countries	A 19-a	
milled rice: tonnage	All countries	A 19-a	
paddy rice: tonnage	All countries	A 19-a	
parboiled rice: tonnage	All countries	A 19-a	
polished rice: tonnage	All countries	A 19-a	
ROLLED STEEL PRODUCTS by kind by source: tonnage	EEC countries	E 5-q	

APPENDIX 2 - IMPORTS BY PRODUCT

	Territorial coverage	Title codes	
ROLLED WHEELS (for railway rolling stock) by source by value in local currency	Main countries	T 4-a	
RUBBER MANUFACTURES shipped ex EEC & non-EEC area by value in $	EEC countries	E 24-a	
RUBBER (natural & synthetic) by source by value in $	World regions	U 23-a	
RUTHENIUM in troy oz	USA	J 6-a	
RYE by source: tonnage	Main countries	B 8-a	
shipped into E European area incl USSR: tonnage	Non-Communist countries (as a group)	A 17-a	
tonnage	All countries	A 17-a	
	European countries	U 35-a	
(unmilled) for production of animal feed: tonnage	UK	P 5-a	
SAFETY GLASS (FOR VEHICLES) by source by value in £	UK	V 1-a	
SAFFLOWER OIL: tonnage	Australia	B 19-a	
SAFFLOWER SEED: tonnage	Japan	B 19-a	
SALT BY KIND: tonnage	All countries	B 15-a	
SANITARY & HOUSEHOLD PAPER: tonnage	OECD countries	D 41-q	
SAUSAGES by source: tonnage	EEC countries	E 47-m	
SAWN HARDWOOD:			
beech & oak by volume in m³	European countries	A 25-a	
by source by volume in m³	European countries	A 13-q	
by volume in m³	Main countries	A 25-a	
ex tropics by volume in m³	European countries	A 25-a2	
SAWN SOFTWOOD by source by volume in m³	European countries	A 13-q	
	W European countries	A 24-a	
SCIENTIFIC INSTRUMENTS by kind by source by value in £	UK	C 24-a	
SELENIUM by source in lbs	UK & USA	T 4-a	
in kg	Main countries	T 4-a	
SEMI-FINISHED ALLOY STEEL PRODUCTS by source: tonnage	Main countries	T 4-a	
SEMI-FINISHED COPPER PRODUCTS: tonnage	Austria & France	T 4-a	
SEMI-FINISHED STEEL PRODUCTS by source: tonnage & value in $	EEC area	E 5-q	
	OECD countries	D 22-a	
by kind: tonnage	Main countries	T 1-a	
SEMI-MANUFACTURED PRODUCTS (total) by value in local currency	African countries	U 44-a	
SEMI-MANUFACTURED PRODUCTS - index nos	OECD countries	D 16-q	
SESAME SEED: tonnage	Main countries	B 19-a	
SESAME SEED OIL: tonnage	Main countries	B 19-a	
SEWING MACHINES by value in $m	All countries	U 38-a	
SHAVING CREAMS (incl SHAMPOOS): tonnage & value in $	OECD countries	D 5-a	
SHEA NUT OIL: tonnage	Sweden	B 19-a	
SHEA NUTS: tonnage	Japan, Sweden & UK	B 19-a	
SHEEP by source: volume	Main countries	B 12-m	
tonnage: live wt	EEC countries	E 1-a	
SHEEPSKINS & LAMBSKINS: tonnage	Main countries	B 9-m	A 18-a
SHEEPSKINS by source: tonnage in value in $	OECD countries	D 18-a	
shipped ex non-OECD area: tonnage	OECD countries	D 18-a	
SHELLFISH: tonnage & value in $m	OECD countries	D 43-a	
SHIPS & BOATS by NIMEXE classes by value in $m	All countries	E 20-a	
SITC classes by value in $m	All countries	U 50-a	U 59-a
by source by CST classes by value in $m	EEC countries	E 21-a	
SITC classes by value in $m	Main countries	D 2-q	
tonnage & value in $m	OECD countries	D 3-a2	
by value in $m	All countries	U 38-a	
SILICO-MANGANESE by source: tonnage	UK	T 4-a	
SILICON (high purity metal) by source: tonnage	UK	T 4-a	
SILK (RAW) incl waste & cocoons in lbs	Main countries	B 10-a	
SILVER (as base & refined bullion) by source in oz	USA	J 6-a	
(beaten, drawn & rolled) in oz	All countries	B 15-a	

•• APPENDIX 2 - IMPORTS BY PRODUCT

Product	Territorial coverage	Title codes	
SILVER BULLION (refined & unrefined) in oz	All countries	B 15-a	
(refined) by source in oz	USA	T 4-a	
(unrefined) by source in oz	UK	T 4-a	
SILVER ORE (incl concentrates) by source in oz	USA	T 4-a	
in oz	All countries	B 15-a	
SILVER ORE & BULLION in oz & by value in $	USA	J 6-a	
SLAB ZINC: tonnage	Main countries	C 12-a	
SLIPPERS (incl HOUSE SHOES) by source by value in $	OECD countries	D 18-a	
in pairs	OECD countries	D 18-a	
SOAP (incl MEDICATED SOAP): tonnage & value in $	OECD countries	D 5-a	
SODA ASH: tonnage	European countries, Japan & USA	U 25-a	
	OECD countries	D 5-a	
SOFTWOOD LOGS by source by volume in m³	Canada, European countries & USA	A 13-q	
SOLDER by source: tonnage	Main countries	C 20-m	
SOLID FUELS (all kinds) tonnage	ECE countries	U 15-a	
SOLID FUELS BY KIND			
by NIMEXE classes: tonnage & value in $	All countries	E 20-a	
SITC classes: tonnage & value in $	All countries	U 50-a	U 59-a
by source by CST classes by value in $	EEC countries	E 21-a	
SITC classes by value in $	Main countries	D 2-q	
tonnage & value in $	OECD countries	D 3-a2	
tonnage	All countries	B 15-a	
SORGHUM: tonnage	Main countries	A 12-a	
SORGHUM & MILLET			
by port of entry: tonnage	UK	B 7-m	P 5-a
shipped into E European area incl USSR: tonnage	Non-Communist countries (as total)	A 17-a	
tonnage	All countries	A 17-a	
	European countries	U 35-a	
SOUND RECORDERS by NIMEXE classes by value in $	All countries	E 20-a	
SITC classes by value in $	All countries	U 50-a	U 59-a
SOYBEAN CAKE & MEAL (as animal feed): tonnage	UK	P 5-a	
by source: tonnage & value in $	W European countries	U 33-a	
SOYBEAN OIL by source: tonnage & value in $	W European countries	U 33-a	
tonnage	Main countries	P 1-a	
SOYBEANS by source: tonnage & value in $	W European countries	U 33-a	
tonnage	EEC countries	B 19-a	
	Main European countries & Japan	B 19-a	
by value in $m	W European countries	U 33-a	
(for production of animal feed): tonnage	UK	P 5-a	
in oil conversion equiv tonnage	UK	P 1-a	
	EEC countries	P 5-a	
(incl soybean oil): tonnage	EEC countries	P 5-a	
	W European countries	B 18-m	
tonnage	Main countries	B 19-a	
SPARE REPLACEMENT PARTS (for vehicles) by source by value in £	UK	V 1-a	
(for works trucks) by source by value in £	UK	V 1-a	
SPECIAL ALLOY STEELS by source: tonnage	EEC countries	E 29-a	
SPICES & ESSENCES by kind: tonnage	Main countries	B 18-q	
SPIEGELEISEN by source: tonnage	EEC countries	E 29-a	
SPINACH by source: tonnage	OECD countries	D 37-a	
SPONGE IRON (incl POWDERS): tonnage	Main countries	T 1-a	
SPONGE METAL (TITANIUM MINERAL): tonnage	USA	J 6-a	
SPUN YARN (cellulosic): tonnage	All countries	A 6-a	
(non-cellulosic): tonnage	All countries	A 6-a	
STAINLESS STEEL INGOTS by source: tonnage	Main countries	T 4-a	
STAINLESS STEEL PRODUCTS by kind: tonnage	Main countries	T 1-a	
by source: tonnage	Main countries	T 4-a	
STATION WAGONS by source: no & value in £	UK	V 1-a	
STATISTICAL MACHINES by value in $m	All countries	U 38-a	

•• APPENDIX 2 - IMPORTS BY PRODUCT

Product	Territorial coverage	Title codes	
STEAM BOILERS by type <u>by source</u> by value in $	EEC countries	B 30-a	
STEAM ENGINES by value in $m	All countries	U 38-a	
STEEL BLANKS (for tubes) <u>by source</u>: tonnage & value in $	EEC countries	E 5-q	
tonnage	Main countries	T 4-a	
STEEL CASTINGS <u>by source</u>: tonnage	Main countries	T 4-a	
tonnage	ECE countries, Japan & USA	U 7-m	U 6-a
	Main countries	H 3-a	T 1-a
STEEL COILS <u>by source</u>: tonnage	EEC countries	E 5-q	E 29-a
	Main countries	T 4-a	
(for re-rolling): tonnage	EEC countries	U 7-m	U 6-a
	Main countries	H 3-a	
STEEL DRAWN WIRE: tonnage	ECE countries	U 7-m	U 6-a
	Main countries	H 3-a	
<u>by source</u>: tonnage	Main countries	T 4-a	
STEEL FORGINGS & PRESSINGS <u>by source</u>: tonnage	Main countries	T 4-a	
tonnage	ECE countries	U 7-m	U 6-a
	Main countries	H 3-a	
STEEL HEAVY SECTIONS <u>by source</u>: tonnage	EEC countries	E 29-a	
STEEL HOOP & STRIP: tonnage	ECE countries	U 7-m	U 6-a
	Main countries	H 3-a	
STEEL INGOTS by quality: tonnage	Main countries	T 1-a	
<u>by source</u>: tonnage	EEC countries	E 29-a	
STEEL INGOTS & CASTINGS <u>by source</u>: tonnage	EEC area	E 5-q	
STEEL MERCHANT BARS <u>by source</u>: tonnage	EEC countries	E 5-q	E 29-a
	Main countries	T 4-a	
STEEL PLATES & SHEETS <u>by source</u>: tonnage	EEC countries	E 29-a	
	EEC area	E 5-q	
by value in $	Indonesia	U 32-m	
STEEL PRODUCTS as % of domestic consumption	Developing countries	U 57-a	
by kind <u>by source</u>: tonnage	EEC area	E 5-q	
	Main countries	T 4-a	
	W Germany	H 3-a	
shipped ex EEC & non-EEC areas (in detail): tonnage	EEC countries	E 30-m	
ex non-EEC area by value in $	EEC countries	E 29-a	
semis & finished products <u>by source</u>: tonnage	OECD countries	D 22-a	
STEEL RAILS <u>by source</u>: tonnage	EEC countries	E 5-q	
STEEL REINFORCING RODS <u>by source</u>: tonnage	EEC countries	E 5-q	E 29-a
	Main countries	T 4-a	
STEEL SCRAP by world regions of supply: tonnage	OECD countries	D 22-a	
STEEL SHEET PILING <u>by source</u>: tonnage	Main countries	T 4-a	
STEEL SHEETS (coated) <u>by source</u>: tonnage	EEC countries	E 29-a	
	Main countries	T 4-a	
(magnetic) <u>by source</u>: tonnage	Main countries	T 4-a	
(under 3mm guage): tonnage	ECE area	U 7-m	U 6-a
	Main countries	H 3-a	
STEEL SLEEPERS (incl fishplates): tonnage	Main countries	T 1-a	
<u>by source</u>: tonnage	EEC countries	E 5-q	E 29-a
	Main countries	T 4-a	
STEEL TUBES (incl fittings): tonnage	ECE countries	U 7-m	U 6-a
	Main countries	H 3-a	
by kind & quality: tonnage	All countries	T 1-a	
<u>by source</u>: tonnage	EEC countries	E 5-q	E 29-a
(welded & seamless) <u>by source</u>: tonnage	Main countries	T 4-a	
STEEL WHEELS, TYRES & AXLES <u>by source</u>: tonnage	EEC countries	E 5-q	
tonnage	ECE countries	U 7-m	U 6-a
	Main countries	H 3-a	
STRAWBERRIES (fresh) <u>by source</u>: tonnage	OECD countries	D 37-a	
STRONTIUM MINERALS: tonnage	All countries	B 15-a	

•• APPENDIX 2 – IMPORTS BY PRODUCT

Product	Territorial coverage	Title codes	
STRUCTURAL STEEL PRODUCTS by source: tonnage	EEC area	E 5-q	
	Main countries	T 4-a	
SUGAR by source: tonnage	Main countries	A 20-a	B 13-a
by value in $	Asian, Far East countries, Australia & New Zealand	U 32-m	
(net imports) ex free markets: tonnage	All countries	C 19-a	
(non-centrifugal): historical table from 1890: tonnage	Main countries	A 20-a	
(quota exempt) for production of alcohol: tonnage	USA	C 19-m	
animal feed: tonnage	USA	C 19-m	
re-export: tonnage	USA	C 19-m	
refining: tonnage	USA	C 19-m	
(raw centrifugal) by source: tonnage	Main countries	C 25-a	
historical table from 1890: tonnage	Main countries	A 20-a	
tonnage	All countries	C 19-a	
(refined) ex EEC & non-EEC areas: tonnage	EEC countries	E 44-a	
historical table from 1890: tonnage	Main countries	A 20-a	
tonnage	Main countries	B 13-a	
SUGAR & HONEY by value in $	OECD countries	D 1-a	
	W European countries	U 33-a	
SUGAR (incl SUGAR PRODUCTS) by NIMEXE classes: tonnage & value in $	All countries	E 20-a	
SITC classes: tonnage & value in $	All countries	U 50-a	U 59-a
by source by CST classes: tonnage & value in $	EEC countries	E 21-a	
SITC classes by value in $	Main countries	D 2-q	
tonnage & value in $	OECD countries	D 3-a2	
shipped ex EEC & non-EEC areas by value in $	EEC countries	E 24-a	
SULPHUR by kind: tonnage	All countries	B 15-a	
SULPHURIC ACID (incl OLEUM): tonnage	ECE countries	U 15-a	
	European countries, Japan & USA	U 25-a	
SUNFLOWER SEED by source: tonnage	EEC countries	B 19-a	
in vegetable oil equiv tonnage	EEC countries	P 5-a	
tonnage	Main countries	B 19-a	
SUNFLOWER SEED OIL: tonnage	Main countries	B 19-a	
SUPERPHOSPHATES (single grade): tonnage	All countries	C 26-a	
SUPPLIER'S SHARE by SITC classes of Communist area imports (value basis)	Main countries	U 23-a	
EEC area imports (value basis)	Main countries	U 23-a	
EFTA area imports (value basis)	Main countries	U 23-a	
SYNTHETIC AMMONIA: tonnage	OECD countries	D 5-a	
SYNTHETIC DETERGENTS by value in $m	Main countries	U 26-a	
SYNTHETIC FIBRE WASTE by source: tonnage	Main countries	K 4-a	
SYNTHETIC FILAMENT YARN: tonnage	Main countries	K 4-a	
SYNTHETIC MONOFIL STRIP by source: tonnage	Main countries	K 4-a	
SYNTHETIC RUBBER (incl substitutes): tonnage	European countries, Japan & USA	U 26-a	
by source: tonnage	Main countries	C 18-m	
	OECD countries	D 5-a	
SYNTHETIC SPUN YARN by source: tonnage	All countries	K 4-a	
tonnage	Main countries	K 4-a	
SYNTHETIC STAPLE carded, combed & tow: tonnage	Main countries	K 4-a	
SYNTHETIC STAPLE & TOW by source: tonnage	Main countries	K 4-a	
tonnage	Main countries	U 26-a	
SYNTHETIC WOVEN FILAMENT FABRICS: tonnage	Main countries	K 4-a	
SYNTHETIC WOVEN SPUN YARN FABRICS: tonnage	Main countries	K 4-a	
TALLOW (incl edible & technical qualities): tonnage	All countries	P 1-a	
TANTALUM in kg	W Germany, UK & USA	T 4-a	
TAR & PITCH: tonnage	Main countries	B 15-a	

APPENDIX 2 – IMPORTS BY PRODUCT

Product / breakdown	Territorial coverage	Title codes	
TEA (black) by source: tonnage	USA	C 11-m	
by NIMEXE classes: tonnage & value in $	All countries	E 20-a	
SITC classes: tonnage & value in $	All countries	U 50-a	U 59-a
by source by CST classes: tonnage & value in $	EEC countries	E 21-a	
SITC classes by value in $	Main countries	D 2-q	
tonnage & value in $	OECD countries	D 3-a2	
in million lbs	Main countries	B 13-a	
passed by Customs examiners for admission: tonnage	USA	C 1-a	
by source: tonnage	Main countries	C 11-m	C 1-a
		P 6-a	
	UK	P 6-m	
by value in local currency	Afghanistan	U 32-m	
consignments retained for domestic consumption by source: tonnage	UK	C 1-a	
domestic consumption: tonnage	All countries	C 1-a	
	Main countries	C 11-m	P 6-a
(green) shipped ex Japan: tonnage	USA	C 11-m	
in million lbs	Main countries	B 13-a	
(Oolong): tonnage	USA	C 11-m	
TELECOMMUNICATIONS EQUIPMENT by source: tonnage & value in $	All countries	U 12-a	
by value in £m	UK	B 24-a	
in $m	All countries	U 38-a	
TELEVISION RECEIVERS by NIMEXE classes by value in $	All countries	E 20-a	
SITC classes by value in $	All countries	U 50-a	U 59-a
by source by CST classes by value in $	EEC countries	E 21-a	
SITC classes by value in $	Main countries	D 2-q	
tonnage & value in $	OECD countries	D 3-a2	
by value in £m	UK	B 24-a	
in $m	All countries	U 38-a	
TEXTILE & LEATHER MACHINERY by value in $	All countries	U 38-a	
TEXTILE FIBRES by kind by NIMEXE classes by value in $	All countries	E 20-a	
SITC classes by value in $	All countries	U 50-a	U 59-a
by source by CST classes: tonnage & value in $	EEC countries	E 21-a	
SITC classes by value in $	Main countries	D 2-q	
tonnage & value in $	OECD countries	D 3-a2	
shipped ex EEC & non-EEC areas by value in $	EEC countries	E 24-a	
by value in $m	W European countries	U 33-a	
in local currency	Japan	U 32-m	
TEXTILE MACHINERY BY KIND by NIMEXE classes: volume & value in $	All countries	E 20-a	
SITC classes: volume & value in $	All countries	U 50-a	U 59-a
by source by CST classes: tonnage & value in $	EEC countries	E 21-a	
SITC classes by value in $	Main countries	D 2-q	
tonnage & value in $	OECD countries	D 3-a2	
TEXTILE MATERIALS by source by value in $m	EEC countries, Japan & USA	U 23-a	
shipped into EEC area by value in $m	Developing countries	U 52-a	
TEXTILE YARNS & FABRICS by source by value in £	UK	B 29-a	
TEXTILE YARNS by kind by NIMEXE classes by value in $	All countries	E 20-a	
SITC classes by value in $	All countries	U 50-a	U 59-a
by source by CST classes: tonnage & value in $	EEC countries	E 21-a	
by source by SITC classes by value in $	Main countries	D 2-q	
tonnage & value in $	OECD countries	D 3-a2	
by value in $m	ECAFE area	U 32-m	
tonnage	OECD countries	D 46-a	
TIMBER & CORK shipped ex EEC & non-EEC areas by value in $m	EEC countries	E 24-a	

692

•• APPENDIX 2 - IMPORTS BY PRODUCT

	Territorial coverage	Title codes	
TIMBER: SAWNWOOD BY KIND			
by NIMEXE classes by value in $	All countries	E 20-a	
SITC classes by value in $	All countries	U 50-a	U 59-a
by source by CST classes by value in $	EEC countries	E 21-a	
SITC classes by value in $	Main countries	D 2-q	
tonnage & value in $	OECD countries	D 3-a2	
TIMBER BY KIND: ROUND LOGS & SAWNWOOD: tonnage	All countries	A 23-a	
TIMBER PRODUCTS (incl furniture) by value in $	Developing countries	U 52-a	
shipped into EEC area by value in $	Developing countries	U 52-a	
TIN by source: tonnage	Main countries	C 20-m	T 4-a
(refined) by source: tonnage	OECD countries	D 21-q	
(unwrought) semis, scrap & alloys: tonnage	All countries	B 15-a	
TIN CONCENTRATES (based on metal content of ore): tonnage	USA	J 6-a	
by source: tonnage	Main countries	C 20-m	
TIN ORE (IN CONCENTRATES) by source: tonnage	Main countries	T 4-a	
TIN PIGS, BLOCKS & BARS: tonnage	USA	J 6-a	
TINPLATE & BLACKPLATE by source: tonnage	EEC area	E 5-q	
TINPLATE, TERNEPLATE & BLACKPLATE by source: tonnage	Main countries	T 4-a	
TINPLATE: tonnage	ECE countries, Japan & USA	U 7-m	U 6-a
	Main countries	C 20-m	H 3-a
TITANIUM DIOXIDE: tonnage	OECD countries	D 5-a	
TITANIUM MINERALS: tonnage	All countries	B 15-a	
TOBACCO (incl tobacco manufactures) by value in $	OECD countries	D 1-a	
TOBACCO by source in million lbs	All countries	B 13-a	
(flue-cured & other types): stripped: tonnage	UK	B 17-a	
unstripped: tonnage	UK	B 17-a	
TOBACCO PRODUCTS			
by kind by NIMEXE classes by value in $	All countries	E 20-a	
SITC classes by value in $	All countries	U 50-a	U 59-a
by source by CST classes: tonnage & value in $	EEC countries	E 21-a	
SITC classes by value in $	Main countries	D 2-q	
tonnage & value in $	OECD countries	D 3-a2	
shipped ex EEC & non-EEC areas by value in $m	EEC countries	E 24-a	
(unmanufactured) by source in lbs	UK	B 17-a	
by value in $m	W European countries	U 33-a	
in lbs million	Main countries	B 13-a	
TOMATO JUICE: tonnage	Main countries	A 7-a	
	OECD countries	B 6-a	
TOMATO PASTE in fresh tomato equiv tonnage	USA	D 36-a	
tonnage	All countries	A 7-a	
TOMATOES (fresh) by source: tonnage	OECD countries	D 37-a	
	Main countries	D 36-a	
tonnage	OECD countries	D 36-a	
imports (net): tonnage	OECD countries	D 29-a	
(processed) by source: tonnage	Main countries	D 36-a	
	OECD countries	D 37-a	
tonnage	OECD countries	D 36-a	
tonnage	USSR	U 20-a	
unit value in $ per ton	Main W European countries	U 20-a	
TOOL STEEL by source: tonnage	Main countries	T 4-a	
TOYS by NIMEXE classes by value in $	All countries	E 20-a	
SITC classes by value in $	All countries	U 50-a	U 59-a
by source by CST classes: tonnage & value in $	EEC countries	E 21-a	
SITC classes by value in $	Main countries	D 2-q	
tonnage & value in $	OECD countries	D 3-a2	
TRANSFORMERS by value in $m	All countries	U 38-a	

APPENDIX 2 – IMPORTS BY PRODUCT

	Territorial coverage	Title codes	
TRANSPORT BY MODE: rail, road, sea & air: tonnage	European countries	U 8-a	
TRANSPORT EQUIPMENT			
by source by value in $m	Main countries	U 23-a	
by value in $m	Main Latin American countries	U 38-a	
	ECAFE countries	U 32-m	
in UA	AASM countries	E 41-a	
TRANSPORT EQUIPMENT – index nos (quantum & value bases)	OECD countries	D 16-q	
TRANSPORT EQUIPMENT BY KIND			
by NIMEXE classes by value in $	All countries	E 20-a	
SITC classes by value in $	All countries	U 50-a	U 59-a
by source by CST classes: tonnage & value in $	EEC countries	E 21-a	
SITC classes by value in $	Main countries	D 2-q	
tonnage & value in $	OECD countries	D 3-a2	
tonnage & value in $	All countries	U 12-a	
shipped ex EEC area by value in UA	AASM countries	E 41-a	
ex EEC & non-EEC areas by value in $m	EEC countries	E 24-a	
TUNG OIL by source: tonnage	EEC countries	B 19-a	
tonnage	Main countries	B 19-a	
TUNGSTEN ORE (incl concentrates): tonnage	Main countries	U 53-q	
by source: tonnage	Main countries	U 53-q	
by value in $m	Main countries	U 53-q	
shipped ex China & USSR: tonnage	All countries	U 53-a	
ex Communist sources: tonnage	All countries	U 53-q	
TUNGSTEN ORE, TUNGSTEN SCRAP & ALLOYS: tonnage	All countries	B 15-a	
TYPEWRITERS by value in $m	All countries	U 38-a	
TYRES (incl INNER TUBES) by source by value in £	UK	V 1-a	
TYRES by source by value in £m	UK	V 1-a	
no & value for motor cars	UK	V 1-a	
for tractors	UK	V 1-a	
for trucks	UK	V 1-a	
UNIVERSAL STEEL PLATES by source: tonnage	Main countries	T 4-a	
URANIUM MINERALS: tonnage	All countries	B 15-a	
VANILLA ESSENCE by source in cwt	France, UK & USA	B 13-a	
VEGETABLE OILS (incl oilseeds by kind) : tonnage	EEC countries	P 5-a	
VEGETABLE OILS by kind by destination: tonnage	Main countries	B 18-m	
by NIMEXE classes: tonnage & value in $	All countries	E 20-a	
SITC classes: tonnage & value in $	All countries	U 50-a	U 59-a
by source by CST classes: tonnage & value in $	EEC countries	E 21-a	
by SITC classes: tonnage & value in $	OECD countries	D 3-a2	
by value in $	Main countries	D 2-q	
in oil conversion equiv	UK	P 1-a	
shipped ex EEC & non-EEC areas by value in $m	EEC countries	E 24-a	
tonnage	EEC countries	E 44-a	
	Main countries	B 19-a	
VEGETABLE PREPARATIONS by kind: tonnage	OECD countries	B 6-a	
VEGETABLES BY KIND			
by NIMEXE classes: tonnage & value in $	All countries	E 20-a	
SITC classes: tonnage & value in $	All countries	U 50-a	U 59-a
by source by CST classes: tonnage & value in $	EEC countries	E 21-a	
SITC classes by value in $	Main countries	D 2-q	
tonnage & value in $	OECD countries	D 3-a2	
VEGETABLES (fresh & frozen) by value in $m	W European countries	U 33-a	
(fresh) by kind: tonnage	OECD countries	B 6-a	
by value in $m	W European countries	U 20-a	
(prepared) by value in $m	W European countries	U 33-a	

•• APPENDIX 2 – IMPORTS BY PRODUCT

Product	Territorial coverage	Title codes	
VEGETABLES: unit value in $ per ton	Main European countries	U 20-a	
VENEER SHEETS by source by volume in m³	European countries	A 13	
by volume in m³	Main countries	A 26-a	
WALNUTS: tonnage	Main countries	P 4-m	
WASHING POWDERS & PREPARATIONS: tonnage & value in $	OECD countries	D 5-a	
WATER MELONS by source: tonnage	Poland	U 20-a	
WEIGHING MACHINERY by value in $m	All countries	U 38-a	
WHALE OIL (incl fish oils & fats): tonnage	Main countries	P 1-a	
tonnage	Main European countries	B 19-a	
WHEAT as % of domestic consumption	World regions	C 27-a	
by port of entry: tonnage	UK	B 7-m	P 5-a
by source: tonnage	Main countries	B 8-a	
by value in $m	W European countries	U 33-a	
(incl wheat flour) by source: tonnage	UK	B 7-m	
tonnage	All countries	A 17-a	
tonnage	All countries	C 29-a	
	Main countries	B 7-q	
(unmilled) for production of animal feed: tonnage	UK	P 5-a	
WHEAT & WHEAT FLOUR by value in $	New Zealand & Pakistan	U 32-m	
tonnage	European countries	U 35-a	
WHEAT BRAN, POLLARDS & SHARPS (as animal feed): tonnage	UK	P 5-a	
WHEAT FLOUR by port of entry: tonnage	UK	B 7-m	
by source: tonnage	Main countries	B 8-a	
shipped into USSR & N Korea: tonnage	Non-Communist countries (as total)	A 17-a	
E European countries & China	Non-Communist countries (as total)	A 17-a	
tonnage	All countries	A 17-a	C 29-a
	Main countries	B 7-q	
WHEY POWDER: tonnage	EEC countries	B 3-a	
WHISKY BY KIND shipped ex UK in proof gallons	Main countries	Z 6-a	
WHITE SPIRIT by source: tonnage	OECD countries	D 31-a	
tonnage	Main countries	B 15-a	C 14-a
WINE by value in $m	W European countries	U 33-a	
by volume in hectolitres	Main countries	A 5-a	
in million gallons	Main countries	B 5-a	
shipped ex EEC & non-EEC areas by value in local currency	EEC countries	E 44-a	
WIRE (copper alloy) by source: tonnage	USA	J 6-a	
(galvanised) by source: tonnage	Main countries	T 4-a	
WIRE ROD by source: tonnage	EEC countries	E 5-q	E 29-a
	Main countries	T 4-a	
tonnage	ECE countries, Japan & USA	U 7-m	U 6-a
	Main countries	H 3-a	
WOLFRAM ORE by source: tonnage	Main countries	T 4-a	
WOOD, LUMBER & CORK by value in local currency	Japan	U 32-m	
WOOD PRODUCTS (incl paper) by source by value in $	Main countries	U 23-a	
WOOD PULP by kind: tonnage	OECD countries	D 41-q	
(chemical): tonnage	Canada, European countries & USA	A 13-q	
(dissolving): tonnage	OECD countries	D 41-q	
(mechanical): tonnage	Canada, European countries & USA	A 13-q	
(sulphate unbleached): tonnage	OECD countries	D 41-q	
(sulphite bleached): tonnage	OECD countries	D 41-q	
(sulphite unbleached): tonnage	OECD countries	D 41-q	
(for paper-making): tonnage	Main countries	J 7-a	
tonnage	World regions	A 5-a	
WOOD-BASED PANELS by kind by volume in m³	Main countries	A 26-a	
WOODEN SLEEPERS by source by volume in m³	European countries	A 13-q	

APPENDIX 2 – IMPORTS BY PRODUCT

Product	Territorial coverage	Title codes
WOOL (ex British Commonwealth countries): tonnage	EEC countries	B 10-a
(greasy raw) by source in lbs million	Main countries	B 10-a
by value in $m	W European countries	U 33-a
tonnage	Main developed countries	U 11-a
	OECD countries	D 46-a
WOOL TOPS: tonnage	OECD countries	D 46-a
WOOL YARN: tonnage	OECD countries	D 46-a
WORKS & INDUSTRIAL TRUCKS by source: no & value in £	UK	V 1-a
WOVEN COTTON FABRICS: tonnage	OECD countries	D 46-a
WOVEN JUTE CLOTH: tonnage	W European countries	C 22-a
WOVEN KNITTED FABRICS: tonnage	All countries	A 6-a
WOVEN TEXTILE FABRICS: tonnage	OECD countries	D 46-a
WOVEN WOOLLEN FABRICS: tonnage	OECD countries	D 46-a
WRAPPING, PACKAGING PAPER & BOARD: tonnage	OECD countries	D 41-q
XYLENE: tonnage	European countries, Japan & USA	U 26-a
YARNS & FABRICS (INCL MADE-UP ARTICLES) by value in $m	Main countries	G 1-a
ZINC METAL by source: tonnage	Main countries	T 4-a
	OECD countries	D 21-q
ZINC ORE (incl concentrates) by source: tonnage	OECD countries	D 21-q
	Main countries	T 4-a
	USA	J 6-a
tonnage	Main countries	U 24-m C 12-a
ZINC ORE, CRUDE METAL & SCRAP: tonnage	All countries	B 15-a
ZINC OXIDE: tonnage	OECD countries	D 5-a
ZINC PIGS (or SLABS) by source: tonnage	USA	J 6-a
tonnage	Main countries	C 30-m
ZINC PLATES, SHEETS & STRIP by source: tonnage	W Germany	T 4-a
ZINC PRODUCTS (rolled): tonnage	USA	J 6-a
ZINC SCRAP by source: tonnage	Main countries	T 4-a
ZIRCONIUM ORE by source: tonnage	Main countries	T 4-a

APPENDIX 3 - INDEX NUMBERS

	Territorial coverage	Title codes	
AGRICULTURAL PRODUCTION	African countries	U 44-a	
	All countries	A 9-a	U 43-a
	Asian & Far East countries	U 32-a	
	EEC countries	B 1-a	E 44-a
	Main countries	E 3-a	R 5-a
	Main ECAFE countries	U 17-a	
	OAS member countries	N 13-a	
	OECD countries	D 1-a	
	World regions & continents	A 11-a	
	World regions	A 1-a	U 60-a
AGRICULTURAL PRODUCTION & % CHANGES (value basis)	Main countries	C 4-a	
	ECE countries	U 15-a	
	E European countries	U 34-a	
all products & per capita	S American countries	U 40-a	
all products & for food	Latin American countries	J 5-a	
all products	World regions	U 23-a	
changes (value basis)	ECE countries	U 34-a	
(less feed & store cattle)	OECD countries	D 1-a	
per capita	African countries	U 44-a	
	Latin American countries	J 5-a	
	Main countries	R 5-a	
	World regions	U 23-a	
AUCTION PRICES: fat cattle, oxen & steers	Main countries	B 11-a	
BUILDING CONSTRUCTION			
activity	OAS member countries	N 14-a	
(all types & residential)	OECD countries	D 26-m	
	World regions	U 60-a	
by type	Main countries	U 43-a	
civil engineering	Main countries	U 58-a	
(non-residential)	Main countries	U 58-a	
(residential)	Main countries	U 58-a	
BUILDING CONSTRUCTION COSTS	Main countries	R 2-m	
	OAS member countries	N 14-a	
	Canada, W European countries, Japan & USA	R 5-a	
labour wages, materials & overheads	OAS member countries	N 14-a	
BUILDING MATERIALS			
prices	Main countries	R 2-m	
CAPITAL FORMATION			
(value basis)	EEC countries	E 32-a	
	World regions	U 60-a	
(volume basis)	EEC countries	E 26-a	
(volume & price bases)	OECD countries	D 30-a	
agricultural machinery industry	ECE countries	U 34-a	
	E European countries	U 34-a	
agriculture (net value basis)	ECE countries	U 34-a	
	E European countries	U 34-a	
farm buildings	E European countries	U 34-a	
	ECE countries	U 34-a	
farmland improvements	E European countries	U 34-a	
motor vehicles industry	UK	B 28	
CHARGES FOR SERVICES PROVIDED	Canada, EEC countries, Japan & USA	D 6-m	
CONSUMPTION: aluminium (volume basis)	EEC countries, Japan & USA	C 12-a	
(primary)	EEC countries, Japan & USA	C 12-a	
(secondary)	EEC countries, Japan & USA	C 12-a	
crude steel (for further processing as semis)	EEC countries	E 30-q	
(for production of metal products)	EEC countries	E 30-q	
fibreboard (compressed)	European countries	A 24-a	
(non-compressed)	European countries	A 24-a	
food (value basis)	EEC countries	E 44-a	
newsprint	European countries (excl USSR)	A 24-a	
paper & paperboard by kind	European countries	A 24-a	
particle & chipboard	European countries	A 24-a	
plywood & blockboard	European countries	A 24-a	
printing paper	European countries (excl USSR)	A 24-a	
sawn hardwood	European countries (excl USSR)	A 24-a	
sawn softwood	European countries (excl USSR)	A 24-a	
wood-based panels by kind	European countries (excl USSR)	A 24-a	
CONSUMPTION PER CAPITA:			
cereals (by income levels)	USA	C 27-a	
farm products	World regions	A 11-a	
food (by income levels)	USA	C 27-a	
food products	World regions	A 11-a	
meat (by income levels)	USA	C 27-a	
steel products	Main countries	U 57-a	
COST OF LIVING	All countries	M 6-a	
	Czechoslovakia, E Germany & Poland	U 16-a	
	OECD countries	R 5-a	
12 month % increases	Main countries	R 2-m	
by kind of personal expenditure	Main countries	R 5-a	
international comparisons	Main countries	R 1-a	
on changed bases: historical table from 1820	Main European countries	Z 1-a	

••• APPENDIX 3 – INDEX NUMBERS

		Territorial coverage	Title codes	
COSTS OF PRODUCTION ON COLLECTIVE FARMS BY PRODUCT		USSR	U 34-a	
CRUDE OIL: PRODUCTION		Oil-producing countries	F 5-m	F 6-q
DELIVERIES:	carpets by manufacturers	UK	B 29-a	
	cotton yarn to textile industry	UK	B 29-a	
	crude steel ingots	EEC countries	E 30-m	
	iron & steel products	EEC countries	E 30-m	
	knitted fabrics to textile industry	UK	B 29-a	
	knitted goods by manufacturers	UK	B 29-a	
	man-made fibre staple to textile industry	UK	B 29-a	
	ready-made clothing by manufacturers	UK	B 29-a	
	textile yarns by kind to textile industry	UK	B 29-a	
	wool yarn to textile industry	UK	B 29-a	
	woven cotton fabrics to textile industry	UK	B 29-a	
	woven woollen fabrics to textile industry	UK	B 29-a	
DEMAND FOR PRIMARY COMMODITIES (PROJECTED TO 1985)		Worldwide	A 1	
DEPRECIATION ALLOWANCES IN AGRICULTURE		ECE countries	U 34-a	
EARNINGS BY SEX				
	(casual daily labour)	Main countries	R 3-a	
	(monthly-paid employees)	Main countries	R 3-a	
	(weekly-paid employees)	Main countries	R 3-a	
EARNINGS DIFFERENTIALS				
	Males in manufacturing industry	Main countries	B 28-a	
	in motor industry	Main countries	B 28-a	
EARNINGS PER HOUR				
	aerospace equipment industry by sex	EEC countries	E 25-a	
	aircraft industry by sex	EEC countries	E 25-a	
	alcoholic drinks industry by sex	EEC countries	E 25-a	
	building & civil engineering industry	EEC countries	E 25-a	
	building materials manufacturing industry	EEC countries	E 25-a	
	cement industry: production workers	EEC countries	E 25-a	
	ceramics industry: production workers by sex	EEC countries	E 25-a	
	chemical industry: production workers by sex	EEC countries	E 25-a	
	clothing industry: production workers by sex	EEC countries	E 25-a	
	coal mining industry: coal-face & pit-head workers	EEC countries	E 25-a	
	coke ovens: coke production workers	EEC countries	E 25-a	
	cotton industry: production workers by sex	EEC countries	E 25-a	
	electrical engineering industry: workers by sex	EEC countries	E 25-a	
	farm machinery & tractor manufacturing industry	EEC countries	E 25-a	
	food industry (excl sugar): workers by sex	EEC countries	E 25-a	
	footwear manufacturing industry: workers by sex	EEC countries	E 25-a	
	foundries (iron & steel): workers by sex	EEC countries	E 25-a	
	furniture manufacturing industry: workers by sex	EEC countries	E 25-a	
	glass industry: workers by sex	EEC countries	E 25-a	
	in industry (in general) by sex	EEC countries	E 3-a	E 25-a
	instrument engineering industry: workers by sex	EEC countries	E 25-a	
	iron & steel industry: workers by sex	EEC countries	E 25-a	
	knitting mills: workers by sex	EEC countries	E 25-a	
	leather goods manufacturing industry: workers by sex	EEC countries	E 25-a	
	machine tools industry: workers by sex	EEC countries	B 31-a	E 25-a
	man-made fibres industry: workers by sex	EEC countries	E 25-a	
	manufacturing industry: workers by sex	OECD countries	D 26-m	
		EEC countries	E 25-a	
	mechanical engineering industry: workers by sex	EEC countries	E 25-a	
	metal fabricating industry: workers by sex	EEC countries	E 25-a	
	metal process workers by sex	EEC countries	E 25-a	
	mining & quarrying	EEC countries	E 25-a	
	motor vehicles manufacturing industry: workers by sex	EEC countries	E 25-a	
	non-ferrous metals industries: workers by sex	EEC countries	E 25-a	
	non-metallic mineral industry: production workers	EEC countries	E 25-a	
	office machinery industry: production workers	EEC countries	E 25-a	
	oil & natural gas industry	EEC countries	E 25-a	
	oil refineries	EEC countries	E 25-a	
	ore mining industry	EEC countries	E 25-a	
	paper & board industry: production workers by sex	EEC countries	E 25-a	
	plastics manufacturing industry: production workers by sex	EEC countries	E 25-a	
	printing & publishing by sex	EEC countries	E 25-a	
	rubber products manufacturing industry: production workers by sex	EEC countries	E 25-a	
	shipbuilding & marine engineering industry	EEC countries	E 25-a	
	solid fuel briquetting industry: production workers	EEC countries	E 25-a	
	structural steel industry: production workers	EEC countries	E 25-a	
	tanning industry: workers by sex	EEC countries	E 25-a	
	textiles manufacturing industry: workers by sex	EEC countries	E 25-a	
	timber & sawmill industry	EEC countries	E 25-a	
	tobacco processing industry: workers by sex	EEC countries	E 25-a	
	transport equipment manufacturing industry by sex	EEC countries	E 25-a	
	woollen textile manufacturing industry: production workers by sex	EEC countries	E 25-a	
ELECTRICITY CONSUMPTION				
	costs in farming	ECE countries	U 34-a	

••• APPENDIX 3 - INDEX NUMBERS

	Territorial coverage	Title codes	
ELECTRICITY CONSUMPTION PER WORKING DAY	EEC countries	E 26-m	
ELECTRICITY GENERATION (see no 2, 5, 8, 11)	Worldwide	U 27-q	
	Latin American countries	J 5-a	
	OAS member countries	N 14-a	
(incl production of gas & water)	OECD countries	D 19-m	D 20-m
EMPLOYMENT: hired farm labour	ECE countries	U 34-a	
in agriculture	Main OECD countries	D 24-q	
	OAS member countries	N 18-a	
building & construction industries	All countries	L 4-a	
	EEC countries	E 26-m	
	European countries & USA	U 5-a	
	OAS member countries	N 18-a	
chemical industries	All countries	L 4-a	
coal mining industry	EEC countries	E 26-m	
food, drink & tobacco industries	All countries	L 4-a	
furniture-making industry	All countries	L 4-a	
gas, water & electricity undertakings	OAS member countries	N 18-a	
industry (by main sectors)	World regions	U 43-a	
	All countries	L 4-a	
	Asian, Far East & Australasian countries	U 45-a	
	OAS member countries	N 18-a	
industry	Developed areas & world regions	U 23-a	
	Main OECD countries	D 24-q	
iron & steel industry	EEC countries	E 26-m	
leather & leather products manufacturing industry	All countries	L 4-a	
manufacturing industry (by sector)	All countries	L 4-a	
manufacturing industry	All countries	L 1-m	U 43-a
	EEC countries	E 26-m	
	Main countries	U 27-m	
	OAS member countries	N 18-a	
	UK	B 28-a	
mechanical engineering industries	All countries	L 4-a	
metal fabricating industries	All countries	L 4-a	
mining & quarrying	All countries	L 4-a	
	OAS member countries	N 18-a	
motor vehicles manufacturing industry	UK	B 28-a	
non-agricultural occupations	Main countries	L 1-m	U 27-m
		L 4-a	N 7-a
non-metallic minerals industry	All countries	L 4-a	
paper & board manufacturing industry	All countries	L 4-a	
printing & publishing	All countries	L 4-a	
public utility undertakings	OAS member countries	N 18-a	
rubber products manufacturing industry	All countries	L 4-a	
textile & clothing manufacturing industries	All countries	L 4-a	
transport & communications	All countries	L 4-a	
transport equipment manufacturing industries	All countries	L 4-a	
wood-working industries	All countries	L 4-a	
on co-operatives & state farms by kind	E European countries	U 34-a	
(total)	All countries	L 1-m	
	OAS member countries	N 18-a	
(total) seasonally adjusted	All countries	F 5-m	F 6-q
EXPENDITURE: on agricultural tractors (new)	ECE countries	U 34-a	
clothing	Canada, Japan, Main European countries & USA	K 4-a	
	OECD countries	D 46-a	
imported animal feeding stuffs	ECE countries	U 34-a	
social welfare per capita	All countries	L 2-a	
social welfare	EEC countries	E 6-a	
EXPENDITURE PER PUPIL			
in primary schools	All countries	U 62-a	
in secondary schools	All countries	U 62-a	
on education (in general)	All countries	U 62-a	
teacher training	All countries	U 62-a	
vocational education	All countries	U 62-a	
EXPENDITURE PER STUDENT			
in universities	All countries	U 62-a	
EXPORT PRICES BY TYPE OF MARKET (see no 3, 6, 9, 12)	Worldwide	U 27-q	
EXPORT PRICES: agricultural products	Worldwide	U 33-q	
agricultural raw materials	Latin American countries	U 18-a	
all products (weighted average)	All countries	F 5-m	F 6-q
aluminium (weighted average main sources)	Worldwide	U 29-q	
animal fats & oils (weighted average main sources)	Worldwide	U 29-q	
bacon (weighted average main sources)	Worldwide	U 29-q	
barley (weighted average main sources)	Worldwide	U 29-q	
basic metals by kind	Latin American countries	U 18-a	
bauxite (weighted average main sources)	Worldwide	U 29-q	
beef (weighted average main sources)	Worldwide	U 29-q	
butter (weighted average main sources)	Worldwide	U 29-q	
cereal (weighted average main sources)	Worldwide	U 29-q	
cheese (weighted average main sources)	Worldwide	U 29-q	
chrome ore (weighted average main sources)	Worldwide	U 29-q	
coal (weighted average main sources)	Worldwide	U 29-q	
cocoa (weighted average main sources)	Worldwide	U 29-q	
coffee (weighted average main sources)	Worldwide	U 29-q	
copper ore (weighted average main sources)	Worldwide	U 29-q	
copper (weighted average main sources)	Worldwide	U 29-q	

••• APPENDIX 3 – INDEX NUMBERS

	Territorial coverage	Title codes
EXPORT PRICES, continued		
cotton (weighted average main sources)	Worldwide	U 29-q
cottonseed oil (weighted average main sources)	Worldwide	U 29-q
crude petroleum (weighted average main sources)	Worldwide	U 29-q
dairy products (weighted average main sources)	Worldwide	U 29-q
eggs (weighted average main sources)	Worldwide	U 29-q
fats & oils (weighted average main sources)	Worldwide	U 29-q
fish (weighted average main sources)	Worldwide	U 29-q
flax (weighted average main sources)	Worldwide	U 29-q
food & beverages by kind	Latin American countries	U 18-a
food products, textiles, minerals & timber	Worldwide	U 54-q
food products (weighted average main sources)	Worldwide	U 29-q
fresh fruit (weighted average main sources)	Worldwide	U 29-q
fuel oil (at ports of exit)	OPEC countries	C 3-a
groundnuts (weighted average main sources)	Worldwide	U 29-q
hemp (weighted average main sources)	Worldwide	U 29-q
hides (weighted average main sources)	Worldwide	U 29-q
iron ore (weighted average main sources)	Worldwide	U 29-q
jute (weighted average main sources)	Worldwide	U 29-q
kerosene (at ports of exit)	OPEC countries	C 3-a
Latin American-produced goods		U 40-q
lead ore (weighted average main sources)	Worldwide	U 29-q
lead (weighted average main sources)	Worldwide	U 29-q
linseed oil (weighted average main sources)	Worldwide	U 29-q
linseed (weighted average main sources)	Worldwide	U 29-q
main export commodities	Main countries	F 5-m F 6-q
maize (weighted average main sources)	Worldwide	U 29-q
manganese ore (weighted average main sources)	Worldwide	U 29-q
manufactured goods (unit value basis)	Worldwide	U 29-q
(weighted average main sources)	Worldwide	U 29-q
meat (weighted average main sources)	Worldwide	U 29-q
metal ores (weighted average main sources)	Worldwide	U 29-q
milk (weighted average main sources)	Worldwide	U 29-q
motor spirit (at ports of exit)	OPEC countries	C 3-a
natural rubber (weighted average main sources)	Worldwide	U 29-q
nickel ore (weighted average main sources)	Worldwide	U 29-q
nickel (weighted average main sources)	Worldwide	U 29-q
non-ferrous metal ores (weighted average main sources)	Worldwide	U 29-q
non-ferrous metals by kind	Worldwide	G 1-a
non-ferrous metals (weighted average main sources)	Worldwide	U 29-q
oil distillates (at ports of exit)	OPEC countries	C 3-a
oilcake & meal (weighted average main sources)	Worldwide	U 29-q
oilseeds, oils & fats by kind	Worldwide	G 1-a
olive oil (weighted average main sources)	Worldwide	U 29-q
palm kernel oil (weighted average main sources)	Worldwide	U 29-q
palm oil (weighted average main sources)	Worldwide	U 29-q
petroleum products	Latin American countries	U 18-a
pork (weighted average main sources)	Worldwide	U 29-q
poultry (weighted average main sources)	Worldwide	U 29-q
primary commodities (see no 3,6,9,12)	Worldwide	U 27-q
(weighted average main sources)	Worldwide	U 29-q
raw materials: non-food farm products	Worldwide	U 29-q
rice by kind (private trade)	Worldwide	A 19-m
(under bilateral contract)	Worldwide	A 19-m
rice (weighted average main sources)	Worldwide	U 29-q
soybean oil (weighted average main sources)	Worldwide	U 29-q
soybeans (weighted average main sources)	Worldwide	U 29-q
sugar (weighted average main sources)	Worldwide	U 29-q
tea (weighted average main sources)	Worldwide	U 29-q
textile fibres (weighted average main sources)	Worldwide	U 29-q
timber (weighted average main sources)	Worldwide	U 29-q
tin ore (weighted average main sources)	Worldwide	U 29-q
tin (weighted average main sources)	Worldwide	U 29-q
tobacco (weighted average main sources)	Worldwide	U 29-q
wheat (weighted average main sources)	Worldwide	U 29-q
wine (weighted average main sources)	Worldwide	U 29-q
wood pulp (weighted average main sources)	Worldwide	U 29-q
wool (weighted average main sources)	Worldwide	U 29-q
zinc ore (weighted average main sources)	Worldwide	U 29-q
zinc (weighted average main sources)	Worldwide	U 29-q
EXPORTS BETWEEN WORLD ECONOMIC REGIONS		
(value basis)		M 4-a
EXPORTS BY COMMODITY CLASSES		
(see no 3, 6, 9, 12)	Worldwide	U 27-q
	World market groups	U 43-a
	World regions	U 43-a
(quantum & value bases)	OAS member countries	N 15-a
(value basis)	Main countries	F 5-m F 6-a
EXPORTS SHIPPED TO NON-EEC AREA		
(value basis)	EEC countries	E 3-a
EXPORTS: (quantum & unit value bases)	All countries	U 27-m
(quantum & value bases)	African countries	U 44-a
	Developed countries	M 4-a
	Developing countries	M 4-a
(quantum basis) & % rate of change	ECE countries	U 15-a

••• APPENDIX 3 - INDEX NUMBERS

	Territorial coverage	Title codes	
EXPORTS, continued			
(quantum basis)	All countries	F 5-m	F 6-q
	Asian & Far East areas	U 32-q	
	ECAFE countries	U 32-m	
	EEC countries	E 22-m	E 24-a
	Main countries	E 24-a	
(unit value basis)	African countries	U 44-a	
	Developed countries	U 18-a	
	Developing countries	U 18-a	
	ECAFE countries	U 32-m	
	Main countries	U 18-a	
	World regions	U 18-a	
	Asian & Far East areas	U 32-q	
	Developed countries	U 23-a	
	Developing countries	U 23-a	
	Main countries	G 1-a	
	Developing countries	U 23-a	
(value basis)	W European countries (as bloc)	R 5-a	
	World (excl W European bloc)	R 5-a	
EXPORTS BY PRODUCT:			
agricultural commodities (value basis)	World regions	A 11-a	
animal feeding stuffs (value basis)	World regions	A 11-a	
building materials (quantum & value bases)	OECD countries	D 16-q	
chemical products (quantum & value bases)	OECD countries	D 16-q	
domestic equipment (quantum & value bases)	OECD countries	D 16-q	
engineering products by kind	Main countries	U 38-a	
fats & oils (quantum & value bases)	OECD countries	D 16-q	
food (quantum basis)	Asian & Far East countries	U 32-q	
(unit value basis)	Asian & Far East countries	U 32-q	
(value basis)	World regions	A 11-a	
food, drink & tobacco (quantum & value bases)	OECD countries	D 16-q	
live animals (quantum & value bases)	OECD countries	D 16-q	
machinery & equipment (quantum & value bases)	OECD countries	D 16-q	
manufactured goods	Main countries	U 27-q	
	OECD countries	D 16-q	D 26-q
mineral fuels (quantum & value bases)	OECD countries	D 16-q	
(quantum basis)	Asian & Far East areas	U 32-q	
(unit value basis)	Asian & Far East areas	U 32-q	
passenger cars (value basis)	UK	V 1-m	
pharmaceutical products (value basis)	Canada, European countries, Japan & USA	U 26-a	
primary products (quantum basis)	Asian & Far East areas	U 32-q	
(unit value basis)	Asian & Far East areas	U 32-q	
raw materials (value basis)	World regions	A 11-a	
(quantum & value bases)	OECD countries	D 16-q	
semi-manufactured products (quantum & value bases)	OECD countries	D 16-q	
tractors all kinds (value basis)	UK	V 1-m	
transport equipment (volume & value bases)	OECD countries	D 16-q	
vehicles by kind (value basis)	UK	V 1-m	
whisky by volume (& by main destinations)	UK	Z 6-a	
FAMILY ALLOWANCES PER CHILD (under 15 yrs of age)	EEC countries	E 6-a	
FARM OPERATING EXPENSES	E European countries	U 34-a	
	ECAFE countries	U 32-m	
	ECE countries	U 34-a	
FARM COSTS: agricultural equipment (incl supplies)	EEC countries	E 44-a	
animal feeding stuffs	ECE countries	U 34-a	
	EEC countries	E 44-a	
	Hungary & Poland	U 34-a	
electricity & fuels	ECE countries	U 34-a	
	Hungary & Poland	U 34-a	
engine fuels (for agricultural machinery)	EEC countries	E 44-a	
fertilisers by kind	W European countries	U 30-a	
fertilisers (chemical)	EEC countries	E 44-a	
fertilisers	All countries	A 2-a	
	ECE countries	U 34-a	
	Hungary & Poland	U 34-a	
livestock management	ECE countries	U 34-a	
machinery maintenance & repairs	ECE countries	U 34-a	
	Hungary & Poland	U 34-a	
oilcakes	W European countries	U 30-a	
pesticides	ECE countries	U 34-a	
	Hungary & Poland	U 34-a	
FARM LABOUR INPUT			
hired labour & family helpers	ECE countries	U 34-a	
FARM SUBSIDIES: costs to government (at current prices)	ECE countries	U 34-a	
FOOD & MANUFACTURED GOODS			
production (value basis)	OECD countries	D 26-q	
FOOD: production & production per capita	African countries	U 44-a	
	Asian & Far East areas	U 32-a	
	Latin American countries	J 5-a	U 40-a
	Australia	U 32-q	
	EEC countries	E 44-a	
(incl drink & tobacco products)	Far East countries	U 32-q	
	Latin American countries	J 5-a	
	OECD countries	D 19-m	D 20-m

APPENDIX 3 - INDEX NUMBERS

	Territorial coverage	Title codes	
FOOD, continued			
production per capita	ECAFE countries	U 17-a	
	Main countries	A 9-a	R 5-a
	World regions	U 43-a	
production	Australia, India, S Korea & Philippines	U 32-q	
	Main countries	A 9-a	R 5-a
	OAS member countries	N 13-a	
	World regions	A 1-a	A 11-a
		U 23-a	
FREIGHT: loaded & unloaded at ports (volume basis)	European countries	U 8-a	
GROSS DOMESTIC PRODUCT			
at factor cost (constant prices)	Czechoslovakia & Poland	U 34-a	
(projected to 1985)	All countries	A 1	
at market prices & per capita	EEC countries	E 44-a	
at market prices	EEC countries	E 32-a	
	OECD countries	D 30-a	
by industrial origin	Country groups	U 43-a	
by kind of economic activity	World regions	U 60-a	
by kind of expenditure	Country groups	U 43-a	
	World regions	U 60-a	
growth rates per capita projected to 1985	All countries	A 1	
per capita (volume basis)	EEC countries	E 32-a	
per capita of employed population	EEC countries	E 26-a	
	Latin American countries	J 5-a	
	World regions	U 60-a	
GROSS NATIONAL PRODUCT			
(volume basis) & per capita	EEC countries	E 26-a	
at market prices	Canada, European countries, Japan & USA	U 38-a	
	Main countries	E 3-a	
per capita (constant prices)	OAS member countries	N 16-a	
(current values)	All countries	U 60-a	
GROSS OUTPUT: agriculture (current values)	ECE countries	U 34-a	
agriculture by product	Asian, Far East & Australasian countries	U 45-a	
per labour unit	E European countries	U 34-a	
	ECE countries	U 34-a	
manufacturing industry	Australasian countries & Far East (incl Japan)	U 32-q	
	World regions	U 60-a	
GROSS PRODUCT: agriculture (current values)	ECE countries	U 34-a	
	E Germany, Hungary & Poland	U 34-a	
agriculture per labour unit	E European countries	U 34-a	
	ECE countries	U 34-a	
IMPLICIT PRICE DEFLATOR	Main countries	N 7-a	
IMPORT PRICES (IN GENERAL)	All countries	F 5-m	F 6-q
	EEC countries	E 26-m	
IMPORT PRICES: iron ore (ex major suppliers)	EEC countries	E 29-a	
	European countries, Canada & Japan	D 22-a	
manganese ore (ex major suppliers)	EEC countries	E 29-a	
IMPORTS & EXPORTS:			
(quantum & value bases)	EEC countries	E 26-m	
(quantum basis)	Asian, Far East & Australasian countries	U 45-a	
(unit value basis)	Asian, Far East & Australasian countries	U 45-a	
IMPORTS: (quantum & unit value bases)	All countries	U 27-m	
(quantum & value bases)	OAS member countries	N 15-a	
	African countries	U 44-a	
	ECE countries	U 15-a	
	EEC countries	E 22-m	E 24-a
(quantum basis) & % rate of change	All countries	F 5-m	F 6-q
(quantum basis)	Main countries	E 24-a	
	Asian & Far East areas	U 32-q	
	ECAFE countries	U 32-m	
	African countries	U 44-a	
	Asian & Far East areas	U 32-q	
	Developed countries	U 23-a	
	Developing countries	U 23-a	
	ECAFE countries	U 32-m	
	EEC countries	E 22-m	
	Main countries	G 1-a	
(unit value basis)	Developing countries	U 23-a	
	W European bloc	R 5-a	
	World (excl European bloc)	R 5-a	
(value basis)		E 3-a	
IMPORTS INTO EEC COUNTRIES EX NON-EEC AREA			
IMPORTS BY PRODUCT:			
agricultural products (value basis)	World regions	A 11-a	
animal feeding stuffs (value basis)	World regions	A 11-a	
building materials (quantum & value bases)	OECD countries	D 16-q	
chemical products (quantum & value bases)	OECD countries	D 16-q	
domestic equipment (quantum & value bases)	OECD countries	D 16-q	
edible offal (quantum basis)	European area	U 36-a	
fats & oils (volume & value bases)	OECD countries	D 16-q	
fibreboard (value basis)	W Germany	A 25-m	

●●● APPENDIX 3 - INDEX NUMBERS

		Territorial coverage	Title codes	
IMPORTS BY PRODUCT, continued				
	food & farm products	World regions	A 14-a	
	food (value basis)	World regions	A 11-a	
	food, drink & tobacco (volume & value bases)	OECD countries	D 16-q	
	live animals (quantum & value bases)	OECD countries	D 16-q	
	machinery & equipment (quantum & value bases)	OECD countries	D 16-q	
	manufactured goods (quantum & value bases)	OECD countries	D 16-q	
	mineral fuels (quantum & value bases)	OECD countries	D 16-q	
	particle board (value basis)	W Germany	A 25-m	
	pharmaceutical products (value basis)	European countries, Japan & USA	U 26-a	
	plywood (value basis)	W Germany	A 25-m	
	raw materials (value basis)	World regions	A 11-a	
	(volume & value bases)	OECD countries	D 16-q	
	semi-manufactured products (volume & value bases)	OECD countries	D 16-q	
	transport equipment (volume & value bases)	OECD countries	D 16-q	
INCOME:	industrial wage earners by sectors & by sex & skills	EEC countries	E 2-a	
	industrial wage earners	All countries	F 5-m	F 6-q
INDIRECT TAXATION LEVIED ON FARMERS		ECE countries	U 34-a	
INDUSTRIAL & MANUFACTURING PRODUCTION		Asian & Far East countries	U 32-q	
INDUSTRIAL PRODUCTION		African countries	U 44-a	
		Asian, Far East & Australasian countries	U 45-a	
		Asian & Far East countries	U 32-q	
		Developed areas & world regions	U 23-a	
		Canada, European countries, Japan & USA	U 38-a	U 49-a
		ECE countries	U 42-m	
		EEC area	E 13-m	
		EEC countries	E 44-a	
		Main countries	E 3-a	N 7-a
			R 5-a	
		OECD countries	D 26-m	
		World regions	U 60-a	
		Worldwide	U 27-a	
		World regions	U 43-a	
		All countries	U 27-m	
		Worldwide	U 27-q	
	by commodity classes (see no 3)	EEC countries	E 28-q	E 27-a
	commodity classes	Latin American countries	J 5-a	
	ISIC groups	Main countries	R 5-a	U 21-a
	sectors (see no 2, 5, 8, 11)		U 43-a	
	sectors	OECD countries	D 26-m	
		OAS member countries	N 14-a	
		Senegal & Zaire	E 41-a	
		World regions	U 27-a	
		EEC countries	E 26-m	
	(excl construction)	Main European countries	Z 1-a	
	historical table from 1801	All countries	F 5-m	F 6-q
	(seasonally adjusted)	European countries	U 16-q	
INDUSTRIAL SHARE PRICE QUOTATIONS		All countries	F 5-m	F 6-q
		ECE countries	U 42-m	
		EEC countries	E 26-m	E 3-a
		Main countries	U 27-m	E 3-a
			R 5-a	U 43-a
			U 18-a	
INTER-EEC EXPORT TRADE (unit price basis)		World regions	U 60-a	
INTERNAL, COMMERCIAL & BUSINESS TRANSACTIONS		Main countries	M 9-a	
INVISIBLE TRADE & PAYMENTS (OVERALL)		Main countries	M 9-a	
INVISIBLE TRADE & RECEIPTS (OVERALL)				
LABOUR COSTS:	engineering industry	Main countries	B 27-a	
	machine tools industry per unit of output	EEC countries	B 20-a	
	manufacturing industry per unit of output	Main countries	B 28-a	
	manufacturing industry	Main countries	B 27-a	
	residential building industry	European countries & USA	U 5-a	
LABOUR FORCE EMPLOYED		OECD countries	D 23-a	
LABOUR INPUTS:	agriculture & industry compared	ECE countries	U 34-a	
	agriculture	ECE countries	U 34-a	
LABOUR PRODUCTIVITY IN NATIONAL ECONOMY		All countries	L 4-a	
LABOUR PRODUCTIVITY:				
	clothing industry	UK	B 22-a	
	industry (by sectors)	World regions	U 43-a	
	industry	All countries	L 4-a	
	machine tools industry	EEC countries	B 31-a	
		All countries	L 4-a	
	manufacturing industry	UK	B 28-a	
	motor vehicles manufacturing industry	UK	B 28-a	
LIVE ANIMALS:	exports (quantum & value bases)	OECD countries	D 16-q	
	imports (quantum & value bases)	OECD countries	D 16-q	
LIVESTOCK POPULATION:				
	cows	Main countries	B 4-a	

APPENDIX 3 – INDEX NUMBERS

	Territorial coverage	Title codes	
LIVESTOCK PRODUCTION (quantum basis)	EEC countries Latin American countries	E 44-a U 40-a	
MATERIAL COSTS: residential building industry	European countries & USA	U 5-a	
MEAT: PRODUCTION: beef, lamb & pig-meat	Main countries	B 11-a	
MILK: production	Main countries	B 4-a	
supply (daily average)	EEC countries	B 3-a	
yield per cow	Main countries	B 4-a	
NET PRODUCT: agriculture & forestry	E European countries	U 34-a	
agriculture (at factor cost)	ECE countries	U 34-a	
per labour unit employed	E European countries	U 34-a	
	ECE countries	U 34-a	
NUMBER OF CERTIFICATES AWARDED IN SECONDARY SCHOOLS	EEC countries	E 3-a	
NUMBER OF HOURS WORKED	Main countries	L 4-a	
NUMBER OF PUPILS: enrolled in schools by grade	World regions	U 62-a	
(female) enrolled in schools by grade	World regions	U 62-a	
NUMBER OF REGISTRATIONS: new motor cars	Main countries	V 1-a	
NUMBER OF TEACHERS BY GRADE OF INSTRUCTION	World regions	U 62	
NUMBER OF TIME CHARTERINGS: vessels by tonnage classes	Worldwide	S 23-q	
NUMBER OF VOYAGE CHARTER FIXTURES: oil tankers by sea routes	Worldwide	S 16-m	
OCEAN FREIGHT RATES			
(average weighted freight basis)	Worldwide	D 28-a	
(time charter basis)	Worldwide	S 16-w	
bulk carriers	W Germany	S 16-m	
by kind & by kind of charter (see no 3, 6, 9, 12)	Worldwide	U 27-q	
dry cargo ships (time charter basis)	Worldwide	D 28-m	S 16-m
		U 37-m	A 9-a
		D 28-a	
(voyage charter basis)	Worldwide	S 16-m	U 37-m
		D 28-q	D 28-a
minerals (time & voyage charter basis)	Worldwide	N 5-q	
oil tankers	W Germany	S 16-m	
tankers (voyage charter basis)	Worldwide	D 28-m	D 28-q
		D 28-a	
tankers by size (incl supertankers)	Worldwide	S 16-m	
tankers: Caribbean ports to USA		S 15-a	
Mediterranean ports to USA		S 15-a	
Persian Gulf to Japan & to UK		S 15-a	
single voyage (dirty load basis)		S 16-m	
world-scale		S 15-a	U 37-a
tankers	Main countries	R 5-a	
	W Germany	S 16-m	
tramp shipping (voyage charter basis)	Worldwide	D 28-m	
by kind of freight	Worldwide	U 37-m	
tonnage	COMECON countries	S 16-m	
tramp shipping	All countries	F 5-m	F 6-q
		R 5-a	
	W Germany	S 16-m	
via European ports (voyage charter)		D 28-m	
(world-scale)		U 37-m	
OLD AGE PENSIONS PER CAPITA paid to population over 60 yrs of age	EEC countries	E 6-a	
OPERATING EXPENSES: agriculture	ECE countries	U 34-a	
ORDERS RECEIVED: iron & steel industry	EEC countries	E 30-m	
OUTPUT PER MAN-YR: iron & steel industry	UK	T 2-q	
PLANT CAPACITY UTILISATION: manufacturing industry	USA	J 2-a	
PLYWOOD: imports (value basis)	W Germany	A 25-m	
POPULATION: historical tables	All countries	A 9-a	
no actively-employed (estimated)	OECD countries	D 23-a	
growth projected to 1985	OECD countries	D 23-a	
	All countries	A 1	
PRICE DEFLATORS FOR FLOWS OF DEVELOPMENT AID	Main countries	D 7-a	
PRICES: Machine tools	W Germany, Italy & UK	B 31-a	
PRICES PAID BY FARMERS FOR FEED, FERTILISERS & MACHINERY	OECD countries	D 1-a	
PRICES POSTED: refined petroleum products by kind	Worldwide	C 3-a	
PRICES RECEIVED BY FARMERS FOR FERTILISERS	All countries	A 2-a	

APPENDIX 3 — INDEX NUMBERS

	Territorial coverage	Title codes	
PRINTING & PUBLISHING ACTIVITY	S American countries	U 40-a	
PRIVATE CONSUMPTION & PER CAPITA	EEC countries	E 26-a	
PRIVATE CONSUMPTION:			
expenditure per capita	EEC countries	E 32-a	
expenditure	EEC countries	E 32-a	
	OECD countries	D 30-a	
	World regions	U 60-a	
PRODUCER PRICES:			
animal products	OECD countries	D 1-a	
arable crops & livestock	EEC countries	E 44-a	
barley	EEC countries	B 3-a	
cereals	OECD countries	D 1-a	
farm products	Australia, India & Japan	U 32-m	
farm products by kind	Main countries	A 9-a	
food products by kind	EEC countries	E 44-a	
milk (fresh)	EEC countries	B 3-m	
	W European countries	U 30-a	
PRODUCTION (value basis)	OECD countries	R 5-a	
PRODUCTION: all goods excl food & tobacco products	EEC countries	E 26-m	
PRODUCTION BY INDUSTRIAL SECTORS	World regions	U 43-a	
PRODUCTION BY KIND OF PRODUCT:			
basic metals	Asian & Far East countries	U 32-q	
	OECD countries	D 19-m	D 20-m
	S American countries	U 40-a	
beverages	Brazil, Chile, Ecuador & Peru	U 40-a	
building materials	ECE countries	U 42-m	
calcium carbide	OECD countries	D 5-a	
capital goods	ECE countries	U 42-m	
carpets	OECD countries	D 46-a	
cattle for slaughter (unit value basis)	W European countries	U 30-a	
caustic soda	OECD countries	D 5-a	
cement	OECD countries	D 4-a	
chemicals	India, Japan, S Korea & Philippines	U 32-q	
	African countries	U 44-a	
	Asian & Far East countries	U 32-q	
	ECE countries	U 42-m	
	EEC countries	E 26-m	
	Canada, European countries, Japan & USA	U 38-a	
	Latin American countries	J 5-a	
	Main countries	R 5-a	
	OAS member countries	N 14-a	
	OECD countries	D 5-a	
	S American countries	U 40-a	
chemicals (incl oil & coal derivatives)	Italy	C 6-a	
	OECD countries	D 19-m	D 20-m
chlorine	OECD countries	D 5-a	
clothing (volume basis)	OECD countries	D 46-a	
	UK	B 22-a	
clothing & footwear	S American countries	U 40-a	
& leather footwear	OECD countries	D 46-a	
coarse grains (volume basis)	Czechoslovakia, Hungary & Poland	U 34-a	
consumer goods (durable & non-durable)	ECE countries	U 42-m	
crops & livestock: changes (value basis)	ECE countries	U 34-a	
crops (constant price basis)	Czechoslovakia & USSR	U 34-a	
(current value basis)	ECE countries	U 34-a	
crude steel per production worker per yr	OECD countries	D 22-a	
eggs (quantum basis)	Czechoslovakia, Hungary & Poland	U 34-a	
electrical machinery & equipment	Main countries	R 5-a	
	S American countries	U 40-a	
electricity & gas by public utilities	Asian countries	U 32-q	
	African countries	U 44-a	
	Australasian, Far East countries & Iran	U 32-q	
	European countries, Japan & USA	U 38-a	
engineering products	Canada, European countries, Japan & USA	U 38-a	
engineering products (excl electrical machinery)	S American countries	U 40-a	
food, drink & tobacco	African countries	U 44-a	
	EEC countries	E 26-m	
	Main countries	R 5-a	
	OAS member countries	N 14-a	
fruit (fresh): quantum basis	Czechoslovakia, Hungary & Poland	U 34-a	
horse meat (volume basis)	European area	U 36-a	
inorganic chemicals	European countries & USA	D 5-a	
investment goods	Main countries	R 5-a	
iron & steel products per man-yr	UK	T 2-q	
iron & steel products	OECD countries	D 19-m	D 20-m
knitted products	OECD countries	D 46-a	
leather goods	EEC countries	E 26-m	
	S American countries	U 40-a	
livestock (constant price basis)	Czechoslovakia & USSR	U 34-a	
(current value basis)	ECE countries	U 34-a	
(volume basis)	Czechoslovakia, Hungary & Poland	U 34-a	
livestock products (excl feed & cattle)	OECD countries	D 1-a	
livestock products	OECD countries	D 1-a	
machine tools	Main countries	R 5-a	

••• APPENDIX 3 – INDEX NUMBERS

		Territorial coverage	Title codes	
PRODUCTION BY KIND OF PRODUCT, continued				
	man-made fibres	OECD countries	D 5-a	
	manufactured goods by kind	Asian & Far East countries	U 32-q	
		S American countries	U 40-a	
		EEC countries	E 26-m	
	manufactured goods (excl food & tobacco)	African countries	U 44-a	
		Latin American countries	J 5-a	
		OECD countries	D 19-m	D 20-m
	manufactured goods per man-hr	UK	B 28-a	
	metal products	Main countries	B 23-a	
		Asian & Far East countries	U 32-q	
		Australia & Philippines	U 32-q	
		Latin American countries	J 5-a	
		Main countries	R 5-a	
		OAS member countries	N 14-a	
		OECD countries	D 19-m	D 20-m
		W Germany	H 3-a	
		ECE countries	U 42-m	
	metallic ores by kind	Latin American countries	U 40-a	
		African countries	U 44-a	
		Asian & Far East countries	U 32-q	
		ECE countries	U 42-m	
		EEC countries	E 26-m	
		Asian countries, Australasia & Iran	U 32-q	
		Latin American countries	J 5-a	
		Main countries	R 5-a	
		Latin American countries	U 18-a	
		OAS member countries	N 14-a	
		OECD countries	D 19-m	D 20-m
	milk (fresh): quantum basis	Czechoslovakia, Hungary & Poland	U 34-a	
	motor vehicles	UK	B 28-a	
	non-electrical machinery	OECD countries	D 19-m	D 20-m
	non-ferrous metals by kind	S American countries	U 40-a	
	non-ferrous metals	OECD countries	D 19-m	D 20-m
	non-metallic mineral products	S American countries	U 40-a	
	non-metallic minerals by kind	Far East countries	U 32-q	
	paper & board products	Asian & Far East countries	U 32-q	
		EEC countries	E 26-m	
		Latin American countries	J 5-a	
		OAS member countries	N 14-a	
		S American countries	U 40-a	
		Australia	U 32-q	
	pharmaceutical products	European countries, Japan & USA	U 26-a	
	pigs for slaughter (quantum basis)	Czechoslovakia, Hungary & Poland	U 34-a	
	(unit value basis)	W European countries	U 30-a	
	potatoes (quantum basis)	Czechoslovakia, Hungary & Poland	U 34-a	
		W European countries	U 30-a	
	poultry (quantum basis)	Czechoslovakia, Hungary & Poland	U 34-a	
	raw materials (quantum basis)	Worldwide	U 27-a	
	by kind (see no 2, 5, 8, 10)	Worldwide	U 27-q	
	rubber products	S American countries	U 40-a	
	soda ash	OECD countries	D 5-a	
	spun & woven materials	OECD countries	D 46-a	
	sugar beet (quantum basis)	Czechoslovakia, Hungary & Poland	U 34-a	
	synthetic rubber	OECD countries	D 19-m	D 20-m
	textiles (fabrics & finished)	African countries	U 44-a	
		Asian & Far East countries	U 32-q	
		Australia, India & Japan	U 32-q	
		ECE countries	U 42-m	
		Australia, European countries & USA	D 46-a	
		Latin American countries	J 5-a	
		Main countries	R 5-a	
		OAS member countries	N 14-a	
		OECD countries	D 46-q	
	textile manufactures, clothing & leather goods	OECD countries	D 19-m	D 20-m
	timber	S American countries	U 40-a	
	tobacco (quantum basis)	Czechoslovakia, Hungary & Poland	U 34-a	
		S American countries	U 40-a	
	transport equipment	Australia, S Korea & Singapore	U 32-q	
		OECD countries	D 19-m	D 20-m
		S American countries	U 40-a	
	vegetables (quantum basis)	Czechoslovakia, Hungary & Poland	U 34-a	
	wheat & rye (quantum basis)	Czechoslovakia, Hungary & Poland	U 34-a	
	wine (quantum basis)	Czechoslovakia, Hungary & Poland	U 34-a	
PRODUCTIVITY:	clothing industry	UK	B 22-a	
	gross output per agricultural worker	ECE countries	U 34-a	
	gross product per agricultural worker	ECE countries	U 34-a	
	manufacturing industry	Main countries	J 2-a	
PUBLIC CONSUMPTION:				
	expenditure	EEC countries	E 32-a	
		OECD countries	D 30-a	
		World regions	U 60-a	
PUBLIC EXPENDITURE ON SOCIAL WELFARE PER CAPITA		EEC countries	E 6-a	
PURCHASING POWER (INTERNAL) OF POUND STERLING		UK	T 4-a	

••• APPENDIX 3 — INDEX NUMBERS

		Territorial coverage	Title codes	
RAIL FREIGHT	(volume basis) see no 1	Continents	U 27-a	
	(volume basis)	World regions	U 43-a	
RENTAL CHARGES (FOR HOUSING)		African countries	U 44-a	
		All countries	L 4-a	
		Canada, EEC countries, Japan & USA	D 6-m	
		European countries & USA	U 5-a	
RETAIL & WHOLESALE TRADE BY KIND (VALUE BASIS)		All countries	U 43-a	
RETAIL PRICES (BASED ON 1958 VALUES)		Main countries	N 7-a	
RETAIL PRICES & COST OF LIVING		Most large cities	U 27-m	
RETAIL PRICES:	all goods, food products, fuel & light	All countries	L 4-a	
	all goods & food products	Australasian & Far East countries	U 32-m	
		Worldwide	U 27-m	
		All countries	L 1-m	U 43-a
		Latin American countries	J 5-a	
		Worldwide	U 27-m	
	all goods & services (excl food)	EEC countries & Japan	D 6-m	
	all goods & services	Canada, EEC countries, Japan & USA	D 6-m	
	all goods (excl food)	E European countries & USSR	U 16-a	
		Canada, EEC countries, Japan & USA	D 6-m	
	all goods, food products & services	OECD countries	D 26-q	
	clothing & footwear	UK	B 22-a	
	clothing	AASM countries	E 41-a	
		African countries	U 44-a	
		All countries	L 4-a	
		Asian, Far East & Australasian countries	U 45-a	
	food products & housing	EEC countries	E 2-a	
	food products, clothing, fuel, rent & rates	Main countries	A 9-a	
	food products & cost of living	AASM countries	E 41-a	
	food products	African countries	U 44-a	
		Asian, Far East & Australasian countries	U 32-m	
		E European countries & USSR	U 16-a	
		EEC countries	B 1-m	
		Canada, EEC countries, Japan & USA	D 6-m	
	footwear	OECD countries	D 18-a	
	fuel & lighting	AASM countries	E 41-a	
		African countries	U 44-a	
		EEC countries	E 17-q	
	fuel oils by grade	Main European countries	Z 1-a	
	historical table from 1820 (on changed bases)	Main countries	C 4-a	
	historical table from 1937	EEC countries	C 9-m	
	pig-meat	Czechoslovakia & Poland	U 16-a	
	public catering	E European countries	U 16-a	
	services			
RETAIL PRICES (IN GENERAL)		AASM countries	E 41-a	
		African countries	U 44-a	
		All countries	F 5-m	F 6-q
			L 2-a	
		E European countries & USSR	U 16-a	
		ECE countries	U 42-m	
		EEC countries	E 2-a	E 3-a
		OECD countries	D 26-m	
RETAIL SALES:	(quantum & value bases)	OECD countries	D 26-m	
	(quantum basis)	ECE countries	U 42-m	
		EEC area	E 13-m	
	butter	UK	B 12-m	
	durable goods (value basis)	OECD countries	D 26-m	
	food products	EEC countries	E 26-m	
RETAIL TRADE:	inventories	OECD countries	D 26-m	
	turnover of co-operative societies	EEC countries	E 26-m	
	of departmental stores	EEC countries	E 26-m	
	of multiple stores	EEC countries	E 26-m	
	textiles, clothing & shoes	EEC countries	E 26-m	
	turnover	Main countries	U 27-m	
SEA FREIGHT:	cargoes carried in bulk in ton-miles	Worldwide	U 37-a	
SICKNESS BENEFITS PER CAPITA PAID OUT BY WELFARE SERVICES		EEC countries	E 6-a	
SOCIAL SECURITY BENEFIT PAID OUT PER CAPITA		All countries	L 2-a	
SOCIAL SERVICES: expenditure per capita		All countries	L 2-a	
		EEC countries	E 6-a	
	receipts per capita	All countries	L 2-a	
TANKER FREIGHT RATES: VOYAGE CHARTER		Worldwide	D 28-m	
TARGET PRICES: MILK (FRESH)		EEC countries	B 3-a	
TERMS OF TRADE: (see no 2, 5, 8, 11)		World regions	U 27-a	
	(unit value basis)	World regions	U 23-a	
TERMS OF TRADE		All countries	M 6-a	
		Asian, Far East & Australasian countries	U 45-a	
		ECE countries	U 42-m	
		EEC countries	E 22-m	E 26-m
			E 24-a	
		Worldwide	M 4-a	

••• APPENDIX 3 – INDEX NUMBERS

	Territorial coverage	Title codes	
TRANSPORT & COMMUNICATIONS ACTIVITY	World regions	U 60-a	
UNEMPLOYMENT: BUILDING INDUSTRY	European countries & USA	U 5-a	
UNEMPLOYMENT: (SEASONALLY ADJUSTED)	EEC countries	E 26-m	
	Main countries	E 3-a	
VALUE ADDED: MANUFACTURE OF FORESTRY PRODUCTS	EEC countries	E 44-a	
WAGES COSTS: Manufacturing industry per unit of output	Main countries	B 23-a	B 27-a
		B 28-a	
WAGE RATES: adult males (minimum per wk)	Australia & New Zealand	U 32-m	
agriculture by sex	W European countries	U 30-a	
building industry	Main countries	R 3-a	
chemical industry by sex	Main countries	R 3-a	
clothing industry by sex	UK	B 22-a	
electrical industry by sex	Main countries	R 3-a	
estate workers (on tea plantations)	Sri Lanka	U 32-m	
hired agricultural labour	ECE countries	U 34-a	
industrial sectors	Asian, Far East & Australasian countries	U 45-a	
	Main countries	R 4-a	
iron steel & metals fabricating industries	Main countries	R 3-a	
machine tools industry by sex	Main countries	R 3-a	
main occupations	Asian, Far East & Australasian countries	U 45-a	
	Main countries	R 4-a	R 5-a
manufacturing industry per hr	ECAFE countries	U 32-m	
	Main countries	C 4-a	
	OECD countries	D 26-m	
mining & quarrying	Main countries	R 3-a	
textile industry by sex	Main countries	R 3-a	
unskilled workers in public employment	Sri Lanka	U 32-m	
WHOLESALE PRICES (IN GENERAL)	African countries	U 44-a	
	All countries	M 6-a	
	ECAFE countries	U 32-m	
	ECE countries	U 42-m	
	Latin American countries	J 5-a	
	Main countries	R 2-m	
	OECD countries	R 5-a	
WHOLESALE PRICES (EXCLUDING VAT)	EEC countries	E 3-a	
WHOLESALE PRICES (BASED ON 1958 VALUES)	Main countries	N 7-a	
WHOLESALE PRICES BY KIND OF GOODS	All countries	U 43-a	
	EEC countries	E 26-m	
	Main countries	U 27-m	R 5-a
WHOLESALE PRICES:			
agricultural commodities	Main countries	A 9-a	
	OAS member countries	N 17-a	
beef, English, Australian & Argentine	UK	B 11-q	
beef, veal & pig-meat	EEC countries	C 9-m	
bricks	Austria, Italy & Switzerland	A 13-a	
building blocks (concrete)	European countries & USA	U 5-a	
(stone)	European countries	U 5-a	
	Greece & Malta	U 5-a	
building materials by kind	OAS member countries	N 14-a	
building materials	Australia	U 32-m	
	European countries	A 13-a	
	Main countries	R 5-a	
	OAS member countries	N 17-a	
butter (normal grade)	Main countries	B 4-a	
cement	Austria, Canada, Italy & Switzerland	A 13-a	
	European countries & USA	U 5-a	
	OECD countries	D 4-a	
chemical products	OECD countries	D 5-a	
	Thailand	U 32-m	
clothing (ready-made)	UK	B 22-a	
confectionery by kind	UK	P 2-a	
consumer goods	Japan & S Korea	U 32-m	
	OAS member countries	N 17-a	
cotton (American)	UK	B 10-m	
cotton textiles	Nepal	U 32-m	
domestic goods	African countries	U 44-a	
dry resin (delivered plant)	European countries	A 26-a	
export products	ECAFE countries	U 32-m	
farm products	S Korea & Thailand	U 32-m	
fat lambs (English & N Zealand)	UK	B 11-q	
fat lambs	Australia, Canada, New Zealand, UK & USA	B 11-a	
fattening compounds (for pigs)	W Germany	C 9-m	
ferrous scrap	OECD countries	D 22-a	
fibre & fibre products	S Korea	U 32-m	
finished goods (home-produced)	ECAFE area	U 32-m	
finished goods & farm products	EEC countries	E 44-a	
flax (ex Belgium)	UK	B 10-m	
food products	ECAFE countries	U 32-m	
	OAS member countries	N 17-a	

APPENDIX 3 – INDEX NUMBERS

	Territorial coverage	Title codes	
WHOLESALE PRICES, continued			
galvanised roofing sheets	Iceland	U 5-a	
hides & skins by kind	OECD countries	D 18-a	
imported goods	African countries	U 44-a	
	ECAFE countries	U 32-m	
iron & steel products	EEC countries	E 29-a	
	W Germany	H 3-a	
iron products (for building industry)	Switzerland	U 5-a	
kerosene	Nepal	U 32-m	
leather by kind	OECD countries	D 18-q	
lime (for building industry)	European countries & USA	U 5-a	
livestock products	OAS member countries	N 17-a	
machine tools (metal-cutting type)	USA	J 2-a	
(metal-forming type)	USA	J 2-a	
man-made fibres	OECD countries	D 5-a	
manufactured goods	All countries	F 5-m	F 6-q
	India & Pakistan	U 32-m	
	OAS member countries	N 17-a	
	OECD countries	D 26-m	
	W Germany	H 3-a	
metal products	Japan & S Korea	U 32-m	
pig-meat	EEC countries	C 9-m	
plywood	W Germany	A 25-m	
potatoes	W European countries	U 30-m	
producer goods	Japan & S Korea	U 32-m	
	OAS member countries	N 17-a	
raw materials (agricultural)	W Germany	H 3-a	
(industrial)	W Germany	H 3-a	
raw materials	OAS member countries	N 17-a	
	OECD countries	D 26-m	
	Pakistan & S Vietnam	U 32-m	
rice & paddy rice	S Vietnam	U 32-m	
roofing tiles	European countries	U 5-a	
roundwood (coniferous)	Main European countries	A 26-a	
(deciduous)	Main European countries	A 26-a	
sand & gravel	European countries & Cyprus	U 5-a	
sawnwood (for building industry)	European countries & USA	U 5-a	
semi-finished products	OAS member countries	N 17-a	
	S Vietnam	U 32-m	
silk raw (ex Japan)	UK	B 10-m	
sisal (ex E Africa)	UK	B 10-m	
steel bars (for building industry)	European countries	U 5-a	
steel sheets	UK	T 2-m	
steel tubes	UK	T 2-m	
textile fabrics	OAS member countries	N 17-a	
textile products	Thailand	U 32-m	
tinplate	UK	T 2-m	
transport equipment	Thailand	U 32-m	
wood panels (for building industry)	Austria	U 5-a	
wool (Merino crossbred)	UK	B 10-m	
WHOLESALE PRICES FROM 1750 (ON CHANGED BASES)	Main European countries	Z 1-a	
WHOLESALE PRICES FROM 1913	Main countries	C 4-a	
WHOLESALE TRADE: TURNOVER BY KIND (VALUE BASIS)	Main countries	U 27-m	
WORLD EXPORT TRADE:			
(quantum basis)	Developed countries	U 23-a	
	Developing countries	U 23-a	
(unit price basis)		U 18-a	
tropical products by kind		B 13-a	
WORLD IMPORT & EXPORT TRADE (VALUE BASIS)		R 5-a	
WORLD INDUSTRIAL PRODUCTION	Communist countries	C 4-a	
	Developed countries	C 4-a	
	Developing countries	C 4-a	
	Non-Communist countries	C 4-a	
WORLD MARKET PRICES:			
agricultural commodities (incl cereals)		A 5-a	
agricultural raw materials by kind		G 1-a	
beef, butter & cereals by kind		G 1-a	
cereals		U 23-a	U 30-a
cocoa beans		G 1-a	
cocoa (ex Ghana) based on US spot prices		B 13-a	
coffee beans		G 1-a	
coffee, cocoa & tea		U 23-a	
coffee (ex Brazil) based on US spot prices		B 13-a	
copper (refined & unrefined)		M 4-a	
copra cake & meal		A 4-m	
cotton (raw)		G 1-a	M 4-a
dairy products		U 30-a	
edible fats & oils & soap		A 5-a	
edible fats & oils		A 4-m	
farm commodities (non-food items)		U 23-a	
fats & oils (all kinds)		A 5-a	
fish & fish products		G 1-a	
food products by kind		G 1-a	
food products, fibres & metals		P 1-a2	
food products		U 23-a	

••• APPENDIX 3 - INDEX NUMBERS

	Territorial coverage	Title codes	
WORLD MARKET PRICES, continued			
fruit (fresh)		G 1-a	
fuel oil		U 23-a	
hides & skins		G 1-a	
iron ore		G 1-a	
lard		A 4-m	
lauric acid oils		A 4-m	
manufactured goods		G 1-a	
marine oils		A 5-a	
meat		U 30-a	
metal ores		U 23-a	
minerals by kind		G 1-a	U 23-a
natural rubber (based on US spot prices)		B 13-a	
natural rubber		G 1-a	M 4-a
non-ferrous metal ores & non-ferrous metals		G 1-a	
oils (soft, hard & marine)		A 5-a	
oils (technical)		A 4-m	A 5-a
oilseed cake & meal		G 1-a	
oilseeds & vegetable oils		U 30-a	
oilseeds, oils & fats		A 4-m	G 1-a
olive oil		A 4-m	
pepper (ex Malabar)(based on US spot prices)		B 13-a	
petroleum (crude) & petroleum products		G 1-a	
primary commodities by kind		G 1-a	
raw materials		U 30-a	
rice (in private trade)		A 10-a	
(under bilateral government contracts)		A 10-a	
soft oils (excl olive oil)		A 4-m	
sugar (based on International Sugar Agreement prices)		B 13-a	
sugar (raw)		G 1-a	M 4-a
tallow, palm oil & fish oils		A 4-m	
tea (based on London auction prices)		B 13-a	G 1-a
textile raw materials		U 23-a	
timber & sawnwood		G 1-a	
tobacco (based on US leaf auction prices)		B 13-a	
tropical products by kind		B 13-a	
tropical products		U 30-a	
wood pulp		G 1-a	
wool (raw)		G 1-a	U 23-a
WORLD PRODUCTION:			
basic metals	World regions	U 38	
chemicals, oil, coal & rubber products		U 38	
coal		N 5-a	
crude petroleum & natural gas		N 5-a	
electricity & gas (5 yr periods)		U 38	
ex mines by manufacturing industry & public utilities		U 38	
manufactured goods (quantum basis)		U 38	U 23-a
metals & engineering products		U 38	
metals & minerals by kind		N 5-a	
non-metallic mineral products		N 5-a	
petroleum, coal products & chemicals		N 5-a	
primary commodities (quantum basis)		U 23-a	
by broad groups		U 43-a	
raw materials (quantum basis)		U 23-a	
tropical products by kind		B 13-a	
WORLD TRADE (QUANTUM & VALUE BASES)	World regions	U 43-a	
WORLD TRADE (see no 2, 5, 8, 11)	World regions	U 27-a	
WORLD TRADE: manufactured goods (quantum basis)		U 23-a	
(unit value basis)		U 23-a	
WORLD TRADE, POPULATION & OUTPUT (COMPARATIVE INDICES)		U 43-a	

APPENDIX 4 — GLOBAL STATISTICS

World consumption by product	711
World maritime fleets	712
World market prices	713
World population	716
World primary energy sources	716
World production	717
World stocks & supply	724
World trade	724
World trade by product	725

WORLD CONSUMPTION BY PRODUCT

	Territorial coverage	Title codes	
aluminium: historical table: tonnage		C 12-a	
(refined): tonnage		C 30-a	
tonnage	All countries	J 6-a	
apparel fibres by kind in lbs & as % of total fibre consumption	Main countries	B 2-a	T 4-a
bananas: tonnage		B 10-a	
cadmium: tonnage	Main countries	B 2-a	
cereals: (3 yr averages): tonnage		C 12-a	C 30-a
	Developed world regions	C 27-a	
	Developing world regions	C 27-a	
coal (incl lignite): tonnage		H 4-a	
cocoa beans: grindings: tonnage	Main countries	B 2-a	
tonnage (raw bean equiv)		B 13-a	
coffee: tonnage	Main countries	B 2-a	
copper: historical table: tonnage		C 12-a	
(refined): tonnage	Main countries	B 2-a	J 6-a
		U 11-a	
	Worldwide	C 30-a	
	All countries	C 12-a	
(unrefined): tonnage	Main countries	J 6-a	
cotton in bales (incl US usage as % of world consumption)		K 1-a	
in lbs (incl cotton as % of usage of all apparel fibres)		B 10-a	
	Main countries	B 10-a	
(raw): tonnage		U 11-a	
	Main countries	B 2-a	
crude petroleum (as % of all energy consumed)		H 4-a	
tonnage		B 30-a	H 4-a
electricity (as % of all energy consumed)		H 4-a	
in coal equiv tonnage		C 14-a	
in kWh		H 4-a	
energy (all kinds) in coal equiv tonnage		C 14-a	
in oil equiv tonnage		U 18-a	
per capita (in kg of coal equiv)		C 14-a	
(in kg of oil equiv)		U 18-a	
fertilisers (nitrogenous) used in agriculture: tonnage		R 5-a	
(phosphate) used in agriculture: tonnage		R 5-a	
(potash) used in agriculture: tonnage		R 5-a	
fibres by kind: artificial fibres projected to 1980: tonnage		B 29-a	
cotton & wool fibres projected to 1980: tonnage		B 29-a	
(incl per capita consumption in kg)		A 6-a	
projected to 1980: tonnage		B 29-a	
synthetic fibres projected to 1980: tonnage		B 29-a	
fuels (liquid) in coal equiv tonnage		C 14-a	
(solid): tonnage		C 14-a	
jute & kenaf manufactures: tonnage	All countries	A 5-a	B 10-a
(raw) & allied fibres: tonnage	World regions	B 10-a	
lead: historical table: tonnage		C 12-a	
(refined): tonnage		C 30-a	U 11-a
	All countries	C 12-a	T 4-a
man-made fibres (incl as % of total usage of all apparel fibres)		B 10-a	
natural gas as % of all energy consumed		H 4-a	
by volume in m³	Main countries	H 4-a	
in coal equiv tonnage		C 14-a	
		C 17-m	C 18-m
		U 11-a	U 26-a
natural rubber: tonnage	Main countries	A 5-a	B 2-a
		B 13-a	

•••• APPENDIX 4 - GLOBAL STATISTICS

WORLD CONSUMPTION BY PRODUCT, continued

Product	Territorial coverage	Title codes	
nickel (refined): tonnage	All countries	C 12-a	C 30-a
	Main countries	T 4-a	
petroleum products (incl bunkers): tonnage		T 3-a	
(refined) in barrels per day		C 3-a	
phosphate rock: tonnage		T 5-a	U 25-a
rayon filament yarn: tonnage (incl as % of usage of all apparel fibres)		B 10-a	
rayon staple fibre: tonnage (incl as % of usage of all apparel fibres)		B 10-a	
rice: tonnage	Main countries	B 2-a	
silk in lbs (incl as % of usage of all apparel fibres)		B 10-a	
silver in oz	Main countries	J 6-a	
(for industrial purposes & the arts) in oz	Main countries	T 4-a	
(for minting of coinage) in oz	Main countries	T 4-a	
sisal & hemp: tonnage	Main countries	B 2-a	
solid fuels: tonnage (incl as % of all energy consumed)		H 4-a	
sugar (raw centrifugal): tonnage		U 11-a	
	All countries	A 20-a	C 25-a
(refined) for human consumption: tonnage		B 13-a	
	Main countries	B 2-a	
sulphuric acid: tonnage	Communist world regions	T 5-a	
	Non-Communist world regions	T 5-a	
synthetic rubber: tonnage	Worldwide excl centrally-planned areas	B 13-a	
		U 26-a	
tea in lbs	Main countries	B 2-a	B 13-a
	Worldwide excl USSR, China & Japan	B 13-a	
tonnage	Main countries	B 2-a	
tin: historical table: tonnage		C 12-a	
(primary): tonnage		C 20-m	
(refined): tonnage	Main countries	B 2-a	C 12-a
		C 20-m	
(secondary): tonnage	All countries excl Communist countries	C 20-m	T 4-a
tonnage	All countries	J 6-a	
tin scrap: tonnage	Main countries	T 4-a	
tinplate: tonnage	All countries	C 20-m	T 4-a
wood pulp (for paper-making): tonnage		J 7-a	
wool in lbs (clean basis) & as % of total fibre consumption		B 10-a	
(virgin) by textile industries: tonnage	World regions	U 11-a	
(clean basis) in lbs (estim)		B 10-a	
zinc (crude slabs): tonnage	All countries	C 12-a	C 30-a
		J 6-a	
historical table: tonnage		C 12-a	
tonnage		U 11-a	
	All countries excl USSR	T 4-a	

WORLD MARITIME FLEETS

	Territorial coverage	Title codes	
% distribution: maritime fleets by kinds of vessels by flag	Worldwide	U 37-a	
by engine type: diesel & diesel-electric motorships: tonnage afloat	Worldwide	D 28-a	
reciprocating steamships: tonnage afloat	Worldwide	D 28-a	
turbine-driven & turbo-electric steamships: tonnage afloat		D 28-a	
by kind: new vessels on order: tonnage	Countries of build	D 28-a	
bulk carriers afloat by type, age & tonnage classes	Worldwide	D 28-a	
distribution of world fleets by flag: tonnage	Countries of registration	U 37-a	
new construction: completions (all types of vessels)	Countries of build	E 14-a	S 1-a
requirements: bulk carriers & combined carriers: tonnage		S 15-a	
projected to 1980: tonnage		D 28-a	
tankers: tonnage		S 15-a	
new vessels on order: tonnage	Countries of build	D 28-a	
under construction: tonnage by flag	Countries of build & registration	D 28-a	
no of vessels afloat: oil tankers (motorships & steamships)	Worldwide	T 3-a	
no & tonnage afloat: all vessels by flag	Countries of registration	S 2-a	
bulk carriers & oil tankers by flag	Countries of registration	S 2-a	
bulk carriers	Worldwide	S 15-a	S 16-a
cargo ships by flag	Countries of registration	S 2-a	S 15-a
		S 16-a	
historical table from 1904 by flag	Countries of registration	S 2-a	
chemical carriers by flag	Countries of registration	S 2-a	
container ships by flag	Countries of registration	S 2-a	
fish factory ships (by size classes)	Worldwide	D 43-a	
fishing vessels & trawlers (by size classes)	Worldwide	D 43-a	S 2-a
liquefied gas carriers by flag	Countries of registration	S 2-a	
oil tankers by age, type & tonnage classes	Worldwide	D 28-a	
by date of build & ownership	Worldwide	S 20-a	
in service by oil companies by tonnage classes	Worldwide	S 19-a	
(total) by flag	Countries of registration	S 2-a	
in service	Worldwide	E 14-a	
under construction	Worldwide	E 14-a	
(used & owned by oil companies)	Worldwide	S 20-a	
(privately-owned)	Worldwide	S 20-a	
ore & bulk cargo carriers (combined) by flag	Countries of registration	S 2-a	
passenger liners by flag	Countries of registration	S 2-a	

•••• APPENDIX 4 - GLOBAL STATISTICS

WORLD MARITIME FLEETS, continued

	Territorial coverage	Title codes	
no & tonnage afloat: research ships by flag	Countries of registration	S 2-a	
tankers (all types) by age groups	Worldwide	C 3-a	S 17-a
vessels (all types): historical table	Worldwide	U 37-a	
laid up (for lack of cargo) by flag (all cargo ships)	Countries of registration	S 23-m	
ocean passenger liners by flag	Countries of registration	S 16-a	
oil tankers by flag	Countries of registration	S 16-a	
ore carriers by flag	Countries of registration	S 16-a	
refrigerated food carriers by flag	Countries of registration	S 16-a	
launched (new construction)	Country of build	E 14-a	S 1-a
steamships & motorships in service by flag	Countries of registration	S 2-a	
tankers (all types) in service by size classes by flag	Countries of registration	S 15-a	S 16-a
tonnage afloat: all vessels by flag	Countries of registration	D 28-a	
as % of world fleets by size classes		D 28-a	
fishing vessels		D 28-a	
general cargo ships		D 28-a	
liquefied gas carriers		D 28-a	
ore carriers		D 28-a	
tankers (all types)		D 28-a	
bulk carriers by flag	Countries of registration	S 4-a	
by age groups as % of world fleets		D 28-a	
by size classes	Worldwide	D 28-a	
by type of vessels by flag	World regions & countries of registration	D 28-a	
(incl % change): combined bulk carriers	Worldwide	D 28-a	
container ships	Worldwide	D 28-a	
non-tanker vessels: historical table	Worldwide	D 28-a	
tankers by flag	Countries of registration	D 28-a	S 4-a
historical table	Worldwide	D 28-a	U 37-a
US reserve fleet		D 28-a	
US reserve fleet: vessels other than tankers		D 28-a	
whale oil factory ships	Japan & USSR	S 4-a	
broken up (for scrap): cargo ships	Worldwide	D 28-a	S 15-a
laid up: tankers: historical table	Worldwide	D 28-a	
vessels (other than tankers): historical table	Worldwide	D 28-a	
under construction by size classes: tankers	Worldwide	S 17-m	

WORLD MARKET PRICES

acrylic "Orlon" fibre in cents per lb		R 2-m	
agricultural commodities as % of EEC area prices		E 44-a	
agricultural commodities - index nos		U 33-q	A 5-a
agricultural raw materials by kind - index nos		G 1-a	
aluminium ingots in £ per ton		E 41-a	
(primary) in cents per lb		R 2-m	
(virgin ingots) in cents per lb		T 4-m	
- index nos (weighted average)		U 29-q	
animal fats & oils - index nos (weighted average)		U 29-q	
feeding stuffs by kind per 100 kg		E 34-m	
bacon (Danish) in £ per 100 kg		E 34-m	
- index nos (weighted average)		U 29-q	
bananas (ex Martinique) in Fr per kg		E 41-a	
barley: world prices as % of EEC area prices		E 44-a	
- index nos (weighted average)		U 29-q	
bauxite - index nos (weighted average)		U 29-q	
beef (hindquarters) ex Argentina per 100 kg		E 34-m	
world prices as % of EEC area prices		E 44-a	
- index nos (weighted average)		U 29-q	G 1-a
butter (ex Denmark) in £ per 100 kg		E 34-m	
(ex N Zealand) in bulk in £ per ton		A 5-a	
in £ per 100 kg		E 34-m	
world prices as % of EEC area prices		E 44-a	
- index nos (weighted average)		U 29-q	G 1-a
castor seed (ex E Africa) in £ per ton		R 2-m	
cattle hides (heavy) in cents per lb		R 2-m	
cereals by kind (incl rice) per 100 kg		E 34-m	
cereals, meat, sugar, tea & coffee - index nos		A 5-a	
cereals - index nos (weighted average)		U 29-q	
cheese: cheddar (ex N Zealand) in £ per 100 kg		E 34-m	
(ex Denmark) in D Kr per 100 kg		E 34-m	
(rindless) ex N Zealand in £ per 40 lbs		A 5-a	
world prices as % of EEC area prices		E 44-a	
- index nos (weighted average)		U 29-q	
chrome ore - index nos (weighted average)		U 29-q	
coal - index nos (weighted average)		U 29-q	
cocoa beans (ex Accra) in cents per lb		E 41-a	
(ex Accra & Bahia) in cents per lb		R 2-m	P 3-a
cocoa - index nos (weighted average)		U 29-q	B 13-a
		G 1-a	
coconut oil in cents per lb		R 2-m	
coffee: Arabica (ex Brazil) in Fr per kg		E 41-a	
(ex Uganda) in cents per lb		E 41-a	
(green) by grade in cents per lb		R 2-m	
(Robusta) ex Angola in Fr per kg		E 41-a	

•••• APPENDIX 4 - GLOBAL STATISTICS

WORLD MARKET PRICES, continued

	Territorial coverage	Title codes	
coffee - index nos (weighted average)		U 29-q	B 13-a
		G 1-a	
copper (electrolytic) in £ per ton		E 41-a	
historical table from 1875 in £ per ton		T 4-a	
in cents per lb		U 18-a	
- index nos (weighted average)		U 29-q	
copper ore - index nos (weighted average)		U 29-q	
copra cake & meal - index nos		A 4-m	
copra (ex Philippines) in £ per 100 kg		E 34-m	
in $ per ton		E 41-a	
in $ per kg		R 2-m	
(ex Madagascar) in Fr per ton		E 41-a	
corn oil (raw) ex tanks in cents per lb		R 2-m	
cotton (ex India) in cents per lb		E 41-a	
(raw) - index nos (weighted average)		U 29-q	G 1-a
cottonseed oil - index nos (weighted average)		U 29-q	
cow hides & calfskins in cents per lb		R 2-m	
crude petroleum (incl freight costs) in $ per barrel		U 16-q	
in $ per 42 gallon barrel	Texas (USA)	R 2-m	
	Algeria	R 2-m	
	Iran	R 2-m	
	Iraq	R 2-m	
	Kuwait	R 2-m	
	Nigeria	R 2-m	
	Saudi-Arabia	R 2-m	
	Venezuela	R 2-m	
crude petroleum - index nos (weighted average)		U 29-q	
dairy produce - index nos (weighted average)		U 29-q	
edible oils & fats by kind - index nos		A 4-m	
eggs: world prices as % of EEC area prices		E 44-a	
eggs - index nos (weighted average)		U 29-q	
fats & oils - index nos (weighted average)		U 29-q	
fibres (all kinds) - index nos		P 1-a2	
fish & fish products - index nos		G 1-a	
fish oil (from herrings ex factory at Liverpool) in £ per ton		E 34-m	
in cents per lb		R 2-m	
fish - index nos (weighted average)		U 29-q	
flax - index nos (weighted average)		U 29-q	
food products - index nos (weighted average)		U 29-q	P 1-a2
		G 1-a	U 23-a
fruit (fresh) - index nos (weighted average)		U 29-q	G 1-a
gold (on London market in sterling) in £ per oz		T 4-m	
US Treasury price in $ per oz		T 4-m	
groundnut oil (ex Nigeria) in £ per ton		R 2-m	
in £ per 100 kg		E 34-m	
oilcake (ex Nigeria) in £ per ton		E 41-a	
groundnuts (husked) ex Nigeria in £ per ton		R 2-m	E 41-a
in £ per 100 kg		E 34-m	
groundnuts - index nos (weighted average)		U 29-q	
hemp (ex E Africa) in £ per ton		E 41-a	
hemp - index nos (weighted average)		U 29-q	
hen eggs (ex Denmark) in D Kr per thousand		E 34-m	
hidex & skins - index nos (weighted average)		U 29-q	G 1-a
iron ore (51.5% iron content) in $ per ton		E 41-a	
iron ore - index nos (weighted average)		U 29-q	G 1-a
jute (raw ex India) in Rs per 400 lbs		R 2-m	
jute - index nos (weighted average)		U 29-q	
lard (ex USA) in £ per 100 kg		E 34-m	
lard - index nos		A 4-m	
lauric acid oils - index nos		A 4-m	
lead in cents per lb		U 18-a	
in £ per ton: historical table from 1875 (average)		T 4-a	
- index nos (weighted average)		U 29-q	
lead ore - index nos (weighted average)		U 29-q	
linseed oil - index nos (weighted average)		U 29-q	
linseed - index nos (weighted average)		U 29-q	
main trading commodities in local currency	Main countries	R 5-a	
maize by grade in cents per 56 lbs		R 2-m	
wholesale prices as % of EEC area prices		E 44-a	
- index nos (weighted average)		U 29-q	
manganese ingots in cents per lb		R 2-m	
ore (high grade) in £ per ton		E 41-a	
- index nos (weighted average)		U 29-q	
manufactured goods - index nos (weighted average)		U 29-q	G 1-a
meat - index nos (weighted average)		U 29-q	
metal ores - index nos		U 29-q	
metals (all kinds) - index nos (weighted average)		P 1-a2	
milk powder in £ per ton		A 5-a	
(ex Netherlands) in Fl per kg		A 5-a	
milk - index nos (weighted average)		U 29-q	
minerals by kind - index nos		G 1-a	
molybdenum concentrates in £ per lb		T 4-m	
natural phosphates in $ per ton		E 41-a	
natural rubber (ex Malaysia) in pence per lb		E 41-a	
(ex Singapore) in M$ per kg		R 2-m	
- index nos (weighted average)		U 29-q	B 13-a
		G 1-a	
nickel ore - index nos (weighted average)		U 29-q	

APPENDIX 4 - GLOBAL STATISTICS

Territorial coverage   Title codes

WORLD MARKET PRICES, continued

	Title codes	
nickel - index nos (weighted average)	U 29-q	
non-ferrous metals - index nos (weighted average)	U 29-q	G 1-a
ores - index nos (weighted average)	U 29-q	G 1-a
non-food commodities & minerals - index nos	U 23-a	
nylon fibre (1.5 denier) in cents per lb	R 2-m	
oilcake & meal - index nos	U 29-q	
oils & fats - index nos (FAO series)	A 5-a	
oils for perfumes (ex Madagascar) in Fr per kg	E 41-a	
oilseed cake & meal - index nos	G 1-a	
oilseeds: world prices as % of EEC area prices	E 44-a	
- index nos	A 4-m	
oilseeds, oils & fats - index nos	G 1-a	
olive oil: world prices as % of EEC area prices	E 44-a	
- index nos (weighted average)	U 29-q	A 4-m
paddy rice: (government contract prices) in $ per ton	A 10-a	
(private trade prices) in $ per ton	A 10-a	
palm kernel oil in Fr per kg	E 41-a	
- index nos (weighted average)	U 29-q	
palm kernels (ex E Africa) in £ per ton	R 2-m	
palm nuts & kernels (ex W Africa) in Fr per kg	E 41-a	
palm oil (ex Malaysia) in £ per ton	E 41-a	
- index nos (weighted average)	U 29-q	
pepper (Malabar Black) in £ per cwt	E 41-a	
- index nos	B 13-a	
petroleum (crude & products) - index nos	G 1-a	
pigs (slaughtered) in D Kr per 100 kg	E 34-m	
polyester: "Dacron" fibre in cents per lb	R 2-m	
pork: world prices as % of EEC area prices	E 44-a	
pork - index nos (weighted average)	U 29-q	
poultry - index nos (weighted average)	U 29-q	
primary commodities by kind - index nos	G 1-a	
primary commodities - index nos (weighted average)	U 29-q	U 23-a
raw coffee (Santos) in $ per 100 kg	E 34-m	
raw materials: jute, cotton & wool - index nos	A 5-a	
non-food farm products - index nos	U 29-q	
rice by grade ex warehouse in cents per lb	R 2-m	
(husked) ex Madagascar in Fr per 100 kg	E 41-a	
world prices as % of EEC area prices	E 44-a	
- index nos (weighted average)	U 29-q	
rye in cents per 56 lbs	R 2-m	
selected main commodities - index nos	P 1-a2	
silk (raw 20-22 denier) in yen per kg	R 2-m	
soft oils (excl olive oil) - index nos	A 4-m	
soybean oil in cents per lb	R 2-m	
in $ per 100 kg	E 34-m	
- index nos (weighted average)	U 29-q	
soybeans (ex USA) in $ per 100 kg	E 34-m	
- index nos (weighted average)	U 29-q	
sugar: contract prices by grade per lb	R 2-m	
(ex Caribbean countries) in cents per lb	B 13-m	
(for bulk shipment) in £ per ton	B 13-m	
International Sugar Agreement price in cents per lb	B 13-m	
in £ per ton	B 13-m	
in cents per lb	E 41-a	
(raw centrifugal) historical table from 1900 in cents per lb	A 20-a	
in £ per ton	B 13-m	C 25-a
in $ per 100 kg	E 34-m	
(refined): world prices as % of EEC area prices	E 44-a	
- index nos (weighted average)	U 29-q	B 13-a
	G 1-a	
tallow in $ per 100 kg	E 34-m	
tallow, palm & fish oils - index nos	A 4-m	
tea: auction price in £ per 100 kg (London market)	E 34-m	
in cents per lb	B 13-a	
tea - index nos (weighted average)	U 29-q	B 13-a
	G 1-a	
technical oils - index nos	A 4-m	
"Terylene" fibre in pence per kg	R 2-m	
textile fibres - index nos (weighted average)	U 29-q	
timber - index nos (weighted average)	U 29-q	G 1-a
tin: historical table from 1875 in £ per ton	T 4-m	
in cents per lb	U 18-a	
tin - index nos (weighted average)	U 29-q	
tin ore (70% metal) in $ per ton	E 41-a	
tin ore - index nos (weighted average)	U 29-q	
tobacco (ex USA) in cents per lb	E 41-a	
- index nos (weighted average)	U 29-q	B 13-a
tropical products by kind - index nos	B 13-a	
tropical wood: mahogany (ex Lagos) in £ per ton	E 41-a	
vanilla (ex Tahiti) in Fr per kg	E 41-a	
vegetable oils by kind - index nos	A 5-a	
wheat, maize & rice - index nos	G 1-a	
wheat (soft) by grade in cents per 60 lbs	R 2-m	
- index nos (weighted average)	U 29-q	
wine - index nos (weighted average)	U 29-q	
wolfram ore in £ per ton	T 4-m	
wood pulp - index nos (weighted average)	U 29-q	G 1-a
wool (raw) - index nos (weighted average)	U 29-q	G 1-a

715

Z*

●●●● APPENDIX 4 - GLOBAL STATISTICS

	Territorial coverage	Title codes
WORLD MARKET PRICES, continued		
zinc: historical table from 1875 in £ per ton		T 4-a
in cents per lb		U 18-a
zinc - index nos (weighted average)		U 29-q
zinc ore - index nos (weighted average)		U 29-q

WORLD POPULATION

in developed regions projected to yr 2000		M 4-a
from 1650 to date		M 4-a
in less developed regions projected to yr 2000		M 4-a
from 1650 to date		M 4-a
% of world population living in developed regions projected to yr 2000		M 4-a
from 1650 to date		M 4-a
in less developed regions projected to yr 2000		M 4-a
from 1650 to date		M 4-a

WORLD PRIMARY ENERGY & MINERAL RESERVES

WORLD MINERAL RESERVES (estim)

	Territorial coverage	Title codes
aluminium: tonnage	Main countries	N 1-a
antimony: tonnage	Main countries	N 1-a
arsenic (white): tonnage	Main countries	N 1-a
asbestos: tonnage	Main countries	N 1-a
barytes: tonnage	Main countries	N 1-a
bauxite: tonnage	Main countries	N 1-a
bismuth: tonnage	Main countries	N 1-a
boron: tonnage	Main countries	N 1-a
cadmium: tonnage	Main countries	N 1-a
cesium ore: tonnage	Main countries	N 1-a
chrome ore: tonnage	Main countries	N 1-a
coal (bituminous) & lignite: tonnage	Main countries	N 1-a
columbite concentrates: tonnage	Main countries	N 1-a
copper ore: tonnage	Main countries	N 1-a
feldspar: tonnage	Main countries	N 1-a
fluorspar: tonnage	Main countries	N 1-a
gold (based on metal content of ore) in oz	Main countries	N 1-a
hydrocarbon fuels: tonnage	Main countries	H 4-a
ilmenite: tonnage	Main countries	N 1-a
indium: tonnage	Main countries	N 1-a
iron ore by kind: tonnage	All countries	U 56-a
tonnage	Main countries	N 1-a
kyanite: tonnage	Main countries	N 1-a
lead: tonnage	Main countries	N 1-a
lithium minerals: tonnage	Main countries	N 1-a
magnesite: tonnage	Main countries	N 1-a
manganese ore: tonnage	Main countries	N 1-a
mercury in flasks	Main countries	N 1-a
minerals by kind: tonnage	All countries	N 5-a
molybdenum: tonnage		N 1-a
nickel: tonnage	Main countries	N 1-a
platinum-group metals in oz	Main countries	N 1-a
potash: tonnage	Main countries	N 1-a
rutile concentrates: tonnage	Main countries	N 1-a
selenium: tonnage	Main countries	N 1-a
sulphur: tonnage	Main countries	N 1-a
tantalum concentrates: tonnage	Main countries	N 1-a
thorium: tonnage	Main countries	N 1-a
tin: tonnage	Main countries	N 1-a
titanium minerals: tonnage	Main countries	N 1-a
vermiculite: tonnage	Main countries	N 1-a
yttrium: tonnage	Main countries	N 1-a

NATURAL GAS RESERVES

by volume in cu ft (estim)	Main countries	N 1-a
in m³ (proven)		C 14-a

PETROLEUM RESERVES

in 42 gallon barrels (estim)	All countries	N 1-a
in barrels million & tonnage	World regions	T 3-a
in barrels million (proven)		C 14-a
by volume in million m³		U 18-a

APPENDIX 4 - GLOBAL STATISTICS

WORLD PRODUCTION

	Territorial coverage	Title codes	
% world growth rates (over 5 yr periods): basic metals production		U 38	
chemicals, oil, coal & rubber production		U 38	
electricity & gas production		U 38	
heavy manufacturing		U 38	
light manufacturing		U 38	
metal & engineering products		U 38	
mining, manufacturing & public utilities		U 38	
abaca: tonnage		K 4-a	
acetate staple & filament: tonnage		D 27-a	
acrylic staple & filament: tonnage		D 27-a	
agaves: tonnage		K 4-a	
agricultural production & farm output per capita - index nos		U 23-a	
agricultural products - index nos		A 11-a	B 1-a
almonds (shelled): tonnage	All countries	P 4-a	
alumina (bauxite): tonnage		N 4-a	
aluminium castings: tonnage	Main countries	T 4-a	
historical table: tonnage		C 12-a	
ingots (unalloyed): tonnage		N 4-a	
(primary): tonnage	All countries	T 4-a	
	Main countries	N 1-a	
(primary & refined): tonnage		C 30-a	
semi-finished products: tonnage	Main countries	T 4-a	
tonnage	All countries	J 6-a	R 5-a
animal fats by kind: tonnage		N 10-a	
anthracite: tonnage		N 1-a	
antimony (based on metal content of ore): tonnage		C 30-a	
tonnage	Main countries	N 1-a	T 4-a
	All countries	C 12-a	
ore (based on metal content): tonnage		C 12-a	
tonnage	Main countries	N 4-a	T 4-a
argon (in gas & liquid form): tonnage		N 1-a	
arsenic (metallic): tonnage		T 4-a	
	Main countries	N 1-a	
(white): tonnage		N 4-a	
asbestos: tonnage		N 4-a	
	All countries	R 5-a	
	Main countries	N 1-a	
babassu oil: tonnage		A 4-a	N 10-a
bananas: tonnage	Main countries	B 2-a	
barite: tonnage		N 4-a	
barley: tonnage & yield per ha in kg (world average)		R 5-a	
tonnage		C 16-a	
barytes: tonnage	Main countries	N 1-a	
basic metals & minerals by kind: tonnage		J 3-a	
- index nos	World regions	U 38	
bauxite: historical table: tonnage		C 12-a	
tonnage	All countries	J 6-a	R 5-a
		T 4-a	
	Main countries	B 2-a	C 30-a
		N 1-a	
beef & veal: tonnage	World regions	A 5-a	
beet sugar: tonnage	All countries	C 25-a	
beryl: tonnage		N 4-a	
beryllium ore: tonnage	Main countries	T 4-a	
incl concentrates: tonnage		C 30-a	
tonnage	Main countries	N 1-a	
bismuth: tonnage	Main countries	N 1-a	N 4-a
		T 4-a	
	Reporting countries only	C 30-a	
bromide: tonnage	Main countries	N 1-a	
buses & coaches: volume		N 8-a	
butter & cheese (based on fat content): tonnage		A 4-a	
& lard: tonnage		U 11-a	
(based on fat content): tonnage		N 10-a	
ex factory: tonnage (incl % share of EEC area)		B 3-a	
butter, lard, edible oils, soap, fats & oils: tonnage		A 5-a	
cadmium: tonnage	Main countries	T 4-a	
		C 30-a	N 4-a
	All countries	C 12-a	
cane sugar: tonnage	All countries	C 25-a	
carbon black: tonnage	Main countries	N 1-a	
castor oil: tonnage		N 10-a	
	All countries	A 4-a	B 18-a
seed: crop tonnage (estim)	All countries	P 1-a	
cattle, calf, buffalo, sheep & goat hides & skins: volume		A 18-a	
cellulosic fibres & filaments: tonnage		R 5-a	
tonnage	All countries	K 4-a	
filament: tonnage		D 27-a	
filament yarn: tonnage	All countries	K 4-a	
staple: tonnage		D 27-a	
cement: historical table from 1913: tonnage		C 4-a	
(hydraulic): tonnage		N 4-a	
tonnage	All countries	R 5-a	
	Main countries	N 1-a	
cereals & coarse grains: tonnage	Main countries	A 5-a	

APPENDIX 4 - GLOBAL STATISTICS

WORLD PRODUCTION, continued

	Territorial coverage	Title codes	
cheese (ex factory): tonnage (incl % share of EEC area)		B 3-a	
chemical fertilisers (based on nitrogen content): tonnage		R 5-a	
chemicals, oil, coal & rubber products - index nos		U 38	
chrome ore (chromite): tonnage		C 30-a	N 1-a
		N 4-a	
	All countries	C 12-a	R 5-a
	Main countries	T 4-a	
cigarettes: volume	All countries	R 5-a	
citrus fruits by kind: grapefruit: tonnage		A 5-a	B 2-a
lemons & limes: tonnage		A 5-a	B 2-a
oranges & tangerines: tonnage		A 5-a	B 2-a
tonnage		U 11-a	
coal (anthracite): tonnage		N 4-a	
(bituminous) & lignite: tonnage		N 1-a	
tonnage		N 4-a	
(incl lignite): tonnage		C 4-a	
coal, lignite & coke: tonnage	All countries	R 5-a	
coarse grains by kind: tonnage	World regions	A 12-a	
cobalt: tonnage	Main countries	N 1-a	T 4-a
	Reporting countries only	C 30-a	
	Worldwide	C 12-a	N 4-a
ore (based on metal content): tonnage		C 12-a	
cocoa beans: tonnage & per capita output in lbs		P 3-a	
tonnage	Main countries	B 2-a	
grindings (incl stock changes): tonnage	Main countries	U 11-a	
historical table from 1946: tonnage		P 2-a	
tonnage	Worldwide	A 3-a	B 13-a
		P 1-a	P 3-a
	All countries	R 5-a	
coconut oil: tonnage		A 4-a	N 10-a
coffee by kind in 60 kg bags	All countries	J 1-a	
(green) in 60 kg bags		B 13-a	B 18-a
	World regions	J 1-a	
	All countries	A 5-a	R 5-a
tonnage	Main countries	B 2-a	
coke (metallurgical): tonnage		N 4-a	
coke oven coke: tonnage	Main countries	U 10-a	
columbite concentrates: tonnage	Main countries	N 1-a	
columbium & tantalum: tonnage	Non-Communist countries	C 30-a	
columbium-tantalum concentrates: tonnage		N 4-a	
commercial vehicles & trucks: volume		N 8-a	R 5-a
		V 1-a	
volume by make	All countries	V 3-a	
commercial vehicles, trucks & buses: volume		V 4-a	
copper-alloy semi-manufactured goods: tonnage		C 30-m	
copper (at smelter plants): tonnage		N 4-a	
	All countries	J 6-a	
(based on metal content of ore): tonnage		B 2-a	C 4-a
		C 12-a	J 6-a
	All countries	R 5-a	
blister: tonnage	All countries	C 12-a	
	Main countries	T 4-a	
historical table from 1897: tonnage		C 12-a	J 6-a
mined, smeltered & refined: tonnage		C 30-a	
(refined) primary & secondary: tonnage	All countries	J 6-a	
tonnage	All countries	C 12-a	R 5-a
		T 4-a	
ore: tonnage	Worldwide	N 4-a	U 11-a
	Main countries	N 1-a	
products (semi-finished): tonnage	All countries	C 30-m	
copra: tonnage	Worldwide	A 4-a	
	All countries	B 18-a	P 1-a
	Main countries	B 2-a	
corn oil: tonnage		A 4-a	N 10-a
corundum abrasive: tonnage	Main countries	N 1-a	
cotton (raw) in lbs		B 10-a	
in bales & US % share of world total		K 1-a	
in bales		P 1-a	
tonnage	Main countries	A 5-a	B 2-a
	World regions	K 4-a	
		U 11-a	
cotton yarn (incl mixtures): tonnage		R 5-a	
cottonseed oil: tonnage		A 4-a	N 10-a
cottonseed: tonnage	All countries	B 18-a	P 1-a
	Main countries	B 2-a	
cow's milk: tonnage (incl % share of EEC area)		B 3-a	
crude petroleum & natural gas liquids: tonnage	All countries	T 3-a	
by volume in m³		U 18-a	
historical table from 1913: tonnage		C 4-a	
in barrels per day	All countries	C 3-a	
in barrels	Worldwide	N 4-a	
	All countries	N 1-a	
in coal equiv tonnage		C 14-a	
projected in barrels per day		U 16-q	
tonnage	Main countries	E 14-a	
crude steel (by process) incl castings: tonnage		T 1-a	
historical table from 1870: tonnage		E 29-a	
from 1913: tonnage		C 4-a	

APPENDIX 4 - GLOBAL STATISTICS

WORLD PRODUCTION, continued

	Territorial coverage	Title codes	
crude steel: ingots & castings: tonnage	Main countries	C 5-a	
tonnage	Worldwide	R 5-a	
	All countries	R 5-a	
crushed stone (ex quarries): tonnage	Main countries	N 1-a	
dairy cows: volume incl % share of EEC area	Main countries	N 1-a	
		B 3-a	
dates, prunes & raisins: tonnage	Main countries	A 5-a	
diamond gems in carats		N 4-a	
diatomite: tonnage		N 4-a	
diesel oil: tonnage		R 5-a	
dried fruit by kind: tonnage	All countries	A 5-a	
edible vegetable oils by kind: tonnage		N 10-a	
electricity generation: (all sources) in kWh	All countries	R 5-a	
by industry & public utility undertakings in kWh		R 5-a	
historical table from 1927 in kWh		C 4-a	
in coal equiv tonnage		C 14-a	
in kWh	All countries	R 5-a	
in nuclear power stations in kWh		R 5-a	
& gas production - index nos		U 38	
energy sources by kind in coal equiv tonnage		C 14-a	
fats & oils by kind: tonnage		A 4-a	
feed grains: tonnage		C 16-a	
feldspar: tonnage	Worldwide	N 4-a	
	Main countries	N 1-a	
fertilisers (nitrogenous): tonnage		N 4-a	
fibreboard: tonnage	All countries	A 5-a	
fish & fish liver oil: tonnage		N 10-a	
& sea oils (excl fish liver oil): tonnage		A 4-a	
meal (incl solubles): tonnage	All countries	A 5-a	
flax fibre (scutched basis): tonnage	All countries	B 10-a	
in lbs		B 10-a	
tonnage		K 4-a	
fluorspar: tonnage		N 4-a	
	Main countries	N 1-a	
food & food production per capita - index nos		U 23-a	
- index nos		A 11-a	
fuel briquettes: tonnage		N 4-a	
gem stones by value in $m	Main countries	N 1-a	
generators (hydroelectric): volume & in MW		T 7-a	
germanium (based on metal content of ore) in lbs		T 4-a	
tonnage	Main countries	N 1-a	
gold (based on metal content of ore) in kg		T 4-a	
tonnage	All countries	R 5-a	
in oz		N 4-a	
	All countries	J 6-a	
	Main countries	N 1-a	
tonnage		C 30-a	
	All countries	C 12-a	
graphite: tonnage	Main countries	N 1-a	
	Worldwide excl USA	N 4-a	
groundnut oil: tonnage		A 4-a	N 10-a
groundnuts: tonnage	All countries	B 18-a	P 1-a
	Main countries	B 2-a	
gypsum: tonnage	Main countries	N 1-a	
	Worldwide excl USA	N 4-a	
hard coal & lignite: tonnage		U 10-a	
hard fibres: hemp, abaca, sisal & henequen: tonnage		B 10-a	
hazelnuts (unshelled): tonnage	All countries	P 4-a	
helium gas (crude & quality gas) by volume in cu ft		N 1-a	
hemp & hard fibres in lbs		B 10-a	
hemp, sisal & henequen: tonnage		K 4-a	
hemp (true & soft) incl sunn hemp: tonnage		B 10-a	
henequen: tonnage		K 4-a	
hides & skins by kind: unit value in $ per kg (worldwide basis)		A 18-a	
value in $m		A 18-a	
volume & tonnage		A 18-a	
ilmenite & rutile minerals: tonnage		T 4-a	
ilmenite concentrates: tonnage		N 1-a	
indium in oz	Main countries	N 1-a	
industrial diamonds in carats		N 4-a	
tonnage	Main countries	N 1-a	
industrial production (total) - index nos	World Economic & Political Regions	C 4-a	
iron castings: tonnage	Main countries	B 25-a	T 4-a
(based on metal content of ore): tonnage		C 4-a	R 5-a
ore: tonnage		C 30-a	E 29-a
		N 4-a	R 5-a
		T 1-a	
	All countries	T 4-a	
	Main countries	N 1-a	
	World regions	U 11-a	U 49-a
		U 56-a	
pyrites: tonnage	All countries	R 5-a	
jute (incl allied fibres): tonnage		A 5-a	B 10-a
		K 4-a	
	All countries	C 22-a	
jute & kenaf manufactures: tonnage		A 5-a	
jute, kenaf & allied fibres: tonnage		U 11-a	

719

●●●● APPENDIX 4 – GLOBAL STATISTICS

WORLD PRODUCTION, continued

	Territorial coverage	Title codes	
kyanite: tonnage	Main countries	N 1-a	
lamb & mutton: tonnage	World regions	A 5-a	
lard: tonnage		A 4-a	N 10-a
lauric acid oils: tonnage		U 11-a	
lead (at smelter plants): tonnage		N 4-a	
	All countries	J 6-a	
		R 5-a	
(based on metal content of ore) incl concentrates: tonnage		U 24-m	C 12-a
tonnage		T 4-a	
		C 12-a	J 6-a
historical table from 1897: tonnage		U 24-m	
(refined): tonnage	All countries	C 12-a	R 5-a
		T 4-a	
tonnage	Main countries	N 1-a	
lead ore (based on metal content): tonnage		C 12-a	
mined & refined: tonnage		C 30-a	
tonnage		N 4-a	
	All countries	J 6-a	
		U 11-a	
& metallic lead: tonnage		U 11-a	
lemons, limes & grapefruit: tonnage		C 4-a	
lignite: historical table from 1913: tonnage		N 4-a	
tonnage	Main countries	N 1-a	
lime: tonnage	World regions	B 2-a	
linseed: tonnage & value in $m	All countries	B 18-a	P 1-a
tonnage		A 4-a	N 10-a
linseed oil: tonnage	All countries	A 5-a	
logs (coniferous & broad-leaved) by volume in m³		J 2-a	
machine tools (metal-cutting type) by value in $m		J 2-a	
(metal-forming type) by value in $m	Worldwide excl USA	N 4-a	
magnesite: tonnage	Main countries	N 1-a	
		C 12-a	
magnesium (based on metal content of ore): tonnage		C 30-a	N 4-a
tonnage	All countries	T 4-a	
	Main countries	N 1-a	
maize: tonnage for ensuing year (estim)		P 1-a	
& yield per ha in kg (world average)		R 5-a	
		C 16-a	
tonnage		R 5-a	
man-made cellulosic fibres & filaments: tonnage		K 4-a	
fibre yarn (synthetic & cellulosic): tonnage		B 10-a	
fibres as % of world industrial fibre production	Canada, European countries, Japan & USA	D 27-a	
by kind: tonnage		K 4-a	
(synthetic & cellulosic): tonnage	All countries	R 5-a	
manganese (based on metal content of ore): tonnage		C 30-a	N 4-a
ore: tonnage		T 1-a	U 11-a
	All countries	C 12-a	T 4-a
manufactured gas (in coke ovens) by volume in m³		R 5-a	
(in gasworks) by volume in m³		R 5-a	
goods – index nos (quantum basis)		U 23-a	U 38
marine oils by kind: fish, whale & sperm oil: tonnage		N 10-a	
meat (all kinds): tonnage	Main countries	R 5-a	
by kind: beef, lamb, pork & poultry: tonnage		A 5-a	
mercury in 76 lb flasks		N 4-a	
	Main countries	N 1-a	
	All countries	T 4-a	
tonnage	All countries	C 30-a	
		C 12-a	
metal & engineering productions – index nos		U 38	
metals (basic) by kind: tonnage		N 5-a	
mica: tonnage		N 4-a	
	Main countries	N 1-a	
milk: tonnage	Main countries	R 5-a	
milk powder (skim): tonnage (incl % share of EEC area)		B 3-a	
(whole): tonnage (incl % share of EEC area)		B 3-a	
mineral fuels by kind (in detail): tonnage		N 4-a	
minerals by kind (in detail): tonnage		N 4-a	
mining, manufacturing & public utilities: world output – index nos		U 38	
molybdenum (based on metal content of ore): tonnage		C 30-a	
tonnage		N 4-a	
ore: tonnage		C 12-a	
	Main countries	T 4-a	
motor spirit & aviation fuel: tonnage	All countries	R 5-a	
vehicles by type & make: volume	All countries	V 3-a	
volume		N 8-a	
historical table: volume	Main countries	V 4-a	
natural & man-made fibres by kind in lbs		B 10-a	
natural gas by volume in cu ft		N 4-a	
	Main countries	N 1-a	
	All countries	C 3-a	
in coal equiv tonnage		C 14-a	
nitrates: tonnage		N 1-a	
phosphates: tonnage	All countries	R 5-a	
rubber: tonnage		C 17-m	A 5-a
		B 13-a	U 11-a
		U 26-a	
newsprint: production capacity: tonnage	All countries	J 4-a	
tonnage	All countries	A 5-a	J 4-a

720

●●●● APPENDIX 4 - GLOBAL STATISTICS

	Territorial coverage	Title codes	
WORLD PRODUCTION, continued			
nickel (all forms): tonnage (estim)		J 6-a	
(at smelters): tonnage	All countries	T 4-a	
(mined & smeltered): tonnage		C 30-a	
(refined): tonnage	All producers	C 12-a	
tonnage		N 4-a	
	Main countries	N 1-a	
nickel ore: tonnage	All countries	T 4-a	
nitrogen (elemental): tonnage	Main countries	N 1-a	
(fixed): tonnage	Main countries	N 1-a	
nitrogen fertilisers: tonnage		T 5-a	
non-cellulosic man-made fibres by type in lbs		B 10-a	
in lbs		B 10-a	
staple fibres in lbs	All countries	B 10-a	
non-metallic minerals by kind (in detail): tonnage		N 4-a	
tonnage		N 5-a	
oats: tonnage & yield per ha in kg (world average)		R 5-a	
tonnage		C 16-a	
oilcake & meal made from copra: tonnage		A 5-a	
from cottonseed: tonnage		A 5-a	
from fish meal: tonnage		A 5-a	
from groundnuts: tonnage		A 5-a	
from linseed: tonnage		A 5-a	
from rapeseed: tonnage		A 5-a	
from sesame seed: tonnage		A 5-a	
from soybeans: tonnage		A 5-a	
from sunflower seed: tonnage		A 5-a	
oils & fats (from seeds & animal fats): tonnage		U 11-a	
(hard): coconut oil (incl Commonwealth share): tonnage		B 19-a	
palm kernel oil (incl Commonwealth share): tonnage		B 19-a	
palm oil (incl Commonwealth share): tonnage		B 19-a	
(soft): cottonseed oil (incl Commonwealth share): tonnage		B 19-a	
groundnut oil (incl Commonwealth share): tonnage		B 19-a	
olive oil (incl Commonwealth share): tonnage		B 19-a	
rapeseed oil (incl Commonwealth share): tonnage		B 19-a	
sesame seed oil (incl Commonwealth share): tonnage		B 19-a	
soybean oil (incl Commonwealth share): tonnage		B 19-a	
sunflower oil (incl Commonwealth share): tonnage		B 19-a	
(technical): castor oil (incl Commonwealth share): tonnage		B 19-a	
linseed oil (incl Commonwealth share): tonnage		B 19-a	
tung oil (incl Commonwealth share): tonnage		B 19-a	
oilseeds by kind: tonnage		P 1-a	
oiticica oil: tonnage		N 10-a	
olive oil: tonnage		N 10-a	
	All countries	A 4-a	B 18-a
		P 1-a	
oranges & tangerines: tonnage		U 11-a	
oxygen (as marketable gas): tonnage	Main countries	N 1-a	
paddy rice: historical table 1909-1962: tonnage	All countries	A 19-a	
tonnage	World regions	A 5-a	C 16-a
		U 11-a	
palm kernel oil: tonnage		A 4-a	N 10-a
palm kernels: tonnage	All countries	B 18-a	P 1-a
	Main countries	B 2-a	
palm oil: tonnage		A 4-a	B 18-a
		N 10-a	
paper & paperboard: tonnage		R 5-a	
	All countries	A 5-a	
particle board by volume in m³	All countries	A 5-a	
passenger cars: volume (incl volume assembled locally)		C 4-a	
volume by make	All countries	V 3-a	
volume		N 8-a	R 5-a
		V 4-a	
	All countries	V 1-a	
peat: tonnage	Main countries	N 1-a	N 4-a
pepper in cwt		B 13-a	
tonnage	All countries	A 5-a	U 11-a
perlite: tonnage	Main countries	N 1-a	
petroleum products in barrels per day		C 3-a	
phosphate fertilisers: tonnage		T 5-a	U 25-a
rock: tonnage		N 4-a	T 5-a
		U 25-a	
	All countries	C 15-a	
	Main countries	N 1-a	U 11-a
pig iron & ferro-alloys: tonnage		C 30-a	N 4-a
		R 5-a	T 1-a
	All countries	R 5-a	
	Main countries	C 5-a	
	World regions	U 11-a	U 49-a
historical table from 1870: tonnage		E 29-a	
tonnage	Main countries	N 1-a	
pig-meat, pork, bacon & ham: tonnage	World regions	A 5-a	
platinum-group metals (from platinum ore): in kg		C 12-a	
in oz		N 4-a	
in kg	All countries	J 6-a	
tonnage	All countries	C 12-a	
		C 30-a	
plywood & blockboard by volume in m³	All countries	A 5-a	

APPENDIX 4 – GLOBAL STATISTICS

WORLD PRODUCTION, continued

	Territorial coverage	Title codes	
polyamide staple & filament: tonnage		D 27-a	
potash fertilisers: tonnage		T 5-a	
potash: tonnage		N 4-a	
potatoes: tonnage & yield in kg per ha (world average)	Main countries	N 1-a	
tonnage	All countries	R 5-a	
poultry (incl game): tonnage	World regions	R 5-a	
primary commodities – index nos (quantum basis)		A 5-a	
pulpwood by volume in m³	All countries	U 23-a	
pumice & volcanic cinder: tonnage	Main countries	A 5-a	
tonnage	Worldwide excl Communist countries	N 1-a	
pyrites (incl cupreous pyrites): tonnage		N 4-a	
	Main countries	N 4-a	
quartz crystal in lbs	Brazil	T 4-a	
railway track material: tonnage		N 1-a	
rapeseed: tonnage	All countries	T 1-a	
rapeseed oil: tonnage		B 18-a	P 1-a
raw materials – index nos (quantum basis)		A 4-a	N 10-a
rayon & acetate continuous yarn & staple in lbs	All countries	U 23-a	
staple fibre in lbs	All countries	B 10-a	
filament staple & yarn in lbs		B 10-a	J 7-a
staple & filament: tonnage		B 10-a	
& yarn: production capacity: tonnage	All countries	D 27-a	J 7-a
fibre in lbs		J 7-a	
rice: tonnage & yield in kg per ha (world average)		B 10-a	
tonnage	Main countries	R 5-a	
rolled-steel products: tonnage		B 2-a	
roundwood (for industrial use) by volume in m³		R 5-a	
rutile concentrates: tonnage	Main countries	A 5-a	
rye: tonnage & yield per ha in kg (world average)		N 1-a	
tonnage		R 5-a	
safflower oil: tonnage		C 16-a	
salt: tonnage		N 10-a	
	Main countries	N 4-a	
sand & gravel: tonnage	USA & others (as total)	N 1-a	
sawnwood (all kinds) by volume in m³		N 1-a	
selenium in kg	All countries	R 5-a	
tonnage	Worldwide excl Communist countries	T 4-a	
	Main countries	C 30-a	N 4-a
sesame seed oil: tonnage		N 1-a	
	All countries	A 4-a	N 10-a
sheepskins: volume	Main countries & world regions	B 18-a	P 1-a
shellac, sticklac & seedlac: tonnage		A 18-a	
silicon: tonnage	Main countries	U 11-a	
silk (raw) in lbs	All countries	N 1-a	
tonnage		B 10-a	
silver (based on metal content of ore): tonnage		K 4-a	
		C 12-a	
in oz	All countries	R 5-a	
		N 4-a	
ore mined: tonnage	All countries	J 6-a	
		C 30-a	
sisal & hemp: tonnage	All countries	B 2-a	
soda ash (natural): tonnage	All countries	N 1-a	
sodium sulphate (natural): tonnage	Main countries	N 1-a	
soft & hard oils: tonnage		U 11-a	
sorghum: tonnage		C 16-a	
soybean oil: tonnage		A 4-a	N 10-a
soybeans: tonnage	All countries	B 18-a	P 1-a
sperm oil: tonnage		N 10-a	
steam turbine generators: volume	All countries	T 7-a	
in MW	All countries	T 7-a	
steel bars, rods & light sections: tonnage		T 1-a	
castings: tonnage	Main countries	B 25-a	
ingots & castings (by process): tonnage		T 1-a	
tonnage		C 30-a	N 4-a
plates & sheets (galvanised): tonnage		T 1-a	
over 3mm gauge: tonnage		T 1-a	
products made of steel by main kinds: tonnage		T 1-a	
(hot-rolled): tonnage		T 1-a	
sections (heavy): tonnage		T 1-a	
sheets under 3mm gauge (uncoated): tonnage		T 1-a	
strip (hot-rolled): tonnage		T 1-a	
tube round & squares: tonnage		T 1-a	
tubes & pipes (seamless): tonnage		T 1-a	
(welded): tonnage		T 1-a	
wire rod: tonnage		T 1-a	
strontium minerals (based on content of ore): tonnage	USA	N 1-a	
tonnage	Worldwide excl Communist countries	N 4-a	
sugar beet (based on sugar content): tonnage		R 5-a	
historical table in 5 yr averages from 1880: tonnage	All countries	A 20-a	
cane: historical table in 5 yr averages from 1880: tonnage	All countries	A 20-a	
(non-centrifugal): tonnage		B 13-a	
(raw centrifugal) from beet & cane: tonnage		A 5-a	
beet: tonnage	All countries	A 20-a	B 13-a
		U 11-a	
cane: tonnage	All countries	A 20-a	B 13-a
		U 11-a	

•••• APPENDIX 4 - GLOBAL STATISTICS

WORLD PRODUCTION, continued

Item	Territorial coverage	Title codes	
sugar (raw centrifugal): tonnage		B 13-a	
	All countries	A 20-a	
	Main countries	B 2-a	
sulphur (all forms): tonnage		T 5-a	
(elemental): tonnage		N 4-a	
(elemental by-products): tonnage		N 4-a	
	Main countries	N 1-a	
sulphuric acid: tonnage	Communist world regions	T 5-a	
	Non-Communist world regions	T 5-a	
sunflower seed oil: tonnage		A 4-a	N 10-a
tonnage	All countries	B 18-a	P 1-a
	Main countries	B 2-a	
superphosphates (concentrated): tonnage	All countries	C 26-a	
(single): tonnage	All countries	C 26-a	
synthetic fibres: tonnage		K 4-a	
filament yarn: tonnage		K 4-a	
rubber: production capacity: tonnage	World regions	B 13-a	
tonnage	Worldwide excl Communist countries	B 13-a	
	Worldwide	U 26-a	
	All countries	C 4-a	
	Main countries	A 5-a	B 2-a
talc soapstone & pyrophyllite: tonnage		N 4-a	
tallow & greases: tonnage		A 4-a	N 10-a
tantalum concentrates: tonnage	Main countries	N 1-a	
tea: tonnage	All countries	A 5-a	R 5-a
		U 11-a	
	Main countries	B 2-a	
technical oils: tonnage		U 11-a	
tellurium in lbs	Main countries	N 1-a	
tonnage	Worldwide excl Communist countries	N 4-a	
	Non-Communist countries	C 30-a	
timber by kind by volume in m³	All countries	A 5-a	
tin (based on metal content of ore) & concentrates: tonnage		R 5-a	
tonnage		C 12-a	
	Main countries	N 1-a	
historical table: tonnage		C 12-a	
(primary): tonnage	Main countries	C 20-m	U 11-a
	All countries	R 5-a	
(refined): tonnage		C 12-a	
(secondary): tonnage		C 20-m	
(smelter): tonnage		N 4-a	
concentrates: tonnage	All countries	B 2-a	
	Main countries	U 11-a	
ore & refined tin: tonnage		C 30-a	U 11-a
in concentrates: tonnage	Main countries	T 4-a	
tonnage	Worldwide excl USA	N 4-a	
		C 12-a	
	All countries	J 6-a	
scrap (secondary): tonnage	Main countries	T 4-a	
tinplate: tonnage		T 1-a	
titanium concentrates: ilmenite: tonnage		N 4-a	
rutile: tonnage		N 4-a	
titanium, ilmenite & rutile: tonnage	Non-Communist countries	C 30-a	
	All countries	C 12-a	
tobacco by kind in lbs		B 13-a	
leaf (unmanufactured) flue & fire cured in lbs		B 13-a	
tonnage	Main countries	A 5-a	B 2-a
(unmanufactured): tonnage	World regions	U 11-a	
tropical products by kind - index nos		B 13-a	
trucks & buses by make: volume	All countries	V 3-a	
tung nuts: tonnage		B 2-a	
oil: tonnage		B 2-a	N 10-a
	All countries	A 4-a	B 18-a
tungsten concentrates: tonnage		N 4-a	
metal: tonnage		C 30-a	
	All countries	C 12-a	
	Main countries	N 1-a	
ore & concentrates: tonnage		U 53-a	
wolfram & scheelite: tonnage		T 4-a	
uranium ore: tonnage	Canada, France, S Africa & USA	T 4-a	
oxide: tonnage	Reporting countries only	C 30-a	
vanadium (based on metal content of ore): tonnage	Worldwide excl Communist countries	N 4-a	
		C 12-a	
	All countries	T 4-a	
tonnage	Worldwide excl Communist countries	N 4-a	
vegetables (all kinds): tonnage	All countries	R 5-a	
vermiculite: tonnage	Worldwide excl Communist countries	N 4-a	
walnuts (unshelled): tonnage	All countries	P 4-a	
water wheels (for hydroelectric generators) in MW		T 7-a	
whale oil (excl sperm oil): tonnage		A 4-a	N 10-a
wheat: tonnage & in bushels	Worldwide incl China	C 29-a	
& yield in kg per ha (world average)		R 5-a	
tonnage	All countries	C 16-a	
	Main countries	A 5-a	P 1-a
	World regions excl China	U 11-a	
	Main countries	A 5-a	U 11-a
wine by volume in hectolitres		J 7-a	
wood pulp (chemical) & paper by grade: tonnage		J 7-a	
(dissolving): tonnage			

•••• APPENDIX 4 - GLOBAL STATISTICS

	Territorial coverage	Title codes	
WORLD PRODUCTION, continued			
wood pulp (mechanical) by value in $m		J 7-a	
tonnage	All countries	A 5-a	
wood-based panels by kind: volume in m³	All countries	A 5-a	
wool (greasy raw) in lbs	Main countries	B 10-a	
tonnage		K 4-a	
	Main countries	A 5-a	
	World economic regions	U 11-a	
in lbs (clean basis)		B 10-a	
(Merino crossbred) in kg		K 6-a	
woollen yarn (incl mixtures): tonnage		R 5-a	
zinc (based on metal content of ore) & concentrates: tonnage		R 5-a	
tonnage		U 24-m	C 12-a
(crude slabs): tonnage	All countries	C 12-a	
historical table from 1897: tonnage		C 12-a	J 6-a
ore & metallic zinc: tonnage		U 11-a	
& slab zinc: tonnage		C 30-a	
tonnage		C 12-a	N 4-a
slabs: tonnage	All countries	J 6-a	R 5-a
smelter: tonnage		N 4-a	
tonnage		R 5-a	
	All countries excl USSR	T 4-a	

WORLD STOCKS & SUPPLY

WORLD STOCKS

butter (end-yr): tonnage		G 1-a
coffee, cocoa & tea (end-yr): tonnage		G 1-a
cotton, jute & wool (end-yr): tonnage		G 1-a
natural rubber (end-yr): tonnage		G 1-a
sugar (end-yr): tonnage		G 1-a
wheat, coarse grains & paddy rice (end-yr): tonnage		G 1-a

WORLD SUPPLY

animal fats & oil by kind: tonnage		B 19-a
butter (based on fat content): tonnage		B 19-a
coffee (green): production & carry-over stocks in bags		J 1-a
cotton in bales & tons (incl US % of total)		K 1-a
(raw) production & carry-over stocks in bales		P 1-a
fish oils (excl fish liver oils): tonnage		B 19-a
lard: tonnage		B 19-a
marine oils by kind: tonnage		B 19-a
natural rubber: tonnage		B 13-a
synthetic rubber: tonnage	Worldwide excl Communist countries	B 13-a
tallow & greases: tonnage		B 19-a
tea: availability & excess over demand: tonnage	Main countries	C 1-a
in lbs	Worldwide excl China, Iran, Japan & USSR	B 13-a
vegetable oils by kind: tonnage		B 19-a
(hard): tonnage		B 19-a
(soft): tonnage		B 19-a
(technical): tonnage		B 19-a
whale oil (excl sperm oil): tonnage		B 19-a
wool (raw) in lbs (clean basis)	Main countries	B 10-a

WORLD TRADE

% changes (based on value)		D 28-a	U 18-a
(based on volume)		U 18-a	
% growth rates (value basis)	World regions	J 5-a	M 3-a
by world regions (value basis)		U 23-a	
% increases in trade: chemical products		U 23-a	
% of aircraft shipped to developed countries		U 25-a	
to developing countries		U 38-a	
% of domestic appliances shipped to developed countries		U 38-a	
to developing countries		U 38-a	
% of electric power equipment shipped to developed countries		U 38-a	
to developing countries		U 38-a	
% of farm machinery shipped to developed countries		U 38-a	
to developing countries		U 38-a	
% of generating equipment shipped to developed countries		U 38-a	
to developing countries		U 38-a	
% of medical apparatus shipped to developed countries		U 38-a	
to developing countries		U 38-a	
% of metal-working machinery shipped to developed countries		U 38-a	
to developing countries		U 38-a	
% of office machinery shipped to developed countries		U 38-a	
to developing countries		U 38-a	

•••• APPENDIX 4 - GLOBAL STATISTICS

	Territorial coverage	Title codes	
WORLD TRADE, continued			
% of passenger cars shipped to developed countries		U 38-a	
to developing countries		U 38-a	
% of railway rolling stock shipped to developed countries		U 38-a	
to developing countries		U 38-a	
% of ships & boats shipped to developed countries		U 38-a	
to developing countries		U 38-a	
% of telecommunication equipment shipped to developed countries		U 38-a	
to developing countries		U 38-a	
% of textile machinery shipped to developed countries		U 38-a	
to developing countries		U 38-a	
% share of world trade: all products imported (value basis)	Communist countries	M 4-a	
	Main countries & world regions	E 45-a	U 23-a
taken by developed countries		M 4-a	
by developing countries		M 4-a	
by oil-exporting countries		M 4-a	
% of world exports shipped to developing countries (value basis)		G 1-a	
to E European Bloc (value basis)		G 1-a	
to industrial countries (value basis)		G 1-a	
% US share of exports of 1109 SITC classes of manufactured goods		N 3-a	
by commodity classes & regions: historical table from 1953 by value		C 4-a	
in $m		C 4-a	U 27-a
in $m (see no 7)		U 27-a	
commodity classes - index nos (quantum & value bases)		U 43-a	
(see no 1, 4, 7, 10)		U 27-a	
economic regions by value in $m		A 1-a	E 45-a
per capita of population in $		E 45-a	
selected commodity classes by value in $m		U 23-a	
SITC classes by value in $m	World economic areas	U 23-a	
source & destination by value in $m		U 43-a	
in $m (see no 6, 12)		U 27-a2	
		G 1-a	R 5-a
value in DM million	World regions	M 3-a	U 23-a
in $m		U 43-a	
	All countries	F 2-a	
	Developed countries	M 4-a	
	Developing countries	M 4-a	
from developing areas to world regions by value in $m		G 1-a	
E European Bloc to world regions by value in $m		G 1-a	
industrial areas to world regions by value in $m		G 1-a	
to & from world regions by value in $m		U 15-a	
developing countries by value in $m		G 1-a	
E European Bloc by value in $m		G 1-a	
industrial countries by value in $m		G 1-a	
trends (comparative): trade, population & production - index nos		U 43-a	
unit prices - index nos		U 18-a	
unit value: agricultural products by kind in $ per ton		A 11-a	
animal feed by kind in $ per ton		A 11-a	
butter & cheese in $ per ton		A 11-a	
cereals by kind in $ per ton		A 11-a	
cotton, jute, hemp & wool in $ per ton		A 11-a	
dairy products by kind in $ per ton		A 11-a	
fibres by kind in $ per ton		A 11-a	
fish & fish products in $ per ton		A 11-a	
forestry products by kind in $ per ton		A 11-a	
fruit (fresh) by kind in $ per ton		A 11-a	
livestock by kind in $ per ton		A 11-a	
meat by kind in $ per ton		A 11-a	
mechanical wood pulp in $ per ton		A 11-a	
natural rubber in $ per ton		A 11-a	
oilseeds by kind in $ per ton		A 11-a	
plantation crops in $ per ton		A 11-a	
potatoes in $ per ton		A 11-a	
sawnwood (hard & soft) in $ per ton		A 11-a	
sugar (raw) in $ per ton		A 11-a	
vegetable oils by kind in $ per ton		A 11-a	

WORLD TRADE BY PRODUCT

	Territorial coverage	Title codes	
accessories & machine replacement parts by value in $m		U 38-a	
agricultural commodities by value in $m		A 5-a	
machinery by value in $m		B 27-a	U 38-a
tractors by value in $m		U 38-a	
air conditioning machinery by value in $m		U 38-a	
aircraft by value in $m		U 38-a	
engines by value in $m		U 38-a	
aluminium (primary): tonnage	Main countries	T 4-a	
antimony: tonnage	Main countries	T 4-a	
ore: tonnage	Main countries	T 4-a	
ball & roller bearings by value in $m		U 38-a	
bananas - index nos (value basis)	Main countries	A 5-a	
tonnage & value in $m		B 2-a	
tonnage	Main countries	A 5-a	U 11-a

•••• APPENDIX 4 - GLOBAL STATISTICS

WORLD TRADE BY PRODUCT, continued

Product	Territorial coverage	Title codes	
batteries & accumulators: % share of exports	Main countries	B 23-a	
by value in $m		U 38-a	
bauxite: tonnage & value in $m		B 2-a	
tonnage	Main countries	T 4-a	
bearings by type: ball, needle & roller by value in $m		B 27-a	
beef & veal (fresh, chilled or frozen): tonnage	World regions	A 5-a	
beryllium ore: tonnage	Main countries	T 4-a	
beverages & tobacco by value in $m	World regions	A 5-a	
boilerhouse plant: % share of exports (value basis)	Main countries	B 30-a	
boilers & boilerhouse plant by value in $m		B 27-a	
buses & commercial vehicles by value in $m		U 38-a	
butter: tonnage (incl EEC area % share)		B 3-a	
cadmium: tonnage	Main countries	T 4-a	
calculating & statistical machines by value in $m		U 38-a	
canned meat: tonnage & value in $m	World regions	A 5-a	
castor oil: tonnage & value in $m	Main countries	B 2-a	
castor oil seed: tonnage & value in $m	Main countries	B 2-a	
cattle & buffalo hides: tonnage	All countries	A 18-a	
cattlehides & skins & sheep & goat skins: tonnage		A 5-a	
cereals, wheat flour & coarse grains: tonnage	Main countries	A 17-a	
cheese: tonnage (incl EEC area % share)		B 3-a	
chemical products & as % of world trade	World regions	U 25-a	
by value in $m	World regions	U 23-a	
chrome ore: tonnage	Main countries	T 4-a	
citrus fruits by kind: tonnage	Main countries	A 5-a	
grapefruit: tonnage		B 2-a	
lemons & limes: tonnage		B 2-a	
oranges & tangerines: tonnage		B 2-a	
coarse grains by kind: tonnage	All countries	C 16-a	
cocoa beans: tonnage (incl % of total)	World regions	P 2-a	
tonnage & value in $m		B 2-a	
tonnage	All countries	A 3-a	
	World producing regions	P 3-a	
coconut oil: tonnage & value in $m		B 2-a	
coffee by grade in 60 kg bags	Main countries	U 11-a	
	All countries	J 1-a	
by value in $m		M 4-a	
in 60 kg bags	Main countries	J 1-a	
(Colombian Mild) in 60 kg bags	Main countries	U 11-a	
(green) by regions of origin in 60 kg bags	World regions	J 1-a	
(home-produced) in 60 kg bags	All countries	B 13-a	
(Robustas) in 60 kg bags	Main countries	U 11-a	
tonnage & value in $m		B 2-a	
(unwashed Arabicas) in 60 kg bags	Main countries	U 11-a	
columbite, tantalite & pyrochlore concentrates: tonnage		T 4-a	
condensers by value in $m		U 38-a	
construction machinery & mining equipment by value in $m		B 27-a	U 38-a
board by destination: tonnage	All countries	D 40-a	
copper blister: tonnage	All countries	T 4-a	
by value in $m		M 4-a	
(refined): tonnage	All countries	T 4-a	
tonnage & value in $m		B 2-a	
copra & coconut oil: tonnage	All countries	A 4-a	
tonnage & value in $m		B 2-a	
cake & meal: tonnage & value in $m		B 2-a	
cotton by destination: tonnage & in bales	All countries	K 1-a	
by value in $m		M 4-a	
imports by source: tonnage & in bales		K 1-a	
(raw) in lbs	Main countries	B 10-a	
tonnage & value in $m		B 2-a	
tonnage	World regions	U 11-a	
tonnage & in bales	Main countries	A 5-a	
	All countries	K 1-a	
cottonseed: tonnage		B 2-a	
crude petroleum by value in $m		M 4-a	
in barrels per day		C 3-a	
cycles by value in $m		U 38-a	
dairying equipment by value in $m		U 38-a	
domestic appliances: % share of exports	Main countries	B 23-a	
(non-electrical) by value in $m		U 38-a	
electrical equipment by value in $m		U 38-a	
electric furnaces by value in $m		U 38-a	
lamps: % share of exports	Main countries	B 23-a	
by value in $m		U 38-a	
power distribution equipment by value in $m		U 38-a	
power machinery & equipment: % share of exports (value basis)	Main countries	B 23-a	T 7-a
by value in $m		U 38-a	
traffic control equipment by value in $m		U 38-a	
electrical equipment (automotive) by value in $m		U 38-a	
electro-magnetic appliances by value in $m		U 38-a	
electron & proton accelerators by value in $m		U 38-a	
engineering products by world economic areas	Main countries	U 38-a	
as % of world trade (value basis)	All countries	U 38-a	
by value in $m		U 38-a	
by type by value in $m		U 9-a	
ferro-alloys: tonnage		T 1-a	
fertilisers by kind: tonnage (incl % change)		A 2-a	
(crude natural) in $m	World regions	U 23-a	

▶▶▶▶ APPENDIX 4 – GLOBAL STATISTICS

WORLD TRADE BY PRODUCT, continued

Product	Territorial coverage	Title codes	
fibreboard: tonnage	Main countries	A 5-a	
fibrous non-wood pulp by destination: tonnage		D 40-a	
fish & fish products by broad classes by value in $m		A 21-a	
by value in $m	All countries	A 5-a	
tonnage	All countries	A 5-a	
fish meal (incl solubles): tonnage	All countries	A 5-a	
fluting paper by destination: tonnage	All countries	D 40-a	
folding box-board by destination: tonnage	All countries	D 40-a	
food & feed grains by value in $m	World regions	A 5-a	
food processing machinery by value in $m		B 27-a	U 38-a
footwear (with leather uppers) by value in $m		A 18-a	
furnaces (industrial) & ovens by value in $m		U 38-a	
galvanised sheets: tonnage		T 1-a	
gas turbines by value in $m		U 38-a	
glass-working machinery by value in $m		U 38-a	
gold (as bullion) in kg	Main countries	T 4-a	
grease-proof paper by destination: tonnage		D 40-a	
groundnut cake & meal: tonnage & value in $m		B 2-a	
groundnut oil: tonnage & value in $m		B 2-a	
groundnuts: tonnage & value in $m		B 2-a	
hides & skins by kind by value in $m		A 18-a	
hot-rolled steel bars: tonnage		T 1-a	
strip: tonnage		T 1-a	
household paper (thin) by destination: tonnage		D 40-a	
ilmenite & rutile minerals: tonnage	Main countries	T 4-a	
insulated wire & cables: % share of exports	Main countries	B 23-a	
by value in $m		U 38-a	
internal combustion engines by value in $m		B 27-a	
iron & steel products by value in $m	World regions	U 23-a	
ore: tonnage & as % of world output		U 56-a	
tonnage (based iron content)	Main countries	U 11-a	
tonnage	All countries	T 4-a	
jute & allied fibres: tonnage	Main countries	A 5-a	
jute manufactures (incl kenaf): tonnage	Main countries	A 5-a	
(raw) & allied fibres: tonnage	Main countries	C 22-a	
kraft lining paper by destination: tonnage		D 40-a	
lead (refined): tonnage	All countries	T 4-a	
leather (made from hides & skins) by value in $m		A 18-a	
liner board by destination: tonnage		D 40-a	
linseed: tonnage & value in $m	Main countries	B 2-a	
cake: tonnage & value in $m	Main countries	B 2-a	
oil: tonnage & value in $m	Main countries	B 2-a	
locomotives (electric) by value in $m		U 38-a	
(steam) by value in $m		U 38-a	
machine tools by value in $m		U 38-a	
(metal-cutting type) by value in $m		J 2-a	
(metal-forming type) by value in $m		J 2-a	
machinery (electrical): % share of exports (value basis)	Main countries	B 23-a	
& transport equipment by value in $m	World regions	U 23-a	
manganese ore: tonnage	All countries	T 4-a	
unit value in $ per ton	Main countries	U 11-a	
manufactured goods as % of world trade	Developed countries	M 4-a	
	Developing countries	M 4-a	
by value in $m	Developed countries	M 4-a	
	Developing countries	M 4-a	
	World regions	U 23-a	
manufactured goods – index nos (quantum basis)		U 23-a	
(unit value basis)		U 23-a	
manufactures by SITC classes by value in $m	Main countries	N 3-a	
measuring apparatus by value in $m		U 38-a	
meat by kind: tonnage		B 11-a	
mechanical engineering products: % share of exports	Main countries	B 23-a	
by value in $m		B 27-a	
handling equipment by value in $m		B 27-a	U 38-a
metal-working machinery by value in $m		U 38-a	
mica (in sheets): tonnage	Brazil, India & Madagascar	U 11-a	
milk powder (incl EEC area % share)		B 3-a	
mineral fuels & lubricants by value in $m	World regions	U 23-a	
mineral processing machinery by value in $m		U 38-a	
minerals, ores & scrap by value in $m	World regions	U 23-a	
motor cycles by value in $m		U 38-a	
natural rubber by destination: tonnage	Main countries	U 11-a	
tonnage & value in $m		B 2-a	
tonnage	Main countries	A 5-a	
newsprint by destination: tonnage		D 40-a	
tonnage	All countries	A 5-a	J 4-a
non-cellulosic man-made fibres: tonnage	Main countries	B 10-a	
non-ferrous metals by value in $m	World regions	U 23-a	
nuclear reactors by value in $m		U 38-a	
ocean freight: goods by kind shipped in bulk: tonnage	Worldwide	D 28-a	
office machinery by value in $m		B 27-a	
packaging & bottling machinery by value in $m		B 27-a	
paddy rice: tonnage	World regions	C 16-a	
paper & paperboard by destination: tonnage		D 40-a	
tonnage	All countries	A 5-a	
pulp machinery by value in $m		U 38-a	
paper-making machinery by value in $m		B 27-a	

●●●● APPENDIX 4 - GLOBAL STATISTICS

WORLD TRADE BY PRODUCT, continued

	Territorial coverage	Title codes
particle & chipboard by volume in m³	All countries	A 5-a
passenger cars by value in $m		U 38-a
pears (fresh) by region: tonnage	World regions	D 34-a
pepper: tonnage & value in $m		B 2-a
petroleum products (refined) in barrels per day		C 3-a
phosphate rock by destination: tonnage		C 15-a
tonnage & value in $m		U 11-a
pig iron by kind by destination: tonnage		T 1-a
power tools by value in $m		U 38-a
transformers by value in $m		U 38-a
primary commodities as % of total world trade (value basis)	Developed countries	M 4-a
	Developing countries	M 4-a
by value in $m	World regions	U 23-a
	Developed countries	M 4-a
	Developing countries	M 4-a
printing & writing paper (coated) by destination: tonnage		D 40-a
(uncoated) by destination: tonnage		D 40-a
& bookbinding machinery by value in $m		B 27-a
machinery by value in $m		U 38-a
product composition by value in $m: capital goods		U 38-a
consumer goods		U 38-a
engineering goods		U 38-a
investment goods		U 38-a
motor vehicles		U 38-a
research equipment		U 38-a
transport equipment		U 38-a
pumps & centrifuges by value in $m		B 27-a U 38-a
radio receivers by value in $m		U 38-a
rail freight cars by value in $m		U 38-a
passenger cars by value in $m		U 38-a
railway equipment by value in $m		B 27-a
raw jute, kenaf & allied fibres: tonnage		U 11-a
raw materials by kind by value in $m	World regions	A 5-a
by value in $m	World regions	U 23-a
refrigerating equipment by value in $m		U 38-a
rice in milled equiv tonnage	All countries	A 19-a
tonnage & value in $m		B 2-a
	World regions	U 11-a
tonnage	All countries	A 10-a
rolling mills by value in $m		B 27-a
rubber (natural) by value in $m		M 4-a
(synthetic): tonnage & value in $m		B 2-a
sack kraft wrapping paper by destination: tonnage		D 40-a
sanitary paper by destination: tonnage		D 40-a
selenium in kg	All countries	T 4-a
sewing machines by value in $m		U 38-a
ships & boats by value in $m		U 38-a
silver bullion in oz	All countries	T 4-a
sisal & hemp: tonnage & value in $m	Main countries	B 2-a
sorghum & millet: tonnage	Main countries	A 12-a
steam boilers: % share of exports	Main countries	B 30-a
engines by value in $m		U 38-a
steel blooms & billets: tonnage		T 1-a
plates: tonnage		T 1-a
sections, angles & shapes: tonnage		T 1-a
wire: tonnage		T 1-a
straw board & paper by destination: tonnage		D 40-a
sugar (all kinds): tonnage & value in $m		B 2-a
tonnage	All countries	B 13-a
by value in $m		M 4-a
(non-centrifugal): tonnage	Main countries	A 20-a
(raw centrifugal & refined) by value in $m		B 13-a
(raw centrifugal): tonnage	All countries	C 25-a
(refined): tonnage	Main countries	A 20-a
tonnage & value in $m	Main countries	A 20-a
	Developing countries	U 11-a
	Developed countries	U 11-a
sunflower seed cake: tonnage		B 2-a
oil: tonnage		B 2-a
superphosphates (single grade) by destination: tonnage		C 26-a
table grapes: tonnage	World regions	A 5-a
tea: tonnage & value in $m		B 2-a
tonnage	All countries	C 1-a
	Main countries	A 5-a
telecommunications equipment by value in $m		U 38-a
television receivers by value in $m		U 38-a
textile & leather machinery by value in $m		B 27-a U 38-a
tin: tonnage	Non-Communist countries	T 4-a
tin concentrates: tonnage & value in $m		B 2-a
tinplate: tonnage		T 1-a
tobacco & cigar leaf: tonnage		U 11-a
(non-Oriental cigarette leaf): tonnage		U 11-a
(Oriental leaf): tonnage		U 11-a
tonnage & by value in $m		B 2-a
tonnage	Main countries	A 5-a
tractors (all types) by value in $m		B 27-a
transport equipment by value in $m		U 38-a
tropical products by kind - index nos (quantum & value bases)		B 13-a

•••• APPENDIX 4   GLOBAL STATISTICS

WORLD TRADE BY PRODUCT,   continued

	Territorial coverage	Title codes	
tubes, pipes & fittings: tonnage		T 1-a	
tungsten ores by kind: tonnage	Main countries	T 4-a	
typewriters by value in $m		U 38-a	
uncoated steel sheets (cold-reduced): tonnage		T 1-a	
valves & tubes (electronic) by value in $m		U 38-a	
vegetable parchment by destination: tonnage		D 40-a	
veneer sheets & plywood by volume in m³		A 5-a	
waste paper by destination: tonnage		D 40-a	
weighing machinery by value in $m		U 38-a	
wheat & wheat flour by destination: tonnage	All countries	C 16-a	U 11-a
shipments (excl inter-EEC deliveries): tonnage		C 29-a	
tonnage	World exporting regions	U 35-a	
	World supplying regions	C 16-a	
wine by volume in hectolitres	Main countries	A 5-a	
wire rods: tonnage		T 1-a	
wood pulp (all kinds) by destination: tonnage		D 40-a	
(chemical) by kind by destination: tonnage		D 40-a	
(dissolving) from fibres by destination: tonnage		D 40-a	
wood by destination: tonnage		D 40-a	
for paper-making by destination: tonnage		D 40-a	
(mechanical) by destination: tonnage		D 40-a	
tonnage	All countries	A 5-a	
wool (greasy raw): tonnage	Main countries	A 5-a	
wrapping paper (all kinds) by destination: tonnage		D 40-a	
zinc: tonnage	Main countries	T 4-a	
ore (incl concentrates) by destination: tonnage	All countries	T 4-a	
zirconium ore: tonnage	Main countries	T 4-a	

LIST OF TITLE CODES

PUBLICATIONS OF THE UN FOOD & AGRICULTURE ORGANISATION (FAO), ROME

Code		Frequency of publication
A 1	Agricultural Commodities – Projections for 1975 & 1985 (Vols 1 & 2)	irregular
A 2	Annual Fertiliser Review (Rapport Annuel sur les Engrais)	annual
A 3	Cocoa Statistics See also "Monthly Supplement" for revisions to statistical data	quarterly
A 4	Coconut Situation	twice yearly
A 5	Commodity Review & Outlook	annual
A 6	Per Caput Fibre Consumption	irregular
A 7	Processed Fruit & Vegetables (Commodity Bulletin Series, No 47)	
A 8	Processed Tropical Fruit (Commodity Bulletin Series, No 51)	
A 9	Production Yearbook For latest data see "Monthly Bulletin of Agricultural Economics & Statistics, FAO"	annual
A 10	Rice Report	annual
A 11	The State of Food & Agriculture	annual
A 12	Survey of Export Markets for Sorghum (Commodity Bulletin Series, No 49)	
A 13	Timber Bulletin for Europe (Bulletin du Bois, pour l'Europe) Compiled in conjunction with Statistical Office of United Nations, New York and contains data also for Canada, USA & USSR	twice yearly
A 14	Trade Yearbook Covers agricultural commodities in SITC Product Classes	annual
A 15	The World Banana Economy (Commodity Bulletin Series, No 50)	
A 16	World Forest Inventory Based on Census taken every 5 years	
A 17	World Grain Trade Statistics	annual
A 18	The World Hides, Skins, Leather & Footwear Economy (Commodity Bulletin Series, No 48)	
A 19	World Rice Economy in Figures, 1909-1963 (Commodity Reference Series, No 3)	
A 20	World Sugar Economy in Figures (Commodity Reference Series, No 1)	
A 21	Yearbook of Fishery Statistics – Fishery Commodities	annual
A 22	Yearbook of Fishery Statistics – Catches & Landings	annual
A 23	Yearbook of Forest Products	annual
A 24	Annual Forest Products Market Review (Supplement to "Timber Bulletin for Europe") Part 1 – Sawn Softwood	annual
A 25	Annual Forest Products Market Review (Supplement to "Timber Bulletin for Europe") Part 2 – Hardwoods & Wood-based panels	annual

LIST OF TITLE CODES

PUBLICATIONS OF BRITISH OFFICIAL & SEMI-OFFICIAL ORGANISATIONS

Code	Title	Frequency of publication
B 1	Agricultural & Food Statistics for the Enlarged Community UK Ministry of Agriculture Fisheries & Food, London	annual
B 2	The Developing Countries Economic Indicators: Part 1 - Commodities UK Foreign & Commonwealth Office, London	annual
B 3	EEC Dairy Facts & Figures UK Milk Marketing Board, London	annual
B 4	Dairy Produce - A Review of Production, Trade, Consumption & Prices Commonwealth Secretariat, London	annual
B 5	Fruit - A Review of Production & Trade Commonwealth Secretariat, London	annual
B 6	Fruit Intelligence Commonwealth Secretariat, London	monthly
B 7	Grain Bulletin Commonwealth Secretariat, London	monthly
B 8	Grain Crops - A Review of Production Trade, Consumption & Prices Commonwealth Secretariat, London	annual
B 9	Hides & Skins Quarterly Commonwealth Secretariat, London	quarterly
B 10	Industrial Fibres - A Review of Production, Trade & Consumption Commonwealth Secretariat, London	annual
B 11	Meat - A Review of Production, Trade, Consumption & Prices Commonwealth Secretariat, London	annual
B 12	Meat & Dairy Produce Bulletin Commonwealth Secretariat, London	monthly
B 13	Plantation Crops - A Review Commonwealth Secretariat, London	annual
B 14	Rice Bulletin Commonwealth Secretariat, London	monthly
B 15	Statistical Summary of the Mineral Industry Institute of Geological Sciences, Mineral Resources Division, London	annual
B 16	Tobacco Consumption in Various Countries Tobacco Research Council, London	irregular
B 17	Tobacco Intelligence Commonwealth Secretariat, London	quarterly
B 18	Tropical Products Quarterly Commonwealth Secretariat, London	quarterly
B 19	Vegetable Oils & Oilseeds - A Review of Production, Trade, Utilisation & Prices Commonwealth Secretariat, London	annual
B 20	British Machine Tools in Europe - A Study of Competition National Economic Development Office, London	
B 21	Industrial Review to 1977 - Chemicals National Economic Development Office, London	
B 22	Industrial Review to 1977 - Clothing National Economic Development Office, London	
B 23	Industrial Review to 1977 - Electrical Engineering National Economic Development Office, London	
B 24	Industrial Review to 1977 - Electronics National Economic Development Office, London	
B 25	Industrial Review to 1977 - Iron & Steel Castings National Economic Development Office, London	
B 26	Industrial Review to 1977 - Machine Tools National Economic Development Office, London	
B 27	Industrial Review to 1977 - Mechanical Engineering National Economic Development Office, London	

LIST OF TITLE CODES

PUBLICATIONS OF BRITISH OFFICIAL & SEMI-OFFICIAL ORGANISATIONS, continued

Code			Frequency of publication
B 28	Industrial Review to 1977 - Motors National Economic Development Office, London		
B 29	Industrial Review to 1977 - Textiles National Economic Development Office, London		
B 30	Steam Boilers & Boilerhouse Plant - Effects of UK Entry into the EEC National Economic Development Office, London		
B 31	UK - EEC Machine Tool Competition in 1971 National Economic Development Office, London		

PUBLICATIONS OF INTERNATIONAL NON-OFFICIAL ORGANISATIONS (NOT COVERED ELSEWHERE)

Code			Frequency
C 1	Annual Bulletin of Statistics & Supplement International Tea Committee, London		annual
C 2	Annual Survey of Wages & Working Conditions, Production & Employment of the Metal Industry International Metalworker's Federation, Geneva		annual
C 3	Annual Statistical Bulletin Organisation of Petroleum Exporting Countries - OPEC, Vienna		annual
C 4	The Belgian & International Economy - Synoptical Tables (L'Eccnomie Belge et Internationale - Tableaux Synoptiques) Université Libre de Bruxelles: Institut de Sociologie, Brussels		irregular
C 5	Bulletin de la Chambre Syndicale de la Sidérurgie Française, Paris	Text in French	monthly
C 6	Compendio Statistico Associazione Nazionale dell'Industria Chemica, Milano (Statistical Review of the Federation of Chemical Industries, Milan)	Text in Italian	annual
C 7	Direct & Total Wage Costs for Workers - International Survey, 1960-1970 Swedish Employers' Confederation, Stockholm		
C 8	The Furniture Industry in Western Europe: A Statistical Digest Furniture Development Council, London		annual
C 9	International Market Survey - Cattle Sheep Pigs Meat & Livestock Commission, London		quarterly
C 10	International Whaling Statistics Committee for Whaling Statistics, Oslo		annual
C 11	Monthly Statistical Summary International Tea Committee, London		monthly
C 12	Metalli Non Ferrosi e Ferroleghe Statistiche (Non-ferrous Metal & Ferro-Alloy Statistics) Azienda Minerali Metallici Italiani - AMMI, Rome	Text in Italian	annual
C 13	Oil - World Statistics Institute of Petroleum, London		annual
C 14	Pétrole Comité Professionnel du Pétrole, Paris	Text in French	annual
C 15	Phosphate Rock Statistics International Superphosphate & Compound Manufacturers' Association Ltd, London		annual
C 16	Review of the World Grains Situation (Examen de la Situation Mondiale des Céréales) International Wheat Council, London		annual
C 17	Rubber Market Report United Baltic Corporation Ltd, London		fortnightly
C 18	Rubber Statistical Bulletin International Rubber Study Group, London		monthly
C 19	Statistical Bulletin International Sugar Organisation, London		monthly
C 20	Monthly Statistical Bulletin International Tin Council, London		monthly

LIST OF TITLE CODES

PUBLICATIONS OF INTERNATIONAL NON-OFFICIAL ORGANISATIONS, continued

Code			Frequency of publication
C 21	Statistical Review of the World Oil Industry British Petroleum Co Ltd, London		annual
C 22	Statistical Yearbook of the European Jute Industry Association of European Jute Industries, Paris		annual
C 23	Statistics (Statistiques: Union Internationale des Producteurs et Distributeurs d'Energie Electrique) International Union of Producers & Distributors of Electrical Energy, Paris Published as special No of the Periodical "L'Economie Electrique"	Text in English & French	
C 24	Statistics of the Instrument Industry Scientific Instrument Manufacturer's Association, London		annual
C 25	Sugar Yearbook International Sugar Organisation, London		annual
C 26	Superphosphate Statistics International Superphosphate & Compound Manufacturers' Association, London		annual
C 27	Trends in Grain Consumption International Wheat Council, London		irregular
C 28	The Working Population & its Structure (La Population active et sa Structure) Université Libre de Bruxelles: Institut de Sociologie, Brussels		
C 29	World Wheat Statistics International Wheat Council, London		annual
C 30	World Metal Statistics World Bureau of Metal Statistics, London		monthly

PUBLICATIONS OF THE ORGANISATION FOR ECONOMIC CO-OPERATION & DEVELOPMENT, PARIS (OECD)

Code			Frequency of publication
D 1	Agricultural Statistics, 1955 - 1968		
D 2	Trade by Commodities - Country Summaries (Series B) Products by SITC Classes (Echanges par Produits - Résumé par Pays - Serie B)		quarterly
D 3	Trade by Commodities - Market Summaries (Series C) Products by SITC Classes (Echanges par Produits - Résumé par Marchés - Serie C)		twice yearly
D 4	The Cement Industry (L'Industrie du Ciment)	Text in English & French	annual
D 5	The Chemical Industry (L'Industrie Chimique)	Text in English & French	annual
D 6	Consumer Price Indices (Indices des Prix à la Consommation)		monthly
D 7	Development Co-operation - Review		annual
D 8	The Electricity Supply Industry: Achievements ... Forecasts (L'Industrie de l'Electricité: Réalisations ... Prévisions)	Text in English & French	annual
D 9	The Engineering Industries in OECD Member Countries: New Basic Statistics, 1963 - 70 (2 Vols)		
D 10	European Monetary Agreement - Annual Report		annual
D 11	Expenditure Trends in OECD Countries, 1960 - 1980		
D 12	Financial Statistics: Vol 1 & Supplements (Bi-monthly)		twice yearly
D 13	Flow of Resources to Developing Countries		irregular
D 14	Food Consumption Statistics		annual
D 15	Forecasts of the Dairy & Beef Situations in 1975 and 1978		
D 16	Statistics of Foreign Trade - Monthly Bulletin (Series A) Products by SITC Classes (Statistiques du Commerce Extérieur - Bulletin Mensuel (Série A)		monthly
D 17	The Growth of Output, 1960 - 1980		
D 18	The Hides, Skins & Footwear Industry in OECD Countries		annual
D 19	Industrial Production - Historical Statistics (Production Industrielle - Statistiques Rétrospectives)		irregular

LIST OF TITLE CODES

PUBLICATIONS OF THE ORGANISATION FOR ECONOMIC CO-OPERATION & DEVELOPMENT, PARIS (OECD), continued

Code			Frequency of publication
D 20	Industrial Production - Quarterly Supplement to "Main Economic Indicators" (Products listed under International Standard Industrial Classification - ISIC)		quarterly
D 21	L'Industrie des Métaux Non Ferreux (Non-Ferrous Metals Industry)	Text in English & French	annual
D 22	Iron & Steel Industry in ... & Trends in ... (L'Industrie Sidérurgique en ... et Tendances en ...)	Text in English & French	annual
D 23	Labour Force Statistics (Statistiques de la Population Active)	Text in English & French	annual
D 24	Labour Force Statistics: Quarterly Supplement (Statistiques de la Population Active: Supplément trimestriel)		quarterly
D 25	Latest information on National Accounts of Less-Developed Countries		irregular
D 26	Main Economic Indicators		monthly
D 27	Man-Made Fibres: Production Consumption Capacity		irregular
D 28	Maritime Transport		annual
D 29	Market Forecasts for 1975 for Certain Fruit & Vegetables: Apples Pears Peaches & Tomatoes		
D 30	National Accounts of OECD Countries		annual
D 31	Oil Statistics: Supply & Disposal		annual
D 32	Paper & Board: Consumption Patterns & Development Trends in OECD Countries, 1950 - 1967		
D 33	Production Consumption & Foreign Trade of Fruit & Vegetables in OECD Countries		irregular
D 34	Production Consumption & Foreign Trade of Fruit & Vegetables in OECD Countries - Pears		irregular
D 35	Production Consumption & Foreign Trade of Fruit & Vegetables in OECD Countries - Peaches		irregular
D 36	Production Consumption & Foreign Trade of Fruit & Vegetables in OECD Countries - Tomatoes		irregular
D 37	Production of Fruit & Vegetables in OECD Member Countries - Country Tables		irregular
D 38	Production & Marketing Structures for Horticultural Produce in Australia & Italy		
D 39	Provisional Oil Statistics		quarterly
D 40	The Pulp & Paper Industry in the OECD Member Countries (L'Industrie des Pâtes et Papiers dans les Pays Membres de l'OCDE)		annual
D 41	Pulp & Paper ... Stocks ... Production ... Trade & Shipments of Market Pulp (Pâtes et Papiers ... Stocks ... Production et Livraisons)		quarterly
D 42	Revenue Statistics of OECD Member Countries		annual
D 43	Review of Fisheries in OECD Member Countries		annual
D 44	Statistics of Energy		annual
D 45	Survey of Electric Power Equipment - Situation & Prospects		annual
D 46	Textile Industry in OECD Countries		annual
D 47	International Tourism & Tourism Policy in OECD Member Countries Contains data for USA		annual
D 48	Uranium Production & Short-Term Demand		irregular

PUBLICATIONS OF THE STATISTICAL OFFICE OF EUROPEAN COMMUNITIES (LUXEMBOURG) & COMMISSION OF THE EUROPEAN COMMUNITIES, BRUSSELS

E 1	Agricultural Statistics (Statistique Agricole) Each issue covers separate groups of products	Text in EEC languages	bi-monthly
E 2	Annuaire de Statistiques Sociales (Jahrbuch der Sozialstatistik) See also "Social Statistics of EEC" (bi-monthly) for current data	Text in French & German	annual

LIST OF TITLE CODES

**PUBLICATIONS OF THE STATISTICAL OFFICE OF EUROPEAN COMMUNITIES (LUXEMBOURG)
& COMMISSION OF THE EUROPEAN COMMUNITIES, BRUSSELS** continued

Code			Frequency of publication
E 3	Basic Statistics of the Community – Comparison with some European Countries Canada, USA, Japan & USSR (Includes statistics for EFTA Countries)		annual
E 4	Balances of Payments (Balances des Paiements)	Table headings in English & French	annual
E 5	Commerce Extérieur de la Communauté – Résultats par Etats Membres (Produits CECA) (Aussenhandel der Gemeinschaft – Ergebnisse nach Mitgliederstaaten (Erzeugnisse EGKS) Covers Foreign trade statistics of the European Coal & Steel Community		annual
E 6	Social Accounts in the European Community (Les Comptes Sociaux dans la Communauté Européenne)		irregular
E 7	La Conjoncture Energétique dans la Communauté: Situation et Prospectives Provides statistics of energy & forecasts for EEC Area	Text in French	annual
E 8	Statistiques Sociales: Coûts de la Main d'Oeuvre dans l'Industrie – Résultats préliminaires (Sozialstatistik – Arbeitskosten in der Industrie) (Social Statistics: Industrial labour costs (preliminary figures): 1962 Enquiry)	Text in English, French & German	irregular
E 9	Statistiques Sociales: Coûts de la Main d'Oeuvre: Banques Assurances Commerce de Detail (Sozialstatistik – Arbeitskosten, Banken, Versicherung, Einzelhandel) (Social Statistics: Labour costs in Banking, Insurance & Retail Trade)	Text in English, French & German	irregular
E 10	Statistiques Sociales: Coûts de la Main d'Oeuvre: Transports Routiers (Sozialstatistik – Arbeitskosten Strassenverkehrsgewerbe) (Social Statistics: Labour costs of Public Road Transport Undertakings)	Text in English, French & German	irregular
E 11	Statistiques Sociales: Coûts de la Main d'Oeuvre dans l'Industrie (Sozialstatistik – Arbeitskosten in der Industrie) (Social Statistics: Industrial Labour Costs)	Text in English, French & German	irregular
E 12	EEC Internal Information – Crop Production		irregular
E 13	The Economic Situation in the Community EEC Commission Publication		quarterly
E 14	Energy Balances – Situation & Forecasts (Bilans Energétiques – Situation et Prévisions)		annual
E 15	Energy Statistics Yearbook	Table headings in English, French & German	annual
E 16	Energy Statistics	Table headings in English, French & German	quarterly
E 17	Energy Statistics: Supplement – Fuel Oil Prices		irregular
E 18	Statistiques Sociales: Enquête par Sondage sur les Forces de Travail (Social Statistics: Sample Survey of the Labour Force)	Text in EEC languages	irregular
E 19	Fonds Européen de Développement – Situation Semestrielle des Projets (Statistics of Projects financed by European Development Fund)		irregular
E 20	Foreign Trade – Analytical Tables (NIMEXE Classes) 12 Vols (Commerce Extérieur – Tableaux Analytiques)	Text in French & German with Summary in English	annual
E 21	Foreign Trade – Analytical Tables: Imports (CST Classes) (Commerce Extérieur – Tableaux Analytiques: Import – CST) See also E 48		annual
E 22	Foreign Trade – Monthly Statistics (Commerce Extérieur – Statistiques Mensuelles)		11 issues per annum
E 23	Trade by Commodity Classes & Main Countries (Supplement to "Foreign Trade: Monthly Statistics")		annual
E 24	Foreign Trade: Monthly Statistics – Special Number (as Supplement)		annual
E 25	Statistiques Sociales: Coûts de la Main d'Oeuvre – Gains Horaires Durée de Travail (Social Statistics: Labour Costs, Hours of Work & Earnings)	Text in English & French	irregular
E 26	Monthly General Statistics Bulletin (Bulletin Mensuel des Statistiques Générales)	Table headings in EEC languages	11 issues per annum
E 27	Industrial Statistics Yearbook (Statistiques Industrielles)		annual
E 28	Industrial Statistics (Statistiques Industrielles)		quarterly
E 29	Sidérurgie Annuaire (Iron & Steel Yearbook)	Text in EEC languages	annual

LIST OF TITLE CODES

PUBLICATIONS OF THE STATISTICAL OFFICE OF EUROPEAN COMMUNITIES (LUXEMBOURG) & COMMISSION OF THE EUROPEAN COMMUNITIES, BRUSSELS continued

Code	Title	Notes	Frequency of publication
E 30	Sidérurgie Statistique Bimestrielle (Iron & Steel Statistics Bi-monthly)		6 issues per annum
E 31	Inventory of Taxes		annual
E 32	National Accounts Yearbook (Comptes Nationaux)	Text in French with Table of Contents in English	annual
E 33	Population & Employment (Social Statistics Series) (Population et Population Active)	Table headings in EEC languages	irregular
E 34	Agrarpreise: Monatliche u. Jährliche Durchschnitte der Preise wichtiger Landwirtschaftliche Erzeugnisse (Prix Agricoles: Moyennes Mensuelles et Annuelles des Prix des Principaux Produits Agricoles) (Farm Prices: Monthly & Annual Averages of Principal Agricultural Products)	Text in French, German, Dutch & Italian	monthly
E 35	Prices Received by Farmers (Agricultural Markets Special Number) (Prix Reçus par les Producteurs Agricoles)	Text in EEC languages	annual
E 36	Public Financing of Research & Development in the Community Countries		annual
E 37	Regional Development in the Community - Analytical Survey		irregular
E 38	Regional Statistics Yearbook		annual
E 39	Statistical Studies & Surveys: Vol 1 1974 - Public Expenditure on Research & Development (Etudes et Enquêtes Statistiques: Vol 1 1974 - Le Financement Publique de la Recherche et du Développement)		
E 40	Statistical Studies & Surveys: Vol 2 1974 - Annual Investments in Fixed Assets in Industrial Enterprises (Etudes et Enquêtes Statistiques: Vol 2 1974 - Investissements Annuels en Actifs Fixes dans les Entreprises Industrielles)		
E 41	Statistical Yearbook of the Associated African Malagasy & Mauritian States (Annuaire Statistique des Etats Africains Malgache et Mauricien Associés)	Table headings in English & French	annual
E 42	Tax Statistics Yearbook (Statistiques Fiscales)	Text in EEC languages	annual
E 43	Transport Yearbook (Transports - Statistique Annuelle)	Text in EEC languages	annual
E 44	Yearbook of Agricultural Statistics (Annuaire de Statistique Agricole)	Text in EEC languages	annual
E 45	Yearbook of Foreign Trade Statistics: Statistical Abstract (Annuaire des Statistiques du Commerce Extérieur: Synthèse)		annual
E 46	Investment in the Community Coalmining & Iron & Steel Industries: Summary Report of the European Coal & Steel Community - ECSC		annual
E 47	Marchés Agricoles - Echanges Commerciaux (CEE Informations)	Table headings in EEC languages	monthly
E 48	Foreign Trade - Analytical Tables: Exports (CST Classes) (Commerce Extérieur - Tableaux Analytiques: Export - CST) See also E 21		annual

INTERNATIONAL TRADE & MONETARY ORGANISATIONS (INCL STOCK EXCHANGE)

Code	Title	Frequency of publication
F 1	Balance of Payments Yearbook International Monetary Fund - IMF	issued monthly in loose-leaf format
F 2	Direction of Trade - Annual Supplement Published jointly by IMF & IBRD, Washington	annual
F 3	Direction of Trade Published jointly by IMF & IBRD, Washington	11 issues per annum
F 4	Financial Statements of the General Account & Special Drawing Account International Monetary Fund - IMF, Washington	quarterly
F 5	International Financial Statistics International Monetary Fund - IMF, Washington	monthly
F 6	International Financial Statistics: Supplement International Monetary Fund - IMF, Washington	annual
F 7	Schedule of Par Values International Monetary Fund - IMF, Washington	annual
F 8	The Stock Exchange Fact Book Stock Exchange, London	quarterly
F 9	Key Figures of European Securities European Banks International - EBIC, Brussels	monthly

LIST OF TITLE CODES

INTERNATIONAL TRADE & MONETARY ORGANISATIONS (INCL STOCK EXCHANGES), continued

Code			Frequency of publication

G 1	International Trade
	    General Agreement on Tariffs & Trade – GATT
	    Covers Trade between Contracting Parties
			annual

GERMAN & ITALIAN UNOFFICIAL SOURCES

H 1	Die Grössten Unternehmen der Welt (The Largest World Enterprises) Schweizerische Bankgesellschaft – Union Bank of Switzerland, Zürich	Text in German	irregular
H 2	Metal Statistics Metallgesellschaft AG, Frankfurt am Main		annual

H 3	Statistisches Jahrbuch der Eisen u. Stahl Industrie
	    (Statistical Yearbook of the Iron & Steel Industry)
	    Wirtschaftsvereinigung Eisen u. Stahl Industrie, Düsseldorf
		Text in German	annual

H 4	Energia ed Idrocarburi – Sommario Statistico
	    (Energy & Hydrocarbon Fuels – Statistical Summary)
	    Ente Nazionale Idrocarburi – ENI
		Text in Italian	annual

PUBLICATIONS OF NORTH AMERICAN-BASED ORGANISATIONS (NOT COVERED ELSEWHERE)

J 1	Annual Coffee Statistics Pan American Coffee Bureau, New York	annual
J 2	Economic Handbook of the Machine Tool Industry National Machine Tool Builders' Association, McLean, Va (USA)	annual
J 3	Metal Statistics American Metal Market – Fairchild Publications Inc, New York	annual
J 4	Newsprint Data – Statistics of World Demand & Supply Canadian Pulp & Paper Association, Montreal	annual
J 5	Statistical Abstract of Latin America University of California, Los Angeles	annual
J 6	Yearbook American Bureau of Metal Statistics, New York	annual
J 7	Wood Pulp Statistics American Paper Institute Inc, New York	annual

PUBLICATIONS OF INTERNATIONAL TEXTILE ORGANISATIONS

K 1	Cotton – World Statistics: Quarterly Bulletin International Cotton Advisory Committee, Washington		quarterly
K 2	European Cotton Statistics Eurocoton, Brussels		annual

K 3	Exporter's Guide to the Wool Textile Markets of the World
	    National Wool Textile Export Corporation, Bradford
	    See also Annual Supplement
			annual

K 4	Information on Man-Made Fibres (Information sur les Textiles
	        Synthétiques et Cellulosiques – CIRFS)
	    International Rayon & Synthetic Fibres Committee, Paris
		Table headings in English, French & German	annual

K 5	International Cotton Industry Statistics International Federation of Cotton & Allied Textile Industries, Zürich		annual

K 6	World Wool Digest
	    International Wool Secretariat, London
	    See also "Wool Intelligence & Fibres Supplement" of Commonwealth
	    Secretariat, London, for similar world-wide data also on monthly basis
			monthly

PUBLICATIONS OF THE INTERNATIONAL LABOUR OFFICE (ILO), GENEVA

L 1	Bulletin of Labour Statistics	quarterly
L 2	The Cost of Social Security	irregular

LIST OF TITLE CODES

PUBLICATIONS OF THE INTERNATIONAL LABOUR OFFICE (ILO), GENEVA   continued

Code		Frequency of publication
L 3	Labour Force & World Population Growth Special Edition for 1974 World Population Year	
L 4	Yearbook of Labour Statistics	annual

PUBLICATIONS OF INTERNATIONAL DEVELOPMENT & FINANCING INSTITUTIONS

M 1	Operations Report Agency for International Development (A.I.D.), Washington	annual
M 2	Annual Report International Finance Corporation (IFC), Washington	annual
M 3	World Bank: Annual Report World Bank, Washington	annual
M 4	Trends in Developing Countries World Bank, Washington	annual
M 5	World Bank Atlas International Bank for Reconstruction & Development (IBRD), Washington	annual
M 6	World Tables International Bank for Reconstruction & Development (IBRD), Washington	irregular
M 7	An International Survey of Interest Rates: Pattern & Differentials Union Bank of Switzerland, Zürich	irregular
M 8	World Currency Charts American International Investment Corporation, San Francisco	annual
M 9	World Invisible Trade Committee on Invisible Exports, London	annual

PUBLICATIONS OF NORTH AMERICAN OFFICIAL & SEMI-OFFICIAL BUREAUX

N 1	Commodity Data Summaries - Appendix 1 to Mining & Mineral Policy US Bureau of Mines, Dept of Interior, Washington	annual
N 2	International Coal Trade US Bureau of Mines, Dept of Interior, Washington	monthly
N 3	Market Share Reports - US Participation in Foreign Markets: Commodity & Country Series US Dept of Commerce, Washington	annual
N 4	Mineral Industry Surveys US Bureau of Mines, Dept of Interior, Washington	annual
N 5	Minerals Yearbook Vol 3 - International US Bureau of Mines, Dept of Interior, Washington	annual

N 6	Projections of the Population of the Communist Countries of Eastern Europe by Age & Sex
	    (Series P 91)
	    US Dept of Commerce, Washington
		irregular

N 7	Rates of Change in Economic Data for Ten Industrial Countries Federal Reserve Bank of St Louis	
N 8	World Motor Vehicle Production & Registration US Dept of Commerce, Washington	annual
N 9	World Military Expenditure US Arms Control Agency, Washington	annual
N 10	Oilseeds Review (La Revue des Grains Oléagineuses) Ministry of Industry Trade & Commerce, Ottawa, Canada	quarterly

N 11	America en Cifras - Situación Física: Territoria y Clima
	    Organización de los Estados Americanos - OAS, Washington
	    Part 1 - Land & Climate
		annual

N 12	America en Cifras - Situación Demografica - Estado y Movimiento de la Población
	    Organización de los Estados Americanos - OAS, Washington
	    Part 2 - Population & Population Movement
		annual

LIST OF TITLE CODES

PUBLICATIONS OF NORTH AMERICAN OFFICIAL & SEMI-OFFICIAL BUREAUX, continued

Code		Frequency of publication
N 13	America en Cifras - Situación Economica: Agricultura, Ganaderia, Silvicultura, Caza y Pesca Organización de los Estados Americanos - OAS, Washington Part 3 - (Vol 1) - Agriculture, Livestock Husbandry, Forestry, Hunting & Fisheries	annual
N 14	America en Cifras - Situación Economica: Industria Organización de los Estados Americanos - OAS, Washington Part 3 - (Vol 2) - Industrial Statistics	annual
N 15	America en Cifras - Situación Economica: Commercio, Transporte, Comunicaciones y Turismo Organización de los Estados Americanos - OAS, Washington Part 3 - (Vol 3) - Trade, Transportation, Communications & Tourism	annual
N 16	America en Cifras - Situación Economica Organización de los Estados Americanos - OAS, Washington Part 3 - (Vol 4) - Balance of Payments & Financial Statistics	annual
N 17	America en Cifras - Situación Economica Organización de los Estados Americanos - OAS, Washington Part 3 - (Vol 5) - Prices, Wages & Consumption Statistics	annual
N 18	America en Cifras - Situación Social Organización de los Estados Americanos - OAS, Washington Part 4 - Social Statistics	annual
N 19	America en Cifras - Situación Cultural: Educación y otros Aspectos Culturales Organización de los Estados Americanos - OAS, Washington Part 5 - Education & Cultural Statistics	annual
N 20	America en Cifras - Situación Politica y Administrativa Organización de los Estados Americanos - OAS, Washington Part 6 - Administrative & Political Statistics	annual

PUBLICATIONS OF BRITISH COMPANIES COVERING EDIBLE PRODUCTS

Code		Frequency
P 1	Annual Review of Oilseeds, Oils, Oilcakes & Other Commodities F Fehr & Co, London	annual
P 2	Cocoa Market Report Gill & Duffus Group Ltd, London	monthly
P 3	Cocoa Statistics Gill & Duffus Group Ltd, London	annual
P 4	Edible Nut Statistics Gill & Duffus Group Ltd, London	monthly
P 5	International Milling & Feed Manual Turret Press, London	annual
P 6	Tea Statistics J Thomas & Co (Private) Ltd, Calcutta	annual

PUBLICATIONS (OFFICIAL) OF THE WEST GERMAN STATISTICAL OFFICE, WIESBADEN

Code			Frequency
R 1	Preise Löhne Wirtschaftsrechnungen - Reihe 10: Internationaler Vergleich der Preise für die Lebenshaltung (International Comparisons of the Cost of Living) Statistisches Bundesamt, Wiesbaden	Text in German	monthly
R 2	Preise Löhne Wirtschaftsrechnungen - Reihe 9: Preise und Preisindices im Ausland (Prices & Price Index Nos for Overseas Countries) Statistisches Bundesamt, Wiesbaden	Text in German	monthly
R 3	Preise Löhne Wirtschaftsrechnungen - Reihe 12 - 1: Arbeitnehmerverdienste u. Arbeitszeiten, Streiks u. Aussperrungen (Employment, Hours of Work, Strikes & Lock-Outs) Statistisches Bundesamt, Wiesbaden	Text in German	annual
R 4	Preise Löhne Wirtschaftsrechnungen - Reihe 12 - 2: Tariflöhne und Lohnindices (Basic Wage Rates & Index Nos of Earnings) Statistisches Bundesamt, Wiesbaden	Text in German	annual
R 5	Statistisches Jahrbuch für die Bundesrepublik Deutschland - Internationale Übersichten (Statistical Yearbook of the Federal German Republic - International Section) Statistisches Bundesamt, Wiesbaden	Text in German	annual

LIST OF TITLE CODES

PUBLICATIONS OF SHIPPING & TRANSPORT ORGANISATIONS

Code		Frequency of publication
S 1	Annual Summary of Merchant Ships Launched in the World Lloyd's Register of Shipping, London	annual
S 2	Lloyd's Register of Shipping - Statistical Tables Lloyd's Register of Shipping, London	annual
S 3	Merchant Shipbuilding Return Lloyd's Register of Shipping, London	quarterly
S 4	Analysis of World Tanker Tonnage Davies & Newman Ltd, London	twice yearly
S 5	Digest of Statistics - Civil Aircraft on Register (Recueil de Statistiques - Immatriculation des Aéronefs Civil) International Civil Aviation Organisation - ICAO, Montreal, Series R	annual
S 6	Digest of Statistics - Financial Data (Recueil de Statistiques - Renseignments Financiers) International Civil Aviation Organisation - ICAO, Montreal, Series F	annual
S 7	Digest of Statistics - Airline Traffic (Recueil de Statistiques - Trafic) International Civil Aviation Organisation - ICAO, Montreal, Series T (2 Vols)	annually & monthly
S 8	Digest of Statistics - Traffic Flow (Recueil de Statistiques - Trafic par Etapes) International Civil Aviation Organisation - ICAO, Montreal, Series TF	monthly
S 9	Digest of Statistics - Airport Traffic (Recueil de Statistiques - Trafic d'Aéroport) International Civil Aviation Organisation - ICAO, Montreal, Series AT	annual
S 10	Digest of Statistics - Non-Scheduled Air Transport (Recueil de Statistiques - Transport Aerien Non Régulier) International Civil Aviation Organisation - ICAO, Montreal, Special Digest	annual
S 11	Digest of Statistics - Fleet Personnel (Recueil de Statistiques - Matériel Volant Personnel) International Civil Aviation Organisation - ICAO, Montreal, Series FP	annual
S 12	Monthly Statistics UK Civil Aviation Authority, London	monthly
S 13	Highway Expenditures: Road & Motor Vehicle Statistics International Road Federation, Geneva & Washington	annual
S 14	International Travel Statistics International Union of Official Travel Organisations, Geneva, - IUOTO	annual
S 15	Review Fernley & Egers Chartering Co Ltd, London	annual
S 16	Shipping Statistics: Monthly Figures of Shipping, Ports & Sea Trade (Statistik der Schiffahrt, Monatszahlen der Schiffahrt, des Schiffbau, der Hafen u. des Seehandels) Institute of Shipping Economics, Bremen	monthly
S 17	Shipping Economics & Statistics H P Drewry Ltd, London	monthly
S 18	Telecommunication Statistics (Statistiques des Télécommunications) Text in English, French International Telecommunications Union, Geneva & Spanish	annual
S 19	Very Large Crude Carriers in Excess of 175,000 dwt E A Gibson Ferguson Wild (Shipbrokers) Ltd, London	annual
S 20	Very Large Crude Carriers in Excess of 175,000 dwt - supplement E A Gibson Ferguson Wild (Shipbrokers) Ltd, London	annual
S 21	World Air Transport Statistics International Air Transport Association - IATA, Geneva	annual
S 22	World Bulk Fleet Fearnley & Egers Chartering Co Ltd, London	monthly
S 23	World Merchant Shipping Laid Up for Lack of Employment Chamber of Shipping of the United Kingdom, London	monthly

LIST OF TITLE CODES

PUBLICATIONS OF SHIPPING & TRANSPORT ORGANISATIONS, continued

Code			Frequency of publication
S 24	World Road Statistics (Statistiques Routières Mondiales) International Road Federation, Geneva & Washington		annual
S 25	The World's Telephones American Telephone & Telegraph Co, New York		annual

PUBLICATIONS COVERING POWER, METAL & OIL STATISTICS (NOT ALREADY LISTED)

Code			Frequency
T 1	International Steel Statistics - World Tables British Steel Corporation, London		monthly
T 2	Iron & Steel Industry - Monthly Statistics British Steel Corporation, London		monthly
T 3	Know More About Oil: World Statistics Institute of Petroleum Information Service, London		
T 4	Metal Bulletin Handbook - formerly Quin's Metal Handbook Metal Bulletin Ltd, London		annual
T 5	Statistical Supplement British Sulphur Corporation, London		twice yearly
T 6	West Indies & Caribbean Yearbook Caribook Ltd, Toronto (formerly Thomas Skinner Directories Ltd)		annual
T 7	The World Market for Electric Power Equipment University of Sussex: Science Policy Research Unit, Brighton		irregular

PUBLICATIONS OF THE UNITED NATIONS & ASSOCIATED UN COMMISSIONS (EXCL FAO), NEW YORK

Code			Frequency
U 1	Annual Bulletin of Electric Energy Statistics for Europe Economic Commission for Europe (ECE) Supplement to "Half-Yearly Bulletin of Electric Energy Statistics"	In English, French & Russian	annual
U 2	Annual Bulletin of Exports of Chemical Products (Bulletin Annuel des Exportations de Produits Chimiques) Economic Commission for Europe (ECE)	Text in English	annual
U 3	Annual Bulletin of Gas Statistics for Europe Economic Commission for Europe (ECE)	Text in English, French & Russian	annual
U 4	Annual Bulletin of General Energy Statistics for Europe Economic Commission for Europe (ECE)	Text in English, French & Russian	annual
U 5	Annual Bulletin of Housing & Building Statistics for Europe (Bulletin Annuel de Statistiques du Logement et de la Construction pour l'Europe) Economic Commission for Europe (ECE)	Text in English, French & Russian	annual
U 6	Annual Bulletin of Steel Statistics for Europe (Bulletin Annuel de Statistiques de l'Acier pour l'Europe) Economic Commission for Europe (ECE)	Text in English, French & Russian	annual
U 7	Quarterly Bulletin of Steel Statistics for Europe Economic Commission for Europe (ECE) Includes data for Canada, Japan, USA & USSR		quarterly
U 8	Annual Bulletin of Transport Statistics (Bulletin Annuel de Statistiques de Transports pour l'Europe) Economic Commission for Europe (ECE)	Text in English, French & Russian	annual
U 9	Bulletin of Statistics on World Trade in Engineering Products (Bulletin de Statistiques du Commerce Mondial des Produits des Industries Mécaniques et Electriques) Economic Commission for Europe (ECE)	Text in English	annual
U 10	Coal Situation in Europe & its Prospects Economic Commission for Europe (ECE)		annual
U 11	Commodity Survey UN Conference on Trade & Development (UNCTAD), New York		annual
U 12	Commodity Trade Statistics: Statistical Papers, Series D - SITC Classes Dept of Economic & Social Affairs, New York Issued in Country Parts: Published irregularly		mainly quarterly

LIST OF TITLE CODES

PUBLICATIONS OF THE UNITED NATIONS & ASSOCIATED UN COMMISSIONS (EXCL FAO), continued

Code		Frequency of publication
U 13	Compendium of Housing Statistics (Recueil des Statistiques de l'Habitation) Dept of Economic & Social Affairs, New York Text in English & French	annual
U 14	Demographic Yearbook Dept of Economic & Social Affairs, New York	annual
U 15	The ECE Region in Figures Economic Commission for Europe (ECE)	irregular
U 16	Economic Survey of Europe - The European Economy in ... Economic Commission for Europe (ECE)	annual
U 17	Economic Survey of Asia & the Pacific Economic & Social Commission for Asia & the Pacific (ESCAP) - formerly ECAFE	annual
U 18	Economic Survey of Latin America Economic Commission for Latin America (ECLA)	annual
U 19	Estimated World Requirements of Narcotic Drugs ... & Estimates of World Production of Opium UN Drug Supervisory Body, Geneva	irregular
U 20	Agricultural Trade in Europe - European Market for Fruit & Vegetables Economic Commission for Europe (ECE)	irregular
U 21	The Growth of World Industry - Vol 1 - General Industrial Statistics Dept of Economic & Social Affairs, New York	annual
U 22	The Growth of World Industry - Vol 2 - Commodity Production Data Dept of Economic & Social Affairs, New York	annual
U 23	Handbook of International Trade & Development Statistics (Manuel de Statistiques du Commerce International et du Développement) UN Conference on Trade & Development, New York See Annual Supplement for latest data	annual
U 24	Lead & Zinc Statistics - Monthly Bulletin UN International Lead & Zinc Study Group	monthly
U 25	Market Trends & Prospects for Chemical Products: Vol 1 Economic Commission for Europe (ECE)	irregular
U 26	Market Trends & Prospects for Chemical Products: Vol 2 Economic Commission for Europe (ECE)	irregular
U 27	Monthly Bulletin of Statistics Dept of Economic & Social Affairs, New York	monthly
U 28	Population & Vital Statistics: Statistical Papers Series A Dept of Economic & Social Affairs, New York	quarterly
U 29	Price Movements of Basic Commodities in International Trade, 1950 - 1970 Dept of Economic & Social Affairs, New York	
U 30	Prices of Agricultural Products & Selected Inputs in Europe Economic Commission for Europe (ECE)	annual
U 31	Coal Statistics for Europe Economic Commission for Europe (ECE) Includes data for USA	annual & quarterly
U 32	Quarterly Bulletin of Statistics for Asia & the Pacific Economic & Social Commission for Asia & the Pacific (ESCAP) - formerly ECAFE	quarterly
U 33	Recent Developments of Agricultural Trade in Europe Economic Commission for Europe (ECE)	annual
U 34	Report on Output Expenses & Income of Agriculture in European Countries Vol 3 - Statistical Annex Economic Commission for Europe (ECE)	irregular
U 35	Review of the Agricultural Situation in Europe Vol 1 - Grain & Dairy Products Economic Commission for Europe (ECE)	annual
U 36	Review of the Agricultural Situation in Europe Vol 2 - Livestock & Meat Economic Commission for Europe (ECE)	annual
U 37	Review of Maritime Transport UN Conference on Trade & Development (UNCTAD), New York	annual
U 38	Role & Place of Engineering Industries in National & World Economies - Vol 2 Economic Commission for Europe (ECE)	irregular

LIST OF TITLE CODES

PUBLICATIONS OF THE UNITED NATIONS & ASSOCIATED UN COMMISSIONS (EXCL FAO), continued

Code	Title	Frequency of publication
U 39	Statistical & Economic Information Bulletin for Africa Economic Commission for Africa (ECA), New York	irregular
U 40	Statistical Bulletin for Latin America Economic Commission for Latin America (ECLA), New York	twice yearly
U 41	Statistical Bulletin for Latin America - Vol IX (Special Issue) Economic Commission for Latin America (ECLA), New York	irregular
U 42	Statistical Indicators of Short-Term Economic Changes in ECE Countries Economic Commission for Europe (ECE)	monthly
U 43	Statistical Yearbook Dept of Economic & Social Affairs, New York	annual
U 44	Statistical Yearbook - Africa (Parts 1-4) (Annuaire Statistique Partie 1-4 - Afrique) Economic Commission for Africa, (ECA), New York	annual
U 45	Statistical Yearbook for Asia & the Pacific Economic & Social Commission for Asia & the Pacific (ESCAP) - formerly ECAFE	annual
U 46	Statistics on Narcotic Drugs & Maximum Levels of Opium Stocks UN International Narcotics Control Board, New York	irregular
U 47	Statistics of Road Traffic Accidents in Europe Text in English, French & Russian (Statistiques des Accidents de la Situation Routière en Europe) Economic Commission for Europe (ECE)	annual
U 48	Statistics of World Trade in Steel Economic Commission for Europe (ECE)	annual
U 49	The Steel Market Economic Commission for Europe (ECE)	annual
U 50	World Trade Annual (5 Vols by Product & 5 Vols by World Regions) SITC Classes Published by Walker & Co under agreement with UN Statistical Office, New York	annual
U 51	Survey of World Iron Ore Resources, 1968 Dept of Economic & Social Affairs, New York	
U 52	Trade in Manufactures of Developing Countries UN Conference on Trade & Development (UNCTAD), New York	annual
U 53	Tungsten Statistics UN Conference on Trade & Development (UNCTAD), New York	quarterly
U 54	World Economic Survey: Current Economic Developments Dept of Economic & Social Affairs, New York	annual
U 55	World Energy Supplies Dept of Economic & Social Affairs, New York	annual
U 56	The World Market for Iron Ore Economic Commission for Europe (ECE)	irregular
U 57	World Trade in Steel & Steel Demand in Developing Countries Economic Commission for Europe (ECE)	irregular
U 58	Yearbook of Construction Statistics Dept of Economic & Social Affairs, New York	annual
U 59	Yearbook of International Trade Statistics UN Statistical Office, New York	annual
U 60	Yearbook of National Account Statistics, Vol 3 Dept of Economic & Social Affairs, New York (See Vols 1 & 2 for details by Country)	annual

PUBLICATIONS OF UNESCO

Code	Title	Frequency of publication
U 62	Statistical Yearbook United Nations Educational Scientific & Cultural Organisations (UNESCO), Paris	annual
U 63	Statistics of Newspapers and other Periodicals United Nations Educational Scientific & Cultural Organisations (UNESCO), Paris	irregular

LIST OF TITLE CODES

PUBLICATIONS OF UNESCO, continued

Code		Frequency of publication
U 64	Statistics of Students Abroad United Nations Educational Scientific & Cultural Organisation (UNESCO), Paris	irregular

PUBLICATIONS COVERING MOTOR VEHICLE INDUSTRY STATISTICS

V 1	The Motor Industry of Great Britain Society of Motor Manufacturers & Traders Ltd, London Includes data for overseas countries	annual
V 2	Répertoire Mondial des Usines d'Assemblage de Véhicles Automobiles Chambre Syndicale des Constructeurs d'Automobiles, Paris World Summary of Statistics of Motor Vehicle Production - includes data for all countries producing over ½ mln vehicles per annum)	irregular
V 3	The World Automotive Market Automobile International - Johnston International Publishing Corp, New York	annual
V 4	World Motor Vehicle Data Motor Vehicle Manufacturers' Association, Detroit	annual

PUBLICATIONS OF THE WORLD HEALTH ORGANISATION (W.H.O.), GENEVA

W 1	World Health Statistics Annual (3 Vols)	annual
W 3	World Health Statistics Report	monthly

MISCELLANEOUS SOURCES OF INTERNATIONAL STATISTICS

Z 1	European Historical Statistics, 1750 - 1970 (B R Mitchell)		
Z 2	Self-Service (Selbstbedienung) International Self-Service Organisation, Cologne International Selbstbedienungs-Organisation, Köln	Text in English, French & German	annual
Z 3	Survey of Europe To-Day, 1970 Reader's Digest Association Ltd, London		
Z 4	Advertising Expenditure Around the World - A Survey of World Advertising Expenditures Starch Inra Hooper & International Advertising Association, New York		irregular
Z 5	Worldwide Operating Statistics of the Hotel Industry Horvath & Horwath International		annual
Z 6	World Whisky Market, 1965-1977 Economic Associates, London		annual